THE OXFORD STYLE MANUAL

The Oxford
Style
Manual

Edited and Compiled by

R. M. RITTER

OXFORD
UNIVERSITY PRESS

OXFORD
UNIVERSITY PRESS

Great Clarendon Street, Oxford ox2 6DP

Oxford University Press is a department of the University of Oxford.
It furthers the University's objective of excellence in research, scholarship,
and education by publishing worldwide in

Oxford New York

Auckland Bangkok Buenos Aires Cape Town Chennai
Dar es Salaam Delhi Hong Kong Istanbul Karachi Kolkata
Kuala Lumpur Madrid Melbourne Mexico City Mumbai Nairobi
São Paulo Shanghai Singapore Taipei Tokyo Toronto

Oxford is a registered trade mark of Oxford University Press
in the UK and in certain other countries

British Library Cataloguing in Publication Data

Data available

Library of Congress Cataloging in Publication Data

Data available

ISBN 978–0–19–860564–5

10 9 8 7

Designed by Jane Stevenson
Typeset in Swift and Arial
by Kolam Information Services Pvt. Ltd, Pondicherry, India
Printed in Great Britain by
Clays Ltd, St Ives plc

Contents

Preface

The *Oxford Style Manual* unites for the first time in one volume the *Oxford Guide to Style* and the *Oxford Dictionary for Writers and Editors*. The *Oxford Guide to Style* is the revised and enlarged edition of Horace Hart's *Rules for Compositors and Readers at the University Press, Oxford*; since 1893 *Hart's Rules* has over the course of thirty-nine editions grown to be the much-loved and respected standard work in its field. The *Oxford Dictionary for Writers and Editors* is an expanded and updated edition of the 1981 original, which was itself successor to eleven editions of the *Authors' and Printers' Dictionary*, first produced by F. Howard Collins in 1905. In joining these two books, the *Oxford Style Manual* offers an unparalleled resource, providing answers to the queries writers or editors are most likely to raise, on every aspect of preparing and presenting the written word.

During the combined total of two centuries that these works have remained in print, succeeding generations have found them to be indispensable. Like an encyclopedia and a dictionary—one arranged by topic, the other by headword—each book supplies its information in a different way, reflecting the disparate requirements of those concerned with the business of putting words into print. Each was the first style guide of its type in any language; both are considered classic works of reference: Peter Sutcliffe, in his *Oxford University Press: An Informal History* (OUP, 1977), describes them as 'two of the most influential books ever published by the Press'.

To understand why the books that make up the *Oxford Style Manual* have enjoyed such longevity and success, one must understand something about the era that produced them. While it is tempting to think that today's technological and information explosions are unique, something not so very different occurred at the turn of the last century. Then, as now, the dissemination of knowledge had entered a new age, which drove the Victorian publishing world into upheaval. Revolutionary surges in technology on almost every front—printing, composing, binding, papermaking, distribution—meant nearly all previous practices for creating the written word had to be radically readjusted or abandoned altogether, sometimes after decades or even centuries of use. In addition the sharp rise in literacy, coupled with the needs of Britain's expanding empire, fuelled a spiralling demand for books around the world. Suddenly, the length of time formerly taken to learn the skills associated with producing books appeared antiquated when measured against the new realities of mechanization and high volume. Traditional training alone—then still frequently via a seven-year apprenticeship—proved progressively less feasible, while rapid standardization and adaptation proved progressively more important. In short, the requirements of the age had outstripped the time-honoured process of training up experts in an ancient craft.

At the same time, English itself was being scrutinized as never before: the compilation of the mammoth *Oxford English Dictionary* (published between 1884 and 1928) generated new thinking about the language and the rules by which it operated, through the application of scientific principles. This in turn led to the pursuit and codification of linguistic right and wrong, which would bring forth such works as the Fowler brothers' *The King's English*. It was against this backdrop that two very different books were conceived, each addressing in its own way the requirements of those for whom change had transformed the language, its precepts, and its dispersal.

Horace Henry Hart (1840–1916), Printer to the University of Oxford and Controller of the University Press between 1883 and 1915, was one of the most influential printers of the last two centuries. Chosen primarily to modernize Oxford University Press (which he accomplished with remarkable success), he devised the first of his *Rules* as a single broadsheet page, which was swiftly followed by enlarged editions in booklet form. Hart originally intended it only for employees of the Clarendon Press, the learned imprint of Oxford University Press, to clarify for his rapidly expanding staff the basic rules of usage and typography by which they should operate. After Hart found, to his amusement, copies of his free booklet on sale in London, he decided in 1904 that it would be prudent for OUP to publish it for the public, as it seemed 'more than complaisant to provide gratuitously what may afterwards be sold for profit'.

The following year saw the publication of the *Authors' and Printers' Dictionary*, by the author and scholar F. Howard Collins (1857–1910). Collins had formed the first draft of his text by accumulating common authorial conundrums, which he amassed with the help of a wide range of writers, academics, publishers, and learned and professional societies. While he relied on the recommendations of the *OED*, he also formulated new rules where no previous guidance existed, particularly concerning capitalization, italicization, and punctuation—realms largely outside the focus of lexicography. He is credited with the 'invention' of the serial comma (the second in e.g. 'red, white, and blue'), with the consequence that in Britain the device is still often called the 'Oxford comma'.

In creating and updating their texts, Hart and Collins benefited greatly from some of the most important names in the scholarly and literary world, such as Sir William Craigie, Sir Sidney Lee, Sir Charles Lyall, Friedrich Max Müller, C. T. Onions, George Bernard Shaw, W. W. Skeat, Herbert Spencer, Sir Leslie Stephen, and Henry Sweet. In particular, the close involvement of Sir James Murray and Henry Bradley, editors of the *Oxford English Dictionary*, meant that changes in both books kept pace with ongoing research in the *OED*: 'Bearing the stamp of their sanction,' said Hart in one preface, the *Rules* carried 'an authority which it could not otherwise have claimed.'

From the moment *Hart's Rules* and the *Authors' and Printers' Dictionary* were published, they assumed lives of their own far beyond the confines of the Press and Oxford. Within a decade OUP's own house style—which from the first was meant to be used by default 'where no special instructions are given' to the contrary—had influenced the house styles of publishers and newspapers in Britain and abroad. The guidance set out in the two texts quickly became incorporated into common practice throughout the English-speaking world. Over time, as the books' volume and authority grew, it became clear that a surprisingly wide range of readers were using them side by side, dipping into one or the other as their needs required. One obvious indication of this is the increasing references in subsequent editions of each work to the other, as well as a gradual harmonizing of the stylistic variations between them; indeed, when Collins died in 1910, Hart himself took charge of producing the fourth edition of Collins's book. Another is the eventual physical transformation of both editions from their original shapes and sizes to, by the middle of the last century, identical formats, which at OUP were limited to these two works. In many ways, then, the *Oxford Style Manual* completes a convergence decades in the making. Publishing today, with its fluid roles, complex technology, and diverse media, would be utterly alien to the world Hart and Collins knew. Nevertheless, the fundamental functions of author and editor, and the basic stages of typescript, proofs, and publication, have not altered—however much their form has—and these both gentlemen would recognize immediately. For no matter what changes occur in the expectations and responsibilities of those who originate, manipulate, and disseminate words, and how they go about it, the goal remains to accomplish each task efficiently and accurately. In part for this reason I use *editor* wherever possible in this manual to denote anyone involved with adjusting text. This term is intentionally vague, to reflect the variety of titles and duties now commonplace in publishing: it is less useful to mark out obligations than ensure the result is as intended, whether on paper, online, or somewhere in between.

Readers familiar with *Hart's Rules* and the *Oxford Dictionary for Writers and Editors* will find minor changes from previous editions. It is quite natural that this should be so: if recreating two such long-lived books teaches one anything it is that the language and its contexts are mutable, and implacably resistant to rationalization. Consequently instances will occur in which the advice given here may not be the best choice, and the prudent author or editor will act accordingly.

Examples and their representation are designed to be as straightforward and intuitive as possible. Within the *Oxford Guide to Style*, italic type is generally used to indicate specific examples of usage. Exceptions occur when some ambiguity might thereby arise, as in passages discussing the use of italic versus roman type. In such cases examples are printed within quotation marks, in italic or roman type as necessary. Conventions governing the *Oxford Dictionary for Writers and Editors* may be found on pages 599–601.

It would be too much to hope that a wide-ranging book devoted specifically to matters that even highly informed people get wrong would itself be free from error, despite the best efforts of others to point the way for me. As such, advice on how any part of this text may be improved or corrected is as welcome now as it has been for previous editions.

Acknowledgements

From the first, *Hart's Rules* and the *Oxford Dictionary for Writers and Editors* always relied on the knowledge of experts in the field, and this new edition is no exception. The text is derived from the archives, experience, and practical knowledge of Oxford University Press, especially the former Arts & Reference Desk Editing Department and the Oxford English Dictionary Department. It also represents the accumulated experience and wisdom of countless people throughout the many editions of this work's precursors. As such my first debt of gratitude is to the generations of compositors, editors, academics, proofreaders, authors, and readers whose labour established and moulded the material included in this book, and whose influence endures on every page.

I should like also to thank those people associated with the Press and University who have generously shared their considerable talents in many areas, in particular Sarah Barrett, Bonnie Blackburn, Kate Elliott, Barbara Horn, Edwin and Jackie Pritchard, Chris Rycroft, J. S. G. Simmons, Della Thompson, George Tulloch, Colin Wakefield, Hilary Walford, John Waś, Connie Webber, Stanley Wells, Ingrid Winternitz, and the late Jenny McMorris.

I have been fortunate in being able to draw upon the extraordinary range and depth of knowledge of my former colleagues at the Press, many of whom have taken considerable time and trouble to help me over the years: the task would have been unthinkable without them. In particular I thank Cyril Cox, Mick Belson, Elizabeth Stratford, Enid Barker, and Milica Djuradjević, all of whom represent an irreplaceable source of editorial expertise. Here I must single out Leofranc Holford-Strevens, whom it has been my great good fortune to count as both colleague and friend, and who has remained a patient and inexhaustible fount of knowledge for this book in particular and OUP in general: in doing so he continues to fulfil the role of a Laudian 'Architypographus'.

Finally—and most importantly—I thank my wife, Elizabeth, who while this book was in preparation endured (with varying degrees of good humour) passive exposure to eleven years of editorial ephemera; and my children, Olivia, James, and Theodore.

R M K

Oxford
Michaelmas Term 2002
http://www.ritter.org.uk

PART I
The Oxford Guide to Style

Contents

Recommended works of reference

The list below represents a selection of some useful editions in their latest, and therefore most accessible, form. Space does not permit inclusion of the many excellent specialist works available for particular fields; similarly, foreign-language dictionaries have not been included. Recommended English-language dictionaries are the *New Oxford Dictionary of English* (Oxford: OUP, 1998) and the *Concise Oxford Dictionary*, 10th edn. (Oxford: OUP, 1999); for US English, *Merriam-Webster's Collegiate Dictionary*, 10th edn. (Springfield, Mass.: Merriam-Webster, 1996) and *The American Heritage Dictionary*, 4th edn. (Boston: Houghton Mifflin, 2000).

R. W. Burchfield (ed.), *The New Fowler's Modern English Usage*, 3rd edn. (Oxford: OUP, 1998).

Judith Butcher, *Copy-Editing: The Cambridge Handbook for Editors, Authors and Publishers*, 3rd edn. (Cambridge: CUP, 1992).

The Chicago Manual of Style, 14th edn. (Chicago: University of Chicago Press, 1993).

Peter T. Daniels and William Bright (eds.), *The World's Writing Systems* (New York: OUP, 1996).

Margaret Drabble (ed.), *The Oxford Companion to English Literature*, 6th edn. (Oxford: OUP, 2000).

H. W. Fowler and F. G. Fowler, *The King's English* (Oxford: OUP, 1973).

Joseph Gibaldi and Walter S. Achtert, *MLA Handbook for Writers of Research Papers*, 5th edn. (New York: Modern Language Association, 1999).

Sir Ernest Gowers, *The Complete Plain Words* (Harmondsworth: Penguin, 1987).

Sidney Greenbaum, *The Oxford English Grammar* (Oxford: OUP, 1996).

Tom McArthur (ed.), *The Oxford Companion to the English Language* (Oxford: OUP, 1992).

Eric Partridge, *Usage and Abusage*, 3rd edn. (Harmondsworth: Penguin, 1999).

R. M. Ritter (ed.), *The Oxford Dictionary for Writers and Editors*, 2nd edn. (Oxford: OUP, 2000).

Allan M. Siegal and William G. Connolly, *The New York Times Manual of Style and Usage*, revised edn. (New York, NY: Times Books, 1999).

Marjorie E. Skillen, Robert M. Gay, et al., *Words into Type*, 3rd edn. (Englewood Cliffs, NJ: Prentice-Hall, 1974).

William Strunk Jr. and E. B. White, *The Elements of Style*, 4th edn. (Needham Heights, Mass.: Allyn & Bacon, 2000).

United States Government Printing Office Style Manual (Washington, DC: US Government Printing Office, 2000).

A complete list of British Standards Institution publications may be found in their yearbook and website. Standards in fields relevant to this guide are as follows:

BS ISO 999:1996 Information and Documentation: Guidelines for the Content, Organization and Presentation of Indexes

BS 1629:1989 Recommendation for References to Published Materials

BS 1749:1985 Recommendations for Alphabetical Arrangement and the Filing Order of Numbers and Symbols

BS 2979:1958 Transliteration of Cyrillic and Greek Characters

BS 4148:1985, ISO 4–1984 Specification for Abbreviation of Title Words and Titles of Publications

BS 4280:1968 Transliteration of Arabic Characters

BS 4812:1972 Specification for the Romanization of Japanese

BS 5261 Copy Preparation and Proof Correction (parts 1–3)

BS 5555:1981, ISO 1000–1981 Specification for SI Units and Recommendations for the Use of their Multiples and of Certain Other Units

BS 5605:1990 Recommendations for Citing and Referencing Published Material

BS 5775–0:1993 (ISO 31–0:1992) Specification for Quantities, Units and Symbols: General Principles

BS 6371:1983 Recommendations for Citation of Unpublished Documents

BS 6505:1982 Guide to the Romanization of Korean

BS 7014:1989 Guide to the Romanization of Chinese

Knowledge is of two kinds. We know a subject ourselves, or we know where we can find information upon it.

SAMUEL JOHNSON

Comme quelqu'un pourrait dire de moi que j'ai seulement fait ici un amas de fleurs étrangères, n'y ayant fourni du mien que le filet à les lier.

MONTAIGNE

CHAPTER 1

The parts of a book

1.1 General principles

A book is composed of three main segments: the preliminary matter (*prelims* or *front matter*), the text, and the endmatter. Each of these is in turn composed of certain items, subject to a given order and presentation. This chapter explains some of the distinctions between these items, which combine in various ways to form a published work. Many of them are shared to some degree with other publications and documents, though it is rare for any work to include all of them. Electronic publications especially will have few of these in the traditional sense, and their arrangement—joined by hyperlinks—may appear very different.

Most publications are based on page extents that are a multiple of thirty-two (sometimes sixteen) pages, which allows for the optimum use of sheets during printing. When planning a book this multiple, called an *even working*, is what publishers aim at—or just under, to be on the safe side: a 256-page book is perfect, a 253-page book is tolerable (a few blank pages at the end do no harm), but a 257-page book is problematic. While fitting a publication to an even working is not normally an author's, or even editor's, concern, both should be aware of the concept, in case an odd fit during setting necessitates adjusting the arrangement of items in the book.

1.2 Preliminary matter

Preliminary matter is any material that precedes the text. Normally it is the part of a work providing basic information about the book for bibliographic and trade purposes, and preparing readers for what follows. It is usually paginated in lower-case roman numerals rather than arabic numbers; however, the introduction can begin the arabic pagination if it acts as the first chapter, rather than falling outside the body of the main text—as in the case where a book is divided into parts, for example.

Publishers try to keep prelims to a minimum: paperbacks and children's books generally have fewer preliminary pages than hardbacks and monographs; journals and other periodicals have fewer still. No rigid rules govern the arrangement of preliminary matter, although publishers routinely develop a house style for its sequence based on the sorts of publication they produce and the combination of preliminary matter common to them. Books in a series should have a consistent order, and those on a single list or subject tend to.

Generally, the more important of the prelim sections start on a new *recto* (right-hand page), sometimes ending with a blank *verso* (left-hand page) if the text is one page in length or finishes on a recto. Others of lesser importance start only on a new page, and two or more sections (especially lists) may be combined to run together on a single page if space demands and logic allows. The decision is based on what preliminary matter is to be included in a given work, how long each section is (often—but not always—equated with how important it is), and the number of pages available.

In addition to space, a consideration is bleed-through from the other side of a page: a one-line dedication or epigraph falling on a recto, for example, often requires a blank verso to avoid the image of the verso's type showing through on a nearly empty preceding page. (Bleed-through is for the most part unnoticeable on pages with similar amounts of text.) Where space permits it is safest to put any dedication or epigraph on a new recto with a blank verso. But a book much pushed for space—to accommodate an even working, for example—may actually demand setting the dedication on the half-title verso.

Assuming sections of standard length and no page restrictions, the following order of preliminary matter may be recommended:

series title	*(new recto)*	table of cases	*(new page)*
publisher's announcements	*(verso)*	table of statutes	*(new page)*
half-title	*(new recto)*	list of illustrations, figures,	
frontispiece	*(new verso)*	plates, maps, etc.	*(new page)*
title page	*(new recto)*	list of tables	*(new page)*
title page verso	*(verso)*	list of abbreviations	*(new page)*
dedication	*(new page)*	list of symbols	*(new page)*
foreword	*(new recto)*	list of (or notes on)	
preface	*(new recto)*	contributors	*(new page)*
acknowledgements	*(new page)*	epigraph	*(new page)*
contents	*(new recto)*	introduction	*(new recto)*

1.2.1 **Endpapers**

Endpapers are the (usually blank) sheets at the beginning and end of a book, half of each pasted to the inside of the cover, half forming a flyleaf. As such they form part of the binding rather than the text. If endpapers are to have printing, such as illustrations or figures, those not solely decorative should be repeated within the text. This is because libraries often conceal or obscure endpapers by fastening labels or dust jackets to them, and may remove them entirely through rebinding. Paperback books have no endpapers, so a hardcover book issued in simultaneous or subsequent softcover will lose this feature.

1.2.2 **Half-title and verso**

The *half-title* (formerly also called the *bastard title*) page is typically on the first recto (p. i) after the flyleaf. It contains only the main title of the volume, not the series title, subtitle, or author's or publisher's name.

Its verso (p. ii) is often blank, although it can hold publisher's announcements, such as series title, list of other titles in the same series, other titles by the same author, or general editors or advisers; exceptionally, it can hold a frontispiece. Some books incorporate the half-title verso into a double-page spread design for the title page.

1.2.3 **Frontispiece**

A *frontispiece* is an illustration that faces the title page when the work is opened. Consequently it is always printed on a verso, which is—unusually—blank on its preceding recto. Primarily a frontispiece illustration is one that warrants being placed in a significant position, customarily because it is an important image representative of the whole of the work (such as a portrait, map, or facsimile relating to the book's subject), because it is the only illustration in the work, or because it requires special treatment. For example, a halftone (photo) frontispiece may need to be printed on glossy art paper to reproduce the image properly; this page is then *tipped in*—fixed to a page by a strip of paste along the inner vertical edge—during printing. A colour halftone must always be tipped in unless the entire work is printed on paper suitable for colour images. All frontispieces not entailing special paper are printed on the same kind of paper as the text. Tipped-in frontispieces are unnumbered; those printed on text paper are numbered and included in the pagination.

A frontispiece should not be set landscape (turned on the page), and may need to be cropped to accommodate this. Like any other illustration, it requires a caption.

Frontispieces may not always be reproduced in all subsequent editions of a work. Tipped-in frontispieces are rare in paperbacks, for example, which also may not use the same quality of paper. For this reason authors should avoid cross-referring to a frontispiece in text.

1.2.4 Title page

The *title page*—properly *full-title page*, as distinct from *half-title page*—is on the first recto after the half-title (p. iii). It contains the full title and subtitle of the work, volume number if any, name of the author(s) or general editor(s), and the publisher's name (imprint). It may also include a series title, translator's name, illustrator's name, place of publication or cities in which the publisher has its main offices, publisher's logo or colophon (*see also* **1.4.6**), and year of publication.

Authors' names should be styled with initials or given name(s) in full as the authors prefer. Styles vary for their presentation: authors' names can appear above or below the title, and may or may not be preceded by *By*, or be followed by degrees or affiliations.

Joint authors need to agree on the order of their names. Authors can be listed in order of seniority, according to the proportion of material contributed, or alphabetically. A volume editor's name is preceded by *Edited by*, *Selected and edited by*, or *General Editor*, as appropriate. A translator's name is preceded by *Translated by*, and an illustrator's name may be preceded by *Illustrations by* or *With illustrations by*.

1.2.5 Title page verso

This page (p. iv) is also referred to as the *full-title verso, copyright, imprint*, or *biblio* page, and contains the essential printing and publication history of the work, including publisher's imprint, date of publication, publishing history, copyright notices, assertion of moral rights, current edition and impression, geographical limitations on sales, cataloguing in publication data (including ISBN etc.), performing rights agencies, and printer's name and location. This accumulation of data has given modern books much more crowded title versos than those of former years, and there is an increasing desire among many publishers to make them less cluttered.

Publisher's imprint

A *publisher's imprint* comprises the name of the publisher (or publishing division if this bears a separate name), its full registered address, place of publication, and date, usually printed at the foot of the title page. It may include the names of associated companies, agencies, or offices, and the cities in which they are located, as on the imprint page in this volume.

Works set wholly in Latin have Latin imprints, in which the place of publication is in the locative form—for example *Londinii* ('at London'), *Oxonii* ('at Oxford'), *Novi Eboraci* ('at New York')—in other languages the nominative has tended to take over: *Paris* for 'À Paris', *Praha* for 'V Praze', etc.

Date of publication

If the date of publication is not included on the title page, it is stated on the imprint page (or both). In this case, it may be combined with the publisher's imprint:

> First published in 2002 by Oxford University Press, Great Clarendon Street, Oxford OX2 6DP

Publishing history

In the case of co-publication, the name and full address of the publisher of a particular edition is stated first, with the name and city of publication of co-publishers following. Thus the imprint page for a co-publication published in Great Britain would read:

> Published in Great Britain in 2002 by Oxford University Press, Great Clarendon Street, Oxford OX2 6DP
>
> Published in the United States in 2002 by Oxford University Press Inc., New York

The imprint page for the same book published in the USA would read:

> Published in the United States in 2002 by Oxford University Press Inc., 198 Madison Avenue, New York, NY 10016
>
> Published in Great Britain in 2002 by Oxford University Press, Oxford

Mention should be made of subsequent publication of the same title, the same work with a different title, a later edition with additional content, or the same work in translation.

Copyright notices

Copyright notices take different forms depending on the country of publication, and whether the work is an original edition, reissue, paperback of original hardback, translation, etc. Different parts of a work may be covered by separate copyrights, such as an introduction or notes, parts of an anthology, or individual chapters in a multi-author text.

Publishers who include such notices normally follow a standard template. The following is an example:

> All rights reserved. No part of this publication may be reproduced, stored in a retrieval system, or transmitted, in any form or by any means, without the prior permission in writing of Oxford University Press, or as expressly permitted by law, or under terms agreed with the appropriate reprographics rights organization. Enquiries concerning reproduction outside the scope of the above should be sent to the Rights Department, Oxford University Press, at the address above.

For general guidelines on copyright *see* **CHAPTER 14**.

Assertion of moral rights

Standardly, this takes the form of a statement such as

> The moral right of [author's name] to be identified as the author of this work has been asserted in accordance with the Copyright Designs and Patents Act 1988.

or simply

> The author's moral rights have been asserted.

For more on moral rights *see* **14.2.4**.

Current edition, impression, and imprint

The edition, impression, and reprint of a work may be listed on the title verso; all three terms are distinct, and require some explanation.

In bibliographical terms, an *edition* is the state of a book or similar creation at its first publication. Separate editions are also counted after each revision, enlargement, abridgement, or change of format (second, third, etc.), or if it becomes revised, enlarged, abridged, paperbacked, or the like. An edition is distinct from a reprinting that contains no substantial alteration, which is an impression or reprint. In trade practice the number of the edition is indicated as *1/e, 2/e, 3/e*, etc. or superscript ^{1,2,3}, etc. following the title, signifying a first, second, third, etc. edition. Any of these three forms can be used in bibliographical references, providing it is imposed consistently.

An *impression* denotes all the copies of a book etc. printed at one press run from the same type, plates, etc. In trade practice this is indicated by *1/i, 2/i, 3/i*, etc. which stands for the first, second, third, etc. impression. *Impression* also has the technical meanings of the product from one cycle of a printing machine, the indentation in the paper by a printing surface, or the pressure between printing and impression surfaces.

In printing, *reprint* has three meanings: a second or new impression of any printed work, with only minor corrections; a reimpression with no corrections at all; or printed matter taken from some other publication for reproduction. When copy is centred, reprints can be indicated on the title verso by a centred line of alternating figures, normally one to ten (*1 3 5 7 9 10 8 6 4 2*); each digit stands for the number of a reprint. One figure is deleted with every subsequent printing so that the smallest remaining digit marks the reprint number: *3 5 7 9 10 8 6 4 2* indicates a second reprint, *3 5 7 9 10 8 6 4* a third reprint, and so forth. When copy is full left, figures are in descending order. More than nine reprints are indicated by higher numbers.

Geographical limitations on sales

The sales of some works may be circumscribed by geographical areas.

Any such limitations are denoted by, say, *For sale only in Canada* or *Not for sale outside the UK.*

Cataloguing in publication (CIP) data

Some national libraries—typically the British Library and the Library of Congress—compile CIP data, which is drawn from a sample of pages sent to them by the publisher before publication. Some publishers include this information, when it is available, or simply state: *Data available.* CIP data cannot be altered in any way; this includes the Library of Congress's US spelling of *cataloging.* Errors of fact can be corrected only with written permission from the issuing library.

International Standard Book Number (ISBN)

The ISBN is a unique number assigned to every edition of every book. Thus a book will have one ISBN for a hardback edition, a different ISBN for a paperback edition, a different ISBN for a revised or new edition, and a different ISBN for a co-publication in another language. Each volume of a multi-volume work will have a separate ISBN if it is for sale separately, as well as an ISBN for the set.

The ISBN is always ten digits divided into four parts, separated by en spaces or hyphens. The first part (one to five digits), called the Group Identifier, identifies the national, language, or geographical area in which the book is published. The Publisher Prefix (one to seven digits) identifies the publisher. The Title Number (one to six digits, depending on the number of digits preceding them) identifies the specific volume or edition of a work. The Check Digit (always one digit, 0–9 or X for ten) is used to check that the number is correct. The ISBN is also part of any bar code found on the back of a work or its dust jacket.

International Standard Series Number (ISSN)

The ISSN is a unique number assigned to a serial publication such as a journal, magazine, yearbook, or monograph series; the number does not vary from issue to issue. If the publication is composed of books, as with some series monographs, each volume is assigned an ISSN as well as an ISBN. The ISBN is printed on the same page as the work's copyright notice, or with the instructions for ordering publications. Since the last letter in *ISBN* and *ISSN* stands for *number*, the phrase *ISBN number* or *ISSN number* is tautological.

Performing rights agencies

Performing rights and copyright organizations license the public performance of non-dramatic musical works on behalf of the copyright owners; their names and addresses can appear on the title verso of printed music and related copy. Common agencies include ASCAP

(American Society of Composers, Authors, and Publishers), BMI (Broad-cast Music Incorporated), and SESAC (Society of European Songwriters, Artists and Composers).

Printer's and binder's names and locations

Some publishers include the name of the printer and binder responsible for producing the work. Where this changes for subsequent versions of the work, the data will need to be adjusted.

Other information

Some publishers may include the font type and size used in the text, though this may also be found (sometimes together with the printer's and binder's names and location) on the bottom of the work's final blank verso. In specialist works this may have a bibliographic interest, though in general it is of most immediate use to anyone who wishes to match the type.

1.2.6   Dedication

A dedication is a highly personal item, for which no rules can be given. Commonly centred on the page, it is open to a variety of typographic treatments, which should suit its subject and satisfy its author. Except when a book is part of a series, there is no reason why a dedication's presentation may not vary between otherwise equivalent volumes. When adjusting prelims to fit the available space, a dedication's size and autonomy often prompts its relocation to a convenient verso, preferably where its significance is not impaired.

1.2.7   Foreword

The foreword is an article about the book written by someone other than the author. The name of its author usually appears at the end, though it may be given under the heading, and may appear in the contents list. The title or affiliation of the foreword writer may also appear under his or her name.

1.2.8   Preface

The preface is the author's introductory address to the reader, in which he or she explains the purpose, prospective readership, and scope of the book, including what the author has decided to include and to omit. It is also the place for a brief acknowledgement to colleagues or advisers in the absence of an acknowledgements section.

A preface may serve the same purpose for the editor of a multi-author book, in which case it is sometimes called an *editor's* or *editorial preface*. It may, but need not, be signed with a date and location.

When a new preface accompanies a new edition, it precedes the original preface, which is then titled *Preface to the First Edition*. The new preface is titled *Preface to the Second Edition, Preface to the Paperback Edition, Preface to the Abridged Edition, Preface to the Student's Edition*, and so forth as appropriate. Successive editions are numbered consecutively and continue to be placed in reverse numerical order. A collection of several prefaces may be distinguished further by adding dates: *Preface to the Thirty-Ninth Edition (1983)*. Works that accumulate many prefaces may have the less significant ones weeded out to conserve space, or include only the first and last of them.

1.2.9 Acknowledgements

Acknowledgements are of two types: those recognizing ideas, assistance, support, or inspiration, and those cataloguing sources of copyright material. The former is a matter of academic integrity, requiring a writer to give credit for another's aid or thoughts—whether or not the same words are used to express them. The latter is a legal requirement, requiring a writer to obtain permission—from the original author or from his or her publisher or copyright holder—if the writer quotes the author's words (otherwise than covered by 'fair dealing'). Acknowledging the source of illustrations (figures, tables, diagrams, etc.) is a function of stating that the writer has obtained permission to reproduce them.

In text it is best to separate the two types of acknowledgement, in keeping with their distinct functions. A work with both types will be likely to have the first integrated into a preface, and the second either as a separate section or at the end of the preface. Copyright acknowledgements most often form a separate section. For acknowledgements in general *see* **14.4.3**; for illustrations acknowledgements *see* **10.8**.

1.2.10 Contents

The contents list is titled only *Contents*, not *List of Contents* or *Table of Contents*. It records the title and beginning page number of every separately titled section that follows it, including all lists in the prelims, parts and chapters, and all endmatter. It may list the frontispiece, but not the dedication or epigraph.

Lists are referred to as *List of*—in the contents list even though their own headings are simply *Illustrations, Abbreviations, etc*.

Use the word *Part* and list the part titles in full, but do not give a page reference if it is the same as that of the first chapter in that part. It is not essential to use the word *Chapter* before each number, even if it appears on the first page of the chapter (the *chapter opening* or *opener*). However, if the word is used in the contents list, it must be used for all chapters, not just the first one. Use *Appendix* before the number and title of each one or, if there are several, list them by number and title only under the heading *Appendices*.

Use roman numerals for part numbers and arabic numerals for chapter numbers: *Part I, Chapter 1*. (Alternatively, part numbers may be spelt out in words—*see* **1.3.2**.)

Chapter numbers should range right and be followed by an en space before the chapter title.

The wording, punctuation, and capitalization of part and chapter titles must be consistent with that used in text, although the designer may subsequently alter the styling, for example using even full capitals or full and small capitals rather than capitals and lower case.

If authors consider it helpful to the reader, they can include the first level of headings ('A' headings), and their numbering if any. Normally a detailed contents list, including titles and hierarchies of sections within chapters, is not necessary: do not list any 'B'-level heading or below; for any more detailed specification the right place is usually the index. In very long or complex works, however, or in the case of textbooks and schoolbooks, the first level or subsequent levels of subheading may also be included—or even set as subsidiary tables of contents at the start of each chapter.

Make sure that all wording and styling (use of italics, hyphens, capitals, etc.) is consistent with the final version of the headings in the edited script, and that all styling is consistent in the list. No full point should be used at the end of any heading, nor leader dots between the title and folio reference.

In multi-author (contributory) volumes, give the names of the author(s) of each chapter. The form for each name, whether initials or full given name and surname, must be consistent with the form in the chapter headings and list of contributors, if any. Each author can use whatever form of name he or she prefers; there is no need to impose consistency on full names or initials.

Editors should mark *allow for double figs* if necessary at the start of the list. Circle any folio numbers, to ensure that they are not printed; and add *000* to be set as page references, to act as a reminder to add the correct references at page proof.

When more than one volume is to be published simultaneously or at short intervals, the first volume should have a contents list and illustrations list, if relevant, for the entire edition. Each subsequent volume should contain a contents list and illustrations list for that volume only.

1.2.11 Table of cases, legislation, citations, etc.

A table of cases, table of legislation, table of citations, and so forth are a typical feature of legal works; some publishers place them instead in the endmatter. Each item is arranged alphabetically on a separate line, with italic components usually switched to roman type for clarity. *See also* **13.2.9**.

1.2.12 List of illustrations

The list of illustrations enables the reader to locate all figures, plates, or maps in a work. It precedes other lists, and is usually included only when readers will want to refer to illustrations independently of the text. Illustrations numbered consecutively in one sequence are presented in a single list titled *Illustrations* (*see* **10.9**). It is better to include the illustrations' sources and copyright acknowledgements in the list rather than in the captions, unless the copyright holder requires otherwise (*see* **10.8**). Alternatively, acknowledgements can be presented in a separate list in the prelims or endmatter.

1.2.13 List of tables

A list of tables is useful only when there are many tables that readers might need to refer to frequently and independently of the text. Only the title, shortened if necessary, and page number are given; the source appears in text under the table itself.

1.2.14 List of abbreviations

The list of abbreviations should contain all the items that will be of use to the readers, and none that are superfluous or common knowledge in the author's discipline. Which abbreviations need to be included varies from work to work, therefore, depending on the subject of the text and the anticipated knowledge of the readership. Common abbreviations that need no explanation in text, such as AD, BC, *ibid.*, UK, and USA, are not included in the list. If a term occurs very sporadically in text, it is preferable to spell it out at each occurrence rather than use an abbreviation.

Arrange the list alphabetically, and ensure each item is consistent with the form used in text: multi-author texts must adopt the same

abbreviations consistently throughout. While there is no absolute requirement for an abbreviation to mimic its expanded form, readers will
find it more logical for an abbreviation to be italic or roman and upper-
or lower-case where the full form appears that way: 'LSJ' for *A Greek–
English Lexicon* by Liddell, Scott, and Jones; *COD* for *The Concise Oxford
Dictionary*; 'hnRNA' for heterogeneous nuclear RNA. For conventions
governing legal abbreviations *see* **13.2.1**.

If the abbreviations cited are used in the text or notes, the list should
appear in the front rather than the back of the work, as it is easier for the
reader to refer to in the prelims. (If it is in the endmatter there is a risk
that some readers will not know it is there, finding it only after finishing
the book.) When the abbreviations cited are used only in the bibliography, endnotes, or an appendix, the list should be placed directly
before the section to which it relates.

1.2.15   List of contributors

This provides a register of the contributors in a given work, to help put
each writer in context. As such the amount and type of information can
vary a great deal, depending upon what data are thought useful for the
reader. While a simple roll of name and affiliation is usually called a *List
of contributors*, the more detailed or discursive the entries are, the more
suitable the title *Notes on contributors* will be, and the more likely it will
fall in the endmatter of the work rather than the preliminary pages.

The volume editor of a multi-author text should compile a list giving all
the contributors in alphabetical order. Each contributor's name should
match the form in the contents list and the chapter headings. This is
followed by the contributors' affiliations, which may include either
partial addresses (city and country) or full postal addresses (including
postal abbreviations and postcodes) and, if applicable, electronic addresses. Street addresses in a foreign language should be left in the
original form, but give the contributor's affiliation, university, and the
name of the country in English where necessary or usual. The addition
of any other information, such as important publications, recent
achievements, or previous posts, should be made as uniform as possible
for each contributor.

1.2.16   Epigraph

An epigraph is a relevant quotation placed at the beginning of a volume,
part, or chapter. It is distinguished typographically from other displayed
quotations. An epigraph referring to the entire volume is placed on a
new page, preferably a recto, before the contents list. Epigraphs for

parts or chapters may be placed on a verso facing, or under the heading of, the part or chapter to which they refer. The use of epigraphs and their positioning must be consistent throughout the work.

Separate two epigraphs in succession by at least a 6-point space. Separate a translation to an epigraph by no more than a 3-point space. Epigraph sources are ranged right under the quotation. If the reference is more than one line long, indent it 1 em from the start of the epigraph, with turn-lines ranged left on the beginning of the source.

The author's name and the title of the work are sufficient reference. Publication details and line numbers are not normally included; since an epigraph is not directly related to a book's subject matter, it is not expected that the readers will be impelled to look up the reference.

1.2.17 Introduction

The introduction should be about the subject matter of the book; it is distinct from a preface, and should not include the topics more at home there. A short introduction that is not vital to understanding the text is part of the prelims, and is paginated in roman numerals and not given a chapter number. An introduction that begins the subject matter and is indispensable to its understanding is part of the text, paginated in arabic numerals, and numbered with the subsequent chapters. Writers in the sciences especially may prefer to number an introduction as Chapter 0, leaving Chapter 1 for the first in the text. (For the effect of parts on an introduction, *see* **1.3.2**.)

1.2.18 Other sections

Any short general information that relates to the whole of a work can be placed in the prelims, as close as possible to the start of the text. This may include items that do not naturally fit elsewhere, such as a conversion table, an explanation of editorial or scholarly conventions, a note on conventions in cross-references or alphabetization, or a 'how to use this book' section. Lengthy subsidiary information, however, is best placed in the endmatter, typically as an appendix.

1.3 Text

An author's approach to a subject and the formation of the narrative often moulds the structure into which the text unfolds. Ideally, this should develop into a form in which each division—volume, part, chapter, section, and subsection—is of a size more or less the same as equivalent divisions. While it is rare to find a work that falls effortlessly into perfectly uniform divisions, and pointless forcing it to do so, a severely unbalanced structure often indicates a lopsided strategy or method. Authors and editors should therefore choose a hierarchy of divisions that most closely mirrors the natural composition of the work, and strive to rectify any aspects that seem unwieldy or sparse.

As part of marking up the text, the editor will normally label the hierarchy of headings *A*, *B*, *C*, etc. for those in text, and *X*, *Y*, *Z* for those in the preliminary matter or appendices. Each will later be styled (often by a design department) to provide an appropriate visual arrangement of section headings and subheadings.

For the presentation of footnotes *see* **2.4.7** and **15.16**; for endnotes *see* **1.4.1**.

1.3.1 Volumes

A *volume* is a set of printed sheets of paper, bound together and forming part or the whole of a work, or comprising several works. Each book of a work published in more than one volume must have its own pagination, index, bibliography, and so forth if it is to act as a wholly independent work in its own right, able to be purchased and used separately from the other companion volumes. Those published to form a subsidiary part of a larger work may share features between several volumes, although ease of use for the reader may be vitiated if several features of a volume are dependent on other volumes.

Books included in a multi-volume work may be identified in several ways. Some are numbered, or numbered and individually titled. Some may not have separate volume numbers, and others (such as the individual volumes making up a collection of correspondence) may be labelled with a year extent alone. Still others divided naturally by subject may have titles but no numbers, to avoid the imposition of an artificial hierarchy or chronology, as for a three-volume set of Shakespeare's works: *Comedies*, *Histories*, and *Tragedies*. In references, volumes are typically styled in lower-case roman numerals, such as *i*, *iv*, *xxvi*, though this style may vary in certain disciplines, circumstances, and languages, and will not be based on the original's typography.

Even if numbering of text pages is consecutive from one volume to the next, the prelim pages of each volume should begin with page i.

Multiple volumes to be published simultaneously or at short intervals should have in the first volume a list of contents and a list of illustrations (if any) for the whole edition. Each subsequent volume should then contain a list of contents and illustrations for that volume only.

A work may be published in instalments called *fascicles* (or *fascicules*) rather than in volumes. Though less common than it was formerly, the practice is still found for some large scholarly works, especially those published over the course of many years. While fascicles are technically separate works with unique ISBNs, they are—unlike volumes—designed to be bound together into a single book once their total is complete. (Fascicles for multi-volume works are arranged and presented accordingly.) An individual book's fascicles are paginated in a single sequence, with prelims or endmatter specific to each fascicle discarded during collation. Typically the first fascicle contains the preliminary matter for the book, just as the last contains any index.

1.3.2 Parts

Arranging a work into parts is useful when a lengthy text falls easily and sensibly into logical divisions of similar length. Parts should be numbered and may also be titled. Ideally, the number and title appear on a recto, and the following verso is blank or illustrated. If there is insufficient room for this arrangement, the part title may appear on the same page as the first chapter in that part, distinguished typographically and with space. In non-fiction, parts are traditionally numbered in roman numerals (*Part I*, *Part II*, *Part III*), though especially in fiction they may be spelt out (*Part One*, *Part Two*, *Part Three*).

Part title pages are included in the arabic pagination, but the numbers are not expressed. Parts are subdivided into chapters, which are numbered consecutively throughout the work, not afresh with each part.

When an introduction, summary, or conclusion addresses the work as a whole rather than one part it is usual, but not mandatory, to leave it unnumbered. For example, if a three-part work with twelve chapters begins with an introduction and ends with a conclusion, the unnumbered introduction will precede Part I and Chapter 1, and the unnumbered conclusion will follow Part III and Chapter 12. When each part has an introduction, summary, or conclusion of its own, it is numbered in the same sequence as other chapters in the work.

Plate sections falling at the end of a work are introduced by their own part title.

1.3.3 Chapters

Most prose works are divided into chapters, which may be given a title, a number (usually in arabic figures), or—especially in non-fiction—both.

The decision is influenced by how useful the form is for the reader, and how many cross-references there might be to that level of division. The use of the word *Chapter* with a number is optional.

The first page of a chapter does not have a running head; its page number appears at the foot of the page (*drop folio*) even when the numbering appears in the head margin on other pages.

Chapter titles

Chapter titles should be a reasonable indication of the contents of the chapter. They should not be too long, as this makes design and running heads awkward.

In a multi-author work, where the chapters are produced by different authors, chapter headings include the name of the contributor (*see* **1.5.1**). This should match that given in a list of contributors.

Chapter openings

Chapter openings may be styled in many ways. Commonly the first line following a chapter head is set full left, with no paragraph indentation. To provide a more finished look to the page, spaced large and small capitals may be used to set the first word or words of a chapter 'THUS' to introduce the text: 'CALL me Ishmael.' Editors should mark up texts according to the following rules:

If the first word is a single capital letter (e.g. I, A), then the second word is spaced small capitals, with no further capital: 'I AM Ishmael.' If the chapter starts with a personal name, then the whole name is spaced capitals and small capitals, *not* just the first name: 'ISHMAEL BLOGGS they call me.' Do not implement this style if any of the chapters contain a subheading preceding the text, whether in words or simply a number like 2.1.

These rules still apply after an epigraph at the start of a chapter. (The epigraph itself starts with ordinary capital and lower-case letters.) If a chapter begins with a displayed quotation, style either the first word(s) of the quotation in spaced capital and small capitals, or the first word(s) of the text that follows at the quotation's end, but not both.

Drop initials

Another typographic device used to start a chapter is the *drop initial*. This is the first letter of a chapter opening, descending two or more lines below the first line, with all lines affected by the drop set shorter to accommodate it. A frequent feature of older typesetting, drop initials fell into disuse because of the setting problems they presented. In the days of hot-metal type, several refinements to the setting of drop initials commonly needed to be made to accommodate the initial letter's shape, which now are made electronically.

THESE three divers
general use in the
have at least four
although known in th
is a solid derived chie
industry was still in it

VIKINGS were kno
especially in the f
they had to use t
areas in which they w
succeeded by selectio
opened up a phase in

WHETHER his fir
but we can be
he did not begi
since it appears to be
that could be employ
either by using a new

YELLOW fields cha
production of cro
the other hand lat
cultivation, once thou
rapid growers must h
shrubs and trees, and

For balance, an initial letter with a projecting left-hand stem should overhang into the margin, unless there are marginal notes or numbers immediately in front of it. If a quotation mark is required before a drop initial, it should be set in the margin in the same size as the text, not the same size as the initial letter.

Where the drop initial is the first letter of a word, avoid a gap between the initial and following letters by kerning. A three-line drop initial, for example, requires that the second and third lines should align and range clear of the letter.

AMONG the results o
the long battle w
in the prohibition
protection against the
uranium, for instance,
for this purpose when

LOCATED at well defi
which break away
the beginning of th
colonies with few rings
but his proposal for the
which was in fact in us

1.3.4 Sections and subsections

Chapters may be divided into sections and subsections by the use of subheadings (*subheads*). There may be one or more levels of subhead; the first level is called the A-head, the second level the B-head, and so on. Some works just have A-heads, and only complex, high-level works will require more than C-heads. Well-structured texts tend to have chapters with parallel structures of subheads, though occasionally this may prove impossible. Too many levels of subhead are more confusing than helpful. Subheads should be short and clearly indicate the contents of the section.

Choosing whether to label each section with a title or number or both is largely a function of how useful it will be to the reader, and how many cross-references there may be to that level of division. The editor will label and mark up section and subsection headings on the *typescript* (the term for a typed or printout manuscript). Variations in placement (e.g. centred, full-left, indented, marginal, run-in) and in type (e.g. bold, italic, small capital, choice of typeface) will later be determined by designers according to the hierarchy appropriate for that book, taking into account any series style. Barring the general rule that larger divisions should be styled to look more important than smaller divisions, there are few regulations governing such choices, although in practice run-in headings are not normally used for subsections longer than a couple of pages. Typically the first line following a section head is set full left and has no paragraph indentation, unless the style is for the text to run into the head.

If there will be extensive cross-references to subheads, they can also be numbered or in 'outline' form (I, A, 1, (a), i). Numbering should reflect the level of heading. For example, the first numeral is that of the chapter. It is followed by a full point and then a number for the A-head: 9.2 is the second A-head in Chapter 9. If the B-heads are also numbered, their reference follows that of the A-head: 9.2.2 is the second B-head under the second A-head in Chapter 9. If the cross-references will be to the individual paragraphs, they can be numbered instead of the subheads, so that 9.2 refers to the second paragraph in Chapter 9. The first line of text under a subhead should not refer back to it with a pronoun; rather the subject should be repeated in full.

1.3.5 Paragraphs

Length

No absolute rules regulate a paragraph's length, since its size is a function of the arrangement and flow of the text it contains. As Fowler says, 'The paragraph is essentially a unit of thought, not of length: it must be homogeneous in subject-matter and sequential in treatment.' To avoid losing the reader's attention or interest, you may need to divide a succession of very long paragraphs, or splice together a succession of very short paragraphs. As a general rule a paragraph in a typescript folio is at least double the length of the same paragraph once set into type in normal measure, so each needs to be at least five lines long to avoid breaking up the finished page too much.

Indentation

It is common not to indent the first paragraph in each chapter (*see* **1.3.3**), or the first new paragraph following a heading, subheading, or line space. In each case the first line of any subsequent paragraph is usually indented only 1 em for full measures; further indentation for subheadings may be designed to be staggered in another 1 em for each level, although complex hierarchies may require more complicated design structuring. Alternatively, a line may be left between paragraphs, which is a common practice in typing and in computer printouts. But this has the disadvantage of failing to show where a paragraph begins at the top of the next page.

In written dialogue, a new paragraph indent is normally required for each new speaker or interruption. (For general guidance *see* **8.1**.)

Numbered paragraphs

Many works—particularly those that need to be updated on a regular basis, such as textbooks and practitioner texts—have numbered paragraphs (*1.1, 1.2, 1.3*, etc.), set either in the margins or at the beginning of headings. Depending on the work's structure, these may be in addition to or instead of section and subsection numbering.

Numbered paragraphs afford greater accuracy in cross-references, index, tables, and supplements, since a paragraph number is usually more specific than a page number.

Authors should assign a number to each section of text that deals with a separate point or concept. There should be a paragraph number next to each heading; paragraphs under that heading which discuss related concepts may also be numbered, but not all grammatical paragraphs need or should be.

The author is normally expected to introduce paragraph numbers as part of the writing process. It is useful to leave the paragraph numbering to the final stage of producing the typescript, should a new paragraph need to be inserted. It is acceptable—and may be preferable from the publisher's point of view—for the paragraph numbers to be written in the margin by hand. Remember also to insert the correct paragraph numbers into cross-references.

1.3.6 Conclusion, epilogue, afterword

A *conclusion* sums up the work's findings and puts them in context; it acts as a final chapter, and is numbered accordingly. An *epilogue* is much shorter than a conclusion, serving only as a brief comment on or conclusion to the preceding text. An *afterword* is much the same, though typically it is written by someone other than the author. The presence of an introduction or foreword does not necessitate the inclusion of any of these sections.

Neither an epilogue nor an afterword bears a chapter number. The headings for each should match the typography for the preliminary headings.

1.4 **Endmatter**

Endmatter, also called *back matter* in the USA, is any supplementary data that follow the text of a work, such as endnotes, appendix, glossary, bibliography, or index. Though endmatter is paginated in sequence with the preceding text, it falls outside the text's internal hierarchy, again like prelims. Endmatter tends to be set in smaller type than the text, in keeping with its subsidiary position.

While publishers try to keep endmatter to a minimum, as with prelims, an even working can result in spare pages at the end of a work. These are sometimes filled with a publisher's advertisements for related books or series.

A plate section too awkward or large to divide and fit into the body of the text may be placed as the final item in the endmatter, preceded by its own part title.

1.4.1 **Endnotes**

Endnotes may replace or supplement footnotes in a work. Where used, they are the first section in the endmatter, typically set one size down from text size. For setting out endnotes *see* **2.4.7**; for running heads to endnotes *see* **1.5.1**.

1.4.2 **Appendix**

An *appendix* (sometimes called an *annexe*, especially with documents) is a section or table of subsidiary matter such as chronologies, genealogical tables, survey questionnaires, or texts of documents, laws, or correspondence discussed in the text. They may be numbered with arabic or roman numerals, or with letters. While appendices are useful for including information that relates directly to the text but which cannot comfortably be incorporated within it, authors should severely limit their content to information that clearly aids understanding of the text, rather than the raw data from which it was derived.

An excursus to a particular chapter normally runs on in text as an appendix to that chapter alone, unless it is relevant to other chapters or especially unwieldy, in which case it is relegated to the end of the whole book.

1.4.3 **Bibliography**

A *bibliography* is an integral part of a book's system of references, and should contain all specific sources mentioned—or mentioned more than once—within that book. If a work has only a handful of references it may be possible to do without a bibliography. Authors who cite a number of works frequently but others only once or twice may find a list of 'Abbreviations and Works Frequently Cited' (in the preliminary matter) sufficient. However, the greater the number and complexity of the references, the greater the need for a bibliography. A bibliography may be of four kinds, designated by different names.

- A straightforward *Bibliography* contains all works cited in the book. Additionally it may contain works not cited, but of oblique influence upon the book, or of potential interest to the reader. An *Annotated Bibliography* contains comments on some or all of the sources.

- A list of *References* or *Works Cited* is limited to all works cited in the book itself. This type (labelled *References*) is appropriate for short bibliographies and books using the author–date (Harvard) system or author–number (Vancouver) system and should not include subdivisions.

- A *Select Bibliography* may be limited to works thought important by the author, or to works mentioned more than once. A headnote may be added explaining the coverage. All works cited by short title must be included.

- A *Further Reading* section is often discursive, and may have the works arranged in paragraphs by chapter or topic rather than by alphabetical order. Often found in textbooks or more general introductory books, it may be subdivided into parts at the end of each chapter rather than assembled as a single section at the end of the book. Normally it will include works not cited but of potential interest to the reader.
  See also **CHAPTER 15**.

1.4.4 Glossary

A *glossary* is an alphabetical list of important terms found in the text, with explanations or definitions. It is not a substitute for explaining them at first occurrence in text, but rather a helpful collection of those terms that the readership would find unfamiliar. A glossary has a separate line for each headword. Those in two columns (headwords on the left, definitions or explanations on the right) are separated by a minimum 1 em space between the longest headword and the second column, with turn-lines not indented. Those with the definitions or explanations run in after the headword have indented turn-lines, to make the headwords more prominent.

1.4.5 Index

An *index* is an alphabetical list by title, subject, author, or other category; these may—but need not—be divided into separate indexes. It is commonly the final element in a work. *See also* **CHAPTER 16**.

1.4.6 Colophon

A *colophon* is a publisher's emblem, device, or imprint, especially one on the title page. Historically it was a statement at the end of a book, typically with a printer's emblem, giving information about its authorship and printing—data now found on the title and title verso pages.

The term is also used to describe a set of any additional facts about the book's publication that are not found on the title verso. These are normally topics considered to be of purely bibliographical interest, such as the history of the edition, typographer's or printer's name, typeface and composing machine, paper, and binding. (The paper and binding may vary between impressions as well as editions, making the information liable to become dated and require correction.) A colophon of this type is typically set at the very back of the book, often on the last recto. Numbering of copies in fine or specialist editions also forms part of the colophon, which is then usually placed in the prelims.

1.5 **Running headlines**

Running headlines, also called *headlines*, *running titles*, *pageheads*, or simply *running heads*, are single lines used to top the pages of the printed book, to help the reader find his or her way around in it. They may take many forms, although most follow standard rules determined by the type of book for which they are designed. Running heads often are on the same line as the numerals of pagination, which are usually set in the outer corners of the spread; technically the entire line is the running head, though in editorial (if not production) work the term commonly describes only the text it contains.

In some publications—such as journals or textbooks—all or part of the running head can be set at the foot of the page, in which case it is called a *running footline* or *running foot*. This is relatively rare in monographs, especially those with footnotes.

1.5.1 Placement and content

Running heads are not set on the following pages: half-title, title, imprint, dedication, epigraph, part title, chapter openings and their equivalents (such as the first pages of the contents, other lists, appendix, notes, and index), and blanks. They are also not used on turned pages (those whose contents are displayed landscape) and those containing tables or illustrations that impinge on the headline space.

Each element in the prelims usually has the same running head on verso and recto. The same is true for elements in the endmatter that are not subdivided, such as a glossary, single appendix, or bibliography. If there is more than one appendix, the verso can carry *Appendix 1* and the recto can carry the appendix title.

Running heads are typically divided between those falling on the recto and the verso; in many books the chapter title is most suitable for both recto and verso. The publication's format constrains the running head's length: in books this means that about forty characters and spaces are available for a royal or demy text, with more or less space available depending also on the size and style of the text. (In most fonts small-capital text, for example, takes up more room than italic text.) Running heads drawn from headings longer than the page width allows must be shortened; for consistency's sake, similar headings should be shortened in similar ways. Long titles that resist paring sometimes can be divided between the heads of both pages, to read across the page spread. Here an appropriate split must be found between verso and recto, so that neither is a nonsense when read in isolation: division at a colon, conjunction, or preposition is usually best.

When listing distinct internal divisions, the larger section is listed on the verso and the smaller on the recto; most often these are set in standard combinations. Single-author books may have the chapter or book title on the verso and the chapter title on the recto. Books with parts may have the part title on the verso and the chapter title on the recto. Multi-author books may have the contributor's name on the verso and the chapter or article title on the recto. Journals and periodicals may incorporate their title, the date or issue number, or both.

Running heads for endnotes should indicate on both recto and verso the inclusive text pages or chapters to which the notes refer. If chapters do not have titles, as is the case with some fiction, there is no need for running heads.

If an editor needs to trim words from an author's chapter titles to create running heads, he or she must supply a list for the author to vet. Ordinarily running heads follow the same capitalization rules as for titles, although they may be designed in various ways.

Where a new section heading falls at the beginning of a recto, its title normally provides the recto running head. Where more than one heading falls on one page, either the first or last title on the page provides the running head, so long as the choice is consistently applied throughout the work. Where the first section heading does not fall directly at the chapter's start, the chapter title should be repeated on the recto until the heading appears in text. Similarly in preliminary matter, or appendices, bibliography, and such—anything with no internal divisions—the title should be repeated recto as well as verso.

1.5.2 Complex running heads

It is best to avoid running heads that rely on combinations of chapter titles and section headings, or on summaries of page content. This is especially true if the sections or subjects are only a few pages long, since a reader searching for the subject of a specific section or subsection would be better served by the index, and running heads that vary with nearly every page are problematic to set and expensive to adjust.

If, however, the work contains an intricate structure with complex hierarchies of headings and subheadings (as with some reference books and textbooks), the reader may need such specific running heads. In this case, it may be useful to include the section number—if any—in the running head along with its heading. Rarely, *shoulder heads* can supplement the running heads: these are additional headlines (usually section, paragraph, or line numbers) that fall either between the running head and the page number on the outside edge, or between the running head and the gutter on the inside edge. A minimum of 1 em separates one element from another. The extra space they demand requires that running heads be even shorter: in practice shoulder heads should be discouraged in all save large-format books and double-column reference works.

1.5.3 Reference works

Running heads in works such as dictionaries, lexicons, encyclopedias, anthologies, and catalogues are typically drawn from the first and last items on each page or spread of pages. Although some dictionaries use only the first three letters of the first and last entries in the running heads, it is best to provide the whole word in each case. In double-column reference works a shoulder head is used on the inner and outer measure of each page, with the page number centred between them. (If necessary the parts of a crowded running headline can be separated by a symbol, such as a vertical or solidus.) In the practice of some UK publishers the first shoulder head on each page formerly was taken from whatever matter continued on from the previous page; now it is more commonly taken from the first full reference on that page.

1.6 **Errata slips**

An *errata slip* list errors and their corrections; use *erratum* (the singular) *slip* if there is only one error. They are expensive to produce and insert, and should be used to correct major errors only: the presence of an errata slip is often more detrimental to a reader's initial judgement of a book than the errors it remedies.

A list of errata should be as concise as possible and should make clear the substance of the error and the form of the correction. Use italic for the editorial directions *for, read,* etc. and spell out *line* so that the abbreviation is not confused with the numeral 1. Do not use full points at the end of the line or quotation marks unless they are part of the error or correction:

> p. 197, line 9: *for* 2.5 mg digoxin PO *read* 0.25 mg digoxin PO
>
> p. 204, line 15: *for* live wire *read* earth wire
>
> p. 399, line 2: *for* guilty. *read* 'not proven'.

Errata can be arranged in tabular form, in which the column headings could equally be *location, erratum,* and *correction*:

page and line number	for	read
p. 197, line 9	2.5 mg digoxin PO	0.25 mg digoxin PO
p. 204, line 15	live wire	earth wire
p. 399, line 2	guilty.	'not proven'.

Some corrections—such as transposition of sentences, figures, or items in a caption or table—do not lend themselves to straightforward text substitution, and may require a more discursive explanation or, exceptionally, the replacement copy in its entirety.

Errata slips are usually inserted loose into books, and for this reason should be labelled with the author's name, book title, and ISBN. Alternatively, errata may be tipped in, or set as part of the endmatter (formerly as part of the prelims), usually in a subsequent imprint or edition where the means or time does not exist to correct the text itself. When fixed to a book the errata may also be called *corrigenda* (singular *corrigendum*).

1.7 **Paper and book sizes**

1.7.1 **Paper sizes**

Originally, paper sizes were determined by the moulds the paper was made in and the use the result was put to. While many hundreds of variations have occurred throughout the centuries, in the main there have seldom been more than six categories of sizes in use since the fourteenth century. These have often come down to us bearing the names of the figures featured in the paper's watermarks, such as *foolscap, elephant, pot*, and *crown*. To enable the creation of smaller sizes from existing larger sizes, the sheets have since the Middle Ages been proportioned with their sides in the ratio of $1:\sqrt{2}$. For example, quarto (4to, formerly 4to) and octavo (8vo, formerly 8vo) sizes are obtained by cutting or folding standard sizes four and eight times respectively.

Former British paper dimensions still used the old sizes before decimalized versions replaced them; US dimensions still retain most of these (untrimmed) paper sizes, in inches. Both are still encountered in specialist and bibliographic work, and in reproducing earlier or foreign formats:

SIZE	STANDARD	4TO	8VO
imperial	22 × 30	15 × 11	11 × 7½
elephant	20 × 27	13½ × 10	10 × 6¾
royal	20 × 25	12½ × 10	10 × 6¼
small royal	25 × 19	12½ × 9½	9½ × 6¼
medium	18 × 23	11½ × 9	9 × 5¾
demy	17½ × 22½	11¼ × 8¾	8¾ × 5⅝
crown	15 × 20	10 × 7½	7½ × 5
post	19 × 15½	18½ × 14½ ('pinched post')	16½ × 21 ('large post')
foolscap	17 × 13½	8½ × 6¾	6¾ × 4¼
pot	12½ × 15½	7¾ × 6¼	6¼ × 3⅞

Metric sizes emulated the original categories of dimensions, and copied many of the old names. Common metric (untrimmed) paper sizes are as follows, in millimetres:

SIZE	QUAD SHEET	4TO	8VO
metric crown	768 × 1,008	252 × 192	192 × 126
metric large crown	816 × 1,056	264 × 204	204 × 132
metric demy	888 × 1,128	282 × 222	222 × 141
metric royal	960 × 1,272	318 × 240	240 × 159

International paper sizes have been standardized still further by the ISO (International Standards Organization), formerly the DIN (Deutsche Industrie-Norme). Its system is divided into three series: A is the commonest, used for business correspondence, xerography, etc.; B is used for posters, wall charts, and similar large items, as well as instances where a size falling between existing A sizes is required; C is used for envelopes and folders to fit A-series sizes, and for envelopes within envelopes. A and B (trimmed) sizes are as follows, in millimetres:

A SERIES		B SERIES	
A0	841 × 1,189	B0	1,000 × 1,414
A1	594 × 841	B1	707 × 1,000
A2	420 × 594	B2	500 × 707
A3	297 × 420	B3	353 × 500
A4	210 × 297	B4	250 × 353
A5	148 × 210	B5	176 × 250
A6	105 × 148	B6	125 × 176
A7	74 × 105	B7	88 × 125
A8	52 × 74		
A9	37 × 52		
A10	26 × 37		

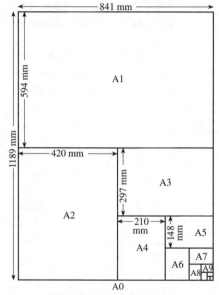

Figure 1.1: **International paper sizes A**

Quantities in paper measures differ according to whether printing paper or writing paper is being gauged:

PRINTING PAPER	WRITING PAPER
516 sheets = 1 ream	480 sheets = 1 ream
2 reams = 1 bundle	24 sheets = 1 quire
5 bundles = 1 bale	20 quires = 1 ream

1.7.2 Book sizes

The following are the standard octavo trimmed, untrimmed, and quad book sizes, in millimetres and inches:

SIZE	MILLIMETRES	INCHES
metric crown 8vo		
trimmed	186 × 123	7.32 × 4.84

untrimmed	192 × 126	7.56 × 4.96
quad	768 × 1008	30.24 × 39.69
metric large crown 8vo		
trimmed	198 × 129	7.80 × 5.08
untrimmed	204 × 132	8.03 × 5.20
quad	816 × 1056	32.13 × 41.57
metric demy 8vo		
trimmed	216 × 138	8.50 × 5.43
untrimmed	222 × 141	8.74 × 5.55
quad	888 × 1128	34.96 × 44.41
metric royal 8vo		
trimmed	234 × 156	9.21 × 6.14
untrimmed	240 × 159	9.45 × 6.26
quad	960 × 1272	37.80 × 50.08
A5		
trimmed	210 × 148	8.27 × 5.83
untrimmed	215 × 152.5	8.46 × 6.00
quad	860 × 1220	33.86 × 48.03

CHAPTER 2

Preparation of copy and proofs

2.1 **General principles**

This chapter will be of interest to authors, editors, and proofreaders. Not all parts will interest all of them equally, but an understanding of the roles of each is essential to a smooth and trouble-free transition to finished page. Sections **2.2** and **2.3** concern the presentation of authors' material, and the editor's role in copy-editing; **2.4** addresses the conventions of spacing and indentation in text, while **2.5** and **2.6** describe proofreading and proof-correction marks and the general principles for typeset matter.

A book or other printed work is made up of *pages*, a typescript from which it is derived is made up of *folios*. (*Typescript* is preferable to *manuscript* when describing copy that is not handwritten.) Throughout this guide, and particularly in this chapter, such terms as *typescript*, *typeset*, *page*, and *print* should be understood to include also the finished products of non-paper media, where applicable. While regard for page breaks, for example, is superfluous where text can be scrolled on screen and margins adjusted, nevertheless many fundamentals of that text's presentation and layout remain applicable, as does the way in which it is produced. Regardless of the method of publication, text in all media tends to jump through the same sequence and sorts of hoops on the way to publication, though the names of the hoops will differ. Consequently, it is still appropriate to consider print publication as offering a broad template for how text can best be produced. The human eye has not altered, nor have readers' basic requirements and expectations.

2.2 **Author's presentation of material**

This section is designed for authors who expect to prepare a typescript for publication; it provides guidelines for submission of copy for general and academic books. Authors can find specific instructions for particular components of a work under various headings throughout this book, and through their own publisher. Every text is unique, and may require different treatment; there is no substitute for authors' contacting their publisher in the first instance, as he or she will be able to offer advice based on the particular set of circumstances in which that work will be published.

2.2.1 Before submission

Check your typescript carefully before it is submitted. This checking applies particularly to quotations, bibliographical details in notes and bibliography (which must match), numerical date, proper nouns, consistency of spelling and capitalization, correct grading of headings, and numbering of tables and figures. It is always worth inspecting the wording in the contents page to ensure that it matches the wording in the text. A typescript that is uniformly and clearly presented allows it to be published more quickly, cheaply, and accurately than one that is not.

Think carefully about your book's structure—its division into parts, chapters, and major and minor sections. Ensure that the hierarchy of sections, subsections, and sub-subsections within chapters is clear. If you find yourself going beyond a third level of heading it may be time to rethink the structure—though the complexity of the subject may demand an elaborate structure.

For every printed work, length is a critical factor; your work's length will usually have been specified in the publisher's agreement. Ever-rising costs of production make it essential that no book should be longer then necessary. If it is, a great deal of time and effort may be needed to put matters right. (Editors of multi-author books (*see* **2.2.7**) are particularly likely to encounter these and kindred problems.) Careful planning of the text and illustrations (which contribute significantly to the total production cost) and equally careful writing will ensure that the work's journey to publication is as trouble-free as possible.

2.2.2 Editorial style

Each element in a book or other publication follows a style, through conscious or unconscious choice, and publishers tend to have a point of view about what that style might entail. Most have preferences about such things as the spelling of certain words; the use of punctuation; the layout of headings, paragraphs, quotations, and lists; the make-up of pages; the order and contents of the preliminary matter; and the construction of notes and references. The experience of those who apply these preferences in editing, designing, and printing works for a given publishing house often combine to establish a set of principles proven to work for that publisher. These principles—passed down, adjusted, and refined over time—evolve naturally into what is commonly referred to as *house style*. While a house style is distinct from the commonly accepted rules of grammar, spelling, and usage—which are for the most part inviolable in good writing—it will draw upon them, and editors will apply both in carrying out their task.

For Oxford University Press publications, the rudiments of these preferences are found in this work and in *The Oxford Dictionary for Writers and Editors* (ODWE). Publishers generally request authors to go along with, or implement themselves, house style wherever they can. Nevertheless, every work presents its own problems, and authors with strong views about particular points can and should raise them with the publisher before editing begins. While a publisher may find it difficult or impractical to comply with every preference, there are a wide range of matters on which an author can be accommodated, depending on the media involved: the uniformity of presentation and tight timetables required by many periodicals—especially those online—often means that editors can be less flexible in matters of style.

2.2.3 Covering note

A covering note with the typescript affords an opportunity for you to explain to the publisher, and by extension your editor, any peculiarities, partiality, or special conventions specific to your discipline—such as an unusual system of reference, capitalization, italics, or notation. With it both publisher and editor are better equipped to understand your wishes from the outset, before editing begins, and iron out any inadvertent deviations from your preferred policy, or warn of problems that you may not have envisaged.

Some authors sensibly set out their weaknesses, the points on which they know they have been inconsistent, and the points which they are not fussy about: all this provides a feel for the extent of editorial intervention that may be necessary or welcome. Likewise, if you quote frequently from books and articles in languages that you do not know thoroughly, it is a good idea to indicate that an editor familiar with these languages should if possible be used.

2.2.4 Presentation of material

Any typescript submitted for publication must be complete. Authors should supply the top copy, as it will be the clearest version and thus

most suitable for the typesetter. You should supply a second, photocopied version of the typescript: this saves time because two departments
(e.g. editorial and design) can then work on the book simultaneously.
You should also, of course, retain another photocopy for yourself.

The text should be on A4 paper (210 × 297 mm) or the nearest equivalent, such as the US 8½ × 11 inches. Use only one side of the paper,
leaving a generous margin on all sides, but especially on the left-hand
side, where much of the mark-up will take place. A golden rule is never
to spare paper: in a book of any complexity it is vital that the arrangement should be clear, and nothing muddles clarity like economy in
paper. Do not fasten copy in a ring binder, spiral binding, or the like.

All copy—notes, appendices, displayed material, bibliography, captions,
as well as main text—must be double-spaced (not 1½-line space), in 12-
point type. If possible, produce your copy with a serif font such as Times
New Roman rather than a sans serif font such as Helvetica, since a serif
face helps the editor to visualize whether or which sorts have been
correctly achieved. Submit all copy unjustified, set full (flush) left with
an uneven (ragged) right-hand margin. Type the first line of text below
all headings without a paragraph indent.

Italic in text can be indicated *thus* or <u>thus</u>, depending on the equipment
at your disposal. Both will be set as italic unless you indicate otherwise.

It is generally preferable for both foot- and endnotes to be supplied on
separate sheets from the main text, either at the end of the chapter to
which they relate or at the end of the typescript: this does *not* oblige the
finished work to have endnotes. While typesetters once found it difficult
or impossible to use files employing the automated footnoting facility
available in word-processing packages, this is less true than formerly.
Nevertheless, editors still find it demanding to style and cross-check a
run of note copy consistently if it is not presented in a single sequence,
particularly when standard footnote settings generate single-spaced
copy smaller than text size. Since many authors find automated footnoting convenient, it is often simplest to ensure that any footnote copy can
be produced double-spaced, text-size, and as endnotes before printing
out the final typescript hard copy (printout). Check to see if your publisher has any preferences in this regard; *see also* **2.2.5**.

Number the preliminary matter in roman numerals, and the rest of the
typescript consecutively in arabic numbers, including notes, bibliography, and any endmatter. Do not number by chapter: if the typescript
is dropped or accidentally shuffled, everything must be able to be re-
ordered. The goal is not to anticipate the pagination of the finished work,
but rather to ensure that every item is accounted for in a single sequence.

Avoid hyphenating words unnecessarily at the end of lines (especially as the result of a word processor's automatic hyphenation mode). It may be difficult to remain consistent in hyphenating words and phrases throughout a text: *multivalent* can rub shoulders with *multi-valent*, *shop worker* with *shopworker*, etc. Ordinarily an editor will impose the publisher's preferences upon the text, unless you have a good reason for a particular preference common in your subject.

Print-ready copy

If you are planning to generate your own print-ready copy (prc) of figures, tables, maps, or similar displayed matter or artwork, discuss this with your publisher, who will provide guidance on presentation, dimensions, typeface compatibility, and styling.

Individual pieces of prc may be stripped into proofs once the text has been typeset. Where prc is to be photographed for reproduction, take care not to mark or write on it, except on wide margins or on labels (usually stuck on the reverse); this is sometimes called *camera-ready copy* (crc). For this reason any prc of illustrations or figures, for example, included for mark-up with a typescript should be supplied as photocopies—*not* the originals. Similarly, demonstrate instructions for cropping on a rough copy.

For general guidelines for illustrations *see* **CHAPTER 10**; for computer-generated copy *see* **2.2.5**.

Contents list

Provide a contents page, listing the chapters in the order in which they appear; this forms part of a work's preliminary matter (*see* **1.2**). It should record the title and page reference of everything that follows it and nothing that precedes it. Include folio numbers relating to the numbered typescript, which makes it easy to locate sections of the text during editing.

Previously published copy

Some material for inclusion in text may already have been typeset; if it is lengthy (e.g. a document for an appendix) or complicated (e.g. equations or concrete poetry), submitting a photocopy of the original may be preferable to reproducing it afresh in text. Authors should ensure that any photocopy is clear, with sufficient margins to allow mark-up. Within the bounds of copyright, a contribution's having been previously published is usually no bar to making it conform to basic house style and the conventions adopted elsewhere, providing that it is to be set anew. However, photographic reproduction of work already generated by different typesetters—as for a multi-author text where the copy is used as crc—makes all editorial changes virtually impossible. Here, only the most rudimentary consistency is imposed, for example in the pagination, chapter titles, and running heads. In either case the volume editor should ask his or her publisher whether permission to reproduce the work will need to be secured.

Bibliography or references section

Like all other references, a bibliography or list of references can vary greatly in presentation and format; this is a function as much of convention as of the information it contains (*see* **1.4.3**). Whatever the format, the information must be presented in a manner that is both uniform and clear. If, in exceptional circumstances, it is advisable to depart from a format familiar to readers, it must be easily intelligible.

Apart from its ultimate use for the reader in looking up references, a bibliography is essential for cross-checking and standardizing references before the book is even printed. Authors should verify all citations just before the preparation of final copy. Once the typescript has been submitted, one of the editor's major tasks is to spot discrepancies between notes and bibliography. The more that are found, the greater will be the delay in completing the editing, since the author will then need to answer more queries. And if one frequently cited reference is found to be incorrect, extensive changes in the typescript will be necessary. Bibliography programs that extract footnotes from a database and generate a bibliography will hinder the useful exercise of cross-checking. When using such programs it is doubly important to make sure that citations are correct in the first place.

2.2.5　**Books prepared on computer**

Many authors find it advantageous to produce their work on computer, which can yield the added benefit of allowing the text to be transferred direct to typesetting equipment from an author's files. If you are considering supplying your text electronically—on floppy disk, CD-ROM, or through other means—consult your publisher, who will advise whether this method is practicable for your book and, if so, provide the necessary information. Many publishers—especially journal and technical publishers—have standard templates for authors to use in producing their submission; many are downloadable from publishers' websites.

Increasingly, authors are submitting electronically captured data for publication in media other than print, such as CD-ROMs or online publishing. These require guidelines appropriate to the project, which authors should request at the earliest planning stages. Authors employing SGML encoding may wish to be involved in developing the DTD (Data-Type Document), and this often can be accommodated.

In print media, setting from computer files is not always preferable to conventional setting: printing costs are such that it may actually be cheaper to key in text manually, especially when the author's software is obscure or outdated, or when the files require many corrections.

Submission

Seek advice from your editor if the text has complicated matter such as equations, unusual diacritics, or other special sorts. You may be asked to provide samples of the output from your system for evaluation, together with a sample of hard copy.

Electronic submission of copy still requires two hard copies, which are subject to all the standard requirements for format and layout. Although many word-processing packages enable the user to approximate the printed page on the final printout, there is absolutely no necessity to do so, even if you know that the published work will follow an established series style: indeed, the extra encoding required to allow different font sizes and styles, complex spacing, full justification, running headlines and footlines, etc. will actually prove a detriment when typesetting on the electronic text begins. (Heading levels may be distinguished simply through upper- and lower-case type, bold and italic, and centred or full-left text.) Similarly, do not add design codes unless specifically asked to do so.

Always ensure that the hard copy you submit to the publisher matches exactly what is on the computer files you supply, otherwise the advantages of time and cost inherent in electronic setting will be lost. If the typesetter encounters even minor discrepancies between electronic files and the edited typescript, it will be necessary to rekey the entire work from the hard copy alone, since the extent of the divergence between file and typescript cannot easily be gauged.

Computer-generated copy

Increasingly, publishers encourage authors having access to technically sophisticated equipment to generate some or all of the text—anything from individual tables or graphical representations to an entire book—in a publishable form. The widespread availability and flexibility of the hardware and software necessary to accomplish this—such as printers capable of producing the minimum acceptable dpi (dots per inch) required for clear reproduction in text, or off-the-shelf systems that accommodate Adobe PostScript or PDF (Portable Document Format) files—means this option has clear advantages for both author and publisher.

On the other hand, it also involves an author in processes more complicated than in the traditional submission of raw text. Since this can require intricate and lengthy interaction between author, editor, production editor, designer, and typesetter, the text as a general rule must be of sufficient complexity for such a process to prove worthwhile. An appropriate instance would be a high-level mathematical text produced in TeX or LaTeX; a complex chemical structure submitted as a ChemDraw, TIFF, EPS, or PICT file; or a text interspersed with hundreds of Chinese characters produced in a specialist font. Any author interested in pursuing this should contact his or her editor as early on as possible to explore the prospect. Such electronic copy should be submitted as files separate from any normal text files. Regardless of size or type, it is in general of two kinds:

Draft copy is text generated by an author and submitted in a provisional form, so that the publisher can intervene as necessary before reproducing it. As with an ordinary typescript, the publisher will arrange for the text to be edited; unlike the case of an ordinary typescript, the author is responsible for correcting the copy, making any editorial and design alterations required by the publisher. Only then is the copy ready to be reproduced. (While any data produced using well-known software equally may be manipulated by the publisher or printer, this in principle is no different from the submission of ordinary text in electronic form.)

Text copy, on the other hand, skips this interim step. It is author-generated copy submitted in its final printable form, so that the publisher can reproduce it directly, perhaps adding only preliminary matter, pagination, and running heads. Text copy is a much more ambitious project than draft copy, since it requires the author to assume many more of the obligations normally shouldered by the publisher. As the publisher will be making no subsequent modifications, an author is responsible for all design specification, page layout, and editorial and proofreading intervention and changes. Thus the final copy an author submits—whether as prc or computer files—must be of a high technical as well as editorial standard.

2.2.6 Additions and alterations to copy

Make small alterations between the lines. Using a prominent colour of ink, draw a line through the characters to be altered and write the revision in the space immediately above. If the typescript has been prepared on computer, make a clear mark, such as an X, in the left-hand margin of the hard copy to draw attention to changes that have *not* been made on the disks you submit. Retype and reprint heavily corrected pages before submission: the publisher requires finished copy, not a typescript covered with handwritten emendations.

Additional matter may be inserted either on the copy itself or, if the addition is too large to be accommodated marginally, on an 'A' page of separate A4-size paper, inserted within the foliation, *behind* the page to which it refers. Mark the point of insertion in the main text clearly and unambiguously, and label added folios so that an addition to, say, folio 123 is numbered 123A and introduced after it, the following folio being 124. If the addition is longer than one page, label subsequent folios 123B, 123C, 123D, for example.

Do not attach copy by paper clips, staples, or sticky tape—avoid the last at all costs, since it makes photocopying difficult, and is well-nigh impossible for an editor to write on. Alternatively, paste can be used to add extra pieces of copy, so long as the entire piece is firmly attached. If any long folios result, cut off the extra piece and stick it onto a new piece of A4 paper, so that all folios of copy are of uniform size. Photocopy any text printed on fax paper before insertion, as fax paper is difficult to mark and its image fades with time.

Authors supplying additional copy to a typescript to be set from computer files need not submit the new copy electronically as well as on hard copy. If the addition is only a few folios or less, it is simpler for a typesetter to key in by hand any supplementary text, providing it is labelled as such and the point of insertion clearly marked. Many such insertions may make electronic setting unfeasible, however.

2.2.7 Multi-author (contributory) texts

Any book involving more than one author is liable to multiply the sorts of problems usually found in a single-author text, and the greater the number of writers, the greater the potential for difficulties. While a single volume written collectively by joint authors can generate problems with scope, consistency, and focus, most often it is a contributory work that requires the greatest amount of effort to avoid complications: here, each chapter might be submitted by a different person and collected under the direction of one or more volume editors, who in turn work with the commissioning editor. This is the case with Festschriften, symposia, or any collection of papers with a common subject.

Volume editor's role

The volume editor is ultimately accountable for the calibre and merit of the chosen contributions, and the academic quality of the book as a whole. Normally it is his or her responsibility to field the editor's queries, either responding to them personally or passing them on to the relevant contributors and collating their replies. Two or more volume editors should clarify any division of responsibilities early on.

The volume editor and the publisher must draft clear and detailed guidelines for contributors, outlining preferred style, spellings and abbreviations, heading and subheading hierarchy, and reference format, and disseminate them as early on as possible, at least with each contributor's contract. The volume editor is responsible for reading and approving each contribution before sending it to the publisher. Those contributions requiring further work can be treated in one of three ways: the volume editor can (*a*) request that contributors rework their texts to conform to the guidelines, (*b*) rework them himself or herself, or (*c*) present the guidelines to the editor with a brief of what needs to be done in each case.

At a number of stages in the publishing process the volume editor may be called upon to authorize small changes in contributors' work which, owing to time constraints, they will not be able to recheck themselves. He or she should therefore make certain the contributors understand that the volume editor will be making decisions on their behalf, and ensure that they agree with this authority. This prevents problems with demands for alterations after the typescript has been set into pages.

Contributors' role

If contributors are asked to answer editing queries and read proofs they should do so promptly, not merely out of compliance to the deadline but out of consideration for their fellow contributors. While some contributors may not mind very much if their chapters ever see the light of day, others may have good reasons—ranging from fear that the work may become outdated to an impending tenure review—for wanting their own published as soon as possible.

Delayed or missing copy

The delivery of contributors' articles to the volume editor should be scheduled to allow the latter time to read and edit the material and, if necessary, to return it to the contributors for revision before it is due for submission to the publisher. Often, multi-author texts require swift publication: a collection of papers may include time-sensitive material, and a Festschrift may need to be published for a specific occasion, such as the honorand's birthday. Where one or two contributions are late in materializing, the already tight publishing schedule can be placed under great pressure, and the volume editor may wish to present the bulk of the typescript for copy-editing with the balance to follow. While on occasion this may be unavoidable, as a matter of policy chapter-by-chapter submissions seldom prove a satisfactory way to hasten the editorial process. In order to impose accurate consistency throughout, an editor must ideally retain the whole typescript until all contributions are accounted for: normally it is difficult (if not impossible) to edit uniformly chunks of text destined for the same book in isolation of one another, since comparisons and cross-checks between them are essential.

Consistency

In terms of the work's framework it is important to standardize the hierarchy of section headings employed throughout, to give a greater sense of continuity between the presentation of individual chapters. In the absence of a set series style, this is largely a question of finding the *via media* among the contributions.

In text a contributor may refer to his or her own or another work as *paper*, *lecture*, *talk*, *speech*, or the like. All such references should be styled alike, preferably substituting *chapter* (where appropriate), although *paper* is possible. However, unless a conscious effort has been made to retain the sense of occasion (*I shall say a few words, as we heard in yesterday's discussion*), change the more obvious conventions of the spoken word to those of the written word.

Many multi-author books are envisaged like journals: a collection of quite possibly diverse and eclectic writings rather than a cohesive work designed to be read from beginning to end. In this case the volume editor and commissioning editor may decide it is unnecessary to impose complete consistency throughout the entire work, and may instead choose to treat each chapter as a 'stand-alone' contribution, to be edited in isolation, unaffected by conventions adopted in other chapters.

Such a policy allows each contribution the freedom to have transliterations, abbreviations, terminology, notes, and bibliographical references that are merely internally consistent, and bear no relation to other chapters. This avoids the troubles inherent in imposing standards that contributors may find Procrustean, such as requiring identical terminology in varied circumstances, rejigging several perfectly adequate reference systems, or telling Contributor A to return to an inconvenient library to verify a work that Contributor B has cited differently.

However, not standardizing contributors' references to a single form throughout a work can have unexpected consequences. For example, in a book of collected essays on Plutarch's works, an editor may be instructed (or inclined) to leave references to the same treatise in the *Moralia* with different titles in two different chapters, for example *Amatorius* and *Eroticus*, or leave citation of the same essay in *Moralia* by its title in one place and by *Mor.* in another. An indexer not familiar with the subject may create two separate index headings for a single subject, and an indexer alive to the pitfalls will have to choose—at the eleventh hour—between two equally acceptable references to create the index heading, and then cross-refer the other to it.

Previously published contributions

Whether the contribution will be set anew or a copy used as crc, the volume editor should ask the commissioning editor whether permission to reproduce the work will need to be secured.

2.2.8 **Converting a thesis for publication**

Many scholarly works originate as theses or dissertations. Before such a work is published, however, the author should take steps to ensure that the text reads like a book rather than a submission for a degree. A candidate is often expected to present material in what can amount to a stilted or artificial form, while an author is free of such formal constraints, which in a book smack of 'thesisitis'—for that which pleases the examiner does not always please the reader. If an author has prepared the text suitably for publication, the only clue that the final book was once a thesis should be a statement to that effect in the preface. Here are some specific guidelines for authors readying theses for publication.

Eliminate matter inserted simply to satisfy the examiners that you know it; the reader will assume you do. In particular, do not retain references to everything that has been said or written on your subject, but cite only what was important in its day or is useful now. If you have consulted archival sources, a bare list of shelf or call numbers is of no use to the reader, though a catalogue of them arranged by content may well be. Notes can often be eliminated or trimmed; it is not necessary to give a source for every fact you mention.

Try to sustain the interest of your readers, whom you should assume to be suitably attentive to your subject. While flowery language is neither expected nor always welcome in an academic book, there is no need for all life to be squeezed out of the writing. In particular, do not be afraid to use personal pronouns instead of repeating proper nouns, and be rigorous in avoiding unnecessary jargon and terms of art, even those established in your discipline. So far as possible do not repeat information, unless you are drawing together disparate threads of an argument: remember that your book will have an index.

The structure and argument of your work should speak for themselves without prior announcement (*In Chapter 6 I shall discuss* or *Chapter 6 will discuss*), frequent self-referentiality, or lengthy recapitulation. An Introduction should put the subject in context; if there is a Conclusion, it should do the same with your findings. Neither needs to justify or précis in turn each chapter's inclusion. Where possible, cross-references should be to chapter and section rather than page; do not cite your notes in text.

The bibliography should be conceived as a service to the reader, not as a record of your own researches: in particular, avoid subdividing the bibliography into categories, as this makes locating references awkward. A division between primary and secondary sources may be acceptable, as the choice of where to look is usually made clear by the reference's type;

other distinctions are rarely so intuitive or helpful. Provided the full details have been given in the notes, it is not always mandatory to include works cited only once—though it is not wrong to do so either.

Books in the bibliography should be cited with the place and date of publication for the original or revised edition (which enables the reader to place them in the history of scholarly debate), *not* of the particular reprint that you have used. It is unnecessary to include a specific edition of a well-known work of literature that is easily available in several editions, unless that particular edition is essential or its page numbers are quoted as the standard form of reference, like those of Stephanus' Plato.

2.2.9 Dialect and transcriptions

Dialect generally is a form of speech peculiar to a particular region, class, or occupation, or a subordinate variety of a language with non-standard vocabulary, pronunciation, or grammar. (The sociolinguistic field recognizes further distinctions.) Imitating dialect in writing is a notoriously hazardous task, which few writers can master in fiction, much less in non-fiction. Except in exceptional circumstances, use standard English spelling for all transcriptions involving dialect, unless the transcription's main purpose is to exhibit phonetic variations—in which case the serious reader is better served by established linguistic symbols. Within a narrow range—where their meaning is clear and their appearance unremarkable—the usual contractions of casual conversation may be copied—*I'd, you've, won't*—but this does not of itself make the work more accessible. Moreover, it is pointless misspelling words in a way that does not alter their pronunciation: *pleeze, dont, sez*.

In creating transcriptions the author must reproduce people's words faithfully. Ordinarily, however, it is far more important to convey their thoughts than to imitate their speech. Approximating non-standard speech through substandard spelling can place unwarranted emphasis on speakers' backgrounds: there is a danger of condescension, since speakers may thereby be portrayed as being less intelligent and articulate than they are. In addition, what they have to say may be unnecessarily lost on readers either unfamiliar with the dialect first-hand or for whom English is a second language: unusual spellings may render the text incomprehensible: *Embro* for 'Edinburgh' would be just as befuddling to a New Yorker as *Lawn Guylant* for 'Long Island' would be to a Scot. Nuances of language and subtlety of dialect manifest themselves not just in pronunciation but in the choice, placement, construction, and rhythm of words, all of which standard spelling can capture and reproduce without the hauteur of intentional misspellings.

Some general considerations can be observed. First, do not interfere with dialect writing done well by a native speaker, unless wholly impenetrable. Secondly, intervene in fiction only when confident that the ethos conveyed by the dialectal passage is not that intended by the author. Thirdly, unless the dialect is essential—for example because it captures an untranslatable essence—prefer indirect speech in reportage to either awkward transcription or falsifying standardization.

2.3 **Copy-editing: the editor's role**

The following section is aimed at any publisher's editor responsible for editing copy—the task generally called *copy-editing* or *line-editing*. The advice offered below presupposes that editors are working in a freelance capacity, but does not exclude those working in house.

The commonly held distinction between editing and proofreading is that editors work on typescripts before they are typeset, the resulting proofs being worked on in turn by proofreaders. While this holds true for the most part now (though it did not in earlier times), editors do 'proofread' their copy—correct misspellings and adjust layout—as part of the editing process, and proofreaders can and do make editorial corrections missed by the editor. Moreover, an editor and proofreader may be one and the same person, performing both roles simultaneously, and in electronic dissemination typescript, proofs, and finished work never exist on paper. Even so, the demarcation between the roles of editor and proofreader remains useful, since the expectations and limits of the roles help define the scope within which each operates.

2.3.1 **The copy editor's job**

During the often years-long writing process, authors are concerned primarily with writing their text rather than editing it. It is not surprising, therefore, that authors' (or their typists') conventions can change through the course of a typescript, which then requires the attention of an impartial and practised eye. As an editor you may be the only person apart from the author to read every word of a text before publication. In this capacity you and the author are working towards the common aim of preparing a text for publication, and your approach to the role should reflect that objective.

Your main aims are to ensure consistency; good grammar, spelling, and punctuation; clarity of expression; and a clear and sensible structure for the book. The result should be a text that is as easy as possible to read and understand. In the short term most editors are marking up for the typesetter's keyboarder, but the more important long-term goal is to ensure that all readers find a well- and clearly written book. Editing is a Zen-like discipline, since the result of all editorial effort should be invisible on the printed page. Most often the only time a reader notices editing is when it is lacking, obtrusive, inconsistent, or awkward: that editor is best who changes—or appears to change—least.

Strictly speaking, subjective modifications are not a copy-editing responsibility. To take the narrowest view—which can be enlarged only within reason—if something is not inconsistent, grammatically wrong, or factually incorrect, it need not be changed. It is vital to think through the ramifications of all changes, and ensure that alterations do no violence to the author's intended meaning.

2.3.2 House style and flexibility

A publisher's house style embodies their stated preference for how copy is produced and set; this allows the efficient output of texts that are as internally consistent and error-free as possible. (*See also* **2.2.2**.) However, the application of any house style is secondary to the main aims outlined above: it is a pragmatic device designed to aid—not supplant— common sense, the generally accepted rules of English, and the conventions common in the author's field. Those instructions given in OUP's own *Hart's Rules* (the precursor to this volume) and the *Oxford Dictionary for Writers and Editors* have grown and altered considerably over the years, suggesting that the Press's own preferences—like those of other publishers—are neither hidebound nor fixed over time. There are countless instances where more than one correct form of a word exists—for example in historical versus modern spellings of place names, or in general versus specialist or scholarly usage of foreign words or technical terms—which the prudent editor will weigh accordingly.

An author's reasonable and consistently applied conventions are welcome, providing they pose no practical difficulties; authors are urged to discuss them initially with their publisher, and submit them in a covering note (*see* **2.2.3**). Similarly, it is important for editors to record conscious departures from the publisher's preferences on a style sheet for submission with the Note to Printer (*see* **2.3.4**), so that the publisher, typesetter, and proofreader can deduce whether something unexpected is intended or a lapse.

Some typescripts will not require or demand thorough editing. In such instances the publisher must be clear to spell out where you should

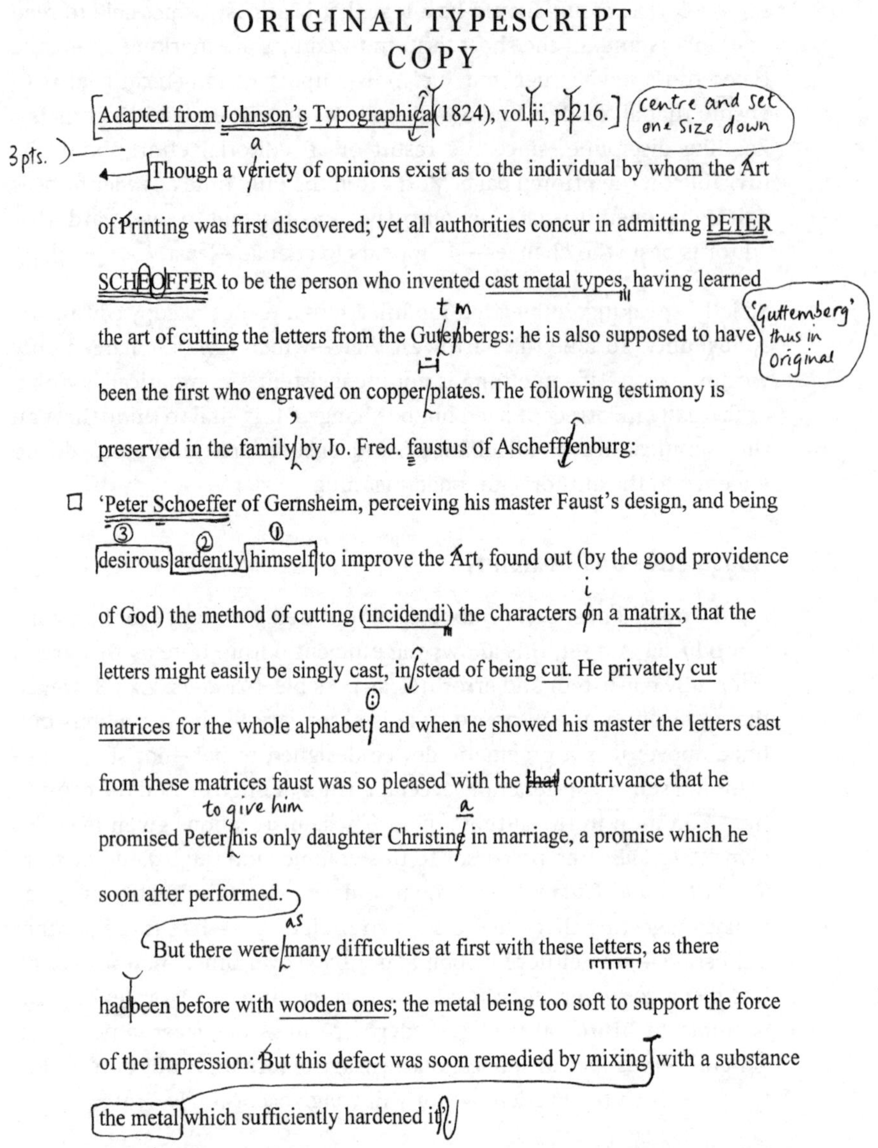

ORIGINAL TYPESCRIPT
COPY

[Adapted from Johnson's Typographia (1824), vol. ii, p. 216.]

Though a variety of opinions exist as to the individual by whom the Art

of Printing was first discovered; yet all authorities concur in admitting PETER

SCHEOFFER to be the person who invented cast metal types, having learned

the art of cutting the letters from the Gutenbergs: he is also supposed to have

been the first who engraved on copper plates. The following testimony is

preserved in the family by Jo. Fred. faustus of Ascheffenburg:

'Peter Schoeffer of Gernsheim, perceiving his master Faust's design, and being

desirous ardently himself to improve the Art, found out (by the good providence

of God) the method of cutting (incidendi) the characters on a matrix, that the

letters might easily be singly cast, instead of being cut. He privately cut

matrices for the whole alphabet and when he showed his master the letters cast

from these matrices faust was so pleased with the that contrivance that he

promised Peter his only daughter Christine in marriage, a promise which he

soon after performed.

But there were many difficulties at first with these letters, as there

had been before with wooden ones; the metal being too soft to support the force

of the impression: But this defect was soon remedied by mixing with a substance

the metal which sufficiently hardened it.

Figure 2.1: **Marked-up typescript copy**

focus your efforts. Commonly they will be restricted to marking up
headings, displayed matter, and references, and ensuring consistency
within those references.

2.3.3 Editorial mark-up

Many of the proof-correction marks (*see* **2.5.3**) are standardly used to
mark up the text for typesetting. The principal distinction between
editorial and proofreading mark-up is one of degree: unless the author
is exemplary and the typesetting execrable, an editor will probably

MARKS USED IN THE CORRECTION OF PROOFS

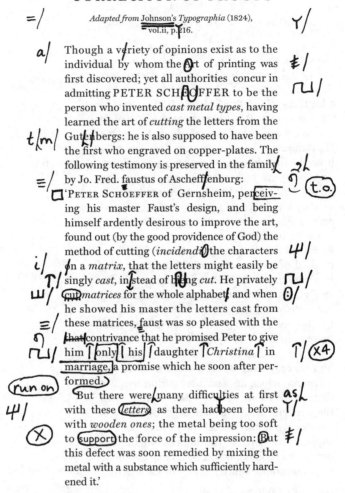

Adapted from Johnson's *Typographia* (1824), vol.ii, p.216.

Though a variety of opinions exist as to the individual by whom the Art of printing was first discovered; yet all authorities concur in admitting PETER SCHOEFFER to be the person who invented *cast metal types*, having learned the art of *cutting* the letters from the Gutenbergs: he is also supposed to have been the first who engraved on copper-plates. The following testimony is preserved in the family by Jo. Fred. faustus of Ascheffenburg:

'PETER SCHOEFFER of Gernsheim, perceiving his master Faust's design, and being himself ardently desirous to improve the art, found out (by the good providence of God) the method of cutting (*incidendi*) the characters on a *matrix*, that the letters might easily be singly *cast*, instead of being *cut*. He privately cut *matrices* for the whole alphabet, and when he showed his master the letters cast from these matrices, faust was so pleased with the that contrivance that he promised Peter to give him only his daughter *Christina* in marriage, a promise which he soon after performed.

But there were many difficulties at first with these *letters*, as there had been before with *wooden ones*; the metal being too soft to support the force of the impression: But this defect was soon remedied by mixing the metal with a substance which sufficiently hardened it.'

Figure 2.2: **Proofread first proof**

make more changes than a proofreader; and unless the typescript copy is excessively cramped (as with photocopies of previously set matter), an editor will probably have more room in which to make those changes. The result of this is that many common copy-editing instructions can be fitted within lines of typescript; and these, depending on their nature and clarity, need not then be stated or reinforced in the margin, as with proofreaders' marks. The prime consideration is that the mark-up on each folio is presented in such a way that a typesetter's keyboarder can implement all the changes while working at speed. Figure 2.1 shows an example of a copy-edited typescript page marked up for setting. Figures 2.2 and 2.3 show the same page as proofs. Marks used in editorial and proof correction are listed in Table 2.1.

THE PROOFREAD PAGE
CORRECTED

Adapted from Jo H N S O N'S *Typographia* (1824),
vol. ii, p. 216.

Though a variety of opinions exist as to the
individual by whom the art of printing was
first discovered; yet all authorities concur in
admitting PETER SCHOEFFER to be the
person who invented *cast metal types*, having
learned the art of *cutting* the letters from the
Guttembergs: he is also supposed to have
been the first who engraved on copper-plates.
The following testimony is preserved in the
family, by Jo. Fred. Faustus of Ascheffenburg:

'PETER SCHOEFFER of Gernsheim, perceiving his master Faust's design, and being
himself ardently desirous to improve the art,
found out (by the good providence of God) the
method of cutting (*incidendi*) the characters
in a *matrix*, that the letters might easily be
singly *cast*, instead of being *cut*. He privately
cut matrices for the whole alphabet: and when
he showed his master the letters cast from
these matrices, Faust was so pleased with the
contrivance that he promised Peter to give
him his only daughter *Christina* in marriage,
a promise which he soon after performed. But
there were as many dificulties at first with
these letters, as there had been before with
wooden ones; the metal being too soft to
support the force of the impression: but this
defect was soon remedied, by mixing the metal
with a substance which sufficiently hardened it.'

Figure 2.3: **Final (revised) proof**

2.3.4 **Typographical mark-up**

Observe a publisher's rules about detailed and consistent mark-up
unless the publisher instructs otherwise. Some general instructions
can be made in a *Note to Printer* (NTP), a sheet presenting typesetting
instructions related to the accompanying typescript, which the editor
submits after editing. The NTP frequently offers a suitable substitute for

repetitious mark-up on the typescript itself, or where detailed mark-up proves unnecessary.

To facilitate design, flexibility, or cross-platform use, publishers may require editors to insert codes or tags during mark-up, either on hard copy or—if the text is held electronically—within the files themselves. Conventions for doing so vary depending on what typesetting (or other) system will be used, and what level of intervention is required; the publisher will supply guidelines for how this should be performed. These codes or tags can delineate simple items like font type, sizes, and special sorts, or classes like headings and layout formats; more complicated parameters are required for metalanguages such as SGML, or CSS for HTML.

2.3.5 Queries

Mention to the author at the start of your queries any general points you wish to bring to his attention: stating a preference and the logic behind it usually preempts an author's needlessly stetting corrections. If you feel there is anything potentially problematic in your editing, an ounce of explanation is worth a pound of eraser shavings. While specific queries should be concise, avoid making them so brief as to appear ambiguous, brusque, or hectoring. Do not bother the author with specific or repetitive queries that are strictly publishing matters, such as points of layout and spacing, specialist terms, or matters covered explicitly in a publisher's preferred style. Conversely, do not sweep genuine problems and qualms under the carpet. If you are not sure whether something should be raised with the author, ask the publisher.

2.3.6 Contacting the publisher and author

The protocol for how and when freelance editors contact their publisher or author varies between publishers, and may vary between authors; publishers normally discuss what is expected before editing begins. For the most part, editors should get in touch with their publisher if they grow worried about the amount of restyling or other intervention they find necessary.

It can be a good idea to send the author a sample chapter or two and see what reaction your changes receive. Unpicking as a result of an adverse reaction is very dispiriting, and this procedure can save a great deal of time. Some publishers encourage experienced freelance editors to telephone, write, or email direct to authors with any general problems or queries that might emerge in the first couple of days of editing, so that things can be sorted out at an early stage in the work. It is important that anything agreed by telephone is confirmed in a letter, and it is vital that the publisher is given copies of all correspondence to and from authors.

2.3.7 Schedules and costs

It is important to treat seriously the schedule a publisher provides, and let them know immediately if the book will be delayed. If the deadline seems impossible as soon as you get the typescript, say so: a publisher may rather have the book back and look for another editor than have the schedule going seriously awry.

It is likewise important to treat seriously the cost estimate for the job. Most publishers base it on past knowledge of what books of a similar nature have cost to edit, combined with an appraisal of the factors unique to that typescript. Nevertheless, if you find that unforeseen difficulties in the work means you are bound to exceed an estimate, always contact the publisher to discuss it. Short of editing the typescript in house beforehand it is impossible for a publisher to set an absolute price. Some books are able to bear extra costs, while others must be kept strictly to budget.

2.4 Spacing and indentation in text

2.4.1 Vertical spacing

The height of type is measured in *points*, a vertical unit of measurement for type sizes and spacing, in the UK and USA reckoned to be 0.351 mm, in Europe 0.376 mm.

Leading

The vertical or interlinear spacing within the body of a page is called *leading*, from the strips of lead formerly inserted between lines of type. This term is used not just for the vertical spacing within the text of a paragraph, for example, but also for that within or around any matter such as headings, displayed poetry or equations, figures, tables, and ornaments. It is normally a function of typographic design, as are the width of the margins around the page.

To provide a suitable proportion, the size of the typeface is normally smaller than the size of the leading, so that for example *11 on 12* refers to an 11-point type with a 12-point space beneath. Some typefaces require more or less leading depending on their look: a fine or flowery type such as Van Djick or Ehrhardt needs more space to allow for the longer ascenders and descenders, while a compact type such as Times or Baskerville needs less. Similarly a blocky type such as Plantin or Bodoni needs more leading to keep the page from looking crowded. While such typographic considerations do not normally concern authors, editors, or proofreaders, it is nevertheless useful to know of their existence and their possible effect on the finished page.

White space

The amount and combination of margins and vertical and horizontal spacing will affect the appearance of the typeset page: the more space, the more open the result seems; the less space, the more compact. The area not printed upon is called *white space*, and the amount of it is normally determined by the type of work being printed. Where space is at a premium, as in dictionaries or encyclopedias, there will be less leading, resulting in a denser-looking page. Where a more open design is called for, as in poetry, art, school-, or fine-edition books, there will be more leading, resulting in greater white space on the page. Altering the leading and margins can affect the length of the final work—sometimes substantially.

In standard academic texts, extra leading between paragraphs is not generally allowed in continuous text, though leading will vary with the weight of headings and the size of the type chosen to set them.

2.4.2 **Horizontal spacing**

When set, copy can be arranged on the page in one of four ways: *ranged* (or *flush*) *left*, so that the left-side is aligned but the right-hand side is *ragged* (uneven); *ranged right*, so that the right-hand side is aligned but the left-hand side is ragged; *justified*, so that both left- and right-hand sides are aligned on the measure; or *centred*, so that each line is balanced on the measure's midpoint. A further refinement of centring is *centred optically*, so that each line is balanced in proportion to what appears to be the centre in relation to itself and surrounding text—which in lopsided or unequal copy may differ from dead centre.

Justified copy is produced by evenly varying spaces between the matter on each line, so that the print fills the space and forms a straight edge at the margin. Spaces that do not vary during justification are *fixed*, that is, of a set width unaffected by proportional spacing.

A *pica* is the standard unit of typographic measurement, equal to 12 points or approximately 4.21 mm (1/6 of an inch). In typewriting it has the additional sense of indicating a size of letter, equal to 10 characters to the inch (about 3.9 to the centimetre.) The pica is used especially for estimating the total amount of space a text will require. In general, the width of a letter in any given font is its *set*; the width of a full line of type or print is its *measure*, typically expressed in picas.

■ An *em* is a horizontal unit of space, calculated as the square of the body of any size of type. Originally it was reckoned as the width of a capital roman M. An *em space* (or *em quad*) has the nickname *mutton*, and is indicated in mark-up by the symbol □. For an *em rule* (—) *see* **5.10.11**. The term *pica em* describes the width of a pica.

■ An *en* is a horizontal unit of space equal to half an em, and approximately the average width of typeset characters. Originally it was reckoned as the width of a capital roman N. An *en space* (or *en quad*) has the nickname *nut*, and is indicated in mark-up by the symbol ◺. For an *en rule* (–) *see* **5.10.9**.

■ A *thin space* is a fifth of an em space. In mark-up it is indicated by the symbol ‡ or ⸮. The fixed thin space should generally be non-breaking. It is used for example between double parentheses to avoid 'nesting', as ')‡)'; between double opening or closing punctuation; and in bibliographies immediately after a 2-em rule:

—— *Principia Mathematica*

■ A *hair space* is a very thin space, thinner (sometimes by half) than a thin space; especially in the USA the term is often used as a synonym for 'thin space'. In the contexts where such small spaces are used they are generally fixed.

2.4.3 Word spacing

Spacing values between words are determined by typographic mark-up. What follows are some general considerations for setting, which for many typefaces will be achieved naturally if the word space defined within the font by the manufacturer is used as the optimum.

Word spacing must be as even (*proportional*) as possible in text that is justified (ranged full left and full right), and constant in text that is *centred* (the width of each line balanced on the measure) or *ragged* (ranged only full left or full right).

For continuous prose, the optimum spacing is 25 per cent of an em in normal bookwork. Thus in 10-point type, the space appearing between words will be 2.5 points. This should be increased to 33 per cent of an em for small type (8 point and below), and for dictionary and reference work setting. Poetry, and verse in plays, should also be set with an optimum 33 per cent word space, unless a very narrow typeface is being used.

Minimum and maximum word-space values for justified setting will vary according to the point size, measure, and typeface, but as a rule the minimum should not be less than 12 per cent of an em, nor the maximum greater than 67 per cent.

For display setting, narrower optimum word spaces can be used. These should relate to the apparent width of the typeface design.

2.4.4 Character spacing

Spacing values between characters should not normally be varied from the typeface manufacturer's metrics, and any unusual kerning pairs supplied with a font should be used at all sizes. Loosely fitted designs may need a reduction in character spacing at display sizes to improve their fit.

Letterspacing (*interspacing*) involves inserting small spaces between letters, typically in capitals or small capitals. It is indicated on typescript by vertical lines between the letters T'H'U'S. It should be used only to improve the appearance of words or lines set in capitals or small capitals; it must not be used as a means of justifying lines of type in hand-setting. The normal value for letterspacing text-size small capitals is 10 per cent of an em. In a line of letterspaced capitals, small capitals, or figures, all characters should be letterspaced, even those normally set close up—for instance there should be a corresponding space each side of a rule or hyphen.

Additional adjustments to character spacing will be required when, for instance, an italic *d* is followed by a roman closing parenthesis. The nature and degree of these will vary from typeface to typeface, and are normally accommodated automatically by modern typesetting equipment, which reconciles the differences in matter that seems when set either to clash or be too far apart. The general term for this adjustment of spacing between characters is called *kerning*; formerly, the part of a piece of metal type that projected beyond the body or shank was called the *kern*.

2.4.5 Normal and other word spaces

In text, use only a single word space after all sentence punctuation. A non-breaking word space should be used between a pair of initials to avoid a line break occurring, for example T. S. | Eliot, *not* T. | S. Eliot. Especially in wide-measure setting the fixed (non-breaking) word space should also be used for the same reason between the abbreviations for *page(s)* and *line(s)* (p., pp., l., ll.) and their following numbers; and, if possible, after the indefinite article *a* and personal pronoun *I*. In apparatus criticus do not end a line with a new line number.

The last line of a paragraph (the *break line*) should be set with the optimum space. Break lines should consist of more than five letters, except in narrow measure (*see also* **2.6**).

An en space will be the width of the figures in many fonts, and therefore may not be exactly half of an em. Use it to separate a number from its text in a heading, for example:

I **The Ferial Set**
   1. Composition of the Set
   2. The Transmission of the Texts
      (*a*) The Numbering System
      (*b*) The Headings
      (*c*) Marginalia

(For lists *see* **9.1.5**.) It may also be used to separate a page reference from its lemma, and the lemma from its gloss, for example:

   234 *his pet wombat*: Rosetti kept a wombat, which he named after Morris.

2.4.6 Indentation

The indentation of the first line of a paragraph is generally 1 em, with any sub-indentation in proportion. The rule for all indentation is not to drive the text too far in, a concern that increases with the narrowness of the measure. There is no indentation in the first paragraph following a heading, epigraph, or dropped initial letter.

In indexes the standard for indentation is for entries to be full out, subentries to be indented 1 em, and all turn-lines indented 2 ems (*see also* **16.2.2**).

For rules on indentation in plays and poetry *see* **13.6** and **13.7**.

2.4.7 Footnotes

Ibid

Do not set 'Ibid.' on the first note of a verso; repeat the reference it is repeating (or its short form) from the previous page.

Spacing

At page make-up, typesetters should leave apparent white space between the end of text and the first line of notes. Footnotes to a short last page of a chapter should be set 12 points below the last line of text, *not* at the bottom of the page.

Footnotes should begin with single digits indented 1 em. Where numbers change to tens or hundreds, figures should range on the inside for that page only (i.e. the room for the additional figure will come out of the em space). Unless there is a special direction to number footnotes beginning from 1 on each page (e.g. when following an older series style), footnotes should be numbered continuously through chapters or, exceptionally, sections. There is no longer any need to begin renumbering after 99: three-figure note cues are no longer cumbersome to set properly.

Short notes

One single-line note on a page should be centred; two or more single-line notes on a page should be ranged on the left, the whole being centred on the longest.

A short note may be set complete in the break-line of another note provided it is set ranged right, with more than 3 ems between the notes. Short notes may be run on in the same line with at least 3 ems between them, the line being centred. Where there are several short footnotes, they should be ranged in columns with a minimum of a 3-em space between the longest lines in the columns. This avoids short notes being stacked into a 'chimney-pot' effect, which looks ugly and squanders space.

Notes overrunning

Once set, a footnote should start on the same page as the text reference, but may overrun on to subsequent pages. If this is necessary, the footnote reference should occur, if possible, in the last line of text of the page in which the footnote starts. In the page(s) on which the note is continued there should be at least three lines of text.

The overrun footnote appears immediately below the text of the following page(s). Where the note overruns from a recto to a verso it is separated from further footnotes by a 3-point space, not a rule. (When footnotes are in double column, use a line space.)

If other notes are turned over as a knock-on effect from the overrun note, insert a catchline at the foot of the first page, ranged full right in the line of white at the foot (i.e. extra to normal page depth):

> [See opposite page for n. 5 cont.]
> [See opposite page for n. 5 cont. and nn. 6 and 7]
> [See p. 123 for n. 5 cont.]
> [See p. 123 for n. cont. and nn. 6 and 7]

Avoid using a final full point, as for a sentence, which may be misunderstood.

Similarly, if the overrun of a footnote jumps one or more pages for any reason (plates, etc.), insert a catchline:

> [cont. on p 123]

An incomplete footnote should not end a page with a full point or other terminal punctuation—in other words, it should be seen to be unfinished.

Notes in columns

Footnotes can be set in two or more columns in wide-measure books. Here, a footnote of one, two, or three single-column lines appearing by itself on one page should be rearranged to full measure and centred. Similarly, two footnotes, one of two lines and one of one line, are treated in like manner. With double-column footnotes, avoid a break-line at the top of the second column where possible.

Notes in textual editions

Where apparatus criticus occurs in addition to footnotes, it appears above the footnotes, separated from them by a 4-em rule, ranged left.

The first line of the apparatus criticus is indented 1 em. If there are also footnotes original to the text, they should appear above both apparatus criticus and editorial notes, separated by a short thin rule, ranged left. Where a single short note occurs below apparatus criticus it is to be set 1 em from the left, not centred.

2.5 **Proofreading and proof-correction marks**

While this section applies primarily to authors, everything within it is of practical significance for proofreaders as well. Proofreading the text is one of the final hurdles authors face before their work is published, and few relish the prospect of revisiting their work one last time: when Gilbert White received the proofs of his *Natural History of Selborne* in 1789, he described this procedure as 'an occupation full as entertaining as that of darning of stockings, tho' by no means so advantageous to society'. Regardless, reading proofs remains a vital last step in ensuring that errors are spotted and eliminated.

2.5.1 **Proofs**

A *proof* is a trial printing of composed matter, taken for correction from type or film. Though fewer varieties persist today than formerly, several different types remain, the most common of which are as follows:

galley proof	a proof taken before the matter is made up into pages
page proof	a proof made up into pages
clean proof	a proof having very few printer's errors
author's proof	a proof supplied to the author for correction

marked proof   a proof on which corrections have been marked

first proof   the first proof taken after setting, with subsequent revised proofs labelled *second proof, third proof*, etc.

foul proof   a marked proof supplied to read against a revised proof

collated proof a proof on which corrections from other proofs are assembled

revised proof   a proof on which corrections from a previous proof have been made

scatter proof   an individual page of proofs on which corrections have been made

final proof   the last proof, which is passed for press (printing); also called *press proof* or *voucher proof*

Authors ordinarily are given a set of proofs to read for correction, along with the original typescript or an up-to-date copy; their proofs may already have been read by a proofreader, or may go off to one to be read subsequently. Especially where time is short more than one set of proofs may be circulated and read simultaneously, and the changes on each collated onto a master set. If the author is not indexing his or her own volume, another set of proofs will be sent to an indexer as well.

Formerly, galley proofs were on sheets about 18 inches long, and represented the text before it was made up into pages, lacking footnotes or artwork. As text is now usually made up into pages from the start, most galleys now look very much like normal proofs, though artwork may be missing. Galleys are rarely produced nowadays except for works with complex layouts or many illustrations. Revised proofs—those incorporating corrections from an earlier set of proofs—are normally dealt with in house. Consequently, after proofreading is complete authors should assume that they will next see their book in final, bound form.

2.5.2 **Corrections**

By the time a text has been typeset into pages it is in an inflexible state, and any corrections marked should be confined to rectifying actual errors by the typesetter: a publisher who gives authors the opportunity to vet their typescript will expect that they have already reread their entire text, examined the editor's work, and made any changes they wished before typesetting began. Although truly unavoidable corrections can and do occur, remember that alterations on proof are extremely expensive: one correction may amount to 30 per cent or more of the composition cost for an entire page. There is no such thing as a 'small' proof correction, since—even with modern equipment—changing so much as a comma might require resetting the whole line in which it occurs, and frequently resetting several lines or an entire paragraph.

Write corrections clearly in the margin by the line to which they refer, in the same left-to-right sequence as they occur there. Use red for type-setter's errors (they may already be marked in green or black by the typesetter's reader). Use blue (or black if not used by the typesetter's reader) for any unavoidable author's change. Never correct in pencil or crayon. Mark the precise point in the proof text where the change is required. Circle all words added to the proof that are not to be printed. If you find a major problem (particularly one that affects pagination), or you are unsure how to correct something, contact the editor or pub-lisher before spending time making extensive corrections.

2.5.3 Proofreading marks

Two marking systems are in current use. The first is espoused in BS 1259 and 5261 Part 2: 1976 and supplements. The second, which pre-dates it, is the main system used in the USA; it remains in wide use in UK and (with many variations) throughout the Continent. Ideally, one system should be used consistently throughout a given set of proofs. However, as each has its strong and weak points, the most pragmatic consider-ation is that the same change not be indicated two different ways, or different ones the same way. Table 2.1 shows the most common forms of proofreading marks, which are acceptable in marking up proofs or typescript copy where space is cramped.

Figure 2.2 shows the folio illustrated in Figure 2.1 as a proofread proof, and Figure 2.3 shows the same page as a final copy.

To cancel a previous alteration, addition, or deletion, write a circled tick mark (✓), or the circled word *stet* (meaning 'let it stand' in Latin), in the margin of a proof; dots also are placed under the affected portion of the text. Ensure there is no ambiguity as to which change is being reversed, and (especially in revised proofs) no danger that a subsequent correction is reversed on the strength of an earlier stet.

2.5.4 Queries

Authors should answer unequivocally all marginal circled queries from the proofreader or printer's reader. To accept a query, strike out the question mark so as to leave the correction to be made; to remove any possible doubt write *Yes* against it. To reject a query, strike out the whole circled query and write *No* against it. Do not use the ambiguous *OK*, which leaves the setter guessing whether you mean 'Very well, do it your way' or 'Copy is correct as it stands'.

2.5.5 **Alterations**

Avoid adding or deleting more than the odd word, as this can have serious consequences in page proofs by upsetting the pagination. Correcting this is very costly and time-consuming, and will affect compilation of the index and any cross-references to pages. If the typesetter has omitted or repeated more than a few words of copy, bring this to the attention of the editor or publisher when, or before, you return the proofs. The typesetter will be responsible for the consequent corrections, but it may be possible—and easiest for all concerned—to limit the damage typographically. If you think an addition or deletion of your own cannot be avoided, remove or add material in the same or adjacent line so that the final text fits into the available space on the page.

2.5.6 **Additional tasks**

Read text and notes carefully against the copy. In addition to this normal reading, the following steps should be taken. It is wise to complete each step separately, rather than risk distraction by combining different procedures.

Footnotes

Check that the right footnotes appear on the right page, and that the corresponding cues appear correctly in the text. Page make-up sometimes demands that the text of long notes runs onto the following page: this is generally acceptable.

Endnotes

Check that the correct cues appear in the text and match the notes at the end. Check also that running heads in the endnotes correctly reflect the copy.

Cross-references

To approximate spacing for cross-references yet to be inserted, the typesetter will have set these as 'p. 000', 'p. ● ● ●', or 'p. ■ ■ ■'. Ensure that the relevant page numbers are inserted in all cases. As these count as author's corrections they should be marked in blue or black.

Contents, list of figures, lists of tables, etc.

Fill in all page numbers, or check that those given are correct. Check that the titles of chapters and sections, and the captions of figures or tables, match those in the text.

Table 2.1: **Proofreading marks**

Proofreading symbols generally in use have been strongly influenced by the British Standards Institution s BS 5261 Part 2: 1976 and supplements. Traditional or alternative symbols are still found, especially abroad; the most common are included here.

Instruction	Textual mark	Marginal mark
Correction is concluded	None	/
Insert in text the matter indicated in the margin	⋏	New matter followed by ⋏
Insert additional matter identied by a letter in a diamond	⋏ Followed by, e.g. ⟨A⟩	The relevant section of the copy should be supplied with the corresponding letter marked on it in a diamond, e.g. ⟨A⟩
Delete	/ through character(s) or ├───┤ through words to be deleted	♂ or ♀
Close up and delete space between characters or words	linking ⌒ characters	⌒ /
Delete and close up	⌒ through character or ├═══╡ through characters, e.g. charaͨcter charaͣacter	♂ or ♀
Substitute character or substitute part of one or more word(s)	/ through character or ├───┤ through word(s)	New character or new word(s) followed by /
Substitute or insert full point or decimal point	/ or ⋏ through character where required	⊙/ or ⊙
Substitute or insert colon	/ or ⋏ through character where required	⊙/ or ⊙
Substitute or insert semicolon	/ or ⋏ through character where required	;/ or ;⋏
Substitute or insert comma	/ or ⋏ through character where required	,/ or ,⋏ or ⌃
Substitute or insert solidus (oblique)	/ or ⋏ through character where required	(/)
Substitute or insert character in superior (superscript) position	/ or ⋏ through character where required	Ɣ or under character e.g. ⌄Ɣ or ⌄ɣ
Substitute or insert character in inferior (subscript) position	/ or ⋏ through character where required	Ⳑ or over character e.g. Ⳑ₂
Substitute or insert opening or closing parenthesis, square bracket, or curly brace	/ or ⋏ through character where required	(/) or {/}, [/], or {/}
Substitute or insert hyphen	/ or ⋏ through character where required	⊢⊣ / or = or ⊢⊣ ⋏
Substitute or insert rule	/ or ⋏ through character, e.g. _2em_	Give the size of rule in marginal mark [1em][4mm]
Set in or change to bold type	⩘⩘ under character(s) to be set or changed	⟮bold⟯ or ⟮bf⟯ or ⩘⩘
Set in or change to bold italic type	⩗⩗ under character(s) to be set or changed	⟮bold ital⟯ or ⟮bf ital⟯ or ⩗⩗
Set in or change to italic	─── under character(s) to be set or changed	⟮ital⟯ or ⊔⊔
Change italic to upright (roman) type	Encircle character(s) to be changed	⟮rom⟯ or ⊔⏌
Set in or change to capital letters	≡ under character(s) to be set or changed	⟮cap⟯ or ≡
Change capital letters to lower-case letters	Encircle character(s) to be changed	⟮lc⟯ or /
Spell out number or abbreviation	Encircle matter to be changed ⟮38pp.⟯	⟮sp⟯
Set in or change to small capital letters	= under character(s) to be set or changed	⟮sc⟯ or ⟮s.cap⟯ or =
Set in or change to capital letters for initial letters and small capital letters for the rest of the word(s)	≡ under initial letters and == under rest of the word(s)	Where space does not permit textual marks, encircle the affected area instead

Instruction	Textual mark	Marginal mark
Change small capital letters to lower-case letters	Encircle character(s) to be changed	(lc) or ≠
Start new paragraph	⌐	(NP) or ⌐ or ¶
Run on (no new paragraph)	⌒	(run on) or ⊃
Transpose characters or words	⊔⊓ between characters or words, numbered when necessary	(trs) or (tr) or ⊔⊓
Transpose lines	5	(trs) or (tr) or 5
Invert type	Encircle character to be inverted	℧
Transpose a number of lines	――――――③ ――――――② ――――――①	To be used when the sequence cannot be clearly indicated otherwise. Rules extend from the margin into the text, with each line to be transplanted numbered in the correct sequence
Centre	[ ] or [enclosing matter to be centred]	
Insert space between characters	| between characters affected	Y or #
Insert space between words	Y between words affected	Y or (more #)
Reduce space between characters	| between characters affected	↑ or (less #)
Reduce space between words	↑ between words affected	↑
Equalize space between characters or words	| between characters or words affected	⅄ or (eq #)
Close up to normal interlinear spacing	(each side of column linking lines)	
Insert space between lines or paragraphs	–(or)–	The marginal mark extends between the lines of text. Give the size of the space to be inserted if necessary
Reduce space between lines or paragraphs	← or →	The marginal mark extends between the lines of text. Give the amount by which the space is to be reduced if necessary
Take over character(s), word(s), or line to next line, column, or page	⌐‾‾‾‾‾	The textual mark surrounds the matter to be taken over and extends into the margin
Take back character(s), word(s), or line to previous line, column, or page	‾‾‾‾‾⌐	The textual mark surrounds the matter to be taken back and extends into the margin
Insert or substitute em space, en space, or thin space	□ (em), ▣ (en), ⧧ or ¶ (thin)	□ (em), ▣ (en), ⧧ or ¶ (thin)
Indent	⊏	⊏
Cancel indent	⊢⊏	⊐
Move matter specified distance to the right	⌐enclosing matter to be moved to the right ⌐→|	⊏
Move matter specified distance to the left	⊢⊏ enclosing matter to be the left ⌐	⊐
Correct vertical alignment	‖	‖ or (align)
Correct horizontal alignment	Single line above and below misaligned matter, e.g. misaligned	= or (align)
Correction made in error. Leave unchanged	under characters to remain _ _ _ _	✓ or (stet)
Remove extraneous mark(s) or replace damaged character(s)	Encircle mark(s) to be removed or character(s) to be changed	✗
Wrong font. Replace by character(s) of correct font	Encircle character(s) to be changed	✗ or (wf)
Refer to appropriate authority anything of doubtful accuracy	Encircle word(s) affected	?

Note: All instructions to the typesetter should be circled as shown above, e.g. (align) (stet) Otherwise they can be mistakenly inserted into the text.

Page numbers and running headlines

Check that the pages are correctly numbered, and ensure that the running headlines appearing at the head of each page of text are properly spelt, accurately ordered, and (where necessary) correctly abbreviated.

Illustrations

Check that all illustrations (figures, maps, plates, etc.) are accounted for and given the correct positions and captions, and that these correspond with any lists in the preliminary matter. The actual artwork may not be shown in the proof: often only a large square or white space takes its place, to indicate its size and placement.

2.6 General principles for typeset matter

In addition to all the tasks, procedures, and considerations laid out for the author in the previous section, proofreaders are charged with ensuring that the page is not simply factually correct and sensibly presented, but pleasing to the eye. To this end printers, typesetters, and publishers have over the years accrued a small clutch of rules generally accepted as producing an attractive printed page. Circumstances and design considerations will determine which of these—or to what extent any—are adhered to, though good proofreaders will be conscious of departures or lapses even while ignoring them.

- Traditionally, printers reckoned that the last line of any typeset paragraph should not be only a syllable or numerals alone and should contain at least five characters, with measures wider than 28 picas requiring more. While nowadays this rule is no longer followed strictly, the last line of a paragraph—even if it is a full line—still should not fall at a page break so that it appears alone at the top of a new page or column: this is known as a *widow*.

  An *orphan* (also called *club line*) is the term for the first line of a paragraph when the page breaks so that the line appears alone at the bottom of a page or column. Ordinarily this is now considered acceptable in most bookwork.

- No more than two successive lines should begin or end with the same word.

- A recto page should not end with a colon that introduces displayed matter.

- Marginal notes should be set on the outside edge of the page and, unless otherwise directed, lines should range on the inside against the text, with at least 1 em separating them.

- Where lines of text are numbered, the numbers (ranged on the inside) should appear on the outside margin in prose works but ranged full right in the measure for poetry. When marginal notes *and* line numbers occur, the marginal notes should appear on the outer edge of the page and line numbers on the inner edge. Where a page number or some other marginal clashes with a line number in the same margin, the next line should be numbered instead; if this is not possible the nearest line to the original numbering should be numbered.

- Pages should all be the same depth, as should columns in multi-column setting. In books of verse, however, it is preferable for pages to be left short rather than be excessively spaced out, since the varying depth is not as noticeable. Complete pages of a body size different from the text (e.g. appendices and extracts) should be made up, to the nearest line, to the depth of the text page. If absolutely necessary to avoid awkward page breaks, facing pages may be made a line long or short.

- Interlinear spacing must be uniform in normal texts.

- In centred displayed headings (chapter titles, section headings, etc.) keep word spaces even and avoid dividing words. Lines should not be forced out to full measure and *each* line should be centred. Where it is possible, and sensible, avoid having a short single word as the last line.

CHAPTER 3

Abbreviations and symbols

3.1 **General principles**

Abbreviations and symbols represent, through a variety of means, a shortened form of a word or words. Abbreviations fall into three categories: only the first of these is technically an abbreviation, though the term loosely covers them all, and guidelines for their use overlap.

- *Abbreviations* are formed by omitting the end of a word or words (*VCR*, *lbw*, *Lieut.*).

- *Contractions* are formed by omitting the middle of a word or words (*I've*, *mustn't*, *ne'er-do-well*).

- *Acronyms* are formed from the initial letters of words (*SALT*, *Nazi*, *radar*), the results being pronounced as words themselves.

Symbols—also called signs—are more abstract representations. They may be letters derived directly from words (Ag, kg, W, T_m), letters assigned to concepts ($\aleph$, μ, Ω, $|Z|$), or special typographical sorts (° % + #). They can be used on their own or in conjunction with words, numbers, or other symbols (πr^2, £6, Rh+, HK$, © OUP).

Abbreviations should be used as a convenience for the reader, not for the writer. In work for a general audience, do not use abbreviations or symbols in running text unless concision is vital—for example, where space is scarce in a narrow measure—or because terms are repeated so often that abbreviations are easier for the reader to absorb. While some abbreviations are so well known that it might seem foolish to spell them out (*USA*, *BBC*, *UN*), the readership should determine which abbreviations these are. Not all readers will be familiar with the same abbreviations, so it is often best to spell out when in doubt.

Use only the best-known shortened forms, and then only those likely to be familiar to the intended audience; in writing aimed at a technical or specialist readership such forms are widespread as space-savers or terms of art (terminology familiar to a profession). In all contexts spell out the rarer ones at first mention in copy, adding the abbreviation in parentheses after it: *the Economic and Social Research Council (ESRC)*, *Commander Submarine Force Eastern Atlantic (COMSUBEASTLANT)*. Normally it is not necessary to repeat this process in each chapter unless the book is likely to be read out of sequence, as in a multi-author work or a textbook. If this is the case, or simply if many abbreviations are used, including a list of abbreviations or a glossary is a good way to avoid repeatedly expanding abbreviations (*see* **1.2.14**).

It is possible to refer to a previously mentioned full name by a more readable shortened form, rather than—or in addition to—a set of initials: *the Institute* rather than *IHGS* for the Institute of Heraldic and Genealogical Studies. In works where terms frequently recur such variation is sensible, and even welcome, but not if confusion or ambiguity results. Ensure, therefore, that each shortened form stands for only one name, and is readily distinguishable: one may use in swift succession *the Association*, *the Organization*, and *the Society* to stand for three different groups in one work, but not without risk of a muddle.

3.2 Usage
....

Abbreviations in running text

Prefer *nineteenth century* to *19th cent.*, and *25 per cent* (two words, no point) to *25%* in text; rules for notes and tabular or parenthetical matter differ. As a general rule, avoid mixing abbreviations and full words of similar terms—though specialist or even common usage may militate against this: *Newark, JFK, and LaGuardia airports, A & E, ICU, Outpatient, Theatre, X-Ray*.

Authors and editors should ensure that comparable units are abbreviated similarly within a single text. For clarity's sake, common single-letter metric abbreviations take a full point (*m.*, *g.*) except in scientific or technical writing, or when a prefix is added (*km*, *mg*); this is not the case in nonscientific US English, where points are the norm.

Punctuation

Traditionally, abbreviations were supposed to end in full points while contractions did not, giving both *Jun.* and *Jr* for Junior, and *Rev.* and *Revd* for Reverend. Handy though this rule is, common usage increasingly fails to bear it out: both *ed.* (for editor or edited by) and *edn.* (for edition) end in a point; Street is *St.* with a point to avoid confusion with *St* for Saint. Further, US English tends to use punctuation more than British

English (*U.S.A.* rather than *USA*), and non-technical English in either country uses more punctuation than technical English (*ml.* rather than *ml*). This means it is difficult to predict with confidence the punctuation following abbreviations, though acronyms and symbols tend to be subject to greater standardization across borders and disciplines. Specific rulings may be found in the individual entries in the *Oxford Dictionary for Writers and Editors*; *e.g.*, *i.e.*, and *etc.* are discussed at **3.8** below.

If an abbreviation ends with a full point but does not end the sentence, other punctuation follows naturally: *Ginn & Co., Oxford.* If the full point of the abbreviation ends the sentence, however, there is no second full point: *Oxford's Ginn & Co.* Abbreviations are more appropriate in marginal or ancillary matter such as appendices, bibliographies, captions, figures, notes, references, and tables, and rules differ for these. For legal abbreviations *see* **13.2.1**, **13.2.3**.

Avoid ampersands except in names of firms that use them, established combinations (e.g. R & D, R & B, C & W), and in some lexicographic work. Occasionally they may be convenient for clarification: in *cinnamon & raisin and onion bagels are available* the ampersand makes clear there are two rather than three types on offer.

Arabic and roman numerical abbreviations take no points: *1st*, *2nd*, *3rd*; but use *first*, *second(ly)*, *third(ly)* in text. Similarly *4to*, *8vo*, *12mo* are found for book sizes, as are such constructions as $II^{\grave{e}me}$ and n^{os} (for the French *deuxième* and *numéros*).

Lower-case abbreviations

Abbreviations usually obey the rules that normally govern punctuation and styling in running text, which means that lower-case abbreviations cannot begin a sentence in their abbreviated form. Normally the same holds true for abbreviations used in notes; a group of exceptions may be allowed however, which have been widely adopted elsewhere: '*c.*', '*e.g.*', '*i.e.*', '*l.*', '*ll.*', '*p.*', '*pp.*' are *always* lower-case in notes, even at the beginning.

Print *a.m.* and *p.m.* in lower case, with two points; use them only with figures, and never with *o'clock*. Correctly *12 a.m.* is always midnight and *12 p.m.* always noon. However, it may be preferable in some contexts to say explicitly *12 midnight* or *12 noon*, or use the more precise twenty-four-hour clock (*see* **7.9**).

Upper- and lower-case abbreviations

Abbreviations and contractions in a mixture of upper and lower case can take full points (*Ph.D.*, *M.Litt.*, *Kt.*, *Sun.*, *Jan.*) or not (*Dr*, *Mr*, *Mrs*, *Ms*, *Mme*, and *Mlle*). Purely scientific abbreviations (*bps*, *PIPES*, *snoRNP*, *TrA*) tend to be printed without full points, as do monetary amounts (*£6 m*, *$220*, *50p*). All British counties with abbreviated forms take a full point (*Oxon.*,

Yorks.). Traditional exceptions were *Hants.* and *Northants.*, whose abbreviations were derived originally from older spellings, but this distinction no longer holds.

All-capital abbreviations

Abbreviations of a single capital letter normally take full points (*J. Bloggs*, *Stage L.*) except when used as symbols (*see* **3.5** below). Those of more than one capital letter normally take no full points in British and technical usage (*TUC, MA, EU, QC, DFC, NW*). It makes no difference whether the capitals are full, small, or italic. This is not true for initials of personal names: initial–name combinations require spaces between the elements (*W. G. Grace, G. B. Shaw, J. R. R. Tolkien*), while all-capital initials are set close up (*W.G.G., G.B.S., J.R.R.T.*). Where an all-capital set of initials has come to assume the status of a name it takes no points, as in *FDR* for Franklin Delano Roosevelt and *LBJ* for Lyndon Baines Johnson.

Where a text is rife with full-capital abbreviations, they can be set all in small capitals to avoid the jarring look of having too many capitals on the printed page. Some abbreviations (AUC, BC, AD) are always set in small captials. (*See* **6.8.2**.)

Italic matter

Italic text (e.g. titles of books, plays, and journals) usually produces italic abbreviations: '*DNB*' (*Dictionary of National Biography*), 'Arist. *Metaph.*' (Aristotle's *Metaphysics*), '*JAMS*' (*Journal of the American Musicological Society*), '*Quad. Ist. Top. Roma*' (*Quaderni dell'Istituto di Topografia antica della Università di Roma*). Follow the forms familiar in a given discipline; even then permutations can exist, often depending on the measure of a line (as in tabular matter, where reduced abbreviations may be used), or on whether the abbreviation is destined for text or note. Shakespeare's *First Part of King Henry IV*, for example, is variously abbreviated to 1 *Henry IV*, 1 *Hen. IV*, and 1H4. (*See also* **13.6.6**.)

3.3 Contractions

Place the apostrophe in the position corresponding to the missing letter or letters (*fo'c's'le, ha'p'orth, sou'wester, t'other*), but note that *shan't* has only one apostrophe. Common verbal contractions, such as *I'm, can't, it's, mustn't, he'll*, are perfectly acceptable in less formal writing, and are frequently found (and may be kept) even in academic works. However, editors should not *impose* them except to maintain consistency within a varying text. (*See* **5.2**.)

There are no points, and no apostrophe, in colloquial abbreviations that have become part of the language, such as *bike, cello, demo, flu, gym, phone, plane, pram, recap,* or *trad.* Retain the original apostrophe only when archaism is intentional, or when it is necessary to reproduce older copy precisely.

In foreign languages, contractions may be indicated with an apostrophe (*commedia dell'arte, j'adore, l'ho vista, wie geht's*), but an exact parallel cannot be drawn with transliterations, where the apostrophe may be there to aid pronunciation (*'amīr, San'yo, t'ai chi ch'uan*).

3.4 **Acronyms**

An acronym is distinguished from other abbreviated forms by being a series of letters or syllables pronounced as a complete word: *NATO* and *UEFA* are acronyms, but *MI6* and *BBC* are not. Acronyms take no points, whether all in caps (*NAAFI, SALT, WASP*), in initial capitals with upper and lower case (*Aga, Fiat, Sogat*), or entirely in lower case (*derv, laser, scuba*). Since they perform as words they can begin sentences, with lower-case forms being capitalized normally: *Laser treatment is* . . . .

Any all-capital proper-name acronym is, in some house styles, fashioned with a single initial capital if it exceeds four letters (*Basic, Unesco, Unicef*). Editors should avoid this rule, useful though it is, where the result runs against the common practice of a discipline (*CARPE, SSHRCC, WYSIWYG*), or where similar terms would be treated dissimilarly based on length alone.

3.5 **Symbols**

Symbols—also called signs—are a shorthand notation signifying a word or concept, and are a frequent feature of scientific and technical writing. The distinction between abbreviation and symbol may be blurred when, like an abbreviation, a symbol is derived directly from a word or words (*Ag* from *argentum, Pa* from *pascal, U* from *uranium*), and in setting they are often treated similarly. Unlike abbreviations, however, symbols never take points, even if a single letter, or used alone or in conjunction with figures or words: *F* for *false, farad, fluorine, phenylalanine,* or *Fahrenheit.*

Do not start a sentence with a symbol: spell out the word or recast the sentence to avoid it: *Sixteen dollars was the price*, *The price was $16*, *Section 11 states*, *As §11 states*.

Symbols formed from words are normally set close up before or after the things they modify (GeV, Σ^+, (*E*)-3-methyl-2-pentanoic acid, H_2SO_4), or set with space either side if standing alone for words or concepts (*A*, 32° F, W chromosome). Abstract, purely typographical symbols follow similar rules, being either close up (° # ¶ ¢ » %) or spaced (♭ ♂ ✳ ✂ ☎ ☺). Authors should provide good examples of any unusual sorts that they cannot achieve satisfactorily on copy; editors should ensure that these are clearly labelled for setting.

Spell out points of the compass in running text: *Woodstock is eight miles north of Carfax*. In notes and tabular matter of nontechnical work, set abbreviated single-letter compass directions as *N.*, *S.*, *E.*, *W.*, with full points. (Outside specialist contexts these are generally treated as abbreviations rather than symbols.) Points are not used in technical work, nor in conjunction with compound directions: *ESE*, *SW–NNE* (an en rule, not a hyphen). In coordinates, the symbols of measurement (degrees, seconds, etc.) are set close up to the figure, not the compass point: *52° N.*, *15° 7′ 5″ W.*

As an alternative to superior numbers the symbols * † ‡ § ¶ | etc. may be used as reference marks or note cues, in that order.

The signs + (plus), − (minus), = (equal to), > ('larger than', in etymology signifying 'gives' or 'has given'), < ('smaller than', in etymology signifying 'derived from') are often used in printing biological and philological works, and not only in those that are scientific or arithmetical in nature. In such instances +, −, =, >, < should not be printed close up, but rather separated by the normal space of the line. For instance, in 'spectabilis, *Bœrl.* l.c. (= Haasia spectabilis)', the = belongs to 'spectabilis' as much as to 'Haasia', and the sign should not be put close to 'Haasia'. (A thin space is also possible, providing it is consistently applied.)

Symbols' uses can differ between disciplines. For example, in philological works an asterisk (*) prefixed to a word signifies a reconstructed form; in grammatical works it signifies an incorrect or nonstandard form. A dagger (†) may signify an obsolete word, or 'deceased' when placed before a person's name (this convention should be used only in relation to Christians). In German a double dagger (⚔) follows the name and signifies 'killed in battle', *gefallen*.

Other special signs and symbols are a feature of writing about, for example, manuscript and early-book references, linguistics, logic, and mathematics and the sciences. For accents and diacritical marks used in foreign languages *see* **CHAPTER 11** under the languages concerned; *see also The Oxford Dictionary for Writers and Editors*, 2nd edn., appendix 4 (Oxford, 2000).

3.6 **The indefinite article with abbreviations**

The choice between *a* and *an* before an abbreviation depends on pronunciation, not spelling. Use *a* before abbreviations beginning with a consonant sound, including an aspirated *h* and a vowel pronounced with the sound of *w* or *y*.

a BA degree	a KLM flight	a BBC announcer
a Herts. address	a hilac demonstration	a YMCA bed
a SEATO delegate	a U-boat captain	a UNICEF card

Use *an* before abbreviations beginning with a vowel sound, including unaspirated *h*:

an AB degree	an MCC ruling	an FA cup match
an H-bomb	an IOU	an MP
an MA	an RAC badge	an SOS signal

This distinction assumes the reader will pronounce the sounds of the letters, rather than the words they stand for (*a Football Association cup match, a hydrogen bomb*). *MS* for manuscript is normally pronounced as the full word, *manuscript*, and so takes *a*; *MS* for multiple sclerosis is often pronounced *em-ess*, and so takes *an*. Likewise 'R.' for rabbi is pronounced as *rabbi* ('a R. Shimon wrote'), but 'R' for a restricted classification is normally pronounced as *arr* ('an R film').

The difference between sounding and spelling letters is equally important when choosing the article for abbreviations that are acronyms and for those that are not: *a NASA launch* but *an NAMB award*. The same holds for names of symbols, which can vary: in America a hash symbol (#) is a 'number sign' or, more formally, an octothorp; in linguistic use an asterisk may be called a 'star' and in mathematics an exclamation mark called a 'factorial', 'shriek', or 'bang', so the correct forms are *a* * and *a* ! rather than *an* * and *an* !. As abbreviated terms enter the language there can be a period of confusion as to how they are pronounced: in computing, for example, *URL* (uniform resource locator) is pronounced by some as an abbreviation (*you-are-ell*) and others as an acronym (*earl*), with the result that some write it as *a URL* and others as *an URL*. Until a single pronunciation becomes generally accepted, the best practice is simply to ensure consistency within a given work.

3.7 **Possessives and plurals**

Abbreviations form the possessive in the ordinary way, with -'s: *CEO's salary, MPs' assistants*. Most abbreviations form the plural by adding -s: *VIPs, MCs, SOSs*. When an abbreviation contains more than one full point, put the -s after the final one: *Ph.D.s, M.Phil.s, the d.t.s*. When it has only one full point, put the -s before it: *eds., nos., Adms. Ramsay and Cunningham*. A few abbreviations have irregular plurals (*Messrs, Mmes*), sometimes stemming from the Latin convention of doubling the letter to create plurals: *pp. (pages), ll. (lines), MSS* (manuscripts).

Weights and measures usually take the same form in both singular and plural:

| oz. | lb. | st. | g. | gr. | bu. | dwt. | pt. | qt. | gal. |
| min. | sec. | in. | ft. | m (miles or metres) |

But insert the plural -s in *hrs., qrs., yrs*. In technical writing, and increasingly in general use, the full point is omitted: *oz, yd, cm, km, mm*, and *lb* now have no points, though the context in which they appear—and the presence of other abbreviated units—will determine how they should be styled. (*See* **CHAPTER 12**.)

3.8 **e.g., i.e., etc.**

Do not confuse 'e.g.' (*exempli gratia*), meaning 'for example', with 'i.e.' (*id est*), meaning 'that is'. Compare *hand tools, e.g. hammer and screwdriver* with *hand tools, i.e. those able to be held in the user's hands*. Print both in lower-case roman, with two points and no spaces, and preceded by a comma. In OUP style 'e.g.' and 'i.e.' are not followed by commas, to avoid double punctuation; commas are often used in US practice.

Although many people employ 'e.g.' and 'i.e.' quite naturally in speech as well as writing, prefer 'for example' and 'that is' in running text. (Since 'e.g.' and 'i.e.' are prone to overuse in text, this convention helps to limit their protusion.) Conversely, adopt 'e.g.' and 'i.e.' within parentheses or notes, since abbreviations are preferred there. A sentence in text cannot begin with 'e.g.' or 'i.e.'; however, a note can, in which case they—exceptionally—remain lower case (*see also* **15.16.3**):

> 22 e.g. Henry Holland, Charles Heathcote Tatham, and Thomas Sheraton.
>
> 23 i.e. the late English neoclassical style of the early 19th c.

Take care to distinguish 'i.e.' from the rarer 'viz.' (*videlicet*, namely). Formerly some writers used 'i.e.' to supply a definition or paraphrase, and 'viz.' to introduce a list of items. However, it is OUP's preference either to replace 'viz.' with 'namely', or to prefer 'i.e.' in every case.

In full 'etc.' is *et cetera*, meaning 'and other things'. Print it in lower-case roman, with a full point; do not use '&c.' except when duplicating historical typography. It is preceded by a comma if it follows more than one listed item: *robins, sparrows, etc., robins etc.* The point can be followed by a comma or whatever other point would be required after an equivalent phrase such as *and the like*—but not by a second full point, to avoid double punctuation.

Use 'etc.' in technical or scholarly contexts such as notes and works of reference. Elsewhere, prefer *such as*, *like*, or *for example* before a list, or *and so on*, *and the like* after it; none of these can be used in combination with 'etc.' It is considered offensive to use 'etc.' when listing individual people; use 'and others' instead; use 'etc.' when listing *types* of people, however. In a technical context, such as a bibliography, use '*et al.*':

> Daisy, Katie, Alexander, and others
>
> duke, marquess, earl, etc.
>
> Smith, Jones, Brown, et al.

Do not write 'and etc.': 'etc.' includes the meaning of 'and'. Do not end a list with 'etc.' if it begins with 'e.g.', 'including', 'for example', or 'such as', since these indicate that the list is to be incomplete. Choose one or the other, not both. As with 'e.g.', normally at least two examples are necessary before 'etc.', in order to establish the relationship between the elements and show how the list might go on. (This is often not the case in very condensed texts such as dictionaries and reference works.)

For lists of abbreviations *see* **1.2.14**; for legal abbreviations *see* **13.2.2**; for abbreviations in or following names *see* **4.2**.

CHAPTER 4

Capitalization and treatment of names

4.1 **Capitalization**

4.1.1 **General principles**

Capital letters in English are used to punctuate sentences and to distinguish proper nouns from other words. This second function in particular has wide discrepancies in practice, and certain disciplines and contexts diverge from the standard style outlined below. Editors should respect the views of authors expressing opinions on the matter, except in cases of internal discrepancies. Both authors and editors should strive for consistency: before writing or editing too much of a work, create a style sheet showing capitalization choices, and stick to it. For capitalization in languages other than English, *see* **CHAPTER 11** under the language concerned; for italics *see also* **6.2**.

4.1.2 **Sentence capitals**

■ Capitalize the first letter of a word that begins a sentence, or the first of a set of words used as a sentence, either initially or after a full point, a question mark, or an exclamation mark:

> He decided not to come. Little wonder!

For the capitalization of sentences between parentheses, *see* **5.11.1**. For capitalization after colons, *see* **5.5**. There is no need to capitalize after dashes—*see* **5.10**.

■ Capitalize the first letter of a syntactically complete quoted sentence, whether or not actual quotation marks are used:

> She replied, 'No more are left.'
> Consider this: 'Thou art the man.'
> Don't say 'That's impossible' till I've explained.
> He mused, Shall I eat this last biscuit?
> The question is, Will he resign?

but:

> Do not follow 'the madding crowd'.

The first word following a question mark should generally begin with a capital letter, except when forming a list of short, syntactically incomplete elements: *Do you prefer sugar? honey? milk or lemon?* (In US style a capital letter follows a question mark or colon in every case, regardless of syntax.)

- Capitalize the first letter of headings and captions, though not of items in lists unless each element in the list forms a complete and separate sentence.

- It is traditional to capitalize the beginning of a line of verse, regardless of whether it corresponds to the beginning of a sentence:

> Thus, though we cannot make our sun
> Stand still, yet we will make him run.

Some modern poets have abandoned this practice, or employ it selectively; editors should follow copy in such cases.

4.1.3 **Place names**

Capitalize names of recognized geographical region, whether topographical, astronomical, political, or merely legendary or popular:

Paris	the Channel	the States
the Black Forest	the Norfolk Broads	the Firth of Clyde
the Sea of Okhotsk	New England	Muswell Hill
the Eiffel Tower	the Straits of Gibraltar	Trafalgar Square
the New World	the Promised Land	the Big Apple
the Eternal City	Saturn	Sirius

the City (*London's financial centre*)

the Coast (*west coast of the US*)

Mexico City (*but* the city (*as metropolis*) *or* the City (*as corporation*) of Birmingham)

London Road (*if so named, but* the London road *for one merely leading to London*)

the Thames Estuary (*but* the estuary of the Thames)

the Milky Way (*but* the earth, the sun, the moon, *except in astronomical contexts and personification*)

- Capitalize compass directions only when they denote a recognized (i.e. titular) geographical or political region:

North Carolina	Northern Ireland (*but* northern England)
the mysterious East	the West End
unemployment in the South	the Western Wall
facing south	the southbound carriageway

- Usage divides where there is doubt whether the area denoted is merely directional or a definite territory, as with the south-east (or South East) of England. Strive for consistency within the text. Beware of anachronistic capitalization: *Romans invaded the Thames Valley; dinosaurs prowled the East Coast of the USA*.

- In a very small number of instances the definite article is always capitalized: *The Hague* (but *the Netherlands*).

- Capitalize *river* when it follows the name: *the East River*, *the Hudson River*, *the Yellow River*, *the Susquehanna River*. It is lower-case where (as in common British idiom) it precedes the name for purposes of description or clarification: *the river Thames*, *the river Dart*, *the river Exe*, *the river Wye*. *The River Plate* is an exception, being a conventional mistranslation of *Río de la Plata* ('Silver River'). Well-known rivers commonly need no such clarification, as there is little risk of confusion: *the Amazon*, *the Liffey*, *the Mississippi*, *the Thames* (archaic or poetic without *the*, as still in place names). A lower-case *river* may be added to any of these names where some clarification is required—to differentiate between the Amazon river and forest, or the Mississippi river and state. The name's context and the readership's expectation will determine whether it is appropriate to omit *river* from less well-known names: *the Cherwell* and *the river Cherwell* are both possible in different works; likewise *the Thames* and *the river Thames* (but *the Thames River Authority*, and *the Thames River* in Canada).

For general considerations in treatment of place names, *see* **4.2.10**.

4.1.4 **Institutions and organizations**

Capitals make a word or words specific in their reference; distinguishing, for instance, between *the white house* (a house painted white) and *the White House* (the US president's official residence), or between *a Christian scientist* (a scientist who is a Christian) and *a Christian Scientist* (a member of the Church of Christ Scientist). Capitalize the names of institutions, organizations, societies, movements, and the adjectives related to them. Follow the usual rules governing titles to determine which words in a single entity's name are capitalized, as in Dickens's *United Metropolitan Improved Hot Muffin and Crumpet Baking and Punctual Delivery Company*:

the Bank of England	the World Bank
the British Museum	the Department of Trade
the House of Lords	the Ford Motor Company
the United Nations	the Charity Organization Society
the Crown	the Campaign for Real Ale
the Cabinet	the Bar
a Nobel Prize	the Right, the Left, the Centre (*as political factions*)

the Navy, the Army, the Air Force (*as titles of particular organizations*)

Marxism	Christianity
Social Democrat	Islam
Buddhism	Judaism
Protestants	Baptists
a Methodist	the Roman Catholic Church

- Some words bear a distinction in capitalization according to their use in an abstract or specific sense. Churches are capitalized for denomination, as *Baptist Church*, but lower-cased for building, as *Baptist church*. Note, however, the distinction between

    the Roman Catholic Church and the Eastern Orthodox Church

    the Roman Catholic and Eastern Orthodox churches

    Oxford University and Cambridge University

    Oxford and Cambridge universities

    where *churches* and *universities* are lower-case since they are descriptive rather than part of a formal name. Similarly, *State* is capitalized in an abstract or legal sense, *separation of Church and State*, but not in a specific sense (except when forming a title): *drove over the New York state line* but *member of the New York State Senate*.

- The historians' common practice of imposing minimal capitalization for titles should be discouraged when it extends to a uniform lower-case treatment for such terms as *catholic, protestant, church, state*. Here, the words' distinct meanings, usually indicated by capital and lower-case forms, may otherwise be obscured.

- In British usage, capitalize *government* when referring to a particular body of persons, the Ministers of the Crown and their staffs, but use lower case for a general concept or body. In US style, *government* is lower-case in all senses.

    Included here are attributes used as recognized names: *a Red*; *he got his Blue for rowing*. Note, however, that *black* and *white* are not capitalized when referring to people by skin colour.

4.1.5 Dates and spans of time

Capitalize the names of days, months, festivals, and holidays:

Tuesday	March	Easter
Good Friday	Holy Week	Ramadan
Passover	Christmas Eve	the Fifth of November
New Year's Day	St Frideswide's Day	

- Those of more than one word that are drawn from other languages are not all treated uniformly, their styling often depending on their mode of transcription. Follow the form most commonly found:

Haru no sanichi	Jamshedi Nau Roz	Laylat al-Qadr
Mahāvīra Jayanti	Rosh ha-Shanah	

- The seasons, spring, summer, autumn/fall, winter, are lower-case, except where personified:

  > I saw old Autumn in the misty morn
  >
  > See, Winter comes to rule the varied year

- Capitalize times and time zones in scientific and British usage; these are lower-case in common US usage (though their abbreviations are not):

Universal Time	International Atomic Time	Greenwich Mean Time
British Summer Time	daylight saving time	eastern standard time

4.1.6 Geological periods and events

Capitalize geological formations and periods, and historical periods and events:

Devonian	Carboniferous	Precambrian
Ordovician	Pleistocene	Palaeozoic
Palaeolithic	Mesolithic	Bronze Age
Stone Age	Early Minoan	the Dark Ages (*but* medieval)
the Age of Reason	the Reformation	the Crucifixion
the Hegira	the Last Supper	the South Sea Bubble

No one rule is applicable to modern periods, which are found with both capitals and lower case. In such cases, follow established usage:

the space age	the age of steam	the Jazz Age
the *belle époque*	the Bronze Age	

- Cultural schools and movements are capitalized when derived from proper names. The tendency otherwise is to use lower case unless it is important to distinguish a specific from a general meaning. Compare, for example

  > classical (*as in period, music, or art*)
  >
  > Classical (*as distinguished from e.g.* Hellenistic *or* Baroque)
  >
  > federal (*as in a federation of states*)
  >
  > Federal (*of the Union side in the US Civil War*)
  >
  > cubist and impressionist (*influences of art upon e.g. literature or design*)
  >
  > Cubist and Impressionist (*the actual historical movements in art*)

Certain disciplines and specialist contexts may require different treatment, depending on how and which terms are used. Classicists, for example, will often capitalize *Classical* to define, say, painting or sculpture in opposition to Hellenistic, or to mean the specific flourishing in Greece during the fifth century BC; editors should not institute this independently if an author has chosen not to do so.

- Use lower case for millennia and centuries: *the first millennium, the six-teenth century.* To denote simple ten-year spans OUP style prefers, for example, *1920s* or *1960s* to *nineteen-twenties* or *nineteen-sixties.* To denote decades of a specific character (say, the Roaring Twenties, the Swinging Sixties) OUP prefers *Twenties* or *Sixties* to *'20s* or *'60s.*

- *War* and equivalent terms are capitalized when it forms part of the name of a specific conflict or campaign:

the Conquest of Gaul	the French Revolution
the American Civil War	the Peninsular Campaign
the Boer War	the Siege of Stalingrad
the Battle of Midway	the Korean Conflict

    After the first mention, any subsequent references to *the war* are in lower case.

    Colloquially, *the War* is a common description for the Second—but *not* the First—World War, if the term cannot in context be confused with any other war, as in *Don't mention the War!* (Prior to the outbreak of the Second World War, the First World War was known as *The Great War.*) However, a distinction in capitals between *the war* (First) and *the War* (Second) would be too subtle in a context that discusses both intermittently, and in formal writing spelling out the full term—*First World War, World War I,* etc.—is preferable.

4.1.7 Titles of rank or relationship, and nicknames:

Auntie Beeb	Lady Mary
the Duke of Wellington	the Prince of Wales
the Prime Minister	the Special Relationship
King Henry	Cardinal Richelieu
Major-General	Assistant Adjutant-General
Vice-President	Chief Justice
Professor Higgins	the Famous Five
HM the Queen	the French Ambassador
the Pope	the Apostles
the Iron Duke	the Prophet
Al 'Scarface' Capone	Old Hickory
Uncle Sam	the Admirable Crichton
Capability Brown	the Lake Poets
Fellow of the Royal Society	the Asbury Jukes

- Titles used as identification or clarification *after* a name normally are not capitalized (especially in US usage):

Miss Dunn, the head teacher	Anne Williams, our managing director
Mr Gladstone, the prime minister	Dr Primrose, the parish vicar

■ Titles used *before* a name are normally capitalized, and are not followed by a comma:

Head Teacher Miss Dunn	Managing Director Anne Williams
the Prime Minister Mr Gladstone	The Reverend Dr Primrose

This extends to all vocatives: *Good evening, General*; *Hello, Father!*

■ When referring back, after the first mention, to a capitalized compound item, the usual practice is to revert to lower case:

Cambridge University—their university	Aunt Jane—her aunt
the Ritz Hotel—that hotel	Lake Tanganyika—the lake
National Union of Mineworkers—the union	Merton College—our college

■ Capitals are preferred, however, when a short-form mention of a title is used as synonym for a specified person, an organization in an institutional or official sense, or a government department:

the Duke	the Princess
the Ministry (of Defence)	the House (of Commons)
the Yard (Scotland Yard)	the University statute
the College silver	the Centre's policy

■ Historians may impose minimal capitalization—particularly in contexts where the subjects of their writing bear titles—*the duke of Somerset, the duke*; *the king of Spain, the king.* (Nevertheless e.g. *King Richard* and *Lord James* should remain thus.) This practice, common in the discipline, avoids a profusion of capitals on the page, and may be followed providing it is imposed consistently throughout a work and it does not introduce ambiguity (*see* **4.1.4**).

Use lower case for referring to all such titles in a general sense:

a French ambassador	most viceroys
the seventeenth-century popes	a visiting professor
every king of England	ask your uncle

■ Capitalize possessive pronouns only when they form part of the titles of a holy person, or of a sovereign or other dignitary:

Her Majesty	Their Excellencies
Our Lady	Your Holiness

Personal pronouns referring to the Sovereign but independent of his or her title (plurals of majesty) are capitalized only in proclamations: 'We', 'Us', 'Our', 'Ours', 'Ourself', etc.

4.1.8 **Titles and subtitles of works**

These include English books, newspapers, plays, films, TV programmes, pictures, the Bible and books of the Bible (*but* biblical), etc. Capitalize the first word and all nouns, pronouns, adjectives, verbs, and adverbs, but generally not articles, conjunctions, or short prepositions.

For Whom the Bell Tolls	*Gone with the Wind*
A Tale of Two Cities	*The Way of All Flesh*
Can You Forgive Her?	*Farmer and Stockbreeder*
Paradise Lost	the Authorized Version
Constable's *The Hay Wain*	Leviticus
the Book of Common Prayer	the Koran

In practice this usually amounts to the first and last words in a title, and any important words in between; very short titles may look best with every word capitalized: *All About Eve*.

Capitalize *The* when it begins a title: *The Origin of Species*, *The Wind in the Willows*, *The Tain*, *The Program Development Process*. For periodicals, capitalize *The* only for one-word titles: *The Times*, *The Spectator* (but today's *Times*, the *Spectator* article); the *New Yorker*, the *Yearbook of English Studies*. (*See also* **6.3**.)

Foreign-language titles and subtitles follow the rules common to that language. (For guidance, *see* under the individual language in **CHAPTER 11**.) Except in general for French and German titles, this consists for the most part of minimal capitalization: capitalizing only the first word in the title and subtitle, and any proper names. Transliterated or romanized titles follow this practice as well. (*See also* **15.2.2**.)

4.1.9 **Musical works**

For the most part song titles in English conform to the rules for capitalizing titles in general:

> 'Three Blind Mice', 'Where the Bee Sucks', 'When a Man Loves a Woman', 'Brown-eyed Girl'

This is irrespective of whether the title forms a sentence with a finite verb:

> 'A Nightingale Sang in Berkeley Square', 'It Don't Mean a Thing (If It Ain't Got That Swing)', 'I Don't Want to Go Home', 'Papa's Got a Brand New Bag'

In contrast, traditional ballads and songs, which customarily draw their titles directly from the first line, follow the rules for poetry where the title forms a sentence. Here, only the first and proper nouns are capitalized:

> 'Come away, death', 'Boney was a warrior', 'What shall we do with the drunken sailor?'

■ For canticles and sections of the Mass, such as the Te Deum and the Kyrie, capitalize a term used in a specific sense and set in lower case when it is used in a general sense:

> Of all Mozart's piano sonatas, the Piano Sonata in A minor is the finest.
> Beethoven's First Symphony is smaller in scale than the Second.
> Mass in D (*genre title*)

Mass 'Gloria tibi Trinitas' (*genre title with plainsong on which it is based*)

Missa Papae Marcelli (*original title*)

- Musical phrases are styled with the following distinctions:

Capitalize the title of a movement: *the Adagio of Mahler's Fifth Symphony.* (A slow introduction to a main movement can be regarded as a movement in its own right.)

Use lower-case initials and single quotation marks to indicate a tempo mark specified by the composer or included in the published version: *the 'andante' gives way after six bars to a spirited 'allegro'.*

Use lower-case initial letters and no quotation marks for the general use of the term: *the vivace character of the trumpet writing.* This also applies to the internal division of a movement: *the second movement, the Intermezzo, has the internal structure andantino–allegro–andante.* This is the most common usage; if in doubt do not add quotation marks.

Titles of musical works in another language follow the rules of that language; *see* CHAPTER 11 under the language concerned. For more on musical works *see* 13.5.

4.1.10 Bills, acts, treaties, policies, and legal documents

the Declaration of Independence, the Bill of Rights, the Corn Laws, Factory and Workshop Act 1911

(For more on legal citations *see* 13.2.)

- Capitals are often obligatory in legal documents:

the Ford Motor Company—The Company shall . . .

4.1.11 Peoples and languages, and their related adjectives and verbs

Englishwoman	Arabs	Austrian	French	Catalan
Cornish	Swahili	Aboriginal	Americanize	Hellenize

- Usage is divided over adjectives based on nationality. Formerly there was a tendency to use lower case where the association was remote or merely allusive, but capitalized where the noun was more closely or more recently linked with the nationality or proper noun. For example:

arabic numbers	roman numerals	italic script
venetian blinds	morocco leather	chinese whispers

but:

German measles	Hong Kong flu	Irish setter
London pride	Turkish delight	Shetland pony
Michaelmas daisy	Afghan hound	Venetian red

This tendency has now halted and in many cases been reversed, as with the current capitalization of *Brussels sprouts, Chinese white, Dutch auction,*

India ink, and *French kissing*, all formerly lower-case. Usage is fluid, but it is important to be aware of the distinction between, for example, the standard English meaning of roman and arabic numbers (indicated by lower case) and those specifically used by Romans and Arabs (indicated by capitals).

4.1.12 **Words derived from proper nouns**

Capitals are used for a word derived from a proper noun, such as a personal name, in contexts where the link with the noun is still felt to be alive:

Christian	Dantesque	Beethovenian
Shakespearian	Homeric	Hellenic
Talmudic	Dickensian	Kafkaesque
Americanize	Christianize	Europeanize

■ Lower case is used in contexts where the association is remote, merely allusive, or a matter of convention:

bowdlerize	galvanize	pasteurize
boycott	wellington boots	protean
quixotic	titanic	stentorian
chauvinistic	gargantuan	mesmerize

■ Some words of this type can have both capitals and lower case in different contexts. This depends on whether the connection with the noun is close or loose or—in the case of a term derived from a personal name—whether the word is being used to evoke a specific person or that person's general attributes:

Byzantine (*of architecture*) *but* byzantine (*complexity*)
Philistine (*of tribe*) *but* philistine (*tastes*)
Machiavellian (*of Machiavelli*) *but* machiavellian (*intrigue*)
Draconian (*of Draco*) *but* draconian (*legislation*)
Bohemian (*of central Europe*) *but* bohemian (*unconventional*)
Stoic (*of Zeno*) *but* stoic (*impassive*)
Lilliputian (*of Lilliput*) *but* lilliputian (*diminutive*)
Platonic (*of philosophy*) *but* platonic (*love*)
Herculean (*of Hercules*) *but* herculean (*task*)
Stentorian (*of Stentor*) *but* stentorian (*loud*)

■ Note the distinction between 'people' and 'things':

an Adonis	a Casanova
a Venus	a Daniel come to judgement

but:

a sandwich	a cardigan	a wellington	a valentine

- Retain the capital letter after a prefix and hyphen:

  pro-Nazi   anti-British   non-Catholic   mid-Atlantic

- Use lower case for scientific units and poetic metres derived from names:

ampere	joule	newton	volt
watt	alcaics	alexandrines	sapphics

- Where compound nouns begin with a capitalized name, the name only is capitalized:

Avogadro number	Halley's comet	Occam's razor
Planck's law	Hodgkin's disease	Angelman syndrome

4.1.13 The deity and religious rites

Use capitals for all references to the monotheistic deity:

God	the Lord	the Almighty	the Supreme Being
Jehovah	the Holy Trinity	Allah	the Holy Spirit

Use lower case for pronouns referring to him, where the reference is clear, unless the author specifies otherwise. In any event, write *who, whom, whose* in lower case. Capitalize *God-awful, God-fearing, God-forsaken.*

Use lower case for the gods of polytheistic religions (*Huitzilopochtli, Aztec god of war*), and for the idiom 'make a god of something'. *Goddess* is always lower case except in titles and at the start of a sentence (*the goddess of blight and mildew, Robigo*).

Capitalization of religious sacraments or rites in different religions (and contexts) is not uniform. Note, for example:

a mass	baptism	compline
bar mitzvah	bhog	ghusl

but:

the Mass	the Eucharist	Anointing of the Sick
Fang Yen-Kou	Agnihotra	Saṁnyāsa

4.1.14 Trade names

Capitalize them if they are proprietary terms:

Hoover	Xerox	Biro
Jacuzzi	Persil	Kleenex
Coca-Cola	Levi's	Stilton

but write e.g. *hoover* and *xerox* as verbs. Where possible it is better as a general policy to employ generic terms both as nouns and verbs, for the sake of (especially foreign) readers unfamiliar with specific brands. Prefer, for example, *vacuum, photocopy, ballpoint pen, whirlpool bath*.

4.1.15 Ships, aircraft, and vehicles

Capitalize references, using italics for individual names but not for types, models, or marques (*see also* **6.4**):

the *Cutty Sark*	HMS *Dreadnought*
The Spirit of St Louis	a 1909 Rolls-Royce Silver Ghost
a Mini Cooper	the airship R. 101

4.1.16 Personification, anthropomorphism, and transcendent ideas

O Fame!	O wild West Wind
Daughter of the Moon, Nokomis	And Joy, whose hand is ever at his lips

Personification is traditional, though sexist, in the case of ships and other craft. It is considered old-fashioned to use *she* of nations and cities in prosaic contexts: prefer, say, 'Britain decimalized its currency in 1971'. The device is still found, and still acceptable, in literary writing:

And that sweet City with her dreaming spires
She needs not June for beauty's heightening

4.1.17 Academic subjects

Capitalize the names of academic subjects only in the context of courses and examinations:

He wanted to study physics, he read Physics, sat the Physics examination, and received a degree in Physics, thereby gaining a physics degree

4.1.18 Sequence

In text it is very common, though not universal, to capitalize words immediately followed by a number or letter to show a sequence, as in *Route 66, Form 3b, Flight 17, Gate 16, Room 101, Act I*.

4.1.19 Postcodes

Postcodes are printed in full capitals, ranging numerals, with no points or hyphens: *OX2 6DP*. Ensure that the letter *O* and the number *0* are distinguished. Where the font has non-ranging numerals, or in a small-capital setting such as a publisher's imprint, small capitals may give a better effect.

For capitalization of abbreviations and acronyms, *see* **3.2**.

4.2 **References to People**

4.2.1 General principles

Use the form of name individuals are most commonly known by, or known to prefer:

> Arthur C. Clarke (*not* Arthur Clarke *or* Arthur Charles Clarke)
>
> k. d. lang (*all lower-case*)
>
> I. M. Pei (*not* Ieoh Ming Pei)
>
> Jimmy Carter (*not* James Earl Carter)
>
> John Wayne (*not* Marion Michael Morrison)

When mentioned in passing, a person's name usually need appear only in the form by which the bearer is best known. For example, a writer's married name or hereditary title is important only if the person wrote under it. In text, authors should clarify titles and names altered by marriage or any other means only to avoid confusion (particularly if someone else is compiling the index):

> Michael (later Sir Michael) Tippett
>
> Laurence (later Lord) Olivier
>
> Sir (later Mr) Anthony Blunt
>
> John Wayne (born Marion Michael Morrison)
>
> George Eliot (pseudonym of Mary Ann, later Marian, Evans)

In any event, avoid combining several permutations at a time:

> Lord Dunglass (then Lord Home, later Sir Alec Douglas-Home, now Baron Home of the Hirsel)

Glossing on this scale is best relegated to a separate parenthetical note.

né(e)

The word *né* (feminine form *née*), meaning 'born' in French, is used to indicate a previous forename or surname for either sex; it is not italic. Strictly speaking it refers only to a surname, which is legally assumed at birth:

> Lord Beaconsfield, né Benjamin Disraeli
>
> Muhammad Ali, né Cassius Marcellus Clay, Jr.
>
> Baroness Lee of Asheridge, née Jennie Lee

Do not use it in conjunction with pseudonyms, aliases, or nicknames, but only where the new name is legally adopted.

In English it is most commonly applied to indicate a married woman's maiden name, after her adopted surname:

> Frances (Fanny) d'Arblay, née Burney
> the Countess of Pembroke, née Mary Spencer

Some writers differentiate between using *née* for a married woman's maiden name and *born* for a person's previous name changed by a process other than marriage. This distinction is acceptable, and should not be changed when consistently applied.

- Do not truncate people's first names—for example, use *George* not *Geo.*, *Robert* not *Robt.*, unless approximating a signature or facsimile. Rules differ in French practice for some names—and for transliterating for example Arabic, Hebrew, and Russian—but the practices customary in those contexts should not be imposed in English texts.

Husbands and wives may jointly be called e.g. *Mr and Mrs Joseph Bloggs*. Strictly speaking the wife is correctly referred to individually as *Mrs Joseph Bloggs*, and using the given name (*Mrs Abigail Bloggs*) is limited to divorcées and widows. Nevertheless, this distinction is no longer obligatory except in the most formal contexts, such as invitations or official lists: *Mrs Abigail Bloggs* is an acceptable form in all day-to-day circumstances.

Do not use an apostrophe in pluralizing names:

> all the Jameses, three Marys, keeping up with the Joneses

4.2.2 Titles

Titles are usually capitalized. Abbreviated titles of honour, such as *MBE*, *FRS*, *MFH*, are usually in capitals, with a comma preceding the first and separating each subsequent title. (Setting the letters all in small capitals may give a better general effect in displayed work, or in contexts where such titles are frequent.) Abbreviated titles composed of all-capital letters have no full points in modern style (e.g. *DFC*, *FRA*, *KCSJ*), but those with a combination of upper- and lower-case letters usually do (e.g. *B.Sc.*, *D.Phil.*, *Dip.Comput.*)—though exceptions exist. The order of titles of honour and decorations may be found in *Debrett's*.

- For the sake of brevity, titles (especially military ranks) are often abbreviated or even ignored in text, whether or not they are used before the surname alone: *Wing Commander Bader*, *W/Cdr Douglas Bader*; *Captain Hornblower*, *Capt. Horatio Hornblower*, *Hornblower*.

- Even at first mention in text, titles do not have to conform to full titles of address, the strict order of which is prescribed in *Debrett's*, *Burke's*, and various books on etiquette. Those cited in references should mirror the form given on the work's title page, although a parenthetical gloss may help the reader if the name under which a book was written is unfamiliar or obscure. Do not use orders, decorations, degrees, or fellowships in title pages, nor normally in text except at first mention—and then only in the proportion required by the subject matter. For example, the Rt. Hon. Ratu Sir Kamisese Kapaiwai Tuimacilai Mara, GCMG, KBE, PC, Tui Nayau, Tui Lau would be best referred to as, say, *Sir Kamisese* or *Mara* in text, and HRH The Prince of Wales, KG, KT, GCB is more simply styled *Prince Charles* or *the Prince*.

■ Internal consistency is most important, with the same person ideally being identified in the same way regardless of honours or ennoblement that during the course of the narrative, so that Joe Bloggs is not referred to in successive parts of a work as *young Joey*, *Joe*, *Dr Bloggs*, *Sir Joseph*, and finally the *Marquess of Bloggshire*.

■ The former distinction is no longer made between using *Mr* for labour-ers or those without a bachelor's degree, and *Esq.* for professional men or those with a bachelor's degree. *Esq.* and *Bt.* precede all other letters following a name; do not combine either with *Mr*. Do not combine *Mr, Mrs, Miss, Ms, Dr, Esq.*, etc. with any other title:

> Joseph Bloggs, Esq.
>
> Mrs Abigail Bloggs
>
> Dr John Bloggs
>
> Mary Bloggs, D.Phil.
>
> Alasdair Bloggs, Bt., CBE, MVO, MFH

■ To aid the reader, it is permissible when making textual references to members of a foreign aristocracy to qualify the family name with an English approximation of their official title, such as *Baron Ito*, *Count von Zeppelin*, *King Geza II*. Take care that the result is not jarring, however, since in some contexts—and for certain readerships—the imposition of a familiar title for a foreign one may seem incongruous.

■ Saints' names can be problematic, as they exist as titles for individuals, as proper nouns, and as surnames. When the place name etc. is in a foreign language, the abbreviation is alphabetized under the full form in that language.

In French, use a capital *S* and hyphen if relating to the name of a place, person, or saint's day, for example *Saint-Étienne*, *Sainte-Beuve*, *la Saint-Barthélemy*, but small *s* with a space after if relating to the person of a saint, for example *saint Jean*; abbreviation *S.*, feminine *Ste*, for the per-sons of Saints; in names of places, of persons other than saints, or of saints' days it is *St-*, feminine *Ste-*.

In German, use *Sankt-*, abbreviated *St.*; for the saints themselves *hl.* (*heilig*).

In Italian, saint before a consonant is masculine *San*, feminine *Santa*; before an impure *S* it is *Santo* ('Santo Stefano'), before a vowel *Sant'*.

In Portuguese, saint is masculine *Sao*; before a vowel it is sometimes *Santo*, feminine *Santa*.

In Spanish, saint is masculine *San*, before *Do-*, *To-* is *Santo*, feminine *Santa*.

4.2.3 Punctuation

Initials before a surname are separated by full points, preferably with a space after each in OUP style: *J. S. Bach, E. H. Shepard, J. R. R. Tolkien.* Normally, names given entirely in initials have points but no spaces (*J.S.B., E.H.S., J.R.R.T.*). Those few people more commonly known by their free-standing initials have neither points nor spaces (*FDR, LBJ*).

Titles that follow a name are separated from it by a comma:

> Millard Fillmore, President of the United States
> Admiral of the Fleet Viscount Lamb, GCB, KBE

Titles of judges (*Justice, Lord Chief Justice, Chief Baron, Master of the Rolls,* etc.) are an exception in their abbreviated form, having no preceding comma: *Kennedy J, Evershed MR* (*see also* **13.2.1**).

There is no comma in some combinations of titles:

> His Grace the Archbishop of Armagh
> His Honour Judge Perkins

Commas are rarely necessary before (or after) names in simple apposition:

> Her husband Henry is a scientist

But further elements may confuse matters. Although context usually clarifies the sense, set off the name in commas if ambiguity is possible:

> Her eighth husband Henry is a scientist. (*Were all eight husbands named Henry?*)
> Her handsome husband Henry (*as opposed to her ugly husband?*)
> His son Theodore (*suggests more than one son*)
> His son, Theodore (*suggests only one son*)

4.2.4 Types of names

Distinguish between adopted names, pseudonyms, nicknames, and aliases.

■ The owner of an **adopted name** uses it for all purposes, and may have adopted it legally. In this case, *born, né(e), formerly,* or the like is suitable:

> Marilyn Monroe, born Norma Jean Mortensen
> Joseph Conrad (formerly Teodor Józef Konrad Korzeniowski)
> Susan Wilkinson (née Brown)

The French use the form *dit(e)* to indicate the better-known name:

Amandine-Aurore Lucille Dupin, baronne Dudevant, dite George Sand

In English this form is often replaced by 'called' or 'known as'.

■ A **pseudonym** is used for a specific purpose, such as a pen-name or *nom de théâtre*, and is not employed outside that sphere; it can be derived from the bearer's true name, or be wholly distinct from it: *Boz* (Charles Dickens), *Q* (Sir Arthur Quiller-Couch), *Æ* (George Russell), *Ranulph Fiennes* (Sir Ranulph Twisleton-Wykeham-Fiennes). Exceptionally, it may be shared by two or more people: *Ellery Queen* (Frederic Dannay and Manfred B. Lee), *Theo Durrant* (Mystery Writers of America, Inc., California Chapter).

■ A **nickname** can supplement or supplant the owner's original name: *the Yankee Clipper* (Joe DiMaggio), *the Sun King* (Louis XIV of France), *the Fat Controller* (Sir Topham Hatt), *Ernest 'Papa' Hemingway*, *Charlie 'Bird' Parker*. Through use it can eventually replace the owner's name, either occasionally (*Old Blue Eyes*, *Il Duce*, *The Wasp of Twickenham*), partially (*Fats Waller*, *Capability Brown*, *Bugsy Siegal*, *Grandma Moses*, *Malcolm X*), or entirely (*Howlin' Wolf*, *Muddy Waters*, *Meat Loaf*, *Twiggy*). While no rules govern whether a nickname is put in quotation marks, the tendency is for quotation marks to be used more often when the nickname is inserted within or precedes another name, and less when used alone.

■ An **alias** is a false or assumed name, borne with an intent for duplicity or fraud. In law-enforcement reports this is indicated by *aka* ('also known as') before the alias.

4.2.5 *Junior* and *senior*

Junior and *senior* are post-positive particles attached to names, to differentiate a son and father with the same name. Each has several abbreviations (*Jr.*, *jun.*, *jnr.*, *jr.*, *junr.*; *sen.*, *senr.*, *snr.*, *sr.*). Use the abbreviation *Jr.* when it forms part of the bearer's name, as in US practice: *John Doe, Jr.* Set it after the surname, before degrees or other titles: *J. Doe, Jr., Esq.*, not *Esq., Jr.* The comma preceding it is sometimes left out; follow the bearer's individual preference, if known. Do not use it with the title only: *Mr John Doe, Jr.*, *John Doe, Jr.*, not *Mr Doe, Jr.* Use *jun.* where it is an ad hoc designation rather than a constituent part of the bearer's name. In this context a comma always precedes it: *John Doe, jun.*

Unlike *junior*, *senior* does not form part of the bearer's name, and therefore is used only as an ad hoc designation. It is not capitalized, and a comma always precedes it: *John Doe, sen.* As for *junior*, set it after the surname, before degrees or other titles.

In French *fils* is an ad hoc designation added after a surname to distinguish a son from a father, as *Dumas fils*; *père* does the same to distinguish a father from a son, as *Dumas père*. Both are italic in English.

4.2.6 **Personal-name particles**

These are prefixes to proper names, like *de*, *du*, *van den*, or *von*, which are sometimes called *nobiliary particles*. Copy signatures and follow the bearer's preference, if known. Within an alphabetical listing supply cross-references where necessary.

de

In accordance with French practice, *de* should not have an initial capital (*de Candolle*, *de Talleyrand-Périgord*), except when Anglicized (*De Quincey*, *De Vinne*) or at the beginning of a sentence. Before a vowel *d'* is used (*d'Alembert*); before a consonant one rule dictates that *de* is used only if the name consists of one syllable, not counting final -*e* or -*es*: *de Gaulle* but *Tocqueville*. (For the purposes of this rule *d'*, *du*, *des* are retained; *de La* becomes *La*.) However, as French practice itself varies, follow established convention or the bearer's preference, where known, ensuring that each name is treated consistently within a work. Names prefixed with a lower-case *de* or *d'* should be alphabetized under the surname: *Alembert, Jean le Rond d'*; *Mairan, Jean-Jacques de*; *Chazelles, Jean-Francois, comte de* (conventions governing some names differ from the norm, as *Corday d'Armont, Charlotte*). French names beginning with a voiced *h* (*aspiré*) take *de* (*de Hainaut*); names beginning with a mute *h* (*non aspiré*) or a vowel take *d'* (*d'Hermies, d'Urfé*). This follows the usual distinction in French that produces e.g. *le haricot* and *La Henriade* on the one hand and *l'homme* and *L'Heptaméron* on the other. As with *de*, alphabetization of names ignores *d'*. British and US names of this form may be dealt with differently by their bearers.

In Dutch the prefix *de* is an article, not a preposition; it is generally not capitalized, and does not form the basis for alphabetization, as *Groot, Geert de*. In Flemish the reverse is true, with *De Bruyne, Jan*.

Particles in Italian names are capitalized—*De Sanctis, Gaetano*; *Della Casa, Adriana*; *Del Corno, Francesco*; *Di Benedetti, Vittorio*—and are the basis for alphabetization. An exception is made for aristocratic names beginning *de'*, *degli*, or *di*: *Medici, Lorenzo de'*; these are capitalized under the name rather than particle. (Some names in this form are still current; to style them with capital *D* is considered a studied insult.)

In Spanish names *de* is lower case and omitted in bare surname references.

de La

In modern French the compound particle *de La* has only one capital (*de La Fontaine, de La Condamine*). The *de* is dropped in the absence of a forename: *La Fontaine said* .... Note that within a French sentence *de La Fontaine* means the possessive 'La Fontaine's', not simply 'La Fontaine'.

This allows Hippolyte Taine's thesis to be titled *Essai sur les fables de La Fontaine*. When Anglicized the prefix may deviate from this practice (*de la Mare*, *De La Warr*); follow established convention or the bearer's preference (if known). Names prefixed with *de La* are alphabetized under *La*: *La Fontaine, Jean de.*

The convention of capitalization for *de La* was not used before the eighteenth century, and was not uniformly imposed afterwards. In the seventeenth century and before some people bearing these particles before their names used lower-case or capital letters indiscriminately. In other cases, however, they adopted a definite preference for one form, which has become fixed in academic usage. Modern French scholarly works may reflect such variations, which should not be regularized.

Du

Du normally has an initial capital, regardless of whether the particle is separated from the name by a space or joined to it. Names are alphabetized under *D* accordingly, *Du Deffand, Marie, marquise*; *Duchamp, Marcel*. Variations exist with lower-case *du*, with the name accordingly alphabetized according to the surname; this is also the case where the surname is actually formed from a title: *Maine, Louise de Bourbon, duchesse du.*

van, van den, van der

As a Dutch prefix to a proper name, *van, van den, van der* are usually not capitalized except at the beginning of a sentence, and therefore are all alphabetized under the main name. In Flemish, however, the reverse is usually true, with a capital *V* used in alphabetizing: Afrikaans employs both conventions. The combined prefix *ver* is usually capitalized and run in: *Vermeer*. In Britain and the USA both upper- and lower-case particles usually form the basis for alphabetizing names of Dutch origin.

von, von der, vom

As a Germanic prefix to a proper name, *von* usually has no initial capital, except at the beginning of a sentence. In some Swiss names the *Von* is capitalized (*Peter Von der Mühll*). Where the surname stands alone *von* is omitted: *Justus von Liebig* but *Liebig*, *Gertrud von Helfta* but *Helfta*; *von* by itself is ignored during alphabetization. The related forms *von der* and *vom* are usually retained, however, and form the basis for alphabetization.

4.2.7 Historical names

Originally, similar names were distinguished by reference to the bearer's location, employment, parents, physical characteristics, or other attributes: for example *Duke Robert the Magnificent* (father of William the Conqueror), *Ralph the Ill-Tonsured* (d. 1062). The originally

Germanic practice of surnaming reached different cultures at different times: in Britain surnames were uncommon before the thirteenth century. Treat historical names according to the conventions of the discipline in which they occur. Sometimes there is no firm agreement as to what constitutes a surname and what a given name—a distinction that may well have puzzled their bearers at the time. Consequently the medieval authors Peter Abelard, William Occam, and Matthew Paris may all be found alphabetized by their last names or their first. The most sensible course is to adopt consistently whatever standard is usual in the context in which a name is found, then provide a suitable gloss in text or cross-reference in the index for those not conversant with the convention. Historical names in other cultures are governed by other rules; guidelines for some are given in the following sections.

Hellenic names

Ancient Hellenic names bear their own set of difficulties. Traditional practice, dating from a time when any educated person could read Latin but few could read Greek, has been to use Greek names in a Latinized form. Until the early nineteenth century this applied even to gods, so that Zeus and Hera would appear as *Jupiter* and *Juno*, a practice no longer acceptable even in writing for the general reader.

Following the lead of the German Romantics, modern Greek scholars often prefer to transliterate the original Greek spellings without Latinizing them, but they are seldom consistent, apart from names of persons known from non-literary sources such as inscriptions, which are nearly always left un-Latinized. Context is the most important test: *Herakles* is used in discussing Greek literature, art, religion, etc. but *Hercules* is used in Roman contexts (he was worshipped by male Romans as a full deity). Similarly, one would discuss the gradual canonification of the twelve labours of Herakles in Greek art and poetry, but in a general allusion one would say *the labours of Hercules*.

Broadly speaking, the rule of thumb is to give familiar names in their traditional English—that is, Latinized—form, but retain the Greek spelling for others; unfortunately, no two scholars seem to agree on which names are familiar and which are not. Consequently it is hard to lay down rules, except that no one should appear in Hellenized spelling who is more of a household name than one who is Latinized. Another rule might be that names should not be spelt in the Greek fashion that are not meant to be so pronounced; but that leaves it open to the author to say yes, he does say *Thoukydides*. When in doubt, editors should request the author either to confirm specific instances or to outline a general policy to be followed.

Editors and indexers can fall foul of scholars who differentiate separate bearers of the same name through Latinizing and Hellenizing alone, casting *Thucydides* for the historian but *Thoukydides* for his uncle the conservative and anti-imperialist politician, *Callimachus* for the scholar-poet but *Kallimachos* for the Athenian general at the time of Marathon. Probably no one would call the philosopher (or even his namesake the comic poet) *Platon*; on the other hand, a lesser light by that name would normally be called *Platon* by modern scholars.

The commonest hybrid forms, which may be regarded as the normal English spellings, are those with *ei* where the strict Latinizers of the past used *i*, for example *Cleisthenes* for *Kleisthenes* or *Clisthenes*; on the other hand a hybrid such as *Teuker* for Greek *Teukros* and Latin *Teucer* is deemed unacceptable. There are also a few purely English forms, such as *Aristotle*: no one would call the philosopher anything else, though another man of the same name would be *Aristoteles* to Hellenizer and Latinizer alike; similarly *Homer* and *Hesiod*.

In the absence of any standardizing authority, the best course of action is for editors to keep an eye out for inconsistency. Provided they can tell Greeks from Romans, even non-classicists will notice that both *c* (as opposed to *ch*) and *k* are being used, and final *-os* and *-us*. Beyond this the task may be likened to the stables of Augeas (or Augeias).

■ Some typical Latinizing changes to Greek names:

  ai = ae

  k = c

  kh = ch (*but* ch *often retained*)

  ei = i (*but* ei *often used in otherwise Latin transcriptions*)

  oi = oe

  os *final* = us, *but* -ros *final after consonant* = er (*with some exceptions:* Phaedrus *not* Phaeder, *though the latter is found in Latin*)

  ou = u (*but* u *occasionally retained*)

  u (*except in diphthongs*) = y (*but* y *sometimes retained*)

The long *e* and *o* are sometimes marked in Greek transcription, but never in Latin. Between vowels, *i* in Greek is the second half of a diphthong, but in Latin a double consonant, which the Romans sometimes spelt *ii*.

■ Some Greek spellings of familiar Latin names:

  Achilleus, Akhilleus = Achilles

  Aias = Aiax (*not* Ae-) = (*English*) Ajax

  Aischines, Aiskhines = Aeschines

  Aischulos, Aischylos, Aiskhulos, Aiskhylos = Aeschylus

  Alkman = Alcman

  Anakreon = Anacreon

  Antipatros = Antipater

  Bakchulides, Bakchylides, Bakkhulides, Bakkhulides = Bacchylides

  Kallimachos, Kallimakhos = Callimachus

Kleisthenes = Cleisthenes (*old-fashioned* Clisthenes)

Lusandros, Lysandros = Lysander

Odysseus = Vlixes, Ulixes = (*traditional English*) Ulysses

Oidipous = Oedipus

Thoukydides, Thoukydides = Thucydides

4.2.8 Foreign names

Problems encountered with foreign names are comparable to those with historical European names, in that the surname does not always have an importance and placement equivalent to modern Western names. Names from countries where the Latin alphabet is not used need transliteration, and for most languages there is no universally accepted system; transliterated forms may therefore vary. The same applies to translated names (Charles *or* Carlos of Spain, Henry *or* Henri of France). Particularly for monarchs the tendency is to translate older (e.g. medieval or early modern) names, leaving more recent names in the vernacular.

In many countries, such as China, Hungary, and Japan, surnames commonly precede given names, though individuals may adopt Western order themselves. This can generate problems in references—especially in translations—as it is not always apparent whether a name has already been transposed, thereby hampering alphabetization for purposes of indexing and references.

Afrikaans

Largely, Afrikaans follows Dutch rules, with *De*, *Du*, *Van*, etc. in names capitalized only when the given name is not given: *Van Riebeeck*, *Van der Post* but *Jan van Riebeeck*, *Sir Laurens van der Post*.

Arabic

Names in the Arabic world were traditionally composed of several elements in addition to personal name or names (*ism*); these were based on tribal affiliation (*nasab* or *nisba*); nickname, honorific, or regnal title (*laqab*); familial relationship (*kunya*); geography; and profession or trade. Since a fully evolved array proved too unwieldy for routine use, people commonly grew to be known by an arbitrary selection of the full form, called the *ʿurf*. This elaborate system has now fallen into disuse, however, and modern Arabic names consist simply of one or two personal names and surname after the European pattern.

In alphabetizing twentieth-century transliterated Arabic personal names the article is ignored and the person is listed under the capital letter of his last name. Thus *Aḥmad al-Jundī* would be listed as *al-Jundī, Aḥmad*, and alphabetized under J; the article is not inverted, and can even be deleted if imposed consistently. (Traditional Arabic practice is to alphabetize by given name, not surname.) Historical names are more complicated, in that the form by which someone is best known (*'urf*) cannot be predicted by any standard practice. Compound names of the type *Shajar al-Durr* would be listed thus, *not* transposed as *al-Durr, Shajar*. Indeed, the preferred form may actually vary from one period to another, so that Ibn Sīnā was in the Middle Ages known as *shaykh Abū 'Alī*.

Transliterated modern Arabic names often employ established Westernized spellings that may not follow normal rules of transliteration: *Hussein* rather than *Ḥusayn, Nasser* rather than *Nāṣir, Naguib* rather than *Najīb*. In each case the most commonly occurring spelling of the bearer's name is acceptable, except in specialist contexts. Transliterated surnames beginning with *al-* are alphabetized with disregard to the particle, although historical convention governs the alphabetization of older Arabic names, which follow different rules analogous to older European names.

Personal names beginning with the definite article *al* should always be joined to the noun with a hyphen: *al-Islām, al-kitāb*. The *a* is capitalized at the start of a sentence, though not (in some styles) at the start of a note. When the noun or adjective defined by *al* begins with one of the fourteen 'sun' letters (*t, th, d, dh, r, z, s, sh, ṣ, ḍ, ṭ, ẓ, l, n*), the *l* of the definite article is assimilated to the 'sun' letter. This is often indicated in transliteration by variations such as *ad-, an-, ar-, as-, at-,* or *az-*. However, the usual scholarly usage is to write the article-noun combination without indicating the resulting pronunciation through spelling. In text this is often encountered in personal names, for example *al-Nafūd* not *an-Nafūd*, and *al-Ṣafī* not *aṣ-Ṣafī*.

Familial prefix elements such as *abū* (father), *umm* (mother), *ibn* or *bin* (son), and *akhu* (brother) are considered to be part of the surname, and therefore determine the alphabetical position: *abu Bekr, ibn Saud*. Another common prefix is *'Abd*, meaning 'slave', which is used in compound names where the second element is one of the names of God: for example *Abdul Aziz* (properly *'Abdul 'Aziz*) means 'Slave of the Mighty'. Note that none of these prefix elements are connected to the following surname by a hyphen.

In historical names these prefixes are usually capitalized when they form part of the *'urf*, and left lower-case when they do not, or when they form part of a modern name. If an author follows this system editors should accept it, unless it appears that the same person has been styled inconsistently. *Ibn* is often abbreviated to 'b.' in indexes and bibliographical references.

Baltic

Formally, Latvian uses honorifics—*kungs* for Mr, *kundze* for Mrs or Miss, *jaunkundze* for children—after the family name, which itself follows the given name. None is capitalized, even in correspondence. In Lithuanian 'Mr' is *Ponas*, 'Mrs' *Ponia*, and 'Miss' *Panelė*, and these follow Western placement. Some Latvian and Lithuanian surnames are in the genitive singular or plural and—like all genitives in those languages—come first: *d'Urbervilles' Tess*, in other words. (This form is particularly favoured for authors' pseudonyms.) Where it is encountered, it should not be altered. The given name also must not be reduced to an initial but must be spelt out in full. Note the distinction between the Latvian suffix *-u* without cedilla (e.g. *Kaudzītes Matiss* (genitive sing.) and *Ligotņu Jēkabs* (genitive pl.)) and the Lithuanian suffix *-ų* with hook left (e.g. *Rygiškių Jonas*).

Burmese

The honorific *U* before the names of Burmese men is equivalent to 'Mr', and should be so treated; *Ko* is used for a man between 30 and 45, and *Maung* for a boy or man younger than 30. *Daw* is used for a woman older than 35, or one with professional status; *Ma* is used for a young woman or girl. Women do not modify their names on marriage.

Chinese

Chinese personal names normally consist of a single-syllable family name, or surname, followed by a two-syllable personal name. In romanization capitals are used for the first letter, both of the family and of the personal name. In the Wade–Giles transliteration system the two elements of the personal name are separated by a hyphen, whereas in the Pinyin system they are run together as a single word. In pre-modern times two-syllable names are frequently to be found, for example *Wang Wei*, *Tai Chên*. Historically, there are a very few surnames that consist of two elements, perhaps because they derive from a civil-service position held by the founder of the line, for example *Ssŭ-ma* (in Pinyin, *Sima*). Names that belong in neither category may be found, for example *Lao-Tzu*, 'old man', a nickname used for a semi-historical figure not to be identified in any other way. For indexing and alphabetization purposes, the form to be adopted is that given in the main body of the text, without transposition.

More recent figures may use a Westernized form of surname, giving the initials for the personal name first and placing the family name last, for example *T. V. Soong*, *H. H. Kung*. In indexing and alphabetizing, the order should be inverted in Western fashion.

Where emperors are known by their era, the name of that era comes first, not last as if a personal name: *the Kangxi Emperor*, not *the Emperor Kangxi*.

When a form of name has a long-established history, for example *Sun Yat-sen*, *Chiang Kai-shek*, this should be preferred. But note the Wade–Giles form *Mao Tse-tung* has now given way to *Mao Zedong* in most contexts.

Dutch

In surnames, the particles *de* and *van* are lower-case and the name is indexed under the main component, though with a bare surname it is acceptable to use the older practice of a capital *De* and *Van*, if consistently applied. However, Flemish names of Belgian citizens since the establishment of the separate kingdom in 1830 should be written *De* and *Van* and indexed under the prefixes; this applies even when such individuals write in French (but *de* in a French name must be treated in the normal way). In English contexts these rules are often ignored: though strictly incorrect, *Vincent Van Gogh* is sometimes found alphabetized under *V. See also* **VAN, VAN DEN, VAN DER** under **4.2.6**.

French

The honorifics *Monsieur* (Mr), *Madame* (Mrs), *Mademoiselle* (Miss) can be used alone or in conjunction with a surname; in speech these forms precede all appointments and titles: *Madame la docteur*. Though outlawed after the Revolution, titles of nobility (*prince, duc, marquis, comte, vicomte, baron*) are still encountered. For possessives and plurals of French names *see* **5.2.1**; *see also* **DE, DE LA, DU** under **4.2.6**.

German

Honorifics are *Herr* (Mr), *Frau* (Mrs), and *Fraulein* (Miss). Formerly *Fraulein* was used of any unmarried girl younger than 18, but in Germany—and to a lesser extent in Austria and Switzerland—*Frau* is used of all but very young girls, and consequently no longer strictly indicates marriage.

Whether individuals include the *Eszett* in their names is a matter of personal style in German or Austrian names, though they are rare in Swiss names. Titles of nobility such as *Prince*, *Graf*, and *Herzog* were outlawed after the First World War, becoming legally—though not socially—just an additional Christian name. Thus Jakob Baron von Uexküll is in the eyes of the law *Herr J. B. von Uexküll*, and Baron Georg Ritter von Trapp simply *Herr G. R. von Trapp*. (No comma precedes the nobiliary particle.) *Baronin* is a baron's wife, *Baroness* his unmarried daughter. *Freiherr* is the north German equivalent of *Baron*, his wife being *Freifrau*.

See also **VON, VON DER, VOM** under **4.2.6**.

Greek

For ancient Greek names *see* **4.2.7** above; for transliteration *see* **11.25**.

Hebrew and Jewish

Standardizing transliterated Hebrew names may be difficult because a variant may represent the personal preference of the individual concerned, or an established convention regarding how his or her name is spelt. For historical and political figures the *Encyclopaedia Judaica* can be a useful point of reference—although avoid adopting its style of transliteration and hyphenation for names if that style is not being used elsewhere. Be aware, too, that many of the names occurring in Jewish studies texts are not in fact Hebrew names; Hebrew-speaking authors may spell them in English as if they were, but they may be the names of Spanish, Italian, or Polish Jews, or indeed Jews of any other nationality. For these names, too, the *Encyclopaedia Judaica* is useful.

Given the range of transliterations, it is not surprising that a Hebrew name may be rendered in English in a variety of ways: *Jacob*, for example, may also be *Ya'acov* or *Ya'akov*; similarly *Haim*, *Hayyim*, *Chaim*, and *Chayim* are all variants. Beyond ensuring that the same person is always referred to in the same way, one cannot standardize automatically throughout a text because any variant may represent the personal preference of the individual concerned or an established convention regarding how his or her name is spelt. Texts relating to earlier periods may refer to the same people in a variety of forms: *Judah the Prince*, *Yehudah Hanassi*, and *Judah the Nassi* are all known variants for the same name, but only one form should be used within a single text. Ensuring this consistency is a particular problem with multi-author works.

Confusion can creep into texts relating to Zionist and Israeli history because many people who went to live in Israel adopted new Hebrew names similar to their original ones: *Victor* became *Avigdor*, *Vivian* became *Haim*, and so on. Old and new names should be properly linked, particularly in indexes, for example, 'Eban, Aubrey *see* Eban, Abba'; 'Herzog, Vivian *see* Herzog, Chaim'.

Until the modern period, Jews often had two personal names rather than a personal name and a surname. Index entries should be under the first personal name; for example, *Menachem Mendel*, or more fully *Menachem Mendel ben Dov Ber*, is indexed under 'Menachem'. Likewise, textual appellation should not subsequently be abbreviated to *Mendel* as a surname would, although the patronymic *ben Dov Ber* can be omitted unless it is required contextually, for example if more than one Menachem Mendel is being discussed. In some cases it may be possible to use just the first of the two names (in this case, *Menachem*), but editors should not do this without consulting the author. If the person is a rabbi he would be referred to in running text as *R. Menachem Mendel*, or perhaps as *R. Menachem*, but not as *R. Mendel*. Famous rabbis are often known by the place they come from, for example *Menachem Mendel of Rymanow*, or by their title and a place name, the latter sometimes in an adjectival form, for example *the Lubavitcher Rebbe* (leader of the Hasidic sect that started in Lubavitch). Check carefully any personal appellations incorporating place names because of the many variations in the contemporary spellings of the pre-war Yiddish names for places in eastern Europe.

The *ben* that occurs in many Hebrew names means 'son of'; this is the traditional Jewish way of naming Jewish males. The female form is *bat* 'daughter of'. In pre-modern times a man would usually be known simply as the son of his father: *Avraham ben David* (Avraham the son of David). In scholarly works this is often abbreviated to *Avraham b. David*. The abbreviation is satisfactory, providing it is used consistently for all *ben* names. For works aimed at a more general readership, the full form is probably clearer. The *Ben* that often figures in modern Israeli names represents a different usage: now part of the surname, it should be hyphenated to it and capitalized, as in *David Ben-Gurion*. The unhyphenated *David Ben Gurion* is wrong, as it suggests that *Ben* is a middle name.

Many pre-modern Jewish personalities were commonly referred to in the Hebrew literature by acronyms formed from the initial letters of their title and name, and these acronyms have effectively become the name by which the person is best known. They can be identified as such by the absence of a first name. The two most frequently occurring acronymic names are undoubtedly *Rashi* (R. Solomon b. Isaac) and *Rambam* (R. Moshe b. Maimon, or Maimonides—not to be confused with Nachmanides, R. Moshe b. Nachman, known as *Ramban*). Unlike the personal appellation derived from acronyms of book titles (as in the case of the Shelah, *see* **15.12.3**), regular acronyms used as names should not be preceded by *the*.

In Hebrew the acronymic nature of the new name is indicated by double quotation marks before the last letter; there is no need to perpetuate this practice in English, as the transliterated form (e.g. *Shada''l*) adds no relevant information. Similarly, avoid capitalizing (*ShaDaL*), or hyphenating (*Sh-D-L*) the consonants of the acronym: *Shadal* is perfectly adequate, and looks neater. People referred to in this way should be fully identified at the first occurrence of the term in the text (*According to Shadal (Samuel David Luzzatto, b. Livorno 1734)...*) or by giving the full name followed by the acronym in parentheses. There should also be suitable cross-referencing in the index ('Shadal, *see* Luzzatto, Samuel David').

Hungarian

In Hungarian, the surname precedes the given name (e.g. *Szabó István*, *Nagy Margit*), and is itself followed by such titles as *úr* ('Mr'), *doktor* (abbr. 'dr'), etc.: *Szabó István dr úr* (cf. 'Herr Doktor'). Traditionally, a married woman is known by her husband's name with the suffix *-né* ('Mrs') attached to the given name: *Szabó Istvánné*; if he has a doctorate, she will be *Szabó Istvánné dr-né*. In contrast to Western countries, where such usages as *Mrs Stephen Taylor* are moribund in common use, the custom is still observed in Hungary, though under challenge from the widespread practice elsewhere of combining the wife's and the husband's surname.

In this case, *-né* is attached to the husband's surname, after which the wife's name follows; on marrying Szabó István, Nagy Margit may choose to become not *Szabó Istvánné* but *Szabóné Nagy Margit*. If he has a doctorate, he is still entitled to recognition of it in his wife's nomenclature: *Szabóné dr-né Nagy Margit*. If the wife has a doctorate in her own right, she will be *Szabóné Nagy Margit dr*; if both husband and wife have doctorates, she will be *Szabóné dr-né Nagy Margit dr*. Some wives, however, include the husband's given name as well: one may thus find such styles as *Szabó Istvánné dr-né Nagy Margit dr*. The combination of a woman's given name with husband's surname does not exist.

Although in other languages Hungarians adopt the normal Western order of names, the given name ought never to be called the forename or first name; the secular counterpart of *keresztnév* 'Christian name' is *utónév* 'last name', the last name in the US sense (sc. surname) being *vezetéknév* or *családnév*, both meaning 'family name'. The literal equivalent of 'forename', *elónév*, denotes the adjective derived from the family estate that preceded a nobleman's surname and was itself preceded by his title, if any: *gróf nagybányai Horthy Miklós*, Count Nicholas Horthy de Nagybánya. It was sometimes abbreviated to an initial: thus P. for *ponori* in the name of the classical scholar *P. Thewrewk Emil* (in Latin *Aemilius Thewrewk de Ponor*), who should in English and other Western languages be called *Thewrewk* for short, not *de Ponor* (note *ew* = ö; Hungarian surnames often exhibit otherwise obsolete spellings).

Except in the most formal circumstances, the rule for expressing such names in Western languages was to omit the forename altogether, in which case *de* or *von* might be put before the surname. The given name would be translated as well as transposed, just as those of Westerners were turned into Hungarian: in a scholarly review published in 1905 Martin Hertz and Fritz Weiss became *Hertz Márton* and *Weiss Frigyes*. In modern usage, however, the given name—though inverted—retains its original form: *Gyula* (not Julius) *Horn*. Some names, indeed, can hardly be translated: *Béla Bartók, Zoltán Kodály*. It is conventional to leave untransposed the name of the latter's most famous work, *Háry János*, and also that of the Transylvanian prince Bethlén Gábor.

Indian

Modern Indian names have the family name last, which is the name used for alphabetizing; married women take their husband's surnames. Formerly a child would be known by a given name, where necessary in conjunction with a clarifying *son of* or *daughter of* followed by the father's given name and surname. So Karam s/o Ravi Ram might have a son and daughter, known as Vijay s/o Karam Ram and Suman d/o Karam Ram respectively. Within recent years the custom increasingly has been to discard the 'son of', 'daughter of' construction in favour of the given name and family name alone, except in official documents, which usually have columns to facilitate this formula.

Irish

O' is an Irish patronymic prefix, meaning 'grandson of'. In their English form use a closing quotation mark (apostrophe), as *O'Brien, O'Neill*. Since this acts as a true apostrophe, it should never be set as an opening quotation mark. In Irish one alternative to this is the capital *O* and full space (not a thin space), another is the more authentic Gaelic *Ó*, followed by a full space: *Ó Cathasaigh, Ó Flannagáin*. In styling follow the bearer's preference, if known.

Historically, variations such as the lower-case *o/ó* (e.g. ó Brian) and *Ua/ ua* are possible as well, although they are most often found in ancient Gaelic literature. When the text itself is in Gaelic, such names would decline: *Ó Néill* (singular), *Uí Néill* (plural). In English text, normal English rules of plurality apply. Nationalism, combined with a minor spelling reform in 1948, caused some people to render previously Anglicized names in a Gaelic form.

In early times an Irishman was commonly identified by a patronymic, 'son of' (*mac*) X, or a papponym 'grandson of' (*ua*) Y; as elsewhere in Europe, but earlier than in most other countries, these became fixed surnames. As such they should be written in Irish as two words, for example *Micheál Mac Mathúna* (or *Mac Mathghamhna*) 'Michael MacMahon', *Pádraig Ó hÓgáin*, 'Patrick Hogan'; in general, names beginning with a consonant are not aspirated after *Ó* or *Mac*, but dialectal differences afford such variations as *Ó Flaithbheartaigh* 'O'Flaherty' versus *Ó Fhlaithbheartaigh* 'O'Lafferty'. Names beginning with a vowel take initial *h* after *O*, but not after *Mac*, which is then sometimes written *Mág*: *Mac/ Mág Aonghusa* '(Mc)Guinness'.

When the given name does not precede, *Mac* may be used as the equivalent of 'Mr', following the entire surname in the genitive: the initial consonant of the basic name is then aspirated, but an initial vowel loses its *h*: *Mac Mhic Mhathúna* 'Mr MacMahon', *Mac Uí Ógáin* 'Mr Hogan'. Their daughters will be respectively *Síle Nic Mhathúna* 'Sheila MacMahon' and *Caitlín Ní Ógáin* 'Kathleen Hogan'; their wives may be known as *Bean Mhic Mhathúna, Bean Uí Ógáin*, 'wife of MacMahon/Hogan', or with the Christian name preceding or replacing *Bean* as *Eibhlín (Bean) Mhic Mhathúna, Máire (Bean) Uí Ógáin*, but the more traditional custom is to retain the maiden name: *Eibhlín Ní Chonaill* (O'Connell; masculine *Ó Conaill*), *Máire Nic Chonmara* (Macnamara, masculine *Mac Conmara*).

There are also adjectival names, *Breathnach* 'Walsh', *Caomhánach* 'Kavanagh', which behave like any other Irish adjective: the sisters of *Seán Breathnach* and *Tadhg Caomhánach* will be *Áine Bhreathnach* and *Bríd Chaomhánach*. Such adjectives may be formed from other surnames, particularly when no personal name is given (*Brianach* 'an O'Brian', with the definite article *an Brianach* 'O'Brien', *na Brianaigh* 'the O'Brians', or in the feminine from *Mac* names (*Siobhán Charthach* = *Nic Charthaigh*, 'Macarthy'; note too that in the south *Ní* may be found for *Nic*). Certain foreign names have no prefix, or only the Norman *de*.

Italian

The honorifics are *Signor* (Mr), *Signora* (Mrs), *Signorina* (Miss); *Signor* adds an -*e* when no name follows, as in conversation. Similarly *Dottor* ('Doctor', though used also of any graduate) adds an -*e* in similar circumstances; the feminine form is *Dottoressa*. Those with higher degrees are *Professore* or *Professoressa*. Abolished officially in 1947, titles of nobility are still used socially as an adjunct to the surname; courtesy titles and bestowed honours are legion, and precede the surname. *See also* DE under **4.2.6**.

Japanese

Japanese names usually take the form of a single surname, followed by a personal name: *Itō Hirobumi*, *Omura Mizuki*. The surname forms the basis for alphabetization. The suffixes -*san* (gender-neutral), -*sama* (polite form), -*chan* (affectionate diminutive), and -*kun* (for addressing an inferior; also used by boys in addressing one another) are used only in speech, or transcriptions of speech.

In Western contexts it is conventional, especially in translations, to transpose the names—*Mizuki Omura*—although it is wise to alert the reader to that fact. Well-known artists are often identified only by the personal name element, leaving out any reference to family, for example *Hokusai*, rather than *Katsushika Hokusai*. Similarly, writers who are well known by their personal name may be so identified: *Bashō*, rather than *Matsuo Bashō*.

Historically, it is common for two elements of a name to be separated by the *kana* 'no', indicating the subordination of the second element to the first: *Ki no Tsurayuki*. Here, too, the name should appear in direct order.

In textual references to members of the Japanese aristocracy for a general audience, it is permissible to qualify the family name with an English approximation of their official title: *Baron Ito*, *Marquis Kido*; avoid this level of normalization in specialist works. Titles of nobility no longer exist except for those associated with the royal family.

Female figures of the remoter past, such as women writers of the Heian period, do not receive a family name and their personal name may be qualified by a court rank, for example *Murasaki Shikibu* (the second element being that of rank). Any such name should be written out in direct order, although it is acceptable for this figure to be referred to as *Lady Murasaki* in normalized contexts. The most usually encountered form of name should be preferred, for example *Murasaki Shikibu, Sei Shonagon*.

Buddhist monks often have several different styles of name. The simplest form of such a name, in a single word, should be preferred, for example *Shinran*. In the case of actors in the kabuki theatre, when the same surname-personal name is used by succeeding generations of performer, the name should be followed by a roman numeral to indicate 'the first', 'the second'.

Korean

These should be expressed in standard romanization (*see* **11.30**), apart from those where a well-established and generally accepted Western form of name exists, for example *Syngman Rhee, Kim Il-Sung, Roh Tae-woo*. Except in the case of Westernized names, the surname precedes the personal name.

There are fifty-five surnames in common use in Korea, of which five are predominant: *Kim, Yi, Pak, Chŏng*, and *Ch'oe*. Over half the population uses these five surnames and more than one in three will use one of the first three. Most surnames are monosyllabic, but a few are bisyllabic—for example *Sŏnu, Namgung*—by far the most common of this genre to be encountered. Personal names may consist of one element, but usually consist of two, normally separated from one another by a hyphen. Surnames and personal names, for the purposes of romanization, should be regarded as separate entities, for example *Pak* (a surname) and *Min-il*. Names of Korean kings should take the form first of a dynastic determinant, to be followed by a reign title, for example *Yi Sejong* (King Sejong of the Yi dynasty). Note here the absence of hyphen in the second element.

Korean names are frequently given in a non-standard romanized form, a source of frustration for editors: the surname that appears as *Yi* in MR (McCune and Reischauer) romanization system may be encountered commonly in the forms *Lee, Rhee*, or other variants. Also, a group of names may appear in the order either of surname–given name or of given name–surname. If it is a case of three elements, any one of these might itself be a monosyllabic surname. This question is quite easy to resolve, but the processes are too complicated to allow for brief description, and good advice as to how to achieve a result is given in BS 6505: 1982, 'Guide to the Romanization of Korean', which has lists of surnames (including variant forms) and of the most common syllables in personal names.

Manx

Manx surnames often show an initial C or Q, from the *c* of *Mac*: for example *Quayle* = Scots Gaelic *Mac Phàil*, 'MacPhail', literally 'son of Paul'.

Portuguese and Brazilian

Honorifics are *Senhor* (Mr), *Senhora* (Mrs or Miss), *Minha Senhora* (a more polite form of Mrs), or *Dona* (Mrs or any older woman). *Menina* (Miss) is used only before a given name. Professional or conferred titles normally fall after the honorific: *Senhor Professor, Senhora Doutora*. Like Spanish names, the surname is normally composed of two elements: the mother's maiden name and the father's surname, the latter forming the basis for alphabetization. Unlike Spanish, however, the mother's maiden name falls before the father's surname, which is therefore alphabetized according to the last element in the surname: *Manuel Braga da Cruz* is ordered as *Cruz, Manuel Braga da*. Brazilian names follow Portuguese rules in the main, except that *Senhorita* is used for 'Miss', and it is considered more polite to use *Senhor* and *Senhora* in conjunction with the first name rather than surname.

Russian

For transliteration *see* **11.38**. The gender-neutral honorific *tovarishch* (Comrade) is now rarely used; it has been supplanted by the pre-Revolution forms *gospodin* (Mr) and *gospozha* (Mrs or Miss), which are used mostly in writing, and then only with the surname following. Russian names follow the patronymic pattern of given name, father's name with the suffix *-ovich* (son of) or *-ovna* (daughter of), and surname. While the surname is inherited, it is rarely used in speech. Correctly, transliterated abbreviated names with initials composed of two letters, one capital and one lower-case, should not be further reduced, as they are derived from a single Cyrillic letter, for example *Ya.* for Yakov, *Yu.* for Yuri, and *Zh.* for Zhores.

Scandinavian

The ancient Scandinavian traditions of alternating patronymic names with each generation (e.g. *Magnus Pálsson* (Magnus, son of Pál) names his son *Pál Magnusson* and his daughter *Guþrún Magnúsdóttir*) are still found in Iceland, although they have not been used consistently elsewhere for the past one or two centuries. In Iceland after 1923 only existing surnames were allowed to be used; Icelandic alphabetization is still by given name rather than surname, with *Finnur Jónsson* under *F* and *Vigdís Finnbogadóttir* under *V*.

Scottish

In Scotland, *Mac* ('son of') is far commoner in names than *O*; the feminine is *Nic*; all are followed by a space in Gaelic contexts. Adjectival forms may be used: *Alasdair Mac Dhomhnuill* or *Alasdair Domhnullach* 'Alexander Macdonald', *Màiri Nic Dhomhnuill* or *Màiri Dhomhnullach*; by itself

Mac Dhomhnuill denotes the clan chieftain (and likewise 'Macdonald' in English, though without the 'the' used in Irish contexts). Some names have no prefix: *Caimbeul* 'Campbell'.

Styling names with *Mac* can lead to problems, depending on whether they are rendered in Gaelic or English forms, or somewhere in between: the diversity possible may obscure inconsistencies. Spelling rests on the custom of the one bearing the name, and variations in English spelling (*MacDonald*, *Macdonald*, *McDonald*, *M'Donald*, etc.) must be followed, even though they do not reflect any variation in the Gaelic forms. As a general rule, leave alone spelling variants found within a text unless you have good reason to believe that the same person's name is being spelt in different ways. However spelt, any name so prefixed is treated as *Mac* in alphabetical arrangement.

Forms of *Mc—McCarthy, McNaughton*—are sometimes formed using a turned comma (opening quotes): *M'Carthy, M'Naughton*; this is an extension of earlier abbreviation using a superscript *c*: *McCarthy, McNaughton*. Occasionally closing quotation marks are used as well, for example *M'Carthy*. (While some newspapers employ this convention in all-capital headlines, it produces a better effect if the *c* or *ac* are put in lower case or small capitals: *McCARTHY, MacDONALD*.) Such variations should be checked, however: although it may be a typographical error, some families and individuals insist on using a closing rather than opening quotation mark in their names.

Spanish

Customs governing surnames in Spanish-speaking countries vary widely; what follows is only a summary of some generalized conventions. Surnames are usually (but not always) composed of two elements, the father's family surname followed by the mother's family surname (derived from her father's family name). So if, for example, Señor Roberto Caballero Díaz marries Señorita Isabel Fuentes López, their son might be *Jaime Caballero Fuentes* (note no hyphens are used). Apart from the change in title from *Señorita* to *Señora*, the wife's name normally does not alter with marriage, though in informal or unofficial contexts the second half of the compound surname may be replaced by the husband's first surname and joined to the maiden first surname by the conjunction *de*, rendering for example *Isabel Fuentes López* as *Isabel Fuentes de Caballero*, or *Señora de Caballero*. (Widows who have adopted their husband's name sometimes add *viuda de* before it.)

Dropping the second element of a compound name is common in informal contexts, or in any situation not requiring a complete legal signature: the full name of Cervantes was *Miguel de Cervantes Saavedra*. Some Spanish names may have *de* or *de la* as part of the surname proper, for example *Luis Barahona de Soto* (alphabetized under B), *Diego de Hurtado de Mendoza* (under *H*), *Lope de Vega Carpio* (under *V*), *Claudio de la Torre* (under *T*), *Juan de la Cruz Varela* (under *V*).

Compound surnames may be joined with a *y*, or—in Catalonia and elsewhere—*i* (e.g. *José Ortega y Gasset, Pío Baroja y Nessi, José de Pellicer de Ossáu Salas y Tovar, Josep Lluís Pons i Gallarza, Antoni Rubió i Lluch*). The second element may be dropped, however: General Franco's full name was *Francisco Franco y Bahamonde*, and Ventura de la Vega's was *Buenaventura José María Vega y Cárdenas*.

In all cases alphabetization is normally according to the first element in the surname or, where there is but one element, the only surname. Beware of mistaking a given name for a surname (e.g. *Gastón Fernando Deligne* is alphabetized under *D*), or for older given names that act as surnames (e.g. *Calderón de la Barca* is alphabetized under *C*); even then, inevitably there are exceptions: *Francisco López de Jerez* is alphabetized under *J*.

It is possible that a person becomes known by another part of the surname: Federico García Lorca and Gabriel García Márquez have become better known in the English-speaking world by the surnames *Lorca* and *Márquez*, though both should be alphabetized under *García* and properly treated as *García Lorca* and *García Márquez*. On the other hand, Pablo Ruiz Picasso, son of José Ruiz Blasco and Maria Picasso, stopped including his father's name in signing works *c*.1900, and therefore should be alphabetized under *Picasso*. (Where confusion is likely, use supplementary index entries to cross-refer to the correct spot.) Note that US or Latin American authors might not have accents on their ostensibly Spanish names.

Thai

In Thailand the personal name comes first and family name last, but as the personal name is usually the one most frequently used, that rather than the family name is employed as the basis for alphabetization. The honorific *Khun* applies to both men and women, and is used only with the personal name.

US

The ethnic diversity of the USA often produces given names and surnames that reflect the bearer's original cultural ties; even so, the result may not always be transliterated or arranged according to traditional or expected rules: *John von Neumann* and *Bas C. Van Fraasen* are alphabetized under *N* and *F* rather than *V*. The use of regnal-style roman—or occasionally arabic—numerals following the surname should be noted, as should the use of *Jr.*, which normally forms part of the name and is not merely an ad hoc designation: either may be preceded by a comma or not, according to the bearer's wishes. (The

Chicago Manual of Style and *New York Times* standardize uniformly without commas, however.)

While double-barrelled names resulting from marriage are common in a single generation, inherited double-barrelled names following the British model are rare. Double-barrelled given names are usually informal (*Billy-Bob*, *Mary-Ann*), though they can be used formally as well.

A traditional or maiden family surname may be employed as a second given name (middle name): *John Foster Dulles*, *F. Scott Fitzgerald*, *Henry Cabot Lodge*. A more widespread practice is to combine the wife's and the husband's surname with no hyphen, as in *Hillary Rodham Clinton*. In neither circumstance should it be used for alphabetization or as a short form: it is *Fitzgerald's novels* not *Scott Fitzgerald's novels*.

Vietnamese

Vietnamese names should not be transposed: although the family name is first, the correct reference is to a person's second given name: *Nguyen Vo Giap* becomes *General Giap*. (This does not apply to *Ho Chi Minh*, which was a Chinese cover name rendered into Vietnamese pronunciation and spelling.)

4.2.9 Sexism

Pronouns

English has no third-person singular pronoun to denote common gender, and no possessive adjective referring to both men and women. This problem is almost without parallel in other languages, many of which are too inflected to grant such variation, and most of which draw upon established conventions that resist mutation.

In English the traditional convention was to use *he, him, his* for both sexes:

> A child learns better from books he likes.
>
> Tell every member to pay his subscription.

While this convention is grammatically correct many consider it to be outmoded; writers may avoid it by several strategies. One is to rephrase the sentence to make it plural, or avoid pronouns altogether:

> Children learn better from books they like.
>
> Tell the members to pay their subscriptions.
>
> A child learns better from congenial books.
>
> Tell every member to pay subscriptions.

The pluralizing form frequently extends to the erroneous use of plural pronouns where the singular is technically correct: *Tell every member to pay their subscription.* Though common in speech it is still substandard usage, and should be avoided in formal writing: necessity may in time establish *they* as an accepted non-gender-specific singular pronoun in English, but this has yet to happen.

Another strategy is to use both masculine and feminine forms: *he or she, her or him.*

> A child learns to read better from books he or she likes.
>
> Tell every member to pay her or his subscription.

This is effective except where too many pronouns are involved, in which case pluralizing or avoidance is best. Regardless, any of these strategies is preferable to the combined forms *s/he, him/her*, which are clumsy and awkward to pronounce.

Since the issue is emotive and mutable, editors should not impose in text any of the strategies cited above without first conferring with the author. In any case, editors must ensure that any attribution expanded to include both sexes is appropriate. Some authors make a conscious effort to redress a perceived masculine bias or gender imbalance, either by using feminine pronouns exclusively or by strictly alternating them with masculine pronouns. An author must be aware of the political statement latent in this choice, and be convinced that the text's subject provides a suitable vehicle for it; he or she has the opportunity to explain any such policy in a preface.

Other words

The policy of avoiding perpetuating or creating gender-linked terms is based on the principle that in most contexts the holder's sex is—or should be—irrelevant. Most occupations are described in asexual terms: *flight attendant* rather than *steward* or *stewardess*; *author, actor,* and *poet* can be either sex, as can *chairperson, spokesperson,* or *salesperson.* Words ending in *-man* or *-master* (*craftsman, postmaster*) can refer to women.

The *-ess* suffix is properly used of animals (*lioness, tigress*) and in female titles of nobility (*princess, duchess*). Some *-ess* and *-ette* words refer to positions which differ from their apparent masculine equivalents: a *governess, ambassadress, priestess, usherette,* or *drum majorette* is not a female governor, ambassador, priest, usher, or drum major. Similarly, a *mayoress* or *ambassadress* is the wife or female consort of a mayor or ambassador— if she holds those positions herself she uses those titles—but a female law lord is properly addressed as 'Lady', not 'Lord'.

Forms such as *murderess, patroness, huntress, shepherdess,* and *sorceress* are acceptable—and usually found—only in a historical or fictional context, although there is less resistance to *horsewoman, hostess,* and *landlady* for *horseman, host,* and *landlord.* Beware of shades of meaning: both *heroine* and *hero* are used of women in different contexts—the former being used for a female protagonist in a fictional work, and the latter for a woman exhibiting heroism.

4.2.10 Foreign place names

The names of countries and the world's main cities and natural features have always been translated into other languages: *Rome* is the English form for the city its inhabitants call *Roma* and the Germans call *Rom*, just as London is *Londres* in French, Spanish, or Portuguese. The following list provides examples of current OUP preference for the names of some foreign cities when given in general—as opposed to specialist or historical—context:

Ankara (*not* Angora)	Beijing (*not* Peking *or* Peiping)
Brussels (*not* Bruxelles *or* Brussel)	Florence (*not* Firenze)
Gdańsk (*not* Danzig)	Geneva (*not* Genève, Genf, *or* Ginevra)
Guangzhou (*not* Canton)	Livorno (*not* Leghorn)
Lyons (*not* Lyon)	Marseilles (*not* Marseille)
Munich (*not* München)	Reims (*not* Rheims)
Sichuan (*not* Szechuan)	Vienna (*not* Wien)

It would be extraordinary if all reference works agreed uniformly on the styling for each geographical feature, but a consensus can often be reached by consulting recent editions of such atlases as *The Times Comprehensive Atlas of the World*, *The Oxford Hammond Atlas of the World*, or *The Rand McNally International Atlas*; similarly, a geographical dictionary—or a general dictionary incorporating place names (such as the *New Oxford Dictionary of English*)—can help resolve discrepancies by furnishing the best-known form.

What is best known is of course subjective: *Birmingham* will mean something quite different to people in Wolverhampton or Alabama, *Georgia* to inhabitants of Tbilisi or Atlanta, or *Wellington* to a New Zealander or Canadian. Newspapers' house styles reflect this subjectivity, and make allowances for the 'local knowledge' expected of their readership: a Midwesterner would assume that *Kansas City* always means the one in Missouri rather than the one in Kansas; the *New York Times* does not require clarification for *White Plains* or *Yonkers*, whereas the *Wall Street Journal*—also published in New York City but aimed at a wider readership—does. When in doubt it is best to err on the side of caution, supplying additional clarification for all but the most famous place names.

In specialist or historical works the difficulty of defining geographical areas increases. Ultimately, a work's subject, historical period, and prospective readership will govern which language or form is used for a particular place name, though the usage for any given region must be consistent; editors should not automatically change a name given in the text to its modern equivalent. When the place name itself—not merely its linguistic form—has changed, do not use the new name retrospectively:

Stalin must defend Tsaritsyn against the Whites, and Field-Marshal Paulus must surrender at Stalingrad, even though since 1961 the city has been Volgograd. This applies no less when the old name is restored: *the Petrograd Soviet* and *the siege of Leningrad* are not to take place in St Petersburg, though naturally '(now St Petersburg)' may be added if readers are thought to need it.

Common practice makes it impossible to treat all foreign place names uniformly, for as well as local forms now universally accepted (e.g. *Ankara*) or well on the way to it (*Beijing, Livorno*), there are local forms still fighting for supremacy (*Guangzhou, Reims*); English forms under threat (*Lyons, Marseilles*); English forms under no threat (*Brussels, Florence, Geneva, Munich, Shanghai*); and changes of language due to a change of state (*Gdańsk*). While blanket edicts are bound to fail, an understanding of the often complex and contentious issues involved will provide a rationale for which form is appropriate.

The tendency to replace English versions of foreign place names by the correct form in the local language sometimes leaves the writer perplexed which to use: to call Calais *Callis* would be obscurantist, to call Munich *München* exhibitionist, but is *Brunswick* or *Lyons* more obscurantist than *Braunschweig* or *Lyon* is exhibitionist? It is likely that after twenty years any balanced list of preferences will seem old-fashioned, but before choosing local forms as those of the future the writer should remember not only that the present reader deserves consideration, but that fashions sometimes go into reverse. The safest advice is to give readers the forms they will expect, unless one has firm reasons for doing otherwise.

The European Union has helped propel the modern tendency towards using the foreign form of certain names that our forebears would have anglicized, whether from traditional usage or a desire to avoid siding linguistically with one or the other of two conflicting cultures. In modern use these include *Frankfurt am Main* (not *Frankfort-on-Main*), *Frankfurt an der Oder* (not *Frankfort-on-Oder*), *Luxembourg* (not *Luxemburg*), *Strasbourg* (not *Strasburg* or *Strassburg*).

Sometimes the choice is not between an English and a foreign form but between two foreign forms. This is the case in certain cities of Germany and Switzerland that were incorporated into revolutionary and Napoleonic France: the traditional English names *Basil, Cullen* (also spelt *Coleyn*), *Mentz* (as in the local dialect), and *Triers* became the Victorians' *Basle* (in French *Bâle*), *Cologne, Mayence*, and *Treves*. The German names are *Basel, Köln, Mainz*, and *Trier*; of these *Mainz* has definitively triumphed, *Trier* hardly less so; *Basel* is gaining popularity, but *Köln* shows little sign of acceptance in English.

When the change of name is due to a transfer of political control, choose the name in official use at the time in question: *Breslau* before 1945, thereafter *Wrocław*. An exception should be made for explicit political statements: for example, authors who prefer writing *Strasbourg* for (neutral) English *Strasburg* should use *Strassburg* for the legitimate period of German rule (1871–1919), but not for the Nazi occupation (1940–5). It follows that authors not writing in a historical context should avoid using German names for Eastern European cities, or Russian names for non-Russian cities in the former Soviet Union: as *Karlovy Vary* is preferable to *Carlsbad*, so *Chişinău* is preferable to *Kishinev*. This applies even when the Russian form is an approximation to the local form adopted in Soviet times in place of the traditional Russian name: write *Tallinn* not *Tallin* (the Tsarist Russian *Revel'* as compared with the German *Reval*).

Names of features such as lakes, oceans, seas, mountains, and rivers can lay traps for the unwary: be careful not to add descriptive terms to foreign names in which it is already present. For example the *yama* or *san* in *Asama-yama* or *Fuji-san* means 'mountain'; the *Hai* in *Huang Hai* means 'sea'; the *mere* in Windermere and *meer* in IJsselmeer mean 'lake'; the rivers *Río Grande, Skellefteälv, Kemijoki, Yangzijiang, and Sumida-gawa* contain the words *río, älv, joki, jiang*, and *gawa*, meaning 'river' respectively in Spanish, Swedish, Finnish, Chinese, and Japanese.

Authors in some specialist subjects may need to wrestle with multiple variations thrown up by politics, culture, language, and alphabet. For example, the Yiddish names Jews used for the Eastern European towns and villages in which they lived often differed from the local names, which themselves have changed—often many times—with subsequent border changes: the Ukrainian town of *Lviv* was known in Polish as *Lwów*; when it was the capital of the Austro-Hungarian province of Galicia it was known by the German name of *Lemberg*; in Yiddish it was always called *Lvov*. The town known in Polish as *Oświęcim* and in German as *Auschwitz* was known in Yiddish as *Oshpitsin*. This is further complicated by the fact that Yiddish place names have often been distorted through oral transmission or, more recently, through transmission in Hebrew. (The index to the *Encyclopaedia Judaica* gives both the Yiddish name and the local name of many settlements, and can be used to check place names.) In such cases a table of equivalence showing alternative contemporary names and/or modern names can help readers unfamiliar with the subject.

Romanization can cause difficulties with place names; some guidance is given under the individual language. Below are guidelines for Chinese, Japanese, Korean, and Israeli place names.

China

Traditionally the authority for geographical names has been the *Postal Atlas of China* (*Chung hua min kuo yu cheng t'u*) (Nanking, 1932), although it is by now very out of date, not only in the matter of transliteration: at that time Beijing (Peking) was not the capital, and was styled *Peip'ing*. Consult a reliable atlas to find the established form, which is increasingly likely to use the Pinyin system rather than Wade–Giles even for well-known cities.

Japan

For a unit below the size of a city, it is best to add the name of the prefecture in which it is located. When mentioning a geographical description that is no longer in use, such as a province or prefecture in pre-modern times, add in parentheses the name of the equivalent modern area, with an explanation. Many areas of the size of a city and above have well-established names that require no modification.

Do not use place names romanized in accordance with the historical (but rarely utilized) government system: prefer *Fukuoka* to *Hukuoka*, *Hiroshima* to *Hirosima*. If a Japanese place name has appended to it an element in Japanese that indicates its nature, such as *gawa/kawa* for river or *yama/san* for mountain, it is normally hyphenated.

Korea

Geographical descriptions, e.g. *san* (mountain) or *to* (island), following a place name are usually joined to this by a hyphen and, for the purposes of MR romanization, regarded as a semantic unit: *Cheju-do* (the Island of Cheju). Similarly, descriptions of geographical entities that are added to place names—such as *si* (city), *kun* (district)—are linked to these by hyphen and romanized similarly: *Yangju-gun*, *Kwach'on-si*. However, this rule is by no means fixed, and the idiosyncrasies of a particular writer may equally well produce such variants as *Chejudo/Cheju to* or *Tokori/Toko-ri*. While it is always best to seek consistency of approach, specialists may have views making this impracticable.

As a general rule, prefer a long-established spelling of a place name to one in what may be more correct romanization: *Seoul* and *Pyongyang* rather than *Sŏul* and *P'yŏngyang*. If reference is being made to an outdated form of place name, add the most modern equivalent in parentheses. Localize very small places wherever possible by adding (after a comma) the larger geographical unit—city, district, village, etc.—to which it may be subordinate.

Israel

The English spelling of most Israeli place names today reflects modern

Hebrew pronunciation, but prefer established English spellings for locations that were well known before the establishment of the State of Israel, such as *Acre, Beersheba, Caesarea, Capernaum, Haifa, Jerusalem, Nazareth, Safed*, and *Tiberias*. (The index to the *Encyclopaedia Judaica* contains an 'Israel Place List', but the system of transliteration used is quite scientific and therefore unsuitable for more general work.)

Where there is a well-established English convention, references to major regions and geographical features within Israel should be in English rather than Hebrew (*the Jordan Valley* not *Emek Hayarden, the Golan Heights* not *Ramat Hagolan, Gethsemane* not *Gat Shemanim*). For lesser-known places there may be no alternative to the Hebrew name, but try to maintain consistency in the style of transliteration.

CHAPTER 5

Punctuation

5.1 General principles

Punctuation exists to clarify meaning in the written word and to facilitate reading. Too much can hamper understanding through an uneven, staccato text, while too little can lead to misreading. Within the framework of a few basic rules (fewer still in fiction), an author's choice of punctuation is an ingredient of style as personal as his or her choice of words. Unless asked to impose their own style upon copy, editors must use great caution in any emendation, the aim in its narrowest scope being to correct grammar, to impose consistency, and to clarify—not alter—meaning. Printers should follow punctuation when so ordered, and always when setting legal texts, facsimiles, or extracts or quotations from any source.

5.2 Apostrophe

The apostrophe has two main functions in English: to indicate possession and to mark contractions. This suppression of letters or syllables—in such medial contractions as *e'en, there'll, I'd, you've, it's* (it is, it has), *William's* (William is, William has)—is always set close up in English.

Spacing varies in other languages. While German follows English, French has a space after an apostrophe following a word of two or more syllables (e.g. *bonn' petite* but *j'ai*). In Italian the apostrophe is set close up where it follows a consonant (e.g. *dall'aver* but *a' miei*). Similar elisions are spaced in, for example, Greek and Latin. For specific guidelines on the use of the apostrophe in a foreign language, see the language concerned.

5.2.1 Possession

Use 's after singular nouns and indefinite pronouns that do not end in *s*:

the boy's job	the bee's knees	Mary's garden
the BBC's policy	one's car	a week's time
nobody's fault	Oxford's bells	Yasgur's farm
the court's decision		

After plural nouns that do not end in *s*:

the children's clothes	people's opinions	women's rights

No single rule governs the possessive form of singular nouns that end in *s*. Euphony is the overriding concern, with the final choice affected by the number of syllables and the letters starting the next word. Consider the following:

the hiss's sibilance	the box's contents
the schnapps' and pastis's taste	the scissors' point
the catharsis' effects	the sparaxis' spathes
the scabies' transmission	the miss's hat
the uraeus' depiction	the syphilis's symptoms

US English is more likely to support such genitive possessives in the first instance, with British English tending instead to transpose the words and insert *of*: *the effects of the catharsis* rather than *the catharsis' effects*.

■ Use an apostrophe alone after singular nouns ending in an *s* or *z* sound and combined with *sake*:

for goodness' sake	for appearance' sake	for conscience' sake

—but *for old times' sake*, since this is a plural.

■ Use an apostrophe after plural nouns ending in *s*:

our neighbours' children	all octopuses' tentacles
three weeks' time	the MPs' salaries,
clouds' movement	authors' and printers' dictionary
doctors' surgery	

■ In compounds and *of* phrases, use *'s* after the last noun when it is singular:

my sister-in-law's car	the King of Spain's daughter
the Duke of Edinburgh's Award	

but use the apostrophe alone after the last noun when it is plural:

a man of letters' erudition	the Queen of the Netherlands' appeal
the Brooklyn Dodgers' best season	

■ Use *'s* after the last of a set of linked nouns sharing 'possession':

Liddell and Scott's *Greek–English Lexicon*, Beaumont and Fletcher's comedies, Auden and Isherwood's collaborations

but repeat *'s* after each noun in the set when the 'possession' is not shared:

Johnson's and Webster's lexicography, Shakespeare's and Jonson's comedies, Auden's and Isherwood's temperaments

- Use 's to indicate residences and places of business: *at Jane's, at the doctor's.* By convention large businesses frequently omit their originally possessive *s,* as it is often interpreted as a plural: *Harrods, Barclays, Debenhams, Boots.* The apostrophe in many brand names—*Pimm's, Jack Daniel's, Levi's, McDonald's*—is frequently but wrongly left out.

- Do not use an apostrophe in the possessive pronouns *hers, its, ours, yours, theirs.*

- Use 's after non-classical or non-classicizing personal names ending in an *s* or *z* sound:

Charles's	Marx's	Dickens's	Leibnitz's
Onassis's	Zacharias's	Collins's	Tobias's

While convention allows latitude in possessives (e.g. the additional *s* is used more in speech than in writing), the possessive misconstruction *Charles Dicken's* is always incorrect.

- An apostrophe alone is also permissible after longer non-classical or non-classicizing names that are not accented on the last or penultimate syllable:

Nicholas'(s)   Barnabas'(s)   Augustus'(s)

Jesus's is acceptable in non-liturgical use. *Jesus'* is an accepted archaism— *Good friend for Jesus' sake forbear*—and *Jesu's* is also possible in older contexts.

- Use an apostrophe alone after classical or classicizing names ending in *s* or *es*:

Arsaces'	Ceres'	Demosthenes'	Euripides'
Herodotus'	Mars'	Miltiades'	Themistocles'
Venus'	Xerxes'	Erasmus'	Philip Augustus'

This traditional practice in classical works is still employed by many scholars. Certainly follow it for longer names (though *Zeus's,* for instance, is possible), as well as for the post-classical Latinate names favoured throughout the Middle Ages. The guiding principle here is that a name reckoned to be consciously styled in the classical mould is governed by the same rules applicable to classical names. For example, the name *Robert Ritter* might be translated as *Hrodebertus Equestrius,* but would not take a final possessive even though its bearer is classical by neither time period nor inclination.

Poetic contexts may require the apostrophe alone where more prosaic contexts would require the additional *s*:

Mars' spear *but* Mars's gravitational force

fair Venus' mirror *but* Venus's atmosphere

great Ajax' shield *but* Teucer takes cover behind Ajax's shield

Note that such names in the genitive alone normally require an additional *s*:

On the whole Marilius' poetry is less elevated than Lucretius's.

- Use *'s* after French names ending in silent *s* or *x*, when used possessively in English:

    Dumas's   Descartes's   Hanotaux's   Crémieux's   Lorilleux's

However, since appending the plural *s* would be grotesque (*Lorilleuxs*) or misleading (*Dumass*), the singular possessive is treated like the plural, for example *both Lorilleux's* (not *Lorilleuxs'*) *cat, the two Dumas's* (not *Dumass'*) *novels*.

- When a singular or plural name or term is italicized, set the possessive *'s* in roman:

    The Times's staff, the *nom de théâtre*'s spelling, *Finnegans Wake*'s allusions

- Do not use an apostrophe in the names of wars known by their length:

    Seven Day War   Seven Years War   Thirty Years War
    Hundred Years War

- Overall it is impossible to predict with certainty whether a place name ending in *s* requires an apostrophe. For example:

    Land's End   Lord's Cricket Ground   Offa's Dyke
    St James's Palace   Martha's Vineyard

but:

    All Souls College   Earls Court   Johns Hopkins University
    St Andrews   Toms River

While the styling of some place names is logical (e.g. *Queen's College, Belfast* and *The Queen's College, Oxford* were each named after one queen, but *Queens' College, Cambridge* was named after two), overall it is best to consult a current atlas or gazetteer, or the *Oxford Dictionary for Writers and Editors*.

5.2.2 **Plurals**

- Do not use the apostrophe when creating plurals. This includes names, abbreviations (with or without full points), numbers, and words not usually used as nouns:

    the Joneses   several Hail Marys   three Johns
    two wet Februarys both the Cambridges   B.Litt.s
    QCs   SOSs   the three Rs
    both Xs   9 yards   sixes and sevens
    the Nineties   the 1990s   whys and wherefores
    Ins and outs   dos and don'ts   tos and fros

Do not employ what is sometimes known as the 'greengrocer's apostrophe', such as *lettuce's* for 'lettuces' and *cauli's* for 'cauliflowers'.

■ Confusion can result when words, letters, or symbols are referred to as objects rather than their meaning, especially when pronunciation may not be immediately clear. Such items are normally either italicized or set in quotes, with the *s* set in roman outside any closing quote:

too many *which*es in that sentence	can't pronounce his *th*s
can't tell her *M*s from her *N*s	subtract all the *x*s from the *y*s
*do*s and *don't*s	four 'X's on the label
*a*s, *e*s, *i*s, *o*s, and *u*s	'a's, 'e's, 'i's, 'o's, and 'u's
the 'dt's	

Common sense and context should determine which style to use and whether it is necessary; complicated text may demand a combination of these solutions.

5.2.3 **Other uses**

■ Use an apostrophe in place of missing letters in contractions, which are printed close up:

won't	we'll	will-o'-the-wisp
shan't	should've	I'd
fo'c'sle	o'clock	g'day

Except when copying older spellings, apostrophes are omitted before contractions accepted as words in their own right, such as *cello*, *phone*, *plane*, and *flu*.

■ When an apostrophe marks the elision of a final letter or letters, such as *o'* or *th'*, it is not set close up to the next character, but rather followed by a full space. This avoids any potential misreading, especially where the elided article and noun could be a word or the context is ambiguous:

o' pen *not* o'pen	o' range *not* o'range
th' ink well *not* th'ink well	th' rough wood *not* th'rough wood

There is no space when the apostrophe elides medial letters within a word, for example *shelt'ring, rhet'ric, learn'd, ev'ry, ma'am, 'em, o'er, e'er*.

■ Formerly *'d* was added in place of *-ed* to nouns and verbs ending in a pronounced vowel sound:

concertina'd	one-idea'd	dado'd
mustachio'd	ski'd	

This practice is now rare in British English, rarer still in US English, as the apostrophe'd result looks odder to a modern eye than the juxtaposition of vowels without it:

subpoenaed	shampooed	hennaed
shanghaied	skied	

The *'d* construction is still found, usually in poetry and older typography, especially to indicate that an *-ed* is unstressed—*belov'd, bless'd, curs'd, legg'd*—rather than separately pronounced—*belovèd, blessèd, cursèd, leggèd*. It is also found in transcriptions of dialogue for the same reason.

- Use an apostrophe to splice a suffix when an abbreviation functions as a verb:

    KO'd   OK's   OD's   SOS'ing

5.3 **Comma**

Commas structure sentences, but they also offer considerable latitude for rhetorical nuance. The modern tendency is towards the use of rather fewer commas. Too few commas can cause confusion, however, just as too many can cause distraction. Since there is a great deal of acceptable variation in their use, they are perhaps the most abused type of punctuation.

- Use the comma to join main clauses that are semantically related, grammatically similar, and linked by one of the coordinating conjunctions *and*, *but*, *nor*, *or*, and *yet*. Such clauses are joined by a comma if they are too long, and too distinct in meaning, to do without any punctuation at all, but not separate enough to warrant a semi-colon:

    Truth ennobles man, and learning adorns him.
    Cars will turn here, but coaches will go straight on.
    I will not try now, yet it is possible I may try again in future.

It may be omitted when the clauses are short and closely linked:

    Do as I tell you and you'll never regret it.
    Dan left but Jill remained.
    I will not try now yet I may in future.

- To give a trenchant sense of contrast, use a comma with no coordinating conjunction to link very short main clauses:

    He doesn't buy antiques, he inherits them.
    Pistols for two, coffee for one.
    I came, I saw, I conquered.

A common error is to use only one comma to join two unrelated main clauses, or those linked by adverbs or adverbial phrases such as *nevertheless*, *therefore*, and *as a result*. This produces a 'comma splice' or 'run-on sentence':

> I like swimming very much, I go to the pool every week.
>
> He was still tired, nevertheless he went to work as usual.

This fault can be corrected by adding a coordinating conjunction or by replacing the comma with a semicolon or colon.

■ Use the isolating comma to separate vocative expressions from the rest of the sentence:

> My son, give me thy heart.
>
> Do you believe her, sir?
>
> Do you believe, sir, that she's telling the truth?
>
> I should like you all, ladies and gentlemen, to raise your glasses.
>
> The question is, Can it be done?

Use it in quotes to separate the speaker from the speech and to introduce direct speech:

> She said, 'You are quite mad.'
>
> 'I think', she said, 'that you are quite mad.'
>
> 'You are quite mad,' she said.
>
> 'You', she said, 'are quite mad.'

■ Use commas as required to isolate interjections, reflexive questions, and brief comments:

> Yes, I'll come.
>
> Oh, how delightful!
>
> You are his brother, aren't you?
>
> She's quite mad, you know.
>
> I can't swim, you see.

■ Use commas with nouns in apposition, where the apposition adds information of the form *and he is, and it was,* or *otherwise known as*:

> They gave us two presents, a bottle of mescal and a tiara.
>
> This is Elizabeth, my wife.
>
> This is my friend, Mr Smith.
>
> George Oakes, a compositor from London, attended the gathering.
>
> My second son, Theodore, is . . .

Do not introduce a comma where what follows has become part of the name:

> Bob the builder, Anne of Cleves, Montgomery of El Alamein

A comma can, but need not, follow *that is* and *namely*. (To avoid double punctuation, no comma follows *i.e.* and *e.g.* in OUP style.) A comma is not required where the item in apposition is restrictive—in other words, when it defines which of more than one item is meant:

> My friend Mr Smith is . . .
>
> The Scottish poet Burns is . . .
>
> My son Theodore is . . .

Note, however, that transposing the names then requires commas:

> Mr Smith, my avatar, is . . .
>
> Theodore, my second son, is . . .
>
> Burns, the Scottish poet, is . . .

- The comma segregates elements that are not an essential part of the sentence, often parenthetical or prepositional phrases. Use a comma to set off a *non-defining* word, phrase, or clause in apposition to a noun, which comments on the main clause or supplies additional information about it. Use a pair of commas when the apposition falls in the middle of a sentence; they function like a pair of parentheses or dashes, though imply a closer relationship with the surrounding text:

> Men, who are bald more often than women, frequently wear hats.
>
> Baldwin II, known as 'the Bald', was father of Arnulf I.
>
> The man, hoping to escape, mingled with the crowd.
>
> Her father, who lives in Spain, has retired.

- Do not use the comma to separate a *defining* (restrictive) word, phrase, or clause, which is one that cannot be omitted without affecting the sentence's meaning:

> Men who are bald frequently wear hats.
>
> Baldwin the Bald ruled Flanders until 918.
>
> The man hoping to escape mingled with the crowd.
>
> Employees who live in Spain are entitled to the usual benefits.

- No comma follows the page number in citing references in text (*see also* **15.16**):

> Motley's *History of the Dutch Republic,* p. 145 refutes this assertion.

- Adverbial material, whether clauses, phrases, or single adverbs, obeys no single rule regarding commas, though the length of the material and what it modifies in the sentence regulates where commas are placed:

> The sermon over, the congregation filed out.
>
> The French, having occupied Portugal, began to advance into Spain.
>
> The Armada being thus happily defeated, the nation resounded with shouts of joy.
>
> Driving as they had been all night, they were relieved to see the sunrise.

(Note there is no comma after *Armada* or *Driving*.)

A subject–verb inversion needs no comma:

> On the burning deck stood a boy.
>
> Behind the temple lay formal gardens of exotic perfume.
>
> Running before the carriage was a small dog.

Adverbs and adverbial phrases that comment on the whole sentence, such as *therefore, perhaps, of course*, are often enclosed in commas, but this is not a fixed rule. Sense may be altered by the comma's placement or presence. Consider the following:

> We'll go to Cornwall, perhaps in the spring. (*perhaps then*)
> We'll go to Cornwall perhaps, in the spring. (*perhaps elsewhere*)
> Again she refused to speak. (*once more*)
> Again, she refused to speak. (*in addition*)
> The ship's captain ordered a change [,] of course. (*indeed?*)

■ Use the comma in 'proportional' expressions of the general form *the...the...*, other than very short ones:

> The bigger the better.
> The longer the subject, the more likely a comma will be inserted.
> The more they charge the customer, the less trouble they seem to take.
> The higher we climbed, the worse the weather became.

■ Do not introduce a comma between subject and verb, or verb and object—even after a long subject, where there would be a natural pause in speech, if only for breath:

> Those who have the largest incomes and who have amassed the greatest personal savings should be taxed most.
> A bear who consumes too much honey at a friend's house and then attempts to leave by way of a small hole may get stuck.

The tendency to add a comma before *should* and *may* in the sentences above manifests itself more in British than US writing, and is often an indication of unbalanced sentence structure. All but the most complex sentences can usually be restructured to trim the subject and shorten its proximity to the predicate:

> Those who make and save the most should be taxed most.
> A bear may get stuck if he consumes too much honey at a friend's house and then attempts to leave by way of a small hole.

■ Use a comma where the same word occurs twice in succession:

> Whatever is, is right.
> All the books I have, have been in storage.
> We wanted to help out, out of compassion.

■ Include a comma even where the structure does not absolutely require one, if necessary for clarification, to resolve ambiguity:

> With the police pursuing, the people shouted loudly.
> As the car pulled up, the demonstrators crowded round.
> Three miles on, the road gets better.
> However, much as I should like to I cannot agree.
> He recognized the girl who opened the door, and smiled.

■ Use a comma to indicate that a word or phrase has been omitted because the context makes it tacitly clear:

> Time seemed plentiful and sluggish in my youth—yet latterly, scarce and fleet.
>
> In summer they wear flip-flops; in winter, snowshoes.
>
> To err is human; to forgive, divine.
>
> At twenty years of age, the will reigns; at thirty, the wit; and at forty, the judgement.

There is usually no need for a comma in short sentences, and in longer ones where the meaning is clear:

> He was as scared of me as I of him.
>
> He turned and ran.
>
> I boiled the kettle and then made tea.
>
> Sarah loved him and he her.

But a writer may use a comma to set a different emphasis or more measured tempo:

> She opened the letter[,] and[,] slowly[,] began to read.
>
> He has lived here for many years [,] and is reluctant to move.

■ Separate a sequence of adjectives by commas when each adjective modifies the noun and could otherwise be followed by *and*:

> an arrogant, impossible man = an arrogant and impossible man
>
> that gentle, amiable, harmless creature = that gentle and amiable and harmless creature

Omit the comma when each adjective modifies the idea expressed by the combination of the subsequent adjective(s) and noun:

> a prominent political commentator, a torn blue cotton fishing cap, a cherubic curly-headed blond toddler

There is a limit to how many adjectives can be added before punctuation is needed for clarity.

See also **5.10**.

■ Use commas in place of conjunctions to separate elements in a list of three or more items. The presence or lack of a comma before *and* or *or* in such a list has become the subject of much spirited debate. For a century it has been part of OUP style to retain or impose this last serial (or series) comma consistently, to the extent that the convention has come to be called the 'Oxford comma'. But it is commonly used by many other publishers both here and abroad, and forms a routine part of style in US and Canadian English. If the last item in a list has emphasis equal to the previous ones, it needs a comma to create a pause of equal weight to those that came before.

> urban, squat, and packed with guile
>
> mad, bad, and dangerous to know
>
> consult a trade union official, a personnel officer, or a staff member
>
> flying through the air, crawling on the ground, and swimming underwater

> she promptly, eagerly, and ostentatiously raised her hand
>
> a government of, by, and for the people

■ The last comma serves also to resolve ambiguity, particularly when any of the items are compound terms joined by a conjunction:

> Touch the smooth grey of the beech stem, the silky texture of the birch, and the rugged pine.

The absence of a comma after *birch* would give the rugged pine a silky texture as well. In the next example, it is obvious from the grouping afforded by the commas that the Bishop of Bath and Wells is one person, and the bishops of Bristol, Salisbury, and Winchester are three people:

> the bishops of Bath and Wells, Bristol, Salisbury, and Winchester

If the order is reversed, however

> the bishops of Winchester, Salisbury, Bristol, and Bath and Wells

then the absence of the comma after *Bristol* would generate ambiguity: is the conjunction or affiliation between Bristol and Bath rather than Bath and Wells? Similarly

> the three Conservative seats of Eastbourne, Ribble Valley, and Kincardine and Deeside

requires the serial comma after *Valley* to clarify that Kincardine and Deeside—not Ribble Valley and Kincardine—is one seat.

Given that the final comma is sometimes necessary to prevent ambiguity, it is logical to impose it uniformly, so as to obviate the need to pause and gauge each enumeration on the likelihood of its being misunderstood—especially since that likelihood is often more obvious to the reader than the writer. Take, for example, the lack of a comma after *beard*:

> The merest suspicion of unorthodox opinions, the possession of foreign newspapers, the wearing of a beard or an anonymous denunciation, sufficed for the arrest and condemnation of a man to years of imprisonment.

Moreover, if one uses the Oxford comma consistently, its intentional absence clarifies the sense instantly:

> He was not above medium height, dapper and handsome.

A comma after *dapper* would compel the *not* to apply to three characteristics, rather than the first alone.

■ In a list of three or more items, use a comma before a final extension phrase such as *etc.*, *and so forth*, *and the like*:

> potatoes, swede, carrots, turnips, etc.
>
> cakes, biscuits, cookies, muffins, and so forth
>
> dukes, earls, barons, and the like

At least three items are required in order to establish the factors that link them, so the reader can predict what related items might follow.

- The listing comma replaces all but the last parenthetic *and* or *or*. Consequently, there are normally no commas where the words are retained:

  > Allah is wise and righteous and full of compassion.
  > Choose whether to go today or tomorrow or early next week.
  > It is neither this nor that nor the other.

- In nontechnical work, use commas to separate numbers into units of three, starting from the right (*see also* **7.6**):

  > 2,016,523,354   £2,200 $9,999.50

  This comma is usually dropped in technical and scientific work, and a thin space is inserted for five-figure numbers and so on: *42 200, 4 200 000*. Do not use commas in four-figure years: *2001*.

- Commas may be used after some salutations in letters (US business letters uniformly use a colon) and before the signature:

  > Dear Sir, . . .   Yours sincerely, . . .   Yours truly, . . .

  On both sides of the Atlantic, however, punctuation is now often omitted.

- Use a comma with names where the surname comes first; and where a name precedes a title:

  > Brown, Tom   Sir Walter Elliot, Bt.   Pooh, Winnie the

- Use a comma to separate the elements in a run-on postal address:

  > Great Clarendon Street, Oxford, OX2 6DP, UK

  There is no comma after the street number. Commas should be omitted altogether if the address is on separate lines, as on an envelope:

  > Great Clarendon Street
  > Oxford
  > OX2 6DP   UK

  The style *Paris, France* is US, not British, which in text employs *in* instead:

  > Richmond in Surrey is architecturally distinct from Richmond in Yorkshire.
  > The parish records of East Hendred in Oxfordshire proved helpful.

  However, a comma may be preferred in three contexts:

  1. Where the address is American: *He lived in Ridgewood, New Jersey, for twenty years.*

  2. Where specific clarification is needed—usually of a university: *a scholarship to Trinity College, Cambridge, was offered* (as opposed e.g. to Trinity College in Oxford or Trinity College in Hartford, Connecticut); but note exceptions such as *University College London, Trinity College Dublin, King's College Cambridge*, each of which chooses not to have commas.

  3. Where in acknowledgements, for example, a quasi-postal address is appropriate: *the librarian who helped me locate the parish records of Irvine, Ayrshire, proved extremely helpful.*

- In dates, use a comma to separate the name of the day from the date: *Wednesday, 12 August 1960*. Do not use one between day, month, and year: *In August 1960*.... In US style, where the month and day are transposed, a comma follows the day: *August 12, 1960*.

5.4 **Semicolon**

- Use the semicolon to punctuate two or more main clauses that are closely related and could have been joined by a coordinating conjunction—such as *and, or, nor, for,* or *but*—or treated as separate sentences:

  The road runs through a beautiful wooded valley; the railway line follows it closely.

  Claret is the liquor for boys; port for men; but he who aspires to be a hero must drink brandy.

  I know the city well; I've lived there all my life.

- The semicolon can also join clauses that complement or parallel each other:

  Truth ennobles man; learning adorns him.

  To be born a gentleman is an accident; to die one, an achievement.

  If youth knew; if age could.

- Where clauses are linked by a conjunction, use a semicolon to impart a greater emphasis to the subsequent clause than either a comma or the conjunction would alone:

  Truth ennobles man; and learning adorns him.

  Economy is no disgrace; for it is better to live on a little than to outlive a great deal.

- In a sentence that is already subdivided by commas, use a semicolon instead of a comma to indicate a stronger division:

  He came out of the house, which lay back from the road, and saw her at the end of the path; but instead of continuing towards her, he hid till she had gone.

- In a list where any of the elements themselves contain commas, use a semicolon to clarify the relationship of the components:

  They pointed out, in support of their claim, that they had used the materials stipulated in the contract; that they had taken every reasonable precaution, including some not mentioned in the code; and that they had employed only qualified workers, all of whom were very experienced.

This is common in lists with internal commas, where semicolons structure the internal hierarchy of its components:

  I should like to thank the Warden and Fellows of All Souls College, Oxford; the staff of the Bodleian Library, Oxford; and the staff of the Pierpont Morgan Library, New York.

> The Inca Empire consisted of three dynasties: the Kingdom of Cuzco, ruled by Manco Capac, Sinchi Roca, Lloque Yupanqui, Mayta Capac, Capac Yupanqui, Inca Roca, Yahuar Huacac, and Viracocha Inca; the Empire, ruled by Pachacuti, Topa Inca, Huayna Capac, Huascar, and Atauhuallpa; and the Vilcabamba State, ruled by Topa Huallpa, Manco Inca, Sayri Tupac, Titu Cusi Yupanqui, and Tupac Amaru.

Semicolons are not needed if other internal punctuation in a list (e.g. parentheses, quotation marks, or dashes) serves to clarify the elements' relationships instead:

> The Inca Empire consisted of three dynasties: the Kingdom of Cuzco (Manco Capac, Sinchi Roca, Lloque Yupanqui, Mayta Capac, Capac Yupanqui, Inca Roca, Yahuar Huacac, and Viracocha Inca), the Empire (Pachacuti, Topa Inca, Huayna Capac, Huascar, and Atauhuallpa), and the Vilcabamba State (Topa Huallpa, Manco Inca, Sayri Tupac, Titu Cusi Yupanqui, and Tupac Amaru).

Complicated lists may benefit from being displayed typographically; *see also* **CHAPTER 9**.

- Since it can be confusing and unattractive to begin a sentence with a symbol, especially one that is not a capital letter, the semicolon can replace a full point in the preceding sentence:

> Let us assume that *a* is the crude death rate and *b* life expectancy at birth; *a* will signal a rise in . . .

- In early manuscripts, the semicolon is known as the *punctus versus* (;). Its use does not uniformly correspond to modern practice, however. The so-called inverted semicolon is the *punctus elevatus* (⁛), which was used in early manuscripts to separate a main from a subordinate clause, or two subordinate clauses from one another.

5.5 **Colon**

- The colon points forward: from a premiss to a conclusion, from a cause to an effect, from an introduction to a main point; from a general statement to an example. It fulfils the same function as words such as *namely, that is, as, for example, for instance, because, as follows,* and *therefore*:

> There is something I must say: you are standing on my toes.
>
> It is available in two colours: pink and blue.
>
> French cooking is the restaurant's speciality: the *suprêmes de volaille Jeanette* was superb.
>
> To: Subject: Your Ref:
>
> She has but one hobby: chocolate.
>
> The weather grew worse: we decided to abandon the piano.

Although grammatically the colon could be replaced by a semicolon in most of these examples, the relationship between the two parts (cause and effect, introduction and subject) would be weakened or altered.

■ Use the colon to introduce a list; a dash does not follow unless you are reproducing antique or foreign-language typography. Follow it with a capital letter only if the list comprises proper names, or more than one (in US English any grammatically complete) sentence:

> You will need the following: a top hat, a white rabbit, and a magic wand.
>
> She outlined the lives of three composers: Mozart, Beethoven, and Schubert.

■ The colon should not precede linking words or phrases in the introduction to a list, and should follow them only where they introduce a main clause:

> She outlined the lives of three composers; namely, Mozart, Beethoven, and Schubert.
>
> She gave this example: Mozart was chronically short of money.

■ Use a colon to introduce direct or paraphrased speech or quoted material more formally or emphatically than a comma would. A capital letter follows:

> Sir Toby: 'Peace, I say.'
>
> Lords, ladies, and gentlemen: Allow me to present tonight's guest of honour.
>
> He asked a simple question: Who was first?
>
> I told them only yesterday: 'Do not in any circumstances tease the cheetah.'

■ A colon may be used optionally in parallel constructions where a semicolon might be equally acceptable:

> Man proposes: God disposes.
>
> To the north lay a boundless forest: to the south, a sandy desert.
>
> Thebes did his green unknowing youth engage: | He chooses Athens in his riper age.

This is usually found in older writing.

■ Regardless of language, a colon is used after the title of a work to introduce the subtitle:

> 'The Methodology of Sabre Fencing: A History'
>
> *Dynamic HTML: The Definitive Reference*
>
> *Hsün Tsu: Basic Writings*
>
> *Baustelle: Eine Art Tagebuch*

Note that italic titles require italic colons. A colon is not needed if the title ends in an exclamation (!) or question (?) mark.

■ Do not use a colon to introduce a statement or a list that completes the sentence formed by the introduction. In the following examples a colon should not be placed after *is*, *include*, and *to*, respectively:

Another Victorian author worth studying is Thackeray.

Other Victorian authors worth studying include Thackeray, Trollope, and Dickens.

He took care to

(*a*) copy all the papers,

(*b*) circulate them to the relevant departments, and

(*c*) record the whole transaction in triplicate.

■ Colons are also used in indexes and biblical and bibliographical references, and have special uses in mathematics and the sciences.

5.6 **Full point**

The full point is also called 'full stop' or, particularly in US use, 'period'. It ends a sentence that is neither a question nor an exclamation; the next word normally takes a capital letter. It is also used at the end of a rhetorical question or where an apparent question functions as a request:

What will they think of next.

May I remind you not to walk on the grass.

Would you kindly turn down the music.

■ Use a full point rather than a question mark when a question is implied by indirect speech:

She wants to know whether you are coming.

He asked could he remind you not to walk on the grass.

We need to know where we shall meet.

■ Do not use a full point in headlines, column headings, or titles of works, even where these take the form of a full sentence:

All's Well that Ends Well

Mourning Becomes Electra

Frankenstein Meets the Wolf Man

■ The full point is not used after signatures except when reproducing facsimiles. It should not appear in the correction of text—'*for* squirrels *read* chipmunks'—unless the stop actually forms part of the correction—'*for* squirrels, the chipmunks *read* squirrels. The chipmunks' (*see also* **1.6**).

■ The full point is used in many abbreviated forms. If the full point of an abbreviation closes the sentence, there is no second point:

They stocked mussels, clams, scallops, oysters, etc.

She was awarded a D.Phil. rather than a Ph.D.

■ It is OUP style to use full points after numbers in lists, though not after items in a displayed list unless one or more of them is a complete sentence:

> He was prosecuted in the court of Aragon on three charges:
> 1. for having caused the death of Escovedo, falsely pretending the King's authority
> 2. for having betrayed secrets of State and tampered with ciphered dispatches
> 3. for having fled from justice when his conduct was judicially investigated

The list above could equally have been styled as a single displayed sentence, with a semicolon at the end of the first element, a semicolon and *and* at the end of the second, and a full point at the end of the last. If every element in a displayed list forms a complete sentence, however, a full point follows each sentence:

> He was prosecuted in the court of Aragon on three charges:
> 1. He caused the death of Escovedo, falsely pretending the King's authority.
> 2. He betrayed secrets of State and tampered with ciphered dispatches.
> 3. He fled from justice when his conduct was judicially investigated.

A decimal point may be used to express dates numerically: *2.11.93*. In British style a full point is used between hour and minutes to express time: *5.17 p.m.*

5.7 **Ellipses**

■ In punctuation, an ellipsis is a series of points (. . .) signalling an omission. Omitted words are marked by three full points (*not* asterisks) printed on the line, normally separated by normal space of the line in OUP style. Points of omission can also indicate missing or illegible parts of a fragmentary original; *see* **8.4**. For guidelines on styling omitted matter in ancient works *see* **8.4.3**.

Where a single initial is to be omitted as unknown—a case that occurs mainly in printing old documents—use only two points. Practice should be uniform throughout a text. Some reference works, such as the *Oxford English Dictionary*, compress entries by employing two- rather than three-point ellipses. This style should not be adopted as a matter of course, however: reinstate the third point whenever drawing examples from such works.

- An ellipsis at the end of an incomplete sentence is not followed by a fourth full point. When an incomplete sentence is an embedded quotation within a larger complete sentence, the normal sentence full point is added after the final quotation mark:

  I only said, 'If we could...'.

- When a complete sentence is to be followed by omitted material, the closing full point is set close up to the preceding sentence, followed by the three spaced points of omission. In British English every sequence of words before or after *four* points should be functionally complete. This indicates that at least one sentence has been omitted between the two sentences. If what follows an ellipsis begins with a complete sentence in the original, it should begin with a capital letter:

  I never agreed to it.... It would be ridiculous.

- Sentences ending with a question or exclamation mark retain these marks, close up, before or after the ellipsis:

  Could we...?
  Could we do it?... It might just be possible...!

- An ellipsis can be used to show a trailing off, interruption of, or pause in speech or thought in order to create dramatic, rhetorical, or ironic effects. (A final dash signals a more abrupt interruption.) Use this technique sparingly, as it can smack of melodrama. In such contexts the ellipsis is sometimes referred to as 'points of suspension', although unlike the French *points de suspension* the ellipsis is set spaced out in English, just as points of omission:

  The door opened slowly...
  I don't...er...understand.
  Their champagne was tolerable enough, and yet...

- Use an ellipsis, like *etc.*, to show the continuation of a sequence that the reader is expected to infer:

  in 1997, 1999, 2001...
  the gavotte, the minuet, the courante, the cotillion, the allemande,...

- The comma before the ellipsis is optional, though its use in similar contexts should be made consistent within a work.

Rules for ellipses in other languages (e.g. French, Italian, Russian, and Spanish) differ from those in English; *see* **CHAPTER 11**.

5.8 **Question mark**

....

5.8.1 **Typical uses**

The question mark is used in place of a full point to show that what precedes it is a question:

> Do you want another piece of lardycake? On Thursday? Know what? She said *that*? Surely he's wrong?

It is used after tag or reflexive questions:

> You're coming, aren't you? It certainly is enormous, isn't it?

- Do not use the question mark when a question is implied by indirect speech. It may—but need not—be used when an apparent question functions as a request. Here, the question mark seems more polite than a full point:

> Would you kindly let us know whether to expect you?
> I wonder if I might ask you to open the window?

These same sentences with full points replacing question marks would imply a virtual command, perhaps even a degree of menace. However, statements framed as questions out of idiom or politeness do not normally take question marks:

> May I take this opportunity to wish you all a safe journey.
> Will everyone please stand to toast the bride and groom.

In some contexts this form may be considered excessively formal or stilted, in which case the sentence can be framed instead as declarative sentences:

> I [take this opportunity to] wish you all a safe journey.
> Please stand to toast the bride and groom.

- Matter following a question mark begins with a capital letter

> Do you want more lardycake? Buns? Muffins?
> You will be back before lunch, right? About noon? Good.

but questions embedded in another sentence are not followed by a capital:

> Where now? they wonder.
> He pondered why me? till his head hurt.

- Embedded questions may or may not themselves be capitalized, depending on the impact intended and on the formality of the context. The question mark follows the question at whatever point it falls in a sentence:

> The question I put to you is, Which of these is best?
> She wondered, why not?
> Why not? she wondered.

- When the question is presented as direct speech (whether voiced or formulated in someone's mind), it should be capitalized and set in quotation marks:

  > 'Why not?' she wondered.
  >
  > She wondered, 'Why not?'

- When the question is a single word in a sentence, there is normally no introductory comma, there may be no question mark, and the word may be italicized:

  > He wondered why.
  >
  > The question is not *whether* but *when*.
  >
  > The questions 'who?', 'what?', and 'where?' remain to be answered.

  See **5.13** for the positioning of a question mark before or after these.

- The question mark can be followed by a dash where necessary:

  > He left—would you believe it?—immediately after the ball.

- The double question mark (??) and the combination (?!), used to add incredulity to a question, should be used very sparingly in formal writing:

  > Do you mean they're coming *today*?!

5.8.2 **Other uses**

- Use a question mark immediately before or after a word, phrase, or figure to express doubt, placing it in parentheses where it would otherwise appear to punctuate or interrupt a sentence. Set a parenthetical question mark closed up to a single word to which it refers, but use a normal interword space to separate the doubtful element from the opening parenthesis if more of the sentence is contentious:

  > The White Horse of Uffington (? sixth century BC) was carved . . .
  >
  > Homer was born on Chios(?).

  Use this device with caution, since it must be evident not merely what, but what aspect, is contentious: in the latter example it is Homer's birthplace that is in question, but a reader might mistakenly think it is the English spelling of what is *Khios* in Greek. Consequently explicit rewording may be preferable:

  > The White Horse of Uffington (sixth or fifth century BC) was carved . . .
  >
  > Homer is believed to have been born on Chios.

- When more of the sentence is contentious, separate the doubtful element from the opening parenthesis with an interword space.

  > The White Horse of Uffington was carved by the indigenous Iceni people (?).

- When giving a span of dates, the question mark must be repeated before each contentious date, as a single question mark is not understood to modify both dates: in *Geoffrey Chaucer (?1340–1400)*, only the date of birth is in doubt. Similarly, if one part of a date is in question it is sometimes not possible to contract in the normal way: *1883–188?* means 'from 1883 till some time between 1883 and 1889'; it cannot be reduced to *1883–8?*, which means 'from 1883 till perhaps 1888'.

Take care to distinguish between a question mark and *c. (circa)* in dates: the former is used where there are reasonable grounds for believing that a particular date is correct; the latter where a particular year cannot be fixed upon, but only a period or range of several years.

■ A question mark in parentheses is sometimes used—and overused—to underline sarcasm:

> With friends (?) like that, you don't need enemies.

■ In chess, *?* denotes a bad move, and *??* a serious blunder; *?!* means an apparently poor move that may work, and *!?* an unusual one that looks impressive but is dangerous: $P \times R!?$

For question marks in foreign languages (especially Greek and Spanish), *see* **CHAPTER 11** under the languages concerned.

5.9 **Exclamation mark**

5.9.1 **Typical uses**

The exclamation mark—called an 'exclamation point' in the USA—follows emphatic statements, commands, and interjections expressing emotion:

> They are revolting! Sit down! If I only had a brain! I'd love to!
>
> What a shame! Ouch! Hurrah! Ho, ho!

It is useful when it adds emphasis or excitement to an otherwise flat statement or instruction

> She's only eighteen!
>
> Would you *mind* not snorting like that!

and can be followed by a dash where necessary:

> His discourse continued—as we feared!—throughout dinner.

■ Use exclamation marks sparingly in serious writing. The doubled or trebled exclamation mark, and the combination of a question mark and exclamation mark to add incredulity to a question, strike a note almost of hysteria:

> I've won!!

Do you mean they're coming *today*?!
Biff!! Pow!!!!

5.9.2 Other uses

■ Within a text, an exclamation mark within parentheses (!) expresses the amusement, surprise, or incredulity of an author or editor. Such a comment in square brackets [!] would be made by a subsequent author or editor:

> At first, Lord Byron consumed Liquorice Allsorts by the box (!).
>
> 'Byron's passion for Liquorice Allsorts [!] was rapidly diminishing.'

When used to mark absurdity, ignorance, or illiteracy its effect can become intrusive, and may appear smug.

■ In mathematics, an exclamation mark is the factorial sign: $4! = 4 \times 3 \times 2 \times 1 = 24$; $4!$ is pronounced 'four factorial'. The sign itself is sometimes called a 'shriek', so in such contexts it would be 'a !' not 'an !'. In computing it is a delimiter symbol, sometimes called a 'bang'.

■ In chess, *!* denotes a good move, and *!!* a very good move indeed; *?!* means an apparently poor move that may work, and *!?* an unusual one that looks impressive but is dangerous: $P \times R!?$

■ In linguistics, *!* denotes the (post)alveolar click, a sound found in the Bantu family of languages and sporadically elsewhere.

For the inverted exclamation marks found in Spanish; *see* **11.42**.

5.10 Hyphens and dashes

The hyphen is of two types. The first, called the 'hard' hyphen, joins words together anywhere they are positioned in the line. The second, called the 'soft' hyphen, indicates word division when a word is broken at the end of a line. On typescripts, editors should use the stet mark on hard hyphens at the end of lines to distinguish them from soft hyphens.

5.10.1 Compound words

A compound term may be open (spaced as separate words), hyphenated, or closed (set as one word). In general the tendency is for new or temporary pairings of words to be spaced, and for new or temporary linkages of a prefix, suffix, or combining form with a word to be hyphenated. As the combination becomes fixed over time, it may pass through the hyphenation stage and finally come to be set as one word. Some compounds are hyphenated where there is an awkward collision of vowels or consonants, particularly one that might lead to mispronunciation (*clear-cut, drip-proof, take-off, part-time*) or to signal an abstract (rather than literal) meaning (*bull's-eye, crow's-feet, cross-question, glassblower*). A specialist sense may mitigate a common form of hyphenation; use a current dictionary to check whether a word is spaced, hyphenated, or closed.

Formerly in British English, the rule governing the combination of a present participle and a noun was that the compound was spaced if the noun was providing the action (*walking wounded* and *walking delegate*) but hyphenated if the compound itself was acted upon (*walking-stick* and *walking-frame*). Though admirably sensible, the so-called 'walking-stick rule' is no longer borne out in common use: *walking stick* and many other such combinations (*clearing house, colouring book, dining room, rallying point, riding habit, sealing wax*) are now set spaced. Nevertheless, the rule remains helpful for styling words in unusual combinations or contexts. When in doubt consult a current dictionary such as the *Concise Oxford Dictionary*.

Formerly it was also normal in British English for a single adjectival noun and the noun it modified to be hyphenated (*note-cue, title-page, volume-number*). This is less common now, but can linger in some combinations.

■ Compound modifiers that follow a noun usually do not need hyphens:

a table of stainless steel	the hand is blood red
the outline is well drawn	the records are not up to date
an agreement of long standing	curls of honey blonde

Hyphenate two or more modifiers preceding the noun when they form a unit modifying the noun:

a stainless-steel table	the blood-red hand
the well-drawn outline	the up-to-date records
a long-standing agreement	honey-blonde curls

■ Do not hyphenate two or more modifiers preceding a noun when the first adjective modifies the complete noun phrase that follows it:

A small scale factory is a small factory that manufactures scales, while a small-scale factory is a factory that produces a small amount of something.

A stainless steel table is a clean table made of steel, while a stainless-steel table is a table made of stainless steel.

A little used car is small and not new, while a little-used car is one that has not been driven a great deal.

A white water lily is a water lily of white, while a white-water lily thrives in fast water.

Until recently in British English, the noun phrases themselves were routinely hyphenated to unify the sense: *small scale-factory, white water-lily*. Although such hyphenation is less common now, editors should leave it where it has been imposed consistently, as it can serve to avoid ambiguity.

■ Do not hyphenate adjectival compounds beginning with adverbs ending in *-ly*:

happily married couple	newly discovered compound
frequently made error	painfully obvious conclusion

■ Do not hyphenate italic foreign phrases (unless hyphenated in the original language):

an *ex post facto* decision	an *ad hominem* argument
the collected *romans-fleuves*	a sense of *savoir-vivre*

Once foreign phrases have become part of the language and are no longer italic, they are treated like any other English words, and hyphenated (or not) accordingly:

an ad hoc decision	the pro bono case
a laissez-faire policy	a bit of savoir-faire

Some roman combinations, such as *a priori*, *a posteriori*, are not hyphenated even attributively.

■ Do not hyphenate capitalized words:

British Museum staff	New Testament Greek
Latin American studies	New Orleans jazz

■ Scientific terms tend not to be hyphenated in technical contexts

liquid crystal display	sodium chloride solution
wavenumber	quasicrystalline
spacetime	tomato bushy stunt virus group

although some scientific terms require hyphens to convey specific meanings.

5.10.2 Prefixes and combining forms

Words with prefixes are often set as one word, but use a hyphen to avoid confusion or mispronunciation, particularly where there is a collision of vowels or consonants:

re-entry	de-ice	anti-intellectual	quasi-scientific
pro-life	semi-invalid	pre-eminent	non-effective
non-negotiable	ex-directory	vice-chancellor	

The hyphen is used less in US practice. Words beginning with *non-* and *re-*, for example, are often set as one word:

noneffective	nonnegotiable	reelect	reenter

■ Use a hyphen to avoid confusion where a prefix is repeated (*re-release*, *sub-subcategory*) or to avoid confusion with another word (*re-form*, *re-cover*, *re-sign*, *re-creation*, *un-ionized*). Set words combined with the prefix *mis-* close up, even before another *s*: (*misspelling*, *misshapen*).

■ Hyphenate prefixes and combining forms before a capitalized name, a numeral, or a date:

anti-Darwinism	pseudo-Cartesian	Sino-Soviet
pre-1990s	mid-August	proto-Foucauldian

■ The prefix *mid-* is now considered to be an adjective in its own right in such combinations as *mid shot*, *mid grey*, *mid range*, and *mid nineteenth century*, though as a combining form it retains its hyphen in *mid-air*, *mid-engined*, *mid-off*, *mid-Victorian*, and other related forms.

5.10.3 Suffixes

Suffixes are always set hyphenated or closed, never spaced. Only some suffixes are governed by rules.

The suffixes *-less* and *-like* need a hyphen if there are already two *l*s in the following word: *bell-less, shell-like*. Use a hyphen in new combinations with *-like*, and with names, but more institutionalized words, particularly if short, are set solid:

tortoise-like	Paris-like	ladylike
godlike	catlike	lifelike
husbandless	deathless	conscienceless

The suffixes *-proof*, *-scape*, and *-wide* usually need no hyphen:

childproof	moonscape	nationwide

5.10.4 Names

Use hyphens in most compound or double-barrelled personal names and their abbreviations, and in compound names that describe single entities, such as companies and places, or when the first element cannot stand alone:

Mary-Anne	Lord Baden-Powell
Domingo Badía-y-Leblich	Zara Plunkett-Ernle-Erle-Drax
J.-J. Rousseau	Rolls-Royce
Alsace-Lorraine	Baden-Württemberg

Use hyphens in compound names where one element modifies the other; for joint creators *see also* **5.10.9**:

Marxist-Leninist theory (Marxist theory as developed by Lenin)

5.10.5 **Numbers**

Use hyphens in spelt-out numbers from twenty-one to ninety-nine (*twenty-three, thirty-fourth, four hundred and sixty-eight, fifty-three thousand*), and in fractions, unless the numerator and denominator are already hyphenated (*one-half, two-thirds, three thirty-seconds, four and five-eighths*).

Hyphens may also be used in a sequence of non-inclusive numbers (*see also* **5.10.8**): *ISBN 0-123-45678-9.*

5.10.6 **Compass points**

Compass points printed in full are hyphenated, and lower-case unless part of a proper name:

south-east	south-by-south-east	south-south-east
south-east-by-south	South-East Asia	

but the compound names of winds are closed:

southeaster   northwester

In US usage individual compass points are compound words:

southeast   south-by-southeast   Southeast Asia

5.10.7 **Other uses**

Use hyphens to indicate stammering, paused, or intermittent speech:

'P-p-perhaps not,' she whispered.
'Uh-oh', he groaned.
The bell went *r-r-r-r-i-n-g-g!* and then fell silent.

Use hyphens to indicate an omitted common element in a series:

three- and six-cylinder models
two-, three-, or fourfold
upper-, middle-, and lower-class accents
ecto-, endo-, and mesomorphs
countrymen and -women

When the common element may be unfamiliar to the reader, it is better to spell out each word: *ectomorphs, endomorphs, and mesomorphs.*

5.10.8 **Word division**

Justified setting and narrow measures may make it necessary to break words at the ends of lines. Words are broken between syllables, but some syllable breaks are better than others, and some are unacceptable. Word breaks must not inconvenience or perplex the reader; consequently both British and US rules governing division are based on a combination of etymology and phonology, since exclusive reliance on either system can yield unfortunate results. The following offers general guidance only; for individual cases, consult a word-division dictionary such as the *Oxford Spelling Dictionary*. For word division in foreign languages, *see* **CHAPTER 11**, under the languages concerned.

- Do not divide one-syllable words (*there, watch, though, prayer, wrought*) or words pronounced as one syllable: (*helped, passed, grasped*). Do not divide letters pronounced as one letter (*ph* as in *atmos-phere*, *gn* as in *poign-ant*, *ea* as in *crea-ture*) or word endings pronounced as one syllable (-*cious*, -*cial*, -*cion*, -*gion*, -*gious*, -*sion*, -*tial*, -*tion*).

- Where possible avoid dividing verbs ending in -*ed*, *ted*, and -*er* even when they are pronounced as separate syllables:

wounded	founded	hunted
sorted	odder	calmer

- Do not break a word to leave a syllable with an unstressed central vowel sound (a schwa):

libel	noble	title	people
li-belled	en-nobled	en-titled	peopled

- Never leave one letter, and try not to leave fewer than three letters, before or after a division. Do not divide words such as *acre, again, event, very, envy, money, woven, hero, holy, holly, hello, iota*. If fewer than three letters must be separated from the rest, two letters are permissible before, rather than after, the break:

in-spire	de-fence	as-phalt

  In very narrow measures, this rule may be excepted for words ending in -*ad*, -*al*, -*an*, -*en*, -*fy*, -*ic*, and -*or*.

- Divide hyphenated words at the existing hyphen. Do not introduce a second hyphen except in the narrowest measures: *counter-|clockwise* not *counter-clock-|wise*.

  In lexical work, a second hyphen at the start of the next line may be used to show that the hyphen in an entry word at the end of the line is a hard hyphen.

- Divide compound words according to etymology, where it is obvious:

tele-vision	trans-port	railway-man
school-master	table-spoon	

  except where it might lead to mispronunciation:

  antipo-des *not* anti-podes, dem-ocracy *not* demo-cracy, chil-dren *not* child-ren

- Division by etymology logically results in word breaks between the root word and the prefix or suffix:

re-organize   un-prepared   dis-interest   help-ful
un-helpful   wash-able   founda-tion   excess-ive

except where it might lead to mispronunciation:

archaeo-logical *but* archae-ologist
psycho-metric *but* psych-ometry
human-ism *but* criti-cism
neo-classical *but* neolo-gism

■ Divide most gerunds and present participles at -*ing*:

carry-ing   divid-ing   tell-ing

■ When the final consonant is doubled before -*ing*, break the word between the consonants:

admit-ting   occur-ring   trip-ping

and when the infinitive ends in *le* and the *e* is an indeterminate vowel (schwa), break the word before one or more of the preceding consonants:

chuck-ling   trick-ling   puz-zling

■ Some scientific terms may cause difficulty if their structure is unfamiliar. It is usually safe to break words after a combining form such as *angio-*, *broncho-*, *cervico-*, *deutero-*, *dia-*, *glycero-*, *ophthalmo-*, *proto-*, or *pseudo-* (but note *pseud-onym*). If in doubt, check a specialist dictionary, or a general one to see whether the prefix is listed as a combining form.

■ When etymology is no help, divide words after a vowel, taking over the consonant:

preju-dice   mili-tate   insti-gate

or between two consonants or two vowels that are pronounced separately:

splen-dour   finan-cier   moun-tain   lam-bent
co-alesce   cre-ate   appreci-ate

■ Avoid divisions that might affect the sound, confuse the meaning, or merely look odd:

exact-ing (*not* ex-acting)   le-gend (*not* leg-end)   lun-ging (*not* lung-ing)
re-appear (*not* reap-pear)   re-adjust (*not* read-just)

This may entail breaking a suffixed word elsewhere than at the suffix:

farm-er *but* charg-er

■ Words that cannot be divided at all without an odd effect should be left undivided:

beauty   sluicing   poker

■ If at all possible, do not end the recto of a typeset page with a divided word.

■ Even where no hyphen is involved, certain constraints must be observed on line breaks.

1. Do not carry over parts of abbreviations, dates, or numbers to the next line.

2. Do not break numerals at a decimal point, or separate them from their abbreviated units, as with *15 kg* or *300 BC*. If unavoidable large numbers may be broken (but not hyphenated) at their commas, though not after a single digit: *493,|000,|000*.

3. Do not break place-names or (especially) personal names, if possible. If it is unavoidable, break personal names between the given name(s) and surname, or initials (there must be at least two) and surname. Do not break between a name and a modifier:

Louis XIV   Daniel P. Daly IV   Samuel Browne, Jr.

Where dividing a single part of a personal name is inescapable—as in narrow-measure work—follow the rules laid out here, and check a spelling dictionary that includes personal names for unusual breaks such as *Beet-hoven*.

5.10.9 **En rule**

The en rule is, as its name indicates, an en in length, which makes it longer than a hyphen and half the length of an em rule.

■ Use the en rule closed up (non-touching) to denote elision in elements that form a range:

pp. 23–36   pp. xi–xvii   1939–45
Monday–Saturday   Tues.–Thurs.   9.30–5.30

Note that it is *the 1939–45 war* but *the war from 1939 to 1945*.

■ Use the en rule alone when the terminal date is in the future: *The Times (1785-)*, *Jenny Bloggs (1960-)*. A fixed interword space after the date may give a better appearance in conjunction with the closing parenthesis that habitually follows it: *The Times (1785-)*, *Jenny Bloggs (1960-)*.

■ Use the en rule closed up to express the meaning of *to* or *and* between words of equal importance. In these cases the words can be reversed in order without altering the meaning. The hyphen must be used when the first element cannot stand on its own:

Dover–Calais crossing   Ali–Foreman match
on–off switch   dose–response curve
editor–author relationship   cost–benefit analysis
Permian–Carboniferous boundary wave–particle duality

■ Use the en rule closed up between names of joint authors or creators to show that it is not the hyphenated name of one person or a modification of one person's work by another: *Einstein–de Sitter universe, Kerr–Sigel hypothesis, Hatch–Slack pathway, Yang–Mills theory.* Thus *the Lloyd–Jones theory* involves two men (en rule), *the Lloyd-Jones theory* one man (hyphen), and *the Lloyd-Jones–Scargill talks* two men (hyphen and en rule). Joint involvement of more than two people may require more than one en rule: *Bouguer–Lambert–Beer law, Hand–Schüller–Christian disease.*

Where possible, do not use en rules to link elements comprising more than one word, such as *the Winston Churchill–Anthony Eden Government,* since the relationship is not immediately clear. Clarifying hyphens are little better (*the Winston-Churchill–Anthony-Eden Government*); prefer instead a shorter form (*the Churchill–Eden Government*). Where a shorter form does not exist, as in *the New York–New Jersey–Connecticut area,* the construction is acceptable, though either a list (*the New York, New Jersey, and Connecticut area*) or abbreviations (*NY–NJ–Conn. area*) are acceptable alternatives, and preferable to hyphenation (*the New-York–New-Jersey–Connecticut area*). Using a solidus (*the New York/New Jersey/Connecticut area*) conveys a different meaning (*see* **5.12.1**).

- Note *Arab–American* (of Arabs and Americans, en rule) but *Arab-American* (of Arab-Americans, hyphen). Compounding forms ending in -o take a hyphen, not an en rule: *Sino-Soviet, Franco-German* but *Chinese–Soviet, French–German.*

- Use the en rule spaced to indicate individual missing letters (*see* **5.10.11**):

    the Earl of H – – w – – d   'F – – – off!' he screamed.

The asterisk is also used for this purpose.

5.10.10 **Dash**

OUP and most US publishers use the unspaced (non-touching) em rule as a parenthetical dash; other British publishers use the en rule with space either side.

- No punctuation should precede a single dash or the opening one of a pair. A closing dash may be preceded by an exclamation or question mark, but not by a comma, semicolon, colon, or full point. Do not capitalize a word, other than a proper noun, after a dash, even if it begins a sentence.

- Use the dash to clarify sentence structure, to express a more pronounced break in sentence structure than commas, and to draw more attention to the enclosed phrase than parentheses:

    The party lasted—we knew it would!—far longer than planned.
    Going—going—gone!
    There is *nothing*—absolutely nothing—half so much worth doing as simply moooing about in boats.

A dash is easily overused in this context, and even a handful can appear jarring on the page. To ensure this does not happen, replace frequent instances with other punctuation such as commas and parentheses.

■ A single parenthetical dash may be used to introduce a phrase at the end of a sentence or replace an introductory colon:

> The people in the corner house are younger than their neighbours—and more outgoing.
>
> She has but one hobby—chocolate.
>
> In England, justice is open to all—like the Ritz Hotel.

It is not used after a colon except in reproducing antique or foreign-language typography.

5.10.11 Em rule

The em rule is, as its name implies, one em in length. Use it spaced to indicate the omission of a word, and closed up to indicate the omission of part of a word:

> We were approaching — when the Earl of C— disappeared.

Such proprietous deletions—found in both seventeenth-century typography and modern-day journalism—vary in execution: sometimes en rules are substituted letter for letter with spaces between each (*see* **5.10.9**) as an aid to the imagination; asterisks or medial rules made up of two or more em rules were—and still are—employed for the same purpose.

> '—— you all,' he said.
>
> the Devonshire village of O—, the Duke of M————, the Earl of H——w——d.

Sometimes an unbroken rule is set (as in the second example), leaving the deleted information nebulous. Where necessary, reproduce as closely as possible the style used in historical typography. In other contexts ensure that consistent treatment is given to similar omissions, keeping in mind that in a work of fiction, the missing word or words may never have been even notionally present.

■ Use the em rule closed up in written dialogue to indicate an interruption:

> 'Warn him not to—', but his words came too late.
>
> 'They couldn't hit an elephant at this dist—'

■ Use the spaced em rule in dictionaries and indexes to indicate a repeated head word or part of a definition.

■ Use the spaced 2-em rule (——) for a repeated author's name in successive bibliographic entries.

5.11 **Brackets**

Brackets is the blanket term for the ( ), [ ], { }, and < > markings. Correctly, the round brackets ( ) are *parentheses*; [ ] are *square brackets* to the British, though often simply called *brackets* in US use; { } are *braces* or *curly brackets*; and < > are *angle brackets*. For more on specialist use of brackets *see* **8.4.3**, **12.4.2**, **12.6.4**, **13.4.1**, and **13.10.2**.

5.11.1 **Parentheses**

Parentheses are the commonest brackets. In many situations paired commas or dashes are an alternative to them, though parentheses suggest more of a *sotto voce* aside to the reader than commas, which provide a closer and more stressed integration with the text, or dashes, which provide a more abrupt break. Ideally, writing should not rely solely on just one of these conventions, since each can become obtrusive through overuse.

Use parentheses for digressions, explanations, glosses, and translations:

> He hopes (as we all do) that the project will be successful.
>
> Zimbabwe (*formerly* Rhodesia)
>
> the 25th Foot (afterwards named the King's Own Scottish Borderers)
>
> Lord Nuffield (William Morris)
>
> They talked about power politics (*Machtpolitik*).
>
> ὁ βίος βραχύς, ἡ δὲ τέχνη μακρή ('The life so short, the craft so long to learn')

Use them to give or expand abbreviations and to enclose ancillary information, references, cross-references, and variants:

> TLS (*Times Literary Supplement*)
>
> £2 billion ($3.6 billion)
>
> a discussion of animal hibernation (*see* p. 61)
>
> lardy(-)cake (*Oxfordshire Glossary* Supplement, 1881)
>
> Geoffrey Chaucer (1340–1400)
>
> *gaulois*(e)

They enclose reference numbers or letters in lists run into text, such as (*a*), (*b*), (*c*) or, (i), (ii), (iii).

5.11.2 **Square brackets**

Square brackets are for comments, corrections, interpolations, parenthetical notes, or translations that a subsequent author or editor has appended to an original text.

> They [the Lilliputians] rose like one man.

Daisy Ashford wrote *The Young Visiters* [*sic*].

He recalled that 'It was true *as far as they knew* [my italics] before they left.'

Square brackets do not *replace* original text, but supplement it. Legal and scholarly works, and textual editions, use them to normalize usage, or to indicate where individual letters have been altered, as at the start of a sentence (*see* **8.1.1**). For the distinction between parentheses and square brackets in legal references *see* **13.2**; for brackets in apparatus critici *see* **13.10.2**.

In quotations—especially those involving translations—always use square brackets to enclose any matter within a quotation that is not present in the original, regardless of the language or form of the insertion:

I would be delighted [he said in a letter to his wife] to accompany you.

This, then[,] is my plan.

However, when the entire quotation is translated with a gloss from the original, use parentheses instead of square brackets:

A brave babe (*infans*), surely, and some god's special care.

Non sine dis animosus infans (babe, child)

Square brackets are also used in mathematics and to enclose stage directions in plays, etymologies in dictionaries, and in linguistic transcriptions:

oleander . . . [med. L]

the sound [z] occurring medially in the word *easy*

In classical work brackets are also used to indicate pseudepigraphia, for example Pseudo-Aristotle becomes [Aristotle].

5.11.3 **Braces**

Braces are used chiefly in mathematics, computing, prosody, and textual notation; their usage varies within each of these fields. Formerly, braces were set horizontally to link displayed items in columns, but this convention is now seldom used in modern typography, rules being used instead. Braces are still found set vertically, as in lists:

Three Johns
$\begin{cases} \text{1. The real John; known only to his Maker} \\ \text{2. John's ideal John; never the real one, and} \\ \quad \text{often very unlike him} \\ \text{3. Thomas's ideal John; never the real John,} \\ \quad \text{nor John's John, but often very unlike either} \end{cases}$

Three Thomases
$\begin{cases} \text{1. The real Thomas} \\ \text{2. Thomas's ideal Thomas} \\ \text{3. John's ideal Thomas} \end{cases}$

5.11.4 **Angle brackets**

Narrow angle brackets 〈 〉 are used to enclose conjecturally supplied words where a source is defective or illegible. Wide brackets < > are used singly in, for example computing, economics, mathematics, and scientific work to show the relative size of entities, the logical direction of an argument, or to enclose code.

5.11.5 **Punctuation with brackets**

Rules governing punctuation are the same regardless of the type of bracket used. A complete sentence within brackets is capitalized and ends in a full point only when it does not occur within another sentence—even when it ends the enclosing sentence:

> The discussion continued after dinner. (This was inevitable.)
> The discussion continued (this was inevitable) after dinner.
> The discussion continued after dinner (this was inevitable).

A complete sentence within brackets that occurs in another sentence is not capitalized but may end in an exclamation or question mark:

> The discussion continued (we knew it was inevitable!) after dinner.

When parenthetical material is not punctuated as a complete sentence, the closing parenthesis precedes any punctuation marks in the enclosing sentence:

> After graduating with a degree in divinity (1533), Caius visited Italy (where he studied under the celebrated Montanus and Vesalius at Padua); in 1541 he took his degree in physic at Padua.

No punctuation precedes the opening parenthesis, except in the case of terminal punctuation before a full sentence within parentheses, or where parentheses mark divisions in the text:

> We must decide (a) where to go, (b) whom to invite, and (c) what to take with us.

As punctuation within parenthetical matter does not affect matter outside it, the following list does not require semicolons after the closing parentheses, since technically there is no internal punctuation within its elements:

> This is typified in the combination of fishing (cod, ling, lobster, and herring), quarries (at Thurso, Olrig, and Halkirk), manufacturing (tweed, rope, and whisky), and employment (coopers, curers, and packers).

While both parentheses and em rules (*see* **5.10.10**) can enclose full sentences, only parentheses can correctly enclose more than one sentence—but keep in mind that the reader's patience will have limits in awaiting the end of an attenuated sentence:

> The discussion continued—we feared it would!—after dinner.

> The discussion continued (we feared it would! Stewart had started another college story) after dinner.
>
> The discussion continued (we feared it would! Stewart had started another college story before the crème brûlée arrived, and Phillips could barely be restrained from climbing onto the table and singing 'Louie, Louie') after dinner.

5.11.6 Nested brackets

In normal running text, avoid using brackets within brackets. This is sometimes inevitable, as when matter mentioned parenthetically already contains parentheses. In such cases OUP prefers double parentheses to square brackets within parentheses (the usual US convention):

> The Chrysler Building ((1928–30) architect William van Alen (*not* Allen))
>
> ὁ βίος βραχυς, ἡ δε τεχνη μακρή (Hippocrates, *Aphorisms* 1.1. (trans. Chaucer))
>
> The album's original title ((*I*) *Got My Mojo Working* (*But It Just Won't Work on You*)) is seldom found in its entirety.

Where two parentheses fall together, as ((or)), editors should mark for them to be separated by a thin space (marked ‡) to avoid 'nesting'.

References to, say, law reports and statutes vary between parentheses and square brackets, even for different series of the same report; the prescribed convention should be followed independent of whether the reference itself falls within parentheses. *See* **13.2.2**.

In mathematics brackets within brackets follow the hierarchy of parentheses, square brackets, braces, angle brackets thus <{[()]}>; this is the US convention in all cases.

5.12 Solidi and verticals

5.12.1 Solidus

This symbol (/) is known by many terms, such as the *slash*, *stroke*, *oblique*, *virgule*, *diagonal*, and *shilling mark*. Although like the bracket not a true mark of punctuation, it is in general used like a dash to express a relationship between two or more things, and similarly is set close up to the matter it relates to on either side. The most common use of the solidus is as a shorthand to denote alternatives, as in *either/or*, *his/her*, *on/off*, *masculine/feminine/neutral*; consequently *the New York/New Jersey/Connecticut area* signifies the area of either New York, New Jersey, or Connecticut, rather than their combined area. Solidi are much abused, however, and are sometimes misused for *and* rather than *or*; hence it is normally best in text to spell out the alternatives explicitly (*his or her, the New York, New Jersey, or Connecticut area*).

In addition to indicating alternatives, the solidus has other uses:

- It forms part of certain abbreviations, such as *A/C* (account), *Bs/L* (bills of lading), *c/o* (care of), *I/O* (input–output), *N/A* (not applicable), *N/V* (non-vintage), *W/Cdr* (wing commander), *W/D* (withdrawal), and *U/w* (underwriter), and *24/7* (twenty-four hours a day, seven days a week).

- It is used to enclose phonemic transcriptions and pronunciations in dictionaries, and in scholarly apparatus and sigla.

- It is used in parenthetical matter, for example in references, tables, figures, diagrams, and other displayed matter.

- It may be used to indicate line breaks when successive lines of poetry are run in as a single line, though it is preferable to use a vertical (|) instead (*see* **5.12.2**).

- To avoid setting difficulties in non-technical work, a complex in-text fraction is usually set in font-size numerals with a solidus between—the so-called *shilling fraction*—such as *99/100* (*see also* **7.3**).

- The solidus replaces the en rule for a period of one year reckoned in a format other than the 1 January to 31 December calendar extent: *49/8 BC, the fiscal year 2000/1*. In some styles (especially in the USA), a solidus may be used in informal or parenthetical contexts to separate the days, months, and years in dates: *5/2/90*: note here that this could mean the second of May, not the fifth of February (*see also* **7.10**).

- In scientific and technical work, the solidus may have different uses, depending on the discipline. In general it is used to indicate ratios, as in *miles/day, metres/second*. In computing it is called a *forward slash*, to differentiate it from a *backward slash* or *backslash* (\)—each of which is used in different contexts as separators. (A backward slash also indicates difference in set theory.)

5.12.2 **Vertical**

The vertical rule (|), also called the *upright rule* or simply the *vertical*, has specific uses as a technical symbol in specialist subjects, such as computing, mathematics, and graphic scansion. (Two verticals together (||) may denote parallel lines or a caesura, for example.) More commonly, it may be used to indicate the separation of lines where text is run on rather than displayed, for instance for poems, plays, correspondence, libretti, or inscriptions:

The English winter—ending in July | To recommence In August.

Christophorus | Codrington | armiger obiit | 1 Aprilis an. dñi | 1710 æt. 44

Editors should ensure that this distinction is clear on text. When written lines do not coincide with verse lines it may be necessary to indicate each differently: in such cases use a vertical for written lines and a solidus for verse.

When more than one speaker or singer is indicated in a run-together extract, the break between different characters' lines is indicated by two verticals (set close up to each other), regardless of whether the names are included:

> LISAURA. Che vidi? || ROSSANE. Che mirai? || LISAURA Gloria precipitosa! || ROSSANE Ambition perversa!
>
> (What have I seen? || Oh, what have I beheld? || Precipitate State of Glory! || O perverse Ambition!)

5.13 **Quotation marks**

Quotation marks, also called 'inverted commas', are of two types: single (' ') and double (" "). British practice is normally to enclose quoted matter between single quotation marks, and to use double quotation marks for a quotation within a quotation:

> 'Have you any idea', he said, 'what "dillygrout" is?'

This is the preferred OUP practice for academic books. The order is often reversed in newspapers, and uniformly in US practice:

> "Have you any idea," he said, "what 'dillygrout' is?"

If another quotation is nested within the second quotation, revert to the original mark, either single-double-single or double-single-double. When reproducing matter that has been previously set using forms of punctuation differing from house style, editors may in normal writing silently impose changes drawn from a small class of typographical conventions, such as replacing double quotation marks with single ones, standardizing foreign or antiquated constructions, and adjusting final punctuation order (*see* **5.2**). Do not, however, standardize spelling or other forms of punctuation, nor impose any silent changes in scholarly works concerned with recreating text precisely, such as facsimiles, bibliographic studies, or edited collections of writing or correspondence.

5.13.1 **Names and titles**

Quotation marks are not used around the names of sacred texts or their subdivisions, musical works identified by description, or houses or public buildings: *Chequers, Cosicot, the Barley Mow.*

■ Use quotation marks and roman (not italic) type for titles of short poems
  and of TV and radio programmes, and for titles of chapters in books and
  articles in periodicals:

> Mr Brock read a paper on 'Description in Poetry'.
>
> Professor Bradley read a paper on 'Jane Austen's Juvenilia'.

But omit quotation marks when the subject of the paper is paraphrased
or a proper name:

> Mr Brock read a paper on description in poetry.
>
> Professor Bradley read a paper on Jane Austen.

■ Use quotation marks to enclose an unfamiliar word or phrase, or one to
  be used in a technical sense. The effect is similar to that of highlighting
  the term through italics:

> 'Hermeneutics' is the usual term for such interpretation.
>
> Our subject is the age of Latin literature known as 'Silver'.

Most often quotation marks should be used only at the first occurrence
of the word or phrase in a work; thereafter it may be considered to be
fully assimilated.

■ Do not use quotation marks around colloquial or slang words or phrases.
  This device, called 'scare quotes', functions simply as a replacement for a
  sniffy 'so-called', and should be used as rarely:

> They have cut down the trees in the interest of 'progress'.
>
> Many of these 'hackers' seem rather clever.

In these examples the quotation marks are used merely to hold up a
word for inspection, as if by tongs, providing a *cordon sanitaire* between
the word and the writer's finer sensibilities. ('You may wish to avert your
eyes, gentle reader, whilst I unveil the word "boogie-woogie".')

5.13.2 **Relative placing with other punctuation**

Except where the matter is quoted for semantic or bibliographic scrutiny, the relationship in British practice between quotation marks and
other marks of punctuation is *according to the sense*. While the rules are
somewhat lengthy to state in full, the common-sense approach is to do
nothing that changes the meaning of the quotation or renders it confusing to read.

In US practice, commas and full points are set inside the closing quotation mark regardless of whether they are part of the quoted material.
The resulting ambiguity can cause editorial problems when using material from US sources in British works.

■ When the punctuation mark is not part of the quoted material, as in the
  case of single words and phrases, place it outside the closing quotation

mark. Usually, only one mark of terminal punctuation is needed. When the quoted matter is a complete sentence or question, its terminal punctuation falls within the closing quotation mark, and is not duplicated by another mark outside the quotation mark:

> They were called 'the Boys from Dover', I am told.
> Why does he use the word 'poison'?
> 'What is the use of a book', thought Alice, 'without pictures or conversations?'
> Alas, how few of them can say, 'I have striven to the very utmost'!
> But boldly I cried out, 'Woe unto this city!'

Where a quotation uses marks of omission or *etc.*, place them within the quotation marks if it is clear that the omitted matter indicated forms part of the quotation.

■ When the requirements of the quotation and the main sentence differ, use the stronger mark. In the examples below, the question mark supersedes the weaker full point:

> She was heard to mutter, 'Did you do it?'
> Can you verify that John said, 'There is only one key to the room'?

■ When the terminal punctuation of the quoted material and that of the main sentence serve different functions of equal strength or importance, use both:

> She had the nerve to ask 'Why are you here?'!
> Did he really shout 'Stop thief!'?

■ When quoting only part of a sentence or phrase, one can standardize punctuation only by ending a grammatically complete sentence with a full point, the full point then falling *within* the closing quote. This is a legitimate change based on the assumption that the reader is more interested in a quotation's meaning in the context into which it is set than in the quotation's original punctuation in the context from which it was taken. The original passage might read:

> It cannot be done. We must give up the task.

One might then quote it as

> He concluded that 'We must give up the task.'
> 'It cannot be done,' he concluded. 'We must give up.'

■ When the quotation is long, or made up of more than one sentence, it is better to attach the closing point to the long sentence:

> Jesus said, 'Do not think that I have come to annul the Law and the Prophets; I have come to fulfil them.'
> Moses told you: 'Do not kill. Do not steal. Do not commit adultery.'

■ When a sentence-long quotation is used as an explanation or specimen, the full point usually does not fall within the closing quotation mark:

Cogito, ergo sum means 'I think, therefore I am'.

We need not 'follow a multitude to do evil'.

Let *A* stand for 'There exists at least one tree in real space'.

He believed in the proverb 'Dead men tell no tales'.

■ When a quotation of a full sentence or longer is followed in text by a reference giving its source in parentheses, the full point falls *outside* the closing parenthesis, rather than inside the closing quote:

'If the writer of these pages shall chance to meet with any that shall only study to cavil and pick a quarrel with him, he is prepared beforehand to take no notice of it' (*Works of Charles and Mary Lamb*, i. 193).

Different rules apply for displayed quotations; *see* **CHAPTER 8**.

5.13.3 **Direct speech**

In direct speech every change in speaker normally requires a new paragraph. A quoted speech may be interrupted at the beginning, middle, or end, by some such interpolation as *he said*. The interpolation is usually—but not always—set off by a comma introducing the speech, or by commas before and after the interpolation:

■ The placement of a comma should reflect the original speech. Three quoted extracts—with and without internal punctuation—might be:

Go home to your father.

Go home, and never come back.

Yes, we will. It's a good idea.

These may be presented:

'Go home', he said, 'to your father.'

'Go home,' he said, 'and never come back.'

'Yes,' he said, 'we will. It's a good idea.'

This last may equally be quoted in the following ways:

He said, 'Yes, we will. It's a good idea.'

'Yes, we will,' he said. 'It's a good idea.'

'Yes, we will. It's a good idea,' he said.

■ The words *yes*, *no*, *where*, and *why* are enclosed in quotation marks where they represent direct speech, but not when they represent reported speech or tacit paraphrasing:

She asked, 'Really? Where?'

He said 'Yes!', but she retorted, 'No!'

The governors said no to our proposal.

When I asked to marry her, she said yes.

Ho did not say why.

■ Thought and imagined dialogue may be placed in quotation marks or not, so long as similar instances are treated consistently within a single work. In dialogue, each speaker's words are set ordinarily within (single or double) quotation marks. In some styles of writing—particularly fiction—opening quotation marks are replaced with em rules and closing quotation marks are omitted (as is done in French); in other styles, marks of quotation are dispensed with altogether, the change in syntax being presumed sufficient to indicate the shift between direct speech and interpolations.

In fiction, dialogue can be employed to delineate the character's identity with each change of speaker. The skill with which this is done is especially important with frequent exchanges of speech, for example in the terse colloquies of Hemingway's novels.

- Displayed quotations of poetry and prose take no quotation marks. In reporting extended passages of speech, use an opening quotation mark at the beginning of each new paragraph, but a closing one only at the end of the last. Formerly in English and some other languages, an opening quotation mark was set at the start of each line of quoted matter to signal the quotation's continuation, but this is no longer used in English typography, although it is still used in French for quotations within quotations.

5.13.4 **Transcript**

A transcript of a person's speech is usually treated like any quotation, providing the context makes the speaker's identity clear. The speech of two or more people needs greater care to clarify each speaker's identity, as in the question-and-answer mode of an interview, or the promptings of a recorder of oral history and his or her subject(s). Transcripts are usually laid out with speakers' names displayed in small capitals. Dialogue can be set out in four ways, depending on the space available, the length of the transcript, and the number and duration of exchanges between speakers. Editors should mark for one of the following:

- Speakers' names can be full left on the measure, with dialogue indented to form a column beginning 1 en from the longest speaker's name. Turn lines and subsequent lines are then hung (aligned) on that measure. A 3-point space is inserted between speakers. As the width available for dialogue is determined by the length of the names, abbreviations or initials are often substituted for full names.

- Speakers' names can be centred on the measure, with dialogue begun on the following new line, set to full measure with a 6-point space between speakers.

- Speakers' names can be set full left followed by a colon or full point and a 1-en space, with dialogue run in on the same line. Turn lines and subsequent lines are then indented 1 em from the left-hand measure. There is no extra space between speakers.

■ Speakers' names can be indented 1 em from the measure (like a paragraph indent), followed by a colon and a 1-en space, with dialogue run in on the same line. Turn lines and subsequent lines are then set full out to the measure. There is no extra space between speakers.

CHAPTER 6

Italic, roman, and other type treatments

6.1 **General Principles**

In most contexts, roman type is the standard face used for text matter, though it can be distinguished, for reasons of emphasis, additional clarity, or common convention, through the use of other typographic styles or forms. Each of these—quotation marks, large capitals, italic, boldface, small capitals, and underlining—has contexts in which it is used to indicate a departure of some sort from normal text.

For quotation marks *see* **CHAPTER 8**; for capitals *see* **CHAPTER 4**. Italics are discussed below at **6.2**; boldface, small capitals, and underlining follow at **6.8**.

6.2 **Italic**

Italic type is a typographic variation of ordinary roman that is used to indicate emphasis or heavy stress in speech; to style titles, headings, indexes, and cross-references generally; and to indicate foreign words and phrases.

6.2.1 **Emphasis and highlighting**

Setting type in italics indicates emphasis by setting off a word or phrase from its context:

> An essay's *length* is less important than its *content*.
>
> I don't care *how* you get here, just *get here*.
>
> The actual *purpose* of her letter remained a mystery.
>
> Such style, such *grace*, is astounding.

Employ italics sparingly for emphasis, since their unrestrained use can seem startling or precious. Prefer to achieve the same effect by making the emphasis clear through the sentence structure, or by using intensifying adjectives and adverbs.

Other languages and styles can emphasize text in other ways. For instance, there is no italic in German Fraktur type, Russian, Greek, or Bernard Shaw's letters or plays; instead, words are set letterspaced (*see* **2.4.4**). For guidance on emphasis in non-English text, *see* **CHAPTER 11**, under the language concerned.

Parts of sentences can be highlighted by italics or by quotation marks. Decide which will be clearest and most intelligible to the reader, and apply that style consistently in comparable contexts:

> the letter *z*   spell *labour* with a *u*
> the past tense of *go* is *went*   the *dos* and *don't*s

Technical terms and words being introduced, defined, or assigned a special meaning often need to be italicized at first mention:

> the doctrine of *determinism*
> the grapes next enter the *crusher-stemmer*
> the outing known as a *wayzgoose* is an old tradition
> here, the punt-till is a *box* rather than a *deck*

When an author or editor adds italics to a quotation for emphasis, indicate that this has been done by adding 'my italics' or 'italics added' in square brackets after the italicized word or words, or in parentheses at the end of the quotation. (Using 'my emphasis' or 'emphasis added' is an acceptable alternative where italics are the only form of emphasis given.)

6.3 **Titles of works**

Titles of works may be given in one of three ways: in italic type, in roman type, and in roman type with quotation marks. If a title is given in a language that the reader is not expected to understand, one may append an English translation of the title in square brackets after the original. An italic title is followed by a translation in quotation marks where it is an ad hoc rendering, but italic where it is the title of a published translation.

■ Use italics for titles and subtitles of books (except for books in the Bible), newspapers, magazines, reviews, and other periodicals:

The Gilded Age: A Story of To-day	*The Electric Kool-Aid Acid Test*
De diversis artibus [*The Various Arts*]	*The New Yorker*
Past & Present	*Tel Quel*
Neuphilologische Mitteilungen	*Južnoslovenski filolog*

■ Use italics for titles and subtitles of plays, films, TV and radio series, and albums and CDs:

A Game at Chesse

The Importance of Being Earnest: A Trivial Comedy for Serious People

Look Back in Anger

West Side Story

It's That Man Again

À nous la liberté

La dolce vita

Have I Got News for You

■ Use italics for long poems (those of book length, or divided into books or cantos):

Childe Harold's Pilgrimage	*The Rubáiyát of Omar Khayyám*
Troilus and Criseyde	*The Ballad of Reading Gaol*

■ Use italics for the titles of paintings, sculptures, and other works of art:

Joseph Stella, *Brooklyn Bridge*

Louise Nevelson, *An American Tribute to the British People* (*Gold Wall*)

Lee Bontecou, *Untitled*

But identificatory descriptions—those titles bestowed by someone other than the artist or sculptor for purposes of description or cataloguing— are in roman, no quotation marks, with only the first word and proper nouns capitalized:

Lioness of Sagunto   Madonna of the rocks   Venus de Milo

So 'Michelangelo's *David*', 'Picasso's *Guernica*' as titles given by the artists but 'the sculpture of David by Michelangelo', 'Picasso's painting of Guernica' as descriptive appellations.

■ Use italics for the descriptive titles of operas, song cycles and collections of songs, symphonic poems, and oratorios, as well as named suites, symphonies, and concertos:

Handel's *Water Music*	Berlioz's *Symphonie fantastique*
Madame Butterfly	*Der fliegende Holländer*
Schoenberg, *Chamber Symphony*	Debussy, *Petite Suite*
Franck, *Variations symphoniques*	Beethoven or Tchaikovsky, *Pathétique*

This includes twentieth-century pieces of this kind that include their instrumentation as part of their published title, such as Bartók's *Music for Strings, Percussion, and Celesta.* This last category—consisting of twentieth-century works only—is comparatively rare. In general the instrumentation after a title should be given in roman, for example 'Three Pieces for cello and piano'; 'Sonata for violin and piano'.

■ Use roman in quotation marks for chapters in books, individual cantos or books within long poems, shorter poems, articles in periodicals, unpublished theses, and individual episodes in broadcast series. Foreign titles may be capitalized according to the rules of English or the original language, depending on the context:

> 'In Which Piglet Is Entirely Surrounded by Water'
> 'My Uncle Toby's Apologetical Oration'
> 'Select Commentary on Aulus Gellius, Book 2'
> 'To Elizabeth, Countesse of Rutland'

■ Use roman in quotation marks for single songs, arias, individual movements and pieces within a suite, and tracks on albums and CDs. This includes 'popular' names (i.e. those not furnished by the composer) of works with a genre title:

> 'Louie, Louie'   'When a Man Loves a Woman'
> 'Les Haricots sont pas salés'   'Ich wollt', ich wär' ein Huhn'
> 'March to the Scaffold'   the 'Rigaudon' from *Le Tombeau de Couperin*
> the 'Jupiter' Symphony   the 'Moonlight' Sonata

This results in the combination of, for example, *Inspector Morse*'s 'The Dead of Jericho' (italic for series, roman in quotation marks for episode); 'Born to Run', from *Born to Run* (roman in quotation marks for song, italic for album).

■ Use roman without quotation marks for an ongoing series of books, journals, and related sequences of publications, if each volume within the series has an individual title (as distinct from e.g. merely a date or volume number):

> Oxford Medieval Texts   Clarendon Aristotle Series
> Studies in Biblical Theology   The Annals of Communism
> Stanford Nuclear Age Series   Leipziger Semitische Studien

If each volume in a series is identified by a date, volume, or series number rather than an individual title, the series title is italic, as for a multi-volume work or periodical.

■ Use roman without quotation marks for generic titles and terms and genre titles like 'Symphony', 'Quartet', 'Piano Sonata', 'Trio', 'Mass', and for variations when 'popular' titles are used:

> Mozart's Piano Concerto No. 27 in B flat
> Beethoven's Symphony No. 5/Fifth Symphony
> the fourth movement of the *Symphonie fantastique*
> Enigma Variations (correctly *Variations on an Original Theme (Enigma)*)

- Overtures may require styling according to context, but in general set the titles of concert overtures in roman without quotation marks, using italics for the part of a title that is an opera or literary source:

  > Overture Leonora No. 3
  > Hebrides Overture
  > Overture *Der Freischütz*, alternatively the *Freischütz* Overture
  > Overture *A Midsummer Night's Dream*

- Use roman without quotation marks for the Bible, the Torah, the Koran, and other religious texts, and their subdivisions; *see also* **13.8**.

  > 2 Thessalonians   Luke 11: 52
  > Beha'alotekha 12: 16   the Cow, second ṣūra of the Qur'ān

6.4 Names

Use italics for the individual names of ships, trains, aircraft, spacecraft, and other means of transport, but keep the definite article, other prefixes, and the possessive 's in roman:

> *Enola Gay*   HMS *Dreadnought*
> the USS *Missouri*'s boiler room   *Challenger*
> the *Spirit of St Louis*   the *Graf Zeppelin*

- Use roman without quotation marks for classes, marques, and models:

  > a Boeing 747 Jumbo Jet   a Supermarine Spitfire Mk 1a
  > the Apollo booster   a Mini Cooper
  > a Ferguson TE 20 tractor   a Type 18 Bugatti

- Use roman without quotation marks for proper nouns, including the names of streets, restaurants, hotels, theatres, organizations, and buildings and monuments, regardless of the original language:

  > Regent Street   rue St Honoré
  > Unter den Linden   the Chrysler Building
  > the Empire Diner   the Eagle and Child
  > the Bibliographical Society   Les Caves du Roy
  > the Globe Theatre   Biblioteca Nazionale Centrale di
  > l'Obélisque in the Place Vendôme Roma

- *The* may or may not begin a title. If it does not, print it in roman lower case unless it starts a sentence; if it does, it should be capitalized and italicized. As a rule, print the definite article in periodicals in lower-case roman type, as in 'the *Oxford Times*', 'the *Washington Post*', 'the *Antiquaries Journal*', 'the *Cleveland Plain-Dealer*', 'the *Frankfurter Allegemeine*'. By long tradition *The Times* and *The Economist* are exceptions to this rule, though this does not extend to similar or related titles, e.g. 'the *Bombay Times*', 'the *New York Times*', 'the *Sunday Times*', or 'the *Times Literary Supplement*'. For consistency's sake it is now OUP style to italicize and capitalize the definite article preceding all one-word periodical titles: *The Scotsman, The Spectator, The Bookseller, The Field, The Library, The Rambler, The Beano.*

- *The*, if it starts the title of a non-periodical work, should be in italic when it is the writer's intention to quote the exact title:

The Origin of Species	*The Comedy of Errors*
The Waste Land	*The Boke of the Lyon*
The Night Café	*The Dream of Gerontius*

However, when the work is merely referred to either as well known to the reader or as having already been mentioned, then the definite article may be either omitted or made roman and lower case:

Darwin's *Origin of Species*	a scene from *Comedy of Errors*
the *Waste Land*'s publication in 1922	the lost *Boke of the Lyon*
van Gogh's *Night Café*	Elgar's *Dream of Gerontius*

Similarly, the article in a title is frequently de-emphasized to indicate a specific physical manifestation of that work:

the *Government of the Tongue* found in the BL

his dog-eared *Golden Bough*

a *Midsummer Night's Dream* production

the manuscript of the *Seven Pillars of Wisdom* lost at Reading Station

6.5 **Foreign words and phrases**

Italic type is used for foreign words and phrases in certain circumstances. When a foreign word becomes naturalized into English, it is printed in roman type like other English words; German nouns may become lower-case.

- Foreign proper names are not italicized, even when cited in their original language:

The French call the English Channel 'La Manche'.

'Mindererus' is the Latinized name of R. M. Minderer.

- When a word is sufficiently assimilated to be printed in roman, it may still retain its accents, as with 'fête', 'pâté', 'plié', and 'crèche'; or it may lose them, as with 'cafe', 'denouement', 'elite', and 'facade'.

Foreign words assimilated into the English language tend to lose the inflections of gender, so that the English 'rentier'—now assimilated into the language in roman type—holds for both male and female, though the French feminine form of *rentier* is *rentière*. While in English the default gender is normally masculine, the feminine form of some words, such as 'employee' or 'blonde', may be applied to males, either correctly (in English, the masculine 'employé' has faded together with its accent) or incorrectly ('blond' is still correct for a man).

■ Convention rather than logic determines when foreign words are sufficiently assimilated into English to be printed in roman type. The best advice is to treat any one item consistently within a given text and follow the newest edition of a suitable dictionary, such as the *Concise Oxford Dictionary*. Take into account also the subject's conventions and the intended reader's expectations: if in doubt over the degree of assimilation of a particular word, the more cautious policy is to italicize, but in a work written for specialists whose terminology it may be a part of, it may be wiser not to.

Conversely, consistency or context may require words normally romanized in general English to revert to italicization (or, as in German, capitalization), to avoid their looking out of place among related but less assimilated foreign words. It is also sometimes important to go on italicizing a foreign word, however familiar, where there is an English word with the same spelling, as with *Land* for a province of Germany, *pension* for a Continental boarding house, or *colon* for a French colonialist.

■ For uncommon words, determining the appropriate style depends on how the words are used. In text, any foreign words may be presented either in italics with their translation in roman type with quotation marks or vice versa:

> In Yoruba *gógórogògòrogògòrògogorò* means 'of several things being tall'.
> In Yoruba 'gógórogògòrogògòrògogorò' means *of several things being tall*.

Complicated contexts will require greater diversity: any sensible system is acceptable so long as it is consistently applied and clear to the reader:

> The Hixkaryana word order is object–verb–subject, so that in the sentence 'Toto yonoye kamara' (The jaguar ate the man), *toto* = 'man' and *kamara* = 'jaguar'.

If an author has taken pains to formulate and apply a logical system of roman quoted versus italic—particularly when juggling awkward juxtapositions—an editor should accept it rather than impose another system in its stead.

■ Use italic type if a foreign term or phrase is used generally, and not as from a specific source. Normally only a few words at most are used in this context, since either no explicit context is implied or the quotation from which the extract derives is alluded to or paraphrased. What is stressed here is the *choice* of the original word or words: they are being held up as if by tongs for clarification, translation, or general inspection:

> As the matter was *sub judice*, they could not discuss it further.
>
> Napoleon said England was a nation of *boutiquiers*.

If a gloss is necessary, it follows in parentheses:

> As the matter was *sub judice* (under judicial consideration), they could not discuss it further.
>
> Napoleon said England was a nation of *boutiquiers* (shopkeepers).

- Use roman type with quotation marks if a foreign term or phrase is used specifically as an extract from a unique source. Normally more than a few words are used, as the particular context would be lost were the extract too truncated. Since it is being presented as a direct quotation it is treated as one, it being immaterial that the words are not in English. What is stressed here is the *meaning* of the original word or words: they form a straight transcription:

> As Horace put it, 'Grammatici certant et adhuc sub judice lis est.'
>
> Napoleon said, 'L'Angleterre est une nation de boutiquiers.'

Some authors prefer to present a short quotation in italics. This is acceptable only if it is not too long, as an extended stretch of italic type quickly becomes tiresome to read. Moreover, an extract of prose longer than about sixty words should be displayed regardless of the language in which it is presented (*see* **8.1.2**), and such displayed extracts normally are not in italic.

- When a gloss is necessary for an entire quotation, it follows in parentheses, without quotation marks:

> As Horace put it, 'Grammatici certant et adhuc sub judice lis est' (Scholars still dispute, and the case is still before the courts).
>
> Napoleon said, 'L'Angleterre est une nation de boutiquiers' (England is a nation of shopkeepers).

Where some familiarity with the language is assumed, and a gloss is necessary for only a word or words, it follows in square brackets as an editorial interpolation:

> As Horace put it, 'Grammatici certant et adhuc sub judice [before the courts, i.e. under judicial consideration] lis est.'
>
> Napoleon said, 'L'Angleterre [England] est une nation de boutiquiers.'

- The reverse of this procedure (a translated quotation with whole or partial glosses in the original language) follows the same format, although the original may be in italic when it forms part of the parenthetical gloss:

> As Horace puts it, 'Scholars still dispute, and the case is still before the courts' (*Grammatici certant et adhuc sub judice lis est*).
>
> Napoleon said, 'England is a nation of shopkeepers' ('L'Angleterre est une nation de boutiquiers').

6.6 **Punctuation and typography**

All internal punctuation within an italic phrase, sentence, or longer extract is set in italic, including colons between titles and subtitles, and exclamation or question marks that form part of the quoted matter. Punctuation not belonging to the italic matter is not set in italic, including opening and closing quotation marks that precede or follow italics, and commas or semicolons that separate italicized words or phrases. Ensure that mark-up on copy or coding on disk is precise.

> Have you read *The French Revolution: A History*, *Moby-Dick, or, The Whale*, and *Westward Ho!*?
> She muttered, 'I think it's called a *propina*.'
> Choose *sometimes*, *always*, or *never*.

- The plurals *s*, *es*, and the possessive *'s* affixed to italicized words are set in roman:

> several old *Economist*s and *New Yorker*s; How many *Yes*es does one have to say?; the *Majestic*'s crew

They are set in italic where (as with emphasized words) they form part of the word, and where (as with some foreign words) the plural is naturally the same as that in English:

> It's not *John's* fault but *Mary's*.
> We fitted several of the *blancs* in our luggage.

- Occasionally it may be necessary to indicate italics in text that is already italicized, especially in titles or foreign text. In this instance the opposite font—roman type—is chosen:

> He hissed, '*Do you have the slightest* idea *how much trouble you've caused?*'
> *La Physiognomonie arabe et le* Kitâb al-Firâsa *de Fakhr al-Dîn al Râzî*
> *Discuss the principle* caveat emptor *in common-law jurisdictions.*
> *Le mot anglais* couplet *ne veut pas dire* «couplet» *mais* «distique».

Where italic type is shown in typescript by underlining or italic type, editors should indicate the opposite font by circling the word or words and writing 'opposite font' (abbr. 'OF') either between the lines or in the margin.

It may look odd in running text to have a title ending in roman type followed immediately by the resumption of roman text:

> I've just finished *A Study of Dickens's* Hard Times. The conclusion was excellent.

As an alternative, some publishers set italics in italicized text by underlining it (*A Study of Dickens's* <u>*Hard Times*</u>) or putting it within quotation marks (*A Study of Dickens's* 'Hard Times').

6.7 **Other uses of italic**

Italic type is also found in the following contexts:

- stage directions in plays
- dictionaries for part-of-speech markers, foreign words in etymologies, comments on formality or subject area, and example sentences
- indicating cross-references such as *see* and *see also*, and other directions to the reader, such as *opposite*, *overleaf*, and *continued*
- enumeration such as (*a*), (*b*), (*c*) in lists
- names of parties in legal cases
- biological nomenclature
- mathematics

6.8 **Other type treatments: boldface, small capitals, and underlining**

Simply put, a denser form of a font produces boldface, a smaller form of its capitals produces small capitals, and normal roman type underscored with a rule produces underlining. The following section explores the most appropriate uses for each.

6.8.1 Boldface type

Often simply called *bold*, **this thick typeface** is indicated in copy by a wavy underline, and where necessary by 'b.f.' in the margin. Where a distinction is to be made between two bold typefaces (e.g. bold and demi-bold), the convention is to use a double wavy line for primary bold and a single one for secondary bold.

Bold is often used for headwords in dictionaries; bibliographies and reference lists; indexing and cross-referencing generally, to distinguish between types of reference or their degree of importance; and titles and headings in tables.

Avoid using bold for emphasis in the course of normal printed matter, as the effect is usually too startling in running text; prefer instead the less obtrusive italic, and then only sparingly.

6.8.2 **Small capitals**

THIS STYLE OF TYPE is about two-thirds the size of large capitals, and is indicated in typescript by a <u>double underline</u>. In typography, the term 'even s. caps.' instructs that the word(s) should be set entirely in small capitals, rather than a combination of capitals and small capitals.

Small capitals are used for displayed subsidiary titles and headings, for signatures in printed correspondence, for cross-references and index-ing, for characters' names in plays, for academic qualifications follow-ing names displayed in a list, and often for postcodes.

They are always used for specifying eras (AD, AM, BC, BCE, BP), even in italics. (Otherwise, small capitals are set only in roman type.) Note, however, that dates before present are sometimes given lower-case ('bp') when they are uncalibrated. (*See* **7.11.2**.)

They are used for roman numerals in references, manuscript sigla, play citations with more than one level, centuries in French (but not if set in italic), and generally in Latin (though sometimes full capitals are used instead in transcriptions of medieval manuscripts).

In text, reproduced all-capital inscriptions, headlines, telegrams, notices, cited titles, and so forth should be set as even small capitals if not reduced to capital and lower case. Formerly, full-capital abbreviations were often set in even small capitals. While this practice has fallen out of widespread use, it remains a convenient alternative for those disciplines routinely requiring full-capital abbreviations in text, which otherwise can look jarring on the printed page. However, retain full capitals in unmodern-ized quotations from sixteenth- or seventeenth-century printing, for there the startling effect of GOD or HERR, for example, was deliberate. In unmodernized quotations from eighteenth-century books, use small capital, or capital and small capital, according to the original; if any distinction in a typescript has been lost through typing, editors should query which words other than names should begin with capitals.

The Tetragrammaton YHVH and its variants are often set thus in small capitals.

Small capitals can be letterspaced (*see* **2.4.4**). Common exceptions to letterspacing include names in a bibliography, abbreviations of eras, and where there is no leading underneath, as in for example an index locorum. Unless instructions are given to the contrary, typesetters should assume that small capitals in display lines are letterspaced, and that any numbers accompanying them are non-ranging (aligning).

The first word or words of chapters may be styled with spaced capital and small capital letters 'THUS' to introduce the text. (*See* **1.3.3**.)

Small capitals are not used in, for example, Greek or Russian. For other foreign languages *see* **CHAPTER 11** under the language concerned.

6.8.3 **Underlining**

Underlining (*underscoring*) in proof-correction marks is indicated by a single underline beneath text matter, which means it should be set in italic. A double underline means it should be set in small capitals, and a treble underline means it should be set in full capitals. Wavy underlining means it should be set in boldface. Technically, underlining matter already in italic directs it to be set in the opposite font (roman type). However, since in editing underlining may be used to reinforce italics—for example where some italic matter is to be set in italic and some not—it is best to reinforce the meaning of this instruction in the margin.

When underlining, ensure that underlining includes all matter that requires setting in italic, but nothing else. Mistakes are particularly common with internal and surrounding punctuation. Consider

'The novel Bell, Book, and Candle', not 'The novel Bell, Book, and Candle.'

'The colours were red, white, and blue', not 'The colours were red, white, and blue.'

Although roman type can be set with an underlining rule in this style, italic type nevertheless should be preferred to underlined type in all circumstances except where the latter is required or uniquely useful, for example in scientific and mathematical notation; as an alternative to the awkward juxtapositions of italic type in opposite font (*see* **6.6**); and in the precise reproduction of a manuscript, inscription, or correspondence, where it is needed to approximate underlining in the original. Editors should flag any instances of this for the typesetter, as it can affect the leading on the page.

CHAPTER 7

Numbers

7.1 **General principles**

When describing an arithmetic value the terms *number*, *numeral*, and *figure* are largely interchangeable, though *figure* signifies a numerical symbol, especially any of the ten arabic numbers, rather than a representation in words. *Number* is the general term for both arabic and roman figures; though BS 2961 recommends the term *numeral*, which many people reserve instead for roman figures. Do not use *figure* where confusion between numbers and illustrations may result.

7.1.1 Ranging (lining) and non-ranging (non-lining) figures

In typography, two different varieties or 'cuts' of type are used to set figures. The old style, also called *non-ranging* or *non-lining*, has descenders and a few ascenders: 0123456789. The new style, also called *ranging*, *lining*, or *modern*, has uniform ascenders and no descenders: 0123456789; these are used especially in scientific and technical work.

Do not mix old- and new-style figures in the same book without special directions. There are, however, contexts in which mixing is a benefit. For example, a different style should be used for superior figures indicating editions or manuscript sigla, to avoid confusion with cues for note references.

7.1.2 Figures or words?

In non-technical contexts, OUP style is to use words for numbers below 100. When a sentence contains one or more figures of 100 or above, however, use arabic figures throughout for consistency within that sentence: print for example *90 to 100* (not *ninety to 100*), *30, 76, and 105* (not *thirty, seventy-six, and 105*). This convention holds only for the sentence where this combination of numbers occurs: it does not influence usage elsewhere in the text unless a similar situation exists.

However, clarity for the reader is always more important than blind adherence to rule, and in some contexts a different approach is necessary.

For example, it is sometimes clearer when two sets of figures are mixed to use words for one and figures for the other, as in *thirty 10-page pamphlets*, *nine 6-room flats*. This is especially useful when the two sets run throughout a sustained expanse of text (as in comparing quantities):

> The manuscript comprises thirty-five folios with 22 lines of writing, twenty with 21 lines, and twenty-two with 20 lines.

Anything more complicated, or involving more than two sets of quantities, is probably presented more clearly in a table.

In technical contexts, OUP recommends spelling out numbers below ten. Similar rules govern this convention: in a sentence containing numbers above and below ten, style the numbers as figures rather than words.

- Use words for indefinite or colloquial amounts, as in *talking twenty to the dozen*; *I have said so a hundred times*; *one in a million*; *with God a thousand years are but as one day.*

- In some contexts it makes better sense to use a rounded number rather than an exact one, such as *a population of 60,000* rather than *of 60,011*. This is particularly true if the idea of approximation or estimation is expressed in the sentence by such words as *some*, *estimated*, or *about*. Rounded figures lend themselves to being spelt out more than do precise ones.

- Spell out ordinal numbers—*first*, *second*, *third*, *fourth*—except when reproducing typography in facsimile, and in notes and references. (They can equally be employed as space-savers in narrow measure, as in columnar work.) Particularly in US legal contexts *second* and *third* may be *2d* and *3d* rather than *2nd* and *3rd*.

- Use figures for a sequence of numbers referring to measurement, percentage, quantity, proportion, etc.:

> a 70–30 split
>
> 6 parts gin to 1 part dry vermouth
>
> Figures for September show the supply to have been 85,690 tons, a decrease for the third consecutive month of over 50 tons.

- Use figures with all abbreviated forms of units, including units of time, and with symbols:

> 6′ 2″   250 BC   11 a.m.   13 mm

- Use figures for parts of books and numbers of periodicals, including chapters, pages, and plates. For numbering of paragraphs, clauses, and lists *see* **9.1.3**. Use figures for scores of games and sporting events, for distances and times of races, for house or building numbers, and for road or highway numbers in a national system, such as *A40*, *M25*, *Route 66*. Note that some numbers are commonly spelt out, such as *Route Nationale Sept*, *Eighth Avenue*, *Nine Mile Drive*.

■ Use figures for ages expressed in cardinal numbers (*a girl of 15, a 33-year-old man*), and words for ages expressed as ordinal numbers or decades (*between her teens and twenties, in his thirty-third year*). In less formal or more discursive contexts (especially in fiction), ages may instead be spelt out, as can physical attributes: *five foot two, eyes of blue; a nine-inch nail; a rambunctious two-year-old.*

■ Use words for all numbers at the beginning of sentences; to avoid spelling out cumbersome numbers, recast the sentence or use periphrasis, for example *The year 1849* instead of *Eighteen forty-nine.*

■ Use words for ordinal numbers in names, and for numerical street names. (No comma follows the figure in a road or street address.)

116 The High	10 Downing Street	37a St Giles
221b Baker St.	1600 Pennsylvania Avenue	Third Reich
Third World	Fourth Estate	fifth columnist
Sixth Avenue	Seventh-Day Adventist	Eight-Day Wonder

Note that the convention for Manhattan addresses is to spell out numbers for avenue names and use figures for street names: *25 W. 43 St., the corner of Fifth and 59th.*

■ Words can supplement or supersede figures in legal or official documents, where absolute clarity is required:

> the sum of nine hundred and forty-three pounds sterling (£943)
> a distance of no less than two hundred yards from the plaintiff

In US style, a figure such as 232 may often be spelt out as *two hundred thirty-two*, without an *and.*

7.1.3 **Punctuation**

■ In nontechnical contexts, use commas in numbers of more than four figures. Although optional, it is OUP style to use the comma in figures up to 9,999, such as *1,863* or *6,523.* Do not use a comma to separate groups of three digits in technical and foreign-language work: Continental languages, and International Standards Organization (ISO) publications in English, use a comma to denote a decimal sign, so that *2.3* becomes *2,3.* Use instead a thin space where necessary to separate numbers with five or more digits either side of the decimal point:

> 14 785 652   1 000 000   3.141 592 65   0.000 025

Four-digit figures are not split with thin spaces—3.1416—except in tabular matter, where four-digit figures are aligned with larger numbers.

■ Use a full point in decimals. (Decimal currencies were formerly considered a special case, with their point set in medial position—£1·17—but this convention is rarely maintained now.) In British English use a full point for times of day: print *4.30*. However, omit the full point if a further decimal is included, for example *0800.02 hours*.

■ There are no commas in page numbers, column or line numbers in poetry, mathematical workings, in or following house or hotel-room numbers, or in library call or shelf numbers: *Harleian MS 24456*, *Pierpont Morgan Library, M. 1039*, *Bibl. Apost. Vat., Vat. lat. 4804*, *Bodl. MS Rawl. D1054*, *1600 Pennsylvania Avenue*.

7.1.4 **Ranges**

For a span of numbers generally, use an en rule, eliding to the fewest number of figures possible: *30–1*, *42–3*, *132–6*, *1841–5*. But in each hundred do not elide digits in the group 10 to 19, as these represent single rather than compound numbers: *10–12*, *15–19*, *114–18*, *214–15*, *310–11*.

When describing a range in figures, repeat the quantity as necessary to avoid ambiguity: *1 thousand to 2 thousand litres*, *1 billion to 2 billion light years away*. The elision *1 to 2 thousand litres* means the amount starts at only 1 litre, and *1 to 2 billion light years away* means the distance begins only 1 light year away.

Use a comma to separate successive references to individual page numbers: *6, 7, 8*; use an en rule to connect the numbers if the subject is continuous from one page to another: *6–8*. OUP prefers references to provide exact page extents; where this is impossible, print *51 f.* if the reference extends only to page 52, but *51 ff.* if the reference is to more than one following page. (*See also* **15.1**.)

Editors should mark for a thin space to be set between the number and the *f.* or *ff.* For eliding manuscript folio references, *see* **15.11**. For elision of dates, *see* **7.10.2**.

7.1.5 **Singular or plural?**

■ Numbers are made plural without an apostrophe both as words and figures: *the 1960s*, *temperature in the 20s*, *twos and threes*, *in the Nineties*. Plural phrases take plural verbs where the elements enumerated are considered severally:

> Ten miles of path are being repaved.
>
> Twenty people are in the lift.
>
> Eight oarsmen and their cox are coming to tea.

Plural numbers considered as single units take singular verbs:

> Ten miles of path is a lot to repave.
>
> The lift's maximum capacity is twenty.
>
> Eight oarsmen and their cox is all the boat will hold.

■ When used as the subject of a quantity, words like *number*, *percentage*, and *proportion* are singular with a definite article and plural with an indefinite:

> The percentage of tourists is increasing, a proportion of whom return regularly.
>
> While a proportion of accidents are inevitable, the percentage continues to fall.
>
> A number of pandas are just over there, so their number is increasing.

7.2 **Units**

■ All units of measurement retain their singular form when they are compounded to form hyphenated adjectives before other nouns:

a one-way ticket	a five-pound note	a nine-inch nail
a two-mile walk	a six-foot wall	a ten-gallon hat
a three-minute egg	a seven-league boot	a 100-metre race
a four-litre engine	an eight-hour journey	a 1,000-megaton bomb

Elsewhere, units are pluralized as necessary, but not if the quantity or number is less than one: *two kilos, three miles, 0.568 litre, half a pint.*

■ The numerals *hundred, thousand, million, billion, trillion*, etc. are singular unless they mean indefinite quantities: *two dozen, three hundred, four thousand, five million* but *dozens of friends, hundreds of times, thousands of petals, millions of stars.*

■ In the USA and now in Britain, a *billion* is a thousand million (10^9), what in Britain was formerly called a *milliard*, or more commonly a *thousand million*. (The German term remains *eine Milliarde*.) In France (since 1948), Germany, and formerly Britain, a *billion* is a million million (10^{12}). A *trillion* is in the USA and Britain a million million (10^{12}), and corresponds to the change in use of *billion*. In France (since 1948), Germany, and formerly Britain, it is a million million million (10^{18}). Be careful to avoid ambiguity, particularly in translations and historical documents.

7.3 **Fractions**

In statistical matter use one-piece (cased) fractions where available (½, ⅔, ¾, ½, ⅔, ¾, etc.). If these are not available, use split fractions (e.g. $\frac{19}{100}$). In non-technical running text, set complex fractions in font-size numerals with a solidus between (*19/100*). Known also as 'shilling fractions', they represent a quantity without needing extra interlinear space to be displayed on more than one line. Decimal fractions are similarly useful: *12.66* rather than *12 2/3*, *99.9* rather than *99 and 9/10*.

■ Spell out simple fractions in textual matter, for example *one-half*, *two-thirds*, *one and three-quarters*. Hyphenate compounded numerals in compound fractions such as *nine thirty-seconds*, *forty-seven sixty-fourths*; the numerator and denominator are hyphenated unless either already contains a hyphen. Do not use a hyphen between a whole number and a fraction: *twenty-six and nine-tenths*. Combinations such as *half a mile*, *half a dozen* contain no hyphens, but write *half-mile*, *half-dozen*, etc. If at all possible, do not break spelt-out fractions at line endings.

7.4 Decimals

Decimal fractions are always printed in figures. They cannot be plural, or take a plural verb. For values below unity, the decimal is preceded by a zero: *0.76* rather than *.76*; exceptions are quantities (such as probabilities and ballistics) that never exceed unity.

Decimals are punctuated with the full point on the line. Formerly decimal currency was treated differently, with the decimal point set in medial position (£24·72). This style has long been out of favour, especially as it may be confused with a medial-dot multiplication symbol, and should not be used unless reproducing a facsimile.

British currency became decimalized on 15 February 1971. For amounts of less than a pound, express as (new) pence: '54p' (roman, no point); for amounts of one pound or more, express as pounds and decimal fractions of a pound (omitting 'p'); amounts using the old decimal halfpenny should be expressed as a fraction.

7.5 Degrees

Degrees are of three types: degrees of inclination or angle, abbr. *d.* or *deg.*; degrees of temperature, symbol °; and degrees of latitude and longitude, abbr. *lat.* and *long.* (no points in scientific work).

■ A degree of inclination or angle is reckoned as 1/360th of a circle. Except in scientific and technical work, express degrees in words, as in *an angle of forty-seven degrees, a ninety-degree slope.* Although not an SI unit, the degree can be used with SI units. Decimal subdivisions of degree are preferred to minute (*1/60 degree*) or second (*1/3600 degree*), as in *60.75°*.

- Express a degree of temperature in figures, such as *40°C* (no point). There is a space of the line (*or* thin space in scientific and technical work) between the figure and degree sign. Since the ° forms part of the temperature unit rather than the figure, it is clarified by and joined to a unit: there is no space between it and the abbreviated unit: *40° C* is wrong. When giving a range of temperatures, print the symbol close up to the abbreviation: *10–15°C.*

  When the scale is understood, however, the symbol is printed close up to the numeral: *10–15°, 35° in the shade*, and can be spelt out in nontechnical contexts: *the temperature rose twenty degrees.*

- In geography, degrees of latitude and longitude are the angular distances on a meridian north or south of the equator (latitude), or east and west of the prime or Greenwich meridian (longitude). They may be expressed in degrees (°), minutes ('), and seconds ("). The degree symbol is set close up to the figure, for example *40° 42′ 30″ N 74° 1′ 15″ W.* In discursive and nontechnical contexts there are generally spaces between each item, though the coordinate should not be broken over a line except following a compass abbreviation. In display work and technical contexts the figures may be close up, and the seconds given as decimal fractions, for example *40° 42.5′ N 74° 1.25′ W.* The *N, S, E*, and *W* (no points) makes the addition of *lat.* or *long.* superfluous in most instances, though especially in precise coordinates the reverse holds, with, for example, *Lat. 40.980818, Long. −74.093665.* Rules vary for geometry.

7.6 **Currency**

British currency

Amounts in whole pounds should be printed with the £ symbol, numerals and unit abbreviation close up: *£2,542, £3 m., £7.47 m.* Print *00* after the decimal point only if a sum appears in context with other fractional amounts: *They bought at £8.00 and sold at £9.50.*

Amounts in pence are set with the numeral close up to the abbreviation, which has no full point: *56p* rather than *£0.56.* Mixed amounts always extend to two places after the decimal point, and do not include the pence abbreviation: *£15.30, £15.79.*

Amounts expressed in pre-decimal currency—*£.s.d.* (italic)—will continue to be found in copy and must be retained. They will naturally occur in resetting books published before 1971, and in new books in which the author refers to events and conditions, or quotations from work dating, before 1971. For example:

> In 1969 income tax stood at 8s. 3d. in the £.
> The tenth edition cost 10s. 6d. in 1956.

In new books, and in annotated editions of reset works, a decision must be made as to whether to introduce decimal equivalents, for elucidation or for ease of comparison (e.g. in statistics). Note the distinction in the pound symbol between the earlier style of, for example, '£44. 3s. 10d.' and the earlier style of '44l. 3s. 10d.'. In both these styles a normal space of the line separates the elements. Note the spelling *fourpence*, *ninepenny*, etc. for amounts in pre-decimal pennies.

US currency

Sums of money in dollars and cents are treated like those in pounds and pence: *$4,542*, $3 m., $7.47 m., *56¢*.

Indian currency

In Indian currency, one hundred thousand rupees is a lakh, punctuated as *1,00,000*; ten million rupees is a crore, punctuated as *1,00,00,000*; in combination they are for example *Rs 25,87,30,000* (25 crore, 87 lakh, 30 thousand). Note the location of the commas in the amounts.

Abbreviation and placement

Amounts of money are either spelt out in words with the unit of currency or printed in numerals with the symbols or abbreviations: *twenty-five pounds*, *thirteen dollars*, *seventy francs*, £25, $13, *F 70*; round numbers lend themselves to words better than do precise amounts, though even these may need to be spelt out where absolute clarity is vital, as in legal documents. For amounts of millions and above, and for thousands in financial contexts, it is permissible to combine symbols, numerals, words, and abbreviations, according to the conventions of the context in which they appear: *£5 million*, *US$15 billion*.

Where symbols or abbreviations are used, such as £ (pounds), $ (dollars), *DM* (Deutschmarks), ¥ (yen or yuan), € (euros), *Pt* (pesetas), *Rs* (rupees), they precede the figures. There is no space after symbols, but some styles use a space after the abbreviations; this is acceptable if imposed consistently within a work. Symbols may be discarded altogether, as with *GBP* and *DFL* for the British pound and Dutch florin.

In text, abbreviations or symbols may need clarification when they are employed by more than one country: for example, the French abbreviation for 'franc' may be rendered in French as *Fr*, F, F., or *f.* before or after the amount. However, in juxtaposition with Swiss or Belgian francs, for example, the abbreviations *FF*, *SF*, and *BF* (or *FFr*, *SFr*, and *BFr*) should be used. Symbols and abbreviations may be used in combination to distinguish different countries using the same system of currency, for example *US$90*, *HK$90*. Any of these approaches is acceptable if it is consistently applied within a work.

Glossing

It is sometimes necessary to gloss one currency in terms of another:

> He lost at least £1 billion ($1.5 billion) in the venture.
>
> Shares were valued at 1.53 trillion lire ($1.2 billion).

Comparison may be required not just between the different currencies at the same time but between the same currency at different times, or different currencies at different times. Whenever this is done, make clear the exchange rate or date that provides the basis for the correlation:

> The bishop of Bayeux held Great Tew, then valued at £40 (£20 in 1066).
>
> A supposed autograph MS of Book 2 of the *Aeneid* was sold in the second century AD for 20 aurei (2,000 senteres).

To establish a comparative rate of exchange, money cited in any historical context usually requires glossing of some sort.

7.7 **Roman numerals**

7.7.1 **General conventions**

The base numerals are I (1), V (5), X (10), L (50), C (100), D (500), and M (1,000). The principle behind their formation is that identical numbers are added (II = 2), smaller numbers after a larger one are added (VII = 7), and smaller numbers before a larger one are subtracted (IX = 9). The I, X, and C can be added up to four times:

> I, II, III, IV, V, VI, VII, VIII, IX, X (10)
>
> XI, XII, XIII, XIV, XV, XVI, XVII, XVIII, XIX, XX (20)
>
> CCCCLXXXXVIIII (499)

Though not required by classical practice, the reductive rule (employing the minimum numerals in each amount) is commonplace today.

Since today the roman system of numbering is considered ungainly and is not always understood, there is an increasing tendency to prefer arabic numerals. Current OUP practice uses roman numerals in the following ways:

- Capitalize roman numerals when used for the chapters and appendices of a book, and for acts of plays or sections of long poems, such as books or cantos. Roman numerals used for volume numbers are not capitalized in references or text when referring to another work, but are capitalized when they refer to the work in which they appear.

  Act I of *The Tempest*   Book V   Chapters III–VIII

- Where a roman-numeral reference cites a section within the present work, it is usually in capitals; where it cites a section within another work, it is usually lower-case or small capitals:

  For more on this, *see* CHAPTER XI.

  Smith discusses this in chapter xi of his two-volume work.

  The division label (part, book, chapter, appendix, etc.) is styled in the same height as the numeral, capital with capital, lower case with lower case, and small capital with small capital. Thus *Chapter XI, chapter xi.*

- Use capital roman numerals after the names of monarchs and popes: *Henry VIII, John Paul II.* No full point follows; the number should not be written as an ordinal (*Henry the VIIIth*)—if the context requires it, use instead *Henry the Eighth.* English style does not follow Continental practice, for example *Heinrich XII., Francois Ier.* In setting, do not divide roman numerals between lines, or separate them from their name.

- Use capital roman numerals similarly in American personal names, where the male of a family bears the same name: *Adlai E. Stevenson III, Daniel P. Daly V, John Paul Getty III.* A male bearing his father's name is styled *Jr.,* whereas a male bearing his grandfather's name—but not his father's—is styled *II.* Strictly speaking *Oscar Hammerstein II* should thus be *Jr.,* although the bearer's preference naturally should be followed.

  No full point follows the numerals and normally no comma precedes them, although some individuals style their names thus.

- Use full capitals for the italicized names of ships, racing cars, spacecraft, etc.: *Gipsy Moth III.*

- Use full capitals where 'LXX' stands for the Septuagint.

- Use words to spell out centuries in English, except in footnotes; but in dating manuscripts, the convention is *s. xi.* In other languages, use figures. These are mostly capital roman, except for the following. In French use small capitals in roman type, full capitals in italic type, followed in either case by superior ^{e} or ^{ème}. In German use arabic followed by full point. (Occasionally capital roman numerals are used; these too must be followed by full point.)

- Small capitals are used whenever a subordinate or intermediate level of roman numeral is needed, normally in conjunction with upper- or lower-case numerals, as in the case of short references:

> here will be an old abusing of God's patience and the King's English. (*The Merry Wives of Windsor*, I. iv. 5)

A full reference to this line would be rendered *Act I, scene iv, line 5*, with the act number restored to a full capital to match the capital *Act*. In contexts where it is important to retain small capital lettering in text, small capital roman numerals are used to match: 'CHAPTER XXII', 'PEACE DECLARED'.

■ Use lower-case roman numerals to number the preliminary pages in a book, and for scenes of plays: '*Hamlet*, Act I, sc. ii.; pp. iii–x'.

■ In tabular matter, roman numerals are ranged on the right if they are meant to be added up, etc., and on the left if they are not.

■ Some Continental countries use lower-case roman numerals for the months in a date: *23. v. 85. See also* **7.10**.

■ Roman numerals in manuscript sometimes have a final or single *i* replaced by a *j*, for example *ij*, *viij*. This style need be retained only when reproducing copy in facsimile.

■ OUP discourages the elision of roman numerals; it is liable to misinterpretation. To save space in certain circumstances (e.g. in narrow measure or repetitive references) two consecutive numerals may be indicated by *f.* for 'following': *pp. lxxxvii–lxxxviii* becomes *pp. lxxxvii f.* (Editors should mark for a thin space between the last numeral and the *f.*) OUP nevertheless prefers arabic figures to be elided.

7.7.2 **Classical contexts**

In editions of Latin texts, roman numerals should generally be set in small capitals. *See also* **11.31** and for the numerals used in Greek *see* **11.25**.

■ Since Roman usage was far more fluid than modern practice, such variations on the modern standard as 'IIX = 8' and 'VIIII = 9' are to be accepted. 500 was I, later corrupted to *D* for 1,000. CIƆ was later reinterpreted as the M of *mille*; similarly 5,000, 10,000, 50,000, and 100,000 may be written 'IƆƆ', 'CCIƆƆ', 'IƆƆ', and 'CCCIƆƆƆ' respectively.

■ Thousands may also be indicated by a bar across the top of a letter: $\bar{V}$ = 5,000 or (improperly) 500,000. Hundreds of thousands were indicated by bars describing three sides of a square (left, top, and right) about the numeral: $|\bar{V}|$ = 500,000. Sometimes the superior bar alone was used, though this could be misinterpreted. *S* was used for a half; other fractions had symbols of their own.

■ German classicists, and Germans generally, nowadays make little use of roman numerals. Even when citing roman page numbers, they often convert them into arabic and add an asterisk, for example *S. 78**

(= p. lxxviii). Classical scholars throughout the world usually adopt this preference, both in classical reference (*Ovid,* Amores *3.1.15* not *III.i.15*) and in volume numbers of books. In classical texts OUP prefers the former, although in general references to classical works roman numerals are still acceptable.

7.7.3 **References**

When roman numerals are used in references, use lower case if there is only one level, small capital and lower case in that order if there are two (*II. i*), full capital, small capital, and lower case in that order if there are three (*III. II. i*). However, small capitals (but not lower case) become full capitals to balance a capital in the item numbered: *2 Henry IV,* IV. *ii. 8* but *Act IV, Scene ii, line 86.* For more on plays and their references *see* **13.6**.

7.8 **Statistical texts**

The rules regarding in-text numbers in heavily statistical, scientific, or technical work vary slightly from normal practice in three respects:

- The symbol %, rather than the spelt-out *per cent*, is permissible in text as well as in peripheral matter such as tables, notes, parenthetical material, and captions.

- Figures in scientific and technical work are usually spelt out up to nine. Although in statistical work figures should still be spelt out up to ninety-nine, this is tempered by common sense if varying the form by type rather than by quantity will make the passage easier to read. For example:

  > Of the 34 respondents, most opt for an intermediate position, with 25 (74%) giving two or three positive answers out of the four. Of that total, however, 1 of the remaining 9 (26%) gave four or five negative answers in addition to that percentage compounded for the original three.

  Each case must be judged on the merits of consistency within the sentence and against accompanying passages, although in very terse, number-laden passages it may even be necessary to vary treatment of figures from one sentence to the next. In general, the closer two different sets of figures are linked in context and proximity, the more likely it is that they should be clarified by some being spelt out and some remaining in arabic, regardless of their amounts.

- In tabular matter, numbers of only four figures have no thin space, except where necessary to help alignment with numbers of five or more figures. In-text numbers, however, use commas unless the work is of a scientific nature, where the convention is to set a thin space for all in-text numbers of four figures and above.

See also **7.2**.

7.9 **Time of day**

- Use words, and no hyphens, with reference to whole hours and to fractions of an hour: *four (o'clock), half past four, a quarter to four.*
- Use *o'clock* only with the exact hour, and with time expressed in words: *four o'clock,* not *half past four o'clock* or 4 *o'clock.* Do not use it with *a.m.* or *p.m.*, but rather write *eight o'clock in the morning,* etc.
- Use figures when minutes are to be included: *4.30.* In North America, Scandinavia, and elsewhere the full point is replaced by a colon: *4:30.* This is found particularly in digital clocks and watches.
- Use figures if *a.m.* or *p.m.* is to be added: 4 p.m.; *see also* **7.1.2**.
- Correctly, *12 a.m.* is midnight and *12 p.m.* is noon; but since this is not always understood, it may be necessary to use the explicit *12 midnight* and *12 noon.* The twenty-four-hour clock avoids the use of *a.m.* and *p.m.*: *12.00* is noon, *24.00* is midnight.
- Some differences exist between British and US ways of referring to time. Americans may use *a quarter of four* for 'a quarter to', and *a quarter after four* for 'a quarter past'. This may give British readers pause, as equally the colloquial British *half four* for 'half past' might give US readers pause and British purists the shudders. *Half four* used to mean 'half past three' (cf. e.g. the German *halb vier* or the Serbo-Croat *pola četiri*).

7.10 **Dates**

7.10.1 **Order**

Dates should be shown in the order day, month, year, without internal punctuation, as *2 November 1993.* A named day preceding a date is separated by a comma: *Tuesday, 2 November 1993.* There is no comma between month and year: *in June 1831.* Four-figure dates have no comma—2001— though those with more do: *10,000* BC. The British all-figure form is

2.11.93, but for clarity's sake months should always be spelt out in text and abbreviated only in notes and references.

- In US style the order is month, day, year: *November 2, 1993*. The all-figure style for a date (separated by solidi in US style) can create confusion in transatlantic communication, since *11/2/93* is 2 November to an American reader and 11 February to a British one.

- The dating system promoted by the ISO is year, month, day, with the elements separated by hyphens: *1993–11–02*. This style is preferred in Japan and increasingly popular in technical, computing, and financial contexts.

- For greater accuracy, precise dates in astronomical work, for example, use days (d), hours (h), minutes (m), and seconds (s) (2001 January 1d 2h 34m 4.8s) or fractions of days (2001 January 1.107).

- Another alternative, common on the Continent and elsewhere, is to use (normally lower-case) roman numerals for the months (*2. xi. 93*). This system serves to clarify which number is the day and which the month in all contexts—a useful expedient when translating truncated dates into British or American English, which may also be of help in very narrow measure.

- Quaker documents always use figures for both days and months, to avoid their pagan names; these should be retained in references. Before 1752, *first month* meant March, but ascertain whether the month or day precedes if it is ambiguous. In medieval and early modern works one may find *viiber* or the like (even *vii*) used for September, and similarly roman or arabic eight, nine, and ten for October, November, December.

- AD and AH precede the year number; BC, BCE, BP, and CE follow it.

- Dates in other calendars should be given in the order day, month, year, with no internal punctuation: *25 Tishri* AM *5757*, *13 Jumada I* AH *1417*. Do not abbreviate months even in notes. In the calendar of Ptolemaic and Roman Egypt it is conventional to put the month first: *Thoth 25, Phaophi 16*.

7.10.2 **Abbreviation**

- Names of days and months should generally be shown in full, but where necessary, as in notes and narrow measure, they are abbreviated thus:

Sun. Mon. Tue. Wed. Thur. Fri. Sat.
Jan. Feb. Mar. Apr. May June July Aug. Sept. Oct. Nov. Dec.

Only *May*, *June*, and *July* escape abbreviation.

- Do not use the endings *st*, *rd*, or *th* in conjunction with a figure, as in *12th August 1960*, unless copying another source: dates in letters or other documents quoted verbatim must be as in the original. Where less than the full date is given, write *10 January* (in notes *10 Jan.*), but *the 10th*. If only the month is given it should be spelt out, even in notes. Elide year spans to the fewest digits (*1804–7, 1914–18, 2001–3*). Do not elide dates involving different centuries; write *1798–1810, 1992–2001*. Use the full form in any display material such as headings, titles, and tables. Where necessary, spell out a year in words at the beginning of a sentence: *Nineteen-forty was the year of the Battle of Britain*. Spans in BC always appear in full, because an elided second date could be misread as a complete year: *185–22* BC is a century longer than *185–122* BC, and dates for, say, Horace (*65–8* BC) might appear to the unwary to express a period of three rather than fifty-seven years.

■ An en rule may be used as a substitute for the word *to*, as in the construction *during the years 1976–9* or *the period 1992–2003*. Do not use the en rule after *from* or *between*, and do not then abbreviate the year: write *from 1976 to 1979* and *between 1992 and 2001*.

■ When a terminal date is in the future, use an en rule alone: *The Times (1785–), Jenny Bloggs (1960–)*. A fixed interword space after the date may give a better appearance in conjunction with the closing parenthesis that habitually follows it: *The Times (1785–), Jenny Bloggs (1960–)*. An alternative for people—*Jenny Bloggs (b. 1960)*—is also possible, as the bare en rule may be seen by some to connote undue anticipation.

■ The solidus replaces the en rule for a period of one year reckoned in a format other than the normal calendar extent: *49/8* BC, *the tax year 1934/5*, AM *5750* = *1989/90*, AH *1414* = *1993/4*, *saka era 1916 (1994/5)*. A span of years in this style is joined by an en rule as normal: *1992/3–2001/2*.

7.10.3 *Circa* and *floruit*

The Latin *circa*, meaning 'about', is used in English mainly with dates and quantities. Set the abbreviation *c.* close up to any figures following (*c.£10,400*), but spaced from words and letters (*c.* AD *44*). In discursive prose it is usually preferable to use *about* or *some* when describing quantities other than dates (*about eleven pints, some 14 acres*). With a span of dates *c.* must be repeated before each date if both are approximate, as a single abbreviation is not understood to modify both dates: 'the logician Adam of Balsham (*c.1105–c.1170*)'.

Distinguish between *c.* and ?: the former is used where a particular year cannot be fixed upon, but only a period or range of several years; the latter where there are reasonable grounds for believing that a particular year is correct. It follows therefore that *c.* will more often be used with round numbers, such as the start and midpoint of a decade, than with numbers that fall between.

A form such as '*c*.1773' might be used legitimately to mean 'between 1772 and 1774' or 'between 1770 and 1775'. As such, it is best in discursive prose to indicate the earliest and latest dates by some other means. Historians employ a multiplication symbol for this purpose: *1996 × 1997* means 'in 1996 or 1997, but we cannot tell which'; similarly, *1996 × 2004* means 'no earlier than 1996 and no later than 2004'. Figures are not to be contracted: *the architect Robert Smith (b.1772 × 1774, d.1855)*.

The Latin *floruit*, meaning 'flourished', is used in English where only an approximate date of activity can be provided, or the only dates known for a subject are those of activities that cannot be related temporally to a birth or death date; in the case of a family, group, or movement, such dates will be irrelevant. Set the abbreviation *fl.* before the year, years, or—where no concrete date(s) can be fixed—century, separated by a space: 'William of Coventry (*fl.*1360)', 'Edward Fisher' (*fl.* 1627–56)', 'Ralph Acton (*fl.* 14th c.)'.

7.10.4 **Decades**

A period capable of being discerned solely by its decade should start with an initial capital. The difference between labelling a decade *the Twenties* rather than *the 1920s* is that the word form connotes all the social, cultural, and political conditions unique to or significant in that decade, while the numerical form is simply the label for the time span. This is not to say the two cannot be used together for variation in text, but in doing so it is useful to attempt some distinction in context between aura and era. So, *jazz- and gin-mad flappers of the Twenties*, but *East Anglian pork production of the 1920s*.

OUP does not use an apostrophe before abbreviated decades. Use either *the Sixties* or *the 1960s*, not *the '60s*. Similarly use *the 1970s and 1980s*, even though *the 1970s and '80s* transcribes how such dates may read out loud.

7.11 **Centuries**

7.11.1 **General conventions**

In written text refer to centuries in words: *the nineteenth century, the first century* BC. Centuries are abbreviated in notes, references, and tabular matter; the abbreviations are *c.* and *cent.*: *14th c., 21st cent.* Both spelt-out and abbreviated forms require a hyphen when used adjectivally: *an eighth-century* [or *8th-c.*] *poem, the early seventeenth-century* [or *17th-c.*] *drama-tists.* In dating medieval manuscripts, the abbreviation *s.* (for *saeculum*, pl. *ss.*) is often used instead: *s. viii.*

- Largely, the ordinal name and the numerical form of a century may be used interchangeably—*the sixteenth century* or *the 1500s*—although strictly speaking they are not quite synonymous, since the 1500s ran from 1500 to 1599, and the sixteenth century from 1501 to 1600. The twenty-first century spans 2001–2100, making the year 2000 the final year of the last century, not the first year of this one.

- Centuries BC run backwards, so that the fifth century BC spanned 500–401 BC. The year 280 BC was in the third century BC.

- Use the phrase *the turn of the century* only where the context makes clear which century is meant, and whether it denotes that century's begin-ning or end.

- Conventions for numbering centuries in other languages vary, though for the most part capital roman numerals are used, with two common exceptions: French uses small capitals in roman, full capitals in italic. In either case the figures are followed by a superior *e* or *ème* to indicate the suffix: *le XVIIe siècle, le XVIIème siècle.* German uses arabic followed by a full point. Occasionally capital roman numerals are used; these too must be followed by a full point.

7.11.2 **Eras**

Some writers prefer to use AD for any date before the first millennium. While this is not strictly necessary, it can be handy as a clarifying label: *This was true from 37* may not instantly be recognized as referring to a year. Any contentious date, or any year span ranging on either side of the birth of Christ, should be clarified by BC or AD: *This was true from 43 BC to AD 18.* Conversely, a date span wholly in BC or AD needs no clarifica-tion, since *407–346* is manifestly different from *346–407*. Otherwise, context usually determines whether BC or AD is required: readers can be relied upon to reflect that the Apostles were active in AD, as were all Roman emperors save Augustus: on the other hand, since Augustus achieved sole power in 31 BC and died in AD 14, dates in his reign usually need to be specified.

Although the era in general use is called *the Christian era*, it is not the only era in use among Christians (even nowadays the Ethiopians reckon the Year of Grace from 29 August AD 8), nor is it used only by Christians (it was made the official era of China by the Communists). Some authors prefer to describe it as *the Common Era*, designating CE instead of AD and BCE instead of BC; the choice is theirs. On the other hand, AC should not be allowed, since it may represent either *ante Christum* (= BC) or *anno Christi* (= AD).

The following eras should be indicated by the appropriate abbreviation before the year:

- *a.Abr.* (the year of Abraham), reckoned from 2016 BC and used in chronicles by Eusebius and Jerome; not written AA.

- AH (*anno Hegirae*), the Muslim era, reckoned from 16 July 622.

- AM (*anno mundi*), 'in the year of the world', will normally represent the Jewish era, reckoned from 7 October 3761 BC; but in suitable contexts it may designate other Creation eras, particularly the Byzantine era (retained in Russia till 1699), reckoned from 1 September 5509 BC.

- AS (*anno Seleuci*), the Seleucid era, variously reckoned from autumn 312 BC and spring 311 BC, formerly current in much of the Near East and still used by the 'Church of the East' in the twentieth century. Use of this abbreviation for the Christian era (*anno salvationis/Salvatoris*) is obsolete.

- AUC (*anno Vrbis conditae*), 'in the year of the foundation of the City', the supposed Roman era from 753 BC, was rarely used by Romans (who had several different dates for the foundation of Rome, and designated the year by the names of the consuls). It is very frequent, especially in respect of BC dates, in German works on Roman history in the nineteenth and early twentieth centuries.

The following eras should be indicated by the appropriate abbreviation after the year:

- BCE (Before Common Era), CE (Common Era) are used mainly by writers who wish to avoid specifying dates in Christian terms.

- BP (Before Present) is used by geologists and palaeontologists for dates not accurate within a few thousand years; AD 1950 is fixed as the conventional 'present'.

For all era abbreviations other than *a.Abr.*, use unspaced small capitals, even in italic. Except in books intended for readers who know or use them, spell out eras other than the above, at least at first mention.

In discussing periods prior to 10,000 years ago it is customary to use BP (before present). Some authors favour BP as a matter of course, since it does not presuppose any Christian reckoning on the reader's part. This is acceptable, provided BP is not intermingled with BC and other references of this kind within the same text. If standardization is necessary, however, be wary of changing dates from one system to another merely by adding or subtracting a round 2,000 years: *60,000–40,000* BP for the late Neanderthal period, for example, is a good deal more general—and intentionally so—than *58,000–38,000* BC, which implies greater precision than a scholar may wish.

Dates before present are sometimes given in lower case (*bp*, *bc*, *ad*) to indicate they have not been calibrated. Follow copy if a distinction has been made; non-specialist texts may need to clarify this convention.

7.12 **Regnal years**

Regnal years are marked by the successive anniversaries of a sovereign's accession to the throne. Consequently they do not coincide with calendar years, which up to 1751 in England and America—though not in Scotland—began legally on 25 March. All Acts of Parliament before 1963 were numbered serially within each parliamentary session, which itself was described by the regnal year or years of the sovereign during which it was held. Regnal years were also used to date other official edicts, such as those of universities.

The abbreviations of monarchs' names in regnal-year references are as follows:

Car. *or* Chas. (Charles)	Hen. (Henry)
Steph. (Stephen)	Edw. (Edward)
Jac. (James)	Will. (William)
Eliz. (Elizabeth)	P. & M. (Philip and Mary)
Wm. & Mar. (William and Mary)	Geo. (George)
Ric. (Richard)	Vic. *or* Vict. (Victoria)

The names of King John and Queens Anne, Jane, and Mary are not abbreviated. OUP prefers to print the monarch's numeral in roman, although arabic is acceptable if consistently applied.

A session starting in one regnal year was renumbered when it passed the anniversary of the monarch's accession. A parliamentary session might, and usually did, extend over parts of two regnal years, for example *9 & 10 Geo. VI* (1945–6), or over parts of two regnal years and the whole of the intervening regnal year, such as *12, 13, & 14 Geo. VI* (1948–9), or even over parts of the regnal years of two sovereigns, such as *15 & 16 Geo. VI and 1 Eliz. II* (1951–2). It was possible to have two Acts passed (sometimes with the same name) within the same parliamentary session but bearing different regnal years.

Because this numbering system proved so confusing, since 1963 Acts of Parliament have been numbered by the calendar year in which they were passed and by the chapter number, with no reference made to the regnal year.

A useful list of regnal years may be found in appendix iii of the *The Oxford*

Companion to English Literature, and appendix a of *The Oxford Companion to the Year*.

7.13 **Calendar**

Variations in time-reckoning systems between cultures and eras can lead both author and editor to error. The following section offers some guidance for those working with unfamiliar calendars; fuller explanation may be found in Blackburn and Holford-Stevens, *The Oxford Companion to the Year* (OUP, 1999).

7.13.1 **Old and New Style**

These terms are often applied to two different sets of facts. In 1582 Pope Gregory XIII decreed that, in order to correct the Julian calendar, the days 5–14 October of that year should be omitted and no future centennial year (e.g. 1700, 1800, 1900) should be a leap year unless it was divisible by four (e.g. 1600, 2000). This reformed 'Gregorian' calendar was quickly adopted in Roman Catholic countries, more slowly elsewhere: in Britain not till 1752 (when the days 3–13 September were omitted), in Russia not till 1918 (when the days 16–28 February were omitted). The discrepancy between the Julian and Gregorian calendars was ten days until 28 February/10 March 1700, eleven days from 29 February/11 March 1700 to 28 February/11 March 1800, twelve days from 29 February/12 March 1800 to 28 February/12 March 1900, and thirteen days from 29 February/13 March 1900; it will become fourteen days on 29 February/14 March 2100.

Until the middle of the eighteenth century, not all states reckoned the new year from the same day: whereas France (which had previously counted from Easter) adopted 1 January from 1563, and Scotland from 1600, England counted from 25 March in official usage as late as 1751; so until 1749 did Florence and Pisa, but whereas Florence, like England, counted from 25 March AD 1, Pisa counted from 25 March 1 BC, so that the Pisan year was always one higher than the Florentine. Thus the execution of Charles I was officially dated 30 January 1648 in England, but 30 January 1649 in Scotland. In Florence—which used the Gregorian calendar—the same day was 9 February 1648, in France and Pisa 9 February 1649. Furthermore, although both Shakespeare and Cervantes died on 23 April 1616 according to their respective calendars, 23 April in Spain (and other Roman Catholic countries) was only 13 April in England, 23 April in England was 3 May in Spain, and in Pisa the year was 1617.

Confusion is caused in English-language writing by the adoption, in England, Ireland, and the American colonies, of two reforms in quick succession. The year 1751 began on 1 January in Scotland and on 25 March in England, but ended throughout Great Britain and its colonies on 31 December, so that 1752 began on 1 January. So, whereas 1 January 1752 corresponded to 12 January in most Continental countries, from 14 September onwards there was no discrepancy.

As a result, many writers treat the two reforms as one, using Old Style and New Style indiscriminately for the start of the new year and the form of calendar, even with reference to countries in which the two reforms were adopted at different times. This is unfortunate: Old Style should be reserved for the Julian calendar and New Style for the Gregorian; the 1 January reckoning should be called 'modern style' (or 'Circumcision style'), that from 25 March 'Annunciation' or 'Lady Day' style (or 'Florentine' and 'Pisan' style with reference to those cities), and others as appropriate, such as 'Easter style', 'Nativity style', 'Venetian style' = 1 March, 'Byzantine style' = 1 September.

It is customary to give dates in Old or New Style according to the system in force at the time in the country chiefly discussed; if the system may be unfamiliar to the reader, a brief explanation should be added. Any dates in the other style should be given in parentheses with an equals sign preceding the date and the abbreviation of the style following it: *23 August 1637 NS (= 13 August OS)* in a history of England, or *13 August 1637 OS (= 23 August NS)* in one of France. In either case, *13/23 August 1637* may be used for short, but when citing documents take care to use this form only when the original itself employs it. On the other hand, it is normal to treat the year as beginning on 1 January: modern histories of England date the execution of Charles I to 30 January 1649. When it is necessary to keep both styles in mind, it is normal to write *30 January 1648/9*, subject to the same qualification when citing documents; otherwise the date should be given as *30 January 1648 (= modern 1649)*. (Contemporary accounts could manage this as well: George Washington's date of birth was recorded in the family Bible as *ye 11th day of February 1731/2*.) Original documents may exhibit the split fraction, for example *172½*; this should be used only when exact transcription is required. For dates in Pisan style between 25 March and 31 December inclusive, write *15 August 1737/6*.

7.13.2 Chinese calendar

The Chinese year consists of twelve or sometimes thirteen months reckoned from the conjunction of moon and sun. Apart from the Christian era, introduced into mainland China in 1949 by the Communist government, years are identified in various ways. The three commonest ways of doing this are as follows:

Imperial reign

During the imperial period, an emperor would proclaim a new era with an auspicious name, usually of two characters; before 1368 emperors proclaimed new eras at will, but in the last two dynasties (Ming and Qing) each emperor announced only one era in his reign, beginning at the next new year after his accession, and was known by the name of that era after death. Hence one should not say *the Emperor Kangxi* (the emperor responsible for the great Kangxi or K'ang-hsi dictionary) or *the Emperor Qianlong* (in whose reign Qianlong or Ch'ien-lung porcelain was produced) but *the Kangxi Emperor, the Qianlong Emperor.*

Sixty-year cycle

A combination of one element from a list of ten ideographs, known as the Celestial Stems, with another element from a list of twelve characters known as the Earthly Branches yields sixty possibilities for assignment to a given year. When these sixty possible forms of date are exhausted, the cycle (which in earlier times was also used for days) begins again with the first combination. The Branches are associated with the animal cycle known with minor variations throughout the Turkic and East Asian world, familiar from such expressions as *the Year of the Rat.* Since any two-character combination can refer to any year in a sixty-year cycle going far back into history, in order to convert a Chinese year to the Christian era it must be placed in its historical context; at the very least the dynasty must be known.

Relation with the start of the Chinese Republic

Dates are reckoned according to the time that has elapsed since the foundation of the Chinese republic at the beginning of 1912. This form of dating is widely used in Taiwan, where it is simply a reapplication of the regnal-era system. The number of the year is prefixed by the characters *Min Kuo* or *Republic.* To convert this to the Western calendar, add 1911 to the number of the year.

It is usually sufficient to give only the Western equivalent for the period of one year. Caution is needed here, however, since lunar years and solar years do not correspond; the lunar year begins at some time in January or February. Those who are not Chinese linguists should seek expert assistance in the use of these reference works.

7.13.3 Greek calendars

Although the ancient Greek cities used calendars based on the moon, in which months contained thirty or twenty-nine days and a thirteenth month was intercalated when the year ran ahead of the sun, uniformity went no further: the beginning of the year, the names of the months, the intercalation of the extra month, the adjustment (or non-adjustment) of the nominal to the actual new moon were each city's business to regulate as it saw fit. Nor in the classical period was there a standard era: years were designated by the name of a magistrate or other office-holder, which meant nothing outside the city concerned. In the third century BC a common framework for historians was found in the Olympiad, or cycle of the Olympic Games, held in the summer every four years from 776 BC onwards. Thus 776/5 was designated the first year of the first Olympiad; 775/5 the second year; and 772/1 the first year of the second Olympiad. When modern scholars need to cite these datings, they are written *Ol. 1, 1*, *Ol. 1, 2*, and *Ol. 2, 1* respectively.

7.13.4 French Republican calendar

The Republican calendar (also called the 'French Revolutionary calendar' or, by the beginning of the nineteenth century, simply 'the French calendar') was introduced by decree of the *Convention nationale* on 5 October 1793, and was discontinued by Senatus-consultum on 19 September 1805, with effect from 1 January 1806. On its introduction it was antedated to begin from the foundation of the Republic (22 September 1792). The year, modelled on that of ancient Egypt as reformed by Augustus, consisted of twelve months of thirty days each; weeks within each month were replaced by three *décades* lasting ten days each. The five days left over were called *sansculottides* (under the Directoire renamed *jours complémentaires*) and observed as national holidays; in years III, VII, and XI a sixth day was kept as the *jour de la Révolution*.

The poet Fabre d'Églantine (guillotined on 16 germinal An II = 24 Nov. 1793) named the months of the new calendar according to their seasonal significance. Though difficult to translate, approximations are included in parentheses:

Autumn	Winter	Spring	Summer
vendémiaire (vintage)	*nivôse* (snow)	*germinal* (seed-time)	*messidor* (harvest)
brumaire (mist)	*pluviôse* (rain)	*floréal* (flowers)	*thermidor* (heat)
frimaire (frost)	*ventôse* (tempest)	*prairial* (meadows)	*fructidor* (fruit)

The months are not now capitalized in French, though they were at the time and may still be so in English. The days making up each *décade* were named in numerical order *primidi, duodi, tridi, quartidi, quintidi, sextidi, septidi, octidi, nonidi,* and *décadi*.

Years of the Republican calendar are printed in large roman numerals: *9 thermidor An II*; *13 vendémiaire An IV*; in English *Year II, Year IV*. If a conversion table is not given, parallel dates in the Gregorian calendar should be supplied for non-specialist readers, for example *from 18 floréal till 10 thermidor, Year II (7 May till 28 July 1794)*.

While English historians use the Republican calendar as much or as little as they like, in France it is still the officially correct way of giving dates from that period, for instance in citing laws passed at that time and still in force.

7.13.5 Japanese calendar

Before 1873 Japan used a lunar calendar based on the same principles as the Chinese, but since the determining longitude was that of Tokyo, not Peking, Japanese and Chinese dates did not always correspond. All dates expressed with reference to this lunar calendar should be converted to the solar equivalent, by consulting specialist reference works. Little used now, this traditional Horeki calendar was in continuous use since the first emperor around 60 BC; the year 2000 is approximately year 2060 in Horeki.

Years are identified according to the regnal era; thus 2000 is known as *Heisei 12*. Since 1868 there has been only one era per reign, but with the difference from China that the period between accession and the next New Year (which since 1873 has been 1 January) is counted as the first year of the reign: hence *Shōwa 1* = 26–31 December 1926, *Shōwa 64* = 1–7 January 1989, and *Heisei 1* = 8 January–31 December 1989. As in the Chinese custom, a deceased emperor is known by his era: Emperor Hirohito, who died on 7 January 1989, is *the Shōwa Emperor*.

Where possible give any translated dates in Western style, with the Japanese equivalent in brackets in the preferred Japanese order of year/month/day.

7.13.6 Jewish calendar

The Jewish year consists in principle of twelve months of alternately 30 and 29 days; in seven years out of nineteen an extra month of 30 days is inserted, and in some years either the second month is extended to 30 days or the third month shortened to 29 days. It follows that the conversion of dates in the Jewish calendar to their Christian equivalent cannot be done accurately without a conversion table or a complex calculation. Day-by-day tables for the Jewish years 5680/1 to 5780/1, corresponding to 1920 to 2020, are printed in the Index volume of the *Encyclopaedia Judaica*. Since the era is reckoned from a notional time of

Creation at 11.11 and 20 seconds p.m. on Sunday, 6 October 3761 BC, the Christian year corresponding to a given Jewish year can be approximated by deducting 3760 from the Jewish year; however, since the Jewish year begins in September, the year of the world (AM) 5760 corresponds not to 2000 but to a period extending from 11 September 1999 to 29 September 2000.

In Hebrew documents the year is indicated by letters used for their numerical value, the thousands normally being omitted. The approximate Christian equivalent can be calculated by adding the numerical value of the letters plus 1240 (since the Jewish year 5000 was Christian 1239/40). For example, the Jewish year תש"ח is equivalent to 1948 (*tav* (400) + *shin* (300) + *chet* (8) = 708 + 1240 = 1948.

7.13.7 Korean calendar

Dates should not prove particularly difficult for editors; nowadays, in both North and South Korea the Western calendar is in general use. In the recent past it was customary to give the date of a book in relation to the era of the legendary founder of Korea, Tangun. This was 2,333 years before our own era, so in order to find the equivalent Western date for the Korean year 4288, for example, this figure is subtracted from it, to give the date as 1955.

7.13.8 Muslim calendar

Before Islam, the Arabs used a lunisolar calendar, in which from time to time, as in the Jewish calendar, an extra month was added; a few years before his death, the Prophet announced that this entailed an impious postponement of the sacred months (Qur'ān, Sūra 9, v. 37). As a result, the Muslim year consists of twelve lunar months, so that thirty-three Muslim years roughly correspond to thirty-two Christian ones. Years are counted from the first day of the year in which the Prophet made his departure, or Hijra, from Mecca to Medina, namely Friday, 16 July AD 622; since the civil day began at sunset, it runs in Western terms from the evening of Thursday, 15 July AD 622. In former times, however, years were often counted from the Thursday just mentioned; this remained the rule amongst astronomers, who began the day at noon.

As set out in the handbooks, the Muslim calendar is one of the simplest and (in lunar terms) most accurate in the world: twelve months of alternating 30 and 29 days, with an extra day added to the last month in 11 years out of 30. However, since the month traditionally began— and in some countries still begins (at least in the case of Ramadan)—not on a pre-calculated day but when the new moon has been observed by reliable witnesses in the night sky, and since cycles of intercalation have varied both as to their length and as to the distribution of leap years within them, the actual date may well fall a day or so earlier or later than the standard conversion tables might suggest. Hence the exact Christian equivalent of a Muslim date given in a text cannot be ascertained for certain unless (as it often is) the day of the week is added, but if it is, it should be believed in preference to that suggested by a table.

The inconvenience of the lunar calendar has caused Muslims to use other systems for civil purposes: notably the Syrian calendar with Julian months reckoned from 1 October and the Seleucid era, and the Western calendar and Christian era (known as *mīlādī*, 'Nativity' dating). In modern Iran, the civil calendar is a solar calendar (*tāqvim-e hejri-ye šāmsi*) reckoned from AD 622; the New Year (Nouruz, a major festival) falls at the vernal equinox on or about 21 March. The first five months are of 31 days, the next six of 30, the last of 29 except in leap year, when it has a 30th day. Leap year normally falls every four years, but is occasionally postponed by a year in accordance with a complex mathematical formula.

CHAPTER 8

Quotations

8.1 **General principles**

A quotation is a group of words taken from a text or speech and repeated in some form by a person other than the original author or speaker. It can be of any length, though there are legal restrictions on how much of someone else's work a person may repeat; for more on copyright *see* **CHAPTER 14**.

8.1.1 **Accuracy and interpolation**

All extracts quoted in a work must be in the exact words of the original; treat any deviation as paraphrasing rather than as a direct quotation. Set words interpolated by anyone other than the original author in square brackets ([ ]) to show that they are not part of the quoted matter. Square brackets can also be used to alter quoted matter to match its placement in text or conventions adopted elsewhere:

> Article 29 requires that '[t]he present Convention . . . be subject to ratification by the signatory [S]tates'.

However, such scrupulous normalization is often unnecessary, so long as the result is not grammatically wrong. Readers will not expect a quotation to conform rigidly to surrounding text:

> Article 29 requires that 'The present Convention . . . be subject to ratification by the signatory states'.

The Latin *sic*, meaning 'thus' or 'so', is used in English as a parenthetical comment by an editor on quoted or copied words, drawing attention to some error of fact or oddity of grammar or spelling. It is printed in italics (roman in an italic context), in square brackets, with no full point. In theory, any error of spelling or sense should be indicated by '[*sic*]'; in practice, however, authors should limit its use in general writing to those contexts in which a reader might genuinely attribute a mistake (such as a misspelling or transposition) not to the original but to its reproduction. Where editorial policy allows latitude for standardizing flaws encountered in the original, an author may prefer to make a silent correction. Often it is unfair and unnecessary to use it to draw attention to what may be no more than dittography or printer's error: unless the mistake has textual significance, transmitting the content of the quoted matter is usually more important than reproducing its original form, warts and all. In cases of violent editorial protest '[*sic*]' is better than '[!]', but use neither device merely to scoff.

To avoid ambiguity, insert '[*sic*]' directly after the matter glossed. For example, in Daisy Ashford's *The Young Visiters* and Steve Katz's *The Exagggerations of Peter Prince*, the title of each work was misspelt in the original (unintentionally in the first instance, intentionally in the second). They may therefore be styled as *The Young Visiters* [*sic*] and *The Exagggerations* [*sic*] *of Peter Prince*.

Punctuation of the extract should be exactly as in the original, with two exceptions. First, when quoting only part of a sentence or phrase, you may standardize punctuation by ending a grammatically complete sentence with a full point, which falls within the closing quotation mark. Secondly, when reproducing matter that previously has been set using forms of punctuation differing from house style, you may silently impose the usual conventions, such as replacing double quotation marks with single, em rules or hyphens with en rules, expanding ampersands to *and*, or otherwise standardizing foreign or antiquated typographical constructions. For example

> Asked to name her greatest love, she replied:—"Chocolate."

can in most contexts be safely altered to

> Asked to name her greatest love, she replied: 'Chocolate'.

Similarly, you may silently correct obvious errors such as a missing full point, or unclosed parentheses or quotation marks.

Do not, however, impose any silent emendations—in spelling, punctuation, or typography—where it is important to reproduce copy in facsimile, as in legal and many scholarly works, or for bibliographical study or textual criticism.

8.1.2 Layout

Quotations can be run on in text or displayed. Those that are run on in text are enclosed in single quotation marks (*see* **5.13**) and are referred to as 'run in' or 'embedded'.

■ Do not break off quotations in text for display unless the matter exceeds sixty words in prose, or about five lines when set in normal type and measure. If the quoted extract comprises fewer than about sixty words, it is run on in the text matter, with quotation marks at the beginning and end.

Short prose quotations may be broken off if the context demands it, for example if the author sets them out as examples or specimens, or if they are comparable in nature to longer quotations treated as extracts, and displaying them would give a more uniform look to the page. Conversely, even longer extracts can be run on in the text within quotation marks if the author weaves the quotations into his or her own paragraphs or even sentences, making it awkward to break them off. In verse quotations even a single line of poetry can be broken off for display (*see* **13.7**), as can epigraphs.

Quotations that are broken off from text are called 'displayed quotations', 'block quotations', or 'extracts'. Displayed extracts are not enclosed by quotation marks, and therefore any quotations within them are enclosed by single quotation marks, not double. They begin on a new line—which is not indented unless the original was—and can appear in various formats: they may be set in smaller type (usually one size down from text size), or in text-size type with less leading; set to the full measure, or to a narrower measure; set with all lines indented from the left, or block centred (indented left and right); or set justified or unjustified. Normal OUP practice in academic books is to set displayed quotations one size down, full measure, and justified.

■ If two or more separate quotations (i.e. not continuous in the original) are displayed to follow one another with none of the author's own text intervening, the discontinuity is shown by leading (usually 3-point vertical spaces) separating each quotation from the next.

8.2 **Foreign-language quotations**

Foreign-language quotations given in English writing follow the same rules as for English quotations: the information a quotation contains is most important. The style of quotation marks can be normalized (e.g. « » or ,, " changed to ' '); so too can the relative order of punctuation surrounding it, though not that within it.

General words or phrases in another language may be treated differently, however, when they are used in isolation or by way of example; for more on this, and for guidelines on translations run in with foreign-language quotations, *see* **6.5**.

■ Languages written right to left, such as Arabic, Aramaic, Hebrew, Persian, and Ottoman Turkish, can pose special problems when they are given in the original characters, particularly in setting turn-lines. If, for example, a Hebrew quotation embedded in an English typescript has to be broken over two lines in the printed English running text, the first word of the quotation—which is in fact the last word from an English perspective—starts on the right-hand side of the uppermost line and fills all the available space to the left. The continuation starts as far to the right as necessary on the next line to ensure that the Hebrew finishes flush with the left margin, as in Example 1. Conversely, if a Hebrew phrase split over two lines in the typescript can be accommodated in the printed English text in a single line, the word order will be as shown in Example 2.

Example 1
Typescript

> The tribulations of the scholar are not new. Ecclesiastes tells us, עשׂות ספרים הרכה אין קץ ולהג הרבה יגעת בשׂר ('Of making many books there is no end; and much study is a weariness of the flesh').

Printed page with line break

> ...new. Ecclesiastes tells us, עשׂות ספרים הרכה אין קץ ולהג הרבה יגעת בשׂר ('Of making many books there is no end; and much study is a weariness of the flesh').

Example 2
Typescript with line break

> ...new. Ecclesiastes tells us, עשׂות ספרים הרבה אין קץ ולהג הדבה יגעת בשׂר ('Of making many books there is no end; and much study is a weariness of the flesh').

Printed page

> The tribulations of the scholar are not new. Ecclesiastes tells us, עשׂות ספרים הרכה אין קץ ולהג הרבה יגעת בשׂר ('Of making many books there is no end; and much study is a weariness of the flesh').

To facilitate this process for non-specialist typesetters and proofreaders, editors can clarify the order by numbering each word in the quotation individually, beginning with the first and working left to the end. This is particularly useful when the quotation is submitted as print-ready copy, and must be stripped into the text by hand.

■ Where a displayed translation is followed by a displayed original—or vice versa—editors should mark for a 3-point vertical space between each extract, with the second of the two quotations set off in parentheses. Where the second of the two displayed quotations is the original, some authors prefer to have it set in italics.

For conventions governing quoted material in foreign-language writing, *see* the language concerned. For quotations drawn from different translations of the Bible *see* **13.8**.

8.3 **Epigraphs**

8.3.1 Types and arrangement

In publishing, an epigraph is a short quotation or saying at the beginning of a book or chapter, intended to suggest its theme. Prose epigraphs are set differently from normal displayed quotations. In OUP's academic books they are set in small type, four picas shorter than text measure and centred on the measure. Verse epigraphs are given the same mark-up as ordinary displayed verse quotations (*see* **13.7**): set in small type, optically centred. Two epigraphs in succession are separated by 6-point spaces. An epigraph is separated from its following translation by a 3-point space.

8.3.2 Sources

Epigraph sources are treated similarly to verse sources: they fall directly beneath the text, ranged right on the epigraph's measure and separated by a 3-point space. (Less space may be needed where the last turn-line is short.) If the reference is very long, it starts 1 em farther in than the start of the epigraph, with turn-lines ranged left on the beginning of the source. Prose and verse epigraphs have about a 3-line drop from their source to the start of text.

> Remember that the most beautiful things in the world are
> the most useless; peacocks and lilies for instance.
>
> (John Ruskin, *The Stones of Venice*)

Publication details are not usually included as part of an epigraph's source, nor even the common bibliographical appendages such as volume, page, act, scene, or canto: since an epigraph is not directly related to a book's subject matter, it is not expected that the reader will need to look up the reference. Obscure sources may be listed in full in the bibliography or a note, and a translation may be given if the reader would benefit from it, either immediately below the epigraph or in a note. Similarly, the date or circumstances of the epigraph, or the author's dates, may be given if they are thought to be germane.

> Ah, la belle chose que de savoir quelque chose. [Knowledge is a fine
> thing.]   (Molière, *Le Bourgeois Gentilhomme*)
> You will find it a very good practice always to verify your references,
> sir!   (Martin Joseph Routh (1755–1854))

8.3.3 Mark-up

If epigraphs are frequent, editors can give them a colour-code analogous to the usual green for prose displayed quotations; interpretation of the coding can be given in a Note to Printer. It is still advisable, however, to provide specific mark-up at least at the first occurrence in a text, or where layout or arrangement is complicated.

8.4 **Omitted matter**

8.4.1 **Prose**

Ellipses (points of omission) are not usually necessary at the beginning or end of either run-in or displayed quotations, as one can assume the reader will know that a quotation is excerpted from another source. (*See also* **5.7**.) This holds even if the quotation does not begin with a capital, since a lower-case first word gives sufficient warning that the quotation begins in mid-sentence. However, an ellipsis must be retained—even at the start or finish—when it forms part of the original material. Never delete an ellipsis within a quotation, even by inserting, say, 'he writes' in its stead, since this might confuse the meaning and will destroy the integrity of the original.

If the preceding sentence ends with a full point, this is placed close up to the final word, and followed by three spaced points of omission. When quoting in text a complete sentence that ends with a full point followed by an ellipsis, do not place another full point outside the closing quotation mark. When quoting an incomplete sentence ending in an ellipsis, place a full point outside the closing quotation mark.

Since a quoted sentence linked to another by an ellipsis does not end in a full point unless the original quotation has one there, it is possible for a new sentence to follow only three points. In the following quotation, the absence of a full point before the ellipsis indicates that *rang* was not the final word in the first sentence:

> We were quietly drinking during the interval when the bell rang...The first half had been quite tedious, but we decided to stay for the 'Mouster Dance'.

An ellipsis used either by the original author as a rhetorical device or by a subsequent author or editor to signal elided text need not be enclosed in square brackets, as in Continental practice. However, where both types of ellipsis occur within a single extract, the latter must be differentiated by square brackets. An editorial ellipsis—that is, one imposed upon a quotation and not part of the original—may be combined with an editorial interpolation. When this occurs, the interpolation can sometimes obviate the need for the ellipsis, where grammatically it is clear that all or some missing matter has been replaced by an editorial gloss. Take, for example, this original sentence:

> The poet's *Scillaes Metamorphosis*, later published as *Glaucus and Scilla*, is the earliest of many Ovidian epyllia in the Elizabethan period.

An editor may alter the text by either adding to or deleting from it:

> The poet's [Thomas Lodge's] *Scillaes Metamorphosis* [1589], later published [1610] as *Glaucus and Scilla*, is the earliest of many Ovidian epyllia [minor epics] in the Elizabethan period.

or

> *Scillaes Metamorphosis* [by Thomas Lodge] . . . is the earliest . . . [minor epic] in the Elizabethan period.

■ Ellipses can show the omission of one or more whole paragraphs of prose. In displayed prose, ordinarily it is unnecessary to indicate the length of the lacuna: it is sufficient to mark the omission by points at either the end of the last text or the beginning of the next—or both— breaking into paragraphs as indicated by the original.

However, in the case of lists or numbered paragraphs, most especially in legal or official documents, a long omission is marked by an ellipsis set full left between paragraphs, with the space between each point increased to 2 ems.

An original sentence or fragment may include an ellipsis, for example as points of suspension, that should not be deleted. For clarity, any later ellipsis inserted in such a passage must be set in square brackets. This passage from *The Importance of Being Earnest*, for example, contains two ellipses:

> The fact is, Lady Bracknell, I said I had lost my parents. It would be nearer the truth to say that my parents seem to have lost me . . . I don't actually know who I am by birth. I was . . . well, I was found.

In the following extract, the square brackets make clear which are in the original and which have been added subsequently:

> The fact is, Lady Bracknell, [. . .] my parents seem to have lost me . . . I don't actually know who I am [. . .]. I was . . . well, I was found.

For general use of the ellipsis *see* **5.7**.

8.4.2 **Poetry**

As verse extracts run into text largely follow the same rules as for prose extracts, similarly ellipses in poetry should be set within square brackets to distinguish them from the poet's own points of suspension (if any). Within displayed poetry, ellipses mark the omission of one or more whole lines by a line of points, separated by 2-em spaces; the first and last points should fall 2 ems inside the measure of the longest line. To indicate the omission of part of a line, use three spaced points of omission if the right-hand part of the line is being chopped off; indicate by ranging (usually right with the next line) if the left-hand part has been cut, with no ellipsis preceding. (*See* **13.7**.)

Two examples follow of displayed quotations from a play. The inclusion of the reference in the first, and the character's name (in spaced small capitals) in the second, reflect the purpose to which each quotation might be put: poetry extract and verse play extract respectively:

> ... even in the dead of night;
> Halloo your name to the reverberate hills,
> And make the babbling gossip of the air
> Cry out, 'Olivia'.
>
> [3-pt. space]
> *Twelfth Night,* I. v. 260–3

and

> VIOLA.   ... even in the dead of night;
> Halloo your name to the reverberate hills,
> And make the babbling gossip of the air
> Cry out, 'Olivia'.

Include stage directions only when the context demands it. For more on setting plays *see* **13.6**.

8.4.3 Ancient works

In works from antiquity, omission of matter is indicated in a variety of ways according to the type and length of the lacuna; the following principles should be followed when indicating absent or indistinct text in copy. They apply in the first instance to Greek and Latin papyri, that is to fragments of manuscripts written in classical antiquity itself; they are also used for inscriptions, and may be extended to descriptions of other damaged sources. Conventions vary for ancient Egyptian literature (*see below*).

Where a character is visible but unidentifiable, its existence is marked by a subscript (inferior) dot, either by itself (.) or beneath the most likely candidate for the indistinct character (e.g. ḥ). There used to be a practice of underlining imperfectly preserved but unambiguous letters; this has been given up because no two scholars could always agree on where to draw the line. Spaces between words are not a normal feature of ancient papyri or inscriptions; where a space does occur, the practice is to write *v.* (for *vacat*). Where spaces between words are common in the original this is indicated by an ordinary space of the line.

Where a line (or part of a line) is illegible but the number of characters is visible, set a subscript dot for every missing character; these points are not spaced (unlike ellipsis points), except that a space may be added after every fifth point for clarity. If the lacunae are so long that points would look unsightly, give the total number of characters in each instance, preceded by *c.(circa)* if there is any uncertainty, for example '[*c.*25]'. Where figures are used, they should be in parentheses if the traces are still visible, in square brackets if they are not.

Where the source has been damaged such that the start or end of a line is absent, use a square bracket to mark the cut-off point. If characters have been lost in the middle of the line, set subscript dots within square brackets for the number of characters estimated to be missing.

When the number of letters is uncertain, use hyphens to indicate a rougher guess than subscript points: whereas .... indicates relative certainty that four letters are missing, - - - - indicates that three or five must also be reckoned with.

A row of points means that the top or bottom of a column is missing; these points are set on the line (not below it), separated by 2-em spaces; the minimum number is two, the maximum five, depending on the width of the column measure. When lines within the column are missing, it is best to put '[*line lost*]', '[*3 lines lost*]', and so on.

Square brackets close up [] may be used to mean 'hole in the papyrus, but not sure it contained anything'.

The following symbols are standard in editing papyri and are used increasingly in editing inscriptions:

( )   = expansion of abbreviation or conventional symbol
< > = wrongly omitted in source, editorially supplied
{ }   = wrongly added in source, editorially deleted
[ ]   = matter lost because writing surface lost or worn smooth, supplied editorially
⟦ ⟧ = deleted by scribe/stonecutter
⌊ ⌋ = matter not preserved in this source, but supplied from others
' '   = written above line

These symbols are also used in editing other texts, such as textual editions, though many people still use [ ] for { }. In the nineteenth century [ ] were used for editorial supplements (now < >), and they still are by modern linguists and other non-classicists; Russian scholars use < > to indicate deletions, [ ] for editorial interventions. In Latin it is no longer normal to mark emendations and expansions by italics.

Angled brackets are used to indicate a phrase omitted by the copyist, but which can be restored: for example, a refrain.

The classicist convention of using one subscript dot for each missing character is not generally used for ancient Egyptian literature. The convention here is to indicate lost matter using dots—*not* subscript, but on the line—within square brackets. Alternatively, a phrase indicating the latter may be supplied:

[6 lines fragmentary, then about 7 lines missing]

[gap of about 12 lines]

CHAPTER 9

Lists and tables

9.1 Lists: general principles

Lists are used to arrange and present related elements of text in a form that is easy for the reader to grasp. As such, it is worth taking the time to ensure that the matter thus enumerated is in its most logical and digestible form, whether run into text or broken off and formally displayed. Tables are used for more complicated data that cannot be accommodated by a list.

9.1.1 Arrangement of elements

Regardless of how they are presented, the elements that constitute a list should refer to things of the same kind: it is inappropriate to write *red, white, spring, and tropical flowers*, confusing colour, season, and habitat. An open-ended list should specify enough items (normally at least three) that are sufficiently similar to show how the list might go on. *Apples, oranges, mangoes, etc.* may clearly be extended to include more types of fruit, but *items such as armadillos, ice cream, and helium* creates a mysterious non sequitur, since no correlation between the items is instantly recognizable.

Lists should be grammatically consistent and structurally parallel. Do not, for example, write *The hindbrain comprises cerebellum, a pons, and the medulla oblongata*. Either the first item alone should have an article (*comprises the [or a] cerebellum, pons, and medulla oblongata*) or all three items should have no article (*comprises cerebellum, pons, and medulla oblongata*). It is usually unnecessary for each item to be preceded uniformly by a definite or indefinite article (*comprises the cerebellum, the pons, and the medulla oblongata*), unless the list is complicated and the reader would benefit from the additional structuring this affords:

> The hindbrain comprises the cerebellum, formed of two spheres—one on each side of the central region (*vermis*)—and overhung by the occipital lobes of the cerebrum; the pons (Pons Varolii), linking the medulla oblongata and the thalamus, bulging forwards in front of the cerebellum; and the medulla oblongata (myelencephalon), the extension within the skull of the upper end of the spinal cord, forming the lowest part of the brainstem.

If the sentence is very complex—or just very long—it may need to be broken off and displayed (*see* **9.1.4**).

9.1.2 Run-in lists

A list occurring as part of a *run-in* (in-text) sentence or sentences follows the same rules governing any other sentence. A straightforward list within a single sentence needs no numbers or letters to aid the reader:

> Rabbits are divided into four kinds, distinguished as warreners, parkers, hedgehogs, and sweethearts.

This is true even of a list of many items:

> Nine different varieties of Cornwall mead are still available: Mead, Sack Mead, Metheglin, Sack Metheglin, Bochet, Pyment, Hippocras, Cyser, and Melomel.

It is usually acceptable to arrange into lists information where each element has only a few simple parts, so long as these are treated unambiguously:

> Indicative (sēo, siehst, sieþ), Subjunctive (sēo, sēo, sēo), Imperative (seoh)
>
> Oxford Bitter (ABV 3.7%, OG 1037), Oxford Mild (ABV 3.7%, OG 1037), Varsity (ABV 4.3%, OG 1041), Graduate (ABV 5.2%, OG 1052), and College (ABV 7.3%, OG 1072)

Information in many run-in lists may equally be displayed, or indeed presented as simple three-column 'open tables' (*see* **9.2.7**).

9.1.3 Numbering

When elements of a list are cited in text, or when a list creates the basis for structuring the text to follow, then providing some form of enumeration clarifies the sense. It is preferable to enumerate lists with lower-case italic letters in roman parentheses—(*a*), (*b*), (*c*), (*d*), etc:

> The Inca Empire consisted of three dynasties: (*a*) the Kingdom of Cuzco, ruled in turn by Manco Capac, Sinchi Roca, Lloque Yupanqui, Mayta Capac, Capac Yupanqui, Inca Roca, Yahuar Huacac, and Viracocha Inca; (*b*) the Empire, ruled by Pachacuti, Topa Inca, Huayna Capac, Huascar, and Atauhuallpa; and (*c*) the Vilcabamba State, ruled by Topa Huallpa, Manco Inca, Sayri Tupac, Titu Cusi Yupanqui, and Tupac Amaru.

Instead of lower-case italic letters, lower-case roman numerals are possible—(i), (ii), (iii), (iv), etc.—though it is preferable to reserve these for enumerating any further subheading within the (*a*), (*b*), (*c*), (*d*) level (*see* **9.1.5**). Roman numerals are normal for displayed proofs in logic, but these are not strictly lists and follow slightly different rules. Excepting necessarily complicated texts, avoid further subheadings.

Numbered paragraphs are styled and indented just like other paragraphs, with the addition of the figures that start each; vertical space between items is not needed. Use a paragraph (1-em) indent before the numeral, but only the space of the line following it; no concession is made to double-digit figures where they occur: each number is indented to the same depth. Mark for an en space to separate the points from the items in the list, and for turn-lines and subsequent lines to be set full out to the margin, not ranged on the start of each line of text as for a hanging list:

> 4.1. *Record-keeping*. Create a hazard-logging and -monitoring system that traces hazards from preliminary hazard analysis through to testing and system validation.
> 4.2. *Safety engineers*. Appoint safety engineers who have explicit responsibility for the safety aspects of the system.
> 4.3. *Safety review*. Use safety reviews extensively throughout the development process.
> 4.4. *Safety certification*. Create a safety certification system, whereby safety-critical components are formally certified for their assessed safety.
> 4.10. *Configuration management*. Use a detailed configuration-management system to track all safety-related documentation and align it with associated technical specifications.

Many publishers prefer to use arabic figures, but other forms of numbering may be used where it is important to follow the style of an official document, legal contract, philosophical treatise, etc., or to correspond to the established hierarchy of numbered sections or paragraphs.

9.1.4 Displayed lists

Lists are usually *displayed* if they are of more than one sentence, or composed of many lengthy or compound elements. A displayed list is broken off from the text (usually by 3-point spaces above and below), and often set one size down from the surrounding text. In general any enumeration of more than five or six items, or any list requiring an additional level of internal structure, will benefit from this treatment. Lists of numbered paragraphs may be broken off to distinguish them from the main text: text with numbered paragraphs throughout is not displayed, because the paragraphs *are* the main text.

The punctuation for a displayed list is treated precisely the same as if the items within it had no number or letter separating them. List items that are complete sentences start with capitals and end in full points, regardless of the length of the sentence or number of subheadings. Sentence fragments do not, and are usually (but not exclusively) lower-case.

Enumerate lists composed of whole sentences with arabic numerals, each figure followed by a full point. Unless the measure is very narrow, mark for a 1-em indent before each number and a 1-en space after, to separate the points from the items in the list. The numbers align on the full point, so also instruct the typesetter to allow for double-digit figures where they occur. In the so-called *hanging list*, turn-lines and any subsequent lines hang from (align on) the start of each line of text:

1. The cerebellum forms two spheres—one on each side of the central region (*vermis*)—and is overhung by the occipital lobes of the cerebrum.
2. The pons (Pons Varolii), linking the medulla oblongata and the thalamus, bulges forwards in front of the cerebellum.
3. The medulla oblongata (myelencephalon), the extension within the skull of the upper end of the spinal cord, forms the lowest part of the brainstem.

Elements in a displayed list may be arranged by means other than a simple numerical hierarchy; for example, this extract from the *Anglo-Saxon Chronicle* is ordered by year:

449 Mauricius and Valentines obtained the kingdom; and reigned seven winters. In their days Hengist and Horsa, invited by Wyrtgeorn, king of the Britons, sought Britain at a place called Ypwines fleot, at first to help the Britons but later they fought against them.
455 Hengist and Horsa fought King Wyrtgeorn in the place called Agæles threp, and Horsa his brother was killed. After that Hengist took the kingdom and Æsc his son.
457 Hengist and Æsc fought the Britons at a place called Crecganford and slew there four thousand men, and the Britons left Kent and fled to London in great terror.
465 Hengist and Æsc fought the Welsh near Wippedes fleot, and there slew twelve leaders of the Welsh, and one of their own thanes was slain whose name was Wipped.
473 Hengist and Æsc fought the Welsh and took countless spoil; and the Welsh fled from the England like fire.
488 Æsc succeeded to the kingdom and was king of the Cantware for twenty-four winters.

Each item in this example list equally could have been ordered by arabic numerals and points rather than by year. The logic governing any non-numerical hierarchy (e.g. chronological, alphabetical) should be immediately apparent.

Lists—particularly short lists where each element is a sentence or less—may use a typographical symbol such as a bullet (●) or square (■)—as in this book—in place of numbers. This device is useful for arranging displayed items without imposing an artificial hierarchy upon them. Here are two examples of unordered lists:

▶ Bulka
▶ Hundertspiel
▶ Špády
▶ Trappola

- The battlements or crenellation (*der Zinnenkranz*)
- The tower platform (*die Wehrplatte*)
- The merlon (*die Zinne*)
- The inner ward or bailey (*der Burghof*)
- The draw-well (*der Ziehbrunnen*)
- The keep or donjon (*der Burgfried*)
- The dungeon (*das Verlies*)

When listed items have no sequential order, arrange them alphabetically, but ensure that you are not disrupting another order (e.g. spatial in the second example) whose arrangement is not immediately apparent. Indent bullets 1 em from the measure, with an en space separating them from the start of the following text. Each typeface has a standard 'bullet' size, so there is normally no need to specify this.

9.1.5 Lists within lists

There are no absolute rules regarding the layout of displayed lists with more than one level, although typically there should be at least two items on each level. Since the goal is to make the hierarchy as clear as possible, each subsequent level should be indented 1 em and, where necessary, its turn-lines hung on that indent, as in any combination of the examples above.

In displayed lists, the first level of element should be an arabic number with a full point and no parentheses. Subsequent levels are the same as those for run-in lists: (*a*), (*b*), (*c*), (*d*), etc. followed by (i), (ii), (iii), (iv), etc.

> Aristotle's hierarchy of citizenship may be ordered thus:
> 1. First-class citizens
>   (*a*) Full citizens
>   (*b*) Immature citizens
>   (i) Boys
>   (ii) Girls
>   (*c*) Superannuated citizens
>   (*d*) Female citizens
> 2. Second-class citizens
> 3. Resident aliens
> 4. Foreign visitors
> 5. Slaves

Editors will need to instruct the typesetter to allow for double- or treble-digit figures where they occur, and for the figures to be ranged on the closing parenthesis. Hierarchies may be enumerated differently, particularly to correspond to numbered sections or paragraphs, or where an awkward or novel page layout suggests a different design.

9.2 **Tables: general principles**

The purpose of a table is to display data—statistical or otherwise—as plainly and concisely as possible. Tables are best used for information that is too complex to be presented clearly in a list or in running text, and particularly for information intended for comparison, either within a single table or between similar tables. There is usually more than one way to arrange tabular information, and marking up table copy for setting can be time-consuming for editors. For these reasons authors should submit all typescript for tables as double-spaced copy, with a minimum of rules—the editor will add them as necessary.

■ Authors and editors should take the time to consider whether each table is in fact necessary in its present form. Could the material it contains be more digestibly presented in a few sentences of ordinary English, or alternatively as a figure or graph? Does it show what it is supposed to show? Even if it does, is that information truly relevant, and if it is, has it all been given in another table, or in text? Could two or more tables be merged, or a larger one split up? If all the information *is* necessary, might it be more usefully gathered in a statistical appendix, where it is less a distraction for the reader than tables scattered every few pages throughout?

■ Tables, being merely a spatial arrangement of text, are normally set by a typesetter. But where tabular matter strays from an uncomplicated presentation in columns and rows it may be difficult to determine when a table leaves off and a figure begins: in other words, what a typesetter will be able to set and what will need to be treated as artwork. It may, for example, be possible to set conventionally a simple truth table, pedigree, matrix, financial statement, or Punnett square composed purely of text and figures, ordered as necessary by vertical and horizontal rules. On the other hand, the complex hierarchy, symbols, and diagonal and dashed rules in, say, a decision tree, extended genealogical table (*see* **FIG. 9.1**), computer data-flow diagram, Venn diagram, or Mendelian genetic chart require careful layout and design, and copy should be prepared as artwork and inserted separately into text as figures. Certainly any table that contains drawn elements, such as arrows, boxes, or tints, will probably need to be numbered and named as a figure. When in doubt authors should flag problematic tables or seek advice from their editor.

■ Normally, the text should not read into a table, to allow flexibility in page make-up (for an exception *see* **9.2.7**). Rather, tables should appear as near to the point of reference as possible—preferably following it. Frequent or large tables may be better placed at the end of the chapter or as an appendix to text.

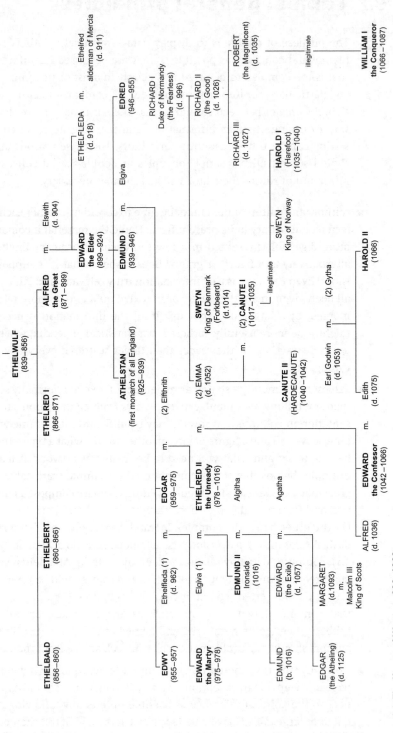

Figure 9.1: **The House of Wessex, 802–1066**

- Most publishers omit as superfluous all vertical rules in tables. If correctly spaced and aligned, presentation is clearer and less cluttered without them: only tables with extremely complex internal structures benefit from them. Horizontal rules should be kept to a minimum, although head and tail rules are included in most cases. In particular, open tables (*see* **9.2.7**) and those tables with only two columns should be set without rules. It is important to distinguish head and tail rules from internal rules: at OUP head and tail rules are both standardly one-half point thick, and internal rules one-quarter point thick.

- Spans in headings must not overlap: *1920–9, 1930–9, 1940–9* or *1–5, 6–10, 11–15* rather than *1920–30, 1930–40, 1940–50* or *1–5, 5–10, 10–15*.

- Capitalize only the first word and proper names in each heading for a column or row; do not number headings unless the numbers are referred to in text. Give units (if any) in parentheses and not as part of the heading: *Income (£/yr)*, not *Annual income in pounds*. Do not repeat the unit or percentage symbol next to each figure in the table.

- Do not abbreviate unnecessarily. Familiar abbreviations are acceptable, such as %, &, country abbreviations, and those well known in the reader's discipline. Abbreviations common in tables include *n/a* for 'not applicable' (or in banking 'no account'), an em rule (—) for 'not available' or 'no answer', and a zero for 'no amount'. Since these all have distinct roles, do not attempt to standardize or amalgamate them, for instance by replacing all em rules with zeros. Repeat information rather than use ditto marks.

  In general, the more cramped the space, the more truncated forms may be required. However, information reduced to telegraphese is both irritating and liable to be misinterpreted; even seemingly unambiguous abbreviations may still prove confusing, and unfamiliar abbreviations must be explained in the notes (*see* **9.2.5**). The reader should be able to understand the table independently of the text.

- Do not include tables within footnotes or endnotes: ancillary data that cannot be incorporated into the text should be relegated to an appendix, either to the chapter or to the whole text.

- When tables are open at the sides, the horizontal rules should not extend beyond the width of the first and last columns.

- Running heads are set normally over full-page portrait (upright) or landscape (turned or broadside) tables, unless the area of the table encroaches on the running head's space.

- Guidelines for table layout are based on giving the greatest clarity in the most common circumstances. Nevertheless, the variety and combination of tabular matter is such that editors may deviate from any of these guidelines if the result is clearer or more visually pleasing on the page.

9.2.1 **Title**

Set a table title at the head of the table, numbered by chapter or section in the order in which each is mentioned; if there are only a few tables they may be numbered in a single sequence throughout the text. Tables in an appendix are numbered separately. Typically the title is centred above the table, as are any turnover lines, and the whole of a short title; alternatively it can also be aligned (ranged) on the left. Titles of tables in academic books may be printed italic, though different treatments are possible. Words in tables are styled the same as in text. For example, if the three types of rice grown in West Bengal appear as *aman*, *aus*, and *boro* in text, they must also appear in italic in the table, or in reverse font if the title is italic. Table titles should match captions for illustrations, if any.

- The descriptive elements to be included in a particular table's title will depend on the other tables in the book, and the context in which they are found. For example, a table in a book on the comparative economics of fruit-growing may need to have *United States: price of apples* . . . , but one in a book on US agriculture will not need *United States* in the title.

- Make the title as clear and concise as possible: a daunting heading like 'Fluctuations in the price of various types of apples (in US dollars per ton) over the period 1954–1976 in different parts of the country' may be distilled to 'Table 15.1. Price of apples, by region, 1954–1976 (*$/ton*)'.

- Give units that apply to the entire table (*00,000*, *$/ton*) in parentheses after the title, in reverse font; they are run in as a continuation of the title, not set on a separate line. Such elements as *by region* or *by date* form part of the title proper and are not given in parentheses. Dates in table titles are presented in full, but are elided in the table's body.

- The style used for the title label will depend on the type of book: at OUP, heavily statistical works (e.g. economics or sociology texts) with many tables may have 'Table' in capital and lower-case letters. Less statistical works (e.g. history or classics texts) with only the occasional table may have 'TABLE' in spaced capital and small capital letters.

9.2.2 **Column headings**

At OUP column headings are usually set in roman capitals and lower case. They should be aligned on the left (turnover lines not indented) and be unjustified. Though they should be set full left in the column, short headings—such as symbols or single or double letters—may look better centred.

Align all column headings on the first line of each column across the page. If an item in the first column has more than one line and is a 'title' that applies to items running across the table, those items should align

Table 9.1: **College housing**

| Housing allowance (£) | College houses | | | Arrangements about capital improvements |
	Rent paid	College responsibility	Responsibility for rates	
356	Nil	Major repairs and decorations	College	Paid by college
269	450, 490, 500, 170, 98, 360, 72, 140	External and major internal repairs	Part paid by college	Interest usually added to reduction
500	300, 360	Structural repairs; external decoration, materials for internal decorations	Fellow if rent paid; college otherwise	College, if of value to future occupants
50 for two fellows with vested interest	—	Maintenance and repairs	Rent free	No fixed policy

horizontally on its first line. Tables should not be spaced out to full measure, but set to give good spacing between columns, with a minimum of 1 em between each column (*See* **TABLE 9.1**).

- Number columns only if the numbers are referred to in the text. These numbers appear in parentheses on the same horizontal line, 3 points below the deepest heading element. Letters can be used instead of numbers, particularly if it makes it easier to impose consistency throughout tables.

- More than one set of data may be compactly presented by arraying the matter beneath more than one level of column head. This arrangement, called nested or decked column heads, is especially useful for comparing related information within the same table. The first level of column head spans subsidiary columns set beneath it, separated by straddle (also called spanner) rules, each of which extends only to the width of the columns it relates to. (**TABLES 9.1, 9.4, 9.6,** and **9.7** employ nested headings.) Formerly a horizontal brace was sometimes used instead of a straddle rule; this is still possible when reproducing antique formats; a vertical brace may be used where spanning the contents or stubs of several rows. While a large and complicated table may contain several levels of nested heads, consider whether the information could be more lucidly presented in two or more tables.

9.2.3 Stub

The stub is the left-hand column of the table, which labels the table's rows, just as the column head labels the columns; only the first word and proper names are capitalized. It may or may not have a heading like other columns, but similar tables should be treated similarly.

- Unrelated items should have some logical order (alphabetical, chronological, size, etc.) imposed on them, as this makes them easier for the reader to use. Do not rearrange items that have no relationship with one another, but whose relationship is clear from scrutinizing the order in other tables meant for comparison with it.

- Items may be grouped under stub headings, which should be typographically distinct (italics, small capitals), but not indented further. No rule or additional space is required, unless the subheads carry totals of their own, in which case they should be preceded by a (usually 3-point) space. Matter set beneath stub headings can be set full left or indented (*see* **TABLE 9.1**).

- Indent turn-lines 1 em. While figures are aligned with the stub's last line, any text within a table aligns with the first line of the stub item to which it applies. (*See* **TABLES 9.1** and **9.3**.)

- Where the stub consists entirely of dates, it often aids clarity to introduce a 3-point space at decade breaks, or at some other logical point.

- Totals may be set off by a 3-point space (not by a rule), and flagged by the word 'TOTAL' in spaced small capitals. Optionally, the word may be indented.

Table 9.2: **New Zealand casualties, 1939–1945**

Branch	Deaths	Wounded	Prisoners	Interned	Total
Army	6,839	15,324	7,863	—	30,026
Navy	573	170	54	3	800
Air Force	4,149	255	552	23	4,979
Merchant Navy	110	—	—	—	—
TOTAL	11,671	15,749	8,469	149	36,038

Source: R. Kay (ed.), *Chronology: New Zealand in the War, 1939–1945* (Wellington, 1968).

9.2.4 **Body**

The body of a table is simply the tabular data introduced and ordered by the columns and stubs; especially in the USA, 'cell' is the term for each intersection of a column and stub, representing a single piece of data.

The unit(s) used in the table should suit the information: for example, national agricultural production figures may well be more meaningful and easier to compare if rounded to 1,000 tons; rounding off large quantities also saves space. Editors should not make wholesale changes without querying them with the author, however. Tables intended to be compared should ideally present their data consistently in similar units—not metres in one, yards in another, and cubits in a third; ensure that abbreviations are consistently applied from one table to another, and all units and percentages are defined. While data drawn from a variety of sources may need to be recast to accommodate comparison, ensure that doing so does not introduce inaccuracy or anachronism, or distort the material's integrity (if the source is in copyright).

■ Turn lines in simple items in columns are indented 1 em, with no extra vertical space between items (*see* e.g. column 2 in **TABLE 9.3**). Turn lines in discursive or run-in items (e.g. data in a chronology) should be set full left in a column as panels or blocks of text, not indented, with a 3-point vertical space between each item (*see* e.g. column 4 in **TABLE 9.3**; columns 3, 4, and 5 in **TABLE 9.1**).

Table 9.3: **Beaufort wind scale**

Force	Description of wind	Mean wind speed (*knots*)	Specification for use at sea
0	calm	less than 1	Sea like a mirror
1	light air	1–3	Ripples with appearance of scales are formed, but without foam crests
2	light breeze	4–6	Small wavelets, still short but more pronounced; crests have a glass appearance and do not break
3	gentle breeze	7–10	Large wavelets; crests begin to break; foam of glassy appearance, perhaps scattered white horses
4	moderate breeze	11–16	Small waves becoming longer; fairly frequent white horses
5	fresh breeze	17–21	Moderate waves, taking a more pronounced long form; many white horses are formed (chance of some spray)
6	strong breeze	22–7	Large waves begin to form; the white foam crests are more extensive everywhere (probably some spray)
7	moderate gale *or* near gale	28–33	Sea heaps up and white foam from breaking waves begins to be blown in streaks along the direction of the wind
8	fresh gale *or* gale	34–40	Moderately high waves of greater length; edges of crests begin to break into spindrift; foam is blown in well-marked streaks
9	strong gale	41–7	High waves; dense streaks of foam; crests of waves begin to topple, tumble, and roll over
10	whole gale *or* storm	48–55	Very high waves with long overhanging crests; the resulting foam, in great patches, is blown in dense white streaks; the sea takes a white appearance; the tumbling of the sea becomes heavy and shock-like; visibility affected
11	storm *or* violent storm	56–63	Exceptionally high waves at sea; the sea is completely covered with white patches of foam; visibility affected
12+	hurricane	64 and above	The air is filled with foam and spray; sea completely white with driving spray; visibility very seriously affected

Sources: Smithsonian Institution, *Smithsonian Meteorological Tables* (1966); Hydrographer of the Navy (UK).

- Related figures in a single column should have the same number of decimal places. Unrelated figures may have a different number of decimal places, but only if reflecting different levels of accuracy. Often it is possible to round them off to a common level for consistency's sake, but editors should query this with the author; percentage totals may vary slightly above or below 100 per cent as a result of rounding.

- Even if four-digit figures are set close up in text, impose commas in tabular matter where they need to align with figures of more than four digits; technical and scientific works use a thin space instead of a comma. Different languages have different conventions regarding commas and full points in figures (*see* **7.1.3**), so tables drawn direct from foreign sources may require closer scrutiny.

- Set mathematical operators (+, −, >, etc.) close up to the following digits. Ensure that minus signs (-) are distinguished from hyphens and from em rules (—) at their first occurrence in each table.

- When statistical matter within each column is unrelated, align it on the left with the column heading, ranged on the first figure or letter in each column (*see* **TABLE 9.4**). Optionally, the longest line can be designed so that it is centred under the heading, if the result suits the material better.
  When statistical matter within the columns is related, align it so that the longest item aligns with the column heading and other items align with the decimal point or with the final digit on the right (*see* **TABLE 9.5**). Align figures horizontally with the last line in the stub item to which they refer.

Table 9.4: **Comparison of four forests with infection present**

	Forest			
	Black	**New**	**Sherwood**	**Speymouth**
Age	20	43	35	69
Area sampled, acres	6.9	11.2	7.5	27.6
No. of trees	10,350	4,702	2,650	945
No. of infected trees	163	98	50	23
Infected trees, %	1.63	0.9	20.3	10.7
Chi-square for observed values	7.83	11.09	4.98	too small

Table 9.5: **Breakdown of the five techniques**

Technique	Output (barrels)	No. of workers	Output per worker-year	Total wage bill
I	34,200	4	12.2	225
II	45,968	10	7.4	364
III	9,732	2	4.7	198
IV	213,427	15	96.3	2,000
V	2,340,646	126	201.9	14,344

■ Centre em rules indicating vacant quantities or data in their columns. Ignore parentheses in aligning columns; they may protrude into the margin between columns where necessary. Plus and minus signs are also usually ignored in such alignment.

9.2.5 **Notes to tables**

Set notes to table width, normally one size down from table size. There are four kinds: general notes, notes on specific parts of the table, notes on level of probability, and source notes; they should appear in this order, though other orders are possible if consistently applied throughout a work. When notes are mixed each different bank of notes is separated by a (usually 3-point) space. Each note should begin on a new line and end with a full point; a wide table (i.e. landscape or in a large-format work) may have room for two columns of notes beneath it. They fall directly beneath the table to which they refer; they are not incorporated with the text's footnote system.

Note cues in a table read across; for example, a cue in the last column of the first row precedes a cue in the first column of the second row. Ensure that notes to a table cannot be mistaken for text recommencing after the table.

■ General notes are uncued, and are preceded by 'Note:' or 'Notes:', with a roman colon. They are aligned on the left and set to table width.

Table 9.6: **Issues of the de luxe edition of Ulysses, *copies 1–1,000***

		Price		
Copies	Paper	France (FF)	UK (£/s./d.)	USA ($)
–100*	Holland handmade	350	7/7/-	30
101–250	Verge d'Arches	250	5/5/-	22
251–1,000†	linen	150	3/3/-	14

* Autographed by Joyce.
† This issue, the cheapest of the three, was still 5–7 times costlier than the average book.

■ Notes on level of probability are treated as a separate bank of notes (see above). Some disciplines use a single asterisk to denote level of probability at the 5 per cent level, a double asterisk at the 1 per cent level, a triple asterisk at the 0.1 per cent level, and so on. When used, this convention should be explained in the relevant note to the table: '*p < .05 **p < .01 ***p < .001'. Editors should not alter the asterisks to superscript italic letters or impose other symbols in their stead.

■ Mark notes on specific parts of the table with a system of indices different from that used in the text (e.g. symbols as in **TABLE 9.6** or superscript italic letters as in **TABLE 9.7**). Note cues should proceed in order, from left to right and down through the table; they are ignored in columnar alignment.

- Source notes are also uncued, and are preceded by '*Source:*' or '*Sources:*', with a roman colon. Align them vertically on the left and to table width, indenting new notes within this section. Their reference structure matches that used elsewhere in the work: author–date, short title, etc.

Table 9.7: **Summary description of local time-series used for Spain**

				Population	
Place	**Province**	**Dates**	**Record type**[a]	**1887**	**1930**
Alicante sample					
Alcolecha	Alicante	1860–1935	P	907	822
Alfaz del Pi	Alicante	1826–1975	P/C	1,200	1,101
Altea	Alicante	1840–1919	P	5,790	5,484
Benidorm	Alicante	1839–1935	P	3,181	3,099
Benilloba	Alicante	1838–1975	P/C	1,392	1,028
Campello	Alicante	1849–1935	P	(2,834)[b]	2,908
Orba	Alicante	1871–1975	C	1,067	1,356
San Juan	Alicante	1871–1975	C	2,973	2,858
Central Spain sample					
Bargas	Toledo	1821–1975	P/C	3,320	3,863
Buitrago de Lozoya	Madrid	1871–1950	C	658	787
Cabanillas de la Sierra	Madrid	1871–1950	C	282	326
Cadalso de los Vidrios	Madrid	1838–1975	P/C	(1,899)[b]	2,289
Calzada de Oropesa	Toledo	1840–1975	P/C	2,246	2,561

Note: The total number of records examined was 20,870.

[a] P = parish register, C = civil register.
[b] These places were integrated into other municipalities when these censuses were carried out, but kept vital registration records of their own. The population estimates are only approximations.

Source: Reher et al. (1997).

9.2.6 **Presentation on the page**

Tables may be placed on the page in portrait or in landscape format. Portrait is used where the table's width is narrower than the measure of the page. Landscape is used where the table's width is greater than the measure of the page; such tables are always printed so that the title is on the left and stub at the foot of the page.

- A table set in portrait is much easier for the reader, since it follows the arrangement of the work's text; however, sometimes the quantity of matter included within a table makes setting in landscape unavoidable. It is often possible to make a wide table fit a page's measure by rewording, using turnover lines, nesting column heads, or reversing the arrangement of column heads and stub heads. Also, tables are normally set in type one or two sizes down from text size, so more table matter can be accommodated on the page than text matter. Conversely, very narrow 'chimney-pot' tables may be presented in two or more columns, so as to increase their width on the page. Consistency is the prime consideration when a table is one of a series, or is meant to be compared with another, so do not rearrange like or related tables into differing structures.

■ If necessary, both portrait and landscape tables may be presented over two or more pages of text. Except in exceptional circumstances fold-out pages are too expensive and impractical to be considered a suitable solution.

When tables will spread onto two or more pages, column widths remain constant on the continuation pages(s). Headings are not repeated where the matter in continued tables can be read across or down a facing page: the recto of a continued table set in portrait does not repeat the verso's stub headings, and recto of a continued table set in landscape does not repeat the verso's column headings.

Use a light (quarter-point) rule above repeated column headings to ensure they are not read as part of the table, omitting tail rules until the table is completed. When tables are landscape, column headings are repeated on the verso pages only.

Insert a 'continued' line, such as 'Table 2 *cont.*', only if the table turns over to a verso page, not if it extends over facing pages. If several continued tables are given in succession it can be helpful to include also a short form of each table's title.

■ Authors are not responsible for determining which tables will need to be set in landscape. Generally, editors need simply to warn the typesetter that landscape setting is permissible where unavoidable, though on tables extending over more than one typescript folio editors can helpfully suggest which may run on horizontally and which vertically, indicating where a split is preferred and where it is unacceptable, and marking which headings are to be repeated on verso pages.

9.2.7 Open tables

An open table is a very simple table with few elements. Used for presenting small blocks of information, no more than four or five rows, it has more impact and accessibility than a run-in or displayed list—its matter is arrayed in columns—but less formality than a full table—it has no number, title, or rules. Particularly in non-technical work, or in texts having no other tables, an open table can serve as a convenient halfway house between list and table, offering data in a readily assimilated visual form.

type of beer	alcohol by volume (%)	original gravity
Oxford Bitter	3.7	1037
Oxford Mild	3.7	1037
Varsity	4.3	1041
Graduate	5.2	1052
College	7.3	1072

An open table typically has only column heads (as in the first example) or a stub (as in the second). Any table with both column heads and stub requires the structure of a formal table, and should be set as such.

Indicative	sēo	siehst	sieþ
Subjunctive	sēo	sēo	sēo
Imperative	–	seoh	–

The size of an open table makes it less likely to be broken over a page when set, so it may be run into text and introduced by a colon:

The de luxe edition of *Ulysses* ran to a thousand numbered copies, printed in three issues on different grades of paper, with corresponding prices in French francs, pounds sterling, and US dollars:

Copies 1–100	Holland handmade paper	350F, £7. 7s., $30
Copies 101–250	Verge d'Arches	250F, £5. 5s., $22
Copies 251–1,000	linen paper	150F, £3. 3s., $14

(This same information is presented more formally in **TABLE 9.6**.)

While running an open table into text can be convenient in some contexts, the table cannot then be moved unless the preceding text is reworded accordingly; and while text must separate one open table from another, several open tables on a page may still pose layout problems for the typesetter.

Do not use open tables in texts in combination with full tables unless the matter they contain is of a type uniformly different from that of their bigger cousins; it would be illogical and confusing to present related matter in a mix of numbered and unnumbered tables differentiated only by size.

CHAPTER 10

Illustrations

10.1 **General principles**

An illustration is any image prepared as artwork and printed in a text, together with a caption—also called *underline*, *cutline*, or *legend*—that explains something about the image. Some publishers, such as the University of Chicago Press, distinguish between a caption and a legend by saying that a caption is never a grammatically complete sentence, while a legend is a sentence or more of explanatory text. OUP does not make this distinction, preferring instead that *legend* be used as an alternative term for *key*.

The main forms of illustration are black-and-white line drawings, halftones (black-and-white photographs), colour transparencies and paintings, and colour artwork. A figure is an illustration integrated into the text, with text flowing above, below, and sometimes around it. A plate is an illustration separate from the text, often printed on glossy art paper. Figures are normally black and white line drawings and halftones; plates can take any form, though they are usually high-quality images that benefit from printing on higher-quality paper.

Before beginning work on illustrations, authors should talk to their editor about the following:

The number and type of illustrations appropriate to your work. Some types of illustration are particularly expensive to reproduce and make a substantial difference to the production costs and thus the final published price of the work. It is important for authors to get advice from their editor at an early stage.

Printing colour illustrations adds enormously to production costs, and is not usually undertaken unless they are considered vital to the work—as they would be, for example, in an art catalogue, dermatology textbook, or field guide. A substantial part of the cost of including colour illustrations is the processing of each picture before printing, not just the printing itself. This means, for example, that one page of colour with four photographs is considerably more expensive to produce than one page with only one photograph.

How the artwork will be prepared. Authors should explain to their editor in advance how they will be producing illustrations: drawing illustrations themselves (either conventionally or using a computer package), using a freelance artist or bureau, taking illustrations from existing publications, or providing illustrations for redrawing or relabelling by the publisher. Illustrations supplied on paper will usually be scanned by the typesetter and inserted into the digital files.

How any redrawing costs will be paid. For most texts the author is expected to supply artwork that is 'press-ready'—that is, suitable for reproduction. If the author is unable to supply print-ready artwork, the publisher can arrange for relabelling or redrawing to be done, but the costs may be chargeable to the author's royalties.

Specimen drawings. Authors preparing their own illustrations should submit some specimen illustrations before undertaking the bulk of the work. This is to make sure that the illustrations will reproduce satisfactorily when printed. It is essential to get the line widths, shading, and size of labelling right, whether the illustration is produced conventionally or via computer, otherwise it may not be possible to use them. Computer drawings can be particularly deceptive, since drawings that look fine on screen or printed on an ordinary printer may still have technical problems when put through a professional output device.

Clearing copyright. The responsibility for clearing copyright typically rests with the author. All artwork reproducing or based on someone else's work needs permission to be cleared for use, unless it has been substantially altered. For guidance *see* **14.4**; *see also* **14.2**. Normally, the author is responsible for clearing permissions to reproduce illustrations from published sources, for paying any reproduction fees, and for preparing the acknowledgements to go in the text. It is important to start work on clearing permissions at a very early stage—before submission of the typescript—because the process can take several months.

10.2 Numbering, presentation, and placement

Numbering

Typically both halftones (black-and-white photographs) and line drawings are numbered decimally by chapter: the first illustration in

Chapter 1 is Fig. 1.1, the second Fig. 1.2, and so on. Alternatively, a work with only a few illustrations may have them numbered in a single sequence throughout: FIG. 1, FIG. 2, FIG. 3, etc. Maps may be included in the same sequence with other illustrations or, if there are many of them, numbered separately. In standard academic works *Figure* is usually abbreviated in text references as well as in notes and parenthetical matter; in the caption itself, it is often styled in capitals and small capitals. (Where *Fig.* is styled in this way, so too is *Plate*.)

Plates are always numbered in a sequence separate from any illustrations in the text, conventionally with roman numerals—PLATE I, PLATE II, PLATE III, etc.—though scientific or technical works often use arabic numbers instead, and upper- and lower-case letters rather than capitals and small capitals. *Plate* is usually not abbreviated, though *Pl.* is possible in narrow measure.

Text references to *Fig.* and *Plate* should be capitalized when the illustration and reference are within the same work; references to other figures and plates should be in lower case.

Presentation

Authors should mark four things on the back of any original artwork: surname, title of the work (a short form will do), figure number (*Fig. 1.1*, *Plate I*, etc.) and an arrow pointing to the 'top' (where confusion might occur). Never use a ballpoint pen for writing on the back of the photograph: it shows up on the other side of the photograph and distorts the image. Use a soft pencil, a chinagraph pencil, or sticky labels. Never attach anything to a print with tape, staples, or a paper clip.

Placement in typescript and proofs

In the typescript, mark the desired approximate positions of the illustrations in the margin of the typescript: FIG. *18.6 near here*. (It is helpful to include a photocopy of each illustration *in situ*, but unfoliated.) The illustration will then be placed as near as possible to that part of the text when the pages are made up. Text must not read into it so as to give it an explicit and fixed introduction, for example 'in the following figure': the final placement is determined by page breaks, which cannot be anticipated before setting, and this makes rewording the text necessary if the illustration does not fit the make-up of the page.

Where high-quality illustrations are printed on glossy paper different from text paper, they are grouped together in a plate section separate from the text. Plate sections are often used for colour illustrations or for black-and-white photographs that demand especially careful printing, or for photographs that supply important background information, such as a facsimile or matter in a scientific biography. If the work includes a plate section, the author should make a list of the plates for the preliminary pages, including a brief description (one or two lines), not a full caption for each plate. Since plate sections are usually placed as unnumbered glossy pages near the middle or at the end of the work, a text reference cannot read into a plate, as in *see* PLATE *XII opposite*. (Authors should also bear in mind that publishers producing a subsequent paperback version of a hardback with plates may be obliged to omit them, and adjust the text accordingly.)

In proofs it is normally the typesetter's responsibility to set artwork correctly on the appropriate page, though frequent illustrations, or complicated or unusual layouts, may require a designer to lay out all or some of the pages beforehand. The following points outline common layout considerations, so that authors and anyone else generating their own page layouts can understand some of the principles involved. In this section, an illustration should be understood to mean the artwork plus any accompanying caption.

- As far as possible an illustration and the in-text reference to it should be kept within a two-page opening, with the illustration falling after the reference.

- Illustrations of approximately half a page or less in depth should be placed slightly above centre, with the page's text divided approximately one-third above and two-thirds below the illustration. Illustrations much greater than half a page in depth can be placed at either the head or foot of the page (preferably the head), to avoid breaking the text into only a few lines above and below the illustration. Five lines of text is the minimum number permitted on such pages.

- Where two full-width illustrations occur within a two-page opening, one illustration should appear on each page. However, if the depth of the illustrations allows, they may be set together on one page with at least a line of white space between. Where three full-width illustrations occur within a two-page opening, two may be set one above the other on one page, with a minimum of four lines of text at the foot of the page and at least a line of white between the two illustrations. Illustrations less than half a page in width should be placed as above, and on the outer edge of the page. The text then runs round on the inside of the illustration. Captions should be set to the width of the illustration.

- Inset artwork—that is, with text flowing around it—should have a line of apparent white space equal to the point size of the surrounding type inserted at the head and side(s) of the artwork. At the bottom it should have one and a half lines, though one line is acceptable where necessary.

Textbooks and the like often avoid running text round a narrow illustration, in which case the captions—if of suitable length—can be placed on the inner side of the artwork. These are aligned at the head for artwork in the upper half of a page, or at the foot for artwork in the lower half of a page, and generally have unjustified lines.

- Centre horizontally an illustration wider than half a page but narrower than a full page, setting the caption to the width of the illustration if it makes two or more lines, or centred below the artwork if it is a single line no wider than the illustration. Illustrations wider than text measure will probably need to be reduced or set landscape (turned sideways). Usually, illustrations should be centred and the captions set to text measure. Place two illustrations side by side if they occur on the same page and are each less than half a page in width. Where two illustrations of similar depth appear side by side on a page, align the bases and/or captions.

- Typesetters should leave between 6 and 9 points white space between the bottom of the artwork's printing area and the caption, with approximately 12 points white space between the caption and any following text.

- Running heads and page numbers are generally omitted from full-page illustrations in books. However, where two or more full-page illustrations occur together and facing pages do not contain a page number, the page number may be centred in parentheses at the top of the page, or at the bottom in texts where the page number normally occurs at the foot of the page. This applies whether or not the illustrations are landscape. In journals, running heads are mostly used with full-page illustrations unless the artwork fills the space for the running head.

- Illustrations should allow a minimum 10 mm border of white space to separate the edges of the illustration from the trimmed page size. Illustrations filling the whole page area (bleeding) must allow 6 mm of additional image area.

- Illustrations that have to be set landscape should always be placed with the head of the illustration turned to the left, whether on a recto or verso page.

- An acknowledgement for a halftone illustration is usually placed either in a list of illustrations or as part of the caption, run in after the acknowledgement heading (if any), following the caption text. An acknowledgement for a figure is set as a separate note below the caption under the heading '*Source:*'.

10.3 **Line drawings**

Line drawings include a broad range of figures such as graphs, charts, plans, diagrams, maps, cartoons, pen-and-ink studies, and woodcuts—typically any black-and-white displayed material that has no tints or shading, and that is neither a photograph nor a table. This category also includes items that are not strictly illustrations, such as any very unusual symbols and characters that cannot be achieved by the typesetter, which must be produced separately as artwork and inserted into text by the typesetter.

Drawings taken from other publications

Authors using a line illustration from another publication should supply a printed copy for the production department to scan. Photocopies are not acceptable for use in direct reproduction—any illustrations provided as photocopies will probably need to be redrawn.

Sketches for redrawing by the publisher

A publisher's art and design department or a freelance artist can redraw from accurate pencil sketches, or from photocopies with any amendments added in pen. While the draughtsperson or artist will be a professional, he or she may not be familiar with the subject of the sketch, and will not be interpreting the content of the rough drawing, but only reproducing an accurate copy of it. It is therefore important for authors to write labels clearly and to add instructions for the draughtsperson: for example, is it vital that two lines are of identical length? Is the random configuration of dots meant to represent shading, an exact figure to be followed, or simply a random pattern? Is an uneven line supposed to be reproduced as an uneven line? Are rough hand-drawn shapes meant to be reproduced as such or symmetrically? Does a pattern of shading need to be preserved because it is mentioned in the text? Circle any instructions to distinguish them from labelling on the figure itself, or write them on a separate list.

Preparing your own artwork

It is preferable, where possible, that authors prepare their own drawings, using a departmental drawing office, or working with a freelance artist or bureau. Authors doing this should prepare some specimen drawings, digital files, or both before undertaking the bulk of the work. What follows are some guidelines for producing specimen artwork. Authors supplying final digital files for printing need the publisher to provide file-format instructions.

Size

The dimensions of the artwork will depend on the format of the text, and whether the text is to be single- or double-column. In general, the more important an illustration, the greater its size. The page dimensions for some common formats are given below, with the text area available for an illustration, and the dimensions for an original destined for a standard reduction to 67 per cent. This means that each linear dimension will be reduced *to* 67 per cent of its original length—not that it will be reduced *by* 67 per cent.

Book format (mm)	Maximum final size dimensions (mm)	Artwork size for reduction to 67% (mm)
Royal octavo (234 × 156)	180 × 113	276 × 176
Demy octavo (216 × 138)	165 × 101	250 × 151
Crown quarto (246 × 189)	178 × 127	265 × 189
Demy quarto (276 × 219)	215 × 156	321 × 233

When considering the dimensions for an illustration, remember to make allowance for fitting in the caption as well. When illustrations span a two-page spread, ensure that nothing of importance is lost in the gutter where the two pages join. Fold-outs are to be discouraged, since they are unwieldy, expensive, and easily torn in use.

Labelling

For many technical and mathematical works the Times Roman typeface is a common choice for labelling: this is a good typeface for distinguishing between the letters i, l, and the roman figure 1. Where this distinction does not need to be made, any clear, solid typeface such as Helvetica (often preferred for chemistry) or Univers is acceptable.

Characters should be large enough not to 'fill in' on printing: as a rough guide, before reduction the letter 'H' should be 4 mm high, and 'x' should be 2.5 mm high. Most often this means using a typeface no smaller than 8 points (with 9-point leading) or, on drawings destined for a 67 per cent reduction, 12 points (with 14-point leading).

Spelling, hyphenation, symbols, and abbreviations for units should match those in the captions, and follow the stylistic conventions used in the text. Use a capital for the first letter of the first word only, followed by lower-case letters for everything else except proper names. There should be no full point at the end of the label. Give units in parentheses at the end of the label where necessary (for example on ordinates and abscissae in graphs). Variables—but not units—should be in italic. When symbols such as circles or triangles are used, they should be solid (filled in) rather than open, since open and half-filled symbols can fill in and appear solid when printed.

Do not include the figure number as part of the illustration: write it instead on the back of the illustration.

An alternative to labelling is to supply the publisher with original line drawings accompanied by photocopies with the labels typed or clearly written in by hand. The editor will mark up the labels to match the editing of the text, and the labels can be added to the original artwork later. This is especially recommended when labelling is heavy or mathematical, since it limits expensive corrections.

Key

The key or legend explains the symbols or tints used on a figure, and is physically part of it; authors should position it within the artwork area as part of the illustration. Do not include the key as part of the caption: the person who creates the figure should generate the key as well, as the typesetter will be unable to reproduce the key's elements. Any captions for illustrations with keys should be provided separately. Where simple letters and numbers (A, B, C, (a), (b), (c), 1, 2, 3, I, II, III) are used to pinpoint parts of a figure, these can be referred to directly in the caption:

> Relief carvings from the Maya ceremonial centre at Yaxchilán, Guatemala. (a) Penitent kneeling before a priest; a calendrical inscription gives a date c. AD 709. (b) Worshipper kneeling before a double-headed serpent deity; the inscription gives a date c. AD 681.

> Reconstruction of a Greek *trapetum* from Olynthus, for crushing olives. A solid column (1) stands in the middle of a large circular basin of lava (2). A square hole on top of this column holds an upright pin (3) fastened with lead. A wooden beam (4) fits over the pin and carries two heavy plano-convex millstones (5), turning on the centre pivot.

Conventional drawing and tints

Use opaque smooth white paper or, ideally, drafting film, which provides the best dimensionally stable base and surface for line drawings: being transparent, it is very useful for tracing from overlays or roughs. Do not use tracing paper; the colour and surface may show up on the scanned version. Technical pens such as Rotring are recommended, in four line weights: 0.25 mm, 0.35 mm, 0.50 mm, and 0.75 mm.

A tint is shading made up of fine dots, like a photograph. Tints are expressed as a percentage of black. Solid black is really 100 per cent tint; white is 0 per cent tint. For all line work, tints should be added by using specialist computer software. Authors can supply the base line artwork, drawn in black, which the publisher can scan in and add tints to. The lowest viable tint for book production is 15 per cent; the highest viable is 80 per cent. (The limitations of the print process make any tint above 80 per cent appear as black.) At least a 20 per cent difference in tint value is required to achieve contrast between areas of different tint, such as three areas with shading tinted at 20 per cent, 40 per cent, and 60 per cent. Do not use solid black for any large area, as it is difficult for the printer to avoid the ink offsetting onto the opposite page, or showing through onto the backing page.

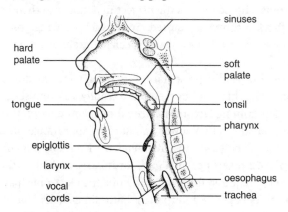

Fig. 10.1: **Nose, mouth, and throat**

Two-colour line drawings

These are black line drawings that have one other colour added to pick out or shade certain areas; they are not commonly used in figures, since the second colour adds greatly to the cost of the work: each colour has to be printed separately, so the whole text may have to be printed twice.

Authors should supply three versions of each illustration: the first is a line drawing of just the material to be printed in black; the second is a line drawing with just the areas to be printed in the second colour; neither should have labels. The third is a photocopy with the two drawings overlaid and photocopied together, demonstrating how the black and colour are to be combined. Write the labels clearly on this copy.

Colour line drawings

Various methods exist for preparing colour line illustrations. The method chosen depends entirely on the style of illustration. It is therefore important for authors to discuss the possibilities with their editor before beginning any work on illustrations of this type. Colour drawings will usually be produced as a four-colour representation. This method may not be able to render the exact colour of the original: for example, fluorescent or metallic colours require special inks at additional cost.

Using a computer package

Using a computer to prepare artwork for publication can save money and time, and facilitate corrections and updating. Many commercially available applications can produce illustrations in a format useful for print or electronic publishing purposes. Simple diagrams, such as graphs or circuit diagrams, are entirely suitable for preparation in this way, though more complicated drawings that require shading or stippling may require greater artistic skills and often a more detailed knowledge of professional-quality software. Before committing a great deal of effort, authors should discuss the project in detail with their editor and confirm the file formats required. Some such drawings may be best handled by a technical artist using specialist graphic software such as Freehand.

Producing images for presentation in a non-paper medium, such as display on a computer monitor, entails a wholly different set of criteria. Here, the determining factor for clarity is not reproduction through ink and paper, but the rather lower standard of appearance on a screen: monitors for all but the most high-end workstations demand only a resolution of 72 pixels per inch (ppi) for images, as against the equivalent of 330 ppi required for print. But while the electronic 'page' differs greatly from its paper counterpart in both dimensions and utility, the underlying considerations for presentation remain, and should be followed so far as possible.

10.4 **Maps**

Maps require many of the same considerations and treatment as other line drawings; their substance ideally should be limited only to those points that are of relevance to the work. Unnecessary features detract from the purpose of a map's inclusion, so authors should ensure that all the features represented will be of use to the reader. This demands careful consideration of the map's scale, perspective, and geographical and political attributes.

Maps must present their necessary information in a clear and uncluttered fashion. The scale of each map must be small enough to include all the locations and features within an applicable scope, but large enough for all details to be distinguished easily.

If the map is to be set in only one colour, do not attempt to present too many disparate data on it, for example by mixing intricate political and geographical material. It is better either to restrict the features offered or to provide two maps divided by subject. If the copy is to be reproduced in its original form and comes wholly or substantially from a previously published source, it is the author's duty to secure copyright permission to produce it, as with any other illustration. If the copy is the author's own creation, or has no copyright restrictions, or is to be significantly altered for inclusion, then no permission is necessary, although the author must provide clear guidance concerning how it is to be altered. When in doubt authors should seek advice from their editor.

Few presses still employ a full cartography department, so maps are likely to be created by design staff from author's copy (usually by computer). If a map is to be (re)drawn by the publisher, the author will need to include the following with his or her rough sketch or copy:

Scale

Authors should state the scale for each rough map (a bar scale is most appropriate). It is useful to include both SI and non-SI readings.

Orientation

In the absence of instructions to the contrary, north is assumed to be at the top of the map (usually the top of the page unless the map will be set landscape).

Text to be included

For roughs, list by category all the text to be labelled (geographical and political features), in capital and lower-case. The spelling of place names must agree with the text. Similarly, supply copy for any key or note to appear on the map, as well as a caption for every map.

Area for inclusion

Indicate where the rough is to be cropped (if necessary), either to allow for enlargement of an area or to minimize peripheral features.

Special distinctions

Two types of distinction are possible: between areas and between groups of names. Even when the finished map will probably be in black and white, distinctions between areas are best shown on the rough by colouring with tints and hatching, either throughout the area or along its boundary. Distinctions between groups of names may be distinguished typographically: a typed list of names should be divided into the relevant groups, and the results shown in the key, for example:

> [Norwich: location only]
> *Oxford*: earldom
> LANCASTER: dukedom

Projection

If known, state the type of projection used for the original.

Features must be easily distinguishable by line weights and treatment of lettering: for example, towns may be presented in roman upper- and lower-case letters, rivers in italic upper- and lower-case letters, and countries and regional features in capitals. Two- and four-colour maps follow the same procedures as those outlined for line drawings in **10.3**.

10.5 Halftone or continuous-tone illustrations (black-and-white photographs)

Quality

Publishers require black-and-white prints to be glossy bromides with good contrast: matt-finish prints do not reproduce as well as glossy, and good contrast is essential for the image to be clear on the printed page. Colour photographs can be converted to black and white, but some quality may be lost, resulting in a rather 'muddy', low-contrast appearance.

Photographs photocopied from or even cut directly out of another publication cannot be reproduced satisfactorily. Instead, authors should ask for a copy of the actual photograph when writing to the author and publisher for permission to use the illustration.

Presentation and identification

Photographs should be on normal photographic paper, not mounted, and should be cut squarely.

Labelling on the photograph

As a guide for the person who will draw any text or symbols to be superimposed on the printed illustration, authors should use a photocopy of the photograph, or an overlay (such as tracing paper), to mark labels. Make a note of any particular areas that should not be obscured by labelling. If only a part of a photograph is to be reproduced, use a photocopy or overlay as well to mark where the photograph is to be cropped. Use scale bars rather than magnification sizes in the caption.

Composite pictures

Present composite pictures—that is, illustrations with more than one part—as individual photographs, clearly identified and accompanied by a photocopy or sketch showing how the illustration is to be set out. Do not paste up original photographs in position.

10.6 **Colour illustrations**

Most publishers require 35-mm (mounted) or larger-format colour transparencies. They can reproduce from colour (glossy) prints if slides are not available, but some contrast will be lost. As with black-and-white photographs, colour photographs cut out of other publications will not reproduce satisfactorily.

Identification, labelling, and cropping resembles that for black-and-white photographs.

10.7 **Captions**

For the most part illustrations require captions, which should indicate the essential content of the illustration. They should not be discursive, though larger images can support more text beneath them without appearing unbalanced.

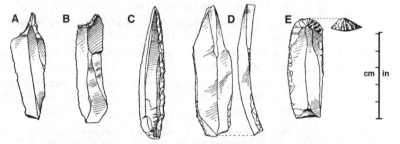

Fig. 10.2: **Upper Palaeolithic blade tools in flint. (A) Solutrean piercer or 'hand-drill', Dordogne. (B) Magdalenian concave end-scraper or 'spoke-shave', Dordogne. (C) Gravettian knife-point, Dordogne. (D) Magdalenian burin, Dordogne. (E) End-scraper, Vale of Clwyd, Wales.**

Authors should present figure captions as a separate list, double-spaced. Do not integrate them with the text or attach them to illustrations, though they can be added to roughs. Make a separate list of captions for illustrations in a plates section. Remember to check that the spellings, hyphenations, and symbols used in the captions correspond to those used in the labelling of the illustration itself (and those used in the text). Where appropriate, give the medium of the illustration's subject, and its dimensions in metric units (height, width, depth); other units of measurement can be added in parentheses as a gloss.

As a typesetter sets the captions, not an artist or draughtsperson, he or she should not be expected to match symbols used in a figure. Captions should be typeset with font, style, layout, and turn lines to match the titles of any tables found elsewhere in the text.

Terms such as *above*, *below*, *top*, *bottom*, *left*, *right*, and *clockwise* can serve to pinpoint elements in an illustration, or components of a group of illustrations. Set in italic when used as labels, the terms are followed by a colon when preceding the subject, and placed in parentheses when following the subject:

> FIG. 1. *Left to right*: Benny Goodman, Teddy Wilson, Lionel Hampton, and Gene Krupa.
>
> FIG. 2. Lionel Hampton (*centre*) and Benny Goodman (*far right*) outside the Paramount, 1937.

The following examples illustrate some of the possible styles of caption; different punctuation and arrangement of elements are possible, providing they are imposed uniformly throughout. All information shown here concerning an illustration's provenance or copyright could equally have been placed in an acknowledgements section or list of illustrations (*see* **10.8**, **10.9**; *see also* **13.5.1.2**).

> PLATE I. Gino Severini, *Dynamic Hieroglyphic of the Bal Tabarin*, 1912. Oil on canvas, with sequins. 162 × 156 cm.
>
> PLATE II. Marcel Duchamp, *The Bride Stripped Bare by Her Bachelors, Even* (*The Large Glass*), 1915–23. Oil and lead wire on glass.
>
> PLATE III. Lee Bontecou, *Untitled*, 1959. Canvas on a frame of welded steel. 251 × 148 × 80 cm.
>
> PLATE IV. Coëtivy Master (Henri de Vulcop?) *Philosophy Instructing Boethius on the Role of God*, from Boethius, *De Consolatione philosophiae*. Loire valley or Bourges, *c.*1465. Pierpont Morgan Library, M. 222.
>
> FIG. 1.1. George V and Queen Mary when they were Duke and Duchess of York, at York House, 1895. Royal Archives, Windsor Castle. Copyright reserved. Reproduced by gracious permission of Her Majesty the Queen.
>
> FIG. 2.1. US Marine Corps sword, 1865 pattern. Blades were typically 68.5–71 cm (27–8 in.) long, with 'USMC' etched on the blade.
>
> FIG. 2.2. Detail from an engraved steel and iron war mask, fifteenth-century Iran. 20 × 16.5 cm. Nasser D. Khalili Collection of Islamic Art, accession no. MTW 1390.
>
> FIG. 3.1. Underside of a Cypriot threshing sled of wood studded with flints. Length about 2.5 m.
>
> FIG. 3.2. Perspective of the Codrington Library and North Quadrangle, as proposed by Hawksmoor in February 1715. *Bodleian Library, MS Gough Plans 7.*
>
> FIG. 3.3. Design by Hawksmoor for the North Quadrangle, showing Gothic tracery in the windows of the Codrington Library. The colonnade of 1703 is shown on the left. *Worcester College Library.*
>
> FIG. 4.1. James Brown (*left, with cape*) and the Famous Flames during the recording of the *Live at the Apollo* album. Courtesy PolyGram/Polydor/Phonogram Records.

FIG. 5.1. 'The Learned Pig relating his Adventures', engraving by R. Jameson, 1 July 1786. By permission of the Houghton Library, Harvard University.

FIG. 5.2. 'Mercy! My state emblems!' Drawing by S. Tsogtbayar and N. Chuluun, *Üg*, No. 32, December 1991.

FIG. 5.3. 'Oh, for heaven's sake! Twenty years from now, will it matter whether the italics are yours or his?' Drawing by Joe Mirachi, © 1981 The New Yorker Magazine Inc.

10.8 **Permissions (clearing copyright) and acknowledgements**

Permission must be obtained in good time from the copyright holder to reproduce any illustrations from published sources. Where there is any doubt (as, for example, when a modified version of an illustration is to be used) it is prudent, as well as courteous, to ask for permission.

Obtaining permissions is the author's responsibility, but the editor publisher can give advice. It is usually best for the author to contact the original publisher. For a model letter *see* **14.4.2**.

If you are intending to modify a drawing, to crop part of a photograph, or to reproduce a colour illustration in black and white, ensure you mention this in your letter. If you are supplying photographs of individuals (for example, photographs of patients in a medical text), ensure that the patient has granted permission for the photograph to be used for publication. Supply details to the publisher if parts of the photograph need to be blocked out to preserve anonymity.

Any reproduction fees should be paid by the author shortly after the work is published. It is the author's responsibility to provide copies of all the permissions letters and invoices. Not all academic publishers charge reproduction fees, but most picture libraries and art galleries do. If any fee seems unusually large, seek advice from your editor.

The text of acknowledgements can appear in an acknowledgements section, or as part of a caption or list of illustrations. *See also* **14.4.3**.

10.9 **List of illustrations**

A list of illustrations enables the reader to locate all the figures, maps, or plates in a work. In it, each numbered item should be described in brief, with just enough information to allow it to be identified. Although the description will probably be drawn from its caption, it need not include the whole caption unless the latter is very short. The term *List of* is used on the understanding that the itemized material merely catalogues illustrations found elsewhere in the work; if the illustrations themselves actually appear collected together beneath the heading, the title should be *Illustrations* alone. When there is just one illustration, such as a frontispiece or map, a list of illustrations is unnecessary; the image can simply be listed in the table of contents.

Particularly where captions are very long, it is best to include the illustrations' sources or copyright information in the list rather than in the caption itself, unless the copyright holder instructs otherwise. If the illustrations are drawn from only a few sources one can acknowledge the sources in a separate note, either following the list itself or in a separate acknowledgements section.

Illustrations numbered consecutively in one sequence or by chapter may be presented in one collective list. Illustrations divided or numbered according to type, or plates grouped in a separate section, need to be presented in separate lists under the broad heading *List of Illustrations*; these are individually labelled *Figures*, *Maps*, *Plates*, etc. with their items numbered beneath. Lists can follow one another, though longer lists can be set on separate pages. If the lists are on the same page or run in one after the other on succeeding pages, the heading is *List of Illustrations*, with *Plates*, *Figures*, etc. as subheadings; if arranged separately on different pages, then use *List of Plates*, *List of Figures*, etc. as full headings and dispense with the umbrella term *List of Illustrations*.

Give the page reference for each illustration on pages counted in the pagination even if it is not expressed on the page; a page of plates, for example, is seldom counted in the pagination. If such illustrations are grouped together, as in a plates section, indicate *between pp. 000 and 000* below the heading *Plates*, or above each section if there is more than one. If the plates are not grouped, refer to *facing p. 000* after the first item in the list, and align the other plates' page references beneath the first.

CHAPTER 11

Languages

11.1 **General principles**

This chapter provides guidelines on the editing and presentation of foreign languages and Old and Middle English, as well as on distinctions between US and British English. Languages are listed alphabetically, either separately or, for clarity and convenience, with related languages. Those grouped together include African languages, Amerindian languages, Baltic languages, Celtic languages (though Welsh is separate), Dutch and Afrikaans, Sanskrit and Indic languages, Scandinavian languages, and Slavonic languages (though Russian is separate).

As any of these languages may be encountered in a wide variety of circumstances, the topics stress common pitfalls and conundrums in orthography, punctuation, diacritics, syntax, and typography, and are intended to offer guidance to users across a broad spectrum of familiarity with the languages. In principle they are restricted to points where practice diverges between English and another language; the context, development, history, or pronunciation of a language is mentioned only where relevant to providing background. Overall, those languages most often met with in English-language publishing are covered in greatest depth, though not all languages of equal frequency are—or can usefully be—addressed equally: with editorial concerns foremost, distinctions between related languages have been highlighted, as this sets a frequent snare for authors, editors, typesetters, and proofreaders.

Help is given on setting non-roman alphabets in English-language texts, as well as transliteration and romanization. Some of the information anticipates fluency on the part of the user, or a work set wholly in another language, or contexts inherent only in scholarly and specialist work. Many points cannot be fully covered by formal rules: a knowledge of the language's word formation and syntax is often essential to reach correct decisions in individual cases.

The information offered in this chapter is distinct from the general topics of the proper display and punctuation of foreign quotations in English text, or their translations (*see* **8.2**). For an overview of translations and transliterations, *see* **13.11**.

11.2 **African languages**

In addition to the Arabic used in the northern African countries, there exist two thousand or so distinct languages in Africa, about a quarter of which have a written form. The vast majority of these use a roman-based orthography supplemented by diacritics, digraphs, 'phonetic' letters— or a combination of these—to accommodate sounds not found in European speech. Some languages (e.g. Malagasy, Hausa, Swahili, Kanuri, and Fulani) were originally, and intermittently still are, written in Arabic, while others (such as N'ko, Vai, and the ancient Ge'ez) employ other writing systems.

Diacritics such as subscript (inferior) dots may be found, for example ạ, ẹ, ọ, ṣ, ṭ. Languages in francophone countries especially employ standard French accents: some, like those of the Ivory Coast, use ä, ï, ö; others in Cameroon use the barred letters ɨ and ʉ.

Swahili uses digraphs such as *ch*, *ng*, *ny*, *sh* rather than diacritics. Digraphs in use elsewhere are *bh*, *bw*, *fy*, *gb*, *gh*, *gw*, *kh*, *kp*, *mb*, *nd*, *ph*, *sw*, *th*, and *tw*. In alphabetizing, accented letters and digraphs normally follow their unaccented or single forms, as in the Yoruba *e*, *ẹ*, *g*, *gb*, *o*, *ọ*, *s*, *ṣ*.

The most frequently used 'phonetic' letter is the Ŋ ŋ (agma), followed by Ɓ ɓ, Ɗ ɗ (hooked *b* and *d*), and occasionally ƙ (hooked *k*—lower case only): note the hooks are to the left on the capitals, to the right on the lower case. Some systems replace the diacritics ạ, ẹ, ọ, ṣ, ṭ with ə, ɛ, ɔ, ʃ, θ, respectively. Hausa also has Ɓ.

Click languages may be represented through many different sorts. For example, the (post)alveolar click forms part of the consonant system in the Nguni and Khoisan languages. It is represented in various ways, most noticeably by an exclamation mark (!) in word-initial position.

11.3 **Albanian**

The Albanian language is a separate branch of the Indo-European language group, spoken in Albania, Kosovo, Greece, and elsewhere. Two main dialects exist, Geg in the north and Tosk (which since 1945 has formed the basis for standard Albanian) in the south. Latin, Greek, Cyrillic, or Arabic script was adapted for writing prior to the introduction in 1909 of a roman alphabet, which includes the diacritics *c*, *ë*; the diacritics *â*, *ê*, *î*, *ô*, *û*, *ŷ* are found in the Geg dialect only. Diacritics and letter combinations are alphabetized as *c c*, *d dh*, *e ë*, *g gj*, *l ll*, *n nj*, *r rr*, *s sh*, *t th*, *x xh*, *z zh*.

11.4 **American English**

11.4.1 **General points**

The success of the English language over the last three centuries has given rise to a remarkable global diversity. The USA, Canada, India, New Zealand, South Africa, the Caribbean, and the Philippines all claim varieties of English that often are as distinct from British English as they are from each other. Of these, US English has for some time been the most codified and dominant, such that the distinction between it and British English is the focus of the greatest attention. For the purposes of this section, the inexact term 'American' means the common English language of the USA, as distinct from—but not necessarily excluding—the English spoken in Canada or elsewhere. Similarly, 'anglicize'—which means technically to render in (any form of) English—here means to render into British English; a more exact but rarer term is 'britannicize'.

As many publishing houses maintain offices on both sides of the Atlantic, maintaining or transforming linguistic differences is of diminishing or merely superficial concern in many quarters. In editing US texts, it is the policy of OUP at Oxford to anglicize at least US spelling and punctuation in the absence of explicit instructions to the contrary. US grammar and vocabulary, on the other hand, are normally kept, though editors should query or alter wording that is impenetrable or misleading. Naturally, phraseology specific to the USA is retained in dialogue and quotations, as are proper nouns. Whether US English is to be preserved or transformed into British English, it is important for authors and editors to be aware of the many differences between the two varieties of writing, since their mutual intelligibility can mask potential problems. A standardized and overarching 'American' style of writing no more exists than does a similar 'British' style: variations can be found within each country. Like any other translation, changing American English to British English—or vice versa—should be undertaken by those proficient in both forms of the language.

What follows is a set of principles illustrating the primary differences between American and British English in their written forms, chiefly in spelling, punctuation, grammar, and vocabulary.

11.4.2 **Spelling**

Many British dictionaries, such as the *Concise Oxford Dictionary* or *Oxford Dictionary for Writers and Editors*, list common US words that can cause difficulty, such as *aluminum, maneuver, pajamas, specialty*. Certain general tendencies should be noted:

> *e* for *ae* and *oe*: *esthete, ameba, estrogen, toxemia, hemoglobin*
> *ense* for *ence*: *defense, offense, pretense, license* (noun and verb)
> *er* for *re*: *center, goiter, theater, ocher, miter, scepter*
> *f* for *ph*: *sulfur, sulfide, sulfate*
> *k* for *c*: *skeptic, mollusk*
> *ll* for *l*: *appall, fulfill, distill, enroll*
> *o* for *ou*: *mold, molt, smolder*
> *og* for *ogue*: *catalog, dialog, demagog, epilog, pedagog*
> *or* for *our*: *color, honor, labor, neighbor, harbor, tumor*
> *z* for *s*: *analyze, paralyze, cozy* but *advise, surprise*

Before a suffix beginning with a vowel, the final -*l* is doubled only where the last syllable is stressed: *labeled, jeweler, counselor, traveling, marvelous, quarreled, rivaled*; but note *fulfill, skillful, thralldom*; *occurred* but *worshiped, kidnaped*. Before a suffix beginning with a vowel, the final -*e* is often omitted where in British usage it is retained, as in *milage* and *salable*. But it is always retained after a soft *c* and *g*, as in British usage.

11.4.3 **Punctuation**

American usage varies slightly for most marks of punctuation, though British editors should generally be able to impose British punctuation on US texts with little difficulty; for more on individual distinctions *see* **CHAPTER 5**.

Most significant is the placement of some punctuation relative to closing quotation marks in US (and often Canadian) English: commas and full points fall *within* quotation marks regardless of whether they are part of the quoted material. This practice means that such texts do not distinguish whether closing punctuation is part of the original quote:

> He considered the theory to be "novel, provocative—the *dernier cri*."

Was 'cri' the last word in the original quotation? In American writing the distinction is lost. While this does not vex Americans very much, the ambiguity can cause editorial problems when transforming American text and transposing closing punctuation.

Americans use the term *parentheses* instead of *brackets* (which for them means 'square brackets'). In all contexts, parentheses within parentheses are set using the mathematical hierarchy of brackets: ([{⟨⟩}]).

11.4.4 **Grammar and structure**

A few verbs inflect differently in American use: *dove* for *dived*, *fit* for *fitted*.

The past participles *kneeled, leaned, learned, spelled*, etc. are preferred to the alternatives *knelt, leant, learnt, spelt*. The participle *gotten* replaces *got* in the sense 'obtain': *She's just gotten a new bathing suit.* (This older usage survives in Britain in *ill-gotten* and *misbegotten.*) But note that the past participle *forgotten* may be treated as *forgot* in the USA.

US writers use the subjunctive form of the verb more widely than is common in British use—*If I were going I would have told you*—even in the negative: *It is better that he not leave.*

Split infinitives are to be avoided on both sides of the Atlantic, although how writers recast a sentence to avoid one may vary. The British tendency is to transpose any separating words before the *to*, while in US style they tend to be transposed after the infinitive, often at the end of the sentence.

US writers rarely use plural verbs and pronouns with 'group' nouns, even if the elements in each are meant severally. This extends to such collective nouns as *audience, committee, crew, family*, where the British might readily use the plural forms: *The jury has argued before coming to its verdict.*

US writers are more inclined to place phrases—especially parenthetical ones—at the beginning or end of a sentence, where their British counterparts would insert them within the body of the sentence. This practice, while sounding odd to a British ear, rarely needs to be altered and, when a phrase is long or complicated, can prove quite useful. For example:

> While sounding odd to a British ear, this practice rarely needs to be altered, and can prove useful when a phrase is long or complicated.

US writers do not place a clarifying comma between a complex subject and its verb except in the event of a parenthetical phrase, in which case two commas—not one—are needed. A British writer might be tempted to do so if too many words fell between the subject and its verb. For example:

> Even an inordinately lengthy or complicated subject of a sentence constructed with all due care and attention by a scrupulous American writer[,] has no comma before its verb.

Instead the tendency would be to rework or reword such a sentence— not a bad idea on either side of the Atlantic, since commas placed thus are considered substandard in British English.

An American question and answer involving the verb *have* usually takes the form *Do you have any brothers? Yes, I do*, rather than *Have you got any brothers? Yes, I have.* Note, however, that using *do* for reinforcement—*He must have done*—is peculiar to British English.

The redundant but idiomatic combination *off* (*of*), as in *It came off of the shelf* or *Get off of the bed*, is considered slang in both British and US English, although it is quite common in US speech. In British English it is non-standard to use *out* for 'out of': *He jumped out of* [not *out*] *the window*; this is not the case in American English, where *out the window* is acceptable usage. (It is acceptable also in British English in a figurative or colloquial sense: *Well, that's my free time out the window.*) By contrast, *outside* is preferable to *outside of* on both sides of the Atlantic: *He stood outside* [not *of*] *the gate*. The use of *outside of* to mean 'apart from' is considered substandard.

Time is reckoned in relation to the following (not preceding) hour: *a quarter of three = two forty-five, five of six = five to six*. The British form is also used interchangeably with the *of* form in the USA. *After* is also used as an equivalent to *past* in specifying a time: *I strolled in about ten minutes after two*.

11.4.5 **Vocabulary**

This is a vast subject, and as the two languages are in constant contact, the boundaries are continually shifting—at even greater and more unpredictable rate thanks to the Internet. Many books deal in depth with the 'common tongue' separating the two countries, and UK and US dictionaries often provide individual references encompassing the other's lexicon. While something in a dictionary labelled 'British English' can safely be assumed to have more currency in Britain than in the USA, it is not clear whether that usage is restricted to Britain or is found elsewhere, e.g. in Australia, New Zealand, or South Africa. Similarly, a term labelled 'American English' may also be in use in Canada or the Caribbean. The fluidity and speed with which the two varieties of English are exchanged provides a cross-pollination that blurs a term's national provenance, thereby making many definitions a moving target.

Since a country's culture affects vocabulary significantly, an author may reasonably expect Americans to understand words taken from baseball terminology more than those taken from cricket, and Britons to feel more at home with an allusion to *the GWR* or *Spaghetti Junction* than *the LIRR* or *Route 66*. More subtly, terms not directly linked to a culture may appear to be in the realm of specialist data in one country but common knowledge in the other. For example, many Britons feel more at home with botanical than medical terminology, while many Americans feel the reverse, the result being that a Briton might have a *heart attack* while planting *antirrhinums*, while an American might have a *myocardial infarction* while planting *snapdragons*.

Many of the differences between the two countries' vocabularies—such as *apartment* for *flat*, *fall* for *autumn*, *zipper* for *zip*, *driver's license* for *driving licence*, *elasticized* for *elasticated*, *elevator* for *lift*, and *windshield* for *windscreen*—are either sufficiently self-evident or familiar that they seldom lead to misunderstanding. Thus readers can encounter *jump rope* for *skipping rope*, *jumper cables* for *jump leads*, and *dog leash* for *dog lead* perhaps without even noticing the difference. Some distinctions seem neatly confined to those technological realms that developed in parallel but independently, for example the nomenclature of the railway, telephone, kitchen, and motor car. Still other differences have entirely dissolved over the years: for example, British Telecom's own title for their telephone directory is now *phone book*, and an engaged line is now *busy*, whereas in 1935 the author of *Modern American Usage* felt obliged to clarify that the British equivalent of the American *tonsorial parlor* was *hairdressing saloon*.

Nevertheless, variation in vocabulary is pre-eminently the area in which an Americanism may cause actual misunderstanding to a British readership. The list beginning p. 244 contains common American terms with their British equivalents. However, the most important and insidious differences in vocabulary concern those words that are superficially intelligible to a British reader but have different meanings in the USA. These include the following:

Billion, trillion. Formerly in the UK a *billion* meant a million million (10^{12}) and a *trillion* meant a million million million (10^{18}). Recently British usage has largely aligned itself with US usage, where a *billion* means a thousand million (10^9), what was formerly called a *milliard* in Britain, and a *trillion* means a million million (10^{12}). In the UK specific amounts of more than one billion or trillion sometimes become plural (*three billions*), while in the USA they always remain singular (*three billion*). In both countries general amounts are normally plural (*trillions of pounds*).

Bomb (noun). (UK) a large sum of money (*costs a bomb*) or a resounding success, especially in entertainment (*went down a bomb*). (US) disastrous failure, a usage derived from its verb form. The natural confusion between the senses of success and failure has in Britain allowed the two forms to exist side by side in uneasy truce. Thus the meaning of each derives only from context, so that a play can be thought *to be a bomb* (be terrible) by one reviewer but *to go down a bomb* (be wonderful) by another.

Brainstorm (noun). (UK) a violent or excited outburst, mental confusion. (US) a sudden bright idea (= *brainwave*). Although British usage has adopted the US verb *brainstorming* to describe a concerted, intellectual, and spontaneous discussion of a problem, the noun form is not used.

Caboose. (UK) a kitchen on a ship's deck. (US) a guard's or workmen's van on a train, usually coupled at the end.

Chicory, endive. (UK) *chicory* a blue-flowered plant, *Cichorium intybus*, cultivated for its flowers and root; *endive* a curly-leaved plant, *Cichorium endivia*, used in salads. (US) these meanings are reversed.

Crank. (UK) (of a person) eccentric. (US) a bad-tempered person.

Dim, dumb. (UK) *dim* obscure or ill-defined, not clear, only faintly visible, with the additional sense of stupid or slow to understand; *dumb* unable or unwilling to speak, having no voice or emitting no sound. In US use *dumb* has the sense of stupid or slow to understand rendered in the UK by *dim*, though the UK has adopted this US sense in e.g. the phrase *dumb blonde*.

First floor. (UK) the first storey of a building. (US) the ground floor.

Foxy. (UK) sly or cunning. (US) slang for (of a person) sexually attractive.

Homely. (UK) simple, plain, unpretentious, cosy. (US) unattractive in appearance, ugly. For the British sense Americans use *homey*.

Inquiry. (UK) an official or formal investigation, *enquiry* being reserved for the act or an instance of seeking information. (US) *enquiry* is not used, so *inquiry* covers both British senses, making no distinction between them.

Knickers. (UK) women's or children's panties or underwear. (US) plus-fours or breeches.

Lumber, timber. (UK) *lumber* cumbersome objects; *timber* dressed or prepared wood for carpentry or building. (US) *lumber* dressed or prepared wood, *timber* rough or partly prepared wood. Thus an American *timber wolf* lives in the woods rather than in either a US *lumber yard* or a British *timber merchants*.

Mezzanine. In theatre contexts (UK) a floor or space beneath the stage. In theatre contexts (US) the dress circle.

Moot point. (UK) something debatable, undecided, open to question. (US) something having no practical significance, abstract or academic.

Nervy. (UK) easily excited or disturbed. (US) bold, impudent. For the British sense Americans use *nervous*.

Nonplussed. (UK) surprised and confused, the former US sense. (US) unperturbed, *not* surprised and confused—a recent and still substandard use of the word.

Off colo(u)r. (UK) not in good health. (US) somewhat indecent.

Pecker. (UK) beak or bill, in the phrase *keep your pecker up* (remain cheerful). (US) vulgar slang for penis (now also common in the UK).

Peckish. (UK) hungry. (US) irritable.

Pokey. (UK) uncomfortably small and cramped, (especially of a car) having considerable power or acceleration. (US) annoyingly slow, also slang for jail.

Redcap. (UK) a member of the military police. (US) a railway porter.

Robin. (UK) a small European bird, *Erithacus rubecula*, which symbolizes

Christmas. (US) a large thrush, *Turdus migratorius*, which symbolizes the coming of spring.

Rubber, rubbers. Certain senses of these terms cause mutually exclusive embarrassment on either side of the Atlantic. *Rubber* meaning eraser is rare in the USA, and *rubbers* meaning galoshes is rare in the UK. In both countries the foreign term is liable to be confused with the colloquial word for condom.

Semi. (UK) the colloquial term for a semi-detached house. (US) the colloquial term for a semi-trailer.

Sherbet. (UK) a sweet, flavoured, effervescent powder, sweet, or drink. (US) a water ice.

Skillet. (UK) a small metal cooking pot with a long handle and (usually) legs. (US) a frying-pan.

Slate. (UK) criticize severely, scold. (US) make arrangements for, schedule, or propose, nominate.

Snifter. (UK) (a glass for) a small drink of alcohol. (US) a balloon glass for brandy etc.

Table (a matter, as in a meeting). (UK) bring forward for discussion or consideration. (US) postpone consideration indefinitely, shelve.

Tenderloin. (UK) the middle part of a pork loin. (US) the undercut of a sirloin.

Trapezium, trapezoid. (UK) a *trapezium* is a quadrilateral with only one pair of sides parallel, and a *trapezoid* is a quadrilateral with no two sides parallel. (US) the definitions are reversed.

Unilateralism. (UK) unilateral disarmament. (US) the pursuit of a foreign policy without allies.

Waffle. (UK) (indulge in) verbose but meaningless talk or writing; avoid committing oneself, prevaricate. (US) only the second definition is in use.

The following list of American words with their British equivalents reflects tendency rather than dogma, and is intended to illustrate differing terms at their widest divergence rather than similar or identical usage in both countries. British and US writers continue to enjoy borrowing from each other's vocabularies, and the appearance of a word in one category does not mean that it is not in occasional—or even frequent—use across the Atlantic. Similarly, there are words in each category that may be considered regionalisms, archaisms, or proprietary rather than generic names. Some of the equivalents given below may be parallel rather than identical, so be wary of treating every pair as exact synonyms.

As with any translation, individual words seldom lend themselves to mechanical substitution, and contexts frequently forbid replacing one word with another. A rote rendering from US to British English will result in false and needless mutation: *the New York Underground* is just as nonsensical as *the New York Métro*—or, for that matter, *the London Subway*. This holds for spelling variations as well: *Pearl Harbour, Piers Ploughman*, and *first draught of a letter* are all well-meaning but meaningless attempts at cisatlantic translation.

about-face = about-turn

alligator clip = crocodile clip

antenna [*radio, TV*] = aerial

apartment = flat

apartment house = block of flats

appointment book, datebook = diary

area code = dialling code

arugula = rocket

aside from = apart from

athlete = track and field sportsman or -woman

automobile/auto [*car*] = motor car/motor

baby carriage = pram

backstretch [*horse racing*] = back straight

back-up lights [*car*] = reversing lights

baggage room = left-luggage office

balcony [*theatre*] = dress circle

bandage/Band-Aid = plaster/Elastoplast

bangs = fringe

bank swallow = sand martin

barrette = hair/-slide, -grip

baseboard = skirting board

bass viol = double bass

bathe [*verb*] = bath

bathrobe = dressing-gown

bathroom = bathroom, lavatory

bathtub = bath

beachfront = seafront

beer = lager

bellhop = bellboy

bell pepper = green pepper

the Big Dipper = the Plough, Charles's Wain

bill [*paper money*] = (bank)note

billboard = hoarding

billfold = wallet

bill of goods = consignment of merchandise

billyclub, nightstick = truncheon

blackjack = pontoon, vingt-et-un

blacktop = asphalt, tarmacadam

bleachers [*sports ground*] = terraces

blender = liquidizer

blind [*hunting*] = hide

blinders [*horse*] = blinkers

blue collar = working class

blue law = Sunday trading law

boardwalk = promenade

bobby pin = hair/-grip, -pin, kirby grip; *not* curler

bookmobile = mobile library

booth [*telephone*] = box, kiosk

botfly = warble fly

boxcar [*railway*] = freight wagon

braces [*teeth*] = brace

brackets [*typography*] = square brackets

brass knuckles = knuckleduster

brights [*car*] = high beams

broil = grill

brook trout, speckled trout = brook charr

buffet [*furniture*] = sideboard

bulletin board = noticeboard

bullhorn = megaphone

bun [*savoury*] = bap, roll

business suit = lounge suit

buzzard = turkey vulture

caboose [*train*] = guard's *or* workmen's van

calico [*animal*] = piebald

call [*telephone*] = ring up

call collect [*telephone*] = reverse charges

calling card = visiting card, business card

can = tin

candy = sweets

candy apple = toffee apple

candy bar = bar of chocolate

candy store = sweet shop, confectioner's

carnival [*with rides and amusements*] = (fun)fair

carom [*billiards, pool*] = cannon

cart [*shopping, tea*] = trolley

cash register = till

casket = coffin
cater-, catty-, kitty-cornered = diagonal(ly)
cell phone = mobile (phone)
charter member = founder member
check, bill [*restaurant*] = bill
checkers = draughts
checking account = current account
check mark = tick
checkroom = cloakroom
chicory = endive
chin-up = pull-up
(potato) chips = crisps
cider = (cloudy) apple juice
citation [*law*] = summons
city editor = local editor
clipping (service) = (press-)cutting (service)
closet = cupboard, wardrobe
clothespin = clothes peg
collect [*telephone*] = reverse charge
(down) comforter = duvet
common stock = ordinary shares
concentrate [*drink*] = squash
conductor [*train*] = guard
connect [*telephone*] = put through
cookie = (sweet) biscuit
corn = maize
cornstarch = cornflour
cot = camp bed
cotton batting = cotton wool
cotton candy = candyfloss
counterclockwise = anticlockwise
countertop [*kitchen*] = worktop
courtyard = yard
cracker = (savoury) biscuit
crawfish = freshwater crayfish
creamer = cream jug
cream of wheat = semolina
crèche = nativity scene
crescent wrench = adjustable spanner
crib = cot
cross tie = railway sleeper
crosswalk = zebra crossing
cuffs [*trousers*] = turn-ups
curb cut = dropped kerb
cutlery = knives

daddy longlegs = harvestman
dashboard [*car*] = fascia
datebook = engagement diary
daycare = crèche
daylight saving time = summer time
dead end = cul-de-sac, close
deck [*cards*] = pack
decorator = interior designer
deductible [*insurance*] = excess
defrost [*car*] = de-ice
denatured alcohol = isopropyl alcohol
derby [*hat*] = bowler
desk clerk = receptionist
dessert = pudding, sweet
detour [*road*] = diversion
devil's bit [*plant*] = blazing star
devil's paintbrush [*plant*] = orange hawkweed
diaper = nappy
divided highway = dual carriageway
doctor's/dentist's office [*practice*] = surgery
doghouse = dog kennel
dormitory [*university etc.*] = hall of residence
downtown = city centre, town centre
draft, selective service [*military*] = conscription
dresser = dressing table, chest of drawers
druggist = pharmacist
drug store = chemist
drygoods store = draper
drywall, wallboard [*building*] = plasterboard
dues [*for club, society*] = subscription
dump [*noun and verb*] = tip
dumpster = skip
dump truck = tipper lorry
duplex = two-storey maisonette, semi-detached
Dutch door = stable door

editorial [*newspaper*] = leader
eggplant = aubergine
egg roll = spring roll
eighth note = quaver
electric cord = flex
elementary school = primary school
elevator = lift
emergency room [*hospital*] = casualty department

endive = chicory

English horn = cor anglais

English muffin [*savoury*] = muffin

entrance/exit ramp = slip road

envision = envisage

eraser = rubber

Erector set = Meccano

exclamation point = exclamation mark

express/way, free-, high- = motorway

face card = court card

fall = autumn

fanny = bottom

faucet = tap

fender [*car*] = wing, mudguard

firecracker = firework, banger

firehouse = fire station

fireplug = fire hydrant

first floor = ground floor

fix = mend

flapjack = pancake

flashlight = torch

flat = puncture

flatware = cutlery

floor lamp = standard lamp

floorwalker = shopwalker

flyover = fly-past

football = American football

freight train = goods train

French door = French window

french fries = chips

frontage road = service road

front desk [*hotel*] = reception

front office = head office

frosting = icing

fusee [*railway*] = signal flare

garbage = rubbish

garbage can, — man, — truck = dust/bin, -man, -cart

garbanzo (bean) = chickpea

garter belt = suspenders, suspender belt

gas(oline) = petrol

gas station = filling station, petrol station

German shepherd = alsatian

gift certificate = gift token

goose bumps = goose pimples

grab bag = lucky dip

grade [*school*] = class, form

grade [*schoolwork, noun and verb*] = mark

grade crossing = level crossing

grade school = primary school

graduate [*adj., noun*] = postgraduate

grain = corn

green thumb = green fingers

grill [*verb*] = barbecue

ground [*electricity*] = earth

ground meat = mince

gutter [*on or in ground*] = gully

gyro = doner kebab

half note = minim

hall(way) = corridor

hardware store = ironmonger

hassock = footstool

hickey = lovebite

highboy [*furniture*] = tallboy

highrise [*noun*] = tower block

hockey = ice hockey

hood [*car*] = bonnet

hope chest = bottom drawer

housebroken = housetrained

hunting [*game*] = shooting

hutch = display cabinet [*with glass doors*], Welsh dresser [*without*]

Information [*telephone*] = Directory Enquiries

intermission = interval

intern [*hospital*] = house officer

Internal Revenue = Inland Revenue

intersection = crossroads

janitor = caretaker

jawbreaker [*sweet*] = gobstopper

jelly roll = Swiss roll

John Doe = Joe Bloggs

jumper = pinafore dress

jumper cables = jump leads

jump rope = skipping rope

jungle gym = climbing frame

kerosene = paraffin

Kleenex = tissues

knickers = plus fours

ladybug = ladybird

laundromat = launderette

laundry = washing

lease, rent [*noun and verb*] = letting, let

leash = lead

legal, public holiday = bank holiday

license plate = number plate

life preserver = life jacket, lifebelt

lightning bug = firefly

lightning rod = lightning conductor

line = queue

line-up [*police*] = identity parade

liquor = spirits

liquor store = off licence

longshoreman = docker

longwearing = hard-wearing

lost and found = lost property

low beams [*car*] = dipped headlights

lumber = prepared [*dressed*] timber

maid of honor = principal bridesmaid

mail [*noun and verb*] = post

mail/box, -man = post/box, -man

Main Street = High Street

mass transit = urban transport

math = maths

matt [*for picture*] = mount

median strip, divider [*road*] = central reservation

mezzanine [*theatre*] = dress circle

milepost = mile marker

mimosa [*drink*] = Buck's Fizz

molasses = black treacle

monkey bars = climbing frame

monkey wrench = adjustable spanner

mononucleosis = glandular fever

mortician = undertaker

motor home = caravan

movie theater = cinema

moving van = removal van, pantechnicon

muffin = American muffin

muffler [*car*] = silencer

mutual fund = unit trust

named for = named after

navy bean = haricot bean

newsdealer, newsstand = newsagent

nipple [*baby bottle*] = teat

normalcy = normality

number [*written cipher*] = figure

numbers [*data*] = figures

oarlock = rowlock

odometer = milometer

of [*time*] = to

office [*doctor, dentist*] = surgery

off of = off

off-ramp = exit ramp

one-way [*ticket*] = single

orchestra [*theatre*] = stalls

ordinance [*law*] = bye-law

outlet [*socket*] = power point

oven = cooker

overalls = dungarees

overly = excessively

over/pass, under- = flyover

pacifier [*comforter*] = dummy

paddle [*table tennis*] = bat

pantry = larder

pants = trousers

pantyhose = tights

paper route = paper round

parentheses = brackets

parka = anorak

parking lot = car park

parquet [*theatre*] = orchestra pit

pass [*vehicle*] = overtake

pavement = road surface

peavey = cant hook

pedestrian crossing = zebra crossing

pedestrian underpass = subway

period = full point, full stop

pharmacy = chemist

phone book = telephone directory

phonograph [*record player*] = gramophone

pigpen = pigsty

pinto [*horse*] = piebald

pit, seed [*fruit*] = stone, pip

pitcher = jug

playbill = (theatre) programme

plexiglas = perspex

pocketbook, purse = handbag

podium [*for speaker*] = rostrum, lectern

popsicle = ice lolly

porch = veranda

Porta Potti = Portaloo

postage meter = franking machine

pot holder = oven glove, oven mitt

powdered sugar, confectioner's sugar = icing sugar

prenatal = antenatal

prep school = public school

principal [*school*] = headmaster, headmistress

private school = prep school *or* public school

pruning shears = secateurs

public school = state school

pull-off [*road*] = lay-by

pump = court shoe

pushpin = drawing pin

push-up = press-up

quarter note = crotchet

Quonset hut = Nissen hut

railroad = railway

raise = pay rise

raisin [*seedless*] = sultana

range [*kitchen*] = cooker

real estate = real property

real estate agent, realtor = estate agent

recess [*school*] = break

reformatory = borstal

restroom = public lavatory

résumé = curriculum vitae

romaine [*lettuce*] = cos

roomer = lodger

round-trip ticket = return ticket

row house = terrace house

rubber = condom

rubbers = galoshes

rubbing alcohol = surgical spirit

rummage sale = jumble sale

run [*hosiery*] = ladder

run [*public office*] = stand

rutabaga = swede

sales clerk = shop assistant

salvage yard = breaker's yard

Saran Wrap, plastic wrap = cling film

scab [*union disputes*] = blackleg

scallion = spring onion

scalper = (ticket) tout

scaup duck = bluebill

Scotch tape = Sellotape/sticky tape

scratch pad = note pad, scribbling block

second floor = first floor

sedan = saloon car

Seeing Eye dog = guide dog (for blind people)

seltzer (water) = soda (water)

semi = HGV, articulated lorry

Senior Citizen = Old Age Pensioner

shade [*window*] = blind

sheers, under drapes = net curtains

shoestring = shoelace

shopping bag = carrier bag

shot [*injection*] = jab

shredded coconut = desiccated coconut

shrimp = prawn

side mirror [*car*] = wing mirror

sidewalk = pavement

silent partner = sleeping partner

silverware = cutlery

sink = wash/basin, hand-

sixteenth note = semiquaver

sixty-fourth note = hemidemisemiquaver

skillet = frying pan

skimmer = darter (dragonfly)

Slavic = Slavonic

sled = sledge

sleeper car, pullman [*train*] = sleeping car

slingshot = catapult

slot machine = fruit machine

slowpoke = slowcoach

snap = press stud, popper

sneakers [*trainers*] = plimsolls

snifter [*glass*] = balloon glass

snow pea(s) = mangetout(s)

soccer = football

soda cracker = cream cracker

specialist [*medicine*] = consultant

spelunking = caving

spool [*sewing*] = cotton reel

sprinkles [*confectionery*] = hundreds and thousands

squib [*newspaper*] = filler

squirt gun = water-pistol

station wagon = estate car

stenography = shorthand

stick shift = gear lever

stockholder = shareholder

stop light, traffic signal = traffic light

store/front, -keeper = shop/front, -keeper

stove = cooker

straight [*drink*] = neat

straight razor = open/cutthroat razor

street/car [*trolley car*] = tram

string bean = green bean

stroller = pushchair

Styrofoam = polystyrene

subway = underground, Tube

suspenders = braces

switch [*railway*] = points

tablet [*paper*] = writing pad

tag [*clothing*] = label

talk show = chat show

tease [*hair*] = backcomb

tempest in a teapot = storm in a teacup

thirty-second note = demisemiquaver

thread [*sewing*] = cotton

thumbtack = drawing pin, pushpin

tick-tack-toe = noughts and crosses

timber = rough [*undressed*] lumber

time payment, installment plan = hire purchase

traffic circle = roundabout

traffic jam = tailback

trailer, mobile home = caravan

trailer park = caravan site

train car = railway coach

training wheels = stabilizers

transom = fanlight

trashbag = bin bag, — liner

truck = lorry

truck farm = market garden

trundle bed = truckle bed

trunk [*car*] = boot

tub [*bathroom*] = bath

tube [*electrical*] = valve

tuition [*education*] = fees

turnout [*car*] = passing place

turn signal [*car*] = indicator

tuxedo = dinner jacket, black tie

ultralight [*aircraft*] = microlight

underpass = subway

undershirt = vest

unlisted [*telephone*] = ex-directory

vacation = holiday

vacationer = holidaymaker

vacuum = hoover

valance = pelmet

vending machine = slot machine

vest = waistcoat

veteran = ex-service/man, -woman

vice [*corruption*] = vice

vise [*workshop*] = vice

visiting nurse = district nurse

wall tent = frame tent

wall-to-wall [*carpet*] = fitted

Wanderjahr = gap year

washcloth = face cloth, flannel

washroom = lavatory

wash the dishes = wash up

wash up = wash one's hands

wastebasket = waste-paper basket

water heater [*electrical*] = immersion heater

water heater [*gas*] = boiler

whole note = semibreve

wholewheat = wholemeal

windbreaker [*jacket*] = windcheater

windshield [*car*] = windscreen

wire [*noun and verb, telegram*] = telegram

wrench [*noun*] = spanner

xerox = photocopy

yard = garden

yarn [*knitting*] = wool

Yield [*sign*] = Give Way

zee [*letter*] = zed

zero [*the figure* '0'] = nought

zip code = postcode

zucchini = courgette(s)

11.5 **Amerindian languages**

Over 900 languages have been recorded as being spoken among the indigenous peoples of North, Central, and South America; it is estimated that several hundred became extinct following post-Columbian colonization. Some of those languages that had not developed their own writing systems were initially recorded, with varied success, by missionaries using largely Spanish- or English-influenced orthography. In the nineteenth century several languages were recorded using newly invented writing systems, either by native or non-native speakers. Many of these writing systems have found continued use. Those employed by native speakers tend to admit of greater variation than those employed by linguists and philologists, who may apply diacritics and other conventions not normally part of the vernacular. In the wake of recent government policy and funding, new scripts are being derived to supplement or replace existing forms, so many existing systems are in a state of reappraisal.

Writing systems derived from Old World orthography do not logically reflect the divisions of New World language families, which in many instances are still contested. The following are some of the many families, with common language representations.

11.5.1 **Algonquian languages**

The Cree syllabary was invented in 1840 to render Cree and Ojibwe (Chippewa). Written left to right in geometric characters derived from shorthand, there is great freedom in which and how shapes of characters are presented, and what spacing, punctuation, and additional diacritics (if any) are used. Lenape (Delaware) is rendered in the same alphabet as English, with the inclusion of digraphs *ll*, *mm*, *tt* and (in some texts) the acute accent and tilde. The Potawatomi alphabet, too, is much like English, and is ordered: a b c d e e' g h i I j k m n o p s sh t u w y z zh. A distinctive feature is the capital *I*, which is distinct from the lower-case *i*.

11.5.2 **Athabaskan languages**

Navajo uses the following diacritics to denote vowel length (superscript dot, macron, or acute), brevity (breve or circumflex), or nasalization (cedilla or tilde), which can be used in combination over a single letter; some are used on consonants as well. The alphabet—which has no capitals—is ordered: a æ b c d e g ǧy gh ǧw h' i j k' kw k ky l ł m n ń o q s sh t t' u w x y z; letter forms are the crossed (Polish) ł and *ae* ligature.

The apostrophe can stand as a separate sound or modify *k* or *t*. Chipewyan and other related languages employ a writing system based on the Cree syllabary.

11.5.3 Central and South American languages

The Aymara alphabet is ordered: a c ch e g i j l m n ñ o p q r s t u v x y z; diacritics are the tilde over *n*, and the acute over vowels. A pictographic script exists as well, though it is not standardized. The Guarani alphabet is ordered: a b c ch d e g i j l jh k m n ñ o p r s t u y; diacritics are the tilde over *n*, and the acute and circumflex over vowels. Quechua, the language of the Inca empire, used quipu strings, a system of recording documents by means of differently coloured and knotted threads; their language is rendered with an alphabet ordered: a c ch f q i j k l ll m n ñ o p r s t u w y. About fifteen Mesoamerican glyphic writing systems existed in the pre-Columbian period, the best known being Maya. The modern Maya language, Yucatec, has several roman-alphabet transliteration systems. Zapotec has its own glyphic writing system; in roman orthography, the Zapotec alphabet is the same as that for English, but without *f* and *w*.

11.5.4 Eskimo-Aleut languages

Though the Eskimo-Aleut peoples are not ethnically Amerindian, their languages are generally considered together with them. Inuktitut (Inuit) is written in a related system (reformed in 1976); its roman orthography uses the additional sort ł, though this is not used in all dialects, which cover an enormous geographical area. It also has a syllabary, based on the Cree, used mainly in Canada. Yupik was before 1937 written in the roman alphabet, with the additional characters ə, ł, ŋ, b, and apostrophe; thereafter it was written in the Cyrillic alphabet, with the additional characters г', к', н', and х'. In the nineteenth century Aleut was written in the Cyrillic alphabet, with additional characters, though both the writing system and language are now moribund.

11.5.5 Iroquoian languages

Cherokee has a writing system invented by a native speaker in the nineteenth century. Its own distinctive alphabet exists in several forms. Alphabetization follows the order of its syllabary, which has more than one order, and may be read according to rows or columns. The Mohawk alphabet is ordered: a d e g h i k n o r s t u v w y; diacritics are the grave over vowels and apostrophe. The Seneca alphabet is ordered: a c œ e ẽ h i k n s t u ũ w y; diacritics are the tilde (ẽ, ũ) and apostrophe.

11.5.6 Muskogean (Sioux) languages

The Choctaw alphabet is ordered: a a̲ ā i̊ ā̊ū b ch e f h hl i i̱ k l ł m n o o̲ p s sh t u u̲ v y. The crossed (Polish) ł is used in addition to a normal l, as are underlined *a*, *i*, *o*, and *u*; the letter *v* is sometimes replaced by *w*. The Sioux alphabet is ordered: a b c ć ç d e g ġ h ḣ i k ķ l m n ŋ o p p̓ s ś ṭ t̠ u w y z ż; variant diacritics that may be found include ɋ, i̧, ṡ, u̧, and ż.

11.5.7 Uto-Aztecan languages

The Nahuatl alphabet is ordered: a c ch e h i l m n o p q t tl tz u x y z. Variations exist, some of which have accents over consonants.

11.6 **Arabic**

11.6.1 Representation

Whether written or typeset, Arabic is composed of a cursive script consisting of twenty-eight letters, all of which are consonants; each has several forms according to position within the word. Many accents are used, representing vowel sounds and other phonetic features: the three long vowels (*ā*, *ī*, *ū*) are usually represented in the script by the so-called 'letters of prolongation'. The three short vowels (*a*, *i*, *u*) and other phonetic features are optionally represented by a system of diacritics in vocalized Arabic: the short-vowel marks and other orthographic signs are *always* written in editions of the Koran, in schoolbooks, and usually in editions of classical poetry. Otherwise they are omitted and employed sporadically only to resolve ambiguity. Augmented forms of the Arabic alphabet are used for Persian, Urdu, and Ottoman Turkish.

Arabic script in English texts

Arabic is read from right to left; hence if any passage is divided, the right-hand words must go in the first line, and the left-hand words in the second line. Therefore wherever two or more Arabic words occur together within English text, each word should be numbered for the printer, to ensure proper placement in the event of turn-lines. (For more on this process *see* **8.2**.) Indexes, glossaries, and copy using Arabic script in tabular form should be set with the Arabic aligned right (rather than left), and the English text, page references, and so on following on at the right.

Numbers

Unlike Arabic script, numbers in Arabic are read from left to right. Derived originally from Sanskrit, they differ from those arabic numerals used in English (for which they formed the basis), and must be used in preference to them where Arabic script is set; 1–9 and 0 is ١ ٢ ٣ ٤ ٥ ٦ ٧ ٨ ٩ ٠. In the countries of the Maghreb (Morocco, Algiers, Libya) the European forms are normally used. Formerly Arabic letters called *abjad* were used as ciphers to render numbers, with each assigned a specific value, as in Greek; they were used especially in, for example, antique astronomical and mathematical works and Persian chronograms, where arranged alphabet numbers form words. They are still used occasionally as the equivalent of roman numerals in the preliminary matter of a book.

11.6.2 Transliteration

There is no standard internationally agreed system of spelling words from Arabic when set into roman type. Indeed, the Arabic script is more widespread than the language itself, being employed as a primary or secondary writing form not just by languages related to Arabic, but by unrelated languages such as Berber, Pashto, Kurdish, Sindhi, Kashmiri, Sulu, Malay, and Malagasy.

Table 11.1: **Arabic transliteration**

Alone	Final	Medial	Initial			Alone	Final	Medial	Initial		
ا	ا			'alif	'	ض	ض	ض	ض	ḍād	ḍ
ب	ب	ﺒ	ﺑ	bā'	b	ط	ط	ط	ط	ṭā'	ṭ
ت	ت	ﺘ	ﺗ	tā'	t	ظ	ظ	ظ	ظ	ẓā'	ẓ
ث	ث	ﺜ	ﺛ	thā'	th	ع	ع	ﻋ	ﻋ	'ayn	'
ج	ج	ﺠ	ﺟ	jīm	j	غ	غ	ﻏ	ﻏ	ghayn	gh
ح	ح	ﺤ	ﺣ	ḥā'	ḥ	ف	ف	ﻓ	ﻓ	fā'	f
خ	خ	ﺨ	ﺧ	khā'	kh	ق	ﻖ	ﻗ	ﻗ	qāf	q
د	ﺪ			dāl	d	ك	ﻚ	ﻛ	ﻛ	kāf	k
ذ				dhāl	dh	ل	ﻞ	ﻟ	ﻟ	lām	l
ر	ﺮ			rā'	r	م	ﻢ	ﻣ	ﻣ	mīm	m
ز	ﺰ			zāy	z	ن	ﻦ	ﻧ	ﻧ	nūn	n
س	ﺲ	ﺴ	ﺳ	sīn	s	ه	ﻪ	ﻫ	ﻫ	hā'	h
ش	ﺶ	ﺸ	ﺷ	shīn	sh	و				wāw	w
ص	ﺺ	ﺼ	ﺻ	ṣād	ṣ	ى	ﻲ	ﻳ	ﻳ	yā'	y

The detail offered in any transliteration depends on the level of audience being addressed; in the main any logical transliteration system is acceptable, provided that it has been consistently applied. None the less, it is preferable to choose one of the several competing 'semi-national' systems that exist, and employ it consistently throughout a single work. The system espoused by the *Encyclopaedia of Islam* is frequently encountered (especially in English, and among those writing on history, religion, or literature), as is that of the *International Journal of Middle East Studies* (IJMES) (favoured by German and French writers, and those writing on linguistics). The system of the US Library of Congress has become increasingly adopted in the English-speaking world: it is the form employed by the automated cataloguing systems of the Bodleian Library and other Oxford libraries, as well as the British Library.

Writers and editors may face the dilemma of incorporating into one work Arabic previously transliterated using different systems. This is often indicated by varied representation of a number of letters: *ṯ* or *th*, *ǧ* (also *dj*) or *j* (*ŷ* in Spanish), *ḵ* or *kh*, *ḏ* or *dh*, *š* or *sh*, *ḡ* (also *ġ*) or *gh*, *ḳ* or *q*. (The *Encyclopaedia of Islam* system recommends underlining the digraphs *dh*, *gh*, *kh*, *sh*, *th*; their *ḳ* is considered obsolete.) Similarly there are two diphthongs, rendered as *ai* or *ay*, *au* or *aw*. In every case choose either the first or second form; do not mix them within the same text.

■ In specialist texts employing transliteration, prefer *a* and *i* to *e*, *ǧ* to *j*, *ai* to *ei*, and *u* to *o* or the Gallic *ou*. The feminine singular ending (*tā' marbūṭa*) should be transliterated as *ah* or *a* rather than variants such as *eh* or *e*; established usage to the contrary is acceptable, however, particularly when recreating colloquial or dialectal forms. In non-technical contexts common proper names are usually best left in their most easily recognizable form: *Bedouin, Emir, Khartoum, Koran, Mecca, Oman, Suez, Yemen*.

■ The definite article *al* should always be joined to the noun with a hyphen: *al-Islām, al-kitāb*. When the noun or adjective defined by *al* begins with one of the fourteen 'sun' letters (*t, th, d, dh, r, z, s, sh, ṣ, ḍ, ṭ, ẓ, l, n*), the *l* of the definite article is assimilated to the 'sun' letter. This is often indicated in transliteration by variations such as *ad-, an-, ar-, as-, at-*, or *az-*. However, the usual scholarly usage is to write the article–noun combination without indicating the resulting pronunciation through spelling. In text this is often encountered in personal names, for example *al-Nafūd* not *an-Nafūd*, and *al-Ṣafī* not *aṣ-Ṣafī*. For more on personal names *see* **4.2.6**.

■ The language spoken throughout the Arabic world varies widely in pronunciation, hence regional variants often occur in transliteration: for example, the Arabic consonant *jīm* is normally pronounced as a soft *j* (as in *jazz*) in standard Arabic, but as a French *j* (as in *bonjour* or *joufflu*) in Syria, and as a hard *g* (as in *girl*) in Egypt; it may be so transliterated in texts concerning Syrian or Egyptian Arabic. Ottoman Turkish can be transliterated according to the modern Turkish roman alphabet that came into being in 1928 (sometimes augmented by diacritics, especially for words of Arabic origin). The Turkish influence in Iraq has resulted in names and local words of Turkish origin, for which the letters *ch*, *e*, and *p* can be used in transliteration. (*See also* **11. 43**.)

11.6.2.1 Accents and diacritics

Diacritics should be limited as much as possible, except in specialized or linguistic works, where underlining (t̲, k̲, d̲), subscript dots (ḥ, ṣ, ḍ, ṭ, ẓ), and háčeks (ǧ, š) are usual. Long-vowel marks should be represented by a macron, not a circumflex or acute: *tawārīkh* not *tawârîkh*, *maʿlūm* not *maʿlûm*, *rubāʿī* not *rubáʿí*.

- Typographically, the transliteration of Arabic ʿ*ayn* and *hamza* corresponds to that of Hebrew ʿ*ayin* and *alef*. These are often represented by Greek asper (ʿ) and lenis (ʾ), respectively, but some typesetters have separate Semitic sorts (ʿ and ʾ), which should be preferred when available. Examples:

  ʿ*ayn*: ʿālim, muʿallim, majmaʿ

  hamza: amīr, muʾallif, dāʾ

  In each case the sort is to be treated as a letter of the alphabet and part of the word, and must not be confused with a quotation mark. Where necessary editors should insert a thin space between the diacritic and a quotation mark, or use double quotation marks; if quotations occur frequently in transliterated material, use guillemets (« ») for quotation marks, as in Arabic or French practice. Note that an apostrophe, denoting elision, usually appears before *l* followed by a hyphen, for example ʿ*Abdu 'l-Malik*. Do not use an opening quotation mark (turned comma) for ʿ*ayn*.

- Like aspers, ʿ*ayns* are often mistyped as opening quotation marks or lenes. If an ʿ*ayn* cannot be correctly achieved on copy, be consistent in imposing its closest approximation, and then instruct the typesetter to replace it with ʿ*ayns* accordingly. The ʿ*ayn* has both capital and lower-case forms (ʿ ʿ). Note the distinction between them and the sorts used in transliterating Ancient Egyptian (*see* **11.16**).

11.6.2.2 Capitalization

Problems of Arabic capitalization occur only in transliteration, since the Arabic alphabet does not distinguish between upper- and lower-case letters. The definite article *al* normally is capitalized only at the beginning of a sentence, but not at the start of a reference title. As with Italian and Spanish, for instance, OUP prefers to capitalize only the first word and proper nouns (e.g. personal or place names) in titles of books and journals, e.g. *Tamhīd al-dalā'il wa-talkhīṣ al-awā'il* rather than *Tamhīd al-Dalā'il wa-Talkhīṣ al-Awā'il*. Authors wishing to capitalize 'important' words in the English fashion may do so if they wish, however, provided that form is consistently employed; this is often preferable for names of organizations.

11.7 **Aramaic**

Aramaic is a branch of the Semitic family of languages, especially the language of Syria used as a lingua franca in Southwest Asia from the sixth century BC. Later dividing into other varieties of languages, including Syriac and Mandaic, Aramaic and its derivations are represented in a variety of scripts, which are also used for Iranian and Altaic languages. Aramaic is one of the three languages in which the Bible was originally written.

11.8 **Armenian**

Armenian is a separate branch of the Indo-European language family. Classical Armenian, called Grabar, remains the ecclesiastical language of the Armenian Church; its distinctive thirty-six-letter script, created in the fifth century and with corresponding numerical values, remains the basis for the modern alphabet. Two mutually intelligible literary dialects—East and West Armenian—are spoken. East Armenian (the language of the ex-Soviet Armenia) has preserved the distribution of voiced and (unaspirated) voiceless stops in the classical language, but West Armenian (largely spoken by those Armenians in the West) has changed them round, so that *Petrosean* (*Petrosjan*) becomes *Bedrosean* (*Bedrossian*). When West Armenians transliterate from other languages they spell according to their own pronunciation, so that the classical or East Armenian *Venetik* becomes *Venedig*.

There are two standard transliteration systems: the Hübschmann–Meillet system (employed by the British Library) was devised for students of the classical language, and therefore follows the classical values; the Library of Congress system reflects West Armenian dialect, and distinguishes between East and West Armenian through the choice of different consonants.

In Hübschmann–Meillet the alphabet is ordered *a b g d e z ē ət' ž i l x c k h j
ł č m y n š o č' p ǰ r̂ s v t r c' w p' k' u ō f*. In the Library of Congress the
alphabet is ordered *a b/p g/k d/t e* (also *y*) *z ē ĕ t' zh i l kh ts/dz k/g h dz/ts gh ch/
j m y* (also *h*) *n sh o ch' p/b j/ch r̄ s v t/d r ts' w p' k' u ō f*. (West Armenian
alternatives follow the solidi.) The opening quotation mark or (preferably) asper follows the letter in both systems. A ligature (*ew̱*) may be
found, though separate letters are normally used.

11.9 Baltic languages

The Baltic languages Latvian and Lithuanian are written in the roman
alphabet, with the addition of diacritics to represent palatal consonants
and long vowels, such as *Rīga* ('Riga'), *Rīgā* ('at Riga'). The diacritics
used for Latvian are *ģ* (capital *Ģ*), *č, š, ž, ķ, ļ, ņ, ŗ, ā, ē, ī, ū*. (In recent
years *ǧ* has become widely used as an alternative for lower-case *ģ*.)
The subscript commas of *ķ, ļ, ņ* are often set as cedillas, so do not
change them on proof if they are consistent. The letters *ch* and *ŗ*
were abolished by the Soviet regime; since independence they have
not been reinstated uniformly, though their use by émigrés has continued uninterrupted. Alphabetize as *a b c č d e f g ģ h i j k ķ l ļ m n ņ o p r ŗ s š
t u v z ž*.

Lithuanian uses the diacritics *ė, č, š, ž, ą, ę, į, ų, ū*; the acute, grave, and
tilde are found in grammars but not in ordinary writing. Alphabetize as
ą c č e ę ė i į y s š u ų ū z ž, ignoring accents on vowels; the digraph *ch* is not
alphabetized separately. The letter *y* counts as *i*. Do not divide the
digraphs *dz, dž, ie, uo* in word breaks.

11.10 Basque

Basque (*Euskara* in Basque) is related to no known language, though it
contains at least some words from the Iberian spoken before the Romans came. The official regional language of the País Vasco (Spain) and
the Pays Basque (France), it is written in the roman alphabet. In standard
modern spelling the only accent used is the tilde on *ñ*; in earlier texts
one may find the acute on any vowel, or on *ŕ*, the grave on any vowel, the
tilde on *ã, ĩ, s̃, t̃*, and the umlaut on *ü*; some sources also distinguish *ll* and
tt from *l* and *t*.

11.11 **Burmese**

Burmese, a Sino-Tibetan language, is written left to right using the Burmese alphabet; spaces do not separate words, and punctuation is normally limited to ၊ (comma or semicolon) and ॥ (full point). The Library of Congress romanization system uses the diacritics ṅ, ḍ, ḷ, ṃ, ṇ, ṭ, ā, ī, ū, ñ; special characters are ' (*hamza*), ' (' *ayin*), ' (prime), and " (double prime). The ordering of consonants in Burmese can vary, though the order of vowels (*a ā i ī u ū e ai o ui*) is standard.

11.12 **Catalan**

11.12.1 **General**

Catalan is now at least on a par with Castilian in Catalonia, where it is the official regional language; it is also the official regional language of Roussillon in France, as well as the official language of Andorra.

Although Catalan was already the official language of the Kingdom of Aragon in the twelfth century, the modern language was standardized only in the early twentieth century: certain features mark it off both from other Iberian languages and from its own earlier literature, such as the use of *-i* as the theme-vowel in the present subjunctive, for which the other languages have *-e* in *-ar* verbs and *-a* in *-er* and *-ir* verbs.

11.12.2 **Alphabet**

The digraph *ll* (called *ella*) has the same value as in Castilian; it is extremely common, being the normal reflex of Latin initial *l-* as well as *-ll-*. However, it is not treated as a separate letter; nor are *ny* (called *enya*, corresponding to ñ) and the modified letter *c* (*ce trencada*).

To *c, g, c, j, qu, gu* before *a, o, u* correspond *qu, gu, c, g, qü, gü* before *e, i*; thus the plural of *boca* 'mouth', *pasqua* 'Easter' is *boques, pasqües*; in contrast to Castilian and Portuguese, *j* in the root is similarly changed, so that *pluja* 'rain' makes *pluges*, and *pujar* 'to rise' makes *puges* 'you (singular) rise', subjunctive *pugi* '(that) I/he rise'. However, *je* is found in a few words, for example *jeure* 'to lie (opposed to stand)'.

Except in *ny*, Catalan does not use *y* outside certain proper nouns. In learned words, Latin or Greek *ll* is represented by *l·l* (*il·legal, metàl·lic*).

Like Portuguese, Catalan (but not Valencian) retains the distinction between voiced and unvoiced sibilants; to voiceless *s* (initial)/*ss* (medial) and *x* correspond voiced *z* (initial)/*s* (medial) and *j*. Some masculine nouns ending in -*s* make their plural in -*ssos*, others in -*sos* (feminines, and masculines not stressed on the final syllable, have no separate plural form). Catalan never had that distinction between *c*, *z* and *ss*, *s*, and therefore writes *Saragossa* for Castilian *Zaragoza*, from the medieval *Çaragoça*.

After a vowel other than *i*, the [ʃ] sound of English *sh* is represented by *ix*, the *i* not being separately pronounced (*baix*, feminine *baixa* 'low', plural *baixos*, *baixes*). In the same circumstances in a stressed final syllable *ig* represents the [tʃ] sound of English *ch*, but changes on inflection to *j* before *a* and *g* or *tg* before *e*: *roig*, 'red' (feminine *roja*, plural *roijs*, *roges*); *lleig* 'ugly' (feminine *lletja*, plural *lleigs*, *lletges*); similarly *mig* 'half', pronounced [mitʃ]. In other circumstances, [ʃ] is written *x* and [tʃ] *tx*.

The group *tll* represents a long *ll* sound (*batlle*, 'mayor'). Before *m*, Catalan writes *com-* (when not reduced to *co-*), *im-*; not *con-*, *in-* as in Castilian and Galician: Catalan *commoció*, Castilian and Galician *conmoción*, Portuguese *comoção*. *B* and *v* are distinguished in some parts of Catalonia, though not in Barcelona.

Object pronouns follow the imperative, infinitive, and gerund; they are attached by a hyphen when they contain a vowel, by an apostrophe when they do not: *creu-me* 'believe me', *creu-nos* 'believe us', but *creure'm* 'to believe me', *anem's-en* 'let us go away'.

The apostrophe is also used before a vowel or *h* in object pronouns preceding the verb, in the preposition *d'* for *de*, and usually in the definite article *l'*, corresponding to *el* masculine and *la* feminine before a consonant; but *el* is retained before a rising diphthong (*el iode* 'iodine', *el hiatus*) and *la* before unstressed (*h*)*i* (*h*)*u* (*la idea*, *la hipotenusa*, *la unió*, *la humanitat*), and in certain cases where the vowels are pronounced separately: *a*- as a negative prefix (*la asimetria*, to avoid confusion with *la simetria*), *la una* 'one o'clock', *la ira* 'wrath', *la host*, 'the host (large number)', *la e i la o* 'the E and the O'. Contrariwise, since initial *s* plus consonant in modern loanwords is pronounced as if it were *es*, 'the snob' is *l'snob*.

11.12.3 Accents

Catalan uses the following accents on vowels to indicate stress, vowel quality, or hiatus: the acute on *e*, *i*, *o*, *u*, the grave on *a*, *e*, *o*, and the diaeresis on *i* and *u*. Words ending in a vowel, or vowel +-*s*, or in -*en* -*in*, have normal stress on the penultimate, others on the final syllable. They take an accent only when a weak vowel capable of forming a diphthong with its neighbour does not do so, and is stressed.

Words with abnormal stress take the grave on *a*, open *e*, and open *o*, the acute on closed *e*, *i*, closed *o*, and *u*. The plural of *caràcter règim* is *caràcters règims*, without change of stress. Diphthongs ending in a weak vowel are held to be falling, and in a final syllable attract normal stress (*canteu* 'you (plural) sing').

A word ending in a consonant followed by a weak vowel itself followed by a strong vowel, strong vowel + *s*, or *-en*, *-in* has normal stress on the weak vowel (*vivia*, *vivies*, *vivien*, but *vivíem*, *vivíeu* with abnormal stress). The accent is written when the stress falls earlier, e.g. *acadèmia*. When three vowels of which the second is weak and the third strong stand together, these two are presumed to form a rising diphthong: *teia* 'torch' with normal stress on the penultimate *te*; *veia* 'I saw' (imperfect), *vèiem* 'we saw'. When a weak vowel capable of forming a diphthong with a neighbouring vowel does not do so, it is written, if unstressed, with a diaeresis (*traïdor* 'traitor', *lloï* '(that) I/he praise', subjunctive). If stressed, then if (given the separate syllables) the stress is normal it is indicated with the diaeresis, if not, with the acute. Thus 'I was pleasing' is *plaïa*, 'we were pleasing' *plaíem*; similarly, the plural of *país* 'country' is *països*. There are, however, exceptions: the suffixes *-isme*, *-ista* do not take the diaeresis (*egoisme*, *panteista*); no diaeresis is used after a prefix (*coincidir*) or in post-tonic syllables (*Màrius*); in verbs in *-uir*, the diaeresis is suppressed in the infinitive (*-uir*), future indicative (*-uiré* etc.), conditional (*-uiria* etc.), and gerund (*-uint*), but added in other forms, e.g. past participle *-uït* (feminine *-uïda*, plural *-uïts*, *-uïdes*), second-person plural present indicative *-uïu*, imperfect *-uïa*.

In the strong forms, verbs in *-iar*, *-uar* are stressed on the *-i* and *-u*; inflectional *i* takes a diaeresis (*canviï*, *evacuï*).

A following object pronoun, whether attached by a hyphen or an apostrophe, has no effect on the spelling of the verb (*posa* 'put', *posa-me-n'hi* 'put some there for me', *compri* 'buy' (polite imperative), *compri'ls* 'buy them').

Adverbs in *-ment* retain a written accent (*ràpidament*). When two adverbs come together, it is the second, not the first, that may lose the suffix; but this is not compulsory.

Contrastive accents are used on words such as *déus* (gods) ~ *deus* (springs), *dóna* (gives) ~ *dona* (woman), *dónes* (you (singular) give) ~ *dones* (women), *féu* (he did) ~ *feu* (you (plural) do), *nós* (we) ~ *nos* (us), *ròssa*, plural *ròsses* (nag) ~ *rossa*, plural *rosses* (blonde), *sí* (yes) ~ *si* (if).

11.12.4 **Word division**

Take over *ll*, but divide *l·l* as *l|l*; take over *ny*, but divide *rr*, *ss*, and other consonant groups (including *tj, tll, tx, tz*) except *b, c, f, g, p* + *l* or *r*, and *dr*, *tr*. Divide *ix* pronounced [ʃ] after the silent *i* (*bai-xos*). Divide compounds: *nos|altres*. Hyphens are not repeated at the start of a new line.

11.12.5 **Punctuation**

The inverted question and exclamation marks are not used.

11.12.6 **Miscellaneous**

The normal polite form of address in urban usage is *vostè*, plural *vostès*, with the third person; but *vós* with the second-person plural may also be used as a polite singular, the plural then being *vosaltres* as in familiar address.

Nouns in *c* or *x* take *-os* in the plural if masculine and stressed on the last syllable, otherwise simply *-s*: so for example *índexs* and the feminines *falcs* 'scythes', *esfinxs* 'sphinxes'.

The 'personal *a*' is incorrect except before an emphatic pronoun, in the expression *l'un a l'altre* 'each other', and after the comparative conjunctions *com* and *que*.

There is no future subjunctive; the *-ra* form, formerly used as in Castilian, is the regular imperfect subjunctive in Valencian but in Catalan proper is now confined to the alternative conditionals *fóra* etc. beside *seria* 'I should be' and *haguera* etc. beside *hauria* 'I should have'.

Haver is used with the past participle to form compound tenses; when the direct object is a non-reflexive pronoun of the third person the participle agrees with it (*l'he vist* 'I have seen him', *l'he vista* 'I have seen her'). But *aquesta cançó, l'he sentit cantar*, 'I have heard this song sung', since *l'* is the object of *cantar*; contrast *l'he sentida cantar*, 'I have heard her sing'.

The very frequent compound tense *vaig cantar* is not a future like French *je vais chanter*, but a preterite, 'I sang'.

For a list of quick identifiers for Iberian languages *see* **11.42.3**.

11.13 **Celtic languages**

The Celtic languages fall into two main groups, Q-Celtic or Goidelic and P-Celtic (Brythonic and the extinct Gaulish), according to whether

Indo-European *qu* was retained or converted into *p* (Indo-European *p* is lost in all Celtic). All these languages are notable for the changes ('mutations') made to initial consonants, and the prefixes added to initial vowels, in certain syntactical relations: the details differ from language to language, era to era, and dialect to dialect, but it should be noted that in four of the six languages 'his' and 'her' (in Irish also 'their') can be distinguished only by their effect on the following noun.

11.13.1 Brythonic: Cornish, Breton, and Welsh (for Welsh *see* 11.45)

Cornish (*Kernowek*) and Breton (*Brezoneg*) are closer to each other than to Welsh (*Cymraeg*). Cornish died out in the eighteenth century but has been revived with a grammar based on the medieval literature and a standardized spelling in which long vowels are sometimes marked in linguistic work by the long mark or the circumflex, and fronted *u* as *ü*. (Formerly the letter *y* was always used rather than *i*, but this is no longer the case.) In contrast to Welsh, there is no *ll* or *rh*, and *w* is not a vowel; *dh* is used for the voiced sound of Welsh *dd* (in the authentic texts *th* is used, but this is now only the voiceless sound as it is in Welsh), *f* and *v* correspond respectively to Welsh *ff* and *f*, *gh* or *h* to *ch* (Cornish *ch* has the English sound, and becomes *j* when lenited), *qu* in loanwords to *cw*, *wh* to Welsh *chw*; *k* is used before *e*, *n*, *y* and at the end of the syllable, *c* before *a*, *h*, *l*, *o*, *r*, *u*, and with the /s/ sound before *e*, *y* in loanwords.

Breton, though generally discouraged by the French authorities, continues to be spoken and written. The letter *c* is used only in *ch* (= French *ch*, English *sh*) and *c'h*, which count as separate letters between *b* and *d*; *q* and *x* are not used. Accented characters additional to those found in French are *ñ*, *ü*, though not all used by all writers; note too the initial *'f*.

11.13.2 Goidelic: Irish, Scots Gaelic, Manx

All three are known to their speakers as 'Gaelic' (Irish *Gaeilge*, before 1947 *Gaedhilge*, Scots Gaelic *Gàidhlig*, Manx *Gailck*, or *Gaelg*); in English the normal terms are as given, except that the Scots form is frequently called 'Gaelic' (pronounced 'gallic'; with Irish reference 'gaylic'); 'Scots' by itself refers to Scottish varieties of English. The name 'Erse'—properly a Scots form of 'Irish'—was formerly used of Scots Gaelic, and sometimes of Irish; it may now be regarded as obsolete.

Both Irish and Scots Gaelic are written in an eighteen-letter alphabet (with no *j*, *k*, *q*, *v*, *w*, *x*, *y*, *z*, except in some modern loanwords); in Irish the lower-case *i* is sometimes left undotted. The orthography of both languages is based on twelfth-century Irish pronunciation, though Irish underwent a mild reform in 1947. Manx spelling, known to us mainly from seventeenth- and eighteenth-century documents, is impressionistically based on English sound values and orthographical conventions.

Until the mid-twentieth century, Irish (but not Scots Gaelic) was often written and printed in insular script, in which the modification of consonants known as lenition or aspiration, expressed in roman script (as also in Scots Gaelic) by adding *h* after the mutated letter, was indicated instead by placing a dot on it, which unlike the *h* was ignored in alphabetization. This represented a standardization of earlier usage, in which either method was employed indiscriminately; in the modified insular script occasionally used for display purposes, *h* may be used as in roman spelling.

Irish marks vowel length with an acute accent (*á, é, í, ó, ú*); Scottish also uses the grave (*à, è, ì, ò, ù*). A special character in Irish, the undotted 'i' (*ı*), was sometimes used instead of normal *i* as more distinct from *í* and closer in character to Gaelic script. Both *ı* and *i* should not be found together. Scots Gaelic makes greater use of the apostrophe: note especially that even a single sentence may, and an extended passage will, contain both *a*—variously 'his', 'her', 'from', the relative particle, or the vocative particle—and *a'* ('the' before *bh, ch, dh, gh, mh*, or the equivalent of '-ing' with a verb beginning with a consonant). In Manx, *ch* (= English *ch*) is distinguished from *çh* (aspirated *c*); in some texts the circumflex will be found on *a, e*, and *o*. However, since the language is now restricted mostly to summarizing the Acts of the Manx parliament, and spelling varies considerably between texts, there is little point in going into further detail here.

In Irish, the mutation known as eclipsis is indicated by writing the sound actually pronounced before the consonant modified: *mb, gc, nd, bhf, ng, bp, dt*; if the noun is a proper name, it retains its capital, the prefixed letter(s) being lower case: *i mBaile Átha Cliath* 'in Dublin', *bliain na bhFrancach* (previously *bliadhain na bhFranncach*) 'the year of the French' (1798). The same combination of initial lower-case letter followed by a capital occurs when *h* or *n* is prefixed to a name beginning with a vowel: *go hÉirinn* 'to Ireland', *Tír na nÓg* 'the Land of the Young', or *t* is prefixed to a vowel or *S*: *an tAigéan Atlantach* 'the Atlantic Ocean', *an tSionnain* 'Shannon'. Before lower-case vowels, *h* is prefixed directly (*na hoíche* 'of the night'), as is *t* before *s* (*an tsráid* 'the street'), but *n* and *t* take a hyphen before a vowel (*in-áit* 'in a place', *an t-uisce* 'the water'). In standard Scots Gaelic, eclipsis is not found with consonants (though it is heard in dialects); prefixed *h-, n-,* and *t-* always take the hyphen: *an t-sràid* 'the street', *Ar n-Athair* 'Our Father', *na h-oidhche* 'of the night', *an t-Òban* 'Oban' (literally 'the Bay'), *Mac an t-Saoir* 'McIntyre' (literally 'son of the carpenter').

11.14 **Chinese**

11.14.1 **Characters and language**

The forms of Chinese spoken in areas occupied by those of Chinese origin differ so widely from one another that many may be deemed to constitute languages in their own right. The principal dialects are Northern Chinese (Pekinese, Mandarin), Cantonese, Hakka, the Wu dialect of Soochow, and the dialect of Min (Fukien). All of these, however, share a common written language consisting of thousands of separate ideographs or 'characters'—the K'ang-hsi dictionary of 1716 contained over 40,000—of which approximately 7,000 are still in regular use. Side by side with modern colloquial Chinese there has existed a language used for the compilation of official documents totally unlike the spoken language—as is the language in which the classic texts of Chinese literature are expressed. For this, also, the same script is adopted.

The structure of individual ideographs can sometimes be very complicated in script, involving the use of as many as twenty-eight separate strokes of the brush or pen. A code of simplified characters is in use on the mainland, but more traditional forms are found in Hong Kong, Taiwan, Singapore, and areas beyond Chinese jurisdiction.

The language is monosyllabic, one ideograph representing a syllable. The syllables are morphemic and some ideographs will be both morphemes and words. Each ideograph is pronounced in a particular inflection of voice, or 'tone'. The National Language uses four separate tones, Cantonese, nine. The National Language is derived from the pronunciation of North China (notably that of the Peking area), which has traditionally been adopted for the transaction of official business—hence the term 'Mandarin', which is sometimes used to categorize it. Alternative names for it are *putonghua* ('speech in common use') or *Kuo-yü* (otherwise *Guoyu*, 'National Language').

11.14.2 **Romanization**

Two romanization systems are currently and commonly in use for the purpose of rendering the National Language: the earlier Wade–Giles and Pinyin. It is desirable to indicate the tone when transcribing; of these, the Pinyin system particularly lends itself to this purpose (though typographically there is the problem of adding the tone mark over the umlaut in the case of the syllable *nü*). Other romanization systems are in less frequent use, notably the Gwoyeu Romatzyh system (GR for short), formerly the official system in Taiwan, which builds the tone into the transcription. Use only one system in a given work. However, if Pinyin is adopted it is permissible to add earlier spellings in parentheses for clarification: *Zhou (Chou)*, *Qing (Ch'ing)*. Some writers prefer not to impose Pinyin retroactively, using the earlier spelling in referring to persons no longer living and Pinyin in the case of the living.

Wade–Giles dates from 1859. Although by current standards somewhat unscientific and unrepresentative of actual pronunciation, this system is still in common use in the production of English-language texts in English-speaking countries. It incorporates certain modifications (the accents *ê*, *ŭ*, and *ü*) to differentiate vowel pronunciation, for example *tsu* and *tzŭ*. The asper ' (frequently replaced by an apostrophe) indicates aspiration in consonants, for example *chên* and *ch'ên*. (Even apostrophes are often omitted in newspapers and non-specialist works, which can lead to ambiguity when converting from one system of transcription to another.) Hyphens are used as syllabic dividers for personal and geographical names. In strict romanization, tone difference can be indicated by the use of a superscript figure [1] [2] [3] or [4], in older texts also [5], following most syllables; toneless syllables may be followed by [0], or left unmarked.

Pinyin was perfected in 1958 and has been in official use in China since 1979. Combinations of characters that have a single meaning when translated into English are transcribed to form a single word, for example *Zhongguo* (China) in contrast to the Wade–Giles *Chung-kuo*.

In strict romanization, the superscript accents ˉ ´ ˇ ` are used to indicate tone over any of the vowels *a*, *e*, *i*, *o*, *u*, and *ü*: contrast *Hanshi wenxian leimu* (without tone markers) and *Hànshǐ wénxiàn lèimù* (with indication of tone). An apostrophe, with no space either side, is used to mark syllabic divisions, which is necessary when a syllable beginning with *a*, *o*, or *e* occurs in the middle of a polysyllabic word, for example *ke'ai* 'lovable', *dang'an* 'archive'.

The *Chicago Manual of Style*, and several websites, have tables for the conversion of Wade–Giles into Pinyin, and vice versa, though these should be used only by those with specialist knowledge.

Although Chinese characters are almost always romanized as if the language of origin is the National Language, it might rarely prove necessary to reproduce a dialect form. With the possible exception of Cantonese, there are almost no standards for scholars to achieve this.

11.14.3 Capitalization

In an English sentence, practice largely follows the standard adopted for European languages, with non-assimilated expressions italicized and in lower case. Names of institutions, schools of thought and religions, etc. are set in roman if they are capitalized or in italics if they are lower-case.

11.14.4 Italicization

Chinese words assimilated into English usage—e.g. 'dim sum', 'kowtow', 'kung fu'—are not italicized, and the vowels carry no tone marks in non-specialist contexts. Proper nouns are italicized only when they would be so treated in English, for example in titles of books and periodicals, films and plays, works of art, ships, and legal cases.

11.14.5 Chinese characters in English text

In producing specialist texts it may be necessary to provide Chinese characters to follow the romanized version of the item they represent. It is normal for typesetters in the West to treat each character as a special sort for the purpose of setting, either accessing the characters from an author's disk (if the characters have been correctly achieved) and inserting them as print-ready copy at proof stage, or sending the relevant copy to a specialist typesetter for setting. If print-ready copy is to be supplied, the editor should ensure that it is of sufficient clarity for the characters to be legible when reduced to text size. Where sufficient reduction is impossible, the relevant lines may need to be set with extra leading to fit in the characters.

It has nowadays become the practice to provide a separate glossary of Chinese terms, arranged in alphabetical order by romanization, that juxtaposes the Chinese characters with the term they depict. This procedure clarifies any problems in romanization, and avoids the necessity of inserting Chinese characters into running text.

11.15 **Dutch and Afrikaans**

Dutch, the language of the Netherlands, belongs to the West Germanic branch of Indo-European languages; it is also the official language of Suriname and the Netherlands Antilles. The Dutch spoken in northern Belgium, formerly called Flemish, is now officially called Dutch (*Neder-lands* in Dutch): Flemish (*Vlaams*) refers only to dialect, Walloon (*Wallon*) only to patois. Afrikaans is one of the official languages of South Africa, and was derived from the Dutch brought to the Cape by settlers in the seventeenth century, combined with French, Malay, and Khoisan languages.

11.15.1 **Dutch**

Alphabet

The alphabet is the same as English, but *q* and *x* are used only in borrowed foreign words. Formerly the combination IJ, *ij* (which developed out of *Ÿ*, *ÿ*) was represented by the one-piece sort IJ, *ij*; this is no longer the case even in Dutch setting, though the letters should be kerned to avoid awkward space between them, and the pair is not separated in letter spacing. In dictionaries *ij* precedes *ik*; in directories and encyclopedias it is sometimes treated as equivalent to *y*; do not follow this usage in English indexes except for books on historical topics in which both spellings may occur. The apostrophe is used in such plurals as *pagina's* 'pages', but not before *s* in the genitive.

Accents

The acute is used to distinguish *één* ('one') from *een* ('a'), and *vóór* ('before') from *voor* ('for'). Otherwise the only accent required—except in foreign loanwords—is the diaeresis: *knieën* 'knees', *provinciën* 'provinces', *zeeën* 'seas', *zeeëend* 'scoter, sea-duck'. Double consonants are not used at the end of words: *stuk* 'piece', but plural *stukken*; double vowels in closed syllables correspond to single vowels in open: *deel* 'part', plural *delen*. In titles and matter quoted from before 1948, double vowels will be found where modern Dutch has single vowels, for example *Mededeelingen* 'communications'; *-sch* (as in *Nederlandsch*) for modern *-s*; and *ph* for *f*. Hence if the title of a periodical appears to be inconsistently spelt, check the dates of the issues before intervening. Early texts may have *ae* for modern *aa*, *oe* for modern *oo* as well as modern *oe*, *ck* for modern *k* or *kk*, and *gh* for modern *g*.

Division of words

Compound words should be broken into their constituent parts; prefixes should be kept together, as should the suffixes *-aard*, *-aardig*, *-achtig*, and all those beginning with a consonant. This applies to the diminutive suffix *-je*, but note that a preceding *t* may itself be part of the suffix: *kaartje* 'ticket', but *paar-tje* 'couple'. Otherwise take over single consonants; the combinations *ch*, *sj*, *tj* (which represent single sounds) and *sch*; and consonant + *l* or *r* in loanwords. In other cases take over the second of two consonants (including the *g* of *ng* and the *t* of *st*), but when more than three come together take over as many as can begin a word. Do not divide double vowels or *ei*, *eu*, *ie*, *oe*, *ui*, *aai*, *eei*, *ieu*, *oei*, *ooi*.

Punctuation

Punctuation is less strict than in, for example, German. Capitals are used for the polite *U*, *Gij* 'you' and *Uw* 'your', for terms indicating nationality

(*Engelsman, Engels*), and for adjectives derived from proper nouns, but not for days or months; in institutional names capitalize all words except prepositions and articles. This practice is often followed for books and periodicals: if copy is consistent it need not be altered, but otherwise impose minimum capitalization as used in official bibliographies. The abbreviated forms of *des* and *het* ('s and 't respectively) take a space on either side except in the case of towns and cities, where a hyphen follows ('s-*Gravenhage*). When a word beginning with an apostrophe starts a sentence, it is the *following* word that takes the capital: 't Is.

11.15.2 Afrikaans

Alphabet, accents, and spelling

There is no *ij* in Afrikaans, *y* being used as in older Dutch; *s* is used at the start of words where Dutch has *z*, and *w* between vowels often where Dutch has *v*. The circumflex is quite frequent; the grave is used on paired conjunctions (*èn...èn* 'both...and', *nòg...nòg* 'neither...nor', *òf...òf* 'either...or') and a few other words; the acute is found in the demonstrative *dié* to distinguish it from the article *die*, and in certain proper nouns and French loanwords. Dutch *zeeëend* is Afrikaans *see-eend*, Dutch *zeeën* Afrikaans *seë* (as distinguished from *seën* 'bless', 'blessing' = respectively Dutch *zegenen, zegen*); but after a *stressed* final *ie* an -*ë* is added: *knieë*. There is no diaeresis with *ae* (*dae* 'days'), since these letters never form a digraph for a single sound.

Since Afrikaans was not generally used in writing till the 1920s, books on early twentieth-century South Africa may quote the same phrases first in Dutch and then in Afrikaans. Word division is largely on Dutch lines, but division according to pronunciation is tolerated.

Capitalization

As in Dutch, when a word beginning with an apostrophe starts a sentence in Afrikaans, the following word is capitalized. This rule is of great importance, since the indefinite article is written '*n*: thus '*n Man het gekom* 'A man has come'. The pronoun *ek* 'I' is not capitalized; otherwise capitalization, in general and in titles of books, matches English practice.

11.16 Egyptian

Egyptian is the language of ancient Egypt up to the time of the Muslim conquest, after which it was replaced by Arabic. Sometimes called Ancient Egyptian to differentiate it from the Arabic of present-day Egypt, it consists of four main forms: Hieroglyphic, a system based on pictographs; Hieratic, a form of abridged hieroglyphics used by priests; Demotic, a simplified, cursive script; and Coptic, which survives as the liturgical language of the Coptic Church.

Hieroglyphic could be written from right to left, left to right, or top to bottom in columns; the Hieratic and Demotic scripts, both derived from hieroglyphs, were written only from right to left. In transliteration Hieratic and Demotic use ś, ḥ ḳ (or q), ḏ (or dj), ẖ (or ch), ṯ (or tš), š (or sh), ḫ (or kh), ḥ̂. The ś and z of Old Egyptian (the language of Old Kingdom texts) coalesced in the Middle Kingdom as s; at a slower pace ḏ was absorbed by d, and ṯ by t.

Special characters are *hamza* ꜣ (capital) and ꜣ (lower case) (sometimes approximated in typescript by a 3), and *'ayn* ꜥ (capital) and ꜥ (lower case) (sometimes approximated in typescript by a 9), 'I i̇ (*aleflenis* combined with I and i, often called the 'lenis-i'). The Ancient Egyptian *alef* and *'ayn* are both larger than the corresponding Arabic characters, and have capital and lower-case forms: ꜥ ꜥ ꜣ ꜣ 'I i̇.

In scholarly works, suffixes known or thought to be derived from independent words are appended by a medial (raised) point: *sḏm·tw·f* (Old Egyptian *śḏm·tw·f*) 'he is heard'. A full point is often substituted in typescript, and even in printing. A hyphen is used only in compounds such as *'Imn-ḥtp* 'Amenhotep' (or better 'Amenhotpe'), literally 'Amun is pleased'.

Nouns and verbs are separated from suffixes by an equals sign, which is often angled. Some writers use a full point instead of an equals sign, and do not mark roots and endings.

The Coptic alphabet, adopted from Greek, is written left to right. In transliteration, Coptic has the digraphs *kh*, *ks*, *ph*, *ps*, and *th*, and the diacritics ḏ, ē, ḥ, k̄, m̄, ñ, ō, ô, r̄, and š.

11.17 **Esperanto**

Esperanto is an artificial universal language invented by Lazarus Ludwig Zamenhof in 1887. It uses the accents ŭ, ĉ, ĝ, ĥ, ĵ, and ŝ. When alphabetizing they fall in the order *c ĉ g ĝ h ĥ j ĵ s ŝ u ŭ*.

11.18 **Estonian**

Estonia having been ruled in turn by Sweden and Russia, Estonian has been heavily dominated and influenced by the languages of these two countries. Estonian uses the roman alphabet with the following accents: č, š, ž (used for foreign words only), õ, ä, ö, ü; these are alphabetized as s š z ž t u v õ ä ö ü (earlier and in Swedish printing ü ä ö õ). The status of č is problematic, with tš often being used to replace it.

11.19 **Finnish**

While Finnish began to be written in the sixteenth century, its status as a national language dates only from 1863, Swedish being previously used. It is set in ordinary roman characters with the accented letters å, š (both used for foreign words only), ä, and ö. In alphabetizing, w is not treated as distinct from v; the order is å ä ö after z. A text with y and yy will be Finnish, and one with ü and üü will be Estonian. Both Finnish and Estonian have long words, doubled vowels, and doubled consonants, but if in any but a very short text the only final consonants are n, s, or t, the language will be Finnish.

11.20 **French**

11.20.1 **Abbreviations**

Such words as *article, chapitre, scène, titre, figure* are abbreviated only when in parentheses, as references; in the text they are set in full. Retain the hyphen when a hyphenated form is abbreviated: *J.-C.* (Jésus-Christ), *J.-J. Rousseau* (Jean-Jacques Rousseau), *P.-S.* (post-scriptum).

When *saint* and *sainte* occur very often, as with names in religious works, they may be abbreviated, taking a capital letter: *S. Louis, Ste Marie.* But in place names, surnames, names of feast days, etc. capital letters and hypens are used (*Saint-Germain-des-Prés, Saint-Domingue, Sainte-Beuve, la Saint-Jean*). Properly these are not abbreviated, but in gazetteers and guide books one may find e.g. *St-Germain, Ste-Catherine, St-Hilaire, la St-Jean, l'église St-Sulpice.*

A full point is not placed after a contraction (i.e. when the last letter of the word and the last letter of the contraction are the same): *St, Ste, Mme, Mlle*, etc.

When not followed by a proper noun the words *monsieur, messieurs, madame*, *mesdames*, *monseigneur*, *messeigneurs*, *mademoiselle*, and *mesdemoiselles* are written in full and all in lower case:

> Oui, madame. Non, monsieur le duc. J'espère que monseigneur viendra. J'ai vu monsieur votre père.

Initial capitals are used before names: *M.* (for *monsieur*), *Mme* (for *madame*), *Mgr* (for *monseigneur*). When followed by another title the words *Sa Majesté* (*S. M.*), *Son Éminence* (*S. É.* or *S. Ém.*), *Leurs Altesses* (*LL. AA.*) are abbreviated as initials, thus *S. M. l'Empereur*; but not otherwise.

When a first name is abbreviated in a French text, if the second letter of the name is an *h*, the *h* is retained, hence *Th. Gautier* (Théophile Gautier), *Ch. Mauron* (Charles Mauron). This style need not be followed in books not printed wholly in French.

The name *Jésus-Christ* is abbreviated only immediately following a date: *337 avant J.-C.* This is sometimes printed *337 av. J.-C.*

Some common examples of abbreviations in French:

abrév.	abréviation	l.c.	loc. cit. (Lat.)
apr.	après	liv.	livre
av.	avant	M.	monsieur
c.-à-d.	c'est-à-dire	Me, M^e	maître
chap.	chapitre	Mlle, Mlle	mademoiselle
Cie, Cie	compagnie	MM.	messieurs
conf.	confer (Lat.)	Mme, Mme	madame
d^o	dito	ms.	manuscrit
Dr	docteur	mss.	manuscrits
éd.	édition	n^o	numéro
etc.	et cætera	p.	page
ex.	exemple	p., pp.	pages
f^o	folio	P.-S.	post-scriptum
Ier, 1er	premier	qqch	quelque chose
IIe, 2e, IIème, 2ème	deuxième	qqn	quelqu'un
ill.	illustration	s., ss., suiv.	suivant
in-4°	in-quarto	s.d.	sans date
in-8°	in-octavo	s.l.	sans lieu
inéd.	inédit	t.	tome
in-f^o	in-folio	v.	voyez, voir
in pl.	in plano (Lat.)	Vve	veuve

11.20.2 Diacritics

The acute (´) is used only over *e*; when two *es* come together the first always has an acute accent, as in *née*. The grave (`) is used over *a*, *e*, *u*; the circumflex (ˆ) is used over any vowel. The cedilla c (ç) is used only before *a*, *o*, *u*. The diaeresis is found on *i* (*naïf*, *ouï-dire*); it is also used on *e* and *y*, in the seventeenth century quite often, but still now in such words as *aiguë*, *ambiguë*, in the classical river *le Caÿstre*, and in the name of the writer Pierre Louÿs. Do not separate the digraph formed by the combination of *o* and *e*.

OUP retains all accents on capital letters. Although there is no uniformity of practice in France, there is a consensus on retaining accents for the letter E: *Étienne*, *Étretat*. The letter *A*, when a capital standing for *à*, is often not accented by French printers when beginning such lines as *A la porte de la maison, A cette époque*, and in full-capital display lines:

HÔTEL A CÉDER

MACHINES A VAPEUR

In all-capital lines accents should be printed: *DÉPÔT, ÉVÊQUE,* and *PRÉ-VÔT*. Small capitals, where used, are accented in the same way as full capitals.

Occitan, the medieval or modern language of Languedoc, includes literary Provençal of the twelfth to fourteenth centuries. It uses a generic spelling based on medieval orthography that can be accommodated to various dialects by assigning the appropriate sound values to letters. The Félibrige orthography, an attempt to represent the various modern dialects in a modified French spelling, uses the diacritics *á, é, í, ó, ú, à, è, ò, ï,* and *ç*.

11.20.3 Capital and lower case

General rules

French surnames beginning with the feminine article *La* take a capital: *La Fontaine, La Rochefoucauld*; but the masculine article *le* with the names of Italian writers and painters is written lower-case (*le Tasse, l'Arioste, le Corrège*—*Le Dante* for Dante follows a mistake sometimes made in Italian). Names beginning *de* or *de La* take lower case in the preposition, but *Du* and *Des* are found besides *du* and *des*. In the nineteenth century *de la* was found, but is now most often *de La*. (For more on French names *see* **4.2.5**.) In case of doubt, consult *Le Petit Larousse*. In place names the article has a lower-case initial (*le Mans, le Havre*) unless starting a sentence.

The first word of a title takes an initial capital letter (*Les Femmes savantes, Le Monde*). However, where an author prefers lower-case *l* for the definite article (*le, la, les*) beginning a title, this style can be adopted. The article is construed with the surrounding sentence: 'les *Femmes savantes* sont le chef-d'œuvre de Molière'. If a substantive in a title immediately follows *Le, La, Les*, it is also given a capital letter (*Les Précieuses ridicules*). If such a substantive is preceded by an adjective, this also is capitalized (*La Folle Journée*); if, however, the adjective follows, it is lower case (*L'Âge ingrat*). If the title begins with any other word than *le*, *la*, *les*, or an adjective, the words following are all in lower case unless they are proper nouns (*Un lâche*, *À la recherche du temps perdu*); so too if the title forms a sentence (*La guerre de Troie n'aura pas lieu*).

In titles of fables and dramatic works the names of the characters have capital initials (*Le Renard et les Raisins*; *Le Lion et le Rat*; *Marceau, ou les Enfants de la République*).

In catalogues or indexes having the first word(s) in parentheses after the noun starting the line, the first word transposed is capitalized (*Homme (Faiblesse de l')*, *Honneur (L')*, *Niagara (Les Chutes du)*); the same rule is followed if the words in parentheses are part of the title of a work (*Héloïse (La Nouvelle)*, *Mort (La Vie ou la)*).

In French usage *rue* is not capitalized in street names (*rue du Quatre Septembre*, *rue de Rivoli*, *rue Royale*). In English contexts, however, it is normal to capitalize *rue*.

Capitals

Use capital letters for words relating to God (*le Seigneur*, *l'Être suprême*, *le Très-Haut*, *le Saint-Esprit*), for religious festivals (*la Pentecôte*), for the pronoun *Elle* referring to *Votre Majesté* etc., for surnames and nicknames (*Louis le Grand*), and for honorary titles (*Son Éminence*, *Leurs Altesses*).

In enumerations, when each item commences a new line, a capital is put immediately after the ordinal figure:

> 1° L'Europe.
> 2° L'Asie, etc.

But when the enumeration is run on, lower-case letters are used (*1° l'Europe*, *2° l'Asie*).

Capitalize the planets and constellations (*la Terre*, *la Lune*, *Mars*, *le Bélier*—but *la terre*, *la lune* in everyday contexts), people of a nation (*les Anglais*, *les Français*), adjectives in geographical expressions (*la mer Rouge*, *le golfe Persique*); and the names of the cardinal points designating an extent of territory (*l'Amérique du Nord*, *aller dans le Midi*).

Capitalize historical events or periods, and people relating to them (*la Révolution*, *la Restauration*, *la Renaissance*, *l'Antiquité*, *la Réforme*, *les Anciens et les Modernes*). Capitalize names of streets, squares, public buildings, churches, etc. (*la rue des Mauvais-Garcons*, *la place de la Nation*, *la place Vendôme*, *la fontaine des Innocents*, *l'Opéra*, *l'Odéon*, *le Moulin-Rouge*). In names of institutions, public bodies, companies, associations, and religious, civil, or military orders, according to strict rules only the first element (or first element after the article) is capitalized: *l'Académie francaise* (but *la Comédie-Francaise*, *le Théâtre-Francais*, and *la Comédie-Italienne*), *la Légion d'honneur*, *le Conservatoire de musique*, *Association francaise de normalisation, Agence nationale pour l'emploi, Compagnie francaise des pétroles*. In practice this is less often followed, with capitalization following the English pattern.

Capitalize *église* when it denotes the Church as an institution (*l'Église catholique*) but not when relating to a building. Capitalize *état* when it designates the nation, the country, or the institution (*La France est un puissant État*, so too *coup d'État*); likewise, the word *Constitution* in its political sense (*La Constitution des États-Unis*).

Capitalize adjectives joined by hyphens to preceding nouns themselves with capitals (*Comédie-Francaise, Palais-Royal*), and trademarks and proprietary names (*un jupe en Tergal, un stylo Bic*), even when used generically.

Lower case

Use lower-case letters for the names of members of religious orders (*un carme* 'a Carmelite', *un templier* 'a Templar'), but the names of the orders themselves take capitals (*l'ordre des Carmes, l'ordre des Templiers*).

Use lower case for days of the week (*lundi, mardi*) and names of months (*juillet, août*), for the names of the cardinal points (*le nord, le sud*), for languages (*le swahili, l'italien*), and for adjectives derived from proper nouns (*la langue francaise, l'ère napoléonienne*).

Members of religious sects, adherents of political movements, and their derivative adjectives are lower-case (*calvinisme, calviniste, chrétien(ne), humaniste, jansénisme, janséniste, les musulmans, protestant(e), romantique, romantisme, socialisme, socialiste*). Note *les juifs* when considered as a religious group, but *les Juifs* when considered as a people; when in doubt prefer the capital.

Objects named from persons or places are lower-case (*un bec bunsen* 'a Bunsen burner', *un verre de champagne*), but *la Bourse* for the French stock exchange, named after the Bruges family Van der Burse.

Plays

The following rules relate to plays set wholly in French; extracts from French plays presented in English-language texts follow the rules for English plays. The dramatis personae at the head of scenes are set in spaced large capitals, and those not named are set in spaced small capitals:

SCÈNE V

TRIBOULET, BLANCHE, HOMMES,

FEMMES DU PEUPLE

In the dialogues use spaced small capitals for the names of speakers, and set them in the centre of the line. When stage directions and the asides are displayed, set them in smaller type, within the text measure; when they are run on in text they follow in italics. If the play is in verse, set directions and asides in parentheses over the words they refer to. If there are two stage directions in the same line, it is advisable to split the line:

> (Revenu sur ses pas.)
> Oublions-les! restons. —
> > (Il s'assied sur un banc.)
> > Sieds-toi sur cette pierre.

Directions not relating to any particular speaker are set, if short, full right:

> Celui que l'on croit mort n'est pas mort. — Le voici!   (Étonnement général.)

11.20.4 **Punctuation and spacing**

In general, French punctuation is rhetorical, not logical, and tends to be lighter than in English: for example, commas are often used where English would have colons or semicolons, and the comma is omitted before *et* in enumerations. However, the comma is more freely used than in English to set off an adverbial phrase at the beginning of a sentence: *Sur la rivière, on voyait un bateau.* Set a space of the line before as well as after a colon.

Dash

The following relates to text set wholly in French. French extracts presented in English-language texts follow rules for English dashes.

Dashes take a thin space before and after them. Unlike the English dash, they are never put close up to a word; similarly, they are never put after colons. They are used to indicate conversational matter in quotations, or to give more force to a point:

> Il avait un cœur d'or, — mais une tête folle; et vraiment, — je puis le dire, — il était d'un caractère très agréable.

They are also used, as in English, for parenthetical matter:

> Cette femme — étrangère sans doute — était très âgée.

Hyphen

Place names containing a medial article or the preposition *en* or *de* should have a hyphen between the component parts (*Saint-Germain-des-Prés, Saint-Valery-en-Caux, Lyons-la-Forêt*); but there is no hyphen between the introductory *le* or *la* and the noun in such names as *la Ferté-Milon, la Ferté-sous-Jouarre.*

Names of places, buildings, or streets to which one or more distinguishing words are added usually take hyphens: *Saint-Étienne du Mont, Vitry-le-Francois, rue du Faubourg-Montmartre, le Pont-Neuf, le Palais-Royal,* but *Hôtel des Monnaies*. Distinguish *Saint-Martin de Tours* (the church of St Martin situated at Tours) and *Saint-Martin-de-Laigle* (where the name of the church is the same as that of the parish in which it is—or was—situated). Composite place names are hyphenated, for example *Saint-Denis-de-la-Réunion*. The hyphen is optional, however, between the first name and the surname in street names: *rue Victor-Hugo* or *rue Victor Hugo*.

Hyphens are used to connect cardinal and ordinal numbers in words under 100 (*vingt-quatre, trois cent quatre-vingt-dix*). But when *et* joins two numbers no hyphen is used, e.g. *vingt et un, cinquante et un, vingt et unième*.

Certain classical names are regularly hyphenated, such as *Tite-Live, Quinte-Curce, Aulu-Gelle*; similarly *Jésus-Christ*. Some that were formerly hyphenated are no longer (*Marc Antoine, Marc Aurèle*).

Compounds of *né* are hyphenated (*nouveau-né, un artiste-né*).

Since 1932, compounds of *grand* with feminine nouns have been spelt with a hyphen: *grand-mère*, not *grand'mère*.

Quotation marks

Texts set wholly in French should use special quotation marks called *guillemets* (« »); these need not be used for French text in English-language books. Space of the line (sometimes a thin space) is inserted inside the guillemets, separating the marks from the matter they contain; most often there is space outside them as well. Spacing with, and direction of, guillemets differs in other languages.

A guillemet is repeated at the head of every subsequent paragraph belonging to the quotation. In conversational matter guillemets are sometimes put at the beginning and end of the remarks, and the individual utterances are denoted by a spaced dash. But it is more common to dispense with guillemets altogether, and to denote the speakers by a dash only.

If the » comes after *points de suspension* (see below), a thin space is put before it (although the French themselves regularly use the space of the line instead):

> La cour a décrété qu' « attendu l'urgence… »

If a passage is quoted in dialogue, the « is put before the dash:

> « —Demain, à minuit, nous sortirons enfin! »

Formerly, in tabular matter the » denoted an absent quantity or nil:

125	15	130	»
10	»	15	25

It does not indicate 'ditto', which may be indicated by an em rule. Where necessary, clarify the older practice, but do not perpetuate it except when repeating older conventions.

When a sentence contains a quotation, the punctuation mark at the end of the quotation is put before the », and the mark belonging to the sentence after (a comma follows close up to the closing guillemet):

« Prenez garde au chien! », lisait-on à l'entrée des maisons romaines.

If the matter quoted ends with a full point, and a comma follows in the sentence, the full point is suppressed:

« Le plus petit croquis vaut mieux qu'un long rapport », a dit Napoléon.

Also, if the point at the end of the quotation is a full point, and the sentence ends with a question or exclamation mark, the full point is suppressed:

Pourquoi a-t-il dit: « Je reviendrai » ?

When quotation and sentence end with the same punctuation mark, only the quotation is given the mark:

Quel bonheur d'entendre: « Je vous aime! »

Pourquoi a-t-il dit: « Qui sait? »

Il a dit: « Je viendrai. »

But if the punctuation at the end of the quotation differs from that of the sentence, both marks are included unless the sentence would take a full point:

Pourquoi a-t-il dit: « Quel grand malheur! » ?

but:

Il a dit: « Quel grand malheur! »

In a quotation within a quotation, the « must stand at the commencement of each line of the enclosed quotation:

On lit dans *le Radical*: « Une malheureuse erreur a été
commise par un de nos artistes du boulevard. Ayant à dire:
« Mademoiselle, je ne veux qu'un mot de vous! », il a fait
entendre ces paroles: « Mademoiselle, je ne veux qu'un
« mou de veau! »

When every line begins with a guillemet, put a thin space after the « commencing each line. Only one » is put at the end of two quotations ending simultaneously.

Spacing

No space precedes, but a space always follows, the *points de suspension*, which are three points set close together (...), denoting an interruption or a rhetorical pause. Ensure that they are distinguished from 'editorial' ellipses, which are spaced and (where necessary) placed within square brackets. Use a thin space before (or after) section marks, daggers, and double daggers. Any asterisks and superior figures referring to notes usually take a thin space before them where they are not enclosed in parentheses. For guillemets see above.

A space follows an apostrophe coming after a word of two or more syllables (*Bonn' petite, Aimabl' enfant!*).

Spaces are put in figures such as *10 h 15 min 10 s* (10 hours 15 min. 10 sec.); formerly this was also printed *10^h 15^{min} 10^s*.

11.20.5 **Word division**

Words should be divided according to spoken syllables, as in what the French call *épellation* (i.e. syllabification), and in only a few cases according to etymology. A single consonant always goes with the following vowel (*amou|reux, cama|rade*), *ch, dh, gn, ph, th*, and groups consisting of consonant + *r* or + *l* counting as single consonants for this purpose (*mé|chant, Prou|dhon, ca|gneux, nénu|phar, Doro|thée, pa|trie, ca|price, li|vraison*). Other groups are divided irrespective of etymology (*circons|tance, tran|saction, obs|curité*), except that a prefix is detached before *h* (*dés|habille*). However, *ll* is always divided even if sounded *y* (*travail|lons, mouil|lé*). Do not divide between vowels except in a compound (*extra|ordinaire* but *Moa|bite*) nor before or after an intervocalic *x* or *y*: *soixante, moyen* are indivisible. Never divide abbreviated words, nor between or after initials, nor after *M., Mme,* or *Mlle.*

Compound words with internal apostrophe are divided by pronunciation: *s'en|tr'aimer, pres-qu'île, aujour|d'hui, pru|d'homme.* When breaking words over a line, avoid ending the line with an apostrophe, as in *Quoi qu'|il dise.* Verbs taking a euphonic *t* should always be divided before the latter (*Viendra-|t-il?*).

In a narrow measure a syllable of two letters may stand at the end of a line (*ce|pendant, in|décis*) but a syllable of two letters must not be taken over to the next line; therefore *élégan|ce, adversi|té* are not permissible. Mute syllables of more than two letters may be turned over to the next line (*ils don|nent, les hom|mes*). Avoid such divisions, however, wherever possible, and avoid ending a paragraph with only the final syllable of a word in the last line.

If a number expressed in figures is too long to go into a line, or cannot be taken to the next without prejudice to the spacing, a part of the number should be put as a word (*100 mil|lions*).

11.20.6 **Italic and roman type**

Titles of works, plays, and journals, names of ships, and titles of tables mentioned in text are put in italic ('La pièce *La Chatte blanche*', 'J'ai vu *Les Rois en exil*', 'On lit dans le *Figaro*', 'le journal *Le Temps*', 'le paquebot *France*').

Words (and short quotations containing words) foreign to French are, as in English, italicized ('*Cave canem!* lisait-on…'); so too are superior letters in italicized words (*Histoire de Napoléon Ier*).

In algebraic formulae, capital letters are always roman and lower-case letters italic. Where the text is in italic the lower-case letters are then roman.

11.20.7 Numerals

Formerly, when cardinal numbers were expressed in lower-case roman numerals, the final unit used to be expressed by a *j*, not an *i*, thus: *ij, iij, vj, viij*; this should be followed when duplicating exactly an earlier style.

In text, numbers are put in words if they only occur occasionally; when they are used statistically, print them in figures. Degrees of temperature, and latitude and longitude, are given as in English: *15° 15'*. Fractions with a horizontal stroke are preferred in mathematical and scientific works; but in ordinary works the solidus can be used, thus: *1/2, 2/3* (½, ⅔).

Age must be given in words (*huit ans*), and also times of day, if expressed in hours and fractions of hours (*six heures, trois heures et quart*). But time expressed in minutes should be set in figures (*6 h 15, 10 h 8 min 30 s*).

As in English, dates, figures, etc. are put in words in legal documents: *l'an mil neuf cent quatre* 'the year one thousand nine hundred and four'. Roman numerals indicating centuries are generally set in small capitals in roman type ('*le* xi*[ème]* [or xi*[e]*] *siècle*') but full capitals in italic ('*le* XI*[ème]* [or XI*[e]*] *siècle*'). Capitalize numerals belonging to proper nouns (*Louis XII*) but not the numbers of the arrondissements of Paris (*le 16e arrondissement*).

Numbers of volumes, books, titles, acts of plays, the years of the Republican calendar, are put in large capitals (*an IV, acte V, tome VI*); *see also* **7.13.4**. Numbers of scenes of plays, if there are no acts, are also put in full capitals ('*Les Précieuses ridicules*, sc. V'); so too chapters if they form the principal division ('*Joseph*, ch. VI'). If, however, scenes of plays and chapters are secondary divisions, they are put in small capitals ('*Le Cid*, acte I, sc. ii'; '*Histoire de France*, liv. VI, ch. vii').

In figures spaces are used to divide thousands (*20 250*); but dates, and numbers in general, are not spaced (*l'an 1466, page 1250, Code civil, art. 1102*).

Note cues for references are generally rendered (1) or [1]. Sometimes an asterisk between parentheses (*) or standing alone *, or italic superior letter, e.g. *[a]*, is used instead. Superior figures not enclosed in parentheses are the best practice from the English point of view. In books or articles written wholly in French, these figures should precede any mark of punctuation. The figure in the note itself is put either 1., (1), or [1]. In many works the reference figure is put [1], and the note figure 1.

11.20.8 Earlier spellings

Texts quoted from previous centuries may show spellings now obsolete: note especially the imperfect and conditional in *-ois*, *-oit*, *-oient*, and similarly *francois*, *anglois*; the omission of *t* in the plural of words ending in *-nt* (e.g. *les tourmens*, now *les tourments*); the acute accent in the ending *-ége*, now *-ège* (*collége*, *Liége* (used in Belgium till 1946), *siége*, etc.), was maintained until 1878, along with the diaeresis in *poëme* (now *poème*). In the seventeenth century there were wider divergences from modern usage: *desir* for *désir*, *pére* for *père*, *teste* for *tête*, also *portés* for *portez* and vice versa. If an author is reproducing exactly the original spelling of a quoted work, follow the copy exactly.

Gaelic *see* CELTIC LANGUAGES 11.13.

11.21 Galician

11.21.1 General

In the Middle Ages Galician was a literary language, used for lyric poetry even by King Alfonso the Wise of Castile, the father of Castilian prose. It was again used for poetry by Rosalía de Castro in the nineteenth century, and since 1982 has been the official language of Galicia.

In many respects Galician is closer to Portuguese than to Castilian, despite basing its orthography on the latter: compare *o cabalo branco* 'the white horse', *o ano* 'the year', *a lúa* 'the moon' with Portuguese *o cavalo branco*, *o ano*, *a lua*; Castilian *el caballo blanco*, *el año*, *la luna*; and Catalan *el cavall blanc*, *l'any*, *la lluna*. Object pronouns are attached to finite verbs, the infinitive may take personal endings (*obedeceren* 'their obeying', 'that they obey'), the *-ra* form is a pluperfect indicative not a subjunctive. However, Galician agrees with Castilian in lacking nasal vowels, in ending third-person singular strong preterites in *-o* not *-e*, and in making little use of the future subjunctive.

Peculiar features include the velar nasal *nh*, for example *unha* 'a, one (feminine)', *inhumano*; the second-person singular pronoun (*see* **11.21.6**); and penultimate stress in the first- and second-person plural of verb forms with tense extensions: imperfect indicative *cantabamos*, *cantabades* against Portuguese *cantávamos*, *cantáveis*, Castilian *cantábamos*, *cantabais*,

Catalan *cantàvem, cantàveu*; similarly pluperfect *cantaramos, cantarades*, conditional *cantariamos, cantariades*, imperfect subjunctive *cantarasemos, cantarasedes* (but in the future subjunctive *cantarmos, cantardes* as in Portuguese).

11.21.2 Alphabet

The Galician alphabet, like the Castilian, recognizes the separate letters *ch, ll, ñ* following *c, l,* and *n* respectively; but *j* and *y* are found only in foreign words.

The distribution of *c/qu, g/gu, gu/gü, z/c* corresponds to that of Castilian; but *g* is never used before *e* or *i*. The letter *c* is not used in Galician words; but note the place name *Valenca* (= Castilian *Valencia*, modern Catalan and Valencian *València*). The letter *x* is extremely frequent, corresponding (with the sound of English *sh*) to Castilian *j*.

The digraph *nh* is not a separate letter; unlike Portuguese *nh*, it does not correspond to Castilian *ñ*, but is pronounced like the *ng* of English *singer*, a value also attaching to *-n* at the end of a word and before consonants other than *b, d, n, p,* and *t*.

Galician deals with doubled consonants in the same manner as does Spanish (*see* **11.42**), including the doubling of initial *r* in composition and the use of *in-* before *m*.

Object pronouns are attached directly to the verb (not only to the same forms as in Castilian but to finite forms in affirmative main clauses); in reflexive forms of the first-person plural, *-s* is lost before *-nos.* but the hyphen is used to attach *-lo, -la, -los, -las* (known as the 'second form' of the definite article) to a preceding verb form or post-verbal pronoun ending in *-r* or *-s* (which is omitted) and to *u* 'where is'; *¿U-los cartos?* 'Where is the money?' (But *ámbolos, ámbalas* 'both' and *tódolos, tódalas* 'all the' are written as one word.) It is also used in some (but not all) compounds of *ad-, inter-, super-* followed by *r*, and of *ab, ob, sub-* before *l* or *r*, to indicate that the syllabic division is respected in pronunciation (*ab-rogar, inter-relación*).

11.21.3 Written accents

Galician uses the same written accents as Castilian, and in general on the same principles; in particular, weak vowel plus strong form a diphthong, for example *Antonio, Galicia,* unless otherwise marked (*vivía, vivías, vivían,* but in contrast to all other Iberian languages *viviamos, viviades,* stressed on the *a*). As in Castilian, some verbs in *-iar* and *-uar* take *í, ú* in the strong forms, others not.

Apart from *carácter, caracteres*, the stress of the singular is always retained in the plural (both *réxime* and *rexime* are acceptable); in contrast to Castilian, the rules governing the use of the acute (sometimes called *til*) permit most words with normal stress ending in a consonant to form their plurals without adding or subtracting an accent. Thus, since final *-ns* (a group not found in Castilian) behaves like its components, the plural of *contracción* and *dolmen* is *contraccións* and *dolmens* (contrast Castilian *contracción, contracciones; dólmen, dólmenes*); but note *compás, compáses; civil, civís*.

Any diphthong ending in a weak vowel is presumed to be falling, and in a final syllable attracts normal stress (*azuis, xerais* (plural of *azul* 'blue', *xeral* 'general')).

When the second of two weak vowels is stressed, it takes the accent: *miúdo* 'tiny', *prexuício* 'damage'; similarly *-uír* in verbs (Castilian *-uir*), for example *construír* 'build', *construíu* 'he built', the syllabic division being *cons-tru-íu*, not *-trui-u*.

When object pronouns or a following definite article are attached to a verb, the group is treated as a unit even across a hyphen: *cantar* 'to sing', *canta-la canción* 'to sing the song', *cantala* 'to sing it', *cantánola* 'to sing it to us'; from *cantas* 'you sing', the corresponding forms are *cánta-la canción, cántala, cántasnola*; after *canta* 'he/she sings', the article remains separate (*canta a canción*) but the pronominal forms are *cántaa, cántanola*. When abnormal stress on the verb becomes normal stress in the group, the written accent is lost: *cantarás* 'you will sing', *cantará* 'he will sing', but *cantara-la canción* 'you will sing the song', *cantarala* 'you will sing it', *cantaraa* 'he/she will sing it'; contrast *cantaras* 'you had sung', *cantara* 'I/he had sung', which make *cantára-la canción, cantárala, cantáraa*. However, contrastive accents on monosyllabic forms are retained (*dámo* 'give it to me' from *dá* 'give').

Adverbs in *-mente* lose the written accent of the adjective (*comunmente, rapidamente*). However, when of two or more adverbs the suffix is added only to the last, the accent is restored in its absence (*cómoda e facilmente* 'conveniently and easily' (Castilian *cómoda y fácilmente*)).

Contrastive accents are used to distinguish certain words otherwise spelt alike, for example:

■ on monosyllables such as *á* 'at/to the (feminine singular)', *a* 'at/to', 'the (feminine singular)'; *ás* 'at/to the (feminine plural)', *as* 'the (feminine plural)'; *có* 'than the (masculine singular)', *co* 'with the (masculine singular)'; *é* 'is', *e* 'and'; *máis* 'more', *mais* 'but'; *nós* 'we', *nos* 'us', 'in the (masculine plural)'; *ó* 'to the (masculine singular)', *o* 'the (masculine singular)'; *pór* 'to put', *por* 'for, by'; *só* 'only', *so* 'under'; *vós* 'you (plural, subject)', *vos* 'you (plural, object)';

- on the disyllables *cómpre* 'it is necessary', *compre* '(that) I/he buy (subjunctive)'; *fóra* 'outside', *fora* 'I/he had been'; *póla* 'branch', *pola* 'hen', 'for/by the (feminine singular)' with their plurals *pólas*, *polas*;

- on other words with open *e* or *o* in the stressed syllable to distinguish them from homonyms with the close vowel (e.g. *tén* 'has, holds', *ten* 'have!, hold!'), but only when the context fails to clarify;

- on interrogatives and exclamations only when ambiguous in context (*dille qué queres* 'tell him/her what you want', *dille que queres* 'tell him/her that you want to'), but not as a matter of course as in Castilian.

The diaeresis is used after a vowel on the *i* of the imperfect indicative endings *-iamos*, *-iades*: thus *caïamos* 'we were falling' (contrast *caiamos* present subjunctive), *constituïades* 'you (plural) were constituting'.

11.21.4 **Word division**

This generally follows Spanish rules. Take over *ch*, *ll*, *rr*, and also *nh* (even *inhumano* should not be divided after *in*), and *tl*. When dividing at a pre-existing hyphen, repeat the hyphen at the beginning of the next line (*canta-|-la*, *inter-|-relación*). Divide prefixes separated by hyphens at the hyphen, which will be repeated on the next line. Otherwise take over the group whole (*su|blime*, *inte|rromper*), except for *dl* (*ad|ligar* 'bind'). Division between vowels is permissible, provided they do not form a diphthong or triphthong (*prexu|ício*).

11.21.5 **Punctuation**

This follows Spanish, including the use of ¿ and ¡.

11.21.6 **Miscellaneous**

The familiar second-person singular pronoun is *ti* for the subject and *te* for the direct object only. The indirect-object form, *che*, is often used as an 'ethic dative'; it must be distinguished from the second-person singular of the preterite in *-ches* (*cántache* 'he sings for you', 'he sings, mark you', *cantaches* 'you sang').

The polite pronouns of address are *vóstede* singular, *vóstedes* plural, with third-person verbs. However, especially in western Galicia the second-person plural may be used as a polite form as in French.

Except before pronouns or in comparisons, the 'personal *a*' before the direct object is a Castilianism frowned on by purists, though grudgingly tolerated before proper nouns.

The verb *haber* is freely used with the infinitive to form compound tenses (*hei* (*de*) *cantar* 'I shall sing', for *cantarei*), but not with the past participle; *ter* is used with the latter when an explicit future perfect or past conditional is required, but not to make a perfect or pluperfect except to express repeated action. The normal equivalents of the English 'I have sung', 'I had sung' are respectively the preterite *cantei* and the pluperfect *cantara*.

Some verbs in -*er* with *e* or *o* in the root have the open vowel in the second- and third-person singular and the third-person plural of the present indicative but the closed vowel in the other strong forms; the only reflection in the spelling is the optional acute on a third-person singular that may in context be confused with the imperative (*bébe* 'drinks', *cóme* 'eats', *bebe* 'drink!', *come* 'eat!'; but *cómeo*, *bébeo* may be either 'eats it', 'drinks it' or 'eat it!', 'drink it!'). Among verbs in -*ir*, some change *e* in the root to *i* in the first-person present indicative, the second-person singular imperative, and the entire present subjunctive, including the first- and second-person plural: *servir* 'to serve', *sirvo* 'I serve', *serve* 'serves', *sirve* 'serve!', *servimos* 'we serve', but subjunctive *sirva*, *sirvamos*; others also change *e* to *i* in the second- and third-person singular, third-person plural present indicative, and second-person singular (e.g. *agride* 'attacks', 'attack!'); some change *u* to open *o* in the second- and third-person singular, and third-person plural present indicative only (*fuxir* 'flee', *foxe* 'flees' but *fuxe* 'flee!').

11.22 **Georgian**

The Georgian language and alphabet moved through two phases: Old Georgian, used in literary and ecclesiastical contexts into the nineteenth century; and New Georgian, used secularly from the thirteenth century, and ecclesiastically till the eighteenth century. They shared the same letters but gave them rather different shapes. The *mkhedruli* ('military') script, used from the eleventh century for administrative purposes, is the only form used for the modern language. It makes no distinction between upper- and lower-case letters.

Several transliteration systems exist, with different sets of diacritics and digraphs. Since aspirated consonants (marked *p'*, *t'*, *k'*, etc., with single opening quotation marks) are much commoner than the unaspirated, some systems leave the aspirated letters unmarked and indicate instead the unaspirated with apostrophes (single closing quotation marks): *t* and *t'* rather than *t'* and *t*. The Deeters–Trubetzkoy system, for example, has

a b g d e v z ē t i k' l m n y o p' ž r s t' w ü p k ɣ q' š č c ʒ c' č' χ q ǯ h ō. (Of these, *ē, y,*
w, q, and *ō* are used only in Old Georgian.) The *ʒ* is not to be set as a yogh,
but is rather the phonetic symbol for *zh,* reassigned to *dz.* Other transliteration systems use, for example, *ey* for *ē, p* or *ṗ* for *p',* *wi* for *ü, ğ* for *ɣ, ǰ*
for *ǯ* and *ow* for *ō.* The Georgian Academy of Sciences system uses the
digraphs *zh, gh, sh, ch, ts, dz, ts', ch',* and *kh;* one favoured by the Library of
Congress marks aspirates, and uses *z̆* (breve).

11.23 German

11.23.1 Diacritics

German requires the diacritics Ä, Ö, Ü, ä, ö, ü, and the special sort *ß*
(*Eszett*). It differs from a Greek beta (*β*), which should not be substituted
for it. No corresponding capital and small capital letters exist for *ß,* and
SS and *s s* are used instead; in alphabetical order *ß* counts as *ss* and not *sz.*
Ligatures and traditional black-letter German types are discussed below.
In early printed texts *å, ô, ú* (superscript *e*), and *ů* may be required.

11.23.2 Orthographic reform

A new orthography agreed by the German-speaking countries came into
force on 1 August 1998. The seven-year transitional period, during
which both systems are official, ends 31 July 2005; after that the older
orthographic forms will be considered incorrect. The reform's main
tendency is to eliminate irregularities that cause difficulty for the native
speaker. At the same time, more variations are permitted than under the
old rules, though these options are restricted: it is not acceptable to mix
and match old and new spellings at will.

Spelling

Under the new orthography, certain words were adjusted to resemble
related words, so that *numerieren* and *plazieren* become *nummerieren* and
platzieren like *Nummer* and *Platz; Gemse* (masculine *Gemsbock*) and *Stengel*
become *Gämse/Gämsbock* and *Stängel* to match *Gams* and *Stange.*

In verbal compounds, nouns and adjectives regarded as retaining
their normal functions are written separately, for example *Rad fahren*
for *radfahren, allein selig machend* for *alleinseligmachend,* but *irreführen* and
wahrsagen as before.

Germanizations of long-established loanwords are imposed (e.g. *Tipp*
for *Tip*), or permitted (e.g. *Portmonee* (one *n*) for *Portemonnaie*), and *ee* for *é*

in such words as *Varietee* for *Variété*, where Germany and Austria will probably prefer *ee*, Switzerland *é*. The optional use of *f* for *ph* will be extended: *Delfin*, *Orthografie*, but not to words deemed more learned: *Philosophie*, *Physik*.

The character *ß* (*Eszett*) was traditionally used at the end of a syllable, before a consonant (whatever the vowel), and after long vowels and diphthongs. The new rules allow the *ß* only after a long vowel (including *ie*) or diphthong: after a short vowel *ss* is to be used (*Fuß*, *Füße* but *Kuss*, *Küsse*; *ihr esst*, *ihr aßt*, like *wir essen*, *wir aßen*). The *Eszett* is considered an archaism in Swiss German, *ss* being preferred in all circumstances. Note that *Geschoß*, which is pronounced with a short *o* in the standard usage of Germany but a long *o* in Austria, becomes *Geschoss* in Germany but remains *Geschoß* in Austria, matching the respective genitive singulars *Geschosses* and *Geschoßes*.

The final *h* of *rauh* is suppressed (*rau*) to match the other adjectives in *au*; however, the abstract nouns *Jäheit* and *Roheit*, derived from *jäh* and *roh*, become *Jähheit* and *Rohheit*.

Advice to editors and proofreaders

In the absence of specific instructions to the contrary, or of evidence from the nature of the text itself (such as teaching matter designed to familiarize pupils with the new orthography), apply the new rules in all matter not by native speakers of German. Before 2005 native speakers will employ both systems, so editors and proofreaders should ascertain which is intended—most rapidly by looking for old *daß* or new *dass*—and correct accordingly. When no intention can be discerned, inconsistent copy should obey the new rules. Quotations from matter published in the old spelling should follow it (except in respect of word division), but new editions will normally modernize. (The principle was already used for nineteenth-century matter: quotations are normally left untouched, even when taken from academic writing that uses lower case for nouns, but literary texts are respelt according to the norms of 1902.)

The new orthography's effects in other areas are mentioned under the headings below.

11.23.3 Abbreviations

Traditionally, German abbreviations in German texts are followed by full points; a full space of the line (previously a thin space) is put after any full points within it: a. a. O. (*am angeführten Ort*), d. h. (*das heißt*), Dr. (*Doktor*), Prof. (*Professor*), usw. (*und so weiter*), z. B. (*zum Beispiel*). There are no full points, however, in abbreviations for metric measures: *m*, *mm*, m^2 or *qm* (now obsolete), m^3 or *cbm* (now obsolete), *hl*, *dz*, *cm*, *l*, *kg*. Nor are there full points generally with abbreviations of recent origin: *AG*

(*Aktiengesellschaft*), *BRD* (*Bundesrepublik Deutschland*), *HO* (*Handelsorganisation*), *DM* (*Deutsche Mark*), *GmbH* (*Gesellschaft mit beschränkter Haftung*).

In texts wholly in German print figures in full, using an em (not en) rule: 27—28, 331—335.

Some other common examples of abbreviations in German:

a. a. O.	am angeführten Ort	o.	oben
Abb.	Abbildung	o. ä.	oder ähnliche(s)
Abt.	Abteilung	o. O.	ohne Ort
Anm.	Anmerkung	R.	Reihe
Aufl.	Auflage	s.	siehe
Ausg.	Ausgabe	S.	Seite
Bd., Bde.	Band, Bände	s. a.	siehe auch
bes.	besonders	s. o.	siehe oben
bzw.	beziehungsweise	sog.	sogenannt
d. h.	das heißt	s. u.	siehe unten
d. i.	das ist	u. a.	und andere(s) unter anderem
ebd.	ebenda, ebendaselbst		
Erg. Bd.	Ergänzungsband	u. ä.	und ähnliches
etw.	etwas	u. ä. m.	und ähnliches mehr
Hft.	Heft	usf., u. s. f.	und so fort
hrsg.	herausgegeben	usw., u. s. w.	und so weiter
Hs., Hss.	Handschrift, Handschriften	verb.	verbessert
Lfg.	Lieferung	Verf., Vf.	Verfasser
m. E.	meines Erachtens	vgl.	vergleiche
m. W.	meines Wissens	z. B.	zum Beispiel
Nr.	Nummer	z. T.	zum Teil

11.23.4 Capitalization

All nouns in German are written with initial capital letters, as are adjectives, numerals, and the infinitives of verbs if used as nouns: *Gutes und Böses, die Drei, Sagen und Tun ist zweierlei*. This style forms the basis for capitalization in German titles.

The basic rule of capitalizing nouns remains untouched by the orthographic reform, but certain exceptions have been abrogated, such as *heute abend* becoming *heute Abend*. Note that *morgen* ('tomorrow') remains lower-case, but *morgen* ('in the morning') becomes *Morgen*: *morgen abend* becomes *morgen Abend*, *gestern morgen* becomes *gestern Morgen*.

Similarly, substantivized adjectives are to be capitalized with fewer exceptions than before: *alles übrige* becomes *alles Übrige* (as commonly in the nineteenth century), the phrase 'to grope in the dark', currently *im Dunkeln tappen* in the literal sense and *im dunkeln tappen* in the metaphorical, will be *im Dunkeln tappen* in all circumstances.

The only difference between the old and new rules for pronouns is that the familiar forms *du, dich, dir, dein, ihr, euch, euer* are no longer to be capitalized in letters and the like; the formality implied by the capital was presumably felt to be dissonant with the familiarity implicit in the choice of pronoun. However, the old rule remains that pronouns given a special sense in polite address are capitalized to distinguish them from their normal value: these are (in medieval and Swiss contexts) *Ihr* addressed to a single person (cf. French *vous*); (in early modern contexts) *Er* and *Sie* (feminine singular), used by servant to master or mistress in the sixteenth century and by master or mistress to servant in the eighteenth; and (nowadays) *Sie* (plural). In all of the above the capital is used also in the oblique cases and in the possessive, but not in the reflexive *sich*.

Capitalize adjectives that form part of a geographical name (*Kap der Guten Hoffnung, Schwarzes Meer*), or the names of historic events or eras (*die Französische Revolution* (of 1789), *der Dreißigjährige Krieg*). Do not capitalize adjectives denoting nationality (*das deutsche Vaterland, die italienische Küste*). Adjectives such as *Berliner* are capitalized because they were originally the genitive plural of the nouns, although *berliner* etc. are found in the nineteenth century.

Traditionally, adjectives derived from personal names were capitalized when they denoted a specific association with the person from whose name they derive: *die Grimmschen Märchen* (*Grimm's Fairy Tales*), *die Lutherische Bibelübersetzung* (Luther's translation of the Bible); but when they were used in a more general sense, the initial capital was dropped: *die lutherische Kirche* (the Lutheran Church), *ein napoleonischer Unternehmungsgeist* (a Napoleonic spirit of enterprise). The new rules, however, make all adjectives derived from personal names lower-case, even in the strict possessive sense (*die lutherische Bibelübersetzung* like *die lutherische Kirche*), except when—in a reversion to nineteenth-century usage— the name is marked off with an apostrophe (*das ohmsche Gesetz* or *das Ohm'sche Gesetz*).

The word *von* in personal names is written with a lower-case initial, but with a capital at the beginning of a sentence unless it is abbreviated to *v.*, when a lower-case initial is used to avoid confusion with the initial of a given name.

11.23.5 **Punctuation**

General

Subordinate clauses of whatever kind are marked off from main clauses by commas, as are most infinitive or participial phrases (but not such encapsulations as *der von dieser Firma getriebene Handel*); note that if *dass* is preceded by a conjunction, the comma is set before the conjunction:

> Ich höre, dass du nichts erspart hast, sondern dass du sogar noch die Ersparnisse deiner Frau vergeudest.
> Er beeilte sich, so dass er den Zug noch erreichte.

Under the new rules, commas will no longer be compulsory before infinitive and participial phrases, but may be used for clarity, or to indicate that the phrase is to be understood parenthetically.

Usually, two clauses linked by *und* or *oder* take a comma between them only if they are main clauses each with its subject indicated. Under the new orthography, even these do not require a comma, though they may take one for clarity's sake.

Sentences containing an imperative normally end in an exclamation mark; the older practice by which the salutation in a letter so ended (*Sehr geehrter Herr Schmidt!*) has largely given way to the use of a comma, after which the letter proper does not begin with a capital unless one is otherwise required.

Square brackets are used for parentheses within parentheses. Em rules (and longer rules) have a space either side.

An exclamation mark is used in preference to *sic*; it is a characteristic device of, for example, Marx and Engels.

Quotation marks

German quotation marks take the form of two commas at the beginning of the quotation, and two opening quotation marks (turned commas) at the end (,, "). Quotations within quotations are marked by a single comma at the beginning and a single opening quotation mark at the end (, '). No space separates the quotation marks from the quotation.

> Er sagte: ,,Kennen Sie Kaiser Augustus' Devise, ,Eile mit Weile!'?"

Commas following a quotation fall after the closing quotation mark, but full points and question and exclamation marks go inside if they belong to the quotation. Some German printers prefer guillemets, called *französische Anführungszeichen*, but—unlike French style—pointing inwards (» «); quotations within quotations are marked by single marks (› ‹).

Apostrophe

The apostrophe is used to mark the elision of *e* to render colloquial usage (*Wie geht's*, *ich komm'*), but not if the elision has been accepted in the literary language (*unsre*, *die andren*). Thus in the present indicative *ich lass'*, but imperative *laß!* (in the new orthography, *ich lass* and *lass!*). When the apostrophe occurs at the beginning of a sentence, the following letter does not therefore become a capital: *'s brennt* (not *'S brennt*).

The apostrophe is also used to mark the suppression of the possessive *s* (for reasons of euphony) after names ending in *s*, *ß*, *x*, *z*: *Voß' Luise, Demosthenes' Reden, Aristoteles' Werke, Horaz' Oden.*

Down to the nineteenth century *'s* was to be found in the genitive singular of proper nouns; Thomas Mann used it throughout his life. The new rules permit, in exceptional circumstances, the apostrophe before the genitive ending *s* for clarity's sake, e.g. to render *Carlo's* more distinct from *Carlos'.*

Hyphen

Traditionally, a noun after a hyphen begins with an initial capital: *Mozart-Konzertabend, Schiller-Museum,* while the new orthography can run words together: *Mozartkonzertabend, Schillermuseum.* When part of a compound word is omitted to save repetition, the hyphen is used to mark the suppression (*Feld- und Gartenfrüchte, ein- und ausatmen*). In this case the hyphen is followed by the space of the line, or preceded by it, as in *Jugendlust und -leid.* When a noun compound is hyphenated the element following the hyphen is capitalized (*80-Pfennig-Briefmarke*).

Traditionally, the hyphen was used to avoid the double repetition of a vowel (*Kaffee-Ersatz*), but not to avoid the similar repetition of a consonant (*stickstofffrei*). The new rules no longer require a hyphen (*Kaffeeersatz*).

German rarely employs the en rule, a hyphen being used instead between words (*Boden-Luft-Raketen, Berlin-Bagdad-Eisenbahn*), and an em rule or hyphen between page extents or dates (*S. 348—349, 1749-1832*), which are never elided. An en rule can, however, be imposed in copy where the work is not wholly in German.

11.23.6 Emphasis and italic

When setting in roman type, German printers use italic, small capitals, or letter-spacing for emphasis. In letter-spaced matter, spaces are put before the punctuation marks excepting the full point. Letter-spacing is also used for emphasizing words in Fraktur type.

In text set entirely in German, italic is not used for foreign words not assimilated into German, and article and book titles; roman is used instead, often without quotation marks. (This does not apply to German titles quoted within an English text.)

11.23.7 Word division

For the purpose of division, distinguish between simple and compound words. Among simple words, do not divide words of one syllable. Divide other simple words by syllables, either between consonants (*Fin|ger, fal|len, An|ker, Red|ner, war|ten, Schif|fer*); or after a vowel followed by a single consonant (*lo|ben*, *tra|gen*, *Va|ter*). This applies even to *x* and mute *h* (*Bo|xer*, *verge|hen*). Germans themselves do not object to taking over only two letters to the next line. (*sechs|te*, *Mau|er*, *dunk|le*).

When a division has to be made between three or more consonants, the last should be taken over (*Vermitt|ler*, *Abwechs|lung*, *Derff|linger*, *kämp|fen*, *kämpf|ten*). But do not separate *ch*, *ph*, *sch*, *ß*, and *th* (representing single sounds): correct examples are *spre|chen*, *wa|schen*, *So|phie*, *ka|tholisch*, *wech|seln*, *Wechs|ler*. Traditionally *st* was included in this group, but under the new rules it is no longer, and should be divided (*Las|ten*, *Meis|ter*, *Fens|ter*).

At the ends of lines, take over *ß* (*hei|ßen*, *genie|ßen*). If *ss* is used instead of *ß*, it should be taken over whole (*genie|ssen* = *genie|ßen*), but *ss* not standing for *ß* should be divided (*las|sen*).

Traditionally, if a word was broken at the combination *ck*, it was represented as though spelt with *kk* (*Zucker* but *Zuk|ker*, *Glocken* but *Glok|ken*). According to the new orthography, the combination *ck* is taken over whole (*Zu|cker*, *Glo|cken*), as it was traditionally after a consonant in proper nouns or their derivatives (*Fran|cke*, *bismar|ckisch*).

Words with suffixes are considered as simple words and are divided in accordance with the rules given above (*Bäcke|rei*, *le|bend*, *Liefe|rung*).

Compound words may be broken into their etymological constituents (*Bildungs|roman*, *Bürger|meister*, *Haus|frau*, *Kriminal|polizei*, *strom|auf*, *Zwillings|bruder*, *Bundes|tag*); the traditional rule against dividing *st* does not apply at the point of junction in compounds—and does not operate under the new orthography.

Prefixes may be separated from the root word (*be|klagen*, *emp|fehlen*, *er|obern*, *aus|trinken*, *ab-wechseln*, *zer-splittern*). A compound may be divided within one of its elements: *Bun|destag* is no less correct than *Bundes-tag*, and should be preferred if it gives better spacing. Under the new orthography, some compounds are no longer felt as such, and may be divided as single words: *wa|rum* besides *war|um*. The new rules also allow greater latitude regarding classical and other foreign loanwords: they may be divided according to normal German principles, or (as historically) according to classical rules: thus *Quad|rat* is now permitted besides *Qua|drat*.

Traditionally, three identical consonants did not precede a vowel, except for *sss* meaning *ßs*, used when an *Eszett* was not available or in capital letters. They sometimes occurred before another consonant: *stickstofffrei* but *Brennessel*, *Schiffahrt*. When such a word was broken, however, the element turned over recovered its initial consonant (*Brenn|nessel*,

Schiff|fahrt); the divisions *Mit|tag*, *den|noch*, and *Drit|teil* were exceptions. Now, except in *Mittag* and *dennoch* (*Dritteil* for *Drittel* is obsolete), groups of three identical consonants are written out even before a vowel (*Brennnessel*, *Schifffahrt*); so too when *sss* results from the abolition of *ß* after a short vowel (*Schlußsatz* becomes *Schlusssatz*). It is permissible to make such compounds more perspicuous by the use of a hyphen (*Brenn-Nessel*, *Schiff-Fahrt*, *Schluss-Satz*).

11.23.8 Ligatures

Set the ligatures *ff*, *fi*, and *fl* where the letters belong together in the stem of a word: *treffen*, *finden*, *flehen*; set *fl* finally (*Aufl.*) and *fi* where *i* begins a suffix (*häufig*). Note that *fi* then takes precedence over *ff*, e.g. *pfäffisch*. Otherwise use the separate letters: *auffällen*, *Schilfinsel*, *verwerflich* (so too *Auflage* despite *Aufl.*), in other words where the letters link elements in a compound, or at the junction of a prefix or of a suffix beginning with *l*. Note too that *fl* should be set separately in words that have related forms with *-fel-*: *zweifle* from *zweifeln*, *Mufflon* from *Muffel*. In foreign compounds set for example *Offizier*, *Effluvium*; but in the proper noun *Effi* use *ff*.

Formerly all German printers had one-piece ligatures, but newer technology has often dispensed with ligatures altogether. Whenever there is any doubt, set separate letters rather than ligatures.

11.23.9 Numerals

A number of more than four figures should be separated with thin spaces by thousands (6 580 340). The comma in German practice marks the decimal point, which is used in writing amounts of money (15,00 DM or 0,75 DM). A full point after a numeral shows that it represents an ordinal number (14. Auflage (14th edition), *Friedrich II. von Preußen*, *Mittwoch, den 19. Juli 1995*). The full point also marks the separation of hours from minutes (14.30 Uhr or 14^{30} Uhr).

Germans use roman numerals rarely: even when citing roman page numbers, they often convert them into arabic and add an asterisk, e.g. S. 78* (= p. lxxviii). This should be distinguished from 1* denoting the first page of an article that is in fact (say) the third or fifth page of a pamphlet, e.g. the *Programm* of a university or *Gymnasium*; the second page will be 4 or 6 as appropriate.

11.23.10 Adjectival endings

German adjectives following the definite article are declined 'weak' (*der gute Mann, die gute Frau, das gute Kind, die guten Leute*); without it, they are generally declined 'strong' (*guter Mann, gute Frau, gutes Kind, gute Leute*). When a title or other quotation is shortened by the omission of the article, the adjective is adjusted accordingly (*Die lustigen Weiber von Windsor* but *Lustige Weiber*). Since the English definite article, unlike the German, does not indicate gender, use the strong form of the adjective after it, so that *das Deutsche Archäologische Institut* in German becomes 'the Deutsches Archäologisches Institut' in English.

11.23.11 Historical and specialist setting

The traditional black-letter German types such as Fraktur and Schwabacher were replaced by the roman Antiqua in 1941, though Antiqua had been common in earlier centuries for technical and scientific printing. Their use was not commonly revived following the war, and they are now found only to a limited extent in German-speaking countries, mostly in decorative or historical contexts, or in approximating earlier typography. Any matter to be set in them should be deemed a quotation. Word division should follow the pre-1998 rules, not the new; in particular the *st* ligature should be taken over. The sorts normally found in Fraktur types are shown below, together with their roman equivalents.

𝔄 𝔄 𝔅 ℭ 𝔇 𝔈 𝔉 𝔊 𝔥   ℨ   𝔎 𝔏 𝔐 𝔑 𝔒 Ö 𝔓 𝔔 𝔥 𝔖 𝔗 𝔘 Ü 𝔙 𝔚 𝔛 𝔜 ℨ
A Ä B C D E F G H I *or* J K L M N O Ö P Q R S T U Ü V W X Y Z

𝔞 ä 𝔟 𝔠 𝔡 𝔢 𝔣 𝔤 𝔥 𝔦 𝔧 𝔨 𝔩 𝔪 𝔫 𝔬 ö 𝔭 𝔮 𝔯 ſ 𝔰 𝔱 𝔲 ü 𝔳 𝔴 𝔵 𝔶 ʒ
a ä b c d e f g h i j k l m n o ö p q r ſ s t u ü v w x y z

ch ck ff fi fl ll ſi ſſ ſt ß tz
ch ck ff fi fl ll si ss st ß tz

The long *s* (ſ) in Fraktur type is used at the beginnings of words, and within them except at the ends of syllables. The short final *s* (s) is put at the ends of syllables and words. However, the long form may be used at the end of a syllable before p (Knoſpe, Weſpe besides Knospe, Wespe) and must be used in the group ſſ (e.g. Laſſen) except at the point of composition (ausſehen, diesſeitig). Never use ſſ for ß (the Fraktur *ß*), which follows the same rules governing the roman *Eszett*.

The ligature combinations ch, ck, ſt, tz are to be regarded as single letters, and must not be spaced apart; normally this does not apply to *ch*, *ck*, *st*, and *tz* in roman. In texts set in Fraktur, foreign words are usually set in roman (ſie kommen in corpore), and titles in Fraktur.

In Fraktur the rules governing ligatures apply also to the ligatures ll (fallen but regellos), ſt, and ſſ (lauſtig, ruſtſich like häuſtg, pfäffſich). Note that ſt, ff, ß, and ſt must not be used across a junction: ausimpfen, ausſehen, ausziehen, austaufchen. Likewise tz must not be used in achtzig (contrast Trotzig from Trotz) or Achtzahl.

Old and Middle High German

The letter *z* in those languages has two values: one, as in the modern language, like *ts*, the other a dental *s* like medieval Spanish *c*. Scholars sometimes distinguish this by attaching a little leftward hook to the bottom right corner: z; its capital form, Z, is used only in all-capital headings. Like the diaeresis used on *e* to indicate a more open sound, this is a matter of modern convention, and is not compulsory.

Long vowels in Old High German are marked—if at all—with a macron, in Middle High German with a circumflex (and in Old Norse with an acute). In Middle High German both *æ* and *œ* ligatures are used; it has not been conventional to use the open italic version of the former (*æ*), but there is no objection to doing so.

11.24 **Gothic**

The language of the Goths is known only through a small number of manuscripts. Originally derived from Greek, the script—also called Visigothic or 'Wulfila's script'—is written left to right; there are no spaces between words; sentences and important phrases are separated by a space, medial point, or colon.

Special characters used in transliteration are þ (thorn) and ƕ (h with upward curl on right leg). In philological work—which most work on Gothic is—the vowels *a*, *u* may be marked with macron or circumflex when long; so too may *e*, *o*, even though they are always long. (No such accent is used with *i*, since the corresponding long vowel is spelt *ei*.) The acute is sometimes used to make etymological distinctions not reflected in Gothic script or probably pronunciation (*ái*, *aí*, *áu*, *aú*).

11.25 **Greek**

11.25.1 **Alphabet**

For setting passages of Greek in English text, or for Greek words or letters used intermittently, a sloping font such as Porson is preferable. ('Porson' is often used as a generic term for sloping fonts in general.) When the actual letter-shape is important, as in discussions of manuscript corruptions, it may be preferable to use a font such as New

Hellenic; moreover, an upright font is best for displayed text such as running heads and speech prefixes, especially in even full capitals.

The standard Greek alphabet consists of twenty-four letters: seventeen consonants and seven vowels (a, ϵ, η, ι, o, υ, ω) in the following order:

A	α	alpha	N	ν	nu
B	β	beta	Ξ	ξ	xi
Γ	γ	gamma	O	o	omicron
Δ	δ	delta	Π	π	pi
E	ϵ	epsilon	P	ρ	rho
Z	ζ	zeta	Σ	σ	(s final) or C c sigma
H	η	eta	T	τ	tau
Θ	θ	theta	Y	υ	upsilon
I	ι	iota	Φ	ϕ	phi
K	κ	kappa	X	χ	chi
Λ	λ	lambda	Ψ	ψ	psi
M	μ	mu	Ω	ω	omega

In reproducing ancient Greek, some scholars prefer the forms C c (lunate sigma), which is normal in papyrological and epigraphic studies, where the editor may not wish to guess whether a sigma followed by lost matter was or was not word-final. In any case, the so-called stigma ς, used for the numeral 6 and in late manuscripts and early printed books for $\sigma\tau$, must be clearly distinguished from s. Hellenists increasingly prefer the lunate forms, though in literature transmitted through medieval manuscripts, layfolk and Latinists may be more comfortable with the traditional Byzantine sigma Σ (capital), σ (lower-case initial and medial), s (lower-case final); in modern Greek only the Byzantine forms are acceptable. The abbreviation for 'scholia' (the marginal commentaries found in some manuscripts) must be Σ.

Older forms of the alphabet found in inscriptions show considerable variations in the shapes and use of letters, some of which are normalized in modern transcription, such as the use in many cities of X for ξ and Ψ for χ, others not, such as the use of H for the aspirate (transcribed with italic *h*) and of E, O for η, ω and certain instances of $\epsilon\iota$, $o\upsilon$ (transcribed as $\bar{\epsilon}$, $\bar{o}$, the long mark being dispensed with when the letter bears the circumflex). In inscriptions, and in dialectal literature, one also finds the letters $\digamma$ (wau or digamma) and $\koppa$ (koppa).

In ancient Greek iota forming a diphthong with long a or with η, ω ceased to be pronounced after the classical period and in Roman times was often omitted; in the traditional minuscule script it is inserted underneath the vowel: α, η, ω ('iota subscript'). Some modern scholars prefer to write $\alpha\iota$, $\eta\iota$, $\omega\iota$ ('adscript iota'), in which case accents and breathings (*see* **11.25.2**) should be set on the first vowel. Since the iota was still pronounced until *c*.300 BC, there is a good case for using ad-script iota in editions of texts written before that date. Since the words in question were often written without the iota after *c*. AD 1, the sub-script is better in editions of works written in the Christian era, and the more so the later they are. In texts edited from papyri or inscriptions the iota must be adscript if written in the source and subscript if not, instance by instance, however inconsistent the result. When the main vowel is capital, the iota must be adscript; hence at the start of a paragraph ῷ̂ will become Ωι, in even capitals ΩΙ.

Since αι may also represent the 'short' diphthong *ai*, which is never written with iota subscript, an editor ignorant of Greek cannot mechan-ically convert adscript iota to subscript. If the author has marked every post-vocalic heterosyllabic iota with a diaeresis, subscript iota may be mechanically converted into adscript; otherwise knowledge of Greek is required, since some sequences that were clearly disyllabic while the subscript iota was being used will become ambiguous when it is made adscript. Hellenists increasingly prefer adscript, though Latinists and others may be more comfortable with subscript.

This issue no longer arises in modern Greek: even in phrases taken from ancient Greek that originally involved such a diphthong the iota is simply omitted.

In texts of papyri and inscriptions any letter—with or without breath-ing, accent, or iota subscript—or any other character may be required to have a dot beneath it.

11.25.2 **Accents and aspirates**

Accents and breathings were devised by grammarians *c*.200 BC, and at first were used only when the word was thought to need clarification. Their routine insertion is a feature of Byzantine minuscule; British writers in the eighteenth century often omitted them. They should not be used with words set entirely in capitals: in such words, adscript iota should always be used (e.g. τῳ but *TΩI*). When the alphabetic nu-merals (*see* **11.25.5**) are set as capitals, ς becomes ΣΤ.

ʼ lenis (smooth)	asper grave
asper (rough)	round circumflex
acute	circumflex lenis
grave	circumflex asper
lenis acute	diaeresis
lenis grave	diaeresis acute
asper acute	diaeresis grave

Instead of the round, breve form of the circumflex ( ) used in the Porson font, for example, some fonts such as New Hellenic use a tilde-like accent (̃). It is never correct to mix the two types.

All words other than enclitics (words that form accentual groups with those immediately preceding) and the four proclitics (words that form accentual groups with those immediately following) ὁ, ἡ, οἱ, αἱ have an accent; even enclitics and proclitics are accented before other enclitics—note too that there are accented forms of the relative pronoun otherwise identical with the proclitics. No word has more than one accent except before an enclitic. Knowledge of the correct accent is a matter for specialists (nor are all scholars accurate).

The acute ( ) is used only on one of the last three syllables of a word; it is not used on the last syllable except in the interrogatives τίς and τί, before punctuation, or when the following word is an enclitic. The grave ( ) can only be used upon the last syllable of a word. The circumflex ( ) occurs upon either the last syllable of a word, or the last but one. The Greek vowels allow of two breathings: the asper or rough ( ), corresponding to the letter h and the lenis or smooth ( ), denoting the absence of the h. All vowels beginning a word have a breathing over them; but upsilon (υ) allows no other than the asper. In diphthongs (αι not standing for ᾳ, ει, οι, υι, αυ, ευ, ηυ, ου, ωυ) the breathing stands over the second vowel (thus: αἰ, οὐ) as do accents. The initial letter ρ takes the asper; double ρρ was formerly printed ῥρ ('horns'), but should now always be ρρ.

The lenis ( ) is used for eliding the vowels α, ε, ι, ο, and sometimes the diphthongs αι and οι, when they stand at the end of a word, followed by another vowel beginning the next word. Elision takes place in all the prepositions, except περί and πρό. The lenis is also used at the beginning of a word when the initial vowel is elided ('prodelision'), for example μη ᾽στι. When the vowel would have been accented, the normal practice is to retain the accent, for example μὴ ᾽χω. Some scholars find this absurd; their preferences should be respected.

Do not set an elided word close up with the word following; it may be set at the end of a line even if it contains only one consonant and the lenis: δ᾽.

When there is 'crasis' (fusion) of two syllables, a 'coronis' (set as a lenis) is placed on the fused vowel or diphthong, the aspirate becoming 'smooth' when the first consonant takes the 'rough' breathing of the second word; for example τὸ ἐπί = τοὐπί; τὸ ιματιον = θοἰματιον; καὶ ἡ = χἠ; πρό + εχω = προυχω.

In classical Greek, the vowels α, ι, υ may be either long or short, but are not so marked (e.g. ᾱ, ᾰ) except in grammars and special contexts; in the standard script, ε, ο are short, η, ω long.

When a Greek word accented grave on its last syllable appears in an English context and is followed by English words, change its grave accent to acute. This does not apply to manuscript readings quoted as such.

In modern Greek, some writers still use the traditional accents and breathings (though the rough breathing on initial rho is generally dispensed with); others retain the acute on final syllables instead of changing it to grave. Many writers nowadays omit all breathings and use only a single accent (properly a filled-in triangle ˈ, but if that is not available an acute will do). In this 'monotonic' system monosyllables, even if stressed, do not bear the accent, save that ἤ 'or' is distinguished from η 'the' (nominative singular feminine), in traditional spelling ἤ and ἡ respectively. Follow copy, especially if the author is Greek.

The diaeresis ( ) is used to separate two vowels from each other, in order to prevent their being taken for a diphthong. Some scholars write a diaeresis on any iota or upsilon following a vowel and not forming a diphthong with it; others do so only when the position of accents or breathings does not make it clear that the iota forms a separate syllable. Either practice is acceptable, but writing the diaeresis every time is safer; if it is written only where needed, it will have to be written more frequently when iota adscript is used (e.g. νῆϊς, since ἦϊ = ῃ). In modern Greek, the diaeresis is used to show that αϊ and οϊ *are* diphthongs, as opposed to the digraphs αι (pronounced ε) and οι (pronounced ι).

11.25.3 Capitalization

In printing ancient Greek, the first word of a sentence or a line of verse is capitalized only at the beginning of a paragraph, but not in verse when the new paragraph is marked by pulling the line out to the left ('ecthesis') instead of indenting it. In modern Greek, capitals are used for new sentences, though not always for new lines of verse.

For titles of works in ancient Greek, it is best to capitalize only the first word and proper nouns, or else proper nouns only; some writers do not capitalize the first word even when they do so in Latin. In modern Greek first word and proper nouns only is the rule in bibliographies, but in running text first and main words tend to be capitalized.

In ancient Greek, it is conventional to capitalize adjectives, and preferably also adverbs, derived from proper nouns, but not verbs: *Ελλην* 'a Greek' (feminine *Ελληνίς*), *Ελληνικός* 'Greek (adj.)', *Ελληνιστί* 'in Greek', but *ἑλληνίζω* 'I speak Greek/behave like a Greek'. In modern

Greek, lower case is the rule: ἑλληνικός (ελληνικὸς) 'Greek (adj.)', ἑλληνικα (ελληνικὰ) 'in Greek'.

11.25.4 Word division

A vowel may be divided from another (λύ|ων) unless they form a diphthong (αι, αυ, ει, ευ, ην, οι, ου, υι). Take over any combination of 'mute' (β, γ, δ, θ, κ, π, τ, φ, χ) followed by 'liquid' (λ, μ, ν, ρ), also βδ, γδ, κτ, πτ, φθ, χθ, or any of these followed by ρ; μν; and any group in which σ stands before a consonant other than σ, or before one of the above groups: ἑλι|κτός, γι|γνώ|σκω, μι|μνή|σκω, κα|πνός, βα|πτί|ζω.

Any doubled consonants may be divided. Apart from the exception for μν, the letters λ, μ, ν, and ρ may be divided from a following consonant; γ may be divided from a following κ or χ; ξ and ψ between vowels should be taken over (δεί|ξειν, ἀνε|ψιός).

In applying these rules to ancient Greek, modern scholars observe an overriding precept that compound words are divided into their parts. Modern Greek word division follows ancient principles, but the consonant groups taken over are those that can begin a modern word; therefore θμ is divided, but γκ, μπ, ντ, τζ, τσ are not.

Some frequent prefixes end in consonants (εἰσ-, ἐν-, ἐξ-, ἐσ-, ξυν-, προσ-, συν-, ὑπερ-; but note that there is also a prefix προ- which may occur before σ); a division after these, even before a vowel, will be correct. The prefixes ἀντι-, ἀπο-, ἐπι-, κατα-, μετα-, παρα-, ὑπο- have their full form before a word-part beginning with a consonant, and are then to be divided as usual (ἀπο|κνίζω, κατα|λύω). Before a word-part beginning with a vowel, however, they become ἀντ- (ἀνθ- if the vowel is aspirated), ἀπ- (ἀφ-), ἐπ- (ἐφ-), κατ- (καθ-), μετ- (μεθ-), παρ-, ὑπ- (ὑφ-), and then it will be right to divide after the consonant (ἀπ|αίρω, καθ|ηκω). Sometimes the initial vowel will be the same as that of the preposition: ἀπ|οκνῶ, παρ|απτομαι. In other compounds, divide for example Ἀλεξ|ανδρος, δημ|αρχος, Διοσ|κόρω, ωσπερ|ανεί.

In ancient times the consonant was often taken over anyway, but so was the final consonant of an elided word, or even a final consonant when the next word began with a vowel; on the other hand σ was often separated from a following consonant within the word.

11.25.5 Numerals

Two systems of numerals were in use. The older, used only for cardinal numbers, is the 'acrophonic' system, in which certain numbers were indicated by their initial letters; this was eventually replaced (at Athens not till 88 BC in official use) by the alphabetic system, which may be used of either cardinals or ordinals:

1	$α'$	14	$ιδ'$	60	$ξ'$	1,000	$,α$
2	$β'$	15	$ιε'$	70	$ο'$	2,000	$,β$
3	$γ'$	16	$ιϛ'$	80	$π'$	3,000	$,γ$
4	$δ'$	17	$ιζ'$	90	$ϟ'$	4,000	$,δ$
5	$ε'$	18	$ιη'$	100	$ρ'$	5,000	$,ε$
6	$ϛ'$	19	$ιθ'$	200	$σ'$	6,000	$,ϛ$
7	$ζ'$	20	$κ'$	300	$τ'$	7,000	$,ζ$
8	$η'$	21	$κα'$	400	$υ'$	8,000	$,η$
9	$θ'$	22	$κβ'$	500	$φ'$	9,000	$,θ$
10	$ι'$	23	$κγ'$	600	$χ'$	10,000	$,ι$
11	$ια'$	30	$λ'$	700	$ψ'$	20,000	$,κ$
12	$ιβ'$	40	$μ'$	800	$ω'$	100,000	$,ρ$
13	$ιγ'$	50	$ν'$	900	$ϡ'$		

$ϛ$ and $ϡ$ are nowadays called 'stigma' and 'sampi' respectively.

Numbers over 10,000 were sometimes indicated by M (for $μύριοι$ or $μυριάς$) with the appropriate multiple above it; other refinements were used for very large numbers. There is also a symbol for a half; other fractions are represented in various fashions.

Modern Greek uses arabic numerals: set these in italic with sloping fonts, but set in roman with upright fonts (e.g. New Hellenic), in both cases ranging. Alphabetic numerals are still employed, however, in much the same way as roman numerals are in Western languages.

11.25.6 Punctuation

The comma, the full point, and the exclamation mark (in modern Greek) are the same as in English; but the question mark (;) is the English semicolon (italic where necessary to match a sloping Greek font), and the colon is an inverted full point (·). Use double quotation marks, or in modern Greek guillemets; but in ancient Greek some scholars may dispense with quotation marks, perhaps using an initial capital instead.

11.25.7 Emphasis

Emphasized words should be underlined; the older practice of letter-spacing was more convenient than underlining in the days of hot-metal printing, but with modern setting methods it is the other way about. Especially in modern Greek, a second Greek font may be used for this purpose, if available, thus avoiding the need for underlining.

11.26 **Hebrew**

This section focuses mainly on Hebrew rather than other related languages, though the general issues are the same.

11.26.1 Alphabet

The Hebrew alphabet is best avoided in English-language publications, even those aimed at a specialist Jewish-studies readership, as it is written from right to left. This can create problems with typesetting and page make-up (*see* **8.2**). Hebrew, Yiddish, and related languages are therefore frequently represented by a transcription or transliteration. However, as setting text in Hebrew characters is sometimes unavoidable, the following points should be noted:

Consonants and vowels

The Hebrew alphabet consists exclusively of consonantal letters. Vowels may be indicated by 'points' above, below, or inside them, but Hebrew is generally written and printed without vowels. The main exceptions are liturgical texts, poetry, and children's books. Hebrew written without vowels is described in English as 'unpointed' or 'unvocalized'.

Each letter has a numerical value. Letters are therefore often used in Hebrew books—especially in liturgical texts and older works—to indicate the numbers of volumes, parts, chapters, and pages. Letters are also used to indicate the day of the week, the date in the month, and the year according to the Jewish calendar. In all cases, the numerical rather than the alphabetical equivalents should be substituted in the English text. (On the calculation of the year according to the Jewish calendar, *see* **7.13.6**.)

Written forms

The consonantal letters are principally found in two different forms: a cursive script, and the block ('square') letters used in printing. A third form, known as Rashi script, is used only in some religious texts. Table 11.2 shows each letter of the alphabet in block and cursive forms, together with its name, a simplified English transcription, its numerical value, and a scholarly transcription (favouring spelling over punctuation). The vowels (the same for all forms of Hebrew) are also shown.

Typesetting

Specialist Hebrew typesetters have no problem in converting the cursive letters of a handwritten text to the square letters of the printed form, and will automatically do so unless instructed otherwise. If a

Table 11.2: **The Hebrew alphabet: a broad transcription for general use**

CONSONANTS

Block*	Cursive*	Name	Simplified transcription	Numerical value	Scholarly transcription
א	א	alef	—†	1	ʾ
ב	ב	beit	b	2	b
ב	ב	veit	v		b̲
ג	ג	gimmel	g	3	g/g̲
ד	ד	dalet	d	4	d/d̲
ה	ה	hé	h	5	h
ו	ו	vav	v	6	w
ז	ז	zayin	z	7	z
ח	ח	chet	ch, ḥ‡	8	ḥ
ט	ט	tet	t	9	ṭ
י	י	yod	y, i§	10	y
כ	כ	kaf	k	20	k
כ ך	כ ך	khaf, khaf sofit	kh‡		k̲
ל	ל	lamed	l	30	l
מ ם	מ ם	mem, mem sofit	m	40	m
נ ן	נ ן	nun, nun sofit	n	50	n
ס	ס	samekh	s	60	s
ע	ע	ʿayin	—†	70	ʿ
פ	פ	pé	p	80	p
פ ף	פ ף	fé, fé sofit	f		p̲
צ ץ	צ ץ	tsadi, tsadi sofit	ts	90	ṣ
ק	ק	kof	k	100	q
ר	ר	resh	r	200	r
ש	ש	shin	sh	300	š
ש	ש	sin	s		ś
ת	ת	tav	t	400	t/t̲

VOWELS

Form	Name
ָ	kamats
	patah
	segol
	tseré
	hirik
	sheva
	kubutz
	hataf patah
	hataf segol
ו	holam
ו	shuruk

* Where two forms are given, the second is that used in final position.
† The letters *alef* and *ayin* are not transliterated in the simplified system. When they occur in intervocalic position an apostrophe is used to indicate that the vowels are to be pronounced separately.
‡ Pronounced *ch* as in the Scottish pronunciation of *loch*.
§ Transliterated 'y' as a consonant, 'i' as a vowel.

non-specialist typesetter is to provide the occasional letter, word, or phrase in Hebrew, copy should be supplied in square letters, and preferably typed rather than handwritten since some letters look very similar—for example, *dalet* and *resh*, *vav* and *yod*. As a further precaution, any ambiguous letters must be clearly labelled. Often the easiest way to do this is to append the full Hebrew alphabet to the typescript with each letter numbered, mark each Hebrew letter in the text with the corresponding number, and give the typesetter a copy of the enumerated alphabet together with the text.

The point size for setting Hebrew should be such that the height of a Hebrew character without ascenders or descenders matches that of a lower-case English character without ascenders or descenders.

For guidance on line breaks in Hebrew *see* **8.2**.

11.26.2 **Transliteration**

Although there may be a case for typesetting Hebrew characters in specialized texts, transliteration is generally preferable, as non-specialists find it easier to read. It is also much easier for typesetters to handle; and even if an author's disks have the Hebrew embedded, not all typesetters have the requisite fonts. (Nevertheless, transliteration may be inappropriate for scholarly biblical, rabbinic, or philological work.)

The transliteration of Hebrew is problematic because certain letters and vowels have no precise English equivalents. Diacritics are therefore inevitable if phonetic distinctions are to be maintained, and to allow the reconstruction of the original. This is reflected in scholarly practice (*see* **TABLE 11.2**, sixth column). For works aimed at non-specialists, however, prefer a broader transcription that aims to reproduce the *sound* of Hebrew rather than the Hebrew alphabet: non-specialist readers are less interested in how a Hebrew word is actually spelt, or its philologically accurate rendering, than in guidance on how to pronounce it intelligibly. A transliteration system with fewer diacritics is also generally cheaper and faster to typeset, because a specialist typesetter is unnecessary.

Different systems of transliterated Hebrew may require the following diacritics: ś (and sometimes the acute is also used on vowels to indicate stress); ā, ē, ī, ō, ū; ê, ô (sometimes used to show the presence of a *mater lectionis*; some writers also use î, û), ă, ě, ŏ (in some systems represented by superiors, ^{a e o}); ḥ, ṣ, ṭ, ẓ (in older system also use ḳ for q); š (less strictly sh, sz); ḇ ḏ, g, ḵ, p̱, ṯ (less strictly bh, dh, gh, kh, ph, th). Special characters are ə (schwa), ' (*alef* or lenis), ʻ (*ʻayin* or asper).

The general transliteration system recommended here (*see* **TABLE 11.2**, fourth column) takes the broad approach to transcription. It aims to reflect the pronunciation prescribed for Modern Hebrew, while at the same time retaining established or conventional spellings that are generally familiar to the average English-speaking reader. This latter criterion means that a small degree of inconsistency within the system as a whole may be unavoidable. Editorial discretion will be required to establish the proper balance in applying these two contradictory principles in a given work, but if individual words are treated consistently, and the inconsistencies occur only when familiar forms are substituted for more 'correct' ones, the overall result is a transliteration that does its job unobtrusively.

All systems aim to transliterate Modern (or Israeli) Hebrew—a language that did not establish itself as a spoken vernacular until the beginning of the twentieth century. Consideration should therefore be given to the possibility that, particularly in the context of the Orthodox Jewish world of central and eastern Europe before the Second World War, a Modern Hebrew rendering of names of people, organizations, ritual objects, festivals, and so on may represent a historical distortion.

For specialized text-based works—where it is important to be able to identify the original Hebrew letters, as in a description of medieval Hebrew liturgical poetry—a more technical system advocated by the Academy of the Hebrew Language in Israel is preferable because it offers great linguistic accuracy. The *Encyclopaedia Judaica* (Jerusalem, 1972) reproduces this as its 'scientific system'. It also has a 'general' system, which has fewer diacritics than the 'scientific system'—but still probably more than the average English-speaking reader requires— and frequent hyphenation that can make the result seem strange to an English eye.

Yiddish transliteration is slightly different; the most widely used system is that advocated by the YIVO Institute for Jewish Research, New York. Yiddish spelling is a mixture of a 'traditional system', used for the Hebrew and Aramaic components (which are spelt as in their languages of origin, though very differently pronounced), and a 'phonetic system', used for the rest (German, Slavonic, etc.). It is possible to transcribe using the philological symbols, but this is unusual, except perhaps for š. The orthography for Aramaic, and such ethnolects as Judaeo-Arabic and Judaeo-Spanish (Ladino), differs as well; explanations and transliterations may be found in *The World's Writing Systems* (New York, 1996).

Consistency

There is more than one established way of transliterating Hebrew; numerous ad hoc spellings are also in wide use. Do not pick and choose between the alternatives available: adopt one system, and apply it

consistently as far as possible within a single work. Authors and translators should not assume that a publisher will take responsibility for
this: certainly an editor who does not know Hebrew cannot be expected
to do so. Moreover, it is much easier and more efficient to use a consistent system of transliteration while writing than to impose one afterwards.

Even when full consistency is impossible to achieve, it is important
always to spell the same Hebrew word in the same way. Differences in
spellings, capitalization, and italicization—e.g. 'Beth Din' and *'beit din'*,
'Sukkoth' and 'Succot', *'halacha'* and *'halakhah'*—can leave readers
wondering whether the two words do in fact represent the same concept; they also cause problems with indexing and with compiling glossaries. Whatever system of transliteration is used, maintain consistency
in spelling individual words. Where this is not possible, as for example
where an official name exists in English—the rabbinical court, or *beit
din*, of London is known in English as the *London Beth Din*—provide the
alternative in parentheses after its first mention in text, as well as
adequate cross-referencing in the index.

The following are common alternative representations of individual
Hebrew letters; if more than one variant in any of the following groups
occurs, the transliteration may not be following a consistent system: *ts/
tz/z, t/ṭ, w/v, ḥ/ch, sh/š/sz, q/k, f/ph*. Similarly, a transliteration should use
either all the diacritics from that system or none. (Another indication of
unsystematic transliteration is when ʿ*ayins* and *alefs* are distinguished
by the special sorts ʿ and ʾ (or by aspers and lenes ʾ), but without any of
the other diacritics that mark a thoroughly scientific transliteration
system. If a scientific system is indeed being used, these letters must
be properly distinguished.)

The best way to achieve consistency is to maintain an alphabetical
style sheet. Editors should include definitions for each word and folio
numbers for each occurrence, so as to identify and deal with inconsistencies. However, some inconsistency may have to be permitted, because
differences in established usages for particular terms may make different conventions 'correct' in different circumstances; this is particularly
true of *ts/tz* and *ḥ/ch* spellings. In each case, the first form represents a
usage fairly well established in academic circles; the second represents a
more popular usage that reflects the influence of German-speaking
Jewry on the transliteration of Hebrew words (as in *barmitzvah, matzah,
Chanukah*, and *chutzpah*) and the names of organizations such as *Hecha-
lutz*. While it may sometimes therefore be necessary to use both forms
within a single text, the spelling of any individual word in running text
should be consistent. (In transliterated bibliographical references, however, it is best to ignore such variations and apply the chosen system of
transliteration rigorously.)

A simple transliteration system for non-specialist works

This section addresses the person responsible for making the transliteration—the author or the translator—rather than the editor trying to ensure the consistency of the text.

In accordance with the general approach of reflecting pronunciation rather than spelling, this transliteration system (or, more accurately, transcription system) does not differentiate between letters that are commonly pronounced in the same way. The only exception is that the distinction is retained between *khaf* and *chet* (or *ḥet*, in works of a more academic nature, where the *ḥ* is well established), using *kh* for the former and *ch* (or *ḥ*) for the latter, because the associated forms are generally familiar to readers even if the distinction is not borne out in pronunciation. (In works of a more general nature, though, there is a case for using *ch* for both *khaf* and *chet*.) With the possible exception of the *ḥ*, then, the use of diacritics is avoided: the *tsadi* is rendered *ts*, and the *shin* by *sh*.

In this system, the (consonantly soundless) *alef* and ʿ*ayin* are indicated only where they occur in intervocalic positions, as their absence might lead an English reader to pronounce the associated vowel cluster as a diphthong or otherwise mispronounce the word. In such instances an apostrophe is inserted between the two vowels to indicate that they are pronounced separately—for example to distinguish *ha'ir* or *pe'er* from the English *hair* or *peer*. The apostrophe is likewise used to disambiguate other vowel clusters that could be mispronounced by an English-speaker, as in *roke'ach*, or *ma'on*. The apostrophe is ignored in alphabetizing. However, following the criterion of retaining established transcriptions for widely used terms, a case can be made for omitting the apostrophe in *Yisrael* and *Shoah*.

A final *hé* is represented by an *h* even though it is not pronounced because, again, many words are conventionally spelt in this way (*Chanukkah*, *Shoah*, etc.); but note that *Rosh Hashana* and *Moshe* (the Hebrew for Moses) are often spelt thus, without representing the final *hé*.

The *dagesh chazak*, represented in some transliteration systems by doubling the letter in which it occurs, is not represented in this system since it in fact has no significant effect on pronunciation. However, the doubled letter is retained in those well-established transcriptions, generally relating to liturgical and religious contexts, that will be familiar to many readers: for example, in such well-known prayers as the *Hallel*, the *Kaddish*, and the *Kiddush*; the terms *kabbalah*, *kibbutz*, and *rabbi*; in the names of familiar biblical and rabbinic figures such as *Hannah, Hillel*, and *Shammai*; and in such holy days as *Sukkot* and *Yom Kippur*. (But note there is no justification whatever for a doubled consonant in *Pessach* or *Rosh Hashannah*—properly *Pesach* and *Rosh Hashanah* in general usage.)

The *sheva na* is indicated by an *e*, as in *devekut* and *berit*, rather than by an apostrophe. Speakers of Modern Hebrew are not consistent about pronouncing the *sheva na* in this way, but this is the prescribed pronunciation. (However, the apostrophe used in the official English names of organizations, such as *B'nai B'rith*, is retained.) The letter *e* is used for the vowels *sheva na*, *segol*, and the diphthong *tseré*, except in the rare cases where the latter occurs at the end of a word, where the use of *é* is preferred (as in *tseré* itself, or *malé*) so as to avoid possible mispronunciations by English-speakers. (This solution is somewhat awkward, since *é* is not conventionally used in transliterating Hebrew. Regardless, the pronunciation of *é* is unambiguous and the alternatives—*eh* or *ey*— would be inconsistent with the system as a whole.)

The *yod* is represented by a *y* when it functions as a consonant at the beginning of a syllable (*yetser*), and by an *i* when it occurs as a vowel (*peri*) or as part of a diphthong (*ein*, *chai*, *noi*). (*Israel* is correctly pronounced 'Yisrael' in Hebrew; *Erets Israel*, the term much used to signify the biblical Land of Israel, confuses the two languages; *Erets Yisrael* is therefore preferable.)

Although Hebrew uses prefixes to indicate the definite article (*ha*, *he*), the relative pronoun (*she*), prepositions (*be*, *le*, *me*, etc.), and conjunctions (*va*, *ve*), the introduction of a hyphen following them in English—as might be done for English prefixes—is not recommended. Those who understand Hebrew recognize the prefix without a hyphen (Hebrew itself does not use a hyphen in such cases); for those who do not, the hyphen adds nothing but distraction, as the following example illustrates:

> A. Grossman, 'Yiḥus mishpaḥah u-mekomo ba-ḥevrah ha-yehudit be-Ashkenaz ha-kedumah', in E. Etkes and Y. Salmon (eds.), *Perakim be-toledot ha-ḥevrah ha-yehudit bi-yemei ha-beinayim u-va'et ha-ḥadashah, mukdashim le-Ya'akov Katz* (Jerusalem, 1980)
>
> A. Grossman, 'Yiḥus mishpaḥah umekomo baḥevrah hayehudit be'Ashkenaz hakedumah', in E. Etkes and Y. Salmon (eds.), *Perakim betoledot haḥevrah hayehudit biyemei habeinayim uva'et haḥadashah, mukdashim leYa'akov Katz* (Jerusalem, 1980)

Where proper nouns are preceded by a prefix, the initial capital of the name is to follow the prefix directly, without any intervening hyphen: Shimon Oren, *MiKineret leKalish: Mikhtavim miYosef Orenstein*.

Word division

There is no simple formula for where to break a transliterated Hebrew word at a line ending. In general terms, the Hebrew syllable consists of consonant + vowel or consonant + vowel + consonant, but the identification of syllables in transliteration can be hampered by the presence of digraphs and doubled consonants. Typesetters should be instructed to avoid hyphenation; word breaks that do occur on proof should be referred to the author or a competent Hebrew-speaker.

Italicization

The extent to which Hebrew terms should be italicized in Jewish-studies texts depends on the intended readership. In a work aimed at scholars, italicization of familiar terms may be intrusive; for the beginner or the general reader it may be distracting if such words are not signalled. Certainly, do not italicize assimilated words of the sort found in the *Concise Oxford Dictionary*, such as *barmitzvah*, *mezuzah*, *kibbutz*, and *rabbi*.

Some Hebrew nouns have English adjectival forms: *halakhic*, *Hasidic*, *midrashic*, and so forth. These terms are not Hebrew, and should not be italicized as such, though setting them in roman suggests that a similar form should be adopted for related words: while *Hasidim*, for example, figure in the *Concise Oxford Dictionary*, their eighteenth-century opponents or *mitnagedim* do not. In a work that discusses both, it makes no sense to italicize—or indeed capitalize—one group and not the other; as much as possible, similar terms should be treated similarly in a given work.

Do not italicize names of people and places, of the deity, of religious festivals, of political and other organizations, of cultural movements, and of wars and other key events for which Hebrew names are used. *Shoah*, when used to denote the Holocaust, is a proper noun and therefore not italicized.

When regular religious services are referred to by their Hebrew names—*shacharit*, *minchah*, and so on—these terms are italicized and in lower case, as any Hebrew common noun would be.

Except in the titles of sources cited in transliteration, transliterated words that are italicized are in general not capitalized, and vice versa.

Capitalization

While Hebrew has no capital letters, all transliterated nouns formerly were capitalized—possibly a consequence of the translation into English of German Jewish texts. This practice is not recommended because it draws too much attention to words that may be of no special significance. However, following the principle of retaining conventions that are familiar to the English-speaking reader, names of people, places, institutions, and religious holidays, etc. are capitalized in the normal way, but as proper nouns they are not italicized. Place names consisting of two words are generally hyphenated in Hebrew, but there is no need to do this in English (*Ramat Gan*, *Tel Aviv*).

Cultural movements can be treated different ways in different contexts. Words used in a specific sense must be capitalized so that the distinction is clear, for example, between the Haskalah movement of the nineteenth century—the Jewish Enlightenment—and the noun *haskalah*, meaning 'education'. As with italicization, establish a pattern for a single work to ensure that similar terms are treated in the same way.

The various institutionalized sectarian groupings within Judaism are usually capitalized: *Conservative Judaism, Liberal Judaism, Orthodox Judaism, Reform Judaism*. As the terms *traditional Judaism, secular Judaism*, and *modern Orthodoxy* are not institutional names they are generally not capitalized. Avoid the value-laden expression *Ultra-Orthodox*; the Hebrew term *charedi* (or *ḥaredi*) is a frequently used alternative, which can be glossed as 'very strictly Orthodox'.

Quotation marks

Because Hebrew has neither italics nor capitals, text submitted by Hebrew-speaking authors often incorporates capitals or quotation marks to emphasize words; follow the English convention and use italics instead. Further, because Modern Hebrew has a smaller vocabulary than English, quotation marks are often used to signal that a word is not being used in the conventional sense (scare quotes). In translations, both these tendencies should be normalized, using italic where necessary for emphasis, and limiting scare quotes wherever possible.

Names of institutions

Do not italicize the proper nouns of institutions, youth movements, political parties, and the like. Translations would usually be of relevance only for a general readership unfamiliar with the bodies in question, who may in any case find it more useful to have the necessary basic information provided systematically in a glossary.

Government and military offices are generally referred to by their English equivalents. As the Israeli army is officially known as the *Israel Defence Forces* (*IDF*), there is no reason to retain the Hebrew acronym *Tsahal*; modern Hebrew military ranks should be converted to their English equivalents. Intelligence services, however, are more generally known by their Hebrew names, such as *Mossad* and *Shin Bet*.

Religious names and terms

The various names of God in Hebrew (*Adonai, Ein Sof, Elohim*, etc.) are capitalized but not italicized, as other names. In works on kabbalah the same system can be followed for the *Shekhinah* (the Divine Presence) and the names of the heavenly spheres or *sefirot*—*Da'at* (Knowledge), *Binah* (Understanding), *Tiferet* (Glory), and so on. This reflects the fact that these represent God in his different aspects—different names of God rather than the mere qualities ascribed to him.

Since the Hebrew names of God are holy, some Orthodox Jewish writers prefer not to spell them out even in English, and will use, for example, *G-d*, *Elokim* (for *Elohim*), or *Hashem* (Hebrew for 'the Name'), and similar variants. An explanation should be provided where such usages will be unfamiliar to the intended readership.

The Tetragrammaton YHVH and its variants is best set thus, in small capitals.

In writing about rabbis who lived before the contemporary period, the title *Rabbi* is often abbreviated to R. (*R. Tarfon and R. Shimon disagreed*), especially in scholarly works. Where an indefinite article is needed, use *a* not *an* (*We have a letter from a R. Moses of Narbonne*). Jewish scholars of pre-modern times are sometimes collectively referred to as *the Rabbis* or *the Sages*; the capitalization is not strictly necessary since contemporary rabbis are considered to be continuing an unbroken tradition. The plurals *tana'im, amora'im*, and *geonim* (singular *gaon*) are technical terms referring to the rabbis of particular periods. In the singular they may be used as titles for particular individuals and would therefore be capitalized rather than italicized ('In the opinion of the Vilna Gaon…').

Since the names of special prayers are often capitalized in English, there is a case for capitalizing the names of specific well-known Hebrew prayers too:

> The Yizkor prayer for the dead is recited during the *shacharit* service on Yom Kippur.
>
> Special paragraphs are inserted into the Birkat Hamazon (Grace after Meals) on sabbaths and festivals.
>
> The Kiddush that is recited over wine on sabbaths and festivals is not to be confused with the Kaddish recited by mourners, which is essentially a doxology.

Less central elements of the liturgy, including the various liturgical poems, are generally referred to by their first line or first few words. Since these phrases effectively function as titles (they have in fact no other titles), treat them typographically as a title, set in italics with the first word and any proper noun capitalized:

> On Chanukah one recites *Al hanisim* in the Amidah and in Birkat Hamazon, but not *Ya'aleh veyavo*.

The decision as to whether to italicize the names of everyday Jewish ritual objects—*mezuzah, tefilin, menorah*, and so on—should be taken contextually, depending mainly on their frequency and that of similar terms, and the intended readership. Although these words are not English, they are so basic to Jewish life—and so untranslatable—that except in the most basic texts, readers will have no alternative but to familiarize themselves with them. In very general books there is a case for italicizing the first occurrence and supplying a gloss, but subsequent references need not be italicized.

11.27 **Hungarian**

Hungarian is written in the roman alphabet, with the accents á, é, í, ó, ú, ő, ű, ö, ü. The alphabet is ordered as *a á b c cs d dz dzs e é f g gy h i í j k l ly m n ny o ó ö ő p q r s sz t ty u ú ü ű v w x y z zs*; *q, w,* and *x* are not found in native words, nor is *y* except as a component of the digraphs *gy, ly, ny,* and *ty.* In alphabetizing, acutes are disregarded, double acutes count as umlauts. The combinations *ccs, ggy, lly, nny, ssz, zzs* count as if *cscs, gygy, lyly, nyny, szsz, zszs*; the combination *dzs* normally falls after *d* in alphabetization (no word begins with *dz*).

11.28 **Italian**

11.28.1 **Diacritics**

Italian uses the same alphabet as English, omitting *k, w, x, y,* and *j* except in names. The use of accents in the Italian language is not entirely consistent; editors should as a general rule follow the author's typescript.

The only firm rule is that stressed final vowels take an accent, and also certain monosyllables: notably *dà* 'gives' (but *da* as a preposition), *è* 'is' (*e* = 'and'), *tè* 'tea' (*te* = 'you'). It is normal to distinguish open *è* from closed *é*, the latter being found in *né* 'nor' (but *ne* as a pronoun), compounds of *che* and *tre*, and the third-person singular preterite indicative of regular verbs in *-ere* (irregular verbs *è*), but on other vowels to use the grave. However, the older practice was to use the grave on all final stressed *e*s, and some printers prefer the acute on *i* and *u*.

Nouns and adjectives ending in *-io* normally take single *-i* in the plural: *vizio* 'vice', plural *vizi*, but in older usage one may find *vizii, vizj,* or *vizî.* The circumflex is still sometimes used, especially to distinguish *principî* 'beginnings, principles', plural of *principio*, from *principi* 'princes', plural of *principe*, but it may also be distinguished by marking the stress *princìpi*. Similarly, other word-pairs differentiated by stress may be distinguished by a written accent on the less familiar word, for example *subìto* 'undergone' versus *subito* 'sudden(ly)', 'at once' (though one may also encounter *sùbito* for the latter). Accents may also be used to distinguish open and close *e* or *o* in otherwise identical words; thus the archaic or poetic infinitive *tòrre* ('to take away'), which has open *o*, may be distinguished by a grave accent from *torre* 'tower', which has closed *o*. (Some, however, would write not *tòrre* but *tôrre*, since it is a contracted form of *togliere*.)

One may also find *dànno* 'they give' distinguished from *danno* 'loss'. All such distinctions are optional, made only when someone has thought them necessary through experience or in a given context; the most regular is *dèi* 'gods' ~ *dei* 'of the', for example *gli dèi dei romani* 'the gods of the Romans'. (It is always *gli*, not *i*, with *dèi*; older Italian would have said *gl'Iddìi de' Romani*.)

In consequence, the appearance in a single text of Italian extracts with several different systems of accentuation may indicate not ignorance or carelessness in the author, but rather scrupulous fidelity to sources. If that is not the case, then although *ì* and *ù* are on the whole more frequent in Italian printing than *í* and *ú*, the acute should be accepted if consistent and imposed if preponderant; the author may be asked to make a consistent distinction between *é* and *è*, in accordance with normal modern practice. Only if neither author nor editor knows Italian should uniform *è*, which by now is archaic, be imposed (in which case *ì* and *ù* must be used). Similarly, the discretional accents mentioned in the previous paragraph should be left alone unless the copy editor is expert in the language and the author is not.

There are other respects too in which Italian spelling is even now less regulated than, say, French. One Italian book, for example, mainly concerned with spelling variants in Latin, mentions in passing the variations *sopratutto* ~ *soprattutto, costatare* ~ *constatare, templi* ~ *témpi* (the plural of *tempio* 'temple'; not to be confused with *tempi*, the plural of *tempo*), *province* ~ *provincie*. Hence zeal for consistency must be tempered by either knowledge or discretion.

11.28.2 Abbreviation

It is increasingly common for Italian abbreviations to be set with an initial capital only rather than in full capitals, with no full point following. Hence *An* for *Alleanza Nazionale, Rai* for *Radiotelevisione Italiana*, and *Lit* for *Lira italiana*. When the expansion does not begin with a capital, neither does the abbreviation, for example *tv* (pronounced *tivù*) for *televisione*.

11.28.3 Capitalization

When citing titles of works, Italian practice is to capitalize only the first word and proper nouns (*I pagliacci, Beatrice di Tenda, La dolce vita*). While all important words in familiar short titles are sometimes capitalized (*La Divina Commedia, Orlando Furioso, Le Quattro Stagioni*), do not follow this practice unless the entire work is to be set in Italian, since the result can appear inconsistent.

When setting in full capitals, accents are generally omitted except when needed to avoid confusion. Roman numerals indicating centuries are generally put in full capitals in both italic and roman (*l'XI secolo*).

11.28.4 Word division

Do not divide the following compound consonants:

bl	br	ch	cl	cr	dr	fl	fr	gh	gl
gn	gr	pl	pr	sb	sc	sd	sf	sg	sl
sm	sn	sp	sq	sr	st	sv	tl	tr	vr
sbr	sch	scr	sdr	sfr	sgh	sgr	spl	spr	str

Divide between vowels only if neither is *i* or *u*. When a vowel is followed by a doubled consonant, the first of these goes with the vowel, and the second is joined to the next syllable; that is, the division comes between the two letters (*lab|bro*, *mag|gio*). Consider the combination *cq* as a doubled consonant (*ac|qua*, *nac|que*, *noc|que*, *piac|que*).

In the middle of a word, if the first consonant of a group is a liquid—i.e. either *l*, *m*, *n*, or *r*—it remains with the preceding vowel, and the other consonant, or combination of consonants, goes with the succeeding vowel (*al|tero*, *ar|tigiano*, *tem|pra*).

Divide words after the prefixes *as-*, *es-*, *dis-*, *tras-* (*as|trarre*, *es|posto*, *dis-|fatta*, *tras|porto*). If assimilation has taken place, we have, according to the foregoing rules, *ef|fluvio*, *dif|ficile*, *dif|fuso*. Divide *dall|l'aver*, *sen|z'altro*, *quaran|t'anni*.

11.28.5 Punctuation

Italian makes a distinction between points of omission (which are spaced) and points of suspension (which are unspaced). The latter equate with the French *points de suspension*, three points being used where preceded by other punctuation, four in the absence of other punctuation.

Both single quotation marks (' ', called *virgolette alte*) and guillemets (« », called *virgolette basse*) are used, sometimes as a mixture; the former being used to highlight terms and the latter for quoted material. Guillemets are used for quotations within quotations. Dialogue is often introduced with an indented em rule and no quotation marks, with subsequent interpolations set off with further em rules.

11.28.6 Spacing

Put the ordinary interword space after an apostrophe following a vowel (*a' miei*, *de' malevoli*, *i' fui*, *ne' righi*, *po' duro*); here, when necessary, the apostrophe may end a line. But there is no space after an apostrophe following a consonant (*dall'aver, l'onda, s'allontana, senz'altro*); in this case the apostrophe may not end a line, but may be taken over along with the letter preceding it. When an apostrophe replaces a vowel at the beginning of a word a space always precedes it (*e 'l, su 'l, te 'l, che 'l*). Down to the nineteenth century the reverse of these rules may be found, for example *a'miei, senz' altro, su'l*.

11.29 Japanese

11.29.1 Characters

Japanese is expressed and printed in ideographs of Chinese origin (*kanji*), interspersed with an alphabet-based script (*kana*), of which there are two versions, the *hiragana* (the cursive form) and the *katakana* (the 'squared' form).

Since the Second World War 1,850 *kanji* have been officially designated for use in textbooks, government documents, etc. Some 1,000 of these are in regular use. *Kanji* will have one or more forms of pronunciation. Some are articulated as an approximation of the original Chinese pronunciation (the so-called *on* reading). Others have a pronunciation of purely Japanese origin (the *kun* pronunciation), which is most typically given to ideographs for some phenomenon commonly found in nature, for example *kusa* 'grass'. Though this is bisyllabic, only one *kanji* is used to express it.

The *kana* are monosyllabic. They consist of a framework of 50 + 1 symbols (*gojuon*) in groups of five, beginning with the vowels in order *a, i, u, e, o*, which are then prefixed successively by the consonants *k, s, t, n, h, m, y, r*, and *w* to form a further nine groupings each of five sounds, and the nasal final *n*.

- *Hiragana* are essential in order to indicate the inflections of Japanese verbs and other grammatical features of the language. Nowadays, they may be used to represent a whole word in place of *kanji* of Chinese origin. Sometimes they may be written beside a *kanji* in order to give the pronunciation of this, in which situation they are known as *furigana*; this practice declined after the official selection of *kanji* was published.

- *Katakana* are used in domestic telegrams, or to express foreign names and foreign words that have entered the Japanese language and have no domestic equivalent, for example *piero* 'pierrot' or *pan* 'bread', or to render onomatopoeia, for example *peta-peta* 'slap, slap'.

Small symbols may be added to the *kana* to permit further variations in pronunciation. Basic Japanese punctuation includes 、 (comma), 。 (full point), 「 (opening quotation mark), and 」 (closing quotation mark); a medial dot · links related elements, such as the parts of a foreign proper noun rendered in Japanese. Question and exclamation marks are as in English. Japanese directories order *kanji* by their *kana* equivalents.

Traditionally, Japanese is written vertically from right to left (*tategaki*), which is still standard for published materials. Modern Japanese can also be written horizontally from left to right (*yokogaki*); a combination of the two is often found, with columns for text coupled with horizontal headlines and captions. The choice of text format determines whether the work itself begins at the left or right.

11.29.2 Romanization

Japanese characters are phonetically transcribed into the roman alphabet according to various systems; the most pervasive system is that used in Kenkyusha's *New Japanese–English Dictionary*, itself only a slight modification of the original Hepburn system. Kenkyusha places an apostrophe after *n* at the end of a syllable when followed by a vowel or the letter *y* (*Gen'e*, *San'yo*). The system operates with the normal English use of *ch*, *f*, *j*, *sh* rather than for example *t/ty*, *h*, *z*, *zy*, *s* (*sy*). The homorganic nasal should be *n* before *b*, *m*, *p*; never, as in unmodified Hepburn, *m*: *shinbun*, not *shimbun*.

A macron (not a circumflex) is used to indicate a long vowel. The inclusion of macrons is optional in non-specialist works, and may be omitted in well-established forms of place names, such as *Hokkaido*, *Honshu*, *Kobe*, *Kyoto*, *Kyushu*, *Osaka*, *Tokyo*. This applies only where names or other words are used by themselves in English text, not when forming part of transliterated titles or other phrases.

Japanese characters inserted in text, as in a gloss or bibliography, fall after their transcription; normally parentheses are unnecessary. If characters will be inserted as print-ready copy at proof stage, editors should leave sufficient space by setting a bullet or asterisk in place of each character. Characters have no descenders as such, and should be equal to ascender height of the accompanying font. Do not mix different types of characters or orthography in similar contexts.

11.29.3 Capitalization

When romanized, only titles preceding a personal name should be capitalized. The words *period* and *era* should appear in lower case when they follow a proper noun (*the Edo period*). English words forming part of a place name (*island, city, village, prefecture*) should be capitalized (*Toyota City*).

Romanized titles of works in Japanese are lower case, except for the initial letter of the first word and any proper nouns they may include. Follow English usage for unitalicized proper nouns (*the Tanaka Faction*).

11.29.4 Italicization

Write Japanese words in common English usage as they appear in standard English dictionaries, for example 'daimyo', 'shogun', 'samurai'. They are not italicized unless being made consistent with less common words mentioned elsewhere.

Proper nouns are italicized only when they would be so treated in English—titles of books and periodicals, films and plays, works of art, ships, legal cases. Ship names end in *Maru*, literally 'sword'.

Do not italicize institutional names unless they are added in parentheses after an English translation that is used to refer to them thereafter. When they are referred to by their Japanese name, it should be in roman with a parenthetical English translation, in quotation marks, at first mention. It is for the translator to decide which system to adopt in each case; the only overall policy is that readers should be able to understand without difficulty why one name was translated and another not.

11.29.5 Word division

In general word division for romanized text follows normal English rules.

11.30 Korean

11.30.1 Characters

The modern orthography of Korean dates from the time of King Sejong, and the *han'gŭl* syllabary then devised must rank as one of the most efficient of all time. It comprises twenty-eight letters, consisting of fourteen basic consonants and fourteen basic vowels. Each syllable must consist at the least of an initial consonant and a vowel.

Some Korean word groups can be written using Chinese characters (*hanmun*). Since Korean contains a large number of homophones, this practice can be useful in clarifying the meaning. Chinese characters are frequently interspersed with *han'gŭl* in books, documents, and newspapers originating in South Korea. In North Korea all texts are in *han'gŭl* and Chinese characters are almost never used, except where they are required in order to clarify a meaning or for historical purposes.

Since the political divide following the Second World War, the orthography of South Korea also differs from that in use in the North, reflecting differences in pronunciation between dialects. The most obvious difference is that the North Koreans still use *n* and *l* (*r*) as initial letters. This usage is absent in South Korea and, in any case, for romanization purposes these initials are dropped.

11.30.2 Romanization

The most universally used system is the so-called MR system devised by George M. McCune and E. O. Reischauer and published in *Transactions of the Royal Asiatic Society*, 29 (1939). It is the system preferred in government agencies, academic libraries, etc. in most countries in the world apart from France and the territories of Eastern Europe. It is not a *transliteration*, but aims to give an approximation of the way a syllable or a series of sounds are to be pronounced. The vowels in the MR system do not change, but consonants will alter quite regularly according to where they stand in relation to adjoining consonants or intervening vowels. To take an extreme example, when the two syllables *kuk* and *min* join together to form a word meaning 'national', the MR romanization becomes *kungmin*. The rules of MR romanization are quite complicated, and those who are not Korean linguists should seek expert advice.

11.30.3 Capitalization

In citing romanized titles of works, practice largely follows the standard adopted for European languages, with only the first word and proper nouns capitalized. Korean expressions used in an English sentence should appear italicized, in lower case. Names of institutions, schools of thought and religions, etc. are set in roman if they are capitalized or in italics if they are lower-case.

11.30.4 Italicization

Write Korean words in common English usage as they appear in standard English dictionaries (*chaebol, jeon, kimchi, tae kwon do*); as with Japanese, they should not be italicized and no accents should be used in non-specialist contexts. Proper nouns are italicized only when they would be so treated in English—titles of books and periodicals, films and plays, works of art, ships, and legal cases.

11.30.5 **Word division**

This is something of a problem in Korean. There has been debate about whether a noun and suffix should be romanized as one word, for example *Han'gugŭi* (= of Korea, Korea's) or two, *Han'guk ŭi*. (Most US libraries choose the second option.) It is debatable whether the Korean term for 'Korean peninsula' should be rendered as *Han pando* or *Hanbando*. Both will be found, depending largely upon the whim of the person who is romanizing. The easiest principle to adopt is to romanize in accordance with the meaning in English. Thus 'Korean peninsula', which makes two words in English, would be best rendered by two words in MR romanization.

11.31 **Latin**

11.31.1 **Alphabet**

The standard Latin alphabet consists of twenty-one letters, *A B C D E F G H I K L M N O P Q R S T V X*, plus two imports from Greek, *Y* and *Z*. *A, E, O, Y* are vowels; *I, V* may be either vowels or consonants. The letter *C* was originally a form of gamma used by early Greek colonists; under the influence of Etruscan (which had no g sound) it acquired that of *k*, its original value being distinguished by the cross-stroke. The original value survives in the use of *C.* and *Cn.* as abbreviations for *Gaius* and *Gnaeus* respectively. The new value of *C* was at first largely confined to the position before *E* or *I*, *K* being preferred before *A* and Q before *O* and *V*.

In classical spelling, *K* is confined to a few words, chiefly *Kalendae*, *Karthago*, and in legal usage *kaput*, but may be found in abbreviations, *K.* = *Caeso* (a praenomen used by patrician Fabii and Quinctii) or *kaput*, *k.k.* = *kalumniae kausa*, and archaizing inscriptions, *kandidatus, karus*. The latter is also found in medieval texts, where *k* also appears for Greek-derived *ch* in *karacter*. Classical spelling, in its standardized form, admits Q only before consonantal *V*: *qui* as opposed to *cui* (earlier spelt *quoi*), where the *u* has its full value. Similarly, one writes *relicuus* in Republican authors, who give the word four syllables, but *reliquus* in Imperial authors, who give it only three.

For some time *O* was used instead of *V* after another *V*; this usage may be found even in modern editions, for example *equos* (nominative singular) instead of *equus*. (It is less usual to retain the other attested spelling *ecus*, even though it best reflects the pronunciation.)

Long *i* is sometimes indicated in inscriptions by a tall character (*I longum*), other long vowels by an acute accent (*apex* 'cap'), or in inscriptions of the late second and early first centuries BC by a doubled letter. However, there is no consistency in the use of such conventions. Long *i* may also be indicated in the late Republic by *EI*, which had originally been used for a different sound, but may also represent its component vowels in separate syllables; the use for ī was revived by archaizers in the second century AD, and is sometimes affected during the Renaissance.

Although aware that *I* and *V* had two values, the Romans saw no need to distinguish them, except that the Emperor Claudius introduced a character for consonantal *V* like an inverted capital *F* (Ⅎ), which is found in official inscriptions from his time and that of his successor, Nero.

The letter *C* is reversed to indicate the feminine name *Gaia* in the formula Ɔ. l. = *Gaiae libertus/ta*, the standard term in the nomenclature for a freed(wo)man liberated by a woman, and in numerals: IƆ 500, CIƆ 1,000.

The ligatures Æ, Œ are not found in classical sources except on the same basis as other space-saving forms in inscriptions. They are found in post-classical manuscripts (where *ae* may also appear as ę or *e*), and in printed books down to the nineteenth century and occasionally beyond. They should not be used unless a source containing them is to be reproduced exactly.

The early modern distinction between vocalic *i*, *u* and consonantal *j*, *v* was formerly applied to Latin; some scholars still retain it with *u/v*, distinguishing *solvit* with two syllables from *coluit* with three (also *volvit* 'rolls/rolled' from *voluit* 'willed'), but others prefer to use *V* for the capital and *u* for the lower case irrespective of value. (However, the numeral must be *v* regardless of case.) By contrast, the use of *j*, except in reproducing early printed matter and in a few tags quoted as such (e.g. *cujus regio ejus religio*), may be regarded as obsolete outside the Roman Catholic Church, though it may be used in special circumstances ('the first syllable of *inice* is long because it was pronounced *injice*').

Between vowels, consonantal *I* was pronounced, and often written, double: *CVIIVS*, *EIIVS*. This is not normal in medieval or modern usage, though some scholars reproduce it in the texts of authors who can be shown to have spelt that way, for example Juvenal, whose manuscripts never exhibit this spelling but frequently exhibit corruptions of it (*il*, *li*, *ll*). Note that the name *Gaius* is not a case in point, but contains three syllables, *Gā-i-us*.

The Greek combinations φθ, χθ, rendered *phth*, *chth* in English and

German, are correctly *pth*, *cth* in classical Latin (the two *h*s being a Renaissance hypercorrection) and *pht*, *cht* in French.

11.31.2 Accents

Apart from the acute accent (*apex*) sporadically used on long vowels, classical Latin employs no accents; they are not normal in modern printing, except for long and short marks in grammars and special contexts. Older printing often indicates adverbs with a grave accent on a final syllable, and distinguishes the long *a* of the ablative singular in the first declension from the short *a* of the nominative by a circumflex; these conventions are no longer current, though in English it is sometimes helpful to use a circumflex to distinguish the plural of fourth-declension nouns such as *hiatus* from the singular.

Older printing uses the diaeresis when *ae* and *oe* do not form diphthongs; this is no longer usual, so that no distinction is made between *aeris* 'of bronze/money', in Victorian printing *æris*, and *aeris* 'of air', in Victorian printing *aëris*; the Romans wrote both as *AERIS*. However, the diaeresis may be used occasionally to indicate less usual pronunciations.

The apostrophe is not used in ancient spelling; elided vowels are either written (the normal practice) or omitted without compensation. Modern scholars, however, sometimes use it to represent a final *s* suppressed in pre-classical verse before a consonant, prodelision of an initial vowel (*bona's* for *bona es*, in which not the *a* but the *e* was silent), and occasionally colloquial apocopes such as *vin'* (more normally written *vin*) = *visne* 'will you?' (a disguised command).

11.31.3 Capitals

Titles of works are capitalized variously. Proper nouns apart, one may find first word only (*De rerum natura*, *De imperio Cn. Pompei*), first and main words (*De Rerum Natura*, *De Imperio Cn. Pompei*), main words only (*de Rerum Natura*, *de Imperio Cn. Pompei*), even proper nouns only (*de rerum natura*, *de imperio Cn. Pompei*). The most sensible recommendation is first word only; otherwise there are too many capitals (e.g. Cicero's lost work on turning Roman law into a proper science, *De Iure Ciuili in Artem Redigendo*)—especially in Renaissance scholarship, and in the titles of doctoral dissertations (which are often cast in the form of an extended indirect question). For general and specialist citation of classical references *see* **15.12**.

Latin titles quoted in English-language works are often treated the same as English titles, with first and main words capitalized. Certainly this is often the case where an English text employs a Latin title: for example, the first words of Psalm 130, *De profundis*, are capitalized thus when used as the title of the mass for the dead; however, the title of Wilde's prose apologia is usually styled *De Profundis* with two capitals.

It is no longer customary to capitalize the first letter in lines of verse; usage varies with sentences.

Small capitals should normally be used for roman numerals rather than full capitals or lower case, though the latter is sometimes correct in transcriptions of medieval manuscripts; roman numerals should similarly be small-capital or lower-case in texts in any language transcribed from manuscripts, unless large lettering is to be reproduced as such.

11.31.4 **Word division**

A vowel may be divided from another (*be|atus*) unless they form a diphthong, as do most instances of *ae* and *oe*, *ei* in words also written with simple *i*, and *au*, *eu* (in early Latin also *ou* = later long *u*); but when *v* is not used, the correct divisions with consonantal *u* are *ama|uit dele|uit*; likewise *i* consonant is taken over (*in|iustus*).

Roman grammarians decree that any group capable of beginning a word in either Latin or Greek shall be taken over. This rule was obeyed by medieval scribes (though not by ancient stonecutters), and is followed by OUP: *fa|ctus*, *di|gnus*, *da|mnum*, *la|psus*, *sum|ptus*. For further details *see* **GREEK 11.25**; but guidance may be had from such learned English words as *ctenoid*, *gnomon*, *mnemonic*, *pneumonia*, *psychology*, and *ptomaine*.

Any doubled consonants may be divided; also, apart from the above exception for *mn*, the letters *l*, *m*, *n*, and *r* may be divided from a following consonant. Take over *x* between vowels (*pro|ximus*) except as below.

In modern practice these rules are subject to the overriding precept that compound words are divided into their parts. Some frequent prefixes end in consonants either always (*ad*, *ob*, *sub*) or in certain contexts (*ab*- besides *a*-, *ex*- besides *e*-, *red*- besides *re*-). The prefix *dis* becomes *dir* before a vowel (*diribeo*, *dirimo*; but *disicio* = *disjicio*, *disieci* = *disjeci*); before a voiced consonant it becomes *di*, but also before *s* + consonant, so that *distinguo* from *dis* + *stinguo* should be divided *di|stinguo* (contrast *dis|tuli*). In noun compounds, divide for example *Alex|ander*, *dem|archus*.

Numerals

For roman numerals *see* **7.7**.

11.32 **Maltese**

Maltese, the national language of Malta, is a Semitic language related to Arabic but much influenced by Spanish, Norman French, and especially Italian, to the extent that the roman alphabet is used together with many Italian spelling conventions. Maltese uses the accents *á, é, í, ó, ú, â, ê, î, ô, û, ċ, ġ, ż, à, è, ì, ò, ù*, and the special characters ' (apostrophe, not lenis or asper) and *ħ* (crossed *h*). The acute and circumflex are used only when it is necessary to distinguish short vowels (as in *zína* 'lechery') from long (as in *zîna* 'ornament'); the grave is used only on end-stressed loanwords, generally from Italian.

The letter *għ* should not be broken, nor should *ie*, though it is not always considered to be a separate letter. In alphabetizing, variation can occur in the placement of certain letters: *għ* can fall after *g* or after *n*, *ħ* can fall before or after *h*, and *ż* can fall before or after *z*; *ġ*, however, is usually before *g*.

11.33 **Mongolian**

A member of the Altaic language family, Mongolian has no accepted standard for transliteration into the roman alphabet: English, German, and French systems differ, for example, and variations exist within each of these. The central reason for this is that Mongolian can be derived from four main sources. The spoken language has many dialects, though the Halh spoken in Mongolia itself is considered the 'central' form. Traditional Mongolian script (written vertically, right to left) exists in several forms, depending on dialect and location, and is often distant from pronunciation. Written Cyrillic Mongolian attempts to follow pronunciation, and alternative spelling still exists for many words. (Some Western scholars approach Mongolian through Russian, and therefore use Russian conventions for rendering certain Cyrillic letters.) Written roman-alphabet Mongolian has numerous variants, some dating back to the brief period in the 1930s when roman characters replaced Cyrillic; several of these versions follow pronunciation, while others attempt to render Mongolian morphology.

Diacritics and special characters likely to be encountered are *ë, ö, ø, ü* (sometimes ɣ), *â* (vowel length), *γ* (sometimes *Γ* or *gh/g*), *ĵ/y/z, c/č, s/š* (sometimes *sh*), and letter groups *ai/ayi, ei/eyi*. Alphabetical order varies depending on the original source.

11.34 **Old and Middle English**

The ash (*Æ*, *æ*) (Old English *æsc* 'ash-tree', originally the name of the corresponding rune) is pronounced as in 'h*a*t'; in Old English texts it should be printed as a single sort, not two separate letters. There are two types of this ligature's italic form, open (*æ*) and closed (*œ*): the open form, employed by the Early English Text Society, is to be preferred, since the closed form is easily mistaken for an italic œ ligature (*œ*). Although the *œ* ligature is not found in standard Old English (West Saxon), it is found in other dialects and also in Old Norse, which is likely to be cited for comparative purposes in Old English studies. (In modern Icelandic, Faeroese, Danish, and Norwegian, where only æ is used, there is no need to use the open italic form, nor is it normal in the countries concerned; but if these languages are quoted in a work for which the open ligature is required—as in this book—then it may be employed for them too.) (*See also* **11.40**.)

The eth or (especially US) edh (*Ð*, *ð*), sometimes called a 'crossed *d*', is pronounced in modern Icelandic and normalized Old Norse 'dh', like the voiced *th* as in 'th*a*t' (or in the name 'e*th*'); in Old English and unnormalized Old Norse it is used indiscriminately for the voiced sound and the voiceless *th* of 'thin'. In Icelandic printing, the lower-case form has a straight but angled cross-bar (*ð*). The form of the lower-case letter preferred by the Early English Text Society has a slight hook (*ð̄*); this is to be used if possible in books on Old and early Middle English, but not in those on Icelandic or Old Norse. The lower-case form with a normal *d* and a straight but horizontal cross-bar (*đ*) is found in Old Saxon and—with a quite different value—in modern Serbo-Croat. (In Old Saxon the bar is required through the ascender of *b* as well as *d*.)

The thorn (*þ*, *þ*), a character borrowed from the runic alphabet, is pronounced in modern Icelandic and in normalized Old Norse with a voiceless *th* as in 'thin'; in Old English and unnormalized Old Norse it is used indiscriminately for the voiceless sound and the voiced *th* of 'that'. (Its Old Norse name was originally *þurs* 'giant'; the designation *þorn* was borrowed from English.) In modern Icelandic printing the plain form with horizontal serifs is used (*P*, *þ*); however, for Old English the Early English Text Society prefers the forms *þ*, *þ*, with a slanted foot serif and a narrower bowl; this is to be used if possible in books on Old and Middle English, but not in those on Icelandic or Old Norse. Authors and editors should ensure that the printer knows which form is intended, and cannot mistake a thorn for a *p* or a wyn. In Old English, furthermore, there is a special character *þ̄*, *þ̄* ('that'-sign) representing the article, pronoun, and conjunction *þæt*.

In printing Old English no attempt should be made to regularize the use of eth and thorn even in the same word; Old English scribes used both letters at random. Whereas eth died out fairly soon after the Norman Conquest, thorn continued in use into the fifteenth century, and even later as the *y* for *th* of early Scots printing and in *ye* or *y*^{e} used for *the* and *yt, y*^{t}*, y*^{at} for *that*; hence *Ye Olde* was originally read *The Old*. (Other combinations included *y*^{ei}*, y*^{m}, and *y*^{u} for *they*, *them*, and *thou*, respectively.) The combination *th* is rare in Old English; editors should avoid it unless it is specified by the author, for example in 'diplomatic' texts. Compounds apart (e.g. *Alpingið*), the modern Icelandic *þ* is always initial, *ð* never.

The wyn (also wynn, formerly also wen, from the Kentish dialect; the name means 'joy') (Ƿ, ƿ) was borrowed from the Runic alphabet to represent the sound of *w* as in 'wyn', in the earliest Old English manuscripts sometimes written *uu*. Except in special circumstances—for example in the few early Middle English works in which both *w* and wyn are used—*w* is normally substituted for the wyn of the manuscript, since it is easily confused with a thorn, though it may be distinguished by the absence of an ascender. Note that a printer may also mistake a wyn for a *p*.

Old English script was borrowed from Old Irish (hence the term 'insular' for this hand); the letter *g* was written ᵹ, ᵹ. According to context, this letter was pronounced hard like Dutch *g* (the voiced equivalent of the German *ach* sound; later at the start of a word like English *g* in *go*) or soft (like *y* in *year*); in early poetry the hard and soft sounds may alliterate with each other. The Norman Conquest brought with it a letter *g* pronounced either as in *go* or as in *gentle*; in Middle English it was conventional to use the Continental shape of the letter for these sounds, but a developed form of the insular shape (ȝ, ȝ) for specifically English values, including the voiceless spirant in *niȝt* 'night' (still heard in Scots *nicht*), previously written *h*; this character acquired the name 'yogh', which combined its two most characteristic sounds. (The loss of the velar spirant that causes certain English persons to call a loch a *lock* and Bach *Bark* induced a pronunciation *yok*; as a result, we find the character called in Latin *iugum* 'yoke'.)

Whereas in modern editions of Old English texts the yogh is normally represented by *g* just as every other insular letter-form is represented by its modern equivalent, ᵹ (the Old English form) should be used only in the few late works in which both letter-shapes occur; in Middle English the distinction must be maintained; in some early Middle English texts ᵹ is permissible, but normally ȝ is to be used for yogh in all Middle English work. In some Middle English texts the same shape is also used for *z* (hence the use of *z* for *y* in early Scots printing and its preservation in dialect forms such as *spuilzie* and names such as *Menzies* (pronounced 'Mingis')); it may even be found, as in the manuscript of *Sir Gawayn*, for inflectional *s*. (It is for the textual editor to decide whether or not to distinguish them.) Note that a printer may mistake a yogh for a g in one form or a 3 or *z* in the other.

In early Latin manuscripts the conjunction *et* (but never its synonyms *ac* and *atque*) is frequently represented by 7, known as the 'Tironian' ampersand (named after Cicero's freedman Tiro, who devised a form of shorthand). In Ireland this character was adopted for the corresponding conjunction *ocus* (also spelt *ocuis, acus*; in modern Irish *agus*); imported into England, it was used for the English equivalent *and* or *ond*. An arabic number 7 from a different font may be substituted if a printer does not have the sort available; a larger form (7) may be used to begin a sentence. Whereas in editing Latin texts it is normal to restore *et*, in Old Irish and Old English the convention is to retain the Tironian character, since the envisaged spelling is uncertain (for a similar reason, roman figures in these and other languages are not replaced by words). The modern ampersand, &, should not be substituted. This was originally a compendium for the letter combination *et*, for example *p&ere* = *petere* ('seek', 'make for'), *hab&* = *habet* ('has'); it was eventually confined to the conjunction, displacing 7, and used for the corresponding English conjunction *and*; regarded as a character in its own right, it was known as 'and *per se* and' = 'ampersand'.

Punctuation

Sometimes called the inverted semicolon, the *punctus elevatus* (⁏), which occurs occasionally in Old English manuscripts and frequently in Middle English manuscripts, is not a semicolon and should not be replaced by one. The *punctus versus* (;) resembles a semicolon, and may be replaced by one; the *punctus interrogativus* (?) resembles a question mark, and may be replaced by one. Editors should not attempt to regularize or correct individual punctuation marks in manuscripts, especially as these marks do not necessarily perform functions equivalent to those of their modern counterparts: in the Old English of the late tenth and eleventh centuries a semicolon was the strongest stop and a full point the weakest.

Alphabetizing

The former convention for alphabetizing Old English was that æ = ae; the new convention is for æ to fall at the end. When alphabetizing, þ = ð; some authors treat as *th*, others as a separate letter after *t*; the prefix *ge* is ignored. In alphabetizing Middle English, *y* = *i*.

11.35 **Persian**

In modern contexts Persian is called Farsi (Fārsī) in Iran, Dari (Dārī) in Afghanistan, and Tajik in Tajikistan. Apart from Tajik (which uses Cyrillic), modern Persian is normally printed in Arabic script with slight modifications, although Old Persian—an earlier form in ancient or medieval Persia—was written in cuneiform until the second century BC, and Middle Persian was written in the Pahlavī alphabet. Middle Persian provided—in less inflected form—the foundation of the modern language, which has been greatly influenced by Arabic and ultimately Greek.

The diacritics used in the Library of Congress transliteration system are á (é in some other systems), ḥ, ṣ, ṭ, ẓ, ẕ (also rendered ż), ā, ī, ū (in classical language also ē, ō), ṣ, ẕ (in classical language also ḏ or δ); and the special characters ' (*hamza*), ' (*'ayn*), ' (prime). In philological transcriptions a háček is used in č, š, ž (popularly *ch*, *sh*, *zh*, in the *Encyclopaedia of Islam* system c͟h, s͟h z͟h), sometimes also ǰ (normally *j* in English). In Middle Persian transcriptions the Greek letter γ may be found.

11.36 **Portuguese**

11.36.1 **General**

The Portuguese of Brazil differs considerably in spelling, pronunciation, and syntax from that of Portugal and the former colonies (European Portuguese)—far more so, even in formal usage, than US English differs from British English. In orthography, a joint accord of 1945 encountered strong resistance in Brazil, which is more radical in its treatment of consonants but more conservative in its use of accents, although it accepted Portuguese reforms in 1972.

11.36.2 **Alphabet**

The digraphs *ch* (pronounced as in French), *lh*, *nh* are not treated as separate letters; nor is *ç* (*cê cedilhado*). To *c*, *g*, *c* before *a*, *o*, *u* correspond *qu*, *gu*, *c* before *e*, *i*; so formerly, and still in Brazil, *gua/güe*. As in Castilian, verbs in *-ger*, *-gir* make *-ja* in the present subjunctive, but verbs in *-jar* make *-je*.

The letter *x*, usually pronounced like *ch*, but sometimes *s* (as in *trouxe*

'I/he brought'), *z* (*êxito* 'success'), or *ks* (*fixar* 'to fix'), is not infrequent, but has not replaced *j* and soft *g* as in Galician.

The letter *y* is used only in foreign words. The devoicing of sibilants has not taken place: to the voiceless *s* (initial)/*ss* (medial) and *ch* correspond voiced *z* (initial)/*s* (medial) and *j*. The distinction between *c*/*z* and *ss*/*s*, present in earlier stages of the language, has now been lost.

Apart from *rr* and *ss*, double consonants are confined to European Portuguese: *accão* 'action, share', *accionista* 'shareholder', *comummente* 'commonly', *connosco* 'with us', in Brazil *acão*, *acionista*, *comumente*, *conosco*. But in Portugal too the negative prefix is reduced to *i*- before *m* and *n* even in learned words: *imaculado* 'immaculate', *inado* 'innate'; *dicionário* 'dictionary', *suceder* 'happen', etc. also have the single consonant.

Several other consonant groups are simplified in Brazil, even in learned words: *acto*, *amnistia*, *excepcão*, *óptico*, *súbdito* ('subject' as opposed to 'sovereign'), *subtil* become *ato*, *anistia*, *excecão*, *ótico*, *súdito*, *sutil*. *Fato* in Portugal means 'suit (of clothes)' (Brazilian *terno*), in Brazil 'fact' (Portuguese *facto*). Most of these distinctions reflect differences of pronunciation: either Portugal still pronounces the consonant outright, or in pretonic position gives the vowel a clearer sound than if there had never been a consonant to close the syllable, but Brazil uses the clear sound anyway.

There is no confusion in pronunciation or spelling between *b* and *v*. In many words the diphthongs *oi* and *ou* are interchangeable; in Brazil the choice is nearly always for *ou*.

11.36.3 **Written accents**

European Portuguese uses four written accents on vowels: acute, grave, circumflex, and til (the Spanish tilde); Brazil has retained a fifth accent, the diaeresis. The acute may be used on any vowel, but on *e*, *o* only when open; the grave only on *a* (but in older usage on any vowel); the circumflex on *a*, closed *e*, and closed *o*, the til on *a* and *o*; the diaeresis on *u* between *q*/*g* and *e*/*i* to show that it is pronounced in its own right.

Normal stress falls on the penultimate in words ending in -*a*, -*am*, -*as*, -*e*, -*em*, -*ens*, -*es*, -*o*, -*os*; in all other cases (including words in -*â*, -*i*, -*u*) on the final syllable. This includes final -*n*: *íman* 'compass' (*im* = 'imam'), plural *ímanes*. The noun *carácter* changes its stress in the plural: *caracteres* (but *regime* is regular).

In contrast to Castilian and Galician, a word ending in a consonant followed by a weak vowel itself followed by a strong vowel, strong vowel + *s*, or -*am*, -*em*, -*ens*, has normal stress on the weak vowel: *vivia*, *vivias*, *viviam* (but *vivíamos*, *vivíeis* with abnormal stress); *averiguo* 'I ascertain'. This is the case even after *q*: *antiquo* 'I render outdated'. The accent is written when the stress falls earlier, for example *vício* 'vice', *bilíngue* (Brazilian *bilíngüe*), *iníquo* 'unjust'. Hence any word ending in *-ia*, *-ie*, *-io*, *-ua*, *-ue*, *-uo* in Castilian may be expected to have accent on the preceding syllable in Portuguese: note however *academia*, which has normal stress in both languages, on *de* in Castilian (and Galician), on *mi* in Portuguese, and verb forms such as *evacuo*. In the standard language, verbs in *-iar* and *-uar* all stress the *-i*, *-u* in the strong forms; a few in *-iar* change *-i* to *-ei*.

The strong subjunctive forms of verbs in *-guar*, *-quar* take an acute on the *-u*: *averigúe*, *averigúes*, *averigúem*, similarly *antiqúe* etc. In the verbs *delinquir* 'transgress', *arguir* 'argue', *redarguir* 'retort' (all formerly—and in Brazil still—spelt with *-üir*), the third-person plural present indicative similarly ends in *-úem* (*delinqúem* 'they transgress'); in the second- and third-person singular present indicative and second-person singular imperative the *e* of the normal endings *-es*, *-e* becomes *i*: *delinqúis* 'you (singular) transgress' (contrast *delinquis* 'you (plural) transgress'), *delinqúi* 'transgresses', 'transgress!' The older spellings were *delinqües*, *delinqüe* (second-person plural *delinqüis*), and similarly *averigüe*, *antigüe* (though stem-stressed forms may be found in Brazil: *averíguo*, *antíquo*; *averígüe*, *antíqüe*).

A weak vowel between a strong vowel and *nh* or syllable-final *l*, *m*, *n*, *r*, *z* takes normal stress: *moinho* 'mill', *adail* 'leader', *Coimbra*, *ainda* 'still', *juiz* 'judge', and in verbs *sair* 'to go out', *sairmos* '(if/when in the future) we go out, our going out', *sairdes* '(if/when) you (plural) go out, your going out'.

A weak vowel between two strong vowels is presumed to make a falling diphthong with the former (*cheio* 'full'). If the second of two weak vowels is stressed, it takes the acute (*miúdo* 'tiny'; contrast *muito* 'much').

Any vowel followed by a weak vowel is presumed to make a diphthong with it and in a final syllable attracts normal stress: *azuis*, *gerais* (plural of *azul* 'blue', *geral* 'general'), *cantais* 'you (familiar plural) sing', *cantáveis* 'you were singing'. Nevertheless, if the diphthongs *-ei*, *-eu*, *-oi* under normal stress have open *e* or *o* it takes the acute: so the plural of nouns in *-el* (*hotéis* 'hotels', *papéis* 'papers'), as opposed both to the abnormal stress of *móveis* 'furniture' (plural of *móvel*) and to the second-person plural future indicative (*cantareis* 'you will sing'), with normal stress and a closed *-e*; similarly *chapéu* 'hat' but *bebeu* 'he drank'. This no longer applies in European Portuguese to words ending in *-eia* (e.g. *ideia* 'idea', in Brazil still *idéia*); contrast *jóia* 'jewel'.

When a weak vowel capable of forming a diphthong with its neighbour does not do so, and is stressed, it takes the accent (*saía* 'I/he was going out').

Notwithstanding any other rule, the third-person singular ending of the preterite -*iu* takes no accent, even after a vowel (*contribuiu* 'he contributed', *saiu* 'he went out').

In words with abnormal stress, the acute is used on *a* (*pátria*) except before *m* or *n* (*circunstância*, *britânico*), and always on *i* and *u* (*empírico*, *dúvida* 'doubt'); on *e* and *o* it is acute or circumflex according to the vowel quality.

Before *m* or *n* followed by a consonant, abnormally stressed *e* and *o* take the circumflex (*paciência*, *cômputo*), except that -*ém*, -*éns* is used word-finally: *alguém* 'someone', *armazém* 'warehouse', plural *armazéns*, *também* 'also'; and -*téns*, -*véns* (second person singular), -*tém*, -*vém* (third person singular) from compounds of *ter* 'have, hold', *vir* 'come' (but third-person plural -*têm*, -*vêm*). In Brazil the circumflex is also used when the *m* or *n* is followed by a vowel (*Nêmesis*, *helênico*, *cômodo*, *sônico*), but European Portuguese, with a few exceptions (e.g. *fêmea* 'female', *cômoro* 'hillock'), has the acute, reflecting a difference in pronunciation (*Némesis*, *helénico*, *cómodo*, *sónico*). Thus to Castilian and Galician *Antonio* correspond *António* in European Portuguese but *Antônio* in Brazil; editors should ensure that any such names are correctly spelt according to their bearers' nationality.

In words with normal stress, it was formerly the custom to mark close *e* and *o* with the circumflex in a great variety of words; since these vowels are normally close before final -*o* but open before -*os*, as well as -*a*, -*as*, one encountered such alternations as *ôvo* 'egg', plural *ovos*. This use of the circumflex lasted longer in Brazil, especially when the open vowel might have been expected, or a similar word had the open vowel. It is now confined to a few instances, mostly contrastive; but note the use of *ê* before final -*em* in the third-person plural verb forms *crêem* 'believe', *dêem* 'give (subj.)', *lêem* 'read', *vêem* 'see', and in Brazil the group *ôo* (e.g. *vôo* 'I fly', 'flight', European Portuguese *voo*).

In European Portuguese a difference is made in first-conjugation verbs (only) between the first-person plural of the present indicative and of the preterite: *falamos* 'we speak', with a closed vowel, *falámos* 'we spoke', with an open vowel; in the verb *dar*, the distinction is between the present subjunctive *dêmos* and the preterite *demos*. In Brazil, the closed vowel being used in both forms, both are spelt *falamos*, *demos*.

Monosyllables in -*a*, -*as*, -*e*, -*es*, -*o*, -*os*, other than unstressed particles, require an accent, whether or not it has contrastive function: for example *vá*, *vás*, subjunctive of *ir*, even though there are no words *va*, *vas*.

Both acute and circumflex—but not til—are omitted on adverbs in -*mente* and suffixes beginning with *z* (*comodamente* (but *cómoda* [Brazilian *comoda*] *e facilmente*); *avozinho* 'grandpa', *avozinha* 'grandma' from *o avô*, *a avó*).

Verbs with suffixed or infixed object pronouns are treated as autonomous units, not as part of a group; their accent is therefore not affected except when -*r* is lost before the third-person pronoun, when in order to restore final stress *a* becomes *á* and *e* becomes *ê* (*invidá-las* 'to invite them (feminine)', *fazê-lo-ei* 'I shall do it'; similarly *compô-la* 'to compose it (feminine)'), whereas no accent is written on -*i* from -*ir*, since this is stressed already. But no accent is written on hyphenated prefixes such as *semi-* and *super-*.

The grave accent is used to represent the coalescence of *a a* in *à*, plural *às* 'at/to the (feminine)', *àquele, àquela, àqueles, àquelas,* neuter *àquilo* 'to that', *àqueloutro, -a, -os, -as*; until 1971 it was used to represent an original acute in adverbs (*ràpidamente*) and before suffixes beginning with -*z* (*sòzinho* 'all alone'). It is also used in representing clear but unstressed vowels in dialect forms.

The accents on *à, às* also contrast these words with *a, as* 'the (feminine)'; similarly the accents on such monosyllables as *dá* 'gives', *dás* 'you give', *dê* '(that) I/he give (subjunctive)', *dó* 'compassion, musical note C', *sé* '(bishop's) see', *sê* 'be!', also distinguish them from *da, das, do* 'the (feminine singular and plural, masculine singular)', *de* 'of', *se* reflexive and 'if'. Contrastive accents are also found in, for example, *avó* 'grandmother', *avô* 'grandfather'; *pára* 'he stoops', 'stop!', *para* 'for'; *pode* 'he can', *pôde* 'he could'; *pólo* (plural *pólos*) '(geographic) pole', *pôlo* (plural *pôlos*) 'falcon'; *pós* (plural of *pó* 'powder'), *pôs* 'he put'; *réis* (plural of *real*) 'reales' (coins), *reis* 'kings'.

Syllable-final *m* and *n* nasalize the preceding vowel; nasality is otherwise marked by the til on *ã* and *õ*. The latter take normal stress in a final syllable, thus distinguishing *cantarão* 'they will sing', stressed on -*rão*, from *cantaram* 'they sang', 'they had sung', stressed on -*ta*. The exceptions are marked with the accent (*bênção* 'blessing; *órfão*, feminine *órfã* 'orphan').

11.36.4 **Word division**

Take over *ch, lh, nh,* and *b, c, d, f, g, p, t, v* followed by *l* or *r*; divide *rr, ss,* also *sc, sc*. Divide prefixed *ab* and *sub* from following *l* or *r* in obvious compounds only: one authority gives the examples *ab|legacão* but *a|blucão* (which is best avoided, as leaving only one letter behind). When a word is divided at a pre-existing hyphen, repeat the hyphen at the beginning of the next line: *dar-lho* is divided *dar-|-lho*.

11.36.5 **Punctuation**

Inverted question and exclamation marks are not normally used.

11.36.6 **Miscellaneous**

In European Portuguese, the polite form of address ranges from *você* (plural *vocês*) between friends or to subordinates, through *o senhor, a senhora, os senhores, as senhoras* (abbreviated *o Sr., a Sra., os Srs., as Srs.*) in normal polite conversation, to *Vossa Excelência* (abbreviated *V. Ex^a.*) and (in writing) *Vossa Senhoria* (abbreviated *V. Sa.*), implying respect. All these take the third person. In Brazil the familiar forms (especially the plural) are almost obsolete, being replaced by *você(s)*.

The 'personal *a*' is used before pronouns and in comparisons.

The future subjunctive is in full everyday use (*se chover amanhã* 'if it rains tomorrow'). The pluperfect indicative in *-ra* competes with a compound tense: *cantara* or *tinha cantado* 'I had sung'; but 'I have sung' is normally expressed by the preterite *cantei*, the compound perfect *tenho cantado* expressing repeated action. *Haver* with the past participle is somewhat literary, but in the future *hei-de* (in Brazil *hei de*) *cantar* is very common.

In some verbs in *-ir*, the *e* or *o* of the root becomes *i* or *u* in the first-person singular present indicative, the second-person singular imperative, and the entire present subjunctive, including the first- and second-person plural: *servir* 'to serve', *sirvo* 'I serve', *serve* 'serves', *sirve* 'serve!', *servimos* 'we serve', but subjunctive *sirva, sirvamos*; others also change *e* to *i* in the second- and third-person singular, and the third-person plural present indicative and the second-person singular imperative (e.g. *agride* 'attacks', 'attack!'); *frigir* 'to fry' makes *freges* 'you fry', *frege* 'fries', 'fry!', *fregem* 'they fry', and several verbs change *u* to *o* in the same forms (*fugir* 'flee', *foges, foge, fogem*); so optionally some but not all verbs in *-struir* (*constróis* besides *construes* 'you build'). Some *-ar* and *-er* verbs also change their vowel quality in strong forms, but without affecting the orthography.

In Brazil, *si* is sometimes used for *se* 'if'; the numbers 16, 17, and 19 are spelt *dezesseis, dezessete, dezenove* against European *deza-*; 14 may be *quatorze* besides *catorze*; 'register' is *registro* against *registo*; 'to furnish' *mobiliar* (note the root-stressed *mobílio* etc.) against *mobilar*. There are also many differences of vocabulary and idiom, such as frequent omission of the definite article after *todo* 'every' and before possessives.

Object pronouns after the verb are attached by hyphens (*dar-lho* 'to give it (masculine) to him/her'); as in Galician, this is normal in affirmative main clauses—though Brazilian usage is fluid—but in the future and conditional the pronouns are infixed between the infinitive and the termination (*dar-lho-ei* 'I shall give it him', *dar-lho-ia* 'I should give it him'). Third-person *o, a, os, as* acquire an initial *n* after a nasal vowel (*condenaram-no* 'they condemned/had condemned him', *condenarão-no* 'they will condemn him'), and an initial *l* after *r* and *s*, which are omitted (*ouvi-la* 'to hear her', *ouve-la* 'you (singular) hear her' (*ouve-a* 'hears her')). Hyphens are also used with prefixes and in compounds more freely than in Castilian, and in set phrases such as *El-Rei* 'the king' (i.e. 'His Majesty', from Castilian *el rey*; contrast *o rei de Frância* 'the king of France').

Elision of *de* is marked more freely than in Castilian, but by contraction, not with an apostrophe: *dum* (feminine *duma*) 'of a'; in the same circumstances *em* 'in' becomes *n-*: *neste livro* 'in this book'.

The names of months and seasons are often capitalized.

For a list of quick identifiers for Iberian languages *see* **11.42.3**.

11.37 **Romanian**

11.37.1 **Derivation and alphabet**

Romanian is a Romance language, derived from Latin and written in roman letters. Its vocabulary, however, shows many Slavonic borrowings and its grammar conforms to Balkan patterns: in particular, the definite article is a suffix and subjunctive clauses are preferred to infinitives. Until the late nineteenth century the Cyrillic alphabet was used, sometimes with an admixture of roman letters; between 1945 and 1989 the Moldavian Soviet Socialist Republic (now the Republic of Moldova) employed a different Cyrillic system for what it claimed was a different 'Moldavian' language.

The Romanian alphabet is as follows (parentheses indicate letters used only in foreign words): a ă â b c d e f g h i î j (k) l m n o p r s ş t ţ u v (w x y) z.

11.37.2 **Accents**

The accented characters (ă, â, î, ş, ţ) count as separate letters; the subscript commas of ş ţ are often set as cedillas (ş ţ), so do not change them on proof if they are consistent. Nineteenth-century texts will show other accented characters, such as ḑ ĕ é ê ĭ ŭ.

11.37.3 **Spelling**

A spelling reform of 1953 abolished â, which had been frequent within words, replacing it with î, which has the same value. (Other changes included the substitution of a hyphen for the apostrophe in such combinations as *s-a* for *s'a*.) However, when the local Communists had successfully purged the Moscow authorities, â was restored in 1963 to *român* and its derivatives, for example *România*; it has now been restored in all contexts. Unless it is important to retain the Cyrillic script, 'Moldavian' texts should be respelt in Romanian.

It may be perfectly correct to have what looks like the same word ending in *-ă* at one place and in *-a* at another: *casă* 'house', *casa* 'the house', *cîntă* 'sings', '(s)he sang', *cînta* '(s)he used to sing/was singing, (to) sing'. Similarly, a masculine plural may end in *-i* (indefinite) and *-ii* (definite): *fraţi* 'brothers', *fraţii* 'the brothers' (note too *fii* 'sons', *copii* 'children', *fiii* 'the sons', *copiii* 'the children'), and the root vowel may change between masculine and feminine (*frumos* 'beautiful', feminine *frumoasă*; *românesc* 'Romanian', feminine *românească*) or in declension (*masă* 'table', *mese* 'table's', 'tables').

11.37.4 Capitalization

Capitalize names of places, events, and the more important political institutions as in English; names of other institutions, and of books and periodicals, are lower-case except for the first word and proper nouns.

11.37.5 Word division

Divide compounds at the point of composition, and do not break within a prefix; otherwise a single consonant, including *x*, should be taken over, as should consonant + *l* or *r*, and *i* or *u* between vowels.

11.38 Russian

This section relates specifically to questions that may arise when editing or setting matter in Russian. For fuller information see, in general, L. A. Gil'berg and L. I. Frid, *Slovar'-spravochnik avtora* (Moscow, 1979); for orthography, see K. I. Bylinskiĭ and N. N. Nikol'skiĭ, *Spravochnik po orfografii i punktuatsii dlya rabotnikov pechati*, 4th edn. (Moscow, 1970), D. E. Rozental' and I. B. Golub, *Russkaya orfografiya i punktuatsiya* (Moscow, 1994), and D. E. Rozental', *Spravochnik po orfografii i punktuatsii* (Chelyabinsk, 1996).

11.38.1 Alphabet

Russian is one of the six Slavonic languages written in Cyrillic script— divided into East Slavonic (Russian, Belorussian (formerly also called White Russian), and Ukrainian), and South Slavonic (Bulgarian, Macedonian, and Serbian). The additional sorts called for by the five non-

Russian languages are omitted from **TABLE 11.3**, but details of them are given in the text.

Additional sorts (including those eliminated in 1918) are used when setting Old Russian texts; Old Church Slavonic also calls for additional sorts, and is usually set in a face that bears the same relation to modern Russian types as black letter does to normal roman faces. Confusingly, printers call this face 'Cyrillic' or 'Slavonic'.

■ **TABLE 11.3** includes 'upright' (*pryamoĭ*) and 'cursive' (*kursiv*) forms and also a transliteration in accordance with the 'British System' as given in British Standard 2979. For further information about transliteration *see* **11.41**.

Table 11.3: **The Russian alphabet**

А	а	*А*	*а*	a		Р	р	*Р*	*р*	r
Б	б	*Б*	*б*	b		С	с	*С*	*с*	s
В	в	*В*	*в*	v		Т	т	*Т*	*т*	t
Г	г	*Г*	*г*	g		У	у	*У*	*у*	u
Д	д	*Д*	*д*	d		Ф	ф	*Ф*	*ф*	f
Е	е	*Е*	*е*	e		Х	х	*Х*	*х*	kh
Ё	ё	*Ё*	*ё*	ë		Ц	ц	*Ц*	*ц*	ts
Ж	ж	*Ж*	*ж*	zh		Ч	ч	*Ч*	*ч*	ch
З	з	*З*	*з*	z		Ш	ш	*Ш*	*ш*	sh
И	и	*И*	*и*	i		Щ	щ	*Щ*	*щ*	shch
Й	й	*Й*	*й*	ĭ		Ъ	ъ	*Ъ*	*ъ*	″
К	к	*К*	*к*	k		Ы	ы	*Ы*	*ы*	ȳ
Л	л	*Л*	*л*	l		Ь	ь	*Ь*	*ь*	′
М	м	*М*	*м*	m		Э	э	*Э*	*э*	é
Н	н	*Н*	*н*	n		Ю	ю	*Ю*	*ю*	yu
О	о	*О*	*о*	o		Я	я	*Я*	*я*	ya
П	п	*П*	*п*	p						

The letter *ë* is not treated as a separate letter in Russian, and is normally written without the diaeresis; neither of these statements is true of Belorussian.

Before 1918 I i (*I i*) was used instead of И и before vowels and й; also in the word мірь 'world' to distinguish it from миръ 'peace'; both are now written мир. Ѣ ѣ (*Ѣ ѣ*) was used mainly on historical grounds in certain words and forms where Е е is now written. Ѳ ѳ (*Ѳ ѳ*) and Ѵ ѵ (*Ѵ ѵ*) were used in Greek loanwords to represent *θ* and *υ/οι*; they are now replaced by ф and и. (Hence, in the genitive case modern мира may represent pre-Revolutionary мира 'of peace', міра 'of the world', and мѵра 'of chrism'.) At the end of a word all consonants were followed by either ъ or ь; the former is no longer written, and serves only to mark off prefixes: съ тѣхъ поръ > с тех пор, but съѣсть > съесть.

The substitution of the apostrophe for the hard sign (ъ), occasionally found in Russian texts, is incorrect. By contrast, the apostrophe is an integral part of the orthography of Ukrainian and Belorussian, serving largely the same purpose in them as does the hard sign in Russian, for example разъезд (Russian) раз'їзд (Ukrainian), раз'езд (Belorussian).

The extra sorts called for by the other languages using Cyrillic are Belorussian i (= *i*) and ў (= *w*); Macedonian ѓ (= *ǵ*), ѕ (= *dz*), ј (= *j*), љ (= *lj*), њ (= *nj*), ќ (= *ḱ*), and џ (= *dž*); Serbian Ђ, ђ (= *đ*), ј (= *j*), љ (= *lj*), њ (= *nj*), Ћ, ћ (= *ć*), and џ (= *dž*); and Ukrainian г (= *g*), є (= *ye*), i (= *i*), and ї (= *yi*).

In some Macedonian and Serbian fonts cursive г, п, and т are in the form of superior-barred cursive *ī*, *ū*, and *w̄* respectively.

Except in certain ancient texts, the term 'Cyrillic' refers to the characters themselves, and not the special font of that name.

11.38.2 **Abbreviations**

Modern Russian non-literary texts abound in abbreviations. Details of these are available in H. K. Zalucky, *Compressed Russian: Russian–English Dictionary of Acronyms… and… Abbreviations…* (Amsterdam, NY, 1991).

In lower-case abbreviations with full points, any spaces in the original should be kept, for example и т. д., и пр., but с.-д. Abbreviations by contraction, such as д-р, have no points. Abbreviations with a solidus are typically (though not exclusively) used in abbreviations of compound words in which the full form is not hyphenated. Compare, for example: к. т. = критическая температура 'critical temperature' (a term with two separate words), к/т = кинотеатр 'cinema' (abbreviation of an unhyphenated compound), к-т = комитет 'committee' (abbreviation by contraction).

Abbreviations consisting of capital initial letters, such as СССР, are set close without internal or final points. If declinable, such abbreviations add flexional endings in closed-up lower case, such as ГОСТа. Commonly used lower-case abbreviations that are pronounced syllabically and declined, e.g. вуз, are not set with points.

Abbreviations for metric and other units used in scientific measurement are usually set in cursive and are not followed by a full point; abbreviated qualifying adjectives do have the full point, however (5 *кв. км* etc.).

11.38.3 **Bibliographical lists**

The author's name should be followed by his or her initials. Titles of books and articles (in upright) and names of publishing houses are *not* given within guillemets. (A detailed account of the Russian method of describing titles in bibliographical lists is given in N. A. Nikiforovskaya's *Bibliograficheskoe opisanie* (Leningrad, 1978).)

> Тимирязев К. А. Земледелие и физиология растений. М.-Л: Книга, 1965. 215 с.
>
> Петрович Г. В. Через ближний космос во вселенную. — Авиация и космонавтика, 1962, № 6, с. 8—12.

Transliterated titles should follow English practice for the use of italic and quotation marks but not of capitals.

11.38.4 **Capitalization**

Capital initial letters are in general rarer in Russian than in English. Capitalize personal names but use lower-case initial letters for nouns and adjectives formed from them (толстовство, марксизм), and for nationalities and names of nationals and of inhabitants of towns (таджик 'Tajik', англичанин 'Englishman', москвич 'Muscovite'). Personal names used to indicate character are lower-case (донжуан 'a Don Juan', меценат 'a Maecenas'), as are ranks, titles, etc. (св. Николай 'St Nicholas', кн. Оболенский 'Prince Obolenskiĭ', проф. Сидоров 'Prof. Sidorov', полковник Иванов 'Col. Ivanov').

Adjectives formed from geographical names are lower-case except when they form part of a proper noun or the name of an institution (европейские государства 'European States', but Челябинский тракторный завод 'Chelyabinsk Tractor Works'). Note the distinction between русский 'ethnically, linguistically, culturally, etc. Russian', also used as a substantive for 'ethnic Russian', feminine русская, and российский 'relating to the Russian state', россиянин 'a citizen of Russia', feminine россиянка.

Names of Union and Autonomous Republics of the USSR are capitalized, but non-proper elements in the titles of administrative areas are lower-case (Курганская область 'Kurgan Region'; but Туркменская Советская Социалистическая Республика 'Turkmen Soviet Socialist Republic'). Capitalize only the first word in titles of international or foreign organizations and societies (Амери-канская федерация труда 'American Federation of Labor'). Each word in names of countries, however, takes a capital (Соединенные Штаты Америки 'United States of America'; so too Организация Объединенных Наций 'United Nations Organization').

Capitalize the first word in titles of Soviet ministries, administrative organs, and Party and public organizations not of a 'unique' nature (Государственный комитет Совета Министров СССР по новой технике; note capitals for the 'unique' Совет Министров). Capitalize the first word in titles of institutions (Академия наук СССР 'Academy of Sciences of the USSR'), but in titles beginning with an adjective only the noun is lower-case (Государственный Исторический музей 'State Historical Museum'). This does not apply consistently in post-Soviet nomenclature (Российская Академия наук 'Russian Academy of Sciences', Санкт-Петербургская государственная академия театрального искусства 'St Petersburg State Academy of the Art of Theatre').

Days of the week and names of the months are lower-case, but note Первое мая and 1-е Мая for the May Day holiday: the capitalization in the latter form is due to the fact that the ordinal number does not count as the 'first word'.

Capitalize only the first word and proper nouns in titles of literary and musical works, newspapers, and journals («Отцы и дети», «Иван Сусанин»).

Geographical terms forming part of the name of an area or place are lower-case (остров Рудольфа 'Rudolph Island', Северный полюс 'the North Pole'), as are the non-proper-name elements in street and similar names (площадь Маяковского 'Mayakovskiĭ Square').

Names of wars are lower-case (франко-прусская война 'Franco-Prussian War'), except for those with titles that refer directly to their character (Великая Отечественная война 'Great Patriotic War').

Capitalize only the first word in names of historical events and battles (Кровавое воскресенье 'Bloody Sunday', Полтавская битва 'the Battle of Poltava'), and names of congresses, agreements, documents, prizes, etc. (Вашингтонское соглашение 'the Washington Agreement', Атлантийская хартия 'the Atlantic Charter', Нобелевская премия 'Nobel Prize').

The pronoun of the first-person singular, я = I, is lower-case (except, of course, when used at the beginning of a sentence). The personal and possessive pronouns of the second person plural (вы, ваш, etc.) take an initial capital when used as polite singulars in letters to individuals or to juridical persons such as institutions (also in advertisements, but not in questionnaires). However, as genuine plurals they remain lower-case even in letters.

The combination of capitals and small capitals may be found in older texts, though not in Soviet typography.

11.38.5 **Dash**

En rules are not used in Russian typography; em rules set close up take their place. Dashes—em rules—are much used in Russian texts, in particular as a substitute for the copula in nominal statements (Волга — самая большая река в Европе 'the Volga is the longest European river'); to indicate omission of the verb (Один рабочий несёт астролябию, другой — треногу 'one of the workmen carries the theodolite, the other the tripod'); and to indicate 'from…to…' (1946—1950, линия Москва—Горький 'the Moscow–Gor'kiĭ line').

Em rules are also used before, and to divide off, statements in dialogue set in paragraphs:

> — Я вас люблю, — сказал князь.
>
> — Простите…
>
> — Что простить? — спросил князь Андрей.

When dialogue is set continuously the direct-speech elements are divided off not only by dashes but also by guillemets (Десятник махнул рукой. «Мищенко вчера свой зкскаватор утопил», — сказал он мрачно. — «Как? — вскипел Правдин. — Так зто же сотни тысяч рублей!» — «Да, конечно!..» — согласился десятник…).

Guillemets alone are used to distinguish occasional spoken words (Она громко закричала: «За мной!»). They are also used if the quoted words are from a letter or soliloquy, though the author's words are nevertheless divided off by dashes in such cases («Боже мой, — подумал Мартин, — зта каналья разъезжает в пульмановских вагонах, а я голодаю!..» — Ярость охватила его).

Note in the above examples the use of the comma in addition to the dash to divide off the quoted from the author's words. Where the quoted words end with omission points or an exclamation or question mark, commas are not required. This rule applies whether or not guillemets are present.

11.38.6 **Word division**

Russian syllables end in a vowel, and word division is basically syllabic. However, there are many exceptions to this generalization, most of which are connected with Russian word formation. (Before the Revolution there was much stricter adherence to etymology.) Consonant groups may be taken over entire or divided where convenient (provided at least one consonant is taken over), subject to the following rules.

Do not separate a consonant from the prefix, root, or suffix of which it forms a part: род|ной, под|бежать, мещан|ство are correct divisions. Divide between double consonants (клас|сами), except where this conflicts with the preceding rule (класс|ный).

Do not divide between initials; try to avoid dividing between initials and a surname. Do not separate abbreviated titles from the name to which they relate, such as проф., ул. (before a street name). Do not divide letter abbreviations (СНГ, Ту-104, и т. д.).

Do not leave at the end of a line—or carry over—a single letter, or two or more consonants without a vowel: к|руглый, ст|рела, жидко|сть are incorrect. The letters ъ, ь, and й should never be separated from the letter preceding them (подъ|езд).

11.38.7 Hyphens

The hyphen is used in nouns consisting of two noun elements, one of which reinforces or qualifies the sense of the other, and which are linked without an interpolated vowel (генерал-губернатор 'Governor-General', but кровообращение 'circulation of the blood').

The hyphen is also used in compound place names, Russian or foreign, consisting of separable words (Каменец-Подольск, Ростов-на-Дону, Рио-де-Жанейро, Ла-Плата (exception: Ламанш 'the Channel'), Сан-Франциско, Соxhо-сквер). If, however, the place name consists of a Russian adjective declined as such and a noun, there are no hyphens (Нижний Новгород, Вышний Волочек). The pre-Revolutionary capital was commonly spelt as one word, Санктпетербург, but modern usage favours Санкт-Петербург.

Hyphens are used in compound points of the compass (nouns and adjectives), as well as in compound adjectives derived from nouns with complementary meanings (журнально-газетный 'periodical and newspaper'), or indicating shades of colour (тёмно-коричневый 'dark brown').

11.38.8 Italic and letter-spacing

Italic (*kursiv*, cursive) and letter-spacing (*razryadka*) are used to distinguish or emphasize a word or words in the text. Of the two methods, letter-spacing is perhaps the more commonly employed for this purpose in works set in Russian, though words cited in Russian linguistic texts are always given in cursive. Guillemets are used to show that a word is being used in an unfamiliar or special sense.

Print titles of books and journals in upright type and not in cursive.

11.38.9 Numerals, dates, reference figures, fractions

Numbers from 10,000 upwards are divided off into thousands by thin spaces, and not by commas (26 453); below 10,000 they are set close up (9999). The decimal comma is used in place of the decimal point

(*0,36578*). Ordinal numbers are followed by a contracted adjectival termination except when they are used in dates (5-й год but 7 ноября 1917 г.).

Inclusive dates are not abbreviated (*1946—1950*). As in English, a financial or academic year that covers parts of two calendar years is expressed with a solidus (*1946/47*).

The form of fraction with a solidus is preferred, e.g. ¾ (except in mathematical or technical work).

In text, superscript footnote-reference figures precede punctuation marks and are followed by a thin space: ...его[1]. In the footnote itself the reference figure or symbol is a superscript and is followed by a space but no point.

11.38.10 **Plays**

In plays set wholly in Russian, the names of the speakers in dialogue usually precede the words spoken and are either letter-spaced or—less often—set in bold. They are also found centred. Stage directions, if set immediately after the name of the speaker or within the body, or at the end, of the spoken words, are set in cursive within parentheses:

> Лопахин. Пришел поезд, слава Богу. Который час?
>
> Дуняша. Скоро два. (*Тушит свечу*) Уже светло.

General stage directions are set in upright but smaller type, either centrally or full left and with their last line centred.

11.38.11 **Punctuation**

The chief points of difference between Russian and English punctuation systems relate to the use of the comma, omission points, and dashes. For the last *see* **11.38.5**; for guillemets *see also* **11.38.5**, **11.38.8**, and **11.38.12**. For punctuation of abbreviations *see* **11.38.2**. The comma is used more often than in English, and always before subordinate clauses introduced by interrogative-relative pronouns and adverbs, participles, and gerunds; and to divide off coordinate clauses joined by conjunctions such as и, да, а, но, или.

It is also used between a principal clause and a subordinate clause introduced by a conjunction. Note that when the conjunction что forms the second element of a compound conjunction, the comma precedes the first part unless it is desired to stress the close causal or temporal connection between the two parts of the sentence:

> Люди умирали, потому что была эпидемия.
> People were dying, for there was an epidemic.

Люди умирали потому, что была эпидемия.

There was an epidemic, so people were dying.

In substantival and adjectival enumerations in which there is single, final и, it is not preceded by a comma.

The three dots indicating an interruption (ellipsis or points of omission) are set in one piece in Russian typography. They are spaced at their open end (except when guillemets precede or follow), and set close at their engaged end (Это… я… умираю; …уже; but «…мы должны отвергнуть»). When ellipses coincide with an exclamation or question mark (but not guillemets), they form one piece with it and are reduced to two points: !.., ?.. It is not mandatory to duplicate this convention in English text quoting only a small amount of Russian, and certainly not necessary when the Russian is transliterated.

A full point never immediately follows points of omission. Quotation marks following points of omission (or an exclamation or question mark) are never followed by a full point («За мной!»).

11.38.12 Quotation marks

Two forms of quotation mark are used in Russian: opening double commas on the line, followed by closing superscript turned double commas (*lapochki*); and (double) guillemets (*ёlochki*). Of the two, guillemets are by far the more common form, but the term is used below to cover both forms of quotation mark.

Apart from their use to indicate direct speech and soliloquy, guillemets are used to show that a word or words are being employed in a special sense, and with titles of literary works, journals, and pictures, and with names of ships, factories, and organizations, except when the latter consist of initials or conventional abbreviations (роман «Война и мир», журнал «Новый мир», картина Репина «Не ждали», завод «Серп и молот», издательство «Книга», but Госиздат, ГЭС).

Quotation marks are not duplicated unless they are of differing design (Он ответил: «Я приехал вчера на пароходе «Казань»—note the final guillemet, which covers both the end of the name of the ship and the end of the sentence); but Он ответил: „Я приехал вчера на пароходе «Казань»“.

11.38.13 Spacing

Except between numerals and when linking extremities, when it is set close up, the dash has a thin space at either end; all other punctuation marks are set close up. For spacing of omission points *see* **11.38.11**.

11.39 **Sanskrit and Indic languages**

11.39.1 **General points**

Sanskrit is the ancient and sacred Indo-Aryan language of the Hindus in the Indian subcontinent; Vedic, the language of the Vedas, is an early form of Sanskrit. Sanskrit is the source of some of the modern languages of that area, such as Hindi, Bengali, Nepali, Sinhalese, and is one of the languages recognized for official use in the modern state of India.

Classical Sanskrit has some fifty letters, with various added vowel marks and ligatures: fourteen vowels and thirty-six consonants, each with an inherent short *a* that is overridden either by a different vowel (in a different form from the free-standing letter) or by being joined to another consonant in a compound letter. There is also a mark of nasalization and another of aspiration after a vowel.

The transliteration system for Sanskrit adopted by the Geneva Congress (*see* **TABLE 11.4**) is more widely accepted and used than that for many other Indian languages. Other systems are now generally considered obsolete in the English-speaking world and elsewhere: these can usually be spotted by such conventions as *c* rather than *ś* (still found on the Continent), and a subscript rather than a superscript dot in conjunction with an *m* (*ṃ* rather than *ṁ*). Similarly, avoid the imposition of *ch* for *c* and *chh* for *ch*, as well as the use of italic letters (*k, kh, g, gh, n*) in otherwise roman type.

Sanskrit is nowadays written left to right in the forty-eight letters of the Devanāgarī script, also called Nāgarī. Historically, however, the written shapes of the alphabet varied from place to place, being the same as those used for the vernacular: the exclusive use of Devanāgarī in its Delhi or Bombay form is a modern development. Since the conceptual scheme remained constant regardless, the same transliteration serves as a basis for most modern languages in India (and some in its cultural environs)—even those such as Tamil and Telugu that belong to a different language family; all the more so since these languages have freely borrowed Sanskrit words and expressions. Nevertheless, certain modifications are needed to reproduce the vernaculars.

In Sanskrit, *e* and *o* are always long, hence no long mark is used in transliteration. Occasionally they are shortened in Vedic, and marked *ĕ, ŏ* in transliteration; these symbols, like *ē, ō* or *ê, ô*, will also be found in transliterations from some modern languages. The candrabindu *ṃ̇* is usually replaced by *ṃ*; the upadhmānīya *ḥ* by *ḥ*, and the underline *ẖ* by *ḫ*.

Table 11.4: **Transliteration of Sanskrit**

Vowels			Consonants			
Initial	Medial	Equivalent	Initial	Equivalent	Initial	Equivalent
अ	—	a	क	k	ध	dh
आ	T	ā	ख	kh	न	n
इ	f	i	ग	g	प	p
ई	ी	ī	घ	gh	फ	ph
उ	ु	u	ङ	ṅ	ब	b
ऊ	ू	ū	च	c	भ	bh
ऋ	ृ	ṛ	छ	ch	म	m
ॠ	ॄ	ṝ	ज	j	य	y
ऌ	ॢ	ḷ	झ	jh	र	r
ॡ	ॣ	ḹ	ञ	ñ	ल	l
ए	ॆ	e	ट	ṭ	ळ	ḻ
ऐ	ॆ	ai	ठ	ṭh	ळ्ह	ḻh
ओ	ो	o	ड	ḍ	व	v
औ	ौ	au	ढ	ḍh	श	ś
			ण	ṇ	ष	ṣ
ं ṅ or ṃ		either true Anusvāra ṅ or the symbol of any nasal	त	t	स	s
			थ	th	ह	h
ः ḥ		symbol called Visarga	द	d		

The characters ळ ḻ and ळ्ह ḻh are peculiar to Vedic.

Mumbai forms अ a आ ā ओ o औ au ण ṇ ल l श्र ś

All consonant letters are deemed to be followed by the vowel a unless another vowel is written (note that f i precedes in writing the consonant it follows in speech). A consonant followed by a pause in speech is marked with the stroke ॒ underneath it; when two or more consonants come together, even in different words, they are combined into a single character. These compound ('conjunct') consonants are too numerous to list; most are based on combinations of the individual components, but note क्ष (Mumbai क्ष) kṣ and ज्ञ jñ.

Digits	
०	0
१	1
२	2
३	3
४	4
५	5
६	6
७	7
८	8
९	9

The vowels transcribed ḷ, ṛ are not used in modern languages, though in the indigenous scripts they will appear in Sanskrit loanwords; on the other hand, the underdotted letters are often used to represent modern consonants not found in Sanskrit. The vowels, when needed, will then be transcribed ḷ, ṛ; these symbols may be used for Sanskrit, and are also normal in Indo-European linguistics.

Transliterations from the Vedas and some grammars use the acute on other letters apart from ś to represent a pitch-accent fully operational in earlier texts but afterwards lost (á, ấ, é, í, î́, ĺ̥, ó, ŕ̥, r̥̂, ú, û́); this is not usually found in classical texts since the accentuation of many words is not known. The Devanāgarī alphabet is ordered a ā i ī u ū ṛ r̥̄ ḷ e ai o au ṃ ḥ k kh g gh ṅ c ch j jh ñ ṭ ṭh ḍ ḍh ṇ t th d dh n p ph b bh m y r l v ś ṣ s h. In modern Indo-Aryan languages ṛ and ṛh follow ṇ. Do not divide the digraphs *ai*, *au*, *bh*, *ch*, *dh*, *gh*, *jh*, *kh*, *ph*, *th*.

11.39.2   Other writing systems based on Sanskrit

Many languages have transcription systems based on Sanskrit principles regardless of whether they are related to Sanskrit; these include Assamese, Avestan, Bengali, Burmese, Gujarati, Hindi, Kannada, Kashmiri, Malayalam, Marathi, Oriya, Pali, Panjabi, Rajasthani, Sindhi, Sinhalese, Tamil, Telugu, Tibetan, Urdu, and Vedic. Such transcriptions may be with the addition of certain special letters and accents such as macron and subscript dot, double subscript dot, double underline, tilde, and diaeresis. The diacritics listed for a particular language may not reflect all those needed in rendering that language, since especially in the older literature almost any Sanskrit word may be borrowed to fill a need or to display the author's erudition. Points related to some of these languages are listed below.

In languages related to Sanskrit, but written with variants of the Persian alphabet, the ḍ, ṣ, ṭ, ẓ, ḥ of Persian and Arabic loanwords are transliterated ḍ, ṣ, ṭ, ẓ, ḥ, to distinguish the first four from inherited ḍ, ṣ, ṭ, ẓ; ḥ is not essential, however, since ḥ is largely confined to Sanskrit loanwords, which are less likely to be used in Muslim than in Hindu cultures. The characters g̱, k̲ may also be found for Arabic *gh*, *kh*; but underlined consonants, and acute and grave accents on vowels, are sometimes used in other modern languages.

11.39.2.1   Avestan

An ancient Iranian language, closely related to Vedic Sanskrit. One of the group of Indo-European languages that includes Persian (Farsi), Pashto, and Kurdish. The diacritics used in transliteration are ā, ē, ī, ū, č, š, ž (sometimes also ǰ), ṭ, ḫ, å (NB å̊ is not used), and ą (ogonek).

Special characters include the shwa, also with acute and macron (ə, ə́, ə̄); agma, also with acute (ŋ, ŋ́) (the curl tends to be kept within the base line). The Greek letters γ, δ, θ are used, as is a superscript v (ᵛ).

11.39.2.2 Bengali and Assamese

Bengali, spoken in Bangladesh and West Bengal, is diglossic and is written in the Bengali alphabet. The Library of Congress uses these diacritics to transliterate Bengali: ś, ṁ, n̐ (candrabindu), ṛ, ṟ, ḻ, ṅ, ẏ, ḍ, ḥ, ṃ, ṇ, ṛ, ṭ, ā, ī, ū, ñ, ṯ; and the special character ' (apostrophe). Assamese is related to Bengali and uses the same alphabet and transliteration system.

11.39.2.3 Gujarati

Gujarati is spoken in Gujarat and Pakistan, and written in the Gujarati alphabet. The Library of Congress's transliteration system uses the diacritics ś, ê, ô, ṛ, ṅ, ḍ, ḥ, ḷ, ṃ, ṇ, ṭ, ā, ī, ū, ñ; special character is ' (apostrophe).

11.39.2.4 Hindi

In its broadest sense, Hindi is the most widespread language of northern India, with a literature in both an eastern and a western dialect, written in the Devanāgarī script. When the Moguls (Mughals) conquered the country, they adopted the central dialect of Delhi (which until then had not enjoyed literary use), writing it in an expanded Arabo-Persian alphabet. They enriched it with borrowings from Arabic (especially terms of religion and philosophy), often mediated through Persian or from Persian itself (especially terms of culture and government), and their own Turkic vernacular, mostly of a military nature. This enriched language was called 'Urdū', from the Turkic word for 'army'.

Like the French, Latin, and Greek loanwords in English, some of these terms remained confined to the literary language, while others penetrated popular speech. It was this popular speech that the British encountered, and called 'Hindustani' (at first spelt 'Hindoostanee'), and it is in this that soldiers and others communicated with the natives. Missionaries, however, and others who wished to communicate at a higher level, knowing that the non-Hindi component of Urdu came from Muslim languages, substituted equivalent terms derived from Sanskrit.

At first the resulting language, which they called 'Hindi' and wrote in Devanāgarī, was an artificial construct less familiar and less comprehensible to most Hindus than the Urdu they were thought not to understand. However, time, education, and nationalism have turned it into a natural and living language, albeit retaining Arabic and other loans that had gained general currency. The Hindustani of the Raj now passes for the popular register of modern Hindi (it is the Delhi dialect of Hindi), rendering the original meaning of the term largely obsolete unless as a name used by linguists for the elements common to both Hindi and Urdu, or as an archaic (and incorrect) synonym for Urdu.

Diacritics used in the Library of Congress system for transliterating Hindi are ś, ăi, ău, ĕ, ŏ, ṁ, n̊ (candrabindu), r, r̄, ḷ, ê, ô, ṅ, ḥ, ṃ, ḍ, ṇ, ṛ, ṭ, ḥ, ṣ, ṭ, gh, kh, gh, ā, ī, ū, ñ; special character: apostrophe '.

11.39.2.5 Panjabi

In India, Panjabi is written in the Gurmukhi script; in Pakistan, the Urdu script is used. Transliteration of Arabic and Persian words may entail the use of underlined letters such as g, ḥ, ḳ. Acutes and graves are used to indicate pitch accent in linguistic work.

11.39.2.6 Urdu

Urdu is a specifically Muslim language related to Hindi but with many Persian words. It is with English the official language of Pakistan, also used in India. Urdu and Hindi have come to be used as lingua francas throughout the subcontinent, although in both Pakistan and India the elite is more at home in English. In many parts of both countries the vernacular is something quite different.

Urdu is written in an extension of the Persian Arabic alphabet, and transliterated with the diacritics á, ḍ, ḥ, r, ṣ, ṭ, ṭ, z̧, ā, ī, ū, g, ḥ, ḳ, ṇ, ṣ, ẓ; and the special characters ' (*hamza*) and ' (*'ayin*).

11.40 **Scandinavian languages**

This group of languages is normally divided by linguists into East Scandinavian (Danish, Swedish) and West Scandinavian (Faeroese, Icelandic, Norwegian). Danish, Norwegian, and Swedish are mutually intelligible; Faeroese and Icelandic are much less so. All these languages derive ultimately from Old Norse, the literary form of Old Icelandic.

11.40.1 Danish, Norwegian, and Swedish

Alphabet

Modern Danish and Norwegian have identical alphabets, the twenty-six letters of the English alphabet being followed by æ, ø, å; in their place Swedish has å, ä, ö. The letter å, found in Swedish since the sixteenth century, was not adopted in Norway till 1907, and in Denmark till 1948; previously these languages used *aa* (cap. *Aa*). Until 1948 Danish nouns were capitalized as in German, a practice also found in nineteenth-century Norwegian. Acute accents are found in loanwords and numerous Swedish surnames, and occasionally for clarity, for example Danish *én* 'one', neuter *ét* (also *een*, *eet*) ~ indefinite article *en*, *et*; the grave may be found in older nynorsk (*see* SPELLING below). The grave accent is sometimes used in Norwegian to distinguish emphatic forms.

Capitalization

The former capitalization of nouns in Danish and Norwegian apart, all languages now tend to favour lower-casing, e.g. for days, months, festivals, historical events, adherents of political parties, and ethnic terms. This also applies to book titles; but periodical and series titles are legally deposited names, complete with their capitals they may have.

Institutional names are often treated as descriptive, or given capitals for only the first word and the last; but in Danish and Norwegian some names begin with the independent definite article, which then must always be included and capitalized, *Den*, *Det*, *De* (= *Dei* in nynorsk). Thus in Danish the Royal Library may be either *Det kongelige Bibliotek* or *Det Kongelige Bibliotek*, but the *Det* is indispensable; it should be retained even when such names are used untranslated in an English sentence. This does not arise in Swedish, where names of that form are not used: the Royal Library in Stockholm is *Kungliga Biblioteket*, the final *-et* being the suffixed article. This may be found in all three languages in various forms: in Norwegian, especially in nynorsk, it may coexist with the independent article: *Det Norske Samlaget*. (In Swedish this applies to ordinary descriptive phrases, but not to names.) Other institutional names have no article at all; this includes, but is not confined to, those containing a genitive case. The safest course is to take over all institutional names into English, but not to put *the* in front of them.

Distinguishing characteristics

While the languages are very similar, they can be distinguished even by the foreigner: thus Swedish uses *ck* and *x* where Danish and Norwegian have *kk* and *ks*; *ä* is used somewhat more frequently in Swedish than *æ* is in Danish, and very much more so than *æ* is in Norwegian. (For the difference between the two forms of italic ae ligature (*æ*, *œ*), *see* **11.34**.) Swedish may also be detected by *och* 'and' = Danish and Norwegian *og*; Danish may be detected by *af* 'from' = Norwegian and (since 1906) Swedish *av*. The infinitive particle is still spelt *at* in Danish, but is *å* in Norwegian and *att* in Swedish; the conjunction 'that' is *at* in Danish and Norwegian, but *att* in Swedish. Hence an extended text in which only *at* is found will be

Danish, but if both *at* and *å* occur it is Norwegian, and *att* indicates Swedish. Danish does not use double consonants at the end of words, but frequently uses the letter *d* after *l* and *n*, and has *b d g* where the other languages have *p t k*.

Word division

Compounds are divided into their constituent parts, including prefixes and suffixes. In Danish *sk*, *sp*, *st*, and combinations of three or more consonants that may begin a word (including *skj*, *spj*) are taken over, but only the last letter in Norwegian or Swedish; *ng* representing a single sound is kept back, and in Swedish *x*; other groups that represent a single sound are taken over (Norwegian *gj*, *kj*, *sj*, *skj*, Swedish *sk* before *e*, *i*, *y*, *ä*, *ö*). In Swedish compounds three identical consonants are reduced to two, but the third is restored when the word is broken: *rättrogen* 'orthodox', divided *rätt|trogen*; in Norwegian the word is spelt with the triple letter *retttroende*, and in nynorsk, *retttruande*. (In Danish, which does not use final double consonants, the word is *rettroende*, divided *ret|troende*).

Pronouns

In Danish and Norwegian the pronouns *De*, *Dem*, *Deres* (*De*, *Dykk*, *Dykkar* in nynorsk) are capitalized when used as a polite second person; so in Danish is the familiar second-person *I*—but not its oblique cases *jer* etc.—to distinguish it from *i* 'in'. In Swedish there is no exact equivalent; the rather condescending second-person plural *ni*, when used as a singular, retains the lower case.

The genitive case always ends in *-s* (after the suffixed article, if present), without apostrophe, and always precedes the word qualified (which has no article); in Danish it may be formed from a word-group as in English (*kongen af Spaniens datter* 'the King of Spain's daughter'; contrast Swedish *kungens av Spanien dotter*). Norwegian, especially nynorsk, tends to replace the genitive with a prepositional phrase; but in all three languages there are set phrases using the genitive, especially after *til* (Swedish *till*) 'to'.

Spelling

Older books in both Danish and Swedish will vary from the modern spellings, and until the 1950s written Swedish used plural verb forms long since given up in speech (*gå* 'go', *gingo* 'went', now *går*, *gick* like the singular); nevertheless both literary languages are now standardized as in other countries.

Norwegian, which until the middle of the nineteenth century used Danish as its literary language, now has two written languages: bokmål (formerly called riksmål, a term sometimes used now for a conservative form of it), which did not abandon Danish spelling conventions till the early twentieth century, and nynorsk (formerly called landsmål), an artificial but highly successful reconstruction of what Norwegian might have been but for the imposition of Danish, each of which has several variants permitting it to approach or keep its distance from the other as the individual writer wishes. Thus 'the book', which in 1900 was *Bogen* as in Danish in riksmål (then called Rigsmaal) and *Boki* in landsmål (then Landsmaal), became normally *boka* in both languages, but *boken* for one group of conservatives and *boki* for another. On the other hand 'a book' is *ei bok* in nynorsk, but *en bok* in all but the most radical bokmål. The only safe rule for the non-expert editor (or indeed author) is to assume that all inconsistencies are correct. Nynorsk is readily identified by the frequency of the diphthongs *au*, *ei*, *øy*, corresponding to ø/ö, *e*, ø/ö in Danish and Swedish; bokmål is far more sparing of them.

11.40.2 Icelandic and Faeroese

Alphabet

In both languages the letter *d* is followed by *ð*; works alphabetized in Icelandic have *þ*, *æ*, *ö* after *z*; those in Faeroese have *æ*, *ø*. The vowels *a*, *e*, *i*, *o*, *u*, *y* may all take an acute accent. Icelandic uses *x*, Faeroese *ks*; the Icelandic *þ* corresponds, to the Faeroese *t*. In Icelandic *z* is very frequent, *é* was formerly written *je*. Unlike continental Scandinavian, Icelandic and Faeroese have preserved most of the Old Norse inflections.

Capitalization

Icelandic capitalization is minimal, for proper nouns only; in institutional names only the initial article (masculine *Hinn*, feminine *Hin*, neuter *Hið*) should be capitalized. Faeroese follows Danish practice, though polite pronouns are not capitalized.

Word division

Compounds are divided into their constituent parts; divide other words after consonants.

Spelling

Old Norse texts are commonly edited in Icelandic spelling, but with additional characters *ǫ*, *ǫ́*, *œ*, which in modern Icelandic have become respectively *ö*, *á*, *æ*; otherwise the most noticeable differences are the ending *-r* after consonants = modern *-ur*, final *-sk* in verbs = modern *-st*, final *-k* in pronouns and *ok* 'and' = modern *-g*, and final *-t* in pronouns, articles, and *at* = modern *-ð*. For Old and Middle English see **11.34**.

11.41 **Slavonic languages**

11.41.1 **General points**

The Slavonic (or Slavic) languages are divided into three branches: East Slavonic, including Russian, Belorussian (or Belarusian, formerly also White Russian), and Ukrainian; West Slavonic, including Polish, Czech, Slovak, and Sorbian; and South Slavonic, including Bulgarian, Macedonian, Slovene (or Slovenian), and Serbian and Croatian (grouped linguistically as Serbo-Croat).

Of the Slavonic languages, Russian, Belorussian, Ukrainian, Bulgarian, and Macedonian are regularly written in the Cyrillic alphabet; Polish, Czech, Slovak, Sorbian (Upper and Lower), and Slovene in the Latin. Serbo-Croat is divided, with Serbs using Cyrillic and Croats using roman. For information on Russian, and on setting Slavonic languages in Cyrillic, *see* **11.38**. In addition the Cyrillic alphabet is or has been used, with adaptations, by more than fifty non-Slavonic languages, such as Moldovan, Tajik, Komi, Azeri, Turkmen, Tatar, Kazakh, Uzbek, Kyrgyz, Abkhaz, Kabardian, and Chukchi. The following guidelines relate to Slavonic languages and, where necessary, their transliteration.

11.41.2 **Transliteration**

Transliteration systems are largely similar for those languages written in Cyrillic. The transliteration system used by the US Library of Congress is in wide use, spurred on by the development of information technology and standardized cataloguing systems. The British Standard scheme may be used with or without diacritics, though in the latter case it loses the advantage of reversibility. If desired, -*y* may be used to express final -й, -ий, and -ый in proper nouns, for example *Tolstoy*, *Dostoevsky*, *Grozny*. Another commonly used British system agrees with the British Standard scheme with the following exceptions: е = *ye* initially and after ъ, ь, or a vowel; ё = *yo* (*o* after ж, ч, ш, or щ); й = *y*; final -ий, -ый = *y* in proper nouns or titles. For philological work the International system described in BS 2979 is also commendable.

Wherever possible, adhere to a single transliteration system throughout a single work. In texts using transliterated Russian, as well as Belorussian, Bulgarian, and Ukrainian, authors and editors should avoid mixing, for example, the usual British *ya*, *yo*, *yu*; the Library of Congress *ia*, *io*, *iu*; and the philological *ja*, *jo*, *ju*. (Note that the transliteration of Serbian and Macedonian operates according to different rules.)

11.41.3 **Belorussian**

Belorussian is closely related to Russian. In standard transliteration the diacritics ĭ, ŭ, è (or ė, é), and ' (soft sign) are used. In specialist texts, the philological system requires č, ë, š, ž. The Library of Congress system requires the ligatures $\widehat{ia}$, $\widehat{io}$, $\widehat{iu}$, $\widehat{zh}$; another form employs a slur beneath (i̯a, i̯o, i̯u). In practice both markings are often replaced by the separate letters, as many non-specialist typesetters have difficulty reproducing the markings; this is the case for all languages that employ this system.

11.41.4 **Bulgarian**

Bulgarian uses the Cyrillic alphabet, and is transliterated with the following diacritics. The Library of Congress transliteration system uses the diacritics ĭ, ŭ (also transcribed ă), and the letter combinations zh, kh, ch, sh, sht. It also requires the ligatures $\widehat{ia}$, $\widehat{iu}$, $\widehat{ts}$; another form employs a slur beneath (i̯a, i̯u, t̯s), but this is often replaced by separate letters.

The philological system requires č, š, ž. The older spelling included the letters ѫ (Library of Congress u̇) and ѣ (ě in the philological system, $\widehat{ie}$ in Library of Congress); since 1945 the former has been replaced by ъ (ŭ) and the latter by either e (e) or я (ja in the philological system, ya in the British Standard, $\widehat{ia}$ in Library of Congress), depending on (East Bulgarian) pronunciation.

The Bulgarian ъ was abolished in 1945 in contexts where it was silent, but continues to be written where it is voiced (like the u in 'but') and as a replacement for the like-sounding ѫ.

11.41.5 **Czech and Slovak**

Czech and Slovak are closely related West Slavonic languages spoken in the Czech Republic and Slovakia. They are written using the roman alphabet, which in Czech is a á b c č d d' e é ě f g h ch i í j k l m n ň o ó p r ř s š t t' u ú ů v y ý z ž; in alphabetizing, ignore accents on vowels and on d, n, and t. The Slovak alphabet is a á ä b c č d d' e é f g h ch i í j k l ĺ l' m n ň o ó ô p r ŕ s š t t' u ú v y ý z ž; in alphabetizing, ignore acute, circumflex, and accents on d, l, n, r, and t.

The diacritics used in Czech are á, é, í, ó, ú, ý, ů, č, d', ě, ň, ř, š, t', ž. The palatalization of d, t is always indicated by a háček in upper case (Ď, Ť) and in lower case either by a háček (ď, ť) or—preferably—a high comma right (d', t'). Slovak uses the diacritics ä, á, é, í, ĺ, ó, ŕ, ú, ý, ô, č, d', l', ň, š, t', ž. The palatalization of d and t is the same as for Czech; that for the Slovak l can be either a háček or high comma right in upper case (Ľ, L') and a high comma right in lower case (l').

11.41.6 Macedonian

Macedonian is written in the Cyrillic alphabet, with a transliteration system similar to that used for Serbian. The diacritics used are ǵ, ḱ, č, š, ž, and the apostrophe; the letter combinations lj, nj, dž should not be broken in word division.

11.41.7 Old Church Slavonic

Also called Old Bulgarian, Old Church Slavonic dates from the ninth century, and is written in the Cyrillic alphabet as well as the older Glagolitic alphabet. It was used in the Bible translation of Cyril and Methodius, and constituted the liturgical language of several Eastern Churches; the Eastern Orthodox Churches still use later forms, broadly labelled 'Church Slavonic'. (This is not one language but several, depending on the particular vernacular by which it was modified, though the best-known is the Russian version.)

The diacritics and ligatures used in the Library of Congress's transliteration of Church Slavonic are ǵ, ĵ, v̇, ẏ, ż, ě, $\widehat{ia}$, $\widehat{ie}$, $\widehat{iu}$, $\widehat{ks}$, $\widehat{ps}$, $\widehat{ts}$, $\widehat{ię}$, $\widehat{iǫ}$ (with hook right on e, o), $\widehat{ot}$, ē, ī, ō, ū, ȳ, ĭ, ę, ǫ (hook right or ogonek). In Russian Church Slavonic, ja/ya/ia may correspond to ę and $\widehat{ię}$, u to ǫ, and ju/yu/iu to $\widehat{iǫ}$. The philological system uses č, š, ž. Special characters are ' (soft sign), " (hard sign), sometimes also replaced by ь and ъ respectively, and in specialist works on Old Church Slavonic by ž and ŭ.

11.41.8 Polish

The Polish language is closely related to Sorbian, Czech, and Slovak. It is written in the roman alphabet, as in English without q, v, and x. It employs the diacritics ć, ń, ó, ś, ź, ż, and Ą, ą, Ę, ę (ogonek, hook right); in addition there is one special character, the crossed (or Polish) l (Ł, ł).

Alphabetical order is: a ą b c ć d e ę f g h i j k l ł m n ń o ó p r s ś t u w y z ź ż. The digraphs ch, cz, dz, dź, dż, rz, and sz are not considered single letters of the alphabet; these letter combinations should not be separated in dividing words.

11.41.9 Serbian and Croatian (Serbo-Croat)

Serbo-Croat was the main official language of the former Yugoslavia, formed from a combination of Serbian and Croatian dialects. Those speaking the Serbian variety use the Cyrillic alphabet, and those speaking the Croatian variety use the roman alphabet. While there is little structural difference (e.g. in declension and conjugation) between the two forms, differences exist in vocabulary and syntax.

There are three main dialects, conventionally identified by the word for *what*: *što*, *kaj*, and *ča*. The standard language is based on the *što* dialect (sometimes called Štokavian), itself divided into subdialects, of which Serbian prefers one, Croatian another. Kajkavian—a transition to Slovene—is the local dialect of Zagreb; the archaic Čakavian is used around Dalmatia.

The roman alphabet used for Croatian is the standard *latinica* that is to be used for transliterating Serbian even for lay readers: thus четници will be *četnici* not *chetnitsi*.

The Cyrillic alphabet is ordered а б в г д ђ е ж з и ј к л љ м н њ о п р с т ћ у ф х ц ч џ ш; both in transliterated Serbian and in Croatian, the *latinica* order is a b c č ć d dž đ e f h i j k l lj m n nj o p r s š t u v z ž.

Diacritics for transliterated Serbian are ć, č, š, ž; special characters are Đ đ. Obsolete Croatian usage allowed ń and a subscript comma on *l* and *g* (superscript and inverted on lower-case *g*): Ļ ļ, Ģ ģ. Except when imitating older typography, the subscript comma may be treated as hook left.

11.41.10 Slovene

Slovene (also called Slovenian) is written in the roman alphabet and uses the háček on č, š, ž; the digraph *dž* is not considered a single letter.

11.41.11 Sorbian

Sorbian is a West Slavonic language still spoken in Lusatia, around Bautzen and Cottbus, eastern Germany. Two languages (or dialects) exist, Upper and Lower Sorbian; both are written in the roman alphabet with accents, though not all accented characters are found in both: Upper Sorbian has ó, ř, and č (which is rare in Lower Sorbian); Lower Sorbian has ŕ and ś. Accented characters in Upper Sorbian are alphabetized c č, d dź, e ě, h ch, ł l, n ń, o ó, r ř, s š, t ć, z ž (formerly also k kh, now written ch). Those in Lower Sorbian are alphabetized: c č ć, d dź, e ě, h ch, ł l, n ń, r ŕ, s š ś, z ž ź. The b́, ḿ, ṕ found formerly are obsolete except in older texts.

11.41.12 Ukrainian

The philological system requires č, š, ž, ī, ï, ′ (soft sign), and the letter combinations *je*, *šč*, *ju*, *ja*. The Library of Congress system requires the ligatures i͡a, i͡e, i͡u, z͡h; another form employs a slur beneath (*i͡a, i͡e, i͡u, z͡h*); as with Belorussian, they are often omitted. The Ukrainian и Is transliterated as *y*, not *i* (which represents Ukrainian і).

11.42 **Spanish (Castilian) and Iberian languages**

....

11.42.1 **The Iberian languages**

This section introduces in general the Iberian languages: Castilian, Galician, Portuguese, and Catalan. Castilian is treated at length at **11.42.2**; the other languages are treated under separate headings. For a list of quick identifiers for Iberian languages *see* **11.42.3**.

In the Middle Ages the Iberian peninsula comprised several different states in which different forms of a common language were spoken: for literary purposes the most important were Castilian (especially in prose and epic), Galician (especially in lyric), and Catalan, a language closely related to Occitan, on which it freely drew in poetry but not in prose. In the later Middle Ages Portuguese established itself as a separate language from Galician, and Catalan (whose centre of gravity had shifted from Barcelona to Valencia) was challenged by Aragonese.

In the sixteenth century, after the union of the Castilian and Aragonese crowns to form the Kingdom of Spain, the standard printed languages were Castilian (commonly called Spanish); Portuguese, which maintained its separate identity even under the sixty years of Spanish rule (1580–1640); and Catalan, which had gone into a steep decline from which it recovered only in the nineteenth-century *Renaixenca*. During the centralizing dictatorship of General Franco its use was discouraged; since then it has asserted itself so vigorously that Castilian-speakers sometimes complain of discrimination. However, Barcelona is not only the capital of Catalonia but the second largest city in Spanish publication. Although any text longer than a few words in either language is unlikely to be mistaken for the other, an editor must not assume that a book published in Barcelona will have a Catalan and not a Castilian title.

The same reaction against Castilian centralism has encouraged regional groups to assert the distinct identity of their own dialects, notably Andalusians, Valencians, and above all Galicians, whose language (*galego*, in Castilian *gallego*) remains closer in many respects (except in its spelling system) to Portuguese than to Spanish.

The four languages have several features in common, notably a distinction between two verbs 'to be', *ser* (Catalan *èsser*) and *estar*, of which the former implies a permanent quality, the latter a transient one, or physical location (but the precise distribution varies from language to language). There are also two prepositions translatable by English 'for', *por* (Catalan *per*) and *para* (Catalan *per a*): in general *por* looks back, as to a cause, *para* forwards, as to a purpose. Latin *h*, though silent, is normally retained in writing.

Each language has characteristics of its own: among the medieval dialects it is Castilian that is the most given to innovation, but if only the modern standard forms are considered, Catalan is the most divergent.

Basque, related to no known language though with at least some words from the Iberian spoken before the Romans came, lies outside the scope of this section.

11.42.2 Castilian

11.42.2.1 General

The language generally called Spanish outside Spain has two names, *castellano* 'Castilian' and *español* 'Spanish'; the former is especially at home with reference to correct usage (*buen castellano*, cf. 'good English') or in contrast to the other languages used in Spain (*diccionario castellano-catalán*; but *diccionario español-portugués* is possible, since Portuguese are not Spaniards).

Despite the strong attachment of Spanish-speakers to their local usages, in language as in other matters, the standard written language of Spain and Latin America remains largely uniform. This is not to say that variations in idiom, vocabulary, and grammar are unknown or ignored. But whereas literature may represent local speech-forms, a reader—and editor—may reasonably expect academic writing in Madrid to be the same as that in Cádiz, La Coruña, Barcelona, Puerto Rico, Mexico City, Bogotá, or Buenos Aires, and anticipate that it should adhere to the rules governing Castilian Spanish. Editors should query any non-standard Spanish title or extract with the author.

11.42.2.2 Alphabet

In Spanish the groups *ch* (pronounced as in English) and *ll* are treated as compound letters, coming after *c* and *l*; *ñ* comes after *n*. The Spanish Academy has recently decreed that *ch* and *ll* should not be indexed as separate letters, but before *ci* and *lm* respectively. Anyone compiling a Spanish-order index (e.g. an index of words to a textual commentary) may wish to retain the old usage for the time being, until it is clear how the new ruling has been received—particularly in Latin America, which takes scant notice of the Academy's views.

Certain consonant sounds are written differently before *a*, *o*, *u* and *e*, *i* (*cu/que*, *ga/gue*, *gua/güe*, *ja/ge* or *je*, *za/ce*). Hence the verbs *sacar* 'take out', *delinquir* 'offend', *pagar* 'pay', *distinguir* 'distinguish', *averiguar* 'verify', *coger* 'get', *cruzar* 'cross', *vencer* 'defeat', in the first/third-person singular present subjunctive, make *saque*, *delinca*, *pague*, *distinga*, *averigüe*, *coja*, *cruce*, *venza*; but *trabajar* makes *trabaje*, since *je* is a legitimate combination, and even makes inroads on *ge* (*injerencia* 'interference', where etymology would require *g*).

Although *ç* was invented in Spain, it is never used in modern Castilian, having been ousted by plain *c* (before *e*, *i*) and by *z* (elsewhere). This is due to the sixteenth-century devoicing of sibilants in Castilian (also in Galician and Valencian, but not in Portuguese or standard Catalan) that abolished the distinction between *c* and *z*, *ss* and *s*, *x* and *j*.

The letters *k* and *w* are used only in words of foreign origin. The letter *q* is used only in the group *qu*, which in turn is used only before *e* and *i* for the sound represented before *a*, *o*, or *u* by *c*; when the *u* is pronounced, *cu* must be written (*cuando* 'when', *cincuenta* 'fifty', *cuidado* 'care'). Distinguish *cuidad* 'take care of (imperative plural)' from *ciudad* 'city'.

The letter *x* is used only before a consonant (*extraño* 'strange', *sexto* 'sixth') or in learned or modern borrowings (*sexo* 'sex'); otherwise it is replaced by *j* (Cervantes' hero is always *Don Quijote* in Spanish), except that Latin American, especially Mexican usage, has retained *México* and *Texas* for what in Spain are *Méjico* and *Tejas*; even King Xerxes is *Jerjes*.

The letter *y* is used initially (*ya* 'now'), medially before a vowel (*reyes* 'kings'), finally (*hoy* 'today'), and by itself in *y* 'and', but never for the Greek upsilon. The letter *z* is very rarely found before *e* and *i* (*Zenón* is a classical name, *zigzaguear* 'to zigzag' is a modern exotic).

At the beginning of a word, the diphthongs *ie* and *ue* are spelt *ye* and *hue*.

Apart from the digraph *ll*, the only doubled consonants in modern Spanish are *cc* before *e* or *i*, *nn* in compounds, and *rr*. Whereas the *ll* of Latin words used in everyday speech yields modern *ll* (*ella* 'she', *caballo* 'horse'), in learned words it becomes single *l*, for example *ilegal*; similarly, whereas inherited *nn* was palatalized to yield modern *ñ* (originally simply a compendious way of writing *nn*), as in *año* 'year', learned *nn* is retained only in some compounds (*innocuo* but *inocente*; note also *innoble*), but otherwise becomes simple *n* (*milenio*). On the other hand, *rr* is extremely frequent; moreover, since initial *r* always has the strong sound (and in the Middle Ages was always written double), it is doubled after a vocalic prefix (*romano* > *prerromano*). In compounds Latin *mm* becomes *nm* (*conmoción*, *inmune*) or simple *m* (*común*).

Since *b* and *v* are always pronounced alike, they are sometimes confused in writing: not every Spanish-speaker knows that *hubo* 'there was' should be written with a *b*, *estuvo* 'was' and *tuvo* 'had' with a *v*. However, it is known that *burro* 'donkey' and *vaca* 'cow' are thus spelt, and these words may be used in enquiring after the correct orthography.

11.42.2.3 Capitalization

Capitals are used for the main words in official names of institutions, organizations, political parties, associations, etc. (*Unión Europea*, *Fútbol*

Club Barcelona, Tribunal de Cuentas, Real Academia Española); historical periods and events, cultural and political movements (*Paleolítico, Renacimiento, Siglo de las Luces, Tercer Reich, Noche de los Cuchillos Largos, Conferencia de Yalta, Mayo del 68*); important sports events, cultural events, or festivities (*Juegos Olímpicos, Exposición Universal, Día de la Madre, Primero de Mayo, Feria de Abril*); names of important buildings and monuments (*Casa Blanca, Arco de Triunfo*); geographical names, and cardinal points and adjectives that are part of the name of a country or region (*Golfo Pérsico, Lejano Oriente, Tercer Mundo, Dakota del Norte*); names of the established powers (*Estado, Gobierno, Administración, Ejecutivo, Iglesia, Ejército*); the first word and proper nouns in titles and subtitles of books, poems, and plays (*Cien años de solidad; Llanto por la muerte de Ignacio Sánchez Mejías; La deshumanización del arte; Doña Rosita la soltera, o El lenguaje de las flores; El ingenioso hidalgo don Quijote de la Mancha*); names of newspapers, magazines, reviews, and classical religious texts (*El País, El Mundo, el Corán*); titles of legal texts when given in full (*Ley de Autonomía Universitaria, Código Penal*); names of registered trademarks (*Peugeot, Sony, SEAT*); names of prizes and medals (*Premio Nacional de Literatura, Orden de Imperio Británico*); names of the highest political or religious authorities—when not followed by their first name—and references to the divinity (*Rey, Reina, Papa, Dios, el rey Carlos III*); and names of the planets, comets, constellations, and other astronomical features (*Neptuno, Vía Láctea, cometa Halley*).

Roman numerals indicating centuries are generally put in full capitals in both italic and roman type (*el siglo XI*).

Lower case is used for names of posts and titles, whether political, religious, professional, or other (*catedrático, doctora, duquesa, general, juez, ministro, presidente*); names of religions and religious orders, races, tribes and their members, and nationalities (*amerindio, católico, francés, oriental, taoísmo*); titles of books, songs, films, etc. except the first letter of the title and of any proper noun (*Las bodas de Fígaro, La educación sentimental, Lo que el viento se llevó*); names of commonly used artistic and literary movements (*romanticismo, gótico, surrealismo*); names of urban thoroughfares, roads, and motorways, except when they have become unique (*calle de Hortaleza, avenida de Navarra, puente de Santiago, la Gran Vía*); names of administrative or territorial divisions and geographical features, and cardinal points when they are not part of a name (*provincia de Toledo, estado de Nueva York, condado de Lancashire, cordillera de los Pirineos, lago Titicaca, el sur de Francia*); and names of the days of the week, months, and seasons (*jueves, sábado, primavera, noviembre*).

11.42.2.4 Accents

The written accent in Spanish does not indicate vowel quality, nor musical pitch, but stress. This is indicated by the acute (´) accent. The only other diacritical marks used are the tilde on the ñ, a separate letter in the alphabet, and the diaeresis on ü, used after g before e or i, where u forms a diphthong with e or i and is not merely used to indicate hard g before e or i. Accents should be set on capitals, but some authors prefer to omit the acute. (In Spanish the word *tilde* may mean 'accent' in general, including the acute.)

There are two kinds of stress, the normal and the abnormal. The normal stress is never indicated by an accent; the abnormal stress is always indicated by the acute. The normal stress falls on either the penultimate or the last syllable, according to the rules given below; any stress on the antepenultimate or earlier syllable is by definition abnormal. Monosyllables never take an accent except for contrastive purposes. (An accent is sometimes used to show that two vowels expected by the modern reader to form a diphthong or triphthong do not do so, as when in Tirso de Molina's play Don Juan says to those who warn him of retribution in the afterlife *¡Qué largo me lo fiáis!* 'What long-term credit you give me!' In modern Spanish *fiais* is a monosyllable, but metre shows that here it is *fi-áis*.)

In words ending in a vowel or in n or s, the normal stress falls on the penultimate syllable, any other position being abnormal: *termino* 'I finish' but *terminó* 'he finished', *término* 'end'; *terminas* 'you (familiar singular) finish', future *terminarás*, *terminan* 'they finish', future *terminarán*. Nouns and adjectives of more than one syllable ending in -n or -s will have an accent in either the singular or the plural but not both; those stressed on the final syllable will lose the written accent in the plural, since the suffix -es restores penultimate stress: *imán* 'magnet', *inglés* 'English', plural *imanes*, *ingleses*; similarly nouns in -ción (= English -tion) have plurals in -ciones. Contrariwise, words stressed on the penultimate will in the plural be stressed on the antepenultimate (*crimen*, *crímenes*); but there is an irregular stress shift in *régimen*, *regímenes*.

In words ending in a consonant other than n or s, the normal stress is on the last syllable (*ciudad* 'city', *reloj* 'clock', but *alcázar* 'castle', *Cádiz*, *Velázquez*). The plural does not affect either the position or the (ab)normality of stress (*ciudades*, *alcázares*); the one exception is *carácter*, *caracteres*. All surnames ending in -ez (originally patronymics) have an acute on the syllable stressed in the corresponding Christian name: usually the penultimate, e.g. *Fernández*, *Gómez*, *González*, *Hernández*, *Jiménez*, *López*, *Márquez*, *Meléndez*, *Sánchez*, *Suárez*, but the antepenultimate in *Álvarez* (often written *Alvarez*).

Final y used instead of i in a diphthong counts as a consonant (*Uruguay*). Names from Catalan and other languages ending in vowel + u do not require the accent (*Palau*).

When a strong vowel (a, e, or o) stands immediately before or after a weak one (*i* or *u*), they are presumed to form a diphthong, rising (i.e. stressed on the second vowel) if the first vowel is weak, as in *lidiar* 'to fight', *igual* 'equal', *tierra* 'land', *abuelo* 'grandfather', *gracioso* 'clown', falling (i.e. stressed on the first vowel) if it is strong, as in *aire* 'air', *pausa* 'pause', *veinte* 'twenty', *deuda* 'debt', *heroico* 'heroic' (*ou* is found only in borrowings from Galician or Catalan). All these words have normal stress; abnormal stress is marked by an accent on the strong vowel: *adiós* (but *a Dios* 'to God', 'God (direct object)'), *vivió* 'lived', *menguó* 'diminished', *estiércol* 'dung', *cláusula* 'clause'. Thus in the familiar second-person plural *cantáis* 'you sing', future *cantaréis*, but imperfect subjunctive *cantarais* stressed on the penultimate (-*ta*-). The diaeresis does not imply hiatus: the -*üe* of *averigüemos* 'let us ascertain' is no less a diphthong than the -*ua*- of the indicative *averiguamos*. (In learned words, a weak vowel followed by a strong vowel under normal stress may remain in hiatus; but that does not affect the written accent.)

A strong vowel between two weak vowels is presumed to form a triphthong with them, subject to the same rules of accentuation (*Chiautla* (Mexican place name), *averiguáis* 'you ascertain', subjunctive *averigüéis*).

When a stressed weak vowel stands next to a strong vowel or diphthong, it takes the accent to mark hiatus (e.g. *período*) even if the stress would otherwise be normal (*egoísta*, *raíz* ('root', plural *raíces*), *Raúl*). Thus in first- and second-person plural imperfects of -*er* and -*ir* verbs and all conditionals: *bebíamos*/*bebíais* 'we/you were drinking', *vivíamos*/*vivíais* 'we/you were living', *cantaríamos*/*cantaríais* 'we should/you would sing', *beberíamos*/*beberíais*, *viviríamos*/*viviríais*.

At the end of a word, or before final -*n* or -*s*, a weak vowel followed by a strong is presumed to form a diphthong with it, the stress falling on the preceding syllable (*noria* 'waterwheel', *agua* 'water', *nadie* 'nobody', *evacue* 'that I/he may evacuate (subjunctive)', *bilingüe*, *necio* 'stupid', *vacuo* 'vacuous'). All these words have normal stress and take no accent; contrast *vivió* 'lived', *averiguó* 'he ascertained', *averigüe* 'I ascertained'. When instead the weak vowel is stressed, it takes the accent: *armonía*, *rocío* 'dew', and so in imperfects and conditionals: *vivía*, *vivías*, *vivía*, *vivían* 'I/you/he was living, they were living', *viviría* 'I should live'.

When two weak vowels come together, the assumption that the diphthong is rising unless marked by an accent on the first vowel (*ruido* 'noise' but *flúido* 'fluid') was abrogated in 1952, except for *iu* in a few Amerindian words; one now writes *fluido*. Even before then, *Luis*, as having a rising diphthong, was written without an accent; contrast Galician and Portuguese *Luís*, Catalan *Lluís*.

The letter *h* between vowels is no longer considered to make hiatus: *rehúso* 'I refuse'; cf. *reúno* 'I collect'.

Some verbs whose infinitives end in *iar* or *uar* stress the *i* or *u* in the strong forms (singular and third-person plural of the present indicative and subjunctive, second-person singular imperative), some do not (*envío* 'I send' but *cambio* 'I change', *continúa* 'continues' but *evacua* 'evacuates').

When object pronouns are attached to a verb, if the stress of the group considered as a whole is abnormal an accent is written even if the verb did not need one by itself (*traiga* 'bring (polite singular)' but *tráiganoslas* 'bring them (feminine plural) to us'). However, if the verb had abnormal stress it retains its accent even if the group-stress is normal (*reírse* 'to laugh', *hablóme* 'he spoke to me'). This does not apply to nominal use (*el acabose* as a noun, 'the end', as in 'that's the end!', from the verbal form *acabóse*).

Infinitives in *aír*, *eír*, and *oír* should be written with the accent, but the preterites *dio* 'he/she/it gave', *fue* 'he/she/it was, went', *fui* 'I was, went', *vio* 'he/she/it saw' without one. (Before 1952 these last were written *dió* etc.; when the accent was omitted it was also omitted in the infinitives, but there it was restored in 1959. The cases are different: since the preterites are monosyllabic, there is no need for an accent on the strong vowel of the diphthong; since the í of the infinitives is a separate syllable, it needs the accent to show that it is not the weak vowel of the diphthong.)

An accented word loses its accent as the first element of a compound (*asimismo* 'likewise', *rioplatense* 'of the Río de la Plata', *sabelotodo* 'know-all'), except for adverbs formed by adding *-mente* to an adjective (*comúnmente*, *rápidamente*).

Strong vowels never form diphthongs with each other: *cae* 'falls', *caer* 'to fall', *lee* 'reads', *leer* 'to read', each count as two syllables, *Feijoo* (proper noun) as three.

Before 1911 the words *a* 'at/to', *e* 'and', *o* 'or', *u* 'or', were written with the accent; this now survives only on ó between arabic numerals, to avoid misreading as 0 (*2 ó 3* but *II o III*, *7 u 8*).

Contrastive accents are used to distinguish the following:

- Interrogative *cuál* ('what', 'which'), *cómo* ('how'), *cuándo* ('when'), *cuánto* ('how many/much'), *dónde* ('when'), *qué* ('what'), and *quién* ('who') take the accent when used as interrogatives or exclamations, but not as relatives or conjunctions (¿*Por qué lo hizo Vd.?* —*Porque conocía a su hermano* 'Why did you do it? Because I knew his brother').

- The demonstratives *éste* ('this'), *ése* ('that [near you]'), *aquél* ('that, yonder') with their feminines, *ésta*, *ésa*, *aquélla* and plurals *éstos/éstas*, *ésos/ésas*, *aquéllos/aquéllas*, when used absolutely without a noun (*éste* 'this one', *este libro* 'this book'); but the neuter forms *esto*, *eso*, *aquello* are never used with nouns.

- A contrastive accent is used to distinguish the following monosyllables: *dé* 'may give', *de* 'of', 'letter D'; *él* 'he', *el* 'the' (but note that 'he who' is *el que* not *él que*, just as 'she who' is *la que* not *ella que*); *más* 'more', *mas* 'but';

mí 'me' after preposition, *mi* 'my'; *sé* 'I know', 'be!' (imperative singular), *se* reflexive (also 'to him/her/it/them' before another third-person pronoun); *sí* reflexive after preposition, 'yes', *si* 'if'; *té* 'tea', *te* 'you' (familiar singular, object), 'letter T'; *tú* 'you' (subject), *tu* 'your'; and the disyllables *sólo* 'only', *solo* 'alone'; *aún* 'still' (of time), *aun* 'even'.

11.42.2.5 Word division

The general rule is that a consonant between two vowels and the second of two consonants must be taken over to the next line. The ñ, which is not a double sound but a pure palatalized *n* (pronounced like French or Italian *gn*, not like English *ni* in 'onion'), is taken over even though only a few colloquial or Amerindian words begin with it.

The combinations *ch*, *ll*, and *rr* are indivisible because they represent single sounds and must be taken over (*mu|chacho, arti|llería, pe|rro*).

The consonants *b, c, f, g, p* followed by *l* or *r* must be taken over with it, since these groups are capable of beginning a word: *ha|blar* 'to speak', *ju|glar* 'minstrel', *lo|grar* 'to achieve', *lú|brico* 'slippery', *re|frán* 'proverb' (cf. *blando* 'soft', *gloria, grande, brazo* 'arm', *frente* 'front'); so must *dr* and *tr*, as in *ma|drugada* 'dawn', *pa|tria* 'fatherland' (cf. *dragón* 'dragon', 'dragoon', *traer* 'bring'); *tl* is taken over in borrowings from Nahuatl used in Mexico and neighbouring countries (*Chiau|tla, cenzon|tle* 'mockingbird', also spelt *cenzonte* or *sinsonte*), but not from Greek (*at|leta* 'athlete', *at|lántico*).

The letter *s* must be divided from any following consonant: *Is|lam, hués|ped* 'guest, host', *Is|rael, cris|tiano* (contrast Italian *cri|stiano*), similarly *Es|teban* 'Stephen', *es|trella* 'star', even in a compound (*ins|tar* 'to urge', *ins|piración*).

Divide compounds into their component parts, except where they contain *s* + consonant or *rr* (*des|hacer* 'to undo', *sub|lunar*, but *circuns|tancia, co|rregir* 'to correct', *inte|rrumpir* 'to interrupt'). Some leeway is admitted with words that are no longer felt to be compounds (*nos|otros* or *no|sotros* 'we'); the non-native speaker is advised to exercise caution.

Never divide diphthongs and triphthongs; if possible, avoid dividing between vowels at all.

11.42.2.6 Punctuation

Most forms of punctuation, such as parentheses, full point, and semicolon, are used in a manner similar to that in English. Some distinctions are given below.

An inverted exclamation mark or question mark is inserted at the place where the exclamation or question begins (*¡Mire!* 'look!' *¿Dónde vas?* 'Where are you going?'). This need not be the start of the sentence (*Si ganases el gordo, ¿qué harías?* 'If you won the jackpot what would you do?').

The hyphen is used to divide a word and to join elements of a loose compound (*guerra franco-prusiana, tratado anglo-francés*), though it is not used when the compound acquires a new meaning (*iberorromano*, *hispanoamericano*). It is also used between the names of the co-authors of something (*pacto Hitler-Stalin*), to separate two or more adjectives that qualify a noun (*enfoque histórico-antropológico*), and between two nouns that refer to a single person or thing (*conde-duque, decreto-ley*). Object pronouns following the verb (regularly the imperative, infinitive, and gerund; occasionally and in older usage other forms, especially in reflexives or at the start of the sentence) are not hyphenated, but rather written as one word with it. The integrity of verb and pronoun is nowadays maintained except in the two cases represented by *sentémonos* 'let us be seated' (for *-mosnos*) and *sentaos* 'be seated (familiar plural)' (for *-ados*; similarly with other reflexive imperatives plural except *idos* 'go away'), but in classical Spanish (the language of the sixteenth- and seventeenth-century Golden Age, *el Siglo de Oro*) one will find *tomallo* 'to take it' for *tomarlo* and *tomaldo* 'take it (plural)' for *tomadlo*.

The em rule indicating parenthetical matter is set close up to the words it introduces or closes, and with a word space between it and the body of the sentence (*la pronunciación figurada —cuyo uso es internacional— debe ser…*). The dash may also be used, close up to the new sentence only, to indicate a change of speaker.

Quotation marks take the form of guillemets (called *comillas*), but in contrast to French usage they are close up on the inside (e.g. *«¡Hola!»*). However, it is more common—especially in fiction—to dispense with *comillas* altogether and denote the speakers by a dash only (a mode sometimes adopted in English and other languages as well); in such cases *comillas* are sometimes reserved for marking a word from another language. Single quotation marks (' ') are used for quotations within quotations, also for definitions and other reference purposes. However, in works not set wholly in Spanish (especially in short extracts) there is no objection to imposing the English system.

Colons are used before a quotation (*Dijo el alcalde: «Que comience la fiesta.»*), in letters (*Querido Pablo:*), and before an enumeration (*Trajeron de todo: cuchillos, cucharas, sartenes*, etc.). A colon is also used before a clause in which we explain the reason for or we draw the conclusion of the previous one (*No creo que debamos invitar a Paulino: seguro que discute con Ana. La música estaba demasiado alta y había demasiado humo: nos fuimos a casa.*)

Points of suspension are used to denote an interruption or a rhetorical pause. These are set close up, as with French *points de suspension*, with space following but not preceding them.

The apostrophe is not generally used in standard Spanish, although the final vowel of one word and the initial vowel of the next are regularly run together in speech (so that *a un* 'at/to a', *de un* 'of a' are only one syllable). This is not marked in writing except in the case of *al* 'at/to the', *del* 'of the', where the words are fused into one. In classical Spanish fusion was more widely used (*daquel* 'of that', *deste* 'of this', *ques* 'which is'); some modern editions use the apostrophe in such cases.

11.42.2.7 Miscellaneous

Immediately preceding a feminine noun beginning with stressed *a* or *ha* the definite article is *el*, not *la* (*el agua* 'water', *el hambre* 'hunger'). This does not apply to letters of the alphabet (*la hache* 'the aitch'), names of women, adjectives (*la árida llanura* 'the arid plain') even when used without a noun (*es más peligrosa la baja marea que la alta* 'low tide is more dangerous than high'), or when sex needs to be specified (*la árabe* 'the Arab woman'); similarly *la ánade* used specifically of the duck and not the drake. In classical Spanish the rule is not always observed; in some regional varieties one may even find *l'*, though otherwise the apostrophe is almost unknown in Castilian spelling.

The normal word for 'or', *o*, is replaced by *u* before initial *o* (*siete u ocho* 'seven or eight') or *ho* (*dioses u hombres* 'gods or men').

The normal word for 'and', *y*, is replaced by *e* before initial *i* (*compases e imanes* 'compasses and magnets') and *hi* (*fluoruros e hidrocarburos* 'fluorides and hydrocarbons'); but *y* is retained before *hie*, which is pronounced like *ye* (*latón y hierro* 'brass and iron').

The preposition *a* is required before a direct object consisting of the proper noun of a person or animal (and normally a place, unless it has the article), a definite person or persons, and in several other circumstances: *vi a Juan* 'I saw John', *los soldados detuvieron a los políticos* 'the soldiers arrested the politicians', *a la guerra sigue la paz* 'war is followed by peace', as against *la guerra sigue la paz* 'war follows peace', *el niño buscaba a su madre* 'the child was looking for its mother'; but *Diógenes buscaba un hombre honrado* 'Diogenes was looking for an honest man', i.e. to see if he could find one: *buscaba a un hombre honrado* would mean that he was looking for a particular honest man of whom he already knew.

In polite address, 'you' is *usted* in the singular and *ustedes* in the plural, both with the appropriate third person form of the verb. They are often abbreviated *Vd.*, *Vds.*, occasionally *Ud.*, *Uds.*

The verb *haber* is used with the past participle to form a complete set of compound tenses: the distinction between the preterite *canté* and the perfect *he cantado* is comparable to that between 'I sang' and 'I have sung', except that the perfect is more normal for actions performed on the day of speaking. However, there is nothing stilted or literary about the preterite as there is in French.

The future subjunctive, which in classical Spanish was normal in conditional, temporal, and relative clauses relating to the future, is now rare outside set phrases: *sea lo que fuere* 'be that as it may', *adonde fueres, haz lo que vieres* 'wherever you go, do as you see' (when in Rome, do as the Romans do), *Al que leyere* 'To the Reader' (literally 'To him who shall read').

In the strong (root-stressed) forms many verbs change stressed *e* to *ie* and *o* to *ue*: *cerrar* 'to close', *cierro* 'I close', *mover* 'to move', *muevo* 'I move'; in initial position *yerro* 'I stray' from *errar*, *huelo* 'I smell' from *oler*. Some verbs in -*ir* instead change their stem from *e* to *i*: *pedir* 'to request', *piden* 'they request', and extend this change to the first- and second-person plural subjunctive *pidamos, pidáis*. Any verb in -*ir* that makes either change will also change *e* to *i*, and *o* to *u*, before a stressed diphthong: *sentir* 'to feel', *siento* 'I feel' (or 'I am sorry'), *sintió* 'he felt', *pedir* 'to request', *pido, pidió*; *dormir* 'to sleep', *duermo, durmió*.

In many words Latin *f* has become *h*: *hacer* 'to do', *hambre* 'hunger', *hierro* 'iron'; in early texts the *f* was still written, and also used for *h* in Germanic or Arabic loanwords. The aspirate was still pronounced, and treated by poets as a consonant, in the early sixteenth century; after that it became silent in standard Castilian, though not in some dialects, notably Andalusian (whence the name *cante jondo* for a style of gypsy song; *jondo* = *hondo* 'deep').

11.42.3 Quick identification: Castilian, Catalan, Galician, and Portuguese

i as a word: Catalan

y as a word: Castilian

che as a word: Galician

lh: Portuguese

ll: not Portuguese; if used initially when Latin has *l*-, Catalan

l·l: Catalan

nh: Portuguese or Galician

ñ: Castilian or Galician

nh (other than initial *inh*-) and *ñ*: Galician

ny: Catalan

tj tll tx tz: Catalan

x very frequent: Galician

x moderately frequent: Portuguese or Catalan

x only in *ex*- or international words: Castilian

y other than after *n*: Castilian

Final -*ía*, -*íe*, -*ío*, -*úa*, -*úe*, -*úo*: Castilian or Galician

Final -*ia*, -*ie*, -*io*, -*ua*, -*ue*, -*uo* with accent on preceding syllable: Portuguese or Catalan

à, às as independent words: Portuguese

à, è, ò before -*mente* or suffixes beginning with -*z*: Portuguese before the later twentieth century

à, è, ò in other circumstances: Catalan

ã, õ: Portuguese

i, ù: Portuguese before later twentieth century

qü: Portuguese (only Brazilian in later twentieth century)

Circumflex accents: Portuguese

Frequent final *-che* and *-ches*: Galician

Final *-d*: Castilian

Initial *h-* when comparable English or French words have *f-*: Castilian

Frequent *-ie-* and *-ue-* when not found in comparable English words: Castilian

Final *-m*: Portuguese

Final *-t*: Catalan

11.43 **Turkish**

11.43.1 **Alphabet**

Though Ottoman Turkish, the language of the Ottoman Empire, was written in an Arabic script, Kemal Atatürk in 1928 decreed the change to the roman alphabet. The resulting diacritics are *c*, *s* (with cedilla), *ğ* (with breve, not háček), *ö*, *ü*, and the apostrophe (not lenis or asper). *I ı* and *İ i* are separate letters; *î* or *ī* in copy should be set as ı, but *â, î, û* are set thus. (Do not use the ligature *fi*—which obscures the distinction between the two types of *i*—set instead *fı* or *fi* as required.) The dotted capital is used in the personal name *İsmet* and the place names *İstanbul, İzmir, İzmit, İznik*, but the undotted letter in *Isparta*. Turkish typesetters often put a dot on upper-case *J* by analogy with dotted upper- and lower-case *i*, but this is not a separate letter and may be ignored.

Pre-1928 texts are normally transcribed in this alphabet; but sometimes it is necessary to indicate the original spelling, which is done with the additional symbols: *ġ, ż, ḥ, ḳ, ṣ, ṭ, ẓ, ḫ, ñ, ṣ, ẓ*, and *ʿ* (asper). These symbols may also be used for transcribing Turkic languages from the Cyrillic alphabet (insofar as they have not yet adopted the roman script), but other scholars prefer symbols of their own, such as *ï* for ı and *л* for *ñ*. (*See also* **11.6.2.**)

11.43.2 **Punctuation**

Since Western conventions do not easily fit the Turkish sentence, punctuation may sometimes seem erratic, but in all save the simplest sentences it is fairly normal to insert a comma between the subject and the predicate, which may save the reader from floundering. Parentheses are often used around quotations or words intended to stand out.

11.43.3 **Spelling**

Some variation of spelling is to be expected: in the 1950s it was fashionable not to mark the devoicing of final consonants; some words, mainly from the Arabic, may appear with dotted or undotted *i*, with umlauted or non-umlauted *u*, with or without circumflex, and with or without apostrophe—never a lenis or asper. In general the use of Arabic and Persian words has decreased (especially in the sciences), and those that remain are nowadays Turkicized, in spelling and declension, more thoroughly than in the early years of the roman script.

11.43.4 **Capitalization**

Practice should largely follow the standard adopted for European languages. Turkish or Persian expressions used in an English sentence should appear italicized, in lower case. Names of institutions, schools of thought and religions, etc. are set in roman if they are to be capitalized or expressed in italics if they are to be lower-case. Titles of books and periodicals should appear in italics, whereas periodical articles should be given in roman with quotation marks.

11.44 **Vietnamese**

The Vietnamese language, properly called Annamite, or in Vietnamese *quốc-ngữ*, uses the roman alphabet with the exception of f, j, w, and z. The alphabet includes certain consonant combinations and the letter Đ, đ, which is typographically similar to the Croatian Đ, đ, but may have the line through the entire body of the capital letter. It is to be distinguished from D, d, which is also found. Although pronunciation varies between the north, central, and south regions, spelling is generally standardized to the Hanoi dialect. Alphabetization is: a ă â b c ch d đ e ê g/gh gi h i k kh l m n ng/ngh nh o ô ơ p ph q r s t th tr u ư v x y.

All morphemes are monosyllabic, so compounds are joined with hyphens. The tone marks are regularly used in all writing, not simply in school texts or sacred writings—as is the case with Pinyin and Serbo-Croat, for example. The six tones are indicated with the following diacritics: level (unmarked), high rising (acute, e.g. á), low (falling) (grave, e.g. à), low rising or dipping-rising (superscript dotless question mark, e.g. ả), high rising broken/glottalized (tilde, e.g. ã), and low constricted/glottalized (subscript dot, e.g. ạ). Accents include the Roman breve (˘) and circumflex (ˆ); there is also a 'horn' (ơ, ư). Each may be used in combination with tone marks. Note that the accents are set above the breve (e.g. ắ, ằ); the acute accent should preferably be set to the right of the circumflex (e.g. ố) and the grave to the left (e.g. ồ). The resulting combinations, which can be bewildering to the uninitiated, are á, ắ, ấ, é, ế, í, ó, ố, ớ, ú, ứ, ý, à, ằ, ầ, è, ề, ì, ò, ồ, ờ, ù, ừ, ỳ, ả, ẳ, ẩ, ẻ, ể, ỉ, ỏ, ổ, ở, ủ, ử, ỷ, ã, ẵ, ẫ, ẽ, ễ, ĩ, õ, ỗ, ỡ, ũ, ữ, ỹ, ạ, ặ, ậ, ẹ, ệ, ị, ọ, ộ, ợ, ụ, ự, ỵ.

11.45 **Welsh**

11.45.1 **Alphabet**

The Welsh alphabet consists of twenty-eight letters, alphabetized as: a b c ch d dd e f ff g ng h i l ll m n o p ph r rh s t th u w y. The letter *j* is used in borrowed words, *k* and *v* are very frequent in medieval texts but are now obsolete.

Note especially the separate ranking of the digraphs *ch*, *dd*, *ff*, *ng*, *ll*, *ph*, *rh*, *th* (but NB not *ngh*, *mh*, *nh*, *nn*, *rr*); the position of *ng*, which follows *g* except when it is two separate letters, in which case ranking between *nff* and *nh*; *rh* counts as a separate letter at the start of a word or syllable only, i.e. after a consonant but not a vowel: *route* comes before *rhad* 'cheap', *cynrychioli* 'to represent' before *cynrhon* 'maggots', but *arholi* 'to examine' before *arian* 'money'; *w* is usually, *y* always, a vowel.

All vowels may take a circumflex; usage is not entirely consistent, but some pairs of words are distinguished only by the accent: *dy dŷ* 'your (familiar singular) house'; *bûm* 'I was' or *bum* 'five' in *Atebwch bum cwestiwn* 'Answer five questions'. There are four different words *a* besides the name of the letter, and three *â*. Acute, grave, and diaeresis are also found: most frequent are *á* in final syllables (*casáu* 'to hate') and *ï* before a vowel (*copïo* 'to copy'); the letter with the diaeresis always precedes or follows another vowel.

A word consisting of an apostrophe followed by a single letter must be set close up to the preceding word: *cerddai'r bachgen a'i fam i'ch pentref* 'the boy and his mother used to walk to your village'.

11.45.2 **Word division**

Do not divide the digraphs *ch*, *dd*, *ff*, *ll*, *ph*, *rh*, *th*. Note that *ng* is indivisible when a single letter, but not when it represents *n* + *g*: this happens most frequently in the verb *dangos* 'to show' and its derivatives, compounds ending in *-garwch* or *-garwr* (*ariangarwr* 'money-lover'), place names beginning with *Llan-* (*Llangefni*), and in *Bangor*. Thus *cyng|aneddol* but *a ddan|goswyd*.

Diphthongs and triphthongs must not be divided: they are *ae, ai, au, aw, ayw, ei, eu, ew, ey, iw, oe, oi, ou, ow, oyw, wy, yw* (in earlier texts also *ay, oy*), and other combinations beginning with *i* and *w*, in which these letters are consonants. The presence of a circumflex or an acute does not affect word division, but it is legitimate to divide after a vowel bearing the diaeresis, as also after a diphthong or triphthong before another vowel. Thus *barddonï|aidd* 'bardic', *gloyw|ach* 'brighter', *ieu|anc* 'young'.

A suffix beginning with *i* plus a vowel must be broken off: *casgl|iad* 'collection'; here the *i* counts as a consonant; so too with *w* plus a vowel (but *an|nwyl, eg|lwys*, and a few other words in which *-wy-* is not a suffix and the *w* is vocalic).

In other cases follow etymology rather than pronunciation. Generally, take back a single consonant other than *h* except after a prefix (especially *di-, go-, tra-*), *g|l* but *s|gl* (and so similar groups), but suffixes should be taken over; take back in doubtful instances when a specialist cannot be consulted. Particularly in narrow measure, two-letter suffixes may have to be taken over, above all the plural *-au*. However, it is always safe to divide *l|rh, ng|h, m|h, n|h* (but *n|nh*), *n|n, n|rh, r|r*, and after a vowel *r|h*. Initial *gwl-, gwn-, gwr-*, and their mutated forms must not be divided, since the *w* is consonantal; *gwlad* 'country', (*hen*) *wlad* '(old) country'; *gwneud* 'to do', (*ei*) *wneud* 'to do (it)'; *gwraig* 'woman', (*y*) *wraig* '(the) woman', cannot be divided.

11.45.3 **Mutations and other changes**

Initial consonants, in certain grammatical contexts, are replaced by others in a process called mutation: *cath* 'cat' but *fy nghath* 'my cat', *ei gath* 'his cat', *ei chath* 'her cat'; *Brymbo, Caerdydd* (Cardiff), *Dinbych* (Denbigh), *Gwent, Penybont-ar-Ogwr* (Bridgend), *Tonypandy* give *i Frymbo* 'to Brymbo' (and *o Frymbo* 'from Brymbo'), *ym Mrymbo* 'in Brymbo'; *i Gaerdydd, yng Nghaerdydd*; *i Ddinbych, yn Ninbych*; *i Went, yng Ngwent*; *i Benybont-ar-Ogwr, ym Mhenybont-ar-Ogwr*; *i Donypandy, yn Nhonypandy*. 'Oxford' is *Rhydychen* (*rhyd* 'ford', *ychen* 'oxen'), but 'from Oxford' is *o Rydychen*; 'University' is *prifysgol*, but 'Printer to the University' is *Argraffwr i'r Brifysgol*. The full range of mutations is *b* to *f* or *m*; *c* to *ch, g*, or *ngh*; *d* to *dd* or *n*; *g* omitted or to *ng*; *ll* to *l*; *m* to *f*; *p* to *b, mh*, or *ph*; *rh* to *r*; *t* to *d, nh*, or *th*. Note that the abbreviations of mutated words are not exempt: where *llinell* 'line' and *llinellau* 'lines' are mutated to *linell* or *linellau*, *ll.* and *llau.* are mutated to *l.* and *lau.* Thus *l.* and *ll.* are both singular.

Initial vowels may acquire a preliminary *h* (*offer* 'tools', *ein hoffer* 'our tools') and changes of stress within a word may cause *h* to appear or disappear and double *n* or *r* to be simplified: *brenin* 'king', *brenhinoedd* 'kings'; *brenhines* 'queen', *breninesau* 'queens'; *corrach* 'dwarf', *corachod* 'dwarfs'; *cynneddf* 'faculty', *cyneddfau* 'faculties'; *cynnin* 'shred', *cynhinion* 'shreds'; *dihareb* 'proverb', *diarhebion* 'proverbs'. But in medieval Welsh we find *brenhin* for 'king', and *breninoedd* was misguidedly written (though not pronounced) in the nineteenth century.

11.45.4 Punctuation

Punctuation and other conventions are as in English with the exception of word division.

CHAPTER 12

Science and mathematics

12.1 **General principles**

12.1.1 Official guidelines

Authors of texts involving the 'harder' sciences, such as astronomy, biology, chemistry, computing, mathematics, and technology, commonly employ practices different from those in the humanities and social sciences—particularly in those texts aimed at a specialist readership. Authors should follow the standards common in their discipline, as well as any set out for specific contexts, such as series or journal articles. In general, authors and editors should follow the relevant practices by the Royal Society and the Système International (SI), particularly those for styling symbols and units, which can still vary between specialities within a single subject. (Many units not recognized by SI are still compatible with SI units.) Internal consistency is vital where more than one standard is acceptable, or where recommendations conflict: for example, the International Standards Organizations (ISO) prefers decimals to be expressed by a comma rather than a full point, and authors writing in languages other than English may draw on different guidelines.

If an author has good reason for using a convention different from the norm, he or she should mention this to the editor early on. As common usage changes more frequently in the sciences than in other disciplines, it is particularly important to clarify variations before editing has begun. Many scientific journals have developed their own house style, each of which will vary according to the subject's conventions and readership's requirements. Authors should be aware that, for reasons of efficiency and speed, this style may be imposed—often by running the text through a computer template—without consulting the author afterwards. (As a requirement of submission, authors may need to download a template from a publisher's website and incorporate it during writing.)

Authors should avoid introducing a novel notation or symbol: do not, for example, embellish characters with superscript dots unless it is specifically necessary to emulate Newtonian notation. If non-standard terms are essential to the notation system, authors should consider including a list of variables in the preliminary matter. If non-standard symbols are used, authors should supply the editor with a printed example of each, so that there is no danger of the typesetter misunderstanding what is intended.

12.1.2 Clarity

Authors and editors should take care that copy is clear and unambiguous, and keep any notation inserted by hand to a minimum. Ensure that the numbers 0 and 1 are distinguished from the letters O and l, single (′) and double (″) primes are distinguished from single (') and double ('') closing quotation marks, the multiplication sign (×) is distinguished from a roman x, and wide angle brackets are distinguished from 'greater than' (>) and 'less than' (<) signs. (In some fonts they may be identical.) Likewise, ensure that any rules above or below odd letters and whole expressions are not mistaken for marking for italic.

Clarify any instances of Hebrew, Greek, or other fonts for the typesetter, ideally providing printed examples of how each character should look when set. For example, mark where there may be danger of confusion between the Greek letters α, β, δ, η, κ, ν, ρ, υ, χ, ω and roman letters a, B, d, n, k, v, p, u, x, w. Do not underline Greek letters to indicate that they are used as symbols (this will be assumed), nor to indicate italic: no italic exists for Greek letters, as their angle is a function of the typeface chosen. When setting Greek OUP prefers to specify an upright typeface for all 'technical' contexts, reserving a sloping typeface for 'literary' or foreign-language contexts.

12.1.3 Numerals

Do not mix technical and non-technical forms. In scientific and mathematical work, figures are set close up, without a comma, in numbers up to 9999. In non-technical work, or in sums of money in technical work, commas are inserted after each group of three in numerals composed of four or more figures (£12,345). In larger numbers thin spaces, or fixed spaces, are introduced after each group of three digits to the right or left of a decimal point (1 234 567.891 011 12); to permit alignment, spaces are also introduced into four-figure numbers in columnar and tabular work. Decimal points are set on the baseline, not medially. Numerals less than one must be preceded by a zero (0.75), except for quantities like probability or ballistics that never exceed unity.

The SI guidelines state that it is preferable to use only numbers between 0.1 and 1 000. It is better, therefore, to write *22 km* rather than *22 000 metres*, or *3 mm³* rather than *0.003 cubic centimetres*. Powers of units can be represented exponentially: for example m^2 for square metre, and cm^3 for cubic centimetre. In many contexts *cc* for cubic centimetre is permissible; in less general work *sq. m.* may be preferable to m^2. There are internationally agreed abbreviations for many units, including all those in the SI; *see also* **3.7**.

Cased fractions (½, ⅔, ¾, , ,) exist for the most common fractions such as quarter, half, one third. Assume, however, that less usual combinations, such as 3/17, will be set with a solidus.

12.1.4 **Punctuation**

Traditionally, any formula or equation—whether occurring in the text or displayed—was regarded in every way as an integral part of the sentence in which it occurred, and was punctuated accordingly. Consequently it ended in a full point, and was interspersed with any internal punctuation required by syntax or interpolated text. This style is now considered by many to be too fussy for use with displayed material: instead no full point ends a displayed formula or equation, and internal punctuation is limited to that in or following any interpolated text, which is instead set spaced (at least 1 em) from the formula or equation.

12.1.5 **Notes**

All important information should be worked into the text, leaving only matter of secondary interest in notes, such as references, interpretations, and corrections. Since authors in many technical subjects choose to use an author–date (Harvard) style of references, footnotes occur infrequently. If a footnote is needed, however, make every effort to avoid adding the cue to a formula or equation, where it can easily be mistaken for part of the notation. For this reason superscript numerical note cues are not used except in non-technical contexts where equations are sparse. Where note cues are required, the cue should be one of the marks of reference († ‡ ¶ ||), in that order, repeated as necessary (††, ‡‡, etc.) throughout the work, chapter, or (in older practice) page. The asterisk (*) reference mark used in other disciplines is not found in scientific or mathematical contexts, where that symbol is assigned special uses.

Since footnotes are usually set in a font some two sizes smaller than the text, the author ought not, as a rule, to include formulae or other displayed matter in it. If, exceptionally, displayed notations must occur in notes, it may be worth considering using endnotes instead of footnotes: these are usually set in a slightly larger type size—about one size down from text size—so there is less restriction on the space available for display, and matter already in smaller type (indices, subscripts, symbols, etc.) is not reduced quite as much.

12.1.6 Eponymic designations

Names identified with specific individuals may be treated in several ways. Traditionally a disease, equation, formula, hypothesis, law, principle, rule, syndrome, theorem, or theory named after a person is preceded by the person's name followed by an apostrophe and s (*Alzheimer's disease*, *Bragg's law*, *Caro's acid*, *Gödel's proof*, *Newton's rings*); any variation follows the normal rules governing possessives (*Charles's law*, *Descartes's rule of signs*, *Archimedes' principle*, *Chagas's disease*, *Fajans's rules*) (see **5.2.1**). An apparatus, coefficient angle, constant, cycle, effect, function, number, phenomenon, process, reagent, synthesis, or field of study named after a person is usually preceded by the name alone or its adjectival form (*Leclanché cell*, *Plank constant*, *Salk vaccine*, *Cartesian coordinates*, *Newtonian telescope*). Eponymic anatomical or botanical parts may incorporate the name either as a possessive (*Cowper's glands*, *Bartholin's gland*, *Wernicke's area*) or adjectivally (*Casparian strip*, *Eustachian tube*, *Fallopian tube*). Something named after two or more people is known by the bare surnames, joined by an en rule (*Cheyne–Stokes respiration*, *Epstein–Barr virus*, *Stefan–Boltzmann law*, *Haber–Bosch process*, *Creutzfeldt–Jakob disease*) (see also **5.10.9**).

Particularly in medical use, British technical practice increasingly is to use bare surnames, so as to avoid the possessive's proprietary effect (*Angelman syndrome*, *Down syndrome*, *Kawasaki disease*, *Munchausen syndrome*, *Rous sarcoma*). This is the typical form for toponymic designations (*Borna disease*, *Coxsackie virus*, *East Coast fever*, *Ebola fever*, *Lyme disease*).

12.1.7 Temperature and calories

The various scales of temperature are Celsius (or centigrade), kelvin, Fahrenheit, and the obsolete Rankine and Réaumur; each may be found in different contexts in general as well as scientific work. Generally, use arabic numerals for degrees of temperature, but words for degrees of inclination (except in technical or scientific contexts), and in ordinary contexts for temperature. The degree symbol (°) is printed close up to its scale-abbreviation, when given: *10.15 °C* (not *10.15° C* or *10°.15C*). When that scale is understood and so omitted, the symbol is printed close up to the number: *35° in the shade*. When the symbol is repeated for a range of temperatures it is printed close up to the figure if an abbreviation does not immediately follow: *15°–17 °C*.

- Degree *Celsius* (abbreviation °C) is used in expressing Celsius temperatures or temperature differences, and is identical in magnitude to the kelvin. (To convert Celsius into kelvin add 273.15.) It is the equivalent of degree centigrade, which it officially replaced in 1948. To convert Celsius into Fahrenheit: multiply by 9, divide by 5, and add 32.

- The *kelvin* (abbreviation K) is used in expressing kelvin temperatures or temperature differences: 0 K = absolute zero, or −273.15 °C. It officially replaced degree Kelvin (abbreviation °K) in 1968 as the SI unit of thermodynamic temperature (formerly called 'absolute temperature').

- Degree *Fahrenheit* (abbreviation °F), common in the USA, is used in expressing Fahrenheit temperatures or temperature differences. Originally calibrated at the ice and steam points, its scale is now generally fixed in terms of the International Practical Temperature Scale (IPTS). To convert Fahrenheit into Celsius: subtract 32, multiply by 5, and divide by 9.

- Degree *Rankine* (abbreviation °R) was formerly used to express thermodynamic temperature or temperature difference: 0 °R is absolute zero, and 1 °R = 1 °F when considering temperature difference (i.e. 0 °R = −459.67 °F, and 0 °F = 459.67 °R).

- Degree *Réaumur* was formerly used to express a scale of temperature at which water freezes at 0° and boils at 80° under standard conditions. For some time obsolete, it is best known now from references to it in the work of Jules Verne.

- The term *calorie* stood for any of several units of heat and internal energy, originally relating to the gram of water and the degree Celsius. Now all deprecated, they should be avoided in favour of the joule. The calorie used in food science is actually a kilocalorie, based on the 15 °C calorie (cal_{15}). Sometimes called a 'large calorie', it is often written with a capital *C* to distinguish it from the 'small calorie'.

12.2 Astronomy

12.2.1 Conventions

Most current astronomy texts follow those recommendations for style set out by the International Astronomical Union (IAU), though other styles may be found, especially in older works. Ensure consistency within a given work, preferring modern to older styles except when reproducing earlier texts.

Capitalize *Earth*, *Moon*, and *Sun* only in contexts where confusion with another earth, moon, or sun may occur. *Galaxy* is capitalized only when it refers to the Milky Way, although *galactic* is lower-case in all contexts. While *minor planet* is preferable to *asteroid* in technical usage, *asteroid belt* is an accepted astronomical term.

12.2.2 Coordinates

Five coordinate systems exist for fixing celestial positions, times, and angles. Most use degrees, subdivided into minutes and seconds (*23° 26′21″*); inclinations may be expressed, for example, as *1°.58* rather than *1°58*. Right ascension coordinates are given in units of time—year (*y*), day (*d*), hour (*h*), minute (*m*), second (*s*)—these abbreviations, formerly given in superscript, are now in normal type (*20h 18m 15s*, or *20h 18.25m*) wherever they cannot be confused with other abbreviations. Southern declinations are denoted by a minus (−) symbol, which must not be omitted: e.g. the zero point of galactic longitude (J2000.0 coordinates) is expressed as *RA 17h 45.6m, dec. −28° 56′.3*. Northern declinations use a plus (+) symbol, or are left unmarked.

For dates in astronomical work *see* **7.10.1**.

12.2.3 Stellar nomenclature

Galaxies, nebulae, and bright star clusters can be designated by names (*Crab Nebula, Beehive Cluster, Sombrero Galaxy*) or by a Messier object number (*M1, M44, M104*).

The eighty-eight constellations have been assigned official names and a three-letter roman abbreviation (no point) by the IAU, so that Andromeda is *And*, Corono Borealis is *CrB*, and Sagittarius is *Sgr*. Many bright stars within these constellations have traditional names (*Sirius, Canopus, Castor and Pollux*), though astronomers tend to avoid them in favour of the Bayer letter system, in which Greek letters are allotted in alphabetical order by brightness as seen from Earth. The letter is followed by the genitive form of the constellation name, each capitalized (*Alpha Centauri, Beta Crucis, Gamma Orionis*). In technical contexts the abbreviated stellar name is usually used: the Greek letter itself is followed by a thin space and the abbreviated constellation name, with no point following (*α Cen, β Cru, γ Ori*). Star names may also be preceded by a Flamsteed number (*61 Cygni, 27 Tauri*). As such, a single bright star is likely to be known by more than one name: Alcor is *80 Ursae Majoris*, Pulcherrima is *Epsilon Boötis*; Betelgeuse is *Alpha Orionis* or *58 Orionis*. Variable stars not already labelled by either system follow a system of capital letters (often doubled), or are identified by a V and a number greater than 335. Fainter stars are usually known only by catalogue numbers.

Distinctions in luminosity between stars of the same spectral type are denoted by a capital roman numeral, separated from the preceding spectral type by a thin space (β *Cet K0 III*, *Sun G2V*). In general contexts Greek letters are often avoided, as readers may be unfamiliar with them.

Constellations and significant stars often have different names in other cultures, most conspicuously features with Greek or Roman names found also in Arabic: Alpha Centari is *Rigil Kent* in Arabic; Alpha Andromedae is *Alpheratz* or *Sirrah*. Colloquial names can cause difficulty: Ursa Major, commonly called the *Plough* or *Great Bear* in Britain, was formerly known as *Charles's Wain*; in the USA it is the *Big Dipper*, and in Germany the *Großer Wagen*. Two stars within Ursa Major are called the *Pointers* in the northern hemisphere, though in the southern hemisphere the term denotes different stars in the constellation Crux.

12.2.4 Planets and satellites

Planetary feature types are for the most part identified in Latin, taking Latin plurals. For example, *fossa* (plural *fossae*) indicates a long, narrow, shallow depression; *mons* (plural *montes*) indicates a mountain. Names of specific features on planets and their satellites follow guidelines drawn up by the IAU, and must be copied exactly: features on Venus, for example, are named after goddesses, those on the Uranus satellite Puck are named after mischievous creatures, and craters on Miranda (another satellite of Uranus) are named after male characters in *The Tempest*. Latin terms are usually capitalized and roman when forming part of a specific name.

Artificial satellites orbiting the Earth are denoted by a catalogue number, name (which follows the style for ships), and international designation, consisting of launch year, launch number, and letter(s) assigned to each type of object derived from the launch (prior to 1963 Greek letters were used). Thus *Vanguard I* has the catalogue number *00005* and the designation *1958 β 2*, and a fragment from the *Ariane 1–11* has the catalogue number *18787* and the designation *1986–19UA*.

12.2.5 Comet nomenclature

The IAU assigns newly discovered comets with a designation consisting of the year of discovery followed close up by a roman a, b, c, etc. in order of discovery (1963c, 2000a). If more than twenty-six new comets are found in a given year, the sequence continues with a subscript number, so that $1987a^1$ follows 1987z. Permanent designations, which are applied later, consist of the year of perihelion passage, a thin space, and a capital roman numeral assigned in order of the perihelion passage's date (*1988 VI, 1989 I*). In general a comet is also named after the person (or people) who discovered it or computed its orbit (*comet IRAS-Araki-Alkock 1983 VII, comet Halley*—colloquially *Halley's comet*). Thus the comet first designated *1973f* became *1973 XIII*, and commonly *comet Kohoutek*. Periodic comets are indicated by a *P/* immediately before the designation (P/Halley, P/Biela, P/Giacobini–Zinner)—not, as formerly, by a *P* after it.

12.2.6 Astronomical abbreviations and symbols, zodiacal signs

a, h	altitude, semi-major axis
A	azimuth; extinction
AU, a.u.	astronomical unit (mean earth–sun distance)
b	galactic or heliocentric latitude
BC	bolometric correction
c	speed of light
CM	central meridian
cpm, c.p.m.	common proper motion
D	aperture (of a telescope, etc.)
dec., Dec., δ	declination
e	eccentricity
ET	Ephemeris Time
f	following
F	focal length
g	acceleration due to gravity
GHA	Greenwich hour angle
GMT	Greenwich Mean Time
GST	Greenwich sidereal time
i	inclination
IC	Index Catalogue
J	Julian epoch
JD	Julian date
l	galactic or heliocentric longitude
l.y., lt-yr	light year
M	absolute magnitude, magnification, mass
m	apparent magnitude
m_{bol}	apparent bolometric magnitude
m_{pg}	apparent photographic magnitude
m_{pv}	apparent photovisual magnitude
m_v	apparent photometric visual magnitude
m_V	photometric visual magnitude
mag	magnitude

MJD	Modified Julian date	
NGC	New General Catalogue	
P, p.a., PA	position angle	
p	preceding	
pc	parsec	
Q	aphelion distance	
q	perihelion distance	
r	radius vector (distance from the Sun in AU)	
RA, α	right ascension	
t	time	
T	time of perihelion passage in an orbit	
T_c	colour temperature	
T_{eff}	effective temperature	
TAI	International Atomic Time (Temps Atomique International)	
TDT	Terrestrial Dynamic Time	
UT	Universal Time	
UTC	Coordinated Universal Time (Universal Temps Cordonné)	
z	zenith distance	
ZHR	zenith hourly rate	
☉	Sun	
●	Moon (new)	
☽	Moon (first quarter)	
○	Moon (full)	
☾	Moon (last quarter)	
☿	Mercury	
♀	Venus	
⊕	Earth	
♂	Mars	
♃	Jupiter	
♄	Saturn	
♅	Uranus	
♆	Neptune	
♇	Pluto	
① ② ③	asteroids in order of discovery (1, 2, 3, etc.)	
✩, ★, ✳	fixed star	
☌	conjunction	
☍	opposition	
☊	ascending node	
☋	descending node	
♈	vernal equinox (first point of Aries)	
♎	autumnal equinox (first point of Libra)	
β	celestial or ecliptic latitude	
Δ	geocentric distance, in AU	
ϵ	obliquity of the ecliptic	

λ	wavelength, celestial or ecliptic longitude
μ	proper motion
ν	frequency
π	parallax
τ	light travel time
φ	latitude
ω	argument of perihelion
ϖ	longitude of perihelion
Ω	longitude of the ascending node
♈	Aries
♉	Taurus
♊	Gemini
♋	Cancer
♌	Leo
♍	Virgo
♎	Libra
♏	Scorpio
♐	Sagittarius
♑	Capricorn
♒	Aquarius
♓	Pisces

Some of these symbols can appear in conjunction with other abbreviations: the planetary signs for earth, moon, or sun can appear as subscripts in conjunction with abbreviations: $M_{\oplus}$, $M_{\circ}$, and $M_{\odot}$, for example, denote terrestrial, lunar, and solar mass respectively.

12.3 Biological and medical nomenclature

12.3.1 Structure

In descending order, the hierarchy of general nomenclatural groups is: kingdom, phylum (in botany, division), class, order, family, genus, species. All organisms are placed in categories of these ranks: the domesticated cat, for example, is described in full as Carnivora (order), Felidae (family), *Felis* (genus), *Felis catus* (species). In addition, intermediate ranks may be added using the prefixes *super*, *sub*, *infra*, and subfamilies may be further divided into tribes. All taxonomic names are Latin in form, though often Greek in origin, except for the individual names of cultivated varieties of plant.

Rules for naming taxonomic groups are specified by the five international organizations: for animals, the International Code of Zoological Nomenclature (ICZN); for wild plants and fungi, the International Code of Botanical Nomenclature (ICBN); for cultivated plants, the International Codes of Nomenclature of Cultivated Plants (ICNP); for bacteria, the International Codes of Nomenclature of Bacteria (ICNB); and for viruses, the International Codes of Nomenclature of Viruses (ICNV).

12.3.2 **Groups above generic level**

Names of groups from kingdom to family are plural and printed in roman with initial capitals (Bacillariophyceae, Carnivora, Curculionidae). The level of the taxon is usually indicated by the ending: the names of botanical or bacteriological families and orders, for example, end in *-aceae* and *-ales*, while zoological families and subfamilies end in *-idae* and *-inae* respectively. (Ligatures are not now used in printing biological nomenclature, though this style has been retained from the first to the second edition of the *OED*.)

12.3.3 **The binomial system**

Living organisms are classified by genus and species according to the system originally devised by Linnaeus. This two-part name—called the binomial or binomen—is printed in italic, and usually consists of the capitalized name of a genus followed by the lower-case specific epithet (for plants) or specific name (for animals). Thus the forget-me-not is *Myosotis alpestris*, with *Myosotis* as its generic name and *alpestris* as its specific epithet; similarly the bottlenose dolphin is *Tursiops* (generic name) *truncatus* (specific name). Other examples are *Primula vulgaris* (primrose), *Persea americana* (avocado), *Equus caballus* (horse), *Erinaceus europaeus* (European hedgehog). Specific epithets and names are often adjectival in form. Zoological specific names are not capitalized even when derived from a person's name: *Clossiana freija nabokovi* (Nabokov's fritillary), *Gazella thomsoni* (Thomson's gazelle), *Myotis daubentoni* (Daubenton's bat). In botany the ending always agrees with the gender of the genus name; in zoology the ending agrees with the gender of the original genus name, which is usually not altered if the species is subsequently transferred to a different genus.

A genus name is printed in italic with an initial capital when used alone to refer to the genus. If, however, it also has become a common term in English for the organism concerned it is printed in roman and lower case (rhododendron, dahlia, tradescantia, stegosaurus); thus '*Rhododendron* is a widespread genus' but 'the rhododendron is a common plant'. Specific epithets are never used in isolation except in the rare cases where they have become popular names (japonica), when they are printed in roman.

Latin binomials or generic names alone may be followed by the surname of the person who first classified the organism. These surnames and their standardized abbreviations are called 'authorities' and are printed in roman with an initial capital: '*Primula vulgaris* Huds.' shows that this name for the primrose was first used by William Hudson; '*Homo sapiens* L.' shows that Linnaeus was the first to use this specific name for human beings. If a species is transferred to a different genus, the authority will be printed in brackets. For example, the greenfinch, *Carduelis chloris* (L.), was described by Linnaeus but placed by him in the genus *Loxia*.

12.3.4 **Abbreviation**

After the first full mention of a species, later references may be shortened by abbreviating the generic name to its initial capital, followed by a full point: *P. vulgaris*, *E. caballus*. However, this is not possible where a single text uses different generic names with identical abbreviations: *E. caballus* and *E. europaeus* must be spelt out entirely if they occur together in the same work. Longer genera may—exceptionally—have expanded abbreviations: for example, *Staphylococcus* and *Streptococcus* become *Staph.* and *Strep.* respectively.

12.3.5 **Subspecies and hybrids**

Names of animal subspecies have a third term added in italic to the binomial, for example *Corvus corone corone* (carrion crow), *C. corone cornix* (hooded crow). Plant categories below the species level may also have a third term added to their names, but only after an abbreviated form of a word indicating their rank, which is printed in roman:

> subspecies (Latin *subspecies*, abbreviation subsp.)
>
> variety (Latin *varietas*, abbreviation var.)
>
> subvariety (Latin *subvarietas*, abbreviation subvar.)
>
> forms (Latin *forma*, abbreviation f.)
>
> subforms (Latin *subforma*, abbreviation subf.)

So '*Salix repens* var. *fusca*' indicates a variety (Latin *varietas*) of the creeping willow, and '*Myrtus communis* subsp. *tarentina*' a subspecies of the common myrtle.

Other abbreviations are occasionally printed in roman after Latin names, such as 'agg.' for an aggregate species, 'sp.' (plural 'spp.') after a genus name for an unidentified species, 'gen. nov.' or 'sp. nov.' indicating a newly described genus or species, and 'auctt.' indicating a name used by many authors but without authority.

The names attached to cultivated varieties of plants follow the binomial, printed in roman within single quotation marks (*Rosa wichuraiana* 'Dorothy Perkins'). The cultivar name may be preceded by the abbreviation 'cv.', in which case the quotation marks are not used (*Rosa wichuraiana* cv. Dorothy Perkins). The names of cultivated varieties may also appear after variety or subspecies names, or after a genus name alone: for example, the ornamental maple *Acer palmatum* var. *heptalobum* 'Rubrum', and the rose *Rosa* 'Queen Elizabeth'. Names of hybrid plants are indicated by a roman multiplication sign ($\times$): *Cytisus* $\times$ *kewensis* is a hybrid species, $\times$ *Odontonia* is a hybrid genus. Horticultural graft hybrids are indicated by a plus sign (+ *Laburnocytisus adamii*).

12.3.6 Bacteria and viruses

Bacterial and viral species are further subdivided into strains. The International Committee on Taxonomy of Viruses (ICTV) has developed a system of classifying and naming viruses. The ranks employed for animal, fungal, and bacterial viruses are *family*, *subfamily*, *genus*, and *species*; as yet there are no formal categories above the level of family. Wherever possible, Latinized names are used for the taxa; hence names of genera end in the suffix *-virus*, subfamilies end in *-virinae*, and families end in *-viridae*. Latinized specific epithets are not used, so binomial nomenclature does not obtain. (The ICTV advocates italicizing all Latinized names, but it is OUP style to italicize only genera and species.) Those genera or higher groups that do not yet have approved Latinized names are referred to by their English vernacular names.

The ranks of genus and species are not used in the taxonomy of plant viruses, which are classified in groups—not families—with the approved group name ending in *-virus*. There is no standardized system for naming individual bacteriophages (i.e. species and isolates). Existing names employ various combinations of Roman or Greek letters, arabic or roman numerals, and super- and subscript characters. Many names are prefixed with a capital P or lower-case *phi* (PM2, ϕ6, ϕX, Pf1). It is important therefore to follow carefully the conventions employed in the original name.

12.3.7 Cytogenetics

Chromosomal and genetic nomenclature is used to describe rearrangements, deletions, or duplications of material within the banding of chromosomal arms. In humans the sex chromosomes are designated X and Y (capital roman); short arms of chromosomes are denoted 'p' and long arms 'q', with banding numbered to establish loci. These are written out without spaces or commas, following the order chromosome number, arm, band, sub-band (14 q32.3). A deletion is designated 'del', a duplication 'dup' (del(1)(q32→q34)); 't' denotes translocations and 'ter' the end of a chromosome. Gain or loss of any chromosome is denoted by a plus (+) or minus (−) respectively. Nomenclature for non-humans is similar, although symbols for chromosome aberrations are italicized (*Df* for deficiency, *Dp* for duplication, *T* for translocation), and symbols for sex chromosomes can be printed in either italic or bold roman type.

12.3.8 Enzymes

Enzyme nomenclature has several forms, depending on context. Most enzyme trivial names are based on the name of the type of reaction they catalyse and the name of the substrate or product they are associated with. Most end in -*ase*, though some do not.

A systematic nomenclature has been devised by the International Union of Biochemistry. In it, each enzyme has a systematic name incorporating its type designation (i.e. group name), the name of its substrate(s), and a unique four-digit numerical designation called the EC (Enzyme Commission) number. For example, the systematic name of glutamate dehydrogenase is L-glutamate:NAD$^+$ oxidoreductase (deaminating), with the designation EC 1.4.1.2.

Because systematic names are so unwieldy, they tend to supplement or clarify trivial names rather than replace them. In most contexts trivial names alone suffice, though the EC number and full systematic name should follow at first occurrence. The reverse holds when an enzyme is named in the title of a work, chapter, or section: here, use the EC number and full systematic name at first occurrence, with the trivial name following and used thereafter.

12.3.9 Genes

For most species the full names of genes are printed in lower-case roman type, irrespective of whether the gene is dominant or recessive. However, in the fruit fly, *Drosophila melanogaster*, the names of dominant mutants are given an initial capital letter, such as Bar, Segregation, or Distorter. The same convention is also applied to certain plants, such as the tomato, which for example has the dominant genes Curl and Lax.

Symbols for genes generally comprise one or more italic letters (or other characters), usually derived from the gene name. In most species, dominant genes have an initial capital letter, while recessive genes are all lower-case. For example, in maize the symbol for the dominant gene 'hairy sheath' is *Hs* (capital italic), while that for the recessive gene 'shrunken endosperm' is *sh* (lower-case italic). In *D. melanogaster* the symbol for the dominant Bar-eye gene is *B*, and that for the recessive eye-colour gene 'carnation' is *car*. However, certain groups of organisms—notably yeasts and humans (*see below*)—follow slightly different rules.

When a gene has only a single locus, the same symbol applies to both gene and locus. When a characteristic is governed by more than one locus, italic arabic numbers are used to distinguish the different loci. For example, the symbols denoting the various loci determining the character 'glossy leaf' (symbol *gl*) in maize take the form *gl3*, *gl8*, *gl10*, etc. (italic, no space). In mice, rats, rabbits, hamsters, and guinea pigs the locus numbers are hyphenated: in mice, glucose phosphate isomerase locus 1 is denoted *Gpi-1* (italic, hyphen).

Conventions vary for distinguishing alleles at the same locus. In *D. melanogaster* and mice such alleles are denoted by italic superscript characters suffixed to the symbol for the particular locus. For example in *D. melanogaster* mutant alleles at the white-eye locus (*w*) are designated w^e (the eosin allele, superscript italic *e*), w^i (the ivory allele), and so forth. Similarly, mutant alleles of the albino gene (*c*) in mice are denoted c^{ch} (chinchilla), c^h (himalayan), and c^p (platinum). Normal alleles are designated by a superscript plus sign; defective mutants may be designated by a superscript minus sign.

Humans

Gene symbols are printed in all-capital italic letters. Loci are designated by italic arabic numbers, and alleles by italic superscript arabic numbers. For example, *PRH* is the symbol for the gene encoding proline-rich protein type H. Loci and alleles can be designated $PRH1^4$, $PRH2^1$, etc. (Exceptions to this convention include the human oncogenes, which vary according to which family they refer to.)

Yeasts and other fungi

Gene symbols for yeasts comprise three italic letters, all capital for dominant and all lower-case for recessive (*MAL*, *gal*); loci are identified by a roman arabic number close up to the gene symbol (*ser1*, *met2*). Alleles at a particular locus are also designated by a roman arabic number, as a hyphenated suffix (*arg2–6*). Complementation groups are designated by a suffixed capital letter (*aro1A*, *aro1B*). Resistance or sensitivity to a drug may be denoted by a superscript roman capital *R* or *S*, attached to the gene symbol and preceding any other characters (CUP^R1, cup^S1). Roman numerals designate linkage groups. In other fungi the three-letter gene notation does not apply, and dominant alleles are designated by an initial capital only.

Bacteria

Genes are designated by italic lower-case three-letter abbreviations derived from the full name of the product of the gene (or operon) or its function. There may be an additional italic letter or letters, usually capital, to distinguish the various member genes of an operon or functionally related group. For example, the genes responsible for the ability of *E. coli* to utilize lactose include *lacZ*, *lacY*, and *lac4*. A cluster of functionally related genes may be written in the form *lacZYA*, the order of the letters specifying the order of the genes on the chromosome. Defective mutants are designated by a superscript minus sign; dominance of such a defective mutant is shown by an additional roman superscript d ($lacI^{-d}$), not by an initial capital, as in eukaryotes. Wild-type alleles are denoted by a superscript plus sign. When a gene has many mutant forms they are simply numbered, all in italic with no spaces (*leuA58*, *leuB79*).

Viruses

Genes are given various designations, all italic, including three-letter abbreviations derived from the full name of the product or function, single capital letters, lower-case letters suffixed by roman numerals, and arabic numbers.

12.3.10 Floral formulae

In botany a graphic representation of a flower's structure may be portrayed through a system of notation. Flower parts are depicted by capital-letter symbols, in the order K (calyx), C (corolla), P (perianth, used instead of K and C when the sepals and petals are indistinguishable), A (androecium), G (gynoecium). Each letter is followed by a figure indicating the number of parts in each whorl: the symbol ∞ is used when there are more than twelve parts, and the number is in parentheses when the parts are fused. If the parts are in distinct groups—or consist of both fused and separate elements—the number is split and linked by a plus sign. If two whorls are united, the respective symbols are linked by a single superscript horizontal brace. A superior ovary is indicated by a line beneath the G number, an inferior ovary by a line above the G number. The formula begins with the symbol $\oplus$ (for actinomorphic flowers) or $\cdot|\cdot$ or $\uparrow$ (for zygomorphic flowers). Thus the primrose (*Primula vulgaris*) is represented as

$$\oplus K(5)\ \overline{C(5)}A5\ G\underline{5}$$

and the tulip (*Tulipa* species) as

$$\oplus P3 + 3\ A3 + 3\ G(\underline{3})$$

12.3.11 Medical terminology

Medical terminology relies on a shorthand system of notation that combines complex modern, pragmatic, and seemingly antiquated forms: HONK (hyperosmolar non-ketotic), NMDA (*N*-methyl-D-aspartate), $t_{1/2}$ (biological half-life), BKA (below-knee amputation), LKKS (liver, right kidney, left kidney, spleen), NAD (nothing abnormal detected), bd (*bis die*), stat (*statim*), qqh (*quarta quaque hora*). Which, and how many, of these abbreviations should be employed in a text depends ultimately on the type of work and its expected readership. In practice, however, a reasonably clear distinction may be drawn between short forms best suited for notes and those acceptable in scholarly writing.

Common symbols used in medical tables and figures may be used in displayed or illustrative material, but not in text:

♂/♀	male to female ratio
−ve	negative
+ve	positive
℞	*recipe* (take)
~	approximately
↓	decreased
↑	increased
↔	normal

Antigens

Blood-group antigens are designated by capital letters, sometimes combined with a lower-case letter or letters, such as A, B, AB, O, Rh. Note that while A, for example, is defined as a blood group, *not* blood type, blood is described as being type A, *not* group A. Genes encoding these antigens are represented by the same letters printed in italic; antibodies corresponding to antigens are designated by the symbol for the antigen prefixed by *anti-* (anti-A).

Haemoglobin

The types of normal human haemoglobin are designated Hb A, Hb A_2, and Hb F (found only in the fetus). Each is composed of two pairs of globin chains with attached haem groups, each chain being designated by a Greek letter (α, β, γ, or δ); subscript numerals indicate the number of chains of the same type occurring in the molecule. Thus the chains of Hb A are designated $\alpha_2\beta_2$ (no space), those of Hb A_2 are $\alpha_2\delta_2$ and those of Hb F are $\alpha_2\gamma_2$. Abnormal haemoglobins are designated either by letters (C–Q, S) or by the name of the place where they were first identified (e.g. Hb Bart's, Hb Chad).

Vitamins

The group of organic compounds that form vitamins may be known by their chemical names or by a system of capital letters; those forming part of a group are identified further by subscript arabic figures. (Dietary minerals are known only by their chemical names.) Use only one form of the name within a single work, treating all vitamins similarly. The most common vitamins are given below:

vitamin A = retinol

vitamin B complex (or B vitamins) any of a group of vitamins which, although not chemically related, are often found together in the same foods, including B^1 = thiamine, B_2 (also vitamin G) = riboflavin, B_5 = pantothenic acid, B_6 = pyridoxine, B^1_2 = cyanocobalamin

vitamin C = ascorbic acid

vitamin D any of a group of vitamins found in liver and fish oils, occurring as D_2 = calciferol, D_3 = cholecalciferol

vitamin E = tocopherol

vitamin H = biotin

vitamin K any of a group of vitamins found mainly in green leaves, including K^1 = phylloquinone, K_2 = menaquinone

vitamin M (especially US) = folic acid (a B-complex vitamin)

Drug nomenclature

In professional or technical contexts, prefer a drug's generic name to its proprietary name, which may differ over time and between countries. Even generic names can vary, however: the humble *paracetamol* is unknown in the USA, where it is *acetaminophen*. To help standardize nomenclature throughout Europe, EC Council Directive 92/27/EEC requires the use of a Recommended International Non-Proprietary Name (rINN) for medicinal-product labelling. For the most part, the original British Approved Name (BAN) and the rINN were the same; where they differed, the rINN is used rather than the BAN: *amoxicillin* not *amoxycillin*, *riboflavin* not *riboflavine*, *secobarbital* not *quinalbarbitone*, *sulfadiazine* not *sulphadiazine*. In some cases—where a name change was considered to pose a high potential risk to public health—the old name follows the new for additional clarity: *alimemazine (trimeprazine)*, *lidocaine (lignocaine)*, *methylthionium chloride (methylene blue)*, *moxisylyte (thymoxamine)*.

Publishers should impose rINN names as a matter of policy, though editors must be aware that it is still useful in certain contexts or markets, and for certain drugs, to add the original names as a gloss. The British National Formulary (BNF) retains former BANs as synonyms in their publications and, in common with the British Pharmacopoeia, continues to give precedence to the original terms *adrenaline* (in rINN *epinephrine*) and *noradrenaline* (in rINN *norepinephrine*)—though this is not the case in the USA or Japan, for example. The BNF website has a complete list of the names concerned.

Early medical texts

Formerly, the formulae in medical books were set in lower-case letters, j being used for i both singly and in the final letter, for example *gr. j* (one grain), ℥*viij* (eight ounces), ʒ*iij* (three drachms), ℈*iij* (three scruples), ℥*iiij* (four minims). This style may also be encountered elsewhere, for example in French.

12.4 **Chemistry**

The International Union of Pure and Applied Chemistry (IUPAC) generates advice on chemical nomenclature, terminology, standardized methods for measurement, and atomic weights. By their recommendations, symbols for the elements are set in roman with an initial capital, no point at the end; spelt-out names of chemical compounds are in lower-case roman; and symbols for the elements in formulae are printed in roman without spaces (H_2SO_4, $Cu(CrO_2)_2$). Other IUPAC recommendations, together with common usage in the discipline, are outlined below.

12.4.1 **Roman and italic**

In certain kinds of name, symbols are printed in italic (*O*-methylhydroxlamine, *fac*-triamine-trinitrosylcobalt(III)). Italic is also used for certain prefixes, of which the commonest are *o-*, *m-*, *p-*, *cis-*, and *trans-* (*o*-tolidine, *p*-diethylbenzene, *cis*-but-2-ene). Retain the italic, but not the hyphen, when the prefix is used as a separate word ('the *cis* isomer', 'position *a* is *ortho* to the methyl group'). The prefixes *d-*, *l-*, and *dl-* are no longer used for labelling stereoisomers, which are expressed either by small capitals or by symbols: D-(+), L-(−), and DL-(±) respectively; for example 'D L-lactic acid', '(+)-tartaric acid'. In each case the hyphens must be retained, although not when expressing their absolute configuration.

12.4.2 **Formulae and structural drawings**

When expressing formulae, the order of brackets in formulae normally follows that in mathematics: $\{[()]\}$. Parentheses are used to define the extent of a chemical group, as in $(C_2H_5)_3N$; square brackets are used to denote e.g. chemical concentration in complex formulae ($[H_2SO_4]$) or a Fraunhofer line ($[D], [H], [K]$). This sequence will vary in certain circumstances, for example in the use of square brackets in denoting coordination compounds, such as $K_3[Fe(CN)_6]$ or $[Ni(CO)_4]$.

In organic chemical nomenclature, it is usual to write a formula as a series of groups ($CH_3COC_2H_5$, RCH_2COOCH_3). If, for purposes of explanation, it is necessary to divide off the groups, the centred dots representing single bonds should be set as medial, not on the line ($CH_3 \cdot CO \cdot C_2H_5$, $R \cdot CH_2 \cdot COOCH_3$). In most other contexts they can be dispensed with altogether, although dots in formulae of addition compounds cannot be dispensed with ($Na_2CO_3 \cdot 10H_2O$).

Indicate a double bond by an equals sign ($CH_3CH=CH_2$), not a colon ($CH_3CH:CH_2$), and a triple bond by a three-bar equals sign ($CH_3C\equiv CH$), not a three-dot colon ($CH_3C:CH$). In chemical equations 'equals' is shown by a 2-em arrow ($\longrightarrow$) rather than a conventional equals sign.

Authors should expect that any formulae or structural drawings will need to be treated as artwork; for details *see* **CHAPTER 10**; *see also* **CHAPTER 2**.

12.4.3 **Superscripts and subscripts**

Super- and subscripts do not occur only singly, or only after what they modify. In specifying a particular nuclide, the atomic (proton) number is printed as a left subscript ($_{12}Mg$). Similarly, the mass (nucleon) number of an element is shown with its symbol and printed as a left superscript (^{235}U, ^{14}C)—not to the right, as formerly. If it is given with the name of the element no hyphen is necessary (uranium 235, carbon 14). Individual transfer RNAs may combine superscript and subscript abbreviations ($tRNA^{Glu}_1$, $tRNA^{Met}_i$).

In inorganic chemical nomenclature the relationship between the super- and subscripts surrounding a chemical symbol is important: superscript expresses the electrical charge and subscript the number of atoms for each molecule. These should be staggered so as to indicate the ions present ($Na^+_2CO_3{}^{2-}$ (sodium carbonate) but $Hg_2{}^{2+}Cl_2{}^-$ (dimercury(I) chloride)). A medial dot is used to indicate coordinated species ($CuSO_4 \cdot 5H_2O$). Ionic charge is shown by a right superscript ($SO_4{}^{2-}$). Indicate complex ions by square brackets ($K^+_3[FeCl_6]^{3-}$).

In names such as 'iron(II) chloride' and 'iron(2^+) chloride' there should be no space before the first parenthesis.

Indicate oxidation states by a small-capital roman numeral, set in parentheses close up to the spelt-out name, e.g. 'manganese(IV)'; or by a superscript roman numeral set in capitals to the right of the abbreviated name, e.g. 'Mn^{IV}'.

Atomic orbitals, designated s, p, d, f, g, are roman, and can have subscript letters with superscript numbers attached (d_{z^2}, $d_{x^2}-d_{y^2}$).

Formerly a hyphen was inserted to indicate that a spelling with *ae* or *oe* was not to be construed as a digraph (*chloro-ethane*). This is no longer the case: all such combinations are run together as one word (*chloroethane*), which is as well because ample hyphenation may exist elsewhere (*1,1-dibromo-2-chloroethane*).

12.4.4 Chemical elements and symbols

Each of the chemical elements has a unique abbreviation derived from its Latin name (copper = *cuprum*, mercury = *hydrargyrum*), which has a single capital and no full point at the end. This abbreviation is used in formulae and tabular matter, and in running text in works for a technical readership.

actinium	Ac	francium	Fr
aluminium	Al	gadolinium	Gd
americium	Am	gallium	Ga
antimony	Sb	germanium	Ge
argon	Ar	gold	Au
arsenic	As	hafnium	Hf
astatine	At	helium	He
barium	Ba	holmium	Ho
berkelium	Bk	hydrogen	H
beryllium	Be	indium	In
bismuth	Bi	iodine	I
boron	B	iridium	Ir
bromine	Br	iron	Fe
cadmium	Cd	krypton	Kr
caesium	Cs	lanthanum	La
calcium	Ca	lawrencium	Lr
californium	Cf	lead	Pb
carbon	C	lithium	Li
cerium	Ce	lutetium	Lu
chlorine	Cl	magnesium	Mg
chromium	Cr	manganese	Mn
cobalt	Co	mendelevium	Md
copper	Cu	mercury	Hg
curium	Cm	molybdenum	Mo
dysprosium	Dy	neodymium	Nd
einsteinium	Es	neon	Ne
erbium	Er	neptunium	Np
europium	Eu	nickel	Ni
fermium	Fm	niobium	Nb
fluorine	F	nitrogen	N

nobelium	No	sodium	Na
osmium	Os	strontium	Sr
oxygen	O	sulfur	S
palladium	Pd	tantalum	Ta
phosphorus	P	technetium	Tc
platinum	Pt	tellurium	Te
plutonium	Pu	terbium	Tb
polonium	Po	thallium	Ti
potassium	K	thorium	Th
praseodymium	Pr	thulium	Tm
promethium	Pm	tin	Sn
protactinium	Pa	titanium	Ti
radium	Ra	tungsten	W
radon	Rn	unnilhexium	Unh
rhenium	Re	unnilpentium	Unp
rhodium	Rh	unnilquandium	Unq
rubidium	Rh	uranium	U
ruthenium	Ru	vanadium	V
samarium	Sm	xenon	Xe
scandium	Sc	ytterbium	Yb
selenium	Se	yttrium	Y
silicon	Si	zinc	Zn
silver	Ag	zirconium	Zr

12.5 **Computing**

The pace at which the computing world evolves can make it difficult to prescribe specific rules governing the presentation of texts on the subject. Nevertheless a few very general characteristics may be observed.

12.5.1 **Terminology**

The influence of the USA on the computing field has resulted in US spelling being adopted for much of the standard vocabulary, such as *analog*, *disk*, *oriented*, and *program* rather than *analogue*, *disc*, *orientated*, *programme* (but note *compact disc*, *laser disc*). Other spellings not forming part of computing terminology should be normalized to British spelling for books intended wholly or mostly for the UK market.

The names of both procedural and functional programming languages vary in treatment. They may be styled in even full capitals (COBOL, FORTRAN, LISP) or—particularly where ubiquitous—even small capitals (COBOL, FORTRAN, LISP), although this style is considered old-fashioned by many. Alternatively they may be styled with an initial capital and lower case (Miranda, Pascal, Prolog). Logically, capitals are used for acronyms and upper- and lower-case for the rest, though this is not universally observed, often through an attempt to impose consistency on all language names. While it is perfectly acceptable to style different language names differently, ensure that the same style is adopted for the same language throughout a work.

12.5.2 Representation

The text of a computer program may be presented in a work in several ways: in whole or in part, displayed or run into text. Not being a prose extract in the traditional sense, any such program is treated rather like an equation, with no minimum size and no small type needed for display.

Where the features of the program require character-literal syntax and precise line breaks, display, indentation, spacing, or special sorts, these must be reproduced exactly. It is wise to insert any lengthy code directly from the source rather than retype it, which can introduce error. For clarity it is often useful to set any selected material in a distinctive typeface—a sans serif font, or a monospace typewriter font like Courier. (It is common to use a font that approximates the form found on the relevant terminal or printout.)

```
<body bgcolor="#000033" text="#000033"
    link="#FF0000" vlink="#66CC33" alink="#FFFF00"
        onLoad="MM_displayStatusMsg ('welcome');
        return
    document.MM_returnValue">
```

Where text is complicated or frequent it may be as well for authors to provide it as print-ready copy—e.g. an ASCII printout—to be inserted into text.

If the font chosen to indicate programming-language text is suffi-ciently different from the font used for normal text, it is unnecessary to delimit it further by quotation marks, even when run into text. If, however, quotation marks are needed, note that computing practice matches standard British usage in the relative placement of punctuation and quotation marks. The punctuation falls outside the closing quota-tion mark, so that in citing parts of

```
begin real S; S := 0;
    for i := 1 step 1 until n do
        S := S + V[i];
    x := s
end
```

in text, the punctuation does not interfere with the syntax: 'begin real S;', 'S := 0;', and 'x := s'. This style, which would be imposed naturally in British publishing, should also be imposed in US computing texts, though not extended to normal quotations. (*See also* **5.13.2**.) US computing books can also reserve British-style single quotation marks for programming-language text, using double quotes for normal quotations.

In-text or displayed formulae and equations are best described and set so far as possible according to the rules governing mathematics. Any visual representations of structures or hierarchical classifications (flow charts, data-flow diagrams, screen shots, tree grammars, Venn diagrams) will be treated as artwork. (*See* **CHAPTER 10**.)

12.5.3 Computing symbols

Mathematical references in computing contexts are usually treated in the same way as in other texts using such references, although the sense of, for example, some logic symbols may differ from standard practice. In programming, the different types of bracket have various specific uses and order, depending on the language. In computing, the solidus (/)—usually called *slash* or *stroke*—is used as a separator, as with directory names. When a *backslash* (\) separator is used, the solidus can be called a *forward slash* to differentiate it further.

Other symbols have various context-specific functions: the asterisk, for example, is a Kleene star in BNF, a multiplication sign in FORTRAN, and a substitute for ∩ in Pascal.

In some computing languages, a combined colon and equals sign (:=) is used as the assignment symbol ('gets' or 'becomes'), in others (::=) means 'is defined as' and (:-) means 'if'. Each of these symbols constitutes a single unit and must be set close up, with space either side:

{A[x] := y, B[u,v] := w}.

⟨decimal fraction⟩ ::= ⟨unsigned integer⟩

Other symbols with unique meanings include the following:

@	'at' sign, display point
=..	a Prolog predicate
↑	up or return
!	cut, comment, 'bang'
==	equality
\=	not equal
°	composition
*	asterisk, superscript star, Kleene star
**	exponention

--	comment
<>	less–greater
<=	subset
=>	superset
+	plus, union
$^+$	superscript plus, Kleene cross

12.6 **Mathematics**

12.6.1 **Notation**

The established style is to use roman type (formerly italic) for all constants and operators, italic for letters expressing a variable, and bold for vectors and matrices. When letters are required for formulae, use capitals and lower case—not small capitals. Each description should be represented by a symbol: do not use abbreviated words. Speed, accuracy, and economy will be achieved if authors can follow, or mark, their notation in this way. Here are some specific guidelines:

- It is common to set the headword of definitions, theorems, propositions, corollaries, or lemmas in capitals and small capitals, with the remaining text in italic. The full text of the proof itself is usually in roman.

- Avoid starting a sentence with a letter denoting an expression, so that there is no ambiguity about whether a capital or lower-case letter is intended.

- Most standard abbreviations, e.g. 'log(arithm)', 'max(imum)', 'exp(onential function)', 'tan(gent)', 'cos(ine)', 'lim(it)', and 'cov(ariance)', are set in roman, with no full points.

- Make clear the distinction between a roman 'd' used in a differential equation, the symbol ∂ for a partial differential, and the Greek lower-case delta (δ). Authors should preclude further potential for confusion by avoiding an italic d for a variable.

- Italic symbols remain italic even when they occur in an italic heading; they do not change to opposite font. In contrast, the exponential 'e' always remains in roman; it is usually preferable to use the abbreviation 'exp' to avoid confusion. The letters i and j are roman when symbolizing pure or imaginary numbers, and italic when symbolizing variables.

- In displayed equations, the integral, product, and summation symbols ($\int \Sigma \Pi$) may have limits set directly above them (upper limit) or below them (lower limit). In running text, place these after the symbol wherever possible (as in the first example) to avoid too great a vertical extension of the symbol:

$$\int_a^b x^2\, dx \quad \sum_{m=0}^{\infty} \quad \prod_{r \geq 1}$$

■ Missing terms can be represented by three dots which are horizontal ($\cdots$), vertical ($\vdots$), or diagonal ($\ddots$), as appropriate. Include a comma after the three ellipsis dots when the final term follows, for example $x_1, x_2, \ldots, x_n$.

12.6.2 Symbols

Operational signs are of two types: those representing a verb ($= \approx \neq \geq$) and those representing a conjunction ($+ - \supset \times$). All operational signs take a normal interword space of the line on either side; they are not printed close up to the letters or numerals on either side of them. Set a multiplication point as a medial point ($\cdot$); it should be used only to avoid ambiguity and is not needed between letters, unless they are vectors. A product of two or more different units may be represented as N m or N·m but not Nm.

Any symbol that involves printing a separate line of type should be avoided when an alternative form is available. So, for angle ABC, prefer $\angle ABC$ to

$\overset{\frown}{ABC}$,

and for vector r, prefer **r** (in bold) to $\overset{\rightharpoonup}{r}$.

A colon used as a ratio sign—as in for example 'mixed in the proportion $1:2$', '$2:4 :: 3:6$'—has a thin space on either side of it, not a normal space of the line.

No more than one solidus should appear in the same expression; use parentheses to avoid ambiguity: $J\,K^{-1}\,mol^{-1}$ or $J/(K\,mol)$, but not: J/K/mol.

Omit the vinculum or overbar—the horizontal rule above the square-root sign: $\sqrt{}2$ is sufficient for $\sqrt{2}$. (Where necessary for clarification the extent covered by the rule may be replaced by parentheses.)

Similarly,

$$\sqrt{\left(\frac{x^2}{a^2} + \frac{y^2}{b^2}\right)}$$

is sufficient for

$$\sqrt{\left(\frac{x^2}{a^2} + \frac{y^2}{b^2}\right)}$$

Although many mathematical software packages enable authors to add the rule, it is still considered superfluous, and it is better printing practice to omit it—especially in running text, where it may encumber the line spacing.

12.6.3 Superscripts and subscripts

Reserve superscript letters for variable quantities (set in italic); reserve subscript letters for descriptive notation (set in roman). Asterisks and primes are not strictly superscripts and so should always follow immediately after the term to which they are attached, in the normal way.

When first a subscript and then a superscript are attached to the same symbol or number, mark the subscript to be set immediately below the superscript in a 'stack'. As it is possible for superscript + and − to appear before a numeral, editors should ensure that they are correctly marked. If it is necessary to have multiple levels of super- or subscripts, the relationships must be made clear for the typesetter.

Wherever possible, it is customary—and a kindness to the reader's eyesight—to represent each super- or subscript description by a symbol rather than an abbreviated word. Those subscript descriptions that are standardly made up of one or more initial letters of the word they represent are set in roman type.

12.6.4 Brackets

The preferred order for brackets is $\{[()]\}$. When a single pair of brackets have a specific meaning, such as $[n]$ to denote the integral part of n, they can, of course, be used out of sequence. The vertical bars used to signify a modulus ($|x|$) should not be used as brackets.

Three further sorts of brackets may be used: double brackets ($[\![\,]\!]$) and narrow ($\langle\,\rangle$) and wide ($<\,>$) angle brackets. (Wide angle brackets have a specific meaning in Dirac bra or ket vector notation, and narrow brackets can indicate value of a quantity over a period of time, but either can be used generally.) Double brackets can be placed outside, and narrow angle brackets inside, the bracket sequence, and are handy for avoiding the rearrangement of brackets throughout a formula or, especially, a series of formulae. Thus for comparison's sake the formula

$$\{1 + [2(a^2 + b^2)(x^2 + y^2) - (ab + xy)^2]\}^2 =$$
$$[\![1 + \{[(a + b)^2 + (a - b)^2](x^2 + y^2) - (ab + xy)^2\}]\!]^2$$

is perhaps better put

$$= \{1 + [(\langle a + b\rangle^2 + \langle a - b\rangle^2)(x^2 + y^2) - (ab + xy)^2]\}^2$$

12.6.5 **Fractions, formulae, and equations**

Displayed formulae three or four lines deep can be reduced to a neater and more manageable two-line form in almost all instances. This form saves time and improves the appearance of the page, making it easier for the typesetter and the reader.

For example,

$\frac{a}{b}$ can be written as a/b, and $\left|\frac{x-1}{3}\right|$ as $|(x-1)/3|$.

Simple fractions such as $\frac{\pi}{2}$, $\frac{x}{3}$, $\frac{a+b}{4}$ can be written as $\frac{1}{2}\pi$, $\frac{1}{3}x$, $\frac{1}{4}(a+b)$.

$$\frac{1-\tan^2\frac{A}{2}}{1+\tan^2\frac{A}{2}} \quad \text{could be written as} \quad \frac{1-\tan^2\frac{1}{2}A}{1+\tan^2\frac{1}{2}A}$$

$$\frac{\sin\frac{(N+1)}{2}\theta\,\sin\frac{N}{2}\theta}{\sin\frac{\theta}{2}} \quad \text{could be written as} \quad \frac{\sin\frac{1}{2}(N+1)\theta\,\sin N\theta}{\sin\frac{1}{2}\theta}$$

Work can be reduced and appearance improved by writing such a formula as

$$\lim_{n\to\infty}\left[1-\sin^2\frac{\alpha}{n}\right]^{\frac{-1}{\sin^2\frac{\alpha}{n}}} \quad \text{in the form} \quad \lim_{n\to\infty}[1-\sin^2(\alpha/n)]^{-1/\sin^2(\alpha/n)}$$

Displayed formulae are usually centred on the page. If there are many long ones, or a wide discrepancy in their length, it may be better to range them all left with a 1- or 2–em indent.

If it is necessary to break a formula—whether displayed or run-in—at the end of a line, it should be done at an operational sign, with the sign carried over to the next line. If an equation takes up two or more lines it should be displayed, with turnover lines aligned on the operational sign (preferably =):

$$\mu_0 = 4\pi \times 10^{-1}\ \text{H m}^{-1}$$
$$= 12.566\ 370\ 614\ 4 \times 10^{-7}\ \text{H m}^{-1} \tag{2.1}$$

Any equation referred to at another point in the text should be numbered; any numbered equation should be displayed. It is usually better to include the chapter number in front of the sequence number, such as 2.1 for the first equation in chapter 2. If, however, the total number of equations is very small, it is possible to use a single sequence of numbers throughout the text. As illustrated above, these numbers are enclosed in parentheses and set full right, aligned on the same line as the final line of the equation.

12.6.6 **Mathematical symbols**

π	pi
e, e, or ε	base of natural logarithms

i, j	imaginary unit: $i^2 = -1$
∞	infinity
=	equal to
≠	not equal to
≡	identically equal to
≢	not identically equal to
≈	approximately equal to
≉	not approximately equal to
≃	asymptotically equal to
≄	not asymptotically equal to
≅	isomorphic to, equal or nearly equal to
≇	not isomorphic to, not equal or nearly equal to
∼	equivalent to, of the order of
≁	not equivalent to, not of the order of
∝	proportional to
→	approaches
⇒	implies
⇐	is implied by
⇔	double implication
>	greater than
≯	not greater than
<	less than
≮	not less than
≫	much greater than
≪	much less than
≥	greater than or equal to
≱	not greater than or equal to
≤	less than or equal to
≰	not less than or equal to
>	has a higher rank or order
≯	has not a higher rank or order
<	has a lower rank or order
≮	has not a lower rank or order
≥	has a rank or order higher or equal to
≱	has not a rank or order higher or equal to
≤	has a rank or order lower or equal to
≰	has not a rank or order lower or equal to
( )	parentheses
[ ]	square brackets
{ }	curly brackets, braces
⟨ ⟩	angle brackets
⟦ ⟧	double brackets
∨	sum of two sets
∧	vector product
⊂	strict inclusion

⊄	not contained in
⊆	inclusion
⊈	is not contained in
⊃, ⊇	contains
⊅, ⊉	does not contain
∪, ⌣	union
∩, ⌢	intersection
\	difference
∅	the empty set
+	plus
⊕	direct sum
−	minus
±	plus or minus
∓	minus or plus
‖	parallel to
⊥	perpendicular to
⇔	equivalent to
⇎	not equivalent to
a, $a \cdot b$, $a \times b$	a multiplied by b
⊗	direct multiplication
a/b, $a \div b$, ab^{-1}	a divided by b
a^n	a raised to the power of n
$|a|$	the modulus (or magnitude) of a
$\sqrt{a}$, $a^{1/2}$	square root of a
$\bar{a}$, $\langle a \rangle$	mean value of a
$p!$	factorial p
′	minute, prime
″	second, double prime
‴	triple prime
°	degree
∠	angle
∟	right angle
∡	acute angle
△	triangle
:	ratio
::	proportion
∴	therefore, hence
∵	because
exp x, e^x	exponential of x
$\log_a x$	logarithm to base a of x
ln x, $\log_e x$	natural logarithm of x
lg x, $\log_{10} x$	common logarithm of x
lb x, $\log_2 x$	binary logarithm of x
sin x	sine of x
cos x	cosine of x

$\tan x$, $\operatorname{tg} x$	tangent of x
$\cot x$, $\operatorname{ctg} x$	cotangent of x
$\sec x$	secant of x
$\operatorname{cosec} x$, $\csc x$	cosecant of x
$\sin^{-1} x$, $\arcsin x$	inverse sine of x
$\cos^{-1} x$, $\arccos x$	inverse cosine of x
$\tan^{-1} x$, $\arctan x$	inverse tangent of x
$\int$	integral
$\oint$	contour integral
Σ	summation
Δ	delta
∇	nabla, del
Π	product
Δx	finite increase of x
δx	variation of x
dx	total variation of x
δf	variation of f
df	total variation of f
$f(x)$	function of x
$f \circ g$	composite function of f and g
$f * g$	convolution of f and g
$\lim_{x \to a} f(x)$	limit of $f(x)$
$\wp$	Weierstrass elliptic function
$\Box$	D'Alembertian operator
h	Planck constant
$\hbar$	Dirac constant

For a list of the symbols commonly used in logic *see* **13.4**.

CHAPTER 13

Specialist subjects

13.1 Collections of correspondence

This section provides a brief guide for editors of collected correspondence, explaining the circumstances in which certain features should be considered. Ultimately the choice is dependent upon the physical state of the collection, the series style (if any), and the editor's chosen approach to the subject.

13.1.1 Introduction

An introduction may contain a brief biography to give the background and setting of the correspondence. It should indicate—but briefly and without venturing into the sort of criticism that will quickly date—the literary and historical value of the correspondence. It should contain a brief statement on the sources, published and unpublished, and on how the editor has handled them; it should not waste space by dwelling on the shortcomings of previous editions. If relevant, it may contain a section on transmission, postmarks, etc.; however, particular problems can be dealt with in appendices (*see* **13.1.10**).

13.1.2 Contents

Where more than one volume is to be published simultaneously or at short intervals, the first volume should have a list of contents and a list of illustrations (if any) for the whole edition. Each subsequent volume should then contain a list of contents and illustrations for that volume only. In a large edition, a chronological list of letters in the preliminary matter between the introduction and contents will help historians and readers to discover quickly whether the edition is worth searching for their requirements.

13.1.3 Chronology

The reader may find a chronology or biographical table useful; it can cover either the whole of the writer's life or (in the case of multiple volumes) that portion of the writer's life represented in the volume.

13.1.4 **Numbering**

The serial numbering of letters aids cross-reference and citation, and avoids possible confusion of reference where there is more than one letter for the same date.

13.1.5 **Running heads**

Where letters run over several openings, use headlines to indicate the recipient and, in mixed correspondence, the sender. The date and number of the letter can also be shown if space permits, though these must be inserted at proof stage and are liable to error if repagination is required.

13.1.6 **The correspondence and text**

Addresses

Give the writer's address, usually at the right-hand side of the letter. If the original address is engraved or embossed, this may be relevant to dating and can be shown by setting it in italic. Give the address of the recipient, where available, at the foot, on the left-hand side, as in modern official communications. Enclose it in square brackets if it is not part of the original manuscript. Where the same address occurs regularly, it may be printed in full at its first occurrence and abbreviated thereafter, only variations being given in full. In such cases provide a note of explanation in the introduction. Not every line of very long addresses need be displayed; some or all can be run together, with a vertical rule used to indicate the divisions of the original.

Dating of letters

Where applicable, give dates in the same place as in the heading of the original. Give editorial dating, whether supplied or in correction, in square brackets, with a note if necessary to indicate the authenticity.

Postmarks

In letters of English provenance all postmarks before 1840 should be printed. After 1840 it can be assumed that all letters go by post, but exceptions, where known, should be stated. Otherwise, after 1840 the postmark need be printed only when it notably diverges from the date of writing. Give information about postmarks concisely, preferably at the foot of the text.

Signatures and subscriptions

Do not display signatures and subscriptions, but run them on, with a vertical line to indicate divisions, if these are worth showing.

Postscripts

Show these as postscripts, wherever they occur in the original. Note anything significant about their position in the original.

Publication

It is sometimes useful to offer a concise indication of whether a letter has been previously published, and where.

Superscript and contractions

Lower to line height superscript letters or words in the text. Silently expand contractions (including the ampersand but excepting those like *Mr* or *Dr*), without the use of square brackets. Exceptions may be made where the writer does not habitually use contractions and the departure from his or her usual practice may be significant, for example as indicating exceptional informality towards a particular correspondent. Omit cancelled words, though where unusually interesting they may be given in a note.

Spelling

Follow the original spelling. Correct occasional misspellings in the text and give the original form in footnotes; where the writer is wildly idiosyncratic, retain the original spelling where it is of interest. Avoid gratuitous editorial interventions such as '[*sic*]'.

Capitalization

Follow the original, but alway capitalize proper nouns and words beginning a new sentence, unless the variation is of special interest.

Punctuation

Follow the original normally, especially if (as in Dickens) the punctuation is deliberately idiosyncratic. Silently correct obvious errors, such as omission of a full point, or unclosed parentheses or quotation marks. Where a writer normally uses only dashes, a lightly modernized punctuation may be substituted: if the excessive use of dashes is occasional only, it may indicate informality or unusual haste and the dashes can be retained. Where a writer dispenses almost entirely with punctuation this should be lightly supplied. Supply or amend paragraphing if the original text is very long and unbroken; where this is done, indicate in the appendices what you have done or give a note in the introduction, with examples.

13.1.7 **Related letters**

It will sometimes be economical of annotation to supply the text of a letter or document related to the correspondence. Where short, it is best to give it in smaller type (usually one size down) in the body of the text, directly after the letter to which it relates, or in a note. Where the document is very long but not susceptible of summary, it is best to give it in a long note at the end of the whole text or in an appendix.

13.1.8 Textual notes (apparatus criticus)

Textual notes should record all substantive alterations to the text and should be at the foot of the page. Where they are numerous the text can be marginally lineated by tens and references can be made by line number. If they are few they need only be by lemma. (*See also* **13.10**.) List any unusual symbols employed as part of a list of abbreviations and symbols.

13.1.9 General notes

The purpose of annotation is to elucidate the text: concision and relevance are essential. Unless very extensive annotation is required, place these notes at the foot of the page, below the textual notes, and—if necessary—separated from them by a rule. Alternatively, the notes may be set in double columns to distinguish them further from the text of the letters.

If an occasional long note is unavoidable, place it at the end of the text as an appendix or an extended note, with a reference on the relevant page of the text. Too many notes can dominate a page, at the expense of a readable text. Where necessary, place extensive annotation as endnotes at the end of the book.

Notes can be numbered by the page, by the letter (except where letters are unusually short), by a renewing series of 1–9, or by reference-mark symbols (* † ‡ § ¶ ||).

Persons

If possible, identify all people mentioned in the correspondence. Those listed in a biographical dictionary such as the *Dictionary of National Biography*, or other easily accessible work of reference, normally need only identification and dates with citation of the appropriate work of reference; if they are not listed, a fuller identification will be necessary for the reader. A brief indication of their particular relation to the writer of the letter is sometimes appropriate.

Places

Identify places mentioned in letters only where they are likely to give difficulty to the reader, for example by being obscure or having changed name. The letter-writer's principal residence may need further treatment; with older writers, contemporary evidence may have to be examined.

Historical evidence

Check references in letters to historical events for date and general reliability; a note should state the name by which the event is customarily known. Specify the writer's source if available and of interest. There need be no comment on the events themselves unless the context demands it.

Language

Give glosses or explanation of words in a foreign language only if they are unavailable in accessible reference books and necessary for elucidation. Translate Greek and Latin quotations in the footnotes, if necessary; translate modern-language quotations if the expected readership is likely to require it. Use a reliable standard translation, if one is available.

Books mentioned

Identify books mentioned in letters so that they may be readily found. Give authors' names with—especially for common surnames—first names in full. After first mention, paraphrase or abbreviate titles, which thereafter need be given at length only if this helps an understanding of the text.

General comment

A general comment should be succinct and strictly related to what is necessary for the understanding of the text. Its subject will probably suggest the most suitable position for it in the text.

13.1.10 Appendices

Limit the number of appendices as far as possible; they should normally be reserved for special topics relevant to the correspondence but too extensive to be dealt with in separate short notes.

13.1.11 Indexes

A single index is usually most convenient for the reader. However, where a collection demands a great deal of biographical and topographical information, it may be preferable to have a biographical or topographical appendix, or separate indexes of people and places.

13.1.12 **Illustrations**

If the author's hand is particularly difficult or varies over his or her lifetime, there may be a case for including one or more facsimiles of autograph letters. These are expensive, however, and in practice those especially interested are likely to prefer to obtain a photocopy of substantial sections of the correspondence for themselves.

Generally, illustration should be limited to those images that offer information which cannot be presented in any other way, and which is worth having in itself. It is usually sufficient to provide good portraits of the writer and principal figures in the correspondence.

13.2 **Law and legal references**

Often the standards adopted in the legal discipline are at variance with those of other subjects—especially as regards basic forms of citing, abbreviating, and italicizing matter. This is compounded by the fact that practices common in one aspect of the law may be unfamiliar in another; for example, an author of a work on common law might be used to, and therefore expect, different presentation of copy from an author of a work on international law or human rights. Nevertheless there should be no reason in principle why the following general guidelines cannot be applied across a broad range of legal studies.

Given the variety of legal citations in use in the UK, the European Community (Union), and elsewhere, this section cannot purport to be wholly definitive, nor resolve every stylistic point that may occur. Options are given for those aspects of citation on which there is no widespread consensus.

13.2.1 **General considerations**

Italics

Law uses more foreign—particularly Latin—words than are common in books on many other subjects. For that reason law publishers may deviate from the usage in general reference works when determining which words and phrases to italicize and which not. Only a handful of foreign-language law terms have become so common in English that they are set as roman in general use. Some publishers use this as a basis for determining styles, so that 'a priori' and 'prima facie' are set in roman, for example, but *inter alia* and *stare decisis* are set in italic. Other publishers develop independent style guides, reflecting their authors' usage or readers' expectations, and impose them uniformly over an entire list or only individual volumes. Still others prefer to set all Latin words and phrases in italic, rather than appear inconsistent to readers immersed in the subject, for whom all the terms are familiar: in a legal context it makes little sense to set 'a priori' in roman and 'a posteriori' in italic simply because the former enjoys more widespread public use than the latter. Regardless of which policy is followed, words to be printed in roman rather than italic include the accepted abbreviations of *ratio decidendi* and *obiter dicta*: 'ratio', 'obiter', 'dictum', and 'dicta'.

Traditionally, the names of the parties in case names are cited in italics, separated by a roman 'v.' (for 'versus') or—especially when displayed—in small capitals with an italic 'v.' (*Smith* v. *Jones*, SMITH v. JONES). Where the italic citation has been used, this is usually reversed for clarity in, say, a table of cases or running heads: to avoid presenting an enormous list of italic cases, the parties' names are given in roman with an italic 'v.' (Smith *v.* Jones). Other styles exist: the 'v.' may match the case-name font, or it may have no full point (*Smith v. Jones*, *Smith v Jones*); any style is acceptable if consistently applied.

Certain textbook references have been accorded such eminence that the name of the original author appears in italics, almost as part of the title: *Chitty on Contracts*, *Kemp on Damages*, *Williams on Wills*, *Dicey and Morris on Conflict of Laws*. After one or two examples when they are frequently referred to in a book, they may be further abbreviated to *Dicey and Morris*, *Chitty*, etc. In full references it is not necessary to give the name of the current editor, although the edition number and the date of that edition must be stated.

Other aspects of italics are mentioned under their individual headings below.

Abbreviations

The use of full points in references is subject to four different schools of thought: (*a*) all points should be put in; (*b*) points should be in abbreviations of fewer than three letters; (*c*) there should be no points at all, or no points only in legal abbreviations; and (*d*) points should not appear between or after capitals, for instance words abbreviated to a single letter, but should appear after longer abbreviations ('Ont. LJ', 'Ch. D' but 'QBD', 'AC'). If the last system is used, it is equally correct to leave the points out of note references to a particular level of court, which should appear in parentheses after the reference, for example '(HL)', '(CA)', '(QBD)', '(ChD)'. As in other subjects, it is permissible to abbreviate familiar references in the text as well as in notes.

In text it is permissible to abbreviate references, especially familiar ones, in the body of the text, but all other matter should be set out in full. Thus, *paragraph, section, chapter,* and the like should only ever be abbreviated in the notes. However, where a term is repeated frequently in a textbook and is unwieldy when spelled out, such as *International Covenant on Civil and Political Rights,* then it is permissible to refer to it at first mention in full with '(ICCPR)' following it, and thereafter simply as *ICCPR.* But be careful that the abbreviations chosen do not confuse institutions with Conventions: for instance it is advisable in notes to use *ECHR* for *European Convention on Human Rights* and *ECtHR* for *European Court of Human Rights.* Both the European Court of Justice and the European Court of Human Rights are frequently and indiscriminately referred to in short as 'the European Court', despite having very different jurisdictions and powers. Therefore it is a good idea for the European Court of Human Rights *always* to be referred to in full, unless the text in question is specifically about human rights and there is no possibility of confusion.

In cases, use *Re* rather than *In re, In the matter of,* etc. Similarly, cases such as *In the matter of the Companies Act 1985* are better expressed as *Re the Companies Act 1985,* while *In re the Estate of Farquar* would be better stated as *Re Farquar's Estate.* Abbreviate *Ex parte* to *Ex p.* with the letter *e* capitalized where it appears at the beginning of a case name but in lower case elsewhere: *R* v. *Acton Magistrates, ex p. McMullen* [1990] 2 All ER 670. When citing a law report, do not include expressions such as *and another* or *and others* that may appear in the title, but use *and anor.* or *and ors.* in cases such as *Re P and ors. (minors)* to avoid the appearance of error. To avoid unnecessary repetition in the discussion of a case, shorten citations in the text following an initial use of the full name. Thus, 'in *Glebe Motors plc* v. *Dixon-Greene*' could subsequently be shortened to 'in the *Glebe Motors* case' (but not 'in *Glebe Motors*'). However, in criminal cases it is acceptable to abbreviate 'in *R* v. *Caldwell*' to 'in *Caldwell*'.

In shipping cases, the name of the ship may be used instead of the full case name (for example, *The Eurymedon*), but in such circumstances provide the full case name in a note (and provide both versions in the table of cases).

Law notes tend to be fairly lengthy, so anything that can be abbreviated should be. Thus, *HL, CA,* etc. are perfectly permissible, as are *s., Art., Reg., Dir.,* %, all figures, *High Ct., Sup. Ct., PC, Fam. Div,* etc. even in narrative notes.

When setting material at length, such as extracts from treaties, contracts, or statutes, indicate any lacuna of a paragraph or more by an ellipsis, with a 1-em space between each of the three dots. This is set full left on a separate line, with a 3-point space above and below. Whether numbered or not, new paragraphs are indented 1 em as usual (unless the author is following a specific form in imitation of the original's typography).

Other aspects of abbreviation are mentioned under their individual headings below.

Capitalization

Capitalize *Act*, even in a non-specific reference, although 'bill' may be lower-case. In text it is better to write *section, subsection, article*, etc. out in full. Unless beginning a sentence, *section* always begins with a lower-case letter. Whether *article* does is largely a matter of taste and house style: many publishers prefer to capitalize it when it refers to, say, supra-national legislation (conventions, treaties, etc.) but leave it lower-case when it refers to, say, a foreign statute or part of a British statutory instrument. (A reference to two subsections of one section cannot be referred to as *sections* or *ss.*: the correct form is *section 14(1) and (2) states . . .* but *subsections (1) and (2) of section 14 state . . . .*)

Court with a capital should be used only for international courts such as the European Court of Justice, European Court of Human Rights, the International Court of Justice, or for relating information specific to a single court. Thus, for instance, in a book about the Court of Appeal, Criminal Division, that court may be referred to as *the Court* throughout. It is a common shorthand convention in US law to refer to the Supreme Court as *the Court*, and to a lesser court as *the court*.

A capital may also be used in transcripts where a court is talking about itself, but not necessarily where it refers to itself in a different compos-ition. Thus, members of a Court of Appeal would refer to *a judgment of the Court* when citing a previous judgment by themselves, but to *that court* when referring to a Court of Appeal composed of others. Where, how-ever, the reference is to a court in general, the *c* should always be lower-case.

Likewise *judge* should always begin with a lower-case letter, unless it is referring to a specific person's title or unless—as a matter of personal taste—the author has contrasted the Single Judge with the Full Court (as in criminal appeals and judicial review proceedings), where they both have specific parts to play and almost constitute separate courts in themselves.

Specific terms such as *Law of Torts* or *Court of Appeal* should have capitals, but not when turned into a more colloquial form, such as *tort law* or *appeal court*.

Other aspects of capitalization are mentioned under their individual headings below.

13.2.2 **References**

Some legal writers cite others' works without a place of publication, or first names or initials. While not followed by all publishers, this *is* an established convention in (at least some parts of) the discipline, the expectation being that the work will be read by those who already are immersed in the relevant texts. (The same thinking is found in other fields, such as classics.) This is permitted where unavoidable, though editors should not impose it, and if the expected readership is more general or more elementary (as in an undergraduate or introductory text) full references must be given.

Continental and US references (except US case references) should be cited with the date and volume number first, followed by the abbreviation of the report or review name, and then—without a comma in between—the page number. Where a specific page within a report or article is referred to, it is a moot point whether the initial page number should be followed by a comma plus the specific page number, or no comma and *at* followed by the specific page number. The decision is a matter of personal choice, but should be made consistent throughout a particular work.

Set the names of books and non-law journals and reports in italic, following the standard format (*see* **CHAPTER 15**). Formerly, abbreviated references to reports were set in roman and those to reviews in italics. However, few modern legal publications (particularly those on the Continent) contain nothing but reports or reviews. Thus the rule now is to set all abbreviated references to reports and reviews in roman—in text, in references, and in lists of abbreviations. Names of law journals and reports are in roman type, its reference follows the date. Set abbreviated titles of works in roman or italic, depending on the style of the expanded version. Abbreviate only titles of extremely well-known books, journals, or reports; all others should normally appear in full. Variations exist in how many periodicals are abbreviated or punctuated—for example the Law Society Gazette may be 'LS Gaz.' or 'Law Soc. Gaz.', and the Solicitors' Journal 'SJ' or 'Sol Jo'. Providing authors are consistent such variations are acceptable; in works for non-specialists, readers may benefit from expanded versions of very terse abbreviations.

When the full title of a reports series or a review is quoted—and only the very obscure ones need to be quoted in full—that full title is always in italics. Setting all abbreviated titles in roman does, however, leave one or two pitfalls, of which one must be wary: 'CMLR', for instance, refers to Common Market Law Reports (which publishes only reports and never articles), while 'CMLRev.' refers to Common Market Law Review. Unfortunately, where authors cite the latter as the former the only clue that they have it wrong is that the reference is to an article.

The list below shows some examples of the preferred style for abbreviated forms of law report series and journals used in citations; in general, spell out in full the name of any journal or report not included here, and all series names. When giving the full name of a journal or law report, certain frequent terms (e.g. Crim., Eur., Intl, J, L, Q, R, Rev., U, Ybk) may be abbreviated. When spelt-out books, journals, reports, or series are referred to very frequently in a particular work, they may after their first occurrence be abbreviated and included in the List of Abbreviations.

Cite a report in *The Times* or *Independent* only if there is no other published report; in references neither is abbreviated or italicized. The form is, for example, '*Powick v. Malvern Wells Water Co.*, The Times, 28 Sept. 1993'.

Advocate General (of the ECJ)	AG
All England Law Reports	All ER
American Journal of Comparative Law	AJCL
American Journal of International Law	AJIL
Anonymous	Anon.
another	anor.
article, articles	art., arts.
Attorney-General	A-G
Borough Council	BC
British Company Law Cases	BCC
British Tax Review	BTR
Brothers	Bros.
Cambridge Law Journal	CLJ
clause, clauses	cl., clauses (*not abbreviated*)
Commissioner	Comr.
Common Market Law Reports	CMLR
Common Market Law Review	CMLRev
Co-operative	Co-op
Corporation	Corp.
County Council	CC
Criminal	Crim.
Criminal Appeal Reports	Cr. App. R
Criminal Appeal Reports (Sentencing)	Cr. App. R(S)
Criminal Law Review	Crim. LR
Crown Prosecution Service	CPS
Current Law	CL
Current Legal Problems	CLP
cwmni cyfyngedig cyhoeddus	ccc
cyfngedig	cyf
deceased	decd.
decision	dec.
directive	dlr.
Director of Public Prosecutions	DPP

District Council	DC
EC Bulletin	EC Bull.
edition	ed. (*not* edn., *as elsewhere*)
Estates Gazette	EG
European	Eur.
European Community	EC
European Competition Law Review	ECLR
European Court Reports	ECR
European Court of Justice	ECJ
European Industrial Relations Review	EIRR
European Intellectual Property Review	EIPR
European Law Review	ELR
European Union	EU
Executor	Exor.
Executrix	Exrx.
Family Law Reports	FLR
Financial Times Law Reports	FTLR
Fleet Street Reports	FSR
Her (or His) Majesty's	HM
Industrial Cases Reports	ICR
Industrial Law Journal	ILJ
Industrial Relations Law Review	IRLR
Inland Revenue Commissioners	IRC
International	Intl.
International and Comparative Law Quarterly	ICLQ
Journal	J
Journal of Business Law	JBL
Journal of Planning and Environmental Law	JPEL
Journal of Planning Law	JPL
Justice of the Peace Reports	JP
Knight's Local Government Reports	LGR
Law	L
Law Journal	LJ
Law Quarterly Review	LQR
Law Reports, Appeal Cases	AC
Law Reports, Chancery Division	Ch.
Law Reports, Family Division	Fam.
Law Reports, King's Bench Division	KB
Law Reports, Probate, Divorce, & Admiralty Division	P
Law Reports, Queen's Bench Division	QB
Law Society Gazette	LS Gaz., Law Soc. Gaz.
Legal Studies	LS
liquidation	liq.
Lloyd's Law Reports	Lloyd's Rep.

Lloyd's Maritime & Commercial Law Quarterly	LMCLQ
Local Government Reports	LGR
Modern Law Review	MLR
New Law Journal	NLJ
Official Journal of the EC	OJ
Order, Orders	Ord., Ords.
others	ors.
Oxford Journal of Legal Studies	OJLS
paragraph, paragraphs	para., paras.
Property and Compensation Reports	P & CR
Proprietary	Pty
Public Law	PL
Quarterly	Q
Railway	Rly
regulation	reg.
Report(s)	R
Reports of Patent Cases	RPC
Review	Rev.
Road Traffic Reports	RTR
rule, rules	r., rr.
Rural District Council	RDC
Scots Law Times	SLT
section, sections	s. (§), ss. (§§)
Session Cases, Court of Session, Scotland	SC
Simon's Tax Cases	STC
Solicitors' Journal	SJ
the sovereign (Queen or King)	R (*not Reg*)
subparagraph, subparagraphs	subpara., subparas.
subsection, subsections	subs. (sub§), subss. (sub§§)
Tax Cases	TC
Times Law Reports	TLR
University	U
Urban District Council	UDC
Vice-Chancellor	V-C
Weekly Law Reports	WLR
Yearbook	Ybk

The appearance of case citations

To indicate a specific page or series of pages of a report, use a comma followed by the page(s) given in full: '*Ridge* v. *Baldwin* [1964] AC 40, 78–9'. Citations should not include letters (A, B, etc.) printed in the margin in some series of reports; reference to the relevant page is sufficient.

There is a rule about the use of square brackets or parentheses in reference dates, which states that a date is in square brackets if it is

essential for finding the report, and in parentheses if it merely illustrates when a case was included in reports with cumulative volume
numbers. For instance

> *R.* v. *Home Secretary, ex p. Hindley* [1998] 2 WLR 505 (QBD)
>
> *Blair* v. *Osborne* [1971] 2 QB 78
>
> P. Birks, 'The English Recognition of Unjust Enrichment' [1991] LMCLQ 473,
> 490–2

but

> *Cobbett* v. *Grey* (1850) 4 Ech. 729
>
> *Badische* v. *Soda-Fabrics* (1897) 14 RPC 919, HL
>
> S. C. Manon, 'Rights of Water Abstraction in the Common Law' (1965) 83
> LQR 47, 49–51

While this rule is not often followed in very recent publications, it does
hold good for those foreign reports derived from common law.

Many reports—for example Appeal Cases, Queen's Bench, Weekly
Law Reports—began by producing cumulative volume numbers, but
realized that this system would give rise to hundreds of volumes (as
in US reports). Gradually they all switched to square-bracket, date-
dependent references, though some—for example Lloyd's Law Reports
and Reports of Patent Cases—made the change much later. A good
number of new and privately published specialist reports do not follow
this system, so that, say, *Estates Gazette* has the date in square brackets,
but volume numbers well into the hundreds. An editor who comes
across unexpected inconsistencies in text should query them with the
author. Most reports illustrate how they should be cited in their running
heads: those for Common Market Law Reports indicate the correct
citation is, say, '[1989] 2 CMLR 351' rather than '(1989) 2 CMLR 351'.

No brackets are used in cases from the Scottish Series of Session Cases
from 1907 onwards, and Justiciary Cases from 1917 onwards: '*Hughes* v.
Stewart 1907 SC 791', '*Corcoran* v. *HM Advocate* 1932 JC 42'. Instead, the
case name is followed by a comma, as it is in US, South African, and
some Canadian cases where the date falls at the end of the reference. It is
usual to refer to Justiciary Cases (criminal cases before the High Court of
Justiciary) simply by the name of the panel (or accused), thus: *Corcoran.*

Unreported cases

When a case has not (yet) been reported, cite just the name of the court
and the date of the judgment. The word 'unreported' should not be used,
for example '*R* v. *Marianishi, ex p. London Borough of Camden* (CA, 13 Apr.
1965)'. Unreported EC cases are handled differently (*see* below).

Courts of decision

Unless the case was heard in the High Court or was reported in a series that covers the decisions of only one court, the court of decision should be indicated by initials (e.g. ECJ, PC, HL, CA) at the end of the reference. References for unreported cases, however, should be made in brackets to the court of decision first (even if it is in an inferior court), followed by the date. Reference is not normally made to the deciding judge ('*per* Ferris J*'*, etc.), except when wishing to specify him or her when quoting from a Court of Appeal or House of Lords decision. The following are examples of correctly cited cases in the preferred style:

> *Blay* v. *Pollard* [1930] 1 AC 628, HL
>
> *Bowman* v. *Fussy* [1978] RPC 545, HL
>
> *Re Bourne* [1978] 2 Ch 43
>
> *Cooper* v. *McKenna, ex p Bishop* [1986] WLR 327, CA
>
> *R* v. *Leeds County Court, ex p Morris* [1990] QB 523, 526–9
>
> *Berk* v. *Hair* (DC, 12 Sept. 1956)
>
> *New Zealand Shipping Co Ltd* v. *Satterthwaite (AM) & Co Ltd* (*The Eurymedon*) [1975] AC 154

As a general rule, a single 'best' reference should be given for each case cited. For UK cases, the reference should, wherever possible, be to the official Law Reports; if the case has not been reported there, then the Weekly Law Reports are preferred, and failing that the All England Reports. Unless there is good cause, references should be from one of these three series, but in certain specialist areas it will be necessary to refer to the relevant specialist series, for example Lloyds Law Reports, Family Law Reports, Industrial Cases Reports, and Reports on Patent Cases.

For pre-1865 cases, both the private reports *and* the English Reports references should be cited, for example: '*Boulton* v. *Jones* (1857) 2 H&N 564, 157 ER 232'.

13.2.3 Primary and secondary legislation

Statutes and Acts of Parliament

A statute's title should always be in roman, even where a US statute is in italics in the original. Do not capitalize 'act' if it does not form part of the title, or when it describes more than one act: 'the Shops and Income Tax acts' describes two different acts. When citing Acts of Parliament, use a capital *A* for Act: *Factory and Workshop Act 1891*, *the Children Act 1995*. Older statutes, without a short title, will require the appropriate regnal year and chapter number. Use arabic numerals for chapter numbers in Public (General) and Private Acts: *3 & 4 Geo. V, c. 12, ss. 18, 19*. Use lower-case roman numerals in Public (Local) Acts: *3 & 4 Geo. V, c. xii, ss. 18, 19*. Scots Acts before the Union of 1707 are cited by year and chapter: *1532, c. 40*. All acts passed after 1962 are cited by the calendar year and chapter number of the act; commas before the date were abolished with retroactive effect in 1963. There is no need for the word 'of' except, perhaps, when discussing a number of acts with the same title, in which case 'of' may be used to distinguish, for example, the Criminal Appeals Act of 1907 from that of 1904. Provided the meaning is clear, it is permissible even in text to refer to 'the 1904 Act'.

A few UK statutes are almost invariably abbreviated, for example *PACE* (Police and Criminal Evidence Act), *the MCAs* (Matrimonial Causes Acts), *the AJAs* (Administration of Justice Acts). Where such abbreviations will be familiar to readers they may be used instead of the full versions, even in text, although it is best to spell a statute out at first mention with the abbreviation in parentheses before relying thereafter simply on the abbreviation. Use an abbreviation where one particular statute is referred to many times throughout the text.

Except at the start of a sentence or when the reference is non-specific, use the following abbreviations: *s, ss* (or *§, §§*), *Pt, Sch.* For example, paragraph (k) of subsection (4) of section 14 of the Lunacy Act 1934 would be expressed as *Lunacy Act 1934, s 14(4)(k)*. There is no space between the bracketed items and no full point after the *s.* In general, prefer *section 14(4)* to *subsection (4)* or *paragraph (k)*; if the latter are used, however, they can be abbreviated to *subs (3)* or *para (k)* in notes.

Statutory instruments should be referred to by their name, date, and serial number, for example:

> Local Authority Precepts Order 1897, SR & O 1897/208
>
> Community Charge Support Grant (Abolition) Order 1987, SI 1987/466

No reference should be made to any subsidiary numbering system in the case of Scots instruments, those of a local nature, or those making commencement provisions. Note that there are no spaces or points in *SI* and *SR.*

Quote extracts from statutes exactly. Even if elsewhere first lines of quotations are set full out, if there is a paragraph indent in the statute it must be reproduced. Most authors like to approximate on the printed page the typographical conventions of the original—double quotation marks, em rules instead of colons, and hanging indents.

13.2.4 Other materials

Reports of Select Committees of the Houses of Lords, Commons, etc.

Refer to such papers by name and number: *HL Select Committee on European Union 8th Report (HL Paper (2000–01) no. 1).*

Law Commission

Cite Law Commission reports by name and Commission number, with the year of publication and any Command paper number; for example:

'Law Commission, *Family Law: The Ground for Divorce* (Law Com No 192, 1990) para 7.41'.

Hansard

Hansard (not italic), the daily and weekly verbatim record of debates in the British Parliament, is published by Her Majesty's Stationery Office. Begun in 1803, Hansard was named after the typesetter Luke Hansard (1752–1828), although since 1892 its formal name has been *The Official Report of Parliamentary Debates*. It was only after 1909 that Hansard became a strictly verbatim report; prior to that time the reports' precision and fullness varied considerably, particularly before the third series. There have been five series of Hansard: first series, 1803–20 (41 vols.); second series 1820–30 (25 vols.); third series 1830–91 (356 vols.); fourth series 1892–1908 (199 vols.); fifth series 1909–.

Since 1909 reports from the House of Lords and the House of Commons have been bound separately, rather than within the same volume. As such, references up to and including 1908 are 'Parl. Deb.', and afterwards 'H.L. Deb.' or 'H.C. Deb.'. Hansard is numbered by column rather than page; do not add 'p.' or 'pp.' before arabic numbers. Full references are made up of the series (in parentheses), volume number, and column number, for example: 'Hansard, HC (series 5) vol. 357, cols. 234–45 (13 Apr. 1965)'. For pre-1909 citations, use the following form: 'Parl. Debs. (series 4) vol. 24, col. 234 (24 Mar. 1895)'.

Command papers

In references, the abbreviations given before the numbers of Command papers vary according to the time period into which the paper falls. Consequently they should *not* be made uniform or changed unless they are clearly incorrect. The series, abbreviations, years, and number extents are as follows, with an example for each:

1st	(*none*)	(1833–69)	1–4,222	(C (1st series) 28)
2nd	C.	(1870–99)	1–9,550	(C (2nd series) 23)
3rd	Cd.	(1900–18)	1–9,239	(Cd 45)
4th	Cmd.	(1919–56)	1–9,889	(Cmd 12)
5th	Cmnd.	(1957–86)	1–9,927	(Cmnd 356)
6th	Cm.	(1986–)	1–	(Cm 69)

The references themselves are set in parentheses. The full points in the abbreviations, while normally dispensed with by those in the legal profession, should be retained in all other contexts.

13.2.5 International treaties, conventions, etc.

Apart from EC treaties, where the short name usually suffices, set out the full name of the treaty or convention with the following information in parentheses: the familiar name; the place and date of signature; the Treaty Series number (if not ratified, the Miscellaneous Series number) or, if earlier, other relevant number; the number of the latest Command Paper in which it was issued; and any relevant protocols. For example, a reference to the European Human Rights Convention should be expressed as follows:

> Convention for the Protection of Human Rights and Fundamental Freedoms (the European Human Rights Convention) (Rome, 4 Nov. 1950; TS 71 (1953); Cmd 8969)

A short title will suffice for subsequent references in the same chapter.

References to the Uniform Commercial Code (UCC) and US Restatements should be set in roman, for example 'UCC §2–203'.

13.2.6 European Community cases

Where available, cite a reference to the official reports of the EC, the European Court Reports (ECR) in preference to other reports. If an ECR reference is not available, the second best reference will usually be to the Common Market Law Reports (CMLR). However, where a case is reported by the (UK) official Law Reports, the Weekly Law Reports, or the All England Law Reports, that may be cited in preference to CMLR, particularly in books intended for readers who may not have ready access to CMLR. For example: 'Case 19/84, *Pharmon BV* v. *Hoechst AG* [1985] ECR 2281'. If the case is not yet reported it should be cited with a reference to the relevant notice in the *Official Journal*, such as 'Case C–134/89, *EC Commission* v. *Ireland* [1989] OJ L145/1'.

The case number should always be given before the name of the case in European Court of Justice cases. (The case number is irrelevant in UK cases.) For many years there was just one European Court, so cases before it were numbered in straight numerical order, e.g. *Case* (always a capital letter because it acts as an alternative title) *109/76*. Following the creation of the European Court of First Instance (CFI) in 1989, cases were numbered and prefixed according to whether they were registered there or at the European Court of Justice (ECJ). Cases registered at the CFI are prefixed by T– (*T* plus an en rule) and cases registered at the ECJ are prefixed C– (*C* plus an en rule). (Do not add a *C* to pre-1989 cases.)

Similarly, the parts of the *European Court Reports* are divided so that C–cases are reported in ECR I– and T– cases are reported in ECR II–. Unusually, the volume number is attached to the page number by an en rule, and follows 'ECR'. Typical European case citations might read

> Case C–34/89, *Psmith* v. *EC Commission* [1993] ECR I–454
> Case T–65/33, *Christy* v. *Mulliner* [1994] ECR II–323

This form may appear awkward when citing passages spanning more than one page, with the elided page reference at the end of, say, '[1993] ECR I-3436, at 3442-3'. (Do not repeat the roman numeral.) Because these cases are cited from ECR, an abbreviated reference to the court of decision at the end of the citation is superfluous; the case and volume numbers clearly signpost the relevant court. When citing from other series of reports, however, it is appropriate to add 'ECJ' or 'CFI' at the end of the citation.

Commission Decisions

Treat Commission Decisions—but not Council Decisions—as cases. For example:

> *Aluminium Cartel* [1985] OJ L92/1, [1987] 4 CMLR 778
>
> *Moosehead/Whitbread* [1990] OJ L100/32, [1991] 4 CMLR 391

Decisions of the Commission's Merger Task Force should also cite the official number given to it by Directorate General IV, for example:

> *Alcatel/Telettra* (Case IV/M042) [1991] OJ L122/48, [1991] 4 CMLR 208

13.2.7 European Community (Union) law

Judgments of the courts are uniformly translated into English from French, sometimes with error: *possibilité* rarely means 'possibility' (more often 'opportunity' or 'chance'), and *jurisprudence* does not mean 'jurisprudence' (which has an esoteric meaning in English), but 'case law'. Thus, if the meanings of such judgments are not clear, it may be feasible to go back to the original French for clarification.

In connection with the European Court, *decision* is only a literal translation from the French, which should be converted into the much more natural *judgment*. One school of thought suggests that *decision* should be retained for adjudications in references from national courts, with *judgment* referring to adjudications in direct cases, but as this is a difficult rule to implement it is simpler to standardize both terms to *judgment*. The *ruling* is that part of the judgment at the very end which summarizes precisely what was decided. In English law, it appears in italics at the end of the judgment, but European Court rulings are longer, and so should appear in roman.

Union institutions should be cited as *EC Commission/EC Council* or *Commission/Council*; *European Court* or *the Court* (always with a capital letter), never *Court of Justice of the European Communities* or the like.

For primary legislation, include both the formal and informal names in the first reference to a particular treaty:

> EC Treaty (Treaty of Rome, as amended), art. 3b
>
> Treaty on European Union (Maastricht Treaty), art. G5c

Cite articles of the treaties without reference to the titles, chapters, or subsections. As part of a reference, abbreviate 'article' to 'art.', in lower-case roman. Cite protocols to the treaties by their names, preceded by the names of the treaties to which they are appended. For example:

> Act of Accession 1985 (Spain and Portugal), Protocol 34
>
> EC Treaty, Protocol on the Statute of the Court of Justice

References to secondary legislation (decisions, directives, opinions, rec-ommendations, and regulations) should be to the texts in the *Official Journal* of the European Communities. The format for citing the *Official Journal* depends on the year of publication. For citations after 1972 the style is [year] + OJ series + OJ number/page ('[1989] OJ L145/1'). Wher-ever possible, references relating to the years 1952–72 (when there was no English edition of the *Journal Officiel*) should be to the Special Edition of the *Official Journal* (produced after the UK joined the European Com-munity), cited as '[1964] OJ Spec Ed 234'. When references must be to the *Journal Officiel*, the format from 1952 to 1967 is 'JO 1312/34', and from 1968 to 1972 is '[1968] JO L332/23'.

The title of the legislation precedes the reference to the source:

> Council Directive (EC) 97/1 on banking practice [1997] OJ L234/3
>
> Council Regulation (EEC) 1017/68 applying rules of competition to transport [1968] OJ Spec Ed 302

While it is always important to state the subject-matter of EC secondary legislation, it is permissible to abbreviate the long official title provided that the meaning is clear. For example, the full title

> Commission Notice on agreements of minor importance which do not fall under art. 85(1) of the Treaty establishing the EEC [1986] OJ C231/2, as amended [1994] OJ C368/20

may be abbreviated to

> Commission Notice on agreements of minor importance [1986] OJ C231/2, as amended [1994] OJ C368/20

Avoid the term *third countries*, as it is inexact and possibly ambiguous, given the common usage of the phrase *Third World*. Prefer either *non-member States* or *non-member countries*.

13.2.8 **European Human Rights cases**

Decisions of the European Court of Human Rights should always cite the relevant reference in the official reports (Series A) and if possible also the European Human Rights Reports, as follows:

> *Young, James and Webster* v. *UK* Series A No 44, (1982) 4 EHRR 38

Decisions and reports of the European Commission of Human Rights (now defunct) should cite the relevant application number, a reference to the Decisions and Reports of the Commission series (or earlier to the Yearbook of the ECHR) and—if available—a reference to the European Human Rights Reports:

> *Zamir* v. *UK* Application 9174/80, (1985) 40 DR 42

13.2.9 US, Commonwealth, and other foreign cases

The citation of foreign laws is too big a subject to cover in any great detail here. Authors and editors unsure of the relevant conventions should consult *The Bluebook: A Uniform System of Citation* (17th edn.), published by the Harvard Law Review Association in conjunction with the Columbia Law Review, the University of Pennsylvania Law Review, and the Yale Law Journal. This is a useful guide to citing legal sources from a wide range of jurisdictions, including the USA, Germany, France, Australia, the EC, Canada, and Japan. What follows are guidelines for some English-language citations.

Use the US style of citation for US cases. Thus, contrary to the general rule that only one 'best' reference need be given, with US cases the reference to the relevant US Federal reports (for Supreme Court cases) or state reports should be followed by a reference to the *National Reporter System*, with a comma separating citations. In the case of lower Federal court cases, a reference to just the Federal Reporter (F) or Federal Supplement (F Supp) suffices. The court (unless it is the Supreme Court) and year are given at the end of the citation. Typical US citations for a state case, a lower Federal court case, and a Supreme Court case respectively might read:

> *Bill* v. *Benn* 9 Ill 2d 435, 134 NE 2d 756 (Ill Ct of Apps, 1957)
> *Bones* v. *Bonar* 550 F 2d 35 (US Ct of Apps (2nd Cir), 1978)
> *Michael* v. *Johnson* 426 US 346, 23 S Ct 118 (1976)

For Australian cases, just one reference is necessary. For cases in the higher courts cite CLR (Commonwealth Law Reports) if available; if not, cite ALJR (Australian Law Journal Reports) or ALR (Australian Law Reports). In state cases, cite the relevant state reports. For New Zealand cases, cite the NZLR (New Zealand Law Reports). For Canadian cases, give two references, if possible: first to SCR (Supreme Court Reports) and then to DLR (Dominion Law Reports). For state provincial cases, cite only DLR.

For all foreign cases, if the report series cited does not make the country or state and the court of decision apparent, then indicate these in parentheses at the end of the reference.

13.2.10 **Tables of cases, legislation, etc.**

Unless it has been otherwise agreed, authors are expected to supply complete lists of cases, legislation, citations, and other material referred to in the work together with the typescript. These will be used as the basis for the tables of cases, legislation, etc. in the published book.

The table(s) of cases are located in the preliminary pages. They should be compiled alphabetically with the 'best' reference cited in the text, followed by all major report citations, but should exclude abbreviated or summary law reports unless they are the only reports available. Thus generally there should be no references to the Solicitors' Journal, Current Law, New Law Journal, or Estates Gazette, but references to Estates Gazette Law Reports are acceptable.

Depending on the number of cases cited overall, divide the tables into separate sections for UK cases, EC cases (distinguishing between ECJ, CFI, and Commission cases), and international cases. Provide a separate table of EC cases arranged in chronological and numerical order in works containing a significant number of such cases. Equally, where there are sufficient international cases to merit it, the table should be subdivided with headings by country.

Invert cases beginning 'Re' or 'In re', and table them under the party's name; for example, table 'In re the Estate of Farquar' or 'Re Farquar's Estate' under 'Farquar's Estate, Re'. Table shipping cases and trade mark cases under the full case name; include also an entry under the name of the ship or the mark, with a cross-reference to the full name.

13.2.11 **Judges' designations and judgments**

In text it is correct either to spell out the judge's title (*Mr Justice Kennedy*) or to abbreviate it (*Kennedy J*). It is best to follow the author's preference, providing it is consistently applied in similar contexts. It is a matter of house style whether or not the abbreviation takes a full point. The following table shows various titles and their abbreviated forms, where they exist:

Mr Justice	J
Messrs. Justice (*this expanded form is not now used*)	JJ
Lord Justice	LJ
Lords Justice	LJJ
Lord Chief Justice Parker	Parker LCJ, Lord Parker CJ
The Master of the Rolls, Sir F. R. Evershed	Evershed MR
His Honour Judge (County Court)	HH Judge

Attorney-General	Att.-Gen.
Solicitor-General	Sol.-Gen.
Lord . . . , Lord Chancellor . . .	LC
Baron (historical, but still quoted)	B
Chief Baron Blackwood	Blackwood CB
The President (Family Division)	Sir Stephen Brown, P
Advocate General (of the ECJ)	Slynn AG
Judge (of the ECJ)	*no abbreviation*

Law Lords are members of the House of Lords entitled to sit on judicial matters; their names are not abbreviated. Do not confuse them with Lords Justice (often wrongly referred to as *Lords Justices*). *Their Lordships* can be a reference to either rank, but *Their Lordships' House* refers only to the Judicial Committee of the House of Lords (its full title). Note there is in legal terms no such rank as *member of the Privy Council*: the Privy Council is staffed by members of the Judicial Committee for legal purposes, such as hearing appeals from the few remaining Commonwealth countries for which it is the final court of appeal.

When extracting a quotation from a transcript that refers to the judge's name or contains a dialogue between judge and counsel, it is usual to set the judge's name either in full and small capitals or in small capitals throughout, followed by his or her designation and a colon. Counsel's name should appear in upper- and lower-case italics, again followed by his or her designation (if any) and a colon. Judges always sit *in* a court (a room) but *on* a bench.

Judgment spelt with only one *e* is correct in the legal sense of a judge's or court's formal ruling, as distinct from a moral or practical deduction (which would take a second *e*). A judge's judgment is always spelt thus, as judges cannot (in their official capacity) express a personal judgement separate from their role. (This stems from the fact that a judge—in the High Court, at any rate—is the embodiment of the monarch: judges in full robes do not stand for the Loyal Toast.) In US style *judgment* is the spelling used in all contexts.

13.3 **Linguistics and phonetics**

Linguistics and phonetics concern the systematic study of language, written or spoken, in any of its forms. Each is subdivided into many fields, including theoretical linguistics, neuro- and psycholinguistics, sociolinguistics, language pathology, child language, and studies of particular languages. A common feature of all these fields is the use of phonetic or grammatical systems of description; authors should supply a list of any symbols or abbreviations used in their text.

13.3.1 Phonetic symbols and abbreviations

A work that includes analysis of spoken language will almost certainly use phonetic symbols; the International Phonetic Alphabet (IPA) includes all the standard symbols representing sounds. Editors should circle or highlight symbols at first occurrence, and identify them on the IPA chart. Authors using additional phonetic symbols should provide a printed example of each. Within a phonetic transcription, it is important that IPA symbols are not mixed with characters from the text font: for example, the IPA versions of [p], [b]—not the text-font versions of those letters—should be used to denote bilabial plosive consonants. In form, some IPA symbols (e.g. ɣ, ɛ, χ) are in some fonts similar or identical to letters of the Greek alphabet (e.g. γ, ε, χ); the IPA version rather than a Greek-font version should be used.

Phonetic transcriptions are conventionally placed between square brackets, phonemic representations between solidi. In typescript some authors may use an ordinary colon rather than the IPA sort : to indicate vowel length, for example /waːnga/ 'speak' versus /wanga/ 'place'. Editors should mark for the proper sort to be inserted.

Linguists usually use some abbreviations of grammatical or other analytical terms in their analysis of language. Since abbreviations are by no means standard within the discipline, readers may be unfamiliar with them. The asterisk, for example, generally denotes unacceptability, say, of the grammar of an utterance, but can also in some branches of the field indicate a reconstructed form. Similarly, *singular* can be abbreviated 'SG', 'S', 'sg.', or 'sing.' and *plural* as 'PL', 'P', 'pl.', or 'plur.'. Moreover, some authors find the need to coin analytical terms for their particular area of study. Authors not following an established series or journal style should submit a list of abbreviations with their typescript, to enable the editor and proofreaders to check for consistency. Book-length works benefit from having such a list printed in the text.

13.3.2 Analysed examples

Some books include numbered examples of utterances. At their most complex, these consist of the utterance, the analytic gloss, and the translation, aligned beneath one another. It is important that the elements in the utterance and the analytic gloss are correctly and evenly aligned, with matching line breaks where necessary. The translation line simply needs to be enclosed within single quotation marks. Such

CONSONANTS (PULMONIC)   © 1996 IPA

	Bilabial	Labiodental	Dental	Alveolar	Postalveolar	Retroflex	Palatal	Velar	Uvular	Pharyngeal	Glottal
Plosive	p b			t d		ʈ ɖ	c ɟ	k ɡ	q ɢ		ʔ
Nasal	m	ɱ		n		ɳ	ɲ	ŋ	N		
Trill	B			r					R		
Tap or Flap				ɾ		ɽ					
Fricative	ɸ β	f v	θ ð	s z	ʃ ʒ	ʂ ʐ	ç ʝ	x ɣ	χ ʁ	ħ ʕ	h ɦ
Lateral fricative				ɬ ɮ							
Approximant		ʋ		ɹ		ɻ	j	ɰ			
Lateral approximant				l		ɭ	ʎ	L			

Where symbols appear in pairs, the one to the right represents a voiced consonant. Shaded areas denote articulations judged impossible.

CONSONANTS (NON-PULMONIC)

Clicks		Voiced implosives		Ejectives	
ʘ	Bilabial	ɓ	Bilabial	'	Examples:
ǀ	Dental	ɗ	Dental/alveolar	p'	Bilabial
ǃ	(Post)alveolar	ʄ	Palatal	t'	Dental/alveolar
ǂ	Palatoalveolar	ɠ	Velar	k'	Velar
ǁ	Alveolar lateral	ʛ	Uvular	s'	Alveolar fricative

OTHER SYMBOLS

ʍ Voiceless labial-velar fricative
w Voiced labial-velar approximant
ɥ Voiced labial-palatal approximant
H Voiceless epiglottal fricative
ʢ Voiced epiglottal fricative
ʡ Epiglottal plosive

ɕ ʑ Alveolo-palatal fricatives
ɺ Voiced alveolar lateral flap
ɧ Simultaneous ʃ and x

Affricates and double articulations can be represented by two symbols joined by a tie bar if necessary.

k͡p t͡s

VOWELS

Where symbols appear in pairs, the one to the right represents a rounded vowel.

SUPRASEGMENTALS

ˈ Primary stress
ˌ Secondary stress   ˌfoʊnəˈtɪʃən
ː Long   eː
ˑ Half-long   eˑ
˘ Extra-short   ĕ
| Minor (foot) group
‖ Major (intonation) group
. Syllable break ɹi.ækt
‿ Linking (absence of a break)

DIACRITICS   Diacritics may be placed above a symbol with a descender, e.g. ŋ̊

̥	Voiceless	n̥ d̥		̤	Breathy voiced	b̤ a̤	
̬	Voiced	s̬ t̬		̰	Creaky voiced	b̰ a̰	
ʰ	Aspirated	tʰ dʰ		̼	Linguolabial	t̼ d̼	
̹	More rounded	ɔ̹		ʷ	Labialized	tʷ dʷ	
̜	Less rounded	ɔ̜		ʲ	Palatalized	tʲ dʲ	
̟	Advanced	u̟		ˠ	Velarized	tˠ dˠ	
̠	Retracted	e̠		ˤ	Pharyngealized	tˤ dˤ	
̈	Centralized	ë		̴	Velarized or pharyngealized	ɫ	
̽	Mid-centralized	e̽		̝	Raised	e̝	(ɹ̝ = voiced alveolar fricative)
̩	Syllabic	n̩		̞	Lowered	e̞	(β̞ = voiced bilabial approximant)
̯	Non-syllabic	e̯		̘	Advanced Tongue Root	e̘	
˞	Rhoticity	ɚ a˞		̙	Retracted Tongue Root	e̙	

Dental t̪ d̪
Apical t̺ d̺
Laminal t̻ d̻
Nasalized ẽ
Nasal release dⁿ
Lateral release dˡ
No audible release d̚

TONES AND WORD ACCENTS

LEVEL			CONTOUR		
e̋ or ˥	Extra high		ě or ˩˥	Rising	
é	High		ê	Falling	
ē	Mid		e᷄	High rising	
è	Low		e᷅	Low rising	
ȅ	Extra low		e᷈	Rising-falling	
↓	Downstep		↗	Global rise	
↑	Upstep		↘	Global fall	

The International Phonetic Association permits (with no limitations or licensing restrictions and at no charge in the form of a license fee or royalties) third parties to use (copy, publicly display, publicly perform, publish/ distribute and create derivative works based thereon) the IPA symbols and IPA charts as part of or in products such as books and software/hardware as long as the third party acknowledges the International Phonetic Association as the copyright owner of the International Phonetic Alphabet and the IPA charts.

Fig. 13.1: **IPA chart The International Phonetic Alphabet (revised to 1993, updated 1996).**

displayed utterances are usually set in text-size type rather than one size down as for normal displayed matter:

(3*a*) [[Omura-san ga   kinendoo   o   kentiksi-yoo   to
    Mr Omura NOM memorial hall ACC construct-VOL COMPL

    keekakusite-iru]   basyo]   wa   takai   desu   ka
    is-planning   place   TOP   expensive is   Q

    'Is the place Mr Omura plans to construct a memorial hall expensive?'

A commonly used system of grammatical analysis employs square brackets to identify specific components of the utterance, and subscript abbreviations, usually in capitals or small capitals, to label the preceding component:

[[The cat]$_{NP}$ [[saw]$_V$ [the queen]$_{NP}$]$_{VP}$]$_S$

Editors can sideline each example in a distinctive colour, to signal basic rules of layout such as spacing or indentation, and thus avoid repetitive mark-up.

13.3.3 Style

Typically italic, small capitals, underlining, and bold type represent specific features in linguistics and phonetics work, so editors should check with the author before changing a consistently imposed style.

- In running text, italic type should be used only for utterances (i.e. samples of language), for example: 'The sentence *John loves Mary* is well formed'. As a general rule, do not use italic for any other purpose, particularly emphasis. In phonetic samples or phonemic representations, utterances should remain in roman type; in numbered examples (*see* **13.3.2**) the utterance should also preferably remain in roman type. Where an utterance is translated or glossed, the translation should follow in single quotation marks, without intervening punctuation, for example: *je me souviens* 'I remember'. (*See also* **6.5**.)

- Small capitals should be used for most grammatical and other analytical abbreviations, for example ABL (ablative), COMPL (complementizer), COP (copula), DEM (demonstrative). Abbreviations for parts of speech, such as NP (noun phrase) or V (verb), should be in full capitals. These conventions apply to examples in both running text and display.

- Normally all underlined copy is set as italic. Where both italics and underlining are required in the text and no distinction exists in the copy—that is, they both appear underscored—the author and editor must distinguish between the two at each occurrence; highlighting one in a distinctive colour usually suffices.

- Avoid the use of bold face wherever possible. It is occasionally necessary, however, in complex analysis where other typographical distinctions (italic, small capitals, underlines) have already been used.

13.4 **Logic**

Works containing philosophical, mathematical, or computer logic often present difficulties in editing and setting, not only because their symbols and conventions are complex but also because their interpretation may vary from writer to writer as well as between disciplines. It may therefore be necessary to depart from the guidelines given below to suit different circumstances.

13.4.1 **Special problems**

Overall, texts containing philosophical logic are more likely to cause problems: although they have shorter formulae and less technical presentation than those with mathematical or computer logic, their notation is usually interspersed with running text and notes, requiring more attention to consistent mark-up and clarification of symbols, variables, etc. In addition to the common concerns shared with mathematical symbols in general (*see* **12.1**), authors and editors should keep in mind the following additional points:

Spacing is sometimes used instead of parentheses; for example one could put: $\bigvee x\ Fx \supset Gx$ or: $(\bigvee x)(Fx \supset Gx)$. The spacing may vary according to the complexity of the expression, just as bracketing may be added or omitted to clarify an expression. Therefore, while editors should attempt to apply consistent spacing in similar contexts throughout a work, the varying syntax of an expression may make this impossible. Dyadic operators ($\&$, $\supset$, etc.) have space either side (except when next to a parenthesis); monadic operators ($\sim$ etc.) are set close up to whatever follows. When used in the context of a clause in English, there should be a space after the colon denoting *such that* (e.g. '$x \subset (x{:}\ x$ is a man $\&\ x$ loves $y)$'), even when a simple predicate variable follows (e.g. '$x{:}\ Fx$'). This avoids any confusion with a ratio symbol.

Normally round brackets are used, although curly brackets ({ }) conventionally denote sets, angle brackets ($<\ >$) denote ordered k-tuples, etc. Embedded brackets should be of the same shape, for example '$(((\ldots)))$', rather than the 'mathematical' hierarchy '$\{[(\ldots)]\}$'. If parentheses rather than $\forall$ are used to denote universal quantification, this should be stated. Avoid using bullets of various shapes to denote brackets, unless it is important to reproduce a historical use exactly. Editors should check to ensure that the number of opening brackets equals the number of closing brackets: if a discrepancy is discovered, raise the point with the author, as a part of the expression may have been omitted along with the missing bracket(s).

Schematic letters or variables may appear in capital or lower-case, roman or italic type; ensure consistency, therefore, in the form used for variables of a particular type. Very broadly, lower-case italic letters from the middle of the alphabet (p, q, r...) are used as propositional variables, or sentential variables; lower-case italic letters from the end of the alphabet (x, y, z...) are used as object variables; lower-case roman letters (n, k, j...) are used to refer to specific numbers; those from the beginning of the alphabet (a, b, c...) also stand for individual constants. Capital roman letters (F, G, R) stand for predicates and relational expressions; capital italic letters (X, Y, Z...) are used on occasion for sets.

Displayed formulae, rules, and proofs in logic are not strictly lists, and therefore follow slightly different rules. They should be indented by 2 to 3 ems (depending on the measure), not centred on the measure. They are set in text-size type (not one size down), and aligned vertically on the closing parentheses numbering each line, to form a column. Any explanatory material is aligned separately in a second column to the right, with a minimum 1–en space separating it from the first.

Here are examples of displayed rules and proofs:

(47) P&—P ∴ Q.

(48) Q ∴ Pv—P.

(49) P&Q ∴ P.

(50) P&Q ∴ Q.

(i)	—(P & Q)	= first assumption
(ii)	P	= second assumption
(iii)	—Pv—Q	from (i) by rule 59
(iv)	— —P	from (ii) by rule 3
(v)	—Q	from (iii) and (iv) by rule 55.

To prove AaB & AaC ∴ CiB (= *Darapti*)

(i)	AaB & AaC	= assumption
(ii)	AaB	from (i) by rule 49
(iii)	AaC	from (i) by rule 50
(iv)	CiA	from (iii) by accidental conversion
(v)	AaB & CiA	from (ii), (iv), from two propositions to their conjunction
(vi)	CiB	from (v) by *Darii*

Therefore from first to last: AaB & AaC ∴ CiB Q.E.D.

There is no extra space between each line of a proof; line turnovers should be indented 1 em further than their hanging column.

In general, avoid abbreviations unless there is a special reason for using them; it is usually preferable to spell out, for example, *ontological commitment* and *substitutional quantification* at every instance, rather than pepper the text with *OC*, *SQ*, and the like, which may be confused for variables by those not well versed in the field. (High-level works may rely on more abbreviations as a matter of course, however.)

13.4.2 Special terminology and punctuation

It is preferable to use *premiss* rather than *premise* to denote a previous statement from which another is inferred. Despite the spelling Hume adopted in his *Enquiry concerning Human Understanding*, prefer *inquiry* in logic, to denote a rigorous intellectual investigation. (This spelling is the norm adopted by US logicians in any event.)

Common editing pitfalls include 'iff', which means 'if and only if', and 'wff' and 'wffs', which mean 'well-formed formula(e)'; neither is a misprint. The signs for 'is not equal to' ($\neq$) and 'is not identically equal to' ($\not\equiv$) are thus, rather than equals signs marked for deletion.

In text an author may maintain a semantic distinction between the use and the mention of a word or words, single quotation marks denoting the 'use' and double quotation marks the "mention". Other authors may choose the reverse marking, the original decision sometimes depending on the form of quotation mark prevalent in a given country; editors should not, however, change this to conform to house style without first checking with the author. Be aware that in such cases the standard system of quotes within quotes may not then apply, as two single quotation marks could appear side by side (separated by a thin space) if a 'used' term nests within another's opening or closing punctuation. Since no universally recognized rules govern this practice, authors employing it are ultimately responsible for its correct implementation. Some authors accomplish the same task by using small capitals for mentioning words: this is preferable to full capitals as it is less distracting on a page, and it allows a further distinction to be made where acronyms are used as well.

Polish notation is an independent and self-contained system that creates logical formulae without brackets or special symbols, using the standard roman alphabet. Within a particular work, its elements should not be interchanged with those from other systems, although it is not normally used nowadays. Again, authors employing such marking are responsible for ensuring that it has been correctly achieved throughout.

Sequences with ellipses have commas only if they would be present grammatically, were all the intermediate terms actually written in. Simple sequences should have commas before and after the ellipsis, such as '$Fx_1, Fx_2, \ldots, Fx_n$'. However, '$Fx_1 \& Fx_2 \& \ldots \& Fx_n$' has no commas; neither does a sequence of elements connected by $\lor$.

It can be difficult to set symbolic formulae properly within running text, as word spacing may break formulae awkwardly over two lines. While logicians consider it bad form to break formulae at all, the requirements of typography may often demand it. Where unavoidable, a break is sometimes tolerable after a symbol corresponding to a verb (e.g. *implies, entails, does not include, equals, is a member of, is not equivalent to, is less than*), but only where that symbol is the main symbol in the formula, not in a subsidiary position enclosed within parentheses. Where a subscript is associated with the symbol, the line is broken after it.

13.4.3 **Logic symbols**

Logic symbolism may vary from logical system to system and work to work: ∀, A, and () may all be used for universal quantification; ∃ and E for existential quantification; -, ¬ and ~ for negation; ∧ and & for conjunction, and so on. One consistent system of symbols should be employed within a single work, though editors should not standardize apparent variations without checking with the author, as there may be valid reasons for the notation's diversity. Here is a list of the most commonly used symbols:

· or & or ∧	and (conjunction)
~ or ¬ or ⁻ or *N*	not (negation)
∈	belongs to, is a member of (a set or class)
∉	does not belong to, negates ∈
Ø	null set, empty set
Λ	older symbol for null set, empty set (prefer Ø)
=	is the same as or equal to, if and only if (strict equivalence)
≠	is not the same as or equal to, negates =
≡ or ↔ or ⟷	is identically equal to, if and only if (material equivalence)
≢	is not identically the same as or equal to, negates ≡
≈	is approximately the same as or equal to
∀	for all (universal quantification)
∃	some, at least one, there exists, i.e. not ∀ not (existential quantification)
∄	there does not exist
□ or *L*	necessarily
◇ or *M*	possibly, i.e. not □ not
⊂	is included in
⊄	is not included in
⊃ → ⇒	includes, implies, if
⊅	does not include, does not imply
∩ or ∨	or (intersection)
∪	union

13.5 **Music texts**

This section gives recommendations concerning works about music, as opposed to music scores (which lies beyond the scope of this volume).

13.5.1 **Music examples**

13.5.1.1 **Positioning in text**

Music examples count as illustrations, so the same rules apply for their placement in text as for other illustrations (*see* **10.2**), though typically captions go *above* music examples but *below* illustrations. Each example should be given a numbered cue, such as *the main theme is given in Ex. 1* or *the opening of the movement (Ex. 2) illustrates this*. Even though it may well prove possible to position the shorter examples in the exact places desired, it is safest to label all examples in this way. The editor should key each example in the margin, circling the note, for example 'Ex. 1 near here'. When examples need to fall at precise places, for example within a quotation from another publication, they must be flagged in text.

13.5.1.2 **Captions**

Authors should supply captions double-spaced on a separate sheet or sheets. 'Caption' denotes anything that will be generated by the typesetter and not the music setter, which in practice means everything except underlaid text in vocal music, tempo or other indications, and occasionally footnote cues.

Each example may have a caption giving brief details of the music quoted, with a broadly consistent level of information. Do not give unnecessary information: for instance, a composer's name is superfluous when the example falls in the middle of a discussion of that composer. Present bar numbers at the head of the first stave.

13.5.1.3 **Numbering**

Examples can be numbered either throughout the typescript (if there are few of them) or by chapter; in the latter case, the example should include the chapter number as well, as *Ex. 3.1* (Chapter 3, Example 1). This last is especially useful in books with frequent cross-reference. Indicate subdivisions of examples by an italicized lower-case letter in parentheses following the number, as 'Ex. 3(*a*)', 'Ex. 6.4(*b*)'.

13.5.1.4 **Presentation**

Authors should discuss with their editor at an early stage whether the music examples will be engraved (now a rare occurrence), set via specialist software (by a music setter or the author), or photographed or scanned from copy already set. If all or most of the examples are from a collected edition, it is probably more economical to photograph or scan them, particularly if the music is complex, such as a dense page of orchestral score. If, however, the examples come from a patchwork of printed sources, it may be decided that they should all be set anew for the sake of consistency. Naturally, examples will have to be set if the music is not readily available from printed sources, or if the existing sources are unsatisfactory.

Authors should supply examples separately from the text, with adequate room left around them for technical mark-up. All examples should be numbered as they are to be in the finished text.

If the examples are to be set:

- Authors should be economical with the use of music examples; reduce the score or quote only the most relevant parts. When supplying photocopies from printed scores, authors should cross out those systems or whole bars that are redundant.

- Add time and key signatures to all examples, even when not quoting from the beginning of a work or movement.

- Where relevant, examples should indicate instrumentation, either to the left of the stave (if in score) or added as necessary to a short score. For examples drawn from operas, oratorios, and the like, authors should ensure that the names of the characters are presented on the music as well (to the left of the stave), if they are not sufficiently indicated in text or caption, for example *The Queen of the Night's opening aria*. The style must match that in the text (i.e. translated or not, as appropriate).

- Texts of examples should be clearly handwritten on the copy (or typed double-spaced on separate pages if the example is cramped, with the handwritten text *in situ*), and consistently divided by syllable. If an example ends in mid-word, the remainder of it should be supplied in square brackets. A translation for vocal music, if required, is added in roman immediately below the example, within parentheses.

Authors should indicate in a covering note any examples that contravene standard rules of musical notation, such as the original beaming or bar division of a manuscript or early printed edition: unless the music setter is informed, he or she will alter to conform to modern usage. Similarly, authors should draw attention to unexpected artwork, such as arrows or crossings-out, that is to be printed—which otherwise an editor may delete as superfluous.

If the examples are to be photographed or scanned:

- Authors should supply either good-quality, high-contrast black-and-white photographs or the scores themselves, with an accompanying photocopy showing clearly which bars are required. During setting it is sometimes possible for the music to be rearranged in a paste-up to make more economical use of space.

13.5.2 Copyright

Authors must obtain permission from the copyright holder to use extracts of music that is still in copyright. Permission must be obtained to reproduce a photographic image if it is in copyright, even if the music itself is out of copyright—for example, a recent image of a sixteenth-century piece.

It is not obligatory to have a lengthy acknowledgement section crediting the copyright holders of musical extracts, if all the necessary source information, including the publisher, is given in either a caption or a footnote. A large number of extracts taken from one source can be covered in the acknowledgements section with a general note, such as 'Extracts of music by Brahms are taken from *Johannes Brahms: Sämtliche Werke*, published by Breitkopf & Härtel.' In this case it is not necessary to credit the publisher in captions or footnotes.

13.5.3 In-text music

Short rhythmic motifs can be illustrated in line in the text without staves, such as 'the repeated ♩♫ ♩♫ pattern'. These do not form part of the numbered sequence of examples; the editor should assign them dummy numbers or letters for reference, usually A, B, C, etc. Do not end a sentence with a motif, as the full point also serves to dot the final note. To avoid layout difficulties, motifs should be no longer than a few notes; it is also often possible to present simple fragments in words. Display longer phrases as separate examples.

13.5.4 Titles of works

The rules for styling titles of musical works basically follow those governing titles in general (for capitalization *see* **4.1.8**; for italicization *see* **6.3**). Nevertheless the diversity of forms in which some titles may be cited can cause problems. Be guided by sense and the context in which it is found, as no rule governs all circumstances. Broadly speaking, refer to a work at its first occurrence in full and in the original language, unless the English translation is the standard way of referring to that work, for example *The Bartered Bride* and not *Prodaná nevěsta*. The more usual form may occasionally be in a language other than English or the original, for example *Les Noces* instead of *Svadebka*. Titles can be shortened thereafter if necessary. There is no need, at the first occurrence, to mark what the short title will be, for example '*Le nozze di Figaro* (hereafter referred to as

Figaro)', unless confusion would otherwise result. If necessary a translation of a foreign title can follow immediately after the title, in which case it should be roman type and in parentheses, for example 'Mahler's *Lieder eines fahrenden Gesellen* (Songs of a Wayfarer)', subsequent references being to the German title; if subsequent references use the English title, this is cited as 'Mahler's *Songs of a Wayfarer (Lieder eines fahrenden Gesellen)*'. (Note the use of italic here for both translation and original.)

References must be consistent, not switching from one language or form to another: not *Die Zauberflöte* here, *The Magic Flute* there, *MF* six folios later, and so on. Slavonic and Oriental languages present the most problems, and as a general rule require more translations. Generally one can assume that the reader will have some familiarity with the main European languages.

13.5.5　Points of style

Period and stylistic terms

The common terms *baroque*, *classical*, and *romantic* are roman, and lowercase when used as a simple adjective (*a baroque fugue*). They are uppercase when used with *era*, *age*, or *period* (*the Classical era*), and also when these words are tacitly understood (*In the Baroque it was rare...*). However, authors tend to use *Baroque* in both contexts, and if they do so consistently this should be left. In its historical sense *Renaissance* should always take an initial capital.

Catalogue numbers

Use a comma after the title and before the catalogue number ('Elgar's *Falstaff*, Op. 68'); use initial capital letters in 'Op. 1 No. 1', with no comma between the two elements. OUP's preferred style is *K.* for Köchel numbers for Mozart's works, with a full point and space before the number ('K. 482', 'K. 622'), except when different editions are referred to in abbreviated form, for example 'K⁶', when the point is omitted. (Ensure that the superscript figure cannot be mistaken for a footnote cue: it is sometimes set as 'K6' to avoid confusion.) Kirkpatrick references to Scarlatti sometimes share the same 'K.' abbreviation—ensure that no ambiguity is introduced in any context where the works of Mozart and Scarlatti are discussed together. Other catalogue abbreviations include 'Hob.' (Hoboken) for Haydn, and 'BWV' (Bach-Werk-Verzeichnis) for J. S. Bach: all are roman, with a space following.

Foreign words

Set most commonly occurring foreign music words in roman type, on the principle that they are part of music's lingua franca. All standard Italian musical phrases are roman ('The crescendo leads to a fortissimo brass chord'); but note that abbreviations of dynamics, such as *pp*, *mf*, *sf*., are italic (and normally require a special sort). Potentially awkward phrases like 'the piano theme, marked piano' can thus be recast as 'the piano theme, marked *p*'.

Foreign genre-words like *ballade*, *chanson*, and *lied* are familiar enough to warrant roman type, without quotation marks ('Schubert's lieder'). More unfamiliar terms, like *durchkomponiert* or *cori spezzati*, or genres like the *dumka*—a little-known Slavonic folk ballad—should be italicized. Treatment of other foreign words falling between these two extremes will depend on their context and the expected readership. Texts not wholly concerning music may need to have more terms italicized.

Key reference

Letters indicating key are upper-case, whether minor or major. There is no hyphen if *flat* or *sharp* is included, for example *E minor*, *D flat major*; *Symphony in B flat major*; *modulating into E flat minor*.

Where it is necessary to abbreviate, as in tables or figures, use *C* and *C m* for C major and C minor (*C m* is separated by a fixed thin space rather than the interword space of the line). An alternative, useful for saving space and preferable in stating chord progressions, is capital *C* for major, lower-case *c* for minor. This convention is common in US music notation; it need not be imposed, but should not be removed.

Musical form

Brief indications of musical form can be rendered with capital roman letters, close up, such as *ABA* = ternary form, whereby the opening material returns at the end after a contrasting middle section. Primes are used to indicate that ideas are reprised but not exactly, and should be labelled to avoid their being set as apostrophes.

Note reference

Reference to notes of indeterminate pitch should appear in upper-case roman type. However, there are several systems to indicate pitch that use both upper- and lower-case letters, with or without primes, for example, the Helmholtz system (where *c′* = middle C): *C,, C, C c c′ c″ c‴ c⁗*. Italic should always be used for the letters here.

Use sharp (♯), flat (♭), or natural (♮) signs with notes of precise pitch; spell out *sharp* or *flat* only when keys are indicated. So: *the note G♯*, *clarinet in E♭*, but *Sonata in E flat*.

Solmization

In the (Oxford) tonic sol-fa system for modern teaching of singing, notes are indicated as 'doh, ray, me, fah, soh, lah, te' (not italic). In historical contexts the syllables created by Guido d'Arezzo are indicated as 'ut, re, mi, fa, sol, la': no seventh syllable exists. The French nomenclature is ut = C, ré = D, mi = E, fa = F, sol = G, la = A, si = B; the Italian is the same except do = C, re = D.

Time signatures

Time signatures in the text should appear cased on one line as 2/4 and not on two lines as

$$\frac{2}{4}$$

The latter style may mean that the size of type must often be too greatly reduced. Simple examples of figured bass can be given as: 'the 6–4 chord' (with an en rule), but a complicated example, such as

$$7\flat$$
$$5$$
$$4\text{–}3$$

needs to be left as here, as there is no satisfactory way of reducing it. Warn the typesetter of places where this occurs (a few sample places if throughout), as it is typographically awkward to have extra-deep vertical matter in the body of a text.

US terminology

US terminology for notes (and *measure* for *bar* in formal contexts) should be retained in works by US authors, as these terms are becoming standard in Britain. Their equivalent names are as follows:

whole note	semibreve
half note	minim
quarter note	crotchet
eighth note	quaver
sixteenth note	semiquaver
thirty-second note	demisemiquaver
sixty-fourth note	hemidemisemiquaver
etc.	

All other stylistic Americanisms should be converted to British English, unless otherwise agreed with the editor.

13.6 **Plays**

. . . .

13.6.1 **General considerations**

Plays should begin on recto pages; acts begin on new pages, recto or verso; scenes are run on. Sometimes the title and list of characters will appear together on the recto, and sometimes the characters will be on the verso of the title, facing the text. Running headlines should include act and scene numbers, usually across the inner shoulders.

Extracts from plays may be treated purely as prose or poetry extracts, with no strict regard given to layout, spacing, or characters' names. While in general the common modern form still reflects eighteenth-century printing style, books of plays vary considerably in presentation, and any sensible pattern is acceptable if consistently applied. A facsimile of an original text, however, must follow precisely the style of speakers' names, indentations, and so on.

13.6.2 Layout

Set characters' names distinctively in entrances, stage directions, and exits, usually in roman even small capitals, letter-spaced. No principles govern how or when names are abbreviated, though it tends to be a consequence of long names or narrow measure.

Unless reproducing a previous edition, set speakers' names in letter-spaced even small capitals, ranged full left; they may end in a full point, though increasingly they do not. In verse plays, run the speaker's name into the first line of dialogue and indent the remainder of dialogue 1 em and turnovers 2 ems. In prose plays, range speakers' names full left, with turnovers indented 1 em.

Where isolated verse such as a song occurs in a prose play it should be centred, following the rules for poetry. It is spaced from prose only if it is a song with a heading. When speakers' names are included in verse play extracts, the verse is not centred, but follows the speaker's name (usually given in small capitals) after an em space; subsequent lines by the same speaker start indented 1 em from the left. Ordinarily such extracts omit all stage directions, unless relevant to the discussion at hand. Where prose and verse alternate in a play, such as *Twelfth Night*, the verse and its speakers' names should be indented or full out to match the style of the prose.

13.6.3 Stage directions

Set exits full right in capital and lower-case italic, with one opening square bracket. Set entrances centred and italic with an initial capital. Entrances and exits tend not to end in full points even if complete sentences, though they do if ending in an abbreviation.

ANTIGONUS.   Well may I get aboard. This is the chase.
I am gone for ever!   [*Exit, pursued by a bear*

> *Enter an Old Shepherd*
>
> CHARLES.   It is well, my friend. Farewell!   [*Exeunt R.*

Set stage directions between the speaker's name and the first word of speech in lower-case italic, without a full point, in square brackets:

> JOHN [*eagerly*]. Do come, by all means.

Set stage directions in the middle of speech in italic with an initial capital, in square brackets. There is no full point if it is not a complete sentence:

> JAMES. Most unpleasant! [*Thunderclap*] Hm! Now we're in for it.

Set end-of-line directions ranged full right, preceded by one square bracket:

> JOHN. Step aside with me, my love.
>   Thou shalt hear my secret wish.   [*Leads her to the right*
> MARGARET. Master, wilt thou trifle yet?
>   Can I believe thou'rt in earnest?

The text measure or length of direction may make it impossible to fit the direction on the appropriate line or turn line. If the stage direction leads on specifically from a character's action, then it is ranged full right as before, on the text line:

> LADY CHILTERN [*with mock indignation*]. Never bonnets, never!
>   [*Lady Chiltern goes out through the door leading to her boudoir*

Note that a stage direction cannot 'nest' on the same short line with the next character's speech, as this would obscure to whom the direction relates.

A stage direction that breaks from the action can be centred on the measure. As its position is sufficiently removed from the dialogue, it does not need an opening bracket—though one is often retained regardless:

> SIR ROBERT. Egad! Is this a lardycake I see before me?
>   [*He startles as the door opens suddenly behind him*

If the direction is longer than the space of the measure, indent the first line 2 ems, with turn lines set to full measure.

>   [*Goes to the corner of the room and pours out a glass of water. While his back is turned Mrs Cheveley steals Lady Chiltern's letter. When Lord Goring returns with the glass she refuses it with a gesture.*

13.6.4 **Complex lines**

Particularly in verse plays, a single line is sometimes made up of the speeches of more than one character, set as more than one line of type. Nevertheless this counts as one line, and demands special treatment.

Align such parts of a line with a space of a line clear to the right of the previous part's end, repeating as necessary.

> PROSPERO For thou must now know farther.
>
> MIRANDA You have often
> Begun to tell me what I am, but stopped
> And left me to a bootless inquisition,
> Concluding 'Stay; not yet'.
>
> PROSPERO The hour's now come.
> The very minute bids thee ope thine ear,
> Obey, and be attentive.

Exceptionally, a single line may be broken several times, as in the following example:

> KING JOHN Death.
>
> HUBERT My lord.
>
> KING JOHN A grave.
>
> HUBERT He shall not live.
>
> KING JOHN Enough.

If the second (or third) part of the line is too long to allow this, the part should be set full right and allowed to run back under the first (or second) part as necessary: turnovers to these parts must be avoided.

13.6.5 **Line numbering**

Lines are numbered in fives, as for poetry. Set the figures on the right-hand edge within the text measure if verse, outside if prose. In plays combining verse and prose, choose one style based on whichever form predominates.

Take care in numbering verse plays where one line of dialogue comprises several lines of type. (The second example above, though five lines, is only one line of verse.) The brackets and line numbers in the following examples illustrate the grouping of typographic lines into metrical lines:

> CAM. Business, my lord! I think most understand (1)
> Bohemia stays here longer.
>
> LEON. Ha! (2)
> CAM. Stays here longer.
>
> LEON. Ay, but why? (3)
>
> CAM. To satisfy your highness and the entreaties (4)
> Of our most gracious mistress. (5)
> LEON. Satisfy!
>
> The entreaties of your mistress! satisfy! (6)

13.6.6 **Styling plays and their references**

When citing the full reference, in text or in notes, the form should be for example '2 *Henry IV*, IV. ii. 86', '*Twelfth Night*, I. v. 289', '*Le Bourgeois Gentilhomme*, II. iv'. The same format is followed when citing a reference without the play's title.

When citing in text all or part of a reference without the play's title, the form is 'Act II, Scene iii, line 4'. Note that the act reference is given in full capitals, rather than the small capitals it would have were it part of a short reference. 'Act' and 'Scene' should have initial capitals if a number follows; 'line' is always lower-case. The logic is that act and scene are assumed to be part of the play's actual structure, whereas the line count is—like a page reference—a function only of typographic setting. (This is especially true in prose plays, where line numbers may vary from edition to edition.)

Capitalizing 'Act' and 'Scene' may appear to run counter to the rule stating that references to elements in another work (volume, part, chapter, section) must be lower case. However, this convention is structured only to avoid confusion between a chapter of another person's work and a Chapter of the work being read. It is assumed that no confusion can result with 'Act' or 'Scene', as a work mentioning these elements would not make use of such elements itself. Keeping 'line' lower-case follows the precedent set by page references.

References cited in the course of running text are styled differently from those cited as short references (either as notes or as parenthetical asides). In running text, a book or act number given in capital roman numerals should be in full capitals, not small capitals, because the capitals used for the numeral should match the height of the capital letter *A* or *B* of *Act* or *Book*. The apparent inconsistency between the two forms is correct, and should not be normalized. Consider the following:

> In Book III he introduces a new character (iii. 20–3).
>
> In Act IV, Scene ii, this character speaks for the first time (IV. ii. 20)
>
> In Act II, Scene iii contains the second scene within that one act in which the mood shifts abruptly (II. iii. 2–4).

The context may fix variations on this rule: if references lacking only the title are frequently cited in running text, the form 'II. iii. 4' may be used, again with full-capital roman numerals for acts. (Two or more together are separated by a semicolon: 'II. iii. 4; V. vi. 7'.) However, in such instances it is most likely that two elements only will be paired: either act with scene or scene with line. In this case, use forms like 'In Act II, Scene iii he says...' or 'In Scene iii, line 4 he says...'.

Some twentieth-century plays will have dispensed with roman numerals for acts, such as 'Act 2, Scene 3, line 4'. It is acceptable to keep that style, though it makes no difference to the hierarchy of elements or to their representation. (This is also true for conventions governing classical texts and for the *Oxford Shakespeare* series, which subscribes to a style very different from that in other OUP books.) In classical texts it is no longer usual to cite by act and scene; continuous lineation is preferred.

Shakespearian references

It is notoriously easy to misquote well-known passages from Shakespeare, since familiarity can breed a certain contempt for checking. As it is a simple matter to verify such passages, authors are encouraged to scrutinize their quotations before their readers do.

The use by scholars and editors of different earlier editions and variant readings has generated many collections with divergent spellings, punctuation, line numbers, and line breaks. In passing references it is generally unnecessary to cite from which edition an extract was drawn; however, specialist texts should state the edition used at the outset, and use that edition consistently. The standard Oxford edition is Stanley Wells and Gary Taylor (gen. eds.), *The Complete Works* (OUP, 1986, compact edn., 1988). (The convention employed within it of using all-arabic for references to acts and scenes is not mandatory in general contexts.)

No single accepted model exists for abbreviating the titles of Shakespeare's plays and poems, although in many cases the standard modern form by which the work is commonly known may be thought to be abbreviated already, since the complete original titles are often much longer. For example, *The First Part of the Contention of the Two Famous Houses of York and Lancaster* is best known as *The Second Part of King Henry VI*, and *The Comical History of the Merchant of Venice, or Otherwise Called the Jew of Venice* as *The Merchant of Venice*.

At a fundamental level, any abbreviation is acceptable providing it is unambiguous and readily intelligible; however, authors are encouraged to implement one of the more commonly found forms used by scholars. One such form (below, column two) is derived from those employed in the *Shorter Oxford English Dictionary* and the *Oxford English Dictionary*; the second (column three) is that specified for the Oxford editions series. A still shorter form (column four) is available, which is useful in marginal or narrow-measure citations, in texts (such as reference books) where space is at a premium, and in the references of specialist texts where familiarity with the conventions is assumed. This last form is derived ultimately from the forms used by C. T. Onions in his *Shakespeare Glossary* (OUP, 3rd edn., 1986). As the longer abbreviations—especially those in column three—function almost as nicknames, authors are encouraged in formal writing to employ the fuller standard modern titles. Abbreviations should be confined to references and peripheral matter; the readership determines which form is chosen, with the shortest form preferred for scholarly texts and the longer preferred for more general texts.

TITLE OF WORK	STANDARD ABBREVIATIONS		SHORT ABBREV.
All's Well that Ends Well	All's Well	All's Well	AWW
Antony and Cleopatra	Ant. & Cl.	Antony	Ant.
As You Like It	AYL	As You Like It	AYL
The Comedy of Errors	Com. Err.	Errors	Err.
Coriolanus	Cor(iol).	Coriolanus	Cor.
Cymbeline	Cymb.	Cymbeline	Cym.
Hamlet	Ham(l).	Hamlet	Ham.
The First Part of King Henry IV	1 Hen. IV	1 Henry IV	1H4
The Second Part of King Henry IV	2 Hen. IV	2 Henry IV	2H4
The Life of King Henry V	Hen. V	Henry V	H5
The First Part of King Henry VI	1 Hen. VI	1 Henry VI	1H6
The Second Part of King Henry VI	2 Hen. VI	2 Henry VI (Contention)	2H6
The Third Part of King Henry VI	3 Hen. VI	3 Henry VI (True Tragedy)	3H6
The Famous History of the Life of King Henry VIII	Hen. VIII	Henry VIII (All Is True)	H8
The Life and Death of King John	(K.) John	K. John	Jn.
Julius Caesar	Jul. (Caes.)	Caesar	JC
King Lear	Lear	Lear	Lr.
A Lover's Complaint	Compl.	Complaint	LC
Love's Labour's Lost	LLL	LLL	LLL
Macbeth	Macb.	Macbeth	Mac.
Measure for Measure	Meas. for M.	Measure	MM
The Merchant of Venice	Merch. V.	Merchant	MV
The Merry Wives of Windsor	Merry W.	Merry Wives	Wiv.
A Midsummer Night's Dream	Mids. N. (D.)	Dream	MND
Much Ado about Nothing	Much Ado	Much Ado	Ado
Othello	Oth.	Othello	Oth.
Pericles	Per.	Pericles	Per.
The Passionate Pilgrim	Pilgr.	P. Pilgrim	PP
The Phoenix and the Turtle	Phoenix	Phoenix	Ph.T.
The Rape of Lucrece	Lucr.	Lucrece	Luc.
The Tragedy of King Richard II	Rich. II	Richard II	R2
The Tragedy of King Richard III	Rich. III	Richard III	R3
Romeo and Juliet	Rom. & Jul.	Romeo	Rom.
Sonnets	Sonn.	Sonnets	Son.
The Taming of the Shrew	Tam. Shr.	Shrew	Shr.
The Tempest	Temp.	Tempest	Tmp.
Timon of Athens	Timon	Timon	Tim.

Titus Andronicus	*Tit. A.*	*Titus*	*Tit.*
Troilus and Cressida	*Tr. & Cr.*	*Troilus*	*Tro.*
Twelfth Night	*Twel. N.*	*Twelfth Night*	*TN*
The Two Gentlemen of Verona	*Two Gent.*	*Two Gentlemen*	*TGV*
The Two Noble Kinsmen	*Two Noble K.*	*Kinsmen*	*TNK*
Venus and Adonis	*Ven. & Ad.*	*Venus*	*Ven.*
The Winter's Tale	*Wint. T.*	*Winter's Tale*	*WT*

Some authors also use 'F1' and 'F2' to mean the First Folio and Second Folio respectively, and 'Q' to mean the Quarto edition.

For guidelines on styling plays in French and Russian *see* **11.20.3, 11.38.10**.

13.7 **Poetry**

13.7.1 **Setting**

A book of poetry, or a play with songs interspersed with the prose, uses full-size type for the poetry. In other contexts, verse quotations (including blank verse) should be set in small type, one size down from text size, and centred on the longest line on each page. If that line is disproportionally long, the text should be centred optically. This can be achieved by striking an average of the longest lines, the aim being to secure a balance of 'white' on the final page. In a book of poems it is common to centre each poem individually, page by page.

Editors should flag displayed verse quotations on typescript with a vertical line in the margin, running from the first to the last line of the quotation. The line may be colour-coded (typically red for displayed poetry, green for displayed prose), or labelled with a mark-up code.

Turnovers in general should be indented 1 em more than the poem's greatest indentation; this must be adjusted to suit the metre of the verse where necessary, or to follow the poet's original concrete structure.

When poetry has to run on to another page, typesetters should avoid splitting short stanzas by carrying part of a stanza on to the next page. Do not separate two paired lines, such as consecutive rhyming lines. Longer stanzas are more likely to need splitting: otherwise the potentially large amount of white space at the bottom of the page may appear to indicate the poem's premature end, when in fact the next stanza continues overleaf.

When lines of poetry are numbered (e.g. in fives), the numbers are to appear on the right-hand edge within the text measure, regardless of whether the page is recto or verso. No points follow the numbers. If a line is too long to allow the number to be inserted, then the next line or, if that is too long as well, the preceding line should be numbered instead. Editors should instruct typesetters accordingly.

13.7.2 In-text quotations

Verse quotations run in with (prose) text are treated like any other quoted matter. It is OUP's preference to indicate the division between each line by a vertical (|) rather than a solidus (/), with a space either side: ''Twas brillig, and the slithy toves | Did gyre and gimble in the wabe; | All mimsy were the borogroves | And the mome raths outgrabe.' When set, the vertical must not start a new turn line (*see also* **5.12.2**).

13.7.3 Displayed quotations

Displayed poetry usually follows the same rules for any displayed text, with no extra space between lines—though unlike prose, which normally requires sixty words or more before being displayed, poetic quotations of only a line or two can be displayed. Nevertheless avoid displaying poetry in notes, especially footnotes (*see* **13.7.8**).

Where displayed poetic quotations are interspersed with prose text and more than one quotation falls on a page, each quotation should be centred separately. However, interspersing too many short displayed lines produces a ragged effect on the printed page, so if the quotations are successive extracts from the same poem, it is usually desirable to have a common indentation for all on each page.

Generally, a line will range on the left with the line(s) with which it rhymes. But where a poem's indentation clearly varies the copy *must* be followed: this is particularly true for some modern poetry, where correct spacing in reproduction forms part of the copyright. In this instance, it is useful to provide the typesetter with photocopies of the original to work from.

Sense breaks between stanzas or groups of lines may be indicated in several ways. A common convention is to use a line of white space, although in books of poetry, ornaments may be used depending on the measure and overall design of the work. When reproducing verse in which a line of medial points has been used to indicate a sense break, distinguish this from a signal that matter has been omitted, either by replacing the dots by a line of white space or, where it is important to reproduce the style of the original, by adding a 3-point space above and below the line of dots (*see also* **13.7.5**).

In Old English manuscripts alliterative verse was run on like prose, even when Latin verse in the same manuscripts was set out line by line. It is therefore conventional to print it with extra space between half-lines.

13.7.4 **Punctuation**

A displayed poetic quotation does not take quotation marks unless they form part of the original quotation; use single quotation marks in such cases.

> 'Beware the Jabberwock, my son!
>   The jaws that bite, the claws that catch!
> Beware the Jubjub bird, and shun
>   The frumious Bandersnatch!'

When run on in (prose) text, however, the quotation is enclosed in single quotation marks, and a quotation within it is enclosed in double quotation marks.

A grave-accented *è* may be used to show that an otherwise mute syllable is to be separately pronounced, as *bell-swarmèd, lark-charmèd, long-leggèd*.

Do not automatically impose capitals at the beginnings of lines: modern verse sometimes has none. In Greek and Latin verse it is usual to capitalize only the first word of each paragraph.

13.7.5 **Omitted matter**

In running text, the omission of matter of any length within a verse quotation is indicated by a 3–point ellipsis, as with prose (*see* **5.7**). The ellipsis can be set within square brackets to distinguish it from the poet's own points of suspension—if any.

In displayed verse, the omission of one or more lines from the original is indicated by a row of medial points set on the next line (no extra vertical space), separated by 2 ems, in which the first and last points fall 2 ems inside the measure of the longest line (*see also* **13.7.3**). The distinction between an authorial ellipsis (a sense break) and an editorial ellipsis (an omission of text) can be clarified by including stanza or line numbers in the source. The omission of matter in the original poem, as in the case of an incomplete or damaged text, can be shown by setting three medial points in square brackets, full left within the measure in place of the omitted stanza(s) or line(s).

13.7.6 **Sources**

If there is sufficient room, a short source—such as a bare book/canto/ line number, or short title—can be placed in parentheses on the same line as the last line of verse. The reference begins 1 em to the *right* of the end of the quotation's longest line.

> The world was all before them, where to choose
> Their place of rest, and providence their guide:
> They hand in hand with wandering steps and slow
> Through Eden took their solitary way.   (xii. 646–9)

(If the longest line is the last line, the source is not taken into account when centring the quotation.) If the source is longer, incorporating for example title, book, and line numbers, place the source on the next line down (no extra space), ranged to the right with the quotation's longest line.

> They hand in hand with wandering steps and slow
> Through Eden took their solitary way.
>   (*Paradise Lost*, xii. 646–9)

In blank-verse extracts starting with a part line, range the end of the source reference on the next full line, not the longest line:

> Speak,
> How low am I? I am not yet so low
> But that my nails can reach unto thine eyes.
>   (*MND* III. ii. 298–9)

13.7.7 **Verse plays**

For guidance on setting out verse plays *see* **13.6.4**.

13.7.8 **In footnotes and endnotes**

Poetic quotations in footnotes ideally should be run on regardless of length, so as to keep footnote height to a minimum: too many lines of poetry in one footnote is less an argument that the quotation should be displayed than an indication that the quotation should be either worked into the text or dispensed with. Where there is no alternative to display, set the matter in the same size type as the footnote, separated from the note's text by a variable half-line space above and below.

Endnotes can accommodate displayed poetic quotations more easily than footnotes, since their format allows for greater vertical space: set these one size down from endnote size, separated from the note's text by a variable half-line space above and below.

13.7.9 **Prosodic notation**

Several systems of graphic notation exist in prosody, employing diacritics, symbols, letters, numbers, schematic formulae, or a combination of these.

Most often diacritical marks are used, either medially by themselves, as representative of a type, or superscript, in combination with the text or transcriptions they relate to. Those used alone may be set larger than those used with text. Metrical units normally will be scanned either in terms of long and short or strong and weak syllables, so that the trochee is indicated in Latin as ˘ – (*antĕ*) and in English as ʹˣ (*sílver*). Be careful that any prosodic notation cannot be confused with diacritics that form part of the text itself, and in setting ensure that they do not clash with them. Common marks are as follows:

    acute (ʹ) for primary stress

    x or cross (ˣ) for weak or no stress

    solidus (/) for any general stress or ictus

    grave (ˋ) for secondary or tertiary stress

    macron (ˉ) for a long syllable

    breve (˘) for a short syllable or weak stress

    vertical (|) for a division between feet

    double vertical (||) for a caesura or major pause within a metrical foot

    superscript dot (˙) above or medial dot (·) following a symbol for relative
       sound lengths

    colon (:) for protracted durations

    circumflex or caret (ˆ) or comma (,) for a pause, omission, or secondary stress

A circumflex coupled with a macron, breve, or one or more dots may be used to indicate relative durations of pauses.

Rhythmic analysis may be indicated through upper- and lower-case roman letters (G, L, M, N, R; F, f, S, o, l, P, p). Another scansion system, based on a lower-case *0*, has the markings o, ó, ò, ȯ, õ, ő, ⸍, and ˄.

In the graphic scansion of Greek, Latin, or Arabic quantitative verse, the macron (–) indicates a long syllable and the breve (˘) a short syllable. An ˣ denotes a syllable of indifferent quantity,   a long that may be resolved into two breves, and   two breves that may be contracted into a long.

Degrees of openness of juncture may use the symbols + | || #. Numbers (1–6) may be used for pitch levels, or position or sequence of stress. Musical notation—either whole or in part—is occasionally used.

Rhyme schemes in stanzas may be indicated by lower-case italic letters, for example *aabba* for a limerick and *ababcdcdefefgg* for a Shakespearian sonnet; subscript numbers may show the number of feet in each line, such as $a_4b_3aa_4b_3$ for the Coleridgean stanza.

13.8 **Sacred works: Christian, Jewish, and Muslim**

13.8.1 **The Bible**

13.8.1.1 **General considerations**

Formerly, biblical references to chapters and verses used lower-case roman numerals for chapter, followed by a full point, space, and verse number in arabic (ii. 34). Though that style is still found, modern practice is to use arabic numbers for the chapter as well, and a colon and space rather than the full point and space (2: 34). Among other benefits, this practice avoids the former possible confusion between roman numerals and the abbreviations for *verse* (v.) and *verses* (vv.).

Set the names of the books of the Bible in roman type but not in quotation marks. Spell out the names in text when used alone, or in discursive or general contexts when only the chapter follows (Ecclesiastes 12); abbreviate names in scholarly contexts, or when chapter and verse follow (Eccles. 12: 12). Elide references to verse numbers within a chapter with an en rule (Ecclesiasticus 5: 15–16) or list them individually with commas (Matt. 5: 3, 14, 37). Divide references in different chapters by semicolons (Acts 17: 18; 26: 24–5); separate extents between chapters by an en rule (Job 1: 6–3: 4).

In specialist works, or in contexts such as references within parentheses or notes, names of the books of the Bible may be abbreviated in various ways, depending on context and available space. The most truncated abbreviations are used exclusively in marginal or narrow tabular matter.

Biblical references vary according to the source, particularly in the arrangement of the Ten Commandments and Apocrypha. The Bible traditionally used in Anglican worship, called the Authorized Version (AV), is an English translation of the Bible made in 1611. The Vulgate, prepared mainly by St Jerome in the late fourth century, was the standard Latin version of both the Old Testament (OT) and New Testament (NT), and the approved Bible of the Roman Catholic Church. The Roman Catholic Bible was translated from the Latin Vulgate and revised in 1592 (NT) and 1609 (OT).

The Septuagint (LXX) is the standard Greek version of the Old Testament, originally made by the Jews of Alexandria but now used (in Greek or in translation) by the Orthodox churches. Neither Septuagint nor Vulgate recognizes the distinction between 'Old Testament' and 'Apocrypha' made by Protestants (who in the matter of biblical translations include the Church of England).

The AV's versions of Greek forms for Hebrew proper nouns in books translated from the Greek (Apocrypha, NT) have long been obsolete except in direct quotation, and should not be followed or imposed elsewhere.

In translating biblical quotations in Latin authors, the standard English Protestant or non-denominational versions—even the Roman Catholic Jerusalem Bible—will often be found to presuppose a different text from that used in the text to be translated. In medieval and modern writing (though not necessarily in the Latin Fathers), this will normally be taken from the Vulgate. The recognized English translations are Richard Challoner's revision of the Rheims–Douay version and the more modern version by Ronald Knox; translators should either follow one of these or make their own translation of the cited passage.

13.8.1.2 Old Testament (Authorized Version)

Pentateuch

Genesis	Gen.
Exodus	Exod.
Leviticus	Lev.
Numbers	Num.
Deuteronomy	Deut.

These five books are collectively known as the Pentateuch (Five Volumes), or the books of Moses: in German they are often called the first to fifth book of Moses, and so abbreviated (e.g. '4. Mos.').

Historical books

Joshua	Josh.	
Judges	Judg.	
Ruth	Ruth	
1 Samuel	1 Sam.	(*LXX* 1 Kingdoms, *Vulg.* 1 Kings)
2 Samuel	2 Sam.	(*LXX* 2 Kingdoms, *Vulg.* 2 Kings)
1 Kings	1 Kgs.	(*LXX* 3 Kingdoms, *Vulg.* 3 Kings)
2 Kings	2 Kgs.	(*LXX* 4 Kingdoms, *Vulg.* 4 Kings)

Abbreviate Kingdoms as 'Kgdms.'; in Vulgate references 'Reg.' may be accepted instead of 'Kgs.'; '3 Kgdms.' is appreciably shorter than '1 Kgs.'/ '3 Reg.'

1 Chronicles	1 Chr.
2 Chronicles	2 Chr.

The abbreviation 'Paral.' (for Paralipomenon, 'Of Things Omitted', the Septuagint and Vulgate name of the books) should be used only when the reader is expected to consult a Greek or Latin Bible.

Ezra	Ezra	(*LXX* 2 Esdras 1–10, *Vulg.* 1 Esdras)

Nehemiah	Neh.	(*LXX* 2 Esdras 11–23, *Vulg.* 2 Esdras)
Esther	Esther	

(*See also* **13.8.1.3**.)

Didactic books

Job	Job
Psalms	Ps. (pl. Pss.)

The numbering of the psalms differs in the Septuagint and the Vulgate: Ps. 9 corresponds to Pss. 9 and 10 of the Jewish and Protestant psalters; thereafter the LXX and Vulgate psalm numbers remain one lower than the Jewish and Protestant reckoning until Pss. 146–7, which correspond to Ps. 147 in the latter. Furthermore, the Vulgate frequently counts a psalm's heading as its first verse, thus raising subsequent verse numbers by 1. The Septuagint contains an additional psalm, sometimes called Ps. 151. Authors must therefore check their source rather than risk introducing errors by miscalculation.

Proverbs	Prov.
Ecclesiastes	Eccles.

Some biblical scholars prefer the abbreviation 'Qo.', from the Hebrew name Qōhelet; editors should accept this if it is encountered in copy.

Song of Songs (*or* Song of Solomon)	S. of S.	(*Also called* Canticles)

'Cant.' is acceptable in reference to LXX or the Vulgate.

Prophetical books: major and minor prophets

The major prophets are

Isaiah	Isa.
Jeremiah	Jer.

The order of chapters in the Septuagint version of this book varies considerably from that in the Hebrew Bible, which is followed by the Vulgate and Protestant versions; hence 'LXX' in Septuagint references should be left even if no Greek is quoted.

Lamentations	Lam.
Ezekiel	Ezek.
Daniel	Dan.

(*See also* **13.8.1.3**.) The Septuagint version was usually replaced by that of Theodotion, represented by the symbol θ.

The minor prophets are

Hosea	Hos.	(*LXX*, *Vulg.* Osee)
Joel	Joel	
Amos	Amos	
Obadiah	Obad.	(*LXX*, *Vulg.* Abdias)
Jonah	Jonah	

Micah	Mic.	(*LXX, Vulg.* Michaeas)
Nahum	Nahum	
Habakkuk	Hab.	(*LXX* Ambakoum, *Vulg.* Habacuc)
Zephaniah	Zeph.	(*LXX, Vulg.* Sophonias)
Haggai	Hag.	(*LXX, Vulg.* Aggaeas)
Zechariah	Zech.	(*LXX, Vulg.* Zacharias)
Malachi	Mal.	

NB: In English the penultimate book is Zechariah, not Zech-.

The Hebrew Bible contains the same books, but in a different arrangement. The Torah has Genesis, Exodus, Leviticus, Numbers, Deuteronomy; Prophets has Joshua, Judges, Samuel, Kings, Isaiah, Jeremiah, Ezekiel, the Twelve; Writings has Psalms, Proverbs, Job, Song of Songs, Ruth, Lamentations, Ecclesiastes, Esther, Daniel, Ezra, Nehemiah, Chronicles. Though nowadays divided as in Christian Bibles, Samuel, Kings, and Chronicles were (and still may be) traditionally counted as one book; similarly Ezra–Nehemiah.

13.8.1.3 Apocrypha

In the Septuagint and Vulgate, the Apocrypha are constituent parts of the Old Testament. The term *apocrypha* means 'hidden away', implying that the texts in question were secret writings known only to the favoured few, but by its use for works of dubious authority it has acquired the sense of 'spurious'. The word used by those who accept some or all of these books as Scripture is *deuterocanonical* ('of the second canon'), *apocrypha* being reserved for texts that no one accepts as Scripture such as the Testaments of the Twelve Patriarchs, the books of Enoch, and the *Protevangelium of James* (sometimes called *pseudepigrapha*, 'works falsely inscribed').

1 Esdras	1 Esdr.	(*LXX* 1 Esdras, *Vulg.* 3 Esdras)
2 Esdras	2 Esdr.	(*not in LXX*; *Vulg.* 4 Esdras)

Sometimes called '3 and 4 Ezra' by biblical scholars; this usage should be accepted. These books are not included in the Roman Catholic canon of Scripture, but are printed in Vulgate Bibles 'so that they might not altogether perish'.

Tobit	Tobit

The corresponding book in the Vulgate (which underlies e.g. paintings of Tobias and the Angel) is called 'Tobias'; it represents a different recension, so that references are not interchangeable.

Judith	Judith
Rest of Esther	Rest of Esth.

These are the parts of Esther found in the Septuagint but not in the Hebrew original. In LXX they are an integral part of the text; in the Vulgate they are added as an appendix (10: 4–16: 24), in English Bibles treated as a separate book, abbreviated 'Rest of Esth.'

Wisdom	Wis.	
Ecclesiasticus	Ecclus.	(*LXX* Wisdom of Jesus the Son of Sirach)

Some biblical scholars prefer the abbreviation 'Sir.', which should be accepted if encountered in copy. The book is also known as 'Sirach'; the name 'Ecclesiasticus' is never used outside the Western churches. The author is normally known as Ben Sira.

Baruch	Baruch
Song of the Three Children	S. of III Ch.

Corresponds to LXX and Vulg. Dan. 3: 24–90.

Susanna	Sus.	(= Vulg. Dan. 13)
Bel and the Dragon	Bel & Dr.	(= Vulg. Dan. 14)
Prayer of Manasses	Pr. of Man.	(= LXX Odes 12)
(in modern versions Manasseh)		

Included in modern editions of the Vulgate on same footing as 3 and 4 Esdras.

1 Maccabees	1 Macc.
2 Maccabees	2 Macc.

13.8.1.4   Septuagint and Vulgate

The Septuagint contains two further books of Maccabees and some other works besides those listed above (all included in the Oxford Annotated Bible). The standard scholarly edition of the Septuagint presents the Old Testament in the following order (English forms of names used for convenience):

> Genesis, Exodus, Leviticus, Numbers, Deuteronomy, Joshua, Judges, Ruth, 1–4 Kingdoms, 1–2 Chronicles, 1 Esdras, 2 Esdras [= Ezra–Nehemiah], Esther, Judith, Tobit, 1–4 Maccabees, Psalms, Odes, Proverbs, Ecclesiastes, Song of Songs, Job, Wisdom, Sirach, Psalms of Solomon, Hosea, Amos, Micah, Joel, Obadiah, Jonah, Nahum, Habakkuk, Zephaniah, Haggai, Zechariah, Malachi, Isaiah, Jeremiah, Baruch, Lamentations, Epistle of Jeremy (= Vulg. Baruch 6), Ezekiel, Susanna, Daniel, Bel and the Dragon

The Vulgate order is as follows:

> Genesis, Exodus, Leviticus, Numbers, Deuteronomy, Joshua, Judges, Ruth, 1–4 Kings, 1–2 Chronicles, 1–2 Esdras [= Ezra–Nehemiah], Tobias, Judith, Esther, Job, Psalms, Proverbs, Ecclesiastes, Song of Songs, Wisdom, Ecclesiasticus, Isaiah, Jeremiah, Lamentations, Baruch, Ezekiel, Daniel, Hosea, Joel, Amos, Obadiah, Jonah, Micah, Nahum, Habakkuk, Zephaniah, Haggai, Zechariah, Malachi, 1–2 Maccabees

In the Vulgate the Prayer of Manasses and 3 and 4 Esdras are added as an appendix after the New Testament. If it is desired to direct the reader specifically to the Vulgate, the books may be abbreviated as follows:

Gen. Exod. Lev. Num. Deut. Jos. Judic. Ruth I–IV Reg. I–II Paral. I–II Esd. Tobias Judith Esth. Job Ps. Prov. Eccle. Cant. Sap. Eccli. Isa. Jer. Lam. [or Threni] Baruch Ezech. Daniel Osee Joel Amos Abd. Jonas Mich. Naum Hab. Soph. Agg. Zach. Mal. I–II Mach.

Matt. Marc. Luc. Joh. Acta Rom. I–II Cor. Gal. Eph. Phil. Col. I–II Thess. I–II Tim. Titus Philem. Heb. Jac. I–II Pet. I–III Joh. Judas Apoc.

Or. Man. III–IV Esd.

In narrow measure or marginal references arabic figures are restored to save space:

Gn Ex Lv Nm Dt Js Jc Rt 1–4 Rg 1–2 Par 1–2 Esd Tb Jdt Est Jb Ps Pro Ec Cn Sap Ecli [or Si] Is Jr Lam Bar Ez Dn Os Jl Am Ab Jn Mic Na Hab So Ag Zc Ml 1–2 Mac

Mt Mc Lc Jo Ac Rm 1–2 Cor Gal Eph Ph Col 1–2 Th 1–2 Tm Tt Phm Heb Jc 1–2 Pt 1–3 Jo Ju Ap

Man 3–4 Esd

13.8.1.5 New Testament

Matthew	Matt.	1 Timothy	1 Tim.
Mark	Mark	2 Timothy	2 Tim.
Luke	Luke	Titus	Titus
John	John	Philemon	Philem.
Acts of the Apostles	Acts	Hebrews	Heb.
Romans	Rom.	James	Jas.
1 Corinthians	1 Cor.	1 Peter	1 Pet.
2 Corinthians	2 Cor.	2 Peter	2 Pet.
Galatians	Gal.	1 John	1 John
Ephesians	Eph.	2 John	2 John
Philippians	Phil.	3 John	3 John
Colossians	Col.	Jude	Jude
1 Thessalonians	1 Thess.	Revelation	Rev.
2 Thessalonians	2 Thess.		

The alternative name for Revelation, 'the Apocalypse', is admissible in continuous prose; the reference 'Apoc.' may be preferred in scholarly or non-Protestant contexts. The plural 'Revelations' is incorrect.

13.8.1.6 Indexing and other references

Biblical books should be indexed according to their order in the version of the Bible studied or, failing that, in the order of one of the above lists, *not* alphabetically. (Other versions of the Bible, such as the Gothic New Testament of Ulfila, will have a different order.) When biblical references are intermingled with those from other sources—for example in a work of classical scholarship—it is acceptable to replace the usual form's colon with a full point (Isa. 23. 12). Some writers favour superior figures for the verse (Isa. 23^{12}), but this form should not be imposed unless specifically requested. There is no need to use 'Ibid.' with biblical references, as it is scarcely briefer than any of the books' abbreviations.

References to pseudepigrapha or other works on the fringes of the Bible (e.g. '1 Clement') should be in non-biblical style except in specialist work; but an author's consistent and valid preferences should be respected. Patristic works are cited according to classical, not biblical, conventions: thus St Ignatius' epistle to the Romans will be italic '*Rom.*' in contrast to 'Rom.' for St Paul's.

In narrow measure or marginal references, the following abbreviations may be used:

> Gn Ex Lv Nu Dt Jos Jg Rt 1–2 S 1–2 K 1–2 Ch Ezr Ne Est Jb Ps Pr Qo Sg Is Jr Lm Ezk Dn Ho Jl Am Ob Jon Mi Na Hab Zp Hg Zc Ml
>
> 1–2 Esd Tb Jdt Rest Ws Si Ba Chi Su Bel Man 1–2 M
>
> Mt Mk Lk Jn Ac Rm 1–2 Co Ga Ep Ph Col 1–2 Th 1–2 Tm Tt Phm Heb Jm 1–2 P 1–2 Jn Jude Rv

13.8.2 Jewish scriptures

13.8.2.1 General considerations

In addition to the standard form of citation used for biblical references (e.g. Gen. 12: 8), references may be given in relation to the sections into which the Torah (Pentateuch) has been divided to create the annual cycle of weekly readings in the synagogue, known as *parashot*.

Indexes of scriptural references are arranged in the order of scriptural writings rather than alphabetically. The order of scriptural writings in the Jewish tradition differs from that in Christian traditions regarding the order of the Hebrew Bible:

Genesis	Ezekiel	Psalms
Exodus	Hosea	Proverbs
Leviticus	Joel	Job
Numbers	Amos	Song of Songs
Deuteronomy	Obadiah	Ruth
Joshua	Jonah	Lamentations
Judges	Micah	Ecclesiastes
1 Samuel	Nahum	Esther
2 Samuel	Habakkuk	Daniel
1 Kings	Zephaniah	Ezra
2 Kings	Haggai	Nehemiah
Isaiah	Zechariah	1 Chronicles
Jeremiah	Malachi	2 Chronicles

Similarly, do not alphabetize indexes of references to the fifty-four *parashot* into which the Pentateuch is subdivided in the Jewish tradition.

13.8.2.2 The Torah

The Torah is the Jewish term for the Pentateuch; it also refers to a scroll containing the Torah, or the will of God as revealed in Mosaic law. Its subdivisions are as follows:

Bereshit (Genesis)

Bereshit 1: 1–6: 8

Noah 6: 9–11: 32

Lekh lekha 12: 1–17: 27

Vayera 18: 1–22: 24

Hayei Sarah 23: 1–25: 18

Toledot 25: 19–28: 9

Vayetsé 28: 10–32: 3

Vayishlach 32: 4–36: 43

Vayeshev 37: 1–40: 23

Mikets 41: 1–44: 17

Vayigash 44: 18–47: 27

Vayehi 47: 28–50: 26

Shemot (Exodus)

Shemot 1: 1–6: 1

Va'era 6: 2–9: 35

Bo 10: 1–13: 16

Beshalah 13: 17–17: 16

Yitro 18: 1–20: 23

Mishpatim 21: 1–24: 18

Terumah 25: 1–27: 19

Tetsaveh 27: 20–30: 10

Ki tisa 30: 11–34: 35

Vayakhel 35: 1–38: 20

Pekudei 38: 21–40: 38

Vayikra (Leviticus)

Vayikra 1: 1–5: 26

Tsav 6: 1–8: 36

Shemini 9: 1–11: 47

Tazria 12: 1–13: 59

Metsora 14: 1–15: 33

Aharei mot 16: 1–18: 30

Kedoshim 19: 1–20: 27

Emor 21: 1–24: 23

Behar 25: 1–26: 2

Behukotai 26: 3–27: 34

Bamidbar (Numbers)

Bamidbar 1: 1–4: 20

Naso 4: 21–7: 89

Beha'alotekha 8: 1–12: 16

Shelah lekha 13: 1–15: 41

Korah 16: 1–18: 32

Hukat 19: 1–22: 1

Balak 22: 2–25: 9

Pinhas 25: 10–30: 1

Matot 30: 2–32: 42

Masei 33: 1–36: 13

Devarim (Deuteronomy)

Devarim 1: 1–3: 22

Va'ethanan 3: 23–7: 11

Ekev 7: 12–11: 25

Re'eh 11: 26–16: 17

Shofetim 16: 18–21: 9

Ki tetsé 21: 10–25: 19

Ki tavo 26: 1–29: 8

Nitsavim 29: 9–30: 20

Vayelekh 31: 1–30

Ha'azinu 32: 1–52

Vezot haberakhah 33: 1–34: 12

13.8.2.3 The Talmud

The Talmud is the body of Jewish civil and ceremonial law and legend, comprising the Mishnah and the Gemara. The Talmud exists in two versions: the Babylonian Talmud and the Jerusalem Talmud. In most non-specialist works only the former is cited, so a reference like 'Pes. 42a' is adequate. Where both works are discussed, take care to distinguish between them: this is normally done by a lower-case prefix, for example 'bPes. 42a' or 'jPes. 42a'. The *j* is sometimes rendered *y* (yPes. 42a) for *yerushalmi*, as it is known in Hebrew.

The following list shows the tractates of the Talmud and Mishnah, with abbreviations, which are conventionally not italicized when in scholarly apparatus:

Zera'im

Berakhot	Ber.	*Pe'ah*	Pe'ah
Dema'i	Dem.	*Kila'im*	Kil.
Shevi'it	Shevi.	*Terumot*	Ter.
Ma'aserot	Ma'as.	*Ma'aser sheni*	Ma'as. Sh.
Ḥallah	Ḥal.	*Orlah*	Orl.
Bikurim	Bik.		

Mo'ed

Shabbat	Shab.	*Eruvin*	Eruv.
Pesaḥim	Pes.	*Shekalim*	Shek.
Yoma	Yoma	*Sukkah*	Suk.
Beitzah	Beitz.	*Rosh hashanah*	RH

Ta'anit	Ta'an.	*Megillah*	Meg.
Mo'ed katan	MK	*Hagigah*	Hag.
Nashim			
Yevamot	Yev.	*Ketubot*	Ket.
Nedarim	Ned.	*Nazir*	Naz.
Sotah	Sot.	*Gittin*	Git.
Kiddushin	Kid.		
Nezikin			
Baba kamma	BK	*Baba metzia*	BM
Baba batra	BB	*Sanhedrin*	Sanh.
Makkot	Mak.	*Shevuot*	Shevu.
Eduyot	Eduy.	*Avodah zarah*	Av. Zar.
Avot	Avot	*Horayot*	Hor.
Kodashim			
Zevahim	Zev.	*Menahot*	Men.
Hullin	Hul.	*Bekhorot*	Bek.
Arakhin	Ar.	*Temurah*	Tem.
Keritot	Ker.	*Me'ilah*	Me'il.
Tamid	Tam.	*Middot*	Mid.
Kinnim	Kin.		
Tohorot			
Kelim	Kel.	*Oholot*	Ohol.
Nega'im	Neg.	*Parah*	Par.
Tohorot	Toh.	*Mikva'ot*	Mik.
Niddah	Nid.	*Makhshirin*	Makhsh.
Zavim	Zav.	*Tevul yom*	TY
Yada'im	Yad.	*Uktzin*	Uk.

13.8.2.4 Classical and rabbinic works

For references to classical texts and primary sources, prefer a transliterated title to a translation, as these works are traditionally referred to by their Hebrew titles. Except for a few famous classics, such as Maimonides' *Guide for the Perplexed*, they are indeed not widely known in any other way. The addition of a translation of the title at the first occurrence, or a gloss explaining the nature of the work where the title is too esoteric to be meaningful in translation, is helpful for non-specialist readers.

For references to rabbinic literature, it is conventional to refer to works by title with no mention of the author, since many famous rabbis are in fact known by the titles of their works. This system works well for specialists, but obviously not for generalists; a workable solution is to provide a suitable annotation in the bibliography, or even a cross-reference to the author. The requisite information is to be found in the

'Index' volume of the *Encyclopaedia Judaica*, under 'Abbreviations Used in Rabbinic Literature'. As an adjective *rabbinic* is sufficient, likewise *halakhic*, *talmudic*, *mishnaic*, and *zoharic*; the use of lower-case for the adjectival form of the rabbinic works *Talmud/talmudic* is consistent with, for example, *Bible/biblical*.

Names of the *parashot* occur quite frequently in references to other works, since many rabbinic commentaries relate to them—for example: 'It is instructive to consult the *Even ha'ezer* on the beginning of "Shemot".' On this form of reference note that, as a *parashah* is part of the Bible rather than a complete work in itself, it should be cited in quotation marks and not italicized.

The tendency to append a definite article to the title of rabbinic works is well established. This may be because they are to some extent regarded as holy writings—like *the Bible*, *the Talmud*, and *the Zohar*, for example—or because they are considered standard sources, like 'the' *Encyclopaedia Britannica* or 'the' *OED*. This is acceptable in the text but not in a note; the equivalent reference in a note would read, 'See *Even ha'ezer*, "Shemot", 44*b*.' References to *the Kabbalah* fall into a different category: there is no book by that name, so the definite article is superfluous: *Kabbalah* is the name used to describe the body of knowledge pertaining to Jewish mysticism, so the capital is similarly superfluous.

Correct any reference to one work being a commentary *to* another— which follows the convention in Hebrew—to the standard English usage of one work being a commentary *on* another.

13.8.3 The Koran, Qur'ān

The Koran (in Arabic and specialist contexts Qur'ān), the sacred book of Islam, is written in classical Arabic, and is divided into 114 unequal units. Each unit is called *sūra* (plural *suwar*) in Arabic. The conventional English rendering is 'sura' or 'surah' (plural 'suwar'), but 'chapter' is also found (though the standard Arabic term for a chapter is *bāb*). In turn, each *sūra* is divided into verses.

Every *sūra* is known by an Arabic name; this is sometimes reproduced in English, sometimes translated, for example 'the Cave' for the eighteenth, *ṣūrat al-Kahf*. The more normal form of reference is by number, especially if the verse follows: '*Sūra* 18, v. 45', or simply '18. 45'. (As with biblical references, 'Ibid.' is not used.) References to *suwar* have arabic numbers with a full point and space before the verse number, though the older style of a roman numeral or colon is also found. Except in *Sūra* 9—which uniquely does not begin with the invocation *bi-smi-'llāhi 'l-raḥmāni 'l-raḥīm* 'In the Name of God the Compassionate, the Merciful'—there is a difference in verse numbering according to whether the invocation is or (more usually) is not included in the count.

The order of the *suwar*, though fixed, is not that of revelation; while each declares in its heading whether it is *makkiyya* (Meccan, i.e. before the Hijra) or *madaniyya* (Medinan, i.e. after the Hijra), the comparative chronology of each of the *suwar* is much debated. The English names of the *suwar* may differ radically according to which translation is followed; while scholars will have their own preferences, references within a single work should present a consistent style. The following list incorporates three sets out of the many in use, with alternatives indicated in parentheses and square brackets:

1. The Opening
2. The Cow
3. The Family of Imran
4. (The) Women
5. The (Dinner) Table [The Food]
6. (The) Cattle
7. The Battlements (The Elevated Places)
8. The Spoils (of War) [The Accessions]
9. Repentance (The Immunity)
10. Jonah
11. Hood (The Holy Prophet) [Hud]
12. Joseph (Yusuf)
13. (The) Thunder
14. Abraham
15. El-Hijr (The Rock)
16. The Bee
17. The Night Journey (The Children of Israel) [The Israelites]
18. The Cave
19. Mary (Mariam)
20. Ta Ha
21. The Prophets
22. The Pilgrimage
23. The Believers
24. (The) Light
25. Salvation (The Distinction) [The Criterion]
26. The Poets
27. The Ant
28. The Story (The Narratives) [The Narrative]
29. The Spider
30. The Greeks (The Romans)
31. Lokman (Luqman) [Lukman]
32. Prostration (The Adoration)
33. The Confederates (The Clans) [The Allies]
34. Sheba (The Saba)

35. The Angels (The Originator) [The Creator]
36. Ya Sin (Yasin)
37. The Rangers
38. Sad (Suad)
39. The Companies (The Companions)
40. The Believers (The Believer) [The Forgiving One]
41. Distinguished (Ha Mim) [Revelations Well-Expounded]
42. (The) Counsel
43. Ornaments (of Gold) [The Embellishment]
44. (The) [Evident] Smoke
45. Hobbling (The Kneeling)
46. The Sand Dunes (The Sandhills)
47. Muhammad
48. (The) Victory
49. Apartments (The Chambers)
50. Qaf
51. The Scatterers
52. The Mount (The Mountain)
53. The Star
54. The Moon
55. The All-Merciful (The Beneficent) [The Merciful]
56. The Terror (The Event) [The Which Is Coming]
57. (The) Iron
58. The Disputer (She Who Pleaded)
59. The Mustering (The Banishment) [The Exile]
60. The Woman Tested (The Examined One) [She Who Is Tested]
61. The Ranks
62. (The [Day of]) Congregation
63. The Hypocrites
64. Mutual Fraud (The Mutual Deceit) [The Cheating]
65. (The) Divorce
66. The Forbidding (The Prohibition)
67. The Kingdom
68. The Pen
69. The Indubitable (The Inevitable)
70. The Stairways (The Ways of Ascent) [The Ladders]
71. Noah (Nuh)
72. The Jinn
73. Enwrapped (The Wrapped-Up) [The Mantled One]
74. Shrouded (The Covered One) [The Clothed One]
75. The Resurrection
76. [The] Man (Time)
77. The Loosed Ones (The Sent Forth) [The Emissaries]
78. The Tiding (The Great Event)

79. The Pluckers (The Draggers) [Those Who Pull Out]
80. He Frowned
81. The Darkening (The Folded Up) [The Cessation]
82. The Splitting (The Cleaving [Asunder])
83. The Stinters (The Deceivers in Measuring) [The Defrauders]
84. The Rending (The Rending Asunder)
85. The Constellations (The Celestial Stations)
86. The Night Star (The Nightly Visitant) [The Night-Comer]
87. The Most High
88. The Enveloper (The Overwhelming Calamity)
89. The Dawn (The Daybreak)
90. The Land (The City)
91. The Sun
92. The Night
93. The Forenoon (The Brightness) [The Early Hours]
94. The Expanding (The Expansion)
95. The Fig
96. The (Blood) Clot
97. Power (The Grandeur) [The Majesty]
98. The Clear Sign (The Clear Evidence) [The Proof]
99. The Earthquake (The Quaking) [The Shaking]
100. The Chargers [The Assaulters]
101. The Clatterer (The [Terrible] Calamity)
102. Rivalry (Vying in Abundance) [Worldly Gain]
103. Afternoon (The Age) [Time]
104. The Backbiter (The Slanderer)
105. The Elephant
106. Koraish (The Qureaish) [The Quraish]
107. Charity (Alms) [The Daily Necessities]
108. Abundance (The Abundance of Good)
109. The Unbelievers (The Disbelievers)
110. (The) Help
111. Perish (The Flame)
112. Sincere Religion (The Unity)
113. [The] Daybreak (The Dawn)
114. [The] Men (The People)

The Sunna (or Sunnah) is a collection of the sayings and deeds of the Prophet; the tradition of these sayings and deeds is called Ḥadīth (or Hadith; plural aḥādith). Hadith references vary according to the scholar responsible for their collection (e.g. Ṣaḥīḥ Bukhārī, Ṣaḥīḥ Muslim, Abū Dāwūd, or Imām Mālik); the citation will include reference to volume (for Bukhari), book, and number. Sīra (the history of the Prophet's life) has also been collected by numerous authors and complied in multi-volume editions, each of which has different forms of reference.

Sharīʿah (or Shariʿah; the Islamic code of law) is based, first of all, on the Qurʾān and the Sunna, and references to it take the form of references drawn from those sources. References to *fiqh* (Islamic schools of jurisprudence) vary according to the collections produced by individual scholars or schools.

Specialist contexts will require terminology distinct from normal usage, as for example the place names Makkah for Mecca and Madinah for Medina (adjectives Makkan and Madinan). The abbreviation for *Anno Hegirae* (AH) may also be rendered simply as H, also in small capitals.

In some texts it is standard practice to use the title 'the Prophet' uniformly in place of 'Muhammad'. Editors should allow this, but not impose it on authors who have not done so themselves. (Note that this leads to the capitalized adjective 'Prophetic'.) Certain terms of respect for Allah and the prophets are a feature of writings on Islamic topics, especially those aimed at a Muslim readership. These are abbreviated in parentheses and follow the name in question, either at first mention in a text, or each time. The name of Allah may have the abbreviation '(s.w.t.)' (*subḥānahu wa-taʿālā* 'the most powerful and the most high'). The name of Muḥammad, or any prophet, may have the abbreviation '(s.a.w.s.)' (*ṣallā ʾllāhu ʿalayhi wa-sallam* 'peace and blessings be upon him'), which equally may be abbreviated in English '(p.b.u.h.)'. Companions of the Prophet and other Messengers mentioned in the Qurʾān may have following their name the abbreviation '(r.)' (*raḍiya ʾllāhu ʿanhu* God's mercy be upon him', *raḍiya ʾllāhu ʿanhā* 'God's mercy be upon her', or *raḍiya ʾllāhu ʿanhum* 'God's mercy be upon them'). Usage is divided as to whether these abbreviations have full points (increasingly they do not); either usage is acceptable if consistently applied.

13.9 **Social sciences**

The USA's predominance in many of the social sciences has influenced the style of writing used within the discipline. As British social scientists will have absorbed large amounts of US writing during their training, the imposition during editing of British (and seemingly unfamiliar) conventions may be less welcome than in other disciplines, even in works aimed at a British readership. In practice this manifests itself in compound adjectives with few hyphens (*see* **13.9.2**) and some 'American' spelling conventions for terms of art, as well as in writers being more inclined towards short sentences and clauses with few conjunctions. Writers are equally inclined to invent verbs, which should be accepted within reason, even if they have yet to be found in a dictionary.

13.9.1 Use of scientific style

Since social science as a discipline resides somewhere between the arts and the 'hard' sciences, a decision must be made for each typescript whether a scientific style should be followed in presenting the text and references. The higher the level of statistical material—as evidenced in economics, econometrics, demography, geography, and the like—the more appropriate a scientific style becomes. In text this usually manifests itself in such matters as spelling out numbers up to ten only (rather than up to one hundred), and using % rather than *per cent*. In references it usually means preferring the author–date form of references rather than the short-title form, and—possibly—imposing minimal capitalization on titles and no quotation marks for article titles. All these styles are acceptable, but editors should not impose them without consulting the author.

13.9.2 Treatment of terms

The tendency in the social sciences to omit hyphens in favour of separating or running together words follows the general trend for the language as a whole, especially in the USA. For example, hyphens previously would have linked two-word terms such as *age set*, *birth rate*, *bride price*, *case study*, *labour market*, and *life table*, and separated one-word terms such as *deskilling*, *multiskilling*, *intergenerational*, *socioeconomic*, *sociolinguistic*, *subsample*, *subset*, and *subsystem*. Two-word compound adjectives are hyphenated only when used attributively, such as *concentric-zone theory*, *primary-sector industry*, or *working-class community*, though US-influenced authors often do not use the hyphen. (Terms that indicate a relationship between two elements of a process, such as *cost–benefit analysis*, require an en rule rather than a hyphen.) Keeping a style sheet will ensure that terminology is treated consistently throughout a work.

13.10 **Textual editions**

The business of editing and publishing a text that derives from a number of sources, even when an original in the author's hand is extant, is a complicated matter that cannot be fully dealt with here. Classicists may choose from a range of well-established conventions, excellently dealt with in M. L. West's *Textual Criticism and Editorial Technique Applicable to Greek and Latin Texts* (Stuttgart, 1973). Scholars working in other fields will generally have the support of existing models that can be adapted for their own purposes, in consultation with the publisher and with colleagues in the discipline. There are different approaches to the question of what the overall purpose of a 'scholarly edition' should be, ranging roughly from the text editor's best guess at the author's intention—regardless of what was actually written down—to the text editor's direct transcript (including even minute and trivial flaws and inconsistencies) of the 'copy text', the version deemed to be the most authoritative of the range of sources available. (Such an edition is essentially a 'diplomatic transcript', producing as faithful a version of the copy text as the exigencies of type will allow.) The first kind is perhaps more deserving of the name '*critical* edition', but the second also has its uses, and indeed in papyrological publications it is established practice to give both on facing pages—or, in large formats, double columns—so that readers can have the raw evidence (without the inconvenience of having to struggle with the difficulties exhibited by the original) as well as the text editor's attempt at providing a readable version of it. (In this section the edition's creator is called the *text editor*, and the publisher's editor—elsewhere called simply the *editor*—is here the *copy editor*.)

13.10.1 General considerations

Classical scholars operate on the assumption that there was originally one authorial text, which they are trying to recover from centuries of miscopying: there is just enough evidence to show that authors revised their texts after first copying, but not enough for us to do anything about it. On the other hand, scholars are not concerned to reproduce the authors' original spelling, let alone their punctuation, even when they have evidence for what it was. (Papyri and inscriptions will be reproduced with greater fidelity, as being themselves ancient documents.) However, late antique and medieval texts sometimes exist in what are quite clearly different recensions: copyists of—say—the *Alexander Romance* or the *History of Apollonius King of Tyre* (source of Shakespeare's *Pericles*) felt free to reword and even renarrate as they saw fit. Often it will be impossible to establish an original version; the choice lies between editing a particular recension, if a reasonably coherent reconstruction can be made, or two or more: the page can be divided horizontally, with the older, or main, recension above the later, or abnormal, one.

Spelling is another problem: if there is only one manuscript, it is normal to follow it rather than impose on a medieval author classical principles he or she did not follow; but if there are several, the text editor may have to reconstruct the author's likely norm. This is even more complex in vernacular texts, when copyists have imposed their own dialect. (In

Middle High German, for example, it has been conventional to impose Lachmann's orthography, based on an early manuscript of Hartmann von Aue's Îwein, but far more regular than anything the authors themselves are likely to have used.)

What is appropriate in each case must be settled at an early stage between a text editor and the publisher. In fact the information given should be about the same regardless: essentially, the reader should be able to re-create the text of any of the reported sources, the information on the readings contained in these sources being distributed between the main text and the textual notes (or apparatus criticus), which are normally and most conveniently given at the foot of the page. The mechanics of the presentation are covered in this section in a general way, but almost all of the specific conventions mentioned below are subject to variation depending on the publisher's preferences, series precedent, and the peculiar requirements of a particular text.

13.10.2 Conventions for apparatus critici

The prelims to the edition should be paginated in roman numerals regardless of length, and should contain a full and lucid discussion of the editorial principles underlying the text. If there have been any routine normalizations of the text that are not separately noted in the apparatus criticus, list them clearly at the outset. It is quite common, for example, to expand the ampersand (&) to *and*, to employ roman parentheses throughout where the source varies between roman and italic (even within the same pair of parentheses), to make all dashes of uniform length, or to impose roman punctuation following an isolated italic word or phrase, particularly if the source text varies unpredictably in its practice. Text editors should record all information in as full a form as possible in the initial stages of preparing a text, and then at an advanced stage of the work decide which items are sufficiently unimportant (both in establishing the history of the text and from the point of view of the reader's convenience) to admit of silent regularization. It is not safe to embark on the work with preconceived notions of what can be normalized, since a minor feature may turn out to be important in establishing some point in the manuscript or printing tradition. For example, the scribe of a manuscript that turns out to be of crucial importance may habitually use a certain abbreviation, or a particular compositor or typesetter may have a habit of neglecting to close parentheses.

The abbreviations for the sources cited in the edition (the *sigla*) should be listed alphabetically in the prelims, preferably close to the start of the text, which will normally coincide with the beginning of arabic pagination. Letters are more convenient and economical than numerals as sigla, since a string such as *ACDE* (accompanying the citation of a variant found in these four sources) can be set close up, whereas *78 83 90 96* (an established convention for citing editions published in, say, 1778, 1783, 1790, and 1796) must be set with a fixed space between each siglum.

The siglum list should also contain all other abbreviations and symbols used, such as ^{corr} or ^{2}: $A^{corr}\ B^2$ is a neat way of indicating that the reported reading is in text A as corrected by the scribe, and in text B in a second hand that can be discerned in the manuscript. Various types of bracket are commonly given a specific editorial function:

( )   May indicate expansion of an abbreviation, for example *N(ether) St(owey)* for the source's *N.St.*

⟨ ⟩   Sometimes used for text added conjecturally or supplied from a source other than the main source of the text. Note that the wide-angled sort of bracket should be used, not the mathematical < and > signs.

[ ]   Often used to indicate text deleted by the text editor (as having been added erroneously to the genuine text). May also be used to enclose supplements where the writing surface has perished (most common in the fields of classical papyrology and epigraphy); often used by modern linguists to indicate insertions.

{ }   Another convention for editorial deletion. Of course the text editor may wish to employ both types of bracket, assigning different functions to each.

⟦ ⟧   Double brackets may be used to indicate deletion in the reported text, where text editors do not wish actually to print text with a line through.
        Successive stages of deletion are awkward to record, but if the situation is not too complex other special sorts such as upper and lower half-brackets ⌈ ⌉⌊ ⌋ may be employed within the ⟦ ⟧ double brackets. If these would not be used frequently, it may be better to document the layers of deletion and revision in a textual note, or in the commentary if the matter is worth discussing at some length. This is better than encumbering the semiotic system for the sake of a few isolated cases.

⌊ ⌋   Used particularly in papyrology to enclose text supplied (usually with a fair measure of confidence) from another source where the papyrus is defective.

` ´   Sometimes used to indicate insertions, particularly supralinear matter, made by the original writer of the text being reported. (Some text editors use ⟨ ⟩ for this purpose rather than the reverse prime and prime, but this should be avoided.)

††   Traditionally used to enclose text judged to be corrupt and beyond hope of emendation.

These are just some examples of the commoner conventions. Text editors will frequently have the choice made for them either by publishing precedent (particularly if the book forms part of a series) or because certain conventions are established in the discipline. It is important to think carefully before employing a novel symbol, or a standard symbol employed in a novel way. The text being edited *may* require special treatment, but it is equally likely that there are conventions already established that will serve the purpose. Do not use symbols unnecessarily: if, for example, only two instances of a scribal deletion need to be reported, it is probably more convenient to offer the information in words rather than introduce the double-bracket sort.

What else goes into the introduction will depend on the kind of text being annotated: literary genre, sources, historical and biographical context, the publication history of the text, and its influence are the kind of topic often included. This is a matter for discussion with the publisher. The prelims will also generally have a list of abbreviations (which may include books and articles frequently referred to), as well as a list of previous editions. A list of abbreviations should precede the use of any of the abbreviations included. Follow the standard conventions for including in the prelims formal bibliographical descriptions of the printed texts on which the edition is based.

13.10.3 Presentation

At an early stage the text editor and publisher need to determine how the text that is being edited should be presented. One generated wholly by the text editor as typescript must be submitted just like any other typescript. Alternatively, the publisher may be able to accept a photo-copy of a previous printing (a so-called *manuscrit belge*), particularly if it requires little alteration for the present edition. On a photocopy, ring any blotches that might be mistaken for punctuation—a particular danger when the original has become flecked. All occurrences of the long 's' need to be marked (e.g. highlighted in a distinctive colour) so that the copy can be set accurately at speed—this usually requires two passes, since the expert is liable to take in the long 's' unconsciously and miss some instances in copy.

In normal scholarly editions the text itself will have the lines numbered, traditionally in fives. These numbers are set in footnote-size type at the right-hand edge and within the measure for poetry, and for prose in the outer margins, 1 en beyond the measure. Lines of prose texts are trad-itionally numbered per page, though works divided into short sections, such as letters or essays, may be numbered through each. (Copy editors should state in the Note to Printer that if a line of poetry is in danger of colliding with the line number when set, the following line should be numbered instead: number line 26, for example, if there is a problem with numbering line 25.) Line numbering of prose texts will obviously vary between copy and proof, and text editors must supply amply spaced copy with plenty of room for the copy editor and designer to add relevant instructions and implement the changes clearly, so as to minimize the risk of typesetting error.

Line numbering can be complicated if there is supplementary matter in the main text not included in the ordinary line numbering: prose pref-aces to poems, stage directions in plays (those preceded by a line break), and footnotes by the original author are common examples. If such items are short, they will not generally require line numbering, but a lengthy original footnote, for example, to which the text editor needs to attach commentary and textual notes will require its own separate numbering in fives.

Where the text editor is transposing lines of poetry from the sequence presented by the sources, or by standard editions, the old numbers should be printed against each of the transposed lines, and the lines surrounding the old position of the passage should also be numbered. Thus if lines 23–5 are being transposed to follow line 14, the right-hand margin will give the line numbers 14, 23, 24, 25, 15, and lines 22 and 26 (now adjacent lines) will also be individually numbered.

When poems or fragments come from disparate sources, ordering becomes an editorial exercise. Text editors should think twice before reordering poems or fragments when a standard already exists: is their evidence so strong that it outweighs the inconvenience of rendering that standard reference obsolete? Avoid renumbering if at all possible: newly discovered items can sometimes be accommodated to their proper place as 222A etc.—this has the advantage of compatibility with existing references, but the disadvantage of suggesting a close connection with 222. If, however, previous numerations reflect untenable views of the facts, then text editors must have the courage of their convictions and renumber. This necessitates a concordance, which should refer both from predecessors' editions to the text editor's and from the text editor's to theirs (*see* **13.10.6**).

Some editions employ a system of cues, such as superscript italic letters, for textual notes. In the case of prose texts this may obviate the need for line numbering at all: notes on the content would then normally have to be cued by a different system, for example the usual [123] numerical cues. This practice is best reserved for cases where the annotation—textual and otherwise—is relatively sparse, otherwise the text will become cluttered with cues and uncomfortable to read.

Original footnotes are generally cued by the sequence of symbols [*†‡§¶‖] (duplicated as [** ††] etc. if necessary), regardless of the practice of the text being edited.

If a particular text exists in a large number of sources that all have a valid claim to be reported more or less fully, there is a danger of textual notes becoming severely cluttered with minutiae such as the font of punctuation following italic words, capitalization of nouns, or changing fashions in spelling. Where this arises a separate register may be created; this is often placed at the end of the volume. It is generally referred to as the 'list of accidentals', or sometimes 'historical collation', and its main purpose is to establish or prove the finer details of the history of a text, particularly one that went through a number of printings with some claim to authority. The notes in this register often look trivial taken individually, but cumulatively a fine matter of punctuation style or layout can establish potentially important information such as the number of copies exhibiting press variants (small changes introduced while a book was actually being printed) or the point at which a new compositor took over. But the distinction between substantive and accidental must be applied historically: the distinctions *loose/lose, than/then, whether/whither*, which are substantive now, were accidental in the seventeenth century, for example. On the other hand, the text editor may wish to discuss in the commentary whether *whether/whither* means modern *whether* or *whither*.

13.10.4 Historical collations

The layout of a historical collation is the same as that of the apparatus criticus. The style discussed below is usual in the absence of particular requirements, differing series precedent, and so forth.

Notes are introduced by the line number to which they refer, followed by a fixed en space; this number must not be broken from its note at the end of a line of type.

Subsidiary matter such as stage directions and original footnotes can be awkward to cue. Possible formats include *12SD* for a stage direction within line 12, $^{-}$*12SD* or *12^{+}SD* for stage directions occurring immediately before or after line 12 (the content of the stage direction itself would determine which of the two logically applies); *12** for an original footnote cued in line 12 (this may need to be altered at setting, if for example the footnote turns out to be the second on the page, cued by †). When specific lines of stage directions need to be identified, a less cumbersome numerical system may be better: *12.3* for the third line of a stage direction immediately following line 12, or a negative form such as $^{-}$*12.3* for a stage direction preceding a line to which it is logically attached—but ensure that the minus sign cannot be mistaken for a hyphen or an en rule marking an extent; $^{-}$*12* may prove useful in either system for notes to characters' names that are set on separate lines above the first line of a speech. The initial stage direction of a scene may be termed *setting, scene heading*, etc., and any apparatus notes can be cued with that term; the alternative numerical system will produce *0.1, 0.2*, etc. A lengthy original footnote may have a succession of notes cued *12***2, 12***4*, etc. The text editor, copy editor, and designer should work together to determine the most apposite system for the subsidiary matter in question. A slightly cumbersome but immediately comprehensible format may be preferable if there are only a very few occasions for its use in a long book; a more economical system will be needed where it arises frequently.

In poetry the $^+$ and $^-$ conventions are useful for recording variants that contain extra material not represented at all in the main text, so that no lemma (*see* **13.11**) is possible:

> 12$^+$ This sure but gives his guilt a blacker dye *B*

indicates that text B contains this extra line between lines 12 and 13 of the text that the text editor has printed. It is also possible to label this line 12*a*.

If a line of drama is split between characters it may prove useful to identify the parts by letters (*12a*, *12b*, etc). But often it will be clear without this refinement which part of the line is being annotated.

The *lemma* (plural *lemmata*) comes after the number and space. It means 'something taken [from the main text]' and must therefore reproduce the form in the text in every way: use of roman and italic, capitals, font of following punctuation, etc. (A partial exception is letter spacing, for example of displayed capital or small-capital matter, which is often not rendered in either lemmata or reported variants, although it may be if that is the text editor's preference.) It is a main task of the copy editor to check that the lemmata have been rendered accurately. The end of the lemma is marked by a closing square bracket] (which, unlike the line number, may fall at the end of the line of type). In annotating a common word like *and*, which may occur several times in a typeset line, give a little more of the context in the lemma, such as the preceding or following word(s); the alternative is to introduce superiors (e.g. *and*^{2}) on copy and correct them at proof, something that is awkward to do—and is easily forgotten at that point. The system of superiors is easier to use with poetic texts, where the lineation will not change, allowing the numerals to be fixed during copy preparation.

The lemma may be omitted if there is no possibility of ambiguity. If there is only one occurrence of the word *honour* in a passage, no harm will be done by '3] honor *1780*', indicating that the 1780 printing used the alternative spelling of the word in line 3 of the present text. (The lemma bracket is frequently omitted as redundant—'3 honour *1780*'— though it may be helpful to the reader to maintain the customary visual rubric as far as possible.) The one place where lemmata are usually omitted naturally—even where the apparatus is not generally adopting the system—is when variants to an entire line of poetry are given, as repeating the whole line from the main text would be superfluous.

Otherwise, omitting lemmata makes the reader work a little harder, and is probably best reserved for cases where the apparatus is very extensive and every possible economy is sought.

The copy editor should highlight in a distinctive colour the parts of a prose text that are being used as lemmata, so that the typesetter knows to make allowance for a textual note in producing paginated text. This should also be done where the textual note dispenses with the lemma, since the typesetter still needs to know that there is a note at this point. In poetic texts it may be sufficient to put a highlighter mark next to each *line* that has one or more textual notes.

After the square bracket come the variant readings from the other sources being reported. Each variant reading is succeeded by the source or sources that have that version of the text. The readings are usually given exactly as found (in citing manuscript texts *italic* represents under-lining and SMALL CAPITALS represent double underlining). If the main text is in a roman alphabet such as English, the sources, and any editorial comments such as '(*illegible*)', '(*in the margin*)', should be given in italic: 'honor *BC*'. The traditional sloping Porson Greek font is deemed to be in italic, so sources are given in roman: "τιμη BC". Where a number of different readings are being cited, use a mark of punctuation such as a roman semicolon or colon (the latter is traditional in classical texts): 'honor *BC*; virtus *D*'.

The swung dash ∼ is often used to avoid repeating those parts of a variant reading that are identical to the lemma (and thus to the main text):

old and sick and feeble] aged ∼ ∼ ∼ weak *B*

It is particularly valuable when the textual note concerns a matter of punctuation:

that,] ∼; *B*

immediately draws attention to the point of difference. Some text editors allow the swung dash to stand for several words, which is acceptable provided that no ambiguity results. It may also be used to draw attention to a variation in the case of the first letter of a word:

fish] F∼ *B*

The base-line caret ʌ indicates absence of punctuation, again drawing the reader's attention to a point which could easily be missed:

animal, which] ∼ʌ ∼

is more quickly taken in than 'animal, which] animal which'.

Normally, a mark of punctuation is omitted from the end of a lemma and its variants if it is identical in all texts: the apparatus should concentrate on the points of difference, excluding superfluous matter.

Employ points of omission with caution. In the case of mutually dependent variants it is better to give

> 12 He . . . his] They . . . their *B*

rather than

> 12 He] They *B* his] their *B*

since that makes it clear that the singular sentence has been turned into a plural one in text B. But when the variants are independent, they should be reported separately:

> 13 God] Heauen *1616* mought] might *1616*

where the first change responds to Puritan sensitivities, the second alters the manner of conjugation.

Where a text editor has identified a group of sources that tend to exhibit the same readings and are therefore supposed to be related in the history of the text, it is often helpful to provide a group siglum, sometimes in a distinctive font such as bold or Greek. It may sometimes be desirable to give the precise version in a particular member of the group if it exhibits a slight variant that is worth recording. For example, if X is being used for manuscripts A, B, C, and D the note might read: 'honor X (honour *C*)'. This is somewhat cumbersome, but better than listing each separate siglum throughout, which would obscure the fact that the four sources are intimately connected and generally in agreement. In evolving such group sigla a text editor should decide, and make clear, at the outset whether (to use the current example) X means 'all manuscripts of this family other than the one specified' or 'the (reconstructed) manuscript from which ABCD descend'; in the latter case the current example would read simply 'honor X', regardless of the existence of 'honour' in any member of the extant group. Either system is legitimate, but the two should not be mixed.

In the textual notes it is not normally necessary to identify the source or sources of the reading being adopted, since the introduction to the edition should have made it clear which sources are being used. The reader will then assume that the text represents the consensus of all reported readings except where there is a textual note giving variants. Thus, if the text editor has stated that the text as printed derives from manuscripts A, B, C, and D, then the reader will deduce from a textual note 'honour] honor *BC*' that A and D read 'honour'. Conjectural emendations that are adopted need to be identified as such, of course: 'virtue] *Malone*; vice *ABCD*'. (Text editors may indicate their own emendations by *ed.* if they are too bashful to use their name.) And where the text editor has stated that the main text essentially follows one particular source— such as an edition privileged because the author is known to have taken great pains with the printing—it will be necessary to draw specific attention to those occasions where the reading of another source has exceptionally been followed: 'forgo] *1802*; forego *1798*'. In such cases some text editors prefer to place the lemma bracket *after* the source, keeping the lemma and its source together; in poetic texts—where it is not necessary to cite the line at all—it is normal, if the source of the line in the main text needs to be specified, to give it before the lemma bracket:

12 *BD*] This sure but gives his guilt a blacker dye *AC*

Displayed matter should be avoided in the apparatus where possible. Two or three complete lines of verse cited from a variant source may be run on, separated by a vertical line (|) with a full space of the line on either side (this may fall at the end but not at the beginning of a line of type); but passages of four lines or more are best displayed. If this comes up very frequently (e.g. if there is a radically different variant source that is so important that it consistently needs to be cited at length) the text editor should consider an alternative solution, such as printing the variant version complete in an appendix, or even on facing pages, opposite the main text (but usually in a smaller size). In the case of, for example, an alternative or breakaway branch of the manuscript tradition, a highly divergent first edition, or a production version of a play that departs radically from the printed text, the version on the recto pages may have an equal claim to validity as a version of the text, in which case it is legitimate to print it in the same size as the verso page, complete with its own apparatus. (An alternative layout, giving one recension above the other on the same page, is mentioned above.) Complex cases like this should be discussed fully with the publisher; it should not be left to the copy editor to invent and implement a solution, particularly one which might involve a radical recasting of the type-script as submitted by the text editor.

Textual notes to different items on the same line are separated by a variable 1½-em space. Only the first textual note on a given line is preceded by the line number; it is separated from the previous textual note by a variable 3-em space. Both these wide spaces disappear when they coincide with a line break at proof. They are expandable (and slightly reducible) to facilitate right-hand justification of the lines, but should retain their proportions: that is, the smaller gap should always be half the size of the larger in any line in which both occur.

Where there are original footnotes, apparatus notes on them should follow the order in which the text should be read: it is supposed that the reader will stop at a note cue in order to read the footnote before returning to the text, and any apparatus notes will be given in that order.

In prose texts it is the typesetter's responsibility to choose the right size of gap between notes, since the distribution of the notes over lines of the printed text can be known only at the typesetting stage. If the typescript is set straight to page, this will be shown on the first proofs, with the true line numbers in place in the apparatus. It is a complex task, since not only do line numbers of the copy have to be converted, but a note in copy that has no preceding line number in the copy because it is not the first note on the line may have to have one introduced (if it is first in the line in the printed text); equally, some line numbers of copy will disappear altogether (where a note is no longer the first in its line).

The apparatus may be divided into paragraphs (each indented 1 em) corresponding to major divisions of the text, such as new poems or new scenes. Sometimes it is useful to follow the paragraph indent with a signal such as 'POEM XIII' (or a bold **13**), 'SCENE IV': as always, ease of reference is paramount. Paragraphing is not otherwise needed, though the traditional style is to start every block of textual notes at the foot of the page with an indent; this may be followed if it is the style of a given series, or specified thus by the designer. It does not apply on any page where a textual note is continued from the preceding page, which is permissible but should be confined to a single page opening.

Copy for textual notes must always be presented on separate sheets from the main text, double-spaced with generous margins. Each note must begin on a fresh line in the typescript, even though notes referring to the same line will be run on without repeating the line number to which they relate.

OUP does not use a rule to separate apparatus criticus from the main text, except where the text itself contains footnotes (i.e. original notes in the text being edited), in which case, to avoid possible confusion, use a quarter-point rule, full left, with a variable 3-point space above and below. This is used only on those pages that contain original footnotes. Sometimes there are further registers of editorial material (generally preceding the apparatus), for example lists of parallel passages or testimonia, both of which may be set out in a style similar to apparatus criticus, with the same 1½-em and 3-em gaps. The quarter-point rule is also used as a separator in these cases, again only on pages where the different registers actually occur. If editorial commentary appears on the same page a separating rule is also used, although it is more usual to set the commentary separately (*see* below).

13.10.5 **Commentary**

The level of annotation required in the commentary is a matter for discussion between text editor and publisher, bearing in mind the intended readership.

While commentary notes are generally given at the end of the volume, those that are not extensive may be printed on the same page as the text, beneath the apparatus criticus. Displayed quotations within the commentary should remain in the same type size, with prose quotations indented 1 em (verse centred as normal); prose quotations should be run on where possible.

A form of cue may be used in the text to indicate a commentary note; this is commoner in popular (as opposed to scholarly) editions, which rely purely on the correlation of line numbers in text and commentary. The same cue, for example a degree sign (°), may be used throughout— several times on the same page if necessary—as the commentary section itself will give a clear reference and lemma drawing the reader's eye to the correct note. As with other conventions, there will frequently be a series precedent to follow, and the precise style to be employed should be discussed with the publisher.

In editions of prose texts where references are cued to line numbers, the copy editor should highlight in the text the lemmata for commentary notes, using a different colour from that used for highlighting lemmata for the apparatus. Where the same piece of text is a lemma for both the apparatus and the commentary, one band of colour should appear beneath the other. This is not required in poetry, where the line numbering is fixed, or in prose texts where references are not by line (e.g. chapter and section).

The text editor should begin each commentary note on a new line of typescript. The first note on a given line of the text begins with the page number followed by an en space and the line number, generally followed by a full point or en space. The lemma, if any, comes next, as with apparatus criticus.

A square bracket may be used to terminate the lemma, though a full point or roman colon (bold point or colon with bold lemmata) is more common. These marks of punctuation are omitted if the lemma itself ends with a question mark or exclamation mark: there is usually no need for a commentary lemma to end with one of the lower marks of punctuation. In some series the lemma ends with *either* a point *or* a colon, depending on whether the commentary note begins with a complete sentence or only a phrase.

Notes to second and subsequent items on the same line normally begin with a paragraph indent followed by the lemma; the line number is not repeated.

Where a commentary note does not start with a full sentence, such as a simple gloss on an unusual word in the text, it may begin with a lower-case letter, except where the commentary lemma is terminated by a full point, exclamation mark, or question mark, where this would look strange. The style of the series—if any—should be followed.

Series precedent, or the publisher's instructions, may have determined the typographic style beforehand, in which case the text editor can submit the typescript with this already in place: generally the line number is in roman type, the lemma in italic, or both line number and lemma in bold. Commentary lemmata do not have to follow the strict rules of lemmata in the apparatus criticus, since their purpose is purely to point the reader quickly to which part of the text is being annotated. Thus all lemmata may be in italic, representing both roman and italic words of the main text. However, if some lemmata consist of text that switches between roman and italic, it is better to reverse fonts, so that italic in the main text becomes roman in the commentary lemma. The square bracket or other punctuation at the end of a lemma is bold if the lemmata are bold. (It is less usual to interfere with capitalization of the text, though there may be a series rule to the contrary.)

The precise typographic layout will be decided by the publisher. Some styles in use include (*a*) an indent on all turn lines, so that the line number stands out to the left on the page; (*b*) ordinary paragraphing (particularly with bold line numbers and lemmata); (*c*) line numbers full left, with (variable) 3-point space to separate the note visually from the preceding note; and (*d*) page and line numbers in a separate column at the left-hand side. In (*d*) the copy editor should indicate the maximum width required for the reference column, for example, *000 00–000 00* with fixed en spaces will allow for a reference such as *110 23–111 16* (from page 110, line 23 to page 111, line 16). An allowance must be made for a gutter (usually 1 en in width) between the reference column and the commentary itself.

For editions of prose texts the most economical course may be not to send the commentary for setting until proofs of the text have been received, so that the line numbers may be inserted and paragraphing determined. This will also involve removing line numbers from the copy and marking for paragraph indents, and introducing line numbers at the start of notes that are now the first note on a given line. This procedure is not necessary if the book is to have page and line numbers in a separate left-hand stub, as described above.

13.10.6   **Appendices**

The commentary on a prose text may be followed by a register of accidental hyphens, recording all cases where an end-line hyphen in the current edition is peculiar to this printing. The reader then knows that all other end-line hyphens are established as part of the text (either because they do not occur at the end of a line in the original printing(s) or because they do but are nevertheless known or deemed to be expressions that would be hyphenated at the time of the original printing). Where it is deemed important or of potential interest, a separate register of accidental hyphens in the original printing may be included. However, these are often not recorded, and the text editor may wish to discuss in the commentary any cases where an end-line hyphen in the original may or may not be intrinsic to the expression in question.

Further endmatter might include a bibliography of the author's works, special indexes (names, works cited, etc.), and a general index. It is less usual to provide a bibliography of secondary literature of the type normal in scholarly monographs. Text editors should discuss all such prospective sections with the publisher.

A concordance of poem or fragment numbers between the present edition and earlier collections also falls in the endmatter. When several numerations have to be surveyed, the most economical form is laid out as in Fig. 13.2 (assuming Bloggs to be the present editor). This means, to take the first line, that Smith's fragment 1 is Bloggs's fragment 2; Jones's fragment 1 is Bloggs's fragment 4; Robinson's fragment 1 is Bloggs's fragment 3; Kunz's fragment 1 is Bloggs's fragment 5; Bloggs's fragment 1 is Smith's fragment 5, Jones's fragment 2, Robinson's fragment 4, and Kunz's fragment 3.

Fragment	Smith	Jones	Robinson	Kunz	BLOGGS				
					BLOGGS	Smith	Jones	Robinson	Kunz
1	2	4	3	5		5	2	4	3
2	3	1	5	4		1	5	3	4
3	4	5	2	1		2	4	1	5
4	5	3	1	2		3	1	5	2
5	1	2	4	3		4	3	2	1
	etc.								

Fig. 13.2: **Concordance of fragment numbers**

13.10.7 Running headlines

The original edition's running headlines should be used where possible to help the reader to correlate main text and endmatter. In the commentary the usual format for prose is *Commentary on pp. 00–00*, and for verse is *Commentary on ll. 00–00*; each can be finalized only on proof. For plays, running heads can be set at first page proof by referring to act, scene, and line numbers, for example '*Commentary on* I. ii. 11–23', or '*Commentary*' on the verso, '*Act* I, *scene* ii, *lines* 11–23' on the recto, for matter covered on the page spread rather than the single page. The latter will be useful only if these subdivisions are clear in the headlines of the main text, for example *Act I* on the inner shoulder of the verso page, and *scene i* across the gutter from it on the inner right-hand shoulder. The text editor should choose a system that is most convenient for the reader.

13.11 **Translations and transliterations**

A *translation* renders the meaning of one language into another. This broad definition covers all tongues, conversion methods, and writing systems, though the specific terms *transliteration*, *transcription*, and *romanization* represent further distinctions. *Transliteration* suggests a system whereby one alphabet is rendered into another, using a one-to-one correspondence of letters or letter groups; the result ideally allows one to reconstruct the spelling of the word in the original alphabet. *Transcription* is a looser system concerned primarily with rendering the proper pronunciation via one's own alphabet; it may be difficult (if not impossible) to reconstruct the original spelling. *Romanization* is the rendering of non-alphabetic languages into the roman alphabet, and is therefore used with such languages as Chinese or hieroglyphs. Again, it is often impossible to reconstruct the original from its romanized form, and those systems that attempt to allow this are often unwieldy and impracticable.

Set against these terms, *translation* tends to be used for converting one roman-alphabet language into another, either strictly or loosely. The first four of the following sections are designed primarily for those translating entire works from the original language into English. However, several aspects are of use to those including foreign-language extracts into English-language works. (For information on setting out quoted matter and translations, *see* **CHAPTER 8**.) The last part of this section is designed for those translating a language that does not use the roman alphabet.

13.11.1 **Translation**

We may all laugh at tales of customs officers forgetting that in French *une grenade* may be a pomegranate, and in Spanish *una bomba* may be a pump; but it is all too easy to make such mistakes ourselves. The task requires not only thorough knowledge of both the original language and

English but also continuous concentration; translators should bear in mind that the text is normally their sole responsibility; editors normally are not accountable for checking the translation.

Translations must include all copy from the source's preliminary matter through to the endmatter. All copy, including notes, bibliography, and index, should be presented double-spaced.

13.11.1.1 Specialist knowledge

Academic works demand more of the translator than a normal linguistic competence. In particular, names (personal and geographical) and technical terms need to be accurately rendered. Mistakes encountered include *Tenare* given as *Tenare* instead of *Taenarum*, *Hennegau* not converted to *Hainaut*, *Stand* mistranslated as 'class' instead of 'estate', and *Thomas Morus* (German for *Sir Thomas More*) left unchanged in English—as was *Rotchina*, i.e. 'Red China' in a work on Balkan affairs, because it looked vaguely Slavonic. Care is all the more important when the original does not use the Roman alphabet: фон Зект has been known to become *fon Zekt* instead of *von Seeckt*. If you do not recognize a name, or understand a technical term, consult the author—if available—or anyone else who may help you: it is no shame not to have known, only to continue not knowing. It is a good idea to consult a few relevant books in English, preferably those used or praised by the author.

Give place names in the English form usual with reference to the period concerned: a Pole will always write *Wrocław*, a German-speaker *Breslau*, but in English it should be *Breslau* up to 1945 and *Wrocław* thereafter. Right-wingers in the former West Germany sometimes used *Ostdeutschland* not for the GDR (which they called *Mitteldeutschland*) but for the lost territories to the east. *Eger* may be either the German name for the scene of Wallenstein's assassination—in Czech called *Cheb* and so to be designated with post-1918 reference—or the Hungarian name for the home of Bull's Blood, to be used for all periods in place of German *Erlau*.

13.11.1.2 Modification of content

You are not responsible for the original author's assertions, opinions, or attitudes, and ought not to propose any alterations (beyond correction of evident misprints, misspellings, or false references), except where factual statements are demonstrably wrong or have been thrown into doubt by subsequent studies. You may, however, propose translator's notes to explain allusions that may not be as familiar to readers of the translation as to those of the original, or facets of language (wordplay, allusions, terms with no English equivalent, etc.) about which the reader needs to be informed. A translator's note should take the form of a footnote—not an endnote—cued by an asterisk or other symbol of a different order from the cues to the author's notes, and enclosed in square brackets: thus, if the original is *le bon roi Dagobert*, you may translate *Good King Dagobert** and add the translator's note:

> *[*Translator's note.* The Frankish king Dagobert I (629–38), whom a traditional song represents as constantly making a fool of himself, notably by donning his breeches inside out.]

However, if the work is still in copyright, no such alteration may be made or note added without the author's or copyright-holder's consent. (*See* **14.2.3**.) Many publishers include in their contracts with translators a clause along the following lines:

> The Translator undertakes to the Publishers that he/she will not introduce into the Translation any matter of an objectionable or libellous nature which was not present in the original work. As consideration for such guarantee the Publishers undertake to indemnify the Translator against all losses and expenses that may be incurred by the Translator arising from any objectionable or libellous material contained in the original Work as translated by the Translator.

13.11.1.3 Approval by author

Before your translation is published, it may be submitted for approval by the author (or copyright-holder), in order to avoid disputes after money has already been spent on copy-editing (time may be saved if the translation is cleared in batches while work is still in progress). He or she may detect errors made from lack of specialist knowledge; on the other hand, do not hesitate to take a firm line, adducing all necessary evidence to assist the editor, if the author objects to your translation where you can show that you are right. He or she may have overestimated his or her English, or failed to appreciate that a literal version will sound silly. (German authors have been known to complain that English translators have lopped off a layer of philosophical understanding.) But if English texts in the field use such language themselves, it is not your duty to reform it.

13.11.1.4 Scope of translation

Your translation must include not merely the text and notes, but also all preliminary matter, tables, illustrations, maps, quotations, footnotes, references, lists of abbreviations, indexes, and bibliographies. For the style of references, and the choice between originals and translations in references without direct quotation *see* **13.11.1.7**. All copy, including that for notes and bibliography, should be double-spaced.

13.11.1.5 Preliminary matter

Preliminary matter should follow normal editorial conventions: at OUP the table of contents should follow the preface irrespective of its original position. If you have been asked to write a translator's foreword, it will precede the preface; if the author has contributed a preface to the translation it will precede the original preface unless conceived as a brief appendage to it. If the structure of the main text departs from standard conventions (e.g. if a single-chapter introduction or conclusion—even the bibliography—is treated as a separate numbered part, or chapters in each new part are numbered from 1), impose standard practice (changing cross-references as may be necessary) unless you know or suspect that retention of original structure will facilitate use of the translation by readers of other works citing the original; in this case, take any specialist advice available and (if necessary) consult the editor.

13.11.1.6 Quotations

For works in English cited in translation, use the English original if it can be traced; retroversion, if unavoidable, must be noted. For works in the author's language already translated into English, use published translations if reliable; if not, translate the extract yourself. Any flaw in the published translation of a particular passage, problem of inter- pretation, or linguistic point lost in English should be recorded in a translator's note: for example on *seventeenth-century** in the text:

> *[*Translator's note*. In the original, 'secentesco'; English translation has 'eighteenth-century', wrongly. Mabillon lived from 1632 to 1707.]

Works in a third language cited by the author may be either in the original or translated into his or her own language. If a work is cited in the original, use an English translation (if available) unless the reader- ship can reasonably be expected to know the original language—consult the editor if in doubt. If it is translated into his or her own language, use the English translation if available; if not, translate directly from the original, or if you do not know the language consult someone who does. If you are unable to determine the merit of a translation (e.g. because you have no access to the original, or do not know the language), consult the author and/or a specialist in the discipline. If a published English translation turns out to be flawed, correct it (inserting translator's notes at the appropriate point), or if necessary translate anew.

Draw your editor's attention to all use of published translations in the original: he or she will advise on any questions of copyright. Similarly, inform him or her of any statement in the author's text that is based on a statement in a translation not borne out by the original. Do not translate from the translation in the author's text unless the source is so skimpily identified that you cannot locate it, or you have no access to it, or neither you nor anyone you know recognize its language. In these circumstances you may need to state in a translator's note that you are translating a translation.

If the quotation is taken from a work of literature—especially poetry—it may be best left in the original, with or without an appended translation: to quote Sidney's *Defence of Poetry*, 'It were as wise to cast a violet into a crucible that you might discover the formal principle of its colour and odour, as seek to translate from one language into another the creations of a poet.' Again, consult the editor if no direct instructions have been given.

If the quotation is rendered in the form of dialect, it is inevitable that some of the impact will be lost: the argot and patois of Zola's Paris or Galdós's Madrid is as remote to modern-day Frenchmen and Spaniards as that of the Dickensian underworld is to us, and replacing the former with the latter may result in text that is still unintelligible to the reader—particularly a speaker of non-British English, or one for whom English is a second language. If translated dialect is necessary, beware also of introducing anachronistic usages.

13.11.1.7 References

All text and footnote references to works cited in one language in the work translated and another in the translation must be adjusted to the page numbers etc. of the edition cited in the translation. If you cannot find a passage because the author has given a false reference, raise the problem with the editor.

If an author writing in English is quoting an extract in the original and also providing a translation, it is entirely a matter of the author's discretion whether the original should stand in text and the translation in the notes, or vice versa. There is no rule, as the choice hinges on the author's appraisal of his or her readership, and whether most readers are expected to understand the original (in which case the translation appears in the notes as an optional extra) or whether the reverse is true. Authors also have the option of providing the original and translation side by side in text, although this works better for smaller extracts than for larger ones. Beyond this lie at one extreme scholarly texts, where knowledge of the language is taken for granted and no translation is required; at the other extreme lie popular works or student texts, where perhaps only the translation is thought necessary.

Where a general survey or work of reference has been cited as the source for an established fact or widely accepted theory, the translator may wish to consider whether it is necessary to provide the original reference, or whether a comparable work in English would provide a more accessible source for those reading the translation.

If a work is cited only in translation, that fact should be mentioned. This is generally done by adding a parenthetical abbreviation, such as *(Heb.)* or *(Jap.)*. This follows the title, or the title of the article or chapter, in the case of a journal or multi-author work, and need be inserted only at the first mention of the source. Where a large number of works are cited in the same language, the abbreviation can be dropped from the notes if a statement to this effect is added in a Note on Translation; retain it, however, in the bibliography.

13.11.1.8 Abbreviations

Substitute current English abbreviations (*NATO* for *O.T.A.N.*, *CIS* for *СНГ*, and find appropriate equivalents for any ad hoc abbreviations devised by the author, unless you consider that spelling them out is preferable. Use italics if and only if the expansion, by English conventions, is italicized. Amend the list of abbreviations accordingly: arrange it in alphabetical order of the abbreviations, not the expansions, and do not separate all-capital abbreviations from others. Consider whether any items included are familiar enough (e.g. BBC, *DNB*) to be omitted from an English list, or any omitted (e.g. KSČ = Komunisktická strana Československa) ought to be added, bearing in mind the degree of knowledge to be expected in the English-speaking reader.

13.11.1.9 Indexes

It is a translator's duty to translate all main and subordinate entries in the index, and to put them in English alphabetical order. Since, from a publisher's point of view, you will count as the author of that edition of the work, normal practice makes you responsible for inserting, or causing an indexer to insert, the correct page numbers from the proofs. If this is unacceptable, please raise the matter when the contract is drawn up. Notify the editor if the original index is so unsatisfactory that a new one must be provided.

13.11.1.10 Figures and tabular matter

Normalize any conventions in the original language that are foreign to English. Change mathematical and logical symbols to those current in the English-speaking world, for example changing the German : to the English ÷, and the Continental *32.174,85* to *32,174.85*. In a table this includes, for example, in French or Italian replacing » with —, in German or Russian eliding numbers and replacing em rules with en rules, and in Hebrew or Arabic reversing the order of columns and labels to read left to right.

13.11.1.11 Bibliographies

Anything in these remarks that would also apply to references in text and footnotes does so apply. If in particular cases good grounds exist for departing from these provisions, consult the editor.

Style of translation

You are required to convert the author's bibliography into the form that an English author's bibliography citing the same works would take. A worked example is given below.

Put all notes, section headings, etc. into English. The names of institutional authors must appear in the same form as they take, or would take, in the main text of the translation. Collections of essays and similar multi-author works must appear under their editors' names and not their titles.

Respell authors' names transliterated from non-roman scripts according to English conventions (*Pouchkine* > *Pushkin*, *Tschechow* > *Chekhov*); retain internationally acceptable scientific systems (*Puškin*, *Čexov*), subject to agreement with the editor. Watch out especially for initials: does initial *S.*, in a Russian name within a German bibliography, stand for Russian *C* (= *S.*) or *3* (= *Z.*)? The Hebrew letter *alef* is the initial letter of such different names as *Avraham*, *Elimelekh*, *Ilan*, *Omri*, and *Udi*; similarly the letter *yod* can also become *I.* or *J.* in English. Also, check English vowels used as initials unless the full name is clear from the text: in many languages, certain letters cannot be reliably represented unless the original associated vowel is known. For Chinese, use Pinyin unless otherwise instructed. The same principle applies to classical or other authors with different forms of name in modern languages: *Tite-Live* > *Livy*, *Kallimachos* > *Callimachus*, *Giuseppe* > *Josephus*, *Jenofonte* > *Xenophon*, *Estrabão* > *Strabo*; the alphabetical order may thus need changing.

Impose English alphabetical order; ignore all diacritics, even if a German author has treated *ä* as *ae* (or, by Brockhaus rules, vice versa), similarly Spanish treatment of *ch* and *ll* as unitary letters. An author's works should be ordered alphabetically if the reference system is to author and short title, chronologically if to author and date. (If the original uses a numbered-reference system, e.g. *Nr. 145, S. 257—283*, meaning pp. 257–83 of item no. 145 in the bibliography, ask the editor whether he or she is prepared to accept it, or wishes another system to be imposed. If it is retained, the original order must be kept unless the editor and you can see a definite case for revision. You would then have to convert *all* references in the book.)

Titles of works cited must follow English rules: italics for published books and titles of journals, roman quoted for articles in journals and unpublished dissertations. (Note that German dissertations are always published, even if in typescript.) Capitalization, however, follows the rules for the language of the title. Continental modes of citation do not generally distinguish article and book titles in the English fashion, but article titles are sometimes followed by *in* before the journal title. (In OUP style this is correct only for separately cited chapters or articles within a book; in journal references 'in' should be replaced with a comma after the closing quote.)

Series titles must appear untranslated, in roman, without quotation marks; but those related to periodicals should appear as for example '*Hesperia*, Suppl. 13'.

All words meaning volume, fascicle, part, page, plate, figure, table, and the like should be put into English, or omitted where the bare figure would be an acceptable reference style: volume and part may be given in the form 'ii/1'; 'vol.' is never used to denote a work's place in a series. (The bare-figure style may enable the translator of a German work to evade the problem of *Heft*, which has no fixed English equivalent.)

Irrespective of the original title page, place of publication should be in English, or—failing an acceptable English equivalent—in the language officially in use there at the time: *Munich* not *München* or *Monaci*; *Breslau* up to 1945, *Wrocław* thereafter, but not *Vratislaviae* (which does not mean Bratislava). (*See also* **4.2.10**.)

Foreign publishers, in general, do not make the English distinction between *edition* (in which the author or another has been given an opportunity to revise the text) and *impression* (a reprint with at most the correction of misprints). The 6. *Auflage* of a German book may be only the second edition in the English sense, after the original and four reprints. Therefore do not translate such expressions, but represent them by a superior figure immediately following the title.

Library names are treated like other institutional names. Leave untranslated all manuscript call marks: *Paris, Bibliothèque nationale, ms. lat. 5765*; *Copenhagen, Royal Library, Gl. kgl. S. 420, 4°* (not *Latin MS, Old Royal Collection*). This is only sensible when one considers the circumstances in which a reader would rely on the call marks cited: translation hinders, not aids, finding a manuscript in its repository.

Originals and translations

Change to the original works in English cited in translation. Change to translations works in the author's language of which good English translations exist. Works in a third language cited by the author can be either in the original or in a published translation into his or her own language. If there is no English version, cite the original, appending an English translation in square brackets if the original is so inaccessible, or its language so unfamiliar, that the English reader will need or prefer to use a translation into the author's language. Translated titles are in quotation marks if an ad hoc designation, in italics if published under that title. Transliterations of titles follow the same principles as those of authors' names. Consult the editor if you think it is sensible to cite a foreign original as well as the English or other translation.

Structure

Retain the structure of the original bibliography unless it is excessively inconvenient. In the event of a numbered bibliography, however, where each work is given a number and cited by it in the text, following the instructions given above may lead to disruption of alphabetical sequence. The translator should then consult with the editor on the advisability of changing the reference system.

Example of bibliography, with translation

Original

Classen, Peter, Kodifikation im 12. Jahrhundert, in: Recht und Schrift im Mittelalter, hg. von Peter Classen, Sigmaringen 1977 (Vorträge und Forschungen 23), S. 311—317.

Die Zisterzienser, Ordensleben zwischen Ideal und Wirklichkeit, hg. von Kaspar Elm u. a., Köln 1980, Ergänzungsbd., hg. von Kaspar Elm u. a., Köln 1982 (Schriften des Rhein. Museumsamtes 10, 18).

Dilcher, Gerhard, Rechtshistorische Aspekte des Stadtbegriffs, in: Vor- und Frühformen der europäischen Stadt im Mittelalter, Tl. 1, hg. von Herbert Jankuhn u. a., Göttingen 1973 (Abh. der Akad. der Wiss. in Göttingen, phil.-hist. kl., 3. Folge 83), S. 12—33.

Duby, Georges, Die drei Ordnungen, Frankfurt am Main 1981.

Grundmann, Herbert, Rotten und Brabanzonen, in: Deutsches Archiv für Erforschung des Mittelalters, 5, 1942, S. 419—492.

Grundmann, Herbert, Bibliographie zur Ketzergeschichte des Mittelalters (1900–1966), Rom 1967 (Sussidi eruditi 20).

Haverkamp, Alfred/Enzensberger, Horst, Italien im Mittelalter, München 1980 (HZ, Sonderheft 7).

Jordan, Karl, Heinrich der Löwe, eine Biographie, München 1979.

Kamp, Norbert, Moneta regis, phil. Diss. masch., Göttingen 1957.

Mayer, Hans Eberhard, Geschichte der Kreuzzüge, 6. Aufl. Stuttgart 1985.

Petrus Abaelardus, Sic et non, hg. von E. L. Th. Henke und G. S. Lindenkohl, Marburg, 1851.

Petrus Abaelardus (1079—1142), hg. von Rudolf Thomas u. a., Trier 1980 (Trierer Theol. Stud. 38).

Planitz, Hans, Die deutsche Stadt im Mittelalter, von der Römerzeit bis zu den Zunftkämpfen, 3. Aufl., Wien 1973.

Runciman, Steven, Geschichte der Kreuzzüge, Bd. 1–3 (München 1957, 1958, 1960).

Turpilii comici fragmenta, hg. von L. Rychlewska, Breslau 1962.

Zimmermann, Harald, Das Mittelalter, Bd. 1—2, Braunschweig 1979.

Zwetajewa, Marina, Isbrannyje proiswedenija (Ausgewählte Werke), hg. von A. Jefron und A. Saakjantz, eingel. von Wl. Orlow, Moskau 1965 (Biblioteka poeta — bolschaja serija).

Translation

ABELARD, PETER, *Sic et non*, ed. E. L. T. Henke and G. S. Lindenkohl (Marburg, 1851).

CLASSEN, PETER, 'Kodifikation im 12. Jahrhundert', in id. (ed.), *Recht und*

Schrift im Mittelalter (Vorträge und Forschungen, 23; Sigmaringen, 1977), 311–17.

DILCHER, GERHARD, 'Rechtshistorische Aspekte des Stadtbegriffs', in Herbert Jankuhn et al. (eds.), *Vor- und Frühformen der europäischen Stadt im Mittelalter*, pt. 1 (Abh. der Akad. der Wiss. in Göttingen, phil.-hist. Kl., 3rd ser., 83; Göttingen, 1973), 12–33.

DUBY, GEORGES, *Les Trois Ordres ou l'imaginaire du féodalism* (Bibliothèque des histoires; Paris, 1979).

ELM, KASPAR, et al. (eds.), *Die Zisterzienser: Ordensleben zwischen Ideal und Wirklichkeit*, with suppl. vol. (Schriften des Rheinischen Museumsamtes, 10, 18; Cologne, 1980, 1982).

GRUNDMANN, HERBERT, *Bibliographie zur Ketzergeschichte des Mittelalters (1900–1966)* (Sussidi eruditi, 20; Rome, 1967).

—— 'Rotten und Brabanzonen', *Deutsches Archiv für Erforschung des Mittelalters*, 5 (1942), 419–92.

HAVERKAMP, ALFRED, and ENZENSBERGER, HORST, *Italien im Mittelalter* (*Historische Zeitschrift*, Sonderheft 7; Munich, 1980).

JORDAN, KARL, *Henry the Lion: A Biography*, trans. P. S. Falla (Oxford, 1986).

KAMP, NORBERT, *Moneta regis* (Phil. Diss., TS, Göttingen, 1957).

MAYER, HANS EBERHARD, *The Crusades*, trans. John Gillingham (2nd edn., Oxford, 1988).

PLANITZ, HANS, *Die deutsche Stadt im Mittelalter: Von der Römerzeit bis zu den Zunftkämpfen 3* (Vienna, 1973).

RUNCIMAN, STEVEN, *A History of the Crusades* (3 vols.; Cambridge, 1951–4).

THOMAS, RUDOLF, et al. (eds.), *Petrus Abaelardus (1079–1142)* (Trierer Theologische Studien, 38; Trier, 1980).

TSVETAEVA, MARINA, *Izbrannye proizvedeniya* [Selected Works], ed. A. Efron and A. Saakyants, introd. V. Orlov (Biblioteka poeta, bol'shaya seriya; Moscow, 1965).

TURPILIUS, SEX., *Turpilii comici fragmenta*, ed. L. Rychlewska (Wrocław, 1962).

ZIMMERMANN, HARALD, *Das Mittelalter* (2 vols.; Brunswick, 1979).

If a decision is made to cite the original titles of translated works, adopt the following style:

JORDAN, KARL, *Heinrich der Löwe: Eine Biographie* (Munich, 1979). [Trans. P. S. Falla, *Henry the Lion: A Biography* (Oxford, 1986).]

MAYER, HANS EBERHARD, *Geschichte der Kreuzzüge*[6] (Stuttgart, 1985). [Trans. John Gillingham, *The Crusades* (2nd edn., Oxford, 1988).]

13.11.2 Transliteration

Transliteration is undertaken either to assist the reader unfamiliar with the original script or to save the expense and likelihood of error incurred in setting a non-roman alphabet. The author may well expect the publisher to urge the latter purpose; but the former requires more detailed consideration.

13.11.2.1 Conventions

If the work is aimed purely at people who do not know the language cited, then it should be translated whenever possible, or—failing that—transcribed in the most pronounceable manner consistent with scholarly convention. If, however, readers are expected to know it, then the choice lies between the original script and strict transliteration (i.e. a transliteration from which the original script may be unambiguously recovered by rule). The policy must depend on the language cited.

Any work that makes significant use of one or more transliterated languages should have a Note on Transliteration to explain both the system adopted and any deviations from it. In many instances more than one transliteration system exists for a single language: so far as possible only one system should be used for each language. While complete consistency in the transliteration may be difficult to achieve, it should nevertheless be the objective. To say, as some authors and translators do, that any transliteration is 'meaningless' is to miss the point that a non-specialist will be confused by the same word spelt differently at different points in the text. For example, Hebrew speakers may recognize *be'er* and *beer* as alternative representations of the same word, but the English speaker has no equivalent prior knowledge on which to base this assumption: after all, *can't* and *cant* are very different.

13.11.2.2 Readership

Readers who know Greek (whether ancient or modern) will find it far harder to understand more than a few words in transliteration than in the Greek alphabet. If the work is intended only for specialists, all Greek should be in the Greek alphabet; if other readers are expected as well, individual words may be transliterated (*history* comes from the Greek word *historiē* 'inquiry'), but continuous phrases or longer texts should remain in Greek script, a translation being added ($H\rho o\delta \acute{o}\tau ov$ $\tau o\hat{v}$ $A\lambda\iota\kappa\alpha\rho\nu\eta\sigma\sigma\acute{e}o\varsigma$ $\dot{a}\pi\acute{o}\delta\epsilon\xi\iota\varsigma$ $\dot{\iota}\sigma\tau o\rho\iota\eta\varsigma$ $\ddot{\eta}\delta\epsilon$ 'This is the record of the investigation by Herodotus of Halicarnassus').

Readers whose specialism is a Slavonic language written in the Cyrillic alphabet will prefer to read it in Cyrillic, but will be able to understand it without much difficulty in transliteration, whether according to the international (philological) system more appropriate if transliteration has been adopted purely on grounds of expense or in a looser transcription, like that used in newspapers, to accommodate non-specialist readers. (The exception is Serbo-Croat, which has a Roman spelling always used in Croatia and a Cyrillic spelling preferred by Serbs.)

Readers who know Hebrew or Arabic, for example, will be familiar with the script, but able to understand strict transliteration. Western-ers—as opposed to native speakers—may well find other languages, such as those of India and the Far East, easier to understand in strict transliteration than in their proper alphabets.

CHAPTER 14

Copyright and other publishing responsibilities

14.1 General principles

This section is not intended to provide legal advice but to act as a general guide only, alerting users to matters on which help may need to be sought from the editor or publisher.

14.2 UK copyright

Copyright is a personal property right that attaches to an 'original' literary, dramatic, musical, or artistic work. Examples include books, articles, letters, examination papers, drawings and logos, sound recording and films, broadcast and cable programmes, page layouts of published editions, and computer programs. It arises when a work is created in permanent form in writing, or by visual, audio, or electronic means, and belongs to the 'author'—the creator of the work—unless made in the course of employment, when it will vest in the employer. In the UK the test of originality is very low so that for example the compilation of a list or simple table will attract copyright. A higher degree of originality is generally required for copyright protection in, for instance, France and Germany.

Copyright can be licensed geographically, temporally, by reference to specific media, or through a combination of these. In the UK, the Copyright Designs and Patents Act 1988 established the copyright period as life of the author plus fifty years from the end of the year in which the author died. As from 1 July 1995 this was increased to life plus seventy years, in compliance with the EC Directive that harmonized the term of copyright protection. A separate copyright, belonging to the publisher and lasting for twenty-five years from the end of the year of first publication, attaches to the typographical arrangement of a literary, musical, or dramatic work, irrespective of whether the underlying content of the work is still in copyright. Accordingly, the copyright in typographical arrangement of a new critical edition of a public-domain work is infringed by making facsimile copies of printed pages from it.

The Copyright Designs and Patents Act 1988, as amended by the Duration of Copyright Regulations 1995, largely altered the position that had applied to unpublished works, namely that such works could attract perpetual copyright. With effect from 1 January 1996, unpublished works have the same copyright period as published works: the life of the author plus seventy years. However, works created before that date are subject to the provisions of the 1956 Copyright Act (fifty years from the date of publication) if it would provide a longer period of protection.

Copyright confers on the owner the exclusive right to authorize certain acts in relation to a work, including copying, publication, and adaptation. Copyright can be transferred by formal written assignment, by testamentary disposition, and—rarely—by operation of law where the courts hold that this is equitable. Copyright protects the expression of ideas, not ideas themselves, although the two do converge: incidents in a story, for example, have been protected.

Subject to the provisions for fair dealing (*see* **14.2.2**), however, copyright is infringed only if the whole or a substantial part of the work is taken. Although the amount used will be relevant, this test is qualitative rather than quantitative. If the essential element of a work is copied, even if this constitutes only a small part of the work, copyright will be infringed.

If an author or editor adapts or adds to a copyright work, and in so doing exercises sufficient skill and care, then a new copyright will arise in the revised work. Nevertheless, if the revised work incorporates a substantial part of the original work without the consent of the copyright owner, copyright in the original work will be infringed. This applies not just to text but to such things as tables, diagrams, and figures.

A joint copyright work is one in which the contributions of two or more authors are commingled. A collective work is one in which the contribution of each author, and initially the copyright for it, is separate from that of the other author(s). For example, a multi-author text, where each chapter is the sole creation of a separate author, constitutes a series of works of individual authorship: the title verso of the text usually has something like © *the various contributors* on it. One party to a joint copyright cannot alone give consent binding on his/her co-authors to use a joint work.

Copyright is subject to national frontiers. Different copyright periods apply, and acts of infringement that take place outside the UK are not actionable in the UK. Proceedings have to be brought in the jurisdiction in question.

14.2.1 Illustrations

Illustrations of any kind that an author wishes to include, but that are not his or her own work, are governed by laws similar to those for writing.

In the main, the copyright for any painting belongs to the artist, and continues with his or her heirs or assigns until seventy years after his or her death. This means that although the owner of the physical painting may do what he or she likes with the work—including selling, altering, or setting fire to it—the owner may not reproduce it in any form without the artist's permission. Formerly the law was completely different for commissioned portraits, engravings, etchings, lithographs, woodcuts, prints, or linocuts: the copyright used to belong to whoever commissioned the work (provided he or she had paid or agreed to pay for it), and lasted until fifty years after that person's death. Since the commencement of the Copyright Designs and Patents Act (1 August 1989), however, the position of such commissioned works is exactly the same as for any other work, with copyright belonging to the creator.

14.2.2 Fair Dealing

The permitted forms of fair dealing provide exceptions to the acts restricted by copyright so long as a sufficient acknowledgement is given. The forms of fair dealing are used for purposes of individual research or private study, criticism and review (whether of that work or another work), and reporting current events.

Photographs are excluded from the provisions for fair dealing relating to the reporting of current events, and fair dealing for the purposes of research and private study does not apply to artistic works (including photographs) as a whole.

The amount of a work that can be copied within the limits of fair dealing will vary, according to the proportion of the whole that it represents. For example, it is unlikely that taking large parts of a long work will come within the ambit of fair dealing, though the reproduction of a large part of a short work might. In each case the author or editor must consider the number and extent of the proposed quotations or extracts in the context of the work in which they are to be incorporated.

For fair dealing to apply the dealing must be undertaken by the copyist for his or her own benefit and not for the benefit of others, and the intention of the copyist must be genuine—that is, use of the material copied must truly be for research purposes. The copyist must use the minimum necessary to achieve his or her purposes. The number of copies made in relation to the copyist's objectives is also relevant. Making and distributing more copies than are necessary will render dealing unfair: for example, it can never be fair dealing to take numerous copies of a work for the purposes of private study.

In the UK commercial use of material may preclude fair dealing. Even though a textbook is intended for private study the fair-dealing exemption will not apply to the reproduction of a substantial part of a copyright work in it, since the dealing will be by the publisher for its own commercial purposes and not by the student.

Fair dealing is not usually available for unpublished material unless—even though unpublished—such material has been made generally available. It is also not usually available for a work that has been prepared in circumstances where there is a duty of confidence.

Separate provisions exist for dealing by librarians, copying for purposes of educational instruction, and examination.

14.2.3 Fair Use

In the UK there are two steps to determining whether the use of a work infringes the copyright in it. First, it must be established whether a substantial part of the work has been used. If so, the second step is to give consideration as to whether such use constitutes fair dealing. There is no such distinction in the USA, which recognizes only one test—that of fair use. Authors of works published or co-published by US authors should seek advice from their US editors.

14.2.4 Moral rights

Under the Copyright Act of 1988, authors and directors have four basic moral rights; many other countries extend similar moral rights to their authors. The rights apply to works entitled to copyright protection, and ownership of copyright is a separate issue: authors can sell their copyright without affecting their moral rights, which cannot be assigned. (The Act itself gives specific information about when and to whom the rights do and do not apply, and how the right of paternity is asserted in the case of non-literary works.)

■ *The right of paternity.* This is the right to be identified as the work's author. The right of paternity needs to be asserted, as it does not exist automatically; it lasts for the same period as the copyright period.

■ *The right of integrity.* This is the right to protest against treatment that 'amounts to distortion or mutilation of the Work and is otherwise prejudicial to the honour or reputation of the author or director'. (Thus something done that is prejudicial to the author's honour or reputation will not be actionable unless there is *also* some modification to the work itself.) The right of integrity does not need to be asserted, as it exists automatically; it lasts for the same period as the copyright period.

■ *The right of false attribution.* This is the right not to have a literary, dramatic, musical, or artistic work falsely attributed to one as author, or a film falsely attributed to one as director. This right lasts for twenty years after the person's death.

■ *The right of privacy of photographs and films.* This does not apply to *all* photographs and films.

Many publishers affirm the author's moral rights as a matter of course in their standard publisher's contract. The statement usually appears on the title verso, taking the form *The moral right of [author's name] to be identified as the author of this work as been asserted in accordance with the Copyright Designs and Patents Act 1988*, or simply *The author's moral rights have been asserted.*

These moral rights do not extend to works reporting current events, or to works where an author contributes to a periodical (e.g. journal, magazine, or newspaper) or other collective work of reference (e.g. dictionary, encyclopedia, or yearbook). In such cases the work may be trimmed, altered, and edited without securing the author's approval.

14.3 **Copyright conventions**

Basically each member nation extends benefit of its own copyright laws to works by citizens of other member nations—the principle of National Treatment—regardless of place of original publication. Anomalies exist, however, because the duration of the copyright period is not the same in all member nations: for example, a work published in Germany would have a copyright period of life of the author plus seventy years, while the same book published in the USA would have a copyright period only of life of the author plus fifty years. (All EU nationals enjoy uniform rights in respect of works first published in the EU.) It is still considered best practice to register copyright in the USA to avoid any potential enforcement problems.

14.3.1 Universal Copyright Convention

First adopted in 1952, the Universal Copyright Convention (UCC) was effective originally in sixteen countries; there are now more than ninety member nations. To claim copyright protection in member nations, the symbol © (which the convention introduced), name of copyright owner, and date of publication must appear in a prominent place—usually the verso of the title page—in every copy of the work.

Any material published before its country of origin became a signatory to the UCC technically should not use the ©, but rather the word *copyright*. Theoretically this means one should try to determine the date of signing for each country represented by an acknowledged work, and maintain the distinction between word and symbol. A publisher's editor or rights department can help with this if need be.

14.3.2 Berne Convention

The Berne Convention was first agreed in 1886, and has been revised several times. There are now 120 members, including the USA (which signed in 1989), and Russia (which signed in 1995). It does not require registration of the book, statement of copyright, or—technically—use of the copyright symbol (©). The author also has the 'moral right' to object to any alteration of his or her work, regardless of copyright ownership.

14.4 **Permissions**

All use of copyright material—whether published or not, and even if covered under fair dealing—requires sufficient acknowledgement. Further, some use requires permission from the copyright holder. Most publishers, including OUP, expect authors to secure permissions to reproduce any copyrighted work in their text. A broad outline follows of what this may entail, with some guidelines for requesting permissions and acknowledging them. Authors requiring further guidance should consult their editor.

14.4.1 **What needs permission**

The Society of Authors and the Publishers Association have set out the following conventions for gauging when permission should be sought. (Note, however, that these conventions do not apply to anthology use, for which *see* **14.4.3**.)

- From a copyright prose work, seek permission for any extract of longer than four hundred words; for a series of extracts totalling more than eight hundred words, of which any one extract has more than three hundred words; and for an extract or series of extracts constituting one-quarter or more of the original work.

- From a copyright work of poetry, seek permission for an extract of more than forty lines; for a series of extracts totalling more than forty lines; for an extract constituting one-quarter or more of a complete poem; and for a series of extracts constituting together one-quarter or more of a complete poem.

- For an illustration, seek permission for any graphic representation (tables, figures, diagrams, photographs, drawings, etc.) or part thereof not generated by the author; and for any such graphic representation adapted by the author.

14.4.2 **Requesting permission**

In requesting permission from copyright holders, authors must first describe the work to be published, so that they have some idea of how, where, and in what circumstances their material will appear. (If necessary, check with your editor to clarify what rights are required, and whom to approach for text, tables, artwork, photos, etc.) Secondly, give them specific information about the work in which the material appeared, to aid identification.

About your book:
- name of author(s) or editor(s)
- title and edition
- proposed publication date
- edition(s) for which rights are needed (hard- and paperback, paperback only, etc.)
- initial print run, by edition if necessary
- projected price
- territory required
- language(s) required
- description (academic monograph, anthology, college text, etc.)

- (for an illustration) size or area of reproduction
- (for an illustration) whether colour or black and white; where and how used if it is to appear on the work's dust jacket or cover

  About their book:
- name of author(s) or editor(s)
- title and edition
- publication date
- exact material to be used (poem, passage, illustration), including line or word count, or figure or table numbers

If the material comes from an unpublished source, give as full a description as possible: shelf mark/call number, folio/negative/catalogue number; it is useful to enclose a photocopy. Ask how the copyright holder wishes to be acknowledged (called the 'credit line' especially in US publishing).

Authors should make clear whether they are translating, redrawing, or modifying copyright material, or are making a model from it (a photocopy of the result is helpful). Ensure that you receive all the territorial rights you need—for example, those for North America or Australasia may be held by the local publisher. Since obtaining permission can take longer than even the more pessimistic of authors may expect, they should embark on the process early on (*see* **FIG. 14.1**)— certainly no later than submission of the typescript.

Crown copyright publications include Bills and Acts of Parliament, Command Papers, Reports of Select Committees, Hansard, non-parliamentary publications by government departments, naval charts published by the Ministry of Defence, and Ordnance Survey publications. Further information can be obtained from Her Majesty's Stationery Office, Copyright Unit, St Crispins, Duke Street, Norwich NR3 1PD.

14.4.3 Acknowledgements

Unless a specific location is stipulated by the copyright holder, the acknowledgement may be placed wherever it is most practicable or logical, given the quantity and variety of material to be acknowledged. Provide the acknowledgement where a reader would reasonably expect to find it, at the place where the material falls in the text, in a separate list of acknowledgements, or as part of a list of illustrations, tables, figures, etc.

When an entire chapter or section is being reproduced, the acknowledgement can appear as an uncued note at the foot of its first page. When a smaller extract or series of extracts is being reproduced, details

Please reply to: [Author's address]

Dear Sir or Madam,

I should like to request permission to use the following material from your book/article:

Author/editor:

Title:

[Journal name, volume number, and page extent:]

Year of publication:

Material:

The material is to be included in the academic [textbook/reference book/ etc.] I am preparing:

Authors/editors:

Title:

To be published by [name of publisher].

Probable publication date:

Estimated number of pages:

[If only a small number of copies is to be printed for a specialized readership, this should be mentioned, as fees may be waived in such circumstances.]

Rights required:

[Typically these will be non-exclusive world rights in all languages.]

Full acknowledgement to the source will be made; please let me know the form you wish the acknowledgement to take, and the fee if one is payable. Any invoice should be sent to me.

If it is necessary to apply to the author also, I should be grateful if you could give me his/her current address.

A duplicate copy of this letter is enclosed for your convenience.

Yours faithfully,

Figure 14.1: **A letter requesting permission to use published material**

can be listed in an acknowledgements section, either in the preliminary matter or—especially with anthologies or collections—at the end of the work.

Acknowledgement of permission to reproduce illustrations, figures, or tables may be incorporated in or appended to a list of illustrations, or added to an acknowledgements section in the preliminary matter of the work. For illustrations, acknowledgements may also be run as part of the caption; for figures and tables they may be set out on a separate note below the caption under the heading *Source:*.

A common alternative in scientific works is to use the author–date formula, for example *From Smith 2001*, for figures, tables, diagrams, or similar graphic representations that have been copied from another work; *After Smith 2001* is used when the representation has been adapted from another work with modifications. This system is suitable if the acknowledgements are short, or if they can be tied easily into the references, since it provides a citation that can be looked up in the bibliography for the complete reference.

The legal and customary requirement is to credit the source, providing the elements in an acknowledgements format along these lines:

> [author], from [title of copyrighted text] [edition, if other than the first], [year of publication], © [copyright proprietor—this can be the author or another party]. Reprinted [*or* Reproduced] by permission of [usually a publisher or agent].

An example of this would be

> Joseph Bloggs, from *A Lardycake Companion* (2nd edn., 2002), © Joseph Bloggs 2002. Reprinted by permission of Crumpet Press.

For examples from an anthology *see* below.

The publisher's name alone is sufficient: no street address, or even city or country, is needed. When it is in a foreign language it should not be translated, although romanization from a non-roman alphabet is acceptable. When copyright illustrations are acknowledged, use *reproduced* instead of *reprinted* (for placement of the acknowledgement in an illustration *see* **10.2**).

Wording, capitalization, and punctuation can be standardized, although not in instances where the copyright holder specifies a particular form of words for the acknowledgement, or its position. Authors must ensure that this is followed exactly, since the copyright holder has the right to make this a condition of granting permission for the text or illustration to be used. This happens most often when dealing with works from modern authors, or with copyright proprietors that are not publishers, for example independent organizations or royal collections. An acknowledgement list may be prefaced by *We are grateful for permission to reproduce the following material in this volume*, to save space and avoid repetition.

The following example illustrates several common features of an acknowledgements section for illustrations:

> Acknowledgement is made to the following for photographs and permission to reproduce illustrations: Alinari 34, 61, 124*a*, 124*b*, 159, 302, 380; Antikensammlungen, Munich 155; Archives Photographiques 148 (top), 222; Arxiv Mas, Barcelona 5, 6, 22, 175, 223, Ashmolean Museum, Oxford 7, 107, 244, 289; Bibliothèque Nationale, Paris 41, 88 (left), 142, 192, 170*a*, 170*b*, 170*c*, 198, 247 (foot), 338; Dean and Chapter of Canterbury Cathedral (Entwistle Photographic Services) 33, 189, 401; Everhard-Karls- Universität, Tübingen, Institut für Ur- und Frühgeschichte 33, 35, Master and Follows of Corpus Christi College, Cambridge 120, 131, 316; Trustees of the British Museum 25, 26, 205, 293, 330.

These could equally have been arrayed in columns, or ordered by page number rather than copyright holder—arguably more useful to the reader—especially where few illustrations share a common source.

Permission must be obtained for *all* copyright material in an anthology, regardless of length. The result is usually a separate acknowledgements section, placed either in the preliminary pages or at the end of the book, before the index. Existing anthologies can provide good patterns to follow, and a publisher's editor or rights department can also provide guidance. Normally the format of an acknowledgement must be in the exact form specified by the copyright holder and not standardized; reprint and copyright years must be given in full where indicated. The following is an extract from an anthology's acknowledgements section, which retains the variations in style stipulated by the copyright holders:

> Evelyn Waugh, from *Men at Arms*, copyright 1952, © renewed 1979 by Evelyn Waugh; from *Put Out More Flags*, copyright 1942, © renewed 1977 by Evelyn Waugh; from *Scoop*, copyright 1937, 1938, © renewed 1965, 1966 by Evelyn Waugh; from *Black Mischief*, copyright 1932, © renewed 1960 by Evelyn Waugh; from *Decline and Fall*, copyright 1928, © renewed 1956 by Evelyn Waugh; all reprinted by permission of Little, Brown and Company and the Peters Fraser & Dunlop Group Ltd.

> H. G. Wells, 'The Truth About Pyecraft', from *The Complete Short Stories of H. G. Wells*, and excerpt from *Kipps*. Reprinted by permission of A. P. Watt Ltd., on behalf of The Literary Executors of the Estate of H. G. Wells.

> Michael Wharton ('Peter Simple'), 'The Way of the World', from the *Daily Telegraph*. Reprinted by permission of Ewan MacNaughton Associates.

> E. B. White, 'Isadora's Brother', from 'The Talk of the Town' feature in *The New Yorker*, 7 Dec. 1929; 'Farewell My Lovely', from *Essays of E. B. White* (Harper & Row); copyright 1936, © 1964 The New Yorker Magazine, Inc. Originally published in *The New Yorker* in 1936 over the pseudonym 'Lee Strout White'. Richard L. Strout had submitted a manuscript on the Ford, and White, with his collaboration, rewrote it. Used by permission.

> P. G. Wodehouse, from *Mike* (1929); from *Ukridge* (1924); 'Came the Dawn', from the *Mulliner Omnibus* (1927); from *Right Ho Jeeves* (1934); from *Something Fresh* (1915); 'Lord Emsworth and the Girlfriend', from *Blandings Castle and Elsewhere* (1935) and brief quotations from other works by P. G. Wodehouse. Reprinted by permission of A. P. Watt Ltd., on behalf of The Trustees of the Wodehouse Trust No. 3 and Century Hutchinson.

> Tom Wolfe, from *In Our Times*, copyright © 1961, 1963, 1964, 1965, 1968, 1971, 1972, 1975, 1976, 1977, 1978, 1979, 1980 by Tom Wolfe. Reprinted by permission of Farrar, Straus & Giroux, Inc.

> Alexander Woollcott, from *While Rome Burns*. Copyright 1934 by Alexander Woollcott. Copyright renewed © 1962 by Joseph P. Hennessey, Executor of the Estate of Alexander Woollcott. All rights reserved. Reprinted by permission of Viking Penguin, a division of Penguin Books USA, Inc.

Naturally there is a necessity for the author's having made a real (and demonstrable) effort to trace and contact copyright owners. When this has proved fruitless, include a disclaimer at the end of an acknowledgements section, along the following lines:

> There are instances where we have been unable to trace or contact the copyright holder. If notified the publisher will be pleased to rectify any errors or omissions at the earliest opportunity.

14.5 **Defamation**

A defamatory statement is one that injures the reputation of another person by exposing that person to hatred, contempt, or ridicule, or is disparaging or injurious to that person in his or her business, or lowers a person in the estimation of right-thinking members of society generally. Libel is the making of a defamatory statement in writing or other permanent form; slander is the making of an oral defamatory statement.

Libel is broadly defined under UK law. In essence an allegation is defamatory if it is untrue and a person's reputation is damaged by it. As far as individuals are concerned it will be actionable whether or not it results in pecuniary loss. The plaintiff need not be named but must be identifiable. The defamatory statement need not be direct; it may be implied or by way of innuendo. A company has a reputation but can sue for libel only if it can demonstrate that an allegation has resulted in financial loss. However, the directors of a company—if named or identifiable—might be able to sue for untrue allegations made against the company even if no financial loss has been suffered.

The dead cannot be libelled, but care must be taken to ensure that in statements about the dead the living are not defamed by association. For example, an untrue allegation that a man was not married to his partner might by implication libel the partner or the offspring of that union.

The intention of the author is irrelevant in determining whether a statement is defamatory. A defamed person is entitled to plead any meaning for the words used that a 'reasonable' person might infer. An example is the word *alleged*. The author might mean no more than 'it has been said against so and so that': the subject of such comment could, however, plead that the word would be understood to mean that he had *done* what was alleged.

The clearest defence against a libel action is that the statements can be proved to be true by direct first-hand evidence. (The defence of fair comment is not available for such statements.) It is no defence to a libel action that the defamatory statements have been published previously, although this might affect the level of damages payable.

Criticism or other expressions of opinion can be defended as fair comment provided (a) the subject matter of the comment is one of public interest, (b) the facts underlying the expression of opinion are true, and (c) the comment is relevant to the facts.

A libel action can be brought in the UK for a libel occurring abroad if the words complained of are defamatory under the laws of the foreign jurisdiction in question, and the plaintiff has a reputation in that jurisdiction.

14.6 **Negligent misstatement**

If an author makes a statement negligently (without due care) in circumstances where it is likely and reasonable that the reader will place reliance on it, the author might be liable for all damage flowing from the statement. There must be sufficient proximity in the relationship between the author and the reader for a duty of care to arise. A 'how to' book as opposed to a purely informational book is more likely to provide such a nexus.

The publisher might be liable for loss resulting from a negligent misstatement if it has failed to exercise reasonable care in checking a work for accuracy in circumstances where it would be reasonable to expect the publisher to check it.

Claims for negligent misstatement are generally successful only where they have resulted in physical injury as opposed to purely financial loss.

14.7 **Passing off**

Passing off is a branch of the intellectual property laws of a number of jurisdictions worldwide—though in some jurisdictions, such as in the USA, the offence falls into the category of unfair competition. Passing off is a particularly well-developed concept in the UK: it often involves the use of similar names or packaging, and is aimed at preventing confusion among dealers or customers that might result from these similarities. In short, no one has the right to represent his or her goods as the goods of somebody else. Passing off is quite separate from the issue of registered trademark or copyright infringement. It is used either where there is no registered trademark at all, or alongside a claim for registered trademark infringement.

Passing-off disputes in the field of publishing can arise in various different ways. Most often they involve similar titles—especially series titles where customers may buy individual books on the strength of the series name; similar dust jacket design, meaning books from different publishers have a similar appearance, logo, or brand. More specific examples include giving the impression that a biography has been authorized by its subject, or that a sequel was authorized or written by the author of the original book.

Authors should notify their editor immediately if they have any reason to suspect that their chosen title or design might lead to a conflict with a third-party publication that is already using, or is about to use, something similar.

CHAPTER 15

References and notes

15.1 **General principles**

Any scholarly book based on primary or secondary sources needs a system of references that is complete, logical, and informative to the reader. It should go without saying that the references must be accurate; no matter how excellent, a book with sloppy citations will perplex or annoy the reader and cast a shadow on the author's reputation. Editing may remove surface blemishes and inconsistencies, but it is the author's responsibility to see that all quotations and references to sources are accurate in the first instance.

The order, presentation, and choice of material included in references and notes is subject to a good deal of variation. While any rational technique is acceptable providing it is clear and consistent, readers will benefit from being presented with a familiar pattern. Several authoritative formats exist, which are favoured by certain disciplines and publishers; choosing one of these will put editors in a better position to impose uniformity where lapses occur. The guidelines below suggest a system of references that is broadly applicable to most subjects; common permutations and problems are highlighted.

Variations aside, references in general should be organized on one of two principles: author–title (*see* **15.18**) or author–date (*see* **15.19**). The former is traditional in humanistic disciplines, and requires foot- or endnotes; the latter is more frequent in the sciences, including the social sciences, and requires in-text references. The author–title system is essential in a bibliography including publications not cited in the work; the author–date system must not be used in a 'Further Reading' section, which should be either discursive or on the author–title plan. A further form of reference—the author–number (*see* **15.20**) system—is also possible, though its utility and scope are limited.

Otherwise, the choice should be guided by the nature of the materials cited, the style of a particular series or journal, and the nature of the materials common in the author's discipline: where works are published once and for all, the Harvard system has the advantage of enabling the reader to follow the progress of debate:

> The contention of Smith (1976) was sharply criticized by Jones (1979), but drew qualified support from Robinson (1982).

It is of less benefit if—as often in the humanities—the Smith citation is from his revised edition of 1994 and the Jones citation from her collected essays of 1987.

No general guidelines can claim to be exhaustive; what follows rather is advice for dealing with frequently used types of citation. For anything not found here the author or editor may devise suitable forms of reference, providing they are imposed consistently and contain all relevant information required by the reader. (*See also* **15.19**.)

Volume and page numbers

In the interest of brevity (a welcome habit in references and notes), certain abbreviations are customary. When specific volumes or pages from a work have been used they should be cited; page numbers are elided as normal. The abbreviation vol. is generally superfluous in notes. Volumes of a multi-volume work are cited in roman numerals followed by a full point, a space, and the page number. The abbreviations p. or pp. can usually be omitted safely as well: the thirty-second and thirty-third pages of the fourth volume is cited as *iv. 32–3*. The page abbreviation is, however, retained before roman numerals when the reference is to roman-numeral preliminary matter, to avoid confusion with a volume number (e.g. pp. iii–xxiv); here, *vol.* should be included to balance *p.* (e.g. *vol. i, p. lxii*).

Even if the work is numbered by column, the bare number will suffice, since the reference will become clear to readers looking up the reference. Exceptionally, citations of works with complex or unusual structures (parts, cantos, sections, lines, etc.) may be used in combination with volume or page numbers to describe a work's hierarchy. In such instances, *vol.* and *p.* or *pp.* are used for clarity's sake, and in uniformity with any other terms.

At first reference to an article, or if it is not in a select bibliography, give the full page extent, since this can give the reader some means of identifying the major articles on a subject. Do so even if only part of it is relevant; in that case add *at* plus the appropriate page numbers.

Do not use *f.* except with roman numerals (*lxxxvii f.*); avoid *ff.* wherever possible. When either *f.* or *ff.* is used—either because the reference cannot be checked or because discussion is too open-ended to assign a definite closing page—editors should insert a thin space between it and the page number.

If a specific page reference is needed the first time a work is cited, it may be given in the following form:

> Mary A. Rouse and Richard H. Rouse, 'The Book Trade at the University of Paris, *c.*1250–*c.*1350', in eid., *Authentic Witnesses: Approaches to Medieval Texts and Manuscripts* (Publications in Medieval Studies, 17; Notre Dame, Ind., 1991), 259–338 at 332.

Notes

A reference to a single note on a page is abbreviated as *n.* (*196 n.*), and to more than one note on the same page as *nn.* (*196 nn.*); in both instances a thin space traditionally separated the page number and abbreviation, but increasingly a word space is used. When the note is cited by its number, a word space precedes and follows the abbreviation (*196 n. 13*; *196 nn. 13–15*).

Dates

Months are abbreviated to the common three- or four-letter form: *Apr.*, *Sept.*, etc. when given as part of a date in a note (*13 Apr. 1975*); in running text the full name is retained (*In March he finally delivered his typescript*). Centuries are abbreviated as *17th cent.* or *17th c.* (*the 17th-c. transept*). Other numerals are treated as in the main text.

15.2　**Books**

References for books form the basis from which other forms of reference are derived. While certain elements of the citation are optional, if they are used they must be used consistently: these are number of volumes, series title, and publisher, which may be omitted from the notes even if given in the bibliography or references.

15.2.1　**Author's name**

A couple of generations ago, British academic authors were known by their initials, and female authors were so rare relatively that the convention of spelling out their names was considered not only gallant but useful, so as to avoid the faux pas of unwittingly referring to a female author as *he*. (Even then the practice was not without pitfalls, as *Chris*, *Evelyn*, *Hilary*, *Kim*, *Jocelyn*, *Lesley*, and *Lindsay* are all names for both sexes.) US custom, however, is to retain whole names for both sexes, and this has much to recommend it: citing forenames by initials only is not a service to the reader, who may wish to look up a book by *J. Smith* in the library.

The recommended practice is to follow the form of the name in the source cited: keep forenames if they are given in the publication; do not force uniformity if initials only are present. Literary names should not be harmonized. While in principle it may be desirable that authors be cited either all with full given names or all with initials, perfect consistency in full names is often unattainable: it may not always be possible to establish the full names of, say, obscure contributors to nineteenth-century journals; and whereas some authors insist on being known by their initials, others object to being cut down.

In English names, first-letter initials suffice: do not, for example, use *Chas.*, *Wm.*, or *Robt.* except when reproducing title pages. This does not apply in foreign—especially transliterated—languages: *Th.*, *Ll.*, or *Ph.*, for example, should not be reduced. Ideally, any accents omitted on capital letters of authors' or editors' names should be restored. This may require some knowledge: a Spanish author called AVILES at the beginning or end of an article should become Avilés in notes and bibliographies.

Three is the maximum number of authors that should be cited in a multi-author or -editor publication; for more than three, use 'et al.' (from *et alii* 'and others', although 'et al.' should be printed in roman type) after the first name:

> Rosemary Stewart et al. (eds.), *Managing in Britain* (London, 1994).
>
> *Theophrastus of Eresus: Sources for his Life, Writings, Thought, and Influence*, ed. William W. Fortenbaugh et al., 2 vols. (Philosophia Antiqua, 54; Leiden, 1991).
>
> Gerald de Vaucouleurs et al., 'The New Martian Nomenclature of the International Astronomical Union', *Icarus*, 26 (1975), 85–98.

List works published under a pseudonym that is an author's literary name under that pseudonym:

> George Eliot, *Middlemarch* (New York: W. W. Norton, 1977).
>
> Mark Twain, *A Connecticut Yankee at King Arthur's Court*, with an introduction by Justin Kaplan (Harmondsworth: Penguin, 1971).

In some contexts it may be useful to add a writer's pseudonym for clarification when a writer publishes under his or her real name:

> C. L. Dodgson (Lewis Carroll), *Symbolic Logic* (Oxford: Clarendon Press, 1896).

In some cases, a work bears the name of someone other than the person who wrote it; when the attribution is known to be false but the true author is unknown, scholars—particularly classicists—prefix the name with *Pseudo-* (shortened to *Ps.-* or *ps.-*):

> Pseudo-Boethius, *De disciplina scolarium: Édition critique, introduction et notes*, ed. Olga Weijers (Leiden, 1976).

In the bibliography the work should be listed as 'BOETHIUS (PSEUDO-)', or in more scholarly works as 'BOETHIUS (Ps.-)'. This system does not distinguish between impersonation by the original author (e.g. Pseudo-Vergil, *Culex*) and wrong guesses by copyists or editors (e.g. Pseudo-Xenophon, *On the Athenian Constitution*).

An alternative, much used in references and occasionally in running text, is to enclose the name in square brackets; a refinement is to use quotation marks where authenticity is still debated (e.g. 'Plato', *Seventh Letter*). When the work is cited together with undoubtedly genuine ones, the brackets or quotation marks may be put round the title (e.g. Pl. *R.*, '*Ep.*' 7, [*Ax.*], meaning spurious *Axiochus*) or the reference number (Demosthenes 18, [59], meaning the genuine speech number 18 and the spurious speech number 59). The latter method may also indicate spurious or doubtful passages of the same work quoted together with genuine ones.

In some cases the traditional 'author' is not believed, and the work is cited under its title:

> *Disticha Catonis*, ed. Marcus Boas and Henricus Johannes Botschuyver (Amsterdam, 1952).

Where the author's name is not given but is known from other sources, it is printed in square brackets:

> [James Balfour], *Philosophical Essays* (Edinburgh, 1768).
>
> [John Gibbon], *Day-Fatality: Or Some Observations on Days Lucky and Unlucky* (London, 1678; rev. edn. 1686).
>
> [Laurence Sterne], *A Sentimental Journey through France and Italy, by Mr. Yorick* (London, 1768).

So, for example, if Sterne's work was cited in a bibliography, it would follow *The Life and Opinions of Tristram Shandy*, and his name would be replaced by a 2-em rule.

For original texts where the author is anonymous, the title is given first:

> *The Book of St Gilbert*, ed. Raymonde Foreville and Gillian Keir (Oxford Medieval Texts; Oxford, 1987).
>
> *Graduale Arosiense impressum*, ed. Toni Schmid (Laurentius Petri Sällskapets Urkundsserie, 7; Malmö, 1959–65).

In a bibliography *Anonymous* may be used, with like works alphabetized accordingly:

> ANONYMOUS, *Stories after Nature* (London: Allman, 1822).

In modern Latin *Anonymus* is used to designate the unknown author himself, such as *Anonymus Iamblichi*, *Anonymus Londinensis*, *Anonymus I*, *Anonymus IV*.

If no author or editor is found, as in some exhibition catalogues, give the title alone:

> *Liber usualis* (Tournai: Desclée, 1956).

Raffaello: Elementi di un mito. Le fonti, la letteratura artistica, la pittura di genere storico (Exhibition catalogue; Florence: Centro Di, 1984).

Editors, translators, revisers

Editors of a multi-author volume should be cited (both in the bibliography and in footnotes) by name followed by *(ed.)* or *(eds.)* (standing for 'editor(s)') as the case may be before the title: Editor (ed.), *Title* (place, date). Editors of literary texts (or of another author's papers) are cited after the title, in the form: Author, *Title*, ed. Editor (place, date); in this case *ed.* (standing for 'edited by') remains unchanged even if there is more than one editor. This practice may also be followed for Festschriften, conference proceedings, and reference works regularly known by their titles rather than their editors; but authors making use of this exception should inform their editor explicitly.

Translators and revisers are similarly named after the title (*tr.*, *rev.*); however, revisers whose contribution is sufficiently substantial for them to count as joint authors and to figure in short-title or name-only references (e.g. Kühner–Blass) are named after the original author: KÜHNER, R., rev. BLASS, F.

15.2.2 Titles and subtitles

Capitalization

Capitalize the first word in titles and then all nouns, strong or main verbs, adjectives, and adverbs, leaving as lower-case any conjunctions, prepositions, and articles not starting the title; pronouns are capitalized according to their importance. Subtitles follow the same formula.

> *The Importance of Being Earnest: A Trivial Comedy for Serious People*
>
> *Punting: Its History and Techniques*
>
> *Twenty Years After*
>
> *Moby-Dick, or, The Whale*
>
> *A Handy Guide to Oxford, Specially Written for the Wounded*

Very short titles may look best with every word capitalized: *All About Eve*. Capitalization of foreign titles follows the rules of the language.

In science and medical books, book titles—whether appearing in the body of the text, including footnotes, or in bibliographies, further reading lists, etc.—are normally printed with initial capital letters for the first word and proper nouns only. While this may be followed for works in disciplines where the convention is common, or where there is strong precedent (such as a series style), it should not be imposed in the absence of specific instructions; similarly, it should not be imposed on subtitles only.

In practice the choice between upper and lower case is usually instinctive, although some titles are more problematic than others, as titles capitalized according to these rules can still look 'wrong'. For example, is it *Can You Forgive her?* or *Can you Forgive Her?*, or something in between? Unless the exact form is of bibliographic or semantic relevance, it is most important to style a title sensibly and consistently throughout a work.

The second (or subsequent) element in a compound is capitalized according to how it would be treated if it stood alone, for example *The Forty-Nine Steps*, *Neo-Classical Art*, *The Well-Beloved* (since the second of each would be upper-case when standing alone); but *Brown-eyed Girl*, *The Lock-out*, *A Pay-off* (since the second of each would be lower-case when standing alone).

Take care to cite titles from the title page, not the dust jacket or the cover of a paperback edition. These can often differ, owing to design or marketing considerations:

> A. L. Poole, *Domesday Book to Magna Carta, 1087–1216* (paperback cover).
>
> Austin Lane Poole, *From Domesday Book to Magna Carta, 1087–1216* (title page).

Spelling

A title's spelling is considered sacrosanct and should not be standardized, or altered to conform to a house style:

> Anonymous, *Primary Colors*
>
> Kenneth Clark, *Civilisation*
>
> Donna J. Haraway, *Modest_Witness@Second_ Millennium.FemaleMan_ Meets_OncoMouse: Feminism and Technoscience*

Similarly, a reference to Carlyle's *History of Mediaeval Political Theory in the West* should be reproduced thus, regardless of imposing the preferred modern spelling *medieval* elsewhere in text. (It is acceptable to change the *æ* ligature to *ae*—or *œ* to *oe*—since in modern English the distinction is typographical rather than phonetic.) *Greenes Groats-Worth of Witte* should not be normalized to *Greene's Groat's-Worth of Wit* unless the reference is not to the 1592 original but to a modern-spelling reprint. Straightforward modernization is acceptable only when it is announced.

The spelling of titles should mirror what is found in the running text. In particular, do not leave classical or modern Greek titles in capitals, even if they were styled thus on the title page: *Γῆς ὀστέα* not *ΓΗΣ ΟΣΤΕΑ*. Add breathings and accents, or accents alone for works in modern Greek using the monotonic system:

> Panayiotis Chrysostomou, "*Οι νεολιθικές έρευνες στην πόλη και την επαρχία Γιαννιτσών κατά το 1991*", Το αρχαιολογικό έργο στη Μακεδονία, 5 (1991), 111–25.

In German, the *Eszett* should be used where appropriate even if the title, being in capitals, used SS (thus GRUNDRISS becomes *Grundriß*, though

GRUNDRISSE remains as *Grundrisse*); in nineteenth-century publications *AE, OE, UE* should become *Ae, Oe, Ue* when initial in words requiring a capital, otherwise *ä, ö, ü* (*UEBER EINE UEBERFLUESSIGE UEBERSETZUNG* will thus become *Ueber eine überflüssige Uebersetzung* rather than modern *Über eine überflüssige Übersetzung*, but not *Ueber eine ueberfluessige Uebersetzung*).

Punctuation

A title's punctuation must follow that on the title page. However, since there is usually a line break rather than any punctuation between the title and subtitle, OUP standardizes to a colon. This applies to all languages, although peculiar or long-winded historical titles with several subtitles may require a more considered approach, perhaps employing full points as well:

> Thomas A. Brady, Jr., Heiko A. Oberman, and James D. Tracy (eds.), *Handbook of European History, 1400–1600: Late Middle Ages, Renaissance and Reformation*, i: *Structures and Assertions* (Leiden: E. J. Brill, 1994).
>
> José Fernández Castillo, *Normas para correctores y compositores tipógrafos: Propuesta y réplica al pliego de enmiendas y adiciones* (Madrid: Espasa-Calpe, 1959).
>
> Louis Duchesne, *Christian Worship: Its Origin and Evolution. A Study of the Latin Liturgy up to the Time of Charlemagne* (London, 1919).
>
> Charles R. Gibson, *The Romance of Electricity: Describing in Non-Technical Language What Is Known about Electricity and Many of Its Interesting Applications* (London: Seeley, 1906).
>
> Daniel I. Vieyra, *Fill 'er Up: An Architectural History of America's Gas Stations* (New York: Macmillan, 1979).

In the first example, both the first comma and the colon have been added to the title, which has no punctuation but is set out in four lines on the title page.

In German books compound words may be divided in displayed matter without a hyphen; these should be returned to their regular form. Thus *DER | SPRACH | BROCK | HAUS* on the cover becomes *Der Sprach-Brockhaus* in a reference. In some cases what looks like a compound word is actually a title and subtitle: the title page *AISCHYLOS | INTERPRETATIONEN* is really U. von Wilamowitz-Moellendorff, *Aischylos: Interpretationen* (Berlin, 1914).

Titles within titles

Book titles within titles are printed in the opposite font, that is, not italicized:

> Lewis White Beck, *A Commentary on Kant's* Critique of Practical Reason (Chicago, 1960).
>
> Antonia Tissoni Benvenuti, *L'Orfeo del Poliziano* (Padua: Editrice Antenore, 1986).

One alternative is to place the book title within quotation marks. This works better when the book title begins or ends the article title, as in the first example above. Titles that themselves use quotation marks should be so reproduced:

> Roderick O'Conor, *A Sentimental Journey through 'Finnegans Wake', with a Map of the Liffey* (Dublin: HCE Press, 1977).

Another alternative—to underline the matter—is possible, though seldom the best option:

> Lewis White Beck, *A Commentary on Kant's Critique of Practical Reason* (Chicago, 1960).

Long titles

In general, long and superfluous subtitles may be discreetly omitted, especially in notes. Titles of older works may retain the original style, and may be shortened if very long-winded:

> Sir Hugh Platt, *Delightes for Ladies To adorne their Persons, Tables, Closets, and Distillatories with Beauties, Banquets, Perfumes and Waters* (London, 1608).

> Henry Burton, *A Divine Tragedie lately acted or... Gods Judgements upon Sabbath-breakers, and other libertines...* (London, 1636).

Where a title is of bibliographical interest, however, it is best to copy it as faithfully as possible, normalizing neither capitalization nor punctuation: for example, vol. iii of Helen Maria Williams's *Letters from France* (1790–6), titled in full *Letters Containing a sketch of the Scenes which passed in various Departments of France during the Tyranny of Robespierre, and of the Events which took place in Paris on the Tenth of Thermidor*; and Paul Kornfeld's intentionally cumbersome *Leben, Meynungen und Thaten von Hieronimus Jobs, dem Kandidaten, und wie Er sich weiland viel Ruhm erwarb, auch endlich also Nachtwächter zu Sulzburg starb* (1784).

Foreign-language titles

Titles in a foreign language may be translated in square brackets, without quotation marks. This is useful in cases where the reader may not understand the language but could make use of the material presented in the book:

> Nissan Motor Corporation, *Nissan Jidosha 30nen shi* [A 30-Year History of Nissan Motors] (1965).

> Mao Zedong, 'Zhonghua suweiai zhongyang zhengfu dui neimenggu renmin xuanyan' [Declaration to the Inner Mongolian People from the Chinese Soviet Government, 20 Dec. 1935], in Zhonggong zhongyang tongzhanbu (compiler), *Minzu wenti wenxian huibian: 1921, 7–1949, 9* (Beijing: Zhonggong Zhongyang Dangxiao Chubanshe, 1991).

If the book contains an abstract or résumé in English (or other language), its title can be cited instead:

Jerzy Pikulik, *Indeks sekwencji w polskich rękopisach muzycznych* [English résumé: 'Sequence index in the Polish musical manuscripts']. *Sekwencje zespołu rękopisów tarnowskich* [English résumé: 'Sequences from the Tarnow manuscript set'] (Warsaw, 1974).

Where the work is a translation of an English-language work, it is helpful to give the original title:

T. E. Lawrence, *Les Sept Piliers de la sagesse* [Fr. trans. of *The Seven Pillars of Wisdom*] (trans. Charles Mauron) (Paris: Payot, 1992).

A. A. Milne, *Pu der Bär* [Ger. trans. of *Winnie the Pooh*] (Potsdam: Williams, 1938).

15.2.3 Editions

Different rules apply to editions of original texts and books and collections of articles edited by modern authors. In general, it is preferable to put editors' names after texts and before studies. If the edition cited is not the first, add (e.g.) *2nd edn.* after the title; if an editor, translator, or reviser is mentioned, the edition number should precede or follow the name according to whether the work is the translation of the subsequent edition or the subsequent edition of the translation.

Sometimes a superscript figure is employed at the end of a title to indicate which edition is cited, especially with foreign works. While this is acceptable, in most other cases it is preferable to give *2nd edn.*, etc., together with the publication information:

J. H. Baker, *An Introduction to English Legal History* (3rd edn., 1990) 419–21.

W. R. Cornish, *Intellectual Property*^{3} (1996) 3–9.

J. D. Denniston, *The Greek Particles* (2nd edn., Oxford, 1954).

J. D. Denniston, *The Greek Particles*^{2} (Oxford, 1954).

Where multiple volumes of a work are cited from different editions, each volume must be listed separately:

E. Zeller, *Die Philosophie der Griechen*, 3 vols. (i/1–2: 6th edn. rev. W. Nestle, Leipzig, 1919–20; ii/1, 5th edn., Leipzig, 1922; ii/2, 4th edn., Leipzig, 1921, iii/1–2; 5th edn. Leipzig, 1923).

Sometimes it is useful to give the date of publication of the first edition, even if quoting from a later edition. This should always be made clear:

J. D. Denniston, *The Greek Particles* (1934; 2nd edn., Oxford, 1954).

J. D. Denniston, *The Greek Particles* (Oxford, 1934; citations are from the 2nd edn., 1954).

Similarly, it can be made clear that the edition cited is a republication by a different publisher:

Bruno Bettelheim, *The Uses of Enchantment: The Meaning and Importance of Fairy Tales* (Harmondsworth: Penguin Books, 1988) (first pub. 1976).

Do not give the original publisher unless this information is of particular bibliographical interest.

In reference works, where a later edition has been undertaken by another editor, the edition number should directly follow the title:

> The Oxford Dictionary of Quotations, 5th edn., ed. Elizabeth Knowles (Oxford, 1999).

Be careful with works printed outside the English-speaking world: the *sechste Auflage* of a German book may be the sixth impression, the sixth edition, or the fourth impression of the second edition. In such cases do not guess, but write 6. *Aufl.* unless you are sure of your facts.

15.2.4 **Reprints, reprint editions, and facsimiles**

Reprint and facsimile editions are generally unchanged reproductions of the original book, although a preface or an index may be added. There is no hard and fast rule to distinguish a reprint edition from a facsimile; works with modern typefaces are more likely to be considered reprints; those emulating works of, say, the mid-eighteenth century or earlier are facsimiles. Facsimiles include the original title page, whereas reprints usually do not.

If possible, give the original place and date of publication:

> C. Adam and D. Tannery (eds.), *Œuvres de Descartes* (Paris: Cerf, 1897–1913; repr. Paris: J. Vrin, CNRS, 1964–76).

> Edward Gibbon, *Decline and Fall of the Roman Empire*, with an introduction by Christopher Dawson, 6 vols. (Everyman's Library; London, 1910; repr. 1974).

> Seemannssprüche: Sprichwörter und sprichwörtliche Redensarten über Seewesen, Schiffer- und Fischerleben in den germanischen und romanischen Sprachen, ed. W. Lüpkes (Berlin: Ernst Siegfried Mittler und Sohn, 1900; repr. Leipzig: Zentralantiquariat der DDR, 1986).

It is also desirable to note a change of title:

> Cyril Hare, *The Wind Blows Death* (London, 1987; first published as *When the Wind Blows*, 1949).

Sometimes only the original date of publication is given in the reprint edition:

> Otto Cartellieri, *The Court of Burgundy: Studies in the History of Civilization* (1925; repr. New York: Haskell House, [1970]).

If publishers are not cited and the place of publication of the reprint is the same, it is not necessary to repeat it:

> C. Adam and D. Tannery (eds.), *Œuvres de Descartes* (Paris, 1897–1913; repr. 1964–76).

A reprint is not necessarily the same as the original version (a second impression normally is, and can be ignored in citations), but sometimes this is not evident from the title page:

> R. W. Southern, *Saint Anselm: A Portrait in a Landscape* (Cambridge: Cambridge University Press, 1990).

Here, the date does not occur on the title page itself. The book was first published in 1990 and reprinted in 1991 and 1993. Only from the 'Preface to the second impression' does it become evident that the 1991 reprint is in fact a corrected reprint. Therefore, the 1991 reprint should be cited in the following form:

> R. W. Southern, *Saint Anselm: A Portrait in a Landscape* (rev. repr., Cambridge: Cambridge University Press, 1991).

An unchanged reprint should not be cited merely because you happen to have used it (an autobiographical fact of no interest to the reader), but only to show that the book, though old, is still in print. On the other hand, it is usually advisable to cite the latest edition, even if the passage cited was already present in the first; if the fact is of importance, state it.

For facsimile editions, give the original date and place of publication in full (the name of the publisher is optional):

> E. Allen, *A Knack to Know a Knave* (London, 1594; facs. edn., Oxford: Malone Society Reprints, 1963).

> Joachim of Fiore, *Psalterium decem cordarum* (Venice, 1527; facs. edn., Frankfurt am Main, 1965).

> Eliza Smith, *The Compleat Housewife: or, Accomplished Gentlewoman's Companion* (16th edn., London, 1758; facs. edn., London, 1994).

If a facsimile edition contains additional material—as is usually the case with edited editions—a different form of citation is needed:

> Kenneth Dewhurst (ed.), *Richard Lower's* Vindicatio*: A Defence of the Experimental Method. A Facsimile Edition Introduced and Edited by Kenneth Dewhurst* (Oxford: Sandford Publications, 1983).

> Horace Hart, *Notes on a Century of Typography at the University Press, Oxford: 1693–1794. A Photographic reprint of the edition of 1900 with an Introduction and Additional Notes by Harry Carter* (Clarendon Press: Oxford, 1970).

There is no point in putting the first title under the author's name (although cross-reference is needed) because the original title is quite different:

> Richard Lower, *Diatribæ Thomæ Willisii Doct. Med. & Profess. Oxon. De febribus Vindicatio adversus Edmundum De Meara Ormoniensem Hibernum M.D.* (London, 1665).

Moreover, the editor has included a modern transcription as well as a facsimile edition and translation, together with an introduction. The rather drawn-out and partially redundant citation is needed to make all these elements clear, though the original publication details can be omitted in the editor's entry. When in doubt, add a cross-reference between author and editor in the bibliography or references.

15.2.5 Co-publications and foreign editions

A co-publication is a simultaneous publication of the same book in different countries by different publishers; a foreign edition is not simultaneous. When a book has, for example, both a British and a US publisher, authors are likely to cite the edition with which they are more familiar, and may not even know there is another. Provided the title is the same this rarely matters unless the precise date is important, though it is disconcerting to readers in one country to see books published there cited as from the other (especially with a different year of publication). In multi-author works with contributors from both sides of the Atlantic, the discrepancy may come to light in copy-editing if it has not already done so in the compiling of a bibliography. The citation may record both editions:

> L. A. Holford-Strevens, *Aulus Gellius* (London: Duckworth, 1988; Chapel Hill: University of North Carolina Press, 1989).

However, this cannot be accomplished if the author–date system is being used: the book must be cited as *Holford-Strevens (1988)* and references to 1989 adjusted.

When works are published in the two countries under different titles, this information may be found with the publishing history, and should be included in the citation; otherwise the reader may fail to recognize the work, or be unable to find it in libraries or bookshops:

> J. D. Salinger, *Nine Stories* (Boston: Little, Brown, 1953), published in the UK as *For Esmé—With Love and Squalor, and Other Stories* (London: Hamish Hamilton, 1953).

15.2.6 Volumes

A multi-volume book is a single work with a set structure. In references, volume numbers are usually styled in lower-case roman numerals (e.g. *i*, *iv*, *xxvi*), although this style may vary in certain disciplines and circumstances, with capital or small capital roman numerals, or arabic figures, being used. The abbreviation *vol.* is generally superfluous, but should be used when the abbreviation *p.* or *pp.* is required. Some multi-volume works do not have separate volume numbers: the individual volumes making up a collection of correspondence, for example, may be labelled with a year extent alone; other works divided naturally by subject may have titles but no numbers, to avoid the imposition of an artificial hierarchy, such as a three-volume set of Shakespeare's works, *Comedies, Histories, Tragedies*.

A reference to a multi-volume book may cite the entire work, giving the particular volume and page number at the end. In this case the number of volumes follows the title directly. Arabic figures are used, in contrast to volume and page references:

> Edmond Vander Straeten, *La Musique aux Pays-Bas avant le XIXe siècle*, 8 vols. (Brussels, 1867–88), ii. 367–8.

Alternatively, only the cited volume may be given. The volume number is placed directly after the title:

> Edmond Vander Straeten, *La Musique aux Pays-Bas avant le XIXe siècle*, ii (Brussels, 1872), 367–8.

When volumes of the same work are produced by different publishers, this can be suggested:

> Heinrich Ritter, *The History of Ancient Philosophy* (trans. Alexander J. W. Morrison), 5 vols. (Oxford: Talboys and London: Bohn, 1838–46).

or made explicit:

> Heinrich Ritter, *The History of Ancient Philosophy* (trans. Alexander J. W. Morrison), 4 vols., i–iii (Oxford: Talboys, 1838–9), iv (London: Bohn, 1846).

When the volumes of a multi-volume work have different (sub)titles, the form is:

> P. Glorieux, *Aux origines de la Sorbonne*, i: *Robert de Sorbon* (Études de philosophie médiévale, 53; Paris, 1966).
>
> A. W. Ward and A. E. Waller (eds.), *The Cambridge History of English Literature*, xii: *The Nineteenth Century* (Cambridge: CUP, 1932), 43–56.

However, if only the subtitle appears on the title page, it makes more sense to cite the book as follows:

> David Hackett Fischer, *Albion's Seed: Four British Folkways in America* (vol. i of *America: A Cultural History*) (New York: Oxford University Press, 1989).

The latter makes sense when the book has many volumes, published over decades, possibly at different locations and by more than one publisher.

In references to works in a foreign language, it is legitimate to translate the term for *volume* or use the numeral only, according to whichever is consistent with the style for English-language titles. For example, a German book may have *Zweiter Band*, *2. Band*, or *Band 2* on the title page, but be cited simply by *ii* after the title. (However, the German *Heft* is best left as such, unless one knows what it denotes in the book in question.)

Do not cite divisions of works—*Part*, *Book*, and so on as found in, say, eighteenth-century novels—with roman numerals; use instead the corresponding words e.g. *Part the First*. Only actual published volumes should be indicated by *i*, *ii*, etc.

15.2.7 Series title

A series is a (possibly open-ended) collection of individual works. In book citations, a series title is optional but useful information. It is always given in roman type; it may be enclosed in parentheses with the publication information, in which case the arabic volume number is followed by a semicolon, or it may be given directly after the book title. Whichever is chosen, all citations within the same work must follow the same style:

> Johannes de Garlandia, *De mensurabili musica*, ed. Erich Reimer, 2 vols. (Beihefte zum Archiv für Musikwissenschaft, 10–11; Wiesbaden, 1972).

> Johannes de Garlandia, *De mensurabili musica*, ed. Erich Reimer, 2 vols., Beihefte zum Archiv für Musikwissenschaft, 10–11 (Wiesbaden, 1972).

> Roger Wright, *Late Latin and Early Romance in Spain and Carolingian France* (ARCA Classical and Medieval Texts, Papers and Monographs, 8; Liverpool, 1982).

In series where the volumes are unnumbered, use the following form:

> E. L. G. Stones (ed. and trans.), *Anglo-Scottish Relations, 1174–1328: Some Selected Documents* (Oxford Medieval Texts; Oxford, 1970).

The Victoria County History series (VCH) requires special consideration. 'The Victoria History of the Counties of England' is the full name of the series as a whole, which has a general editor heading a committee. Every volume in the series is in turn under the control of an editor, who collects the contributions for that volume. There is no general editor for all the volumes concerning a given county. The series follows its own style guide, set out in a handbook for authors and editors.

Each volume in a county's series is published when it is completed, so volume numbers are not in chronological order by publication date. The full title of each volume is *A History of the County of . . . .* 'VCH' may be set in roman as an in-text series abbreviation, but should be italicized when used in references as part of a title, as should the county name: the common form is, say, *VCH Oxfordshire*. (This is contrary to the normal style for series titles, but without it such a bibliographical entry would seem to have no title.) The convention for an entry to a contribution in a volume is to omit the general editor altogether and conflate the series and volume titles thus:

> Tringham, N. J., 'Seisdon Hundred, Southern Division: Bobbington', in M. W. Greenslade (ed.), *VCH Staffordshire*, xx (Oxford, 1984), 64–76.

15.2.8 Place of publication

The place of publication is usually placed in parentheses, in the bibliography as well as the notes. The place of publication should normally be given in its modern form, using the English form where a separate one exists, such as *Brunswick* (Braunschweig), *Munich* (München), *Turin* (Torino). However, when a town or city now belongs to a different state, one should use the form obtaining at the time (e.g. *Breslau* → *Wrocław*); and actual changes of name (e.g. *Christiania* → *Oslo*, *St Petersburg* → *Petrograd* → *Leningrad* → *St Petersburg*) cannot be made retrospective. Except for well-known places it is helpful to add the modern name in square brackets: *Kolberg [Kołobrzeg]*. For more information, *see* **4.2.10**.

Where no place of publication is given, *n.p.* is used instead:

> Marchetto of Padua, *Pomerium*, ed. Giuseppe Vecchi (Corpus scriptorum de musica, 6; n.p., 1961).

It is sufficient to cite only the first city named by the publisher on the title page. (Note, however, the University of California Press, which prefers *Berkeley and Los Angeles*.) While other cities from which that imprint can originate may also be listed there, it is the custom for publishers to put in first place the branch responsible for originating that book. For example, an OUP book published in Oxford may have *Oxford · New York*; one published in New York reverses this order, one published in Australia puts Melbourne first and Oxford second, and so forth.

For books published in the USA, Canada, and Australia, cite the city rather than the state or province: *Baltimore* not *Maryland*, *Bendigo* not *Victoria*. In contexts where no danger exists of confusing different cities with the same name, the city alone may be cited: *Princeton, New Haven, Berkeley*. In other cases the name of the state should be added: *Albany, NY*; *Birmingham, Ala.*; *Cambridge, Mass.*

The list below is of US cities that normally do not need the state appended to them in text or references. Authors creating books in US style destined for a wholly US or North American readership may wish to expand this list accordingly, just as those writing for other readerships may wish to compress it.

Anchorage	Colorado Springs	Madison	Omaha
Ann Arbor	Dallas	Memphis	Philadelphia
Atlanta	Denver	Miami	Pittsburgh
Baltimore	Detroit	Milwaukee	Princeton
Berkeley	Fort Worth	Minneapolis	St Louis
Boston	Honolulu	Nashville	Salt Lake City
Buffalo	Houston	New Haven	San Diego
Chicago	Indianapolis	New Orleans	San Francisco
Cincinnati	Iowa City	New York	Seattle
Cleveland	Los Angeles	Oklahoma City	Washington

While *Washington* should be able to stand on its own in references, as cities, not states, are given as place of publication, it is nevertheless common usage to include *DC* in such contexts. Where the name of the publisher (where given) includes a state or province—as in the case of many university presses—the name need not be repeated:

> Albany: State University of New York Press
> Austin: University of Texas Press

Edmonton: University of Alberta Press

Norman: University of Oklahoma Press

Traditionally, abbreviations of states follow the official rather than the postal designation, though increasingly the postal abbreviation is used in all contexts for both US states and Canadian territories. Official and postal state abbreviations are as follows:

Alabama (Ala., AL)	Montana (Mont., MT)
Alaska (Alas., AK)	Nebraska (Nebr., NE)
Arizona (Ariz., AZ)	Nevada (Nev., NV)
Arkansas (Ark., AR)	New Hampshire (NH)
California (Calif., CA)	New Jersey (NJ)
Colorado (Col., CO)	New Mexico (N. Mex., NM)
Connecticut (Conn., CT)	New York (NY)
Delaware (Del., DE)	North Carolina (NC)
Florida (Fla., FL)	North Dakota (N. Dak., ND)
Georgia (Ga., GA)	Ohio (OH)
Hawaii (HI)	Oklahoma (Okla., OK)
Idaho (Ida., ID)	Oregon (Ore., OR)
Illinois (Ill., IL)	Pennsylvania (Pa., PA)
Indiana (Ind., IN)	Rhode Island (RI)
Iowa (Ia., IA)	South Carolina (SC)
Kansas (Kan., KS)	South Dakota (S. Dak., SD)
Kentucky (Ky., KY)	Tennessee (Tenn., TN)
Louisiana (La., LA)	Texas (Tex., TX)
Maine (Me., ME)	Utah (Ut., UT)
Maryland (Md., MD)	Vermont (Vt., VT)
Massachusetts (Mass., MA)	Virginia (Va., VA)
Michigan (Mich., MI)	Washington (Wash., WA)
Minnesota (Minn., MN)	West Virginia (W. Va., WV)
Mississippi (Miss., MS)	Wisconsin (Wis., WI)
Missouri (Mo., MO)	Wyoming (Wyo., WY)

For several states the official and postal form are identical; two states— Hawaii and Ohio—have no official non-postal abbreviation. In US style the official form can include points in capital two-letter abbreviations (e.g. *N.C.*, *N.H.*, *N.J.*, *N.Y.*, *R.I.*, *S.C.*), the only distinction from their postal form. In informal or historical contexts more than one abbreviated variant may be found, for example *Pa.*, *Penn.*, and *Penna.* for Pennsylvania. These should be made to conform to standard conventions.

15.2.9 Publisher

The name of the publisher may be included if desired; the examples in this section vary intentionally to reflect this, though in practice references should be made uniform throughout a single work. As a general rule one should give names of all publishers or none at all; however, it is a pity where nearly every name is given to erase all this additional information during editing for the sake of the handful of references for which publishers cannot easily be found. For earlier editions, information should be given when available—sometimes this will be the printer, who formerly fulfilled the publisher's role. While the inclusion of publishers is not generally essential—especially now that publishers of current books may easily be found in various reference works both in print and online—the practice is gaining universal acceptance: formerly, inclusion was more common practice in US than in British referencing (perhaps because in many US institutions it was a requirement for the Ph.D. dissertation).

The preferred order is place of publication, publisher, and date, presented in parentheses thus: (*Oxford: Oxford University Press, 1990*). However, if consistently applied, the order publisher, place of publication, and date is acceptable: (*Oxford University Press: Oxford, 1990*). University presses whose names derive from their location can be abbreviated (*Oxford: OUP, Cambridge: CUP, Harvard: HUP, Princeton: PUP*, etc.), providing this is done consistently; avoid combinations such as *Oxford UP*.

Although *The* may be part of the publisher's formal name, it is dropped in bibliographical references: *University of Chicago Press*, not *The University of Chicago Press*.

Retain the ampersand if the publisher uses it (e.g. *Budlong & Bloom, Harper & Row, Kiepenheuer & Witsch*), but do not impose it if the publisher does not use it (e.g. *Faber and Faber, Simon and Schuster, Thames and Hudson*).

Publishers' names may be reduced to the shortest intelligible unit; unless variation is of bibliographical interest, this means reducing the distinction between, say, Charles Scribner, Charles Scribner and Sons, and Charles Scribner's Sons to *Scribners*; this holds for foreign publishers as well: *Firmin Didot* instead of *Firmin Didot Frères*; *Teubner* instead of *Druck und Verlag von B. G. Teubner*; *Laterza* instead of *Gius. Laterza & Figli*. Similarly, *Ltd*, *& Co.*, and *plc* are dropped.

15.2.10 Date of publication

The date is usually found on the title page or the copyright page; for older books it may appear only in the colophon. Dates given in roman numerals should be rendered into arabic figures. Years not reckoned from 1 January are commonly left unadjusted.

When no date of publication is listed, use the latest copyright date. Ignore the dates of printings or impressions, but when citing a new or revised edition, use that date.

Particularly for works in languages other than English, publication dates reckoned by non-Western calendars should be retained where it is clear what system is used. Typically the Western date follows as a gloss, separated by a solidus: *Cairo, 1298/1881, Damascus, 1418/1998.*

When no date can be found, use *n.d.* instead. Alternatively, if the date is known from other sources, it can be supplied in square brackets.

When the book or edition is still in progress, an open-ended date is indicated by an em space after the en rule:

> W. Schneemelcher, *Bibliographia Patristica* (Berlin, 1959–   ).

Cite a book that is to be published in the future as 'forthcoming'; *see also* **15.11**.

15.2.11 Original texts by a named author

The author's name comes first, and the editor's name follows the title:

> Guillaume Dufay, *Opera omnia*, ed. Heinrich Besseler (Corpus mensurabilis musicae, 1; Rome, 1950–66).
>
> Paul Oskar Kristeller, *Renaissance Thought and Its Sources*, ed. Michael Mooney (New York: Columbia University Press, 1979).
>
> Sibrandus Schafnaburgensis, *De dentiscalpiis corcodillorum*, ed. Joseph Bloggs and Heinz Kunz (Edinburgh, 1953).

When the author's name is part of the title, for example *Johannes Regis opera omnia* or *The Collected Works of Joseph Bloggs*, the name may be separated from the title and set in roman: 'Johannes Regis, *Opera omnia*', 'Joseph Bloggs, *Collected Works*'; however, in a bibliography of the subject's works, the full form should be retained. Thus, in a book about Shelley:

> *The Letters of Percy Bysshe Shelley*, ed. F. L. Jones, 2 vols. (Oxford, 1964).

An edition may be cited in different ways depending on the context. In the following example, Sarah Wister is the author of the journal, but not of a publication called *Occasional Writings*. Therefore it would be better to place the editor's name first:

> Kathryn Zabelle Derounian (ed.), *The Journal and Occasional Writings of Sarah Wister* (Rutherford, NJ, 1987).

However, if the reference is in a book about eighteenth-century diarists, it would be more logical to cite it under the author's name:

> Sarah Wister, *The Journal and Occasional Writings of Sarah Wister*, ed. Kathryn Zabelle Derounian (Rutherford, NJ, 1987).

15.2.12 Multi-author works

It is preferable to list the editor(s) first in volumes comprising the edited works of a number of authors, or a collection of documents, essays, congress reports, etc.:

A. Ashworth, 'Belief, Intent, and Criminal Liability', in J. Eekelaar and J. Bell (eds.), *Oxford Essays in Jurisprudence* (3rd ser., 1987), 1, 6.

Katherine Bucknell and Nicholas Jenkins (eds.), *W. H. Auden, 'The Map of All My Youth': Early Works, Friends, and Influences* (Auden Studies, 1; Oxford, 1990).

M. L. Gatti Perer (ed.), *Atti del Congresso internazionale sul Duomo di Milano*, 2 vols. (Milan, 1968).

E. Ruspini, P. Bonissone, and W. Pedrycz (eds.), *Handbook of Fuzzy Computation* (London: Institute of Physics Publishing, 1998).

Rodney Sampson (ed.), *Early Romance Texts: An Anthology* (Cambridge, 1980).

Don Yeates, Maura Shields, and David Helmy (eds.), *Systems Analysis and Design* (London: Pitman Publishing, 1994).

The Bucknell volume, for example, contains a considerable amount of unpublished material by Auden, but it would be misleading to list the volume under his name; *W. H. Auden* is part of the title.

Textual editions in which a variety of matter by various authors has been gathered together by the editor are often cited as if the editor were author:

B. J. Whiting, *Proverbs, Sentences, and Proverbial Phrases from English Writings mainly before 1500* (Cambridge, Mass., 1968).

D. L. Page, *Poetae Melici Graeci* (Oxford, 1962).

though in a list of abbreviations one might find:

PMG   *Poetae Melici Graeci*, ed. D. L. Page (Oxford, 1962)

Often it makes more sense not to list the editor first. For example, reports of congresses other than those organized by individual initiative; in particular when the congress itself is numbered, for example:

Proceedings of the XIV International Congress of Papyrologists: Oxford, 24–31 July 1974 (London, 1975).

An editor's name may be appended with *ed.* when given on the title page, but should not otherwise be sought out.

This is also the case with Festschriften, in which the glory should belong to the honorand, not the editor:

'Owls to Athens': Essays on Classical Subjects for Sir Kenneth Dover, ed. Elizabeth Craik (Oxford, 1990).

Often, indeed, there is no one editor, but either a committee or a collective designation such as *former pupils*; furthermore, the work is likely to be catalogued under the name of the honorand.

15.2.13 Organizations

In the absence of an author or editor, an organization acting in the role of author can be treated as such:

Amnesty International, *Prisoners without a Voice: Asylum Seekers in the United Kingdom* (London, 1995).

Cardiac Society of Australia and New Zealand, 'Clinical Exercise Stress Testing: Safety and Performance Guidelines', *Medical Journal of Australia*, 164 (1996), 282–4.

Government of Botswana, *A Human Drought Relief Programme for Botswana* (Gaborone: Ministry of Local Government and Lands, 1980).

International Astronomical Union, *Transactions of the International Astronomical Union, Rome*, 12–20 May 1922 (London: Imperial College Bookstall, 1922), 1.52–3.

Penal Affairs Consortium, *An Unsuitable Place for Treatment: Diverting Mentally Disordered Offenders from Custody* (London, 1998).

UNICEF, *The State of the World's Children* (Oxford: Oxford University Press, 2000).

15.2.14 Reference books

Works of reference are more likely to be known by their title, which should come first. In the absence of any general editor's name, those reference works produced by a publisher's staff sometimes have the publisher's name as 'editor':

American Heritage College Dictionary, ed. Houghton Mifflin (Boston, 1993).

Chicago Manual of Style (Chicago: University of Chicago Press, 1993).

Handbook of Chemistry and Physics, 50th edn. (New York: Chemical Rubber Publishing, 1969).

Oxford History of the Classical World, ed. John Boardman, Jasper Griffin, and Oswyn Murray (Oxford, 1986).

However, some reference works are more likely to be remembered by their author's name:

John Russell Bartlett, *Dictionary of Americanisms: A Glossary of Words and Phrases Usually Regarded as Peculiar to the United States* (Boston: Little, Brown, 1859).

John Ciardi, *A Browser's Dictionary: A Compendium of Curious Expressions and Intriguing Facts* (New York: Harper & Row, 1980).

H. W. Fowler, *A Dictionary of Modern English Usage* (Oxford: Clarendon Press, 1926).

15.2.15 Translations

The original author's name comes first, the translator's name after the title:

Bernhard Bischoff, *Latin Palaeography: Antiquity and the Middle Ages*, trans. [*or* tr.] Dáibhí Ó Cróinín and David Ganz (Cambridge, 1990).

Joanat Martorell, *Tirant lo Blanc*, trans. with foreword David H. Rosenthal (London, 1984).

> Jacobus de Voragine, *The Golden Legend: Readings on the Saints*, trans. William Granger Ryan, 2 vols. (Princeton, 1993).

If important, the date of original publication may be added in parentheses at the end: (*first pub. 1979*). Or both the original edition and the translation may be cited (*see also* **15.1**):

> Bernhard Bischoff, *Paläographie des römischen Altertums und des abendländischen Mittelalters* (Berlin: Erich Schmidt Verlag, 1979); trans. Dáibhí Ó Cróinín and David Ganz as *Latin Palaeography: Antiquity and the Middle Ages* (Cambridge: Cambridge University Press, 1990).
>
> Joanat Martorell, *Tirant lo Blanc* (Valencia, 1490), trans. with foreword David H. Rosenthal (London, 1984).
>
> José Sarrau, *Tapas and Appetizers*, trans. Francesca Piemonte Slesinger (New York: Simon & Schuster, 1987); orig. pub. as *Tapas y aperitivos* (Madrid: Ediciones Sarrau, 1975).

Note, however, that a translation with the same or similar title may have different contents:

> Edgar Wind, *The Eloquence of Symbols: Studies in Humanist Art*, ed. Jaynie Anderson, with a Biographical Memoir by Hugh Lloyd-Jones (Oxford, 1993) (first pub. 1983).
>
> Edgar Wind, *L'eloquenza dei simboli. La* Tempesta: *Commento sulle allegorie poetiche di Giorgione*, ed. Jaynie Anderson, trans. Enrico Colli (Milan, 1992).

The latter contains an additional essay, 'L'eloquenza dei simboli' (which gave the title to the first book but was not reprinted there), and comprises two separate publications by Wind; hence the full point rather than a colon after the first part of the title.

15.3 Chapters and articles in books

The chapter or article title is followed by a comma, the word *in*, and the title of the book:

> John Shearman, 'The Vatican Stanze: Functions and Decoration', in George Holmes (ed.), *Art and Politics in Renaissance Italy: British Academy Lectures* (Oxford: Clarendon Press, 1993), 185–240.
>
> W. B. Todd, 'David Hume: A Preliminary Bibliography', in id. (ed.), *Hume and the Enlightenment: Essays Presented to Ernest Campbell Mossner* (Edinburgh: Edinburgh University Press, 1974).

When the article appears in the author's own book or a collection of his or her writings, it should be cited in the following form (the date of original publication is optional):

> G. Frege, 'On Sense and Reference', in id., *Philosophical Writings*, trans. and ed. P. T. Geach and M. Black (Oxford: Blackwell, 1952) (originally pub. 1892).

Note that *id.* is not strictly necessary; the same authorship may be assumed if no other author is given.

Often it is more helpful to the reader—especially with recent books—to refer to both the original publication and the reprinted version, since the original may be more easily available than the author's collected writings. In this case, make clear which version is being cited, since the page numbers are usually different. Two possible ways:

> G. E. L. Owen, 'Philosophical Invective', in id., *Logic, Science, and Dialectic*, ed. M. Nussbaum (Ithaca, NY: Cornell University Press, 1986), 347–64. From *Oxford Studies in Ancient Philosophy*, 1 (1983), 1–25.

> G. E. L. Owen, 'Philosophical Invective', *Oxford Studies in Ancient Philosophy*, 1 (1983), 1–25 = *Logic, Science, and Dialectic*, ed. M. Nussbaum (Ithaca, NY: Cornell University Press, 1986), 347–64.

It is clear in the first example that the author is using the later publication. In the second, if individual pages are cited, this should be done for both versions.

Articles in yearbooks without volume number

When an article appears in a yearbook that had no identifying volume number, the year of publication takes the place of the volume number, and is not placed in parentheses:

> M. Boyce, 'The Parthian *Gsn* and Iranian Minstrel Tradition', *Journal of the Royal Asiatic Society*, 1957, 10–45.

> Carl Dahlhaus, 'Miszellen zur Musiktheorie des 15. Jahrhunderts', *Jahrbuch des Staatlichen Instituts für Musikforschung Preußischer Kulturbesitz, 1970* (Berlin, 1971), 21–33.

Articles in dictionaries and encyclopedias

If more than one article is cited, it is useful to abbreviate the source and include it in the list of abbreviations. Articles then can be cited with 's.v.' (*sub verbo*, 'under the word'); page (and volume) numbers are not necessary:

> *Oxford English Dictionary*, s.v. 'Tawdry'   *OED*, s.v. 'Tawdry'
>
> *RE*, s.v. 'Pharsalos'   *COD*, s.v. 'pip⁵'

This convention is useful also for citing electronic sources that lack pagination, where references instead cite the closest internal division (*see also* **15.15.3**):

> Renaissance Studies Resources, s.v. 'Seminars'

15.4 **Articles in periodicals**

15.4.1 **Names and titles**

Authors' and editors' names in periodical titles are treated the same as those for books.

Give the part number of a journal volume only if each part begins at page 1. Separate it from the volume number with a solidus: *15/2* refers to the second part of volume 15. When there are several series of a journal, describe them as, say, *6th ser.*

Give the full page-extent of all articles and chapters, not just first page and *ff.*

When two or more articles by the same author are cited from the same journal, repeat the title; only if it is very long should you use 'ibid.' (printed in roman).

Periodical references generally fit the following structure: Author, 'Article Title', *Periodical Title*, volume/issue (year), page extent. Titles of articles—whether English or foreign—are always given in roman within single quotation marks. Quotation marks within quoted matter become double quotation marks. (If single and double quotation marks appear in conjunction, editors should insert a thin space between them.)

> Halil Inalcik, 'Comments on "Sultanism": Max Weber's Typification of the Ottoman Polity', *Princeton Papers in Near Eastern Studies*, 1 (1992), 49–72.
>
> Luise Schorn-Schütte, ' "Gefährtin" und "Mitregentin": Zur Sozialgeschichte der evangelischen Pfarrfrau in der frühen Neuzeit', in Heide Wunder and Christina Vanja (eds.), *Wandel der Geschlechterbeziehungen zu Beginn der Neuzeit* (Frankfurt am Main, 1991), 109–53.
>
> Anne Jacobson Schutte, 'Irene di Spilimbergo: The Image of a Creative Woman in Late Renaissance Italy', *Renaissance Quarterly*, 44 (1991), 42–61.

In scientific works, titles of articles are commonly printed without quotation marks, and with capital initials for proper nouns only. But where scientific papers are cited in non-scientific works (and vice versa) their titles should be made to conform to a single prevalent style. For example, in a scientific work:

> Miller Christy, The common teasel as a carnivorous plant, *Journal of Botany*, 61 (1922): 13–18.
>
> Robert Goldblatt, Diodorean modality in Minkowski space-time, *Studia Logica*, 39/3 (1973): 219–36.
>
> Alain Tschudin et al., Comprehension of signs by dolphins (*Tursiops truncatus*), *Journal of Comparative Psychology*, 115/1 (2001): 100–5.

And in a non-scientific work:

Miller Christy, 'The Common Teasel as a Carnivorous Plant', *Journal of Botany*, 61 (1922), 13–18.

Robert Goldblatt, 'Diodorean Modality in Minkowski Space-Time', *Studia Logica*, 39/3 (1973): 219–36.

P. M. Greenfield and E. S. Savage-Rumbaugh, 'Perceived Variability and Symbol Use: A Common Language–Cognition Interface in Children and Chimpanzees (*Pan Troglodytes*)', *Journal of Comparative Psychology*, 98 (2002): 201–18.

Always give titles of newspapers, journals, and magazines in italics. It is normal practice to drop the definite or indefinite article at the beginning (*see also* **6.4**). Place a comma between the journal title and volume number if the journal title is given in full, or in an abbreviated form consisting of or ending in a whole word. The date follows; it is not enclosed within parentheses unless a volume or issue number is added. Page and column numbers for newspaper articles can be included, though they need not, since they may differ between issues:

Taylor Downing and Andrew Johnston, 'The Spitfire Legend', *History Today*, 50/9 (2000), 19–25.

Peter Drucker, 'Really Reinventing Government', *Atlantic Monthly*, 275/2 (1995), 49–61.

A. W. Greeley, 'Will They Reach the Pole?', *McClure's Magazine*, 3/1 (1894), 39–44.

Alan Lee, 'England Haunted by Familiar Failings', *The Times*, 23 June 1995.

Unattributed articles are listed under the title:

'One Thing and Another', *New York Times*, 8 Sept. 1946, sec. 2 p. 7, cols. 2–3.

'Solar Photon Thruster', *Journal of Spacecraft and Rockets*, 28/4 (July–Aug. 1990), 411–16.

'Who's Excellent Now?', *Business Week*, 5 Nov. 1984, 76–86.

In the titles of French articles, dates in roman numerals are set in small capitals (but full capitals in italic matter):

Georges Benoît-Castelli, 'Un processional anglais du xivème siècle: Le processional dit "de Rollington"', *EL* 75 (1961), 281–326.

G. Devailly, *Le Berry du Xe siècle au milieu du XIIIe siècle* (Paris, 1973).

Robert Mantran, *Istambul dans la second moitié du XVIIe siècle: Essai d'histoire institutionelle, économique et sociale* (Paris, 1962)

If a book contains more than two or three articles from the same journal it is advisable to abbreviate the journal title. In some disciplines (e.g. classics) the standard abbreviations are well known and do not need to be listed under Abbreviations. Some seemingly abbreviated names are in fact the journal's official title: *PMLA, ELH*. When the journal title is abbreviated no comma precedes the volume number, unless the last word of the abbreviated title is itself unabbreviated:

H. J. Wolff, 'The Origins of Judicial Litigation among the Greeks', *Traditio*, 4 (1946), 34–9.

> B. Lindars, 'Ezechiel and Individual Responsibility', *VT* 15 (1965), 452–67.
>
> N. Wilson, 'A Serbo-Croatian Translation of Apicius', *Class. Cook. Review*, 2 (1979), 89–95.

Articles that fill an entire issue may be cited as follows:

> John Hersey, 'Hiroshima', *New Yorker*, 31 Aug. 1946.
>
> C. Bec (ed.), *Italie 1500–1550: Une situation de crise?* = *Annales de l'Université Jean Moulin*, 1975/2 (Langues étrangères, 2; Lyon, 1976), 99–109.
>
> F. Trisoglio, *Gregorio di Nazianzo in un quarantennio di ricerche (1925–1965)* = *Rivista lasalliana*, 40 (1973).

Supplements published as separate entities should be described accordingly:

> X. Zhentao, K. K. C. Yau, and F. R. Stephenson, 'Astronomical Records on the Shang Dynasty Oracle Bones', *Archaeoastronomy*, 14 (1989); Supplement to *Journal for the History of Astronomy*, 20, pp. S61–S72.

Greek article titles should be in double quotation marks if the journal title is also in Greek, but not otherwise. In modern Greek guillemets may be used instead:

> G. A. Megas, «*Ο Αηβασίλης ο ζευγολάτης*», *Λαογραφία*, 27 (1971), 290–4.

15.4.2 Periodical volume numbers

The volume number is given in arabic numerals, even if it appears in roman numerals in the journal itself: '*Renaissance Quarterly*, 47', not 'XLVII'.

Part numbers of volumes are usually superfluous, unless the pagination begins afresh at page 1, as is the case with some magazines:

> Steve Neale, 'Masculinity as Spectacle', *Screen*, 24/6 (1983), 2–12.

Part numbers may be cited as 24/1 or 24: 1, both meaning the first part of volume 24. There is no need to make the volume number bold. The style '24 (1)' should not be used in the author–title system because the parentheses will clash with another set enclosing the date.

> David A. Garvin, 'Japanese Quality Management', *Columbia Journal of World Business*, 19/3 (1984), 3–12.

However, it is well suited to the author–date system, since the next element is the page number or page extent, and parentheses help separate the volume number from the page numbers:

> Garvin, David A. (1984), 'Japanese Quality Management', *Columbia Journal of World Business*, 19 (3): 3–12 [*or* 19/3: 3–12].

In periodicals with no volume number (or where the volume number is not commonly cited), give the date instead:

Roderic H. Blackburn, 'Historic Towns: Restorations in the Dutch Settlement of Kinderhook', *Antiques*, Dec. 1972, 1068–72.

Seth J. Putterman, 'Sonoluminescence: Sound into Light', *Scientific American*, Feb. 1995, 32–7.

Follow the form used on the periodical itself: if the issue is designated *Fall*, do not change this to *Autumn*, nor attempt to adjust the season for the benefit of readers in another hemisphere, as the season forms part of the work's description rather than being an ad hoc designation.

Cite an as-yet unpublished article as *to be published in* before the journal's name, with the expected date.

15.4.3 Series

Where there are several series of a journal, describe them as, say, *6th ser.* (a superior figure attached to the title is another way of indicating the series number). 'New series' is abbreviated NS in small capitals and followed directly by the volume number. OS is occasionally found for 'original' or 'old' series. (For German periodicals, owing to other associations of this abbreviation, retain NF, standing for 'Neue Folge'.)

J. Barnes, 'Homonymy in Aristotle and Speusippus', *Classical Quarterly*, NS 21 (1971), 65–80.

D. Daube, 'Error and Accident in the Bible', *RIDA*² 2 (1949), 189–213.

A. Ludwich, 'Nachahmer und Vorbilder des Dichters Gregorios von Nazianz', *RhM*, NF 42 (1887), 233–8.

15.4.4 Reviews

Reviews are listed under the name of the reviewer; the word *review* has a lower-case *r*. The place of publication and date of the book reviewed are helpful but not mandatory.

F. Ames-Lewis, review of Ronald Lightbown, *Mantegna* (Oxford, 1986), in *Renaissance Studies*, 1 (1987), 273–9.

J. Dean, review of Philippe Basiron, *My Early Life* (Bourges, 1994), in *Res facta*, 17 (1995), 56–9.

G. Fine, review of T. Penner, *The Ascent from Nominalism*, in *Noûs*, 25 (1991), 126–32.

If the review has a different title, cite that, followed by the name of the author and title of the book reviewed:

H. D. Jocelyn, 'Probus and Virgil', review of Maria Luisa Delvigo, *Testo virgiliano e tradizione indiretta* (Pisa, 1987), in *CR*, NS 39 (1989), 27–8.

Roy Porter, 'Lion of the Laboratory: Pasteur's Amazing Achievements Survive the Scrutiny of his Notebooks', review of Gerald L. Geison, *The Private Science of Louis Pasteur* (Princeton, 1995), in *TLS*, 16 June 1995, 3–4.

15.5 **Theses and dissertations**

Citations of theses and dissertations should include the degree for which they were submitted, and the full name of the institution as indicated on the title page. Titles should be printed in roman within single quotation marks. (Most German and some other universities and academic institutions require that dissertations be published as a degree requirement; references to such works are correctly set in italics.)

15.5.1 **Terminology**

The terms *dissertation* and *thesis* are not interchangeable; use whichever appears on the title page of the work itself. The distinction between them is normally one of convention: at Oxford one writes a *doctoral thesis*, but some other degrees require a *dissertation*; in many US universities one writes a *master's thesis* but a *doctoral dissertation*. Authors should take care to reproduce the term given, and editors should not normalize the usage unless they are certain something is amiss.

Some universities use the form *D.Phil.*, others *Ph.D.*; do not change these. German and Dutch dissertations may be cited simply as *Diss.*, and the name of the institution must be given if a city has more than one university (if not published; place of publication may be different):

> Bonnie J. Blackburn, 'The Lupus Problem', Ph.D. diss. (University of Chicago, 1970).
>
> Patrick Collinson, 'The Puritan Classical Movement in the Reign of Elizabeth I', Ph.D. thesis (University of London, 1957).
>
> L. A. Holford-Strevens, 'Select Commentary on Aulus Gellius, Book 2', D.Phil. thesis (Oxford University, 1971).
>
> H. F. R. M. Oosthout, 'Wijsgerig taalgebruik in de redevoeringen van Gregorius van Nazianze tegen de achtergrond van de Neoplatoonse metafysica', Diss. (Nijmegen, 1986).
>
> G. M. Sutherland, 'Étude littéraire comparée de la poésie latine et francaise de Joachim Du Bellay', doctoral thesis (Paris, 1952).
>
> B. Watterson, 'The Dynamics of Interbeing and Monological Imperatives in *Dick and Jane*: A Study in Psychic Transrelational Gender Modes', MA diss. (Università degli Studi, Bologna, 2001).

The degree may also be placed within the parenthesis:

> V. Berridge, 'Popular Journalism and Working-Class Attitudes, 1854–1886: A Study of *Reynold's Newspaper*, *Lloyd's Weekly Newspaper*, and the *Weekly Times* (Ph.D. thesis, University of London, 1976).
>
> R. R. Liddell, 'The Library of Corpus Christi College, 1517–1617' (B.Litt. thesis, Oxford University, 1936).
>
> B. A. Smith, 'The Influence of the RC Church on Anglican Doctrine' (MA thesis, University of Leeds, 1936).

15.5.2 **University names**

The British convention is that the original Latin of, for example, *Universitas Oxoniensis* can be rendered as either *Oxford University* or *University of Oxford*. However, US and most modern institutions have one official form, which must be followed exactly. Particular care must be taken with universities having similar names: in references these should not be abbreviated to the point of bewilderment. For example, there exist the University of Washington, Eastern Washington University, Central Washington University, Western Washington University, and Washington State University (all in Washington), but also Washington University (in Missouri), Washington College (in Massachusetts), George Washington University (in Washington DC), Washington and Lee University (in Virginia), and Washington and Jefferson College (in Pennsylvania). And recall that the University of Miami is in Florida, whereas Miami University is in Oxford, Ohio, and the State University of New York campus at Buffalo and the State University of New York's Buffalo State College are separate institutions.

Hitherto it was common to cite theses and dissertations from the universities of Oxford, Cambridge, and London by the city only. However, with the proliferation of British universities one may no longer assume that, for example, *Oxford* means Oxford University rather than Oxford Brookes University, and so the institution should always be identified. In multi-campus universities, cite the campus as well; the name can take more than one form (*University of California at Berkeley*, *University of California, Berkeley, UC Berkeley*; *State University of New York at Oswego, State University of New York, Oswego, SUNY Oswego*), which should be made consistent within a single text.

15.6 **Unpublished books and articles**

While the reader may find references to unpublished works more exasperating than helpful—especially when prefaced *see*—it is useful to cite a work that will be published in the near future. The titles of such works should be cited in roman within single quotation marks. If the work has been delivered in the final form and accepted by a publisher, it is legitimate to say *in press* in parentheses (or if an article, *to be published* in [*name of journal*]), with the expected year of publication. If publication is expected within one year from the date of writing one may say *forthcoming*, and put the title in italics.

Unpublished papers presented at conferences may be cited in roman and quotation marks. The place and date can be in parentheses, but are better out so as not to suggest publication. Cite either the date(s) of the conference or the exact date on which the cited paper was read:

> Leofranc Holford-Strevens, 'Humanism and the Language of Music Theory Treatises', paper given at the 65th Annual Meeting of the American Musicological Society, Kansas City, Mo., 4–7 Nov. 1999.

Once published, they match the style of the medium in which they are published:

> E. H. Gombrich, *Art and Scholarship*, Inaugural Lecture, University College London, 14 Feb. 1957 (London: H. K. Lewis, 1957).
>
> Roy Jenkins, *The Chancellorship of Oxford: A Contemporary View with a Little History*, Romanes Lecture, 14 Nov. 1996 (Oxford: Clarendon Press, 1997).

15.7 Orations, addresses, lectures, and speeches

Orations whose names are derived from a place or time are capitalized but not in quotation marks:

> Sermon on the Mount   Gettysburg Address

Those derived from a time are neither capitalized nor in quotation marks:

> Easter sermon   speech in the House of Lords, 18 March 1751

An actual title or *incipit* will be in quotation marks, as will famous phrases ('I have a dream') even if translated ('Blood and Iron', from Bismarck's 'Eisen und Blut') or misquoted ('Rivers of Blood'—not Powell's exact words). Capitalization can vary, depending on the nature and familiarity of the title, though similar titles should be treated similarly.

15.8 Poems

In English, verse titles follow the same rules as for other titles. However, where the poem's title is drawn directly from the first line (either by the poet or as an ad hoc designation), it is traditional to use minimal capitals, especially when the title forms a sentence with a finite verb, for example 'Hark, hark! the lark at heaven's gate sings', 'What shall we do with a drunken sailor?', 'Do not go gentle into that good night'. Many modern poems do not follow this form, even when the title is drawn from the first line.

Citations for long poems are styled with full capital roman numeral (book, in practice very rare), small capital roman numeral (canto), lower-case roman numeral (stanza), and arabic number (line number).

> Spenser, *Faerie Queene*, II. VI. xxxv. 7

The elements are separated by full points and spaces; in some styles the entire reference is set closed up, and may be uniformly in arabic figures.

If citing a stanza rather than a line, it is best to identify the stanza number as such, rather than attempt to incorporate its number into an abbreviated sequence, for example:

> Spenser, *Faerie Queene*, II. VI, stanza iii [or better bk. ii, canto vi, stanza iii]
>
> Byron, *Don Juan*, iv. 10 [= canto the fourth, line 10]
>
> Byron, *Don Juan*, canto iv, stanza ii

The form of citation may differ from that in running text, for example

> In Act III Hamlet finally comes face to face with Ophelia (III. i. 88).
>
> Towards the end of Book I Satan addresses the other fallen angels (i. 622–62).

Italicize the titles of book-length poems or long poems divided into books and cantos. Give titles of other poems in roman in single quotation marks.

> W. H. Auden, 'Es regnet auf mir in den Schottische Lände' [*sic*], in 'The German Auden: Six Early Poems', trans. David Constantine, in Katherine Bucknell and Nicholas Jenkins (eds.), *W. H. Auden, 'The Map of All my Youth': Early Works, Friends, and Influences* (Auden Studies, 1; Oxford, 1990), 1–15 at 6.
>
> William of Blois, 'The Quarrel of the Flea and Fly' (*Pulicis et musce iurgia*), trans. in Jan M. Ziolkowski, *Talking Animals: Medieval Latin Beast Poetry, 750–1150* (Middle Ages Series, ed. Edward Peters; Philadelphia: University of Pennsylvania Press, 1993), 274–8.

15.9 **Plays**

For references to plays *see* **13.6**.

15.10 **Religious works**

For references to the Bible *see* **13.8**. For citations of Jewish religious works *see* **13.8.2**; in general *see also* **15.12**. For citations of the Qur'ān *see* **13.8.3**.

15.11 **Manuscript and other documentary sources**

15.11.1 **General considerations**

References to unpublished or original manuscripts (as distinct from the printed editions of them), documents, unpublished letters, personal communications, and so on are set in roman without quotation marks.

Bibliographical references to manuscripts and early books take a variety of forms, largely reflecting the structure into which the original work was arranged. Each entry should specify the city, the library or other archive, the collection and any series or sub-series, and the volume (or file, bundle, box, etc.) As with all references, the goal is to provide the information sufficient to allow a reader to find the specific extract in the original; thus any peculiarities of foliation or cataloguing must be faithfully rendered: a unique source is permitted a unique reference, if that is how the archive stores and retrieves it.

If the language of the archive is not English, retain in the original everything—however unfamiliar—except the name of the city. (You may add an English translation in parentheses.) Otherwise you will leave future researchers to retranslate 'new series' or 'loose file' into Magyar or Estonian.

Do not use abbreviations (apart from those that are very well known or used by the libraries themselves, for example *Gl. kgl. S.* in Copenhagen), unless they appear on a list of abbreviations in the prelims. If abbreviations are provided—either in the preliminary matter or at the start of the bibliography if not cited elsewhere—shorter versions such as *BL MS Rawl. D 810, fo. 25* and *BL Add. MS 2787* are possible; for sigla *see* **15.11.2**.

Below are some examples and guidelines for citing such works, as well as the various systems of foliation employed:

> Oxford, Bodleian Library, MS Rawlinson D. 520, fo. 7
> (*possible abbreviation*: Oxford Rawl. D. 520)
>
> Paris, Bibliothèque nationale de France, MS fonds francais 146
> (*possible abbreviation*: Paris fr. 146)
>
> All Souls College, Warden's MS 1, fos. 35–6, 49
>
> Bodl. MS Rawlinson D. 520, fo. 7
>
> BL MS Cott. Vitellius A. xiv, fos. 123^v–125^r
>
> BL Royal 15 E. vi
>
> British Library, Lansdowne MS civ
>
> Kent Archives Office, Maidstone, U269/A1/1
>
> MS Bodley 34, fo. 14^{r-v}

Paris, Bib. Nat., ital. 72

Pierpont Morgan Library, M. 366, fo. 150^v–52^r

Public Record Office, State Papers, Foreign Series, Elizabeth, Holland, xxxvi

PRO PROB 11/113, q. 1

PRO Scottish Documents, Exchequer (E 39), 4/5

PRO Ancient Petitions 325/E672

Personal letter to the author, 2 May 2001

Lieut. Frewin's Diary, 3 June 1916

For this last, note that the diary is unpublished; italic for *Diary* would imply that it was published.

In citations of folio numbers, *fo. 7* of itself indicates recto and verso; *fo.* [not *fos.*] 7^{r-v} is also used. Otherwise recto and verso are designated separately as *fo. 7^r*, *fo. 7^v*. When the abbreviations are used, the figures are not contracted: *fos. 117^v–121^r*. In English-language work, the Continental alternative of superscript 'a' and 'b' may safely be replaced by superscript 'r' and 'v' respectively. (*See also* **15.11.4**.)

In references to modern unpublished sources, *mimeo* is often used as an umbrella term for *copy*, whether reproduced by xerography or mimeography. While strictly speaking this is a misuse of the word, most people are aware of the general concept, however outmoded and inexact the term. (Mimeograph machines have not seen extensive use since the 1960s.) Also, in references of an older vintage a mimeo might be precisely what *is* meant. Unless there is specific reason to suppose that a photocopy or printout is more likely than a mimeo, and the distinction is important, then *mimeo* can stand. Do not, however, impose it simply for the sake of standardization.

When reproducing underlined words in handwritten texts, underlined text should be used only if it is important to approximate as far as possible the look of the original; otherwise, italic is adequate for the purpose of indicating stress.

15.11.2 Library sigla

Where manuscripts are cited frequently, it is advisable to use sigla or abbreviations rather than to spell out the country, city, depository, and shelf mark or pressmark at each instance. Library sigla are abbreviated references to libraries and other archives, established for use in manuscript citations; they should be explained in the list of abbreviations (unless well known to readers of the book) or in a separate section in the preliminary matter. Letters in sigla should be full capitals and roman numerals in small capitals, or alternatively lower-case.

Sigla designed for music consist of capital letters indicating country and city or town, followed by lower-case letters indicating the library. For example:

GB-Ob = Great Britain, Oxford, Bodleian Library

A-Wn = Austria, Vienna, Österreichische Nationalbibliothek

The letter(s) indicating country are, however, frequently omitted. Lists of common music sigla may be found in volumes of the *Répertoire international des sources musicales (RISM)* and *The New Grove Dictionary of Music and Musicians*, but authors may devise their own abbreviations for particular archives, providing they are explained in a list of abbreviations.

15.11.3 **Early manuscripts and books**

When it is necessary to reproduce the spellings and printed forms of fifteenth- to seventeenth-century works, the following rules should be observed: Initial *u* is printed *v*, as in *vnderstande*, also in such combinations as *wherevpon*. Initial and medial *j* is printed *i*, as in *iealousie*, *iniurie*, but in roman numerals *j* may be used finally, as in *viij*. In capitals the *U* is nonexistent, and should always be printed as a *V*, initially and medially, as *VNIVERSITY*. This is true regardless of whether the capitals are then styled in text as full or small capitals. The second letter in y^e (*the*) and y^t (*that*) should be a lower-case superscript, with no full point. Medial *v* is printed *u*, as in *haue*, *euer*. Old manuscripts, however, are often inconsistent in the use of *u* and *v*; where exact reproduction is preferred over standardization, follow the copy.

15.11.4 **Conventions in foliation**

Both manuscript and typeset books were ordinarily foliated as a guide as much for the binder as for the reader. The first sheet of each signature would be numbered, for example, *A*, *B*, *C*, *D* (or *a*, *b*, *c*, *d*, especially in prelims) in sequence, to help the signatures to be ordered correctly when the book was assembled. When the alphabet was exhausted the letters were duplicated, as *AA*, *AAA*, etc.

Usually this marking was made on the bottom right-hand corner of a leaf. Signatures were most commonly denoted by the twenty-three letters of the Latin alphabet. (*I* or *J*, *U* or *V*, and *W* were omitted: the two pairs were at that time variant forms of the same letter; even when it was agreed to distinguish them by value they were interfiled till at least the eighteenth century.) The twenty-fourth sheet might then be signed *Aa*, the forty-seventh *Aaa*, and so on. Subsequent leaves would be numbered, but only the first half of the signature and only the recto of each page, so that a sixteen-page signature, for example, could be numbered *A*, *Aij*, *Aiij*, *Aiiij*, followed by four unnumbered leaves. The following new signature would then be numbered B, *Bij*, *Biij*, *Biiij*, with four more unnumbered leaves, and so on.

Many such books were also foliated or paginated *passim*, but this numbering is not always reliable, and may at times prove spectacularly wrong. Scholars therefore often supply the signature number instead. The result of this numbering system is that text on all versos and on the second half of any given signature would be unnumbered. References to both recto (r) and verso (v) are cited in superscript, as *fo. 12^r*, *fo. 12^v*. (Formerly only versos were indicated; an unmarked folio reference was assumed to be to a recto.) When citing both sides of a folio the formula is, for example, *fo. 12^{r-v}*, folio extents spanning more than one leaf are *fos. 12^v–17^r*. Where an author needs to cite text on an unnumbered leaf, he or she provides the numbering in square brackets according to the system already in place; consequently, the citation for the twelfth page of the third sixteen-page signature would be *c [vii]^v*. (The modern pagination equivalent would be *p. 44*.)

A variety of numbering conventions were followed—capital and lower-case letters, numbers and numerals—with the sequence repeated or modified through need or (sometimes) carelessness. No attempt should therefore be made to 'standardize' folio references, even when drawn from the same work: it may be possible to have *sig. BB iiij^r* and *sig. c* referring to different parts of one book. Additionally, typographical sorts (¶, *, §, ★) can be pressed into service to define signatures making up a book's preliminary matter. These should be left and indicated as special sorts where necessary.

Editors should not substitute arabic numbers for roman numerals without first checking with the author. While the substitution is acceptable and generally correct, some authors take exception to this, as they may have taken great pains to transcribe the original system, even down to the old forms of roman numerals. It does not follow, however, that all letters denoting signatures should be made uniformly capital or lower-case; as mentioned above, these may vary within the same book, to say nothing of between books.

15.12 Classical, post-classical, and Jewish and Hebrew references

While classical and post-classical references follow very general rules, the conventions for citing individual authors and works can vary considerably, and cannot be listed here fully. Beyond the broad guidelines below, authors and editors without specialist knowledge should follow the forms commonly found in the discipline, standardizing references only where they are obviously inconsistent. Jewish and Hebrew references follow certain conventions that may cause similar problems to those unfamiliar with their form.

15.12.1 Classical references

References to classical authors are found both in non-classical works and in specialist books solely concerned with classical subjects. Perhaps surprisingly, many classicists use arabic figures to the exclusion of roman numerals, which they considered old-fashioned. Nevertheless, in general works the traditional convention of roman numerals may be maintained—though not imposed—since both classical and post-classical works should be consistently styled in the form most familiar to the general reader. Thus in a non-classical work 'Juvenal's *Satire VI*' is correct, though the number is not in italic.

In specialist references, however, use arabic numerals, separated by full point and space of line, for every element of the reference; lower-case roman numerals for book numbers are considered old-fashioned in classical references. Commas separate different references to the same work; semicolons separate references to different authors. Semicolons should also be used to separate references to different works by the same author unless commas can be used with no risk of confusion. (For rules regarding the use of roman numerals in Latin texts *see* **7.7.2–3**.) In German the roles of comma and full point are reversed; some authors use German style, which needs to be corrected.

Some principal exceptions exist to these general rules:

- References to Plato, Plutarch, and Athenaeus are normally made to the pages of old editions divided vertically into lettered sections (also used in some volumes of *Patrologia Graeca* and *Patrologia Latina*). The traditional style is to use small capitals preceded by a thin space (173 E3, 539 D), though the simple form of lower-case letters set close up is also acceptable (*173e3, 539d*)—but be careful not to mistake *539f* for *539f.* (meaning 539–40).

- When line numbers are given in Plutarch and Athenaeus, the simple form is *1052d4*; the more complicated form is *1052 D4* (but editors should not expect all references to be in this form). The small-capital letters in these references are preceded by a thin space.

- Use the lower-case superscript letters (461^a20, 1089^u24) for Aristotle and Photius references, where [a] and [b] refer to columns of a standard edition.

It is possible to elide a reference to, for example, *173b3–5*, *464ᵃ20–ᵇ6*, or *464ᵃ⁻ᵇ*; the reference *173e3–174a2* should not be elided to *173e3–4a2*.

- Strabo references have a capital *C* (*260 C*, *432 C*), which stands for an editor's name (Casaubon).

- Cite Plautus and Terence references according to the continuous lineation, never by act, scene, and line. In other classical references, such as *fr. 42 W*, initials stand for editor's names and should be in full capitals.

- Greek letters are sometimes used to identify the books of the *Iliad* (capitals), the *Odyssey* (lower-case), and some works by Aristotle. Do not use capital roman numerals to identify books of the *Iliad*, and lower-case for books of the *Odyssey*, as small capitals are not always distinct from lower-case, and full capitals are too big.

15.12.2 Post-classical references

Styling references to authors writing in the post-classical period can cause some difficulties, for the reasons explained above. Roman numerals are still standardly found in many such references, and it would be incorrect to alter them all to arabic, particularly in contexts where readers are used to them in roman, and classical references are rare. Conventions vary between writers and works. By way of example, here are guidelines for references to works by St Thomas Aquinas, which illustrates some of the variety possible:

The *Summa Theologica* has three elements: part, question/answer, and article. The use of the abbreviations *q.* and *a.* obviates the need for punctuation between elements. The part number is set in full capitals: 'Summa Theologica, I q. 1 a. 3'. Where the part number has more than one element itself, the roman numerals are joined by an en rule (also styled as a hyphen): 'Summa Theologica, I–II, q. 4 a. 7'. The part numbers can also take the form: 'Summa Theologica, Ia IIa q. 3 a. 9'. Some references to this work have a fourth element, the objection: 'Summa Theologica, I–II q. 2 a. 4 ad 6'.

The *De Veritate* is cited similarly, but has no part numbers: 'De Veritate, q. 4 a. 1 ad. 8'. The *Commentary on the Nicomachean Ethics* usually has three elements: book, lecture, and note. The book number is set in small capitals: 'Commentary on the Nicomachean Ethics, VII lec. 9 n. 247'. The *De Anima* is cited in the same way, but lacks the final note element: 'De Anima, II lec. 1'. The *Summa contra Gentiles* has books, chapters, and notes: 'Summa contra Gentiles, lib. 1 d. 3 n. 6'. The *Commentary on the De Trinitate of Boethius* has the usual style for classical references, with arabic numbers for every element: 'Commentary on the De Trinitate of Boethius, 16. 5. 1'.

For rules governing an index locorum (index of passages cited), *see* **16.4.4**.

15.12.3 **Jewish and Hebrew references**

References to sources published in Hebrew

Apart from the option of setting Hebrew sources in Hebrew characters—which is generally suitable only in specialist contexts—there are three ways of referring to sources published in Hebrew: (*a*) with the title both transliterated and translated; (*b*) in transliteration only; and (*c*) in translation only. Which option is used depends on the type of source being cited—contemporary works or primary sources—and on the intended readership. (Editors need to consider also what style the author has already imposed.) Titles of journals and periodicals are always given in transliteration. Where the publication in question has a masthead in Latin characters, use that title even when contrary to the transliteration rules applied elsewhere.

References to modern sources

The standard recommendation on the citation of sources in non-roman alphabets is to give the transliterated title first with the translation following it in parentheses. While this allows readers who want to take up the references to find them easily while also giving the non-specialist an idea of what the source is about, it can prove cumbersome; especially in a heavily annotated work it may be preferable to opt for translation only or transliteration only, depending on the intended readership.

Book titles as personal names

In traditional Jewish society, rabbis were so closely associated with the ideas they had expressed in writing that many became known by the name of their major work. Thus, Rabbi Elimelekh of Lyzhansk, whose most famous work is called *No'am Elimelekh*, is known as the Noam Elimelekh; when a book title becomes used as a personal appellation in this way, it is always preceded by *the*, and is not italicized. Sometimes an author's major work is referred to only by an acronym formed from the letters of the Hebrew title: for example, *Shenei luchot haberit*, by Rabbi Isaiah b. Abraham Halevi Horowitz, is known as 'the *Shelah*'—and he in turn is frequently referred to as 'the Shelah'.

References to an author may be interspersed with references to his work; to avoid the same name appearing in text in both roman and italic typefaces, wording should—as far as possible—be recast to style references to the author in roman type, with the title of the work (i.e. the italicized form of the name) given only in notes. Alternatively, the author can be referred to by his original name—but the advisability of doing so would depend on the intended readership. For a non-specialist readership unfamiliar with the practice of referring to people by the titles of their works, this is probably the preferred solution; it also facilitates further research, since personal names are the form invariably used in indexes and reference works.

Except in very specialized works, full information on people who are otherwise identified only by the title of their work should be given at the first occurrence of the term in the text ('According to the Divrei Chayim (R. Chayim b. Leibush Halberstam, d. Sanz 1876)...') and there should be a suitable cross-reference in the index ('Divrei Chayim, the, *see* Halberstam, Chayim'). The addition of the place and date of birth—or more commonly, as here, the place and date of death—in the text is recommended as a way of fixing these writings in a historical context.

15.13 **Legal references, and government and official papers**

For legal references, and government and official papers, *see* **13.2.2**. For the citation of US public documents, *see also The US Government Printing Office Style Manual* and *The Chicago Manual of Style*.

15.14 **Audio and visual broadcasts and recordings**

Audio and visual broadcasts and recordings are often difficult to deal with because no universally accepted form of citation exists. Moreover, the order of a reference may change according to the subject; sound recordings, for example, might be listed under the name of the conductor, the name of the composer, or even the name of the ensemble, depending on the focus of the work in which the reference appears, or the element the reader is most likely to search for. As with all citations, sufficient information should be given to enable the reader to understand what type of work it is, and then to find it. Bear in mind that for non-book materials the finding is not likely to take place in a library.

15.14.1 **Audio recordings**

The title is always given in italics. The recording company, number of the album, and date (when included; often this will be the copyright date, but dates are frequently omitted on recordings) should always be given. Other information, such as the exact type of recording (e.g. wax cylinder, 78 rpm, stereo, quadraphonic, compact disc, MP3), is optional, though of increasing importance if the medium is unusual or scarce. Sometimes it may be necessary to specify exactly what medium is involved, since a record, tape, video cassette, or compact disc may have the same title.

Music recordings may be listed under the composer, the conductor, the performer, or the ensemble. Often the title will be the best choice, especially if the works are anonymous:

> Francois Couperin, *Pièces de clavecin: Huit préludes de L'Art de toucher le clavecin. Livre I. Troisième et quatrième ordres*, Huguette Dreyfus (Valois, MB 797, 1970).
>
> *Comedian Harmonists* (EMI Electrola, 1 C 148-31-094/95, n.d.).

(In this example, the name of the album is the same as that of the performers.)

> *Le Chansonnier Cordiforme*, Consort of Musicke, dir. Anthony Rooley; edition and project supervision by David Fallows (Decca Record Company Ltd.: Éditions de l'Oiseau-lyre, 1980) (four-record album).

or (if the reference is destined for a book about musical ensembles):

> Consort of Musicke, dir. Anthony Rooley, *Le Chansonnier Cordiforme*; edition and project supervision by David Fallows (Decca Record Company Ltd.: Éditions de l'Oiseau-lyre, D 186 D 4, 1980) (four-record album).

In recording numbers a hyphen rather than an en rule is the norm. Other examples:

> Scott Joplin, 'Maple Leaf Rag' (Scott Joplin), in *The Smithsonian Collection of Classic Jazz*, selected and annotated by Martin Williams, Record Side One, no. 1 (Smithsonian Institution; Columbia P 11892-7).
>
> Paul Hillier, *Proensa* (ECM Records compact disc ECM 1368, 1989).
>
> Lightnin' Hopkins, *The Complete Aladdin Recordings* (EMI Blues Series, CDP-7-96843-2) (two-volume compact disc set).
>
> *The Mirror of Narcissus: Songs by Guillaume de Machaut*, Gothic Voices, dir. Christopher Page (Hyperion compact disc CDA 66087).
>
> Claudio Monteverdi, *L'Orfeo*, The Monteverdi Choir, The English Baroque Soloists, His Majesties Sagbutts & Cornetts, dir. John Eliot Gardiner (Archiv audio cassette 419 250-4, 1987).
>
> *Music from Renaissance Coimbra*, A Capella Portuguesa, dir. Owen Rees (Hyperion compact disc CDA66735, 1994).
>
> *Musique de la Grèce antique*, Atrium Musicae de Madrid, dir. Gregorio Paniagua (Harmonia Mundi compact disc HMA 1901015, 1979).
>
> Raymond Scott, *The Music of Raymond Scott: Reckless Nights and Turkish Twilights* (Columbia compact disc CK 53028, 1992).
>
> Bruce Springsteen, 'Live at the Bottom Line' (bootleg audio cassette tape recording, 15 Aug. 1975).

Spoken recordings may be listed under the name of the author or the speaker, or under the title:

Albert Schweitzer: A Self-Portrait. Albert Schweitzer Speaking in German,
recorded at Lambarene by Erica Anderson, 1963 (Caedmon TC 1335, n.d.).

C. S. Lewis, *The Lion, the Witch, and the Wardrobe,* read by Sir Michael
Hordern (2 audio cassettes, TO1611, 1981).

Martin Buber, *Professor Martin Buber spricht* (excerpts from the Old
Testament) (Christophorus-Verlag Herder, Freiburg im Breisgau, CLP
72106-7, n.d.).

15.14.2 Films, video recordings, and slides

References to these media vary so much in format that it is impossible to
give specific instructions, apart from making the titles italic and ensuring that the date, producer, distributor, and catalogue or order number
(if any) is reproduced. It is useful to remember that—unlike for a book or
periodical—a reader interested in obtaining a copy of such a recording is
likelier to approach the publisher or distributor than a library. Give
whatever information is useful for the context, specifying what the
medium is if it is likely to be unclear. Again, the amount and position
of the information given will vary according to the context in which the
reference appears, and the other types of reference supplied. The formats of the examples below differ accordingly:

The Ashes: Victory in Australia (BBCV 4040, 1987).

Casablanca (Warner Brothers, 1942), Michael Curtiz (dir.).

Casablanca (1942) (PAL DVD, Warner Home Video D065008, 2000) ASIN:
B00004I9PZ, run time: 98 minutes.

Charles Chaplin (dir.), *Modern Times* (United Artists, 1936).

Leningrad Cowboys Go America (Villealfa Filmproductions, 1989), dir. and
screenplay by Aki Kaurismäki, story by Sakke Järvenpää, Aki Kaurismäki,
Mato Valtonen.

'Percy and Harold and Other Stories', *Thomas the Tank Engine and Friends*
series (Britt Allcroft 5-014861-100224, 1986).

This is Spinal Tap: A Rockumentary by Marti Di Bergi, dir. Rob Reiner
(Embassy Pictures, 1983).

Cite films held in proprietary electronic media other than DVD as
electronic sources (*see* **15.15**).

15.14.3 Television and radio programmes

The title of a single programme should be in italics; programmes
forming an episode from a series are in single quotation marks,
followed by the series title in italics. The information that follows is
determined by whatever may be relevant to the author's purpose
(author, narrator, producer, director, conductor, singers, actors, etc.): it
should not be included for its own sake. Finally, list the network and
date of transmission: it is increasingly necessary—especially in the
USA—to list the station, time zone, city, or a combination of these,

since the same programme may be broadcast at different times from different locations. In some cases, such as the dramatization of a novel, the author's name should come first:

> *Sunday Grandstand*, BBC2, 17 Sept. 1995.
>
> 'Secrets of Lost Empires', *Nova* (PBS), KHET Honolulu, 26 May 1998.
>
> Ellis Peters, *Dead Man's Ransom* (1984), BBC Radio 4 serial, Episode 3, 21 Sept. 1995.
>
> *Un Cœur in Hiver*, Canal+ (Paris), 15 May 2001, 23.40 CET.
>
> 'Pine Barrens', *The Sopranos*, Episode 39, HBO, 9 May 2001, 22.00 EST (USA).

15.15 **Electronic Data**

15.15.1 **General considerations**

A number of approaches exist to citing sources held as electronic data, and these are evolving in tandem with the media they reflect. Certain disciplines favour specific styles, though fundamentally any sensible and consistent approach is admissible if it offers enough information about the source to access or retrieve it. The following guidelines are suited to most contexts, and should be adopted to fit the reference style in which the other sources are cast: as much as possible, make notes and references correspond with each other and to other types of citations, including the same presentation and levels of information most useful to the reader. (The International Standard ISO 690B2 guidelines for citing some electronic documents detail more than a dozen required fields.) This may prove unfeasible in practice: not all elements of a citation will be uniformly available for all references, and even similar references may provide different levels of information. It can be difficult or impossible to find the basic facts that fit naturally into categories normally associated with print publications, such as author, title, place and date of publication, and publisher. Moreover, the medium in which the data are held might not be immediately apparent as it is in printed works: the same data can exist, and be retrievable, in more than one format or platform.

The ephemeral nature of online material means it may be procurable only for a short time. Since readers may be unable to find the material subsequently, it is good practice for authors to download locally or print any material from online sources, to provide a tangible record of the information in case it becomes inaccessible from its original source. When making citations for references with more than one online source, choose the one that is most likely to be stable and durable (*see also* **15.15.4**). Authors should test links to their sources before publication, even if their citations will appear only in print.

Electronic books, journals, magazines, newspapers, and reviews should be treated as much as possible like their print counterparts; however, aspects such as pagination and publication date can differ between hardcopy and electronic versions, so the reference must make clear which is meant. Where print versions exist they can—but need not—be cited; similarly, citing electronic versions of printed media is not mandatory. Providing both does, however, offer the reader another option for pursuing the reference. Authors should always give precedence to the most easily and reliably accessible form: for example, journal references drawn from back issues available on a CD-ROM should be cited with the journal itself as the source rather than the CD-ROM, unless the CD-ROM is the best way to access it (as for particularly old or obscure periodicals).

15.15.2 **Representation**

In principle, it is immaterial whether the work in which a citation appears will itself be available electronically: the presentation of online sources in references is the same for print and electronic dissemination. Consequently, a hypertext link given in an electronic medium must display the entire text of the linked address if it is to function as a reference.

Particularly in references destined for electronic dissemination (e.g. on-line publishing), represent all italic matter as italic rather than through underlining, which is frequently used to indicate hypertext links. In print, do not use underlining to mimic hypertext links to, say, an email address or website URL (Universal Resource Locator), especially as those citations that use underlined spaces will not reproduce well in print.

A basic template for many electronic references might include the following classes of information:

> Author or editor name, 'Title of article or section used', *Title of complete work* [type of medium], (date created, published, or posted (day month year)) <address of electronic source> pagination or online equivalent, date accessed

This would appear as

> Barbara Quint, 'One Hour to Midnight: *Tasini* Oral Arguments at the Supreme Court', *Information Today* [online journal], 18/5 (May 2001) <http://www.infotoday.com/newsbreaks/nb010330-1.htm>, accessed 1 July 2001

Parentheses help delimit different classes of information. Use punctuation sparingly; in particular do not use full points when a reference ends in an address link, especially when angle brackets are not used around addresses.

In keeping with the principle that electronic references should reflect the format of other references in a work, adopt the same style for capitalization, italics, and quotation marks; the examples given should be adjusted accordingly (*see also* **15.15.3**). Electronic references in the author–date (Harvard) system follow the normal order: put the year the reference was originated immediately after the author's or editor's name, with *a*, *b*, *c*, etc. as necessary; this forms the basis of the in-text citation. Unlike print sources, however, the full date (day, month, and year) should be given again following the title, either in addition to or instead of the date it was accessed.

Media

Where the context or content does not make obvious the format or platform in which the data is held, give additional clarification (typically in square brackets), such as '[CD-ROM]', '[newsgroup article]', or '[abstract]'. Different types of sources and readerships will require different levels or types of glosses; keep in mind also that the rate of technological change might render some bare references unintelligible within a generation. There is no need to add *online* or *available from* to the citation, since this will be apparent from the inclusion of an address, just as it is apparent that a work is available from a cited publisher or an article in a cited journal. (Some guides, however, make the distinction between *at* for a unique source and *available at* for a parallel or supplementary one.) It is helpful to mention whether the source is available in alternative forms or locations; this is usually placed at the end of the entry.

When citing references accessible only through a fee, subscription, or password (as for many databases, online periodicals, or downloadable electronic books), include its source (typically a URL) and how it is accessed.

Addresses

It is common, though not universal, to delimit addresses in print by enclosing them within angle brackets (< >); alternatively, it is possible to differentiate addresses by setting them in a different (typically sanserif) font (*see also* **12.5.2**). It is still considered necessary to retain the protocol prefix 'http://' in Internet addresses, even though most browsers do not require it, since other protocols—such as gopher, ftp, and telnet—exist. (The secure form 'https://' is also possible.) Addresses given in electronic media do not need special treatment if they form hypertext links that are differentiated typographically from surrounding text (e.g. the typical default of blue type and underlining).

Time and dates

It is unnecessary to give dates in the order stipulated by ISO 8601 (e.g. 2002–07–04), or to extend this date to include hours, minutes, or seconds, unless writing in disciplines where readers will be familiar with and expect this convention, and frequent daily revisions or updates make it a practical requirement. In such contexts it may be necessary to allow for the time difference in hours plus or minus Universal Standard Time (GMT), such as '15:22:11 +0500'.

Two dates are important in online media. The first is the date the source was posted, published, or last updated, clarified if necessary as, say, '(posted 10 Oct. 2001)'. Cite it if the date is evident (again, this may be found in the source code); if no date is given, this can be signalled with 'n.d.'. The second is the date you last accessed the source, preceded by 'accessed'. In most instances it is unnecessary to cite both, though it is not incorrect—and may be safer—to do so. Online books or periodicals that exist in print may also require separate dates for online and hardcopy publication, if the citation encompasses both.

Line breaks

Never hyphenate an address at the break between lines, or at hyphens. Divide URLs only after a solidus (slash) or a %; where this is impossible, break the URL *before* a punctuation mark, carrying it over to the following line. Where space and measure allow, setting a URL on a separate line can prevent those of moderate size from being broken.

15.15.3 Forms of reference

Internet (World Wide Web) sites

There is no distinction in format between a personal and a professional site. (Indeed, there may be no practical distinction between such sites themselves.) If citing the whole of a document that is a series of linked pages—as most websites are—give the highest-level URL; this is most often the contents or home page:

> R. M. Ritter, 'About the Oxford Guide to Style', *Oxford Editorial* [website], (updated 10 Oct. 2001) <http://www.ritter.org.uk/Oxford_Editorial/AboutOGS.html>

> William Strunk, Jr., *The Elements of Style* (1st edn., Geneva, NY: W. P. Humphrey, 1918), published online Jul. 1999 <http://www.bartleby.com/141>, accessed 14 Dec. 1999

Many Web documents do not explicitly cite an author, though occasionally it may be given as part of the header in the HTML code itself, which can be viewed through all popular browsers. Otherwise treat the item as an anonymous work.

In notes, cite the level of information consistent with the information referred to in text. If citing matter from a single page within that document, cite only the URL from which the matter is drawn:

> William Strunk, Jr., 'Introductory', para. 4, *The Elements of Style*, (published online Jul. 1999) <http://www.bartleby.com/141/strunk1.html>, accessed 14 Dec. 1999

On this, consider the following article:

> Erdmute Heller, 'Venezianische Quellen zur Lebensgeschichte des Ahmed Pasa Hersekoğlu', *Electronic Journal of Oriental Studies*, 3/4 (2000), 1–85.

The URL <http://www.let.uu.nl/oosters/EJOS/EJOS-III.4.html> has links to the entire article, held as four PDF files. Citing this address provides a reference to the entire article; citing the URL of one of the four pdf files (e.g. <http://www.let.uu.nl/oosters/EJOS/pdf/Heller1.pdf>) enables a reference to be made to a single page number within the article. In a bibliography, the entire work would be cited.

Citing pages or sections in the traditional print sense can prove awkward when neither is enumerated, as is generally the case for Web pages. Locating a reference by number of paragraphs from the top rapidly becomes tedious for long documents, while doing so by number of screens from the top presupposes that both writer and reader have the same size monitor. Reference to the nearest relevant internal sub-heading or division may have to suffice. Alternatively, the main browsers (and PDF readers) have the option of searching a document for a unique word or word string: offering readers a searchable item preceded by 's.v.' (*sub verbo* 'under the word'), as in dictionaries, may be a more efficient way of directing them quickly to a specific reference once they have accessed the source:

> Maggie Powell, 'Cyberchat interview' with Southside Johnny Lyon (n.d.) <http://www.southsidejohnny.org/chatinterview.htm>, s.v. 'trigonometry', accessed 23 May 2002

References to hyperlinked notes can be given by the specific URL

> <http://www.parliament.the-stationery-office.co.uk/pa/ld200001/ldselect/ldeucom/31/3102.htm#note2>

In some cases it may be neither advisable nor possible to cite the specific page of a document: some pages exist only as pop-up windows linked to another, and URLs with control codes may be excessively long, as for some journal articles or search results. Reprinting the entire string is of little use, as it is unrealistic to expect a reader to key the entire series into a browser. Instead, include enough of the URL to identify the source, so that the author's steps may be retraced. For example, the URL beginning

> <http://docsonline.wto.org/gen_searchResult.asp?searchmode=simple &collections=&restriction_type=&synopsis=&subjects=&organizations= &products=&articles=&bodies=&types=&drsday=&dreday= &meet_date=&dpsrday=&dupeday=&mh=&c2=@meta_Symbol&c3 ...

leads to a page with a link to a WHO document as a pop-up HTML page with no URL of its own. In this case, provide a reference to whatever URL clearly contains or leads to the page cited, or a search facility to locate it:

> World Health Organization, 'Committee on Technical Barriers to Trade—Notification—Mexico—Tequila' [online WHO notification], document G/TBT/Notif.00/168, serial number 00–1336 (3 Apr. 2000) <http://docsonline.wto.org>, accessed 9 Apr. 2000

Many websites require that hypertext links be made only to their home pages, and then only with their consent. Logically this extends to URLs recorded in print media as well: where necessary this can be clarified by adding '(home page)' after the closing angle bracket, lest the reader thinks the address leads directly to the cited material. Where the site provides a search facility and regularly archives material, this is not the burden it may seem, since often the original direct link is quickly broken.

Some online sources offer examples of how they wish to be cited. Since the format usually is that of an acknowledgement rather than a citation, it can within reason be standardized to conform with other citations.

Online electronic books, monographs, and transcriptions of printed works

> George Borrow, *The Zincali: An Account of the Gypsies of Spain* [online text], Project Gutenberg <ftp://ftp.ibiblio.org/pub/docs/books/gutenberg/etext96/zncli10.txt>
>
> James Joyce, *Ulysses*, chapter 9, [online text], *On-Line Books Page* <ftp://ftp.trentu.ca/pub/jjoyce/ulysses/ascii_texts/ulys9.txt> (also available in WordPerfect 5)
>
> M. F. Maury, *The Physical Geography of the Sea* (Harper: New York, 1855), ['Making of America' digital library] <http://moa.umdl.umich.edu/cgi/sgml/moa-idx?notisid=AFK9140>

Online journal articles, abstracts, reviews, and databases

> Brent Cunningham, 'The World Sees News through New York Eyes', *Columbia Journalism Review*, Mar./Apr. 2001 <http://www.cjr.org/year/01/2/cunningham.asp>
>
> L. Lehane, 'Paralytic shellfish poisoning: A potential public health problem', *Med J Aust* 175:1 (2 Jul. 2001), 29–31; PubMed National Library of Medicine [abstract] ID 11476199 <http://www.ncbi.nlm.nih.gov>
>
> 'University Performance, 2001 League Tables: Firsts and Upper Seconds', *Times Higher Education Supplement*, Statistics page (published online 31 May 2001) <http://www.thesis.co.uk/main.asp> (home page), accessed 31 May 2001
>
> Alan D. Woolf, 'Absinthe', *Clinical Toxicology Review*, 18/4 (Jan.1996), Massachusetts Poison Control System <http://www.mapoison.org/ctr/9601absinthe.html>, accessed 17 April 2001

The form varies for citing information from databases such as ProQuest, Ovid, Lexis–Nexus, and EBSCOHOST, depending on how they are accessed (e.g. online, CD-ROM, hard drive).

> Gray, J. M. & Courtenay, G. (1988) *Youth cohort study* [computer file]. Colchester: ESRC Data Archive [distributor]
>
> 'United States v. Oakland Cannabis Buyers' Cooperative', 2001 US Supreme Court case, US LEXIS 3518, LEXIS/NEXIS (online database) (14 May 2001)
>
> Steven W. Colford, 'Government Ready to Set New Telecom Rules: Mergers a Hot Topic at ComNet Conference', *Advertising Age*, p. 16, in LEXIS/NEXIS [online database], LEXIS 2000 (Research Ver. 2.5 for DOS), Mead Data Central, Inc. 1991.

Online images and animations

Include the name of the image's creator (if known). Titles of images follow the same rules as those governing other images (*see* **6.3**). It is a kindness to readers to offer the size of large downloadable files.

> Charles Trenet, 'Poèmes' (reminiscences to Olivier Royat, 2 May 1993), (audio file, 1.5 mb) <http://parismatch.tm.fr./news/trenet2202/trenet.mp3> accessed 3 Sept. 2001
>
> 'Edge-on spiral galaxy NGC 891' by E. Kopan (2MASS/IPAC), 24-30 Nov. 1998 <http://www.ipac.caltech.edu/2mass/gallery/n891atlas.jpg> accessed 29 May 1999
>
> Erich Karkoschka et al., 'Rotation at Uranus', *Hubble Space Telescope News*, STScI-PRC99-11, 29 Mar. 1999 (online animation, 18.04 mb) <http://oposite.stsci.edu/pubinfo/pr/1999/11/content/9911a.mpg> accessed 5 Jun. 2002
>
> 'UNESCO Director-General Koïchiro Matsuura with UNESCO Goodwill Ambassador Claudia Cardinale' (7 Mar. 2000) [online image] <http:// www.unesco.org/opi/eng/dg/photos/cardinale.tif> accessed 22 Aug. 2000

Online reference sources

This is for online journals, encyclopedias, and other texts available electronically.

> 'Attorney General', *Microsoft Encarta Online Encyclopedia 2001* <http:// encarta.msn.com> 1997–2001 Microsoft Corporation. All rights reserved.
>
> Philip Hoehn and Mary Lynette Larsgaard, 'Dictionary of Abbreviations and Acronyms in Geographic Information Systems, Cartography, and Remote Sensing' (UC Berkeley Library) <http://www.lib.berkeley.edu/EART/ abbrev.html> accessed 25 Jul. 2001
>
> 'Knight bachelor', Encyclopaedia Britannica 2002 <http://www.britannica.com/eb/article?eu=46863>

FTP, Gopher, and Telnet sites

These represent different protocols for accessing information; their form differs from that for Web-based addresses:

Dorothy Parker, 'Marie of Roumania' [poem] <gopher://ftp.std.com/00/obi/book/Dorothy.Parker/Marie.of.Roumania> accessed 3 Mar. 2002

R. Braden et al., 'Request to Move STD 39 to Historic Status', Network Working Group, *The Internet Society*, RFC 3109 (May 2000) <ftp://ftp.isi.edu/in-notes/rfc3109.txt> accessed 16 Jun. 2001

Telnet addresses are unlikely to form part of traditional references. To be useful, any such reference would require path information including a host, user ID, password, and program. It may be more helpful to provide an associated Internet URL, where possible:

<telnet://tecfamoo.unige.ch 777> <http://tecfa.unige.ch/tecfamoo.html>
<telnet://ariane@ariane.ulaval.ca:23/> <http://arianeweb.ulaval.ca/>

Newsgroup articles, Usenet, email discussion boards, and newsletters

Where email list servers archive (and therefore move) discussions, the main address becomes that of the server itself.

John Bruder, 'HTML Lists: 1.1, 1.2,…?' [newsgroup article], *comp.infosystems.www.authoring.html, comp.infosystems.www.authoring. stylesheets* <jmb@megatelco.com>, 5 Mar.1999, Message-ID: <34FF0B22.3A21A0A6@megatelco.com>

Ian Kingston, 'Too much memory is bad for Windows', *Online Grapevine* 204 [email discussion list] (15 May 2001) <*i.kingston@ntlworld.com*>

'N-Dimensional Thinking & Magical Numbers', in *Developer.com Update* [email newsletter] (19 Jan. 2001) <journal@developer.com>

Personal communications

A wide range of electronic sources are, in practical terms, difficult or impossible for readers to retrieve from the original source cited. In this they are akin to personal correspondence, or papers or records held privately. Note that data-protection and copyright regulations require you to secure the sender's permission before quoting from an electronic message. (As emails can be counterfeited, this is a sensible precaution in any case.)

Email messages are the most frequently cited type of personal communications. Where necessary, specify the recipient(s):

R. M. Ritter, 'Revised proofs' [email to H. E. Cox], (1 Aug. 2001) <OGS@ritter.org.uk> accessed 3 Aug. 2001

Synchronous (real-time) communications such as IRC, MUD, MOO, or text messaging are transient and unlikely to form the basis of a reference except as a personal communication: a transcript derived from a chatroom discussion, for example, is cited as a hardcopy document. Where archived, the address will be an http:// URL.

CD-ROMs

Bob the Builder: Can We Fix It? [multimedia game] PC CD-ROM (Windows 95, 98) (BBC Multimedia, 2000), ASIN: B0000507NN

Peter Morris and William Wood, *The Oxford Textbook of Surgery*, 2nd edn. [Windows CD-ROM], (Oxford: OUP, 2001)

Pokémon Project Studio: Blue Version [graphics software] (Crawley: The Learning Company, 2000) CD-ROM (Windows 95, 98) PKB844AB-CD

15.15.4 Persistent identifiers

Several international efforts are currently under way to address the problem of the impermanence of links to electronic data, since intellectual property available as digital content can change ownership or location (e.g. a new copyright holder or server) during the course of its life. New technology, and the extensibility and interoperability of existing systems, wireless applications, broadcasting media, and Internet applications, mean that in future existing data will be accessed in new ways. Current protocols for persistently identifying a digital object include DOI (Digital Object Identifier), PURL (Persistent URL), and URN (Uniform Resource Name). Some forms of data, such as newsgroup articles, already have unique message IDs, which can be—though seldom are—cited in references.

No agreed guidelines exist as yet for how references to these initiatives will look, or their level of granularity. Some will look very much like URLs, while metadata for DOI, for example, may include within its code several types of labels. For now, any identifiers should be given in addition to the more common references, as in the example below:

Karen W. Gripp, Elaine H. Zackai, and Catherine A. Stolle, 'Mutations in the Human *TWIST* Gene', *Human Mutation* 15/2 (2000), pp. 150B5 (published online 25 Jan. 2000)

<http://www3.interscience.wiley.com/cgi-bin/abstract/69501452/START>, accessed 3 Feb. 2000

<DOI 10.1002/(SICI)1098-1004(200002)15:2<150::AID-HUMU3> 3.0.CO;2-D>

15.16 **Notes**

15.16.1 Presentation in text

As the main mechanism in the author–title system—or as an auxiliary part of the author–date or author–number systems—notes are used for citing references, or for any matter supplemental to the text. They can be set at the foot of the page on which their cue occurs (footnotes) or gathered together under the heading *Notes*, either at the end of the relevant chapter or at the end of the work (endnotes). Especially in multi-author works, endnotes can also go at the end of the chapter; endnotes gathered together at the end of a work have running heads specifying the pages to which they refer. It is possible to use both foot- and endnotes for different purposes in the same work, for example footnotes for parenthetical remarks closely related to the text, and endnotes for references.

Footnotes are to be recommended in many contexts, especially if the citations are discursive. Some authors specify endnotes on the grounds that they will not disrupt the flow of the narrative. The opposite is often the case: the reader deliberates whether it is worthwhile to look up this or that note, and soon finds either that he or she need not bother (in which case the author–date system might be a better choice) or that he or she must disrupt the flow of the narrative by flipping back and forth between notes and text. It takes much less time to glance at the foot of the page; the saving in aggravation is immeasurable. Nevertheless, there are cases where endnotes are preferable—such as with long notes or notes containing displayed matter.

15.16.2 Content

Since notes are ancillary to the text, the rules they follow differ from those for normal running text: in keeping with their parenthetical nature they tend to (though need not always) be briefer in style, and generally employ more abbreviations and symbols than in the text; in general, cite the smallest number of the work's divisions that is consist- ent with clarity.

The manner of citation in footnotes and endnotes is the same, although more information—publisher, date of first edition, etc.—might be found in the bibliography. The same format can sensibly be used in the bibli- ography, apart from reversing the author's name. Thus citations in notes and bibliography are largely identical.

The first time any reference is cited, it must be given in full. Thereafter if the work includes a bibliography, a short title is sufficient; otherwise the complete citation should be used again at the first appearance in each chapter. If there are several full references to the same book, a bibliog- raphy—or at least a list of abbreviated references—is best. On the other hand, articles (unless following the author–date or author–number system) rarely have bibliographies. If cross-references are widely spaced, it is helpful to add a cross-reference back to the full title, in the form:

[116] Citarella, 'Relations of Amalfi with the Arab World' (above, n. 13), 47.

As a rule, publishers prefer authors to avoid references to note numbers in the main body of the text. Similarly, avoid wherever possible—or keep to a strict minimum—cross-references by page number, since each involves an expensive change at proof stage. An expedient is to use the form *See Ch. 3 at n. 6*, which refers to the text at that point.

15.16.3 Abbreviations

Many abbreviations are used in note references, to aid or direct the reader as succinctly as possible. For the most part, a lower-case abbreviation that begins a note is capitalized, whether or not the note is a complete sentence. A handful of common abbreviations are, however, exceptions to this rule: *c.*, e.g., i.e., l., ll., p., pp. are always lower-case in notes, even at the start:

[20] *c.*1344, according to Froissart.

[21] e.g. service outside the jurisdiction.

[22] i.e. Copyright, Designs & Patents Act 1988, § 4.

[23] p. 7.

[24] ll. 34–44 (Miller edn.).

The following abbreviations are commonly used with the author–title system. Authors not confident of correctly using these forms should avoid them: in the case of 'id.' and its associates, a copy editor will not normally have the information necessary to adjust any errors of usage, especially if initials only are used in citations. Authors who have moved notes around while writing must be careful that these abbreviations still refer to the authors and passages intended. Apart from '*i.q.*' (*idem quod*) all the abbreviations should be printed roman; all are lower-case except when beginning a sentence or note.

■ 'Ibid.' in Latin, *ibidem* means 'in the same place'. Its preferred abbreviation is 'ibid.', though 'ib.' is also found; 'in ibid.' is ungrammatical. 'Ibid.' is used in place of the author's name and the title when this would otherwise duplicate the citation in the immediately preceding note. (When the second reference falls at the top of a verso page during setting, it should be replaced with a short title.) If the reference is exactly the same, 'ibid.' suffices. A comma is unnecessary if a volume and/or page number follows; however, if any other matter follows, a comma is required:

Stratford, *Apple Crumble*, 21.

Ibid. 28.

Ibid.

Belson, *Lardy Cake*, ii. 93, pl. xv.

Ibid. i. 101.

Ibid., app. A.

'Ibid.' may also be used to replace the name of a journal or other source cited in the immediately preceding note, though it is preferable to

repeat the title unless it is very long. It cannot be used to replace information in a note that does not directly precede it.

Avoid producing a long string of notes that merely repeat 'ibid.'. If a
paragraph draws generally on one source, it may be sufficient to say:
'For what follows, see Stratford, *Apple Crumble*, 10–31.' Alternatively, the
page or line numbers may be cited in the text.

■ 'Op. cit.', short for *opere citato* ('in the work cited'), and 'art. cit.', short for
articulo citato ('in the article cited'), can often be false friends, since they
require readers to look back through the text to locate the preceding
citation; they are best removed in favour of surname and short title.
Either is acceptable when used in the same note after an intervening
reference or in the succeeding note, where a repetition would be otiose:

> Studies have shown (Stratford, *Apple Crumble*; Belson, *Lardy Cake*) that
> departmental morale was measurably amplified by the occasional and
> unexpected provision of baked goods; on the acceptance of traditional
> variants see Stratford, op. cit.

Do not use them in conjunction with author–title references; if consistently used by an author, a construction such as 'op. cit. (n. 13)' is
acceptable, but editors should not impose it.

■ 'Loc. cit.', short for *loco citato* ('at the place referred to'), is appropriate
only for the exact page number of an earlier citation at short range.

■ *Idem quod* means 'the same as', and is abbreviated in italic as *i.q.*

■ 'Id.' and 'Ead.' 'Id.', short for *idem* ('the same' or 'as mentioned before'), is
used generally to avoid repeating an author's name in notes or bibliographical matter, when citing in uninterrupted succession more than
one work by the same man. It cannot be used to refer to a female author,
who is 'ead.' (for *eadem*). Two or more female authors are referred to as
'eaed.' (for *eaedem*), and two or more authors of whom at least one is
male are referred to as 'eid.' (for *eidem*).

> T. W. M. Ritter, *A History of the New York Cheesecake*, 156.
> Id., 'Geographical Distribution of Later Variants of the New York
> Cheesecake', 223.
> E. Wells, 'East Hendred', 276.
> Ead., *A White Horse Childhood*, 43–69.

In notes, cross-references to other foot- or endnotes are given in the
form *(p.) 90 n. 17* (with a full point after the *n*); the note number is not
given where only one note falls on the page cited: *(p.) 90 n.* A normal
interword space of the line is inserted between page number and note
number in all cases: to improve the clarity of the reference a thin space
was formerly inserted between page number and *n.* when no number
followed, but this convention seldom applies except to note references
cited in indexes, where exceptionally a thin space is used.

15.16.4 **Length**

Avoid also footnotes exceeding one paragraph, since they may cause problems in page layout. Instead, part of the note can sometimes be moved into the text, but extensive discussion of a subsidiary matter may be better placed in an appendix or annexe. Do not place in footnotes displayed quotations, music examples, figures, tables, or mathematical equations, unless they are very brief. If these are unavoidable, endnotes may be useful.

It is important that the copy for each footnote is of a limited size—one folio or less—since lengthy footnotes are unwieldy and difficult to set and read. Longer notes can usually be avoided through the use of one or more of the following options: (a) insert the bulk of the material into the running text to which it refers; (b) change some of the notes into an appendix; (c) make selected footnotes into chapter endnotes, each with a footnoted cross-reference to it in the form *See Note A following this chapter*; or (d) delete superfluous or extraneous portions of the notes' text.

15.16.5 **Cues**

Note references can be cued in several ways. The most common is by superscript figures or letters. Place in-text footnote cues outside punctuation, but inside the closing parenthesis when referring solely to matter within the parentheses. Normally cues fall at the end of a sentence unless referring only to part of the sentence: a cue at the end of a sentence represents the whole of the sentence:

> Causes for infection were initially thought to be isolated.[16] (This was rapidly discredited.[17]) Even so, specialists in England[18] and Wales[19] reached different conclusions during subsequent tests.

Reference marks are used as cues in several instances: when there are relatively few notes; as an alternative to superior figures for note references where cues made up of superscript figures or letters may be confused with technical notation (as in mathematical or scientific setting); as an alternative to a notation system used simultaneously (as in tables, or in works using both foot- and endnotes); or in facsimile setting and fine editions to approximate antique printing practices. Their traditional order is *, †, ‡, §, ¶, ||, repeated in duplicate as **, ††, etc. as necessary. Other symbols are possible, such as the degree mark (°) or star (*). Single and double asterisks are not used in scientific work and in probabilities, where they may be confused with notation for statistical significance.

In general, cue references in text by superscript (superior) arabic figures. Do not use numerical cues in mathematical setting of any kind, as cues attached to equations or other mathematical symbols, since they may be mistaken for superscript figures.

For mathematical setting, or for a second set of cues, use symbols or lower-case superior italic letters. (For footnotes to tables *see* **9.2.5**.) A second set may be necessary where differentiating between footnotes and endnotes or, in the case of scholarly editions, between original footnotes and those supplied by the volume editor.

There are three exceptions to standard note-cue style. The first is the uncued first note in the text or chapter, which is reserved for giving details of the chapter's original source. The second is also the first note, uncued or cued typically by an asterisk (normally set against the chapter title) where all other notes are arabic numbers; this cites acknowledgements associated with the text. (Apart from these, avoid attaching note cues to headings or subheadings, as the disparate sizes of type look awkward on the printed page.) The third is marginal notes, which appear in the foredge margin directly beside the passage they gloss, précis, or otherwise comment on. Their proximity to the text they relate to makes cues unnecessary. Nevertheless they are seldom used, as they demand wide margins, making them difficult to set and suitable mostly for large-format works.

15.16.6 Numbering

When there are endnotes, or substantial numbers of footnotes, number them consecutively through each chapter. This allows cross-references between notes in the form *see Ch. 3 n. 6*. When there are a very few notes they may be numbered consecutively throughout the whole work, or their sequence repeated anew on every page, so that the first cue on each page is *1*, *a*, or *, the second *2*, *b*, or †, and so on.

For guidance on setting footnotes *see* **2.4.7**.

15.17 Bibliographies

For a general description of the types of bibliographies and reference sections *see* **1.4.3**. For bibliographies in translation *see* **13.11.1.11**. Within a bibliography or other reference section, entries typically begin full left, with turn-lines indented one em, and end in a full point. Except for the inversion of the authors' names, the form of citations in bibliographies does not differ from that in the notes.

15.17.1 **Organization**

The bibliography may be alphabetical throughout, or with subdivisions. (For the author–date (Harvard) system *see* **15.19**; for the author–number (Vancouver) system *see* **15.20**.) In general writers should refrain from subdividing bibliographies into categories or chapters: this renders them difficult to use, since the reader (or editor) must then be able to predict or recall accurately into which class or section a given work falls. There are two exceptions to this: a division into primary and secondary sources, and a separate list of manuscripts and documents.

A division into primary and secondary sources is appropriate, for example, in biographies or works on literary criticism, separating works *by* and works *about* an author. Primary sources may be listed chronologically (as in the case of the works of a single author) or alphabetically.

Manuscripts and documents follow the same guidelines in bibliographies as in notes (*see* **15.16** above). List manuscripts and documents separately, since neither falls naturally into an alphabetical listing by author. Arrange manuscripts according to depository and collection; pressmarks should follow strictly the usage of the library concerned, otherwise it will be difficult for the reader to find the source. List documents by department and—if necessary—country. The form of citation should match that used in the body of the work.

While it is possible that a bibliography may contain primary, secondary, manuscript, and document sources, even the longest or most complex bibliography nevertheless should—if carefully arranged—require no more than two or three categories or subdivisions.

15.17.2 **Order of entries**

Alphabetization follows the same principles as in indexing. Authors' names are presented surname first, followed by a comma and the given names or initials, in full and small capitals:

ELIOT, T. S.

Make sure that all names are correctly spelt according to the bearers' preference, even when this is unusual; take particular care with such variants as *MacDonald*, *Macdonald*, or *McDonald*; *Mueller* or *Müller*.

Alphabetize according to English rules (*ch* before *ci* even if the name is Spanish or Czech) and ignore all accents (index *Müller* as Muller, not as Mueller); treat *Mc* as *Mac* and *St* as *Saint*. With prefixes such as *de* or *De*, follow the correct usage for the language in question: the general rule is to put them first if written with a capital ('DE QUINCEY, THOMAS'), otherwise to postpone them (thus *Jean de La Fontaine* becomes 'LA

FONTAINE, JEAN DE'). For more on names *see* **4.2**; for more on alphabetizing *see* **CHAPTER 16**.

Names from an older period do not necessarily follow modern rules; German names may exhibit fluctuation between umlaut and written-out *e*; Italian names with *del* and *della* may be regularly written lower-case when the given name precedes (Italian indexes were often sorted by given name down to the nineteenth century). Likewise, English-speaking scholars with non-English surnames may not abide by the rules of the original language.

In multiple-author or -editor works, the names are all uniformly inverted. These are displayed like those of single authors, although the conjunction is not in small capitals. With more than one author a comma (not a semicolon) follows the initials of the first:

> DOE, J., and SMITH, T....

If initials only are provided, without a surname, do not invert them even if the bearer's full name is known. Hence *G.E.C.* for the *Complete Peerage* is alphabetized under *G*, even though the author's name is known to be George Edward Cokayne. (*See also* **16.3.4**.)

Single author

Entries by the same author may be ordered alphabetically by title, ignoring articles, or chronologically by year, earliest first, and alphabetically within a single year. The former is advisable when many works of one author are cited, but the latter may be preferred if it is important to show the sequence of works, for example *Further Thoughts on* ... or *Reply to* .... In second and subsequent works by the same author replace the name with a 2-em rule, followed by a fixed thin space. In marking up a typescript, editors should indicate that the rule should be replaced by the author's full name if it falls at the top of a left-hand page.

Multiple authors

It is usual to alphabetize works by more than one author under the first author's name. Some presses follow the convention of grouping numbers of authors together, for example one-author works, followed by two-author works, three-author works, four-author works, and so forth. OUP, however, prefers straight alphabetical listings. Regardless, if another style has been followed consistently and successfully, it need not be altered.

Replace the names of authors common to subsequent works by a 2-em rule for each name, according to how many names are restated. There is a thin space after each rule, with no punctuation between or following them:

AUTHOR, A. N., *First Book Title* (London, 1999).

—— and AUTHOR NO. 2, *Second Book Title* (Oxford, 2000).

———— *Third Book Title* (Cambridge, 2002).

———— and AUTHOR NO. 3, *Fourth Book Title* (New York, 1998).

When there is more than one citation to the same author, group references within these three categories:

- works written by a single author, in alphabetical order
- works written by the same author with one co-author, in alphabetical order; different works with the same authors are listed in chronological order
- works written with two or more co-authors, in chronological order

This last group is not listed in alphabetical order because the names of more than two co-authors do not appear in text ('et al.' is used instead), so references listed by alphabetical order of co-author will not help the reader, who will be looking only for the year of publication. Here is an example of the order for a complex collection of authors:

HORNSBY-SMITH, M. P., *Roman Catholic Beliefs in England: Customary Catholicism and Transformations of Religious Authority* (Cambridge, 1991).

—— and DALE, A., 'Assimilation of Irish Immigrants', *BJS* 39 (1988).

—— and LEE, R. M., *Roman Catholic Opinion* (Guildford, 1979).

———— and TURCAN, K. A., 'A Typology of English Catholics', *SR* 30 (1982), 43–9.

———— and REILLY, P. A., 'Social and Religious Change', *Sociology*, 18 (1984), 53–5.

———— 'Common Religion and Customary Religion', *RRR* 26 (1985), 244–52.

—— TURCAN, K. A., and RAJAN, L. T., 'Patterns of Social Change', *ASSR* 64 (1987), 137–55.

—— FULTON, J., and NORRIS, M., *Power in Religion* (London, 1991).

Works edited by an author are listed in a separate sequence following all works written by him or her, singly or with co-authors; works edited in collaboration are arranged according to the same rules as for multiple authors. Alternatively, it is possible to list all publications associated with a single person in a single sequence, ignoring the distinction between author and editor.

Edited volumes

If the bibliography includes works both by and edited by the same author, place the edited books at the end of the entry, following their own alphabetical or chronological organization. These precede multi-author works (*see also* **15.19.1**).

15.17.3 **Arrangement according to the author–date system**

This system is frequently used in scientific journals. Citations in text merely refer to author's surname (with initials if necessary) and date of publication, distinguishing more than one work per year with *a, b, c*, etc. The entries in the bibliography must then be arranged with the date following the author's name rather than the place of publication, and placed in chronological order. The same basic information is used in author–date bibliographical references as for the author–title system, but the order of some of the elements differs.

15.17.4 **Name variants and titles**

When more than one form of the author's name appears in the sources cited, for example the full name in a book but initials only in an article, use the most complete form available for the first entry.

If works of one author are cited under different names, use the latest form, with the former given after it in parentheses, and a cross-reference if necessary:

> JOUKOVSKY, F., *Orphée et ses disciples dans la poésie francaise et néolatine du XVIe siècle* (Publications romanes et francaises, 109; Geneva, 1970).
>
> ——(= JOUKOVSKY-MICHA, F.), 'La Guerre des dieux et des géants chez les poètes francais du XVIe siècle (1500–1585)', *BHR* 29 (1967), 55–92.

If the bibliography contains works under the author's true name as well as a pseudonym, include both, with a cross-reference under the pseudonym:

> Coulange, *see* Turmel.
>
> TURMEL, J., 'Histoire de l'angélologie du temps apostolique à la fin du Ve siècle', *RHL* 3 (1898), 299–308, 407–34, 533–52.
>
> ——('P. Coulange'), *The Life of the Devil*, trans. S. H. Guest (London, 1929).

For styling names in a bibliography, anything that counts as an integral part of the author's name is included in the large and small capitals, but titles of nobility are given in upper and lower case only, although the rest of the name is still in large and small capitals. (Academic titles or degrees are not included in references.) Such particles as *de, of, von, z*, and so on preceding a place name or surname will therefore appear in small capitals when they divide one name-element from another:

> JOHN OF SALISBURY, *Historia Pontificalis*, ed. Marjorie Chibnall (Oxford Medieval Texts; Oxford, 1986).
>
> GOETHE, JOHANN WOLFGANG VON, *Gedichte*, ed. Erich Trunz (Munich, 1974).
>
> MUSSET, ALFRED DE, *Contes d'Espagne et d'Italie* (Paris, 1830).

but:

> BISMARCK, OTTO, Fürst von, *Gedanken und Erinnerungen*, 3 vols. and 2
> appendices (Stuttgart, 1898–1919); new edn., 2 vols. (Stuttgart, 1921).

After the First World War all German titles of nobility (e.g. *Fürst, Graf,
Ritter*) were no longer titles in their own right, but subsumed into the
given name. In a bibliography such titles should match the name, in full
and small capitals:

> LAMBSDORFF, HANS GEORG GRAF, and HÜBNER, ULRICH,
> *Eigentumsvorbehalt und AGB-Gesetz* (Cologne, 1982).

However, if the title is translated (*Prince, Count, Kt.*) it should be styled in
capital and lower case.

Authors who publish under their title should be cited under their family
name (if known), with the title following, for example:

> STANLEY, EDWARD, 14th Earl of Derby, *The Iliad of Homer, rendered into
> English Blank Verse, to which are Appended Translations of Poems
> Ancient and Modern*, 13th edn., 2 vols. (London, 1894).

15.17.5 Volume editors

When editions of original works of literature are cited, the entry is given
under the original author, followed by the title and then the editor's
name, preceded by *ed. Ed.* means *edited by* and is invariable. For collections of essays, by contrast, the editor's name is given first, followed by
ed. in parentheses. For two or more editors the form is *eds.*, preferable to
edd. In the following entries, note first the change in the treatment and
placement of *ed.*, and secondly how the editors' names are arranged:

> BROWNING, ROBERT, *The Ring and the Book*, ed. Richard D. Altick
> (Harmondsworth: Penguin, 1971).
>
> *Debussy Letters*, ed. Francois Lesure and R. Nichols (Harmondsworth:
> Penguin, 1971).
>
> LESURE, FRANCOIS, and NICHOLS, R. (eds.), *Studies in Debussy*
> (Harmondsworth: Penguin, 1971).

In the second example, *ed.* indicates that the *Debussy Letters* were edited
by Lesure and Nichols; in the third, *(eds.)* indicates that they were the
editors of *Studies in Debussy*.

For exceptions, *see* **15.2.12**.

15.17.6 Organizations as authors

An organization may choose to publish under the umbrella title of its
own name rather than that of its members. This name is set in upper
and lower case, since the length of such names often makes them
unwieldy when set in large and small capitals:

Department of Education and Science, *Falling Numbers and School Closures*, Circular 5/77, HMSO (London, 1977).

US Department of Energy, *Preliminary Report on the Assessment of Health Risks From the United States Nuclear Weapon Facilities*, DOE Report #88–805P (Washington, DC: Department of Energy, 1988).

US National Academy of Sciences, *Diet and Health* (Washington, 1989).

A preponderance of organizations in a bibliography is grounds for putting *all* names—authors and organizations both—into upper- and lower-case style. This is particularly the case in those disciplines that tend to cite many organizations, such as the social sciences. An organization's name need not be spelt out in full if it has appeared in a list of abbreviations elsewhere, either at the start of the text (for those organizations cited in text) or at the start of a bibliography (for those cited only in the bibliography).

15.17.7 Short titles

If two or more articles are cited from a volume of essays by different authors, the volume itself may appear in the bibliography, allowing the book title to be abbreviated in the citation of the article:

JACKSON, W. H., 'Tournaments and the German Chivalric *Renovatio*: Tournament Discipline and the Myth of Origins', in Anglo (ed.), *Chivalry*, 77–91.

15.18 **Author–title system**

If a work is cited more than once, the second and all subsequent references within the chapter—or, alternatively, all further references, if there is a bibliography—may be limited to the author's surname and a succinct version of the title. This is commonly known as the author-title or short-title system of references. Exceptionally, even the first full reference may be dispensed with if it is essential to keep the work within a tight page limit. Full references given in a separate list of abbreviations count as first mention, and need not be repeated in the text.

Use an author's initials only when citing works by different authors with the same surname. The short title selected should be meaningful and unique. Normally it consists of the first words of the title, minus any initial article:

Leach, *God Had a Dog* = Maria Leach, *God Had a Dog: Folklore of the Dog* (New Brunswick, NJ, 1961).

Yates, 'Cock-and-Fox Episodes' = Donald N. Yates, 'The Cock-and-Fox Episodes of *Isengrimus*, Attributed to Simon of Ghent: A Literary and Historical Study' (Ph.D. diss., University of North Carolina at Chapel Hill, 1979).

However, if the essence of the work can be conveyed better by later words, it is proper to do so:

Kramer, *Sumer* = Samuel Noah Kramer, *History Begins at Sumer* (Philadelphia, 1981).

Snow, 'Guerrero in Guatemala' = Robert J. Snow, 'Music by Francisco Guerrero in Guatemala'.

In titles that do not lend themselves to obvious abbreviation, a different short title may be chosen and specified at the first occurrence:

J. van Benthem, 'Was "Une mousse de Biscaye" Really Appreciated by L'ami Baudichon?', *Muziek & Wetenschap*, 1 (1991), 175–94 (cited hereafter as 'Mousse').

Ira Flatow, *They All Laughed . . . From Light Bulbs to Lasers: The Fascinating Stories behind the Great Inventions that have Changed our Lives* (New York, 1992) (cited hereafter as *Light Bulbs to Lasers*).

If the references are widely scattered, such short titles should be listed in the Abbreviations if there is no bibliography.

When only one work of the author is cited—and that frequently—the title may be omitted:

Snow 115–16.

When a book title is abbreviated there is no need for a comma before the volume reference:

Stubbs, *Constitutional History*, ii. 95–8.

Stubbs, *Const. Hist.* ii. 95–8.

If the author's name and the title have been cited in the text, it is superfluous to repeat them in a footnote, but advisable to do so in an endnote. The note is thought of as a continuation:

³ (London: Macmillan, 1980).

⁴ (Cambridge, Mass., 1946), 17.

Short titles derived from foreign-language works follow the same criteria as for English. In creating a truncated form, ensure that the result is sensible: for example, a Hebrew title such as *Miflegot hayamin babechirot ha'acharonot* ('Parties of the right in the last elections') cannot be shortened to *Miflegot*, which means 'Parties of'. It is helpful for authors to prepare a list of suitable abbreviations, to aid editors not familiar with the language.

15.19 **Author–date system**

The author–date reference system—also called the Harvard system—is the most commonly used reference method in the physical and social sciences. It provides the author's name and year of publication within parentheses in text, and the full details at the end of the work in a list of references. It is in contrast to the author–title (short-title) system, which provides this information with a combination of footnotes or endnotes and the full reference at the end of the work. Within the in-text parentheses the minimum amount of information is supplied to make the reference unique, ensuring a single possible match in the reference section (*see* **15.19.2**).

Some sample in-text references:

> This is held by Barnes (1982: 15–17) and Hankinson (1988*a*: 93, 96; 1989: 72); see generally Annas (1983); it was 'the best of all possible worlds' (Hankinson 1989: 43; cf. 76). I discuss the point in Chapter 2. Summaries of the working party's conclusions may be found in Mason et al. (1994). According to another study, 'the effect of the proposals on the community would be disastrous' (P. Smith, forthcoming *b*: i. 24). (The World Health Organization (WHO 1975) takes a different view.)

Adhered to strictly, this system may cause sentences to become unduly clogged:

> Both economic (Peters and Jenkins 1985*a*, 1985*b*: 57–64; Jenkins and Peters 1987*b*: 26–37; Witherspoon and Worrall 1994: 36–51) and educational (Peters and Jenkins 1985*b*: 65–79; Richardson and Shigemitsu 1988; O'Connell et al. 1995) factors have been invoked to account for the observed (Willoughby and Banarji 1954; Gershon and Shirazi 1969; Al-Kabir et al. 1983) and anecdotal (Powell 1968) differences.

In such cases it is better to rewrite, or use footnotes.

15.19.1 **References in text**

Each time a reference is made to any document, its author's surname and the year of its publication are given in parentheses, with no punctuation separating the two:

> Depression is more heterogeneous in the old than in the young (Blumenthal 1971).

When the citation is given at the end of a sentence, it is printed before the full point. (When it is given at the end of a displayed quotation, it follows the full point.)

The author's name and year of publication are placed at their most logical and unambiguous spot within the sentence—not necessarily at the end of the sentence in which the reference occurs. If the author's name already exists naturally elsewhere in the sentence it is superfluous in the reference, so only the year is given in parentheses:

> At the ARP colloquium Daly asserted (1978) that...

When using the possessive, write *Spinelli's demonstration (1976)* not *Spinelli's (1976) demonstration.*

A string of references cited together in text may be listed in chronological or alphabetical order. References to works by different authors are separated by semicolons:

> Four controversial experiments in the late 1970s (Stamatos 1975; McNamee 1977; O'Donnell 1978; Rosengren 1979)...
>
> Four controversial experiments in the late 1970s (McNamee 1977; O'Donnell 1978; Rosengren 1979; Stamatos 1975)...

Author–date references should be placed in text wherever possible; place a group of references in a footnote only if it is very lengthy. Author–date references should never be given in endnotes because of the inconvenience to the reader.

When the same author has published more than one cited work in the same year, avoid ambiguity by adding a lower-case letter, often italic (*a*, *b*, *c*, etc.), placed close up to the year of publication. Thus two works by the same author, both published in 2001, are identified as 2001*a* and 2001*b* (not 2001 and 2001*a*). Assign the letters in the order in which the works are referred to in text:

> As Jones (1979*a*) stated...He went on to disclaim (1979*b*)...

When such references are cited together in text, they fall within the same set of parentheses, separated by commas:

> Jones's research (1977, 1979*a*, 1979*b*) points to...

When there are two authors or editors, give both surnames before the date:

> effects of positive reinforcement (Bohus 1981; De Kloet and De Wied 1980)...

An ampersand is also possible (*De Kloet & De Wied*). When there are three or more authors or editors, the name of the first author only is given in text, followed by 'et al.':

> Three investigations (Lloyd-Evans et al. 1979; Dencker and Lindberg 1977; Feris et al. 1908) showed that...

If possible, all authors' names should be given in the corresponding bibliographical entry, up to the usual limit of three (though twice that number is possible), after which 'et al.' should be used. (*See also* below.)

If in the same year an author collaborates with the same group of two or more co-authors, they are distinguished from one another with lower-case '*a*', '*b*', '*c*', etc. as for two works produced by the same single author or pair of authors in the same year. Again, letter labels follow the order of the references' appearance in text; the alphabetical order of co-authors is ignored.

When an author has written one work and been editor of a multi-author work in the same year, add *ed.* or *eds.* before the date to distinguish the author's editorial role. The abbreviations are not in parentheses of their own as they would be in author–title references:

> Others (Rowland 1961, ed. 1961; Wells and Wiley eds. 1967; Dohnert 1954*a*, et al. eds. 1956) still maintain . . .
>
> Rowland (1961, ed. 1961), Wells and Wiley (eds. 1967), and Dohnert (1954*a*, et al. eds. 1956) still maintain . . .

When there are references by two or more authors with the same surname, include their initials in the text reference where there is danger of confusion:

> (P. Jones 1994; L. Jones 1996)

If the reference section lists works by more than one author with the same surname, that surname should always be preceded by the appropriate initial(s) in citations—not just where the names are in direct conjunction in the text.

When the work has been produced by an organization and no author's name is given, use the organization's name in place of the author's. Cite the organization by the common abbreviated form in text (*WHO 1986*) and list it alphabetically by that abbreviation in the reference section, adding the full name in parentheses:

> WHO (World Heath Organization) (1986), *Nutrition and Development in East Africa (WHO, Geneva).*

Cite anonymous works as such, with letters as necessary:

> (Anonymous 1952*a*)

When citing an unsigned editorial in a journal or other periodical, use the name of the periodical and the date, which is listed in the reference section according to the periodical's name:

> (*Lancet* 2001)   (*The Times* 1953)

When different parts of a document are cited at different points in the text, give the appropriate page or section numbers in the citation, following the year. Prefer a colon—rather than a comma and *p.* or *pp.*—to separate the year and page:

> Harris (1985: 73) shows . . .
>
> It has been found (Harris 1985: 56) that . . .
>
> One source (Harris 1985: ch. 3) finds . . .

Label theses as such within the citation, and give further details in the reference section:

The work of Wells (thesis, 1925) has led us to query...

In her thesis (1925) Wells expressed some doubt...

Similarly, label personal communications within the citation, although further details need not be given in the reference section:

There is some evidence (Daly, personal communication) that...

When a work is to be published in the future use *forthcoming* rather than *in press*:

One source (Rowland, forthcoming) now states...

Rowland (forthcoming) now states...

There is an important distinction between the two terms: *forthcoming* means written or being written, *in press* means under contract and due to be published in the future. Nevertheless it may be best if *forthcoming* is employed throughout, as the status of a work may change from the first to the second (or even back again) so quickly that it is difficult to divine which will be appropriate by the time the citation appears in print. When the typescript is in proof, the author should check whether the work cited has been published yet, and update the reference accordingly both in text and in the reference section.

When a work is cited as part of a parenthetical statement in text, one set of parentheses suffices:

We will argue below that high fertility rates are a strategic response to the economic environment. (The general argument has been explored by Dasgupta 1993.) On the other hand, there is failure at the collective level. A number of reasons have been identified in the recent research (see e.g. Dasgupta 1993: ch. 12). (For a general discussion of Africa, see Guyer 1981; for the developing world, see Folbre 1986.)

When a work is cited as part of an acknowledgement (e.g. for a table or figure), only the date is in parentheses:

Source: Clark (2001)

Since the author–date system is best suited to modern works and secondary sources, some may find it awkward fitting historical, archival, or literary sources into its form, as this entails citing the edition used rather than the first edition, for example 'in Freud's *Jokes and their Relation to the Unconscious* (1963)', or 'When Shakespeare (1992) penned ...'. Singling out by date a subsequent edition of a work available in several editions suggests to the unwary that this is the sole standard work, and to the naive that this is the original publication date. To avoid such seeming anachronisms in text, mention of a well-known work may have either no date or—if placing it in context is important—the original date of publication. This may be placed instead of the reprint date or before it, either in square brackets ([1905] 1963) or separated by a solidus (1905/1963).

Alternatively, it is acceptable to use the author–title system in conjunction with the author–date system:

> Johnston (1904: 396) and Apuleius Platonicus (*Herbarium*, fo. 26^v) treat the same subject . . .

Within the reference section all works remain uniformly in the author–date format, however. For the full form of such citations in the reference section, and the relationship between multiple-edition citations and their references, *see* **15.19.2** below.

15.19.2 **Reference section**

Apart from the location of the year of publication and the ordering of authors, co-authors, editors, and co-editors, author–date-system references are presented in the same way as those for the author–title system. The only typographic difference is that in the author–date system the authors, editors, etc. are seldom set in capital and small-capital letters, but rather in upper- and lower-case. (This may be because small capitals take up more room than upper- and lower-case letters, and when organizations with long names are listed as authors—a frequent occurrence in the physical and social sciences—the result is unwieldy.)

The order of the elements in references differs most markedly from those in the ordinary author–title system in that the year of publication falls immediately after the author's name, so that the reader can find the appropriate entry easily. Publishers tend to be included less often in author–date references than in author–title references, though there is no reason why they cannot be included. References are listed in alphabetical order by author, and each author's publications are listed chronologically within the following groups: first, single-author works; second, works the author wrote with one other person; and third, works the author wrote with more than one other person.

Some sample references:

> Annas, J. (1983) (ed.), *Oxford Studies in Ancient Philosophy*, i (Oxford).
>
> Barnes, J. (1982), *Aristotle* (Past Masters; Oxford).
>
> —— and Griffin, M. T. (1989) (eds.), *Philosophia Togata: Essays on Philosophy and Roman Society* (Oxford).
>
> Hankinson, R. J. (1988*a*), 'Stoicism, Science, and Divination', in Hankinson (1988*b*: 88–102).
>
> —— (1988*b*) (ed.), *Method, Medicine, and Metaphysics* (Edmonton, Alta.).
>
> —— (1989), 'Galen and the Best of All Possible Worlds', *CQ* NS 39: 43–76.
>
> Hollingsworth, T. H. (1957), 'A Demographic Study of the British Ducal Families', *Population Studies*, 11/1: 4–26; repr. in D. V. Glass and D. E. C. Eversley (eds.) (1965), *Population in History* (London), 354–78.
>
> Marx, K. (1867), *Capital: A Critique of Political Economy*, i, trans. B. Fowkes (New York, 1977).

Mason, J. B. (1984), 'Introduction', in Mason et al. (1984*b*: 1–15).

——Habicht, J. P., and Tabatabai, H. (1984*a*), 'Notes on Nutritional Surveillance', paper delivered to the WHO conference.

—————— and Valverde, V. (1984*b*), *Nutritional Surveillance* (Geneva).

Office of Population Censuses and Surveys (1979*a*), *Area Mortality Tables: The Registrar-General's Decennial Supplement for England and Wales 1969–1973*, Series DS, No. 3 (London).

——(1979*b*), *Projections of the New Commonwealth and Pakistani Population*, OPCS Monitor PP2 79/1 (London).

Pritchard, E., and Pritchard, J. (1990), 'A Reply to Drèze', unpub. paper.

Smith, P. (forthcoming *a*), 'The Case of Tigray', in Smith (forthcoming *b*: ii. 76–94).

——(forthcoming *b*), *Gender and Famine*, 2 vols. (London).

Smith, T. (1988), *Famine and Gender* (New Haven, Conn.).

WHO (1983): World Health Organization, *Primary Health Care: The Chinese Experience* (Geneva).

——(1988), 'Nutrition: Sex Bias of Nutritional Status of Children 0–4 Years', *Weekly Epidemiological Record*, 20 May.

In single-author works, arranged chronologically, the author's name is replaced by a 2-em rule in the second and subsequent listings:

Jones, F. (1970)...

——(1991)...

In an ordinary bibliography *Jones ed. (1970)* would precede *Jones (1991)*; however, in an author–date reference section, edited works follow in a separate group, or may be placed individually in chronological order following works written by the author. In this case the author's name must be repeated each time his or her designation changes.

Jones, F. (1970)...

Jones, F. ed. (1970)...

Jones, F. (1991)...

——(1992)...

Jones, F. ed. (1999)...

Either system is acceptable if it is consistently applied.

Double-author works are arranged in alphabetical order by second author, then chronologically:

——and Smith, P. (1991)...

——and Thomas, G. (1980)...

——and Veevers, L. (1974*a*)...

————(1975*b*)...

————(1975)...

Each repeated name is replaced with a 2-em rule, according to how many names are restated. There is a thin space but no punctuation between or following names. If the original date of the work cannot be given, cite the year of the edition used:

> Aristotle (1976), *Metaphysics: Books M and N*, trans. with introd. by J. Annas
> (Oxford: Clarendon Press).

Alternatively, the work may be cited and listed as *Aristotle (1976 edn.)* (*see* **15.19.1**). When the original date of publication has been cited in text, that date is repeated in the reference, in addition to the year of the edition used. It can either follow the edition-year within the parentheses or fall at the very end of the reference; including the original publisher is optional:

> Bede, C. (Edward Bradley) (1982, first pub. in three parts, 1853, 1854, 1857),
> *The Adventures of Mr Verdant Green* (Oxford: Oxford University Press).
>
> Orwell, G. (1962, first pub. 1938 by Martin Secker & Warburg), *Homage to
> Catalonia* (Harmondsworth: Penguin).
>
> Bede, C. (Edward Bradley) (1982), *The Adventures of Mr Verdant Green*
> (Oxford: Oxford University Press), first pub. in three parts, 1853, 1854,
> 1857.
>
> Orwell, G. (1962), *Homage to Catalonia* (Harmondsworth: Penguin), first
> pub. 1938 by Martin Secker & Warburg.

Either format is acceptable, provided it is employed consistently throughout.

Matching citations to references requires more consideration when using more than one edition. For example, a newspaper article Marx originally wrote in 1848 is not readily available in that form; it appears in the first volume of the standard collection of his work, published in German in 1956, and appears in later collections, among them one published in English in 1977. The in-text form *(Marx 1848)* properly corresponds in references to the article:

> Marx, K. (1848), *Rheinische Zeitung* (23 Oct.), 1.

but is not accessible to the reader without a protracted archival search. A citation to the same article as part of the standard work *(Marx 1956: i. 177)* or English translation *(Marx 1977: 24)* is possible when the reference properly relates to one or the other edition. The page reference in text directly follows the date of the work to which it refers:

> Marx, K., Engels, F. (1956), *Werke* (Berlin), 41 vols.
> McLellan, D. (1977) (ed.), *Karl Marx: Selected Writings* (Oxford), 24.

An author wishing to retain the original date and a more accessible citation (in this case the English translation) may give both dates in text *(Marx [1848] 1977: 24)*, with the reference:

> Marx, K. (1848), *Rheinische Zeitung* (23 Oct.); in D. McLellan (1977) (ed.),
> *Karl Marx: Selected Writings* (Oxford).

Equally, the standard work may be cited instead of the original article, in text *(Marx [1956] 1977: 24)* and in references:

> Marx, K., Engels, F. (1956), *Werke* (Berlin); in D. McLellan (1977) (ed.), *Karl
> Marx: Selected Writings* (Oxford).

15.20 **Author–number system**

Mainly confined to scientific journals, the author–number system—often called the Vancouver system—is similar in form to the author-date, but each publication is numbered and the reference in text is merely to the number:

> By mid-century both Ryle[12] and Wittgenstein[18] were advocating forms of logical behaviourism.

In the list of references at the end of the article the works will be ordered by number and author and cited as follows:

> 12. Ryle, G., *The Concept of Mind* (New York: Barnes & Noble, 1949).
>
> 18. Wittgenstein, L., *Philosophical Investigations* (Oxford: Blackwell, 1953).

Alternatively, each author's publications may be consecutively numbered in chronological order and cited as follows:

> By mid-century both Ryle (2) and Wittgenstein (5) were advocating forms of logical behaviourism.

The references will then be arranged by author and number:

> Ryle, G. (2), *The Concept of Mind*...
>
> Wittgenstein, L. (5), *Philosophical Investigations*...

Editors should not impose the author–number system unless specified by the author or a pre-existing series style. When it is used, any addition to or subtraction from the list of works cited will entail renumbering all subsequent items and references thereto.

15.21 **Cross-references**

Generally, cross-references direct the reader to related points of substantive discussion in another part of a work. Ensure that each cross-reference is clear, accurate, unambiguous, and—above all—essential. Implement a consistent system that relies on the text's own internal structure, and avoid sending the reader elsewhere when the point or reference could economically be restated on the original page. While authors may occasionally find it necessary to explain where else within their text information is found or a concept developed, extensive cross-referencing can denote poorly arranged material. Repeatedly guiding a reader back and forth throughout a text becomes tedious, and produces writing that appears elliptical and self-referential.

15.21.1 **Structure and elements**

Capitalize the labels of all internal citations, to indicate that the components are structures *within* the text:

see Part I, Chapter 2, Plate III, Fig. 4.5, Table 5.6, Appendix 7, Section 8.9

Do not capitalize any component that is not a specific structure, such as *page* or *note*. Cross-references to foot- or endnotes are possible only if the notes are numbered by chapter or throughout the text, not by page. Capitalize labels only when they are used attributively, so *developed in Chapter 2* but *developed in the preceding chapter*; *in Table 5* but *in the following table*; *see Section 2.2* but *see the next section*. Set in small capitals text references to capital symbols in plates and line blocks, except in scientific work, where full capitals are used. In legal or technical contexts, *Section* and *Sections* may be replaced by the symbols § and §§ respectively.

Avoid making cross-references to note numbers in the main text.

Cross-references to sections take the same form whether referring to another section in the same or a different chapter, for example *For further discussion see Section 4.4.2*. Such a reference is not called *Chapter 4.4.2*, as the number relates to the subdivision number, not the chapter.

Wherever a citation is to an entire section or other component of a book, cross-references should be to that component, reduced to the smallest common level. This system has the advantage of avoiding potential problems with page cross-references, but only if it demands that the sections and subsections are numbered down to the lowest heading cited, to facilitate the reader's search. When frequent cross-references to numbered sections are unavoidable, include the numbers—possibly with shortened section titles—in the running headlines, or as additional shoulder headlines.

When it is necessary to refer to any text extent smaller than the smallest subsection, page cross-references are most useful to a reader. However, since each page number must be introduced at proof stage, this form of cross-reference is not just expensive to insert and correct but prone to error—especially if repagination is necessary during proofs. Where page cross-references are unavoidable and comparatively rare, editors should insert noughts in copy to approximate the number of digits to be inserted on proof—*p. 00*, *pp. 000–0*—and flag each occurrence in the margin of the typescript, with the applicable folio number (if any).

The abbreviation *cf.* (*confer* 'compare') is used to signal that one item is to be compared with another elsewhere (*cf. Phipps (n. 16 above) 34–40*). Do not confuse 'cf.' with 'see', which has a broader purpose. Editors encountering only the former in references may be right in thinking the author has made no distinction between the two forms.

15.21.2 **Cross-references in notes**

To avoid repeating citations, cross-references can be made from one note to another in the same chapter. Keep such cross-references to a strict minimum: the savings in space are rarely great, and seldom offset the reader's inconvenience. Do not make them to a note in a different chapter (repeat the information instead), and confine them to occasions where the repeated reference would be in very close proximity to an earlier reference—usually on the same page. In notes a shortened version of the reference may be given initially, with a subsequent 'pointer' to the full reference:

> R. Phipps, *The Law of Banking* (3rd edn., 1970).
> Phipps (n. 16 above), 42–5.

15.21.3 *Above* and *below*

Use *above* and *below* to refer to what was or will be mentioned on an earlier or later page, or higher or lower on the same page:

> the figures quoted above   the above statement   the remarks below

Avoid this device in matter intended to be read aloud. Alternatives that work equally well in text are such constructions as *the previous/preceding/earlier statement*.

Do not use *above* and *below* where a more exact indicator is already supplied: *in Chapter 5* or *on page 43* is sufficient—readers can discern whether that chapter or page is before or after the one they are reading at the moment. Similarly with section subheadings: in Chapter 4, Section 3 it should be obvious which way to turn for Chapter 1, Section 2.

Wherever possible, cross-references to related discussion should refer to the relevant chapter or section of the book rather than to a specific page, as this avoids having to add in or check the page number at proof stage. In books with paragraph numbering, the cross-reference should be to the relevant paragraph number(s):

> See the discussion in Chapter 2.
> For the position in Scotland, see paras 6.12–6.15.

Even in legal and official documents, avoid *above-mentioned* or *above-named*, as well as *supra*, *infra*, *ante*, *post*, and so on.

It is, however, a kindness to the reader to have *above* and *below* for cross-references to section headings *within* a chapter where no subsections occur, or where they are unnumbered. The logic is that if no chapter number is cited, the reference must be within the present chapter, and so can take *above* or *below*. Either *see n. 7 below* or *see below, n. 7* is acceptable, providing the style is consistent. Direction is also useful where ambiguity might otherwise arise ('see O'Brien, *History of the Nairn Family*, 237, and below, 238'), though this situation is better avoided by transposition ('see p. 238 below and O'Brien, *History of the Nairn Family*, 237').

CHAPTER 16

Indexing

16.1 General principles

A good index enables the user to navigate sensibly through the work's main topics and facts. How long it need be to accomplish this depends on the size and complexity of the work and the requirements and expectations of the readership. In general, a short index for a general book can account for as little as 1 per cent of the text it catalogues, while an exhaustive index for a specialist book can take up as much as 15 per cent. Although extremely short indexes are of limited use to a reader, it does not necessarily follow that a long index is better than a short one; authors should familiarize themselves with the indexes of related works in their field, and consult their editors regarding an agreed length.

Since an index normally requires proof pages before it can be started, it is chronologically one of the last publishing stages involving the author. The index is nevertheless a vital component of the work, and one that directly affects the text's usefulness for the reader. This chapter provides guidance for authors wishing to produce an index for their book, including what to index, how to arrange it, and how the result should look. Professional indexers are available for this purpose who are skilled at choosing, compiling, and ordering an index's content; nevertheless they may find it helpful for authors to suggest common themes and a rough structure for the indexer to work from. Many publishers prefer authors to generate their own indexes where possible, considering that they are best placed to produce copy appropriate to what may be a highly technical or specialist text.

16.2 What to index

Enter all items of significance (names, places, concepts), with correct page numbers and spelling, always keeping in mind the user of the index, particularly in terms of what and where things will be sought.

Usually a single index will suffice, so do not provide subsidiary indexes without good reason, and without agreeing it with your editor before-hand. (For indices locorum and other sorts of indexes, *see under* **16.4**.) An index of authors cited may be useful in the absence of a bibliography, though incorporating it into the main index removes the need to enter separately authors both cited and discussed or quoted, or indeed to determine into which category each mention fits.

Indexes are made up of individual *entries*, each comprising a *headword* and some indication of where that word may be found in text, by way of either one or more references (to a page, section, clause, or some other division) or a cross-reference to another headword. Entries complicated enough to require further division may have *subentries*; the entries within which they fall are sometimes called *main entries* to distinguish them. In all but the most complex indexes, subentries within subentries (*sub-subentries*) should be avoided.

Editors of multi-author works must ensure as far as possible that contributors' terminology and sources have been standardized to a single form throughout a work, otherwise the subsequent index may require frequent cross-references to guide the reader between variants.

16.2.1 Main entries

Main entries are those most likely to be first sought by the reader, and should be in a form that anticipates where the reader will look for them. They should be concise, and consist of nouns that may if necessary be modified attributively by adjectives, verbs, or other nouns; they should start with a capital letter *only* if the word is capitalized in text. Choose either the singular or plural form of a word if both are found in text, though where unavoidable both can be accommodated through paren-theses: *cake(s)*. In English, headwords of 'countable' nouns are usually plural, though those in foreign-language indexes (e.g. French and German) are usually singular.

Ignore passing or minor references that give no information about the topic. Do not include entries from the preface, contents, introduction, and other preliminary matter unless they contain information not found elsewhere that is relevant to the subject of the work. There is no need to index bibliographies or reference lists. There is usually no need to augment an entry's heading with supplementary information from the text, particularly for an item with only a single page reference, though in some cases a gloss or other clarification in parentheses may prove necessary.

If it is necessary to create main entries that echo the title or subtitle of the book, ensure that these are succinct. Use cross-references or subentries where a single reference spans ten or more pages, or where lengthy strings of page numbers threaten to clutter the layout: an array of unqualified or undifferentiated page numbers several lines deep is tiresome and unhelpful to the reader, and any string ideally should be reduced to six or fewer numbers. In biographies or collections of letters, keep subentries relating to the subject to a reasonable minimum, confining them to factors of relevance.

16.2.2 **Subentries**

Subentries and sub-subentries are used chiefly to analyse a complex subject heading made up of two or more discrete categories:

> cakes:
>> in antiquity 1–3, 30
>> decoration of 3, 4–9
>> in different cultures 1–2, 30–4
>> as gifts 22–35
>> types of 1–5, 19

Run together a simple heading with no general page references and only one category: *cakes, decoration of 3, 4–9.*

It may not always be possible, or practical, to use subentries and sub-subentries to avoid long strings of page numbers in an exhaustive index—such as one containing numerous references to authors of cited publications, a separate index of authors, or an index of musical works.

16.2.3 **Notes**

Notes should be indexed only if they give information not found elsewhere in the text. When there is a reference to a topic and a footnote to that topic *on the same page*, it is usually sufficient to index the text reference only.

16.2.4 **Cross-references**

Cross-references are used to deal with such things as synonyms, near-synonyms, pseudonyms, abbreviations, variant or historical spellings, and closely related topics; they fall into two classes. The first, introduced by *see*, directs attention from one possible entry to a synonymous or analogous one, under which the references will be found:

> Canton, *see* Guangzhou
> farming, *see* agriculture
> Dodgson, C. L., *see* Carroll, Lewis
> restrictive conception of an event (RCE), *see* event, restrictive conception of

The second, introduced by *see also*, extends the search by directing attention to one or more closely related entries or subentries. Two or more cross-references are given in alphabetical order, separated by semicolons:

> adab ('manners') 52, 78, 126; *see also* belles-lettres
>
> clothing 27, 44–6, 105–6; *see also* costume; millinery
>
> housing 134–9, 152; *see also* shelter, varieties of
>
> tread depth 109; *see also* routine maintenance; tyre condition, indicators

Do not cross-refer to an entry that takes up the same space occupied by the cross-reference itself. In

> authors, *see* writers
>
> writers 25, 36–8

the reader would find it easier if the page references were repeated after both headwords. Equally, do not cross-refer simply to the same references listed under a different heading, nor bewilder the reader by seemingly capricious or elliptical cross-referring:

> authors 13, 25, 36–8, 50; *see also* writers
>
> writers 25, 36–8, 50, 52; *see also* authors

There must be no 'blind' cross-references: in other words, ensure that every cross-reference is to an existing entry. Cross-references to general areas rather than specific headwords are often in italic: 'authors, *see under the individual authors*'.

16.2.5 Tables of cases and statutes

As part of their scholarly apparatus, legal books usually—but not invariably—contain a Table of Cases, a Table of Statutes, or both. These are simply a form of index enabling readers to identify passages of text by means of the significant cases and statutory provisions discussed in them, arranged alphabetically. Any such tables should therefore be treated exactly like indexes, except that they often appear as part of the preliminary pages following the table of contents. Their layout and form will be fashioned according to the style of the work as a whole.

16.3 **Alphabetical order**

16.3.1 Systems of alphabetization

The two systems of alphabetizing words are *word-by-word* and *letter-by-letter*, with minor variations in each. The British Standard

(BS ISO 999:1996) advocates word-by-word, which is the system usually employed in general indexes in Britain. Letter-by-letter is preferred in British encyclopedias, atlases, gazetteers, and some dictionaries, and is more common in the USA.

In both systems a single root word precedes the same word with a suffix (e.g. *fertilize* before *fertilizer, garden* before *gardening*), and hyphens are treated as spaces. Alphabetizing ignores apostrophes, all accents and diacritics, and parenthetical descriptions, and continues until a comma indicates inverted order.

For compound terms, the word-by-word system alphabetizes up to the first word space and then begins again, so separated words precede closed compounds (e.g. *high water* before *highball*). In both systems *High, J.* is treated as a simple entry; *high (light-headed)* is also simple, as descriptions in parentheses are disregarded. The two parts of a hyphenated compound are treated as separate words, except where the first element is not a word in its own right (e.g. *de-emphasis, iso-osmotic, proto-language*). In the letter-by-letter system alphabetization proceeds across spaces, so separated and hyphenated words are treated as one word, and hypens in proper names ignored.

The examples below consist of simple and compound entries; simple names precede compound names. In both systems identical entries are ordered as follows:

people:	New York, Earl of
places:	New York, USA
subjects, concepts, and objects:	New York, population
titles of works:	*New York, New York*

Science-related texts and some dictionaries and directories may reverse the order of these classes, so that lower-case words (things) appear before capitalized words (people):

barker, sideshow	Barker, Enid
barrow, long	Barrow, Isaac
bell, Lutine	Bell, Gertrude
bow, violin	Bow, Clara

For examples of complex hierarchies of names, *see* **16.3.4**.

Word-by-word	*Letter-by-letter*
High, J.	High, J.
high (light-headed)	high (light-headed)
high chair	highball
high-fliers	highbrow
high heels	high chair
High-Smith, P.	Highclere Castle

high water	high-fliers
High Water (play)	high heels
highball	highlights
highbrow	Highsmith, A.
Highclere Castle	High-Smith, P.
highlights	high water
Highsmith, A.	*High Water* (play)
highways	highways

In both systems, letter groups are treated as one word if—like 'NATO' and 'NASA'—they are pronounced as such. Otherwise, the word-by-word system lists all sets of letters before any full word, ignoring any full points:

Word-by-word	Letter-by-letter
I/O	I/O
IOU	iodine
IPA	IOU
i.p.i.	Iowa
IPM	IPA
i.p.s.	IP address
IP address	Ipanema
Ipanema	i.p.i.
iodine	IPM
Iowa	i.p.s.

Definite and indefinite articles at the beginning of entries are transposed: *Midsummer Night's Dream, A*; *Vicar of Wakefield, The*.

In works written in English, foreign words are conventionally alphabetized by ignoring accents and diacritics, so for example ö and ø are treated as *o*. Foreign names are treated in the form familiar to the reader, so there is a comma in *Bartók, Béla* even though in Hungarian the surname comes first.

Foreign languages have their own rules of alphabetization. For example, in Danish and Norwegian æ, ø, and å are listed after *z*, whereas in Swedish å, ä, and ö are after *z*; in Faeroese æ and ø are after *z*, and in Icelandic þ, æ, and ö. In Spanish and Welsh *ch* goes after *c*; Czechs and Slovaks place it after *h*. Take these conventions into account only when indexing a work written wholly in another language. (Exceptionally, a specialist text in English may follow foreign-language conventions if the readers are thought to expect and be fully conversant with them; where this has been done, note it at the start of the index.) For more guidance, *see* under the individual languages in **CHAPTER 11**.

Alphabetize indexes of poem titles as for book and periodical titles, disregarding definite or indefinite articles that may begin them. Alphabetize indexes of first lines (e.g. of poems, stanzas, quotations, or lyrics) word by word, rather than letter by letter:

> A chestnut tree stands in the line of sight
>
> 'A cold coming we had of it'
>
> A curious tale that threaded through the town
>
> Abstracted, sour, as he reaches across a dish
>
> Acts passed beyond the boundary of mere wishing

16.3.2 Scientific terms

If the first character or characters in a chemical compound is a prefix or numeral, such as O-, *s*-, *cis*-, it is ignored for alphabetizing but taken into account in ordering a group of similar entries. For example, '2,3-dihydroxybenzene', '2,4-dihydroxybenzene', and '*cis*-1,2-dimethylcyclohexane' would all be found under *D*, and the abbreviation '(Z,Z)-7,11-HDDA', expanded as '*cis*-7,*cis*-11-hexadecadien-1-yl acetate', would be alphabetized under *H*. In chemical notation, disregard subscript numerals except when the formulae are otherwise the same:

> vitamin B_1
>
> vitamin B_2
>
> vitamin B_6
>
> vitamin B_{12}

Greek letters prefixing chemical terms, star names, etc. are customarily spelt out (and any hyphen dropped); for example, α Centauri, α chain, and α-iron are alphabetized as *Alpha Centauri*, *alpha (α) chain*, and *alpha iron*. Similarly, the bacteriophage λ is alphabetized as *lambda (λ) phage*. However, Greek letters beginning the name of a chemical compound are ignored in alphabetization, for example 'γ-amniobutyric acid' is spelt thus but alphabetized under *A* for 'amnio', not *G* for 'gamma'.

16.3.3 Symbols and numerals

Arrange signs and symbols that begin an entry as if they were spelt out, alphabetizing '=' as *equals,* '£' as *pounds,* '⇒' as *implies,* and '&' as *ampersand*—though they can equally be listed before the alphabetical sequence, as the British Standard advises. (An ampersand within an entry is best treated as *and* or ignored.) Double coverage is helpful where the names of symbols may be problematic, with an umbrella heading for symbols (e.g. *rules of inference, linguistic symbols, coding notation*) in addition to alphabetical listings.

Treat numerals as if spelt out, with *1st Avenue* as if written *First*, and *10 Downing Street* as if *Ten*. However, the British Standard suggests that

numbers should precede the alphabetical sequence in numerical order
(the policy adopted in the telephone directory):

> 1st Cavalry
>
> 2/4 time
>
> 3i plc
>
> 42nd Street Nite Klub

16.3.4 **Names**

People bearing the same surname are conventionally listed with initials
preceding full names. Ignore numbers, rank, sanctity, material in parenthesis, and particles such as *de*, *of*, *the*, and *von*; a name with a title that
is otherwise identical with one without should follow it:

> Meynell, A.
>
> Meynell, Dr A.
>
> Meynell, Alice
>
> Meynell, F.
>
> Meynell, Sir F.
>
> Meynell, W.
>
> Meynell, W. G.

Personal names given only by surname in text require a fuller form in
the index, even if mentioned only in passing: *Shepard's illustrations* is
therefore expanded to the headword *Shepard, E. H.* Bare surnames should
be avoided wherever possible: particularly for specialist subjects an
author should anticipate inserting missing names in an index generated
by an indexer, or checking for accuracy those the indexer supplies.

Personal names given only by initials can be alphabetized by the *last*
letter, when it can be assumed that it is the surname; in such a case *W. H.*
goes under *H.*, not *W.* (This is the system used by Pollard's *Short-Title
Catalogue* and the BL catalogue, although not by the Bodleian Library.)
However, initials given not as a name but as a designation or arbitrary
collection of letters are alphabetized by the *first* letter: *ABC* goes under *A*,
not *C.* When it is difficult to discern what initials stand for, adopt a
single pattern for all similar initials within a list: in a book on cricket,
'MCC' might stand for Michael Colin Cowdrey or Marylebone Cricket
Club. Initials used as an ad hoc shorthand to avoid repetition in an
index—for example of the subject of a biography or collection of
letters—are alphabetized letter by letter.

Although alphabet takes precedence over rank, personal names in a
single numbered (usually chronological) sequence should be recorded
in that sequence in spite of any surnames or other additions. (*See also*
16.4.2.) Beware the omission of a number, especially of *I*; if others in the

sequence appear duly numbered, restore the number when listing. Hence Frederick Barbarossa becomes *Frederick I Barbarossa* and precedes Frederick II, and the Byzantine emperors John Tzimisces, John Comnenus, John Palaeologus, and John Cantacuzene are listed

> John I Tzimisces
>
> John II Comnenus
>
> John V Palaeologus
>
> John VI Cantacuzene

List names prefixed with *Mc*, *Mac*, or *M'* as if they were spelt *Mac*:

> McCullers
>
> MacFarlane
>
> M'Fingal
>
> McNamee

Where appropriate—especially for the period before *c.*1300—index people by their Christian or given names, with their titles, offices, etc. provided with suitable cross-references. (Some bodies, such as the Oxford Medieval Texts series editors, recommend that *son of* be preferred to *Fitz*, which should be used only where it forms a genuine surname, as in the case of Robert Fitz Ralph, bishop of Worcester 1191–3, who was son of William son of Ralph.) The following alphabetical listing illustrates several of these points:

> Henry
>
> Henry (of France), archbishop of Reims
>
> Henry, chaplain
>
> Henry I, count of Champagne
>
> Henry (the Lion), duke of Saxony
>
> Henry, earl of Warwick
>
> Henry II, emperor and king of Germany
>
> Henry IV, emperor and king of Germany
>
> Henry VI, emperor and king of Germany
>
> Henry I, king of England
>
> Henry II, king of England
>
> Henry, king of England, the young king
>
> Henry, scribe of Bury St Edmunds
>
> Henry, son of John
>
> Henry de Beaumont, bishop of Bayeux
>
> Henry of Blois, bishop of Winchester
>
> Henry Blund
>
> Henry of Essex
>
> Henry the Little
>
> Henry de Mowbray
>
> Henry Fitz Robert

List *St* as if it were spelt *Saint*, for both personal and place names. In alphabetical arrangement, saints considered in their own right as historical figures are indexed under their names, the abbreviation *St* being postponed: *Augustine, St, bishop of Hippo, Margaret, St, queen of Scotland, Rumwald, St, of Kings Sutton.*

When a place or a church is named after a saint, or the saint's name complete with prefix is used as a surname, alphabetize it under the word *Saint* as if spelt out, not under *St*. Thus for example *St Andrews, Fife, St Peter's, Rome,* and *St John, Olivier* are all treated as if they were written *Saint —*.

> Saint, J. B.
> St Andrews, Fife
> St Benet's Hall
> St James Infirmary
> St John-Smythe, Q.
> Saint-Julian
> St Just-in-Roseland

When the saint's name is in a foreign language, alphabetize its abbreviation under the full form in that language (for forms *see* **4.2.2**).

Alphabetize natural geographical features (mountains, lakes, seas, etc.) according to whether the descriptive component forms part of the name:

> Graian Alps
> Grampians, the
> Granby, Lake
> Granby River
> Grand Bérard, Mont
> Gran Canaria
> Grand, North Fork
> Grand, South Fork
> Grand Canyon
> Grand Rapids
> Grand Ruine, La
> Grand Teton

Always retain the component if it is part of the official name:

> Cape Canaveral
> Cape Cod
> Cape of Good Hope
> Cape Horn

Where confusion may result—in atlases, for example—cross-references or multiple entries are common.

16.3.5 **Subentries**

Arrangement of subentries should normally be alphabetical by key words, ignoring leading prepositions, conjunctions, and articles in alphabetical ordering. Ensure that subentries are worded so that they are unambiguous and 'read' from or to the headword in a consistent pattern. Arrange subentries beneath related or similar headwords in parallel. Cross-references given as subentries fall at the end of all other subentries:

> value:
> > -added 19, 22, 28
> > as amusement 21, 37, 73
> > of gossip xxxix, 70, 73, 75, 77
> > historical (relative) 73
> > magical 21, 37, 73
> > relative 212, 214–19
> > scales of 218
> > snobbery 73 n. 41, 75
> > versus worth 33, 97–8
> > *see also* fact as value-constituted; valuation

16.4 **Non-alphabetical order**

Some matter will call for ordering on some basis other than alphabetical, such as numerical, chronological, or hierarchical. Where this matter forms part only of an occasional group of subentries within an otherwise alphabetical index it may be ordered as necessary without comment; however, where a significant amount needs to be included in the form of headwords it should be placed in a separate index where similar elements can be found and compared easily. Never arrange entries or subentries themselves by order of page references, as this is of least help to the reader.

16.4.1 **Numerical**

An index of telephone numbers or US postal codes, for example, would be ordered in strict numerical hierarchy.

16.4.2 **Chronological**

Chronological ordering is useful in arranging entries or subentries, for example arranged according to the life and times of the subject in a biography rather than the order of reference in the work:

dynasties, early:

Legendary Period (prehistoric)   1–33, 66, 178

Xia (*c*.2100–1600 BC)   35–60, 120

Shang (*c*.1600–*c*.1027 BC)   61–84

Zhou (*c*.1027–256 BC)   12, 85–100, 178

Quin (221–207 BC)   109–135

Han (206 BC–AD 220)   132, 136–7, 141

Hart, Horace:

birth 188

apprenticeship 192, 195

in London 195–9

in Oxford 200, 201–60

retirement 261

illness and death 208, 277–9

16.4.3 **Hierarchical**

Subjects may be ordered according to some other recognized system of classification (e.g. *BA, MA, M.Phil., D.Phil.* or *duke, marquess, earl, viscount, baron*). Indexes of scriptural references are arranged in their traditional order rather than alphabetically, and species may be ordered according to their taxonomy.

16.4.4 **Index locorum**

Commentaries and some other works—such as those concerned with classical, biblical, or medieval subjects—may have an index locorum (index of passages cited) as one of the indexes. This is set out in columns, with passages cited on the left and followed by the page references, which may be arranged in one of three ways: (*a*) indented 1 em space (with or—especially in biblical citations—without a colon separating the entry from its page reference); (*b*) set in another column at least 1 em space apart from the longest passage; or (*c*) set full right in the column, again with a minimum of 1 em separating the elements:

(*a*)	(*b*)		(*c*)	
Homer	Homer		Homer	
Iliad	*Iliad*		*Iliad*	
1. 1–3: 14–56, 221–36, 329	1. 1–3	14–56, 221–36, 329	1. 1–3	14–56, 221–36, 329
1. 30: 8	1. 30	8	1. 30	8
1. 197: 40 n. 125	1. 197	40 n. 125	1. 197	40 n. 125
2. 11: 51, 140	2. 11	51, 140	2. 11	51, 140
2. 53–4: 41	2. 53–4	41	2. 53–4	41
. . .	. . .		. . .	

23. 175–6: 77	23. 175–6	77	23. 175–6	77
24. 720: 44	24. 720	44	24. 720	44
Odyssey	*Odyssey*		*Odyssey*	
1. 22–4: 140	1. 22–4	140	1. 22–4	140
1. 183: 12	1. 183	12	1. 183	12
3. 154: 79 n. 104	3. 154	79 n. 104	3. 154	79 n. 104

It is usually possible to accommodate at least two such columns within the measure of most works, and more columns in works with wider formats. Alternatively, it is possible where space is tight to run in the entries and page references to the margin width, with each locus in parentheses:

> HOMER, *Iliad* (1. 1–3) 14–56, 221–36, 329; (1. 30) 8; (1. 197) 40 n. 125
> (2. 11) 51, 140; (2. 53–4) 41

When two or more successive entries have the same starting point but different finishing points, they should be ordered in descending order of length:

> HOMER
> *Iliad*   1 [= the whole book]
>   1. 1–3   14–56, 221–36, 329
>   1. 1–2   472–9
>   1. 1   312–17

This is the principle of *digniora sint priora* 'let things worthier precede'.

Works including an index locorum may also have other types of indexes, which may be set along similar lines. These include an index rerum (subject index), index nominum (index of names), and index verborum (index of words). Normally the contexts in which they are found make the use of Latin terms appropriate, the plural of each beginning 'indices —'. The indexes are placed in that order, with the index locorum between the index rerum and the index nominum.

16.5 **Presentation of index copy**

Print all copy in a single column on A4 paper. It *must* be double spaced— for both entries and subentries—so as to leave plenty of room for editorial mark-up before setting. An index's intricate structure and un-intuitive content means that errors introduced during typesetting are comparatively easy to make and difficult to catch; consequently, an author who creates an index on a computer is encouraged to submit it electronically, to enable direct setting from the file.

16.5.1 **Style**

Begin each entry with a lower-case letter unless the word is capitalized in the text (other than at the start of a sentence). Check carefully hyphenation, italics, spelling, and punctuation for consistency with the text. Instructions for cross-referring (*see*, *see also*) should be printed out in italic, or underlined if copy is typed. However, 'see' and 'see also' commonly appear in roman when they are followed by italicized text:

> Picq, Charles Ardent du, see *Études sur le combat*
>
> Plutarch's *Lives*, see *Parallel Lives*; *see also* biographies; Dryden
>
> *Poema Morale*, see *Selections from Early Middle English*
>
> *Poetics, see* Aristotle

Usually there is an en space between the entry and the first page number; there is no need to put a comma between them, though formerly this style was commonplace (and remains for cross-references). If an entry ends with a numeral (*B-17*, *Channel 13*, *M25*, *Uranium 235*), place the numeral in parentheses, or add a colon between it and the page reference. Insert a space after *all* punctuation (particularly in names), except for those abbreviations printed close up in the text. Separate an entry followed by a cross-reference with a comma; separate more than one cross-reference with a semicolon. There is no punctuation at the end of entries apart from the colon used after a headword with no page numbers, where it is followed by a list of subentries:

> earnings, *see* wages
>
> earnings, *see* income; taxation; wages
>
> earnings:
>> income 12, 14–22, 45
>>
>> taxation 9, 11, 44–9
>>
>> wages 12–21, 48–50

16.5.2 **Number references**

In references to pagination and dates, use the least number of figures consistent with clarity (*see* **7.1.4**; **7.10.1**); so *30-1*, *42-3*; but *10-11* or *116-18*, not *10-1* or *116-8*; *1789-1810* or *1999-2001*, not *1789-810* or *1999-001*.

Be as specific as possible in your references. For this reason, do not use section or clause numbers instead of page numbers unless they are frequent and the entire index is to be organized that way. (More than one section or clause on each page will provide references that are even more specific than page references.) Avoid using *f.* and *ff.*; give instead the first and last pages of the material: *123-5*, for example, denotes one continuous discussion spanning three pages, whereas *123, 124, 125* denotes three separate short references. Avoid *passim* ('throughout') unless there are a large number of general references to a person or topic in one section of a book. Avoid indexing a whole chapter; where this is impossible, cite the page extent, not *Ch. 11*.

Except where each page has a great deal of text, it is normally unnecessary to indicate when an entry is mentioned more than once on a page. It can, however, be useful in a large-format or densely spaced work; this is done either by adding the Latin terms *bis* ('two times'), *ter* ('three times'), *quater* ('four times'), *quinquies* ('five times'), etc. after the page number, or (rarely) by a superscript number: '90 *bis*', '90^2'.

An index to a large-format or densely spaced work—especially in two or more columns—may benefit from page references followed by lowercase italic or small-capital letters indicating relative placement on the page, such as '412*a*' for the top of the first column on page 412 and '412*d*' for the bottom of the second column. This convention is found most often in encyclopedias and other reference works, and requires an explanation at the start of the index.

Give references to foot- and endnotes in the form '*word* 90 n. 17' for one note and '*word* 90 nn. 17, 19' for two or more; each has a full point and a normal space of the line after the abbreviation. There is no need to give the note number where there is only one note on the page cited; in such instances it is OUP style to insert a thin space between page number and 'n.' to improve the clarity of the reference: '*word* 90 n.' (A thin space also separates the page reference and the abbreviation where 'f.' and 'ff.' are unavoidable.)

To provide the most effective help to the reader, a general index serving more than one volume must include the volume number as part of each page reference, regardless of whether the volumes are paginated in a single sequence or begin anew with each volume. Volume numbers may be styled in roman numerals, often in small capitals, separated by a full point: '*word* III. 90'. Indexes to a group of periodicals may have both the series and volume number as part of the page reference.

It is usual to mark figures denoting references to illustrations in italic or boldface, or with some typographic symbol (e.g. an asterisk or dagger), and provide a key at the start of the index in the form *Italic/bold numbers denote reference to illustrations*. Some authors use a similar treatment to flag passages that are particularly significant or include definitions; again, explain this practice at the start of the index.

16.6 **Setting**

The first or only index in a work typically begins on a new recto, though subsequent indexes can begin on a new page. Index matter is set in small type, one or two sizes down from text size, usually set left-hand justified (ragged right) in two or more columns, with a minimum 1 fixed em space between each column. Turn-lines are set 2 ems from the left-hand margin. Subentries are indented by 1 em, or run on after a semicolon; sub-subentries are always run on.

A variable line of white space between alphabetical sections is normally sufficient; there is no need to print each letter at the beginning of its alphabetical section. Typically, the running heads are *Index* on both recto and verso, though two or more indexes can be differentiated according to their title, such as *General Index, Index Locorum, Index of First Lines*.

16.6.1 **Layout**

The samples below show the two basic styles of typographic design for indexes, the subentries being either *set-out* (*indented*) or *run-on* (*run-in*). The set-out style uses a new (indented) line for each subentry; it is therefore clearer than the run-on style, though it takes up more room. In it, avoid further subdivision of subentries if possible, as this can result in complicated and space-wasting structures. In the run-on style, subentries do as the name suggests: they run on and are separated from the main entry—and each other—by a semicolon. They are indented appropriately to distinguish them from the heading. Take particular care that the arrangement is logical and consistent, since the style's density makes it more difficult to read.

Set-out

iconoclasm 111, 297, 430, 437
  of Modern Movement in
  architecture 329, 362

idylls 115, 152–4, 160, 163

imitation 183, 186, 200
  as allusion 179
  architectural 343
  of Latin poetry 350
  in rhetoric 287, 288, 290
    theatrical 245 n., 247, 251
    and Virgil 112, 167 n., 192

  see also irony; satire

imperialism, *see* conquest

Indo-European 370

Run-on

iconoclasm 111, 297, 430, 437; of
  Modern Movement in architecture
  329, 362

idylls 115, 152–4, 160, 163

imitation 183, 186, 200; as allusion
  179; architectural 343; of Latin
  poetry 350; in rhetoric 287, 288,
  290; theatrical 245 n., 247, 251;
  and Virgil 112, 167 n., 192; *see also*
  irony; satire

imperialism, *see* conquest

Indo-European 370

Which style a publisher chooses depends on the length and number of subentries in the final index copy, and the conventions of related works. If you feel that one or the other style is particularly suitable for your index, tell your editor. Regardless, index copy must be submitted for setting with all entries and subentries in the set-out form for mark-up: it is easier for the typesetter to run these on afterwards, if necessary, than it is to set out an index from copy that was presented run-on.

Turn-lines (where text runs to more than one line of typescript) should be indented consistently throughout, in what is called the *flush-and-hang* style in the USA; in a set-out format that indentation should be deeper than all the subentry indents. The beginning of each subentry must be easily identifiable on the left.

To save space, sub-subentries—where unavoidable—are generally run-on even in otherwise set-out indexes. However, they can most effectively be bypassed by denesting the subentry into a separate main entry of its own, cross-referring to it as necessary. For example, in the following

> experience:
>> ideal, as disjunctive totality of elements 168
>> immediate 6, 39–40, 47–51, 70, 165–6, 172, 181–92
>>> beatification of 28
>>> as indivisibly one with finite centres 44
>>> non-conceptual structure of 82, 182
>>> as unintelligible 191
>> visual 83, 184; *see also* felt contents

the subentry of 'immediate experience' under 'experience' can be changed to a cross-reference 'immediate, *see* immediate experience', leading to a headword entry with subentries of its own. Where sub-subentries cannot be avoided, they may be run together with the rest of the subentries' page references, either following on or interspersed within parentheses:

> immediate 6, 39–40, 47–51, 70, 165–6, 172, 181–92; beatification of 28; as indivisibly one with finite centres 44; non-conceptual structure of 82, 182; as unintelligible 191
>
> immediate 6, (beatification of) 28, 39–40, (as indivisibly one with finite centres) 44, 47–51, 70, (non-conceptual structure of) 82, 182, 165–6, 172, 181–92, (as unintelligible) 191

16.6.2 **Continuation**

When an entry breaks across a page—most especially from the bottom of a recto to the top of a verso—the heading or subheading is repeated and a continuation note added during typesetting:

experience (*cont.*)

visual 83, 184; *see also* felt contents

16.7 **Schedules**

Authors should try to send in their completed index when they return their proofs to the publisher; if a word processor has been used, authors who submit a disk must remember to label it with their name and computer format details. Be sure to include with the index copy a note of any special systems of organization, alphabetical order, etc. that have been adopted.

The methodical compilation of an index demands a level of scrutiny that often yields errors—usually of consistency—in the proofs. While the nature of the error and the timetable and budget of the work will help determine whether and which corrections can be made, it is vital to avoid any changes to pagination that would throw out the index's references.

If completion of the index copy is likely to delay the return of the proofs, please warn your editor: it may be better to send the proofs back in advance of the index, so that correction of the text can proceed in the interim.

Publishers have different procedures for dealing with index proofs: while authors may not need to see a typeset proof of an index they have produced themselves and submitted on disk, most are given an opportunity to vet an index produced by an indexer.

PART II
The Oxford Dictionary for Writers and Editors

Contents

*Ταράσσει τοὺς ἀνθρώπους οὐ τὰ πράγματα, ἀλλὰ τὰ
περὶ τῶν πραγμάτων δόγματα.*

Epictetus, *Manual*

('Not things, but opinions about things, trouble folk.')

How to use this dictionary

Arrangement of the text and cross-references

1. ARRANGEMENT. Entries are ordered alphabetically, letter by letter.

2. CROSS-REFERENCES. Cross-references are set in normal boldface type **thus.** Semicolons are always used to separate references, so as to distinguish those with internal commas. So the cross reference

    See also **Mac-, Mc-, Mᶜ**

    refers to only one entry, and the cross-references

    See also **Smith; Smythe**

    are to two entries. In addition to these cross-references, the direction 'cf.' (meaning 'compare') may be used in text to cite another entry or entries.

    cf. **assurance; assure; ensure**

    cf. **de La; du; van, van den, van der**

Conventions used in the text

1. BOLD. Boldface type is used for headwords, cross-references, and for all approved forms and spellings; a rejected form or spelling is printed in light face except when it stands as a headword cross-referring to the preferred form. Italic boldface is used for words to be printed in italics.

2. SOLIDUS. A solidus (/) is used to mark the end of that part of the headword to which boldface elements introduced with a dash (*see* **3**) or a hyphen (*see* **4**) later in the same entry should be attached. Thus the entry

    collegi*/*um ... pl. *-a*

    shows that the plural form should be *collegia*, and the inflections given as

    gallop/ ... **-ed, -er, -ing**

    are to be understood as *galloped*, *galloper*, and *galloping*. Only boldface elements follow this rule; note for example in the entry

    metal/, **-led, -ling, -lize** ... *not* -ise

    that **-led, -ling,** and **-lize** join the headword, forming *metalled*, *metalling*, and *metallize*, but the rejected termination -*ise* is independently given.

3. DASH. An em-rule dash is used to stand for the repetition of a single headword already given, and the solidus again marks the end of a common element. Thus in the entry

    paddle/ **boat, — steamer, — wheel** (two words)

    the three combinations are *paddle boat*, *paddle steamer*, and *paddle wheel*.

In the entry

> **Einstein,/ Albert** (1879-1955) German phys-
> icist, naturalized US citizen 1940; — **Alfred**
> (1880–1952) German musicologist, natural-
> ized US citizen 1945

the names are *Albert Einstein* and *Alfred Einstein.*

Use of more than one dash indicates the repetition of a corresponding number of words.

4. HYPHEN. In headwords the hyphen serves two purposes: to indicate that a compound is normally hyphenated whenever used, and to introduce a further second element to form a compound with a first element marked off earlier in the entry by means of a solidus. In the second case the intended form of that compound will be clear from scrutiny of the first compound given, and by recourse to the comment given in parentheses at the end of the sequence, e.g. '(hyphen)', '(hyphens)', '(one word)'. The entry

> **bird/cage, -seed** (one word)

therefore indicates that *birdcage* and *birdseed* are both to be written as one word, and the entry

> **multi/-role, -stage, -storey, -user** (hyphens,
> one word in US)

indicates that *multi-role*, *multi-stage*, *multi-storey*, and *multi-user* are all to be written with hyphens in British English (but as one word in US English—*see* 8).

5. PARENTHESES. These are used to supply information directly after the headword, portraying the discipline, context, or language the headword may be found in, or describing some special aspect of its spelling, formation, or use. Where a foreign word is not assimilated into the English language, its gender and case are given, as required. This information has been dispensed with as irrelevant where a foreign word has been assimilated into English and is no longer given in italic, unless the original and assimilated forms differ:

> **gateau/** cake, pl. **-s**; (Fr. m.) *gâteau/*, pl. *-x*

In addition to their normal function, parentheses are used to formulate a concise definition that will serve two or more parts of speech, the part in parentheses being included or omitted as appropriate. Thus the definition

> **oxytone** (Gr. gram.) (a word) with an acute
> accent on the last syllable

covers both the noun ('a word with an acute accent on the last syllable') and the adjective ('with an acute accent in the last syllable'). Similarly, the definition

> **Cherokee** (of or relating to) (a member of) a
> Native American tribe, or the language of this
> people

encompasses the adjectival and noun forms, as well as the singular and collective forms, of the headword.

6. FULL POINT. The full point or period is used in the normal way to mark an abbreviated form, where appropriate, or the end of a sentence. Entries are normally not in complete sentences, and do not end in full

points: this enables the user to determine at a glance whether an abbreviation that occurs as the last word in an entry—as is frequently the case—ends in a full point:

cosine (math., no hyphen) abbr. **cos**

cosmogony, cosmography abbr. **cosmog.**

7. RESTRICTED USAGES. If the use of a word is restricted in any way, such as limited to a specific geographical area (e.g. Austral., Can., NZ), register (e.g. colloq., derog., sl.), or field of activity (e.g. gram., her., math.), this is indicated by any of various labels set within parentheses (*see* the List of abbreviations, p. xi). These refer only to the definition immediately following, so that in

FA (statistics) factor analysis, (Fr.) Fédération
Aéronautique, Fine Art, Football Association

the label '(statistics)' refers only to factor analysis, and '(Fr.)' refers only to Fédération Aéronautique, not to Fine Art or Football Association.

8. BRITISH AND US ENGLISH VARIANTS. 'US' indicates that the use is found chiefly in US English (though often including e.g. Canadian, Australian, and New Zealand English) but not in British English except as a conscious Americanism. Other geographical designations restrict uses to the areas named.

whole note (US) = **semibreve**

Where an exact British equivalent exists this is set (following an equals sign) in boldface whether it forms a headword or not; where no exact British equivalent exists, a short definition follows instead:

muffin/ a light flat round spongy cake, eaten
toasted and buttered; (US) a round cake made
from batter or dough; a British — = US
English — (savoury), a US — = British **American** — (sweet)

Where the word and meaning are the same, but the spelling or treatment differs, this is indicated parenthetically:

color *use* **colour** (except in US)

colourant *not* color- (US)

empanel/ enrol, *not* im-; **-led, -ling** (one l in US)

tender-hearted/, **-ness** (hyphen, one word in
US)

9. DATES. All dates given in the dictionary are AD unless otherwise specified.

List of abbreviations

Abbreviations used regularly are listed below; others are given in the text itself. Abbreviations of subjects (anthropology, botany, etc.) are also valid for their corresponding adjectival forms (anthropological, botanical, etc.).

abbr.	abbreviation	dép.	*département*
adj.	adjective	derog.	derogatory
adv.	adverb	Du.	Dutch
Afr.	Africa(n)	dyn.	dynamics
Afrik.	Afrikaans	eccl.	ecclesiastical
alt.	alternative	econ.	economics
Amer.	American	elec.	electrical
anat.	anatomy	Eng.	English
anthrop.	anthropology	esp.	especially
Apocr.	Apocrypha	Est.	Estonian
apos.	apostrophe	f.	feminine
approx.	approximately	fig.	figurative(ly)
Arab.	Arabic	Fin.	Finnish
arch.	archaic	Fl.	Flemish
archaeol.	archaeology	*fl.*	*floruit* (flourished)
archit.	architecture	Fr.	French
astr.	astronomy	Gael.	Gaelic
attrib.	attributive	gen.	general
Austral.	Australian	geog.	geography
AV	Authorized Version	geol.	geology
b.	born	geom.	geometry
bibliog.	bibliography	Ger.	German
bind.	binding	Gr.	Greek; Greater
biol.	biology	gram.	grammar
bot.	botany	Heb.	Hebrew
Brazil.	Brazilian	her.	heraldry
Brit.	British	Hind.	Hindi
c.	century	hist.	historical
c.	*circa*	hort.	horticulture
Can.	Canadian	Hung.	Hungarian
cap.	capital	Icel.	Icelandic
cc.	centuries	Ind.	India(n)
Cent.	Central	indep.	independent
cf.	compare	intr.	intransitive
chem.	chemistry	Ir.	Irish
Chin.	China, Chinese	It.	Italian
Co.	County	ital.	italic
colloq.	colloquial	Jap.	Japan(ese)
comput.	computing	joc.	jocular
contr.	contraction	Lat.	Latin
cook.	cookery	lit.	literally; literary
d.	died	m.	masculine
Dan.	Danish	math.	mathematics

ME	Middle English	Port.	Portuguese
mech.	mechanics	prep.	preposition
med.	medicine	print.	printing
meteor.	meteorology	pron.	pronounced
mil.	military	propr.	proprietary
mod.	modern	pseud.	pseudonym
MS	manuscript	psychol.	psychology
mus.	music	pt.	point
myth.	mythology	q.v.	*quod vide* (which see)
n.	neuter	RC	Roman Catholic
naut.	nautical	relig.	religion
NEB	New English Bible	rep.	republic
NODE	*New Oxford Dictionary*	rhet.	rhetoric
	of English	Rom.	Roman
Norw.	Norwegian	rom.	roman
NT	New Testament	Russ.	Russian
NZ	New Zealand	Sc.	Scottish
obs.	obsolete	sci.	science, scientific
OE	Old English	SI	Système International
OED	*Oxford English Dictionary*		d'Unités
off.	official	sing.	singular
offens.	offensive	Skt.	Sanskrit
opp.	opposite, opposed	sl.	slang
orig.	original(ly)	Sp.	Spanish
ornith.	ornithology	spec.	specifically
OT	Old Testament	Swed.	Swedish
Pak.	Pakistan	theat.	theatre
parl.	parliamentary	theol.	theology
part.	participle	tr.	transitive
Pers.	Persian	trad.	traditional(ly)
philol.	philology	trans.	translated
philos.	philosophy	TS	typescript
photog.	photography	Turk.	Turkish
phys.	physics, physical	typ.	typography
physiol.	physiology	US	United States (style)
pl.	plural	var.	variant
poet.	poetical	Vulg.	Vulgate
Pol.	Polish	zool.	zoology

Note on trade marks and proprietary status

This guide includes some words that have, or are asserted to have, proprietary status as trade marks or otherwise. Their inclusion does not imply that they have acquired for legal purposes a non-proprietary or general significance, nor any other judgement concerning their legal status. In cases where some evidence exists that a word has proprietary status this is indicated by the word 'propr.', but no such judgement concerning the legal status of such words is made or implied thereby.

A Advanced (level examination), ampere, *avancer* (on timepiece regulator); the first in a series

₳ austral (currency of Argentina)

A. Academician, Academy, Acting (rank), alto, amateur, answer, artillery, Associate

a are (unit of area), atto-, year (no point)

a. accepted (Fr. *accepté*, Ger. *acceptiert*) (on bills of exchange), acre, active (in grammar), adjective, anna, area, arrive, (Lat.) *ante* (before)

Ä, ä in German, Swedish, etc. should *not* be replaced by *Ae, ae* (except in some proper names), or *A, a,* or *Æ, æ*. Only the first of two vowels takes the umlaut, as *äu*

Å angstrom

Å, å the 'Swedish *a*', used in Danish, Norwegian, and Swedish

@ at, the 'commercial *a*' used in calculating from prices; used in the domain name in email addresses

A0 ('A nought' or 'A zero') a paper size; *see* **DIN**

A1 first class (originally of ships)

AA Advertising Association, Alcoholics Anonymous, anti-aircraft, Architectural Association, Associate in Arts, Automobile Association; a film-censorship classification

AAA (US) Agricultural Adjustment Acts *or* Administration; Amateur Athletic Association, American Automobile Association

AAC *anno ante Christum* (in the year before Christ) (small caps.)

Aachen Germany; cf. **Aix-la-Chapelle**

AAF (US) Army Air Force; Auxiliary Air Force (till 1957)

AAG Assistant Adjutant General

AAIA Associate of the Association of International Accountants

Aalborg Denmark, in Dan. **Ålborg**

Aalto, (Hugo) Alvar (Henrik) (1896–1976). Finnish architect and designer

A. & M. agricultural and mechanical; (Hymns) Ancient and Modern

A. & N. Army and Navy (Stores, Club)

A. & R. artists and recording, artists and repertoire *or* repertory

a. a. O. (Ger.) *am angeführten Orte* (at the place quoted) (spaces in Ger.)

AAR against all risks (insurance)

aard/vark, -wolf different animals (one word)

Aarhus Denmark

AAS *Academiae Americanae Socius* (Fellow of the American Academy of Arts and Sciences), *Acta Apostolicae Sedis* (Acts of the Apostolic See), Agnostics' Adoption Society

A'asia Australasia

aasvogel a vulture

AAU (US) Amateur Athletic Union

AB able-bodied (seaman), Alberta, *Artium Baccalaureus* (US Bachelor of Arts), a blood type

ab (Lat.) from

ABA Amateur Boxing Association, American Bankers' Association, American Bar Association, Antiquarian Booksellers' Association, Association of British Archaeologists

aba a sleeveless outer garment worn by Arabs; *not* abaya, abba

ABAA Associate of British Association of Accountants and Auditors

abac/us a counting frame, (archit.) a plate at the top of a column; pl. **-uses**

Abaddon hell or the Devil; *see also* **Apollyon**

Abailard, Peter *see* **Abelard, Peter**

abalone a shellfish

à bas (Fr.) down with

abattoir a slaughterhouse (not ital.)

Abb. (Ger.) *Abbildung*

abb. abbess, abbey, abbot

Abbasid (of) a member of a dynasty of Baghdad caliphs ruling 750–1258, *not* Abassid

abbé (Fr. m.) an ecclesiastical title (not ital.)

Abbevillian (of) the culture of the earliest palaeolithic period in Europe

Abbildung/ (Ger. typ. f.) an illustration (cap.), pl. **-en**; abbr. **Abb.**

Abbotsinch Airport Glasgow

abbr. abbreviat/ed, -ion

abbreviat/e, -or *not* -er

abbreviation in general do not use points in abbreviations with several full or small caps.: BBC, MA, QC; with numbers: 1st, 4to; of units of measurement: lb, yd (*but* in.), cc, mm, °C, °F. Use full points with initials of personal names (H. G. Wells) and in abbrs. with mixed upper- and lower-case letters: Sun., Jan.; and with lower-case initials: l. 5, p. 7 (*but* p for pence); abbr. **abbr.**; *see also* individual entries; **acronym**; **contraction**

ABC the alphabet; Argentina, Brazil, and Chile; Associated British Cinemas, Audit Bureau of Circulations, Australian Broadcasting Corporation (*formerly* Commission)

ABCA Army Bureau of Current Affairs, *now* **BCA**

ABC Guide (no points)

abdicat/e, -ion, -or

abecedarian (adj.) arranged alphabetically, (noun) a person learning the alphabet

à Becket, Thomas *use* **Thomas Becket**

Abelard, Peter (1079–1142) French dialectician and theologian, in Fr. **Pierre Abé-**

lard; learned spellings include **Abailard** and **Abaelard** (more authentically **Abaëlard**); editors may accept this spelling but should not impose it

Abendlied (Ger.) an evening song (cap., ital.)

Aberdeen/ Angus (two caps.), — **terrier** (one cap.)

Aberdonian (adj. and noun) (a native or citizen) of Aberdeen

Abergavenny Gwent

Abernethy biscuit (one cap.)

Aberystwyth Dyfed, *not* -ith

abest (Lat.) he, she, *or* it, is absent; pl. *absunt*

abett/er, in law **-or**

ab extra (Lat.) from outside

abgekürzt (Ger.) abbreviated; abbr. **abgk.**, **abk.**

Abhandlungen (Ger. f. pl.) Transactions (of a society), abbr. **Abh.**

abide past tense **abided** *not* abode (except in arch. usage)

Abidjan Ivory Coast

abigail a lady's maid

Abilene Kans., Tex.

abîme (Fr. m.) abyss, in literary or heraldic sense *use* **abyme**; *see also* *mise en abyme*

ab incunabulis (Lat.) from the cradle

Abingdon Oxon. and Va.

Abington Cambs., Northants., Strathclyde, Co. Limerick; Mass.

ab/ initio (Lat.) from the beginning, abbr. *ab init.*; — *intra* from within

abjure renounce on oath; cf. **adjure**

Abl. (Sp.) *abril* (April)

abl. ablative

ablaut variation in the root vowel of a word (e.g. *sing, sang, sung*)

able-bodied (hyphen)

ABM anti-ballistic missile

ABMM anti-ballistic-missile missile

Åbo Swed. for **Turku**

A-bomb atomic bomb (hyphen, no point)

aboriginal (adj.) indigenous (with initial cap., in technical sense in Australia); **aborigin/es** (pl. noun, for sing. *use* **-al**) also with initial cap. in Australia

ab origine (Lat.) from the beginning

ABO Area Beat Officer, — **system** a system of four types (A, AB, B, and O) used to classify human blood

aboul/ia loss of will power, *not* abulia; **-ic**

about-face noun and verb (hyphen)

above/-board, -mentioned, -named (hyphens)

ab ovo/ (Lat., from the egg) from the beginning, — — *usque ad mala* (Lat., from egg to apples) from (the) beginning to (the) end

Abp. Archbishop

abr. abridged, abridgement

abracadabra a supposedly magic word, a spell or charm

abrégé (Fr. m.) abridgement

abréviation (Fr. f.) abbreviation

abridgement abbr. **abr.**

ABS *Antiblockier-System* (Ger. n.), an antilocking brake system

abs. absolute(ly), abstract

abscess a swollen area accumulating pus within body tissue

Abschnitt/ (Ger. typ. m.) section, part, chapter, or division (cap.); pl. **-e**

absciss/a (math.) pl. **-ae**

abseil (noun and verb) (US) = **rappel**

absenter *not* -or

absente reo (Lat.) the defendant being absent, abbr. *abs. re.*

absent-minded/ (hyphen); **-ly, -ness**

absinth/ the plant, **-e** the liqueur

absit/ (Lat.) let him, her, *or* it, be absent; — *omen* (Lat.) let there be no (ill) omen, may what is threatened not become fact

absolute(ly) abbr. **abs.**

absorb/ soak up, incorporate, consume; **-able, -ability, -ent** *but* **absorption, absorptive** (*not* -btion, -btive); cf. **adsorb**

abs. re. *absente reo*

abstract abbr. **abs.**

absunt see abest

abt. about

ABTA Association of British Travel Agents

Abteilung (Ger. f.) division, abbr. **Abt.**

Abu Dhabi United Arab Emirates

abulia *use* **abou-**

ab/ uno disce omnes (Lat.) from one (sample) judge the rest; — *urbe condita*, abbr. **AUC** (but **A.V.C.** in printing classical Latin texts), from the foundation of the city (Rome), 753 BC (small caps.)

Abu Simbel the site of Egyptian rock temples built by Rameses II

abusus non tollit usum (Lat.) abuse does not take away use, i.e. is no argument against proper use

abut/, -ment, -ted, -ter (law), **-ting**

ABV alcohol by volume

abyme (Fr. m., lit., her.) *not* abîme; *see also* *mise en abyme*

abys/s a deep cavity, **-mal**

abyssal at or of the ocean depths or floor, (geol.) plutonic; cf. **abysmal**

Abyssinia *now* **Ethiopia**

AC (hist.) Aircraftman, Alpine Club, Assistant Commissioner, Athletic Club, Companion of the Order of Australia

A/C account current, in printing *use* **acct.**; air conditioning (also **a/c**)

AC *anno Christi*, in the year of Christ, occasionally useful to distinguish chronologies based on non-standard Nativity dates from normal AD reckoning, but otherwise inadvisable because also used in the past for *ante Christum* (before Christ) (small caps.)

Ac actinium (no point)

a.c. (elec.) alternating current, author's correction

ACA Associate of the Institute of Chartered Accountants in England and Wales (*or* Ireland)

Academe originally a garden near Athens sacred to the hero Academus (*or* Hecademus), the site of Plato's Academy; now refers to the academic community, world of university scholarship (cap.)

Academician abbr. **A.**

Académie française (one cap.)

Academy a learned body, abbr. **A.**, **Acad.** (cap.)

Academy, the the Platonic school of philosophy; *see also* **Academe**

Acadian of Nova Scotia (Fr. **Acadie**), *not* Ar-

a capite ad calcem (Lat.) completely

a cappella (It.) (mus.) unaccompanied, *not* alla cappella

Acapulco/ Mexico, *in full* **— de Juárez**

ACAS Advisory, Conciliation, and Arbitration Service

ACC Army Catering Corps

acc. acceptance (bill), according (to), accusative

Acca Israel, *use* **Acre**

Accademia (It.) Academy

Accademia della Crusca an Italian literary academy

Accadian *use* **Akk-**

acced/e, -er *not* -or

accedence a giving consent

accelerando/ (mus.) accelerating; as noun, pl. **-s**; abbr. **accel.**

accelerat/e, -or *not* -er

accepᵒⁿ acceptance (bill)

acceptance abbr. **acc.**

accept/er in law and science **-or**

accessible *not* **-able**

access/it (Lat.) he, she, *or* it, came near; pl. **-erunt**

accessory (noun and adj.) *not* -ary

access time (comput.)

acciaccatura (mus.) a grace note

accidence inflections of words

accidental (mus.)

accidentally *not* -tly

accidie listlessness

acclimat/e, -ize *not* -ise

ACCM Advisory Council for the Church's Ministry (*formerly* **CACTM**)

Acco Israel, *use* **Acre**

accommodat/e, -ion (two *c*s, two *m*s)

accompanist *not* -yist

accouche/ment, -ur, -use (ital.)

account abbr. **A/C**, in printing *use* **acct.**

Accountant-General abbr. **A.-G.**

accoutre/, -ment; *not* accouter (US)

Accra Ghana, *not* Akk-

acct. account, *or* account current

accumulat/e, -or (two *c*s)

accusative abbr. **acc.**, **accus.**

ACE after Common Era (in place of AD) (small caps.); *see also* **BCE**; **CE**

acedia *use* **accidie**

ACF Army Cadet Force

ACGB Arts Council of Great Britain

ACGBI Automobile Club of Great Britain and Ireland

ACGI Associate of the City and Guilds of London Institute

Achaean of or relating to Achaea in ancient Greece, (lit., esp. in Homeric contexts) Greek

Achaemenid (*also* **Achaemenian**) of or relating to the dynasty ruling in Persia from Cyrus I to Darius III (553–330 BC); a member of this dynasty; *not* Achai-

acharnement (Fr. m.) bloodthirsty fury, ferocity; gusto

Acheson, Dean (**Gooderham**) (1893–1971) US diplomat

Acheulian (of or concerning) the culture of the palaeolithic period following the Abbevillian and preceding the Mousterian; *not* -ean

à cheval (Fr.) on horseback

Achilles/ heel, — tendon (no apos.)

Achin Sumatra, Indonesia; *not* Atch-

Achnashellach Highland, *not* **Auch-**

achy *not* -ey

ACI Army Council Instruction

ACIA Associate of the Corporation of Insurance Agents

ACIB Associate of the Corporation of Insurance Brokers

acid rain (two words)

ACII Associate of the Chartered Insurance Institute

ACIS Associate of the Institute of Chartered Secretaries and Administrators

ack-ack anti-aircraft gun, fire, etc. (hyphen)

ackee a tropical tree, fruit, *not* ak-

acknowledgement *not* -ledgment (US)

Acland, Sir Antony Arthur (b. 1930) British diplomat

ACLU American Civil Liberties Union

ACMA Associate of the Institute of Cost and Management Accountants

acolyte *not* -ite

Açores (Port.) **Azores**

acoustics (noun sing.) the science of sound, (noun pl.) acoustic properties

ACP Associate of the College of Preceptors; Association of Clinical Pathologists; Association of Correctors of the Press, part of **NGA**

acquit/, -tal (verdict), **-tance** (settlement of debt)

Acre Israel; *not* Acca, Acco

acre abbr. **a.**

acriflavine an antiseptic, *not* -vin

Acrilan (propr.)

acronym a word formed from initials, as *Anzac, laser, scuba,* pron. as words; *see also* **abbreviation; contraction**

acrylic (chem.)

ACS American Chemical Society, Association of Commonwealth Students

ACSA Associate of the Institute of Chartered Secretaries and Administrators

ACT Australian Capital Territory

act. active

Actaeon (Gr. myth.) a hunter

ACTH adrenocorticotrophic hormone

actini/a (zool.) pl. **-ae**

actinium symbol **Ac**

actinomy/ces (bot.) pl. **-cetes**

actionnaire (Fr. m.) shareholder

active abbr. **a., act.**

actor (person) *but* **one-acter** (play)

acts of a play titles, when cited, to be in italic; in text use cap. *A* for Act only when a number follows: *Hamlet,* Act I, Scene ii, *but* 'in the second act'

Acts of Parliament (two caps.)

Acts of Sederunt (Sc. law)

Acts of the Apostles (NT) abbr. **Acts**

ACTT Association of Cinematograph, Television and Allied Technicians

actualité (Fr. f.) present state

actuel/ (Fr.) f. ***-le*** present

acushla (Ir.) darling

ACW (hist.) Aircraftwoman

AD (*anno Domini*) precedes numerals, *but* follows numbers written as words: 'AD 250', '16 July AD 622', 'the first century AD'; use only when using BC dates as well, or where there is some other reason to fear misunderstanding (small caps.); *see also* **BC, CE**

ad advertisement (no point)

ad. adapted, adapter (point)

a.d. after date

a.d. *ante diem* (before the day)

Ada (propr. comput.) a real-time programming language

adagio/ (mus.) slow; as noun, pl. **-s**

Adams,/ Ansel (Easton) (1902–84) US photographer; — **John** (1735–1826) US statesman, President 1797–1801; — **John Quincy** (1767–1848) his son, President 1825–9

Adam's Peak Sri Lanka

adapt/able, -er (person), **-or** (device)

adaptation *not* adaption (US)

a dato (Lat.) from date

ADC aide-de-camp, analogue–digital converter

ad captandum vulgus (Lat., to catch the rabble) claptrap, applied to unsound arguments

ADD *American Dialect Dictionary*

Addams,/ Charles (Samuel) (1912–88) US cartoonist; — **Jane** (1860–1935) US social worker and writer, Nobel Peace Prize 1931

Addenbrooke's Hospital Cambridge

addend/um something to be added, pl. **-a** (not ital.)

addio (It.) goodbye

Addis Ababa Ethiopia

additive (something) in the nature of an addition

addorsed (her.) *not* ador-, -ossed

adducible *not* -eable

Adélie/ Land Antarctica (two caps.), — **penguin** (one cap.)

Adenauer, Konrad (1876–1967) German statesman, Chancellor of W. Germany 1949–63

ad eundem (gradum) (Lat.) to the same degree at another university

à deux/ (Fr.) of (or between) two, — ***temps*** *see* **valse**

ad/ extra (Lat.) in an outward direction; — ***extremum*** to the last; — ***finem*** near the end, abbr. ***ad fin.***; — ***hanc vocem*** at this word

ad hoc for this (purpose) (roman)

ad/ hominem to the (interests of the) person, personal; — ***hunc locum*** on this passage, abbr. ***a.h.l.***; — ***idem*** to the same (point)

adieu/ pl. **-s** (not ital.); in Fr. ***adieu***, pl. ***adieux***

ad infinitum (Lat.) to infinity (not ital.)

ad interim (Lat.) meanwhile, abbr. ***ad int.***

adios (Sp.) goodbye (not ital., no accent)

Adirondack Mountains a mountain range in New York State, part of the Appalachians, *not* -dac

Adj. Adjutant

Adj. Gen. Adjutant General

adjectiv/e abbr. **a., adj.**; **-al, -ally**

adjudicator *not* -er

adjure charge or request (a person) solemnly or earnestly; cf. **abjure**

adjutage a nozzle, *not* aj-

Adjutant/ abbr. **Adj.** (cap. as rank); — **General** (two words) abbr. **AG, Adj. Gen.**

adjuvant (adj.) helpful, auxiliary; (noun) an adjuvant person or thing

Adler, Alfred (1870–1937) Austrian psychologist

ad lib (adv., noun, and verb)

ad/ libitum (Lat.) at pleasure, — **litem** appointed for a lawsuit

ad locum (Lat.) to or at the place, abbr. **ad loc.**, pl. **ad locos**, abbr. **ad locc.** (abbr. not ital.)

Adm. Admiral, Admiralty

admin short for administration (no point)

adminicle a thing that helps, (Sc. law) collateral evidence of the contents of a missing document

administrable *not* -atable

administrat/or abbr. **admor.**, **-rix** abbr. **admix.**

Admiral abbr. **Adm.**, in Fr. **amir/al** pl. **-aux**

Admiralty, the abbr. **Adm.**; *see* **MOD**

ad misericordiam (Lat.) appealing to pity

admissible *not* -able, *but* **admittable**

admix. administratrix

ad modum (Lat.) after the manner of

admonitor/ *not* -er, **-y**

admor. administrator

ad nauseam (Lat.) to a sickening degree (not ital.), *not* -um

ado work, trouble (one word)

adobe a form of sun-dried brick (not ital.)

Adonai (Heb.) the Lord; *see also* **Yahweh**

Adonais Keats, in P. B. Shelley's elegy, 1821

Adonis (Rom. myth.) a youth beloved of Venus

adopter *not* -or

adorable *not* -eable

Adorno, Theodor (Wiesengrund) (1903–69) German philosopher, sociologist, and musicologist; b. **Theodor Wiesengrund**

adorsed, adossed (her.) *use* **addorsed**

ADP adenosine diphosphate, automatic data processing

ad patres (Lat.) deceased (not ital.)

ad personam (Lat.) personal

ADR American Depository Receipt

ad/ referendum (Lat.) for further consideration, — **rem** to the point

adrenalin *not* -ine; in US, **adrenaline** is the hormone, **Adrenalin** (propr.) the synthetic drug

adresse (Fr. f.) address

Adrianople *use* **Edirne**

à droite (Fr.) to the right

A.d.S. Académie des Sciences

adscriptus glebae (Lat.) bound to the soil (of serfs)

adsor/b hold as condensation a gas, liquid, or solute on the surface of a solid; **-bable, -pent, -ption**; cf. **absorb**

adsum (Lat.) I am present

adulator *not* -er

ad/ unguem (Lat.) perfectly; — **unum omnes** all, to a man; — **usum** according to custom, abbr. **ad us.**

adv. adverb, -ially; advocate

adv. (Lat.) adversus (against)

ad valorem (Lat.) according to value, abbr. **ad val.**

adverb/, -ially abbr. **adv.**

ad verbum (Lat.) to a word, verbatim

adverse (often followed by *to*) contrary or hurtful: 'adverse reaction to the drug'; cf. **averse, aversion**

adversus (Lat.) against, abbr. **adv.**

advertise *not* -ize

advertisement abbr. **ad, advt.**; pl. **ads, advts.**

advis/e *not* -ize; **-able** *not* -eable

advis/er *not* -or; **-ory**

ad/ vitam aut culpam (Lat.) for lifetime or until fault, — **vivum** lifelike

ad voc. *use* **s.v.**

advocaat a liqueur

advocate abbr. **adv.**

Advocate General abbr. **AG**

Advocates, Faculty of (law) the Bar of Scotland

advocatus diaboli (Lat.) devil's advocate (ital.)

advt/., -s. advertisement, -s

adyt/um the innermost part of an ancient temple, pl. **-a**

adze *not* adz (US)

AE Air Efficiency Award

A.E. or **AE** (originally and properly **Æ**) pseud. of George (William) Russell (1867–1935) Irish poet, playwright, and journalist

Æ (numismatics) = copper (Lat. *aes*)

AEA Atomic Energy Authority

Aeaea (Gr. myth.) an island inhabited by Circe

AEC Army Educational Corps (*now* **RAEC**), (US) Atomic Energy Commission (*since* 1975 **ERDA**)

aedile *not* e-

AEF Allied (*or* American *or* Australian) Expeditionary Force, Amalgamated Union of Engineering and Foundry Workers

Aegean Sea the Mediterranean between Greece and Turkey

aegis a shield, protection; *not* e-

aegrot/at he *or* she is ill (a certificate that an examination candidate is ill, or the degree thus awarded), pl. **-ant**

AEI Associated Electrical Industries

Ælfred *prefer* **Alfred**

Ælfric (*c*.955–*c*.1010) English writer, also called **Grammaticus** in the 17th–18th cc.

Ælfthryth (*c*.945–*c*.1000) wife of King Edgar and mother of Ethelred the Unready

Aelia Laelia an insoluble riddle

Ælla a tragic interlude by Chatterton, 1768–9

Aemilius a character in Shakespeare's *Titus Andronicus*

Aeneas, *Aeneid*

Aeolian, Aeolic (caps.) *not* E-

aeon *not* eon (except in scientific use)

aepyornis (zool.) *not* epi-, epy-

aequales (Lat.) equal (pl. adj.), (pl. noun) equals (in age or performance); abbr. **aeq.**

AERA Associate Engraver, Royal Academy

aerate etc. *not* aë-

AERE Atomic Energy Research Establishment (Harwell), *now* **UKAEA**

AERI Agricultural Economics Research Institute (Oxford)

aerial *not* aë-

aerie *use* **eyrie**

aer/ify, -obic *not* aë-

aerodrome *use* **airfield**

aero/dynamics, -elasticity, -foil, -gramme, -logy (one word)

aeronaut/, -ical, -ics *not* aë-

aero/nomy, -phagy, -phone (one word)

aeroplane (US **airplane**) superseded by **aircraft** in some contexts

aerosol *not* air-

aerospace (one word)

aeruginous of the nature or colour of verdigris

Aeschylus (525–456 BC) Greek playwright

Aesculapi/us Latin form of the Greek god Asclepius, **-an** of or relating to medicine or physicians; *not* E-

Aesir the collective names of the gods in Scandinavian mythology

Aesop (6th c. BC) Greek fable-writer

aesthete, etc. *not* e-

aestiv/al, -ation *not* e- (US)

aet. *or* **aetat.** *anno aetatis suae* (of age, aged)

aetheling *use* **atheling**

aether in all meanings *use* **e-**

aetiology *not* e- (US)

Aetna *use* **Etna**

AEU Amalgamated Engineering Union

AEU (TASS) Technical, Administrative, and Supervisory Section of the AEU

AF audio frequency

AFA Associate of the Faculty of Actuaries

Afars and Issas, French territory of the *formerly* French Somaliland, *now* **Djibuti**

AFAS Associate of the Faculty of Architects and Surveyors

AFC Air Force Cross, Association Football Club

AFDCS (UK) Association of First Division Civil Servants (cf. **FDA**)

aff. affirmative, affirming

affairé (Fr.) busy (accent)

affaire d'amour (Fr. f.) love affair

affaire (de cœur) affair of the heart

affaire d'honneur duel

affenpinscher a small breed of dog (not ital.)

afferent (physiol.) conducting inwards or towards

affettuoso (mus.) with feeling

affidavit abbr. **afft.**

affranchise *not* -ize

Afghan a breed of hound (cap.), a blanket or shawl (not cap.)

Afghanistan abbr. **Afghan.**

aficionado/ an enthusiast for a sport or hobby, pl. **-s** (not ital.)

afield (one word)

AFL-CIO American Federation of Labor and Congress of Industrial Organizations (hyphen)

AFM Air Force Medal

à fond/ (Fr.) in depth, in detail, thoroughly (cf. **au fond**); **— de train** at full speed

aforethought (one word)

a fortiori with stronger reason, *not* à (not ital.)

Afr. Africa, -n

A.F.R.Ae.S. Associate Fellow of the Royal Aeronautical Society

afreet a demon in Muslim mythology; *not* afrit, efreet

African-American (adj. and noun) term preferred in most contexts to e.g. **black** (q.v.) or Afro-American

Africander a S. African breed of cattle or sheep; *not* Afrikander, Afrikaner

Afridi a people of Cent. Asia

Afrikaans a S. African Dutch language, abbr. **Afrik.**

Afrikaner an Afrikaans-speaking white S. African, *formerly* -cander; *not* -caner

after/birth, -care (one word)

after/-effect, -image (hyphens, one word in US)

afternoon abbr. **aft., p.m.**

after/shave, -taste, -thought (one word)

after-wit *see* **esprit de l'escalier**

AFV armoured fighting vehicle

AG Adjutant General, Air Gunner, (Ger.) *Aktiengesellschaft* (public limited company), Attorney General

A-G Accountant-General, Agent-General (of Colonies)

Ag argentum (silver) (no point)

Agadah *use* **Hagga-**

Aga Khan the leader of Ismaili Muslims

Aganippides (the) (Gr. myth.) alternative name for the Muses

agape gaping, open-mouthed; a love-feast, divine love (one word)

à gauche (Fr.) to the left

age group (two words)

ageing *not* agi- (US)

age/ism, -ist *not* agism, agist

agenda/ list of items for discussion, pl. **-s**; formally, **agend/um** (things to be done) is preferred, pl. **-a**

agent abbr. **agt.**

Agent General abbr. **A-G**

agent/ provocateur (not ital.) pl. **-s provocateurs**

ages *use* numerals for specific ages: 'a girl of 3', or 'a 3-year-old girl', *not* 'a girl of 3 years old'; *but* write 'in his fortieth year', 'in his forties'; in more literary contexts, 'a man of forty', 'a three-year-old'

aggiornamento (It.) bringing up to date

aggrandize *not* -ise

aging *use* **ageing** (except in US)

agitato (mus.) hurried

agitator *not* -er

AGM Advisory Group Meeting, Annual General Meeting

agma the symbol ŋ, or the sound represented by it

agnail *use* **hangnail**

agnostic/, -ism (not cap.)

à gogo in abundance, e.g. 'whisky à gogo' (two words, not ital.) (in US, a-go-go, no accent)

agonize *not* -ise

agouti a S. American rodent; *not* -y, agu-

agreeable in Fr. *agréable*

agric. agricultur/e, -al, -ist

agriculturist *not* -alist

agrimony (bot.)

agronomy rural economy

AGSM Associate of the Guildhall School of Music

agt. agent

Ag^to (Sp.) *agosto* (August)

Aguascalientes a city and state, Mexico

Agulhas, Cape S. Africa, *not* L'A-

aguti *use* **agou-**

AH *anno Hegirae*, the Muslim era; precedes the year number (small caps.); *see also* **hegira**

ah when it stands alone, takes an exclamation mark (!); as part of a sentence usually followed by a comma, the ! being placed at the end of the sentence: 'Ah, no, it cannot be!'

AHA American Heart Association, American Historical Association

aha an exclamation of surprise; *see also* **ha ha**

ahem an interjection used to attract attention, gain time, or express disapproval

ahimsa (Skt.) in the Hindu, Buddhist, and Jainist tradition, respect for all living things and avoidance of violence towards others

a.h.l. (Lat.) *ad hunc locum* (on this passage)

Ahmad/abad, -nagar India; *not* Ahmed-, Amed-

Ahmadu Bello University Nigeria

AHMI Association of Headmistresses, Incorporated; *see also* **IAHM**

à huis clos (Fr.) in private

Ahura Mazda (Old Pers.) the Zoroastrian spirit of good; *not* the many variants, although **Ormuzd** (Middle Pers.) is a common later and lit. form

a.h.v. (Lat.) *ad hanc vocem* (at this word)

Ahvenanmaa (Fin.) **Åland Islands**

AI American Institute, Anthropological Institute, artificial insemination, artificial intelligence

AIA American Institute of Aeronautics, American Institute of Architects, Associate of the Institute of Actuaries, automated image analysis

AIAA Architect Member of the Incorporated Association of Architects and Surveyors

AIAC Associate of the Institute of Company Accountants, Association internationale d'archéologie classique

AIAS Surveyor Member of the Incorporated Association of Architects and Surveyors

AIB Associate of the Institute of Bankers

AICC All India Congress Committee

AICS Associate of the Institute of Chartered Shipbrokers

AID Army Intelligence Department, artificial insemination by donor

Aida an opera by Verdi, 1871 (no diaeresis)

aide-de-camp abbr. **ADC**, pl. **aides-de-camp** (not ital.)

aide-memoire aid to memory, pl. **aides-memoires** or (properly) **aide-memoires** (not ital.); in Fr. m. *aide-mémoire*, pl. same

Aids acquired immune deficiency syndrome (one cap.); **AIDS** (four caps.) in technical use

aigrette a spray; *not* ei-, -et; *see also* **egret**

aiguillette (Fr. f.) a thin slice of meat, *not* an-

AIH artificial insemination by husband

ail/ (Fr. m.) garlic; *-e* (Fr. f.) bird's wing

Ailesbury, Marquess of; *see also* **Ayl-**

A.I.Loco.E. Associate of the Institute of Locomotive Engineers

aimable (Fr.) amiable

A.I.Mech.E. Associate of the Institution of Mechanical Engineers

A.I.Min.E. Associate of the Institution of Mining Engineers

AIMM Associate of the Institution of Mining and Metallurgy

AIMTA Associate of the Institute of Municipal Treasurers and Accountants

Ain a dép. of France

ʿ*ain* (Arab.) *prefer* ʿ*ayn*

ain/*é* (Fr.) f. *-ée* elder, senior; opp. to *puîné*, f. *puînée* or *cadet*/, *-te* younger

A.Inst.P. Associate of the Institute of Physics

AIQS Associate of the Institute of Quantity Surveyors

Air, Point of Clwyd; *see also* **Ayre**

air/ **bag, — bed, — bladder** (two words)

air/**borne, -brick** (one word)

Airbus (cap., propr., one word)

Air Commodore abbr. **Air Cdre**; *see also* **Commodore**

air condition/, **-ed, -er, -ing** (two words)

aircraft/ sing. and pl. (one word), **— carrier** (two words)

aircraft/**man, -woman** *not* aircrafts- (one word)

Airedale/ W. Yorks.; a terrier; **Baron —**

air/**field, -flow** (one word)

Air Force, Royal *see* **Navy, Army, and Air Force**

airgun (one word)

Air Gunner abbr. **AG**

air/**lift, -line, -mail** (one word)

Air Ministry *now* in **MOD**

airplane (US) *use* **aircraft** or **aeroplane**

airport (one word)

air raid (two words)

air/**ship, -sick, -space, -tight** (one word)

air-to-air (adj., hyphens)

airworthy of aircraft (one word)

AISA Associate of the Incorporated Secretaries Association

Aisne a dép. of France

ait an islet, *not* eyot (cap. when part of name)

aitchbone (one word) *not* H-, edge-

Aix-la-Chapelle (hyphens) the Fr. name for **Aachen**

Aix-les-Bains (hyphens)

Ajaccio Corsica

Ajax pl. **Ajaxes**

ajutage *use* **adj-**

AK Alaska (postal abbr.), Knight of the Order of Australia

aka also known as (used before an alias)

AKC Associate of King's College (London)

akee *use* **ack-**

akimbo (one word)

Akkadian of Akkad in ancient Babylonia, or its Semitic language; *not* Acc-

Akkra Ghana, *use* **Acc-**

Akmola cap. of Kazakhstan, *formerly* **Almaty**

Aktiengesellschaft (Ger. f.) public limited company, abbr. **AG**

akvavit *use* **aquavit** except when describing a specific (e.g. Scandinavian) variety

AL Alabama (postal abbr.), autograph letter

Al aluminium (no point)

al- an Arabic article, used in proper names (hyphen)

ALA Associate of the Library Association

Ala. Alabama (off. abbr.)

à la short for *à la mode* (Fr., in the manner of); the *la* does not need to agree with the gender of the person or thing to which it refers: *à la reine, à la maître d'hôtel*

Alabama off. abbr. **Ala.**, postal **AL**

à la carte (a meal) that may be ordered from a wide range of available dishes (not ital.); *see also* **table d'hôte**

Aladdin *not* Alladin

Alanbrooke, Viscount (one word)

Åland Islands Baltic Sea, in Fin. **Ahvenanmaa**

à la page (Fr.) up to date

alarm/ *not* alarum except in 'alarums and excursions', **— clock** (two words)

à la russe (Fr.) in the Russian style (not cap.)

alas when it stands alone, takes an exclamation mark (!); as part of a sentence, usually followed by a comma, the ! being placed at the end of the sentence: 'Alas, it is true!'

Alaska/ postal abbr. **AK**; **baked —** (one cap.)

Alb. Albania, -n

Alba. Alberta, *use* **Alta.**

alba Provençal for **aubade** (not ital.)

Alban. *formerly* the signature of the Bishop of St Albans (point), *now* **St Albans:** (colon)

Albania/ republic, abbr. **Alb.**; **-n** (of or related to) (the people or language) of Albania

albedo/ a fraction of radiation reflected, pl. **-s**

Albee, Edward (**Franklin**) (b. 1928) US playwright

albeit though (one word, not ital.)

Albigens/es a S. French Manichaean sect, 12th–13th c.; **-ian**

albin/o pl. **-os**, f. **-ess**; **-ism** *not* -oism; **-otic**

Ålborg Dan. for **Aalborg**

Albrighton Shropshire

album/en the natural white of an egg, **-in** its chief constituent; adj. **-inous**

Albuquerque N. Mex.

Albury Herts., Oxon., Surrey

Alcaeus of Mytilene (b. *c.*620 BC) Greek lyric poet

alcahest *use* **alka-**

alcaic a form of verse metre in four-line stanzas

alcaide (Sp. m.) governor, jailer

alcalde (in Spain) a magistrate, mayor

Alcatraz a former US prison, San Francisco Bay, Calif.

alcázar (Sp.) palace, fortress, bazaar

Alceste an opera by Gluck, 1767

Alcestis *not* Alk-

alcheringa (Aboriginal myth.) the 'dreamtime' or golden age when the first ancestors were created

Alcibiades *not* Alk-

ALCM Associate of the London College of Music

Alcoran *use* **Koran**

Alcyone (Gr. myth.) daughter of Aeolus and wife of Ceyx, *not* Hal-; *see also* **halcyon**

Aldborough Norfolk, N. Yorks.

Aldbrough Humberside

Aldbury Herts.

Aldeburgh Suffolk

al dente cooked but not soft (not ital.)

Alderbury Wilts.

Alderman abbr. **Ald.**

Aldermaston Berks.

Alderney Channel Islands, in Fr. **Aurigny**

Aldiborontiphoscophornia character in *Chrononhotonthologos*

Aldine (adj.) printed by the Manutius family, who introduced italic type

Aldis lamp a hand lamp for signalling

Aldsworth Glos., W. Sussex

Aldus Manutius printer, *see* **Manutius**

Aldworth Berks.

aleatoric depending on the throw of a die or on chance; *not* -ory except in music and the arts, where it describes stochasticism

Alecto (Gr. myth.) one of the three Furies

alef (Heb.) a smooth-breathing mark ('), typographically largely equivalent to the Arab. *hamza* or Gr. lenis (ital.); *not* -eph

alehouse (one word)

Alençon lace (cedilla)

Aleutian Islands Bering Sea

A level 'advanced level' examination (no hyphen)

alexandrine a metrical line of verse having six iambic feet

ALF Animal Liberation Front, Arab Liberation Front (Iraq)

Alf Automatic Letter Facer (Post Office sorting machine)

Alfa-Romeo an Italian make of car (hyphen)

Alford Grampian, Lincs., Som.

Alfred 'the Great' (849–99) King of Wessex; abbr. **A.**, **Alf.**

alfresco (adj. and adv.) (one word, not ital.)

Alfreton Derby.

Alg. Algernon, Algiers

alg/a (bot.) pl. **-ae** (not ital.)

Algarve, (the) Portugal

algebra abbr. **alg.**

ALGOL (comput.) Algorithmic Language

algology (bot.)

Algonkian (geol.) US term for the **Proterozoic** era

Algonqui/an of a large group of Native American Indian tribes or their languages; **-n** (of or concerning) one people in this group or their language, a dialect of Ojibwa; *not* -nki-

Algonquin Round Table the name given to the informal meetings of a group of literary wits at the Algonquin Hotel (New York City), mainly 1920–40

alguacil a mounted official at a bullfight in Spain, a constable or officer of justice in Sp.-speaking countries; *not* -zil (not ital.)

Alhambr/a a Moorish palace at Granada; **-esque**

alia (Lat. pl.) other things

alias/ (adv. and noun) pl. **-es**

alibi/ (noun) pl. **-s**

alienator *not* -er

Aligarh Uttar Pradesh, India

Alighieri the family name of **Dante**

align/, -ment *not* aline

alii (Lat. pl.) other people

alimentative/, -ness *not* alimentive, -ness

A-line (of a garment) having a narrow waist or shoulders and flared skirt (cap., hyphen)

aline *use* **-ign**

alinéa (Fr. m.) paragraph

Alipore India

Alipur India, Pakistan

Alitalia the Italian national airline

ali/us (Lat. m.) another person, pl. **-i**

Aliwal E. Punjab, India; S. Africa

alkahest *not* alca-

alkali/ pl. **-s**

alkalize *not* -ise

Alkestis, Alkibiades *use* **Alc-**

Alkoran *use* **Koran**

alla breve (mus.) two or four minims in bar

alla cappella (mus.) *use* **a cappella**

Alladin *use* **Aladdin**

Allahabad Uttar Pradesh, India

Allah il Allah corruption of Arab. *lā ilāha illa'llāh*, There is no god but God (Muslim prayer and war cry)

Allan-a-Dale a companion of Robin Hood and minstrel hero

allargando (mus.) broad, spread out

allée (Fr. f.) alley, avenue

Allegany Pittsburgh, Pa.

Allegheny US mountains, river, and airline

allegretto/ (mus.) fairly brisk; as noun, pl. **-s**

allegro/ (mus.) brisk, merry; as noun, pl. **-s**

allele one of the alternative forms of a gene; *not* -l, -lomorph

alleluia Lat. form (also liturgical) for Heb. and biblical **hallelujah**

allemande the name of several German dances

Allen, (William) Hervey (1889–1949) US novelist, *not* Harvey

Allendale Northumb.

allerg/y a sensitivity to certain foods, pollens, etc.; **-ic**

alleviator *not* -er

Alleynian a member of Dulwich College

All Fools' Day (caps., no hyphen)

allgemein (Ger.) general (adj.); abbr. **allg.**, **allgm.**

All-Hallows All Saints' Day, 1 Nov. (caps., hyphen)

Allhallows Kent (one word)

allineation alignment, *not* alin-

Allingham, Margery (1904–66) English novelist

allodium an estate held in absolute ownership, *not* alo-

allons! (Fr.) let us go!, come!

allot/, -ment, -table, -ted, -ting

all' ottava (mus.) an octave higher than written, abbr. **all' ott.**

all ready completely or entirely prepared; cf. **already**

all right *not* alright, all-right

all round (prep., two words) ('all round the Wrekin')

all-round/ (adj., hyphen) ('an all-round man') **-er** noun

All Saints' Day 1 Nov.

all/seed, -spice (one word)

All Souls College Oxford (no apos.), **— Souls' Day** 2 Nov., **— Souls' Eve** 1 Nov. (caps., no hyphens)

all together (in a body) *but* **altogether** (entirely)

alluvi/um pl. **-a**

Alma-Ata former Russian name of **Almaty**

almacantar *use* almu-

Alma Mater fostering mother, one's school or university

almanac *but* **Oxford Almanack,** *Whitaker's Almanack*

Almanach de Gotha an annual publication (in Fr.) giving information about European royalty, nobility, and diplomats, published in Gotha 1763–1944; a smaller-scale version was revived in Paris in 1968 (ital.)

Alma-Tadema, Sir Lawrence (1836–1912) Dutch-born English painter

Almaty former cap. of Kazakhstan

Almighty, the cap. except when used attributively, e.g. 'an almighty bang'

Almondbury W. Yorks.

Almondsbury Avon

almucantar *not* alma-

Alnmouth Northumb.

Alnwick Northumb.

alodium *use* **allod-**

A.L.O.E. A Lady of England, pseud. of **Charlotte M. Tucker** (1821–93)

à l'outrance *use* *à outrance*

ALP Australian Labor Party

Alpes-de-Haute-Provence a dép. of France (hyphens)

Alpes-Maritimes a dép. of France

Alphaeus the father of Apostle James 'the Less'

alphanumeric (comput.) of instructions containing alphabetic, numerical, and other characters (one word)

alpha/ the first letter of the Gr. alphabet (*A*, α); **— particle, — ray** (two words)

Alpinist (cap.)

already (adv.) before the time in question (I knew that already), as early or as soon as this (already at the age of 6); cf. **all ready**

alright *use* **all right**

ALS Associate of the Linnean Society, autograph letter signed

Alsace-Lorraine (hyphen)

Alsirat (Arab.) the bridge to paradise

Alsop en le Dale Derby. (four words)

alt. alternative, altitude (point)

Alta. Alberta, Canada; *not* Alba.

alter/ ego (Lat.) one's second self, pl. **— egos** (not ital.)

alter idem another self

Altesse (Fr. f.), **Altezza** (It.) Highness

Althing the Icelandic Parliament, in Icel. **Alþingi**

Althorpe Humberside

Althorp/ House, — Library, — Park Northants.

Althusser, Louis (1918–90) French philosopher

altitude abbr. **alt.**

alto/ (mus.) pl. **-s**, abbr. **A.**

altogether *see* **all together**

alto-relievo/ high relief, pl. **-s**; Anglicized version of It. *alto rilievo*

aluminium symbol **Al** (no point) *not* -num (US)

alumn/us pl. **-i**; f. **-a**, pl. **-ae**; abbr. **alum.**

AM Academy of Management, air mail, Air Ministry, Albert Medal, amplitude modulation, *Artium Magister* (US Master of Arts), *Ave Maria* (Hail, Mary!), Member of the Order of Australia (caps.)

A.-M. Alpes-Maritimes

AM *anno mundi* (in the year of the world) (small caps.)

Am americium (no point)

Am. America, -n

a.m. (Lat.) *ante meridiem* (before noon) (lower case, points)

AMA American Management/Marketing/Medical/Missionary Association; Assistant Masters' Association, *now* **AMMA**

amadavat *use* ava-

amah a child's nurse, esp. in the Far East and India (not ital.)

Amalek *not* -ech, -eck

amanuens/is pl. **-es**

amateur abbr. **A.**

Ambala India, *not* Umbal(l)a

ambassad/or f. **-ress**

ambergris a waxy secretion from the intestine of the sperm whale, used in perfumery

ambiance Fr. spelling of **ambience**, used in English esp. of accessory details in a work of art (ital.)

ambidextrous *not* -erous

ambience the surroundings (*not* -cy); *see also* **ambiance**

ambivalen/t, -ce

amblyop/ia impaired vision, **-ic**

Amboina Indonesia, *properly* **Ambon**; *not* -oyna (except in hist. contexts)

amboyna a type of decorative wood

ambry *use* aum-

AMDG *ad majorem Dei gloriam* (for the greater glory of God)

ameba *use* amoeba

Amedabad, Amednagar India; *use* Ahmad-

âme damnée (Fr.) a 'cat's-paw', a devoted adherent (lit. 'damned soul')

Ameer *use* only with reference to British India; *use* **Amir** for Arabic titles, **Emir** for Turkish and Indian titles

amend correct an error, make minor improvements; cf. **emend**

amende/ honorable (Fr. f.) honourable reparation, pl. **-s honorables**

a mensa et toro (Lat.) 'from board and bed', legal separation, *not* thoro; cf. **a vinculo matrimonii**

Amer. American

amerc/e (law) punish by fine *or* punish arbitrarily; **-ement, -iable**

American Indian (of or relating to) a member of the aboriginal peoples of America or their descendants or languages; *prefer* Native American

Americanize *not* -ise

American plan (US) = **full board** (of hotels)

American Revolution (US) = **War of American Independence**

America's Cup, the a yachting race and trophy

americium symbol **Am**

Amerind/ (also **Amerindian**) American Indian; **-ic**

à merveille (Fr.) perfectly, wonderfully

AMG(OT) Allied Military Government (of Occupied Territory) (Second World War)

Amharic the official language of Ethiopia

amiable friendly and pleasant in temperament, likeable; in Fr. **aimable**

amicable showing or done in a friendly spirit, peaceable; in Fr. **amiable**

amic/us curiae a friend of the court, a disinterested adviser; pl. **-i curiae** (not ital.)

amidships *not* -ship (one word)

amigo (Sp.) friend (not ital.)

amino acid (chem., two words)

Amir (in Arab. *'amīr*) Arabic title, cap. when forming part of the name; *see also* **Emir**; **Ameer**

Amis,/ (Sir) Kingsley (1922–97) English novelist and poet; **— Martin** (b. 1949) his son, English novelist

Amish (of or relating to) a strict US Mennonite sect

AMMA Assistant Masters' and Mistresses' Association, *formerly* AMA

Ammal (Ind.) a suffix used to indicate that a name belongs to a woman, e.g. Dr E. K. Janaki Ammal

Amman Jordan

Ammergau Bavaria

ammeter for measuring electric current

amoeb/a pl. **-as** (not ital.), *not* ame-

à moitié (Fr.) half

amok *not* amuck, amock

Amoor *use* **Amur**

amorett/o (It. m.) a cupid, pl. **-i**

amortize *not* -ise

Amos (OT) do not abbreviate

amour-propre (Fr.) self-respect, proper pride

amp amperage, ampere, amplifier

Ampère, André Marie (1775–1836) French physicist (accent)

ampere an electric unit of current (no accent); abbr. **A** (sing. and pl.) *or* **amp** (no point)

ampersand = **&**, used in some formulae, references, and lexicographic work, in Acts of Parliament, and in business names. Since it may imply a closer relationship than *and*, the ampersand can be useful in grouping items: 'cinnamon & raisin and onion' are two, not three, types of bagels. However, in general *prefer* **and**. For **&c.** *use* **etc.**, except when reproducing antique typography

amphetamine (med.) a synthetic drug used esp. as a stimulant

amphibian (zool.) a member of the Amphibia; a vehicle adapted for land and water

amphor/a a jar, pl. **-ae**

ampoule a glass container for hypodermic dose; *not* -pule (US), -pul

Amritsar India, *not* Umritsur

amt. amount

amuck *use* **amok**

Amundsen, Roald (1872–1928) Norwegian explorer, S. Pole 1911

Amur Siberia, *not* -oor

amygdalin *not* -e

AN Anglo-Norman, autograph note

ana/ anecdotes or sayings, collective pl.; or sing. with pl. **-s**

-ana a suffix denoting anecdotes or other publications concerning, as Shakespeariana, Victoriana

anacoluth/on (gram.) a sentence or construction that lacks grammatical sequence (e.g. 'while in the garden the door banged shut'), pl. **-a**; **-ic**; *not* -outhon, -koloulthon, -koloulthon

Anacreon (6th c. BC) Greek poet, abbr. **Anacr.**

anacreontic (noun and adj.) (a poem written) after the manner of Anacreon, convivial and amatory in tone; a classical verse form

anaemi/a, -c *not* anemi/a, -c (US)

anaerob/e, -ic

anaesthetist a doctor specializing in administering anaesthetics = (US) **anesthesiologist**; in the USA an anesthetist may be either a nurse or a doctor with a subordinate role

anaesthetize *not* ane- (US), -ise

anal. analog/y, -ous; analys/e, -er, -is; analytic, -al

analects (also **analecta**) a collection of short literary extracts

analog (comput.) the use of physical variables to represent numbers; cf. **digital**

analog/ous, -y abbr. **anal.**

analogue an analogous or parallel thing, *not* -log (US); *see also* **analog**

analys/e, -er, -is pl. **-es**, abbr. **anal.**; *not* -lyze (US)

analyst

analytic/, -al abbr. **anal.**

Anam *use* **Annam**

anamorphos/is pl. **-es**

anapaest (prosody) a foot of three syllables, *not* -pest (US)

anastase *use* anat-

anastomos/is communication by cross-connections, pl. **-es**; **-ist**

anastrophe (rhet.) the inversion of the usual order of words or clauses

anat. anatom/y, -ical

anatase a mineral, *not* anast-

anathema/ a curse (not used with an article), pl. **-s**; **-tize**

anatomize dissect, *not* -ise

anatom/y, -ical, -ist abbr. **anat.**

anatta (bot.) *use* **annatto**

ANB *American National Biography*

ANC African National Congress, Army Nurse Corps, Australian Newspapers Council

anc. ancient, *not* anct.

ancest/or if a feminine form is required, *use* **-ress**, *not* -rix

anchor/ite hermit, *not* -et; **-etic**

anchylosis *use* ank-

ancien régime (Fr. m.) the old order of things (not caps.); of France before 1789 (caps.)

ancient abbr. **anc.**, *not* anct.

Ancient Mariner, Rime of the a poem by Coleridge, 1798

Ancient Order of/ Druids abbr. **AOD**, — — — **Foresters** abbr. **AOF**, — — — **Hibernians** abbr. **AOH**

Ancrene/ Wisse *also called* — **Riwle**, *not* Ancren

Andalusia a region of Spain, in Sp. **Andalucía**

andante (mus.) moving easily, steadily

andantino/ (mus.) rather quicker (*formerly* but erroneously slower) than andante; as noun, pl. **-s**

Andersen, Hans Christian (1805–75) Danish writer

Andhra Pradesh an Indian state

Andoni Basque for **Anthony**

and/or signifying either or both of the stated alternatives; useful in legal, official, and business contexts—'soldiers and/or sailors'—as it compresses a lengthier clarification; avoid elsewhere

Andrea del Sarto (1486–1531) Italian painter

Androcles *not* -kles (except in specialist use)

androgen/ic, -ous (adj.) capable of developing and maintaining male characteristics

androgynous (adj.) of ambiguous gender

Andropov, Yuri (**Vladimirovich**) (1914–84) President of the USSR 1983–4

anent (prep.; arch., Sc.) concerning; a legal term used in Scottish law courts

aneurysm *not* -ism

Angeles, Victoria de los (b. 1923) Spanish soprano

Angelico, Fra (*c.*1400–55) Florentine painter and Dominican friar, *born* **Guido di Pietro**

Angelman syndrome *not* Angelman's

Angers, Marie-Louise-Félicité (1845–1924) French-Canadian novelist, pseud. **Laure Conan**

Angevin a native or inhabitant of Anjou; a Plantagenet, esp. any of the English kings from Henry II to John; certain kings and queens of Naples and Hungary

anglais/ (Fr.) f. *-e* English (not cap.); *but **Anglais*/, *-e* English/man, -woman

angle the sign ∠, angle between the two lines ∧, right angle ∟, two right angles ⊥

angle brackets <> (wide), ⟨⟩ (narrow)

Anglesey/ Gwynedd, *not* -ea; in Welsh **Ynys Môn**; **Marquess of —**

Angleterre (Fr. f.) England

anglice in English (not ital., no accent); abbr. **angl.**

Anglicize *not* -ise (cap.)

Anglo- prefix meaning 'English', although commonly used to encompass 'British'; can sometimes be replaced by 'British' to avoid offending non-English Britons

Anglo/-American; **-French** abbr. **AF**; **-Norman** abbr. **AN** (hyphens)

Anglophile *not* -phil

anglophone (not cap.)

Anglo-Saxon abbr. **AS**; as a language, **Old English** is now usually preferred; avoid as a term for 'English-speaking', except in disciplines where its use has become entrenched

Angora Turkey, *now* **Ankara**

Angostura *now* **Ciudad Bolívar**, Venezuela; — **Bitters** (propr., caps.) a kind of tonic

angostura/ (in full — **bark**) an aromatic bitter bark used as a flavouring

angst fear, anxiety; from (Ger. f.) *Angst*, ultimately from (Dan.) *Angest*, *now* **angst**

angstrom a unit of length equal to 10^{-10} metre (no accents), abbr. **Å**; now largely replaced by the **nanometre**

Ångström/, Anders Jonas (1814–74) Swedish physicist, created the — **pyrheliometer**

anguillette (Fr. f.) eel, *not* ai-

aniline a source of dyes (also adj.)

animalcule/ pl. **-s**, *not* -ae

animalcul/um *pl.* **-a**

animé a W. Indian resin, (Fr. mus.) animated (not ital.)

anion (elec.) an ion carrying a negative charge

Ankara Turkey, *formerly* Angora

ankylos/is the fusion of bones, pl. **-es**; *not* anch-

Anmerkung/ (Ger. f.) a note (cap.), pl. *-en*; abbr. **Anm.**

ann. annals, *anni* (years), *anno*, annual

anna/ (Ind., Pak.) *formerly* one-sixteenth of a rupee, *now* replaced by decimal coinage; pl. **-s**; abbr. **a.**

annales (Fr. pl. f.) annals, abbr. *ann.*

annals abbr. **ann.**

Annam/ *not* Anam; *formerly* a kingdom within French Indo-China, *now* merged in Vietnam; **-ite** the formal name for the Vietnamese language

Annan Dumfries & Galloway

Ann Arbor Mich.

annatto (bot.) an orange-red dye; *not* an-, -a

Anne,/ **Queen** (1702–14) (b. 1665); — **Saint**

Anne of Cleves (1515–57) fourth wife of Henry VIII of England

Anne of Geierstein a novel by Scott, 1829

annex verb, **annexe** noun (except in US, where 'annex' is both noun and verb)

anno/ (Lat.) in the year, abbr. *ann.*; — *aetatis suae* aged, abbr. *aet.*, *aetat.*; — *Domini* (cap. A, D) abbr. **AD** (small caps); — *Hegirae* (Muslim era) abbr. **AH** (small caps.); — *mundi* in the year of the world, abbr. **AM** (small caps.); all three abbrs. to be placed *before* the numerals

annonce (Fr. f.) advertisement

annotat/ed, -or *not* -er; abbr. **annot.**

annual abbr. **ann.**

annul/ar ringlike; **-ate, -ated, -et, -oid**

ann/us (Lat.) year, pl. *-i*; *-us horribilis* terrible year; *-us mirabilis* remarkable year

anonymous abbr. **anon.**

anorexic *not* -ectic

Anouilh, Jean (1910–88) French playwright

anschluss unification, esp. *Anschluss* (Ger. m.), the annexation of Austria in 1938 by Germany

ANSI American National Standards Institute

answer abbr. **A.**, **ans.**

answerphone (not cap.)

Ant. Anthony, Antigua

ant. antonym

Antaeus (Gr. myth.) a giant with whom Hercules wrestled

antagonize *not* -ise

Antananarivo Madagascar

Antarctic/ -a

ante a stake in card game (not ital.)

ante/ (Lat.) before, — **bellum** before the war

ante-bellum (adj., hyphen, not ital.) occurring or existing before a particular war, esp. the US Civil War (one word in US)

antechamber *not* anti-

ante diem (Lat.) before the day, abbr. **a.d.**

antediluvian (one word)

ante mediem (Lat.) before the middle, abbr. **ante med.**

antemeridian (one word)

ante meridiem (Lat.) before noon, abbr. **a.m.**

ante-mortem (adj., hyphen)

antenatal (one word)

antenn/a (zool.) pl. **-ae**; (US) radio or television aerial, pl. **-s**

ante-post in racing (hyphen)

ante-room (hyphen; one word in US)

anthelmintic a drug or agent used to destroy parasitic worms, *not* -thic

Anthony abbr. **Ant.** Anglicized from Lat. **Antonius**, from which came the variant **Antony** (NB *Antony and Cleopatra*); also **Antain(e)** (Ir. Gael.), **Antal** (Hungarian), **Antoine** (Fr.), **Andoni** (Basque), **Anton** (Ger., Russ.), **Antoni** (Catalan, Polish), **Antonio** (Castilian Sp., Galician, It.), **António** (European Port.), **Antônio** (Brazil. Port.), **Antonín** (Czech)

anthropolog/y -ical abbr. **anthrop.**

anthropomorphize *not* -ise

anthropophag/us a cannibal, pl. **-i**; adj. **-ous**

antichamber *use* ante-

Antichrist (cap.) *but* **antichristian**

anticline (geol.)

anticlockwise (one word)

antifreeze (one word)

Antigua abbr. **Ant.**

anti-hero a principal character noticeably lacking traditional heroic qualities (hyphen, one word in US)

antilogarithm (one word) abbr. **antilog**

antimacassar a covering put over furniture for protection (not cap.)

antimatter (one word)

antimony symbol **Sb**

antinomy conflict of authority

antinovel a novel in which formal conventions are studiously avoided (one word)

anti-nuclear (hyphen)

antiparticle (one word)

antipathize *not* -ise

antiq. antiquar/y, -ian

antiqs. antiquities

Antiqua (Ger. typ. f.) roman type (cap.)

antique paper a moderately bulky, opaque book paper with roughish surface

antisabbatarian (one word)

anti-Semit/e, -ic, -ism (hyphen, one cap.)

antistrophe a stanza corresponding to the strophe in a Greek dramatic chorus

antistrophon (rhet.) a retort

antitetanus (adj., one word)

antithes/is pl. **-es**

antithesize *not* -ise

antitoxin (one word)

antitype that which is represented by a type or symbol, *or* a person or thing of the opposite type; *not* ante-

António (European Port.), **Antônio** (Brazil. Port.)

antonym a word of opposite meaning, abbr. **ant.**

Anvers Fr. for **Antwerp**, in Fl. **Antwerpen**

Anwick Lincs.

any- pronouns and adverbs beginning with *any-*, *every-*, and *some-* are single words ('anyone you ask', 'everything I own', 'somebody to talk to'), *but* where each word retains its own meaning, the words are printed separately ('any one item', 'every thing in its place', 'some body in motion').

any/body, -how (one word)

any more (two words, one in US)

any/one, -place, -thing (one word)

anyway one word in conventional sense, *but* 'you can do it any way you like' (two words)

anywhere (one word)

Anzac Australian and New Zealand Army Corps (First World War)

Anzeige/ (Ger. f.) notice, advertisement; pl. **-n**

Anzus Australia, New Zealand, and the USA, as an alliance for the Pacific area (one cap.)

AO Accountant Officer, Army Order, Officer of the Order of Australia

AOB any other business

A.O.C.-in-C. Air Officer Commanding in Chief

AOD Ancient Order of Druids, Army Ordinance Department

AOF Ancient Order of Foresters

AOH Ancient Order of Hibernians

A-OK (caps., hyphen)

AOR adult-oriented rock, advance of rights, album-oriented radio

aorist abbr. **aor.**

aort/a (anat.) pl. **-ae**

Aotearoa (Maori) a poetic name for New Zealand, meaning 'land of the long white cloud', originally referring solely to the North Island

août (Fr. m.) August (not cap.)

à outrance (Fr.) to the bitter end, *not à l'outrance*

AP anti-personnel, *à protester* (Fr., on bills of exchange), armour-piercing, Associated Press

Ap. Apostle

ap. (Lat.) *apud* (quoted in)

a.p. above proof, author's proof

Apache a Native American people (cap.), a Parisian ruffian (not cap.)

apanage *not* app-

à part (Fr.) apart

apartheid (Afrik.) segregation (not ital.)

apatosaurus a huge herbivorous dinosaur of the Jurassic period, *formerly* called brontosaurus

ap/e, -ed, -ing, -ish

Apelles (4th c. BC) Greek painter

Apennines Italy (one *p*, three *ns*), in It. **Appennini**

aperçu an outline (not ital.)

aperitif/ an alcoholic drink taken as an appetizer, pl. **-s** (not ital., no accent)

APEX Association of Professional, Executive, Clerical, and Computer Staff

Apex (often attrib.) a system of reduced fares, abbr. of Advance Purchase Excursion (one cap.)

apex/ pl. **-es**, adj. **apical**

apfelstrudel a dish of baked apples in pastry (not cap., not ital.)

aphaere/sis the omission of a sound from the beginning of a word as a morphological development, pl. **-ses**; **-tic**

apheli/on (astr.) pl. **-a**, symbol **Q**

aphid/ pl. **-s**

aphi/s pl. **-des**

APL (comput.) A Programming Language

à plaisir (Fr.) at pleasure

apnoea the temporary cessation of breathing, *not* -nea (US)

Apocalypse (NT) abbr. **Apoc.**

apocalypse a grand or violent event; a revelation, esp. of the end of the world (not cap.)

Apocrypha (cap.) abbr. **Apoc.** (for abbr. of books *see* under names), adj. **apocryphal**

apodictic clearly established, *not* -deictic

apodos/is (gram.) pl. **-es**

apog/ee (astr.) abbr. **apog.**; **-ean**

Apollinaire, Guillaume born **Wilhelm Apollinaris de Kostrowitzky** (1880–1918) French poet and critic

Apollinaris (water) a mineral water from Ahr Valley, Germany

Apollin/arius (*sometimes* **-aris**) (c.310–c.390) Christian heretic, **-arianism**

Apollo/ a Greek god, **-nian**; **— Belvedere** a statue in the Vatican

Apollonius Rhodius (c.250 BC) Greek poet

Apollos a follower of St Paul (Acts 18: 24)

Apollyon the Devil

apologize *not* -ise

apophthegm a pithy maxim, *not* apothegm (US)

a-port (hyphen)

apostasy *not* -cy

apostatize *not* -ise

a posteriori (reasoning) from effects to causes (not ital., hyphen in attrib.); cf. **a priori**

Apostle abbr. **Ap.**, pl. **App.**

Apostles' Creed (caps.)

Apostroph/ (Ger. m.) apostrophe, pl. **-e** (cap.)

apostrophize *not* -ise

apothecaries' weight, signs ℳ minim; ℈ scruple; ʒ drachm; ℥ ounce; print quantities in lower-case letters close up behind symbol: final *i* becomes *j*, as vij = 7, j = 1

apothegm *use* **apophthegm** (except in US)

apotheos/is pl. **-es**

apotropaic averting ill luck

App. Apostles

app. appendix

appal/, -led, -ling

Appalachia/, -n Mountains, -n Trail E. North America; this mountain system includes the Adirondacks, Alleghenies, Catskills, and Great Smoky Mountains

appanage *use* **apan-**

apparatchik/ a member of a (usually Communist) party administration, esp. one who executes policy; pl. **-s, -i** (not ital.)

apparatus/ pl. **-es**, *not* -ati (*but* use an alternative, e.g. appliances, when possible)

apparatus criticus a collection of variants accompanying a printed text, abbr. **app. crit.**

apparel/, -led, -ling

apparitor an officer of ecclesiastical court, *not* -er

app. crit. apparatus criticus

appeal/, -ed, -ing

appeasement *not* -sment

appell/ant, -ate, -ation, -ative

append/ix pl. **-ices** for the supplement, **-ixes** for the anatomical organ, abbr. **app.**, pl. **apps.** (in all senses)

appetiz/e *not* -ise; **-er, -ing**

applesauce (one word)

appliqué/ (noun, adj., and verb) **-d**

appoggiatura (mus.) a type of grace note, leaning note

appraise estimate value

appreciat/or *not* -er; **-ive, -ory**

apprentice abbr. **appr.**

apprise inform

apprize (arch.) esteem highly

appro (on) approval (no point)

appro. approbation

approver one who turns Queen's evidence; the term is virtually obsolete in British law, but still used elsewhere (e.g. Pakistan)

approximat/e, -ely, -ion abbr. **approx.**

appurts. appurtenances

APR annual percentage rate (of interest), annual progress report

Apr. April

APRC *anno post Romam conditam* (in the year after the building of Rome in 753 BC) (small caps.), *but use* AUC

apr. J.-C. (Fr.) *après Jésus-Christ* (= AD)

après/ (Fr.) after, **— coup** after the event, **— -midi** afternoon (hyphen), **— moi** (or **nous**) **le déluge** after me (*or* us) the deluge

après-ski (of) the time after a day's skiing

April abbr. **Apr.**

April Fool's Day (one fool) *not* Fools' (US)

a/ primo (Lat.) from the first, **— principio** from the beginning

a priori (reasoning) from causes to effects (not ital., hyphen in attrib.); cf. **a posteriori**

apriorism the doctrine of a-priori ideas (one word, not ital.)

apropos (adj. and adv.) (one word, no accent)

à propos de bottes (Fr.) beside the mark

APS Aborigines' Protection Society, American Philosophical Society, American Physics Society, Associate of the Philosophical Society

apse/ a semicircular recess, esp. in a church; pl. **-s**

apsis/s in an orbit, point of greatest or least distance from central body; pl. **-des**

APT advanced passenger train, advanced process technology, Association of Polytechnic Teachers, Association of Printing Technologists, automatic picture transmission (from satellites)

apud (Lat.) according to, in the work, *or* works, of; abbr. **ap.**

Apuleius, Lucius (2nd c. AD) Roman satirist

Apulia a region of Italy, in It. **Puglia**

aqua/ fortis, — regia (chem.) (two words, not ital.)

aquarium/ pl. **-s**

à quatre mains (Fr. mus.) for two performers (lit. 'for four hands')

aquavit an alcoholic drink; *see also* **akvavit**

aqua vitae (two words, not ital.)

Aquinas, St Thomas (*c.*1225–74) Italian theologian

AR Arkansas (postal abbr.)

AR *anno regni* (in the year of the reign) (small caps.)

Ar argon (no point)

a/r all risks

ARA Associate of the Royal Academy, London

Arabi/a, -an, -c abbr. **Arab.**

Arabian Nights' Entertainments, The

Arabic the Semitic language of the Arabs, now spoken in much of N. Africa and the Middle East

arabic numerals the numerals used in ordinary computation, as 1, 2, 3 (not cap.)

arach. arachnology

arachnid (zool.) a member of the Arachnidae

arachnoid (bot.) having long hairs, (anat.) one of meninges

ARAD Associate of the Royal Academy of Dancing

Aragon a region of Spain, *not* Arr-; in Sp. **Aragón**

Araldite (propr.)

ARAM Associate of the Royal Academy of Music

Aramaic abbr. **Aram.** a Semitic language, esp. that of Syria; written in Hebrew characters

Aran, Island of Co. Donegal; *see also* **Arran**

Aran Islands Galway Bay, Ireland; *see also* **Arran**

ARAS Associate of the Royal Astronomical Society

ARB Air Registration Board, Air Research Bureau

ARBA Associate of the Royal Society of British Artists

arbalest a crossbow, *not* arblast

arbit/er, -rary, -ration abbr. **arb.**

arbiter elegantiae (Lat.) a judge of taste

arbitrageur *not* -ger

arbitrament *not* -ement

arbitrator a legal or official word for arbiter

arbor a spindle, axis

arboret/um (bot.) a tree garden, pl. **-a**

arboriculture abbr. **arbor.**

arbor vitae a conifer

arbour a bower, *not* -or (US)

ARBS Associate of the Royal Society of British Sculptors

ARC Aeronautical Research Council, Agricultural Research Council, Architects' Registration Council

Arc, Jeanne d' (Fr.) **Joan of Arc** (1412–31)

ARCA Associate of the Royal College of Art

Arcades ambo (Lat.) two with like tastes

arcan/um pl. **-a**

Arc de Triomphe Paris

arced (elec.) *not* arck-

arc-en-ciel (Fr. m.) rainbow, pl. ***arcs-en-ciel***

arch. archa/ic, -ism; archery, archipelago; architect, -ural, -ure

Archaean of or relating to the earlier part of the Precambrian era, *not* -hean (US)

archaeolog/y, -ical, -ist abbr. **archaeol.**, *not* arche- (US)

Archangel Russia, in Russ. **Arkhangelsk**

archangel (one word, cap. when part of name)

Archbishop abbr. **Abp.**

Archd. Archdeacon, Archduke

archetype *not* archi-

archidiaconal of or relating to an archdeacon, *not* archide-

archiepiscopal of or relating to an archbishop

Archimedean *not* -ian

archipelago/ pl. **-s**, abbr. **arch.**

Archipiélago de Colón off. Sp. name for **Galápagos Islands**

architect/, -ural, -ure abbr. **arch., archit., archt.; orders of classical architecture** Doric, Ionic, Corinthian, Tuscan, and Composite

architype *use* arche-

arcing (elec.) *not* arck-

ARCM Associate of the Royal College of Music

ARCO Associate of the Royal College of Organists

ARCS Associate of the Royal College of Science

arctic (not cap.) cold

Arctic Circle (two caps.)

Arctic regions (one cap.)

Arctogaea (zool.) the land mass including Europe, Asia, Africa, and N. America; cf. **Neogaea; Notogaea**

Ardleigh Essex

Ardley Oxon.

ARE Arab Republic of Egypt, Associate of the Royal Society of Painter-Etchers and Engravers

are a unit of square measure, 100 sq. m.

areol/a a small area, pl. **-ae** (not ital.); *not* au-

Arequipa Peru

arête a sharp mountain ridge (not ital.)

argent (her.) silver, abbr. **arg.**

Argentina the country, *or* **Argentine Republic** (in very formal discourse), *not* 'the Argentine'

Argentin/e (adj.) *also* (noun) the inhabitant; *also* **-ian** *not* -ean

argentum silver, symbol (chem.) **Ag**, (numismatics) **AR**

argon symbol **Ar**

argot slang (not ital.)

arguable *not* -eable

argumentum ad/ crumenam (Lat.) argument to the purse; — — ***hoc*** argument for this (purpose); — — ***hominem*** argument to the person's interests; — — ***ignorantiam*** argument based on the adversary's ignorance; — — ***invidiam*** argument to hatred or prejudice; — — ***rem*** argument to the purpose; — — ***verecundiam*** appeal to modesty; ***argumentum baculinum*** or — — ***baculum*** argument of the stick, club-law; ***argumentum e silentio*** argument from silence

argy-bargy a dispute, wrangle; *not* argle-bargle (hyphen)

Argyle Minn.

Argyll/ and Bute District, — and Sutherland Highlanders, — and the Isles (Bishop of), Duke of —

Argyllshire a former county of Scotland

Århus (Dan.) **Aarhus**

Arian (theol.) a follower of Arius, (one) born under Aries

ARIBA Associate of the Royal Institute of British Architects

ARICS Professional Associate of the Royal Institution of Chartered Surveyors

Ariège a dép. of France

Aristotelian *not* -ean

Arius (*c*.250–*c*.336) Christian heretic

Ariz. Arizona (off. abbr.)

Arizona off. abbr. **Ariz.**, postal **AZ**

Ark. Arkansas (off. abbr.)

Arkansas off. abbr. **Ark.**, postal **AR**

Arlay dép. Jura, France

Arle Glos.; *not* -s

Arles dép. Bouches-du-Rhône, France

ARM adjustable-rate mortgage

ArM Master of Architecture (from Lat. *Architecturae Magister*)

Arm. Armenian, Armoric

armadillo/ pl. **-s**

armchair (one word)

Armenia/ an ancient country, a former Soviet Socialist Republic, now an independent republic; **-n** (of or related to) (the people or language) of Armenia

armes blanches (Fr.) side arms (bayonet, sabre, sword)

armful/ pl. **-s**

armhole (one word)

Arminians followers of Arminius

Arminius, Jacobus Latinized form of **Jacob Harmen** (1560–1609) Dutch theologian

armory heraldry, (US) = **armoury**

armoury a collection of arms

armpit (one word)

ARMS Associate of the Royal Society of Miniature Painters

arm's length (two words)

Army/ Dental Corps *now* **RADC**; — **Nursing Service** abbr. **ANS**; — **Order** abbr. **AO**; — **Ordnance Corps** *now* **RAOC**; — **Service Corps** *later* **RASC**, *now* **RCT**; — **Veterinary Department** abbr. **AVD**, *now* **RAVC**

arnotto *use* **annatto**

Arola Piedmont, Italy

Arolla Switzerland

Arolo Lombardy, Italy

Aroostook War settled the border of Maine and New Brunswick, 1842

ARP air-raid precautions

arpeggio/ (mus.) the striking of notes of chord in (usually upward) succession, pl. **-s**

ARPS Associate of the Royal Photographic Society, Association of Railway Preservation Societies

arquebus *use* **harq-**

ARR *anno regni Regis* or *Reginae* (in the year of the King's, *or* Queen's, reign) (small caps.)

arr. arranged; arriv/e, -ed, -es, -als

Arragon *use* **Aragon**

Arran, Earl of

Arran, Isle of Scotland; *see also* **Aran**

arrant utter, notorious; cf. **errant**

arrester a device for slowing an aircraft during landing, *not* -or

arrêt (Fr. m.) decree

Arrhenius, Svante August (1859–1927) Swedish scientist

arrière/-garde (Fr. f.) rearguard; — **-pensée** ulterior motive or mental reservation, pl. **-pensées** (hyphens)

arrivis/me (Fr. m.) ambitious behaviour, **-te** one who behaves thus

arrondissement (Fr. m.) a subdivision of a *département*, district, or province

arrowhead (one word)

Arrows of the Chace by Ruskin (1880), *not* Chase

arroyo/ a brook, stream, or gully; pl. **-s**

ARSA Associate of the Royal Scottish Academy, Associate of the Royal Society of Arts

ARSCM Associate of the Royal School of Church Music

arsenic symbol **As**

ars est celare artem (Lat.) the art is to conceal art

ARSL Associate of the Royal Society of Literature

ARSM Associate of the Royal School of Mines

ARSW Associate of the Royal Scottish Society of Painting in Water Colours

art. article, artillery, artist

art deco a decorative art style of 1920s (not cap.)

artefact *not* arti- (US)

artel an association of craftsmen, peasants, etc. in the former USSR

arteriosclerosis hardening of the arteries (one word)

arthropod/ a member of Arthropoda, animals with jointed body and limbs; pl. **-s**

article abbr. **art.**

articles of roup (Sc. law) conditions of sale (by auction)

articles, titles of (typ.) when cited, to be roman, quoted

artifact (US) *use* **arte-**

artillery abbr. **A.**, **art.**

artisan *not* -zan

artiste a professional singer, dancer, or other performer of either sex; *different from* **artist**

artizan *see* **artis-**

art nouveau a late 19th- to early 20th-c. ornamental art style (not cap.)

art paper a high-quality coated paper used for illustrations

art. pf. artist's proof

Arts and Crafts movement (two caps.)

artwork (one word) abbr. **a/w**

Arundel W. Sussex

Arundell of Wardour, Baron title now extinct

ARV (Bible) American (Standard) Revised Version

Arva Co. Cavan, *not* Arvagh

ARWS Associate of the Royal Society of Painters in Water Colours

Aryan Indo-European, *not* -ian

AS Academy of Science, Admiral Superintendent, Advanced Supplementary (level, in education), Angelman syndrome, Anglo-Saxon

AS (Lat. *anno Seleuci*) in the year of Seleucus (era beginning 312/11 BC); formerly also used for *anno salutis*, in the year of salvation, or *anno Salvatoris*, in the year of the Saviour, both equivalent to AD (small caps.)

As arsenic (no point)

As. Asia, -n, -tic

ASA Advertising Standards Authority, Amateur Swimming Association, Associate Member of the Society of Actuaries, Associate of the Society of Actuaries (USA)

asafoetida (med.) an ill-smelling gum resin; *not* ass-, -fetida (US)

Asahi Shimbun a Japanese newspaper

Asante the modern form of **Ashanti**

asap as soon as possible (no points)

Asbjörnsen, Peter Christian (1812–85) Norwegian writer

ascendan/ce *not* -ence; **-cy, -t**; cap. when referring to a specific period of Irish history

ascender (typ.) the top part of letters such as b, d, f, h, k, l

Ascension/ Day (caps., two words), **— Island** S. Atlantic

ascetic austere

Ascham, Roger (1515–68) English writer

ASCII (comput.) American Standard Code for Information Interchange (caps. or small caps.)

ascites (sing. and pl.) abdominal dropsy

Asclepiad a verse metre, *not* Ask-

Asclepius the Greek hero and god of healing, *not* Asklepios (except in specialist contexts); *see also* **Aesculapius**

a/s de (Fr.) *aux soins de,* = **c/o**

ASDIC Anti-Submarine Detection Investigation Committee, used for a form of hydrophone; *later* **Asdic,** *now* officially **sonar**

ASE American Stock Exchange, Associate of the Society of Engineers

ASEAN Association of South East Asian Nations

as follows: (use colon only, *not* :—)

Asgard the heaven of Norse mythology

ASH Action on Smoking and Health

ash Old English letter **æ** also used in phonetic script, Danish, and Norwegian

Ashanti Ghana, *not* -ee; *now also* **Asante**

Ashby de la Zouch Leics. (no hyphens)

Ashgabat the capital of Turkmenistan, *formerly* Poltoratsk in Russ. **Ashkhabad**

Ashkenazi/ a Jew of N. or E. European descent, pl. **-m** (cap.); cf. **Sephardi**

ashlar (archit.) *not* -er

Ashmolean Museum Oxford

Ashtar/oth, -eth in biblical and Semitic use, otherwise *use* **Astarte**

Ashton/-in-Makerfield, -under-Lyne Gr. Manchester (hyphens), *not* -Lyme; **— upon Mersey** Gr. Manchester (no hyphens)

ashtray (one word)

Ash Wednesday first day of Lent (two words)

ASI air-speed indicator, Association soroptimiste internationale

Asian (adj. and noun) of Asia; *not* Asiatic except for e.g. 'Asiatic cholera'

A-side the main side of a gramophone record

asinin/e like an ass, *not* ass-; **-ity**

Asir ('the inaccessible') former name for Saudi Arabia

askance *not* askant

Asklepi/ad *use* **Asclepiad**; **-os** *see* **Asclepius**

a.s.l. above sea level (points)

Aslef Associated Society of Locomotive Engineers and Firemen (one cap.)

Aslib Association of Special Libraries and Information Bureaux (one cap.)

ASM air-to-surface missile

Asnières a Paris suburb

Asola Lombardy, Italy

Asolo Venetia, Italy

asper (Gr.) a rough-breathing mark ('), typographically largely equivalent to the Arab. ʿ*ayn* or Heb. ʿ*ayin* (not ital.)

asperg/e (Fr. f.) asparagus, **-é** (Fr.) sprinkled with (something)

asperges (noun sing.) a sprinkling with blessed water

asphalt *not* ash-, -e

asphodel an immortal flower in Elysium

asphyxia an interruption of breathing

aspic a savoury jelly

aspic (Fr. m.) an asp, a serpent

ASPR Anglo-Saxon Poetic Records

ASR (comput.) answer send and receive

ass a donkey, a stupid person; (US) = arse

ass. assistant

assafoetida *use* asa-

assai (mus.) very

assailant a person who attacks another physically or verbally, *not* -ent

Assam/ NE India, **-ese** (of or related to) a native or the language of Assam

assassin the killer of a political or religious leader (not cap.); (hist.) any of a group of Muslim fanatics sent on murder missions in the time of the Crusades (sometimes cap.), *properly* **Nizari Ismaili**

assegai a spear, *not* assa-

Assembly (Church of Scotland) (cap.) *properly* **General Assembly** (also in other Presbyterian Churches); *see also* **Church Assembly**

assent/er one who assents, **-or** one who subscribes to a nomination paper

Asserbaijan, -i *use* **Azer-**

assert/er one who asserts, **-or** an advocate

assess/able *not* -ible, **-or** *not* -er

ASSET Association of Supervisory Staffs, Executives, and Technicians

assign/ee one to whom a right or property is assigned, **-or** one who assigns

Assiniboine Canada, *not* Assinn-

Assisi Italy

assistant abbr. **ass., asst.**

assize (hist.) a court sitting at intervals in each county of England and Wales to administer civil and criminal law

assizer an officer with oversight of weights and measures; *not* -ser, -sor, -zor

assoc. associat/e, -ion

ASSR (hist.) Autonomous Soviet Socialist Republic

asst. assistant

Assuan *use* **Aswan**

assurance the insurance of life (the technical term); *see also* **life insurance**

assure convince or make certain of; *see also* **ensure; insure**

assymmetry *use* **asy-**

Assyr. Assyrian

AST Atlantic Standard Time

a-starboard (hyphen)

Astarte a Syro-Phoenician goddess; *not* Ashtaroth, -eth

astatine symbol **At**

Asterabad Iran

asterisk a symbol (*); in specialist linguistic use a 'star', so a word is 'starred' *not* 'asterisked'; consequently, 'a *' *not* 'an *'

Asti/ an Italian white wine; **— spumante** a sparkling form of this, from Asti in Piedmont (one cap., not ital.)

ASTMS Association of Scientific, Technical, and Managerial Staffs; *now* part of the **MSF**

astr. astronom/y, -er, -ical

astrakhan lambskin from Astrakhan (not cap.)

astrol. astrolog/y, -er

Astronomer Royal (caps., no hyphen)

astronomical unit a unit of length reckoned as 1.496×10^{11} m; *not* an SI unit (though it may be used with SI units); has no internationally agreed symbol; abbr. **AU**

astrophysic/s (pl. noun, treated as sing.) **-al, -ist** (one word)

AstroTurf (propr.) (one word, two caps.)

Asturias Spain, *not* The —

Asunción Paraguay

ASVA Associate of the Incorporated Society of Valuers and Auctioneers

Aswan Egypt, *not* the many variants

asymmetry *not* ass-

asymptote a line approaching but not meeting a curve

asyndet/on the omission of a connecting word (usually a conjunction), **-ic**

Asyut Egypt

AT (Ger.) *Altes Testament* (the Old Testament)

At astatine (no point)

at. atomic

Atahualpa the last Inca

Atalanta (Gr. myth.) a great huntress

atar *use* **attar**

Atatürk, (Mustapha) Kemal (1881–1938) Turkish statesman, President 1923–38

ATC Air Traffic Control, Air Training Corps

Atchin Sumatra, Indonesia; *use* **Ach-**

ATCL Associate of Trinity College of Music, London

atelier a studio (not ital.)

a tempo (mus.) in time; it indicates that, after a change in time, the previous time must be resumed

Athabasca Sask., Canada; *not* -ka

Athanasi/us, St (d. 373) Greek patriarch, **-an**

atheling a prince, lord, or member of a noble family in Anglo-Saxon England; *not* aeth-, although **æth-** is acceptable

Athenaeum a London club; (ital.) a British literary review, 1828–1921

Athene (Gr. myth.) goddess of wisdom, war, and handicrafts, patron of Athens, in which contexts *use* **Athena**

Atheneum publishers, *not* -ae-

Athol New Zealand; Mass.

Atholl/, Duke of; **—** *also* forest, Sc.

Atholville New Brunswick, Can.

Atl. Atlantic

Atlanta Ga.

ATM automated (*or* automatic) teller machine

atm. atmosphere, atmospheric

atmosphere the gaseous envelope around the Earth and other planets, the pressure exerted by it; abbr. **atm.**

at. no. atomic number

atoll a ring-shaped coral reef surrounding a lagoon

atomize *not* -ise

atonable *not* -eable

ATP adenosine triphosphate

atri/um the hall of a Roman house or a central court in a modern building, pl. **-a**; a cavity in the body, esp. one of two in the heart, pl. **-ums**

Atropos (Gr. myth.) the Fate that cuts the thread of life

ATS Auxiliary Territorial Service (*superseded by* **WRAC**), (Austral.) Amalgamated Television Services

attaché/ pl. **-s** (not ital.)

attar (as of roses) *not* atar, ott-, otto

Attawapiskat a Canadian river

Att. Gen. Attorney General

Attic salt delicate wit (one cap.)

Attila (*c*.406–43) king of the Huns

attitudinize *not* -ise

Attlee, Clement (Richard) (1883–1967) British politician, Prime Minister 1945–51; created earl 1955

attn. for the attention of

atto- (as prefix) 10^{18}, abbr. **a**

attorn (law) to transfer

attorney-at-law (hyphens)

Attorney General (two words) abbr. **AG**, **Att. Gen.**

attractor *not* -er

ATV all-terrain vehicle, Associated Television (*now* **ITV**)

Atwood, Margaret (b. 1939) Canadian writer

Atwood's machine (phys.) *not* Att-

at. wt. atomic weight

AU (US) Actors' Union, angstrom unit, astronomical unit

Au aurum (gold) (no point)

aubade a dawn-piece

AUBC Association of Universities of the British Commonwealth

auberg/e (Fr. f.) inn, **-iste** (m. *or* f.) innkeeper

aubergine the fruit of the eggplant; in the USA the fruit is called eggplant as well

Aubigné dép. Deux-Sèvres, France

Aubigny dép. Nord, France

aubrietia a dwarf perennial, *not* -retia

AUC (**AVC** in classical transcriptions) *anno urbis conditae* (in the year from the building of the city of Rome in 753 BC), also *ab urbe condita* (from the foundation of the city) (small caps.; no points except in Latin composition)

Auchinleck, Field-Marshal Sir Claude (**John Eyre**) (1884–1981) British soldier

Auchnashellach Highland, *use* **Ach-**

au/ contraire (Fr.) on the contrary, **— courant de** fully acquainted with

Audenarde *see* **Oudenarde**

Audi a German make of car

audio/ frequency, — typist (two words)

audio-visual (hyphen, one word in US)

Auditor-General abbr. **Aud.-Gen.**

auditori/um pl. **-ums, -a**

Audubon, John (**James**) (1785–1851) US ornithologist and artist

AUEW/ Amalgamated Union of Engineering Workers, **— (TASS)** Amalgamated Union of Engineering Workers (Technical and Supervisory Section)

au fait (Fr.) thoroughly conversant (not ital.)

Aufklärung (Ger. f.) enlightenment, esp. the 18th-c. intellectual movement

Auflage/ (Ger. f.) edition, impression; pl. **-n** (cap.); abbr. **Aufl.**; note the 'fl' is set as a ligature in Ger.; **unveränderte — reprint, verbesserte und vermehrte —** revised and enlarged edition; *see also* **Ausgabe**

au fond (Fr.) at the bottom; used in Eng. to mean basically, in reality, in fact; cf. **à fond**; **dans le fond**

Aufsteiger (Ger. m.) social climber

auf Wiedersehen (Ger.) till we meet again, goodbye

Aug. August

aug. augmentative

Augean (Gr. myth.) (stables) filthy (cap.)

auger a tool for boring; cf. **augur**

aught anything (cf. **naught**)

au grand sérieux (Fr.) in all seriousness

au gratin browned with cheese etc. (not ital.)

augur (noun) a Roman soothsayer, (verb) foresee, portend; cf. **auger**

August abbr. **Aug.**

Augustan of the Roman Emperor Augustus (63 BC–AD 14); or an era compared to this, most usually the early to mid-18th c. in England

Augustine an Augustinian monk, **St —** (354–430) Bishop of Hippo, **St —** (d. 604) first Archbishop of Canterbury

Augustinian a monk of an order following St Augustine of Hippo

au jus (Fr.) in gravy

auk a diving bird, *not* awk

auld lang syne (caps., quotation marks for song title)

Auld Reekie literally 'Old Smoky', i.e. Edinburgh

aumbry a closed recess in the wall of a church, *not* ambry

Aumerle, Duke of a character in Shakespeare's *Richard II*

au mieux (Fr.) on excellent terms

au naturel in its natural state, plainly cooked

Aung San/ (1914–47) Burmese nationalist leader, **— — Suu Kyi** Burmese political leader, daughter of Aung San

auntie *not* -y; a nickname for the BBC (cap.)

au pair (Fr.) at par, on mutual terms

au pair a person helping with childcare, housework (not ital.)

au pied de la lettre (Fr.) literally

Aurangzeb (1618–1707) Mogul Emperor, *not* the many variants

aurar pl. of **eyrir**

aurea mediocritas (Lat.) the golden mean

aureole a saint's halo, a circle of light; *also* **aureola**; *not* ar-

au reste (Fr.) besides

au revoir till we meet again, goodbye

Aurignacian a flint culture of the palaeolithic period in Europe, following the Mousterian and preceding the Solutrean

Aurigny Fr. for **Alderney**

aurochs an extinct wild ox, ancestor of domestic cattle; *not* urus; cf. **wisent**

auror/a australis (astr.) pl. **-ae australes, -a borealis** pl. **-ae boreales**

aurum gold, symbol (chem.) **Au** (no point)

Aus. Austria, -n

Auschwitz a town and a German concentration camp in Poland in Second World War, in Pol. **Oświęcim**; Poles use the Ger. for the camp and the Pol. for the town *au/ secours* (Fr.) a cry for help, **—** *sérieux* seriously

Ausgabe (Ger. f.) edition (refers to the form, not to a revision), abbr. **Ausg.** (cap.); *see also* **Auflage**, and the compounds *Buch-*; *Pracht-*; *Volks-*

auspicious of good omen, favourable, prosperous; *not* a synonym for notable, significant, important

Aussie Australian; *not* -y, Ossie, Ozzie, or other variants

Austen, Jane (1775–1817) English writer

Austin/ an English form of the name Augustine; **—, Alfred** (1835–1913) Poet Laureate 1896–1913; **—, John Langshaw** (1911–60) English philosopher; **—** Tex.

austral/ southern (not cap.); of Australia or Australasia (e.g. 'Austral English') (cap.); a basic unit of currency in Argentina; pl. **-es** (not cap.)

Australasia abbr. **A'asia**, a collective term, referring either to (*a*) Australia, New Zealand, and the islands of Melanesia, *or* to (*b*) Australia, New Zealand, Fiji, and Western Samoa; **Oceania** includes Micronesia and Polynesia as well

Austral/ia, -ian abbr. **Austral.**

Australian Capital Territory abbr. **ACT**

Australian Labor Party *not* Labour

Austrasia a Frankish kingdom of 6th–8th cc.

Austria abbr. **Aus.**

Austria-Hungary (*but* **Austro-Hungarian**), hyphen *not* en rule, 1867–1918, in Ger. **Österreich-Ungarn**

Austro- combining form of Austrian (e.g. *Austro-Hungarian*) *or* Australian (e.g. *Austro-Asiatic*)

Austronesian a family of *c.*600 languages spoken in the S. Pacific, also called **Malayo-Polynesian**

AUT Association of University Teachers

autarchy absolute sovereignty

autarky self-sufficiency

Auteuil a Paris suburb

auteur/ (Fr. m.) author, also (esp. in cinema) used of a person who controls all aspects of the creative process, hence *-iste*

auth. authentic; author, -ess, -ity, -ized

author refer to oneself in writing as 'I', *not* 'The author'; avoid using *author* or *co-author* as a verb where *write* or *co-write* will serve

author–date system a form of referencing, often called the Harvard system (en rule)

authorize *not* -ise

Authorized Version (of the Bible) (caps.) abbr. **AV**

autis/m a mental condition obstructing response to environment, **-tic**

autobahn/ a German motorway, pl. **-s**, in Ger. **Autobahn/**, pl. **-en** (not ital.)

autochthon/ an original inhabitant, pl. **-s**; **-ous**

autocracy absolute monarchy

autocue (propr.)

auto/-da-fé (Port.) pl. **autos-da-fé**, 'act of the faith', burning of heretic by Inquisition (not ital.); (Sp.) *auto de fe* (ital.)

autogiro an early form of helicopter, *not* -gyro

autolithography (typ.) printing by lithography from stones or plates prepared by the artist personally

automat/on a piece of mechanism with concealed motive power, a person who acts like such a piece; pl. **-a, -ons**

autonomy self-government

autonym a book published under an author's real name

autopista a Spanish motorway (not ital.)

autore (It.) author, abbr. *aut.*

autoroute a French motorway (not ital.)

autostrad/a an Italian motorway, pl. **-e** (not ital.)

autres temps, autres mœurs (Fr.) other times, other manners

AUT(S) Association of University Teachers (Scotland)

autumn (not cap.)

Auvergne (Fr.) *not* The —

Auvers dép. Seine-et-Oise, France

Auverse dép. Maine-et-Loire, France

auxiliary abbr. **aux., auxil.**

Auxiliary Forces (caps.)

N (numismatics) = gold (Lat. *aurum*) (no point)

AV audio-visual, Authorized Version (of the Bible)

a/v *ad valorem*

av. average

avadavat *not* **ama-**

avant/-courier in Fr. m. *-courrier* or *-coureur*, f. *-coureuse* forerunner

avant-gard/e the advanced guard, the innovators; **-ism, -ist**

avant-propos (Fr. m.) preface, pl. same (hyphen)

avaunt (arch.) begone

av. C. (It.) *avanti Cristo* (BC)

avdp. avoirdupois

ave. avenue, average

ave atque vale (Lat.) hail and farewell

Ave Maria (Hail, Mary!) abbr. **AM**

Avenue abbr. **Ave.**

Avenue of the Americas off. name of Sixth Avenue, New York City

average abbr. **av.**

Averroes (1126–98) Spanish-Muslim physician, astronomer, philosopher; *also* **-ës** (though less correct); *also called* **Ibn-Rushd** *or* **the Commentator**

averse, aversion opposed or disinclined: 'he is not averse to grumbling', 'Mary-Jane's aversion to rice pudding'; cf. **adverse**

avertible *not* -able

avertissement (Fr. m.) notice, warning

aviculture the rearing of birds

Avignon dép. Vaucluse, France

a vinculo matrimonii (Lat.) 'from the bond of marriage', full divorce (cf. **a mensa et toro**)

avis au lecteur (Fr.) notice to the reader

avizandum (Sc. law) a judge's consideration of case in private

av. J.-C. (Fr.) *avant Jésus-Christ* (BC)

AVM Air Vice-Marshal

avocad/o pl. **-os**

avocet a bird, *not* -set

Avogadro/, Amedeo (1776–1856) Italian scientist, *not* Avro-; — **constant** (symb. *L*, N_A) 6.022 1367 × 10^{23} mol^{-1}, *not* Avogadro number (no apos.); *but* **Avogadro's hypothesis**

avoirdupois/ (*in full* — **weight**) a system of weights based on a pound of 16 ounces or 7,000 grains, abbr. **avdp.**

à volonté (Fr.) at pleasure, at will

Avon/ a county of England, and name of several English rivers; **Earl of —**

à votre santé (Fr.) (here's) to your health!

avril (Fr. m., not cap.) April

a/w (typ.) artwork

AWACS Airborne Warning And Control System (a long-range radar system for detecting enemy aircraft)

Awdry, Revd W(ilbert Vere) (1911–97) children's author, creator of the 'Railway Series' (Thomas the Tank Engine)

awesome *not* aws-

awhile (adv.) *but* for a while

awing (part. of **awe**) *not* aweing

awk *use* **auk**

awk. awkward

AWOL absent without (official) leave

AWRE Atomic Weapons Research Establishment

ax. axiom

axe *not* ax (US)

axel a jumping movement in skating

ax/is pl. **-es**; (cap., hist.) the German alliance formed in 1939

ay/ yes: 'Ay, ay, sir'; pl. **-es**: 'The ayes have it'

ayah an Indian nursemaid

ayatollah a Shi'ite religious leader in Iran (cap. when used as title)

Aycliffe Dur., 'new town', 1947

aye ever: 'For ever and for aye'

Ayer's Cliff Quebec, Canada (apos.)

Ayers Rock Australian Western Desert (no apos.), in Pitjantjatjara **Uluru**

AYH American Youth Hostels

ʿayin (Heb.) a rough-breathing mark (ʾ *properly* ʿ), typographically largely equivalent to the Arab. ʿayn or Gr. asper (ital.); also expressed as **ayin** (no accent)

Aylesbury Bucks. *See also* **Ail-**

ʿayn (Arab.) a rough-breathing mark (ʾ *properly* ʿ), typographically largely equivalent to the Heb. ʿayin or Gr. asper (ital.); *not* ain

Ayr Strathclyde

Ayr. Ayrshire

Ayre, Point of IoM

Ayub Khan, Muhammad (1907–74) Pakistani soldier and politician, President 1958–69

AZ Arizona (postal abbr.)

az. azure

Azerbaijan/ a province of NW Iran and former Soviet Socialist Republic, **-i** (adj); **-ian** *or* **Azeri** the language, formerly written in the Arabic or (later) Cyrillic alphabet, now in the roman alphabet; *not* Asser-

Azikiwe, (Benjamin) Nnamdi (1904–96) Nigerian leader, President 1963–6

Azilian a transitional period between the palaeolithic and neolithic ages in Europe

Azores in Port. **Açores**, 'Islands' no longer forms part of the name

Azov, Sea of *not* -off, -of

Azrael the Muslim angel of death

AZT azidothymidine, a drug intended for use against the Aids virus

Aztec (a member) of, *or* concerning, a people dominant in Mexico before the Spanish conquest; adj. same, *not* -ian; *see also* **Nahuatl**

Bb

B bel, (mus.) B flat in German system, (chess) bishop, (pencils) black (*see also* **BB**, **BBB**), boron, the second in a series

B. Bachelor, Baron, bass, basso, Bay, Blessed (*Beat/us, -a*), British

b (phys.) barn, (compass) by

b. base, (Heb.) ben, billion, (meteor.) blue sky, book, born; (cricket) bowled, bye; (Arab.) ibn

BA Bachelor of Arts, Booksellers Association, British Academy, British Airways, British America, British Association

Ba barium (no point)

BAA British Airports Authority, British Astronomical Association

Baader–Meinhof Group (en rule, hyphen in Ger.)

Baalbek Syria

baas (Afrik.) master, boss

baaskap (Afrik.) domination, esp. of non-whites by whites

Ba'ath an Iraqi and Syrian political party, in Arab. *Ba'ṯ*; a loose transliteration for non-technical contexts is **Baath**

Babbitt/ by Sinclair Lewis, 1922 (roman in allusive use, as character's name); **-ry**

babel not cap., except in **Tower of Babel**

babiroussa a wild hog; *not* baby-, -russa

babu an Indian title of respect, *not* -boo except in hist. use

Babygro (propr.) an all-in-one garment for babies

babysitter (one word)

BAC British Aerospace Corporation

baccalaureate the university degree of bachelor (not ital., no accent); *baccalauréat* (Fr. m.) the Fr. equivalent of A levels (ital., accent)

baccarat a card game; in Fr. m. *baccara*

Bacchanalia/ the festival of Bacchus, strictly pl. but used in Eng. as sing.; **-n** (not cap.) riotous or drunken (revelry)

bacchant/ a male or female follower of Bacchus, **-e** female only

Bach,/ German musical family, more than fifty in number in seven generations, of whom the greatest was — **Johann Sebastian** (1685–1750) (of the fifth generation) composer of orchestral, instrumental, and choral music; also important were his father's cousin, — **Johann Christoph** (1642–1703) composer; and of J.S.B.'s twenty children, — **Wilhelm Friedemann** (1710–84); — **Carl Philipp Emanuel**, usually referred to as **C. P. E.** (1714–88), developer of sonata and symphony form; — **Johann Christoph Friedrich** (1732–95); — **Johann Christian** (1735–82) 'the English Bach'

Bacharach/ a small (wine-producing) Rhineland town, —**, Burt** (b. 1929) US composer

Bachelier ès/ lettres (Fr.) Bachelor of Letters, abbr. **B. ès L.**; — — *sciences* Bachelor of Science, abbr. **B. ès S.** (no hyphens)

Bachelor/ abbr. **B. — of Agriculture**, abbr. (US) **B.Agr.**; — — **Architecture**, abbr. **B.Arch.**; — — **Arts**, abbr. **BA**; — — **Art of Obstetrics**, abbr. **BAO**; — — **Canon and Civil Law**, abbr. **BUJ**; — — **Civil Engineering**, abbr. **BCE**; — — **Civil Law**, abbr. **BCL**; — — **Commerce**, abbr. **B.Com.**; — — **Dental Surgery**, abbr. **BDS**, **B.Ch.D.**; — — **Divinity**, abbr. **BD**; — — **Education**, abbr. **B.Ed.**; — — **Engineering**, abbr. **BE**, **B.Eng.**, (Dublin) **B.A.I. Dub.**; — — **Law**, abbr. **BL**; — — **Laws**, abbr. **B LL** (no point, thin space); — — **Letters**, abbr. **B.Litt.**, **Litt.B.**; in Fr. **B. ès L.**; — — **Medicine**, abbr. **BM, MB**; — — **Metallurgy**, abbr. **B.Met.**; — — **Mining Engineering**, abbr. **BME**; — — **Music**, abbr. **B.Mus., Mus.B.**; — — **Obstetrics**, abbr. **BAO**; — — **Philosophy**, abbr. **B.Phil.**; — — **Science**, abbr. **B.Sc.**, (US) **BS**, in Fr. **B. ès S.**; — — **Surgery**, abbr. **BC, B.Ch.**, **BS, Ch.B.**; — — **Technical Science**, abbr. **B.Sc. Tech.**; — — **Theology**, abbr. **B.Th.**

bacill/us pl. **-i** (not ital.)

back (typ.) the margin of a book nearest the binding; *see also* **margins**

backbench(er) (Parliament) (one word)

Backhuysen, Ludolf (1631–1708) Dutch painter, *not* Bakhuisen

backing up (typ.) printing on the second side

backstreet (one word)

back-up (noun, hyphen, one word in US)

backwoodsman (one word)

baclava *use* **baklava**

Bacon,/ Sir Francis (*often incorrectly* Lord) (1561–1626) Baron Verulam and Viscount St Albans; — **Francis** (1909–92) Irish painter; — **Roger** (*c.*1214–94) English philosopher, scientist, and Franciscan friar

Baconian pertaining to Roger Bacon, *or* to Sir Francis Bacon, *or* to the theory that Sir Francis Bacon wrote Shakespeare's plays

bacshish *use* **baksheesh**

bacteri/um a microscopic organism, pl. **-a**; **-cide**

bade see **bid**

Baden-Baden Germany (hyphen)

Baden-Powell,/ Robert (Stephenson Smyth), Baron (1857–1941) founder of Boy Scouts, 1908, and, with his sister — **Agnes** (1858–1945), Girl Guides, 1910 (hyphen)

Baden-Württemberg a German *Land* (hyphen) (two ts); *see also* **Württemberg**

badinage humorous ridicule (not ital.)

badlands (geog.) (one word, cap, as place name)

Baedeker, Karl (1801–59) guidebook publisher

Baffin/ Bay, — Island, NE America: *not* -ns, -n's

BAFU Bakers', Food, and Allied Workers' Union

bagarre (Fr. m.) scuffle, brawl

Bagehot, Walter (1826–77) English economist and writer

bagel *not* beigel

Baghdad Iraq, *not* Bagd-

Bagnères/ de Bigorre dép. Hautes-Pyrénées, France; **— de Luchon** dép. Haute-Garonne, France

bagnio/ a bathing-house, oriental prison, brothel; pl. **-s**

Bagnoles dép. Orne, France

Bagnols dép. Gard, France

bagpip/e(s), -er (one word)

B.Agr. (US) Bachelor of Agriculture

Baha'/i a religion initiated by Bahá'u'lláh (1817–92), **-ism**

Baham/as W. Indies, indep. 1973; **-ian**

Bahasa Indonesia the official language of Indonesia

Bahrain islands, Persian Gulf; *not* -ein

Baiae Naples

B.A.I. Dub. Bachelor of Engineering, University of Dublin

baignoire (Fr. f.) a theatre box at stalls level

Baikal, Lake Russia

bail (noun) a security for the appearance of prisoner, a cross-piece over stumps in cricket, (hist.) the outer line of fortifications; (verb) deliver goods in trust, secure release on bail, (naut.) scoop water out of; cf. **bale**

bailee (law) one to whom goods are entrusted for a purpose

bailer (naut.) one who bails water out, a scoop used for bailing; cf. **bailor; bale**

bailey the outer wall of a castle; **Old Bailey** London's Central Criminal Court

bailie/ (Sc.) an alderman; **-ry** the jurisdiction of a bailie, *not* -iary

bailiwick the office or jurisdiction of a bailiff

Baillie, Joanna (1762–1851) Scottish poet

Baillière Tindall Ltd publishers (accent)

bailor (law) one who entrusts goods to a bailee; cf. **bailer**

Baily's/ Magazine, — Directory (apos.)

bain-marie a double boiler, pl. **bains-**

Bairam/ either of two annual Muslim festivals; **Greater —** falls at the end of the Islamic year, **Lesser —** falls at the end of Ramadan

Baireuth Bavaria, *use* Bay-

Bairut Lebanon, *use* **Beirut**

Bakelite (propr.)

Bakewell/ tart *properly* **— pudding**

baklava a Turkish pastry, *not* bac-

baksheesh (Arab., Turk.) a gratuity or alms, *not* the many variants (not ital.)

bal. balance

balaclava (in full **— helmet**) *not* -klava (not cap.)

balalaika a Russian stringed instrument

balanceable *not* -cable

Balboa, Vasco Núñez de (1475–1519) Spanish explorer and discoverer of the Pacific Ocean

Balbriggan Co. Dublin, also knitted cotton goods

baldachin *not* -quin

bale/ (noun) a package, abbr. **bl.**, pl. **bls.**; (arch.) destruction, woe; (verb) make into a package; **— out** escape from an aircraft by parachute; cf. **bail**

Bâle Fr. for **Basle**

Balearic Islands a group of Spanish islands in the Mediterranean

Balfour,/ Baron, of Burleigh; **— Baron, of Inchrye**; **— Earl of** three distinct titles

Bali/ Indonesia, **-nese**

Baliol an Anglo-Norman family; *see also* **Balliol**

balk *use* **baulk** (except in US)

Balkan Mountains Bulgaria

Balkhan Mountains Transcaspia

Ball/aarat Victoria, Australia; *use* -arat

ballade a medieval French poem, also its imitation (esp. in the 19th c.)

Ballantine,/ James (1808–77) Scottish artist and poet; **— William** (1812–86) English serjeant-at-law

Ballantyne/, James (1772–1833) and **—, John** (1774–1821), Sir W. Scott's printers and publishers; **— Press** founded by them in 1796; **—, R(obert) M(ichael)** (1825–94) Scottish writer for boys

Ballarat Victoria, Australia; *not* -aarat

ballet dancer (two words)

ball game (two words)

Balliol College Oxford; *see also* **Baliol**

ballistic/ (adj.), **-s** (pl., usually treated as sing.) the science (two ls)

ballon/ d'essai (Fr. m.) an experiment to see how a new policy etc. will be received, pl. **-s** *d'essai*

ballot/, -ed, -ing (one *t*)

ballpark/ (one word), **— figure** an approximately correct number

ballroom (one word)

Ballsbridge Co. Dublin (one word)

ballyhoo commotion, sensational publicity

Balnibarbi the country of the 'projectors' in Swift's *Gulliver's Travels*

baloney humbug, blather, drivel, *not* boloney; a type of sausage, *use* **bologna**

BALPA British Air Line Pilots' Association

Baluchi a native of Baluchistan; *not* Be-, Bi-

baluster an upright supporting a rail, commonly of stone and outdoors, the whole structure being a **balustrade**; cf. **banister**

Balzac/, Honoré (self-styled) **de** (1799–1850) French writer, **-ian**; **—, Jean Louis Guez de** (1596–1654) French writer

Bamberg Germany, *not* -burg

bambin/o (It. m.) baby, pl. **-i**; f. **-a** pl. **-e**

Bamburgh Northumb.

banal commonplace

Banaras Hind. for **Benares**

Band (Ger. m.) a volume, pl. **Bände**; abbr. **Bd.**, pl. **Bde.**

bandanna a handkerchief, *not* -ana

Banda Oriental (hist.) Uruguay

Bandaranaike, Sirimavo Ratwatte Dias (b. 1916) Sinhalese stateswoman, Prime Minister of Sri Lanka 1960–5, 1970–7, and since 1994

b. & b. bed and breakfast

bande/ dessinée (Fr. f.) a comic strip, pl. **-s dessinées**, abbr. **BD**

banderole *not* banderol

bandolero a Spanish brigand

bandolier a belt for cartridges; *not* -oleer, -alier

Bandung Indonesia, *not* Bandoeng

bang an Indian hemp, *use* **bh-**

Bangalore Mysore, India

Bangkok Thailand, *not* Bank-

Bangladesh 'Land of the Bengalis', formerly E. Pakistan (one word)

banian *use* **banyan**

banister an upright supporting a rail, commonly of wood, used indoors on a staircase, the whole structure being **banisters** (pl.); *not* bannister; cf. **baluster**

banjo/ pl. **-s**

bank abbr. **bk.**

banking abbr. **bkg.**

banknote (one word)

Bankok *use* **Bang-**

bank paper a thin, strong paper

banlieue (Fr. f.) precinct, suburb

banneret/ (law) a knight commanding his own troops in battle, *or* a knight made on the field of battle; **-te** a small banner

bannister *use* **bani-**

banns *not* bans

banquet/, -ed, -ing (one *t*)

banquette a raised way behind a firing-rampart, a seat; (S. US) a pavement

banshee a wailing female spirit, in Ir. **bean sidhe**

Bantu designating a large group of Cent., E., and S. African native peoples and languages

banyan an Indian fig tree, *not* -ian

Banyoles Catalonia, Spain

banzai a Japanese battle cry; a greeting used to the Japanese emperor (not ital.)

BAO Bachelor of Art of Obstetrics

BAOR British Army of the Rhine

baptism the religious rite symbolizing admission to the Christian Church; cf. **christening**

Baptist abbr. **Bapt.**

baptistery *not* -try

baptize *not* -ise, abbr. **bap.**

Bar (law) called to the (cap.); a unit of pressure, 10^5 newtons per sq. m., approx. one atmosphere (not cap.)

bar. barleycorn; baromet/er, -ric; barrel

Barbad/os *not* -oes; abbr. **Barb.**, adj. **-ian**

barbarize *not* -ise

Barbary N. Africa

barbecu/e *not* -que; **-es, -ed, -ing**

barbed wire (two words), *not* barbwire (US)

barberry a shrub of genus *Berberis*, *not* ber-, -ery

barbet a tropical bird

barbette a gun platform

Barbirolli, Sir John (1899–1970) English conductor

barbitone a sedative drug, *not* barbital (US)

barbiturate any derivate of barbituric acid

Barbour (propr.)

barcarole a Venetian gondolier's song, in Fr. **barcarolle**

B.Arch. Bachelor of Architecture

Barclays Bank plc. (no apos.)

Barclays de Zoete Wedd a British financial company, abbr. **BZW**

bard (hist.) a Celtic minstrel; the winner of a prize for Welsh verse at an Eisteddfod; a poet (not cap.); **the Bard (of Avon)** Shakespeare (cap.)

Bareilly Uttar Pradesh, India; *not* -eli

Barenboim, Daniel (b. 1942) Argentinian-born Israeli musician

Barents Sea N. of Norway and Russia; *not* -'s, -'z

bargain/er a haggler; **-or** (law) the seller

bargepole (one word)

Bar Harbor Me.

Baring-Gould, Revd Sabine (1834–1924) English author (hyphen)

barite (US) = **barytes**

baritone (mus.) *not* bary- (except for Gr. accent)

barium symbol **Ba**

bark a vessel (arch., poet.), in the technical sense *use* **barque**

barkentine *use* **barquen-** (except in US)

Barkston Lincs., N. Yorks.

barleycorn (one word) abbr. **bar.**

bar/maid, -man (one word)

Barmecide (one who offers) illusory benefits, *not* -acide

bar mitzvah the Jewish initiation rite for boys; *see also* **bat mitzvah**

Barmston Humberside

barn (phys.) a unit of area, abbr. **b**

Barnaby Bright St Barnabas' Day, 11 June; the longest day in the Old Style calendar

Barnard, Dr Christiaan (b. 1922) S. African surgeon

Barnardo, Dr Thomas John (1845–1905) British philanthropist

Barnstable Mass.

Barnstaple Devon

baro/graph a recording barometer; **-gram** the record; **-logy** science of weight; **-meter, -metric**, abbr. **bar.**

baron member of the lowest order of British nobility; cap. with name (*but* **Lord** more common); lower case with a foreign name (*but* cap. in Ger.); abbr. **B.**

baron*/** (Fr.) Baron, f. ***-ne (not cap.)

baron and feme (law) husband and wife regarded as one

baronet/ a member of the lowest hereditary titled British order; cap. with name; abbr. **Bt.**; **-age** baronets collectively, or a book about them; **-cy** the patent or rank of baronet

Barons Court London (no apos.)

baroque (not cap., not ital.) highly ornate style, esp. of architecture, music, and other arts, of the 17th and 18th cc.; cap. when followed by 'age', 'era', or when this is to be understood

barouche a four-wheeled carriage, *not* baru-

barque a vessel, *not* bark (except in poet. senses)

barquentine a three-masted vessel with foremast only square-rigged and remaining masts fore-and-aft rigged; *not* -antine, barke- (US)

barr. barrels, barrister

barrac/uda a large and voracious tropical marine fish of the family *Sphyraenidae*, **-outa** only with reference to *Thyrsites atun* (Austral. and NZ)

barrator (law) a malicious litigant; *not* -ater, -etor

barratry (marine law) a master's or crew's fraud or negligence, (law) vexatious litigation, (hist.) trade in the sale of Church or State appointments

Barrault, Jean-Louis (1910–94) French actor, director, producer

barré a method of using a finger to raise the pitch of a (guitar) chord (not ital., in rock and pop music no accent)

barrel/, -s abbr. **bar., barr., bl., bls.**

barrel/led, -ling (one *l* in US)

barrico/ a small cask, pl. **-es**

Barrie, Sir James Matthew (1860–1937) Scottish novelist and playwright

barrister abbr. **barr.**

Barrow-in-Furness Cumbria (hyphens)

Bart. Baronet, *use* **Bt.**

bartender (one word)

Barth,/ Heinrich (1821–65) German explorer; **— John** (b. 1930) US writer; **— Karl** (1886–1968) Swiss theologian

Barthes, Roland (1915–80) French writer and critic

Bartholomew Day 24 Aug. (caps., two words for London local terminology *but* **St Bartholomew's Day** for the massacre, 1572)

Bartók, Béla (1881–1945) Hungarian composer; in Hung. **Bartók Béla** (surname and given name transposed)

Bartolommeo, Fra (1475–1517) Italian painter

Bartolozzi, Francesco (1727–1813) Italian engraver

Bart's St Bartholomew's Hospital, London

Baruch (Apocr.) not to be abbreviated except in narrow measure or marginal notation

baruche *use* **barou-**

barytes a mineral form of barium sulphate, *not* barite (US)

barytone *use* **bari-** except for the Greek accent

bas bleu (Fr. m.) a bluestocking

base abbr. **b.**

baseball US national game, played by two teams of nine; the ball used in it

baseboard (US) = **skirting board**

Basel Ger. for **Basle**

bashaw *use* **pasha**

Bashi-Bazouk (hist.) a Turkish mercenary of the 19th c. (hyphen)

Bashkirtseff, Marie K. *properly* **Mariya Konstantinovna Bashkirtseva** (1860–84) Russian diarist

BASIC (comput.) Beginners' All-Purpose Symbolic Instruction Code

Basic English (two caps.) a simplified form of English proposed by C. K. Ogden, 1929

Basildon Essex, 'new town', 1949

basinet a light steel headpiece, *not* bass-

bas/is pl. **-es**

Baskerville, John (1706–75) typefounder and printer, designer of Baskerville type

Basle Switzerland; in Fr. **Bâle**, Ger. **Basel**; the trad. Eng. form was **Basel** until the 19th c., when **Basle** replaced it; now being replaced by **Basel**

Basque (of or relating to) one or more members of a people of the Western Pyrenees, or their language (cap.); a close-fitting bodice (not cap.)

Basra Iraq, *not* -ah

bas-relief *not* bass-

Bas-Rhin a dép. of France (hyphen)

bass the lowest part in music, the common perch, *not* -e

bassinet a (wicker) cradle, perambulator; *not* basi-, -ette, berceaunette (except in Fr.)

basso/ (mus.) abbr. **B.**, **— profundo** (It. mus.) the lowest male voice

basso-rilievo (It.) bas-relief, pl. **bassi-rilievi** (hyphen)

bastaard (S. Afr.) a person of mixed white and black parentage, whether legitimate or not (not ital.)

bastardize *not* -ise

bastard/ **size** (typ.) a non-standard size, **— title** *see* **half-title**

Bastille (Fr. f.) a Paris district and prison

bastille a fortified tower, *not* -ile

bastinado/ *not* basto-, pl. **-s**

Basuto/, **-land** S. Africa, *now* **Lesotho**

Batak an Austronesian language of Sumatra, Indonesia, also called **Toba Batak**

bateau/ (Fr. m.) a boat, *not* batt-; pl. **-x**

Bath: et Well: the signature of the Bishop of Bath and Wells (two colons)

Bath/ **brick, — bun, — chair, — chap** (not chop), **— Oliver, — stone** (one cap., two words)

bath/os an anticlimax through an unintentional shift from sublime to ridiculous mood, adj. **-etic**; cf. **pathos**

bat mitzvah the Jewish initiation rite for girls; *see also* **bar mitzvah**

baton a music conductor's stick, a twirler's rod

Batswana (sing. and pl.) inhabitant(s) of Botswana

battalion abbr. **battn., bn.**

battels an account for provisions etc. in Oxford colleges

batter (typ.) a damaged letter

batterie de cuisine (Fr. f.) a set of cooking utensils

battery abbr. **batt., bty.**

battle/axe, -cruiser (one word)

battle cry (two words)

battle/dress, -field, -ground, -ship (one word)

Batumi Georgia; *not* -oum, -um

baud (comput.) abbr. **Bd**, pl. same

Baudelaire, Charles (1821–67) French poet, *not* Beau-

Bauhaus a German school of architectural design 1919–33, founded by Walter Gropius

baulk *not* balk (US)

Bavaria/, **-n** abbr. **Bav.**, in Ger. **Bayern**

bawbee (Sc.) a halfpenny, *not* bau-

bayadère a Hindu dancing girl

Bayard, Pierre de Terrail, Chevalier de (1475–1524) 'The knight without fear and without reproach'

Bayern Ger. for **Bavaria**

Bayeux Tapestry a linen embroidery depicting the invasion of England, 1066

bayonet/, **-ed, -ing**; **— fitting, — plug** (elec.) two words

Bayreuth Bavaria, *not* Bai-; *see also* **Beirut**

Bayrût Arab. for **Beirut**

bazaar (one z, two as)

BB (pencils) double black, *also* **2B**

BBB (pencils) treble black, *also* **3B**

BBC British Broadcasting Corporation

bbl. barrels (esp. of oil)

BC Bachelor of Surgery, Board of Control, British Columbia (Canada)

BC before Christ, to be placed *after* the numerals: 250 BC, the second century BC (small caps.); *see also* **BCE**

b.c. (meteor.) partly cloudy sky

BCA Bureau of Current Affairs

B.C.B.G. (Fr. abbr.) **bon chic bon genre** (points in Fr.)

BCC British Copyright Council, British Council of Churches, British Crown Colony

BCD (comput.) binary coded decimal

BCE Bachelor of Civil Engineering

BCE before Common Era (small caps.); *see also* **ACE; BC; CE**

BCG bacillus of Calmette and Guérin (anti-TB inoculation)

B.Ch., B.Chir. Bachelor of Surgery

B.Ch.D., BDS Bachelor of Dental Surgery

BCL Bachelor of Civil Law

B.Com., B.Comm. Bachelor of Commerce

B.Com.Sc. Batchelor of Commercial Science

BCP Book of Common Prayer

BD Bachelor of Divinity, *bande dessinée*

Bd. baud; (Ger.) *Band* (a volume)

bd. board, bond, bound

BDA British Dental Association

Bde. (Ger.) *Bände* (volumes)

Bde. Maj. Brigade Major

bdg. binding

bdl. bundle, pl. **bdls.**

Bdr. Bombardier

BDS Bachelor of Dental Surgery (*also* **B.Ch.D.**), Bomb Disposal Squad

bds. (bound in) boards

BE Bachelor of Engineering

Be beryllium (no point)

b.e. bill of exchange

BEA British Epilepsy Association, British Esperanto Association, (hist.) British European Airways

Beach-la-mar (one cap.) *use* **Bislama**

beard (typ.) the space between the bottom of the **x-height** and the upper edge of the shank

beargarden (one word)

Béarnaise a rich white sauce (cap.)

bearskin a military cap (one word)

beastings *use* **bee-**

beasts of the/ chase (law) buck, doe, fox, marten, roe; — — — **forest** (law) boar, hare, hart, hind, wolf; — — — **warren** (law) cony and hare; **beasts of venery** (law) = **beasts of the forest**

beatae memoriae (Lat.) of blessed memory, abbr. **BM**

Beata/ Maria, or — *Virgo* (Lat.) the Blessed Virgin, abbr. **BM**, **BV** (no points); *see also* **BMV**; **BVM**

beat generation (not cap.)

Beatles, the a pop group, 1960–70

beat music (not cap.)

beatnik a member or follower of the beat generation

beau/ pl. **-x** (not ital.)

Beauclerc the sobriquet of Henry I

Beauclerk family name of the Duke of St Albans

Beaudelaire *use* **Baud-**

beau-fils (Fr. m.) son-in-law, stepson; (two words) beautiful son

Beaufort scale of wind force (one cap.)

beau/ idéal the highest type of excellence or beauty, *not* beautiful ideal (not ital.); pl. **-x idéals**

beauidealize *not* -ise (one word)

Beaujolais a red or white burgundy

Beaulieu Hants.

beau monde the fashionable world

Beaune a burgundy

beau-père (Fr. m.) father-in-law, stepfather; (two words) beautiful father

Beauvoir, Simone de (1908–86) French author

beaux arts (Fr. pl. m.) (noun) fine arts, (attrib.) relating to the rules and conventions of the École des Beaux-Arts in Paris (later, Académie des Beaux-Arts); therefore *beaux-arts* is historically acceptable

beaux/ esprits (Fr. pl. m.) brilliant wits; sing. *bel esprit*; — *yeux* good looks

bebop (mus.) (one word)

beccafico/ a small edible Italian bird, *not* beca-; pl. **-s**

béchamel (Fr. cook.) a white sauce named after Béchamel, steward of Louis XIV (not cap.)

bêche-de-mer the sea slug, a Chinese delicacy

Bechstein,/ Friedrich Wilhelm Carl (1826–1900) German pianoforte maker, — **Johann Matthäus** (1757–1822) German naturalist

Bechuana/, -land *see* **Botswana**

Becket, Thomas (?1118–70) Archbishop (one t); *not* à Becket

Beckett, Samuel (1906–89) Irish writer

Becquerel/, a French family of physicists: —, **Antoine César** (1788–1878) father of —, **Alexandre Edmond** (1820–91) father of —, **Antoine Henri** (1852–1908) discoverer of radioactive — **rays** *now* **gamma rays**

becquerel a unit of radioactivity, abbr. **Bq**

bed (typ.) the part of the press on which the forme lies

B.Ed. Bachelor of Education

Bedaw/een, -i, -in *use* **Bedouin**

bed/bug, -chamber, -clothes (one word)

Beddgelert Gwynedd, *not* Beth-

bedel in Oxford the official form of beadle, at Cambridge and London **bedell**

Bedfordshire abbr. **Beds.**

Bedouin a desert Arab, *not* the many variants; pl. same; in specialist usage, *prefer* sing. **Bedu** and pl. **Beduin**

Bed/owy *use* **Bedouin**

bed/pan, -post, -ridden, -room (one word)

Beds. Bedfordshire

bed/sitter (one word), *but* **-sittingroom** (one hyphen)

bed/sore, -time (one word)

Beduin *see* **Bedouin**

Beeb (preceded by **the** *or* **Auntie**) (Brit. colloq.) the BBC

beefsteak (one word)

beehive (one word)

beer glass (two words)

beerhouse (law) where beer is sold to be drunk on or off the premises

beer mat (two words)

beershop (law) where beer is sold to be drunk off the premises

beestings the first milk from a mammal (pl. also treated as sing.); *not* bea-, bie-

beeswax (noun and verb)

Beethoven, Ludwig van *not* von (1770–1827) German composer; divide **Beet-hoven**

beeves pl. of beef, *not* beets (US)

BEF British Expeditionary Force

be/fall *not* -fal, past **-fell**

Beggar's Opera by John Gay, 1728; *not* -s'

Begin, Menachem (1913–92) Israeli politician, Prime Minister 1977–84

begum a Muslim lady of high rank, in the Indian subcontinent; (cap.) the title of a married Muslim woman, equivalent to **Mrs**

behemoth a biblical animal (Book of Job), thought to be the hippopotamus

Behmenism concerning the doctrines of the German mystic Jakob Boehme

Behn, Aphra (1640–89) English novelist and dramatist

behoof (noun) benefit

behove (verb) be incumbent on, *not* behoove (US)

Behring, Emil von (1854–1917) German bacteriologist

Behring/ Isle, — Sea, — Strait *use* **Ber-**

beigel *use* **bag-**

beignet (Fr. m.) a fritter

Beijing (Pinyin) **Peking**

Beinn Bhuidhe near Inveraray, Strathclyde; cf. **Ben Buie**

Beirut Lebanon, *not* Ba-, Bai-, Beyrout(h); in Arab. **Bayrūt**; *see also* **Bayreuth**

bel a unit of sound pressure levels equivalent to ten decibels (**decibel** is more often used), abbr. **B**

Belalp Switzerland (one word)

Bel and the Dragon (Apocr.) abbr. **Bel & Dr.**

Belarus formerly **Belorussia**, *properly* **Belarus´**

bel canto (not ital.)

beldam (arch.) a hag, *not* -e

Belém Brazil, *formerly* Pará

bel/ esprit (Fr. m.) a brilliant wit, pl. *beaux esprits*; *— étage* the first floor, *not* belle

belge (Fr.) Belgian (not cap., unless used as a noun)

Belgic of the ancient Belgae of N. Gaul *or* of the Low Countries

Belgique (Fr. f.) Belgium

Belg/ium, -ian, -ic abbr. **Belg.**

Belgrade Serbia, capital of the former Yugoslavia; in Serbo-Croat **Beograd**

believable *not* -eable

bélinogramme (Fr. Canadian m.) a cablegram or fax, abbr. *bélino*

Belisha beacon (one cap.)

Belitung Indonesia, *not* Billiton

Belize/ Cent. America, *formerly* British Honduras; **-an**

Bell,/ Acton, — Currer, — Ellis *see* **Brontë**

belladonna (bot.) deadly nightshade (one word)

belle (not ital.)

belle/ amie (Fr. f.) female friend; *-de-jour* (bot.) convolvulus; *-de-nuit* (bot.) marvel of Peru

Belleek Co. Armagh, Co. Fermanagh, N. Ireland; also name of a type of china

belle/ époque (Fr. f.) before 1914; *-fille* (hyphen) daughter-in-law, stepdaughter; (two words) beautiful girl

Belle-Île-en-Mer dép. Morbihan, France (hyphens)

Belle Isle, Straits of between Newfoundland and Labrador

Belleisle Co. Fermanagh

belle/ laide (Fr. f.) fascinatingly ugly woman; *-mère* (hyphen) mother-in-law, stepmother; (two words) beautiful mother

belles-lettres literature, pl. but treated as sing. (hyphen)

belletris/t one devoted to belles-lettres, **-m, -tic** *not* -ettr-

Bell Island off NE coast of Newfoundland

Bell Rock North Sea; *also* **Inchcape Rock**

bell-wether *not* -weather (hyphen)

Bel/oochee, -uchi *use* **Baluchi**

Belorussia/ (White Russia) a former Soviet Socialist Republic, *not* Bye-; *now* **Belarus´, -n** of or relating to the country, language, or inhabitants of Belarus´

Beltane an ancient Celtic festival celebrated on May Day

Belvedere Kent; Calif.

belvedere (It.) a raised building, *not* belvi- (not ital.)

Belvidere Ill.

Belvoir Castle Leics.

BEM British Empire Medal

Benares India, officially **Vārānasī**; in Hind. **Banaras**

Benavente y Martínez, Jacinto (1866–1954) Spanish playwright and critic

Ben Buie Mull, Strathclyde; cf. **Beinn Bhuidhe**

benchmark (one word)

Ben Day (typ.) a mechanical method for producing shading and stippling effects

Benedic a canticle from Psalm 103

Benedicite the 'Song of the Three Children' (Apocr.), as canticle

benedick a confirmed bachelor newly married, *not* -ict (from a character in Shakespeare's *Much Ado about Nothing*)

Benedictus the Canticle of Zacharias (Luke 1: 68 ff.), or a choral passage in the mass, beginning *Benedictus qui venit* (Matt. 21: 9)

benefactor *not* -er

beneficent *not* -ficient

benefit/, -ed, -ing (one *t*)

Benelux Belgium, the Netherlands, Luxembourg

Beneš, Edvard (1884–1948) Prime Minister of Czechoslovakia 1921–2; President 1935–8, 1939–45 (in exile), 1946–8

Benet an English form of the name Benedict; used of St Benedict and institutions bearing his name, e.g. St Benet's Church, St Benet's Hall

Benét,/ Stephen Vincent (1898–1943) and — **William Rose** (1886–1950) his brother, US poets

Bene't Street Cambridge

ben for (Dan.) = **lbw**, abbr. **bf** (no points)

B.Eng. Bachelor of Engineering

Bengali/ (of) person born in, language of, Bengal; *not* -ee; pl. **-s**; abbr. **Beng.**

Benghazi Libya, *not* -gasi

Ben-Gurion, David (1886–1973) Israeli statesman, Prime Minister 1948–53, 1955–63

Ben-Hur historical novel by Lew (Lewis) Wallace, 1880; Hollywood films, 1925, 1959 (hyphen)

Ben/ Lawers Tayside, — **Macdhui** Grampian

Bennet/ the family name of the Earl of Tankerville; a family in Austen's *Pride and Prejudice*; —, **John** (*c*.1600) English madrigalist

Bennett,/ (Enoch) Arnold (1867–1931) English writer; — **Richard Rodney** (b. 1936) and — **William Sterndale** (1816–75) English composers

benth/al of ocean depths exceeding 6,000 feet; **-os** the flora and fauna of the sea bottom; cf. **plankton**; adj. **-ic** *not* -onic

Bentham,/ George (1800–84) botanist; — **Jeremy** (1748–1832) English political philosopher

ben trovato (It.) well invented, characteristic if not true

Ben Venue Central (two words)

ben venuto (It.) welcome

Ben/ Vorlich, — Vrackie Tayside

Benzedrine (med.) propr. term for an inhalant or nerve stimulant, *not* -in (cap.)

benzene a liquid obtained from coal tar, petroleum, etc.

benzine a mixture of liquid hydrocarbons obtained from petroleum

benzoin an aromatic resin from various E. Asian trees

benzol crude benzene, *not* -ole

benzoline benzine

benzoyl, benzyl two different chemical radicals

Beowulf an Anglo-Saxon epic

bequeather a testator

Béranger, Pierre Jean de (1780–1857) French poet

Berber (of or relating to) (a member of) the indigenous mainly Muslim Caucasian peoples of N. Africa, or their languages; in Arab. *barbar*

berberry *use* **bar-**

berceau (Fr. m.) a cradle

berceaunette *use* **bassinet** (except in Fr.)

berceuse (Fr. f.) a lullaby

Beretta an Italian arms manufacturer, *not* Bir-

Berg/ (Ger. m.) a mountain, pl. **-e** (cap.)

berg (Afrik.) a mountain

Bergamask a native of Bergamo, Lombardy; **bergamasque** a rustic dance attributed to the Bergamasks

bergamot a tree of citrus family, a type of pear or herb; *not* burg-

Bergerac/ dép. Dordogne, France; wine made there; —, **Savinien Cyrano de** (1619–55) French writer

Bergman,/ Ingmar (b. 1918) Swedish film and theatre director; — **Ingrid** (1917–82) Swedish actress

bergschrund a crevasse or gap at the head of a glacier or névé (not cap.)

Bergson, Henri (1859–1941) French philosopher

beriberi a tropical disease, *not* -ria (one word)

Bering, Vitus Jonassen (1680–1741) Danish navigator

Bering/ Isle, — Sea, — Strait *not* Beh-, -ings

berk a fool, *not* burk

Berkeleian of the philosopher Berkeley

Berkeley/ Calif.; —, **George, Bishop** (1685–1753) Irish philosopher; —, **Sir Lennox** (1903–89) English composer

berkelium symbol **Bk**

Berkhamsted Herts.

Berks. Berkshire

Bermudian a person from Bermuda, *not* -dan

Bernard, Claude (1813–78) French physiologist

Bernardine Cistercian, from St Bernard of Clairvaux (1091–1153)

Berne/ a Swiss canton and town, in Ger. **Bern**; — **Convention** 1886, with later revisions; deals with copyright; each of the more than 110 member states extends benefit of its own copyright law to works by citizens of other member states; *see also* **Universal Copyright Convention**

Berners,/ Gerald Hugh Tyrwhitt-Wilson, Baron (1883–1950) English composer; — **John Bourchier, Baron** (1467–1533) English translator; — **Dame Juliana** wrote *Boke of St Albans*, first edn. 1486

Bernhardt, Sarah, b. **Henriette Rosine Bernhard** (1845–1923) French actress

ber/noose, -nouse *use* **burnous** in general use

Bernoulli a family of Swiss mathematicians, *not* -illi

bersaglier/e (It.) a rifleman, pl. **-i**

Berthelot, Pierre Eugène Marcellin (1827–1907) French chemist and statesman

Berthollet, comte Claude Louis (1748–1822) French chemist

Berwickshire a former county in Scotland

Berwick-upon-Tweed Northumb. (hyphens)

beryllium symbol **Be**

Berzelius, Jöns Jakob, baron (1779–1848) Swedish chemist

B. ès A. *now* **B. ès L.**

Besançon dép. Doubs, France

beseech (past and past part.) **besought**

B. ès L. (Fr.) *Bachelier ès lettres* (Bachelor of Letters)

beso/ las manos (Sp.) 'I kiss the hands' (frequently said or written), **—** *los pies* 'I kiss the feet'

B. ès S. (Fr.) *Bachelier ès sciences* (Bachelor of Science)

Bessarabia (hist.) a district in Moldavia and Ukraine, ceded by Romania to USSR 1940

Bessbrook Co. Armagh

Bessemer process in steel manufacturing (one cap.)

Besses o' th' Barn Gr. Manchester

bestialize *not* -ise

beta/ the second letter of the Gr. alphabet (*B*, *β*); **— blocker, — coefficient, — decay, — particle, — ray** (two words)

betatron an apparatus for accelerating electrons

betel the leaf of a betel pepper, chewed in the East and Far East

Betelgeuse (astr.) a red star in Orion, *not* -x

betel nut a misnomer for the areca nut, chewed with betel

bête/ noire (Fr. f.) one's pet aversion, *not noir*; pl. *-s noires*

bethel a Nonconformist chapel (not cap.)

bêtise (Fr. f.) a foolish or ill-timed remark or action, stupidity

Betjeman, Sir John (1906–84) English poet and writer on architecture, appointed Poet Laureate 1972

betony (bot.) *not* bett-

better one who bets, *not* -or

Betws-y-coed Gwynedd (hyphens)

BeV (abbr.) billion (10⁹) electron volts, *also called* **GeV**

Bevan, Aneurin (1897–1960) Welsh politician who introduced the National Health Service 1948; *see also* **Bevin**

bevel/, -led, -ling (one *l* in US)

Beveridge, William Henry, Baron (1879–1963) English economist

Beverley Humberside

Beverly Miss.

Beverly Hills Calif.

Bevin, Ernest (1881–1951) English politician; *see also* **Bevan**

bevy the proper word for a company of ladies, larks, maidens, quails, or roe deer; also in general use

Bewick, Thomas (1753–1828) English engraver

Bexleyheath London (one word)

bey (hist.) the title of a provincial governor in the Ottoman Empire; **Bey of Tunis** (hist.) the ruler of Tunisia (cap.)

beylik the jurisdiction of a bey, *not* -ic

Beyrout/, -h Lebanon, *use* **Beirut**

bezahlt (Ger.) paid, abbr. **bez.**

bezant a gold coin first struck at Byzantium; a gold roundel in heraldry; *not* by-

beziehungsweise (Ger.) respectively, abbr. **bzw.**

bezüglich (Ger.) with reference to, abbr. **bez.**

BF Bachelor of Forestry, Banque de France, Belgian franc

bf (Dan.) *ben for* = **lbw**

b.f. bankruptcy fee, beer firkin, bloody fool, (typ.) boldface, brought forward

BFA Bachelor of Fine Arts

BFBS British and Foreign Bible Society

BFI British Film Institute

BFPO British Forces' Post Office

BGC bank giro credit

Bhagavadgītā a philosophical dialogue in the Hindu epic *Mahābhārata*

B'ham Birmingham

bhang Indian hemp, *not* ba-

bharal a Himalayan wild sheep, *not* burhel

BHC British High Commissioner

b.h.p. brake horsepower (points)

BHS British Home Stores

Bhutan/ a protectorate of the Republic of India since 1949, **-ese**; **-i** the official language of Bhutan, *properly* **Dzonghka**

Bhutto,/ Benazir (b. 1953) Pakistani politician, Prime Minister 1988–90, 1993–6; daughter of **— Zulfikar Ali** (1928–79) Pakistani politician, President 1971–3, Prime Minister 1973–7

Bi bismuth (no point)

Biafra the name taken by the provinces seceding from eastern Nigeria 1967–70

biannual twice every year, every six months, cf. **biennial**

bias/, -ed, -ing

Bib. Bible

bib. biblical

bibl. *bibliotheca* (library)

Bible abbr. **Bib.**

Biblia Pauperum a medieval 'Bible of the poor', in pictures (caps.)

biblical (not cap.) abbr. **bib.**

bibliograph/er, -ic, -ical, -y abbr. **bibliog.**

bibliomancy foretelling the future by the analysis of a randomly chosen passage from a book, esp. the Bible

bibliopeg/y bookbinding as a fine art, **-ist**

bibliophile *not* -phil

bibliopole a seller of (esp. rare) books

biblio/theca (Lat.) a library, *-thécaire* (Fr. m., f.) a librarian, *-thèque* (Fr. f.) a library

Bibliothek/ (Ger. f.) a library, *-ar* (Ger. m.) a librarian (caps.)

Bibliothèque nationale/ Paris, *now* — — de France

bicenten/ary a 200th anniversary; **-nial** of or relating to a bicentenary, (esp. US) = **bicentenary**

Bickleigh Devon

Bickley Ches., London, N. Yorks.

bid past **bid** *or* **bade**, past part. **bid** *or* **bidden**; *use* bid for the past and past part. in context of auctions and card-playing; and *bade, bidden* for archaic meanings 'command', 'invite', 'utter', or 'proclaim'

Biedermeier a German bourgeois artistic and literary style 1815–48

biennial every two years; cf. **biannual**

bienni/um a two-year period, pl. **-ums**

bienséance (Fr. f.) propriety

bienvenu/ (Fr.) f. **-e** (a) welcome

Bierce, Ambrose (Gwinnett) (1842–?1914) US journalist and author

BIF British Industries Fair

biff/é (Fr.) f. **-ée** cancelled

Big Dipper, the (US astron.) = **the Great Bear**

Bigelow,/ Erastus Brigham (1814–79) US inventor and industrialist, **— John** (1817–1911) US journalist and diplomat

Biglow Papers, The anti-slavery poems 1848 and 1857–61, by James Russell Lowell

bigot/, -ed (one *t*)

bijou/ (Fr. m.) a jewel, trinket; in the general sense of something small and elegant, not ital.; pl. *-x*

bijouterie (Fr. f.) jewellery, a jeweller's shop

Bilbao Spain

bilberry (*Vaccinium myrtillus*), *not* bill-

bilbo/ a Spanish sword or rapier, pl. **-s**

bilboes pl. fetters

Bildungsroman (Ger. m.) a novel of early life and development

bill (parl.) (cap. when part of title)

Billericay Essex

billet/, -ed, -ing

billet-doux a love letter, pl. **billets-doux** (hyphens, not ital.)

billiard/ ball, — cue, — table, etc., *not* billiards- (two words)

billion in the USA and now largely in Britain, a thousand million (10^9), or what formerly was a **milliard**; in France and Germany, a million million (10^{12}). Be careful to avoid ambiguity, particularly when writing for a transatlantic audience; pl. *billions* used only for general sense of a very large number ('billions of years'); abbr. **bn.**; *see also* **trillion**

Billiton Indonesia, *use* **Belitung**

bill of/ exchange abbr. **b.e.**; — — **lading** abbr. **b.l.**; — — **sale** abbr. **b.s.**

Biloxi Miss.

biltong (Afrik.) sun-dried meat

Biluchi *use* **Bal-**

BIM British Institute of Management

bimanal *not* bimanous

bimbo/ pl. **-s,** *not* -es

bimetall/ic, -ism, -ist

bimillenary (designating) a period of 2,000 years; a 2,000th anniversary

bi-monthly avoid as ambiguous; *prefer* (adj. or adv.) fortnightly, semi-monthly or (adv.) twice a month, every two months, as appropriate

bindery a bookbinder's establishment

binnacle (naut.) a compass stand

binocle a field glass

binocular/ (adj.) for two eyes, **-s** (pl. noun) field or opera glasses

Binstead IoW

Binsted Hants., W. Sussex

Binyon, Laurence (1869–1943) English poet

biochemist/, -ry (one word)

biocoenos/is an association of or relationship between different organisms forming a community, pl. **-es**; *not* -cenosis (US)

biodegradable (one word)

biograph/er, -ic, -ical, -y abbr. **biog.**

biolog/y, -ical abbr. **biol.**

bio/mathematics, -physics (one word)

Bipont/, -ine books printed at **Bipontium** (Zweibrücken), Germany

bird bath (two words)

bird/cage, -seed (one word)

bird's-eye view (one hyphen)

birdsong (one word)

bird table (two words)

biretta a square cap worn by (RC) clergymen, *not* bar-, ber-

Birmingham/ abbr. **Birm., B'ham; — Small Arms** abbr. **BSA**

Birnam Tayside, immortalized in Shakespeare's *Macbeth*

Biro (Brit. propr.) a kind of ballpoint pen (cap.)

Birstall Leics., W. Yorks.

birth/ certificate, — control (two words)
birthmark (one word)
birthplace abbr. **bpl.**
birth rate (two words)
birthright (one word)
BIS Bank for International Settlements
bis (Fr., It., Lat.) twice, encore; in references, space from preceding figure: '12 *bis*'
bis. bissextile
Biscayan pertaining to Biscay, Spain; Basque; abbr. **Bisc.**
bis dat qui cito dat (Lat.) he gives twice who gives quickly
bise (Fr. f.) dry, cold N. wind in Switzerland, S. France, etc.
BISF British Iron and Steel Federation
Bishop abbr. **Bp.,** (chess) **B**
Bishopbriggs Strathclyde
Bishop *in partibus infidelium* a RC bishop taking title from an ancient see situated 'in territory of unbelievers', *now* termed **Titular Bishop**
Bishop Rock a lighthouse, Scilly Isles
Bishop's/ Castle Shropshire, — **Cleeve** Glos., — **Frome** Hereford, — **Lydeard** Som. (apos.)
bishop's signature usually consists of Christian name and diocese (John Birmingham); for special spellings and punctuation, *see* individual entries
Bishop's Stortford Herts. (apos.)
Bishopsteignton Devon (one word)
Bishopston Avon, W. Glam.
Bishopstone Bucks., Hereford, Kent, E. Sussex, Wilts.
Bishop's Waltham Hants. (apos.)
Bishopthorpe the residence of the Archbishop of York (one word)
Bishopton Dur., N. Yorks., Strathclyde
bisk *use* **bisque**
Bislama the pidgin English of W. Pacific, also called **Beach-la-mar**
Bismarck, Karl Otto Eduard Leopold, Fürst von (1815–98) German statesman, *not* -ark
bismillah (Arab.) 'in the name of God', *not* biz-
bismuth symbol **Bi**
bison either of two wild oxen of the genus *Bison*, native to Europe (*B. bonasus*) or to N. America (*B. bison*) (pl. same). Where the latter inhabits the plains rather than forests, it is usually called **buffalo** (pl. same)
bisque in tennis, croquet, golf; unglazed white porcelain; rich soup (not ital.)
bissextile (noun and adj.) leap year, abbr. **bis.**
bistoury a surgeon's scalpel
bistro a small restaurant (not ital.)
bit (US) 12½ cents (used only in multiples of two); (comput.) binary digit; *see also* **byte**

bitts (naut., pl.) a pair of posts on deck for fastening cables etc.
bitumin/ize, -ous
bivouac/, -ked, -king
biweekly avoid as ambiguous; prefer (adj. or adv.) 'semi-weekly' *or* 'fortnightly', (adv.) 'twice a week' *or* 'every two weeks', as appropriate
bizarre, bizarrerie (not ital.)
Bizet, Georges (1838–75) French composer
Bjørnson, Bjørnstjerne (1832–1910) Norwegian writer
Bk berkelium (no point)
bk. bank, book
bkg. banking
bkt. basket, pl. **bkts.**
BL Bachelor of Law, Bachelor of Letters, Bachelor of Literature, (hist.) British Leyland, British Library
bl. bale, barrel; pl. **bls.**
b.l. bill of lading
black (not cap.) preferred term for people having dark-coloured skin, except for those from the Indian subcontinent, who are usually referred to generally as *Asian*; avoid *coloured*, *Negress*, and *Negro* (cap.) except as a specific ethnologic term; *African-American* is commonly used to describe a black person in the USA
black (typ.) a space inked in
Blackburn: signature of the Bishop of Blackburn (colon)
blackcock *see* **black game**
Black/foot (of or relating to) (a member of) a Native American tribe, or the language of this people; pl. **-feet**
Blackfriars London
black game (two words) black grouse; m. **blackcock** (one word), f. **greyhen**
black letter (typ.) a general term for Gothic or Old English (q.v.) type; *see also* **Fraktur**
blacklist (noun and verb, one word)
Black Maria a prison van (two words, caps.)
Blackmoor Hants.
Blackmore/ Essex, Shropshire; **—, Richard Doddridge** (1825–1900) English writer
blackout (adj., noun, one word)
black out (verb, two words)
Blackrock Co. Cork, Corn., Co. Dublin, Gwent, Co. Louth
Blackrod Gr. Manchester
Black Rod abbr. for 'Gentleman Usher of the Black Rod'
blackshirt/ a Fascist, **-ed** (one word)
blad (print.) a booklet of sample pages from a forthcoming book, used for promotion purposes
blaeberry Sc. and N. Eng. for **bilberry**

Blaenau Ffestiniog Gwynedd (no hyphen), *but* the **Festiniog Railway**

blague*/** (Fr. f.) humbug; **-*ur (m.) hoaxer, pretentious talker

Blairadam Fife (one word)

Blair Atholl Tayside (caps., no hyphen)

Blairgowrie Tayside (one word)

Blairs College Aberdeen (no apos.)

blameable *not* blamable (US)

blancmange (cook.) (one word, not ital.)

Bland, Edith *see* **Nesbit**

Blandford, Viscount title of eldest son of the Duke of Marlborough

blanket/, -ed, -ing (one *t*)

blanquette (Fr. cook. f.) white meat in white sauce

Blantyre Strathclyde, Malawi

blas/é bored through overfamiliarity or a surfeit of pleasure (not ital.); f. **-ée** (not usually used in English)

blastula/ pl. **-e** (US pl. -s)

blather/, -skite *not* blether, -skate

Blatherwycke Northants.; *not* -wyck, -wick

bldg. building, pl. **bldgs.**

bleed (typ.) an illustration going to the trimmed edge

bleed (bind.) overcut the margins and mutilate the printing

Blenheim Orange a type of golden-coloured apple (two caps.)

Blériot, Louis (1872–1936) French aviator, first to cross the English Channel in an aeroplane, 1909

blesbok (Afrik.) an antelope, *not* -buck

blessed *not* blest, blessèd (except in poet.)

bletherskate *use* **blatherskite**

Blighty England *or* home

blind (noun, US) = **hide**

blind/ (typ.) a paragraph mark with solid loop, a pilcrow; symbol ¶; **— blocking** *or* **— tooling** (bind.);͏ *see also* **blocking**

Blindheim Ger. for **Blenheim**

B.Lit. Bachelor of Literature

B.Litt. *Baccalaureus Literarum* (Bachelor of Letters)

blitzkrieg (not ital.) a swift, intense military campaign; **blitz** (colloq. Eng.) any violent attack; **the Blitz** the German air raids on London in 1940 (cap.)

Blixen, Karen (**Christentze**), Baroness Blixen-Finecke (1885–1962) Danish novelist and short-story writer; born Karen Dinesen; pseud. **Isak Dinesen**

blk. (typ.) block, -s

BLL Bachelor of Laws (no point, thin space following 'B')

bloc (Fr.) a combination of nations or parties

Bloch, Ernest (1880–1959) Swiss-American composer

block (typ.) a letterpress printing plate for an illustration, (brass) a stamp to impress book-cover; (US) the area between streets in a town or suburb, often used as a measure of distance

Block, Maurice (1816–1901) French economist

blocking/ (bind.) impressing lettering or a design into the case of a book; **blind —** without foil or colour, **gold —** with gold foil

Bloemfontein Orange Free State, S. Africa

Blok, Aleksandr (**Aleksandrovich**) (1880–1921) Russian poet

blond/ fair-complexioned, light-coloured (of hair); f. **-e** (not ital.)

blood/ bank, — cell, — count (two words)

blood group (two words) antigens are designated by capital letters, sometimes combined with lower-case letter(s), such as A, B, AB, O, Rh; while defined as groups, blood is described as types, e.g. type A, *not* group A; genes encoding these antigens are represented by the same letters printed in italic; antibodies corresponding to antigens are prefixed by 'anti-', e.g. anti-A

blood pressure (two words)

blood sport (two words)

bloodstain/, -ed (one word)

bloodstream (one word)

blood supply (two words)

bloody hand (her.) the armorial device of a baronet

Bloody Mary (two caps.)

Bloomsbury Group (two caps.)

Blot on the 'Scutcheon, A a tragedy in blank verse by R. Browning, 1843

blottesque painting with blotted touches (not ital.)

blow past part. **blown**, *but* **blowed** in the sense of 'cursed' ('Well I'm blowed')

blow-up (noun) an enlarged picture (hyphen, one word in US)

blow up (verb) enlarge (two words)

blowzy coarse-looking, *not* blou-, -sy

Blubberhouses N. Yorks. (one word)

Blücher, Gebhard Leberecht von (1742–1819) German field marshal

Blue a person who has represented a university in a sport, esp. Oxford or Cambridge, *also* **Full Blue, Half Blue** (caps.)

bluebell (one word)

Blue Book a parliamentary or Privy Council report (two words, two caps.); cf. **Green Paper**; **White Paper**

blueing *use* **bluing**

blueish *use* **bluish**

bluejacket a RN sailor (one word)

Bluemantle one of four pursuivants of the English College of Arms

blueprint/ a photographic print, **-ing** this process (one word)

blues, the (mus.) (a piece of) melancholic music, usually in 12-bar sequence (pl. same); depression

bluestocking *but* **Blue Stocking/ Circle, — — Ladies, — — Society**

bluey bluelike

blu/ing, -ish *not* blue-

Blundellsands Merseyside (one word)

blurb a résumé of a book, printed on the jacket

Blu-Tack (propr.)

Blut und Eisen (Ger.) blood and iron

Blyth Northumb.

Blyth Bridge Borders

Blythebridge Staffs.

BM Bachelor of Medicine, Bachelor of Music, *Beata Maria* (the Blessed Virgin), *beatae memoriae* (of blessed memory), benchmark, British Museum

BMA British Medical Association

BME Bachelor of Mining Engineering

B.Met. Bachelor of Metallurgy

BMJ *British Medical Journal*

BMR (med.) basal metabolic rate

B.Mus. Bachelor of Music

BMV *Beata Maria Virgo* (Blessed Virgin Mary)

BMW Bayerische Motorenwerke

BMX organized bicycle racing on a dirt track, esp. for youngsters; abbr. of bicycle motocross

bn. battalion, billion

B'nai B'rith sons of covenant, a Jewish fraternity (two apos.)

BNB British National Bibliography

BNC Brasenose College, Oxford

BO body odour

b.o. box office, branch office, broker's order, brought over, buyer's option

BOA British Optical Association, British Olympic Association

Boabdil the last Moorish king of Granada 1482–92 (d. *c.*1533)

Boadicea a fierce woman; *use* **Boudicca** for the historical figure

Boanerges sing. or pl., loud preacher(s)

boarding/ house, — school (two words)

Board of Trade (hist.) abbr. **B.o.T., B. of T.**, absorbed in **Department of Trade and Industry** 1970

boat although usually small, a *boat* can be of any size; a *ship* is a sea-going vessel capable

of carrying smaller craft. The Royal Navy classes submarines as *boats*

boatswain contr. and pron. **bo's'n** *or* **bosun**

boatyard (one word)

Bobadil a braggart, from Bobadill in Jonson's *Every Man in his Humour*

bobby pin (US) = **hairpin**, *but* **hairpin turn** in both countries

bobby socks (cotton) ankle socks *but* **bobby-soxer** (hist.) for a teenage girl

bobolink a N. American songbird

bobsleigh (one word), *not* bobsled (except in US)

bobwhite the American quail

bocage the representation of silvan scenery in ceramics (not ital.)

Boccaccio, Giovanni (1313–75) Italian writer (four *c*s)

Boccherini, Luigi (1743–1850) Italian composer

Boche a German, esp. a soldier of the First World War (cap.)

BOD biochemical oxygen demand

Bod Tibetan for **Tibet**

bodega a cellar or shop selling wine and food, esp. in a Sp.-speaking area (not ital.)

Bodensee Ger. for **Lake Constance**

Bodhisattva in Mahayana Buddhism and Hinduism, a person able to reach nirvana

bodhrán a shallow one-sided Irish drum (not ital.)

bodh tree *use* **bo tree**

Bodicote Oxon.

Bodleian Library abbr. **Bod. Lib., Bodl., Bodley**

Bodoni, Giambattista (1740–1813) Italian printer and punch-cutter, designer of Bodoni type

body (typ.) the measurement from front to back of the shank of a piece of type; in the Anglo-American system 12 pt. = 0.166 in.; *see also* **Didot**

body blow (two words)

body/builder, -guard (one word)

Boehme, Jakob (1575–1624) German mystic philosopher

Boeotia/ a district of central Greece, **-n** stupid

Boerhaave, Herman (1668–1738) Dutch naturalist

Boethius, Anicius (470–525) Roman statesman and philosopher

bœuf (Fr. m.) beef, bull

B. of T. Board of Trade

bogey/ in golf, ghost; pl. **-s**; *not* bogy

bogie a wheeled undercarriage

Bogota NJ

Bogotá Colombia, S. America

bogy *use* **-ey**

Bohême (Fr. f.) Bohemia (the territory)

bohème (Fr. m., f.) bohemian person, (f.) collective noun for non-traditional artists

Bohemian/ (a native) of Bohemia (cap.); socially unconventional person, **-ism** (not cap.)

bohémien/ (Fr.) f. *-ne* Bohemian, Gypsy

Bohr,/ Niels (Hendrik David) (1885–1962) and his son — **Aage** (b. 1922) Danish physicists

Boïeldieu, François Adrien (1775–1834) French composer

boilermaker (one word)

boiler/ room, — **suit** (two words)

boiling point (two words) abbr. **BP, b.p.**

Bokhara river, NSW, Australia; *see also* **Bu-**

bokmål the literary language of Norway, *formerly* **riksmål**, which is now sometimes used to denote a more conservative form of it (not cap.)

boldface type heavy, **as this**, abbr. **b.f.**

Boldizsár, Iván (b. 1912) Hungarian writer

bolero/ a Spanish dance, a woman's short jacket; pl. **-s**

Boleyn, Anne (1507–36) second wife of Henry VIII of England

bolivar a Venezuelan monetary unit

Bolívar, Simón (1783–1830) S. American patriot

Bolivia/, -n abbr. **Bol.**

Böll, Heinrich (Theodor) (1917–85) German writer

Bologna Italy, in Lat. **Bononia**; adj. **Bolognese**, *but* **spaghetti bolognese**

bolometer a radiation measurer

boloney humbug, *use* **bal-**; a type of sausage, *use* **bologna**

Bolshevik an advocate of proletarian dictatorship by soviets; a member of the majority group of the Russian Social Democratic Party, later the Communist Party, opp. to **Menshevik**

bolshie uncooperative

bolts (bind.) the three outer edges of a folded sheet before trimming

Boltzmann constant (phys.) symbol *k*

bolus/ a large pill, soft ball of chewed food, pl. **-es**

bomb (colloq. noun) a large sum of money or a resounding success in British slang, but a disastrous failure in US slang

Bombardier cap. as title, abbr. **Bdr.**

Bombay India, in Maratha and properly **Mumbai**

bombazine a fabric; *not* -basine, -bazeen, -bycine

bombe (Fr. cook. f.) a conical confection, often frozen

bona/ fide (Lat.) genuine(ly), — **fides** good faith (no accent, not ital.)

Bonaparte a Corsican family, *not* Buonaparte

bona/ peritura (Lat.) perishable goods, — *vacantia* (law) unclaimed goods

bon-bon/ a kind of sweet (one word in US), **-nière** a box for sweets (not ital.)

bon chic bon genre (Fr.) (of a person) well dressed, well bred; abbr. **B.C.B.G.**

bon/-chrétien a pear, pl. **-s-chrétiens**

bond abbr. **bd.**

bondholder (one word)

bond paper a hard, strong paper

Bonduca *use* **Boudicca**

Bo'ness (originally **Borrowstounness**) Central Scotland (apos.); *see also* **Bowness**

Boney a sobriquet of Napoleon; cf. **bony**

bon/ goût (Fr. m.) good taste; — *gré, mal gré*, whether one likes or not

Bonheur, Rosa (1822–99) French painter

bonhomie geniality, good nature

bonhomme (Fr. m.) pleasant fellow, friar

Bonhomme, Jacques a personification of the French peasant

bonhomous full of bonhomie (not ital.)

bonjour (Fr. m.) good day (one word)

bon marché (Fr.) a cheap shop, cheap (two words)

bon/ mot a witticism, pl. **-s mots** (two words, not ital.)

bonne (Fr. f.) a maid

bonne/ bouche (Fr.) a dainty morsel, pl. *-s bouches*; — *foi* good faith; — *fortune* success, pl. *-s fortunes*; — *grâce* gracefulness, pl. *-s grâces*

bonnet/, -ed, -ing (one *t*)

bonnet rouge (Fr. m.) a Republican's cap

Bononia (Lat.) Bologna, Italy

bonsai (Jap.) a dwarfed tree or shrub

bonsoir (Fr. m.) good evening, goodnight (one word)

bontebok (Afrik.) a pied antelope, *not* -buck

bon ton (Fr. m.) good style

bon vivant/ one fond of luxurious food (no hyphen, not ital.), pl. **-s**; the feminine, **bonne vivante**, is not in French usage

bon viveur a pseudo-Fr. substitute for **bon vivant** (not in French usage)

bon voyage! pleasant journey!

bony of or like bone, *not* -ey; cf. **Boney**

boob tube (sl.) a woman's close-fitting, strapless top; (US sl., usually preceded by **the**) television (two words)

Booerhave *see* **Boerhaave**

boogie/, -d, -ing, -s; -woogie (hyphen)

book abbr. **bk.,** pl. **bks.**

bookbind/er, -ing (one word)

bookcase a cabinet with shelves for books (one word)

book case (print.) an outer covering for a book (two words)

bookend (one word)

bookkeep/er, -ing (one word)

bookmak/er, -ing (one word)

bookmark/, -er (one word)

bookmobile (US) = **mobile library**

Book-of-the-Month Club (US) (hyphens)

bookplate (one word)

book-rest (hyphen)

books, titles of when cited, to be in italic; *but* series titles roman, no quote marks

book/seller, -shop, -stall (one word)

Booksellers Association, abbr. **BA**

books of Scripture (typ.) not to be italic, nor quoted; for abbrs. *see* separate entries

book trim (bind.) standard trim is approx. 3 mm off head, foredge, and tail margins

bookwork (one word)

Boole/, George (1815–64) English logician and mathematician, **-an**

Boone, Daniel (1735–1820) American explorer and colonizer

bootee a small (e.g. baby's) boot, *not* -ie

Boötes (astr.) a northern constellation containing Arcturus

booze (to) drink; *not* -se, cf. **bouse**

Bophuthatswana a former black homeland, S. Africa

bor. borough

Borak, Al the winged horse on which Muhammad, in a vision, ascended to heaven

Bordeaux/ dép. Gironde, France; a claret or any wine of Bordeaux; — **mixture** of lime and copper sulphate, to kill fungus and insect parasites on plants

border (typ.) an ornament

bordereau. (Fr. m.) a memorandum, docket

borderland (one word)

Borders a region of Scotland

bordure (her.) a border round the edge of a shield

Boreas (Gr. myth.) the god of the north wind

Borehamwood Herts.

Borges, Jorge Luis (1899–1986) Argentinian writer

Borghese an Italian family

Borgia,/ Cesare (1476–1507), — **Lucrezia** (1480–1519), — **Rodrigo** (1431–1503)

born/ of child, with reference to birth, abbr. **b.**; **-e** carried, also of birth when 'by' (with name of mother) follows

born/é (Fr.) f. **-ée** narrow-minded

Borodin, Aleksandr (**Porfirevich**) (1834–87) Russian composer and chemist

boron symbol **B**

borough abbr. **bor.**

borscht a Russian soup, *not* bortsch; in Russ. *borshch*

Borstal (hist.) an institution for reformative training (cap.); *now* called detention centre, young offender institution, or youth custody centre, although **borstal** (not cap.) remains as a slang term to describe any of these

borzoi/ a Russian wolfhound, pl. **-s**

bosbok Afrik. for **bushbuck**

Boscán de Almogáver, Juan (*c.*1487–1542) Italian-born Spanish poet

Bosch, Hieronymus (?1450–1516) Dutch painter

bo's'n, bosun contr. of **boatswain**

Bosnia-Hercegovina a republic of the former Yugoslavia, in Serbo-Croat **Bosna i Hercegovina**

Bosporus strait separating European and Asian Turkey, *not* Bosph-

Bossuet, Jacques Bénigne (1627–1704) French bishop and writer

Boswellize write a laudatory biography (cap.)

B.o.T. Board of Trade

botanize *not* -ise

Botany merino wool, esp. from Australia (cap.)

botan/y, -ical, -ist abbr. **bot.**; genera, species, and varieties to be ital., all other divisions roman: order, family, cultivar

botfly (one word), *not* -tt-

bothy (Sc.) a hut, *not* -ie

bo tree the sacred tree of India, *not* bodh —

Botswana S. African rep. *formerly* Bechuanaland

Botticelli, Sandro (1445–1510) Florentine painter

bottle bank (two words)

bottle/-brush, -feed, -fed, -green (hyphens)

bottle/neck, -nose dolphin (one word)

Boucher de Perthes, Jacques (1788–1868) French archaeologist

Boucicault, Dion (1822–90) Irish playwright

Boudicca (d. AD 61) queen of the Iceni; the name is reconstructed as **Boudikā** in British, **Boudicca** in Tacitus' Latin, and miscopied as **Bonduca**; *see also* **Boadicea**

boudoir (not ital.)

bouffant puffed out, as a dress (not ital.)

bougainvillea a tropical plant

Bouguereau, William Adolphe (1825–1905) French painter

bouillabaisse a thick fish soup (not ital.)

bouilli (Fr. m.) stewed meat (ital.)

bouillon broth (not ital.)

boul. boulevard

Boule a legislative council in an ancient Greek city state

boule a French game akin to bowls (not ital.)

boule, boulle (inlay) *use* **buhl**

boulevard/ abbr. **boul.**; **-ier** a 'man about town'

boulevers/**é** (Fr.) f. **-ée** overturned, **-ement** (m.) a violent inversion

Boulez, Pierre (b. 1925) French composer

Boulogne déps. Haute-Garonne, Pas-de-Calais, France

bounceable *not* -cable

bouncy *not* bouncey

bound abbr. **bd.**

bouquetin the ibex

bouquinist a second-hand bookseller, (Fr. m.) *bouquiniste*

bourgeois/ (Fr.) f. **-e** one of the middle class, **-ie** the middle class (not ital.)

Bourn Cambs.

bourn a stream, (arch.) a limit; *not* -ne

Bourne Lincs.

Bournemouth Dorset

Bournville Birmingham

bourrée an old lively dance, the music for this (not ital.)

bourse a foreign money-market, esp. in Paris

bouse (naut.) haul, *not* -wse; cf. **booze**; **bowser**

boustrophedon written from left to right and right to left on alternate lines, esp. in Gr. or Etruscan inscriptions

boutonnière a spray of flowers worn in a buttonhole (accent, not ital.)

Boutros-Ghali, Boutros (b. 1922) Egyptian diplomat and politician

bouts-rimés rhymed endings

Bouvet Island (Norw.) Antarctic Ocean

bowdlerize expurgate, from **Dr Thomas Bowdler** (1754–1825) (not cap.)

bowled (cricket) abbr. **b.**

Bowness Cumbria; *see also* **Bo'ness**

bowser a tanker used for fuelling aircraft etc.; cf. **booze**; **bouse**

Boxing Day the first weekday after Christmas Day (caps.)

box/ number; **— office** abbr. **b.o.** (two words)

box/room, -wood (one word)

boyar (hist.) a member of the old aristocracy in Russia

boycott exclude from society or business (not cap.), from **Capt. Charles C. Boycott** (1832–97)

boyfriend (one word)

Boy Scout *now* **Scout**

BP boiling point, British Petroleum, British Pharmacopoeia

BP before present (calibrated) (small caps.), to be placed *after* the numerals; *but note* **bp** before present (uncalibrated) (lower case)

Bp. Bishop

b.p. below proof, bills payable, blood pressure, boiling point

BPC British Pharmaceutical Codex

B.Phil. Bachelor of Philosophy

b.p.i. (comput.) bits (*see* **bit**) per inch

BPIF British Printing Industries Federation

bpl. birthplace

Bq becquerel

BR (hist.) British Rail, *formerly* — Railways

Br bromine (no point)

Br. British, Brother (monastic title)

bra formerly common colloquialism and now the usual term for **brassiere** (no point)

'Brabançonne, La' the Belgian national anthem

bracket/, -ed, -ing

Bradford: the signature of the Bishop of Bradford (colon)

Braggadochio a character in Spenser's *Faerie Queene*

braggadocio empty boasting (not ital.)

Brahe, Tycho (1546–1601) Danish astronomer

Brahma the supreme Hindu god (not ital.)

brahma/, -putra an Asian domestic fowl (not cap.)

Brahman/ a member of the highest Hindu caste, whose members are traditionally eligible for the priesthood; pl. **-s**; adj. **-ical** (cap.); *not* Brahmin

Brahmaputra a river flowing through Tibet, India, and Bangladesh

Brahmi one of the two oldest alphabets in the Indian subcontinent; cf. **Kharoshthi**

Brahmin/ (US) a socially or intellectually superior person; pl. **-s**; *not* Brahman

Brahmoism a reformed theistic Hinduism

brail haul up

Braille signs composed of raised dots replacing letters, for the blind (cap.)

Braine, John (1922–86) English novelist

braise (cook.) *not* -ze; cf. **braze**

brake/ (for wheel, a large vehicle, etc.) *not* break, **— horsepower** (two words)

Br. Am. British America(n)

Bramah/, Ernest (1867–1942) English writer, **—, Joseph** (1749–1814) English inventor of **— lock** etc.

brand new *not* bran

Brandt, Willy (1913–92) German statesman, Chancellor of W. Germany 1969–74

Brandywine a battle of the American War of Independence, 1777

brant goose *use* **brent-** (except in US)

Brantôme, Pierre de Bourdeille, Seigneur de (1540–1614) French writer

Brasenose College Oxford

Brasília new capital of Brazil, 1960

brass/, (binder's) (typ.) a die for blocking book cases, pl. **-es; — rule** (typ.) for printing simple borders or lines between columns of type

brassard a badge worn on the arm

brasserie a beer garden, licensed restaurant; *brasserie* (Fr. f.) *also* a brewery

brassie a golf club with a brass sole, *not* -y

brassiere a woman's undergarment supporting the breasts, a **bra** (no accent)

brassière/ (Fr. f.) (baby's) vest or undershirt, (Fr. Can. f.) bra; **— *de sauvetage*** life jacket; cf. *soutien-gorge*

bratticing (archit.) open carved work, (coal-mining) wooden shaft-lining or screen

Brauneberger a white wine

Braunschweig Ger. for **Brunswick**

brav/al (It.) 'well done!' (to a woman); **-o** (to a man)

bravo/ a desperado, pl. **-es**; a cry of 'well done!', pl. **-s**

braze to solder; *not* -ise, -ize; cf. **braise**

brazier a worker in brass, a pan for holding lighted coal; *not* -sier

Brazil/, -ian abbr. **Braz.**

Brazzaville capital of Republic of Congo, Cent. Africa

BRCS British Red Cross Society

BRD (Ger.) *Bundesrepublik Deutschland,* Federal Republic of Germany

bread/board, -crumb, -fruit, -line (one word)

break/ (typ.) the division into a fresh paragraph, **-line** the last one of a paragraph (hyphen); *see also* **brake**

breakdown (noun) a collapse, analysis of statistics (one word)

Breakspear, Nicholas Pope Adrian IV 1154–9, *not* -eare

breakthrough (noun, one word)

breakup (noun, one word)

Breathalyser (noun) a device for testing amount of alcohol in the breath; *not* -iser, -izer, -yzer (US) (cap.); **breathalyse** (verb) carry out test, *not* -yze (US) (not cap.)

breathing/ (typ.) either of two signs in Greek, Arabic, Hebrew, and other languages indicating the presence (**rough** ') or the absence (**smooth** ') of an aspirate

breccia a rock composed of angular fragments, *not* -cchia

Brechin Tayside

Brecht/, Bertolt (1898–1956) German playwright; *not* -th-, -d; adj. **-ian**

Brecon Powys

breech birth (two words)

Breeches Bible the 1560 Geneva Bible, with *breeches* for *aprons* in Gen. 3: 7

breeches buoy a life-saving apparatus (two words)

Bren gun a light machine-gun (two words)

brent goose *not* bra- (US)

Brescia Lombardy, Italy

Breslau Ger. for **Wrocław** (Poland)

Bretagne/ Fr. for **Brittany, Grande —** Great Britain

Breton (an inhabitant) of Brittany, abbr. **Bret.**

Bretton Woods NH (UN Monetary Conference, 1944)

bretzel *use* **pretzel**

Breughel *use* **Brueghel** *or* **Bruegel**

brev. brevet, -ed

breve a curved mark (˘) to indicate a short vowel or syllable

brevet d'invention (Fr. m.) a patent

breveté s.g.d.g. (Fr.) patented without government guarantee (*sans garantie du gouvernement*)

breviary a book containing RC daily service

Brezhnev, Leonid (Ilich) (1906–82) General Secretary, USSR Communist Party 1964–82; President of the Supreme Soviet 1977–82

bri/ar *use* **-er** in all senses, *but* (US) briar pipe, **Sweet Briar College,** Sweet Briar, Va.

Briarean many-handed, like **Briareus,** of Greek myth.; *not* -ian

bribable *not* -eable

bric-a-brac (hyphens, no accent)

brick/bat, -work (one word)

Bridge End Cumbria, Devon, Lincs., Shetland

Bridgend Corn., Cumbria (near Patterdale), Co. Donegal, Glos., Lothian, Mid Glam., Strathclyde, Tayside

Bridge of Allan Central

Bridge of San Luis Rey, The novel by Thornton Wilder, 1927

Bridgeport Ala., Calif., Conn., Nebr., Pa., Tex.

Bridges, Robert (Seymour) (1844–1930) English poet, Poet Laureate 1913–30

Bridges Creek Va., birthplace of George Washington

Bridgeton Glasgow; NJ

Bridgetown Corn., Som., Staffs., Co. Wexford, Barbados; NS, Canada; W. Australia

Bridgewater/ NS, Canada; **Duke of —** (1736–1803), projector of the **— Canal; Earl of —** (1756–1829), founder of the **— Treatises**

Bridgnorth Shropshire

Bridgwater Som., *not* Bridge-

bridle path (two words)

bridle-road (hyphen)

bridleway (one word)

brier/, -root (hyphen); *not* briar, brere

brier rose (two words) *not* briar, brere

Brig. brigad/e, -ier

Brillat-Savarin, Anthelme (1755–1826) French gastronome

brimfull (one word)

bring up (typ.) to underlay or interlay a block to bring it to printing height

brio (mus.) fire, life, vigour

briquette a block of compressed coal dust, *not* -et

brisling a Norwegian sprat, *not* brist-

Bristol: the signature of the Bishop of Bristol (colon)

Bristol-board a cardboard used by artists (hyphen; two words, not cap. in US)

Brit. Britain; Britann/ia, -icus, -ica; British

Britain *more correctly* Great Britain, the land mass of England, Scotland, and Wales, with some of its immediately surrounding islands. The United Kingdom adds Northern Ireland to these, though not the Isle of Man and Channel Islands; British Isles is a geographical, not a political, term, and includes the Republic of Ireland, the Isle of Man, and the Channel Islands

Briticism idiom current in Britain, *not* Britishism

British/ abbr. **Brit.**; — **Academy,** — **Association** abbr. **BA**; — **America** abbr. **Br. Am.**; — **Columbia** abbr. **BC**; — **Guyana** *now* **Guyana**; — **Honduras** *now* **Belize**; — **Library** abbr. **BL**; — **Museum** abbr. **BM**; — **Rail** abbr. **BR**; — **Standard** abbr. **BS** (*see* **BSI**)

Britisher *use* **Briton**

British Indian Ocean Territory a group of 2,300 islands in the Indian Ocean, governed as a British colony from Diego Garcia

britschka *use* **britzka**

Britt. (on coins) Britanniarum, 'of the Britains' (Roman *Britannia Inferior* and *Britannia Superior*)

Brittany in Fr. **Bretagne**

Britten, (Edward) Benjamin, Baron (1913–76) British composer

britzka a Polish open carriage, in Pol. *bryczka*

Bro. Brother (monastic title)

bro. brother, pl. **bros.**

Broad-Churchman (caps., hyphen)

Broad Haven Dyfed, Co. Mayo

Broadmoor a psychiatric hospital, Crowthorne, Berks.

Broad Oak Cumbria, Dorset, Hereford, E. Sussex

Broadoak Corn., Dorset, Glos., Kent, Shropshire

broadside (US typ.) (adj.) = **landscape**

Brobdingnag the land of giants in Swift's *Gulliver's Travels*, 1726; *not* -dig-

broccoli a hardy cauliflower; It. pl., but Eng. sing. *or* pl.

brochet/ (Fr. m.) freshwater pike; **-te** (Fr. f.) (food cooked on) a skewer

Broderers a livery company

broderie anglaise open embroidery on white linen or cambric (not ital.)

broil (US) = **grill**

Bromberg Ger. for **Bydgoszcz**

bromine symbol **Br**

bronch/i pl. the main forks of the windpipe (sing. **-us**), **-ia**, pl. ramifications of the above; **-ioles** their minute branches

bronco/ a type of Mexican horse, *not* -cho; pl. **-s**

Brontë,/ Anne (1820–49) pseud. **Acton Bell,** — **Charlotte** (1816–55) pseud. **Currer Bell,** — **Emily** (1818–48) pseud. **Ellis Bell,** English writers

brontosaurus former term for **apatosaurus**

Bronx, the a borough of New York City

bronzing (typ.) printing in yellow and then dusting with bronze powder to imitate gold

brooch *not* -ach

Brooke/ Leics., Norfolk; **Baron** —; —, **Rupert** (1887–1915), English poet

Brookings Institution Washington, DC; *not* Institute

Brookline Mass.

Brooklyn a borough of New York City

Brooks's Club London, *not* -es's

broomstick (one word)

Brother (monastic title) abbr. **Bro.**

brother/ abbr. **b., bro.**; pl. **-s, brethren,** abbr. **bros.**; — **german** having same parents; **-in-law,** pl. **brothers-in-law,** — **uterine** having same mother only

brougham (hist.) a horse-drawn closed carriage or motor car with an open driver's seat (not cap.), pron. 'broom'

brouhaha a commotion, uproar (not ital.)

Brown/, Ford Madox (1821–93) English painter, —, **John** (1800–59) US abolitionist, —, **Lancelot** (called **Capability** —) (1716–83) English landscape gardener; —, **Robert** (1773–1858) Scottish botanist

Brown University RI, abbr. **BU**

Browne,/ Charles Farrar *see* **Ward**; — **Hablot Knight** (1815–82) English artist, pseud. **Phiz,** illustrated Dickens; — **Sir Thomas** (1605–82) English physician and author

Brownian motion of particles (observed by Robert Brown)

Brownie a junior Guide (cap.); a Scottish house-spirit (not cap.)

browse to read desultorily, eat; *not* -ze

BRS British Road Services

Bruckner, Anton (1824–96) Austrian composer

Bruegel, Pieter (*c*.1520–69) Flemish painter; **Brueghel, Pieter** (1564–1638) and **Jan** (1568–1625) his sons, also painters; *not* Breu-

Bruges Belgium, in Fl. **Brugge**

Brummagem derogatory form of Birmingham, abbr. **Brum**; (adj.) tawdry

Brummell, George Bryan, 'Beau' (1778–1840)

Brummie from or relating to Birmingham

brummy (Austral. and NZ) counterfeit, showy, or cheaply made

Brunei NW Borneo

Brunel/, Sir Marc Isambard (1769–1849) and **—, Isambard Kingdom** (1806–59) his son, British engineers; **— University** Uxbridge

Brunelleschi, Filippo (1377–1446) Italian architect and sculptor

brunette a woman with dark brown hair *or* this colour of hair; the masculine form is **brown, brunet** being seldom used

Brünhild (Ger. (orig. Burgundian) myth.) the queen won by Siegfried for Gunther; (Norse myth.) spelt **Brynhild**, won by Sigurðr for Gunnar; variations include (Middle High Ger.) **Brünhilt** (in Bavarian **Prünhilt**); the Anglicized form most familiar from Wagner is **Brunhilda**, *properly* **Brünnhilde**

Brunonian (noun) an alumnus of **Brown University**; (adj.) of the system of medicine of Dr John Brown of Edinburgh (1736–88)

Brunswick Eng. for **Braunschweig**, Germany

Brussels capital of Belgium; in Fl. **Brussel**, Fr. **Bruxelles**

Brussels sprouts (one cap., no apos.)

brut (Fr.) unsweetened

brutalize *not* -ise

Bruxelles Fr. for **Brussels**

bryczka (Pol.) **britzka**

Brynhild a Norse heroine, *see* **Brünhild**

Brynmawr Gwent

Bryn Mawr College Philadelphia

bryology the study of mosses, abbr. **bryol.**

bryozoan (of or relating to) any aquatic invertebrate animal of the phylum Bryozoa, properly *not* polyzoan

Brython Welsh for Briton, a S. British Celt

Brythonic (the language) of the Celts in Britain or Brittany

Brzezinski, Zbigniew (b. 1928) Polish-born US academic and statesman

BS Bachelor of Surgery *or* (US) Science, Blessed Sacrament, British Standard (*see also* **BSI**)

b.s. balance sheet, bill of sale

BSA Birmingham Small Arms, British School at Athens

BSC British Steel Corporation

B.Sc. Bachelor of Science; **B.Sc.(Econ.)** Bachelor of Science in faculty of Economics; **B.Sc.(Eng.)** Bachelor of Science Engineering, Glas.; **B.Sc.Tech.** Bachelor of Technical Science

BSE bovine spongiform encephalopathy, a usually fatal disease of cattle; commonly called 'mad cow disease'

b.s.g.d.g. *see* *breveté s.g.d.g.*

BSI British Standards Institution; a complete list of British Standards is in the BS Yearbook

B-side the secondary side of a gramophone record

BSJA British Show Jumping Association

BSR British School at Rome

BST British Summer Time (before 1968 and from 1972), British Standard Time (1968–71) (both 1 hr. ahead of GMT)

Bt. Baronet, *not* Bart.

BTA British Tourist Authority

B.Th. Bachelor of Theology

B.th.u. *or* **B.t.u.** *or* **BTU** British Thermal Unit(s)

bty. battery

BU Baptist Union; Boston University, Mass.; Brown University, RI; Bucknell University

bu. bushel, -s

buccaneer *not* -ier

Buccleuch, Duke of *not* -gh

Bucellas a white wine from Bucellas, near Lisbon

Buch (Ger. n.) book, pl. *Bücher*

Bucharest Romania, in Romanian **Bucureşti**; *not* Buka-

Buchausgabe (Ger. f.) edition of a book

Buckinghamshire abbr. **Bucks.**

Bucknall Lincs., Staffs.

Bucknell Oxon., Shropshire; also a university at Lewisburg, Pa.

buckram a coarse fabric, (bind.) a good quality cloth

Budapest Hungary, *not* -pesth (one word). Collective name for two towns, Buda and Pest, fused in the 19th c.

Buddha (Skt.) a title (meaning 'The Awakened One') denoting the founder of Buddhism, **Siddhārtha Gautama** (*c*.490 BC–*c*.410 BC); as this is a title rather than a personal name, it should be preceded by **the**

Buddh/ism, -ist if necessary divide as shown, abbr. **Budd.**

budgerigar a parakeet

budget/, -ed, -ing

buen/as noches (Sp.) goodnight; **-as tardes** good afternoon; **-os días** good day, good morning

Buenos/ Aires cap. of Argentina; also in Panama, *use* **— Ayres** in titles of Argentinian railway companies

buffalo/ pl. **-es**

buffer state (two words)

buffet/, -ed, -ing (one *t*)

buffo (noun) a comic actor, esp. in Italian opera (ital.); (adj.) comic, burlesque (not ital.)

Buffon, Georges Louis Leclerc, comte de (1707–88) French naturalist

Bugatti a sports car manufacturer

buhl (inlaid with) brass, tortoiseshell, etc.; Ger. form of *boule*, from **André Charles Boule** (1642–1732) cabinetmaker to Louis XIV

Bühnenaussprache (Ger. f.) a standard pronunciation of German, free of dialectal variations

building abbr. **bldg.**, pl. **bldgs.**

BUJ (*Baccalaureus utriusque juris*) Bachelor of Canon and Civil Law

Bukarest *use* **Buch-**

Bukhara Uzbekistan; *see also* **Bo-**

buksheesh *use* **bak-**

bulbul (Pers.) the Asian song-thrush, the literary counterpart of a nightingale; a singer or poet

Bulfinch's Mythology *not Bull-*

Bulgaria/, -n abbr. **Bulg.**

bulgur a wholewheat cereal food; *not* -gar, -ghur

bulletin (not ital.) abbr. **bull.**

bullfight/, -er, -ing (one word)

bullring (one word)

bull's-eye the centre of a target, a lantern, a peppermint sweet (apos. and hyphen)

bull terrier (two words)

bulrush *not* bull-

bulwark a defence; *not* bull-, -work

Bulwer-Lytton,/ Edward George Earle Lytton, first **Lord Lytton** (1803–73) English novelist; **— Edward Robert** first **Earl of Lytton** (1831–91) his son, English poet and diplomat, pseud. **Owen Meredith**

bumbag (one word)

bumblebee (one word), *not* humble-

bumf papers, *not* bumph

bumkin (naut.) a projection from bows or stern of ship

bumpkin a yokel

bump out (typ.) increase word or letterspacing to fill a line, or line spacing to fill a page

Bumppo, Natty the hero of James Fenimore Cooper's 'Leather-Stocking Tales'

bun/combe *use* **-kum**

Bundesanstalt a German official institution since 1945; *see also* **Reichsanstalt**

Bundesrat, Bundestag (Ger.) the upper and lower houses of the German Parliament

bundle abbr. **bdl.**, pl. **bdls.**

Bunker Hill Mass., a battle of the American War of Independence, 1775, actually fought at neighbouring Breed's Hill; *not* -er's

bunkum *not* -combe

Bunsen burner (one cap.)

Buñuel, Luis (1900–83) Spanish-born film director

Buonaparte *use* **Bona-**

buona sera (It.) good evening, **buon giorno** good day

buoyan/t, -cy

BUPA British United Provident Association

bur a clinging seed vessel or catkin; cf. **burr**

Burckhardt, Jacob Christoph (1818–97) Swiss historian

Burdett-Coutts, Angela Georgina, Baroness (1814–1906) English philanthropist

bureau/ a writing-desk with drawers, (US) a chest of drawers; pl. **-x** (not ital.); **-cracy, -crat**, adj. **-cratic**

Bureau Veritas a maritime underwriters' association at Brussels (two caps.)

burette a graduated glass tube used in chemical analysis, *not* buret

burg. burgess, burgomaster

burgamot *use* **ber-**

Burgerbibliothek Berne, *not* Bü-

burgess abbr. **burg.**

burgh (hist.) Scottish borough or chartered town; status abolished in 1975

burgomaster (one word) abbr. **burg.**

burgrave a governor, *not* burgg-; in Ger. *Burggraf*

burgundy a wine (not cap.)

burhel *use* **bharal**

burial/ ground, place, — service (two words)

burk *use* **be-**

Burkina Faso W. Africa, *formerly* Upper Volta

burl a lump in cloth

burl. burlesque

Burleigh, William Cecil, Lord (1520–98) English statesman, chief minister to Elizabeth I; also spelt **Burghley**

Burlington House London, headquarters of the Royal Academy, British Association, and other artistic and learned bodies

Burm/a *not* -ah (in Burmese and strict official use **Myanmar**); **-ese** a native, national, or the language of Burma; pl. same; *not* -an, -ans

Burmah Oil Co. *not* Burma

Burne-Jones, Sir Edward Coley (1833–98) English painter (hyphen)

Burnett, Frances Eliza Hodgson (1849–1924) US writer

burnous an Arab or Moorish hooded cloak; *not* -e, bernouse, -noose; in Arab. *burnus*

Burntisland Fife (one word)

burnt sienna an orange-red pigment, *not* siena

burr a rough edge, a rough sounding of the letter *r*; a kind of limestone; cf. **bur**

burrito a flour tortilla rolled round a savoury filling

burro a donkey

burro (It.) butter

Burroughs,/ Edgar Rice (1875–1950) US novelist, — **John** (1837–1921) US naturalist and poet, — **William** (1914–97) US novelist

bursar the treasurer of a college, *not* -er

Burton upon Trent (no hyphens)

Burundi Cent. Africa

Bury St Edmunds Suffolk (no apos., no hyphen)

bus/ *not* 'bus; pl. **-es**; as verb **-ed, -ing**

bushbuck (S. Afr.) an antelope, in Afrik. **bosbok**

bushel abbr. **bu.** (sing. and pl.)

Bushey Herts., *not* -hy

bushido the code of the samurai or Japanese military caste

Bushire Iran

Bushy Park London

businesslike (one word)

business/man, -people, -person, -woman (one word)

buss/ (arch. or US colloq.) a kiss, pl. **-es**; as verb, **-ed, -ing**

busybody *not* busi-

busyness the state of being busy, distinct from business

Buthelezi, Chief Mangosuthu (Gatsha) (b. 1928) S. African politician

Butler, Samuel/ (1612–80) English poet (*Hudibras*), — — (1835–1902) English writer (*Erewhon*)

Butte Mont.

butter/fingers, -milk (one word)

buttonhole (one word)

buyer's option abbr. **b.o.**

buyout the purchase of a controlling share in a company etc. (one word; two words as verb)

Buys Ballot, Christoph Hendrik Didericus (1817–90) Dutch meteorologist (no hyphen)

BV *Beata Virgo* (the Blessed Virgin)

B.V. pseud. of **James Thomson**

BVM *Beata Virgo Maria*, the Blessed Virgin Mary

BWI British West Indies *now* **WI**

BWV *Bach-Werke-Verzeichnis*, a prefix to enumeration of J. S. Bach's compositions

by- (as prefix) tends to form one word with the following noun, but hyphen still sometimes found in the cases below

by and by, by and large (no hyphens)

by-blow a side blow, bastard (hyphen)

Bydgoszcz Poland, in Ger. **Bromberg**

bye/, -s (cricket) abbr. **b.**

bye-bye a familiar form of goodbye (hyphens)

by-election (hyphen)

Byelorussia *now* **Belarus** (since 1991)

by-form (hyphen)

bygone (one word)

by-lane (hyphen)

by-law (hyphen, one word in US), *not* bye-

byline in journalism and football (one word)

byname a sobriquet (one word)

by/pass, -path, -play (one word)

by/-plot, -product *not* bye- (hyphens)

by/road, -stander (one word)

by-street (hyphen) *but* Masefield's *The Widow in the Bye Street*

byte (comput.) a group of eight bits (*see* **bit**)

by the by (three words)

by/way, -word (one word)

byzant *use* **be-**

Byzantine cap. when referring to Byzantium, the Eastern Roman Empire, *or* its architecture, painting, or people; not cap. when referring to something extremely complicated, inflexible, or underhand

BZW Barclays de Zoete Wedd

bzw. (Ger.) *beziehungsweise* (respectively)

C carbon, Celsius *or* centigrade, centum (a hundred), (elec.) coulomb, (comput.) a programming language, the third in a series, (mus.) common time

₵ cedi (currency of Ghana), colón (currency of El Salvador)

C. Cape, Catholic, century, chairman, chief, Church, Command Paper (q.v.) (1870–99) with number following, congressional, Conservative, consul, contralto, Council, counter-tenor, Court, Gaius

c (as prefix) centi-

c. (cricket) caught, cent, -s; centime, century, chapter (esp. in legal works or where indicating *caput*, otherwise prefer **ch.**), city, (meteor.) cloudy, colt, conductor, constable, copeck, cubic

C (ital. cap.) symbol for capacitance

c. *circa* (about), set close up to figures, spaced from words and letters

Ɔ (inverted 'C') 500

CA California (postal abbr.), Central Africa, Central America, Member of the Institute of Chartered Accountants of Scotland, Chief Accountant, chronological age, Civil Aviation, College of Arms, commercial agent, Consumers' Association, Controller of Accounts, Court of Appeal

C/A capital account, commercial account, credit account, current account

Ca calcium (no point)

ca. (law) cases

ca. *circa* use **c.**

CAA Civil Aviation Authority

Caaba use **K-**

caaing-whale *use* **ca'ing-**

CAB Citizens' Advice Bureau, (US) Civil Aeronautics Board

cabal a secret faction

caballero/ a Spanish gentleman, pl. **-s** (not ital.)

cabana (US) a hut or shelter at a beach or swimming pool, from (Sp.) *cabaña*

cabbala Hebrew tradition; *not* k-, cabala, -alla

Cabell, James Branch (1879–1958) US novelist

cabinet a piece of furniture or a small room (not cap.); the committee of senior ministers responsible for controlling government policy (usually cap.)

Cable, George Washington (1844–1925) US writer

cable (naut.) one-tenth of a sea mile

cabochon a gem polished but not faceted, *en cabochon* (of a gem) treated in this way

Cabot Lodge *see* **Lodge**

cabotin/ (Fr.) fem. **-e** a second-rate actor, a strolling player

Cabul *use* **K-**

CAC Central Advisory Committee

ca'canny (Sc.) go carefully!; the practice of 'going slow' at work to limit output

cacao a tropical tree, *Theobroma cacao,* from whose roasted and ground seeds **cocoa** (q.v.) and chocolate are made; *see also* **coca, cocco**

cache/mere, -mire *use* **cashmere**

cachet a distinctive mark, a capsule containing medicine

cachinnate (lit.) laugh loudly

cachou a lozenge to sweeten breath, *not* cashew

cachucha a Spanish dance

caciqu/e a W. Indian and S. American chief, political boss; **-ism**; *not* caz-

caco/demon, -daemon an evil spirit or malignant person (not ital.)

cacoethes/ (Lat. from Gr.) an urge to do something inadvisable (not ital.); **— loquendi** an itch for speaking, **— scribendi** an itch for writing (ital.)

caco/graphy bad handwriting or spelling, **-logy** bad choice of words or pronunciation, **-phony** dissonance, discord

CACTM Central Advisory Council for the Ministry, *now* **ACCM**

cact/us (bot.) pl. **-i**

CAD computer-aided design

c.-à-d. (Fr.) *c'est-à-dire* (that is to say)

cadastral of or showing the extent, value, and ownership of land for taxation

caddie a golf attendant

caddis/-fly, -worm *not* -ice (hyphens)

caddy a box for keeping tea etc.

cadi a Muslim judge, *not* k-

Cadiz city and port, SW Spain; in Sp. **Cádiz**

Cadmean/ of Cadmus of Thebes, *not* -ian; **— victory** a ruinous one

cadmium symbol **Cd**

cadre a nucleus of personnel (not ital.)

caduce/us the wand of Hermes or Mercury, pl. **-i**

caducous (bot.) tending to fall

Cædmon (d. 670) English poet, *not* Ce-

Caenozoic (geol.) *use* **Cen-**

Caermarthen *use* **Car-**

Caernarfon Gwynedd; *not* Car-, -von

Caerns. Carnarvonshire, former county in Wales

Caerphilly Mid Glam., also the cheese; in Welsh **Caerffili**

caerulean *use* **ce-**

Caesar/, -ean *not* Cesarian (US)

Caesarea name of several ancient cities

caesium symbol **Cs**, *not* ce- (US)

caesura a division of a metrical line, *not* ce-

CAF (US) cost and freight

café a coffee house etc. (not ital.)

café/ au lait (Fr. m.) coffee with milk, — *noir* strong coffee without milk

Caffre *use* **Kaffir** *or* **Kafir**

caftan *use* **k-**

cag/ey shrewd, *not* -gy; adv. **-ily**, noun **-eyness**

cagoule a waterproof outer garment, *not* ka-

cahier/ (Fr. m.) a paper book, sheets of a MS, an exercise book; — *de doléances* a register of grievances presented to the States-General in 1789 (cap.)

CAI computer-assisted (or -aided) instruction

Caiaphas a Jewish high priest, Luke 3: 2

caiman *use* **cay-**

Cainan a grandson of Seth; *see also* **Canaan**

Caine, Sir Thomas Henry Hall (1853–1931) Manx novelist

ca'ing-whale the round-headed porpoise, *not* caa-

Cainozoic (geol.) *see* **Cenozoic**

caique a Bosporan skiff or Levantine sailing ship, *not* caïque

'Ça ira' ('It will be!') a French revolutionary song; lit. 'It will go!', i.e. the revolutionary process

Caius/ a Roman praenomen, *use* **Gaius** *but* abbr. **C.**; — (*properly* **Gonville and Caius**) **College**, Cambridge, pron. 'keys'; abbr. **Cai.**, **CC**

Cajan *use* **-un**

cajole/ persuade by flattery, noun **-ry** (one *l*)

Cajun a Lousianian descended from French-speaking Acadian immigrants *or* their language; *see also* **Creole**

caky *not* -ey

CAL computer-assisted learning

Cal. (California) *use* **Calif.**

cal calorie (no point)

cal. (mus.) calando; calendar

calamanco/ a woollen stuff, pl. **-es**

calamar/o (It.) a squid, pl. **-i**; the pl. form is found on most English menus for sing. or pl., often rom.; the older form, **calamary**, is still sometimes used

calando (mus.) volume and rate diminished, abbr. **cal.**

calcareous chalky, *not* -ious

calcedony *use* **chal-**

calceolaria a slipper-like flower, *not* calci-

calcium symbol **Ca**

calcspar *use* **calcite**

calculator *not* -er

calcul/us a stony concretion in the body, pl. **-i**, adj. **-ous**; a system of computation, pl. **-uses**, adj. **-ar**

Calderón de la Barca, Pedro (1600–81) Spanish playwright and poet

caldron *use* **caul-**

calecannon *use* **colc-**

calendae calends, *use* **k-**

calendar an almanac, abbr. **cal.**; *not* -er; *not* k- except in some church contexts

calend/er make smooth (cloth, paper, etc.), a machine that does this; **-erer** one who does this, *not* -ar, k-

calender (Pers., Turk.) a dervish, *not* k-

calends/ the first day of a Roman month, **the Greek —** a time that never comes; *not* k-

calf/ abbr. **cf.**; **— leather, — love** (two words)

calfskin (one word)

Caliban/ a character in Shakespeare's *The Tempest*; **'— upon Setebos'** a poem by R. Browning, 1864

calibre *not* -er (US)

Caliburn King Arthur's sword; *not* Cala-, Cale-; *also* **Excalibur**

calico/ pl. **-es** *not* -s

California off. abbr. **Calif.**, postal **CA**

californium symbol **Cf**

caligraphy *use* **calli-**

caliper *use* **calli-** (except in US)

caliph/ a Muslim chief civil and religious ruler (common spelling), in Arab. *ḵalīfa*; **-ate**; **kali/f, -ph** are more learned forms

calisthenics *use* **callis-** (except in US)

cal/ix (physiol., biol.), a cuplike cavity or organ, pl. **-ices**

calk (US) = **caulk**

Callaghan, Leonard James (b. 1912) British statesman, Prime Minister 1976–9

Callander Central

called abbr. **cld.**

calligraphy *not* cali-

Calliope (Gr. myth.) the muse of eloquence and epic poetry (cap.); a steam organ at a fairground (not cap.)

calliper a metal leg-support, (pl.) compasses for measuring diameters of objects; *not* cali- (US)

Callirrhoe (Gr. myth.) the wife of Alcmaeon

callisthenics gymnastic exercises, *not* cali- (US)

callous unfeeling, insensitive; (of skin) hardened or hard

call/us thick skin, pl. **-uses**, adj. **-ous**

Calmann-Lévy publishers

calmia, Calmuck *use* k-, **Kalmyk**

Calor gas (propr.) (cap., two words)

calori/e a unit of heat or energy (not now in scientific use), abbr. **cal**; **-meter** a measurer of heat; **-motor** a voltaic battery (one word)

calotte an RC skullcap

Caltech California Institute of Technology

caltrop (mil.) a horse-maiming iron ball with spikes; *not* -throp, -trap

calumet a Native American peace pipe

calumniator *not* -er

Calvé, Emma (1866–1942) French operatic soprano

Calverleigh Devon

Calverley/ Kent, W. Yorks.; **—, Charles Stuart** (1831–84) English writer

calves-foot jelly *not* -f's, -ves', -feet

cal/x the residue from burning, pl. **-ces**

Calypso (Gr. myth.) a sea nymph in the *Odyssey*, **calypso/** a W. Indian song, usually about current affairs, pl. **-s**

caly/x (bot.) pl. **-ces**, *not* -xes

camaraderie good-fellowship

Camargue, the S. France

Camb. Cambridge

Cambodia Indo-China, *not* Kam-, -oja; in Fr. **Cambodge**

Cambrensis, Giraldus *see* **Giraldus Cambrensis**

cambric a fine white linen or cotton fabric

Cambridge/ abbr. **Camb., Cantab.**; **— University** abbr. **CU**; **— — Press** abbr. **CUP**

Cambridgeshire abbr. **Cambs.**

Cambridge University Press abbr. **CUP**

camel the two-humped Bactrian camel, *Camelus bactrianus*; cf. **dromedary**

camellia a flowering shrub, *not* -elia

camelopard (arch.) the giraffe, *not* -leo-

Camelopardalis (astr.) a northern constellation between Ursa Major and Cassiopeia

Camembert a French cheese (cap.)

cameo/ pl. **-s**

camera/ pl. **-s**; **— obscura** *not* — oscura

camera-ready copy (typ.) material ready for photographing for reproduction; (US) = **mechanical**; abbr. **crc, CRC**

Camera Stellata the Star Chamber

Cameroon/, United Republic of Cent. Africa; *not* the Cameroons; **-ian**; in Fr. **République du Cameroun**

Cammaerts, Émile (1878–1953) Belgian poet

Camões, Luís Vaz de (1524–80) Portuguese poet, *not* Camoëns; the older Eng. form is **Luiz Vas de Camoens**

camomile a medicinal plant, *not* cha- (US)

Camorra a Neapolitan secret society, practising violence and extortion; *see also* **Mafia**

Campagna di Roma the plain around Rome

campanile/ a bell tower, pl. **-s**

campbed (one word)

Campbell-Bannerman, Sir Henry (1836–1908) British statesman, Prime Minister 1905–8 (hyphen)

Campbeltown Strathclyde

Campeche/ Bay, — City, — State Mexico, *not* -peachy

campfire (one word)

camp/o (It.) open ground, pl. **-i**; **campo santo** (It., Sp.) a cemetery

campsite (one word)

Campus Martius the field of Mars in ancient Rome

CAMRA Campaign for Real Ale

Can. Canada, Canadian, Cantoris

can. canon, canto

Canaan a son of Ham; the biblical promised land; *see also* **Cainan**

Canad/a, -ian abbr. **Can.**

Canadian River Okla.

canaille (Fr. f.) the rabble, populace

canaker *use* **kanaka**

Canaletto,/ Giovanni Antonio real surname **Canal** (1697–1768) Italian painter; name also used by his nephew **— Bernardo Bellotto** (1720–80) Italian painter

canalize *not* -ise

canapé/ pl. **-s**

Canar/a, -ese *use* **K-**

canard an absurd story (not ital.)

canasta a card game

canaster a tobacco, *not* k-; cf. **canister**

cancan a high-kicking Parisian dance (one word)

cancel (typ.) incorrect matter, a new-printed leaf correcting this (its signature is preceded by *)

cancel/, -lation, -led, -ler, -ling (one *l* in US)

cancellate (biol.) porous, marked with cross-lines

cancelled abbr. **cld.**

Candahar *use* **K-**

candela a standard unit of light intensity, abbr. **cd**

candelabr/um pl. **-a**; also sing. **-a**, pl. **-as**

Candide, or Optimism by Voltaire, 1759

candlelight (one word)

Candlemas Day 2 Feb.

candle/power, -stick, -wick (one word)

candour *not* -or (US)

C. & W. country and western

canephor/us (archit.) a sculptured youth or maiden with a basket on the head, pl. **-i**

caneton (Fr. m.) a duckling

canister a small metal box; cf. **canaster**

cannabis Indian hemp, *not* cana- (not cap. except for the bot. genus)

cannelloni (two *n*s, two *l*s)

Cannes dép. Alpes-Maritimes, France

cannibalize *not* -ise

Canning,/ George (1770–1827) and his son — **Charles John, Earl** (1812–62) English statesmen

cannon ball (two words, one word in US)

cannon-bone (hyphen, two words in US)

cannon fodder (two words)

canoe/, -d, -ing, -ist

cañón (Sp.) a gorge, canyon

canonize *not* -ise

'Canon's Yeoman's Tale' by Chaucer

Canopic (cap. except in US)

Canosa Apulia, Italy

Canossa/ Emilia, Italy, the scene of penance of Emperor Henry IV before Pope Gregory VII, 1077; hence **to go to —** 'to eat humble pie'

Canova, Antonio (1757–1822) Italian sculptor

canst (no apos.)

Cant. Canterbury, Canticles

cantabile (mus.) in a singing, graceful style

Cantabrigian of Cambridge, *not* -dgian

Cantabrigiensis (Lat.) of Cambridge (University), abbr. **Cantab.**

cantaloupe a musk melon, *not* cante-, -loup

Cantate Psalm 98 (97 in Vulg.) as a canticle

cantatrice (Fr. and It.) a professional woman singer

cante hondo (Sp.) a mournful song

Canterbury/ abbr. **Cant., — bell** a flower (one cap.)

canticle a hymn, abbr. **cant.**

Canticum Canticorum 'The Song of Songs', *also* **Canticles**; abbr. **Cant.**; same as the Song of Solomon

cantilever *not* canta-, -liver

Cantire Strathclyde, *use* **Kintyre**

canto/ a division of a long poem, a song; pl. **-s**, abbr. **can.**

Canton the capital of Guangdong Province, China; in Pinyin **Guangzhou**, in Wade–Giles **Kuang-chou**

Cantonese of Canton or the Cantonese dialect of Chinese (also called **Yue**); (of) a native of Canton (pl. same)

cantonment military quarters

cantoris of the precentor, i.e. on the north side of the choir; abbr. **Can.**

Cantor Lectures Royal College of Physicians, and Society of Arts

Cantuar. *Cantuarius, Cantuariensis* (of Canterbury)

Cantuar: the signature of the Archbishop of Canterbury (colon)

Cantuarian of Canterbury

cantus firmus (mus.) the basic melody in counterpoint, pl. **cantus firmi**; in It. **canto fermo**, pl. **canti fermi**

Canute Eng. variant of **Cnut**, not to be used in serious hist. work; *see also* **Knut**

canvas/ a coarse linen; **-ed, -es**

canvass/ solicit votes; **-ed, -er, -es**

canyon a gorge, in Sp. **cañón**

Can You Forgive Her? a novel by Anthony Trollope, 1864–5

caoutchouc unvulcanized rubber

CAP Common Agricultural Policy (EC)

Cap (Fr. geog. m.) Cape

cap. capital letter, chapter, foolscap

cap-à-pie from head to foot (accent, hyphens, not ital.)

Cap d'Ail dép. Alpes-Maritimes, France

Cape/ cap. when with name, abbr. **C.; — Breton** NS, Canada, *not* Briton, Britton, abbr. **CB; — Canaveral** Fl. (called **Cape Kennedy** 1963–73); **— Coloured** (S. Afr.) *see* **coloured**; **— of Good Hope** abbr. **CGH; — Province** (of S. Africa) abbr. **CP**

apek,/ Josef (1887–1945) and his brother — **Karel** (1890–1938) Czech writers

capercaillie *not* -lzie

Cape Town S. Africa (two words)

Cape Verde/ Islands off W. Africa; *not* — Verd, — de Verd; **-an**

Cap Haitien Haiti

capias (law) a writ of arrest

Capital Gains Tax abbr. **CGT**

capitalize *not* -ise

capital letter abbr. **cap.**

capitals,/ large indicated in copy by three lines underneath the letter, abbr. **cap.; — small** abbr. (typ.) **s.c.; small cap.,** pl. **small caps.; s. cap.,** pl. **s. caps.;** *see also* **even small caps.**

Capitol the hill in ancient Rome, in Lat. **Capitolium**; the temple of Jupiter was the temple of **Capitoline Jove**; Congress building, Capitol Hill, Washington, DC

capitulary a collection of ordinances, esp. of the Frankish kings

capitulum (bot., anat.) a small head, knob

Cap'n slang abbr. of **Captain**

cappuccino coffee made frothy with milk (not ital.)

capriccio/ (mus.) a short fanciful work, pl. **-s**; adj. **-so**

caps. and smalls (typ.) set in small capitals with the initial letters in large capitals, abbr. **caps.** (*or* **c.**) **and s.c.**

Capsian (of) a palaeolithic culture of N. Africa and S. Europe

capsiz/e *not* -ise, noun **-al**

Captain abbr. **Capt.**

caption (typ.) descriptive matter printed above or below an illustration; (also US) heading of a chapter, page, or section

Captivity, the of the Jews (cap.)

Capuchin a Franciscan friar of the new rule of 1529, *or* a cloak and hood formerly worn by women (cap.); a S. American monkey (not cap.)

caput/ (Lat.) head, — **mortuum** the worthless residue after distillation

Car. Carolus (Charles)

car. carat

carabineer (hist.) a soldier with a carbine; *not* carb-, -ier; *but* **Carabiniers & Greys**

Carabineers, the Royal Scots Dragoon Guards

carabinier/e an Italian gendarme, pl. **-i**

Caracci a family of painters, 1550–1619; *not* Carr-

Caractacus (*fl.* AD 50) King of Silures, ancient Britain; in hist. writing *use* **Carat-**

caracul *use* **karakul**

carafe a glass container for water or wine; *not* -ff, -ffe

¡caramba! (Sp.) wonderful!, how strange! (turned exclamation mark before, unturned after)

carat a unit of weight for precious stones, 200 mg; *not* caract, caret, carrat, karat; abbr. **K.**, **car.**; cf. **caret**; **karat**

caratch *use* **kharaj**

Caravaggio, Michelangelo Merisi da (1569–1609) Italian painter

caravanserai an Eastern inn with courtyard used as halting-place for caravans; *not* -sary, -sery, -sera; *see also* **khan**

caravel a type of Spanish ship, *not* carvel

caraway *not* carra-

carbineer *use* carab-

carbon symbol **C**

carbon copy abbr. **c.c.**

carbon dating (two words)

carboniferous producing coal (not cap.); the fifth period in the Palaeozoic era (cap.)

carbonize *not* -ise

carburet/ted, -ting, -tor *not* -ed, -ing, -or (US), *not* cr

carcass/ *not* -ase; pl. **-es**

Carcassonne dép. Aude, France

carcinom/a a cancer, pl. **-ata**

card. cardinal

cardamom *not* -mon, -mum

Cardigan Dyfed; *see also* **Ceredigion**

card index (two words as noun, hyphen as verb)

cardphone (one word)

card-sharp (hyphen)

card table (two words)

Carducci, Giosuè (1835–1907) Italian poet

CARE Christian Action for Research and Education, computer-aided risk evaluation, Cooperative for American Relief Everywhere (*originally* Cooperative for American Remittances Europe)

careen (US) = **career** (swerve about)

carefree (one word)

carême (Fr. m.) Lent

care of abbr. **c/o**

caret an insertion mark (∧, ⋀), the mark over a letter (e.g. ê) in musical (Schenkerian) analysis; cf. **carat**; **karat**

caretaker (one word)

Carew,/ **Richard** (1555–1620) English poet, — **Thomas** (1595–?1639) English poet and courtier

car/ex a sedge, pl. **-ices**

Carey/, Henry (?1690–1743) English poet and composer; —, **Henry Charles** (1793–1879) US economist, son of —, **Mathew** (one t) (1760–1839) US publicist; — **Street** London, synonymous with the Bankruptcy Court; *see also* **Cary**

cargo/ pl. **-es**

Carib an aboriginal inhabitant of the southern W. Indies or the adjacent coasts, the language of this people

Caribbean Sea W. Indies, *not* Carr-

Cariboo Mountains BC, Canada

caribou a N. American reindeer, pl. same; *not* -boo

Caribou Highway BC, Canada

Caribou Mountain Ida.

carillon (a chime of) bells

Carington *see* **Carrington**

Carinthia Austria and Slovenia; in Ger. **Kärnten**, in Slovenian **Koroško**

carioca a Brazilian dance, the music for this; a native of Rio de Janeiro (not cap.)

cariole *use* carr-

Carisbrooke IoW

carità (It. art) a representation of maternal love

Carleton, William (1794–1869) Irish novelist

Carlile,/ **Richard** (1790–1843) English reformer and politician; — **Revd Preb. William** (1847–1942) founder of Church Army; *see also* **Carlisle**; **Carlyle**

Carliol: the signature of the Bishop of Carlisle (colon)

Carlisle/ Cumbria, **Earl of —**; *see also* **Carlile**; **Carlyle**

Carlist a supporter of the Spanish pretender Don Carlos (1788–1855)

Carlovingian *use* **Carolin-**

Carlsbad *use* Czech **Karlovy Vary**

Carlsbad Caverns National Park N. Mex.

Carlskrona Sweden, *use* **K-**

Carlsruhe Germany, *use* **K-**

Carlton Club London

Carlyle, Thomas (1795–1881) Scottish writer; *see also* **Carlile**; **Carlisle**

Carlylean *not* -eian, -ian

Carmagnola Piedmont, Italy

'Carmagnole, La' a French revolutionary song and dance

Carmarthen Dyfed, *not* Caer-; in Welsh **Caerfyrddin**

Carnarvon/ Gwynedd, *use* **Caernarfon**; *but* **Earl of —**

Carnatic Madras, India, *not* K-

Carnaval/ a suite of piano pieces by Schumann, 1834–5; *— des animaux, le* a suite for small orchestra by Saint-Saëns, 1886; *— romain, le* overture by Berlioz, 1844; *see also* **Carnival**

'Carnaval de Venise, le' (mus.) a popular type of air and variations, early 19th c.

Carnegie/, **Andrew** (1835–1919) Scottish-born US millionaire and philanthropist; **— Institute** Pittsburgh, Pa.; **— Institution** Washington, DC

carnelian *use* **cor-**

carnival in Fr. m. *carnaval*, in Ger. n. *Carneval*

Carnival an overture by Dvořák, 1891; *see also* **Carnaval**

Carnoustie Tayside

carol/, **-led, -ler, -ling**

Carol/ine of the time of Charles I or II, *also* **-ean**

Carolingian of the Frankish dynasty of Charlemagne; *not* Carlovingian, Karl-

Carolus Lat. for Charles, abbr. **Car.**

carom (US) = **cannon** in billiards

Carothers, Wallace Hume (1896–1937) US scientist

carous/e drink heavily, **-al**

carousel (US) merry-go-round, tournament, rotating conveyor system; *not* carr-; *see also* **Carrousel, place du**

car park (two words)

Carpathian Mountains E. Europe, not K-

carpe diem (Lat.) seize the day

carpet/, **-ed, -ing**

carport (one word)

carp/us the wrist, pl. **-i**

Carracci *use* **Cara-**

carrageen Irish moss; *not* — moss, -gheen; from Carragheen, near Waterford

Carrantuohill Co. Kerry, the highest mountain in Ireland

Carrara N. Italy, a source of marble

carrat *use* **carat**

carraway *use* **cara-**

carriageway (one word)

Carribbean *use* **Cari-**

Carrigtohill Co. Cork (one word)

Carrington, Baron family name **Carington** (one *r*)

carriole a carriage, *not* cariole

Carroll, Lewis pseud. of **Charles Lutwidge Dodgson** (1832–98) English author

carrousel use **caro-**

Carrousel, place du Paris, from Fr. *carrousel* (m.) a tilting-match

Carrutherstown Dumfries & Galloway (one word)

carry/all, -cot (one word)

carry-on excitement, fuss (hyphen)

carry-out (US) = **take-away**

carsick (one word)

carte (fencing) *use* **quarte**

Carte, Richard D'Oyly *see* **D'Oyly Carte**

carte blanche full discretion (not ital.)

carte-de-visite (not ital.)

Cartesian *see* **Descartes**

carthorse (one word)

cartouche (archit.) a scroll ornament, (archaeol.) a ring enclosing hieroglyphic royal name; *not* -ch

cartridge paper a firm, strong paper

cart/wheel, -wright (one word)

carvel-built (naut.) with smooth planking

Carver (US) a chair with arms, a rush seat, and a back having horizontal and vertical spindles; named after **John Carver**, first Governor of Plymouth Colony in America (cap.)

carver the principal chair, with arms, in a set of dining chairs, intended for the person who carves (not cap.)

Cary,/ **Alice** (1820–71) and **— Phoebe** (1824–71) US sisters, poets; **— Henry Francis** (1772–1844) English translator of Dante; **— (Arthur) Joyce (Lunel)** (1888–1957) English novelist; **— Lucius** Lord Falkland (1610–43); *see also* **Carey**

caryatid/ a female figure as a column, pl. **-s**

CAS Chief of the Air Staff

Casabianca, Louis de (?1755–98) French seaman

Casablanca Morocco

Casa Grande a prehistoric ruin in Arizona; *see also* **Casas Grandes**

'Casa Guidi Windows' by Elizabeth Barrett Browning, 1851

Casals, Pau (1876–1973) Catalan cellist, in Sp. **Pablo**

Casanova de Seingalt, Giovanni Jacopo (1725–98) Italian adventurer

Casas Grandes a Mexican village with famous ruins; *see also* **Casa Grande**

Casaubon/, Isaac (1559–1614) French scholar and theologian; **—, Méric** (1599–1671) his son, clergyman; **Mr —** a character in G. Eliot's *Middlemarch*

casava *use* **cass-**

casbah *use* **k-**

case/ (bind.) bookbinding consisting of two boards joined by a flexible spine, and usually covered with cloth etc.; **upper —** (typ.) capitals; **lower —** small letters (hyphens when attrib.)

case-bound (bind.) bound in a hard cover

case history (two words)

casein milk protein, *not* -ine

case law (two words)

cases (law) abbr. **ca.**

case study (two words)

casework (one word)

cash card (two words)

Cashmer/, -e *use* **Kashmir**

cashmere a soft wool fabric; *not* -meer, cachemere, -ire; cf. **kerseymere**

cash register (US) = **till** (two words)

Casimir-Perier, Jean Pierre Paul (1847–1907) French President 1894–5 (no accent)

casine *use* **casein**

casino/ pl. **-s** (not ital.)

Caslon, William (1693–1766) typefounder, cutter of Caslon type

Cassandra a prophet of disaster, esp. one who is disregarded (from **Kassandra** (Gr. myth.))

cassata an Italian ice cream (not ital.)

Cassation, Cour de highest court of appeal in France

cassava the manioc; *not* cas-, -ave

Cassel Germany, *use* **K-**

Cassell publishers

cassimere *use* **kerseymere**; *see also* **cashmere**

Cassiopeia (astr.) a constellation

Cassivellaunus (*fl.* 50 BC) British prince

cast the actors in a play

caste a hereditary class

Castellammare Campagna and Sicily, Italy

Castelnuovo-Tedesco, Mario (1895–1968) Italian composer

caster one who casts (cf. **castor**), (typ.) a casting machine

Castil/e Spain, *not* -ille; **-ian** (of or related to) a native or the language of Castile

cast iron (noun), **cast-iron** (adj.)

Castle Cary Som.

Castlecary Central, Co. Donegal

Castlerea Co. Roscommon

Castlereagh, Robert Stewart, Viscount (1769–1822) British statesman

Castleton Borders, Derby., Gr. Manchester, Gwent, N. Yorks.

Castletown Cumbria, Dorset, Highland, IoM, Staffs., Tyne & Wear

cast off (typ.) to estimate amount of printed matter copy would make, **cast-off** the result of this estimate

castor a beaver (hence **castor oil**) or its fur, a small wheel for furniture, a small pot with perforated lid (hence **castor sugar**); cf. **caster**

Castor and Pollux stars, twins in classical myth., also patrons of sailors

castrat/o (mus.) a castrated male soprano, pl. **-i**

casual incidental, not regular; *see also* **causal**

casus/ belli (Lat.) the cause of war, **— foederis** a case stipulated by treaty, **— omissus** a case unprovided for by statute

CAT College of Advanced Technology, (typ.) computer-assisted typesetting, (med.) computerized axial (*or* computer-assisted) tomography

Cat. Catalan, Catullus

cat. catalogue, catechism

cataboli/c, -sm *not* k-

cataclasm a violent disruption

cataclysm/ a deluge, a violent event; **-al, -ic, -ist** *not* -atist

Catalan (of or relating to) (a person from) Catalonia or the language of Catalonia, abbr. **Cat.**

Catalina Sp. for **Catherine**

Cataline *use* **Catiline**

catalogu/e abbr. **cat.**; **-ed, -er, -ing**; *not* -log (US); 'Cataloging in Publication Data' is the correct spelling for Library of Congress data on the title verso of a work

catalogue raisonné an explanatory catalogue (not ital.)

Catalonia in Catalan **Catalunya**, Sp. **Cataluña**

catal/yst, -yse *not* -yze (US); **-ysis, -ytic**

catamaran a raft, a two-hulled boat

catarrh an inflammation of the mucous membrane

catarrhine narrow-nosed (of monkeys), *not* -arhine

Catawba a Native American tribe, a US variety of grape *or* wine made from it

Catch, Jack *use* **Ke-**

catch/-all, -as-catch-can (hyphens)

catchline (typ.) a short line of type containing catchword(s), signature letter, running head-line, etc.

catchphrase (one word)

catchpole a sheriff's officer, *not* -poll

catch-22 an inescapable dilemma, after a novel by Joseph Heller, 1961 (not cap. except in title)

catchup *use* **ketchup**

catchword (typ.) the first word of next page printed at bottom of preceding page, word(s) printed at head of dictionary page as guide to its contents

Câteau Cambrésis, Peace of 1559

catechism teaching by question and answer, abbr. **cat.**

catechiz/e, -er, -ing *not* -is-

catechumen a convert under instruction before baptism

categorize classify, *not* -ise

caten/a a connected series of patristic comments on Scripture, a series *or* chain, pl. **-ae**

cater-cousin a good friend, *not* qua-

caters (campanology, pl.) changes on nine bells

Cath. Catherine, Catholic

cath. cathedral

Cathar/ a member of a medieval sect seeking great spiritual purity, pl. **-s** *or* **-i**

Catharine Kan., NY, Pa.; *see also* **Catherine**; **St Catharine**; **St Catherine**

cathars/is purging, pl. **-es**

Cathay poetical for China, *not* K-

cathedral cap. when with name, as Ely Cathedral; abbr. **cath.**

cathemeral (biol. adj.) applied to an organism equally active by day and by night

Catherine/ abbr. **Cath.**; **St** — hence — **pear** and — **wheel**; — **I** and **II** empresses of Russia; — **of Aragon**, — **Howard**, — **Parr** first, fifth, and sixth wives of Henry VIII of England; — **de' Medici** (1519–89) Queen of France, in Fr. — **de Médicis**; *see also* **Katherine**

cathisma *use* **ka-**

cathod/e a negative electrode; **-e ray tube** abbr. **CRT**; **-ic, -ograph**; *not* k-

Catholic abbr. **C.**, **Cath.**; cap. only when referring to the RC religion (the Catholic Church)

catholic/ism, -ize *not* -ise

Catiline the Eng. form of (**Lucius Sergius**) **Catilina** (108–62 BC) Roman conspirator, *not* Cata-

cation (elec.) an ion carrying positive charge of electricity, *not* k-

cat-o'-nine-tails (hyphens)

cat's/ cradle a children's game; **-eye** a precious stone (hyphen), reflective stud in road (cap., propr., hyphen)

Catskill Mountains NY

cat's-paw a person used as a tool, (naut.) a light breeze; *not* catspaw, cats-paw

catsuit (one word)

catsup *use* **ketchup**

Cattegat *use* (Dan.) **Kattegat**, (Swed.) **Kattegatt**

Cattleya an orchid genus

Catullus, Gaius Valerius (?84–?54 BC) Roman poet, abbr. **Cat.**

Cauchy, Augustin Louis (1789–1857) French mathematician

caucus a political clique, (US) a political meeting

Caudillo Sp. for 'leader', the title assumed by Gen. Franco after the Spanish Civil War

caught (cricket) abbr. **c.**

cauldron *not* cal-

caulk make watertight, *not* calk (US)

caus. causa/tion, -tive

causal having to do with a cause; cf. **casual**

causa/tion, -tive abbr. **caus.**

cause/ célèbre a famous law case, pl. **-s célèbres** (not ital.)

causerie (Fr. f.) informal article or talk, esp. on a literary subject

cauterize *not* -ise

Cavafy, Constantine (1863–1933) Greek poet, *not* K-, -is; **Konstandinos Kavafis** in a Modern Gr. transcription

Cavalleria rusticana ('rustic gallantry') an opera by Mascagni, 1890

cavass *use* k-

caveat a formal warning (not ital.)

caveat/ actor (Lat.) let the doer beware

caveat emptor let the buyer beware (not ital.)

caveat/ venditor (Lat.) let the seller beware, — **viator** let the traveller beware

caviar *not* -iare, -ier

cavil/ make trifling objections; **-led, -ler, -ling** (one l in US)

Cavour, Count Camillo (1810–61) Italian statesman

Cawnpore Eng. hist. form, *now* **Kanpur**

Caxton, William (c.1422–91) the first English printer

Cayenne the capital of and district in French Guiana (cap.), a type of hot pepper (not cap.)

cayman/ a type of American alligator; *not* cai-, kai-; pl. **-s**

Cayman Islands W. Indies

cazique *use* **cacique**

CB Cape Breton, Cavalry Brigade, Chief Baron, citizens' band (radio), Coal Board, Common Bench, Companion (of the Order) of the Bath, (naval) Confidential Book, confined to barracks, cost–benefit, County Borough, (mus.) *contrabasso* (double bass)

CBA cost benefit analysis, Council for British Archaeology

CBC Canadian Broadcasting Corporation

CBE Commander (of the Order) of the British Empire

CBEL *Cambridge Bibliography of English Literature* (also rom. as abbr.)

CBI Confederation of British Industry, (US) Cumulative Book Index

CC 200, Caius College, Central Committee, Chamber of Commerce, Chess Club, Circuit Court; City Council, -lor; Civil Court, Common Councilman, Companion of the Order of Canada, Consular Corps, Countryside Commission, County Clerk, County Commissioner; County Council, -lor; County Court, Cricket Club, Cycling Club

cc cubic centimetre (no points)

cc. *capita* (chapters)

c.c. carbon copy

CCC 300, Corpus Christi College, Oxford and Cambridge

CCCC 400

CCCCCC Corpus Christi College, Cambridge, Cricket Club

CCF Combined Cadet Force

C.Chem. chartered chemist

CCP Code of Civil Procedure, Court of Common Pleas, credit card purchase

C.Cr.P. Code of Criminal Procedure

CD 400, Civil Defence, compact disc

Cd cadmium (no point)

cd candela (no point)

Cd. Command Paper (1900–18) with number following

c.d. cum dividend (with dividend)

CDC Commonwealth Development Corporation (till 1963 Colonial Development Corporation)

Cdr. Commander

Cdre. Commodore (naval)

CD-ROM (comput.) compact disc read-only memory

CE Chief Engineer, Church of England, Civil Engineer

CE Common (*or* Christian) Era, used instead of AD in non-Christian contexts; follows the numerals: '250 CE', 'second century CE' (small caps.)

Ce cerium (no point)

ceasefire (noun, one word)

Ceauşescu, Nicolae (1918–89) President of Romania 1967–89

cedar a tree

ceder one who cedes; cf. **Seder**

cedilla a mark under a letter, as ç

Cedron *see* **Kidron**

Ceefax (propr.) the BBC teletext service

CEGB Central Electricity Generating Board

ceilidh (Ir. and Sc.) gathering for music, dancing, etc. and stories

Celanese (propr.) an artificial silk

cela/ va sans dire (Fr.) needless to say, — **viendra** that will come

Celebes *now* **Sulawesi**

Celebrated Jumping Frog of Calaveras County, The sketch by Mark Twain 1865

celebrator *not* -er

celestial hierarchy based on the two enumerations of St Paul, St Gregory the Great arranged the nine orders of angelic beings as seraphim, cherubim, thrones, dominations, principalities, powers, virtues, archangels, and angels; Dionysius the Pseudo-Areopagite transposed virtues and principalities

celiac (US) = **coeliac**

cellar *not* -er

Cellini, Benvenuto (1500–71) Italian goldsmith and sculptor

cell/o a violoncello, pl. **-os**; **-ist** the player

cellophane (propr.) a transparent wrapping material

Celsius a temperature scale (cap.) (*prefer to* centigrade), abbr. **C**

Celt/, -ic, -icism *not* K-, abbr. **Celt.**

celt (archaeol.) stone or metal prehistoric implement with a chisel edge (not cap.)

cembal/o a harpsichord, pl. **-os**; **-ist** the player

CEMS Church of England Men's Society

C.Eng. chartered engineer

cenobite *use* **coe-** (except in US)

Cenozoic (geol.) the most recent era of geological time; in specialist use **Caino-** (cap.)

censer an incense vessel

censor (noun) an official with power to suppress (parts of) books etc.; (verb) act as a censor

censure criticize harshly, reprove

cent/, -s a US etc. coin (no point); abbr. **c.**, **ct.**, **cts.**; symbol ¢ (the solidus may be vertical or slanted) close up to the figure, e.g. 49¢, and used only with amounts less than a dollar

cent. central, century; *see also* **per cent**

cental/ a corn measure of 100 lb, pl. **-s**; abbr. **ctl.**

centauromachy (a representation of) centaurs fighting

centaury a plant

centenarian one who is 100 years old

centen/ary a 100th anniversary; **-nial** of or relating to a centenary, (esp. US) = **centenary**

centennial (adj.) lasting for 100 years, (noun) = **centenary**

center *use* **-re** (except in US)

centering a framing for an arch, *not* -reing; *see also* **centre**

Centers for Disease Control a US national medical research facility, Atlanta, Ga.; *not* Center

centesimal reckoning or reckoned by hundredths

centi a prefix meaning one-hundredth, abbr. **c**

centigrade (not cap.) abbr. **C**, *use* **Celsius**

centigram *not* -gramme, abbr. **cg** (no point)

centilitre abbr. **cl** (no point)

centime/ one-hundredth of French franc, pl. **-s**; abbr. **c., cts.**

centimetre 0.394 inch, *not* -er (US); abbr. (sing. and pl.) **cm** (no point)

Cento (hist.) Central Treaty Organization

cent/o writing composed of scraps from various authors, pl. **-os**

Central region of Scotland

central abbr. **cent.**

centralize *not* -ise

Central Provinces (India) *now* Madhya Pradesh

centr/e, -ed, -ing (typ.) set matter in middle of line, measure, etc.; *not* center- (US); *see also* **centering**

centre/board, -fold (one word)

centre-notes (typ.) those between columns

centrepiece (one word)

cents abbr. **c., cts.**

centum 100, abbr. **C** (no point); *see also* **per cent**

centumvir/ a Roman commissioner, pl. **-i**

centurion the commander of a company in the Roman army, *not* -ian

century abbr. **c.** *or* **cent.**

ceorl (hist.) a freeman of the lowest rank in Anglo-Saxon England

cephalic of the head, *not* k-

Cephalonia a Greek island, ancient name **Cephallenia**; in Modern Gr. **Kefallinia**

ceramic etc., *not* k-; abbr. **ceram.**

Cerberus (Gr. myth.) the three-headed dog at the gate of Hades

cerebell/um the hind brain, pl. **-a**; adj. **-ar**

cerebro/spinal, -vascular (one word)

cerebr/um the brain proper, pl. **-a**; adj. **-al**

cere/cloths, -ments grave clothes, originally dipped in wax; *not* sere-

Ceredigion a district of Wales, *formerly* Cardiganshire

Cerenkov/, Pavel (**Alekseevich**) (1904–90) Russian physicist, discoverer of — **radiation**, created — **counter**; *not* Che-

cerge *use* **cie-**

ceriph (typ.) *use* **serif**

cerise (Fr. f.) cherry

cerise a colour

cerium symbol **Ce**

CERN (*formerly* Conseil Européen [*later* Organisation Européenne] pour la Recherche Nucléaire); *now* the European Laboratory for Particle Physics

cert (colloq.) abbr. of certainty (no point)

cert. certificate, certify

Cert. Ed. Certificate in Education

certiorari (law) a writ removing a case to a higher court (not ital. except in legal works)

cerulean blue; *not* cae-, coe-

Cervantes (**Saavedra**)**, Miguel de** (1547–1616) author of *Don Quixote*

cervelas (Fr. m.) saveloy sausage

cervelle (Fr. f.) brains

Cervin/ (Fr. m.) the Matterhorn, in It. **-o**

cervi/x (anat.) pl. **-ces**, adj. **-cal**

Cesarean *use* **Cae-** (except in US)

cesare/vitch, -witch *use* **tsarevich**

Cesarewitch an annual Newmarket horse race

cesium *use* **cae-** (except in US)

cesser (law) the coming to an end

c'est/-à-dire (Fr.) that is to say, **— la guerre** it is according to the customs of war, **— le premier pas qui coûte** it is the first step that is difficult

Cestr: the signature of the Bishop of Chester (colon)

Cestrian of Chester

cestui/ que trust (law) a beneficiary, pl. **cestuis que trust** (*not* trustent); **— que vie** he on whose life land is held, pl. **cestuis que trust**

cesura *use* **cae-**

CET Central European Time

cetera/ desiderantur *or* **— desunt** (Lat.) the rest are missing

ceteris paribus (Lat.) other things being equal, abbr. **cet. par.**

Cetinje former capital of Montenegro; *not* Cett-, Zet-, -inge; *see also* **Podgorica**

Ceylon *now* **Sri Lanka**; adj. **Sri Lankan**; *see also* **Sinhalese**

Cézanne, Paul (1839–1906) French painter

CF Chaplain to the Forces

Cf californium (no point)

cf. calf, *confer* ('compare' *not* 'see') (not ital.)

c.f. carried forward

CFA Communauté Financière d'Afrique (African Financial Community)

CFC/ chlorofluorocarbon, pl. **-s** (no apos.)

CFE college of further education

CG Captain of the Guard, coastguard, Coldstream Guards

C.G. Captain General, Commissary General, Consul General

cg centigram, -s (no point)

c.g. centre of gravity

CGM Conspicuous Gallantry Medal

CGPM Conférence Générale des Poids et des Mesures (General Conference of Weights and Measures)

CGS Chief of General Staff

cgs centimetre-gram-second

CGT Capital Gains Tax, Confédération Générale du Travail (General Federation of Labour)

CH clearing house, Companion of Honour, courthouse, custom house

Ch. chaplain; Chin/a, -ese; (Lat.) *Chirurgiae* (of surgery), (mus.) choir organ, Church

ch not to be divided in most languages; a separate letter in Spanish and Welsh (following *c* in the alphabet) and Czech, Slovak, and Serbian (following *b* in the alphabet)

ch. chapter, chief; child, -ren; chorus

Chablis a white burgundy

cha-cha a ballroom dance, originally cha-cha-cha (hyphens)

chaconne a dance

chacun/ à son goût (Fr.) everyone to his taste (properly — *son goût*), — *pour soi* everyone for himself

Chad/ Cent. Africa; **-ian**; **Lake** — in Sudan, in Fr. **Tchad**; English saint (also spelt **Ceadda**)

chador (Ind.) a Muslim overgarment worn by women; *not* chadar, chuddar

Chagall, Marc (1889–1985) Russian painter

chaîné (ballet) a quick step or turn from one foot to another, or a series of these, performed in a line

chain/ gang, — **mail** (two words, hyphen when attrib.), — **reaction** (two words)

chain-smok/er, -ing (hyphens)

chair/, -man, -person, -woman (one word), abbr. **C.**

chaise/ longue a couch, daybed; pl. **-s longues** (not ital.)

chal (Romany) a Gypsy, f. *chai*

chalaz/a (biol.) a string attached to the yolk of an egg, pl. **-ae**

chalcedony *not* calce-, chalci-

Chald/aea Babylonia (*but* -ea in AV); **-aic, -aism** (*not* -ism), **-ean, -ee**; abbr. **Chald.**

Chaldee the language of the Chaldaeans *or* a native of ancient Chaldaea; the Aramaic language as used in OT books

chalet *not* châ- (not ital.)

Chaliapine (*strictly* **Shalyapin**), **Fyodor** (**Ivanovich**) (1873–1938) Russian bass singer

chalkboard (US) = **blackboard**

Châlons-sur-Marne dép. Marne, France; battle, 451

Chalon-sur-Saône dép. Saône-et-Loire, France

chamb. chamberlain (cap. as a title of office)

chambermaid (one word)

chamber/ music, — pot (two words)

Chambers's/ (*Edinburgh*) *Journal,* — *Encyclopaedia*

Chambertin a dry red burgundy

chambray a gingham cloth

chambré (of red wine) brought to room temperature

chameleon a lizard of changeable colour, *not* chamae-

chamois-leather *not* shammy-

chamomile *use* cam- (except in US)

Chamonix dép. Haute-Savoie, France; *not* -ouni, -ounix, -oisny

champagne a sparkling wine from the Champagne region of France

champaign flat open country

champerty (law) an illegal agreement, *not* -arty

champignon (Fr. m.) a mushroom or toadstool, *not* -pinion

Champigny-sur-Marne a Paris suburb (hyphens)

Champlain, Lake between NY and Vt.

Champlain, Samuel de (*c.*1570–1635) French founder of Quebec, Can.

champlevé a kind of enamel

Champollion, Jean François (1790–1832) French Egyptologist

Champs-Elysées Paris

chancellery *not* -ory

chancellor (cap. as title) abbr. **chanc.**

chance-medley (law) a form of homicide (hyphen)

Chancery abbr. **Chanc.**

chancre an ulcer, esp. venereal

Chandler's Ford Hants.

Chanel, Gabrielle 'Coco' (1883–1971) French couturier

change/able, -ability

changeover (one word)

Chang Jiang Pinyin for the **Yangtze River**

channel/, -led, -ling

Channel Islands *not* Isles, abbr. **CI**

chanson/ (Fr. f.) a song, *-nette* (f.) a little song, *-nier* (m.) singer or songwriter in cabaret; — *de geste* a medieval French epic poem, pl. *-s de geste*

chant/ singing; *-er* of a bagpipe, *not* chau-

chanteuse a female singer of popular songs (not ital.)

Chantilly dép. Oise, France

Chantrey/, Sir Francis Legatt (1781–1841) sculptor; — **Fund** Royal Academy of Arts, London

chantry an endowed chapel

chanty *use* **shanty**

Chanukkah a scholarly and US var. of **Hanukkah**

chap. chapel, chaplain, chapter

chaparajos (pl.) a cowboy's leather protection for the front of the legs, *not* -ejos; abbr. **chaps**

chapatti *not* chupatty

chapbook (one word)

chapeau/ (Fr. m.) a hat, pl. *-x*; *-x bas!* hats off!; *-bras* a three-cornered hat carried under arm (hyphen)

chapel/ abbr. **chap.**; (typ.) smallest organized union group in printing and publishing offices; **father/mother of** — elected head of a chapel, abbr. **FOC, MOC**

Chapel-en-le-Frith Derby. (hyphens)

chapelle ardente (Fr. f.) a chapel lighted for a lying-in-state (no hyphen)

Chapel/ Royal pl. *-s Royal*

chaperone *not* -on, -onne

Chap.-Gen. Chaplain-General

chaplain abbr. **chap.**

Chapman, Geoffrey publisher

Chapman & Hall publishers

Chappell, William (1809–88) music publisher

chaps *see* **chaparajos**

chapter/, -s abbr. **c., cap., ch., chap.**

char/, -red, -ring

char a small trout, *not* -rr

charabanc/ a motor coach, pl. *-s*; *not* char-à-banc

characteriz/e *not* -ise; *-able, -ation, -er*

chargé *more fully* **chargé d'affaires**, pl. **chargés** (not ital.)

charisma/, adj. *-tic*, pl. *-ta*

charivari a mock serenade, *not* shivaree (US); *The London Charivari*, former subtitle of *Punch*

Charlemagne (742–814) king of the Franks from 768, Holy Roman Emperor from 800, adj. **Carolingian**

Charles abbr. **C., Chas.**

Charles's Wain (astr.) the seven stars of Ursa Major = US the Big Dipper

Charleston Ill., SC (source of the dance), W. Va.

Charlestown Mass.; Nevis Island, St Kitts-Nevis

Charlottenburg a Berlin suburb

charlotte russe (cook.) a custard or cream enclosed in sponge cake (not ital.)

Charollais a breed of cattle, *not* -olais

Charon (Gr. myth.) the ferryman of the Styx

charpoy an Indian bedstead

charr *use* **char**

chartbuster (one word)

charter/ flight, — member, — party (two words)

Charters Towers Queensland, Australia (no apos.)

chartreuse a liqueur first made at Carthusian monastery near Grenoble (cap. only as propr.)

Chartreux a Carthusian monk

Charybdis (Gr. myth.) a personified whirlpool supposedly in the Straits of Messina; *see also* **Scylla and Charybdis**

Chas. Charles

Chasid/, -ic *use* **Has-**

Chasles,/ Michel (1793–1880) French mathematician; — **Philarète** (1798–1873) French literary critic

chasse (Fr. f.) a liqueur taken after coffee

châsse (Fr. f.) a reliquary, a rim or frame

chassé/ (Fr. m.) a gliding dance step (not ital.), — *croisé* double chassé (ital.)

chassis a framework as of a motor car; a window sash; pl. same (not ital.)

chastis/e *not* -ize; *-ement, -ing*

chateau/ a castle, pl. *-x* (not ital., no accent)

Chateaubriand, François-René, vicomte de (1768–1848) French writer and statesman (no accent on surname)

chateaubriand (Fr. cook.) a fillet of beef, cut thick and grilled (no accent, no cap.)

Châteaubriant dép. Loire-Inférieure, France

Châteaudun dép. Eure-et-Loir, France

Châteauguay Que., Canada

Château/ Lafite, — Latour, — Margaux clarets (two words)

châteaux en Espagne (Fr.) = 'castles in the air'

chatelain/ a lord of the manor, f. *-e*

Chattanooga Tenn.; site of a battle in the US Civil War

Chatto & Windus publishers

Chaucer/, Geoffrey (?1345–1400) English poet, *-ian*

chaud-froid a dish of cold cooked meat or fish in jelly or sauce (not ital.)

chauffeu/r f. *-se*

chaunt/, -er *use* **chant** (except when copying older spelling)

chaussée (Fr. f.) a causeway, the ground level

chaussures (Fr. f. pl.) boots, shoes, etc.

Chautauqua a celebrated resort in New York State; (not cap.) (hist.) a school or similar educational course

chauvin/ism, -ist (not cap.)

Ch.B. *Chirurgiae Baccalaureus* (Bachelor of Surgery)

Ch.Ch. Christ Church, Oxford; *also* **Ch:Ch:** (after a former style of abbreviation)

Chebyshev, Pafnuti (Lvovich) (1821–94) Russian mathematician, *not* Tch-

Chech/nya *formerly* the Chechen-Ingushetian Autonomous Republic; **-en** a native or inhabitant of Chechnya, pl. **-ens**

check *see* **cheque**

checkers (US) = **draughts**

check/-in (noun, hyphen)

checking account (US) = **current account**

check/list, -out (one word)

check-up (noun, hyphen)

Cheddar cheese *not* -er

Cheeryble Brothers characters in Dickens's *Nicholas Nickleby*

cheese/board, -cake, -cloth (one word)

cheesy *not* -ey

cheetah *not* chet-

chef (Fr. m.) a cook; *chef/ de cuisine* head cook; — *d'orchestre* leader of the orchestra; — *d'œuvre* a masterpiece, pl. *chefs-d'œuvre*

cheir- *use* **chir-**

Cheka (hist.) Soviet 'Extraordinary Commission (against counter-revolution)', 1917–22; *see also* **KGB**

Chekhov, Anton (Pavlovich) (1861–1904) Russian playwright and story-writer, *not* the many variants

CHEL Cambridge History of English Literature (also rom. as abbr.)

Chelonia an order of reptiles comprising tortoises and turtles, *not* Testudinata

Chellean *use* **Abbevillian**

Chelmsford: the signature of the Bishop of Chelmsford (colon)

Chelyabinsk Siberia

chem/ical, -ist *not* chy-; abbr. **chem.**

chemical elements no point after symbols; *see also* individual entries

chemico-physical (hyphen)

chemin de fer (Fr. m.) railway, a form of baccarat

chemistry abbr. **chem.**

Chemnitz Germany, called **Karl-Marx-Stadt** under the GDR

cheque a written money order, *not* check (US)

chequer (noun) a pattern of squares; (verb) variegate, interrupt (*not* -ck-)

Chequers the Prime Minister's official country house in Bucks.

Cherbourg dép. Manche, France

chercheu/r (associée) (Fr. m.) (associate) researcher, f. *-se*

cherchez la femme (Fr.) lit. 'look for the woman', i.e. find the woman indirectly responsible for otherwise inexplicable acts or occurrences

chère amie (Fr. f.) a sweetheart

Cherenkov *use* **Cerenkov**

chér/i (Fr.) f. *-ie* darling

Chernenko, Konstantin (Ustinovich) (1911–85) General Secretary of Communist Party of the Soviet Union, President of the USSR 1984–5

Chernobyl Ukraine, the site of a nuclear accident 1986

chernozem a Russian black soil

Cherokee (of or relating to) (a member of) a Native American tribe, the language of this people

chersonese a name applied to various peninsulas, cap. when used as name (esp. of Thracian peninsula west of Hellespont)

cherub/ an angelic being, pl. **-s**, Heb. pl. **-im**; the practice in the AV of -*im* as sing. and -*s* as pl. should not be imitated

Cherubini, (Maria) Luigi (1760–1842) Italian composer

Cherwell a river, Oxon.; pron. 'char-well'

Chesapeake Bay between Md. and Va.

che sarà sarà (It.) what will be, will be

Cheshire abbr. **Ches.**

Chesil Beach Dorset

chess/board, -man (one word)

chess/ piece, — player, — problem (two words)

Chester the formal name for Cheshire, now only in hist. use, esp. in 'County palatine of Chester'

Chester-le-Street Co. Durham (hyphens)

chestnut *not* chesnut

chetah *use* **chee-**

chetniks Serbian guerrilla forces during Second World War, now used of Serbian irregulars or pejoratively of Serbian troops in general; in Serbo-Croat *četnici*

cheval/ (Fr. m.) a horse, pl. **chevaux**; — *de frise* (mil.) an obstacle to cavalry advance, usually in the pl. *chevaux de frise*

cheval glass a tall mirror on a frame

Chevalier,/ Albert (1861–1923) English music-hall artiste; — **Maurice** (1888–1972) French entertainer

chevalier/ (Fr. m.) knight, — *d'industrie* a swindler

Chevallier, Gabriel (1895–1969) French novelist

cheville a violin peg; a stopgap word in a sentence or verse

chèvre goat's-milk cheese (not ital.)

chevreau/ (Fr. m.) kid goat, pl. *-x*

chevreuil (Fr. m.) roe deer, (cook.) venison

chevrotain a deerlike animal, *not* -tin

Chevy abbr. of Chevrolet, US make of car

chevy *use* **chivvy**

Chevy Chase Md.

Chevy Chase, The Ballad of 15th-c. Eng. ballad

Cheyenne Wyo.; also a Native American tribe, the language of this people

Cheyne–Stokes respiration (en rule)

Cheyne Walk Chelsea

chez (Fr.) at the house of

chi/ the twenty-second letter of the Gr. alphabet (*X*, χ); **-square** a method of comparing statistical experiment with theory (hyphen)

Chi. Chicago

Chiang/ **Ching-kuo, General** (1910–88) President of Taiwan 1978–87, son of — **Kai-shek** (1887–1975) Nationalist Chinese statesman and first President of Taiwan 1950–75

Chianti an Italian wine (cap.)

chiaroscuro/ light and shade, pl. **-s**

chias/**mus** inversion in the second of two parallel phrases of the order followed in the first (e.g. 'He saved others; himself he cannot save'), **-tic**

chibouk a Turkish pipe, *not* -bouque

chic stylish(ness) (not ital.)

Chicago Ill.; abbr. **Chi.**

chiccory *use* **chicory**

Chichele Oxford professorships, *not* -ley

Chichén Itzá Mexico, site of antiquities

Chickahominy Va.

Chickamauga Ga.; battle, 1863

Chickasaw a Native American people

chickenpox (one word)

Chico Calif., often erroneously altered to Chicago in references

chicory *Chichorium intybus*, cultivated for its flowers and root; *not* chicc-; (US) = **endive**

chief abbr. **C.**, **ch.**; **Chief**/ **Accountant** abbr. **CA**; — **Baron** abbr. **CB**; — **Justice** (caps., no hyphen) abbr. **CJ**; — **of General Staff** abbr. **CGS**

chield (Sc.) a young man, *not* chiel

chiffonier a sideboard, *not* -nnier (not ital.)

chiffre (Fr. m.) figure, numeral, monogram

chignon a coil of hair

chigoe a W. Indian parasite; *not* jigger, chigger (except in dialect)

child/**bed, -birth, -care** (one word)

Childe Harold's Pilgrimage a poem by Byron, 1811–17

Childermas 28 Dec.

child/**like, -minder, -proof** (one word)

Chile/ S. America, *not* Chili; **-an**

chile *use* **chilli** (except in US)

Chilianwala Pakistan; *not* -wallah, Killian-

chilli/ a red, *or* Guinea, pepper; *not* chile, chili (US), chilly; pl. **-es**

Chiltern Hundreds (noun pl.) a Crown manor, whose administration is a nominal office for which an MP applies as a way of resigning from the House of Commons

chimaera *use* **chimera**

Chimborazo Ecuador

chimera a creation of the imagination, (biol.) an organism with two cells of two or more genetically distinct types; *not* -aera

chimere a bishop's upper robe, *not* -er

chincapin dwarf chestnut; *not* -kapin, -quapin

chin-chin a drinking toast

Chindits the British troops behind Japanese lines in Burma 1943–5

Chinese abbr. **Ch.** *or* **Chin.**

Chinese Classics the sacred books of Confucianism

chinoiserie imitation Chinese decorative objects

chin-up (US) = **pull-up**

chipmunk a N. American ground squirrel, *not* -uck

Chipping Campden Glos.

chi-rho the monogram of ΧΡ (☧), first letters of Gr. *Khristos*

chiromancy palmistry, *not* cheir-

Chiron (Gr. myth.) a centaur, *not* Cheir-

chiropodist one who treats hands and feet; *not* cheir-, -pedist

chiropract/**ic** removal of nerve interference by manipulation of spinal column, **-or** one who does this

Chiroptera the bat order

chirosophy palmistry, *not* cheir-

chirrup/, **-ed, -ing**

chirurgiae (Lat.) of surgery, abbr. **Ch.**

chisel/, **-led, -ling**

Chişinău cap. of Moldavia, *not* Kishinev; in Russ. **Kishinyov**

chit, chitty (Anglo-Ind.) a letter

Chittagong Bangladesh

chivvy harass; *not* che-, chivy

chlorine symbol **Cl**

chlorodyne a medicine containing chloroform, *not* -ine

chlorophyll (bot.) the green colouring matter of plants; *not* -il, -yl

Ch.M. *Chirurgiae Magister* (Master of Surgery)

chm. chairman (m. and f.)

choc. chocolate

chock/-a-block, -full (hyphens)

Choctaw (of or relating to) a Native American people, their language

choir a part of a church, singers; *not* quire

cholera morbus acute gastroenteritis

cholesterol a fatty substance found in parts of the body, *not* -in

choliamb (prosody) a Greek or Latin metre of limping character, esp. a trimeter of two iambuses and a spondee or trochee; also called **scazon**

Chomsk/y, (Avram) Noam (b. 1928) US linguist and writer, **-yan** *also* **-ian**

choosy *not* -ey

Chopin, Frédéric François (1810–49) Polish composer

'Chops of the Channel' the west entrance to the English Channel

chop suey (two words)

choreograph/y ballet design, **-er** the arranger

chorography description of districts (intermediate between geography and topography)

chorus/ pl. **-es, -ed**

chose (law) a thing

Chose, Monsieur (Fr.) Mr So-and-so

chose jugée (Fr. f.) a matter already decided

chota hazri (Anglo-Ind.) a light early breakfast

Chota Nagpur Bihar, India

chota peg a small measure of spirits (usually whisky)

chou/ (Fr. m.) cabbage, puff (pastry), a dress rosette; pl. **-x**; *-fleur* cauliflower (hyphen), pl. *choux-fleurs*; *choux de Bruxelles* Brussels sprouts; *chou marin* sea-kale

Chou En-lai in Pinyin **Zhou Enlai**

choux a rich light pastry

chow mein (two words)

Chr. Christ, Christian, Chronicles

Chr. Coll. Cam. Christ's College, Cambridge

Chrétien de Troyes (12th c.) French poet

Christ Church Oxford, *not* — — College; abbr. **Ch.Ch., Ch:Ch:** (older)

Christchurch Dorset, and NZ

Christe eleison (eccl.) 'Christ, have mercy'

christening the act of giving a Christian name during the rite of **baptism**

Christian/ -ity (cap.)

Christiania former name of Oslo, Norway (sometimes **K-**); a type of turn in skiing, abbr. **Christie**, *not* -y

Christianize *not* -ise (cap.)

Christie, Manson, & Woods auctioneers ('**Christie's**')

Christmas Day/ (caps.), **Old** — — 5 Jan. (1753–1800), 6 Jan. (1801–1900), 7 Jan. (1901–2100)

Christoff, Boris (1919–93) Bulgarian bass singer

Christ's College, Cambridge abbr. **Chr. Coll. Cam.**

chromatography (chem.) technique for separation of a mixture

chrome yellow a pigment

chromium symbol **Cr**

chromo/ (typ.) (no point) abbr. of **chromolithograph** a picture printed in colours from stone or plates, pl. **-s**

chromolithography (one word)

chromo paper one with a special heavy coating for lithographic printing

chromosome (biol.) a structure carrying genes in cell

chromosphere the gaseous envelope of the sun

chron. chronolog/y, -ical, -ically; chronometry

Chronicles, First, Second Book of (OT) abbr. **1 Chr., 2 Chr.**

chronological age abbr. **CA**

Chrononhotonthologos a burlesque drama by Henry Carey, 1734

chrysal/is pl. **-ides**

Chrysaor (Gr. myth.) the son of Neptune

Chryseis (Gr. myth.) the daughter of Chryses, a Trojan priest

chryselephantine (Gr. sculpture) overlaid with gold and ivory

Chrysler/ a US make of car, — **Building** New York City

chrysoprase green chalcedony, *not* -phrase

Chrysostom, St John (347–407) Greek patriarch

chthon/ian, -ic (Gr. myth.) dwelling in the underworld, *not* -ean

chuddar *use* **chador**

chukka a period of play in polo, *not* -er

Chunnel a portmanteau slang word for the *Channel tunnel* (cap., not in official use)

chupatty *use* **chapatti**

Chur Graubünden, Switzerland; in Fr. **Coire**

Church institutions or organizations of Christianity, e.g. the Church of England, the Methodist Church (cap.); a building for (usually Christian) worship (not cap.); in the NT 'church' (*ekklesia*, othewise trans. 'congregation' or 'assembly') is lower case, as not yet a formal title or entity; abbr. **C., Ch., ch.**

Church Assembly (*properly* National Assembly of the Church of England) set up 1920, absorbed into the General Synod 1970

Church Commissioners *formerly* Ecclesiastical Commissioners and Queen Anne's Bounty

church/goer, -going (one word)

Churchill,/ Winston (1871–1947) US writer; — **Sir Winston Leonard Spencer** (1874–1965) British statesman, Prime Minister, grandfather of — **Winston Leonard** (b. 1940) British politician

church mouse (two words)

church/warden, -yard (one word)

churinga a sacred object, esp. an amulet, among the Australian Aboriginals

Churrigueresque a lavishly ornate Spanish baroque style

chute a slide

chutney *not* -nee, -ny

chutzpah (Yiddish) shameless audacity, cheek (not ital.)

Chypre Fr. for Cyprus

chypre (Fr. f.) a heavy perfume made from sandalwood (not ital.)

CI Channel Islands, Chief Inspector, Chief Instructor, Commonwealth Institute, Communist International

Ci curie (no point)

CIA (US) Central Intelligence Agency

ciao (It.) hello, goodbye (not ital. in Eng.)

Cibber, Colley (1671–1757) Poet Laureate 1730–57

Cic. Cicero

cicad/a tree cricket; *not* cig-, -ala; pl. **-ae** (biol.), **-as** (general)

cicatri/ce a scar, pl. **-ces**; (med.) **-x**, pl. **-ces**

cicatrize *not* -ise

Cicero, Marcus Tullius, 'Tully' (106–43 BC) Roman orator, abbr. **Cic.**

cicero (typ.) Continental type-measure of 12 **Didot** points

ciceron/e a guide, pl. **-i**

Cicestr: the signature of the Bishop of Chichester (colon)

cicisbe/o (It.) a married woman's gallant, pl. *-i*

CID Criminal Investigation Department

Cid (Campeador), El (*c.*1040–99) Spanish warrior

ci-devant (Fr.) formerly

CIE Companion of the Order of the Indian Empire

Cie (Fr. abbr.) *compagnie* (company) (no point)

cierge a large candle; *not* cer-, ser-

c.i.f. cost, insurance, and freight

cigala *use* **cicada**

ci-gît (Fr.) here lies

CIGS Chief of Imperial General Staff

CII Chartered Insurance Institute

cili/um a hairlike appendage, pl. **-a**; **-ary, -ate, -ation**

cill *use* **sill**

Cimabue, Giovanni (*c.*1240–1302) Italian painter

cimbalom a dulcimer

cim/ex a bedbug, pl. **-ices**

Cimmerian intensely dark; (pl.) a nomadic people, 7th c. BC (cap.)

C.-in-C. Commander-in-Chief (no hyphens in US)

Cincinnati Ohio

Cincinnatus, Lucius Quinctius (5th c. BC) Roman hero

cine-camera (hyphen)

CinemaScope (propr., one word, two caps.)

cinematheque a film library or archive *or* a small cinema

cinéma-vérité art or process of making realistic films

cinerari/a a plant with ash-coloured foliage, pl. **-as**

cinerari/um a niche for urn with ashes of the deceased, pl. **-a**

Cingalese *use* **Sinhal-**

cingul/um a girdle *or* zone, pl. **-a**

Cinquecento 1500–99, and the Renaissance art of that century (usually cap. in It. and often in Eng.)

Cinque Ports Hastings, New Romney, Hythe, Dover, and Sandwich, plus Winchelsea and Rye

cinques (campanology pl.) changes on eleven bells

cion *use* **scion**

cipher *not* cy-

cipolin (one l) veined white and green marble; in It. *cipollino*

Cipriani, Giambattista (1727–85) Italian painter and engraver

circ. *circiter* (about), *prefer* abbr. **c.**

circa (Lat. prep.) about, in Eng. used mainly with dates and quantities; abbr. **c.** (set close up to figures)

circa mediem (Lat.) about the middle (as of a work), abbr. **circa med.**

Circean of Circe, *not* -aean *but* **Circaeus** in Lat.

circiter (Lat. adv.) about, approximately; abbr. **c.**

circle sign ○; **arc of a circle** sign ∩

Circuit Court abbr. **CC**

circuit edges (bind.) limp covers turned over to protect the leaves

circulariz/e issue circulars, *not* -ise; **-ing**

circum (Lat.) about; in Eng. used as a (roman) prefix meaning around, surrounding (no hyphen)

circumcise *not* -ize

circumflex (typ.) the accent ^

circumflexion *not* -flect-

Cirencester Glos.

cire perdue (Fr. f.) the lost-wax process of bronze-casting

cirque a (natural) amphitheatre or arena, a ring; (geol.) a hollow or gully at the head of a valley or on a mountainside (not ital.)

cirrhos/is a liver disease, pl. **-es**; 'cirrhosis of the liver' is a tautology

cirriped a marine crustacean, *not* -de

cirr/us (bot.) a tendril, (zool.) a slender appendage, (meteor.) a tuftlike cloud formation; pl. **-i**

CIS Confederation of Independent States

cis- prefix meaning 'on this side of'

cis- (chem.) a prefix denoting a type of isomer, e.g. *cis*-decalin (ital., always hyphenated); *not syn-*

cisalpine on the Roman side of the Alps (not cap. except in **Cisalpine Gaul**)

cisatlantic on this side of the Atlantic

cislunar on the side of the moon facing Earth

cispontine on the north side of the Thames; *see also* **transpontine**

cist (archaeol.) a tomb or coffin, *not* k-; cf. **cyst**

cit. citation, cited, citizen

citizens' band (radio) abbr. **CB**

Citlaltépetl a dormant Mexican volcano

citoyen/ (Fr.) f. *-ne* citizen

citrine lemon-colour(ed)

Citroën a French make of car

cittadin/o (It.) a citizen, pl. *-i*; f. *-a*, pl. *-e*

city abbr. **c.**, **the City** London's financial centre

City Company a corporation descended from an ancient trade guild (caps.)

City editor the supervisor of financial reports, *but* (US) **city editor** the editor of local news

ciudad (Sp.) city, *not* cui-

Ciudad Bolívar Venezuela, *formerly* Angostura

Ciudad Trujillo *now* **Santo Domingo**, capital of Dominican Republic

civ. civil, -ian

civics (pl. used as sing.) the study of citizenship

Civil/ Court abbr. **CC**, **— Engineer** abbr. **CE**

civiliz/e *not* -ise; **-able**, **-er**

Civil/ Servants, — Service (caps.) abbr. **CS**

Civitavecchia Italy (one word)

CJ Chief Justice

Cl chlorine (no point)

cl. class, clause, cloth; centilitre, -s (no point)

Clackmannan a district and former county of Scotland (three *n*s)

Clairaut, Alexis Claude (1713–65) French mathematician, *not* -ault

claire-cole *use* **clearcole**

clairvoyant/ f. **-e** (not ital.)

clam/ to clog, smear; **-miness, -my**

clamjamphrie (Sc.) rubbish, a mob; *not* the many variants

clam/our *not* -or (US), *but* **-orous**

clampdown (noun, one word)

clang/our *not* -or (US), *but* **-orous**

Claparède, Jean Louis (René Antoine Édouard) (1832–70) Swiss naturalist

claptrap empty words (one word)

claque/ hired applauders, **-ur** a member of a claque (not ital.)

clar. (mus.) clarinet, (typ.) clarendon

clarabella (mus.) an organ stop, *not* clari-

Clarenceux (her.) the second King of Arms (q.v.), *not* -cieux

Clarendon/ Press named after **— Building** a former printing house of the University Press at Oxford; hence an imprint on certain learned books published by OUP

claret red wine of Bordeaux

clarinet/, -tist *not* -ionet, -ist; abbr. **clar.**

Clarissa Harlowe the heroine of the novel *Clarissa* by S. Richardson, 1748

class abbr. **cl.**

class. classic, -al; classification

classes (bot., zool.) (typ.) to be in roman with capital initials

classic of acknowledged excellence, remarkably typical, outstandingly important, *or* simple and harmonious, as in art, music, etc.

classical of ancient Greek or Latin literature or art, or having the linguistic form used by ancient standard authors; serious or conventional *or* following traditional principles; within disciplines *classical* may have a sense that is more temporal and less qualitative: in music studies 'classical music' refers to the period after Baroque and before Romantic; in Greek studies 'classical Greek' is Hellenic (rather than modern or Byzantine)

clause (typ.) lower case as part of a name, e.g. 'clause 3.2'; abbr. **cl.**, pl. **cll.**

Clausewitz, Karl von (1780–1831) Prussian military writer

clayey of the substance of clay

cld. called, cancelled, cleared (goods or shipping), coloured

clean (typ.) said of proofs or revises with few errors, or pulled after matter has been corrected

clearcole (noun and verb) (to paint with) a coating of size, *not* claire-

clear-cut (adj., hyphen)

clear days time to be reckoned exclusive of the first and last

cleared (goods or shipping) abbr. **cld.**

clear/-eyed, -headed (hyphens)

clearing bank (two words)

clearing house (two words, one word in US) abbr. **CH**

clear-sighted (hyphen)

clearstory *use* **clere-**

clearway (one word)

clef (mus.) three are in use: the C clef 𝄡 (movable), the treble clef 𝄞, and the bass clef 𝄢

cleistogam/ic, -ous (bot.) permanently closed and self-fertilizing, *not* k-

Clemenceau, Georges Eugène Benjamin (1841–1929) French politician, *not* Clé-

Clemens, Samuel Langhorne (1835–1910) US writer, pseud. **Mark Twain**

clench secure (a nail or rivet), grasp firmly; the action or result of these; cf. **clinch**

clepsydra/ an ancient water clock, *not* k-; pl. **-s**

cleptomania *use* **k-**

clerestory (archit.) the upper part of wall with row of windows, *not* clear-

clerihew a short comic verse on a famous person

clerk abbr. **clk.**

Clerke, Agnes Mary (1842–1907) English astronomer

Clerk-Maxwell, James *see* **Maxwell, James Clerk**

Clerk/ of the Closet, — of Parliaments, — of the Peace abbr. **CP, — of the Privy Council** abbr. **CPC** (caps.)

Clermont-Ferrand dép. Puy-de-Dôme, France (hyphen)

Cleveland a county of England

clevis/ a U-shaped iron at end of beam for attaching tackle, pl. **-es**

clew a ball of thread, (naut., verb *or* noun) (draw up) the lower corner of a sail; cf. **clue**

cl. gt. (bind.) cloth gilt

cliché (typ.) a block or stereotype, hackneyed phrase or opinion

clicker (typ.) the former title of foreman of a companionship

Clicquot, Veuve a brand of champagne

clientele clients collectively (no accent, not ital.)

cliffhang/er, -ing (one word)

climacteric/ (pertaining to) a critical period, **grand —** the age of 63

climactic pertaining to a climax

climatic pertaining to climate

clinch make fast a rope in a special way, embrace, settle conclusively; the action or result of these; cf. **clench**

clincher-built *use* **clinker-**

Clinker, Humphry *not* -ey, a novel by Smollett 1771

clinometer an instrument for measuring slopes, *not* k-

Clio (Gr. myth.) the muse of history

cliometrics (pl. used as sing.) a statistical method of historical research

clippings (US) = **cuttings** (from a newspaper etc.)

cliqu/e, -ish, -ism, -y *not* -eish, -eism, -ey (not ital.)

clish-ma-claver (Sc.) gossip (hyphens)

C.Lit. Companion of Literature

Clitheroe Lancs.

clitor/is (anat.) a part of the female genitalia, **-al**

clk. clerk

cll. clauses

Cllr. Councillor

Cloaca Maxima the major sewer of ancient Rome (caps.)

cloche (hort.) a translucent cover for plants, a woman's close-fitting hat (not ital.)

clock/ face, — radio, — tower (two words)

clock/wise, -work (one word)

cloff an allowance on commodities, *not* clough

cloisonné (Fr.) a kind of enamel finish

close (typ.) the second of any pair of punctuation marks, as ']); pron. 'kloze'

close/ up (typ.) push together, remove spacing; **— matter** unleaded *or* thinly spaced

close-up (noun)

closure a stopping, esp. of debate in Parliament; in Fr. f. **clôture**

Clos Vougeot a burgundy

clotbur (bot.) burdock; *not* clote-, cloth-

clote (bot.) burdock and similar burry plants, *not* clote bur

cloth/ abbr. **cl.; — of Bruges** gold brocade

Clotho (Gr. myth.) the Fate that draws the thread of life

clôture (Fr. f.) closure

clou (Fr. m.) point of chief interest

cloud-cuckoo-land in general senses, hyphens, no cap.; in direct reference to Aristophanes' *Birds*, one word, one cap.

cloudy (meteor.) abbr. **c.**

clough a ravine

clove hitch a knot (two words)

cloze text a comprehension exercise

clubbable sociable

club foot a congenital malformation (two words, one word in US)

club/house, -land (one word)

club line (typ.) *see* **orphan**

clue information to be followed up; cf. **clew**

Cluniac (a monk or nun) of a branch of the Benedictine order stemming from Cluny, France

Clwyd a river and county, N. Wales

Clydebank Strathclyde

Clytaemestra (Gr. myth.) the wife of Agamemnon, *also* **Klytaimestra** (in Gr. contexts); do not impose the trad. Eng. spelling **Clytemnestra** (with an *n*), but do not alter in hist. contexts

CM Certified Master *or* Mistress, *Chirurgiae Magister* (Master of Surgery), (mus.) common metre, Corresponding Member, Member of the Order of Canada

Cm curium (no point)

Cm. Command Paper (1986–) with number following

c.m. *causa mortis* (by reason of death)

cm centimetre(s) (no point)

Cmd. Command Paper (1919–56) with number following

cmdg. commanding

Cmdr. Commander

Cmdre. Commodore

CMG Companion of (the Order of) St Michael and St George

Cmnd. Command Paper (1956–86) with number following

CMP Commissioner of the Metropolitan Police

CMS Church Missionary Society

CNAA Council for National Academic Awards

CND Campaign for Nuclear Disarmament

Cnossus *use* **Knossos**

cnr. corner

Cnut (995–1035) king of Norway, Denmark, and England; this more correct (OE) form of **Canute** is favoured by historians; *see also* **Knut**

CO Colorado (postal abbr.), Commanding Officer, conscientious objector, criminal offence, Crown Office

Co cobalt (no point)

Co. Colón, Company, County

c/o care of

coad. coadjutor

coaetaneous *use* **coe-**

coagul/um a clot, pl. **-a**

Coalbrookdale Shropshire

coal dust (two words)

coal/face, -field, -man (one word)

coal mine/, -r (two words)

coalmouse (ornith.) the coal titmouse, *not* cole-

coal pit (two words)

Coalville Leics.

Coast, the (US) the Pacific coast of the USA, usually California

coastguard an individual *or* the organization (one word), abbr. **CG**

coat of arms (three words), *properly* **achievement of arms**

co-author acceptable as a noun, to be avoided as a verb (hyphen)

coaxial (one word)

cobalt symbol **Co**

Cobbe, Frances Power (1822–1904) British social writer

coble boat, *not* cobble

Coblen/ce, -z Germany, *use* **Koblenz**

COBOL (comput.) common business oriented language; caps. *or* even small caps.

cobra de capello an Indian snake; *not* da, di

Coburg/ Ia.; Saxe- — Germany; *not* -ourg, -urgh

coca a tropical American shrub whose leaves yield cocaine; cf. **cocoa**

Coca-Cola (propr.) abbr. **Coke** (cap.)

Cocagne *use* **Cockaigne**

cocaine *not* -ain, popular abbr. **coke** (not cap.)

cocco (bot.) a Jamaican plant tuber; *not* coco; cf. **cocoa**; **coca**

coccy/x (anat.) the end of the spinal column, pl. **-ges**

cochle/a the ear cavity, pl. **-ae**

cochon de lait (Fr. m.) sucking pig

Cockaigne an imaginary land of luxury and idleness, the 'land of cakes'; in the 19th c. applied humorously to London as the country of the cockneys; *not* Cocagne, Cockayne

cock-a-leekie (Sc.) a soup; *not* cockie-leekie, cocky-leeky

cockatiel a small crested Australian parrot, *not* -teel

cockatoo/ a large crested Australian parrot, pl. **-s**

cockatrice a fabulous serpent

Cockcroft, Sir John Douglas (1897–1967) British nuclear scientist

Cocker, Edward (1631–75) reputed author of *Arithmetic*, thus **'according to Cocker'**, accurate

cockney a native of E. London, esp. one born within the sound of Bow Bells (not cap.)

cockscomb a plant; *see also* **coxcomb**

cockswain *use* **cox-**

Cocles, Horatius (Rom. hist.) kept the Sublician Bridge

cocoa the common name for **cacao** (q.v.), (a drink made from) cacao seeds

COCOM Coordinating Committee for Multinational Export Controls

COCOMO (comput.) constructive cost model, also **CoCoMo**

coconut *not* coker-

Cocos Islands (**Keeling Islands**) Bay of Bengal, an external territory of Australia

cocotte a small dish, (arch.) a prostitute

Cocytus a river in Hades

COD cash on delivery

COD Concise Oxford Dictionary

cod. codex

CODASYL Conference on Data Systems Languages

Code Napoléon (Fr. m.) a civil code promulgated 1804–11

cod/ex an ancient MS, abbr. **cod.**; pl. **-ices**, abbr. **codd.**

codfish (one word)

codling a small cod, an elongated apple

cod liver oil (three words)

Cody, William Frederick, 'Buffalo Bill' (1846–1917), US frontiersman and showman

co-ed (a girl at a) co-educational (institution), (no point; hyphen, one word in US)

co-education/, -al (hyphen, one word in US)

coefficient (one word)

coelacanth a large bony marine fish, formerly thought to be extinct

Coelebs in Search of a Wife a novel by Hannah More, 1809, *but* **caelebs** Lat. for bachelor

Coelenterata a zool. phylum (not ital.)

coeliac abdominal, *not* ce-

coenobite a member of a monastic community, *not* cen- (US)

co-equal (hyphen, one word in US)

coerulean *use* ce-

coetaneous of the same age, *not* coae-

coeternal (one word)

Cœur de Lion Richard I of England ('the Lionheart'), *or* Louis VIII of France (no hyphens)

coeval of the same age (one word)

coexist/, -ence (one word)

coextensive (one word)

C. of E. Church of England

coffee/ bar, — bean, — cup, — house, — pot, — table (two words)

cofferdam a watertight enclosure

cogito, ergo sum (Lat.) I think, and therefore I exist (the motto of Descartes)

cognac a high-quality brandy (not cap.)

cognate abbr. **cog.**

cogniz/e become conscious of, *not* -ise; **-able, -ance, -ant**

cognoscent/e (It.) a connoisseur, pl. **-i**; *not* con-

cognovit (**actionem**) (law) an acknowledgement that the action is just

coheir/, -ess (one word)

COHSE Confederation of Health Service Employees

COI Central Office of Information

COID Council of Industrial Design, *now* Design Council

coiff/eur, f. **-euse** hairdresser; **-ure** (f.) headdress, hairstyle (not ital.)

coign of vantage a favourable position

Cointreau (propr.) an orange-flavoured liqueur (cap.)

Coire Graubünden, Switzerland; *use* **Chur**

coits *use* **quoits**

Coke abbr. for **Coca-Cola** (cap.)

coke popular abbr. for **cocaine** (not cap.)

Coke, Sir Edward (1552–1634) Lord Chief Justice of England, pron. 'cook'

cokernut *use* **coco-**

Col. Colonel, Colossians

col. colonial, column

cola a W. African tree and its seed, *not* k-

colander a strainer; *not* colla-, culle-

colcannon an Irish dish; *not* calc-, cole-

cold composition *see* **hand-setting**

Cold Harbor Va.; scene of three Civil War battles

Cold Harbour Lincs., Oxon.

Coldharbour Dorset, Glos., Surrey

cold/ metal, — type (typ.) sorts cast up for hand composition or correction; (compositing) *see* **strike-on**

Coldstream/ a town, Borders; **— Guards** *not* The Coldstreams, abbr. **CG**

cold war, the (not caps.)

colemouse *use* **coal-**

Coleoptera (zool.) the beetles

cole-pixy *use* **colt-pixie**

Colerain NC

Coleraine Co. Londonderry

Coleridge,/ Hartley (1796–1849) English minor poet and critic, son of next; **— Samuel Taylor** (1772–1834) English poet and critic; **— Sara** *not* -ah (1802–52) English writer

Coleridge-Taylor, Samuel (1875–1912) English composer

coleslaw (one word)

Colette pseud. of **Sidonie Gabrielle Claudine Colette** (1873–1954) French writer

colic/, -ky

Coligny, Gaspard de (1519–72) French Huguenot leader

Coliseum London theatre; *see also* **Coloss-**

coliseum a large stadium

coll. colleague; collect/ed, -ion, -or; college

collage art composition with components pasted onto a surface

collander *use* **colan-**

colla/ parte *or* **— voce** (mus.) adapt to the principal part or voice; abbr. **col. p.**, **col. vo.**

collapsar (astron.) an old star that has collapsed to form a white dwarf, neutron star, or black hole; *not* -er

collapsible *not* -able

coll'arco (mus.) with the bow

collar of SS *see* **SS, collar of**

collat. collateral, -ly

collat/e, -or *not* -er

colla voce *see* **colla parte**

colleague abbr. **coll.**

collect. collectively

collectable *not* -ible

collectanea (Lat. pl.) collected notes

collect/ion, -or abbr. **coll.**

collections/ an examination at some universities

college abbr. **coll.** (cap. when used as part of name)

Collège de France (m.)

College of Arms abbr. **CA**

College of Justice (Sc.) supreme civil courts

collegi/an a member of a college, **-ate** belonging to a college

collegi/um an ecclesiastical body uncontrolled by the State, pl. **-a** (not cap., ital.); the name for the orchestra at some US universities (cap., not ital.)

col legno (mus.) with the wood of the bow

Colles fracture (med., of the wrist)

collie a dog, *not* -y

Collins a letter of thanks for hospitality (from the character in Austen's *Pride and Prejudice*)

collogue talk confidentially

collop a piece of meat

colloq. colloquial, -ly, -ism

colloqui/um a conference, pl. **-a**

colloqu/y talk, pl. **-ies**; **-ize** *not* -ise

collotype (typ.) a printing process

Colo. Colorado (off. abbr.)

Cologne Germany, in Ger. **Köln**

Colombia, Republic of S. America; *see also* **Colu-**

Colombo capital of Sri Lanka, *not* Colu-

Colón Cent. America, abbr. **Co.**; *see also* **Columbus**

Colonel/ abbr. **Col.**; **— Blimp** a pompous, jingoistic person; **— Bogey** (golf) the imaginary good player, eponymous subject of a marching song (ital.)

colonial abbr. **col.**

coloniz/e *not* -ise; **-able, -ation**

colonnade a row of columns

colophon (typ.) publisher's device or imprint

colophony rosin

color *use* **colour** (except in US)

Colorado off. abbr. **Colo.**, postal **CO**

coloration *not* colour-

Colosseum Rome, *properly* the **Flavian Amphitheatre**; *see also* **Colis-**

Colossians (NT) abbr. **Col.**

coloss/us pl. **-i**

Colossus of Rhodes (cap.)

Colour, Trooping the *not* Colours

colourant *not* color- (US)

coloured/ (S. Afr.) of Asian or mixed ancestry, speaking Afrikaans or English as the mother tongue (adj.); **-s** Cape Coloured people (cap.); *see also* **black**

colourist *not* colorist (US)

Colour-Sergeant *not* -jeant; abbr. **Col.-Sgt.**, **Col.-Sergt.**

col. p. (mus.) **colla parte**

colporteur a hawker of books, esp. bibles (not ital.)

Colquhoun pron. 'ko-hoon' (stress on second syllable)

colt abbr. **c.**

colter *use* **cou-** (except in US)

colt-pixie a mischievous fairy, *not* cole-pixy

colubrine snakelike

columbari/um a dovecote; a place for cremation urns; pl. **-a**

Columbia, British Canada, abbr. **BC**

Columbia, District of USA, abbr. **DC** (no points); comma precedes: 'Washington, DC'; *see also* **Colo-**; **Washington**

columbium *now* **niobium**

Columbo *use* **Colombo**

Columbus, Christopher (1451–1506) Genoese navigator, in Sp. **Cristóbal Colón**

column abbr. **col.**

colure (astr.) each of two great circles of the celestial sphere

Colville of Culross, Viscount

col. vo. (mus.) **colla voce**

COM computer output on microfilm *or* microfiche

Com. Commander, Communist

com. comedy, comic, commercial; commission, -er; committee; common, -er, -ly; commun/e, -ity; communicat/e, -ed, -ion

coma/ (med.) stupor, pl. **-s**; (astr.) the nebulous envelope round head of comet, (bot.) a tuft of hair; pl. **-e**

comb. combin/e, ed, -ing

combat/, -ed, -ing, -ive

Combermere, Viscount

combin/e, -ed, -ing abbr. **comb.**

Comdr. Commander

Comdt. Commandant

come-at-able accessible (hyphens)

come back (verb, two words; noun, one word)

Comecon Council for Mutual Economic Assistance, a former economic association of Communist countries

Comédie-Française, La official name of **Le Théâtre français** (caps.)

Comédie Humaine, La a series of novels by Balzac, 1842–8

comédien/ (Fr.) actor, f. *-ne*

comedy abbr. **com.**

comedy of manners (no caps.)

come/ **prima** (mus.) as at first; — **sopra** as above, abbr. **co. sa.**

comfit (arch.) a sweet consisting of a nut, seed, etc., coated in sugar; cf. *confit*

comfrey (bot.) any of various plants of the genus *Symphytum*; *not* cum-

comic abbr. **com.**

comillas (Sp. f.) quotation marks « », equivalent to guillemets

Comintern the Communist (Third) International 1919–43; *not* Kom-

comitadji a band of irregulars in the Balkans; *not* k-, -aji

comitatus (Lat.) a retinue, a county or shire; pl. same

comitia (Lat. pl.) a Roman assembly

Comitia/ (pl.) a meeting of the Senate of Dublin University; — *Aestivalia* the same in summer; — *Hiemalia* the same in winter; — *Vernalia* the same in spring

comity of nations international courtesy

Comm. (naval) Commodore

comm. commentary, commerce, commonwealth

commandant abbr. **comdt.**

commandeer seize for military or other service

Commander/ abbr. **Cdr.** (Admiralty), **Com.**, **Comdr.**; **-in-Chief** (hyphens) abbr. **C.-in-C.**; — **of the Faithful** a title of a caliph

commanding abbr. **cmdg.**, **Commanding Officer** abbr. **CO**

commando/ (a member of) a body of troops, esp. shock troops; pl. **-s**

Command Paper a paper laid before Parliament by command of the Crown; abbr. **C.** (1870–99), **Cd.** (1900–18), **Cmd.** (1919–56), **Cmnd.** (1956–86), **Cm.** (1986–), with number following

comme ci, comme ça (Fr.) indifferently, so-so

commedia dell'arte Italian Renaissance comedy

comme il faut (Fr.) as it should be, properly

Commemoration at Oxford, an annual ceremony in memory of founders and benefactors

commencement the ceremonial conferring of university degrees, as at Cambridge and US universities (often cap. as the name of the ceremony)

commendam an ecclesiastical benefice held *in commendam*, i.e. without duties

commentary abbr. **comm.**

commentator *not* -er

commerce abbr. **comm.**

commère a female compère (not ital.)

commingle *not* comingle

Commissary-General (hyphen) abbr. **CG**

commission/, **-er** abbr. **com.**

commissionaire a uniformed door-attendant (not ital.); the Fr. m. *commissionnaire* is less specific in meaning

commit/, **-ment**, **-table** (*not* -ible), **-tal**, **-ted**, **-ting**

committee (collective sing., with sing. verb), abbr. **com.**

committ/**er** one who commits, **-or** (law) a judge who commits someone to the care of a **-ee** (stress on final syllable)

Commodore (naval) abbr. **Cdre**, **Cmdre**, **Comm.**

common/, **-er**, **-ly** abbr. **com.**

Common Bench abbr. **CB**

common law (two words, hyphen when attrib.)

Common Market now **European Community**

common metre (mus.) abbr. **CM**

commonplace/ (adj.) (one word), — **book** (two words)

Common Pleas abbr. **CP**

common sense noun, hyphen when attrib.

commonsensical (adj.) (one word)

Common Serjeant *not* -geant; abbr. **CS**, **Com.-Serj.**

common stock (US) = **ordinary shares**

common time (mus.) abbr. **C**

Common Version (of the Bible) abbr. **CV**, **Com. Ver.**

commonwealth (cap. when part of name) abbr. **comm.**

Commonwealth (Austral.) abbr. **Cwlth**

Commonwealth, the *not* the British Commonwealth

Communard (hist.) a supporter of the Paris Commune (cap.)

communard a member of a commune

Commune, the (hist.) communalistic government in Paris in 1871 (cap.)

commune a communal group (esp. sharing accommodation), a small territorial division (France and elsewhere); abbr. **com.**

communicat/e, -ed, -ion abbr. **com.**

communications satellite *not* -ation (two words)

communiqué an official report

Communis/m the specific communistic form of society established in the former USSR and elsewhere, *or* any movement or political doctrine advocating communism; **-t** a member of a Communist Party (cap.)

communis/m the political theory derived from Marx, **-t** a person advocating or practising the general theories of communism (not cap.)

Communist/ abbr. **Com.,** — **Party** abbr. **CP**

communize make common, *not* -ise

commutator an apparatus for reversing electric current

commuter one who travels regularly to work in a town

Comor/o Islands Indian Ocean, indep. 1975; adj. **-an**

comp. comparative, comparison; compil/e, -ed, -er, -ation; compos/er, -ite, -ition, -itor; compounded

compagnie (Fr. f.) company, abbr. *Cie*

compagnon de voyage (Fr. m.) travelling companion

Companies Act (no apos.)

companionship (typ.) the former name of a group of compositors working together under a clicker (q.v.), abbr. **'ship**

company abbr. **Co.,** (mil.) **Coy.** (point); *see also compagnie*

comparative abbr. **comp.**

compare abbr. **cf.** (*confer*) or **cp.**

comparison abbr. **comp.**

compass points (typ.) not caps. unless part of an accepted geographical designation: *the mysterious East, the West End, Northern Ireland, the South Bronx* (but e.g. *the south of the Bronx*); the compound points, when printed in full, to be hyphenated: *south-south-east* (but in US *south-southeast*); no points for abbreviation of compound points: *SSE*

compendi/ous comprehensive but fairly brief; **-um** pl. **-a**

compère a master of ceremonies

competit/or f. **-ress**

Compiègne dép. Oise, France

compil/e, -ed, -er, -ation abbr. **comp.**

complacen/t self-satisfied, **-cy**

complaisan/t obliging, **-ce**

Compleat Angler, The by Izaak Walton, 1653

complement (verb and noun) make complete, that which makes complete

completor/ium (Lat.) compline, pl. **-a**

complexion *not* -ction

compliment (to) praise, flatter(y)

compline the last service of the day (RC), *not* -plin

compos/er, -ite, -ition, -itor abbr. **comp.**

compos mentis (Lat.) in one's right mind

compote stewed fruit

compound/, -ed abbr. **comp.**

compound ranks *or* **titles** each main word to be cap., as Assistant Adjutant-General, Vice-President

comprehensible that can be understood, intelligible; *not* -able

comprehensive complete; including all or nearly all elements, aspects, etc.

compromise *not* -ize

compte/ (Fr. m.) an account; — *rendu* official report, pl. **-s rendus**

Comptes Rendus reports of the French Academy (caps.)

Compton-Burnett, Dame Ivy (1884–1969) English novelist (hyphen)

comptroller retain when citing official title that has it, otherwise *use* **controller**

Comptroller-General of the National Debt Office, Comptroller-General of the Patent Office (caps., hyphen)

computer *not* -or

computerize *not* -ise

Com. Serj. Common Serjeant

Comsomol *use* **K-**

Comt/e, Auguste (1798–1857) French philosopher; **-ian, -ism, -ist**

comte (Fr.) a count, f. *comtesse* (not cap.)

Con. Consul

con/ to direct a ship's course, *not* -nn (US); examine, swindle; *not* -un; **-ning**

con. conclusion, conics, conversation

con. contra (against, in opposition to)

Conakry Guinea

con amore (It.) with affection (not ital. in mus.)

Conan, Laure pseud. of **Marie-Louise-Félicité Angers**

con brio (mus.) with vigour

conc. concentrat/ed, -ion

Conceição the name of many places in Portugal and Brazil

concensus *use* **conse-**

concentre *not* -er (US)

Concepción the name of many Cent. and S. American places (*but* **Conceição** in Brazil)

Concertgebouw Orchestra Amsterdam

concert-go/er, -ing (hyphen, one word in US)

concert hall (two words)

concertina/, -s, -ed *not* 'd, **-ing**

concertino/ (mus.) a group of soloists, a short concerto; pl. **-s**

concert master (two words)

Concert/meister, -stück (Ger. mus.) *now* **Konzert-** (cap.)

concerto/ (mus.) pl. **-s** (but **concerti grossi**), abbr. **cto.**

concessionaire a holder of a concession or grant (not ital.), in Fr. m. ***concessionnaire***

conch/ a shell, pl. **-s**

conch. conchology

conchie *not* -y; *see* **conscientious objector**

concierg/e a caretaker, **-erie** (no accent) a caretaker's flat

Conciergerie, La a former Paris prison

concinnity elegance or neatness of literary style

concision conciseness (esp. of literary style)

conclusion abbr. **con.**

Concord Calif., Mass., NC, NH

concordance an index of words or phrases used in a book or by an author

concordat an agreement (not ital.)

Concorde a make of aircraft

concours/ (Fr. m.) a competition, **— *d'élégance*** parade of vehicles

concur/, -red, -ring

conde (Sp., Port.) a count, *not* -dee

Condé, Louis II de Bourbon, Prince de, 'The Great' (1621–86) French general

condensed type a narrow typeface

condominium (law) the joint control of a State's affairs by other States, (US) a building complex containing individually owned flats or houses

condottier/e (It.) a captain of mercenaries, pl. ***-i***

conductor *not* -er, abbr. **c.**

conduct/us (medieval mus.) pl. ***-uses*** or ***-ûs***, *not* -i

con espressione (mus.) with expression, *not* ex-; abbr. **con esp.**

coney *use* **cony**

Coney Island NY

conf. conference

confection/ery (noun), **-ary** (adj.)

Confederacy (US hist.) the league of seceding states in the Civil War

Confederation of Independent States abbr. **CIS**

confer/, -red, -ring, -rable, -rer *but* **-ee, -ence, -ment**

confer (Lat.) compare, abbr. **cf.** (not ital.)

conference abbr. **conf.**

conférence (Fr. f.) lecture

Confessio Amantis a poem by Gower, 1393

confetti bits of coloured paper etc.

confidant/ a trusted friend, f. **-e**

confit/ (Fr. m.) a preserve or conserve, either sweet or savoury; **-ure** (Fr. f.) jam, or preserves; cf. **comfit**

confrère a colleague (not ital.)

Confucius (551–479 BC) Chinese sage; latinized as **Kongfuze** (Pinyin), **K'ung Fu-tzŭ** (Wade–Giles)

con fuoco (mus.) with passion

cong. congregation, -al, -alist, -ist; congress, -ional

congé/ (Fr. m.) leave, dismissal; **— *d'élire*** leave to elect, *not* **— *de lire***

Congo, Democratic Republic of Cent. Africa, *was* **Zaire** 1971–97

Congo/, Republic of the Cent. Africa, *formerly* French Middle Congo, People's Republic of the Congo; **-lese**

congou a black tea; *not* -o, kongo

congregation/, -al, -alist (cap. as religious denomination) abbr. **cong.**

Congresbury Avon

Congress India, the political party; US, the legislative body (cap.); spell out the number, as 'fifty-fourth Congress', not '54th'

congress/, -ional abbr. **C., cong.**

conics the geometry of the cone and its sections, abbr. **con.**

conjugation the inflections of a verb, abbr. **conj.**

conjunction connection, abbr. **conj.**; (astr.) apparent proximity of two heavenly bodies, symbol ☌

conjunctiv/a the mucous membrane between eyelid and eyeball, pl. **-ae** (not ital.); **-itis** an inflammation of this

conjuror a magician, *not* -er

con moto (mus.) with movement

Conn. Connecticut (off. abbr.)

Conna Co. Cork

Connacht a province of Ireland containing the counties of Galway, Leitrim, Mayo, Roscommon, and Sligo

Connah's Quay Clwyd

connect/er one who connects, **-or** that which connects

Connecticut off. abbr. **Conn.**, postal **CT**

connection *not* -xion except in use by Wesleyans and other related Methodist associations to describe the concept of 'religious society' or 'denomination'; also for Lady Huntingdon's Connexion

connivance tacit assent, *not* -ence

connoisseur a well-informed judge in matters of taste (not ital.)

connotation that which is implied by a word, phrase, etc. in addition to its literal or primary denotation

conoscente *use* **cogno-**

conquistador/ a conqueror, esp. of Mexico and Peru; pl. **-es** (not ital.)

Conrad, Joseph pseud. of **Teodor Józef Konrad Korzeniowski** (1857–1924) Polish-born English novelist, *not* K-

Cons. Conservative

cons. consecrate(d), conservation, consonant, constable; constitution, -al

Conscience, Hendrik (1812–83) Belgian novelist

conscience' sake *not* -e's

conscientious objector abbr. **CO**, (First World War colloq.) **conchie**

consenescence general decay

consensus/ *not* -census, -pl. **-es**

Conservative cap. when referring to specific groups so called, e.g. the British political party, or to Conservative Judaism; lower case for other meanings: conservative in dress; a conservative estimate; abbr. **Cons.**

conservatoire a school of music or other arts, *not* -tory (US)

conservat/oire (Fr. m.), **-orio** (It., Port., Sp.), **Konservatorium** (Ger. n., cap.)

consol. consolidated

console (archit.) a bracket; the key-desk of an organ, a cabinet for radio etc.

Consolidated Annuities abbr. **Consols**

consommé a clear soup (not ital.)

consonant abbr. **cons.**

consonantize make consonantal, *not* -ise

con sordino (mus.) with a mute

conspectus (Lat.) a general view (not ital.)

con spirito (mus.) spiritedly

constable abbr. **c., cons.**

Constance a lake (in Ger. **Bodensee**) and town (in Ger. **Konstanz**), Switzerland

Constans/ Roman Emperor (337–50); — mythical king of Britain

Constant,/ Benjamin (in full **Henri Benjamin Constant de Rebecque**) (1767–1830) French-Swiss political novelist, — **Benjamin Jean Joseph** (1845–1902) French painter

Constantino/ple *now* **Istanbul**; **-politan**

Constitution of a country (cap.)

constitution/, -al abbr. **cons.**

construction abbr. **constr.**

Consuelo a novel by George Sand, 1842

consuetude (law) a custom, esp. one having legal force in Scotland

Consul diplomat, abbr. **C., Con.**; Lat. **consul**/, as Roman magistrate, abbr. **cos.**; pl. **-es**, abbr. **coss.**

Consul-General abbr. **C.-G.**

Consumers' Association abbr. **CA**

consummat/e (verb) to perfect or complete; (adj.) perfect, complete; noun **-ion**

consummatum est (Lat.) it is finished

cont. containing, contents, continent; continue, -d; *not* con't (US)

contadin/o an Italian peasant, pl. **-i**; f. **-a**, pl. **-e**

contagi/um contagious matter; pl. **-a**

containing abbr. **cont.**

contakion *use* **k-**

contang/o (Stock Exchange) a charge for carrying over, pl. **-os**

conte (Fr. m.) a short story, a medieval narrative tale; (It. m.) a count

contemptible deserving contempt, despicable; *not* -able

contemptuous showing contempt, scornful

contents abbr. **cont.**

conterminous coextensive; having a common boundary or border; cf. **coterminous**

Contes drolatiques by Balzac, 1832–7

contessa (It.) a countess

Continent/, -al cap. when referring to mainland Europe as distinct from Britain, lower case when referring to countries that are also continents, such as Australia; *continental USA* is the USA excluding Hawaii but including Alaska; abbr. **cont.**

continual constantly or frequently recurring; cf. **continuous**

continuance (US law) = **adjournment**

continu/e, -ed abbr. **cont.**

continuo/ (mus.) an improvised keyboard accompaniment, pl. **-s**

continuous unbroken, uninterrupted, connected throughout in space or time; cf. **continual**

continu/um (philos., phys.) a continuous quantity, pl. **-a**

cont-line (naut.) a spiral space between rope strands, a space between stowed casks

contr. contract, -ed, -ion, -s; contrary

contra against, in opposition to; abbr. **con.**

contrabasso (It. mus.) the double bass, abbr. **CB**; in Eng. **contrabass**

contract/, -ed, -ion, -s abbr. **contr.**

contracting-out (noun, hyphen)

contraction a word shortened by elision; verbal forms use an apostrophe to mark omission (e.g. *cannot = can't*); nouns usually are not punctuated (e.g. *Mister = Mr*); *see also* **abbreviation; acronym**

contractor *not* -er

contrafagotto (It. mus.) the double bassoon (one word)

contra jus gentium (Lat.) against the law of nations

contralto/ (mus.) the lowest female voice, pl. **-s**; abbr. **C.**

contra/ mundum (Lat.) against the world, — *pacem* (law) against the peace

contrariwise *not* -ry-

contrary abbr. **contr.**

contratenor (mus.) a singing part, abbr. **Ct** (no point)

Contrat social, Le by Rousseau, 1762

contretemps a mishap (not ital.)

control/, -led, -ling

controller *see* **comptroller**

Controller-General *but* **Comptroller-General**, National Debt Office, Patent Office

Controller of Accounts abbr. **CA**

conundrum/ a riddle, pl. **-s**

convector an apparatus for heating by convection

convenances, les (Fr. f. pl.) the conventional proprieties

convener a caller of a meeting

convention/, -al abbr. **conv.**

conventionalize *not* -ise

conversation abbr. **con.**

conversazione/ a meeting for learned conversation, pl. **-s**

converter *not* -or

convertible *not* -able

convey/er (person), **-or** (thing) esp. in **conveyor belt**

Convocation a provincial assembly of the Church of England, a legislative assembly of certain universities

convolvulus/ a flower, bindweed; pl. **-es**

Conwy a river and town, Gwynedd

cony/ a rabbit, *not* coney, pl. **conies**

Conyngham, Marquess

Cooch Behar India, *not* Kuch

cooee (a) call (one word); *not* -ey, -hee, -ie

Cook,/ Captain James (1728–79) British explorer, — **Thomas** (1808–92) English travel agent

cookie (Sc.) a bun, (US) a sweet biscuit; *not* -ey, -y

coolabah an Australian gum tree, *not* -ibah

coolie (Ind., Chin.) a native hired labourer, *not* -y

Coomassie Ghana, *use* **Kumasi**

Cooper, James Fenimore (1789–1851) US novelist, (one *n*)

cooperat/e, -ion, -ive (one word); *but* **co-operative society** (hyphen), abbr. **co-op**

Coopers & Lybrand Deloitte British accountancy firm

co-opt (hyphen)

coordinat/e, -ely, -ion, -ive, -or (one word)

Cop. Copernican

cop. copper, copulative

copaiba (med.) a balsam from a S. American tree, *not* -va

coparcen/ary (law) joint heirship to an undivided property, *not* -ery; **-er** a joint heir

COPEC Conference on Christian Politics, Economics, and Citizenship

copeck a hundredth of a rouble; *not* -ec, -ek, ko-; abbr. **c.**

Copenhagen capital of Denmark, in Dan. **København**

Copernican abbr. **Cop.**

copier *not* copyer

Copland, Aaron (1900–90) US composer, *not* Cope-

copper abbr. **cop.**, symbol **Cu** (cuprum)

copperas ferrous sulphate, green vitriol

copperize to impregnate with copper, *not* -ise

copro- (in compounds) dung-, *not* k-

Copt a native Egyptian in the Hellenistic and Roman periods, a native Christian of the independent Egyptian Church

Coptic the language of the Copts, now used as the liturgical language of Egyptian Christians; abbr. **Copt.**

copul/a (gram., logic, anat., mus.) that which connects; pl. **-as, -ae**

copulative abbr. **cop.**

copy (typ.) matter to be reproduced in type

copy/book, -cat (one word)

copy editor a person who edits copy for printing (two words, one word in US), *but* **copy-edit/, -ing** (verb, one word in US)

cop/yer *use* **-ier**

copyholder (typ.) a stand or clasp holding sheets of copy, *formerly* a proofreader's assistant; (hist.) a type of feudal tenant (one word)

copyreader (one word)

copyright notice the symbol ©, date of publication, and name of copyright owner must appear (usually on title-page verso) in every copy of a publication claiming protection under the Universal Copyright Convention; *see also* **Berne Convention**

copy typist (two words)

copywriter (one word)

coq/ (Fr. m.) cock, — **au vin** chicken cooked in wine (not ital.), — *de bruyère* black game

coquet/ f. **-te** a flirt; **-ry, -ting, -tish**

coquille (Fr. typ. f.) a misprint

Cor. Corinthians

cor. corpus; (mus.) cornet, corno (horn); coroner

coram/ (Lat.) in presence of, — *judice* (law) before a judge, — *nobis* before us, — *paribus* before one's equals, — *populo* before the people

Coran *use* **K-**

cor anglais (mus.) an instrument of the oboe family

coranto *use* **courante**

Corbière, (Édouard Joachim) Tristan (1845–75) French poet

Corbusier, Le *see* **Le Corbusier**

Corcoran Gallery of Art Washington, DC

Corcyra the ancient name of **Corfu**

Corday, Charlotte (1768–93) French revolutionist

cordillera/ a mountain chain, pl. **-s**

Córdoba in Eng. **Cordova** (as in *cordovan*) (cf. **Cordova** in Alabama, Arkansas, and Maryland); in Sp., **Córdoba** (Spain, Argentina, Colombia, Mexico) or **Córdova** (Peru); in Lat. **Corduba**; in Arab. **Qurtuba**

córdoba monetary unit of Nicaragua

cordon bleu (cook.) pl. **cordons bleus** (not ital., two words)

cordon-bleu (ornith.) an African waxbill, pl. **cordon-bleus** (hyphen)

cordon sanitaire pl. **cordons sanitaires** (not ital., two words)

CORE (US) Congress of Racial Equality

Corea/, -n *use* **K-**

co-respondent in divorce case (hyphen, one word in US)

cor/f a lobster cage, pl. **-ves**

Corfe Castle Dorset, castle and village

Corflambo the giant in Spenser's *Faerie Queene*

Corfu a Greek island, ancient name **Corcyra**; in Modern Gr. **Kerkyra**

Corinthians, First, Second Epistle to the (NT) abbr. **1 Cor., 2 Cor.**

Corn. Cornish, Cornwall

corncrake a bird (one word)

Corneille, Pierre (1606–84) French playwright

cornelian *not* car-, -ion

cornemuse French bagpipe

cornerstone (one word)

cornet (mus.) abbr. **cor.**

cornett/o (mus.) an old form of woodwind instrument, pl. **-i**

corn/ field -flour, -flower (one word)

Corniche, La the coast road from Nice to Genoa, in It. **La Cornice**

Cornish/ abbr. **Corn.**, — **gillyflower** a variety of apple

Corn Laws (caps.)

corn/o (mus.) a horn, pl. **-i**; **-o inglese** (It.) cor anglais (ital.)

cornstarch (US) = **cornflour**

cornu/ (anat.) a hornlike process, pl. **-a**

Cornubia (Lat.) Cornwall

cornucopia/ horn of plenty, pl. **-s**, adj. **-n**

Cornwall abbr. **Corn.**, in Cornish **Kernow**, in Fr. f. **Cornouailles**

corolla/ (bot.) pl. **-s**

coron/a (archit., bot., anat., astr.) pl. **-ae**

coroner (cap. as title) abbr. **cor.**

coronis a mark of contraction (crasis) in Gr.

Corot, Jean Baptiste Camille (1796–1875) French painter

Corp. (US) corporation

Corporal abbr. **Cpl.**

corpor/al of the human body; **-eal** physical, as opposed to spiritual

corporealize materialize, *not* -ise

corposant St Elmo's fire

corps sing. and pl.

corps/ d'armée (Fr. m.) army corps

corps de ballet company of ballet dancers (not ital.)

corps de bataille the central part of an army, — **d'élite** a picked body, — **des lettres** (Fr. typ.) the body of the type, — **diplomatique** diplomatic body

corp/us body, pl. **-ora**, abbr. **cor.**

Corpus Christi the festival of institution of the Eucharist, on the Thursday after Trinity Sunday

Corpus Christi College Oxford and Cambridge, abbr. **CCC**

corpus delicti (law) the facts constituting an alleged offence

corp/us luteum (physiol.) an ovarian body, pl. **-ora lutea**

corp/us vile worthless substance, pl. **-ora vilia**

corr. correct/ion, -ive, -or; correspond, -ence, -ent, -ing; corrupt, -ed

correcteur (Fr. typ. m.) corrector of the press

correct/ion, -ive, -or abbr. **corr.**

Correggio, Antonio Allegri da (1494–1534) Italian painter

corregidor (Sp.) a magistrate

correlative abbr. **correl.**

correspond/, -ence, -ent, -ing abbr. **corr.**

Corresponding Member abbr. **CM, Corr. Mem.**

Corrèze dép. France

corrida a bullfight (not ital.), **corrida de toros** (Sp.) a bullfight (ital.)

corrigend/um a thing to be corrected; pl. **-a**; *see also* **erratum**

Corr./ Mem. Corresponding Member, — **Sec.** Corresponding Secretary

corroboree an Australian aboriginal dance; *not* -bery, -boric, -bury

corrupt/, -ed, -ion abbr. **corr.**

corrupter *not* -or

Corsica abbr. **Cors.**, in Fr. f. **Corse**

corslet (armour) a cuirass, *not* -elet

corso (It.) (horse) race, a street for it

Corstorphine Edinburgh

cort. cortex

cortège a (funeral) procession

Cortes the legislative assembly of Spain

Cortés, Hernando (*or* **Cortez, Hernán**) (1485–1547) Spanish conqueror of Mexico

cort/ex bark, pl. **-ices**; abbr. **cort.**

Corunna in Sp. **La Coruña**

corvée feudal forced labour, drudgery (not ital.)

corvette a small naval escort vessel

Coryate, Thomas (?1577–1617) English traveller

corybant/ a Phrygian priest, pl. **-es** (not ital.); adj. **-ic** frenzied

Corycian nymphs the Muses

coryphae/us a chorus leader, *not* -eus; pl. **-i**

coryphée a leading dancer in a corps de ballet (not ital.)

COS Chief of Staff

Cos Greek island, *use* **K-**; *but* **cos lettuce**

cos (math.) cosine (no point)

co. sa. (mus.) come sopra, as above

Cosa Nostra (US) a criminal organization resembling and related to the Mafia

cosec (math.) cosecant (no point)

cosh (math.) hyperbolic cosine (no point)

cosh/ar, -er (Heb.) *use* **kosher**

Così fan tutte ('All women are like that') an opera by Mozart 1790

co-signatory (hyphen, one word in US)

cosine (math., no hyphen) abbr. **cos**

cosmogony, cosmography abbr. **cosmog.**

COSPAR Committee on Space Research

coss. *consules* (consuls)

cosseted pampered, *not* -etted

co-star (hyphen, one word in US)

cost–benefit (**analysis**) (en rule)

costumier a person who makes or deals in costumes, *not* -mer

cosy *not* -zy (US)

cot a small bed with high sides, esp. for a baby or small child; (US) a small folding bed

cotangent (math., no hyphen) abbr. **cot**

cote a shelter, esp. for animals or birds; a shed or stall

cote (Fr. f.) market quotation, figure, mark, share

côte (Fr. f.) hillside, shore

côté (Fr. m.) side

Côte d'Azure the eastern Mediterranean coast of France

Côte-d'Or dép. France

côtelette (Fr. f.) a cutlet

coterie an exclusive 'set' of persons (not ital.)

coterminous coextensive; having the same or coincident boundaries; cf. **conterminous**

Côte-rôtie (Fr. f.) a red wine

côtes de bœuf (Fr. f.) ribs of beef

Côtes-du-Nord dép. France

cotillion a dance, in Fr. m. **cotillon**

cotoneaster a rosaceous shrub with berries

cottar a peasant, *not* -er

cotter a pin, wedge, etc.

Cotter's Saturday Night, The a poem by Burns, 1786

Cottian Alps France and Italy

cottier a cottager

cotton candy (US) = **candyfloss**

Cottonian Library in British Library, Reference Division

cotton/tail American rabbit (one word); — **wool** raw cotton (two words)

cottonize to make cotton-like, *not* -ise

couch a kind of grass; *see also* **cutch**

coudé (astr.) a telescope with its light path bent at an angle

Couéism psychotherapy by auto-suggestion, named after **Émile Coué** (1857–1926)

cougar (US) a puma

couldst (no apos.)

coulé (mus.) a slur

coulée a stream of molten or solidified lava; (US) a deep ravine or gulch (not ital., no accent in US), *not* cooley

couleur/ (Fr. f.) colour, — **de rose** roseate (fig.)

coulis a fruit purée thin enough to pour (not ital.)

coulisse/ a place of informal discussion or negotiation; **-s** (pl.) the wings in a theatre, 'behind the scenes'

couloir a gully

Coulomb, Charles Augustin de (1736–1806) French physicist; **coulomb** (elec.) a unit of charge, abbr. **C**

coulter a plough blade, *not* col- (US)

council/ assembly; **-lor** member of a council (one *l* in US), abbr. **Cllr.**

council/ estate, — flat, — house (two words) properties owned by council *or* a place in which a council meets

Council of Europe an association of European states, independent of the European Union, founded in 1948 to safeguard the political and cultural heritage of Europe and promote economic and social cooperation

counsel/ advice, a barrister; **-led, -ling; -lor** one who counsels (one *l* in US)

count/, -ess (cap. as title) abbr. **Ct.**

countdown (noun, one word)

counter (typ.) space wholly or mainly enclosed within a letter, e.g. the centre of 'O'

counter/act, -balance, -charge, -claim (one word)

counterclockwise (US) = **anticlockwise**

counter/-culture, -espionage, -intelligence, -intuitive (hyphens, one word in US)

counter-quarte (fencing) (hyphen) *not* -carte

counter/-reformation (caps. with hist. reference); **-revolution** (hyphens)

counter-tenor (mus.) a singing-voice, abbr. **C.**; cf. **contratenor**

Countesthorpe Leics.

Counties palatine Ches. and Lancs. (one cap. only)

countrif/y, -ied *not* country-

country/ dance, — house (two words)

country/side, -wide (one word)

county abbr. **Co.** (as part of name)

County Council/, -lor abbr. **CC**

County court (one cap.) abbr. **CC**

coup a stroke, esp. a political revolution

Coupar Angus Tayside (no hyphen) *not* Cu-

coup/ de foudre (Fr. m.) stroke of lightning; *— de fouet* (fencing) a 'beat', lit. a lash of the whip; *— de grâce* a finishing stroke; *— de main* sudden attack to gain a position; *— de maître* a master stroke; *— de pied* a kick; *— de poing* blow with the fist; *— de soleil* sunstroke; *— d'essai* first attempt; *— d'état* sudden or violent change in government (often not ital. in Eng.); *— de théâtre* sudden sensational act; *— d'œil* a glance, wink

coupe a shallow dish

coupé a covered motor car, usually for two (not ital.)

coupee in dancing, a salute to the partner

couper (Sc.) a dealer

Couperin the name of a French musical family, esp. **François** (1688–1733) composer

coup manqué (Fr. m.) a failure

courante (music for) a dance with a gliding step, *not* coranto

Cour de Cassation *see* **Cassation**

courier in Fr. m. *courrier*

Court abbr. **C., Ct.**

Courtauld Institute of Art London

court bouillon (Fr. cook. m.) a fish stock

Courtenay the family name of the Earl of Devon

courthouse (one word), abbr. **CH**

Courtmantle *use* Cu-

court/ martial (noun, two words) pl. **-s martial**; **court-martial** (verb, hyphen)

Court of/ Appeal abbr. **CA**, — — **Common Pleas** abbr. **CCP**, — — **Probate** abbr. **CP**, — **St James's** (apos.), — — **Session** abbr. **CS**

Courtrai Belgium, *not* -ay; in Fl. **Kortrijk**

Courts of Justice (caps.)

courtyard (one word)

couscous a NW African dish of granulated flour steamed over broth; *see also* **cuscus**

cousin/ german *not* -aine, -ane; pl. **-s german**

coûte que coûte (Fr.) at any cost, *not qui*

Coutts & Co. bankers, pron. 'coots'

coutur/ier, -ière a dressmaker

Covenanter (Sc. hist.)

covenantor (law)

Coventry: the signature of the Bishop of Coventry (colon)

cover girl (two words)

covering letter *not* **cover letter** (US)

Coverley, Sir Roger de a character described in the *Spectator* by Addison and Steele; a dance

cover-up (noun, hyphen)

covin (law) conspiracy to commit a crime etc. against a third party; (arch.) fraud, deception

Coward, Sir Noel (Pierce) (1899–1973) English actor, dramatist, and composer; *also* sometimes **Noël**

Cowling Lancs., N. Yorks.

Cowlinge Suffolk

Cowper, William (1731–1800) English poet

cowrie a shell, used as money in Africa and S. Asia; *not* -ry; cf. **kauri**

Cox a variety of eating apple, in full **Cox's orange pippin**

coxcomb a fop; *see also* **cocks-**

coxswain (naut.) *not* cocks-, colloq. **cox**

Coy. (mil.) company

coyote a N. American prairie wolf

coypu a S. American aquatic rodent, source of nutria fur; *not* -ou

cozen cheat, defraud, beguile

cozy *use* **cosy** (except in US)

CP Cape Province (of S. Africa); Central Provinces, *now* Madhya Pradesh (India); Chief Patriarch, Civil Power, Civil Procedure, Clarendon Press, Clerk of the Peace, Code of Procedure, College of Preceptors, Common Pleas, Common Prayer, Communist Party, *Congregatio Passionis* (Passionist Fathers), Court of Probate

cp. compare, *prefer* **cf.**

c.p. candlepower, carriage paid

CPC Clerk of the Privy Council

c.p.i. characters per inch

Cpl. Corporal

c.p.l. characters per line

c.p.m. characters per minute

CPO Chief Petty Officer, Compulsory Purchase Order

CPR Canadian Pacific Railway

CPRE Council for the Protection of Rural England

CPS *Custos Privati Sigilli* (Keeper of the Privy Seal)

c.p.s. characters per second, cycles per second

CPSA Civil and Public Services Association

CPU (comput.) central processing unit

CR *Carolina Regina* (Queen Caroline), *Carolus Rex* (King Charles), *Civis Romanus* (Roman citizen), Community of the Resurrection, credit rating, current rate, *Custos Rotulorum* (Keeper of the Rolls)

Cr chromium (no point)

Cr. credit, -or; Crown

cr. created

Crabb, George (1778–1854) English philologist

Crabbe, George (1754–1832) English poet

Cracow Anglicized spelling of **Kraków**, Poland

Craigton Glasgow

crampon *not* -oon (US)

Crane,/ (Harold) Hart (1899–1932) US poet, — **Stephen** (1871–1900) US novelist and poet

cranesbill plant of the genus *Geranium* (one word)

crani/um the skull, pl. **-a**

crank an eccentric person, esp. one obsessed by a particular theory; (US) a bad-tempered person; adj. **-y**

crap/e a (usually black) gauzelike fabric, for mourning; adj. **-y**; *see also* **crêpe**

craquelure a network of fine cracks in a painting or its varnish

crash/ helmet, — pad (two words)

crassa negligentia (law) criminal negligence

crawfish a large marine spiny lobster, pl. same

crayfish a freshwater crustacean, pl. same

crc, CRC camera-ready copy

cream/-laid a writing paper with wire marks, **-wove** a writing paper without wire marks (hyphen)

created abbr. **cr.**

Creation, the (cap.)

crèche a day nursery, (US) a representation of a Nativity scene

Crécy, battle of 1346, *not* Cressy, Créci

credible believable, convincing

creditable bringing credit or honour

credit/, -or abbr. **Cr.**

credit card (two words)

crédit/ foncier (Fr. m.) a society for loans on real estate, **— mobilier** a society for loans on personal estate

credo/ creed; capitalize as part of title, e.g. Apostles' *or* Nicene Credo; pl. **-s**

creese *use* **kris**

Crefeld Germany, *use* **K-**

Creighton, Mandell (1843–1901) bishop and historian

cremator/ium pl. **-a**

crème/ anglaise, — brulée, — caramel, — de cassis, — de la crème the very best, **— de menthe, — fraîche** (not ital.); *not* crê-

Cremona Italy, also a violin made there (cap.)

crenate (bot.) notched (of leaves)

crenellate(d) (mil.) furnish(ed) with battlements

crenulate (bot.) finely notched

Creole in strict use, a pure-blooded descendant of French, Spanish, Portuguese settlers in W. Indies, Louisiana, Mauritius, Africa, and E. Indies, in loose use (cap.) a Creole–Negro speaking a Spanish or French dialect, a black person born in the USA, or a pidgin grown more sophisticated through use (not cap.); *see also* **Cajun; pidgin**

creosote *not* k-

crêpe/ (Fr. m.) crape fabric other than black, (f.) pancake; **— de Chine** raw silk crêpe; **— lisse** smooth crêpe; **— Suzette** small pancake; *see also* **crape**

crescendo/ (mus.) growing in force; abbr. **cres., cresc.**; (non-technical) gradually increasing noise; pl. **-s**

Cressy *use* **Crécy**

crest (her.) a device above the shield and helmet of a coat of arms

cretaceous chalky, *not* -ious; (cap.) of or relating to the last period of the Mesozoic era

Cretan of Crete

cretin (a person affected by) a type of physical and mental handicap; in Fr. m. *crétin*, f. *crétine*

cretonne a cotton cloth

Creusot, Le dép. Saône-et-Loire, France; *not* -zot

Creutzfeldt–Jakob disease (en rule)

crevasse a large fissure, esp. in the ice of a glacier

Crèvecœur, Michel Guillaume Jean de (1735–1813) French-born US writer (ligature)

crève-cœur (Fr. m.) heartbreak, pl. same

crevette (Fr. f.) prawn

crevice a small fissure

crib (US) a small bed with high sides, esp. for a baby or small child (UK = **cot**)

Criccieth Gwynedd

Crichton/, James, 'the Admirable' (1560–?1585) Scottish scholar and soldier

cricket/, -er, -ing

cri de cœur (Fr. m.) a passionate appeal

crim. con. (law) criminal conversation, adultery

crime passionnel (Fr. m.) a crime caused by sexual passion (two *n*s)

crimplene (propr.) bulked Terylene

cring/e, -ing

crinkum-crankum intricate, crooked; *not* -cum -cum

cris/is pl. **-es**

crispbread a thin biscuit (one word)

crit. critic/al, -ized

criteri/on standard of judgement, pl. **-a**

criticaster a petty critic

criticize *not* -ise

critique a review (not ital.)

Critique of Pure Reason by Kant, 1781, in Ger. *Kritik der reinen Vernunft*

CRMP Corps of Royal Military Police

Crna Gora Serbo-Croat for **Montenegro**

Croat/ a native of Croatia, in Serbo-Croat **Hrvat**; *not* Croatian (US); **-ia** a republic of the former Yugoslavia, in Serbo-Croat **Hrvatska**

crochet/ hooked-needle work; **-ed, -ing**

Crockford in full *Crockford's Clerical Directory*, the 'Who's Who' of the clergy

Crockford's a London club

crocus/ pl. **-es**

Croesus (6th c. BC) a rich king (and the last) of Lydia

croissant *not* croisant

Croix de Guerre a French military decoration

Cro-Magnon/ (anthrop.) of a prehistoric race, from remains found at –, dép. Dordogne, France

Cromartie, Earl of

cromesquis (Fr. cook. m.) *see* **kromesky**

Crome Yellow by Aldous Huxley, 1921

Cronos *use* **K-**

Crookback sobriquet of Richard III, *not* Crouchback

Crookes, Sir William (1832–1919) English physicist

Croonian Lecture of the Royal Society

croquet/ a game (not ital.), as verb **-ed, -ing**

croquette rissole (not ital.)

crore (Ind.) ten million, point thus: 1,00,00,000; *see also* **lakh**

crosette *use* **crossette**

crosier a bishop's or archbishop's staff, *not* -zier

croslet *use* **crosslet**

cross/ (typ.) a proof-correction sign for a battered sort; **Greek** +; **Latin** †; **Maltese** ✠; **tau** — of St Anthony T; *see also* **crux**

crossbar (one word)

cross-bench(er) (parl.) (hyphen)

crossbill a passerine bird (one word)

cross-bill (law) a promissory note given in exchange, a bill brought by defendant against plaintiff in a Chancery suit (hyphen)

crossette (archit.) a ledge, *not* crose-

Crossgates Cumbria, Fife, Powys, N. Yorks.

Cross Gates W. Yorks.

cross-heading (typ.) a heading to a paragraph printed across a column in the body of an article in a newspaper, journal, etc.

Crosshill Fife, Strathclyde

Cross Hill Derby., Shropshire

Crosskeys Co. Antrim, Co. Cavan, Gwent

Cross Keys Kent, Wilts.

crosslet (her.) a small cross, *not* cros-

cross-link (hyphen)

crossmatch (one word)

cross-reference abbr. **x-ref.**

crossroad(s) (one word)

cross section (noun, two words)

crosswalk (US) = **pedestrian crossing**

crossways *not* -way, -wise (US)

crosswind (one word)

crossword (puzzle)

crotchet/ a musical note, a whim; **-ed, -ing, -y**

Crouchback *use* **Crook-**

croupier a gaming table attendant

crouton a bit of crust or toast, in Fr. m. *croûton*

Crowland Lincs., Suffolk, *not* Croy-

Crown, the (cap. C) abbr. **Cr.**

crown a former British coin equal to five shillings (25p); a former size of paper, 15 × 20 in.; **crown 4to** 10 × 7.5 in.; **crown 8vo** 7.5 × 5 in. (untrimmed); the basis for size of **metric crown** is 768 × 1008 mm

Crowner's quest dialectal for Coroner's inquest (one cap. only)

Crown Office abbr. **CO**

Crowther-Hunt, Baron (hyphen)

crozier *use* **cros-**

CRP *Calendarium Rotulorum Patentium* (Calendar of the Patent Rolls)

CRR Curia Regis Roll

CRT cathode-ray tube

cru (Fr. m.) a French vineyard or wine-producing region, the wine produced from it, a specific growth (no accent)

Crucifixion, the (cap.)

crudités an hors d'oeuvre of mixed raw vegetables, in pl. (not ital.)

Cruft's Dog Show *not* -s'

Cruikshank, George (1792–1878) English caricaturist and illustrator

crumhorn Eng. spelling of **krummhorn**

cruse a jar, *not* cruise

crush/ bar, — barrier (two words)

Cruso NC

Crusoe, Robinson by Defoe, 1719

cru/x (of an argument) the decisive point at issue, pl. **-xes** *or* **-ces** (not ital.)

crux/ ansata cross with a handle, †; — *commissa* tau cross, ⊤; — *decussata* cross of St Andrew or St Patrick, ×

cruzeiro former monetary unit of Brazil, from 1986 one-thousandth of a **cruzado**

Crying of Lot 49, The novel by Thomas Pynchon, 1966

cryogenics the study of low-temperature refrigeration

cryptogam/ (bot.) any member of the Cryptogamia, flowerless plants; **-ous**

crypto/gram anything written in code; **-grapher, -graphic, -graphy**

crypton (chem.) *use* **k-**

cryptonym a private name

crystal. crystallography

crystalliz/ation, -e *not* -is-; **-ed, -ing**

CS Chemical Society (now part of Royal Society of Chemistry), Civil Service, Clerk to the Signet, College of Science, Common Serjeant, Court of Session, *Custos Sigilli* (Keeper of the Seal)

Cs caesium (no point)

c/s cycles per second

Csar etc., *use* **Ts-**

csárdás a Hungarian dance, pl. same; *not* cz-

CSC Civil Service Commission, Conspicuous Service Cross (*now* DSC)

CSE Certificate of Secondary Education, replaced in 1988 by GCSE

CS gas a gas used to control riots etc. (two caps.)

CSI Companion of the Order of the Star of India

CSM Company Sergeant Major

CSU Civil Service Union

CT Connecticut (postal abbr.)

Ct. Count, Court

ct. cent

CTC Cyclists' Touring Club

Ctesiphon city of ancient Mesopotamia

ctl. central, -s

cto. (mus.) concerto

cts. centimes, cents

CU Cambridge University

Cu cuprum (copper) (no point)

cu. cubic

cube root (two words)

cubic abbr. **c., cu., cub.**

cubicul/um (archaeol.) burial chamber, pl. **-a**

Cúchulainn (Ir. myth.) warrior hero

cuddl/y tempting to cuddle, given to cuddling; **-lier, -liest**

cudgel/, -led, -ling (one *l* in US)

CUDS Cambridge University Dramatic Society

cue/, -ing; cf. **queue**

cuffs (US) = (**trouser**) turn-ups

Cufic *use* **K-**

cui bono? (Lat.) who gains by it?

cuidado (Sp. m.) danger, care, worry; *not ciu-*

Cuillins mountains in Skye

cuirass/ body armour, **-ier** a soldier wearing it

cuisine cookery (not ital.)

culch oyster spawn, *not* cultch

cul-de-sac pl. **culs-de-sac**

cul/ex a gnat, pl. *-ices*

cullender *use* **colan-**

Cullinan a famous diamond

Culpeper/, Nicholas (1616–54) English herbalist; — Va. from **Thomas, Lord** — (1578–1662) former Governor

cultivar (bot.) a variety made by cultivation, abbr. **cv.**

Culzean Castle Strathclyde

CUM Cambridge University Mission

cum (Lat.) with (not ital.)

Cumaean of Cumae, near Naples

Cumbernauld Strathclyde

Cumbria a county of England

cum dividend with dividend, abbr. **c.d.**

cumfrey *use* **com-**

cum grano salis (Lat.) with a grain of salt

cumin a plant with aromatic seeds (one *m*)

cum laude/ (Lat.) with distinction, *magna —* — with high distinction, *summa — —* with highest distinction

cummerbund a waistbelt; *not* cumber-, ku-, -band

Cummings, E(dward) E(stlin) (1894–1962) US writer and poet who renounced use of capital letters; thus properly **e. e. cummings**

cum multis aliis (Lat.) with many others

cum. pref. cumulative preference

cumquat *use* **k-**

cumul/us (meteor.) a cloud form, pl. **-i**; abbr. **k.**

cuneiform wedge-shaped; *not* cunif-, cunef-

Cunninghame Graham, Robert Bontine (1852–1936) British writer (no hyphen)

CUP Cambridge University Press

Cupar/ Fife; — **Angus** Tayside, *use* **Coupar Angus**

cupbearer (one word)

Cup Final *but* **cup-tie**

cupful/ the amount held by a cup, esp. (US) a half-pint or 8-ounce measure in cookery (one word); pl. **-s**; *but* 'cups full' (two words)

cupronickel an alloy of copper and nickel (one word)

cuprum copper, symbol **Cu**

cur. currency, current

curable not -eable

curaçao a liqueur named after the Caribbean island, *not* -oa (not cap.)

curare a drug; *not* -a, -i, urari

curb for verb, and part of a bridle (used for all senses in US); cf. **kerb**

curbstone *use* **kerb-**

curé/ French priest (not ital.), *petit* — French curate (ital.)

cure-all a universal remedy (hyphen)

curfuffle *use* **ker-**

Curia/ the papal court (cap.); — *advisare vult* the court desires to consider, abbr. *c.a.v.*

Curie,/ **Marie Sklodowska** (1867–1934) and her husband — **Pierre** (1859–1906) French scientists

curie a unit of radioactivity, abbr. **Ci** (cap.); *now* replaced by **becquerel**

curio/ an object of art, pl. **-s** (not ital.)

curium symbol **Cm**

curlicue a decorative curl; *not* -eque, -ycue

curly brackets (typ.) braces { }

currach a coracle, *not* -agh

Curragh, The Co. Kildare

curren/**cy**, **-t** abbr. **cur.**

current (elec.) abbr. **cur.**; symbol *I*, *i* (ital.)

currente calamo (Lat.) easily, fluently

curricul/**um** pl. **-a**; **-um vitae** pl. **-a vitae**, abbr. **CV**, **c.v.** (not ital.)

Currie Lothian

Curry Co. Sligo

cursor (comput.) a movable indicator on a VDU screen, identifying the active position

curtain-raiser (theat.) in Fr. *lever de rideau*

Curtiss, Glenn Hammond (1878–1930) US pioneer aviator

Curtmantle sobriquet of Henry II, *not* Cou-

curts/**y** *not* -sey, **-ied**, **-ies**, **-ying**

curvilinear (one word)

Curwen, John (1816–80) pioneer of tonic sol-fa

cuscus/ a marsupial, — **grass** of India; *see also* **couscous**

Cushitic (of or pertaining to) a group of E. African languages of the Hamitic type

custodia legis (Lat.) in the custody of the law

custom house (two words) abbr. **CH**

cust/*os* (Lat. m.) a custodian, pl. **-odes**

Custos/ *Privati Sigilli* Keeper of the Privy Seal, abbr. **CPS**; — *Rotulorum* Keeper of the Rolls, abbr. **CR**; — *Sigilli* Keeper of the Seal, abbr. **CS**

cut and dried (adj., no hyphens)

cutback (noun, one word)

Cutch India, *use* **K-**

cutch catechu, an extract of Indian plants, the tough paper sheets used by gold-beaters; *not* k-; *see also* **couch**

cut/**-off**, **-out** (nouns), **-price** (adj.) (hyphens)

cuts (typ.) illustrations

cut-throat (hyphen)

Cutty Sark a famous clipper, now in dry dock at Greenwich

cutty-stool a stool of repentance

cuvée a vatful, jugful, or sort of wine

Cuyp Dutch artists, *not* K-

CV curriculum vitae

cv. (bot.) cultivar

CVO Commander of the Royal Victorian Order

Cwlth (no point) Commonwealth (Australian)

Cwmbran Gwent

Cwmcarn Gwent

c.w.o. cash with order

CWS Co-operative Wholesale Society

cwt. hundredweight (no point in scientific and technical work)

cybernetics the study of communication processes in animals and machines (sing. treated as pl.)

cyc. cycloped/ia, -ic

Cycle of the Saros (astr.) $6,585\frac{1}{2}$ days

cyclo-cross cross-country bicycle racing

cycloped/**ia**, **-ic** *but use* -paed- in quoting titles using that form; abbr. **cyc.**

Cyclop/**s** a giant with one eye, pl. **-es**; adj. **-ean**

cygnet a young swan, *not* cig-

Cym. Cymric

cyma (archit.) a moulding of the cornice

cymbalist a cymbal-player; cf. **cembalo**

cymbal/**o** a dulcimer, pl. **-os**

cymbiform boat-shaped, *not* cymbae-

Cymmrodorion, Honourable Society of (two *m*s)

Cymrae/**g** (Welsh) the Welsh language, **-s** a Welsh woman

Cymreig/ (Welsh, adj.) Welsh, **-esau** Welsh women

Cymric Welsh

Cymr/o (Welsh) a Welshman; **-u** Wales; **-y** Welshmen, the Welsh nation; *not* K-

CYMS Catholic Young Men's Society

Cynewulf (8th c.) Anglo-Saxon poet

cynghanedd a form of Welsh poetic alliteration, pl. **cynganeddion**

cynocephalus (classical myth.) a dog-headed creature

Cynthia the moon

Cynthius an epithet of Apollo

cypher *use* **ci-**

cy près (law) as near as possible to a testator's intentions

Cyprian/ of Cyprus and Cypriot; — **Aphrodite** Venus, — in Lat. **Thascius Caecilius Cyprianus** (*c.*200–58) Christian writer and martyr

Cypriot an inhabitant or the language of Cyprus

Cyprus indep. rep. 1960

Cyrenaic pertaining to Cyrene *or* its school of philosophy

Cyrillic (pertaining to) the alphabet used by Slavonic peoples of the Eastern Church (two ls)

cyst/ (biol.) a sac, **-ic**; *not* ci-

Cytherean pertaining to Aphrodite, *not* -ian

CZ Canal Zone (Panama)

Czar etc., *use* **Ts-** (except in US)

czárdás *use* **cs-**

Czech (of or relating to) (a native) of the Czech Republic, or Bohemia, *or* the language of this people

Czechoslovak (hist.) (a person) belonging to the former **Czechoslovakia**; *not* -ian, *now* **Czech** *or* **Slovak**

Czech Republic formed 1993

Czerny, Karl (1791–1857) Austrian composer

Dd

D 500, deuterium (= heavy hydrogen), the fourth in series

D. (US) Democrat, Deputy, *Deus* (God), *Dominus* (Lord), Duke, prefix to enumeration of Schubert's works (*see* **Deutsch**)

đ a lower-case letter found in Old Saxon and (with quite different value) modern Serbo-Croat

d (prefix) deci-

d. date, daughter, day, dead, degree, departs; desert/ed, -er; died, dime, dioptre, dose; (Fr.) *douane* (customs), *droite* (the right hand); (It.) *destra* (right), (Lat.) *decretum* (a decree), *denarii* (pence), *denarius* (penny); (meteor.) drizzling

d' as prefix to an un-Anglicized proper name should, in accordance with Fr. practice, be lower case and *not* cap., as 'd'Arsonval', except at beginning of sentence; it is always cap. in It., as 'D'Annunzio'. Signatures to be copied

Đ ð Icelandic, Norse, OE (lower case ð), and phonetic letter, pron. like the soft *th* in '*that*'; *see also* **eth**

∂ (math.) sign of partial derivative

δ (typ.) delete

DA deposit account, (US) District Attorney

Da. Danish

da (prefix) deca-

DAB *Dictionary of American Biography*

da/ ballo (mus.) a dance style; — **capo** *or* — **capo al fine** repeat from the beginning to the word *fine*, abbr. **DC**; — **capo al segno** repeat from the beginning to the sign 𝄋, abbr. **DS**; — **capella** *or* — **chiesa** in church style

DAC digital–analogue converter

Dacca *use* **Dhaka**

d'accord (Fr.) I agree

dacha a country house or cottage in Russia (not ital.)

Dachau a Nazi concentration camp, 1933–45

dacoit an Indian robber; *not* dak-, dec-

dactyl/ (prosody) a foot of three syllables (- ˇ ˇ), -**ic**

Dada/ unconventional art, literature, music, and film *c.*1920; -**ism**, -**ist**, -**istic**

daddy-long-legs the crane-fly (of the family *Tipulidae*) or the harvestman (of the family *Opilionidae*), *not* daddy longlegs (US)

dado/ pl. -**s**

Daedalus (Gr. myth.) the builder of the Cretan labyrinth and father of Icarus; cf. **De-**

daemon *use* **demon** except for the sense in Greek mythology of a supernatural being or indwelling spirit, *not* dai- (except when using Hellenic transcription)

daffadowndilly a daffodil; *not* daffi-, daffo-, daffy (one word)

Dafydd Wales, Welsh for **David** (the saint is **Dewi**); *not* Daff-

Dagapur Ethiopia

dagger/ (†), **double —** (‡) (typ.) in Eng. before (in Ger. after) a person's name signifies 'dead' or 'died'; this should be used only of Christians. When in Ger. ✗ follows the name it signifies 'killed in battle'; the normal double dagger should not be used for this symbol

daggle-tail *use* **draggle-**

Dagonet, Sir King Arthur's fool

Daguerre, Louis Jacques Mandé (1789–1851) French pioneer of photography

daguerreotype (not cap.)

dahabeeyah a Nile sailing boat

Dahomey W. Africa, *now* **Benin**

Dáil Éireann the Lower House of the Irish Parliament

d'ailleurs (Fr.) besides, however

daimio/ a Japanese noble, pl. -**s**

Daimler a make of motor car

daimon Hellenistic transcription of **daemon**; *see also* **demon**

daiquiri a rum-based cocktail (not cap.)

dais a small platform, *not* daïs

dakoit *use* **dac-**

Dakota (**North, South**) off. abbrs. **N. Dak.**, **S. Dak.**, postal **ND**, **SD**

Dalai Lama the Grand Lama of Tibet, spiritual head of Tibetan Buddhism

Dalarö Sweden, *not* — Island, as the suffix -ö indicates 'island'

Dalí, Salvador (1904–89) Catalan painter

Dalila *see* **Delilah**

Dallapiccola, Luigi (1904–75) Italian composer

Dalmatian a breed of spotted dog, of Dalmatia; *not* -ion

dal segno (It. mus.) repeat from the sign 𝄋, abbr. **DS**

damageable *not* -gable

Damara/, -land SW Africa, *now* **Namibia**

damascen/e (noun, verb, adj.) (of or relating to) ornament in metal; *not* -keen, -kin; -**er**

Dame the title given to a woman with the rank of Knight Commander or holder of the Grand Cross in the Orders of Chivalry

Dame aux camélias, La a play by Dumas *fils*, 1848

Damien de Veuster, Joseph, 'Father Damien' (1840–89) Belgian priest to a leper colony in the Hawaiian Islands

damnosa hereditas (Lat.) an inheritance involving loss

damnum absque injuria (Lat.) damage without wrong

Damon and Pythias (Gr. myth.) model friends; the correct spelling is **Phintias**

Dan. (Book of) Daniel

Dan/aë (Gr. myth.) the mother of Perseus, also an asteroid; **Danaea** a fern genus; **-aïd** a daughter of Danaus; **-aus** the son of Belus

d. and c. dilatation (of the cervix) and curettage (of the uterus)

Dandie Dinmont a breed of Scottish terrier, from **Andrew Dinmont** a farmer in Scott's *Guy Mannering*

dandruff scurf, *not* -riff

Dane/geld *not* -lt; **-law** (one word)

Daniel, Book of (OT) abbr. **Dan.**

Daniell's battery (elec.) usually called a **Daniell cell**

Danish abbr. **Da.**

danke schön (Ger.) many thanks

Dannebrog the Danish national standard, *also* an order of knighthood; *not* Dane-

D'Annunzio, Gabriele (1864–1938) Italian writer (cap. *D*)

danse macabre (Fr. f.) dance of death

dans/eur a male dancer, **-euse** a female dancer (not ital.)

dans le fond (Fr.) basically, in fact; cf. *au fond*

Dant/e Alighieri (1265–1321) Italian poet; **-ean, -esque, -ist** (caps.)

Danzig Ger. for **Gdańsk**

daou *use* **dhow**

DAR Daughters of the American Revolution

d'Arblay, Mme (1752–1840) the English novelist **Fanny Burney**

Darby and Joan a devoted old married couple, *not* Derby

d'Arc, Jeanne (Fr.) **Joan of Arc**, alphabetized **Arc, Jeanne d'**

Darcy de Knayth, Baroness

Dardanelles the strait linking the Sea of Marmara to the Aegean, in antiquity called **Hellespont**

daredevil (one word)

dare say (two words)

Dar es Salaam the former capital of Tanzania (no hyphens)

Dar the modern Persian language of Afghanistan

Darjeeling *not* Darji-

Dark Ages, the the period of European history preceding the Middle Ages, especially the 5th–10th cc. Beware of using the term too liberally, since not all European cultures underwent the same degree of unenlightenment during this period, or feel the same about it: the traditional French right wing holds the age in high esteem

darkroom (one word)

darshan (Hind.) seeing a revered person

Darwen Lancs., *not* Over –

Darwin/, Charles Robert (1809–82) author of *Origin of Species*; **—, Erasmus** (1731–1802) English physician and poet, grandfather of Charles; **-ian, -ism, -ist**

das (Ger.) the (n. sing. nominative and accusative), *also* that (demonstrative); *see also* **das heißt**; **dass**

dashboard (one word)

das/ heißt (Ger.) that is to say, abbr. **d. h.**; **— ist** that is, abbr. **d. i.** (spaces in Ger. abbrs.)

dass (Ger.) that (conjunction)

DAT digital audio tape

dat. dative

data (pl.) in computing and related fields, treated as collective noun taking singular verb; *see also* **datum**

data bank (two words)

database (one word)

datable capable of being dated, *not* -eable

data processing (hyphen when attrib.)

data-set (hyphen)

date/ abbr. **d.**, **-line** (hyphen)

dative the indirect object, abbr. **dat.**

Datta, Michael Madhusudan (1824–73) Bengali poet and dramatist

Datta, Sudhindranath (1901–60) Indian poet

datum a thing known or granted, pl. **data**

daube a braised meat stew

Daudet,/ Alphonse (1840–97) French novelist, **— Léon** (1867–1942) French writer and politician

daughter/ abbr. **d.**, **dau.**; **-in-law**, pl. **daughters-in-law** (hyphens)

Daumier, Honoré (1808–79) French painter

Dauntsey's School Devizes

dauphin the eldest son of the King of France 1349–1830; **Dauphiné** his traditional lands in SE France; **dauphiness** his wife, in Fr. *dauphine*

Dav. David

D'Avenant, Sir William (1606–68) English playwright and poet, Poet Laureate 1660–8; also spelt **Davenant**

Davies,/ Sir Henry Walford (1869–1941) musician, **— William Henry** (1871–1940) poet

da Vinci, Leonardo *see* **Leonardo da Vinci**

Davis, Jefferson (1808–89) US senator and President of the Confederate States 1862–5

Davis/ apparatus for escape from a submarine, **— Cup** a tennis trophy

Davy/, Sir Humphry *not* -ey (1778–1829) English chemist, inventor of the **— lamp**

Davy Jones's locker the seabed

Dawley Shropshire

Day, John (1522–84) English printer, also spelt **Daye, Daie**

day abbr. **d.** (typ.) initial caps for days of the week, and of fasts, feasts, festivals, holidays; abbr., when necessary, to **Sun., Mon., Tue., Wed., Thur., Fri., Sat.** In Fr., no caps., as *lundi*

Dayak *use* **Dyak**

daybed (one word)

daybook (one word), abbr. **d.b.**

day-boy (hyphen)

day/break, -dream (one word)

day-girl (hyphen)

Day-Glo (propr.) (of) a make of fluorescent paint or other colouring

Day-Lewis, Cecil (1904–72) Poet Laureate 1968–72 (hyphen), wrote under the name **C. Day Lewis** (no hyphen)

daylight (one word)

Daylight Saving Time (US) one hour in advance of local US time, largely equivalent to British Summer Time (three words); abbr. **DST**

day/-long (hyphen)

day/ nursery, — room (two words)

dayside (one word)

day's journey (Heb.) about 17 miles

daytime (one word)

Dayton Ohio

Daytona Beach Fla.

DB Domesday Book

dB decibel (no point)

d.b. daybook, double bed, double-breasted

DBE Dame Commander of the Order of the British Empire

dbk. drawback

dbl. double

DBS direct-broadcast satellite, direct broadcasting by satellite

DC 600, (mus.) da capo (from the beginning), deputy-consul, direct current (*not* d.c.), District of Columbia (USA)

DCB Dame Commander of the Order of the Bath

DCC digital compact cassette

D.Ch. Doctor of Surgery

DCL Doctor of Civil Law

DCM Distinguished Conduct Medal

DCMG Dame Commander of the Order of St Michael and St George

DCVO Dame Commander of the Royal Victorian Order

DD direct debit, *Divinitatis Doctor* (Doctor of Divinity)

D.d. *Deo dedit* (gave to God)

dd in Welsh a separate letter, not to be divided

dd. delivered

d.d. *dono dedit* (gave as a gift)

DDA Dangerous Drugs Act

D-Day 6 June 1944 (hyphen)

DDD *dat, dicat, dedicat* (gives, devotes, and dedicates); *dono dedit dedicavit* (gave and consecrated as a gift)

DDR (Ger.) *Deutsche Demokratische Republik* (German Democratic Republic) East Germany, 1949–90

DDS Doctor of Dental Surgery

DDT dichlorodiphenyltrichloroethane (an insecticide)

DE Delaware (postal abbr.)

de (as prefix to proper name) not cap. ('de Candolle', 'de Talleyrand-Périgord'), except when Anglicized ('De Quincey', 'De Vinne') or starting a sentence; where lower-case, alphabetize by surname ('Mairan, Jean-Jacques de', 'Chazelles, Jean-François, comte de'), though Anglicized names may be treated differently by their bearers. In Sp. and Port. not cap. ('Figueiredo, Adelpha Silva Rodrigues de') and omitted in bare surname references, as for It. ('Medici, Lorenzo de'') unless of Lat. form ('De Sanctis'). In Du. generally not cap. and not used in alphabetizing ('Groot, Huijg de'); in Flemish the reverse is true ('De Bruyne, Jan'); Afrikaans varies; follow established convention or the bearer's preference; cf. **de La**; **du; van, van den, van der**

deacon/al, -ate *use* **diac-**

dead abbr. **d.**

dead/beat, -bolt, -eye, -fall (one word)

dead-head (hyphen)

dead heat (noun), **dead-heat** (verb)

dead/line, -lock, -pan (one word)

dead reckoning (naut.) calculating a ship's position from the log, compass, etc. when observations are impossible; often inexact, and the term should not be used in contexts where precision is meant; abbr. **DR**

deadweight (one word, two in US), abbr. **dw**

deaf-and-dumb alphabet *use* **sign language** unless this specific system is meant

dean *not* a synonym for **doyen**; *see also* **dene**

Dean of Faculty (Sc.) (*not* of the) president of the Faculty of Advocates, abbr. **DF**

Dear/ Madam, — Sir in printed letter full left

deasil (Sc.) clockwise, opp. to **widdershins**

deathbed (one word)

death/ blow, — knell, — mask, — penalty, — rate, — rattle, — roll, — row, — squad, — tax, — threat, — toll, — trap, — warrant (two words)

death-watch beetle (hyphen, two words in US)

death wish (two words)

deb (colloq.) debutante (no point, no accent)

deb. debenture

debacle a downfall (no accents)

débat (Fr. m.) discussion, debate; (poet.) a poem in the form of a debate between two characters representing opposed principles (ital.)

debatable *not* -eable

debauchee a libertine

debenture/ abbr. **deb.**, **-holder** (hyphen, two words in US)

debonair gaily elegant, *not* -aire; in Fr. **débonnaire**

Debrett (Peerage)

debris ruins (no accent), in Fr. m. **débris**

debut/, -ant f. **-ante** (not ital., no accent); *see also* **deb**

Dec. Decani, December, (archit.) Decorated

dec. deceased, declaration, declared, declension, declination, decorative

dec. (mus.) decrescendo

déc. (Fr.) *décéd/é*, f. *-ée* (deceased); *décembre* (not cap.) (December)

deca- prefix meaning ten, abbr. **da**

décade (Fr. f.) a period of ten days, substituted for a week in the French Republican calendar 1793–1805

decalitre 10 litres, abbr. **dl** (no point)

Decalogue the Ten Commandments

Decameron, The by Boccaccio, 1352

decametre 10 metres, abbr. **dm** (no point)

Decan India, *use* **Decc-**

decani dean's or south side of a choir (north side in Durham Cathedral), abbr. **Dec.**; opp. to **cantoris**

decanter a bottle to hold decanted liquor

Deccan India, *not* Decan

deceased abbr. **dec.**

décéd/é (Fr.) f. **-ée** deceased, abbr. **déc.**

December abbr. **Dec.**; in Fr. m. **décembre**, abbr. **déc.** (not cap.), *also* **X**ᵇʳᵉ

decenni/um a decade, pl. **-a**

decentralize *not* -ise

decern (Sc. law) to judge; *see also* **discern**

deci- a prefix meaning one-tenth, abbr. **d**

decibar one-tenth of a bar

decibel a unit for comparing intensity of noises, power, etc.; abbr. **dB**; *see also* **bel**

Decies, Baron

decigram one-tenth of a gram, *not* -mme; abbr. **dg** (no point)

decilitre one-tenth of a litre, abbr. **dl** (no point)

decimalize *not* -ise

decimal point (two words)

decimate kill or remove one in ten, kill a large proportion of; do not use to mean 'exterminate totally', or when any other proportion is specified

decimator one who decimates, takes every tenth part or person; *not* -er

decimetre one-tenth of a metre, 3.937 in.; *not* -er; abbr. **dm** (no point)

decimo-octavo (typ.) 18mo (not ital.); *see* **eighteenmo**

deckle edge the ragged edge of handmade paper, *not* -el

declar/ation, -ed abbr. **dec.**

Declaration of/ Independence USA, 4 July 1776 (caps.); — — **Indulgence** a royal proclamation of religious liberties, esp. under Charles II in 1672 and James II in 1687 (caps.)

déclass/é f. **-ée** who (or that) has fallen to an inferior status (not ital.)

declension (gram.) a system of case-endings, abbr. **dec.**

declinable *not* -eable

declination (astr.) the angular distance from the celestial equator, abbr. **dec.**; (US) a formal refusal

Deco, deco *use* **art deco**

decoit *use* **dac-**

decollate behead; **Decollation** of St John the Baptist, 29 Aug.

décollet/age a low neckline on a woman's dress etc.; **-é** having a low neckline (not ital.)

decolorize *not* -colour-, -ise

decolour render colourless, *not* -or (US)

deconstruct/-ion, -ionist, -ing, -ive (philos. and lit. theory) (one word, not cap.)

decor stage or room furnishings and fittings (no accent)

decorat/e, -or

Decoration Day (US) *see* **Memorial Day**

decorative abbr. **dec.**

decorum propriety of conduct

découpage (not ital.)

decree nisi (law) the first stage in the dissolution of a marriage (not ital.)

decrepit decayed, *not* -id

decrescendo/ (mus.) decreasing in loudness; abbr. **dec.**, **decres.**; as noun, pl. **-s**

decret/um (Lat.) a (papal) decree, pl. **-a**; abbr. **d.**

Dedalus, Stephen a character in Joyce's *A Portrait of the Artist as a Young Man*, 1914–15, and *Ulysses*, 1922; cf. **Dae-**

Dedlock, Sir Leicester *and* **Lady** characters in Dickens's *Bleak House*, *not* Dead-

deducible able to be inferred, *not* -eable

deductible able to be subtracted, *not* -able

de-emphasize (hyphen)

deemster a judge in the Isle of Man, *not* demp-

de-escalat/e, -tion (hyphens)

def. defective, defendant, deferred (shares), defined, definite, definition, defunct

de facto (Lat.) in actual fact (not ital.)

defecat/e, -or *not* defae-

defector *not* -er

defence *not* -se (US), *but* **defensive, defensible**

Defence of Poetry, A an essay by P. Sidney, 1579–80; original title *The Defence of Poesie*

Defence of Poetry an essay by P. B. Shelley, 1821

defendant abbr. **def.**

défense/ d'afficher (Fr.) stick no bills, **— *de fumer*** no smoking, **— *d'entrer*** no admittance

defens/ive *not* -cive; **-ible** *not* -ceable, -sable

defensor* f¹*dei (Lat.) Defender of the Faith, abbr. **DF**

defer/, -ence, -rable, -red, -rer, -ring

deferred (shares) abbr. **def.**

de fide (Lat.) authentic, to be believed as part of the (Christian) faith

definable *not* -eable

defin/ed, -ite, -ition; abbr. **def.**

deflate remove air, reverse economic inflation

defle/ct bend away, **-ction** this act or process

Defoe, Daniel (1661–1731) English writer, *not* de Foe

defunct abbr. **def.**

deg. degree(s)

dégag/é f. **-ée** easy, unconstrained (not ital.)

Degas, Hilaire (Germain Edgar) (1834–1917) French painter (no accent)

de Gaulle, Charles *see* **Gaulle, de**

degauss/, -ing a device or method for neutralizing magnetism

degradable *not* -eable

degree/ abbr. **deg.**, symbol °, set close up to the scale (10 °C) or, where none, figure (35°)

dégringolade (Fr. f.) rapid deterioration

de/ haut en bas (Fr.) contemptuously, **— *haute lutte*** with a high hand

de Havilland, Sir Geoffrey (1882–1965) English aircraft designer and manufacturer

Deïaneira (Gr. myth.) the wife of Hercules; *also* an asteroid

de-ic/e, -er (hyphens)

deictic (philol., gram.) (a word that is) pointing, demonstrative

Dei/ gratia (Lat.) by the grace of God, abbr. **DG**; **—*judicium*** the judgement of God; *see also* **Deo**

Deity, the the one God (cap.)

déjà vu seen before (not ital.)

déjeuner/ (Fr. m.) breakfast or lunch; ***petit —*** coffee and rolls on rising; **— *à la fourchette*** meat breakfast, early lunch

de jure (Lat.) by right (often not ital. in legal contexts)

Dekker, Thomas (*c.*1570–1640) English playwright

de Klerk, F(rederik) W(illem) (b. 1936) President of S. Africa 1989–94

de Kooning, Willem (b. 1904) Dutch-born US painter

del (math.) the symbol ∇

Del. Delaware (off. abbr.)

del. delegate, delete

del. delineavit (drew this)

de La (as prefix to proper name) one cap. ('de La Condamine'), two if starting a sentence; *de* is dropped in the absence of a forename; alphabetized under *La* ('La Fontaine, Jean de'). When Anglicized, the prefix may deviate from this practice ('de la Mare', 'De La Warr'); follow established convention or the bearer's preference; cf. **de; du**

Delacroix, Ferdinand Victor Eugène (1799–1863) French painter

de La Fontaine *see* **La Fontaine**

de la Mare, Walter (1873–1956) English poet, novelist, and critic

de la Ramée, Marie Louise (1839–1908) English novelist, pseud. **Ouida**

De la Roche, Mazo (1885–1961) Canadian novelist

Delaroche, Paul (1797–1856) French painter

de La Tour *see* **La Tour**

Delaware off. abbr. **Del.**, postal **DE**

De La Warr, Earl (three caps.)

dele (typ.) delete

deleatur (Lat.) let it be deleted

delegate abbr. **del.**

delenda (Lat.) things to be deleted

delft/, -ware glazed earthenware made at Delft (*formerly* Delf) in Holland

Delibes, Léo (1836–91) French composer

delicatesse delicacy (not ital.), in Fr. f. ***délicatesse***

delicatessen a shop or department selling prepared foods

Delilah (OT) *but* Dalila in Milton's *Samson Agonistes*

delineable that can be delineated

delineavit (Lat.) drew this; abbr. ***del.***

delirium/ a disordered state of mind, with hallucinations, pl. **-s**; **— tremens** delirium with trembling induced by heavy drinking, abbr. **d.t., d.t.s**

De L'Isle, Viscount

deliverer *not* -or

Della Cruscan (noun and adj.) (a member) of the Florentine Accademia della Crusca, concerned with the purity of the Italian language, 16th c.; or of an English poetical group in Florence, late 18th c.

Della Robbia an enamelled terracotta invented by Luca della Robbia; *see also* **Robbia**

Delph/i Greece, the site of an ancient oracle, in Gr. **Delphoi**; **-ic**, *not* -ian

delta/ the fourth letter of the Gr. alphabet (*Δ*, δ); — **rays,** — **rhythm,** — **wing** (two words)

deltiology the collecting and study of post-cards

de luxe luxurious (not ital., two words, one word in US)

dem (Ger.) to the, for the (m. and n. sing., dative)

Dem. (US) Democrat

dem. (typ.) demy

demagog/ue *not* -gog (US); **-y, -uery, -ic**

dem/ain *use* **-esne**

de mal en pis (Fr.) from bad to worse

demarcate mark the limits of, *not* -kate

demarch the chief officer of an ancient Attic deme, a modern Greek mayor

démarche political step or initiative (not ital.)

demean to lower in dignity

demeanour bearing towards another

démenti (Fr. m.) official denial of a rumour etc.

dementia mental enfeeblement (not ital.)

demesne *not* -ain

demi/god, -goddess, -john (one word)

demilitarize *not* -ise

demi/-mondaine (Fr. f.) a woman of the *demi-monde*; *-monde* a class of women considered to be of doubtful social standing and morality, esp. those in 19th-c. France; *-pension* accommodation with one main meal per day; *-saison* spring or autumn fabric (ital., hyphens)

demise death, bequeath; *not* -ize

demi-sec (of champagne or other wines) moderately sweetened (hyphen)

demisemiquaver also called (esp. US) **thirty-second note**

demitasse a small coffee cup, in Fr. f. *demi-tasse*

demiurg/e, -ic (one word)

demo/ (colloq.) demonstration, pl. **-s** (no point)

demobilize discharge from the army, *not* -ise; colloq. **demob**

Democrat/ cap. for US political party; abbr. **D.**; lower case for a believer in a government of social equality, adj. **-ic**

democratize *not* -ise

Democrit/us (5th c. BC) Greek philosopher, adj. **-ean**

démod/é (Fr.) f. **-ée** out of fashion

demoiselle a young lady (not ital.)

Demoivre, Abraham (1667–1754) French mathematician (one word)

demon an evil spirit or devil, *or* a cruel or destructive person; *see also* **daemon**; **daimon**

demon. demonstrative

demonetize divest of value as currency, *not* -ise

demon/ic, -ize *not* dae-

demonstrable *not* -atable

demonstrator *not* -er

demoralize *not* -ise

De Morgan,/ Augustus (1806–71) English mathematician; — **William Frend** (1839–1917) his son, English novelist

de mortuis nil nisi bonum or *bene* (Lat.) speak nothing but good of the dead

demos the people (not ital.)

demotic the popular colloquial form of a language (not cap.); the later form of Ancient Egyptian cursive writing, or the form of the language used in such texts (cf. **hieratic**); the normal spoken form of modern Greek (cf. **katharevousa**)

dempster *use* **deem-**

demurr/able (law) **-age, -er**

dem/y a scholar at Magdalen College, Oxford; pl. **-ies**

demy/ (pron. 'dĕ-meye', with stress on second syllable) (typ.) former size of paper, $17\frac{1}{2}$ × $22\frac{1}{2}$ in.; — **4to** $11\frac{1}{4}$ × $8\frac{3}{4}$ in.; — **8vo** $8\frac{3}{4}$ × $5\frac{5}{8}$ in. (untrimmed); basis for size of **metric** — 564 × 444 mm

den (Ger.) the (m. sing., accusative), to the (pl., dative)

Den. Denmark

denar *use* **din-**

denar/ius (Lat.) an ancient Roman silver coin, often translated as a penny; pl. **-ii**; abbr. **d.** (ital.)

denationalize *not* -ise

dene a wooded valley, *not* dean

D.Eng. Doctor of Engineering

dengue not — fever, denga, -gey

Deng Xiaoping (1904–97) Chinese Communist statesman, Vice-Premier 1973–6 and 1977–80, Vice-Chairman of the Central Committee of the Chinese Communist Party 1977–80; even after retirement in 1989 was effective leader of China until death; in Wade–Giles **Teng Hsiao-P'ing**

Denholm Borders

Denholme W. Yorks.

deniable *see* **deny**

denier a unit of silk, rayon, or nylon yarn weight; (hist.) one-twelfth of a French sou

denim a twilled cotton fabric

Denmark abbr. **Den.**

de nos jours (Fr.) of our time (placed after the noun)

denouement a final unravelling, as of a plot or complicated situation *not* the climax of a story etc. (no accent, not ital.)

denounce give notice to terminate (treaty)

de nouveau (Fr.) afresh

de novo (Lat.) afresh

dent. dent/al, -ist, -istry

dentelle (Fr. f.) lacework

dentil one of the toothlike blocks under the bed-moulding of a cornice; *not* -el, -ile

dentine a hard, dense, bony tissue in teeth; *not* -tin (US)

den/y, -iable, -ial, -ier

deoch an doris (Sc.) a drink taken at parting, a stirrup cup; *not* the many variants (no hyphens, not ital.); in Gaelic *deoch an doruis*, in Ir. *deoch an dorais*

deodand (law, hist.) a personal chattel that has caused death, forfeited to the Crown for religious or charitable use

deodar an E. Indian cedar

deodoriz/e *not* -ise, -er

Deo/ favente (Lat.) with God's favour; — *gratias* (we give) thanks to God; — *volente* God willing, abbr. **DV**; *see also Dei*

dep. departs, deposed, deputy

dép. (Fr.) *département*, *député* (deputy)

département (Fr. m.) shire, county; abbr. **dép.**

department abbr. **dept.**, *not* dep't

departmentalize *not* -ise

Department for Education and Employment abbr. **DFEE** (no points)

Department of/ — **Health** abbr. **DoH** (no points); — — **the Environment** abbr. **DoE** (no points); — — **Social Security** abbr. **DSS**; — — **Trade and Industry** abbr. **DTI**

dépays/é (Fr.) f. -ée out of one's habitual surroundings

dependant (noun) a person who relies on another, esp. for financial support; *not* -ent (US)

dependen/t, -ce, -cy depending, conditional, or subordinate; *or* unable to do without (esp. a drug)

de pis en pis (Fr.) from bad to worse

de plano (law) clearly

depolarize *not* -ise

deposed abbr. **dep.**

depositary a person to whom something is entrusted

deposition the act or an instance of deposing *or* (law) testimony under oath; cap. for the taking down of the body of Christ from the Cross, or its representation

depositor *not* -er

depository a storehouse

depot in Fr. m. *dépôt*

depressible *not* -able

Depression, the Great the depression of 1929–34 (caps.)

De profundis (Lat.) out of the depths; the first words of Psalm 130, used as the title of the mass for the dead (one cap.); *De Profundis* a prose apologia by Wilde, 1905 (two caps.)

de proprio motu (Lat.) of his, *or* her, own accord

dept. department

député a member of the lower French Chamber

deputize *not* -ise

deputy abbr. **dep.**

Deputy Lieutenant abbr. **DL**

De Quincey/, Thomas (1785–1859) English essayist, -an

der (Ger.) the (m. sing., nominative) of *or* to *or* for the (f. sing., genitive and dative, or m., f, and neut. pl., genitive)

der. deriv/ation, -ative, -ed

derby (US) = **bowler** (hat)

Derbyshire abbr. **Derby.**

de règle (Fr.) in order, proper

de rigueur according to etiquette or custom (not ital.)

derisible laughable, *not* -able

derisory derisive, scoffing

deriv/ation, -ative, -ed abbr. **der.**

derm the true skin, *also* **derm/a, -is**

dernier/ (Fr.) last, — *cri* the very latest, — *ressort* a last resource

Derrid/a, Jacques (b. 1930) French philosopher, -ean

derrière the buttocks (not ital.)

derrière (Fr. m.) the buttocks, behind (prep.)

derring-do daring action, *not* -doe

derringer a small large-bore pistol (three *r*s), invented by **Henry Deringer** [*sic*] (1786–1868) (not cap.)

Derry postally acceptable abbr. of **Londonderry** (city or county)

der Tag (Ger.) the (great) day

derv a fuel oil for diesel-engined road-vehicles (not cap.)

des (Fr.) of the (pl.); as prefix to a proper name, treat as **de**

dès (Fr.) since

des (Ger.) of the (m. and neut. sing., genitive)

Descartes/, René (1596–1650) French mathematician and philosopher, adj. **Cartesian**, possessive —'s

descend/ant (noun) a person or thing descended, -ent (adj.) descending

descender (typ.) the lower part of letters such as g, j, p, q, y, which extends below the line

descendible that may descend or be descended, *not* -able

desert a wilderness, to abandon; *see also* **dessert**

desert/ed, -er abbr. **d.**

déshabillé (Fr. m.) a state of being only partly or carelessly clothed, undressed; *not déshabille; see also* **dishabille**

desiccate to dry, *not* dessicate

desiderat/um something desired, pl. **-a** (not ital.)

desirable *not* -eable

desktop (one word)

D. ès L. (Fr.) Docteur ès Lettres

desman/ pl. **-s**, *not* -men

Des Moines Ia.

desorb, desorption release from adsorbed state

despatch *use* **dis-**

desperado/ a desperate man, pl. **-es** (not ital.)

despicab/le vile, (morally) contemptible; **-ly**

despise *not* dis-, -ize

Des Plaines a city and river, Ill.

despot in Byzantine times used for territorial rulers subject to an overlord, e.g. 'Despot of Morea'; cap. in such hist. contexts only

despotize act like a despot, *not* -ise

des Prez *see* **Josquin des Prez**

des res a desirable residence (no points)

D. ès S. (Fr.) Docteur ès Sciences, *also* **D. ès Sc.**

D. ès Sc. Pol. (Fr.) Docteur ès Sciences Politiques

dessert a dinner course; *see also* **desert**

dessertspoonful/ pl. **-s** (one word)

dessicate *use* **desicc-**

destra/ (It.) right-hand side, abbr. **d.**; — *mano* (mus.) the right hand, abbr. **DM**

destructible *not* -able

destructor a refuse-burning furnace, *not* -er

desuetude a state of disuse

desunt/ cetera (Lat.) the rest are missing, — *multa* many things are wanting

Detaille, Jean Baptiste Édouard (1848–1912) French painter (no accent)

detector (person or thing) *not* -er

de te fabula narratur (Lat.) of thee is the story told

detent a catch (mechanical)

détente easing of strained relations between states (not ital.)

détenu/ (Fr.) f. **-e** one detained in custody

deterrent *not* -ant

detestable *not* -ible

detonat/e, -or

detour a circuitous way, in Fr. m. *détour*

detract/or f. **-ress**

detritus debris (not ital.)

de trop not wanted, superfluous (not ital.)

Deus/ (Lat.) God, abbr. **D.**; — *avertat!* God forbid; — *det* God grant

deus ex machina an unexpected power or event that saves a seemingly hopeless situation, esp. in a play or novel (not ital.)

Deus misereatur God be merciful

deuteragonist the person second in importance to the protagonist in a drama

deuterium/ symbol **D** (no point), — **oxide** heavy water

Deutero-Isaiah the supposed later author of Isaiah 40–55

Deuteronomy (OT) abbr. **Deut.**

Deutsch,/ André, Ltd publishers; — **Otto Erich** (1883–1967) compiler of a thematic catalogue of Schubert's works, *see* **D.**

Deutsche Mark chief monetary unit of Germany; usually written and spoken in Eng. **Deutschmark** *or* **D-Mark**; abbr. **DM** (no point), set close up to following (also preceding) figure; *see also* **mark**; **Ostmark**

Deutsches Reich (Ger.) the official name of Germany 1871–1945 (including the Weimar period)

Deutschland (Ger.) Germany as a geopolitical entity, and the shorthand term for the political entity (*formally* **Bundesrepublik Deutschland**)

de Valéra, Éamon (1882–1975) US-born Prime Minister of Ireland 1932–48, 1951–4, 1957–9; President 1959–73

Devanagari the alphabet used for Indian languages; more properly transcribed as **Devanāgarī**, also called **Nāgarī**.

develop/, -able, -ment *not* -pe

devest *see* **divest**

deviat/e, -or *not* -er

devil not cap. unless referring to Satan

devilling a young devil

devilled *not* -viled (US)

devilling working as a hack, *not* -iling (US)

devilry *not* -try

devil's advocate an official at papal court appointed to challenge proposed canonization (officially the *Promotor Fidei*); a person who opposes a proposition to test it

Devil's Island a penal settlement, French Guiana; in Fr. **Île du Diable**

Devils/ Playground, — Postpile Calif. (no apos.)

Devils Tower Wyo. (no apos.)

devis/e *not* -ize, **-er** one who devises (non-legal)

devis/ee one who is bequeathed real estate, **-or** one who bequeaths it

devitalize render lifeless, *not* -ise

devoir an act of civility (not ital.)

Devon/ the official name of the county; **Earl of** — *but* **Duke of Devonshire**

Devonian of or relating to Devon; (of or relating to) the fourth period of the Palaeozoic era

Devonshire abbr. **Devon.**

De Vries, Hugo (1848–1935) Dutch botanist

DEW Distant Early Warning

Dewalee *use* **Diwali**

dewan the prime minister or finance minister of an Indian state

dewar a vacuum flask (not cap.)

De Wet, Christian Rudolph (1854–1922) Boer general and statesman

Dewey/, George (1837–1917) US admiral; **—, John** (1859–1952) US philosopher; **—, Melvil** (1851–1931) US librarian, inventor of the **— decimal system**, a library classification using three-figure numbers to cover the major branches of knowledge; **—, Thomas Edmund** (1902–71) US politician

De Witt, Jan (1625–72) Dutch statesman

dexter/ (her.) the shield-bearer's right, the observer's left, opp. of **sinister**

dextrous/ *not* -erous; **-ly**

DF *Defensor Fidei* (Defender of the Faith), Dean of Faculty; direction-find/er, -ing

DFC Distinguished Flying Cross

DFEE Department for Education and Employment

DFM Distinguished Flying Medal

dft. draft

DG *Dei gratia* (by the grace of God), *Deo gratias* (thanks to God), Director General, Dragoon Guards

dg decigram(s) (no point)

d. h. (Ger.) *das heißt* (that is to say) (space in Ger. abbr.)

Dhaka Bangladesh

dhal (a dish made with) a kind of split pulse, a common foodstuff in India; *not* dal

dharma (Ind.) social custom, the right behaviour; the Buddhist truth; Hindu social or moral law

dhobi an Indian washerman

dhooly *use* **doolie**

dhoti a loincloth worn by male Hindus; *not* -ee, -ootie

dhow a lateen-rigged ship used on the Arabian sea (accepted misspelling of **dow**), *not* daou, daw

DHSS (hist.) Department of Health and Social Security

Dhuleep *use* **Du-**

dhurra *use* **durra**

dhurrie an Indian cotton fabric, *not* durrie

DI Defence Intelligence

d. i. (Ger.) *das ist* (that is) (space in Ger. abbr.)

dia. diameter

diablerie devilry, *not* -ry (not ital.)

diachylon a plaster; *not* -um, -culum

diaconate the office of deacon, *not* de-

diacritic a sign (e.g. accent, diaeresis, cedilla) used to indicate different sounds or values of a letter

diaeresis (typ.) a sign (¨) over the second of two vowels, showing that it is to be pronounced separately, as in 'naïve'; *not* die-

Diaghilev, Sergei (**Pavlovich**) (1872–1929) Russian ballet impresario

diagnos/is pl. **-es**

dial/, -led, -ling

dialect/, -al, -ic, -ical abbr. **dial.**

dialectic/ pl. **-s** (usually treated as sing.); **-al, -ian**

diallage (rhet.) a figure of speech in which various arguments are brought to bear on one point; (mineralogy) a brown, grey, or green mineral similar to augite

dialling/ code, — tone *not* dial tone (US) (two words)

dialogue conversation in drama, novels, etc., not necessarily between two persons only; *not* -log (US)

dialyse (chem.) separate by filtration through a membrane; *not* -ize, -yze (US)

dialys/is pl. **-es**

diamanté (not ital.)

diameter abbr. **dia., diam.**

diarchy rule by two authorities (esp. in India 1921–37), *not* dy-

diarrhoea *not* -hea (US)

diaspora a dispersal, (cap.) that of the Jews among the Gentiles mainly in the 8th–6th cc. BC

diatessaron (mus.) Greek and medieval name for the perfect fourth, hence metaphorically a harmony of the four Gospels (not cap.)

diathes/is (med.) a constitutional predisposition to a certain (esp. diseased) state, pl. **-es**

DIC Diploma of Membership of Imperial College, London

dic/ey risky, *not* -cy; **-ier, -iest**

dichotom/y a division into two classes, parts, etc., a sharp or paradoxical contrast; does not mean *dilemma* or *ambivalence*; **-ize** divide into two parts, *not* -ise

Dichter/ (Ger. m.) an author, esp. one of superior merit (suggesting, but not confined to, a writer of verse), f. **-in**; cf. **Schriftsteller**; **Verfasser**

Dickens/, Charles (1812–70) English novelist, **-ian**

Dickens House London, headquarters of the Dickens Fellowship (no apos.)

dickey *use* **-ky**

Dicksee, Sir Frank (1853–1928), English painter, FPRA 1924–8

dicky a rear seat (usually a folding type), a false shirt-front, a small bird; *not* -ey

dict. dictator, dictionary

Dictaphone (propr.)

dictionnaire (Fr. m., two *n*s) dictionary

dict/um a saying, pl. **-a**

dicy *use* **-cey**

didactyl two-fingered, *not* -le

didgeridoo an Australian Aboriginal musical wind instrument of long tubular shape, *not* -jeridoo

didicoi (sl.) a gypsy, an itinerant tinker; *not* didakai, diddicoy

Didot (typ.) a European system for type measurement; 12 pt. Didot = 4.512 mm; *see also* **body; cicero**

didrachm a coin worth two drachmas

didst (no apos.)

die (Ger.) the (f. sing., and m., f., and neut. pl., nominative and accusative)

diecious *use* **dioe-**

died abbr. **d.**; *see also* **dagger**

diehard (one word)

dieresis *use* **diae-**

dies (Lat.) day(s)

diesel a compression-ignition engine

dies/ fausti (Lat.) auspicious days, *— infausti* inauspicious days, *— irae* day of wrath (cap. **D** as Latin hymn sung in a mass for the dead)

dies/is (mus.) variously used for 'quartertone' and sharp sign, (typ.) a rare name for the double dagger (‡); pl. **-es**

dies/ juridicus (Lat.) a day on which courts sit; *— nefasti* blank days (*properly* days on which the Roman praetor did not hear lawsuits, popularly (in Rome) unlucky days); *— non* (law) a day on which no business is done, or that does not count for legal purposes

die-stamping (typ.) an intaglio process leaving a raised impression

dietitian *not* -cian

'Dieu et mon droit' God and my right (English royal motto)

'Die Wacht am Rhein' (Ger.) the Watch on the Rhine, a famous German patriotic song

differ/, -ence abbr. **diff.**

différance (Fr. m.) a term coined by philosopher Jacques Derrida to combine two senses of the French verb *différer* (to differ, and to defer or postpone) in a noun, to indicate simultaneously two senses in which language denies us the full presence or identity of any meaning

differenti/a a distinguishing mark, esp. between species within a genus; pl. **-ae**

diffuser *not* -or

digamma the sixth letter (Ϝ, ϝ) of the early Greek alphabet; original name *wau*

Digest, the the compendium of Roman law compiled in the reign of Justinian (6th c. AD)

digester a person or instrument, *not* -or

digestible *not* -able

digital/ something giving a reading by means of displayed digits; (comput.) operating on data represented as a series of binary digits or in similar discrete form, *see also* **analog;** **— audio tape** a magnetic tape on which sound is recorded digitally, abbr. **DAT**

digitiz/ation (comput.) electronic reduction of characters, by scanning, to a series of digital signals; **-ed font** font so prepared stored electronically in photosetter (also called **ECM**)

diglot (a book containing text) using two languages, *not* -lott

digniora sint priora (Lat.) let things worthier precede

dignitary *not* -atory

Dijck, Christoffel Van (1601–?1669) type founder; his work (now largely lost) served as the model for Caslon and for the Monotype 'Van Dijck' (1935)

dike *use* **dy-** in all senses (except in US for the sense of a long wall, embankment, etc.)

diktat a categorical statement (not ital.); *but* **Diktat** (Ger. n.) the German view of the Treaty of Versailles, 1919 (cap., ital.)

dil. dilute

dilapidat/e, -ed, -ion *not* de-

dilatable *not* -eable

dilat/ation widening or expansion, *not* dilation; **-or, -ator**

dilemma/ a position involving a choice between two unsatisfactory lines of argument or action, *not* simply a synonym for 'problem'; pl. **-s**

dilettant/e (It.) a lover of the fine arts, an amateur dabbler in the fine arts; pl. **-es** *or* **-i** (not ital.)

Dilhorne, Viscount family name Manningham-Buller

diligence (hist.) a public stagecoach, esp. in France (not ital.)

Dillon, Viscount

diluvi/um (geol.) an aqueous deposit, pl. **-a**; **-al** of a flood, esp. of the Flood in Genesis or the Glacial Drift formation in geology (not ital.)

dim. *dimidium* (one half), diminutive

dim. diminuendo

DiMaggio, Joe (1914–99) US baseball player

dime (US) ten cents, abbr. **d.**

diminuendo (It. mus.) getting softer, abbr. *dim.*

dim sum a meal or course of savoury Chinese-style snacks, *not* dim sim

DIN (Deutsche Industrie-Norm) (hist.) a series of technical standards used internationally, esp. to designate electrical connections, film speeds, and paper sizes; *now* **ISO** (International Standards Organization)

Dinan dép. Côtes-du-Nord, France

Dinant Belgium

dinar a Byzantine gold coin (*denarius*, in Arab. *dīnār*); a unit of currency in Bosnia-Hercegovina, Macedonia, and various Middle East and N. African countries; *not* de-

Dinard dép. Côtes-du-Nord, France

d'Indy, Paul Marie Théodore Vincent (1851–1931) French composer

Dinesen, Isak pseud. of **Baroness Karen Blixen** (1885–1962) Danish writer

Ding an sich (Ger. philos. n.) thing in itself

ding-dong (hyphen)

dinghy a small boat; *not* -gey, -gy

dingo/ an Australian native dog, pl. **-es**

dingy grimy; *see also* **dinghy**

dining/ car, — room, — table (two words)

dinner jacket abbr. **DJ**

dioces/e, -an abbr. **dioc.**

dioecious (bot.) *not* die-

Diogenes (412–323 BC) Cynic philosopher

Diogenes Laertius (*c.* AD 200) biographer of philosophers

dionym a binomial, as *Homo sapiens*

Dionysia (pl. noun) the orgiastic and dramatic festival(s) of Dionysus

Dionysi/ac of Dionysus, **-an** of Dionysius

Dionysius (430–367 BC) and his son (*fl.* 350 BC) tyrants of Syracuse

Dionysus the Greek god of living growth, wine, and ecstasy

dioptre a unit of a lens's refractive power, abbr. **d.**; *not* -ter (US)

Dioscuri, the (Gr. myth.) Castor and Pollux

DIP/ (comput.) a form of integrated circuit, **— switch** an arrangement of switches on an electronic device for selecting an operating mode (abbr. of *dual in-line package*)

Dip. Diploma

Dip. A.D. Diploma in Art and Design

Dip. Ed. Diploma in Education

Dip. H.E. Diploma of Higher Education

diphtheria *not* dipth-

diplomaed *not* -a'd, *but prefer* 'with a diploma'

diplomat *not now* -matist, abbr. **dipl.**

diplomate (esp. US) one holding a diploma, esp. in medicine; in Fr. **diplôm/é** f. **-ée**

Diplomatic Lectureship in, *not* Diplomatics

dipsomania/, -c *not* dyp-

diptych *not* -tich

Dirac constant (math.) Planck constant divided by 2π, pron. 'h bar'; symbol $\hbar$

Directoire the French Directory of 1795–9; (adj.) of the dress or furniture of the period (cap.)

directress female director; *not* -ice, *but prefer* **director**

directr/ix (geom.) a fixed line used in describing a curve or surface, pl. **-ices**

dirham the principal monetary unit of Morocco and the United Arab Emirates

Dirichlet series (math.)

dirigible capable of being guided; a dirigible balloon or airship

dirig/isme economic control by the State, **-iste** (not ital.)

dirndl an Alpine peasant bodice and full skirt

dirt track (two words, hyphen when attrib.)

dis. discipline; discontinu/e, -ed; discount, (typ.) distribute

disaffirm (law) reverse (a previous decision); repudiate (a settlement)

dis aliter visum (Lat.) the gods (have) thought otherwise

disappoint (one *s*, two *p*s)

disassemble take (a machine) apart; cf. **dissemble**

disassociate *use* disso-

disbound (of a pamphlet etc.) removed from a bound volume

disburden *not* -then

disbursement *not* -sment

disc/ a flat thin circular object, a mark of this shape, a layer of cartilage between vertebrae, a gramophone record; **compact —** and **optical —, — brakes**; *see also* **disk**

disc. discover/ed, -er; discount

discern/ to see; **-ible**; *see also* **decern**

discerpt/ible able to be plucked apart, divisible; **-ibility**

discerption (arch.) (an instance of) a pulling apart, severance; a severed piece

disciplinary *not* -ery

discipline abbr. **dis.**

discipular disciple-like

disc jockey abbr. **DJ**

disco/ pl. **-s**

discobol/us a discus thrower, *not* -ulus; pl. **-i** (not cap.); the 'Discobolus' (cap.) is the lost statue by Myron, of which **discoboli** are copies

discoloration *not* discolour-

discolour/, -ed, -ment *not* discolor (US)

discombobulate (US) disturb, disconcert

discomfit/, -ed, -ing disconcert, thwart; **-ure**

discomfort lack of ease, to make uneasy

disconnection *not* -xion

discontinu/e, -ed abbr. **dis.**

discothèque (not ital., no accent in US)

discount/ abbr. **dis.**, **— rate** (US) the minimum lending rate, **— store** a shop that sells goods at less than the normal retail price

discover/ed, -er abbr. **disc.**

Discovery Day (US) = **Columbus Day**

discreet tactful, judicious

discrete distinct, separate

discus/ pl. **-uses**

disect *use* **diss-**

disenfranchise *or* **disfranchise** not -ize

disenthral/ *not* -enthrall (US), -inthral(l); **-led, -ment**

disenthrone *use* **dethrone**

disentrain (mil.) get off a train

diseu/r (Fr. m.) f. *-se* artist entertaining with monologues

disguis/e, -er

dishabille Eng. form of *déshabillé*

dishevel/led with hair or dress in disorder, *not* -eled (US); **-ling** *not* -eling (US)

dishonour/, -able *not* -or, -orable (US)

disinterested impartial; cf. **uninterested**

disjecta membra (Lat.) scattered remains, *but* 'disiecti membra poetae' (Horace)

disk/ (US) = **disc**; (comput.) **— drive, floppy —, hard —, magnetic —; -ette**; *see also* **disc**

diskette (comput.) a floppy disk

dismissible *not* -able

Disneyland Anaheim, Calif.

Disney World Orlando, Fla.

disorganiz/e, -er *not* -ise

disorient/ed, -ing *prefer to* **disorientat/ed, -ing**; *see also* **orientate**

dispatch/, -er, -ing *not* des-

dispensable *not* -ible

dispensary abbr. **disp.**

Dispersion, the the Diaspora

display/ (typ.) the setting and leading of titles, advertisements, etc., *or* a direction to set in this style; **— type** of a size or cut suited to this

Disraeli,/ Benjamin (1804–81) Earl of Beaconsfield; **— Isaac** (1766–1848) writer, father of the foregoing, originally spelt his surname **d'Israeli**

dissect/, -ion, -or *not* dise-

disseis/e dispossess wrongfully, *not* -ze; **-ee, -in, -or, -oress**

dissemble conceal (one's thoughts or intentions); cf. **disassemble**

disseminat/e scatter abroad, **-or**

dissension disagreement giving rise to discord, *not* -tion

Dissenter from Church of England (cap.)

dissertation abbr. **diss.**

dissociate to separate, *not* disasso-

dissoluble able to be disintegrated, loosened, or disconnected; *not* -uable

dissolvable *not* -ible

dissyllable *use* **disy-**

dissymmetry *not* disy-

dist. distance, distilled; distinguish, -ed; district

distension *not* -tion

distich/ a pair of verse lines, a couplet; pl. **-s**

distil/ *not* distill (US) *but* **-lation, -led, -ling**; abbr. **dist.**

distingu/é (Fr.) f. *-ée*, having a distinguished air

distinguish/, -ed abbr. **dist.**

distrait/ f. **-e** absent-minded (not ital.)

distraught extremely agitated or distracted

distributary one of the streams of a river delta

distributor one who or that which distributes

district abbr. **dist.**

District/ Attorney (US) abbr. **DA**; **— Court** abbr. **DC**; **— of Columbia** the seat of the US federal government, covering the same area as the city of Washington, abbr. **DC**; **— Registry** abbr. **DR**

disulphide *not* -sulfide (US)

disyllab/le, -ic, -ize of two syllables, *not* diss-; in Fr. m. *dissyllabe*

disymmetry *use* **diss-**

dit/ (Fr. m) ditty; (verb) called, used after a name to indicate a better-known pseudonym etc., f. *-e*

ditheism belief in two gods, *not* dy-

dithyramb a wild hymn of Bacchic revellers, *not* dythi-

ditto/ abbr. **do.**, often represented by ,, under the word or sum to be repeated; **-graphy** (an example of) a copyist's mistaken repetition of a letter, word, or phrase

div. divide, -d; dividend, divine, division, divisor, divorce, (Fr.) *divers* (diverse)

dive-bomber (hyphen)

divers sundry

diverse different

diverticul/um a byway, esp. of the intestines; pl. **-a**

divertiment/o (mus.) a light and entertaining composition, often in the form of a suite for chamber orchestra; pl. **-i**, *not* -os

divertissement a diversion, an entertainment; a short ballet

Dives a rich man, from the Vulgate translation of Luke 16

divest *not* de- (except in law, as *devest out of*)

divi *use* **divvy**

divid/e, -ed, -end abbr. **div.**; sign for divide ÷

divided highway (US) = **dual carriageway**

divide et impera (Lat.) divide and rule

Divina Commedia, la by Dante, 1300–18; *not* a Come-

diving/ bell, — board, — suit (two words)

Divis (Ger. typ. n.) the hyphen

divisi (mus.) in several parts

divisible *not* -able

divisim (Lat.) separately

division mark ÷

divisor (math.) a factor, *not* -er; abbr. **div.**

divorc/é (Fr.) f. *-ée* a divorced person; Eng. **divorcee** is common gender

divvy *not* divi

Diwali a Hindu festival with illuminations, held between September and November; *not* Dewalee

dixi (Lat.) I have spoken (marking the end of a speech)

Dixie/ *or* **-land** (one word) the US Southern states

DIY do it yourself

DJ dinner jacket, disc jockey

Djakarta Indonesia, *use* **Jak-**

djellaba a hooded woollen Arab cloak; *also* **jellaba**

djib/ba, -bah *use* **jibba**

Djibouti *not* Jibuti

djinn *use* **jinnee**

DL Deputy-Lieutenant

dl decilitre(s) (no point)

D.Lit. Doctor of Literature, **D.Litt.** Doctor of Letters; *see also* **Lit.D.**; **Litt.D.**

DLM (mus.) double long metre

DM Deputy Master, (It. mus.) *destra mano* (the right hand), Deutsche Mark (Ger. currency), Doctor of Medicine (Oxford), (Fr.) *Docteur en Médecine* (Doctor of Medicine)

dm decimetre(s) (no point)

D-Mark *see* **Deutsche Mark**

D.Mus. Doctor of Music

DMZ (US) Demilitarized Zone

DN *Dominus noster* (our Lord)

DNA deoxyribonucleic acid

DNB *Dictionary of National Biography*

Dnieper River Belarus–Ukraine, in Russ. **Dnepr**

Dniester River Ukraine, in Russ. **Dnestr**

D-notice a government notice to news editors not to publish items on specified subjects, for reasons of security

DNS (typ.) do not set

do (noun) pl. **dos**, *not* do's

do (mus.) *use* **doh** in the tonic sol-fa system

do. ditto, the same

DOA dead on arrival

doat *use* **dote**

Dobbs Ferry NY (no apos.)

Dobermann pinscher a German breed of hound, *not* -man (US)

doc. document(s)

Docent (Ger. m.) a university teacher, now *Doz-*

doch-an-doris *use* **deoch an doris**

docket/, -ed, -ing

docklands (not cap.) but **Docklands** E. London

dockyard (one word)

Docteur ès/ Lettres (Fr. m.) Doctor of Letters, abbr. **DèsL**; **— — Sciences** Doctor of Science, abbr. **DèsS** *or* **DèsSc**; **— — Sciences Politiques** Doctor of Political Science, abbr. **DèsScPol**

Doctor abbr. **D.** but 'Dr' before name (although not in combination with any of the following after the name); **Doctor of/ Canon Law** *or* **Civil Law DCL**; **— — Dental Surgery DDS**; **— — Divinity DD**; **— — Laws LLD**; **— — Letters D.Litt., Lit(t).D.**; **— — Literature Lit.D.**; **— — Medicine MD, DM**; **— — Music D.Mus., Mus.D.**; **— — Philosophy Ph.D., D.Phil.**; **— — Science D.Sc., Sc.D.**; **— — Veterinary Science** *or* **Surgery DVS**

Doctors' Commons London, where marriage licences were formerly issued by the Bishop of London's Registry (apos.)

doctrinaire an unpractical theorist or political extremist; theoretical and unpractical (not ital.)

docudrama a dramatized television film based on real events (one word)

document/, -ation abbr. **doc.**

documentary (noun) a factual report or film

DOD (US) Department of Defense

dodecaphonic (mus.) of the twelve-note scale

dodgem a funfair car

dodo/ an extinct flightless bird, pl. **-s**

DoE Department of the Environment

doek (S. Afr.) a cloth, esp. a head-cloth

dogana (It. f.) custom house

dogaressa the wife of a doge (not ital.)

dogate the office of doge, *not* -eate (not ital.)

dog/ cart, — days hottest period of the year (two words)

doge the chief magistrate of Venice (not ital.)

dog/fight, -fish (one word)

doggerel unpoetic verse, *not* grel

Doggett's Coat and Badge trophies of Thames Watermen's championship

dogg/ie a pet name for a (little) dog, **-y** of or like a dog; *see also* **dogie**

doghouse (one word)

dogie (US) a motherless or neglected calf

dog Latin barbarous Latin (two words)

dogma/ authoritative doctrine, pl. **-s**

dogmatize *not* -ise

dogsbody (naut. sl.) a junior officer, a general drudge

dog-star (hyphen)

DoH Department of Health

doh (mus.) *not* do

Dohnányi/, **Ernő** (1877–1960) Hungarian composer (double acute on first name, *not* umlaut), *formerly* known as **Ernst von** —

doily a napkin; *not* -ey, doyley, -ly, d'oyley, -ie

Dolby (propr.) an electronic noise-reduction system used to reduce tape hiss in recording

dolce (mus.) sweetly

dolce/ **far niente** (It.) delightful idleness, — **vita** sweet life

doleful *not* -ll

Dolgellau Gwynedd, *not* -ey

Dolittle, Dr John the hero of a series of children's books by Hugh Lofting (1886–1947)

dollar mark $ *or* $, to be before, and close up to, the figures, as $50. Various dollars should be differentiated as $A (Australian), $CAN (Canada), $HK (Hong Kong), $US

Dollfuss, Engelbert (1892–1934) Austrian politician, Chancellor 1932–4

doll's house *not* -s' house, dollhouse (US)

Dolly Varden a character in Dickens's *Barnaby Rudge*, 1841; a type of woman's large hat; a brightly spotted char of western N. America

dolman a Turkish robe, a hussar's jacket, a woman's mantle

dolmen a prehistoric megalithic tomb

dolorous doleful, *but* **dolour** *not* -or (US)

DOM *Deo optimo maximo* (To God the best and greatest), *Dominus omnium magister* (God the Master, or Lord, of all)

Dom (Ger. m.) cathedral; (Russ.) house (not cap.)

dom (Port.) a title of nobility, (Brazilian) a title of respect, as for priests (= **don**); f. **dona**, *not* doña (cap. as part of name), abbr. **D.** (m. and f.); also a title prefixed to the names of some Roman Catholic dignitaries and Benedictine and Carthusian monks, e.g. Dom Gasquet, Dom Pérignon; *see also* **don**

dom. domestic, dominion

domaine a vineyard

Domenichino real name **Domenico Zampieri** (1581–1641) Italian painter

Domesday Book *not* Dooms-; abbr. **DB**

domestic abbr. **dom.**

domicile *not* -cil

Domine dirige nos (Lat.) O Lord, direct us (motto of the City of London)

Dominica one of the Windward Islands, W. Indies

Dominican Republic W. Indies, the eastern portion of the island of Hispaniola

dominie (Sc.) headmaster

dominion abbr. **dom.**

Dominion Day Canada, 1 July

domino/ pl. **-es**

Dominus/ (Lat.) Lord, abbr. **D.**; — **noster** our Lord, **DN**

Domus Procerum (law) the House of Lords; abbr. **DP, Dom. Proc.**

don/ a Sp. and S. American title prefixed to a forename, and in It. used with a priest's Christian name and with certain noble families (cap. as part of name, except in Peru); (Port. f.) *dona*, (Sp. f.) **doña**, (It. f.) **donna**; abbr. **D.** (m. and f.); *see also* **dom**; — a university teacher, by convention reserved for a senior member of a college, esp. at Oxford or Cambridge

Donegal Ireland

Donegall/, **Marquess of**; — **Square**, — **Street** Belfast

dong the chief monetary unit of Vietnam

dongle (comput.) a security attachment required by a computer to enable protected software to be used

Donizetti, Gaetano (1797–1848) Italian composer

donjon the great tower or innermost keep of a castle; cf. **dungeon**

donna (It.) a lady (ital.), the title of such a lady (cap., not ital.)

Donne, John (1573–1631) English poet

donnée (Fr. f.) a basic fact, the subject or theme of story etc.

Don/ **Quixote** a novel in two parts (1605, 1615) by Cervantes; in Sp. — **Quijote** (in full *El ingenioso hidalgo don Quijote de la Mancha*, and alphabetized under 'Q')

donut *use* **dough-**

doohickey (US) a small (esp. mechanical) object

doolie (Ind.) a litter, palanquin; *not* dhooley, -lie, -ly, dooly

Doolittle,/ **Eliza** the heroine of Shaw's *Pygmalion*, — **Hilda** (1886–1961) US poet

Doomsday Book *use* **Domes-** *not* the — —

doorkeeper (one word)

doormouse *use* **dor-**

Doornik Fl. for **Tournai**

dop (Afrik.) cheap brandy, a tot

Doppelgänger/ (Ger. m.) an apparition or double of a living person, pl. same; f. **-in**, pl. **-innen**; in Eng. not cap., not ital., and takes an *s* for the plural

Doppelpunkt (Ger. typ. m.) the colon

Dopper (S. Afr.) a member of the Ge-reformeerde Kerk

doppio (*movimento*) (It.) double (speed)

Doppler effect (phys.) apparent change of frequency when source of vibrations is approaching or receding, from **Christian Johann Doppler** (1803–53) Austrian physicist; *not* -ö-

dopy *use* -pey

Dor. Doric

DORA Defence of the Realm Act, 1914

Doré, Paul Gustave (1833–83) French painter and engraver

Dori/an of or relating to the Dorians in ancient Greece, or to Doris in Cent. Greece; **-c** (of) the dialect of the Dorians, (of) a rustic accent, (archit.) (of) the oldest Greek order

dormeuse (Fr. f.) a settee, nightcap, travelling sleeping carriage

dor/mouse *not* door-, pl. **-mice**

dormy (golf) as many up as there are holes to play, *not* -ie

Dorneywood Bucks., a country house used as the official residence by any minister designated by the Prime Minister

doronicum (bot.) leopard's bane

dorp (Afrik.) village, country town

d'Orsay, Alfred Guillaume Gabriel, Count (1801–52) 'the last dandy'

Dorset *not* -shire

dory a fish, (US) a flat-bottomed boat; *not* -ey

DOS (comput.) disk operating system

dos-à-dos (Fr.) back to back, a sofa made for sitting so; also a kind of bookbinding

dosage the size or the giving of a dose, *not* -eage

dos and don'ts *not* do's and don't's

dose an amount of medicine taken at one time, abbr. **d.**

do-se-do/ pl. **-s**; *not* do-si-do

dosimeter *not* dose-

Dos Passos, John (**Roderigo**) (1896–1970) US novelist

dossier papers referring to some matter (not ital.)

Dostoevsky, Fyodor (**Mikhailovich**) (1821–81) Russian novelist

dot (Fr. f.) a woman's dowry

dot/e show great fondness, *not* doat; **-age, -ard**

dots (...) *see* **ellipsis**

Douai/ dép. Nord, France; *not* -y; **— School** *but* **Douay Bible** the RC translations

douane a foreign custom house, abbr. **d.**

double (typ.) a word etc. erroneously repeated

double agent (two words)

double-barrelled (hyphen) *not* -eled (US)

double bass (mus.) (two words)

double/ bill, — bluff, — boiler, — bond (two words)

double/-book, -breasted, -check (hyphens)

double/ concerto, — cream (two words)

double-cross, (hyphen)

double dagger (typ.) the reference mark ‡, formerly called a diesis (two words)

double/-dealer, -decker (hyphens)

double entendre a word or phrase of two meanings, one of them usually indecent (obs. Fr., now Anglicized (hyphen in US); the modern Fr. is *double entente, un mot à*)

double obelus (typ.) a double dagger (‡)

double/-stopping, -talk (hyphens)

doublethink (one word)

double-tonguing (mus.) (hyphen)

doubloon (hist.) a Spanish gold coin

doublure (Fr. typ. f.) ornamental inner lining (usually of leather) to a book cover

doubting Thomas an incredulous or sceptical person (after John 20: 24–9) (one cap.)

doucement (Fr. mus.) sweetly

douceur (Fr. f.) a gratuity

douche a jet of water directed at the body (not ital.)

doughboy (US) a dumpling; a US infantryman, esp. in the First World War (one word)

doughnut (one word) *not* donut

Douglas/ fir, — pine, — spruce (one cap.)

Doukhobors *use* **Dukh-**

Dounreay Highland, atomic research station

douse drench with water, extinguish; cf. **dowse**

douzaine (Fr. f.) dozen, abbr. *dzne.*

dove (US past and past part.) = **dived**

dovecote *not* -cot

dow *use* **dhow**

dowager a widow with a dower or retaining her title, abbr. **dow.**

dowel/ (fasten with) a headless pin, usually of wood; **-led, -ling** (one *l* in US)

dower a widow's life-interest in her husband's property

Dow-Jones New York Stock Exchange index (hyphen)

Down a county of N. Ireland

down/beat, -cast (one word)

Downe, Viscount

down/fall, -grade, -hearted, -hill, -land, -load, -market, -pour, -right, -scale, -side, -stairs, -state, -stream (one word)

down-stroke (hyphen)

Down syndrome *not* 's — (*see* **syndrome**); *not* mongol, -oid

down time (two words)

downtown (US) the more central or business part of a town or city, = **city centre** (one word); cf. **uptown**

down/trodden, -turn (one word)

down wind (noun), **downwind** (adj. and adv.)

dowry money or property brought by a bride to her husband

dowse use a divining rod; cf. **douse**

doyen/ the senior member of a society (not ital.), f. **-ne**

d'oyl/ey, -ie *use* doily

D'Oyly Carte, Richard (1844–1901) English theatrical impresario

dozen/, -s abbr. **doz.**

Dozent (Ger. m.) a university teacher, *not now Doc-* (cap.)

DP data processing, displaced person (refugee), (law) *Domus Procerum* (the House of Lords)

DPAS Discharged Prisoners' Aid Society

DPH Diploma in Public Health

D.Phil. Doctor of Philosophy; Ph.D. is the more usual title

DPP Director of Public Prosecutions

DR (naut.) dead reckoning, dispatch rider, District Railway, District Registry, (Ger.) *Deutsches Reich* (German Empire)

Dr doctor (before name)

dr. drachm, -s; drachma (dram *or* coin), -s; dram, -s; drawer, drive, debtor

drachm a weight or measure formerly used by apothecaries, sign ʒ, abbr. **dr.**; for other senses *use* **dram**

drachma/ the chief monetary unit of Greece; pl. **-s**, abbr. **dr.**

draconian very harsh or severe, esp. of laws and their application (not cap.); of or relating to Drako, 7th-c. BC Athenian legislator (cap.)

draft a deduction in weighing, a military party, a money order, a rough sketch; *or* to draw off, sketch (US) = **draught**; abbr. **dft.**; cf. **draught**

draftsman one who drafts documents; cf. **draughtsman**

drafty (US) = **draughty**

dragée a sweetmeat enclosing a drug or nut or fruit

draggle-tail a slut, *not* daggle-

drag/line, -net (one word)

dragoman/ an Arabic, Turkish, or Persian interpreter; pl. **-s**, *not* -men

dragonfly (one word)

dragonnade the French persecution of Protestants from 1681; *not* -onade, -oonade

Dragoon Guards abbr. **DG**; these are not 'Guardsmen'

drag/ queen, — race (two words)

drainboard (US) = **draining board**

dram 60 grains, one teaspoonful, 60 minims, small drink; *see* **drachm**; pl. **-s**, abbr. **dr.**

dramat/ic, -ist abbr. **dram.**

dramatis personae (a list of) characters in a play, abbr. **dram. pers.** (not ital.)

dramatize *not* -ise

Drambuie (propr.) a Scotch whisky liqueur

Drang nach Osten (Ger.) desire for expansion eastwards

Drapier's Letters by Swift, 1724

draught the act of drawing or drinking, a take of fish, 20 lb of eels, a dose, a vessel's depth in water, a current of air, liquor 'on draught'; cf. **draft**

draughtsman one who makes drawings, plans, etc.; a piece in the game of draughts; cf. **draftsman**

Dravidian (of or relating to) (a member of) a dark-skinned aboriginal people of S. India and Sri Lanka, including the Tamils and Kanarese; any of the languages spoken by this people

drawback in technical meaning of excise duty remitted, abbr. **dbk.**

drawbridge (one word)

drawer abbr. **dr.**

drawing/ board, — paper, — pin, — room (two words)

draw-on cover (bind.) a limp cover glued to the back of a book

Drdla, Franz (1868–1944) Czech composer

dreadnought (hist.) a type of battleship (from the name of the first, launched in 1906) (cap.); *not* -naught

Dred Scott (19th c.) black slave, subject of US law case, 1857

Dreiser, Theodore (1871–1945) US novelist

Dresden china (one cap.)

dressing/ case, — down, — gown, — room, — station, — table (two words)

drey a squirrel's nest, *not* dray

driblet a trickle, *not* dribb-

dri/er (adj.), **-est, -ly**; *but* **dry/ish, -ness**; cf. **dryer**

drift/-ice, -net (hyphens)

driftwood (one word)

drily *not* dryly (US)

drip/-dry, -proof (hyphens)

drivable *not* -eable

drivell/ed, -er, -ing (one *l* in US)

drive out (typ.) to set matter with wide word spacing, such setting

driving licence (two words), *not* driver's — (US)

drizzling (meteor.) abbr. **d.**

droit/ moral and legal right; **— de seigneur** (not ital.)

droite (Fr. f.) the right hand, abbr. **d.**

dromedary the one-humped Arabian camel, *Camelus dromedarius*; cf. **camel**

Drontheim *use* **Trond-**

drop initial (typ.) the first letter of a chapter opening etc., descending one or more lines below the first line

drop kick (two words)

drop-leaf, -out (hyphens)

dropped head (typ.) an opening title of chapter etc. set lower than first line of text on other pages

droshky (Russ. pl. ***drozhki***) a low four-wheeled open carriage, *not* -sky

drought/, -y arid(ity), *not* drouth

DRP *Deutsches Reichspatent*, a German patent

drug/gist (US) a pharmacist, **-store** (US) a chemist's shop (one word)

Druid/ f. **-ess** (cap.)

drum/beat, -fire, -head (one word)

drum major/ an NCO commanding regimental drummers, a baton-twirling leader of a marching band, f. **-ette**

drum set (US) = **drum kit**

drumstick (one word)

drunkenness (three *n*s)

Druze a member of a political or religious sect linked with Islam and living near Mount Lebanon, *not* Drus, -e

Dryasdust a dull pedant (character in prefaces of Scott's novels) (one word, cap.)

dry/er (noun) one who or that which dries, *not* drier; **-est** *use* **dri-** (except in US); *see also* **drier**

dry/ish, -ness *not* dri-

dryly *use* **drily** (except in US)

dry point an etching needle, the work produced by it (two words)

DS (mus.) dal segno (from the sign), disseminated sclerosis

Ds. *dominus*, at Cambridge, a Bachelor of Arts

DSC Distinguished Service Cross

D.Sc. Doctor of Science

DSIR Department of Scientific and Industrial Research

DSM Distinguished Service Medal, (mus.) double short metre

DSO (Companion of the) Distinguished Service Order

d.s.p. *decessit sine prole* (died without issue)

DSS Department of Social Security

DST (US) Daylight Saving Time

d.t., dt's delirium tremens

Du. Dutch

du (as prefix to proper name) where cap. ('Du Deffand, Marie, marquise', 'Duchamp, Marcel'), used in alphabetizing; where not cap.

(except when starting a sentence), alphabetized by surname, even if formed from a title ('Maine, Louise de Bourbon, duchesse du'); follow established convention or the bearer's preference; cf. **de**; **de La**

Dual Monarchy (caps.)

Duarte, José Napoleón (1925–90) President of El Salvador 1972, 1980–2, 1984–9

dub. *dubitans* (doubting), *dubius* (dubious)

Du Barry, Marie Jeanne Bécu, comtesse (1746–93) favourite of Louis XV of France

dubbin a grease for leather, *not* -ing

Dubček, Alexander (1921–92) Czechoslovak politician

Dublin/ abbr. **Dubl.**, **— Bay prawn** (two caps.)

Dubois-Raymond, Emil (1818–96) German physiologist, *not* du Bois

Dubonnet (propr.) a sweet French aperitif

duc (Fr.) Duke, f. ***duchesse*** (not cap., not ital. as part of name)

duces tecum (Lat.) a subpoena (lit. 'you will bring with you')

du Chaillu, Paul Belloni (1837–1904) French-American explorer in Africa

duchess a duke's wife or widow, *or* a woman holding the rank of duke in her own right (cap. as title); in Fr. ***duchesse*** (not cap.)

duchesse/ a soft heavy kind of satin, a dressing table with a pivoting mirror; **— lace, — potatoes, — set** (two words)

duchy a dukedom, **the Duchy** the royal dukedom of Cornwall or Lancaster (cap.)

duckbill (one word), *but* **duck-billed platypus** (one hyphen)

duckboard (one word)

duck-rabbit (philos.) *see* **hare-duck**

duckweed (one word)

ductus (Lat. med.) a duct, pl. same (*not* -i)

Dudevant *see* **Sand, George**

dudgeon a feeling of offence, resentment; *not* dun-

duel/ler, -ling, -list (one *l* in US)

duello the rules or practice of duelling

duende an evil spirit, personal magnetism, inspiration (not ital.)

duenna a chaperon (not ital.), in Sp. ***dueña***

Dufay, Guillaume (*c*.1400–75) Franco-Flemish composer, *also* **Du Fay**

duffel/ a coarse woollen cloth, *not* -le; **— bag, — coat** (two words)

Dufy, Raoul (1877–1953) French painter

dugout (one word)

Duguesclin, Bertrand *see* **Guesclin, du**

duiker (Afrik.) a small antelope, *not* duy-

duke cap. as title, abbr. **D.**; in Fr. ***duc*** (not cap.)

Dukhobors a Russian sect, *not* Doukh-

Duleep Singh *not* Dhuleep, Dulip

dulia (RC) the reverence accorded to saints and angels (not ital.)

dullness *not* dul-

Dulong and Petit, law of (phys.)

Duma a Russian council of State

Dumas/, Davy de la Pailleterie, Alexandre (1762–1806) French general, father of — **Alexandre** (1802–70) French writer; — *fils*, **Alexandre** (1824–95) his son, French writer; —, **Jean Baptiste André** (1800–84) French chemist

du Maurier,/ George (**Louis Palmella Busson**) (1834–96) English artist and author; — **Sir Gerald** (1873–1934) his son, actor-manager; — **Dame Daphne** (1907–89) his daughter, author

Dumbarton Strathclyde

Dumbarton Oaks/ an estate in Washington, DC, at which — — **Conference** was held, 1944

dumb-bell (hyphen)

dumbfound/, -ed, -er, -ing *not* dumf-

dumdum bullet (no hyphen)

Dumfries & Galloway a region of Scotland

dummy (print.) a prototype

dump truck (US) = **tipper lorry, dumper truck**

dum sola (*et casta*) (law) while unmarried (and chaste)

Dunbarton a former Scottish county; *see also* **Dumbarton**

Dunblane Central, *not* Dum-

Duncan-Sandys, Baron (hyphen)

Dunelm: the signature of the Bishop of Durham (colon); of Durham University (no point, no colon)

dungaree/ a coarse calico material, **-s** overalls made of this; *not* -eree(s)

dungeon an underground cell for prisoners, *not* dud-; cf. **donjon**

dunghill (one word)

duniwassal (Sc.) a Highland gentleman, *not* dunni-

Dunkirk dép. Nord, France; in Fr. (and often now in Eng.) **Dunkerque**

Dún Laoghaire port and suburb of Dublin

Dunnottar Castle Grampian

Duns Scotus, Johannes (*c.*1266–1308) metaphysician

duodecimo/ *or* **twelvemo/** (typ.) a book based on twelve leaves, twenty-four pages, to the sheet; pl. **-s**; abbr. **12mo**

duologue a (stage) conversation between two

duotone (print.) a half-tone illustration in two colours from the same original with different screen angles

Du Pont a family of American industrialists

duppy (W. Ind.) a malevolent spirit or ghost

du Pré, Jacqueline (1945–87) English cellist

Duquesne/, Abraham, marquis (1610–88) French admiral; **Fort** — French fort, 1754, renamed Fort Pitt (Pittsburgh, Pa.) on its capture by the English in 1758

dur (Ger. mus.) major

dura *use* **durra**

durab/le, -ility

durchkomponiert (mus.) having different music for each stanza in a song

Dürer/, Albrecht (1471–1528) German painter; **-esque**

duress constraint, *not* -e

Durex (propr.) a condom

D'Urfey, Thomas (1653–1723) English playwright

Durham abbr. **Dur.**

Durkheim, Émile (1858–1917) French sociologist

durra a kind of sorghum, = **jowar**, *not* dhurra, dura

Dürrenmatt, Friedrich (1921–90) Swiss playwright, novelist, and critic

durrie *use* **dhurrie**

Dushanbe capital of Tajikistan

Dussek, Jan Ladislav (1760–1812) Bohemian composer

Düsseldorf Germany

dustbin (one word)

dust bowl an area denuded of vegetation by drought or erosion (two words, not cap.); the region along the western edge of the Great Plains, USA (caps.)

dustcart (one word)

dust jacket (two words); the parts of a dust-jacket are usually divided into front, front flap, back, back flap, and spine

dust/man, -pan (one word)

dust sheet (two words)

dust-shot (hyphen, two words in US)

dust storm (two words)

dust-trap (hyphen, two words in US)

Dutch of, relating to, or associated with the Netherlands; (US arch.) German; abbr. **Du.**

Dutchess County New York State

Dutch Guiana *now* **Suriname**

dutiable subject to duty

duumvir/ one of a pair of Roman officials, Eng. pl. **-s**

dux a top pupil at certain schools (not ital.)

dux/ (Lat.) a leader, pl. *duces*; — *gregis* leader of the flock

duyker *use* **dui-**

DV *Deo volente* (God willing)

Dvořák, Antonín (1841–1904) Bohemian composer

Dvr. Driver

DVS Doctor of Veterinary Science (*or* Surgery)

dw deadweight, delivered weight

dwale *use* **belladonna**

dwarf/ pl. **-s**, *not* -ves (except in Tolkien and other fantasy writing)

dwt deadweight tonnage, pennyweight, -s; 24 troy grains; *not* pwt.

Dy dysprosium (no point)

dyad a pair, a group of two, (math.) an operator that is a combination of two vectors

Dyak (an indigenous inhabitant) of Borneo or Sarawak, *not* Day-

dyarchy *use* **di-**

dybbuk/ a malevolent spirit in Jewish folklore, pl. **-im**

Dyce Airport Aberdeen

dyeing colouring cloth etc.; cf. **dying**

dye-line (print.) a diazo print (hyphen)

dyestuff (one word)

Dyfed a Welsh county

dying ceasing to live; cf. **dyeing**

Dyirbal (of or relating to) (a member of) an Aboriginal people of northern Queensland, Australia, or their language

dyke *not* di- (US, for a long wall, embankment, etc.)

dynamics the science of matter and motion (sing.), abbr. **dyn.**

dynamo/ pl. **-s**

dyne a unit of force, abbr. **dyn** (no point); in SI units 10 μN

dyotheism *use* **dith-**

dys- a prefix meaning difficult or defective; distinguish it from **dis-**, meaning apart

dysentery a severe infection of the intestines

dyslex/ia a disorder marked by difficulty in reading and spelling, adj. **-ic**

dyspep/sia chronic indigestion, *not* dis-; **-tic**

dysphasia (med.) a lack of coordination in speech, owing to brain damage

dysphoria a state of unease or mental discomfort

dysplasia (med.) the abnormal growth of tissues etc.

dyspno/ea (med.) difficult or laboured breathing, *not* -nea (US); **-eic**

dysprosium symbol **Dy**

dyss/ a megalithic chambered tomb of a kind found in Denmark, pl. **-er**; in Dan. *dysse*

dytheism *use* **di-**

dythiramb *use* **dithy-**

dziggetai a Mongolian wild ass, *not* the many variants

dzne. (Fr.) *douzaine* (dozen)

dzo a cow–yak hybrid, pl. same; *not* the many variants; in Tibetan *mdso*

Dzonghka *also* **-gka** a Tibetan dialect, also called **Bhutani**, the official language of Bhutan

D-Zug (Ger. m.) *Durchgangszug* (an express train)

Ee

E Egyptian (as in £E), (prefix) exa-, the fifth in a series

E. Earl; east, -ern; English

e a symbol used on packaging (in conjunction with specification of weight, size, etc.) to indicate compliance with EC regulations

€ symbol for the euro

e (It., Port.) and

e. (meteor.) wet air but no rain

e eccentricity of ellipse, (dyn.) coefficient of elasticity, (elec.) electromotive force of a cell

e, e, or **ϵ** (math.) the base of natural or Napierian logarithms

é (Port.) is

è (It.) is

è (**e grave accent**) to be used in Eng. for the last syllable of past tenses and participles when that otherwise mute syllable is to be separately pronounced, as 'Hence, loathèd Melancholy!'

each abbr. **ea.**

eadem (Lat.) the same (female) author, abbr. **ead.**, pl. **eaedem**, abbr. **eaed.** (not ital., not cap. except to begin a sentence or note); see also **eidem**; **idem**

EAEC European Atomic Energy Community (now **Euratom**)

eagre a tidal wave, not -er

E. & O. E. errors and omissions excepted

ear/ache, -bash (one word)

ear drops (two words)

ear/drum, -ful (one word)

Earhart, Amelia (1898–1937) US aviator

earl (cap. as title) abbr. **E.**

Earl Grey a type of tea flavoured with bergamot

Earl Marshal the officer presiding over the College of Heralds

ear lobe (two words, except in US)

Earl Palatinate (hist.) an earl having royal authority within his country or domain (caps.)

Earls Court London (no apos.)

ear/mark, -muff, -phone, -piece, -plug, -ring, -shot (one word)

earth, the cap. only in astronomical, poetical, mythological, and anthropomorphic contexts; not cap. and not preceded by 'the' in electrical contexts; symbol ⊕

earthwork (one word)

east abbr. **E.**; see also **compass points**

eastbound (one word)

East Bridgford Notts.

East Chester, Eastchester two different towns in NY

East End London (caps.)

East Ender (two words) but the television programme is **EastEnders** (one word)

Easter Day the first Sunday after the ecclesiastical full moon on, or next after, 21 Mar.

eastern abbr. **E.**; see also **compass points**

easternmost (one word)

East Indiaman (hist.) a large ship engaged in trade with the East Indies

East Kilbride Strathclyde

easy chair (two words)

easygoing (one word)

eau/ de Cologne (three words); **-de-Nil, -de-vie** (hyphens); — **forte** nitric acid, also an etching; — **fortiste** an etcher; — **sucrée** sugar and water (not ital.)

Eaudyke Lincs.

EB Encyclopaedia Britannica

Ebbets Field a baseball stadium, New York (no apos.)

Ebbw Vale Gwent, in Welsh **Glynebwy**

ebd. (Ger.) ebenda, ibid.

Eblis the chief of the fallen angels in Muslim mythology, also **I-** (following Persian pron.)

ebonize not -ise

Ebor. Eboracum (York)

Ebor: the signature of the Archbishop of York (colon)

EBU European Broadcasting Union

eburnean like ivory, not -ian

EC East-Central (postal district of London), Education(al) Committee, Electricity Council, Engineer Captain, Episcopal Church, Established Church, European Community, Executive Committee

écarté a two-person game of cards or a position in classical ballet (not ital.)

ECB English Cricket Board

Ecce Homo 'Behold the Man' (John 19: 5)

eccentric/, -ally, -ity; for mathematical sense see **excentric**

Ecclefechan Dumfries & Galloway, birthplace of Carlyle

Ecclesiastes (OT) abbr. **Eccles.**

ecclesiastical/ abbr. **eccles.**; — **signs**; Greek Cross ☩ used in service books to notify 'make the sign of the cross', also before signatures of certain Church dignitaries; in service books use ℞ response, ℣ versicle, * words to be intoned; see also **cross**; **crux**

Ecclesiasticus (Apocr.) abbr. **Ecclus.**; also called **Sirach, Sirah, Ben Sirach**

ECG electrocardiogram

ECGD Export Credits Guarantee Department

Echegaray, José (1833–1916) Spanish poet, playwright, economist, mathematician, and statesman

echelon (not ital., no accent)

echo/ pl. **-es**, *not* -os

echt (Ger.) genuine

éclair a small pastry filled with cream

éclaircissement (Fr. m.) explanation

éclat a brilliant display, dazzling effect, *or* social distinction, universal renown (not ital.)

eclectic borrowing freely from various sources

eclogue a short pastoral poem

ECM electronic character master; *see also* **digitization**

Eco, Umberto (b. 1932) Italian academic and writer

ecology the study of organisms in their environment, *not* oe-; abbr. **ecol.**

econometrics (pl. noun, usually treated as sing.)

Economist, The (cap. T) the definite article is traditionally included in references

economize *not* -ise

econom/y, -ical, -ics, -ist abbr. **econ.**

écossais/ (Fr.) f. **-e** Scottish (not cap.)

écossaise an energetic dance (not ital.)

ecphras/is (lit.), **-tic** a description used as a device to halt a narrative so as to include ancillary information; in Gr. **ekph-**

ecraseur a surgical instrument (no accent)

écrevisse (Fr. f.) crayfish

ecru an unbleached linen colour (no accent, not ital.)

ECSC European Coal and Steel Community

ecstas/y rapture, *not* ex-, -cy; (cap., sl.) a powerful stimulant and hallucinatory drug, MDMA; **-ize** *not* -ise

ECT electroconvulsive therapy

ecu (hist.) European currency unit (*also* **ECU**)

écu (Fr. m.) a French coin; (Fr. her.) a shield or escutcheon (ital.)

Ecuador/ *not* Eq-; abbr. **Ecua.**

ecumenic/, -al belonging to the entire Christian Church, *not* oec- except in specialist uses, e.g. Oecumenical Council

eczema a skin inflammation

ed. edited, editor

EDD English Dialect Dictionary

Edda/ a collection of Icelandic legends, pl. **-s**; **The Elder** (*or* **Poetic**) — a collection of poems, 11th c. and earlier; **The Younger** (*or* **Prose**) — 13th-c. stories, prosody, and commentary

Eddy, Mary Morse Baker (1821–1910) founder of Christian Science

Eddystone/ Lighthouse, — Rocks off SW coast of Britain

edelweiss an Alpine plant

edema/, -tous *use* **oed-**

Edgbaston Birmingham, *not* Edge-

edge tool *not* edged

edgeways *not* -way, -wise (except in dialect)

Edgeworth,/ Maria (1767–1849) Irish novelist; **— Richard Lovell** (1744–1817) her father, Irish educationist

Edgware/ London, **— Road**

edh alternative (esp. US) spelling for **eth**

edidit (Lat.) edited this

edile *use* **aed-**

Edinburgh abbr. **Edin.**, **E'boro**

Edipus *use* **Oe-**

Edirne *formerly* Adrianople, Turkey

Edison, Thomas Alva (1847–1931) US inventor

édit/é f. **-ée**; *édité*(e) *par* (Fr.) published by

éditeur (Fr. m.) publisher, *not* editor; *édité par* is now used in Fr. also to describe the role of a volume editor, as distinct from e.g. a publisher's editor; cf. *rédacteur*

edition (print.) abbr. **edn.** (*not* ed.), pl. **edns.** (*not* eds.) the state of a book (also the copies, or any one copy, so printed) at its first publication, and after each revision, enlargement, abridgement, or change of format (2nd, 3rd, etc.); *not* a reprint containing no substantial alteration; *see also* **impression**; **reprint**

édition de luxe (Fr.) sumptuous edition (ital.)

editio/ princeps first printed edition, pl. **-nes principes**

editor abbr. **ed.**; pl. **eds.** (preferred) *or* **edd.**

edn. edition, pl. **edns.**

edn. cit. the edition cited

Edo a former name for Tokyo; *see also* **Yeddo**

EDP electronic data processing

EDS English Dialect Society

EDT (US) Eastern Daylight Time

educ/ate, -able

educationist *not* -alist

educ/e, -ible

Eduskunta the Parliament of Finland

EE Early English

ee (Sc.) eye, pl. **een**

E.E. & M.P. Envoy Extraordinary and Minister Plenipotentiary

EEC European Economic Community (the Common Market); *see also* **European Community**; **European Union**

EEG electroencephalogram

eerie weird, *not* -y; **eerily**

Eestimaa (Est.) **Estonia**, *also* **Meiemaa**

EETPU Electrical, Electronic, Tele-communications, and Plumbing Union

EETS Early English Text Society

effect/er one who effects, **-ive** having a definite or desired result, **-or** (biol.) an organ that effects a response to a stimulus, **-uate** cause to happen (*prefer* **effect**)

effendi/ a man of education or standing in eastern Mediterranean or Arab countries, (cap.) a former title of respect or courtesy in Turkey; *not* -dee; pl. **-s**

Efficients a 19th-c. economic school (cap.)

effluvi/um the vapour from decaying matter, pl. **-a**

effluxion that which flows out, *not* -ction

EFL English as a Foreign Language

Efrog (Welsh) York, *also* **Caer** —; — **Newydd** New York

Efta (*also* **EFTA**) European Free Trade Association

e.g. (Lat.) *exampli gratia* (for example) (not ital., comma before)

egg/cup, -head (one word)

eggplant (US) = **aubergine** (one word)

eggshell (one word)

ego/ (psychol.) the self that is conscious and thinks, pl. **-s**

egotize act egotistically, *not* -ise

egret the lesser white heron; *see also* **aigrette**

Egypt/, -ian *see* **United Arab Republic**

Egyptolog/ist, -y abbr. **Egyptol.** (cap.)

eh to be followed by exclamation mark when used as an exclamation, by question mark when used as a question

Ehrenburg, (Ilya Grigorevich) (1891–1967) Russian writer and poet

ehrenhalber (Ger.) honorary, abbr. **eh.**

Eid/ (*correctly* **Id**) either of two Muslim festivals; (in full) — **ul-Fitr**, marking the end of the fast of Ramadan, or (in full) — **ul-Adha**, marking the culmination of the annual pilgrimage to Mecca

eidem (Lat.) the same authors (at least one of whom is male), abbr. **eid.** (not ital., not cap. except to begin a sentence or note); *see also* **eadem**; **idem**

eidol/on a phantom, pl. **-a**

Eifel Mountains Germany

Eiffel/, Alexandre Gustave (1832–1923) French engineer; — **Tower** Paris, in Fr. **Tour Eiffel**

eigen/frequency, -function, -value (math., phys.; one word)

Eigg Inner Hebrides, Scotland

eighteenmo/ (typ.) a book based on eighteen leaves, thirty-six pages, to the sheet; also called **octodecimo, decimo-octavo**; pl. **-s**, abbr. **18mo**

Eighteenth Amendment to the Constitution of the USA, 1920, introducing prohibition of intoxicating liquor; repealed by Twenty-First Amendment, 1933

8vo octavo

eigret/, -te *use* **aigrette**; *see also* **egret**

eikon *use* **icon**

Eikon Basilike a pamphlet (1648/9) reputedly by Charles I, more probably by John Gauden (1605–62), bishop and writer; another, written by Titus Oates, dedicated to William III and attacking James II

Eileithyia the Greek goddess of birth

ein (Ger.) a, an *or* one, a person, they; to differentiate between indefinite article and pronoun in Ger., the latter is sometimes styled with an acute (*éin*); the use of cap. (*Ein*) or letterspacing (*e i n*) is now considered old-fashioned

einschließlich (Ger.) including, inclusive; abbr. **einschl.**

Einstein,/ Albert (1879–1955) German physicist, naturalized US citizen 1940; — **Alfred** (1880–1952) German musicologist, naturalized US citizen 1945

einsteinium symbol **Es**

Éire in Gaelic means 'Ireland'; former off. name of the Republic of Ireland (or 'the Irish Republic'); note the accent, as **eire** in Gaelic means 'burden'

eirenicon a peace proposal, *not* ir-

Eisenhower, Dwight David (1890–1969) US general, Supreme Commander of Allied Expeditionary Force in the Second World War; US President 1953–61

Eisenstein, Sergei (Mikhailovich) (1898–1948) Russian film director

eisteddfod/ a congress of Welsh bards, a national or local festival for musical competitions; pl. **-s, -au** (in Welsh); not cap. except as part of title

eiusdem/ (Lat.) of the same, abbr. **eiusd.**; — **generis** of the same kind; *also* (esp. in law) **ejusdem**

ejector *not* -er

ejemplo (Sp.) example, abbr. **ej.**

EKG (US var., Ger.) electrocardio/gram, -graph

ekphrasis *use* **ecph-**

El (Heb.) God

el (Sp. m.) the

él (Sp.) he (*but* **el que** (no accent) for 'he who', as *el* is the article)

Elagabalus (204–22) Emperor of Rome 218–22; *not* Elio-, though Helio- is found in late Roman sources

El Al Israel Airlines, Ltd

El Alamein Egypt; battle, 1942

élan dash, spirit (accent, not ital.)

élan vital life force (ital.)

elasticated *not* -cized (US)

E-layer a layer of the ionosphere able to reflect medium-frequency radio waves, *not* E-region

Elbrus, Mount Caucasus; *not* -ruz, -urz

Elburz mountains, Iran, *not* -bruz

elchee Anglicized version of *elçi*, a Turkish ambassador

Elder Brethren of Trinity House (caps.)

eldorado/ any imaginary country or city abounding in gold, a place of great abundance; in specialist use (hist.) **El Dorado** (two words, not ital.); pl. **-s**

elec. electricity, electrical, electuary

elector (hist.) a German prince electing an emperor (cap. as title); a member of a US electoral college, a voter, *not* -er

Electra complex the f. analogue of **Oedipus complex**

electress *not* -toress

electro/ electrotype (no point), pl. **-s**

electrocute *not* -icute

electroencephalograph an instrument recording the electrical activity of the brain (one word), abbr. **EEG**

electrolyse break up by electric means, *not* -yze (US)

electrolyte a solution able to conduct electric current

electromagnet/ic, -ism (pertaining to) electricity and magnetism (one word)

electro/meter an electricity measurer, **-motive** producing electricity, **-motor** an electric motor (one word)

electron spin resonance (no hyphen) abbr. **ESR**

electronvolt a unit of energy (one word), abbr. **eV** (one cap.)

electrotype a duplicate printing plate made by copper electrolysis (one word), abbr. **electro**

electuary a sweetened medicine, abbr. **elec.**

eleemosynary of or dependent on alms; charitable, gratuitous

eleg/y a funeral song, a pensive poem; **-iac**; **-ist** the writer of an elegy, *not* -iast; **-ize** write elegy, *not* -ise; *see also* **elogy; eulogy**

elementary abbr. **elem.**

elements (chem.) no point after symbols

elench/us (logic) a refutation, pl. **-i; elenctic** *not* -chtic

Elephantine Egypt, famed for archaeological yields

elevator *not* -er

Elgin Marbles transported to British Museum from Athens, 1805–12, by the Earl of Elgin

El Giza Egypt, site of the pyramids; *use* **Giza**

Elia pseud. of **Charles Lamb**

Elias Gr. form of Elijah used in NT (AV)

Elien: the signature of the Bishop of Ely (colon)

eligible *not* -able

Eliogabalus *use* **Ela-**

Eliot/ family name of the Earl of St Germans; **—, George** (1819–90) pseud. of **Mary Ann** (*later* **Marian**) **Evans**, English novelist; **—, T(homas) S(tearns)** (1888–1965) US (naturalized British) poet; *see also* **Elliot; Elyot**

elision (typ.) the suppression of letters or syllables in contractions

elite (not ital., no accent)

Elizabeth abbr. **Eliz.**, in Fr. and Ger. **Elisabeth**, in It. **Elisabetta**, in Sp. **Isabel**, in Scandinavian languages **Elisabet**

Ellice a river in NW Canada

Ellice Islands the former name of **Tuvalu**, W. Pacific

Elliot in the family name of the Earl of Minto; the family in Jane Austen's *Persuasion*; *see also* **Eliot; Elyot**

ellips/is the omission of words, pl. **-es**; symbol ...

Ellis Island the former immigration centre in New York Bay

éloge (Fr. m.) an oration of praise, Anglicized as **eloge** (no accent)

elogi/um pl. **-a, elogy** a (funeral) oration of praise, also **eloge**; *see also* **elegy; eulogy**

Elohim (Heb.) the Deity

eloin (law) abscond, *not* -gn

Elois/a, -e *see* **Héloïse**

E. long. east longitude

El Paso Tex.; *not* -ss-

El Salvador Cent. America, capital San Salvador

Elsass-Lothringen *use* **Alsace-Lorraine**

Elsevier *see* **Elze-**

Elsinore trad. Eng. (as in *Hamlet*) for Dan. **Helsingør**

ELT English language teaching

elucidator one who makes clear, *not* -er

elusive difficult to grasp, mentally or physically; cf. **illusory**

elver a young eel

Elyot, Sir Thomas (?1499–1546) English writer; *see also* **Eliot; Elliot**

Élysée palace, Paris

Elysium (Gr. myth.) the abode of dead heroes (cap., not ital.), also **Elysian Fields**

elytr/on the hard wing-case of a beetle, pl. **-a** (not ital.)

Elzevier a Dutch family of booksellers and printers, in business ?1583–1712, *not* -vir, although the form is found in some bibliographical sources; the name of the modern publisher is **Elsevier**

EM Earl Marshal, Edward Medal, *Equitum Magister* (Master of the Horse)

Em. Emmanuel, Emily, Emma

em (typ.) a horizontal unit of space, the square of the body of any size of type, originally figured as the width of a capital M; *also* the standard unit of typographic measurement, equal to 12 pt., the 'pica' em; *see also* **em rule**, **en**

'em them

EMA European Monetary Agreement

email electronic mail, *also* **e-mail** (hyphen), *not* E-mail

ém/ail (Fr. m.) enamel, pl. *-aux*, adj. *-aillé*

email/ ink a type of ink used on glass, porcelain, etc.; **— ombrant** a process in which the impressions of the design appear as shadows (two words, not ital.)

Emanuel School Wandsworth

embalmment the preservation of a dead body (three *ms*); **embalming** is the more usual noun

embargo/ a temporary ban on trade, pl. **-es**

embarkation *not* -cation

embarras/ (Fr. m.); **— de richesse(s)** a superfluity of good things; **— de voitures** traffic jam; **— du choix** difficulty of choosing, *not* de

embarrass/, -ment

embassy *not* am- (not cap.)

embathe *not* im-

embed/, -ded, -ding *not* im-

embezzlement *not* -lment

emblaz/e, -onry *not* im-

embod/y, -ied, -ier, -iment *not* im-

embolden *not* im-

embonpoint plumpness (not ital.)

embosom receive into one's affections, *not* im-

emboss raise in relief, *not* im-

embouchement a river mouth (not ital.)

embouchure (mus.) the shaping of the mouth, a mouthpiece (not ital.)

embower shelter with trees, *not* im-

embrangle entangle, confuse; *not* im-

embrasure a door or window recess, widening inwards; *not* -zure

embrocation a liquid used for rubbing on the body to relieve muscular pain etc.; cf. **imbrication**

embroglio *use* im-

embroil confuse, involve in hostility; *not* im-

embrue *use* im-

embryo/ pl. **-s**

embryology abbr. **embryol.**

embue *use* im-

emcee (*also* **MC**) a master of ceremonies, compère

em dash (typ.) = **em rule**

emend alter or remove errors in a text etc.; *see also* **amend**

emerit/us retired and retaining one's title as an honour, pl **-i**, f. **-a**

emerods *use* **haemorrhoids**

Emerson, Ralph Waldo (1803–82) US poet, essayist, and philosopher

emeu (bird) *use* **emu**

émeute (Fr. f.) insurrection

emf electromotive force

EMI Electrical and Musical Industries (Ltd.)

-emia (suffix) *use* **-aemia** (except in US)

emigra/te leave one's own country to settle in another, **-nt** one who does this; cf. **immigrate**

émigr/é f. **-ée** an emigrant, esp. a political exile (not ital.)

éminence grise (Fr. f.) power behind the throne, confidential agent

eminent distinguished, notable, remarkable; cf. **immanent; imminent**

Emir a Turkish title (cap.), not cap. in non-specific Eng. contexts; *see also* **Ameer, Amir**

Emmanuel/ College Cambridge; **— (I–III)** Kings of Italy, *properly* **Emanuele**

Emmental a Swiss cheese, *not* -thal

emmesh *use* **enm-**

Emmet, Robert (1778–1803) Irish patriot

emollient softening or soothing the skin

emolument a salary, fee, or profit from employment or office

Emp. Emperor, Empress

empaestic connected with embossing, *not* -estic

empanel/ enrol, *not* im-; **-led, -ling** (one l in US)

empassion *use* im-

Emperor abbr. **Emp.**

emphas/is pl. **-es**

emphasize *not* -ise

emplane *not* en-

empolder *use* im-

empori/um a centre of commerce, a large shop; pl. **-a**

emprise (arch.) a chivalrous enterprise, *not* -ize

emptor a purchaser

empyre/an the highest heaven, **-al**

empyreum/a the 'burnt' smell of organic matter, *not* -ruma; pl. **-ata**

em rule (typ.) a rule (—) the width of an em, set with no space either side in OUP style; *see also* **em; en rule**

EMS European Monetary System

EMU European Monetary Union

emu an Australian running bird, *not* emeu

e.m.u. electromagnetic unit(s)

emulator rival, *not* -er

en (typ.) a horizontal unit of space equal to half an em, originally the width of a capital N; *see also* **em**; **en rule**

enactor *not* -er

enamel/led, -ler, -ling

enamorato *use* **in-**

enamoured inspired with love

en/ arrière (Fr.) behind, — **attendant** meanwhile, — **avant** forward

en bloc in the mass (not ital.)

en brosse bristly cut

enc. enclos/ed, -ure

Encaenia Commemoration at Oxford University, *also* the Graeco-Latin name for Hanukkah; *not* -cenia (not ital.)

encage, encapsulate, encase *not* **in-**

encephalin *use* **enk-**

enchase put in a setting, engrave; *not* **in-**

enchilada (Mexican cook.) a tortilla with chilli sauce and a filling

enchiridi/on a handbook or manual; pl. **-ons**, **-a** (not ital.)

en clair (Fr.) in ordinary language (i.e. not in cipher)

enclos/e, -ure *not* in- (*but* **Inclosure Acts**)

encomi/um a eulogy; pl. **-ums, -a** (not ital.)

encore again (not ital.)

encroach intrude usurpingly, *not* **in-**

encrust *not* in-, *but* **incrustation**

encrypt (comput.) convert (data) into code, esp. to prevent unauthorized access; conceal by this means

encumber to hamper, burden; *not* **in-**

Encyclopaedia Britannica abbr. **EB, Ency. Brit.**

encycloped/ia, -ic, -ical, -ism -ist, -ize abbr. **ency.**, *but use* **-paed-** in quoting titles where that spelling was followed

Encyclopédie the French encyclopedia edited by Diderot, 1751–72; **encyclopédiste** a writer for it (not cap.)

en dash (typ.) = **en rule**

endemic regularly found in a specified place; cf. **epidemic**

endemn/ify, -ity *use* **in-**

endent/, -ure *use* **in-**

en/ dernier ressort (Fr.) as a last resource, — **déshabille** in undress

endive a curly-leaved plant, *Cichorium endivia*, used in salads; (US) = **chicory**

end leaves *see* **endpapers**

endnote a note printed at the end of (a section of) a book

endors/e write on the back of, *not* in-; **-able** *not* -eable, -ible

endpapers (bind.) the sheets at the beginning and end of a book, half of each pasted to the inside of the cover, half forming a flyleaf

endue to invest, *not* in-

endur/e, -able, -ed, -er, -ing *not* in-

endways *not* -wise

Endymion (Gr. myth.) lover of Selene; **Endymion**, a poem by Keats; *also* Disraeli's last novel

ENE east-north-east

ENEA European Nuclear Energy Agency

enema/ pl. **-s** (not ital.)

Enemy, the cap. to denote Satan only, *not* the other side in a conflict

energize *not* -ise

enervate deprive of vigour or vitality, *not* in-; cf. **inn-**

en/ face (Fr.) facing, — **famille** with one's family

enfant/ gâté (Fr. m.) spoilt child, — **prodigue, l'** the prodigal son, — **terrible** indiscreet person

enfeoff (hist.) transfer land to possession of a subordinate tenant; *see also* **fee; feoffee**

en fête (Fr.) in festivity

enfin (Fr.) finally (one word)

enfold *not* in-

enforce/, -able *not* in-

enfranchis/e, -able, -ement, -ing *not* -ize

ENG electronic news-gathering

Eng. England, English

eng. engineer, -ing; engrav/ed, -er, -ing

Engadine Switzerland, in Ger. **Engadin**

engag/é (Fr.) f. **-ée** morally committed

en garçon (Fr.) as a bachelor

Engels, Friedrich (1820–95) German socialist, associate of Karl Marx

engineer/, -ing abbr. **eng.**

engine room (no hyphen)

Engl/and, -ish abbr. **Eng.**, *not* a synonym for **Britain, British**

English horn *use* **cor anglais**

engraft *not* in-

engrain to dye in the raw state, *not* in; cf. **ingrain**

en grande/ tenue or — — **toilette** (Fr.) in full dress

en grand seigneur magnificently

engross *not* in-

engulf *not* in-, -gulph

enigma/ a riddle, pl. **-s**

enjambment (prosody) the continuation of a sentence without a pause beyond the end of a line, couplet, or stanza (not ital.); in Fr. (m.) **enjambement**

enkephalin either of two morphine-like peptides occurring naturally in the brain, *not* ence-

en masse in a body (not ital.)

enmesh entangle; *not* emm-, imm-

Enniskillen/ Co. Fermanagh, **Earl of —**, *see also* **Inniskilling**

ennui boredom (not ital.)

ennuy/é f. **-ée** bored (not ital.)

ENO English National Opera

enoculate *use* **in-**

enology *use* **oen-** (except in US)

enormity extreme wickedness *or* error; *not* immensity, of great size, for which *use* **enormousness**

en pantoufle (Fr.) relaxed

en/ passant by the way, in passing; a kind of pawn capture in chess, abbr. **ep** (no points); **— pension** as a boarder or resident (ital.)

enplane *use* **em-**

en/ poste (Fr.) in official position, **— prince** in princely style, **— prise** (chess) in a position to be taken

enquir/e (Brit.) ask, **-y** a question; cf. **inquire**

en/ rapport (Fr.) in sympathy; **— règle** as it should be, in order; **— revanche** in revenge

enrol/, -ment *not* enroll (US), *but* **-led, -ler, -ling**

en route on the way (not ital.)

en rule (typ.) a rule (–) half the width of an em, in OUP style set with no space either side; it is longer than a hyphen (-) and distinct from it in purpose; *see also* **em rule**; **en**

en/s (Lat.) an entity, pl. **-tia**

En Saga ('A Saga'), a tone poem by Sibelius, 1892

Enschede the Netherlands, *but* **Enschedé en Zonen** a printing house at Haarlem

ensconce *not* ins-, es-

en secondes noces (Fr.) by second marriage

ensemble (not ital.)

ensheath *not* -the

ensilage the storage of green fodder in pits or silos

ensnare/, -ment *not* in-

en somme (Fr.) in short

ensuing *not* -eing

en suite to match, forming a unit (not ital.)

ensuite (Fr.) after, following (one word)

ensure make safe or certain; *see also* **assurance**; **assure**; **insure**; **insurance**

enswathe wrap, *not* in-

ENT (med.) ear, nose, and throat

entablature the upper part of a classical building supported by columns or a colonnade

entablement a platform supporting a statue, above the dado and base

entail *not* in-

entente a group of States having an **entente cordiale** (not ital.)

entente/ meaning; **— cordiale** cordial understanding, (caps., not ital.) that between Britain and France, 1904 onwards; **un mot à double —** a word or phrase with two meanings, pl. **mots à double —**; *see also* **double entendre**

enterprise *not* -ize

enthral/ *not* -ll (US), **-led, -ler, -ling, -ment**

enthron/e, -ization *not* in-

entitle *not* in-; *see also* **intitule**

entomology the study of insects, abbr. **entom.**

entourage (not ital.)

en-tout-cas (Fr.) an umbrella-cum-parasol, **En-Tout-Cas** (propr.) a type of hard tennis court

entozo/on an internal parasite, pl. **-a** (not ital.)

entr'acte/ (a performance in) the interval between two acts, pl. **-s**

en train (Fr.) in progress

entrain go or put aboard a train, carry or drag along

entrain (Fr. m.) heartiness

entrammel/ entangle; **-led, -ling** (one *l* in US)

entrap/, -ped, -ping *not* in-

entreat beseech, *not* in-

entrechat (not ital.)

entrecôte (cook.) a boned steak cut off the sirloin (not ital.)

entrée a dish served between the fish and meat courses, (US) the main dish of the meal; the right of admission (not ital.)

entremets side dishes (ital.)

entrench *not* in-

entre nous (Fr.) confidentially

entrepôt a market (not ital.)

entrepreneur/ a person in control of a business enterprise, a contractor (not ital.); **-ial**

entresol a low storey between the ground floor and first floor, mezzanine (not ital.)

entrust *not* in-

entryism infiltration into a political organization to change or subvert its policies or objectives, *not* entrism; (noun) **entrist**

entryphone (propr.) an intercom device at an entrance to a building

en/twine, -twist *not* in-

E-number the letter *E* followed by a code number, designating food additives according to EU directives

enunciat/e, -or

enure *use* **in-**

envelop/ (verb), **-ed, -ment**

envelope (noun)

Enver Pasha (1881–1922) Turkish political and military leader

Env. Extr. Envoy Extraordinary

enweave *use* **in-**

enwrap/, -ped, -ping *not* in-

enwreath *not* in-

enzootic endemic in animals

enzyme (chem.) a protein with catalytic properties

EO Education Officer, Entertainments Officer, Equal Opportunities, (US) Executive Officer, Executive Order

EOC Equal Opportunities Commission

Eocene (geol.) (of or relating to) the second epoch of the Tertiary period (cap., not ital.)

e.o.d. entry on duty, every other day

e.o.h.p. except otherwise herein provided

eo ipso (Lat.) by the fact itself

EOJ (comput.) end of job

EOL (comput.) end of line

eolian *use* **aeo-** (except in US)

eon *use* **aeon** (except in US and scientific use)

Eōthen ('From the East') an account of travels by Kinglake, 1844

EP electroplate, extended play (gramophone record)

Ep. Epistle

ep (chess) *en passant*

EPA (US) Environmental Protection Agency

épat/ant (Fr.) shocking, **-er les bourgeois** shake up the hidebound

epaulette a shoulder-piece, *not* -et (except in US)

EPCOT Experimental Prototype Community of Tomorrow, Fla.

EPDA Emergency Powers Defence Act

épée a sharp-pointed duelling-sword, used (with blunted end) in fencing

epeirogenesis (geol.) the regional uplift of extensive areas of the Earth's crust, *not* -geny

epenthes/is the insertion of a letter or sound within a word (e.g. *b* in thimble), pl. **-es**

epergne a table ornament to hold flowers or fruit (not ital., no accent)

Épernay a French white wine

epexeges/is the addition of words to clarify meaning (e.g. *to do* in 'difficult to do'), the words added; pl. **-es**

Eph. Ephesians, Ephraim

ephah a Hebrew measure, *not* epha

ephedrine *not* -in

ephemer/a *same as* **-on**, pl. **-as** (not ital.)

ephemer/is an astronomical almanac, pl. **-ides**

ephemer/on an insect that lives for a day, pl. **-ons** (not ital.); (bibliog.) a printed item intended for transient use (e.g. theatre programme, bottle label), pl. **-a**; **-ist** a collector of ephemera

Ephesians (NT) abbr. **Eph.**

ephod a Jewish priestly vestment

ephor/ a Spartan magistrate, pl. **-s**

ephphatha (Aramaic) 'Be opened'

epicedi/um a funeral ode, pl. **-a**

epicentre the point over centre of earthquake, *not* -er (US)

Epicoene, or the Silent Woman a play by Ben Jonson, 1609

epicure/ a person with refined tastes, esp. in food and drink; **-an** (noun and adj.) (one) devoted to (esp. sensual) enjoyment

Epicurean a philosopher who identifies pleasure with virtue, following the Greek **Epicurus** (342–270 BC)

epideictic adapted for display, *not* -ktic

epidemic (a disease) breaking out locally and lasting only for a time; cf. **endemic**

epidermis the outer skin or cuticle

epigon/e one of a later (and less distinguished) generation; pl. **-es, -i**

epigram a short, witty poem, *or* a pointed remark

epigraph an inscription on a statue or coin, or at the head of a chapter, section, etc.

epilogue the concluding part of a literary work

epiornis *use* **aepy-** (except in US)

epiphany the manifestation of a god; (cap.) 6 Jan., the manifestation of Christ to the Magi; *properly* the Baptism of Christ with the revelation in the heavens, the connection with the Magi being confined to the Western churches

epiphyte a plant that lives on the surface of another

'Epipsychidion' a poem by P. B. Shelley, 1821

Epirot an inhabitant of Epirus, *not* -te

episcopal/ belonging to bishops, abbr. **episc.**; (cap.) the title of Anglican Churches in Scotland and USA; **-ian**

epistem/e the accepted mode in a hist. period of acquiring and arranging knowledge, **-ic**, **-ology**; in Michel Foucault's work it is spelt (Fr. f.) *épistème*; the original Gr. is *epistēmē*, with different technical uses in both Plato and Aristotle

'Epithalamion' a hymn by Spenser, 1595

epithalami/um a nuptial song, pl. **-a**

epitheli/um surface tissue, pl. **-a**

epitomize *not* -ise

epizo/on (zool.) an animal that lives on the surface of another, pl. **-a**; **-otic** epidemic in animals

e pluribus unum (Lat.) out of many, one (motto of the USA)

EPNS electroplated nickel silver

EPOS electronic point-of-sale (of retail outlets recording information electronically)

eppur si muove (It.) and yet it does move (ascribed to Galileo, after his recantation)

épreuve (Fr. typ. f.) proof

épris/ (Fr.) f. **-e** enamoured

epsilon the fifth letter of the Gr. alphabet (*E*, ε)

Epstein, Sir Jacob (1880–1959) English sculptor

épuis/**é** (Fr.) f. **-ée** exhausted, out of print

epylli/**on** a miniature epic poem, pl. **-a**

epyornis *use* **ae-** (except in US)

eq. equal

equable uniform, not easily disturbed; *see also* **equatable**

Equador *use* **Ecu-**

equal/ *to* (not *with*), **-led, -ling** (one *l* in US)

equaliz/**e, -ation** *not* -ise

equal sign (typ.) = (normal interword space before and after, *not* set close up)

equanimity evenness of mind or temper

equatable able to be regarded as equal; *see also* **equable**

Equator/, **-ial** abbr. **Eq.**

Equatorial Guinea W. Africa

equerry *not* -ery

equestri/**an** a horseman, f. **-enne**

equilibri/**um** balance, pl. **-a**

equinoctial *not* -xial

equinox/ pl. **-es**

equivalent abbr. **equiv.**

equivocator a user of misleading words, *not* -er

equivoque a quibble (not ital.)

ER Eastern Region, *Edwardus Rex* (King Edward), *Elizabetha Regina* (Queen Elizabeth)

Er erbium (no point)

eraser one who, *or* that which, rubs out; *not* -or

Erasmus, Desiderius (1466–1536) Dutch scholar

Erato (Gr.) the lyric muse

erbium symbol **Er**

Erckmann–Chatrian joint pseud. of two French writers collaborating from 1848 to 1870 (en rule)

Erdgeist (Ger. myth.) an earth spirit

Erechtheum a temple at Athens

erector one who, *or* that which, erects; *not* -er

E-region *use* **E-layer**

erethism (med.) excitement, *not* ery-

Erevan Armenia, *use* **Yere-**

Erewhon a novel by Butler, 1872

erf (Afrik.) a plot of ground, pl. **erven**

erg/ a unit of energy and work, now largely replaced by the joule (in SI units $10^{-1}\mu J$), pl.

-s; an area of shifting sand dunes in the Sahara; pl. **-s, areg**; in Arab. ʿ*irj*

ergo therefore

Erie one of the Great Lakes (USA and Canada)

Erin (arch., poet.) Ireland, in Ir. Gael. **Éireann**

Érin go brágh (Ir.) Ireland for ever

Eriny/**s** (Gr. myth.) any of the three Furies, Eumenides, or avenging deities; pl. **-es**

Eris/ the Greek goddess of discord; **-tic** of or characterized by disputation, aiming at winning rather than at reaching the truth (not cap.)

erl-king (Ger. myth.) a bearded giant who lures small children to the land of death, in Ger. **Erlkönig** (roman quoted as title of poem by Goethe and of songs by Loewe, Schubert, and others)

ERM exchange-rate mechanism

erne (poet.) a sea eagle, *not* ern (US)

Ernie a device for selecting weekly and monthly winners in Premium Savings Bonds

'Eroica' Symphony by Beethoven, 1804

Eros the Greek god of love

erpetolog/**y, -ist** *use* **h-**

errant erring, deviating from an accepted standard; (lit., arch.) travelling in search of adventure, 'a knight errant'; cf. **arrant**

errat/**um** an error in writing or printing, pl. **-a** (not ital.)

erroneous wrong, *not* -ious

errors (on proof) alterations to proofs are marked in different colours of ink, depending on who makes them and why. Normal convention is for printing errors marked by the printer to be in *green*, printing errors marked by the proofreader to be in *red*, and all other errors (or alterations or inclusions) to be in *blue* or *black*

ersatz (Ger.) substitute (not ital.)

Erse of the Highland or Irish Gaelic language

erstens (Ger.) in the first place, **erstgeboren** first-born

Erté (1892–1990) Russian-born French fashion designer and illustrator, born **Romain de Tirtoff**

Ertebølle (archaeol.) a late Mesolithic culture in the Westen Baltic

erup/**t** break out suddenly or dramatically; **-tion** cf. **irrupt**

erven *see* **erf**

erysipelas a skin disease, St Anthony's fire, *not* -us

erythism *use* **ere-**

Erzurum Turkish Armenia; *not* -oum, -om

ES (paper) engine-sized

Es einsteinium (no point)

ESA European Space Agency

escalade mount and enter by a ladder

escalat/e rise, steadily and inevitably, like an escalator; **-ion**

escallop a shellfish, *use* **scallop** (except in heraldry)

escalope a thin slice of boneless meat (not ital.) (US) = **scallop**

escargot an edible snail

escarp/, -ment a steep slope, *not* -pe

Escaut Fr. for **Schelde**

eschalot *use* **shallot**

eschatology (theol.) the doctrine of last things

escheator an official who watches over forfeited property, *not* -er

eschscholtzia a yellow-flowered plant

esconce *use* **ens-**

Escorial, El Spain, *not* Escu-

escritoire *not* -oir (not ital.)

escudo/ the principal monetary unit of Portugal and Cape Verde; pl. **-s**

Esculap/ius, -ian *use* **Ae-**

escutcheon a heraldic shield, a plate for keyhole, etc.; *not* scut- except for *A Blot on the 'Scutcheon* by Browning

Esdras, First, Second Book of (Apocr.) abbr. **1, 2 Esd.**

ESE east-south-east

esker a long ridge of post-glacial gravel in river valleys, *not* -ar

Eskimo/ a native inhabitant of N. Canada, Alaska, Greenland, and E. Siberia; pl. same *or* **-s**; in Fr. **Esquimau/**, pl. **-x**; *prefer* **Inuit**; *see also* **Inuk; Yupik**

ESN educationally subnormal

esophag/us, -eal *use* **oes-** (except in US)

esp. especially

ESP extrasensory perception

espagnol/ (Fr.) f. **-e** Spanish

espagnolette the fastening for a french window

espalier a latticework, a trained fruit tree (not ital.)

especially abbr. **esp.**

Esperanto an artificial universal language invented by L. L. Zamenhof, 1887

espièglerie roguishness (not ital.)

espionage spying, in Fr. **espionnage**

espressivo (mus.) with expression, *not* ex-

espresso an apparatus for making coffee under pressure, the coffee thus produced; *not* exp- (not ital.)

esprit/ (Fr. m.) genius, wit; **— de corps** members' respect for a group; **— de l'escalier** tardy inspiration for an apt retort or clever remark; **— fort** a strong-minded or free-thinking person, pl. **-s forts** (ital.)

Esquimalt Vancouver Island, Canada; *not* -ault

Esquimau Fr. for **Eskimo**

Esquire abbr. **Esq.** a title appended to a man's surname only in the absence of any other form of address preceding or following a name, esp. in (usually Brit.) correspondence. Except in the case of e.g. 'Jr.' or 'III' (which it follows), it is placed immediately after the name; in the USA it is often used in writing to denote a lawyer of either sex

ESR electron spin resonance

ess the name of the letter *s*, pl. **esses**

ess. essences

essays (typ.) cited titles to be roman quoted unless published as a separate work

Essene a member of an ancient Jewish ascetic sect

Essouan *use* **Aswan**

EST (US) Eastern Standard Time

established abbr. **est.**

Established Church the Church recognized by the State as the national Church (caps.), abbr. **EC**

Establishment, the (the values held by) the established sector of society (cap.)

estamin a woollen fabric, *not* ét-

estaminet (Fr. m.) a small café selling alcoholic drinks

estanci/a (Sp.-Amer.) a cattle farm, **-ero** its keeper

Estate/s of the Realm the Parliament of Scotland before union with England in 1707; **the Three Estates** Lords Spiritual (i.e. bishops, the Church of England), Lords Temporal (the House of Lords), Commons (the House of Commons); **the Third** — French bourgeoisie before the Revolution (cap.); **the fourth** — the press (not cap.)

Esther (OT) not to be abbr., *but* **Rest of Esth.** (Apocr.)

esthet/e, -ic *use* **aes-**

estimator *not* -er

estiv/al, -ate, -ation *use* **aes-** (except in US)

Estonia a Baltic republic and former Soviet Socialist Republic, *not* Esth-; in Est. **Eestimaa**, *or* **Meiemaa; Eesti**, in Ger. **Estland** (*formerly* Ehstland, *earlier* Esthland), in Latvian **Igaunija**

estoppel *not* -ple, -pal

estr/ogen, -us *use* **oe-** (except in US)

ESU English-Speaking Union

e.s.u. electrostatic unit(s)

Eszett (Ger.) the character ß, representing a double *s*

ET English translation

ETA estimated time of arrival, Basque separatist movement (Euzkadi ta Azkatasuna, 'Basque homeland and liberty')

eta the seventh letter of the Gr. alphabet (*H*, η)

et alibi (Lat.) and elsewhere, abbr. **et al.**

et alii (Lat.) and others; abbr. **et al.**, *not* et als.

etalon (phys.) an interference device (no accent, not ital.)

étamin *use* **est-**

état-major (Fr. m.) a staff of military officers

et cetera and other things (not ital.), abbr. **etc.**; comma before if more than one term precedes

etceteras extras, sundries (one word)

Eternal City, the Rome

Etesian winds NW winds blowing each summer in the E. Mediterranean (cap.)

eth *or* (esp. US) **edh** OE, Icel., and Norse letter (Ð, ð), also used in phonetic script; lowercase OE form *properly* ð; distinguish from **thorn** and **wyn**

ether a medium filling all space, *not* ae-

ethereal/, **-ity**, **-ly** *not* -ial

Etherege, Sir George (?1635–91) English playwright

ethics the science of morals (treated as sing.)

Ethiopi/a the modern name of Abyssinia; **-c** the liturgical language of the Ethiopian Coptic Church

ethn/ic concerning races, or national or cultural traditions; **-ology, -ological** abbr. **ethnol.**

et hoc genus omne (Lat.) and all this kind of thing

ethology the study of character formation or human or animal behaviour

etiology *use* **ae-** (except in US)

etiquette (not ital.)

Etna Sicily, *not* Ae-

étrier a short rope ladder (not ital.)

et sequen/s and the following; abbr. **et seq.**, **et sq.** (not ital.); pl. **-tes**, n. **-tia** abbr. **et sqq.** (not ital.)

étude a study (not ital.)

étude de concert (mus.) concert study (ital.)

étui a case for small articles such as needles, *not* etwee (not ital.)

etymolog/y the study of derivations; **-ical, -ically, -ist, -ize**; abbr. **etym.**

etym/on a root-word, pl. **-a**

EU European Union

Eu europium (no point)

eucalypt/us (bot.) pl. **-uses**

euchre a card game; *not* eucher, eucre

Euclid/ (*c.*300 BC) Athenian geometer, his treatise (cap.); **-ean** (cap.)

eudemon/ a good angel; **-ic** conducive to happiness, **-ism** a system of ethics that bases moral obligation on the likelihood of actions producing happiness; *not* -dae-

Euer (Ger. m.) your, abbr. **Ew.**

Eugène/ a French given name (è); **Prince — of Savoy** (1663–1736) Austrian general

Eugénie, Empress (1826–1920) wife of Napoleon III (é)

eulogium/ a eulogy, pl. **-s**

eulogize *not* -ise

eulogy (**a** *not* an) spoken or written praise; *see also* **elegy**; **elogium**

Eumenides (Gr. myth.) the avenging Furies: Alecto, Tisiphone, and Megaera; (ital.) a play by Aeschylus

euonymus (**a** *not* an) a plant of genus *Euonymus*, e.g. spindle tree

euphem/ism (**a** *not* an) a mild term for something unpleasant, **-istic(ally)**; abbr. **euphem.**

euphemize *not* -ise

euphonize *not* -ise

euphony (**a** *not* an) an agreeable sound

euphorbia (bot.) any plant of the genus *Euphorbia*, including spurges

euphor/ia a feeling of well-being, **-ic**

Euphues a prose romance in affected style, 1579, by John Lyly; hence **euphuism** an affected or high-flown style of writing or speaking

Euratom European Atomic Energy Community

Eure-et-Loir Fr. dép., *not* Loire; not to be confused with Fr. dép. **Eure**

eureka I have found (it), *not* heu- (not ital.); *see also* **heuristic**

eurhythmic *not* eury- (US)

euro the single European currency, symbol €; the common wallaroo (not cap.)

Euro- prefix denoting Europe(an); usually capitalized and occasionally hyphenated (**Eurocentric, Euro-sceptic, Eurotrash**); terms in specialist financial or economic usage (*eurobond, eurocredit, eurocurrency, eurodeposit, euroequity, euronote*) are usually not cap.

Europe abbr. **Eur.** geographically ends at the Urals, and includes Scandinavia and the British Isles

European (**a** *not* an) abbr. **Eur.**

European Atomic Energy Community abbr. **Euratom**

European Bank for Reconstruction and Development to assist formerly state-controlled economies in eastern Europe and the Soviet Union to make the transition to free-market economies

European Coal and Steel Community established 1952 to regulate pricing, transport, etc. for the coal and steel industries of the member countries; abbr. **ECSC**

European Commission the initiator of European Community action and the guardian of its treaties; appointed by agreement among the governments of the European Community

European Commission for Human Rights part of the Council of Europe, created under the European Convention on Human Rights to examine complaints of alleged breaches of the Convention

European Community abbr. **EC**, formed from the ECSC, EEC, and Euratom; since 1993 called the **European Union**

European Conventions any of the international agreements established by the **Council of Europe**

European Court of Human Rights part of the Council of Europe, separate from the UN and EU, but working in conjunction with the European Commission for Human Rights

European Court of Justice an EU body dealing with disputes between member states

European currency unit ecu

European Economic Community *formerly* the Common Market, *now* part of the EC; abbr. **EEC**

European Free Trade Association a trade association of countries not members of the EC, abbr. **EFTA**

Europeanize *not* -ise (cap.)

European Monetary/ System an EC programme designed to harmonize and stabilize member states' currencies, as a prelude to monetary union, abbr. **EMS**; — — **Union** an EU programme intended to work towards full economic unity in Europe, abbr. **EMU**

European Organization for Nuclear Research *see* **CERN**

European Parliament the Parliament of the European Community

European Recovery Program the Marshall Plan

European Space Agency devoted to advancing space research and technology; formed from the European Space Research Organization and the European Launcher Development Organization; abbr. **ESA**

European Union an organization of Western European countries, *formerly* the **European Community**

europium symbol **Eu**

Europoort a major European port facility near Rotterdam

eurythmic *use* **eurhy-** (except in US)

Euskar/a the Basque language, **-ian**

Euterpe (Gr. myth.) the muse of music

eV electronvolt

evangelize inform about the gospel, *not* -ise

Evans-Pritchard, Sir Edward (**Evan**) (1902–73) English anthropologist

evaporimeter an instrument to measure evaporation, *not* -ometer

evening abbr. **evng.**

even pages (typ.) the left-hand, or verso, pages

even small caps. (typ.) word(s) set entirely in small capitals

everglades (US) tracts of low swampy ground; (cap.) a large area like this in Fla.

evermore for ever, always (one word)

Everyman the eponymous character in a 15th-c. morality play, later applied generally to an ordinary or typical human being (cap., one word); ital. for title of the play, *but* Jonson's plays are *Every Man in his Humour* (1598) and *Every Man out of his Humour* (1599)

evildoer (one word)

Ew. (Ger.) *Euer* etc. (your)

ewe (**a** *not* an) a female sheep

ewer (**a** not an) a jug

Ewigkeit (Ger. f.) eternity

ex (Lat.) out of, excluding (not ital.)

ex. example, executed, executive

exa- prefix meaning 10^{18}, abbr. **E**

exactor one who exacts, *not* -er

exaggeration (two gs)

exalt/ raise in rank, power, etc.; praise highly; **-er** *not* -or; cf. **exult**

examination/ colloq. **exam, — paper** the questions, **— script** the answers

examplar *use* **exem-**

example abbr. **ex.**, pl. **exx.**; in Fr. m. *exemple*

exanimate lifeless, depressed

ex animo (Lat.) from the mind, earnestly

ex ante (Lat.) as a result of something done before

exasperate irritate, *not* -irate

Exc. Excellency

exc. excellent; except, -ed, -ion

exc. *excudit* (engraved this)

Excalibur King Arthur's sword; *not* -bar, -boor (not ital.); *also* **Caliburn**

ex cathedra (Lat.) with full authority

excavator *not* -er

excellence/ superiority; pl. **-s**, *not* -cies

Excellenc/y pl. **-ies** (persons), abbr. **Exc.**

excellent abbr. **exc.**

excentric (math.) used instead of *eccentric* to avoid the sense of 'odd'

except/, -ed, -ion abbr. **exc.**

exceptionable open to objection

exceptional out of the ordinary

exceptis excipiendis (Lat.) with the necessary exceptions

excerpt an extract

exch. exchange, exchequer

exchange/ abbr. **exch.**, **Stock —** (caps.) abbr. **St. Ex.**

exchangeable *not* -gable

exchequer abbr. **exch.**

excisable liable to excise duty, removable by excision; *not* -eable

excise (verb) *not* -ize

Excise Office *now* Board of Customs and Excise

excit/able *not* -eable, **-ability** *not* -ibility

exciter one who, or that which, excites; (elec.) an auxiliary machine supplying current for another; *not* -or

excitor (anat.) a nerve stimulating part of the body, *not* -er

exclamat/ion, -ory abbrs. **excl., exclam.**

exclamation mark *not* — point (US)

excreta (pl.) excreted matter (not ital.)

excudit (Lat.) engraved this, abbr. **exc.**

ex curia (Lat.) out of court, not *-â*

excursus/ a detailed discussion of a special point in a book (usually in an appendix) *or* a digression in a narrative, pl. **-es** (not ital.)

excusable *not* -eable

ex-directory (hyphen)

ex dividend without next dividend; abbr. **ex div., x.d.**

exeat/ 'let him depart', a formal leave of temporary absence; pl. **-s** (not ital.); *see also* **exit**; *exit*

execut/ed, -ive abbr. **ex.**

execut/or one who carries out a plan etc.; (law) a person appointed to execute a will, *not* -er; abbr. **exor.**; f. **-rix**, abbr. **exrx.**, pl. **-rices**

exege/sis an explanation, pl. **-ses** (not ital.); **-tic**

exemplaire (Fr. m.) a specimen, a copy; (Ger. n.) *Exemplar*

exemplar a pattern, *not* exa-

exemple (Fr. m.) example

exempli gratia (Lat.) for example, abbr. **e.g.**

exempl/um an example or model, esp. a moralizing or illustrative story; pl. **-a**

exequatur/ an official recognition by a foreign government of a consul or other agent, pl. **-s** (not ital.)

exequies (pl.) a funeral ceremony (not ital.)

exercise *not* -ize

Exeter in Lat. *Exonia*, abbr. **Exon.**; *see also* **Exon:**

exeunt/ *see* **exit**, **— omnes** (Lat. stage direction) they all leave

ex gratia voluntary (not ital.)

exhibitor *not* -er

exhilarat/e enliven; **-ing, -ion**

ex hypothesi (Lat.) according to the hypothesis proposed

exigen/cy urgency, **-t** urgent

exiguous small, scanty

ex interest without next interest; abbr. **ex int., x.i.**

existence *not* -ance

existentialism the philosophy that individuals are free and responsible agents determining their own development (not cap.)

exit/ a way out, pl. **-s**

exit (Lat. stage direction) he, *or* she, goes out, pl. **exeunt** they go out (ital.); *see also* **exeat**

ex/ lege (Lat.) arising from law, **— lex** beyond or outside the law

ex-libris (sing. and pl.) 'from the library of', a bookplate (not ital.); abbr. **ex-lib.**

ex new without the right to new shares; abbr. **ex n., x.n.**

ex nihilo nihil fit (Lat.) out of nothing, nothing comes

Exocet missile (propr., one cap.)

exodi/um the conclusion of a drama, a farce following it; pl. **-a**; Anglicized as **exode**; cf. **exordium**

exodus a departure, esp. of a body of people; (cap., OT) the departure of Israelites from Egypt, a biblical book, abbr. **Exod.**

ex officiis (Lat.) by virtue of official positions

ex officio by virtue of one's official position (not ital.)

exon an officer of the Yeomen of the Guard

Exon: the signature of the Bishop of Exeter (colon)

exor. executor

exorcize expel an evil spirit from, *not* -ise

exordium/ the introductory part of a discourse, pl. **-s**; cf. **exodium**

exp. export, -ation, -ed; express

expanded type (typ.) a type with unusually wide face

ex parte (law) in the interests of one side only or of an interested outside party

ex pede Herculem (Lat.) judge from the sample

expedient advantageous, advisable on practical rather than moral grounds; suitable

expeditious acting or done with speed and efficiency, suited for swift performance

expendable able to be sacrificed

expense *not* -ce

experimenter *not* -or

expertise (noun) expert skill, knowledge, or judgement

expertize (verb) give an expert opinion, *not* -ise

experto crede (Lat.) believe one who has tried it

expi/ate, -able

explanation abbr. **expl.**

explicit (Lat.) (here) ends; as noun, the conclusion (of a book)

export/, -ation, -ed abbr. **exp.**

exposé an explanation, exposure (not ital.)

expositor one who expounds, *not* -er

ex post facto (Lat.) after the fact

expostulator one who remonstrates, *not* -er

ex-president (caps. as title)

express abbr. **exp.**

expressible *not* -able

expressivo (mus.) *use* **es-**

expresso *use* **es-**

exrx. executrix

ex silentio (Lat.) by the absence of contrary evidence

ext. extension, exterior; external, -ly; extinct, extra, extract

extasy, extatic *use* **ecs-**

extempore (adj., adv.) unprepared, without preparation (not ital.)

extemporize *not* -ise

extender *not* -or

extendible *not* -able, *but* in general *use* **extensible** *not* -able

extension abbr. **ext.**

extensor a muscle, *not* -er

extent (typ.) the amount of printed space, expressed in ens (*see* **en**) or pages, filled by a given batch of copy

exterior abbr. **ext.**

external/, -ly abbr. **ext.**

externalize *not* -ise

externe a non-resident hospital physician, a day-pupil

exterritorial *use* **extra-**

extinct abbr. **ext.**

extirpator one who destroys completely, *not* -er

extol/, -led, -ler, -ling

extra, extract abbr. **ext.**

extractable *not* -ible

extractor *not* -er

extra/marital outside marriage, **-mural** outside the scope of ordinary teaching (one

word); *but* **Extra-Mural Studies** (of Brit. universities)

extraneous brought in from outside, *not* -ious

extrasensory perception abbr. **ESP**

extraterritorial not under local jurisdiction, *not* exter-

extraversion *see* **extroversion**

extremum/ (math.) the maximum or minimum value of a function, pl. **-s**

extrover/sion, -sive, -t, -ted *not* extra- (except in Jungian psychology)

exult be greatly joyful, feel triumphant; cf. **exalt**

ex ungue leonem (Lat.) judge from the sample

exuviae cast coverings of animals

ex-voto/ an offering made in pursuance of a vow, pl. **-s**

exx. examples

Exxon Corporation *formerly* Esso, originally Standard Oil of New Jersey

Exzellenz (Ger. f.) Excellency, abbr. *Exz.*; *not* Exc-

Eyck *see* **Van Eyck**

eye/ball, -bath, -bright, -brow, -ful, -glass (one word)

eyeing *not* eying

eye/lash (one word)

eye/ lens, — level (two words, hyphen when attrib.)

eye/lid, -liner (one word)

eye muscles (two words)

eye/patch, -piece (optics), **-shadow, -sight** (one word)

eye socket (two words)

eye/sore, -wash, -witness (one word)

eyot an islet, *use* **ait**

eyrie *not* aerie, eyry

eyrir a coin of Iceland, one-hundredth of a króna; pl. **aurar**

Ezekiel (OT) abbr. **Ezek.**

Ezra (OT) not to be abbr.

Ff

F Fahrenheit, fail, farad, (on timepiece regulator) fast, (pencils) fine, fluorine, (photog.) focal length, (math.) function, the sixth of a series

F. fair, Fellow, felon; formul/a, -ae; Friday, all proper names with this initial except those beginning ff

f femto-, (math.) function

f. farthing, fathom, female, feminine, filly, (photog.) focal length (cf. **f-number**), (meteor.) fog, following, franc, free, from, furlong

f (mus.) forte (loud); (Du.) guilder(s) (no point, space between abbr. and amount), *see also* **fl.**

f. (Lat.) *fortasse* (perhaps), (Ger.) *für* (for)

FA (statistics) factor analysis, (Fr.) Fédération Aéronautique, Fine Art, Football Association

Fa. Florida, use **Fla.**

fa (mus.) use **fah**

FAA (US) Federal Aviation Administration, Fleet Air Arm

Faber & Faber publishers

Fabian/ism, -ist (cap.)

fabliau/ a metrical tale in French poetry, pl. **-x**

fabula in Lat. lit. the name for several types of play, e.g. *fabula Atellana* and *fabula palliata*; in Russ. Formalism, the 'raw material' of a story's events; cf. **sjužet**

fac. facsimile, use **facs.**; *see also* **fax**

façade (not ital.)

face (typ.) the printing surface of type, the design of a particular font

facet/ one side or aspect; **-ed, -ing** *not* -tt-

facetiae pleasantries, witticisms; (in book-selling) pornography (not ital.)

facia/ the instrument panel of a motor vehicle, *or* any similar panel or plate for operating machinery; the upper part of a shopfront with the proprietor's name etc.; pl. **-s**; cf. **fascia**

facies (med., geol.) general aspect, features

facile princeps (Lat.) easily best (ital.)

facilis descensus Averni (*not* Averno) (Lat.) easy is the descent to Avernus

façon de parler (Fr.) mere form of words

facsimile/ an exact copy, pl. **-s**; abbr. **facs.**; *see also* **fax**

facta, non verba (Lat.) deeds, not words

factional of or characterized by faction, belonging to a faction

factious characterized by, or inclined to, faction

factitious specially contrived, artificial

factorial (math.) (of) the product of a number and all the whole numbers below it (factorial four = 4 × 3 × 2 × 1); symbol **!** (as in 4!)

factorize *not* -ise

factotum/ a servant or employee who attends to everything, pl. **-s** (not ital.)

factum/ (law) an act or deed, a statement of the facts; pl. **-s**

factum est (Lat.) it is done

facul/a a bright solar spot or streak, pl. **-ae**; *not* fae-

fado/ a Portuguese folk song, pl. **-s**

faec/es (pl.) excrement, **-al**; *not* feces (US)

faerie (arch., and poet.) fairyland, the (realm of) fairies, esp. as represented by Spenser in *The Faerie Queene*, 1590–6; *not* faery, faërie, fairy

Faeroe/ Isles Danish, in N. Atlantic; use **the Faeroes**, adj. **Faeroese**; in Dan. **Færøerne**, in Faeroese **Føroyar**, in Fr. **les îles Féroé**, in Ger. **Färöer, -se** the language of the Faeroes

fag end (two words)

faggot/ a bundle of sticks etc., a seasoned meatball; (Brit.) derog. name for a woman, (US) derog. name for a male homosexual; *not* fagot (US); **-ted, -ting** (one *t* in US), **-y**

fah (mus.) in the tonic sol-fa system, *not* fa

Fahrenheit abbr. **F**

FAIA Fellow of the Association of International Accountants

faience glazed pottery; *not* faï-, fay-

fainéant idle, idler (not ital.)

faint ruled (paper) use **feint**

fair abbr. **F.**

fair and square (no hyphens except when attrib.)

fair copy a transcript free from corrections, abbr. **f. co.**

fair game (two words)

fairground (one word)

Fair Isle Shetland, and knitting design

fair/ name, — play, — rent, — sex (two words)

fair-spoken (hyphen)

fairway *not* fare- (one word)

fairyland (one word)

fairy/ story, — tale (two words, hyphen when attrib.)

fait accompli an accomplished fact, pl. **faits accomplis** (not ital.)

faith heal/er, -ing (two words)

Faizabad Uttar Pradesh, India; *not* Fyz-

fakir a Muslim or (rarely) Hindu religious mendicant or ascetic, *not* the many variants (Arab. *faḳīr*)

falafel use **fela-** (except in US)

Falang/e, -ism, -ist (a member of) the Fascist movement in Spain; cf. **Phalange**

faldstool *not* fold- (one word)

Falernian wine of ancient Campania

Falkland/ Islands S. Atlantic, in Sp. **Islas Malvinas; Viscount —**

Falk Laws 1874–5, German anti-Catholic laws introduced by Adalbert Falk

fall (US) = **autumn** (although both terms are used in US)

Falla, Manuel de (1876–1946) Spanish composer

fal-lal a piece of finery, *not* fallol; collective noun **fallallery**

fallible liable to err, *not* -able

Fallodon, Edward, Viscount Grey of (1862–1933) English statesman, *not* -en

fallout (noun) (one word)

falsa lectio (Lat.) a false reading, abbr. *f.l.*

falsetto/ pl. **-s**

falucca *use* **fel-**

falutin *see* **high-falutin**

FAM Free and Accepted Masons

fam. familiar, family

familiarize *not* -ise

famille/ a Chinese enamelled porcelain with a predominant colour, e.g. **— jaune, — noire, — rose, — verte**

family abbr. **fam.**; *see also* **botany; zoology**

famul/us (hist.) an attendant on a magician or scholar, pl. **-i**

fan/ belt, — club, — dance (two words)

fandango/ a Spanish dance or its music, pl. **-es** (not ital.)

Faneuil Hall a historic building, Boston, Mass.

fanfaronade arrogant talk, *not* -nnade; in Fr. f. *fanfaronnade*

fanlight (one word)

fanny/ (Brit. coarse sl.) the female genitals, (US sl.) the buttocks; usually considered a taboo word in Britain, but mild slang in the USA **— pack** (US) = **bumbag** (two words)

fantasia/ (mus.) a free composition (not ital.), pl. **-s**

fantasize *not* -ise

fantasmagoria *use* **phantas-**

fantas/t, -y *not* ph-

Fanti (of or relating to) (a member of) a tribe native to Ghana, the language of this people; *not* -te, -tee

Fantin-Latour, Henri (1836–1904) French painter

fantoccini (It.) marionettes

fantom *use* **ph-**

FAO Food and Agriculture Organization (of UN), for the attention of

FAP First Aid Post

faqu/eer, -ir *use* **fakir**

far. farriery, farthing

farad/ (elec.) a unit of capacitance, abbr. **F** (no point); **-ic current** inductive, induced; *not* -aic

Faraday/, Michael (1791–1867) English chemist; **— cage, — constant, — effect**

farandole a lively Provençal dance or its music

farceur a joker, wag, writer of farces (not ital.)

fareway *use* **fair-**

farewell (one word)

far/-fetched, -flung (hyphens)

Far from the Madding Crowd a novel by Hardy, 1874; *not* Maddening (orig. a line from Gray's *Elegy*)

farinaceous starchy, *not* -ious

Faringdon Oxon., *not* Farr-

farm/hand, -house, -stead, -yard (one word)

Farne Islands N. Sea; *not* Farn, Fearne, Ferne

far niente (It.) doing nothing; *see also* **dolce**

Faro Brazil, Canada, Chad, Portugal

Fårö Sweden

Faroe Denmark, *use* **Faeroe**

farouche sullen from shyness (not ital.)

Farquhar, George (1678–1707) Irish dramatist

farrago/ a hotchpotch, *not* fara-; pl. **-s**

Farrar, Frederick William, Dean (1831–1903) English divine and writer

Farrar, Straus & Giroux publishers (one comma)

farriery horse-shoeing, abbr. **far.**

Farringdon/ Within, — Without wards of the City of London

Farsi the modern Persian language of Iran

far-sighted having foresight, prudent; (esp. US, one word) = **long-sighted**

farthing abbr. **f., far.**

FAS Fellow of the Anthropological Society, Fellow of the Antiquarian Society

Fas Arab. for **Fez**

fasces (pl.) a bundle of rods, the symbol of power

fasci/a (archit.) a long flat surface between mouldings on the architrave in classical architecture, *or* a flat surface covering the ends of rafters; pl. **-ae**; cf. **facia**

fascicle an instalment of a book, usually not complete in itself; a bunch or bundle; *not* -icule

fascicul/us (anat.) a bundle of fibres, pl. **-i**

Fasc/ism, -ist (noun, adj.), **-istic** (adj.) cap. when referring to the principles and organization of the extreme nationalist movement in Italy (1922–43); lower case when referring generally to any similar movement

Fassbinder, (Rainer) Werner (1946–82) German film actor, director, and writer

Fastens/-een, -eve, -even (Sc.) Shrove Tuesday, *not* Feastings-

Fastnacht (Ger. f.) Shrove Tuesday

fata Morgana a mirage seen in the Straits of Messina (ital.)

Fates, the Three (Gr. myth.) Atropos, Clotho, and Lachesis

Father/ (relig.) abbr. **Fr.**; **the** — as Deity (cap.)

father-in-law pl. **fathers-in-law** (hyphens)

fatherland (one word)

father of (the) chapel *see* **chapel**

fathom abbr. **f.**, **fm.**

fatigu/able, -e, -ed, -ing

Fatiha the short first sura of the Koran, used by Muslims as a prayer; *not* -hah

Fatimid a descendant of Fatima, the daughter of Muhammad; a member of a dynasty ruling in N. Africa in the 10th–12th cc.; *not* -mite

fatstock livestock fattened for slaughter (one word)

fatwa (in Islamic countries) an authoritative ruling on a religious matter (not ital.)

faubourg (Fr.) a generic (Parisian) suburb, cap. when with the full name

Faulkland a character in Sheridan's *The Rivals*

Faulkner/, William (1897–1962) US novelist, **-ian**

fault-find/er, -ing (hyphen)

faun/ (Rom. myth.) a rural deity, pl. **-s**

fauna/ (collective sing.) the animals of a region or epoch, pl. **-s** (not ital.)

Faure, François Félix (1841–99) French statesman

Fauré, Gabriel (1845–1924) French composer

faute de mieux (Fr.) for want of a better alternative

fauteuil/ (Fr.) armchair, membership of the French Academy; pl. **-s**

Fauves, Les a group of painters led by Matisse; **fauv/ism, -ist** (concerning) the style of painting associated with them (not cap.)

faux pas a blunder, tactless mistake; pl. same (two words, not ital.)

favela (Port.) a Brazilian shack, slum, or shanty town

favour/, -able, -ite, -itism *not* favor- (US)

Fawkes, Guy (1570–1606) Catholic rebel and conspirator

fawn a young deer, its colour; (verb) grovel

fax (dispatch) (a copy produced by) facsimile transmission via electronic scanning (not cap.); *see also* **facs.**

fayence *use* fai-

FBA Fellow of the British Academy, *not* FRBA

FBAA Fellow of the British Association of Accountants and Auditors

FBCS Fellow of the British Computer Society

FBI (US) Federal Bureau of Investigation

FBIM Fellow of the British Institute of Management

FBOA Fellow of the British Optical Association

FC Football Club, Free Church (of Scotland)

FCA Fellow of the Institute of Chartered Accountants in England and Wales (*or* Ireland) (off.)

FCC (US) Federal Communications Commission

FCGI Fellow of the City and Guilds of London Institute

FCIA Fellow of the Corporation of Insurance Agents

FCIB Fellow of the Corporation of Insurance Brokers

FCII Fellow of the Chartered Insurance Institute

FCMA Fellow of the Institute of Cost and Management Accountants

FCO Foreign and Commonwealth Office

f. co. fair copy

FCP Fellow of the College of Preceptors

fcp. foolscap

FCS *see* **FRSC**

FCSA Fellow of the Institute of Chartered Secretaries and Administrators

FCSP Fellow of the Chartered Society of Physiotherapy

FCST Fellow of the College of Speech Therapists

FD *fidei defensor* (Defender of the Faith)

FDA (UK) First Division (Civil Servants) Association (cf. **AFDCS**); (US) Food and Drugs Administration

FDIC (US) Federal Deposit Insurance Corporation

Fe *ferrum* (iron) (no point)

Fearne Islands *use* **Farne**

feasible practicable, *not* -able

Feastings- *use* **Fastens-**

feather bed (noun, two words; verb, hyphen)

feather-brain (hyphen)

feather edge (two words)

featherfew *use* **fever-**

featherweight paper a light but bulky book paper

February abbr. **Feb.**

fecal, feces *use* **fae-** (except in US)

fecerunt (Lat. pl.) made this, abbr. **ff.**

fecial *use* **fet-**

fecit (Lat.) made this, abbr. **fec.**

fedayeen Arab guerrillas (pl.), in colloq. Arab. *fidā'iyīn*

Federalist abbr. **Fed.**

federalize *not* -ise

fee/ (law) an inherited estate of land, **— simple** estate unlimited as to class of heir, **— tail** estate so limited (two words); *see also* **fief**

feed/back, -stock (one word)

feeoff/ *use* **fief**, **-ee** *use* **feoffee**

feff/ *use* **fief**, **-ment** *use* **feoffment**

Fehmgericht/ a medieval German secret tribunal, Anglicized as **Vehmgericht**; (Ger. pl.) **-e**

Feilding the family name of the Earl of Denbigh; *see also* **Fie-**

feint (noun) a sham attack, (verb) pretend

feint ruled (paper) *not* faint

felafel *not* fala- (US), in Arab. **falāfil**

feld/spar a rock-forming mineral, *not* felspar; **-spathic**

Félibre a member of **Félibrige**, a school of Provençal writers

Felixstowe Suffolk

Fell a general term used to describe the typefaces and ornaments secured by **John Fell** (1624–86) Dean of Christ Church and Bishop of Oxford

fellah/ an Egyptian peasant; pl. **-in**, *not* -s, -een; *see also* **Fulahs**

Fellini, Federico (*not* Fr-) (1920–93) Italian film director

fellmonger a hide dealer

felloe a wheel rim, *not* felly

Fellow abbr. **F.**; in Lat. *socius*, in the Royal Society *sodalis*

fellow/ citizen, — feeling, — men (two words)

fellow-traveller (hyphen)

felly *use* **felloe**

felo de se (Anglo-Lat.) suicide, pl. **felos de se**

felon abbr. **F.**

felspar *use* **felds-**

felucca a small Mediterranean sailing vessel; *not* fal-, fil-

fem. feminine

female (bot., zool., sociology) abbr. **f.**, sign ♀

feme/ (law) wife, *not* -mme; **— covert** a married woman; **— sole** a woman without a husband, e.g. spinster, widow, or (esp.) divorcee (two words); *see also* **femme**

Femgericht (Ger.) *use* **Fehm-**

feminine abbr. **f.**, **fem.**

feminize make feminine, *not* -ise

femme/ de chambre (Fr. f.) chambermaid, lady's maid; pl. **-s de chambre**, *see also* **feme**

femme fatale a dangerously attractive woman (not ital.); *see also* **feme**

femme/ galante (Fr. f.) a prostitute, **— incomprise** an unappreciated woman, **— savante** a learned woman; *see also* **feme**

femto- a prefix meaning 10^{-15}, abbr. **f**

fem/ur pl. **-ora** (not ital.); **-oral**

fencible able to be fenced, (hist., noun) a soldier liable only for home service; *not* -able

Fénelon, François de Salignac de La Mothe (1651–1715) French ecclesiastic and writer, *not* Féné-

fenestr/a (anat.) a small hole in a bone etc., pl. **-ae** (not ital.)

feng shui in Chinese thought, a system of influences in natural surroundings (not ital.)

fenugreek a leguminous plant, *not* foenu-

feoff *use* **fief**

feoff/ee (hist.) one enfeoffed, *not* feeo-; **-ment** act of enfeoffing; *see also* **enfeoff**; **fee**; **fief**

ferae naturae (law, adj.) wild (of animals), literally 'of a wild nature'

Ferd. Ferdinand

Ferdausi *use* **Fir-**

fer de lance a venomous snake (Cent. and S. Amer.)

Ferghana Cent. Asia, *not* -gana

Feringhee in the Orient, a European, esp. a Portuguese; *not* the many variants

Fermanagh a county of N. Ireland, abbr. **Ferm.**

fermata (mus.) an unspecified prolongation of a note or rest, a sign indicating this

Fermi, Enrico (1901–54) Italian-American physicist

Fermi–Dirac–Sommerfeld law (en rules)

fermium symbol **Fm**

Ferne Islands *use* **Farne**

Ferrara/ Italy; **—, Andrea** (16th c.) Italian swordsmith

Ferrari, Paolo (1822–89) Italian dramatist

Ferrero, Guglielmo (1871–1942) Italian historian

ferret/, -ed, -er, -ing

Ferris wheel (one cap.)

ferrule a metal cap or band on the end of a stick or tube (two *r*s); *not* ferrel, ferule

ferrum iron, symbol **Fe**

ferryman (one word)

fertilize *not* -ise

ferule a cane or rod for punishment (one *r*); *see also* **ferrule**

fess/ (her.) a horizontal stripe across the middle of a shield, *not* fesse; **— point** (two words)

festa (It.) festival

Festiniog Railway Wales, *not* Ffest-

Festschrift/ (Ger. f.) a collection of writings published in honour of a scholar, pl. **-en** (cap., not ital.)

feta cheese *not* -tta

fêt/e entertainment, **-ed** (not ital.)

fête champêtre an outdoor entertainment, a rural festival (not cap.); **Fête-Dieu** feast of Corpus Christi, pl. **Fêtes-Dieu** (ital., caps., hyphen)

fetial ambassadorial, *not* fec-

fetid ill-smelling, *not* foe-

fetish/ *not* -ich, -iche; **-eer, -ism, -ist** (not ital.)

fetor a bad smell, *not* foe-

fet/us pl. **-uses; -al, -ation, -icide,** *not* foe-

feu/ (Sc.) a perpetual lease at a fixed rent, the land so held; pl. **-s**

feu/ (Fr.) f. **-e,** late, deceased; note *la feue reine* but *feu la reine*

Feuchtwanger, Lion (1884–1958) German novelist

feud. feudal

feudalize make feudal, *not* -ise

feu/ d'artifice (Fr. m.) firework, pl. *-x d'artifice*; **— de joie** a salute by firing rifles etc., pl. *-x de joie*

feu-duty (hyphen)

feuille (Fr. typ. f.) sheet

Feuillet, Octave (1821–90) French novelist and playwright

feuillet/ (Fr. typ. m.) leaf, **— blanc** blank leaf

feuilletage (Fr. cook. m.) puff pastry

feuilleton fiction, criticism, light literature, etc. (not ital.); in Fr. m. the part of newspaper etc. devoted to this

Feulhs *use* **Fulahs**

feverfew (bot.) a herb, *Chrysanthemum parthenium*; *not* feather-, fetter-, -foe

février (Fr. m.) February, abbr. **fév.** (not cap.)

Fez Morocco; in Arab. **Fas,** in Fr. **Fès**

fez/ a cap, pl. **-zes** (not ital.); **-zed**

FF *Felicissimi Fratres* (Most Fortunate Brothers), Fianna Fáil, French Franc

ff, cap. **Ff** in Welsh, a separate letter, not to be divided, alphabetized after 'f'

ff (typ.) as initial letters for a proper name, follow the bearer's preference in capitalization: ffolkes, Fforde, Ffowcs, ffrench

ff. folios; following pages etc. (pl.) preferred to *et seqq.*

ff (mus.) fortissimo (very loud), to be set as a special music sort in scores

ff. *fecerunt*

FFA Fellow of the Faculty of Actuaries (Scotland)

FFAS Fellow of the Faculty of Architects and Surveyors

Ffestiniog Wales, *not* Fest-

fff (mus.) fortississimo (as loud as possible), to be set as a special music sort in scores

F.F.Hom. Fellow of the Faculty of Homoeopathy

FFPS Fellow of the Faculty of Physicians and Surgeons

FFR Fellow of the Faculty of Radiologists

Ffrangcon-Davies, David (Thomas) (1855–1918) Welsh baritone, *not* ff-, -çon

FG Fine Gael

FGS Fellow of the Geological Society

FH fire hydrant

FHA (US) Federal Housing Administration, (UK) Fellow of the Institute of Health Service Administrators

FHS Fellow of the Heraldry Society

FIA Fellow of the Institute of Actuaries

FIAC Fellow of the Institute of Company Accountants

fiacre a four-wheeled cab

FIAI Fellow of the Institute of Industrial and Commercial Accountants

fianc/é f. **-ée** one betrothed (not ital.)

fianchetto/ (chess) placing the bishop on long diagonal, pl. **-es** (not ital.)

fianna the militia of Finn and other legendary Irish kings; **Fianna/** (pl.) the Fenians, **— Éireann** the Fenians of Ireland, **— Fáil** an Irish political party

F.I.Arb. Fellow of the Institute of Arbitrators

FIAS Fellow Surveyor Member of the Incorporated Association of Architects and Surveyors

fiasco/ a failure, pl. **-s**

Fiat Fabbrica Italiana Automobile Torino (Italian motor car, company, and factory)

fiat a formal authorization (not ital.)

fiat/ justitia (Lat.) let justice be done, **— lux** let there be light

FIB Fellow of the Institute of Bankers

F.I.Biol. Fellow of the Institute of Biology

fibre/board, -glass (one word) *not* -er (US)

fibrin blood protein appearing as network of fibres, *not* -ine

fibul/a a leg bone, a brooch; pl. **-ae**

FICE Fellow of the Institute of Civil Engineers

fiche a microfiche, pl. same

fichu a woman's small triangular neckerchief (not ital.)

FICS Fellow of the Institute of Chartered Shipbrokers, Fellow of the International College of Surgeons

fictile of pottery

fic/tion, -titious abbr. **fict.**

fictionalize *not* -ise

fictive/ly, -ness

FID Fellow of the Institute of Directors

fidalgo (Port.) a noble

fiddle-de-dee nonsense (hyphens)

Fidei Defensor (Lat.) Defender of the Faith; abbr. **FD**, **Fid. Def.**

fides Punica (Lat.) Punic faith, bad faith

fidget/, -ed, -ily, -ing, -y (one *t*)

Fido Fog Intensive Dispersal Operation, to enable aeroplanes to land

fidus Achates (Lat.) a trusty friend, devoted follower

FIEE Fellow of the Institution of Electrical Engineers

fief (hist.) land held by tenant of a superior, *not* feoff; *see also* **enfeoff**; **fee**; **feoffee**

field/-book, -cornet (hyphens)

field/ day, — glasses (two words)

field hockey (US) = **hockey**

Fielding, Henry (1707–54) English novelist; *see also* **Fei-**

field marshal (two words, caps. as title) abbr. **FM**

field officer (two words, caps. as title) abbr. **FO**

fieldwork/, -er (one word)

Fiennes, Sir Ranulph (Twisleton-Wykeham) (b. 1944) English explorer (one hyphen); *see also* **Twisleton-Wykeham-Fiennes**

fieri facias (Lat.) 'see that it is done', a writ; abbr. **fi. fa.**

FIFA International Football Federation (Fr. Fédération internationale de football association)

FIFST Fellow of the Institute of Food Science and Technology

fifth/ column, columnist (two words, not cap.)

Fifth/ Monarchy the last of the five great kingdoms predicted in Dan. 2: 44 (two caps.); **— -monarchy-man** (hist.) a 17th-c. zealot expecting the immediate second coming of Christ (one cap., hyphens)

fift/y, -ieth symbol **L**

fifty-year rule (hist.) *now* **thirty-year rule**

fig. figure; figurative, -ly

figura a person or thing representing or symbolizing a fact etc.

figural figurative, relating to figures or shapes, (mus.) florid in style

figurant/ (Fr. m.) ballet dancer appearing only in a group, pl. **-s**; f. **-e**, pl. **-es**; in It. (m. or f.) **-e**, pl. **-i**

figure/ (typ.) a numeral, esp. arabic; an illustration, abbr. **fig.**, pl. **figs.**

figurehead (one word)

figure skat/er, -ing (two words)

FIHE Fellow of the Institute of Health Education

F.I.Inst. Fellow of the Imperial Institute

FIJ *use* **FJI**

Fiji/ W. Pacific; adj. **-an** only of Polynesians, otherwise **Fiji**

filagree *use* **fili-**

Fildes, Sir Luke (1844–1927) English painter

filemot a yellowish-brown, 'dead leaf' colour; *not* filamort, filmot, phil-

filet (cook.) a fillet of meat or fish

filfot *use* **fy-**

filibeg (Sc.) a kilt, *not* the many variants; in Gaelic **feileadh-beag**

filibuster *not* fill-

filigree/ ornamental metallic lacework, **-d**; *not* fila-, file-; **— letter** (typ.) an initial with filigree background

filing cabinet (two words)

Filipin/as Sp. for Philippine Islands; (m.) **-o(s)**, (f.) **-a(s)** native(s) of the islands; *see also* **Pilipino**

fille de/ chambre (Fr. f.) chambermaid, lady's maid, pl. **filles de chambre**; **— — joie** a prostitute

fillet/ in Fr. m. *filet*; **-ed, -ing**

fillibeg *use* **fili-**

filling station (two words)

fillip/ a stimulus; **-ed, -ing**

fillipeen *use* **philippina**

fillister a kind of plane tool (two ls)

filmot *use* **file-**

filmsetting (typ.) typesetting on photographic film (one word)

filo a thin pastry, *not* phyllo (US)

Filofax (propr.)

filoselle floss silk (not ital.)

fils (Fr. m.) son, junior, added to a surname to distinguish a son from a father, as 'Dumas *fils*'; *see also* **père**

filter/ a device for separating solid matter from liquid, **-able** *not* filtrable; **-bed, -paper** (hyphens); cf. **philtre**

filucca *use* **fel-**

FIMBRA (UK) Financial Intermediaries, Managers, and Brokers Association

F.I.Mech.E. Fellow of the Institution of Mechanical Engineers

Fin. Finland, Finnish

finable liable to a fine

finale a conclusion (not ital.)

finalize *not* -ise

fin de/ siècle (Fr. f.) (characteristic of) the end of the (19th) century, decadent; **— — millénaire** (characteristic of) the end of the millennium

fine (mus.) end of the piece

fine champagne old liqueur brandy

Fine Gael an Irish political party

fine-paper edition abbr. **FP**

fines herbes mixed herbs used in cooking

finesse subtlety (not ital.)

fine-tooth comb (one hyphen)

fingerboard (one word)

finger bowl (two words)

finger/mark, -nail (one word)

finger/-paint, -painting, -plate (hyphens, two words in US)

finger/print, -tip (one word)

finick/ing, -y over-particular, fastidious

finis the end (not ital.)

finis (Lat.) the end (as of a work), abbr. *fin.*

Finistère a dép. of France

Finisterre/ a weather-forecast sea area, **Cape** — Spain

Finland in Fin. **Suomi**

Finn a native or national of Finland, or a person of Finnish descent

finnan haddock smoked haddock (two words), *not* the many variants

Finnegans Wake a novel by Joyce, 1939 (no apos.)

Finnish/ abbr. **Fin.**

Finno/-Karelia *formerly* the Karelian Soviet Socialist Republic; **-Ugric** (or **-Ugrian**) (belonging to) the group of Ural-Altaic languages including Finnish, Estonian, Sami, and Magyar

fino a light-coloured dry sherry

Fin. Sec. Financial Secretary

F.Inst.P. Fellow of the Institute of Physics

FIOB Fellow of the Institute of Building

FIOP Fellow of the Institute of Printing

fiord *use* **fj-**

fioritura (mus.) decoration of melody

FIPA Fellow of the Institute of Practitioners in Advertising

FIQS Fellow of the Institute of Quantity Surveyors

fir. firkin, -s

Fırat (Turk.) the Euphrates (undotted *ı*); *not* Frat, Furāt

Firbank, Ronald (1886–1926) English novelist

Firdausi (?930–1020) Persian poet; *not* Fer-, -dousi, -dusi

fire alarm (two words)

fire/arm(**s**)**, -back, -ball, -box, -brand** (one word)

fire brigade (two words)

fire/cracker (US) an explosive firework, **-dog** (one word)

fire-drake a fire-breathing dragon in Teutonic myth. (hyphen)

fire/ drill, — engine, — escape (two words)

fire/fighter, -fighting, -fly, -guard (one word)

fire hose (two words)

fire hydrant abbr. **FH** (two words)

fire insurance (two words)

fire/light, -man (one word)

Firenze (It.) Florence

fire-opal a girasol (hyphen, two words in US)

fireplace (one word)

fire-plug (hyphen, one word in US) abbr. **FP**

fire/proof, -side (one word)

fire station (two words)

firestorm (one word)

fire trap (two words, one word in US)

fire/water, -wood (one word)

firkin/ a small cask for liquids, pl. **-s**; abbr. **fir.**

firman/ an edict, pl. **-s**

firn névé, granular snow not yet compressed into ice at the head of a glacier (not ital.)

first aid (two words)

first/-born, -class (adj. and adv.) (hyphens)

first floor (two words, hyphen as adj.)

first-fruit(**s**) (hyphen)

first-hand (adj., hyphen) *but* **at first hand** (two words)

first proof (typ.) the first impression taken

first-rate (hyphen)

First World War 1914–18 (caps.) is common British style; **World War I** is common US style

firth an estuary, *not* fri-

fir tree (two words)

FIS Fellow of the Institute of Statisticians

FISA Fellow of the Incorporated Secretaries Association

Fischer, Bobby (**Robert James**) (b. 1943) US chess grand master

Fischer-Dieskau, Dietrich (b. 1925) German baritone

fisgig *use* **fiz-**

fish/ pl. same, unless describing differing types or species, in which case *use* **-es**

fish cake (two words)

Fisher,/ Andrew (1862–1928) Australian statesman, Prime Minister 1908–9, 1910–13, 1914–15; **— Sir Ronald Aylmer** (1890–1962) British statistician and geneticist

fish finger (two words)

fishing/ line, — rod (two words)

fish/monger, -net, -pot, -tail, -wife (one word)

fissile able to undergo fission, *not* fissionable

FIST Fellow of the Institute of Science Technology

fist (typ.) the ☜ or ☞, used to draw attention to a note

fisticuffs *not* fisty-

fistul/a the opening of an internal organ to the exterior or to another organ; pl. **-as, -ae** (not ital.)

fit past **fitted** (except in US)

fit (arch.) a section of a poem, *not* fytte

FitzGerald/ the family name of the Duke of Leinster; —, **Edward** (1809–83) English poet and translator (one word); —, **George Francis** (1851–1901) Irish physicist, devised the theory of — **contraction**, in full **Lorenz–FitzGerald contraction** (en rule); cap. *G*

Fitzgerald,/ **Ella** (1918–96) US singer and composer; — **F(rancis) Scott (Key)** (1896–1940) US novelist, surname *not* Scott Fitzgerald; lower-case g

Fitzwilliam/ College, — Museum Cambridge

fivefold (one word)

Five Towns, the in the novels of Arnold Bennett: Tunstall ('Turnhill'), Burslem ('Bursley'), Hanley ('Hanbridge'), Stoke-on-Trent ('Knype'), and Longton ('Longshaw'); *see also* **the Potteries**

fix (US verb) mend, prepare (food or drink)

fixed star (astron.) sign ✰ or ✶

fizgig a flirtatious girl, a small firework, (Austral. sl.) a police informer; *not* fis-, fizz-

fizz a sound, *not* fiz

FJI Fellow of the Institute of Journalists, *not* FIJ

fjord (Norw.) a deep arm of the sea (not ital.), *not* **fi-**

FL (naval) Flag Lieutenant, Florida (postal abbr.)

Fl. Flanders, Flemish

fl. florin, fluid, (Du. etc.) gulden (space between abbr. and amount); *see also* **f**

fl. *flores* (flowers), *floruit* (flourished)

f.l. *falsa lectio* (a false reading)

FLA Fellow of the Library Association

Fla. Florida (off. abbr.)

flabbergast/, -ed dumbfound(ed), *not* flaba-, flaber-

flabell/um (eccl., bot.) a fan, pl. **-a**

flack *use* **flak**

flag-boat (hyphen)

flag day a day on which money is raised for a charity by the sale of small paper flags (two words); (US, caps.) 14 June, the anniversary of the Stars and Stripes in 1777

flageolet (mus.) a small flute, (bot.) a French kidney bean; *not* -elet (not ital.)

flagitious deeply criminal

flag-officer (hyphen)

flagpole (one word)

flag-rank (hyphen)

flag/ship, -staff, -stone (one word)

flair instinct for selecting or performing what is excellent, useful, etc.; a talent or ability; cf. **flare**

flak anti-aircraft fire, *not* -ck

flambé (cook.) served in flames (not ital.)

flambeau/ a torch, pl. **-s** (not ital.)

flamboyant showy, (archit.) with flame-like lines (not ital.)

flame/less, -like (one word)

flamenco/ a type of song or dance performed by Spanish gypsies, pl. **-s** (not ital.)

flameproof (one word)

flame-thrower (hyphen, two words in US)

flame tree (bot.) any of various trees with brilliant red flowers (two words)

flamingo/ a tropical bird, pl. **-s**

flammab/le inflammable, **-ility**; negative form = **non-flammable**

Flamsteed, John (1646–1719) first English Astronomer Royal, 1675–1719; *not* -stead

flanch slope inwards, *not* -aunch

Flanders abbr. **Fl.**; in Fl. **Vlaanderen**, in Fr. **Flandre**, in Ger. **Flandern**

flân/erie (Fr. f.) idling, idleness; **-eur** f. **-euse** an idler, a lounger

flannelette a cotton imitation of flannel, *not* -llette

flannel/led, -ling (one l in US), **-board** (one word)

flapjack a biscuit-like cake made from oats, golden syrup, etc.; (esp. US) a pancake

flare a sudden outburst of flame, a bright light or signal, or a gradual widening; cf. **flair**

flash/back, -bulb (one word)

flash/ burn, — flood (two words)

flash/gun, -light, -point (one word)

flat (mus.) sign ♭

flatback (bind.) *see* **square back**

flat/fish, -ware, -worm (one word)

Flaubert, Gustave (1821–80) French novelist

flaunch *use* **flanch**

flautist *not* flut- (US)

flavour/, -ed, -ing, -less *not* -or (US) but **flavorous**

F-layer the highest and most strongly ionized region of the ionosphere (one cap.)

flèche (Fr. f.) an arrow, (archit.) a slender spire

flection *use* **flexion** (except in US)

fledgling *not* -geling

Fleming a native of medieval Flanders, or a member of a Flemish-speaking people inhabiting N. and W. Belgium; cf. **Walloon**

Fleming,/ **Sir Alexander** (1881–1955) Scottish bacteriologist, discovered penicillin; — **Ian (Lancaster)** (1908–64) thriller writer and journalist

flense cut up, flay (a whale or seal); *not* -ch, **flinch**

fleur-de-lis a heraldic lily, *not* fleur-de-lys, flower-de-luce; pl. **fleurs-de-lis** (not ital.); no hyphens in Fr.

fleuret an ornament like a small flower

fleuron a flower-shaped ornament in a type-face, or on a building, coin, etc.

fleury (her.) decorated with fleurs-de-lis, *not* -ory

flexible *not* -able

flexion *not* -ction (US)

flexitime the system of working variable hours, *not* flext-

flexography (print.) a rotary letterpress technique using rubber or plastic plates and synthetic inks or dyes for printing on fabrics, plastics, etc., as well as on paper

flibbertigibbet a gossiping or frivolous person

fliegende Holländer, Der (*The Flying Dutchman*) an opera by Wagner, 1843; but e.g. 'Wagner's *Fliegender Holländer*' when the article is omitted

flier *use* **flyer** in all senses

flintlock (one word)

floatage *but* **flotation**

floccul/us (Lat.) a small tuft, (astr.) a small solar cloud, (anat.) a small lobe in the cerebellum; pl. **-i**

Flood, the in Genesis (cap.)

flood/gate, -light, -plain (one word)

flood tide (two words)

floor in Brit. usage, the *ground floor* is the floor of a building at ground level, the floor above it being the *first floor*. In US usage, the ground floor is called the *first floor*, the floor above it being the *second floor*. Most Continental languages agree with British usage, Russian with US

floor/board, -cloth (one word)

floorlamp (US) = **standard lamp** (one word)

floor/ manager, — plan, — sample, — show (two words)

floozie *not* -sie, -zy

flophouse (US) = **dosshouse**

flor. *floruit* (flourished), *prefer* ***fl.***

flora/ (collective sing.) the plants of a region or epoch, pl. **-s** (not ital.)

floreat may he, she, *or* it, flourish (not ital.)

Floren/ce in It. **Firenze**; **-tine**

flores (Lat.) flowers, abbr. ***fl.***

florescen/ce, -t

floriat/e, -ed florally decorated, *not* -eate

Florida off. abbr. **Fla.**, postal **FL**

florilegi/um an anthology, pl. **-a**

florin abbr. **fl.**, (Du.) **f**

floruit (Lat.) flourished; abbr. ***fl.*** (preferable), ***flor.*** (not ital. when used as noun); use only to precede approx. date of activity for a person whose birth or death date is unknown: 'William of Coventry (*fl.* 1360)', 'Edward Fisher (*fl.* 1627–56)', 'Ralph Acton (*fl.* 14th c.)'; *see also* **circa**

flotation *not* float-.

flotsam and jetsam (naut.) floating wreckage and goods thrown overboard; rubbish

flourished abbr. ***fl.*** (*floruit*)

flow chart (two words, one word in US)

flower-de-luce *use* **fleur-de-lis**

FLS Fellow of the Linnean Society (off. spelling), *not* Linnae-

Flt. Lt. Flight Lieutenant

Flt. Sgt. Flight Sergeant

flu influenza (no apos., no point)

fluffing (typ.) a release of paper fluff or dust during printing

Flügel, Johann Gottfried (1788–1855) German lexicographer

flugelhorn (mus.) a kind of cornet

flugelman *use* **fugle-**

fluid abbr. **fl.**

fluidize *not* -ise

fluky *not* -ey

flummox confound; *not* -ix, -ux

flunkey/ pl. **-s**, *not* -ky

fluoresce/, -nce, -nt be made luminous

fluoridate add fluoride to

fluorinate introduce fluorine into

fluorine *not* -in, symbol **F**

fluoroscope an instrument for X-ray examination, with fluorescent screen

fluorspar (chem.) calcium fluoride as mineral

flush/ (typ.) set to the margin of columns or page; **— left, — right** text is aligned to left or right margin

Flushing the Netherlands, in Du. and Ger. **Vlissingen**, in Fr. **Flessingue**; Queens, New York City

flustr/a a seaweed, pl. **-ae** (not ital.)

flutist *use* **flautist** (except in US)

fluty flutelike, *not* -ey

fluxions (math.) *not* -ctions

flyer *not* -ier

flyleaf (print.) a blank leaf at beginning or end of a book; the blank leaf of a circular (one word)

flyover a bridge carrying one road or railway over another (one word)

flysheet (print.) a two- or four-page tract (one word)

fly/weight, -wheel (one word)

FM field magnet, Field Marshal, Foreign Mission, frequency modulation

Fm fermium (no point)

fm. fathom

FMS Fellow of the Medical Society

fn. footnote, *but prefer* **n.** (except in contexts requiring a distinction between footnotes and other notes)

f-number (photog.) the ratio of the focal length to the effective diameter of a lens (e.g. f5)

FO Field Officer, (naval) Flag Officer, (RAF) Flying Officer, (hist., in UK) Foreign Office

fo. folio

f.o.b. free on board

FOC father of the chapel; *see* **chapel**

focalize *not* -ise

Foch, Ferdinand (1851–1929) French general

fo'c'sle *use* **forecastle**

focus/ pl. **-es**, (sci.) **foci**

focus/ed, -es, -ing *not* -uss-

foehn *use* **föhn**

foenugreek *use* **fe-**

Foerster, Friedrich Wilhelm (1869–1966) German philosopher and political writer

foet/id, -or *use* **fe-**

foetus *use* **fe-**

fog (meteor.) abbr. **f.**

Fogg, Phileas the hero of J. Verne's *Around the World in Eighty Days*

foggy obscured by fog

fog/y one with antiquated notions; *not* -ey, -ie; pl. **-ies**

föhn a warm Alpine south wind, *not* foehn

FOIA (US) Freedom of Information Act

foie (Fr. m.) liver

Fokine, Michel (1880–1942) Russian-born US ballet dancer and choreographer

fol. folio (*use* **fo.**), following

-fold as a suffix forms one word (e.g. threefold), except after numerals (10-fold)

fold-out an oversize page in book, unfolded by the reader (hyphen)

foldstool *use* **fald-**

foliaceous leaflike, *not* -ious

Folies Bergère (not ital.)

folio/ (typ.) a sheet of MS or TS copy; a page number; a book based on two leaves, four pages, to the sheet; pl. **-s**; as verb, **-ed** *not* -'d; abbr. **fo.**, *not* fol.

foli/um (Lat.) a leaf, pl. **-a**

folk/ art, — dance (two words)

Folketing the Danish Parliament, *not* -thing

folk-like (hyphen, one word in US)

folklor/e, -ism, -ist, -istic (one word)

folk singer (two words, one word in US)

folk song (two words)

folk tale (two words, one word in US)

folkways (one word)

follic/le (bot., med.) a small sac, *not* -cule; *but* **-ular, -ulated**

following abbr. **f., fol.**

fonda (Sp.) an inn

fondant a soft sweet of flavoured sugar

fondue a dish of melted cheese, eggs, chocolate, etc.; *not* -du

fons et origo (Lat.) source and origin

font a receptacle in a church for baptismal water; (typ.) a set of type of one face or size; cf. **fount**

Fontainebleau dép. Seine-et-Marne, France

fontanelle *not* -el (US)

Fontarabia *use* **Fuenterr-**

Fonteyn, Dame Margot (1919–91) English prima ballerina, born **Margaret Hookham**

foodstuff (one word)

foolproof (one word)

foolscap a former size of paper, $17 \times 13\frac{1}{2}$ in.

foot 30.48 cm; abbr. (sing. and pl.) **ft**, sign '; not now in scientific use

foot-and-mouth disease (hyphens)

foot/ball, -board, -brake, -bridge, -hills, -hold, -lights (one word)

footline, running (typ.) a running headline set at the foot of a page

foot/loose, -man (one word)

footnote (typ.) a note printed at the foot of a page; *see also* **reference marks**

foot/pad, -path, -plate, -print, -rest (one word)

Foots Cray London

Footscray Victoria, Australia

foot/sore, -step, -stool, -way, -wear, -work (one word)

for. foreign, forestry

f.o.r. free on rail

fora pl. of **forum**

foram/en (anat., bot.) an orifice, pl. **-ina**

forasmuch (arch., one word)

foray a raid, *not* forr-

forbade *see* **forbid**

for/bear abstain, past **-bore**, past part. **-borne**; cf. **forebear**

Forbes-Robertson, Sir Johnston (1853–1937) Scottish actor

for/bid past **-bade**, past part. **-bidden**, present part. **-bidding**

force majeure (Fr. f.) irresistible compulsion or coercion, an unforeseeable course of events excusing a person from the fulfilment of a contract

forcemeat meat or vegetables finely chopped and seasoned, *not* forced- (one word)

forceps surgical pincers, pl. same

forcible *not* -eable

Ford, Ford Madox, b. **Ford Hermann Hueffer** (1873–1939) English writer

forearm (noun and verb, one word)

forebear an ancestor; cf. **forbear**

forebod/e, -ing *not* forb-

forecast predict, *not* forc-

forecastle *not* fo'c'sle

foreclose *not* forc-

foredge (typ.) the margin of a book opposite the binding, *not* fore-edge; *see also* **margins**

fore-edge (hyphen in non-technical uses)

fore-end *not* forend

forefend *use* **forf-**

fore/finger, -front (one word)

foregather *not* forg-

fore/go to go before, past **-went**, past part. **-gone**, present part. **-going**; cf. **forgo**

fore/head, -hock (one word)

foreign abbr. **for.**

Foreign and Commonwealth Office formed 1968 from the two separate Offices, abbr. **FCO**

Foreign/ Mission abbr. **FM**; — **Office** (caps.) abbr. **FO**, *now* **FCO**

forel an early vellum-like covering for books, *not* forr-

fore/leg, -lock, -mast, -play (one word)

fore/run past **-ran**, past part. **-run**; -runner (one word)

fore/said, -see, -shadow, -shore -shorten, -sight, -skin, -stall *not* for- (one word)

Forester, C(ecil) S(cott) (1899–1966) English novelist

foretell *not* fort-, fortel

for ever for always (two words, one word in US); **forever** continually (one word)

forewarn *not* for- (one word)

foreword (of book) *not* forw-, -ward; an introduction to a book by someone other than the author or editor

forfeit/, -able, -ure

forfend (US) protect by precautions, (arch.) avert; *not* fore-

forgather *use* **fore-**

forget/, -ting, past **forgot**, past part. **forgotten** *or* (esp. US) **forgot**; **-table**

forget-me-not (bot.)

forgivable *not* -eable

for/go abstain from, past **-went**, past part. **-gone**, present part. **-going**; cf. **forego**

forint the chief monetary unit of Hungary

formalin a germicide or preservative, *not* -ine

formalize *not* -ise

format/ (typ.) the size (octavo, quarto, etc.) of a book, periodical, etc.; (loosely) its general typographic style and appearance; (comput.) a defined structure for holding data etc.; as verb, past **-ted**, past part. **-ted**, present part. **-ting** (one *t* in US)

forme (typ.) a body of type secured in the frame called a chase; *not* form (US)

former the first of two; *see also* **latter**

Formica (propr.) (cap.)

formul/a pl. **-ae** (in math., sci., and scholarly uses), **-as** (in common usage, esp. in US) (not ital.); abbr. **F.**

forray *use* **foray**

forrel *use* **forel**

forsaid *use* **fore-**

Fors Clavigera a series of letters by Ruskin, 1871–84

Forster,/ John (1812–76) English biographer (*see also* **Foster**), — **E(dward) M(organ)** (1879–1970) English novelist

forsw/ear, past **-ore**, past part. **-orn**

forsythia an ornamental shrub

Fort cap. when part of a name; abbr. **Ft.**

fort. fortification, fortified

forte/ person's strong point (not ital.); (mus.) strong and loud, abbr. *f*; **-piano** loud, then immediately soft (hyphen), abbr. *fp*; **-piano** an early form of pianoforte (one word)

fortell *use* **fore-**

FORTH (comput.) a programming language (caps. or even small caps.)

fortissimo/ (mus.) very loud; as noun, pl. **-s**; abbr. *ff*

fortississimo/ (mus.) as loud as possible; as noun, pl. **-s**; abbr. *fff*

fortiter in re (Lat.) bravely in action; cf. *suaviter in modo*

Fort-Lamy *now* **N'Djamena**, Chad

Fortran (comput.) Formula Translation, a programming language; *also* **FORTRAN** or even small caps

fortuitous due to or characterized by chance; *not* fortunate or well-timed

forty-eightmo (typ.) a book based on forty-eight leaves, ninety-six pages, to the sheet; abbr. **48mo**

for/um a place of or meeting for public discussion; pl. **-ums**, (in Rom. or legal contexts) **-a**

forward/ (adj., noun, adv., and verb), **-s** common alt. adv. meaning towards the front, in the direction one is facing, or in the direction of motion

forwarn *use* **fore-**

forzando (mus.) forced, abbr. **fz** (no point); *see also* **sforzando**

fos. (abbr.) pl. of **fo.** (folio)

foss/a (anat.) a cavity, pl. **-ae**

fosse a ditch, *not* foss

fossilize *not* -ise

Foster,/ Birket (1825–99) English painter, — **John** (1770–1843) English essayist (*see also* **Forster**), — **Stephen Collins** (1826–64) US songwriter, — **Sir Harry Hylton-** *see* **Hylton-Foster**

Fotheringhay Castle Northants., 1066–1604

Foucault,/ Jean Bernard Léon (1819–68) French physicist, — **Michel** (**Paul**) (1926–84) French philosopher and historian of ideas; **Foucaldian**

Foucquet *use* **Fouq-**

fouetté (ballet) a quick whipping movement of the raised leg (not ital.)

foul/, -ly; **-up** (hyphen as noun)

Foulahs *use* **Ful-**

foulard a thin, soft material (not ital.)

foul proof (typ.) a proofreader's marked proof as opposed to the corrected proof that succeeds it

foundry/ *not* -ery, — **proof** a final proof from a forme that has been prepared for plating

fount a source of a desirable quality or commodity; cf. **font**

Fouqué, Friedrich, Baron de la Motte (1777–1843) German poet and dramatist

Fouquet,/ Jean (1416–80) French painter, — **Nicolas** (1615–80) French statesman; *not* Foucq-

four-colour process (typ.) printing in yellow, magenta, cyan, and black to give a complete colour reproduction

fourfold (one word)

4GL (comput.) Fourth-Generation Language

Four Horsemen of the Apocalypse Conquest, Slaughter, Famine, and Death, riding white, red, black, and pale horses respectively (Rev. 6: 1–8)

Fourier/, François Marie Charles (1772–1837) French socialist, hence **-ism, -ist, -ite**; —, **Jean Baptiste Joseph** (1768–1830) French mathematician and physicist, hence **— series**

four/score, -some (one word)

four-stroke (hyphen)

fourth estate (joc.) the press, journalism; *see also* **Estates**

Fourth of July US Independence Day (caps.)

Fourth of June George III's birthday, a day of celebration at Eton

4to quarto

Fowler,/ F(**rancis**) **G**(**eorge**) (1870–1918) English lexicographer; — **H**(**enry**) **W**(**atson**) (1858–1933) English lexicographer, author of *Modern English Usage* and joint author, with brother F. G., of *The King's English*

Fox,/ Charles James (1749–1806) English politician; — **George** (1624–91) English preacher, founder of Society of Friends (Quakers)

Foxe, John (1516–87) English clergyman and martyrologist

foxed paper stained with brown spots

fox/glove, -hole, -hound (one word)

fox/-hunt (hyphen)

fox terrier (two words)

foxtrot (one word)

foxy of or like a fox, sly or cunning, reddish-brown; (of paper) damaged, esp. by mildew; (US sl.) (of a woman) attractive

foyer an entrance hall (not ital.)

FP Fine Paper (the best edition of a work), fire-plug, (Sc.) former pupil(s)

f.p. freezing point

fp (mus.) forte-piano

FPA Family Planning Association, Foreign Press Association

F.Ph.S. Fellow of the Philosophical Society of England

FPS Fellow of the Pharmaceutical Society of Great Britain

Fr francium (no point)

Fr. Father, France, French, Friar, Friday, (Ger.) Frau (Mrs, wife), (It.) *Fratelli* (Brothers)

fr. fragment, franc, from, (Ger.) *frei* (free)

Fra (It.) brother, friar (no point)

fracas a noisy quarrel, pl. same (not ital.)

fractal (math.) a curve having the property that any small part of it, enlarged, has the same statistical character as the whole

fractile fragile, of or relating to breakage; (statistics) *use* **quantile**

fractionalize *not* -ise

fractious irritable, peevish, unruly; cf. **factious, factitious**

FRAD Fellow of the Royal Academy of Dancing

fraenu/lum, -m *not* fre-

F.R.Ae.S. Fellow of the Royal Aeronautical Society

F.R.Ag.Ss. Fellow of the Royal Agricultural Societies

FRAI Fellow of the Royal Anthropological Institute

fraise/ (Fr. f.) strawberry; — *des bois* wild strawberry, — *de veau* (Fr. cook.) calf's mesentery or caul

Fraktur (typ.) a German style of black-letter type, as 𝔉𝔯𝔞𝔨𝔱𝔲𝔯

FRAM Fellow of the Royal Academy of Music

framable *not* -eable

framboesia (med.) yaws, *not* -besia (US)

framework (one word)

franc (Fr. m.) abbr. **F**, **f.**, **fr.**; pl. same; the chief monetary unit of France, Belgium, Switzerland, Luxembourg, and several other countries (not ital.); in general contexts to be put *after* numerals, as 10 f. 50 c., or 10.50 fr. In financial contexts, *use* **Fr** (pl. same) close up *before* numerals; may be clarified further by country, e.g. 'BFr15' (Belgian franc), 'FFr15' (French franc), 'SwFr15' (Swiss franc)

française, à la (Fr.) in the French style (not cap.)

France abbr. **Fr.**

France, Anatole pseud. of **Jacques-Anatole-François Thibault** (1844–1924) French novelist and critic

Franche-Comté a region of France

franchise *not* -ize

Francic of or pertaining to the ancient Francs or their language

francisc a kind of battleaxe used by the ancient Francs

francium symbol **Fr**

Franck, César Auguste (1822–90) Belgian-born French organist and composer

Franco (y Bahamonde), Gen. Francisco (1892–1975) Spanish head of state 1939–75, titled *el Caudillo*

Franco- of France, French (hyphen) cap. in e.g. 'Franco-Prussian', 'Francophile', *but* 'francophone'

François Premier designating the styles of architecture, furniture, etc. or the characteristics of the reign of Francis I of France (1515–47)

franc-tireur (Fr. m.) guerrilla, partisan; (fig.) freelance; pl. *francs-tireurs*

franglais (Fr. m.) French regarded as including too many borrowings from English

Frankenstein (in Mary Shelley's novel, 1818) the maker of the monster, not the monster itself

Frankfort Ind., Ky.

Frankfurt/ am Main, — an der Oder Germany (no hyphens); *not* -fort, -on-Main, -on-Oder; in Fr. **Francfort**

Frankfurter Allgemeine Zeitung a German newspaper, *not* Frankfor-, -für-; familiarly **FAZ**

Franz Josef Land an archipelago, Arctic Ocean (Russia)

frappant (Fr.) striking, affecting

frappé (Fr.) iced, an iced drink (ital.); (US) a thick milk shake (not ital.)

FRAS Fellow of the Royal Asiatic Society, Fellow of the Royal Astronomical Society

Fraser the family name of Barons Lovat, Saltoun, and Strathalmond; *see also* **Frazer**

Fraser River BC, Canada

frat/e (It.) a friar, pl. *-i*; *-ello* brother, pl. *-elli*; in N. It. dialect these meanings are reversed

fraternize *not* -ise

Frau/ (Ger. f.) Mrs, wife, woman; *not* Fräu; abbr. **Fr.**; pl. *-en*; in Ger. used of any adult woman

Fräulein (Ger. n.) Miss, unmarried girl; pl. same; abbr. **Frl.**

Fraunhofer/, Joseph von (1787–1826) German optician and physicist, discoverer of — **diffraction, — lines** (no umlaut)

Frazer, Sir James George (1854–1941) English anthropologist; *see also* **Fraser**

FRBS Fellow of the Royal Botanic Society, Fellow of the Royal Society of British Sculptors

FRCGP Fellow of the Royal College of General Practitioners

FRCM Fellow of the Royal College of Music

FRCO Fellow of the Royal College of Organists

FRCOG Fellow of the Royal College of Obstetricians and Gynaecologists

FRCP Fellow of the Royal College of Physicians, London

F.R.C.Path. Fellow of the Royal College of Pathologists

FRCS Fellow of the Royal College of Surgeons, England

FRCVS Fellow of the Royal College of Veterinary Surgeons, London

F.R.Econ.S. Fellow of the Royal Economic Society

Fred. Frederic, Frederick; no point when it is a full name, or a diminutive

Fredericton NB, Canada; *not* -ck-

free and easy (three words)

free/base, -board, -booter, -born (one word)

freedman an emancipated slave; cf. **freeman**

Free/fone (US propr.) *also* **-phone**

free-for-all (adj.) (hyphens)

free/hand, -hold, -holder (one word)

free house an inn or public house not controlled by a brewery (two words)

freelance/ (verb, adj., adv.), **-r** (noun) one word except in hist. sense of a medieval mercenary

freeman one to whom the freedom of a city has been given; cf. **freedman**

Freemantle *use* **Frem-**

Freemason/, -ry (cap., one word)

Freepost (cap.)

free-range (adj., hyphen)

freest the superlative of **free** (no hyphen)

freethink/er, -ing (one word)

free verse *vers libre*

freeway (US) an express highway, esp. toll-free or with controlled access

free will the power of self-determination (two words), **free-will** (adj., hyphen)

freeze convert to ice; cf. **frieze**

freezing point abbr. **f.p.**

Frege/, Gottlob (1848–1925) German mathematician, logician, and philosopher; **-an**

frei (Ger.) free, abbr. **fr.**

Freiberg Saxony, Germany

Freiburg/ im Breisgau Baden, Germany; Ger. abbr. **— i. B.**

Freiburg Ger. for **Fribourg**

Freightliner (propr.) (one word)

Freiherr Ger. title, abbr. *Frhr.*

Freischütz, Der an opera by Weber, 1819

freize *use* frieze

Fremantle W. Australia, *not* Free-

French abbr. Fr.

French/ chalk, — cricket (cap.)

french fries (US) = (potato) chips (not cap.)

French groove (bind.) an extra space between the board and spine

French horn (cap.)

Frenchified (cap.)

French/ kiss, — knickers, — leave, — letter (two words, cap.)

Frenchlike (one word, cap.)

French/ mustard, — polish (noun, hyphen as verb), — polisher, — seam, — toast, — vermouth, — windows (two words, cap.)

frenetic delirious, frantic; *not* ph-

frenu/lum, -m *use* frae- (except in US)

freon (propr.) any of a group of halogenated hydrocarbons (not cap.)

freq. frequent, -ly, -ative

frère (Fr. m.) brother, friar

FRES Fellow of the Royal Entomological Society

fresco/ a watercolour done on damp plaster, pl. -s (not ital.)

freshman a first-year student of either sex at university, college, polytechnic, or (N. Amer.) high school (one word)

fresh water (noun, two words; adj. one word)

Fresnel/, Augustin Jean (1788–1827) French optical physicist; — biprism, — diffraction, — rhomb (one cap.), — lens (not cap.)

Freud/, Sigmund (1856–1939) Austrian neurologist and founder of psychoanalysis, -ian

Freytag, Gustav (1816–95) German writer

FRG Federal Republic of Germany, 1949–90, W. Germany

FRGS Fellow of the Royal Geographical Society

F.R.Hist.S. Fellow of the Royal Historical Society

Frhr. (Ger. title) *Freiherr*

FRHS Fellow of the Royal Horticultural Society

Fri. Friday

friable easily crumbled; cf. fryable

friar's balsam tincture of benzoin, *not* -s'

FRIBA Fellow of the Royal Institute of British Architects, pl. FFRIBA

Fribourg Switzerland, in Ger. Freiburg

FRIC Fellow of the Royal Institute of Chemistry, now FRSC

fricandeau/ a braised and larded fillet of veal, pl. -x (not ital.)

fricassee/ a white stew, pl. -s (not ital., no accent)

FRICS Fellow of the Royal Institution of Chartered Surveyors

Friday abbr. F., Fr., Fri.

fridge (colloq.) a refrigerator, *not* frig

Friedman, Milton (b. 1912) US economist

frier one who fries, *use* -yer

Friesian a breed of cattle, *not* Fris-; (in US) = Holstein

frieze a cloth, (archit.) the part below the cornice; *not* frei-

Friml, Rudolf (1879–1972) Czech-born US pianist and composer

FRIPHH Fellow of the Royal Institute of Public Health and Hygiene

frippery tawdry finery

Fris. Frisia (Friesland, an area comprising the NW Netherlands and adjacent islands), Frisian; *see also* Friesian

frisbee (propr.) (not cap.)

frisson an emotional thrill, a shudder (not ital.)

frit/ (Fr. cook.) fried, pl. -s; f. -e, pl. -es

frith an estuary, *use* firth

fritto misto (It.) mixed grill

Friuli-Venezia Giulia a region of Italy

frivol/led, -ling (one *l* in US)

frizz curl, roughen; *not* friz

Frl. (Ger.) Fräulein (Miss)

F.R.Med.Soc. Fellow of the Royal Medical Society

F.R.Met.S. Fellow of the Royal Meteorological Society

FRMS Fellow of the Royal Microscopical Society

FRNS Fellow of the Royal Numismatic Society

fro as in 'to and fro' (no point)

froe (US) a cleaving tool, *not* -ow

Froebel/ a kindergarten system developed by Friedrich Fröbel (1782–1852) German teacher and educationist, -ian

frolic/, -ked, -king

fromage/ (Fr. m.) cheese; — *de tête* pig's head, — *de porc* brawn

Fronde a French rebel party during minority of Louis XIV

frondeur a member of Fronde, political rebel

Frontignan a muscat grape or wine (not ital.)

frontispiece (print.) an illustration facing the title page of a book or of one of its divisions (one word)

frontmatter (print.) pages preceding the text proper (one word)

frost/bite, -bitten (one word)

frosting (US) = icing (on food)

Froude, James Anthony (1818–94) English historian

Froufrou a comedy by Meilhac and Halévy, 1869

frou-frou a rustling of a dress; frills or frippery (not ital.)

frow *use* **-oe**

frowsty musty, stuffy

frowzy unkempt, slatternly

FRPS Fellow of the Royal Photographic Society

FRS Fellow of the Royal Society, in Lat. **SRS** (*Societatis Regiae Sodalis*)

frs. francs

FRSA Fellow of the Royal Society of Arts

FRSC Fellow of the Royal Society of Chemistry

FRSE Fellow of the Royal Society of Edinburgh

FRSH Fellow of the Royal Society of Health

FRSL Fellow of the Royal Society of Literature

FRSM Fellow of the Royal Society of Medicine

FRST Fellow of the Royal Society of Teachers

frumenty hulled boiled wheat with milk, sugar, etc.; *not* the many variants

frust/um (geom.) the lower portion of inter- sected cone or pyramid, pl. **-a**; *not* -rum

FRVA Fellow of the Rating and Valuation Associ- ation

fry/able able to be fried (cf. **friable**), **-er**; *not* fri-

FSA Fellow of the Society of Antiquaries

FSAA Fellow of the Society of Incorporated Accountants and Auditors

FSB 'Federal Service of Security' (Federal´naya Sluzhba Bezopasnosti); successor to the KGB in Russia, 1992–; *see also* **KGB**

FSE Fellow of the Society of Engineers

FSIAD Fellow of the Society of Industrial Artists and Designers

FSS Fellow of the Royal Statistical Society

FSVA Fellow of the Incorporated Society of Valuers and Auctioneers

ft foot *or* feet (no point except in US)

Ft. fort

ft. feint (paper), flat, fortified

FTCD Fellow of Trinity College, Dublin

FTCL Fellow of Trinity College (of Music), Lon- don

FTI Fellow of the Textile Institute

FTP (comput.) File Transfer Protocol

Fuad/ I (1868–1936) King of Egypt 1923–36; **—** **II** (b. 1952) King of Egypt 1952–3

fuchsia (bot.) *not* fuschia (not ital.)

fuc/us a seaweed, pl. **-i** (not ital.)

Fuehrer (Ger.) *use* **Füh-**

fuelled *not* -eled

Fuenterrabia Spain, *not* Fontarabia

fugleman a leader in military exercises; *not* flugel-, flugle-, fugal-, fugel-; in Ger. m. *Flügelmann*

fug/ue (mus., psychol.) (not ital.), **-al**

Führer leader, the title assumed by Hitler in Nazi Germany, 1934; *not* Fue-

Fujiyama extinct Japanese volcano, *not* Mount Fujiyama; *properly* **Fujisan** *or* **Fuki-no-Yama**; *not* Fuzi-

-ful a suffix denoting amounts, pl. **-fuls**

Fula a W. African language; *not* Ful, Fulfulde

Fulahs Sudanese; *not* Felláh, Fellani, Feulhs, Foulahs, Fulbe; *see also* **fellah**

Fulbright/, (**James**) **William** (1905–95) US senator, responsible for the **—** **Act** 1946, which provided the foundation for the **—** **scholarship**

fulcr/um the point of leverage, pl. **-a** (not ital.)

fulfil/, -led, -ling, -ment *not* fulfill/, -ment (US)

fulgor splendour, *not* -gour

full-bound (bind.) completely cased in the same material (hyphen)

full capitals (typ.) large capital letters

fuller's earth (not cap.)

full/ left, — right (typ.) set text to align with respective margin of a page, same as **range**; cf. **ragged/ left, — right**; *see also* **full out**

full/-length not shortened, **-scale** not reduced (hyphens)

fullness *not* ful-

full out (typ.) set to the margin of a column or page, not indented

fulmar a petrel

fulness *use* **full-**

fulsome excessive and cloying; *not* full-

fumatory a place for smoking or fumigation; cf. **fumitory**

fumigator *not* -er

fumitory (bot.) any plant of the genus *Fumaria*, esp. *F. officinalis*; cf. **fumatory**

function (math.) abbr. **F**, **f**; symbol *f*

funfair (one word)

fung/us pl. **-i**, adj. **-ous** (not ital.)

funnel/led, -ling (one l in US), **-like** (hyphen)

funny bone (two words)

funny-face (hyphen)

fur. furlong

für (Ger.) for, abbr. *f.*

Furat *use* **Fırat**

furbelow a flounce, *not* -llow

furfuraceous scaly

furlong one-eighth of mile; abbr. **f.**, **fur.**

furmenty *use* **fru-**

Furness,/ Christopher, Baron (1852–1912) English shipping magnate, **— Horace Howard** (1833–1912) or his son (1865–1930) US Shakespearian scholars

Furniss, Harry (1854–1925) English cari- caturist and illustrator

Furnivall, Frederick James (1825–1910) English philologist

furor (Lat.) rage (ital.)

furore uproar (not ital.); *not* -or (US)

Fürst/ (Ger. m.) ruling or reigning prince (not necessarily of the blood royal), pl. *-en*; f. *-in* pl. *-innen* (cap.; not ital. as part of title, no comma preceding); cf. *Prinz*

furth/er (adv., adj., and verb), **-est** (adv. and adj.)

Furtwängler,/ Adolf (1853–1907) German archaeologist; — **Wilhelm** (1886–1954) his son, German conductor

fusable *use* **fusi-**

fus/e, -ee, -elage *not* fuz-

fusible *not* -able

fusil a musket, *not* -zil

fusilier *not* -leer

fusillade *not* -ilade

fut. future

futhorc the Scandinavian runic alphabet; *see also* **rune**

futur/e, -ism (often cap. as a specific hist. movement), **-ist, -istic, -ity**

fuz/e, -ee, -elage, -il *use* **fus-**

Fuzhou (Pinyin) Foochow, China

Fuziyama *use* **Fuji-**

f.v. *folio verso* (on the back of the page)

FWA Family Welfare Association

fwd forward

f.w.d. four-wheel drive, front-wheel drive

fylfot (typ.) the swastika, esp. when used as a decorative page-filler rather than a political or religious emblem; *not* fil-

fyrd the English local militia before 1066

fytte *use* **fit**

Fyzabad *use* **Faiz-**

fz (mus.) forzando

FZS Fellow of the Zoological Society

Gg

G gauss, the seventh in a series, (as prefix) giga-, Group

ɢ guarani (currency of Paraguay)

G. Graduate, Grand, Gulf, (naval) gunnery

g (dyn.) local gravitational acceleration; gram(s)

g. (meteor.) gale; (Fr.) *gauche* (left), *gras, -se* (big); guinea, -s

GA General Assembly (Sc. Church); Georgia, USA (postal abbr.)

Ga gallium (no point); a language spoken in Ghana

Ga. Gallic; Georgia, USA (off. abbr.)

gabardine a durable cotton cloth; cf. **gaber-**

gabbey *use* **gaby**

gabbro/ (geol.) an igneous rock, pl. **-s**

gaberdine (hist.) a loose, long cloak worn esp. by Jews and almsmen; cf. **gabar-**

Gabon/ W. Africa; **-ese**

Gaborone Botswana

gaby a simpleton; *not* -ey, gabbey, gawby

Gadarene (adj.) involving or engaged in headlong or suicidal rush or flight as in Matt. 8: 28–32

Gaddafi *see* **Qaddafi**

Gaddi a family of Florentine painters, 1259–1396

Gadhel *use* **Goidel**

Gaditanian of Cadiz, SW Spain

gadolinium symbol **Gd**

Gadshill Kent, site of **Gad's Hill Place**, Charles Dickens's residence 1860–70; character in Shakespeare's *1 Henry IV* (one word)

Gaekwar the title of the prince of Baroda, India; *not* Gaik-

Gaelic (of or relating to) any of the Celtic languages spoken in Ireland, Scotland, and the Isle of Man; abbr. **Gael.**

Gaeltacht any region of Ireland where the vernacular language is Irish

gaff a hooked or barbed fishing spear

gaffe a blunder, an indiscreet act or remark

gaga senile, incapable (one word)

Gagarin, Yuri (**Alekseevich**) (1934–68) Russian cosmonaut, first to orbit earth, 1961

gage a, *or* to, pledge; cf. **gauge**

Gaia/, Gaea, Ge (Gr. myth.) personification of the Earth; later, the Earth-goddess, daughter of Chaos; **Ge** is the classical Attic and commonest prose form; **Gaia** (Latinized as **Gaea**) the epic and poetic form normally preferred in general discussion of myth. or in (sci.) viewing the Earth as a vast living organism; **— hypothesis, -n**

gai/ety, -ly; *not* gay-

Gaikwar *use* **Gaek-**

gaillardia (bot.) a plant

gairfish *use* **gar-**

gairfowl *use* **gare-fowl**

gairish *use* **gar-**

Gair Loch Strathclyde, *use* **Gare Loch**

Gairloch Highland, *not* **Gare-**

Gaitskell, Hugh Todd Naylor (1906–63) British statesman

Gaius a Roman praenomen, *not* Caius; abbr. **C.**

gal a unit of acceleration, with numbers **Gal** (no point)

Gal. Galatians

gal. gallon, -s

gala/ a festive occasion, pl. **-s** (not ital.)

galaena *use* **-lena**

galangale *use* **gali-**

galantine white meat served cold in aspic, *not* gall-

Galantuomo, Il Re King Victor Emmanuel I of Italy

galanty show a shadow pantomime; *not* -tee, gallantee, -ty

Galápagos Islands in the Pacific Ocean, official Sp. name **Archipiélago de Colón**

Galatea, Acis *or* **Pygmalion and** (Gr. myth.)

Galaţi Romania; *not* -acz, -atch, -atz

Galatia Asia Minor

Galatians (NT) abbr. **Gal.**

galaxy (astr.) any of the many independent systems of stars, gas, dust, etc. held together by gravitational attraction (not cap.); the galaxy of which the solar system is part, the Milky Way (cap.)

galena lead ore, *not* -aena

galera (Sp. typ.) a galley

galère/ (Fr. f.) galley (ship), **qu'allait-il faire dans cette —?** how did he get into this scrape? (with the implication 'by his own stupid fault')

Galician (of or relating to) (a person from) Galicia, or the language of Galicia

Galilean of Galilee, of Galileo

Galileo Galilei (1564–1642) Italian astronomer and mathematician; **Galileo** is the given name, **Galilei** the surname; in Fr. **Galilée**, It. and Ger. **Galilei**

galingale *not* gala-

galiot a vessel, *use* **gall-**

galipot a resin; cf. **gall-**

galivant *use* **galli-**

gall. gallon, -s

gallantine *use* **gal-**

gallanty show *use* **gala-**

gallaway *use* **gallo-**

gall bladder (two words)

Galle Sri Lanka, *formerly* Point de Galle

Galles, le pays de Wales; adj. **gallois**/ f. **-e**

galley/ (typ.) oblong tray for set type, **— proofs** those supplied unpaginated

Gallic of Gaul, French; abbr. **Ga.**

gallice in French

Gallic/ism a French idiom; **-ize** make Gallic or French, *not* -ise

Galli-Curci, Amelita (1889–1963) Italian soprano

galliot a Dutch cargo-boat

Gallipoli S. Italy, Turkey; in Turk. **Gelibolu,** which should be used for modern references, but **Gallipoli** for the First World War campaign

gallipot a small jar; cf. **gali-**

gallium symbol **Ga**

gallivant gad about; *not* gala-, gali-

gallon/, **-s** abbr. **gal., gall.**

galloon a dress trimming

galloot *use* **gal-**

gallop/ a horse's movement; **-ed, -er, -ing;** cf. **gal-**

gallopade a Hungarian dance; *not* galop-, gallopp-

Gallovidian of Galloway

Galloway SW Scotland

galloway a breed of cattle; *not* galla-

gallows treated as sing.

gallstone (one word)

Gallup/, Dr George Horace (1901–84) founded the American Institute of Public Opinion, 1936; **— poll** a measure of public opinion (two words, one cap.)

galoot an awkward fellow; not gall-, geel-

galop a dance; cf. **gall-**

galosh/ an overshoe; *not* gol-, -oshe; **-ed**

galumph move noisily or clumsily

galv. galvan/ic, -ism

Galvani, Luigi (1737–98) discoverer of galvanism

galvanize *not* -ise

Galway W. Ireland

Galwegian of Galloway

Gama, Vasco da (1467–1524) Portuguese navigator, first round Africa to India

gambade/ a horse's leap or bound, a fantastic movement, an escapade; *not* -do; pl. **-s**

Gambia, The W. Africa; no definite article in US

Gambier Ohio

gambier a gum; *not* -beer, -bir

gamboge yellow pigment, *not* -booze

gambol/ to frisk; **-led, -ling** (one l in US)

Game at Chesse, A an allegorical comic play by Middleton, 1624

game bird (two words)

game/book, -keeper (one word)

game/ machine, — plan, — point, — show, — theory, — warden (two words)

gamin/ f. **-e** a street urchin (not ital.)

gamma/ the third letter of the Gr. alphabet (Γ, γ); unit of magnetic flux density, in SI units 1 nT; **— globulin** a protein; **— ray** (two words)

gammon a cured ham, *not* gam-

gamy having the flavour or scent of game left till high, *not* -ey

Gand Fr. for Ghent, Belgium

Gandhi,/ Mohandas Karamchand ('Mahatma Gandhi') (1869–1948) Indian nationalist leader; **— Mrs Indira** (1917–84) Prime Minister of India 1966–77, 1980–4, daughter of Pandit Nehru, not related to preceding; **— Rajiv** (1944–91) Prime Minister of India 1984–9, her son

gangli/on a knot on a nerve, pl. **-a**

gangue rock or earth in which ore is found

gangway (one word)

ganister a hard stone, *not* gann-

ganja marijuana

gantlet (US) a stretch of railway track where two lines of track overlap; *see also* **gauntlet**

gantry platform to carry travelling crane etc.; *not* gau-

Ganymede (Gr. myth.) cup-bearer to the gods, fourth moon of Jupiter

gaol/, **-bird, -break, -er** *use* **jail**/ except in hist. contexts

Garamond a typeface

Garamont, Claude (c.1500–61) French type-designer, -cutter, and -founder

garbage can (US) = **dustbin**

García Lorca, Federico (1898–1936) Spanish poet and playwright, often alphabetized under **Lorca**

García Márquez, Gabriel (b. 1928) Colombian novelist

Garcilaso de la Vega/ (1503–36) Spanish poet, **— — — —** ('the Inca') (1540–1616) Spanish historian

garçon (Fr. m.) waiter, boy, bachelor (ital.)

Garda Síochána (Ir.) the police force of Ireland; **garda**/ a member of that force, pl. **-í** (not cap.)

Garde nationale (Fr.) national guard (one cap.)

gardenia (bot.) (not ital.)

Gardens abbr. **Gdns.**

gare (Fr. f.) railway station

garefish *use* **gar-**

gare-fowl the great auk; *not* gair-, gar- (hyphen)

Gare Loch Strathclyde, *not* Gair

Gareloch Highland, *use* **Gair-**

garfish similar to pike; *not* gair-, gare-

gargantuan enormous (not cap.)

gargoyle (archit.) *not* -ile, -oil

Garhwal Uttar Pradesh, India

gari *use* **gharry**

garish gaudy, *not* gair-

garlic *but* **-licky**

Garmisch-Partenkirchen Germany

garni/ (Fr.) f. **-e** furnished

garrott/e to throttle, or the apparatus used; *not* -ote (US), garo-; **-er**

garryowen a type of high kick in Rugby Union, in League Rugby called an **up-and-under** (not cap., one word)

garter belt (US) = **suspender belt**

Garter King of Arms a chief herald (at the College of Arms), *not* -at-

Gascogne Fr. for Gascony

Gascon a native of Gascony

gascon a braggart, *gasconnade* (Fr. f.) boasting

gaseous *not* -ious

Gaskell, Mrs Elizabeth (**Cleghorn**) (1810–65) English novelist

gasoline a volatile liquid from petroleum, esp. (chiefly US and technical) petrol; *not* -ene

Gaspé a peninsula, cape, and town, Que., Canada

gas poisoning (two words)

gas station (US) = **filling station**

Gast/haus (Ger. n.) an inn, pl. *-häuser* (cap.)

Gast/hof (Ger. m.) a hotel, pl. *-höfe* (cap.)

gastroenteri/c, -tis (one word)

gastropod any member of the Gastropoda, mollusc class (not ital.); *not* -ster-

gât/é (Fr.) f. **-ée** spoiled

gateau/ cake, pl. **-s**; (Fr. m.) *gâteau*/, pl. *-x*

gatecrash/, **-er** (one word)

gate/fold a folded oversize page (one word)

gate/house, -keeper, -leg, -post, -way (one word)

gather (bind.) assemble the printed and folded sections in sequence

Gatling gun a machine gun with clustered barrels (cap.)

GATT General Agreement on Tariffs and Trade

gauch/e awkward, **-erie** awkwardness (not ital.)

gauche (Fr.) left, abbr. **g.**

gaucho/ a cowboy from the S. Amer. pampas, *not* gua-; pl. **-s**

Gaudí (**y Cornet**), **Antonio** (1853–1926) Catalan architect

Gaudier-Brzeska, Henri (1891–1915) French sculptor

gauge a measure; not gua-; cf. **gage**

Gauguin, (Eugène Henri) Paul (1848–1903) French painter

Gaul ancient France; adj. **Gallic**, (Fr.) *gaulois*/, f. **-e**

gauleiter a regional party official governing a district under Nazi rule, a local or petty tyrant (not ital.)

Gaull/e, General Charles (**André Joseph Marie**) **de** (1890–1970) French President 1944–5, 1959–69; **-ist**

Gauloise (propr.) a French cigarette

gauntlet/ a long glove, *not* gant-; **-ed**

gauntr/ee, -y *use* **gantry**

gaur an Indian ox, *not* gour

Gauss, Karl Friedrich (1777–1855) German mathematician and physicist

gauss a unit of magnetic induction, abbr. **G**; pl. same

Gautama Buddha *see* **Buddha**

Gauthier-Villars publishers

Gautier, Théophile (1811–72) French writer

gauzy *not* -ey

gavel/ a president's or auctioneer's hammer; **-led, -ling** (one l in US)

gavial *use* **gharial**

gavotte a dance, music for it

gawby *use* **gaby**

gay/ety, -ly *use* **gai-**

Gay-Lussac, Joseph Louis (1778–1850) French chemist and physicist

gaz. gazett/e, -ed, -eer

gazebo/ a summer-house, belvedere; pl. **-s**

gazett/e, -ed, -eer abbr. **gaz.**

gazpacho a cold vegetable soup

gazump raise the price to a would-be buyer after agreement but before completion

GB gigabyte, Great Britain

GBE Knight, *or* Dame, Grand Cross (of the Order) of the British Empire

GBH grievous bodily harm (caps.)

G.B.S. George Bernard Shaw (1856–1950) Irish-born British dramatist and critic

GC George Cross, Golf Club

GCA Ground Controlled Approach (radar)

GCB Knight, *or* Dame, Grand Cross (of the Order) of the Bath

GCE General Certificate of Education

GCF *or* **g.c.f.** (math.) greatest common factor

GCHQ Government Communications Headquarters

GCI Ground Controlled Interception (radar)

GCIE Knight, *or* Dame, Grand Commander (of the Order) of the Indian Empire

GCLH Grand Cross of the Legion of Honour

GCM general court martial, (math.) greatest common measure

g.c.m. (math.) greatest common measure

GCMG Knight, *or* Dame, Grand Cross (of the Order) of St Michael and St George

GCSE General Certificate of Secondary Education

GCSI Knight, *or* Dame, Grand Commander (of the Order) of the Star of India

GCVO Knight, *or* Dame, Grand Cross of the Royal Victorian Order

GD Grand Duchess, Grand Duchy, Grand Duke

Gd gadolinium (no point)

Gdańsk Poland, *formerly* Danzig

Gdns. Gardens

GDP gross domestic product

GDR (hist.) German Democratic Republic; *see* **DDR**

Gdsm. Guardsman

Ge germanium (no point)

g.e. (bind.) gilt edges

gearbox (one word)

gear lever (two words)

gearwheel (one word)

geboren/ (Ger.) born, **-e** = née (e.g. 'Jenny Marx, geb. von Westfalen'); abbr. **geb.**

gebunden (Ger.) bound, when used of a stringed instrument the term is retained in Eng.; abbr. **geb.**

GEC General Electric Company

gecko/ any of various house lizards, pl. **-s**

gee-ho a call to horses, *not* jee-

geeloot *use* **gal-**

gee-string *use* **G-string**

gee-up a call to horses, *not* jee-

Ge'ez the classical literary language of Ethiopia, surviving as **Ethiopic**

geezer (sl.) an old man, *not* geyser·

gefallen (Ger.) killed in battle, abbr. ***gef.***; symbol ✕ (follows the name); cf. ***gestorben***

gefuffle *use* **ker-**

Geg one of two main dialects of Albanian, *not* Gheg; *see also* **Tosk**

Gehenna (NT) hell

Geiger counter (*in full* **Geiger–Müller counter**) an instrument for detecting radioactivity

Geisenheimer a white Rhine wine

geisha a trained Japanese hostess, pl. same

Geissler/**, Heinrich** (1814–79) German physicist, inventor of — **tube**

gel (phys.) (form) a semi-solid colloidal suspension or jelly

gelatin/, **-ize, -ous** *not* -e, -ise

Geld (Ger. n.) money (cap.)

Gelderland E. Netherlands, *not* Guel-

gelder rose *use* **gue-**

gelée (Fr. f.) frost, jelly

Gelée, Claude *see* **Lorrain**

Gelert a faithful dog of Welsh legend

Gellert, Christian Fürchtegott (1715–69) German poet

Gelsemium (bot.) *not* -inum

Gemara second part of the Talmud

gemm/**a** a bud, pl. **-ae**

gemütlich (Ger.) leisurely; agreeab/le, -ly; comfortab/le, -ly

Gemütlichkeit (Ger. f.) geniality, friendliness

Gen. General, Genesis

gen. gender, genera; general, -ly; genitive, genus

gendarme/ pl. **-s**; **-rie** a body of soldiers used as police (not ital.)

gender abbr. **gen.**

gên*/*e (Fr. f.) constraint; **-é**, f. **-ée** constrained

gene/ the unit of heredity, pl. **-s**

genealog/**y** a family's pedigree, *not* -olog-; **-ical**

genera *see* **genus**

General abbr. **Gen.**

General Assembly (Sc. Church) abbr. **GA**

general election (not caps.)

generalia (Lat. pl.) general principles

generalissimo/ supreme commander, pl. **-s**

generalize *not* -ise

generator *not* -er

Genesis (OT) abbr. **Gen.**

genes/**is** the origin of a thing, pl. **-es** (not cap.)

genet a catlike mammal of genus *Genetta*, *not* -tte; cf. **jennet**

Geneva/ Switzerland, in Fr. **Genève**, Ger. **Genf**, It. **Ginevra**; adj. **Genevan**; **Genevese** (sing. and pl.) native(s) of —, in Fr. ***genevois***/, f. **-e**(**s**)

genev/**a** (lit.), **-er** Dutch (Hollands) gin

Geneva Convention an international agreement governing the status and treatment of captured and wounded military personnel in wartime, 1864, revised 1950, 1978

Geneviève, Saint (*c*.422–*c*.512) patron saint of Paris

Genghis Khan (1162–1227) Mongol conqueror of N. China and Iran, *not* Jenghiz; in Mongolian **Chingiz Khan** *or* **Čingiz Khan**

genie/ (Muslim myth.) a spirit, pl. **-s** *see also* **jinnee**

genit *use* **jennet**

genitive abbr. **gen.**, **genit.**

geni/us since the Romantic era, (a person of) consummate intellectual power, pl. **-uses**; *previously* innate disposition *or* (Roman myth.) personal spirit, pl. **-i**; *see also* **genie**

geni/us loci (Lat.) the pervading spirit of a place, pl. *-i loci*

Gennesaret, Sea of *not* -eth

gennet *use* **j-**

Geno/a Italy; in Fr. **Gênes**, It. **Genova**; **-ese** *not* -ovese (except in It.)

genre (not ital.)

gen/s a clan, pl. **-tes**

Gens de Lettres, Société des French society of authors

Gensfleisch *see* **Gutenberg**

Gent Fl. and Ger. for **Ghent**, Belgium

gent a gentleman

genteel/ affectedly refined, **-ly**

Gentele's green a colour

gentil/ (Fr.) f. *-le* gentle, kind

Gentile (a person who is) not Jewish (*see also* **goy**), not Mormon; *or* of or relating to a nation or tribe (cap.); (gram.) a word indicating nationality (not cap.)

gentilhomme (Fr. m.) nobleman (by ancestry rather than creation), gentleman; pl. *gentilshommes*

gentleman-at-arms (hyphens)

Gentleman's Magazine UK periodical 1731–1914; *not* -men's

Gentlemen's Quarterly US periodical, *now called* **GQ**; *not* -man's

Gents, the men's lavatory (cap., no apos.)

genuflection a bending of the knee, *not* -xion

genus pl. **genera**, abbr. **gen.**

Geo. George

geod. geode/sy (large-scale earth measurement), -tic

Geoffrey-Lloyd, Baron

Geoffroy Saint-Hilaire, Étienne (1772–1844) French zoologist, *not* -frey (one hyphen)

geog. geograph/er, -ical, -y

geographical qualifiers forming everyday terms often have lower-case initials, as chinese white, roman type, venetian blinds; *but* Brussels sprouts, India ink, London pride

geol. geolog/ical, -ist, -y

geological *not* geologic (US)

geologize *not* -ise

geology the names of formations to have caps., as Old Red Sandstone

geom. geome/ter, -trical, -try

Geordie a native of Tyneside

Georg Ger. for George

George abbr. **Geo.**

George/ Cross (also — **Medal**) decorations for bravery awarded esp. to civilians, instituted by King George VI

George Town Bahamas, Cayman Islands, Malaysia, and many places in Australia, Canada, and USA

Georgetown Guyana, and many places in Australia, Canada, and USA (one word)

Georgia USA, off. abbr. **Ga.**, postal **GA**; a Caucasian state, *formerly* a Soviet Socialist Republic

Georgian of or characteristic of the time of Kings George I–IV (1714–1830), esp. architecture; *or* of the time of Kings George V and VI (1910–52), esp. of the literature of 1910–20; of or relating to (the language of) Georgia in the Caucasus, *or* a native thereof; of or relating to Georgia in the USA, *or* a native thereof

Georgium sidus (astr.) an old name for Uranus

Ger. German, Germany

ger. gerund, -ial

geranium/ (bot.) pl. **-s** (not ital.)

Gerard, John (1545–1612) English botanist, *not* -arde

gerbil a mouselike desert rodent of the subfamily *Gerbillinae*, distinct from the **jerboa**; *not* jer-

gerfalcon *use* **gyr-**

Géricault, Jean Louis André Théodore (1791–1824) French painter

gerkin *use* **ghe-**

German abbr. **Ger.**

german (placed after *brother* or *sister*) having both parents the same; (placed after *cousin*) having both grandparents the same on one side

germane relevant

germanium symbol **Ge**

Germanize *not* -ise

German/ measles, — shepherd (esp. US) = **alsatian, — silver** (two words, one cap.)

Germany abbr. **Ger.**

germon *use* **albacore**

Gernika (Basque) **Guernica**

Gérôme, Jean Léon (1824–1904) French painter

gerrymander manipulate an electoral district unfairly, *not* je-

gerund/, -ial abbr. **ger.**

Ges. (Ger.) *Gesellschaft* (cap.)

gesammelte Werke (Ger. pl.) collected works (one cap.)

Gesellschaft (Ger. f.) a company or society (cap.), abbr. **Ges.**; *see also* **GmbH**

gesso/ gypsum used in art, pl. **-es**

gest. (Ger.) *gestorben*

gestalt (psychol.) an organized whole that is perceived as more than the sum of its parts (not cap., not ital.)

Gestapo the German secret police under Hitler

Gesta Romanorum (Lat. pl.) a medieval collection of anecdotes

gesticulator one who moves his hands and arms in talking, *not* -er

gestorben (Ger.) deceased, abbr. **gest.**; symbol † (follows the name); cf. **gefallen**

Gesundheit (Ger.) expressing a wish of good health (said before drinking or to one who sneezes)

get-at-able accessible (hyphens)

getaway an escape (one word)

gettable (two *t*s)

Getty, Jean (*not* John) **Paul** (1892–1976) US oil businessman

Gettysburg Pa.; scene of battle and of Lincoln's address, 1863

Geulinex, Arnold (1625–69) Dutch philosopher

GeV giga-electronvolt

Gewandhaus (Ger. n.) Clothworkers' Hall, a concert hall and orchestra in Leipzig

gewgaw a gaudy plaything (one word)

geyser a hot spring, water heater (not ital.); *not* geezer

G5 Group of Five

GFS Girls' Friendly Society

GG Girl Guides, Governor-General, Grenadier Guards

Gg gigagram

g.gr. a great gross, or 144 dozen

GGSM Graduate of the Guildhall School of Music

Ghadames Libya

Ghana/ W. Africa; adj. and noun **-ian**

Ghandi *use* **Gandhi**

gharial a large Indian crocodile, *not* gavi-

gharry a vehicle used in India, *not* gari

ghat (Anglo-Ind.) a mountain pass, steps to a river; *not* ghât, ghát, ghaut

Ghazi a Muslim fighter against non-Muslims

ghee Indian clarified butter, *not* ghi

Gheel a Belgian commune known for its treatment of mentally ill people, in Fl. **Geel**

Gheg *use* **Geg**

Ghent Belgium; in Fr. **Gand**, Fl. and Ger. **Gent**

gherao (Ind., Pak.) a lock-in of employers

gherkin a small cucumber; *not* ge-, gi-, gu-

ghetto/ pl. **-s** (not ital.)

ghi *use* **ghee**

ghiaour *use* **gi-**

Ghibelline one of the Emperor's faction in medieval Italian states, opposed to Guelf; *not* -in, Gib-, Guib-

Ghiberti, Lorenzo (1378–1455) Italian sculptor, painter, goldsmith

ghillie *use* **gill-**

Ghirlandaio, Domenico (1449–94) Italian painter

Ghizeh *use* **Giza**

Ghom Pers. pronunciation of **Qom**

Ghonds *use* **Gonds**

Ghoorkas *use* **Gurkhas**

ghost/-write (hyphen, one word in US), — **writer** (two words, one word in US)

ghoul an evil spirit; *not* -ool, -oule, -owl

GHQ General Headquarters

Ghurkas *use* **Gurkhas**

GI (US) Government Issue, (colloq.) serviceman

Giacometti, Alberto (1901–66) Swiss sculptor, painter, poet

giallo antico (It.) a rich yellow marble

Giant's Causeway Co. Antrim, *not* -ts'

giaour (derog.) Turk. name for a non-Muslim; *not* ghiaour, giaur; in Turk. now **gâvur**

Giaour, The a poem by Byron, 1813

Gib Gibraltar

gibber to chatter, *not* j-

gibbet/, -ed, -ing

Gibbon, Edward (1737–94) English historian

Gibbons,/ Grinling (1648–1720) English carver, — **Orlando** (1583–1625) English composer

gibbo/us humpbacked, convex; **-sity**

gib/e to sneer; **-er, -ing**; cf. **gybe**

Gibeline *use* **Ghibell-**

Gibraltar/ abbr. **Gib**; **-ian**

Gibran, Khalil (1883–1931) Lebanese-born US writer and artist, *not* Jubran

gibus an opera hat (not ital.)

Gide, André Paul Guillaume (1869–1951) French writer

Gideon a biblical character, a member of a body distributing bibles

Gielgud, Sir (**Arthur**) **John** (b. 1904) English actor, director, and producer

giga- a prefix meaning one thousand million (10^9), abbr. **G**

gigabyte (comput.) a unit of information, equal to 2^{30} bytes; abbr. **GB**

GIGO (comput.) garbage in, garbage out

gigolo/ pl. **-s** (not ital.)

gigot/ (cook.) leg of mutton or lamb, — **sleeve** (two words); *not* j-

gigue a lively dance

Gilbert, Sir William Schwenck (1836–1911) English librettist

Gil Blas a picaresque satire by Le Sage, 1715

gild an association, *use* **gui-**

Gilead/ a mountainous district east of River Jordan, 'balm in –' (Jer. 8: 22)

gill a quarter of a pint; a deep ravine, narrow mountain torrent, *not* ghy-

Gill, (Arthur) Eric (Rowton) (1882–1940) artist, sculptor, and type designer

Gillette/, King Camp (1855–1932) US inventor of safety razor, **— William** (1857–1937) US actor and writer

gillie (Sc.) a man or boy attending a person hunting or fishing, (hist.) a Highland chief's attendant; *not* ghi-

Gillray, James (1757–1815) English caricaturist

gillyflower a clove-scented flower, *not* jilli-

gilt abbr. **gt.**

gimcrack trumpery, *not* jim-

gimlet a tool, *not* gimb-

gimmick a contrivance, device

gimp a trimming, a fishing line; *not* gui-, gy-

Ginevra It. for Geneva

ginger/ ale, — beer (two words)

gingerbread (one word)

ginger/ nut, — snap (two words, one word in US), **— wine** (two words)

ginglym/us (anat.) a hingelike joint such as the elbow, pl. **-i**; **-oid**

ginkgo an oriental tree, *not* gingko

ginn *see* **jinnee**

Gioconda, La *see* **Mona Lisa**; an opera by Ponchielli, 1876; a play by D'Annunzio, 1898

Giorgione, Giorgio Barbarelli da Castelfranco (1475–1510) Italian painter

Giott/o di Bondone (1266–1337) Italian painter and architect, **-esque**

gipsy *use* **gyp-**

Giraldus Cambrensis (de Barri) (*c.*1146– *c.*1220) Welsh churchman and historian

girandole a firework (not ital.)

girasol a fire opal, *not* -ole

Giraudoux, Jean (1882–1944) French novelist and playwright

girkin *use* **ghe-**

girlfriend (one word)

Girl Guide *now* **Guide**

giro a system of money transfer, *not* gy-

Girobank (cap., one word)

Girond/e a dép. of France, **-ist** a French moderate republican 1791–3

Giscard d'Estaing, Valéry (b. 1926) President of France 1974–81

gismo *use* **giz-**

gitan/ (Fr.) f. **-e** Spanish gypsy

gitan/o (Sp.) f. **-a** gypsy

gîte (Fr. m.) a rural holiday house in France

Guilia an Italian name, *not* Gui-

Giulini, Carlo Maria (b. 1914) Italian conductor

Giulio an Italian name, *not* Gui-

Giulio Romano (*c.*1499–1546) Italian architect

giuoco piano (It.) quiet play (a chess opening, 'the Italian game'); *giuoco* is in modern It. *gioco*, but the older spelling is retained in Eng. refs.

Giuseppe an Italian name, *not* Gui-

giveable *not* givable

given name a name given in addition to a surname; *prefer to* 'Christian name', which implies that Christian baptism is the norm; and to 'forename', since it includes names that follow the surname (e.g. Hungarian, Chinese, and Japanese)

Giza Egypt; *not* El-Ghiz-, -eh

gizmo *not* gis-

Gk. Greek

glace (Fr. cook. f.) ice

glacé glazed (not ital.)

gladiol/us (bot.) pl. **-i** (not ital.)

Gladstone/ bag, — cap (two words)

Gladstonian *not* -ean

Glagolitic of or relating to the alphabet ascribed to St Cyril, formerly used in writing some Slavonic languages

glair the white of an egg, *not* glaire

Glam. Glamorgan

glamorize *not* -ise

glamorous/, -ly *not* -our-

glamour *not* -or (even in US)

glandular fever = **(infectious) mono-nucleosis** (the usual US term)

glan/s the rounded part forming the end of the penis or clitoris, pl. **-des**

Glas. Glasgow

glaserian fissure (anat.) *not* glass-

glasnost (in the former Soviet Union) the policy or practice of more open government and greater information (not ital.), in Russ. *glasnost'*

glassful pl. **glassfuls**

glasshouse greenhouse, (sl.) military prison

Glaswegian of Glasgow

Glauber/, Johann Rudolf (1604–68) German chemist; **—'s salt** a cathartic (apos.), *not* salts

glaucoma an eye condition

glaucous greyish green or blue; (bot.) covered with a bloom

Glazunov, Aleksandr (Konstantinovich) (1865–1936) Russian composer

GLC (hist.) Greater London Council

Glen written separately when referring not to a settlement but to the glen itself, as Glen Almond, Glen Coe

Glenalmond Tayside

Glencoe Highland, *but* **Glen Coe** (pass)

Glendower, Owen (*c.*1354–*c.*1416) Welsh chieftain; in Welsh **Owain Glyn Dŵr**, *also called* **Owain ap Gruffydd**

Glenealy Co. Wicklow

Gleneely Co. Donegal

Glenfarclas, Glenfiddich, Glenforres whiskies

glengarry a Scottish cap

Glenlivet/ a Speyside village; *not* -at, -it (one word); **The —, Braes of —** whiskies

Glenmorangie a whisky

Glenrothes Fife

glissade a slide down a steep slope (not ital.)

glissand/o (mus.) slurred, in a gliding manner; pl. **-os** *not* -i

glissé a sliding step in dance (not ital.)

glockenspiel/ an orchestral percussion instrument, pl. **-s**

Gloria/ (liturgy) pl. **-s**

Gloria/ in Excelsis, — Patri hymns

Gloria Tibi glory to Thee (two caps.)

Glorious Twelfth, the (UK) 12 Aug., the start of grouse-shooting season

Glos. Gloucestershire

gloss a superficial lustre, a marginal note

gloss. glossary, a collection of glosses

glosseme (not ital.)

Gloucestershire abbr. **Glos.**

Gloucestr: the signature of the Bishop of Gloucester (colon)

glovebox (one word)

glove/ compartment, — puppet (two words)

glower gaze angrily, *not* -our

glow-worm (hyphen)

gloxinia/ (bot.) pl. **-s** (not ital.)

Gluck, Christoph Willibald Ritter von (1714–87) German composer, *not* Glü-

glu/e, -ed, -ey, -ing

glue/-pot, -sniffer (hyphen)

glut/en *not* -in; *but* **-inize, -inous**

glutton one excessively greedy (esp. for food); a voracious animal, *Gulo gulo*, called **wolverine** in N. Amer.

glycerine *not* -in (US)

Glyn Dŵr *see* **Glendower**

GM genetically modified, George Medal, Grand Master

gm. gram, *use* **g** (no point)

gm² *properly* **g/m²** grams per square metre, *use* **gsm**

G-man (US colloq.) a special agent of the FBI

GmbH (Ger.) *Gesellschaft mit beschränkter Haftung* (limited liability company)

GMC General Medical Council

Gmelin, Leopold (1788–1853) German chemist

GMT Greenwich Mean Time

GMWU General and Municipal Workers' Union

gn. guinea

gnamma (Austral.) a waterhole; *not* n-

GNC General Nursing Council

gneiss (geol.) a laminated rock (not ital.)

gnocchi small dumplings (not ital.)

gnos/is the knowledge of spiritual mysteries, pl. **-es**; **-tic** having spiritual knowledge

Gnosticism an eclectic philosophy of the redemption of the spirit from matter through knowledge; cap. when referring to the ancient world, but lower case for more modern systems

GNP gross national product

Gnr. (mil.) gunner

gns. guineas

gnu/ antelope, pl. **-s**

GO general order, great (*or* grand) organ

goalkeeper (one word)

goal/ kick, — line (two words)

goal/mouth, -post, -tender (one word)

goatee a chin-tuft like a goat's beard

goat/herd (one word)

goat's-beard a plant or fungus (hyphen)

goat/skin, -sucker (bird) (one word)

goaty goatlike

gobbledegook pompous jargon, *not* -dyg- (US)

Gobbo/, Launcelot a character in Shakespeare's *The Merchant of Venice*; **Old —** his father

Gobelin tapestry *not* -ins

gobemouche/ a credulous person, pl. **-s**; (Fr. m. sing. and pl.) *gobe-mouches*

Gobi a desert in Mongolia and E. Turkistan

gobsmack/, -ed, -ing (one word)

goby a fish (not ital.)

GOC General Officer Commanding

go-cart *use* **-kart**

God cap. when referring to the monotheistic deity, but lower case for pronouns referring to him; lower case for the gods of polytheistic religions and for the idiom 'make a god of something'

God-awful (hyphen, cap.)

god/child, -dam (one word)

god-daughter (hyphen, one word in US)

goddess (not cap.)

godfather (one word)

godhead divine nature, *but* **the Godhead** (cap.)

godless (one word)

Godley, Arthur *see* **Kilbracken**

godlike (one word)

god/mother, -parent (one word)

God's acre a burial ground (apos., one cap.)

god/send, -sent -son (one word)

Godspeed (one word, cap.)

Godthåb *use* **Nuuk**

Goebbels, Joseph (**Paul**) (1897–1945) German minister of propaganda 1933–45, *not* Gö-

Goehr,/ Alexander (b. 1932) German-born composer; — **Walter** (1903–60) his father, German conductor

Goering, Hermann (1893–1946) German field marshal, *not* Gö- (except in Ger.)

Goeth/e, Johann Wolfgang von (1749–1832) German poet and playwright; *not* Gö-, Got-; **-ean**

Goetheaner (Ger. m.) a follower of Goethe

gofer (US sl.) a person who runs errands, a dogsbody; cf. **goffer, gopher**

goffer to crimp, emboss; *not* gau-; animal, wood, *use* **goph-**

Goffs Oak Herts. (no apos.)

Gogh, Vincent (**Willem**) **Van** (1853–90) Dutch painter; in Eng. sometimes alphabetized under 'Van'

Gogmagog (Br. myth.) a giant, named **Göemot** by Spenser in the *Faerie Queene*

goi *use* **goy**

Goidel a member of Goidelic peoples (Irish, Highland Scottish, Manx), a Gael; *not* Gadhel; *Gaidheal* in Sc. Gaelic

goitre *not* -er (US)

go-kart a miniature racing car, *not* -cart (hyphen)

Golconda a rich source of wealth (from a ruined city near Hyderabad)

gold symbol **Au**

gold-digger (hyphen, two words in US)

gold dust (two words)

Golders Green NW London (no apos.)

goldfield (one word)

gold leaf (two words, hyphen when attrib.)

gold mine (two words)

Goldsmiths College University of London (no apos.)

golf/ bag, — ball, — cart (two words)

golf/ club the implement, the premises, or the association, — **course**, — **links**, — **match**, — **player** (two words)

Goliath a Philistine giant, a type of crane; *not* -iah

Gollancz,/ Sir Israel (1864–1930) English writer, — **Sir Victor** (1893–1967) British publisher and writer

golliwog *not* golly-

golosh *use* **gal-**

GOM Grand Old Man (esp. W. E. Gladstone)

Gomorr/ah (OT); **-ha** (AV NT) *but* **-ah** in NEB

Goncharov, Ivan (**Aleksandrovich**) (1812–91) Russian novelist

Goncourt/, Edmond Louis Antoine (1822–96) and his brother —, **Jules Alfred Huot** (1830–70) French novelists; **Prix —** (named after Edmond)

gondola/ pl. **-s** (not ital.)

Gonds a people of Cent. India, *not* Gh-

Gongo a tributary of the Zaïre

Góngora y Argote, Luis de (1561–1627) Spanish poet

gongorism a Spanish form of euphuism

gonorrhoea *not* -hea (US)

Gonville and Caius College Cambridge, *see also* **Caius**

good afternoon (salutation) (two words)

goodbye (one word), *not* -by

good/ day, — evening (salutations) (two words)

Good Friday (caps., two words)

good humour (two words), **good-humoured** (hyphen)

good morning (salutation) (two words)

Good-Natur'd Man, The a comedy by Goldsmith, 1768

good nature (two words), **good-natured** (hyphen)

goodnight (salutation) (one word)

good-quality (adj.)

Good/ Samaritan, — Templar (caps.)

goodwill of a business etc. (one word)

Goorkhas *use* **Gur-**

gooroo *use* **guru**

goose pl. **geese**, (in tailoring) **gooses**

gooseberry (one word)

goose/ bumps (US) = **gooseflesh**, — **egg** (US) a zero score in a game

gooseflesh (one word)

goose pimples (two words)

goose/-skin, -step (hyphens)

goosey a diminutive of goose; *not* -sie, -sy

Goossens a 19th–20th-c. Anglo-Belgian family of musicians

GOP Grand Old Party (Republican Party in USA)

gopher a burrowing animal, a kind of wood; cf. **gofer**; **goffer**

Gorbachev, Mikhail (**Sergeevich**) (b. 1931) General Secretary of Communist Party of the USSR 1985–91, President of the Supreme Soviet of the USSR 1988–91, President of the USSR 1990–1

Gordian knot tied by Gordius, cut by Alexander the Great

Gordonstoun School Elgin, Grampian

Gordonstown Grampian

Gorgio/ the Gypsy name for a non-Gypsy, pl. **-s**

Gorgonzola a cheese (cap.)

Gorky Russia, *formerly*, and once again, **Nizhni Novgorod**

Gorky, Maxim pseud. of **Aleksei Maksimovich Peshkov** (1868–1936) Russian writer and playwright

gormand *use* **gour-**

gormandize eat greedily; *not* gour-, -ise

gors/e furze, **-y**

Gorsedd/ a meeting of Welsh bards and druids, pl. **-au**

Goschen, Viscount

Göschen, Georg Joachim (1752–1828) German publisher (accent), grandfather of the first **Viscount Goschen** (1831–1907) (no accent)

Goshen a land of plenty, name of several towns in the USA and Canada

go-slow (noun, hyphen)

gospel cap. only when referring to the record of Christ's life and teaching in the first four books of the NT, *or* the north side of the altar (*Gospel side*)

gospodin (Russ.) Lord, Mr; f. **gospozha**; Russian practice now is to use initials instead of the title; *see also* **grazhdanin**

Goss, Sir John (1800–80) English organist and composer

Gosse,/ Sir Edmund William (1849–1928) English writer; — **Philip Henry** (1810–88) his father, English naturalist

gossip/, -ed, -er, -ing, -y (one *p*)

Göteborg Sweden, in Ger. **Gothenburg**

Gotham/ a village proverbial for the folly of its inhabitants, sometimes applied to Newcastle; **wise men of** — i.e. fools; — **City** (US colloq.) New York City, **-ite** a New Yorker

Gothic architecture, writing, etc. (cap.); abbr. **Goth.**

Gothic (typ.) a loose name for (esp. bold) sans serif faces, *formerly* OE black-letter faces

gotten past part. of **get**; *use* **got** except in the common expression 'ill-gotten gain', and in US

Götterdämmerung (Twilight of the Gods) the last part of Wagner's *Ring des Nibelungen*, 1876

Göttingen University Germany

Gouda a Dutch cheese

gouge a concave chisel

goujons deep-fried strips of chicken or fish (not ital.)

gouk *use* **-wk**

gour an Indian ox, *use* **ga-**

gourmand/ a glutton; **-ise** indulgence in gluttony; *see also* **gormandize**

gourmet a connoisseur of good food

goût (Fr. m.) taste

Goutte d'or a white burgundy wine

gov. govern/or, -ment

Government meaning the State (cap.), abbr. **Govt.**

Governor General abbr. **Gov. Gen.**, **GG**

Gowers, Sir Ernest (1880–1966) English civil servant, author of *Plain Words*, reviser of Fowler's *Modern English Usage*

gowk a cuckoo, a fool; *not* -uk

goy/ (derog.) Jewish name for a Gentile, pl. **-im**

Goya (y Lucientes), Francisco José de (1746–1828) Spanish painter

GP general practitioner, Graduate in Pharmacy, Grand Prix, Gloria Patri (glory be to the Father)

Gp. Group

g.p. great primer

Gp/Capt (RAF) Group Captain (no points)

GPO (hist.) General Post Office, (US) Government Printing Office

GPS Global Positioning System

GPU the Soviet 'State political administration for struggle against espionage and counter-revolution' (1922–3); *see also* **KGB**

GR *Georgius*, or *Gulielmus, Rex* (King George, or William)

Gr. Grand, Greater, Grecian, Greece, Greek

gr. grain, -s; *for* gram *use* **g**; gross, grey

Graaff, Robert Jemison van de *see* **van de Graaff**

Graafian follicle in ovary

Graal *use* **-ail**

Grabar the classical Armenian language

graben (Geol.) a depression of the Earth's surface between faults, pl. same

Gracchus,/ Gaius Sempronius (153–121 BC) and his brother — **Tiberius Sempronius** (163–133 BC), the **Gracchi,** Roman reformers

grace note (mus.) (two words)

Gracián, Baltasar (1601–58) Spanish moralist

gradatim (Lat.) step by step

gradine a tier of low steps or seats, a ledge at the back of an altar; *not* -ine

gradus ad Parnassum (Lat.) step(s) to Parnassus, Lat. or Gr. poetical dictionary, any series of graded exercises; in short **gradus** (not ital.)

Graeae (Gr. myth.) three sisters who guarded the abode of the Gorgons

Graec/ism a Greek characteristic, *not* Grec- (US); **-ize, -o** (combining form), **-ophile**

Graf/ (Ger.) a count (equivalent to an earl), pl. **-en**, f. **Gräfin/**, pl. **-nen** (cap.; not ital. as part of title, no comma preceding)

graffit/o scribbling, usually on a wall; pl. **-i**; cf. **sgraffito**

Grahame, Kenneth (1859–1932) English author

Graian Alps France and Italy

Grail, the Holy *not* Graal, Graile

grain apothecaries', avoirdupois, or troy weight, all 0.0648 gram; abbr. **gr.**

Grainger, Percy (**Aldridge**) (1882–1961) Australian-born US composer

gram a unit of mass, abbr. **g**; in SI units 0.001 kg

gram. gramm/ar, -arian, -atical

gramaphone *use* **gramo-**

graminivorous feeding on grass, *not* gramen-

gramm/ar, -arian, -atical abbr. **gram.**

grammar school (two words)

gramme *use* **gram**

Grammont E. Flanders, Belgium

Gramont, Philibert, comte de (1621–1707) French courtier, adventurer, and soldier; *not* Gramm-

gramophone *not* grama-, grammo-

Gram's stain (bacteriology) (cap.)

Granada Spain, a British television network

granadilla *use* **gren-**

Gran Chaco, El a region in Bolivia, Paraguay, and Argentina

Grand abbr. **G., Gr.**

grandad *use* **-ddad**

grandam grandmother, old woman; *not* -dame

grand aunt (two words) *prefer* **great-aunt**

Grand Canyon Ariz.

grandchild (one word)

Grand Coulee Dam Wash.

granddad *not* grandad, grand-dad

granddaughter (one word)

Grand/ Duchess, — Duchy, — Duke (two words, both caps. if used as title) abbr. **GD**

grande dame (Fr.) a dignified lady

grande/ passion violent love affair, **— tenue** or **— toilette** full dress

grandeur (not ital.)

grandeur naturelle (Fr. f.) life-size

grandfather (one word)

Grand Guignol a sensational or horrific drama (not ital.)

grandiloquence pompous or inflated language, *not* -elo-

grand jury (not caps.)

grand mal a serious form of epilepsy (not ital.)

grand master a chess player of highest class

Grand Master (caps.) abbr. **GM**

grand-messe (Fr. f.) high mass (hyphen), before 1932 *grand' messe* (apos.)

Grand Monarque, le Louis XIV

grand monde, le (Fr.) the court and nobility

grandmother (one word)

grand/-nephew, -niece (hyphen)

Grand Old Party (US) the Republican Party, abbr. **GOP**

grandparent (one word)

Grand/ Prix an international motor-racing event, pl. **-s Prix** (not ital.); abbr. **GP**

Grand Rapids Mich.

grand siècle a classical or golden age, esp. the 17th c. in France

grand signior one of high rank (not cap.), the Sultan of Turkey (caps.); in Fr. *grand seigneur*, It. *gran signore*, Sp. *gran señor*

grandson (one word) abbr. **g.s.**

grand uncle (two words)

Grant Duff, Sir Mountstuart Elphinstone (1829–1906) Scottish politician (no hyphen)

granter one who grants

Granth the Sikh scriptures, *not* Grunth

grantor (law) one who makes a grant

gran turismo (It.) touring car

Granville-Barker, Harley (1877–1946) English playwright, producer, and actor

grapefruit pl. same

grapey *not* -py

graphology the study of character from handwriting, *not* graphio-

gras/ (Fr.) f. *-se*, fat; **— double** tripe; cf. *gros*

Grasmere Cumbria

Grass, Günter (**Wilhelm**) (b. 1927) German writer

Grasse dép. Alpes-Maritimes, France

grass/hopper, -land (one word)

gratia Dei (Lat.) by the grace of God

gratin *see* **au gratin**

gratis for nothing, free (not ital.)

Grattan, Henry (1746–1820) Irish statesman and orator

Gratz Pa.

Gratz Austria, *use* **Graz**

Grätz Czech Republic, *use* **Hradec Králové**

Grätz Poland, *use* **Grodzisk**

Graubünden a Swiss canton; in Fr. **Grisons**, in Romansh **Grisun**, in It. **Grigioni**

grauwacke *use* **grey-**

gravam/en the essence or most serious part of an argument, or a grievance; pl. **-ens**, *properly* **-ina**

grave (mus.) slow, solemn

grave accent (`)

gravel/, -led, -ling (one *l* in US)

Graves a Bordeaux wine

Graves' disease exophthalmic goitre (apos.)

grave/stone, -yard (one word)

gravitas (Lat.) solemn demeanour

gravure (typ.) the intaglio printing process (from photogravure)

gravy/ boat, — train (two words)

gray a colour, *use* **grey** (except in US)

gray a unit of absorbed radiation dose, abbr. **Gy** (no point); in SI units 1 J/kg

Gray,/ Asa (1810–88) US botanist, — **Louis Harold** (1905–65) English radiobiologist, — **Thomas** (1716–71) English poet; *see also* **Grey**

grayling a fish, *not* grey-

Gray's Inn London

graywacke *use* **grey-** (except in US)

Graz the capital of Styria, Austria, *not* Gratz

grazhdan/in (Russ.) citizen, f. **-ka**, pl. **-e**; formal term, often replaced by **tovarishch**

grazier one who pastures cattle, *not* -zer

GRCM Graduate of the Royal College of Music

greasy not -ey

great-aunt (hyphen)

Great Britain abbr. **GB**; *see also* **Britain**

Greater Manchester a metropolitan county

great gross 144 dozen, abbr. **g.gr.**

Great Lakes between USA and Canada: Superior, Huron, Michigan, Erie, Ontario

great/-nephew, -niece (hyphen)

Great Power (caps. only with hist. reference)

Greats the Oxford BA final examination for honours in Lit. Hum.

great-uncle (hyphen)

Grecian/ *use* **Greek** except as an adj. referring to architecture and facial outline, and as a noun for a boy in the top form at Christ's Hospital, or a Greek-speaking Jew of the Dispersion; also — **bend, — knot, — slippers**; abbr. **Gr.**

Grec/ism, -ize, -ophile *use* **Grae-** (except in US)

Greco, El (1541–1614) Spanish painter, born in Crete, real name **Domenico Theotocopuli** *or* **Kyriakos Theotokopoulos**

Greece abbr. **Gr.**

greegree *use* **gris-gris**

Greek abbr. **Gr., Gk.** (to avoid confusion with abbr. for 'German')

Greek calends, at the never, in Lat. *ad kalendas Graecas*

Greeley, Horace (1811–72) US journalist and politician

Greely, Adolphus Washington (1844–1935) US general and Arctic explorer

Green, John Richard (1837–83) English historian

Greenaway, Kate (1846–1901) English artist and illustrator of children's books

green/back (US) a note of legal tender, **-bottle** (one word)

Green Cloth (in full **Board of Green Cloth**) the Lord Steward's department of the Royal Household

Greene,/ Sir Conyngham (1854–1934) British diplomat, — **Graham** (1904–91) English novelist, — **Harry Plunket** (1865–1936) English singer, — **Nathanael** (1742–86) American Revolutionary War general, — **Robert** (1560–92) English dramatist and pamphleteer

green fee (golf) *not* **greens fee** (US)

green/gage, -grocer, -house (one word)

Greenland/ in Dan. **Grønland**, in Inuit **Kalaallit Nûnaat**; **-er, -ic**

Green Paper (UK) a consultative preliminary report of government proposals, for discussion (two caps.); cf. **Blue Book; White Paper**

green room a room off stage for actors

greensand/ a sandstone (not cap.), **Lower —** and **Upper —** two strata of the Cretaceous system (caps.)

green thumb (US) = **green fingers**

Greenwich Mean Time (caps.) abbr. **GMT**

greetings card *not* greeting (US)

gregale the Mediterranean NE wind; *not* -cale, grigale (not cap.)

grège a colour between beige and grey, *not* grei-

Gregorian/ calendar, — chant, — telescope (one cap.)

Greifswald university town, Germany

Grenada W. Indies

grenadilla a passion fruit, *not* gran- (not ital.)

grenadine a syrup made from pomegranates or currants; a loosely woven silk fabric; (cook.) a dish of veal or poultry fillets, (Fr. m.) *grenadin*

Grenadines, The chain of islands between Grenada and St Vincent, W. Indies

Gresham/'s Law 'bad money drives out good', from **Sir Thomas —** (1519–79) English financier

Grétry, André Ernest Modeste (1741–1813) French composer

Greuze, Jean Baptiste (1725–1805) French painter

Grévy, François Paul Jules (1807–91) French President 1879–87

grey colour, *not* gray (US)

Grey, Lady Jane (1537–54) proclaimed Queen of England 1553, deposed, beheaded; *see also* **Fallodon; Gray**

greybeard an old man, large jug, clematis (one word)

Greyfriars College Oxford

greyhen a female black grouse

greyhound/ (one word), — **racing** (two words)

greyling *use* **gray-**

grey matter (two words)

greywacke (geol.) a sedimentary rock; *not* grau-, gray- (US) (not ital.)

Grieg, Edvard (*not* Edward) **Hagerup** (1843–1907) Norwegian composer

Grieve *see* **MacDiarmid**

grievous *not* -ious

griffin a fabulous creature; *not* -on, gryphon

griffon a vulture, a breed of dog

grigale *use* **gre-**

Grigioni It. for **Graubünden**

grill cook under or on a grill etc.

grille a grating, a latticed screen, *not* -ill (except in US) (not ital.)

grill/é f. **-ée** (Fr. cook.) broiled, grilled

Grimm,/ Jakob (1785–1863) and his brother — **Wilhelm** (1786–1859) German philologists, collectors of fairy tales

Grimm's Law deals with consonantal changes in Germanic languages

Grimsetter Airport Orkney

grimy begrimed, *not* -ey

Grindelwald Switzerland, *not* Grindle-

grindstone (one word)

gringo/ a foreigner, esp. a Brit. or N. Amer. in a Sp.-speaking country (derog.); pl. **-s** (not ital.)

Griqua/ a child of Cape Dutch and Khoikhoi parents, **-land**, S. Africa (one word)

grisaille a method of decorative painting (not ital.)

Griselda a patient wife (after Boccaccio and Chaucer), in Sc. **Grizel**

grisette a working-class French girl

gris-gris/ an African *or* voodoo charm or fetish, **— bag, — maker, — man** (hyphen, two words); *not* greegree, gri-gri

grisly terrible, *not* grizz-

Gris-Nez, Cap dép. Pas-de-Calais, France (hyphen)

Grisons Fr. for **Graubünden**, in Romansh **Grisun**

grissini (pl.) long sticks of crispbread

gristly having or like gristle, *not* -ey

Grizel Sc. form of **Griselda**

grizzly/ grey-haired, **— bear** (two words)

gro. gross

groat (hist.) a silver coin worth four old pence, a small sum ('don't care a groat')

groats hulled or crushed grain, esp. oats

Grodzisk Poland, *not* Grätz

groin the fold between belly and thigh, (archit.) line of intersection of two vaults; cf. **groyne**

grommet not gru-

Gromyko, Andrei (**Andreevich**) (1909–89) Soviet Foreign Minister 1957–85, President of the Supreme Soviet 1985–8

Gropius, Walter (1883–1969) German architect

gros/ (Fr.) f. **-se** big; cf. **gras**

grosbeak (ornith.) the hawfinch

Groschen (Ger. m.) an Austrian and old German small coin, pl. same

grosgrain a corded silk fabric

gros point (Fr. m.) cross-stitch embroidery on canvas

gross (144) is sing. and pl., abbr. **gro.**

Grosse Point Mich.

Grosseteste, Robert (1175–1253) Bishop of Lincoln

grosso modo (It.) approximately

Grote, George (1794–1871) English historian of Greece

grotesque (typ.) a 19th-c. sans-serif typeface, abbr. **grot.**

grotesquerie *not* -ery (not ital.)

Grotius, Hugo (1583–1645) Dutch jurist and statesman (Latinized form of De Groot)

grotto/ pl. **-es**

ground/ floor, — level (two words, hyphen as adj.)

ground/ plan, — rent (two words)

ground/sheet, -sman, -water, -work (one word)

Group of/ (econ.) various combinations of industrial nations that meet to consider economic and trade concerns; **— — Three** (abbr. **G3**); **— — Five** (abbr. **G5**); **— — Seven** (abbr. **G7**); **— — Ten** (abbr. **G10**)

grovel/, -led, -ler, -ling (one *l* in US)

grove of Academe (one cap., not pl.) from Milton's *Paradise Regained*, refers specifically to Plato's Academy; *see also* **Academe**

Grove's Dictionary of Music and Musicians the current edn. is ***The New Grove Dictionary of Music and Musicians***, usually abbr. ***New Grove***

grown-up (adj. and noun) (hyphen)

groyn/e a breakwater, *not* -in (US); **-ing**; cf. **groin**

GRSM Graduate of the Royal Schools of Music (the Royal Academy and the Royal College)

GRT gross registered tonnage

Grub Street haunt of literary hacks and impoverished authors, later Milton Street, now demolished

gruelling (one *l* in US)

Gruffydd *see* **Glendower**

grummet *use* **gro-**

Grundy, Mrs in Thomas Morton's *Speed the Plough*, 1798, an embodiment of conventional propriety

Grunth the Sikh scriptures, *use* **Gra-**

Gruyère a cheese (cap., not ital.)

Gruyères Switzerland

Gryphius, Sébastien (1491–1556) German-born French printer, *not* Gryptinus

gryphon *use* **griffin**

grysbok (Afrik.) an antelope, *not* -buck

GS General Secretary, General Service, (mil.) General Staff, Grammar School

gs (hist.) guineas

g.s. grandson

G7 Group of Seven

GSM Guildhall School of Music

gsm grams per square metre, metric method for measuring weight of paper and card (no points)

GSO General Staff Officer

GSP (naval) Good Service Pension

G/-string the garment, a string for a violin etc.; **-suit** (hyphens)

GT Good Templar, *gran turismo*

gt. gilt, great, gutta

g.t. (bind.) gilt top

G10 Group of Ten

gtt. guttae

gu. gules

guacho *use* **gau-**

Guadalajara Mexico, Spain

Guadalupe/ Spain; — **Hidalgo** Mexico, *formerly* **Gustavo A. Madero**; — **Mountains** Texas and New Mexico

Guadeloupe W. Indies

guage *use* **gau-**

guaiacum (bot.) a tropical American tree, the resin obtained from it; *not* guaiac

Guaira, La Venezuela, *not* Guay-

Guam Marianas Islands; *not* Guaham, Guajam

guana a lizard, shortened from **iguana**

Guangdong (Pinyin) a Chinese province, *also* **Kwantung**

Guangzhou (Pinyin) a Chinese province, *not* Canton

guano fertilizer from seabirds' excrement

Guarani a member of a S. American Indian people, their language (cap.)

guarani the monetary unit of Paraguay (not cap.), symbol **G** *or* **₲**

guardhouse (one word)

Guardia Civil (Sp.) national guard (two caps.)

guard rail (two words)

guardroom (one word)

guards are *mounted*, **sentries** are *posted*

guard-ship (hyphen)

guardsman (one word)

Guareschi, Giovanni (1908–68) Italian novelist

Guarneri violin makers; *not* -nieri, -nerius

Guatemala Cent. America

Guayaquil Ecuador

Guayra *use* **La Guaira**

guazzo (It.) = **gouache**

Guedalla, Philip (1889–1944) British writer

Guelderland *use* **Geld-**

guelder rose *not* ge-

Guelf one of the Pope's faction in medieval Italian states, opposed to Ghibelline; *also* **Guelph**

Guenevere, Defence of by W. Morris, 1858; *see also* **Guinevere**

Guernica Spain, in Basque **Gernika**; subject of painting by Picasso, 1937

Guernsey a Channel Island, in Fr. **Guernesey**

guernsey a heavy knitted woollen pullover; the jersey worn by Australian footballers

guerre (Fr. f.) war

guerrilla/ a person or body engaged in — **warfare** irregular fighting by small bodies; *not* -eri-, gor-

Guesclin, Bertrand du (1314–80) Constable of France

guesstimate (colloq.) an estimate based on a mixture of guesswork and calculation, *not* guest-

guesswork (one word)

guest house (two words)

Gueux a league of Dutch rebels 1565–6

Guevara (de la Serna), Ernesto 'Che' (1928–67) leader of the Cuban revolution, *not* 'Ché'

Guggenheim/ Fellowship; — **Museum** (*formerly* **Solomon R. — Museum**) NYC

Guglielmo (It.) **William**

Gui, Vittorio (1885–1975) Italian conductor and composer

Guiana/, British *now* **Guyana**, — **Dutch** *now* **Suriname**

Guibelline *use* **Ghi-**

guide/book, -line, -post (one word)

Guides a girls' organization (cap.) (US) = **Girl Scouts**

Guido (It.) **Guy**

Guilbert, Yvette (1869–1944) French *diseuse*

guild an association, *not* gild

guilder a silver florin, the chief monetary unit of the Netherlands, abbr. **f**; in Du. **gulden**

Guildford Surrey, *not* Guilf-

Guildford: the signature of the Bishop of Guildford (colon)

guildhall *not* gi-; *but* **Guildhall**, London (*not* the —), York, and elsewhere (cap.)

Guilford, Earl of

Guili/a, -o It. names, *use* **Giu-**

Guillaume (Fr.) **William**

guillemets (typ.) quotation marks (« ») used in Fr., Ger., Russ., Sp., etc. (not ital.)

guillemot a seabird

Guillermo (Sp.) **William**

guilloche an architectural ornament (not ital.)

guillotine a beheading apparatus, a paper-cutting machine, a device for terminating parliamentary debates

guimp *use* **gi-**

Guinea/ W. Africa, adj. **-n**; — **Bissau** W. Africa; **New** — E. Indies; **Equatorial** — W. Cent. Africa

guinea/ (Brit. hist.) 21 shillings (21/-, £1.05), used esp. in determining professional fees; pl. **-s**; abbrs. **g.**, **gn.**, **gns.**, **gs.**

guinea fowl (two words)

guinea pig a small S. American rodent; the subject of an experiment (two words)

Guinevere the wife of King Arthur; *see also* ***Guenevere***

Guiranwala Pakistan

Guisborough Cleveland

Guiscard, Robert (11th c.) Norman leader

Guiseppe an Italian name, *use* **Giu-**

Gujarat/ an area in W. India, *not* Guze-; **-i** (of or relating to) (a native or the language of Gujarat

Gujrat Pakistan

Gulag (Russ. acronym) Chief Administration for Corrective Labour Camps, the Soviet network of these camps, or a camp or prison within it (cap., not ital.); originally transliterated as **GUlag**

gulden *see* **guilder**

gules (her.) red (usually placed after the noun), abbr. **gu.**

Gulf/ cap. when with name, as Gulf of Corinth, Persian Gulf; abbr. **G.**; — **Stream** (no hyphen)

Gulielmus (Lat.) William

gullible easily cheated, *not* -able

Gulliver's Travels a novel by Swift, 1726

gully a channel, *not* -ey

GUM a Moscow department store (caps.)

gum arabic (two words)

Gumbo a patois of blacks and Creoles spoken esp. in Louisiana (cap.)

gumbo/ okra, a kind of soup thickened with these; pl. **-s** (not cap.)

gum/boil, -boot, -shield (one word)

gum tree (two words)

gun. gunnery

gun/ barrel, — battle (two words)

gunboat (one word)

gun/ bore, — carriage, — dog (two words)

gun/fight, -fire (one word)

gung-ho enthusiastic, eager (hyphen)

Gungl, Josef (1810-89) Hungarian composer

gun/lock, -man, -metal (one word)

gunnel *use* **gunwale**

gunnery (naval) abbr. **G.**, **gun.**

gunny sacking

gun platform (two words)

gun/point, -powder, -room (one word)

gun-runner (hyphen)

gun/ship, -shot (one word)

gun-shy (hyphen)

gun/slinger, -smith, -stock (one word)

Gunter's chain a surveyor's chain, 66 ft long

Gunther a character in the *Nibelungenlied* (no umlaut)

gunwale *not* gunnel

gurdwara a Sikh temple

Gurkhas Nepali soldiers in Ind. or Brit. service; *not* Ghoor-, Ghur-, Goor-

gurkin *use* **gher-**

Gurmukhi the alphabet in which Punjabi is written

gurnard a fish, *not* -net

guru a religious teacher; *not* gooroo

Gutenberg (*or* **Gensfleisch**), **Johann** (*c.*1399-1468) German inventor (so generally assumed) of movable metal types

gutt/a a drop, abbr. **gt.**; pl. **-ae**, abbr. **gtt.**

gutta-percha a hard rubber-like substance (hyphen, not ital.)

gutter (typ.) the space between imposed pages of type allowing for two foredge margins; in a book, the inner space between two columns or pages

guttural connected with the throat

Guyan/a S. America, **-ese**; *not* Gui-

Guyot, Yves (1843-1928) French economist

Guy's Hospital London (apos.)

Guzerat India, *use* **Gujarat**

Gwalior India

Gwent a Welsh county

GWR Great Western Railway

Gwyn, Nell (1650-87) (born **Eleanor Gwynne**) English actress, mistress of Charles II; *not* -nne

Gwynedd a Welsh county

Gwynn, Stephen (1864-1950) English writer

Gy gray (no point)

gybe (naut.) change course, *not* ji- (US); cf. **gibe**

gym (colloq.) gymnasium (no point)

gymkhana an athletic display, a pony-club competition; *not* -kana (not ital.)

gymnasium/ pl. **-s** (not ital.), colloq. **gym**

gymnot/us the electric eel, pl. **-i** (not ital.)

gymp *use* **gi-**

gymslip (one word)

gynaeceum (Gr., Rom.) the women's apartments in a house

gynaecology the study of women's diseases, *not* gyne- (US); abbr. **gyn.**

gynoeci/um (bot.) the female organ of a flower, pl. **-a**

gypsum hydrated calcium sulphate

Gypsy a member of a nomadic people of Europe and N. America speaking Romany (cap.); *not* Gip-; a person resembling or living like this people (not cap.)

gyrfalcon a large falcon; *not* ger-, jer-

gyro money transfer, *use* **gi-**

gyro/ short for gyroscope, -compass, pl. **-s**

gyr/us a fold or convolution, esp. of the brain; pl. **-i**

gyttja (geol.) a lake deposit of a usually black organic sediment

Hh

H henry (unit of inductance), hydrogen, (pencils) hard (*see also* **HH, HHH**), (mus.) B natural in German system, the eighth in a series

H. harbour, hydrant

h hour, -s (in scientific and technical work), (as prefix) hecto-

h. hardness, height, husband, (meteor.) hail

H. (Ger.) *Heft* (number, part)

h Planck constant

ħ Planck constant divided by 2π, also called the Dirac constant, pronounced 'h bar'

HA Historical Association, Horse Artillery

Ha hahnium (no point)

ha. hectare(s) (no point)

h.a. *hoc anno* (in this year), *hujus anni* (this year's)

Haag, Den informal Du. for **The Hague**; cf. **'s-Gravenhage**

Haakon the name of seven Norwegian kings; in Old Norse **Hákon**, in Modern Norw. **Håkon**

haar a raw sea-mist (E. coast of England and Scotland)

Haarlem Netherlands; cf. **Harlem**

hab. habitat

Habakkuk (OT) abbr. **Hab.**

Habana, la Sp. for **Havana**

habeas corpus a writ to produce a person before court, abbr. **hab. corp.** (not ital.)

Habeas Corpus Act 1640 (amended 1679), 1816, 1862

habendum (law) part of deed defining estate or interest granted

Haberdashers' Aske's School Elstree

habet (Lat.) he is hit (lit. he has); *see also* **hoc habet**

habile skilful, able; *not* -ille (not ital.)

habitat the normal abode of an animal or plant (not ital.), abbr. **hab.**

habitu/é f. **-ée**, a frequenter (not ital.)

Habsburg, House of the Austrian Imperial family, *not* Hap-

HAC Honourable Artillery Company

háček a diacritic mark (ˇ) placed over letters to modify the sound in some Slavonic and Baltic languages

Hachette publishers

hachis (Fr. cook. m.) minced meat, hash

hachisch *use* **hashish**

hachure a line used in map hill-shading (usually in pl.)

hacienda (not ital.)

hackberry the bird cherry, *not* hag-

Hackluyt *use* Hak-

hackney/ (verb) make trite, **-ed**; (noun) a horse pl. **-s**; — **carriage** off. term for 'taxi'

hacksaw (one word)

hac lege (Lat.) on these terms

Hades (Gr. myth.) the abode or god of the dead (cap.)

Hadith a body of traditions relating to Muhammad, in Arab. *ḥadīt*

hadj/, -i *use* **haj**

Hadramaut S. Arabia, *not* Hadhra-

haecceity (philos.) the individual quality of a thing that makes it unique

Haeckel, Ernst Heinrich (1834–1919) German philosopher, *not* Hä-

haem/, -al, -atin, -atite *not* heme, hem/al, -atin, -atite (US)

haema-, haemo- prefix meaning blood, *not* hema-, hemo- (US)

haemorrh/age, -oids *not* hem- (US)

haere mai (Maori) welcome (not ital.)

Haffner a serenade and symphony by Mozart

hafiz a Muslim who knows the Koran by heart

Hāfiz (d. 1388) Persian poet, real name **Shams ud-din Muhammad**

hafnium symbol **Hf**

Hag. Haggai

hagberry *use* **hack-**

Haggad/ah a legend etc. used to illustrate a point of the Law in the Talmud; a book recited at the Seder; *not* Agadah, Hagada, -ah; **-ic**

Haggai (OT) abbr. **Hag.**

haggard wild-looking; an untamed hawk

haggis a Scottish dish; *not* -ess, -ies

Hagiographa last part of the Hebrew Scriptures (cap.)

hagio/grapher, -graphy, -latry, -logy (not cap.)

Hague, Cap de La NW France

Hague, The in Du. **'s-Gravenhage** *or* **Den Haag**, in Fr. **La Haye** (caps.) Amsterdam is the capital of the Netherlands; The Hague is its seat of government. The definite article in 'The Hague' is cap. in running text, unlike that in 'the Netherlands'

ha ha laughter (two words)

ha-ha a trench dug as a garden boundary; *not* aha, haw-haw (hyphen)

hahnium symbol **Ha**

Haidarabad *use* **Hyder-**

haik an outer covering for head and body worn by Arabs, *not* haick, -ek

haiku a Jap. verse form, pl. same; *not* hokku

Haile/ Selassie I (1892–1975) Emperor of Ethiopia 1930–74; *also* — **Sellassie**

Haileybury College Herts.

hail-fellow-well-met (adj.) friendly, often excessively (three hyphens)

hail/stone, -storm (one word)

Hainault London

Hainaut a province, Belgium

hair/bell, -brain *use* hare-

hairbreadth (adj. one word), *but* **hair's breadth** (noun, two words)

hair/brush, -cloth, -cut (one word)

hairdo/ a coiffure (one word), pl. **-s**

hairdress/er, -ing (one word)

hairdryer *not* -drier

hair/grip, -like, -line (one word)

hairlip *use* hare-

hair/net, -piece, -pin (one word)

hair's breadth *see* **hairbreadth**

hair shirt (two words, hyphen when attrib.)

hairslide (one word)

hair space (typ.) a very thin space, thinner than a thin space (hyphen); (US) = **thin space** (two words)

hair/-splitter, -splitting (hyphens, one word in US)

hair/spray, -spring, -style, -stylist (one word)

hair-trigger (hyphen, one word in US)

Haiti W. Indies, *not* Hay-; *formerly* the island of Hispaniola, *now* its western part

haj/ the Islamic pilgrimage to Mecca, **-i** a Muslim who has been to Mecca as a pilgrim (cap. used as a title); *not* hadj, -i, hajj, -i

Hakenkreuz (Ger. n.) the swastika

hakim (in Ind. and Muslim countries) a physician, in Arab. *ḥakīm*; also a judge, ruler, or governor, in Arab. *ḥākim*; *not* -keem

Hakluyt/, Richard (c.1552–1616) English historian and geographer, — **Society**; *not* Hack-

Hákon, Hákon *see* **Haakon**

Halach/a Jewish law and jurisprudence, based on the Talmud; **-ic**; *not* -kah

halal/ (verb) kill (an animal) as prescribed by Muslim law, (noun) the meat thus prepared; **-led, -ling**; in Arab. *ḥalāl*; *not* -llal

halberd/ (hist.) combined spear and battleaxe, *not* -ert; **-ier**

Halcyone (Gr. myth.) *use* **Al-**

Halevi, Judah (c.1085–1140) Spanish-Jewish philosopher and poet

Halévy,/ Élie (1870–1937) French historian; — **Jacques François Fromental Élie** (1799–1862) his great-uncle, French composer; — **Joseph** (1827–1917) French traveller; — **Ludovic** (1834–1908) father of Élie, French playwright and novelist

half a dozen etc. (no hyphens) *but* **half-dozen** (hyphen)

half-and-half (hyphens)

half an hour (no hyphens) *but* **half-hour** (hyphen)

half/-binding (bind.) when the spine and corners are bound in a different material from the sides (hyphen), **-bound** (hyphen)

half-breed (hyphen)

half-brother (hyphen, two words in US)

half/-caste, -cut, -deck, -hardy, -hearted (hyphens)

half/ hitch, — holiday (two words)

half/-hour, -hourly, -life, -light (hyphens)

half/ mast, — measures (two words)

half-moon (hyphen)

half nelson (two words, no caps.)

half note (esp. US mus.) = **minim**

half past, — pay (two words)

halfpenny (one word)

halfpennyworth (one word) colloq. **ha'p'orth**

half-price (hyphen)

half-sister (hyphen, two words in US)

half/-term, -timber, -timbered, -time (hyphens)

half-title (typ.) the short title printed on the leaf before the full title (hyphen, two words in US); *also called* **bastard title**

half-tone (typ.) reproduction in which tones are produced by varying sizes of dots, a black-and-white photograph; (esp. US mus.) = **semitone** (hyphen)

half/-track, -truth (hyphens)

halfway (one word)

half/wit (one word), **-witted** (hyphen)

half-year(ly) (occurring at) an interval of six months, biannual

Haliburton, Thomas Chandler (1796–1865) Canadian-born British writer, pseud. **Sam Slick**

haliotis a type of edible gastropod mollusc

halitosis bad breath

hallabaloo *use* **hulla-**

hallal *use* **halal**

Hallé/, Sir Charles (1819–95) German-born Mancunian pianist and conductor (born **Karl Halle**), founded — **Orchestra** 1857, — **Concerts**

Halle an der Saale Germany, abbr. **Halle a/S.**

hallelujah *see also* **alleluia**; 'Hallelujah Chorus' in Handel's *Messiah*

Halles, Les Paris, former central market

Halley, Edmond (1656–1742) English astronomer, *not* -und

halliard *use* **haly-**

Halliwell-Phillipps, James (**Orchard**) (1820–89) English Shakespearian scholar

hallo *use* **he-**

halloo/ (a cry) inciting dogs to the chase; **-ed, -s**

Hallow/e'en 31 Oct. (no apos. in US); **-mas** (one word) 1 Nov., All Saints' Day

Hallstatt (of or relating to) the early Iron Age in Europe, *not* -stadt

hall/ux the great toe, pl. **-uces**

halm a stalk or stem, *use* **haulm**

halo/ a ring of light round moon, head, etc.; **-ed, -es**

Hals, Frans (1582/3–1666) Dutch painter

halva a sweet confection of sesame flour and honey, *not* -ah

halves pl. of **half**

halyard (naut.) a rope for raising sail; *not* halli-, hauly-

hamadryad/ a wood nymph, a king cobra; pl. **-s**

hamadryas a large Arabian baboon, pl. same

hamba (S. Afr.) go away, be off (not ital.)

Hambleden/ Bucks., **Viscount —**

Hambledon Hants., Surrey

Hambleton Lancs., Leics., N. Yorks.

Hambros Bank, Ltd (no apos.)

Hamburg/ Germany; a fowl, a grape (not cap.), **-er** (not cap.)

'Hamelin, The Pied Piper of' a poem by R. Browning, 1842

ham/-fisted, -handed (hyphens)

Hamit/es a group of peoples in Egypt and N. Africa, by tradition descended from Noah's son Ham; **-ic** (of or relating to) a group of African languages

hammam a Turkish bath; *not* hummum, -aum

Hammarskjöld, Dag (**Hjalmar Agne Carl**) (1905–61) Swedish statesman, Secretary-General of the UN 1953–61

hammer/beam, -head (one word)

Hammergafferstein, Hans pseud. of **Henry W. Longfellow**

Hammerklavier (Ger.) former name of the pianoforte, as opposed to harpsichord; Beethoven labelled Op. 101 and Op. 106 'für das Hammerklavier'; Op. 106 is popularly known as the *Hammerklavier* Sonata

Hammerstein II, Oscar (1895–1960) US lyricist and playwright

Hammett, (Samuel) Dashiell (1894–1961) US writer of detective novels

Hampden, John (1594–1643) English patriot and statesman

Hampshire abbr. **Hants.**

Hampton Court London

hamsin *use* **kham-**

ham/string past and past part. are correctly **-stringed**, but **-strung** is favoured by usage

Hamtramck Mich.

hamza (Arab.) a glottal-stop mark ('), typographically largely equivalent to the Gr. lenis or Heb. *alef* (ital.)

hand/bag, -bell, -bill, -book, -brake (one word)

Hand/buch (Ger. n.) a handbook (cap.), pl. **-bücher**

hand/clap, -cuffs (one word)

Handel, George Frederick (1685–1759) German composer resident in England, in Ger. **Georg Friedrich Händel**; *see also* **Handl**

Handels/blatt (Ger. n.) trade journal (cap.), pl. **-blätter**

handful/ *not* -ll, pl. **-s**

hand grenade (two words)

hand/grip, -gun, -hold (one word)

handicap/, **-per, -ping**

handiwork *not* handy-

handkerchief/ pl. **-s**, abbr. **hdkf.**

Handl, Jacob (1550–91) Slovenian composer, *not* Hä-; also known as **Gallus**; *see also* **Handel**

hand/list, -made, -maid(**en**) (one word)

handout (noun, one word)

hand-pick/ (verb, hyphen), **-ed** (adj., one word in US)

handrail (one word)

Handschrift/ (Ger. f.) MS, abbr. **Hs.**; pl. **-en**, abbr. **Hss.** (caps.); printer's copy is usually **Manuskript** (Ger. n.)

handsel/, **-led, -ling** (one *l* in US); *not* hans-

handset a combined mouthpiece and earpiece (one word)

hand-setting (typ.) manual composition (hyphen)

hand/shake, -spike, -spring, -stand, -writing (one word)

handyman (one word)

handywork *use* **handi-**

hangar/ a large shed (cf. **hanger**), **-age**

hangdog shamefaced (one word)

hanged past tense or past part., used of capital punishment; other senses *use* **hung**

hanger one who, *or* that which, hangs; a sword, a wood; cf. **hangar**

hang-glid/e, -er, -ing (hyphen, two words in US)

hanging/ **paragraph** *or* **— indent** (typ.) set with second and following lines indented under first line

hangnail *not* agnail

Hang Seng/ Bank, — — index Hong Kong

hang-up (noun, hyphen)

hanky-panky (hyphen)

Hanover/ in Ger. **Hannover, -ian** of or relating to the British sovereigns from George I to Victoria (1714–1901)

Hans/ (Du., Ger.) Jack, **— Niemand** 'Mr Nobody'

Hansa a medieval guild of merchants, the entrance fee to a guild; *not* -se

Hansard the verbatim record of debates in Parliament (not ital.)

Hanseatic League a medieval political and commercial league of Germanic towns

hansel *use* **hand-**

hansom a two-wheeled horse-drawn cab

Hants. Hampshire, *not* Hants

Hanukkah the Jewish festival of lights; *see also* **Chanukkah**

hanuman/ an Indian langur; (cap.) (Hindu myth.) the monkey-god; pl. **-s** *not* -men

hapax legomenon/on a word found once only (not ital.) pl. **-a**

haphazard (one word)

ha'p'orth (colloq.) a halfpennyworth

happi a loose Japanese coat

happy-go-lucky (hyphens)

happy hunting ground (no hyphen)

Hapsburg *use* **Hab-**

hara-kiri (Jap.) ritual suicide by disembowelment with a sword; *not* hari-, -kari, hurry-curry; the more refined term is **seppuku**

haram a Muslim sacred place, forbidden to non-Muslims; *not* -em

harangu/e address like an orator, **-ed**

Harare the capital of Zimbabwe

harass *not* harr-

harbour/, -age abbr. **H., har.**; *not* -or, -orage (US)

Harcourt Brace Jovanovich publishers (no commas)

hard (pencils) abbr. **H**

hard/-a-lee, -a-port, -a-starboard, -a-weather (two hyphens each)

hardback (of) a book bound in stiff covers

hard/ball, -bitten, -board (one word)

hard-boiled (hyphen)

hard copy (comput.) printed material produced by computer (two words); cf. **soft copy**

Hardecanute accepted var. of **Harthacnut** (1019–42) King of Denmark and England

hard hat (two words)

hard hit severely affected (hyphen when attrib.)

Hardie, James Keir (1856–1915) British socialist

hardi/hood, -ness *not* hardy-

Harding, Baron, of Petherton

Hardinge/, Viscount; Baron — of Penshurst

hard/line unyielding, **-liner** a person who adheres rigidly to policy (one word)

hardness (mineralogy) abbr. **h.**

hard rock (two words)

hards coarse flax, *not* hur-

hardshell (attrib. one word)

hard shoulder on motorway (two words)

hard sign (typ.) a double prime (″), used in e.g. transliterated Russ.; cf. **soft sign**

Hardt Mountains Bavarian Palatinate; cf. **Harz**

Hardwicke, Earl of

hard-wired (hyphen)

hardwood (one word) *but* **hard-wooded**

hard-working (hyphen)

harebell (bot.) *not* hair- (one word)

hare-brain/, -ed *not* hair- (hyphens)

hare-duck (philos.) in Wittgenstein's illustration of ambivalent diagrams; *not* rabbit-duck, duck-rabbit (hyphen)

Harefoot the sobriquet of Harold I

Hare/ Krishna (a member of) a sect devoted to the worship of the Hindu deity Krishna, pl. **— Krishnas**

harelip *not* hair- (one word)

harem the women of a Muslim household living in a separate part of the house; their quarters; *not* -am, -eem, -im (not ital.)

harem-scarem *use* **harum-scarum**

Hargreaves, James (1720–78) English weaver, inventor of the spinning jenny

haricot a variety of French bean

haricot/ de mouton Irish stew, **-s blancs** haricot beans, **-s d'Espagne** scarlet runners, **-s rouges** kidney beans, **-s verts** French beans

haridan *use* **harr-**

harier *use* **harr-**

Harijan a member of the caste of untouchables in India (cap.)

hari-kari *use* **hara-kiri**

harim *use* **-em**

Haringey Greater London borough, 1965; *not* -ay; *see also* **Harringay**

Harington, Sir John (1561–1612) English poet and pamphleteer; *see also* **Harri-**

hark/ (arch.) listen attentively, **-en** *use* **hearken**

harl a fibre, *not* -le

Harlech Gwynedd, *not* -ck

Harleian of Harley or his manuscript collection

Harlem New York; cf. **Haarlem**

Harlequin/ a character in pantomime and in It. *commedia dell'arte* (cap.); **-ade** (not cap.); **— duck** an Icelandic duck (not cap.)

Harlesden London

Harleston Devon, Norfolk, Suffolk

Harlestone Northants.

Harley,/ Robert (1661–1724) first Earl of Oxford, statesman and bibliophile; **— Edward** (1689–1741), his son, the second Earl

Harlow (1911–37) US film actress

harmattan a parching dusty land-wind of the W. African coast; in Fanti or Twi *haramata*

Harmen *see* **Arminius**

harmonize *not* -ise

HarperCollins publishers (one word)

Harper's Bazaar a US fashion magazine, founded 1867; Brit. version, founded 1929, *now* *Harpers & Queen* (*H&Q*)

Harpers Ferry W. Va. (no apos.)

Harper's Magazine a US magazine, founded 1850

harquebus/ (hist.) an early type of portable gun; *not* -ss, arque-; **-ier**

Harraden, Beatrice (1864–1936) English writer

harrass *use* **har-**

harridan a haggard old woman, *not* hari-

harrier a hound for hunting hares, a hawk; (cap. as pl.) group of cross-country runners; *not* har-

Harringay N. London; *see also* **Haringey**

Harrington, Earl of, *see also* **Hari-**

Harris Manchester College Oxford, *formerly* Manchester College

Harris tweed a kind of tweed woven by hand in Harris in the Outer Hebrides

Harrogate N. Yorks., *not* Harrow-

Harrovian a member of Harrow School

harrumph clear the throat or make a similar sound, esp. ostentatiously

Hart, Horace (1840–1916) Printer to the University of Oxford 1883–1916

hartal the closing of Indian shops or offices as a mark of protest or sorrow

Harte, (Francis) Bret (1836–1902) US novelist and story-writer

hartebeest a large African antelope, *not* hartb-; in Afrik. *hartebees*

Hartford Conn.

Harthacnut a more correct form of the commonly spelt **Hardecanute**; **Hǫrðaknútr** the technically correct Old Norse form

Hartlepool Cleveland

hartshorn (one word)

Hart's Rules for Compositors and Readers at the University Press, Oxford 1st (pub.) edn. 1904, 39th edn. 1983

Hartz Mountains *use* **Harz**; cf. **Hardt**

harum-scarum reckless (hyphen), *not* harem-scarem

Harun-al-Rashid (763–809) Caliph of Baghdad, hero of the *Arabian Nights*; (two hyphens) *not* -oun, -ar-, -sch-

harusp/ex a Roman religious official who interpreted omens from the inspection of animals' entrails, pl. **-ices**

Harvard references an author–date system of referencing sources

Harvard University at Cambridge, Mass.; abbr. **Harv.** or **HU**

harvestman *see* **daddy-long-legs**

Harv/ey, William (1578–1657) English physician, discovered blood circulation; **-eian** *not* -eyan

Harz Mountains Cent. Germany, *not* Hartz; cf. **Hardt**

has-been/ a person or thing that is no longer of importance or use, pl. **-s** (hyphen)

Hašek, Jaroslav (1883–1923) Czech novelist and satirist

Hashemites an Arab princely family

hashish hemp smoked or chewed as a drug; *not* hach-, hasch-, -eesh, -isch

Hasid/ a member of any of several mystical Jewish sects; adj. **-ic**, pl. **-im**; *not* Hass-, Ch-

Haslemere Surrey; *see also* **Haz-**

Hasse, Johann Adolph (1699–1783) German composer

Hassler, Hans Leo (1564–1612) German composer

hatable *not* -eable

hat/band, -box (one word)

hatch/back, -way (one word)

hatha yoga a system of exercises in yoga

hatpin (one word)

Hatshepsut (*c*.1500 BC) Queen of Egypt

hatt short form of *hattı humayun* or *hattı şerif* a Turkish edict made irrevocable by a Sultan's mark

hat-trick (hyphen)

hauberk (hist.) a coat of mail

hauler one who or that which hauls

haulier (Brit.) a firm or person engaged in road transport, a miner who moves coal

haulm (bot.) a stalk or stem, *not* halm

haulyard *use* **hal-**

Hauptmann,/ Gerhart (1862–1946) German poet and dramatist, — **Moritz** (1792–1868) German composer

Hausa (of or relating to) (a member of) a people of W. Africa and the Sudan, or the language of this people, widely used in W. Africa as a lingua franca; pl. same; *not* -ssa, Housa

hausfrau/ housewife (not cap.); in Ger. f. *Hausfrau/* pl. **-en**

Haussmann, Georges Eugène, baron (1809–91) Paris architect

haussmannize open out and rebuild

haut/bois, -boy (hist. mus.) *use* **oboe** in an orchestral or chamber context

haute bourgeoisie (Fr. f.) upper middle class

haute/ couture high fashion; — **cuisine** cooking of a high standard (not ital.)

haute école advanced horsemanship

Haute/-Garonne a dép. of SW France, **-Loire** a dép. of Cent. France, **-Marne** a dép. of E. France (hyphens)

Hautes-Alpes a dép. of SE France (hyphen)

Haute/-Saône a dép. of E. France (hyphen)

Haute-Savoie a dép. of SE France (hyphen)

Hautes-Pyrénées a dép. of SW France (hyphen)

hauteur haughty demeanour (not ital.)

Haute-Vienne a dép. of Cent. France (hyphen); cf. **Vienne**

haute volée (Fr. f.) the upper ten

haut-goût (Fr. m.) high flavour

haut monde (Fr. m.) fashionable society

Haut-Rhin a dép. of E. France (hyphen)

Hauts-de-Seine a dép. of N. France (two hyphens)

Haüy, René Just (1743–1822) French mineralogist and crystallographer

Havana Cuba; *not* -ah, -annah; in Sp. **la Habana**

Havas a French news agency

Havel, Václav (b. 1936) Czech playwright and politician, President of Czechoslovakia 1990–3, President of Czech Republic 1993-

haver (Sc.) talk nonsense (*not* vacillate)

Haverfordwest Dyfed

Havergal, Frances Ridley (1836–79) English hymn-writer

Havering-atte-Bower Essex

haversack a bag for carrying food, *not* -sac

havoc/ (noun); as verb, **-ked, -king**

Havre France, use **Le Havre** (always cap. *L* in Eng., lower case in Fr.)

Hawaii/ one or all of the Hawaiian Islands, or the US state comprising most of them, *properly* **Hawai'i**; off. and postal abbr. **HI**; adj. **-an**

haw-haw *use* ha-ha

Haw-Haw, Lord nickname of William Joyce, American-born German propagandist in the Second World War, executed 1946

hawk-eyed (hyphen)

hawksbill a small turtle, *not* hawk's-bill

hawse/ (naut.) part of ship's bows; **-hole, -pipe** (hyphens)

Hawthorne,/ Julian (1846–1934) US writer; — **Nathaniel** (1804–64) his father, US novelist

hay/ a country dance, *not* hey (*but Shepherd's Hey*, by P. A. Grainger); **-box, cock** (one word)

Haydn,/ Franz Joseph (1732–1809) and his brother — **Johann Michael** (1737–1806) Austrian composers; — **Joseph** (d. 1856) compiled *Dictionary of Dates*

Haydon, Benjamin Robert (1786–1846) English painter

hay fever (two words)

hay/field, -maker, -rick, -seed, -stack -wire (one word)

hazel-hen (hyphen)

hazelnut (one word)

Hazlemere Bucks.; *see also* **Has-**

Hazlitt,/ William (1778–1830) English essayist, — **William Carew** (1834–1913) English bibliographer

hazy indistinct, *not* -ey

HB (pencils) hard black

Hb haemoglobin (no point)

HBM Her, *or* His, Britannic Majesty('s)

H-bomb hydrogen bomb (no point, hyphen)

HC habitual criminal, Heralds' College, High Church, Holy Communion, Home Counties, (Fr.) *hors concours* (not competing), House of Commons, House of Correction

h.c. *honoris causa*

HCF *or* **h.c.f.** (math.) highest common factor; **HCF** (Brit.) Honorary Chaplain to the Forces

hd. head

hdkf. handkerchief

H. Doc. (US) House of Representatives Document

hdqrs. headquarters

Hdt. Herodotus

HE His Eminence; His, *or* Her, Excellency; high explosive

He helium (no point)

head (typ.) the blank space at the top of a page; *see also* **margins**

headach/e (one word); **-y** *not* -ey

headband a band worn round head, (bind.) strengthening band of multicoloured silk etc. sewn or stuck to head (and sometimes tail) of back of book

headbang/er, -ing (one word)

head-butt (hyphen)

head/board, -count, -dress, -gear (one word)

headhunt/, -er, -ing

head/lamp, -land (one word)

Headlesscross N. Lanarkshire (one word)

headlight (one word)

headline *see* **running heads**

head/lock, -long, -man a chief (one word)

head/master, -mistress as general term (one word, no caps.); off. title at certain schools (two words, caps.), abbr. **HM**

headnote a summary at the head of a chapter or page, (mus.) a tone produced in the head register (one word)

head-on (hyphen)

head/phone(s), -piece (one word)

headquarters used as sing. of the place, pl. of the occupants (one word); abbr. **HQ, hdqrs.**

head/rest, -room, -sail, -scarf (one word)

head sea waves from forward direction (two words)

headship the position of chief (one word)

headsman an executioner (one word)

headstock the bearings in a machine (one word)

head/stone, -strong (one word)

head teacher (two words)

head voice the high register of the voice in speaking or singing (two words)

head/water, -way, -wind (one word)

headword (typ.) an emphasized word opening a paragraph or entry etc. (one word)

headwork (one word)

heal *see* **hele**

health/ centre, — certificate, — farm, — food (two words)

healthful *not* -ull

health/ officer, — service, — visitor (two words)

Heap *see* **Heep**

hear, hear! an exclamation of agreement; *not* here, here!

hearken *not* hark-

Hearn, Lafcadio (1850–1904) US author

heart/ache, -beat (one word)

heartbreak/, -er, -ing (one word)

heartbroken (one word)

heartburn pyrosis (one word)

heart-burn jealousy (hyphen)

heart/ disease, — failure (two words)

heartfelt (one word)

hearth/rug, -stone (one word)

heartland (one word)

heart/-rending, -searching (hyphens)

heartsease *or* **heart's-ease** a pansy

heart/sick, -sore, -strings (one word)

heart/-throb, -warming (hyphen)

heartwood (one word)

Heath Robinson (a contraption) having absurdly ingenious and impracticable machinery (no hyphen); (US) = **Rube Goldberg**

heatproof (one word)

heat-resistant (hyphen)

heat/stroke, -wave (one word)

heave ho! (two words)

Heaven cap. when equivalent to the Deity; lower case when a place

heaven/-born, -sent (hyphens)

Heaviside/, Oliver (1850–1925) British electrical engineer; **— layer** (in full **Heaviside–Kennelly layer** (en rule)) the E-layer, a stratum of the atmosphere that reflects radio waves; *not* Heavy-

heavy/-duty, -footed, -handed, -hearted (hyphens)

heavy/ metal, — water, — weather (two words)

heavyweight (one word)

Heb. Hebrew, -s; Epistle to the Hebrews (NT)

hebdomad/ a group of seven, a week; *not* -ade; **-al**

Hebraize make Hebrew; *not* -ise, -aicize

Hebrew abbr. **Heb.**

Hebrews (NT) abbr. **Heb.**

Hebridean *not* -ian

Hecat/e the Greek goddess of dark places, **-aean**

hecatomb a great public sacrifice, originally of 100 oxen

heckelphone (mus.) a bass oboe

Heckmondwike W. Yorks.

Hecla a mountain, Western Isles; *not* Hek-; cf. **Hekla**

hectare 10,000 sq. m.; abbr. **ha** (no point)

hecto- prefix meaning 100; abbr. **h**; **hectogram** (**hg**) *not* -gramme; **hectolitre** (**hl**) *not* -liter (US); **hectometre** (**hm**) *not* -meter (US)

Hedda Gabler a play by Ibsen, 1890

hedgehog/ adj. **-gy**

hedgerow (one word)

hedgrah *use* **hegira**

hee-haw (noun, verb) bray, *not* he-

heel *see* **hele**

Heep, Uriah a character in Dickens's *David Copperfield, not* Heap

Heer (Ger. n.) army (cap.)

Heft (Ger. n.) number, part; abbr. **H.**

Hegel/, Georg (*not* -e) **Wilhelm Friedrich** (1770–1831) German philosopher, **-ian**

hegemon/y leadership, esp. political; **-ic**

hegira a general exodus or departure; (cap.) denotes the flight of Muhammad from Mecca to Medina, 16 July AD 622, from which the Muslim era is reckoned; *not* hedgrah, heijira (not ital.), in Arab. *hijra*

Heidegger, Martin (1889–1976) German philosopher

Heidelberg a university town, Germany

Heidsieck a champagne

Heifetz, Jascha (1901–87) Russian-born US violinist

heighday *use* **hey-**

heigh-ho an audible sigh, *not* hey-

heijira *use* **heg-**

heil (Ger.) hail!

Heiland, der (Ger.) the Saviour (cap.)

heilig (Ger.) holy, abbr. **hl.**

Heilige Schrift (Ger. f.) Holy Scripture (caps.), abbr. **Hl. S.**

Heimskringla 'the round world', a history of Norse kings by Snorri Sturluson

Heimweh (Ger. n.) homesickness

Heine/, Heinrich (*but* signed **Henri** when in France) (1797–1856) German poet, **-sque**

Heinemann, William publishers

Heinrich Ger. for Henry

Heinz Ger. for Harry

heir apparent a legal heir, whoever may subsequently be born (two words); abbr. **heir app.**

heir presumptive the legal heir if no nearer relative should be born (two words), abbr. **heir pres.**

Heisenberg/, Werner Karl (1901–76) German physicist, discoverer of — **uncertainty principle**

Hejaz 'the boundary', *not* Hi-; *see also* **Saudi Arabia**

hejira *use* heg-

Hekla a volcano, Iceland, *not* Hec-; cf. **Hecla**

Hel (Norse myth.) originally, the abode of the dead; later, the abode of the damned, as opposed to Valhalla; later still, the goddess of the dead (in Ger. and Lat. **Hela**)

Hela a Polish holiday resort, in Polish **Hel**

HeLa a strain of human cells (one word, two caps.)

Heldentenor (Ger. m.) 'hero-tenor', with robust operatic voice

hele to set (plants) in the ground; *not* heal, heel

Helensburgh Strathclyde, *not* -borough

Helicon (Gr. myth.) a mountain range in Boeotia, home of the Muses, site of fountains Aganippe and Hippocrene

Heliogabalus *use* **Elag-**

heliport a landing pad for helicopters (one word)

helium symbol **He**

hel/ix a spiral curve like the thread of a screw, pl. **-ices**

hell (not cap.)

hell (Ger.) clear, bright

Helladic of or belonging to the Bronze Age culture of mainland Greece

hell-bent (hyphen)

hellcat (one word)

Helle (Gr. myth.) the sister of Phrixus, fell from the golden ram into the strait afterwards named **Hellespont** (the Dardanelles)

Hellen (Gr. myth.) the son of Deucalion and Pyrrha, progenitor of the Greek people

Hellen/e a (modern or ancient) Greek, pl. **-es**; **-ic** (cap.)

Hellenist one skilled in Greek; one who has adopted Greek ways, esp. a Jew of the Dispersion

Hellenistic denoting the Greek language and culture of the period after Alexander the Great

Hellenize make Greek, *not* -ise

Hellespont *now* **the Dardanelles**

hell/fire, -hole, -hound (one word)

hell-like (hyphen)

hello *not* ha-, hu-

helmet/, -ed (one *t*)

Helmholtz, Hermann Ludwig Ferdinand von (1821–94) German scientist

helmsman one who steers (one word)

Héloïse (1101–64) beloved of Peter Abelard; *not* El-, -sa, *but* Pope's poem is 'Eloisa to Abelard', 1717

helpline (one word)

helpmate *not* -meet (one word)

Helsingør (Dan.) **Elsinore**

Helsinki Finland, in Swed. **Helsingfors**

helter-skelter (hyphen)

Helvellyn a mountain, Cumbria

Helvetia/ (Lat.) Switzerland (used as a linguistically neutral term), **-n** a native of Switzerland

Hely-Hutchinson/ an Irish name, the family name of the Earl of Donoughmore (hyphen); —, **Victor** (1901–47) British composer

hema- prefix, *use* **haema-** (except in US)

Hemel Hempstead Herts. (two words)

hemidemisemiquaver (mus.) a sixty-fourth note; *not* semidemi-

Hemingway, Ernest (**Miller**) (1899–1961) US novelist and journalist

hemistich (prosody) half a line, *not* -itch

hemo- prefix, *use* **haemo-** (except in US)

hemstitch (one word)

hence/forth, -forward (one word)

hendiadys the expression of one idea by two words connected with *and*, instead of one modifying the other, e.g. 'nice and warm' for 'nicely warm'

henge a prehistoric monument consisting of a circle of massive stone or wood uprights

henna/ an oriental shrub, its leaves used for dyeing hair; **-ed**

henpeck/, -ed (one word)

Henri Fr. for Henry

Henry abbr. **Hy**

Henry, O. pseud. of **William Sydney Porter** (1862–1910) US short-story writer

henr/y the SI unit of inductance, pl. **-ies**; abbr. **H**

Henschel, Sir George (1850–1934), German-born English musician

Henslow, John Stevens (1796–1861) English botanist and geologist

Henslowe, Philip (d. *c*.1616) English theatrical manager

heortology the study of (Church) festivals

Hephaestus (myth.) *not* -aistos, except in Greek contexts

Hepplewhite/ an 18th-c. style of furniture, from **George** — (d. 1786); *not* Heppel-

Heptateuch the first seven books of the OT

her. heraldry

her. *heres* (heir)

Herakles *use* **Hercules**

heraldry abbr. **her.**

Heralds' College the College of Arms, abbr. **HC** (apos.)

Hérault a dép. of France

Herausgeber (Ger. m.) editor (of a text)

herbaceous *not* -ious

herbari/um a collection of dried plants, a book, room, or building for these; pl. **-a** (not ital.)

Herbart, Johann Friedrich (1776–1841) German philosopher and educationist

Hercegovina/ a region in the former Yugoslavia; **Bosnia-** — (hyphen); *not* Herz-

Herculaneum a Roman town overwhelmed by Vesuvius, AD 79; *not* -ium

Herculean strong, difficult

Hercules *not* -akles, except in Greek contexts

Hercynian (geol.) of a late Palaeozoic mountain-forming time in the E. hemisphere

herd book (two words)

here/about(s), -after, -by, (one word)

Hereford: the signature of the Bishop of Hereford (colon)

Hereford and Worcester a former county of England (1974–98)

here, here! *use* **hear, hear!**

herein/, -after, -before (one word)

here/of, -on, -out (one word)

here/s (Lat.) heir, pl. *-des*; abbr. *her.*

here/to, -tofore, -under, -unto, -upon (one word) formal and antiquated terms meaning 'to this matter', 'before this time', 'below', 'to this', and 'after (*or* 'in consequence of') this'; *prefer* the more familiar modern words

herewith (one word)

Hergesheimer, Joseph (1880–1954) US novelist

Heriot-Watt University Edinburgh

heritor (Sc. law) a person who inherits

heritrix an heiress; *not* -tress, here-

Her Majesty('s) (caps.) abbr. **HM**

hermeneutic/ concerning interpretation, esp. of Scripture or literary texts; **-s** the science of interpretation (treated as sing.)

hermetic *not* -ical

hernia/ a rupture, pl. **-s**

hero/ (**a** *not* an) pl. **-es; -ic**

Herodotus (*c*.484–*c*.420 BC) Greek historian; abbr. **Hdt., Herod.**

heroi-comic combining the heroic with the comic, in Fr. *héroï-comique*; *not* heroic-comic, -al

heroin a drug, *not* -ine

heroine a heroic woman, chief female character in story etc.

heroize make a hero of, *not* -ise

hero-worship/, -ped, -per, -ping (one *p* in US)

herpes a skin disease; *herpes zoster* shingles

herpetolog/y the study of reptiles, **-ist**; *not* er-

Herr/ (Ger. m.) Mr, Sir; pl. **-en**

Herr, der (Ger.) the Lord (cap.)

herr (Norw., Swed.) Mr, abbr. **hr.**

herre (Dan.) Mr, abbr. **hr.**

Herrenvolk (Ger. n.) master race, (in Nazi ideology) the German people

Herrgott (Ger.) Lord God

herringbone a stitch or pattern (one word)

Herrnhuter a member of a Christian Moravian sect (not ital., not -ü- even in Ger.)

Her Royal Highness (caps.) abbr. **HRH**

hers (no apos.)

Herschel,/ Caroline Lucretia (1750–1848) German-born English astronomer; — **Sir John Frederick William** (1792–1871) English astronomer, son of — **Sir William,** b. **Friedrich Wilhelm** (1738–1822) German-born English astronomer

Herschell, Baron

Herstmonceux E. Sussex, former site of the Royal Observatory; *not* Hurst-

hersute *use* hir-

Hertfordshire abbr. **Herts.**

Herts. Hertfordshire

Hertz/, Heinrich Rudolf (1857–94) German physicist, discoverer of **-ian waves**, used in radiocommunication

hertz an SI unit of frequency, pl. same; abbr. **Hz**

Hertzog, James Barry Munnik (1866–1942) S. African statesman, Prime Minister 1924–39; *not* Herzog

Herz (Ger. n.) heart (cap.)

Herzegovina *use* Herce-

Herzog/ (Ger. m.) duke, pl. *Herzöge;* *-in* (f.) duchess, pl. *-innen; -tum* (n.) duchy, *not* -thum (caps.)

Herzog, Werner (b. 1942) German film director, b. **Werner Stipetic**

Hesperian (poet.) western, (Gr. myth.) of or concerning the Hesperides

Hesperis a genus of plants

Hesperus the evening star, Venus

Hesse a German state, in Ger. **Hessen**; **Hessian** an inhabitant of Hesse, in Ger. **Hess/e**, f. **-in**

Hesse, Herman (1877–1962) German-born Swiss writer

hessian a strong coarse sacking

het (Du. n.) the; abbr. **'t**, as van 't Hoff

hetaer/a a courtesan or mistress of ancient Greece, pl. **-ae**; **-ism**; *not* -tair-, -tar-

heterogeneous dissimilar, *not* -nous

heteroousian (theol.) (a person) believing the Father and Son to be of unlike substance, *not* heterou-; cf. **homoiousian**; **homoousian**

het/man a Polish or Cossack military commander, pl. **-men**

Hetton-le-Hole Tyne & Wear (hyphens)

heu (Lat.) alas!

heureka *use* **eu-**

heuristic/ allowing or assisting to discover (an educational method), **-s** the science of heuristic procedure (treated as sing.); *see also* **eureka**

HEW US Department of Health, Education, and Welfare

hex (verb) practise witchcraft, bewitch; (noun) a magic spell, a witch

hex- Gr. prefix for six, in Lat. **sex-**

Hexateuch the first six books of the OT

hey *see* **hay**

heyday the flush or full bloom of youth, prosperity, etc. (one word); *not* heigh-

heyduck a Hungarian of an ennobled military class; in Hung. *hajdú*, pl. *hajdúk*

Heyerdahl, Thor (1914–2002) Norwegian ethnologist (*Kon-Tiki* expedition, 1947)

hey-ho *use* **heigh-**

hey presto a conjuror's exclamation (two words)

HF (pencils) hard firm, high frequency, Home Fleet, Home Forces

Hf hafnium (no point)

hf. half

h.f. high frequency

HFRA Honorary Fellow of the Royal Academy

HG His, *or* Her, Grace; High German, Home Guard, Horse Guards

Hg *hydrargyrum* (mercury) (no point)

hg hectogram, -s (no point)

HGV (Brit.) heavy goods vehicle

HH His, *or* Her, Highness; His Holiness (the Pope); (pencils) double-hard, *also* **2H**

hh. hands (measure of horse's height)

hhd. hogshead, -s

HHH (pencils) treble hard, *also* **3H**

HI Hawaii (official and postal abbr.), Hawaiian Islands, *hic iacet* (here lies)

hiatus/ pl. **-es** (not ital.)

Hiawatha the Native American hero of Longfellow's poem

hibernate (of some animals) spend the winter in a dormant state; *not* hy-

hic (Lat.) this, here

hiccup/ *not* -cough, -kup; **-ed, -ing** (one *p*)

hic et ubique (Lat.) here and everywhere

Hichens, Robert Smythe (1864–1950) English novelist

hic iacet/ (*or* **jacet**) (Lat.) here lies; — — **sepult/ us**, f. — — **-a** here lies buried; abbr. **HIS, HJS**

hidalgo/ a Spanish gentleman by birth, pl. **-s**

hide-and-seek a game (hyphens)

hideaway (noun)

hidebound narrow-minded (one word)

hieing *not* hy-

hier (Ger.) here, *hier spricht man deutsch* German spoken here

hieratic priestly; of the ancient Egyptian writing used by priests (cf. **demotic**); of Egyptian or Greek traditional styles of art

hieroglyph/ a stylized figure representing a word; **-ic(s)**, **-ist**, **-ize**, *not* -ise

hierogram a sacred inscription or symbol, *not* -graph

hierology sacred literature or lore

hierophant an interpreter of sacred mysteries or esoteric principles

hifalutin *use* **high-**

hi-fi high fidelity (no points), pl. **hi-fis**

higgledy-piggledy haphazard, in confusion

highball (one word)

highboy (US) a type of tallboy; cf. **lowboy**

highbrow (one word)

high chair (two words)

High Church abbr. **HC**; **High Churchman** (caps., two words)

high-class (adj., hyphen)

High Commission an embassy from one Commonwealth country to another

high dudgeon *see* **dudgeon**

highfalutin bombast(ic); *not* -en, -n', -ng, hifa-

high fidelity reproducing sound with little distortion; colloq. **hi-fi/** pl. **-s**

high/-flown, -flyer, -flying (hyphens)

high frequency (hyphen when attrib.)

high hat a top hat, (mus.) a pair of foot-operated cymbals (*also* **high-hat**)

highjacker *use* **hi-**

high jump (two words)

Highland a region of Scotland

highlight/, -er (one word)

high-minded (hyphen)

high pressure (hyphen when attrib.); abbr. **HP, h.p.**

high priest abbr. **HP** (two words)

high-rise (a building) having many storeys (hyphen)

high/-risk (adj., hyphen), **— road** (two words)

high school (Eng.) a grammar school, (US, Sc.) a secondary school

high seas, the outside territorial waters (two words)

high/ table, — tea, — tech (hyphen when attrib.), **— tide, — treason** (two words)

high water mark (three words) abbr. **HWM**

highway/, -man (one word)

HIH His, *or* Her, Imperial Highness

hijack/ seize control of aircraft etc., steal goods in transit; **-er, -ing**

Hijaz *use* **Hej-**

hijira/, -h *use* **heg-**

Hil. Hilary

Hilary a session of the High Court of Justice, the university term beginning in January, esp. at Oxford and Dublin universities; from St Hilary of Poitiers (d. *c.*367), festival 13 Jan.

hill cap. with name, as Boars Hill, Box Hill, Bunker Hill

Hillary, Sir Edmund (Percival) (b. 1919) NZ explorer and mountaineer, climbed Everest 1953

hillbilly (one word)

hill fort (two words)

Hillingdon W. London

Hillington Norfolk, Strathclyde

hillside (one word)

hill station (two words)

hill/top, -walker, -walking (one word)

HIM His, *or* Her, Imperial Majesty

Himachal Pradesh an Indian state

Himalaya/ *or* **the -s** India and Tibet; **-n**

Hinayana Skt. for **Theravada**

hinc/ (Lat.) hence, **— illae lacrimae** hence those tears

Hinckley Leics., *not* Hink-

Hind. Hindu, -stan, -stani

Hindi *not* -dee (not ital.)

hind leg (two words)

hindmost (one word)

Hindoo *use* **Hindu**

hindquarters (one word)

hindrance *not* -erance

hindsight (one word)

Hindu/ *not* -doo, abbr. **Hind.** (not ital.); **-ism, -ize**

Hindu Kush mountains, Afghanistan

Hindustani abbr. **Hind.**, *not* Indo-

hing/e, -ed, -ing

Hinkley Point Som., the site of a nuclear power station

Hinshelwood, Sir Cyril Norman (1897–1967) British chemist

hinterland the (often deserted or uncharted) areas beyond a coastal district or a river's banks, a remote or fringe area (one word)

hip/ bath, — bone, — flask, — joint (two words)

hip-length (hyphen)

hippie *use* **-y** in all senses

hippo/ hippopotamus, pl. **-s**

hip pocket (two words)

Hippocrat/es (*fl.* 400 BC) Greek 'Father of Medicine', **-ic**

Hippocrene a fountain on Mt. Helicon sacred to the Muses, a term for poetic or literary inspiration

hippogriff a fabulous monster, *not* -gryph (not ital.)

hippopotamus/ pl. **-es**

hipp/y a person of unconventional appearance, associated with a rejection of conventional values; *also* a person with broad hips; pl. **-ies**

hiragana the cursive form of Japanese syllabic writing or kana; cf. **katakana**

hirdy-girdy (Sc.) in disorder; cf. **hurdy-gurdy**

hireable obtainable for hire, *not* -rable

hire car (two words)

hire purchase (two words) abbr. **HP, h.p.**

hirly-birly *use* **hurly-burly**

Hiroshima Japan

Hirschhorn Museum Washington, DC

hirsute hairy, *not* her-

HIS *hic iacet sepult/us, -a* (here lies buried)

His/ Eminence abbr. **HE, — Excellency** abbr. **HE, — Majesty('s)** abbr. **HM** (caps., not ital.)

Hispanic of or relating to Iberia or Spain and other Spanish-speaking countries; a Spanish-speaking person, esp. one of Latin-American descent, living in the USA

Hispanicize render Spanish, *not* -ise

Hispanist an expert in or student of the language, literature, and civilization of Spain; *not* -icist

His Royal Highness (caps.) abbr. HRH

hist. histor/ian, -ic, -ical

Hitchens, Sydney Ivon (1893–1979) English painter

hitch-hik/e, -er, -ing (hyphen, one word in US)

Hitchin Herts., *not* -en

hi-tech *use* **high tech** (hyphen when attrib.)

HIV human immunodeficiency virus, a retrovirus that causes Aids; 'HIV virus' is tautologous

HJ *hic jacet* (here lies)

HJS *hic jacet sepult/us, -a* (here lies buried)

HK Hong Kong; House of Keys, Isle of Man

HL House of Lords

hl hectolitre(s) (no point)

hl. (Ger.) *heilig* (holy)

Hl. S. (Ger.) *Heilige Schrift* (Holy Scripture)

HM Head Master, Head Mistress; Her, *or* His, Majesty('s); Home Mission

hm hectometre(s) (no point)

h.m. *hoc mense* (in this month), *huius mensis* (this month's)

HMC Headmasters' Conference; Her, *or* His, Majesty's Customs; Royal Commission on Historical Manuscripts

HMG Her, *or* His, Majesty's Government

HMI Her, *or* His, Majesty's Inspector

HMP *hoc monumentum posuit* (erected this monument)

HMS Her, *or* His, Majesty's Service, *or* Ship

HMSO Her, *or* His, Majesty's Stationery Office; *not* the —

HMV His Master's Voice

HNC, HND Higher National Certificate, Higher National Diploma

HO Home Office, (Ger.) *Handelsorganisation* (state shop in GDR, taken over in 1990)

Ho holmium (no point)

ho. house

Hoangho *use* **Hwang-Ho**

hoard a store of money or possessions, to save these; cf. **horde**

hoar frost (two words, one word in US)

hoarhound *use* **hore-**

hoarstone (Brit.) an ancient boundary stone, *not* hore-

Hobbema, Meindert (1638–1709) Dutch painter

Hobbes,/ John Oliver pseud. of **Pearle Mary Teresa Craigie** (1867–1906) English writer, — **Thomas** (1588–1679) English philosopher

hobbledehoy a raw youth, *not* the many variants

hobby horse (two words)

hobnob (one word)

hobo/ (US) a migrant worker or tramp, pl. **-es**

Hoboken NJ

hoboy (mus.) *use* **oboe**

Hobson-Jobson/ism (hyphen) the assimilation of adopted foreign words to the sound-pattern of the adopting language, e.g. *Sir Roger Dowler* for the 18th-c. Indian prince Siraj-ud-Dawlah

Hobson's choice a choice between taking the thing offered or nothing, *not* between two

equally unacceptable or unpleasant alternatives

hoc/ age (Lat.) attend!; — **anno** in this year, abbr. **h.a.**

Hoccleve, Thomas (?1370–?1450) English poet, *not* O-

hoc/ genus omne all of this kind, — **habet** he has a hit (of gladiators)

hochepot (Fr. cook. m.) hotchpotch, stew, ragout

Ho Chi Minh/ adopted Chinese name of **Nguyen That Thanh** (1890–1969) Vietnamese politician, President of Vietnam 1945–54 and North Vietnam 1954–69; — — — **City** Vietnam, *formerly* Saigon

hock/ a joint of a quadruped's hind leg; a Rhineland white wine (properly from Hochheim); (esp. US) (verb) pawn, pledge, **in** — in pawn or in debt

hockey/ in Britain this general term suggests **field** —, in the USA it suggests **ice** —

Hocking,/ Joseph (1855–1937) and his brother — **Silas Kitto** (1850–1935) British novelists

hoc/ loco (Lat.) in this place; — **mense** in this month, abbr. **h.m.**; — **monumentum posuit** erected this monument, abbr. **HMP**; — **sensu** in this sense, abbr. **h.s.**; — **tempore** at this time, abbr. **h.t.**; — **titulo** in, or under, this title, abbr. **h.t.**

hocus/ to hoax, drug; **-sed, -sing**

hocus-pocus deception, trickery (hyphen)

Hodder & Stoughton publishers

hodgepodge *use* **hotchpotch** (except in US)

Hodgkin's disease a malignant disease of lymphatic tissues, named after **Thomas Hodgkin** (1798–1866) English physician

hodmandod a snail

hodograph (math.) a curve

hodometer *use* **od-**

Hoe Plymouth

Hoe,/ Robert (1784–1833), — **Richard March** (1812–86) his son, — **Robert** (1839–1909) his grandson, all US printers

hoeing *not* hoing

Hofer, Andreas (1767–1810) Tyrolese patriot

Hoff, Jacobus Hendricus van 't (1852–1911) Dutch physicist and chemist

Hoffmann,/ August Heinrich (1798–1874) German writer ('Hoffmann von Fallersleben'; *Deutschland über Alles*, 1841); — **Daniel** (1576–1601) German theologian; — **Ernst Theodor Amadeus** (originally **Wilhelm**) (1776–1822) German writer and composer, source of Offenbach's *Tales of Hoffmann*; — **Friedrich** (1660–1742) German chemist; *see also* **Hofmann**

Hoffnung (Ger. f.) hope (cap.)

Hoffnung, Gerard (1925–59) English humorous artist and musician

Hofmann,/ August Wilhelm von (1818–92) German chemist, — **Johann Christian Conrad von** (1810–77) German theologian, — **Josef Casimir** (1876–1957) Polish pianist and composer; *see also* **Hoffmann**

Hofmannsthal, Hugo von (1874–1929) Austrian poet, librettist of some operas by Richard Strauss

hog a castrated pig

hogan a Navajo Indian hut of logs etc.

hoggin a gravel mixture

Hogmanay (Sc.) the last day of the year

hogshead/ a large cask; pl. **-s**, abbr. **hhd.**

Hogue, La dép. Manche, France

Hohenzollern, House of the Prussian Imperial family

Ho Ho Kus NJ (three words)

hoiden *use* **hoy-**

hoing *use* **hoe-**

hoi polloi (Gr.) the masses; *not* oi, *not* the − −, as *hoi* = the (not ital.)

hokey (US sl.) sentimental, melodramatic, artificial; *not* -ky

hokey-cokey a communal dance performed in a circle with synchronized shaking of the limbs in turn

hokey-pokey (hist.) ice cream, *not* hoky-poky (hyphen)

hokku *use* **haiku**

hokum stage business used for cheap effect

Holbein, Hans 'the Elder' (1465–1524), 'the Younger' (1497–1543) both German painters

Hölderlin, Johann Christian Friedrich (1770–1843) German poet

hold-up (noun) a delay, a robbery (hyphen)

holey having holes

Holi a Hindu religious festival

Holiday, Billie born **Eleanora Fagan** (1915–59) US jazz singer

holidaymaker (one word)

holily in holy manner

Holinshed, Raphael (d. *c*.1580) English chronicler; *not* -ings-, -head

Holland/ *use* **the Netherlands; North —, South —** (provinces), **Parts of —** (former division of Lincs.)

holland a linen (not cap.)

hollandais/ (Fr.) f. **-e** Dutch (not cap.)

hollandaise a creamy sauce (not ital.)

Hollands Dutch gin (cap.)

hollow (bind.) a paper reinforcement of the back, and sometimes the spine, of a book

hollowware hollow articles of metal, china, etc. such as pots, kettles, jugs, etc. (one word)

hollyhock a plant

Hollywood Los Angeles, Calif.

Holman-Hunt, William (1827–1910) English painter (hyphen)

Holmes, Oliver Wendell (1809–94) US professor, author, and essayist; and his son (1841–1935) US jurist, Associate Justice of the US Supreme Court 1902–32

holmium symbol **Ho**

Holm Patrick, Baron

holocaust a whole burnt offering, wholesale sacrifice or destruction (cap. with hist. reference to the mass murder of the Jews by the Nazis, 1939–45)

Holocene (of or relating to) the most recent epoch of the Quaternary period; also called **Recent**

Holofernes an Assyrian general (-ph- in NEB); a pedantic and pretentious teacher in Rabelais's *Gargantua*, 1534, and Shakespeare's *Love's Labour's Lost*, 1598

hologram (a photograph of) a three-dimensional image formed by the interference of light beams from a coherent light source

holograph (a document) wholly written by hand by the person named as the author

Holstein (US) = **Friesian**

holus-bolus all at once (hyphen)

Holy Communion (caps.), abbr. **HC**

Holy Cross Day (three words, caps.), Holy Rood Day, feast of the Exaltation of the Cross, 14 Sept.

Holy/ Family, — Ghost, — Land (two words, caps.)

Holyoake,/ George Jacob (1817–1906) English writer and agitator, — **Rt. Hon. Sir Keith Jacka** (1904–83) Prime Minister of New Zealand 1960–72

holy of holies the inner chamber of the Jewish tabernacle (not caps.)

Holy Roman Empire (caps.) abbr. **HRE**

Holy Rood Day *see* **Holy Cross Day**

Holyroodhouse, Palace of Edinburgh

Holy Saturday the day before Easter Sunday (caps.)

Holy Spirit as Deity (caps.)

holystone (naut.) (scour decks with) soft sandstone (one word)

Holy Thursday Ascension Day in English Church; but Thursday in Holy Week, or Maundy Thursday, in Roman Church

Holy Week the week before Easter (two words, caps.)

Holywood Co. Down

Hom. Homer

homage public acknowledgement of allegiance, in Fr. *hommage* (m.)

homard (Fr. m.) lobster

hombre (Sp. and US sl.) man (not ital.)

Homburg a soft felt hat

Home/ a surname, pron. 'Hume'; **— of the Hirsel, Baron**

homebody (one word)

home/ boy, -girl someone from the same hometown, community, or neighbourhood

home/-brew, -brewed, -brewing (hyphen, two words in US)

homecoming (one word)

Home Counties, the the counties closest to London, i.e. Essex, Herts., Kent, Surrey; sometimes includes Berks., Bucks., Sussex; abbr. **HC**

home/-grown (hyphen, one word in US)

Home Guard (two words, caps.) (a member of) the British citizen army, 1940–57; abbr. **HG** (no points); *see also* **LDV**

home/land, -like (one word)

homely suggesting home, cosy; (US) unattractively plain, ugly

home-made (hyphen, one word in US)

home/maker (one word), **-making** (hyphen, one word in US)

Home Office the British government department

home of lost causes Oxford University (from Arnold's *Essays in Criticism*) (not cap.)

homeopath/, -y *use* **homoeo-** (except in US)

Homer (*c*.9th c. BC) Greek poet, abbr. **Hom.**

homeroom (US) (one word)

Home Rule (two words, caps.), abbr. **HR**

homesick/, -ness (one word)

homespun (one word)

home town (two words, one word in US)

homework (one word)

homey homelike

homing *not* -eing

homin/id a member of the family *Hominidae*, **-oid** a humanlike animal

Hommage/ d'auteur, — de l'auteur (Fr.) with the author's compliments; **— d'éditeur, — de l'éditeur** with the publisher's compliments, *not* editor's (*but see* **éditeur**)

homme/ d'affaires (Fr.) businessman, *not* des; **— de bien** a respectable man; **— de cour** a courtier; **— de lettres** author; **— de paille** man of straw; **— d'épée** a military man; **— de robe** lawyer; **— d'esprit** man of wit; **— d'État** statesman; **— de tête** man of resource; **— du monde** man of fashion

Homo (zool.) genus of humans

hom/o (Lat.) human being, pl. **-ines**

homoeopath/y the treatment of diseases by minute doses of drugs that excite similar symptoms; **-ic, -ist**; *not* homeo- (US)

homogene/ous of the same kind, consistent, uniform; (math.) containing terms all of the same degree; **-ity**

homogenize to make (milk) homogeneous, *not* -ise

homogen/ous, -etic (biol.) having a common descent or origin

homogeny (biol.) similarity due to common descent

homograph a word spelt like another but of different meaning or origin

homoiothermic warm-blooded

homoiousian (theol.) (a person) believing the Father and Son to be of like substance (not ital.); cf. **heteroousian; homoousian**

homolog/ue a homologous thing, *not* -log (US); **-ize** be or make homologous, *not* -ise

homonym a homograph or homophone; *not* -me

homoousian (theol.) (a person) believing the Father and Son to be of the same substance, *not* homou- (not ital.); cf. **heteroousian; homoiousian**

homophone a word having the same sound as another but of different meaning or origin (e.g. *pair, pear*)

Homo sapiens (zool.) the species modern humans

homosexual (a person of either sex) feeling (or involving) sexual attraction only to persons of the same sex

Homs Syria

homy *use* **homey**

Hon. Honorary, Honourable (son or daughter of a peer, MP)

Honble. Honourable (former Indian title)

honch/o (US sl.) the person in charge, an admirable man; pl. **-os**; in Jap. **han'chō**

Hondura/s Cent. America, **-n**

Honegger, Arthur (1892–1955) French-born Swiss composer

honey/ badger, — bee, — buzzard (two words)

honey/comb, -dew (one word)

honeyed sweet, *not* -ied

honey/moon, -suckle (one word)

Hong Kong S. China (no hyphen), abbr. **HK**

HongKong and Shanghai Banking Corporation *not* Hong Kong, abbr. **HSBC**

Honi soit qui mal y pense shamed be he who thinks evil of it (motto of the Order of the Garter)

honnête homme (Fr. m.) a decent, cultivated man

honor/, -able *use* **honour-** (except in US)

Honorable (US) abbr. title for a congressman or judge, abbr. **Hon.**

honorand one to be honoured

honorarium/ a voluntary fee for professional services, pl. **-s** (not ital.)

honorary/ (of office etc.) bestowed as an honour, unpaid; **— secretary** abbr. **Hon. Sec.**

honorific (utterance) expressing honour or respect

honoris/ causa or *— gratia* (Lat.) for the sake of honour

Honourable title for the son or daughter of a peer (used with name) or for an MP (used with constituency, e.g. 'the Hon. Member for —'), abbr. **Hon.**; for Indian title abbr. **Honble.**; *see also* **Honorable**

Hons. Honours

Hon. Sec. honorary secretary

hoodwink (one word)

hoof/ usual pl. **-s**, *not* -ves

Hooghly India, *not* Hugli

Hook, Theodore Edward (1788–1841) English humorist; *see also* **Hooke**

hookah an oriental pipe, *not* the many variants

hook and eye (no hyphens)

Hooke/, Robert (1635–1703) English physicist, **—'s law**; *see also* **Hook**

Hooker,/ Sir William Jackson (1785–1865) and **— Sir Joseph Dalton** (1817–1911) his son, English botanists

hooping cough *use* wh-

hoopoe S. European bird

hoor/ah, -ay *use* **hurr/ah, -ay**

Hooray/ Henry a rich but ineffectual young man, esp. one who is fashionable, extrovert, and conventional; f. **— Henrietta**

Hoover/ (propr.) a vacuum cleaner (cap.); (not cap.) to vacuum-clean, **-ed, -ing**

hooves *use* **hoofs**

hophead (US sl.) a drug addict, (Austral. and NZ sl.) a drunkard

Hopi/ (of or relating to) (a member of) a Native American tribe, or the language of this people; pl. **-s**; *not* -ki, -qui

Hopkins/, Gerard Manley (1844–89) English poet; **—, Johns** (*not* John) (1795–1873) US financier; **Johns — University Medical Center** Baltimore, Md. (no apos.)

hop-o'-my-thumb a dwarf (hyphens)

hop-picker (hyphen)

Hoppner, John (1758–1810) English painter

hopscotch a children's game (one word)

hor. horizon, -tal

hor/a (Lat.) hour, pl. *-ae*

Horace (in Lat. **Quintus Horatius Flaccus**) (65–8 BC) Roman poet, abbr. **Hor.**

horae/ canonicae hours for prayer, *— sub-secivae* leisure hours

Horatius Cocles (Rom. hist.) who kept the Sublician Bridge

horde a troop of nomads, a crowd of people; cf. **hoard**

horehound a plant; *not* hoar-

horizon/, -tal abbr. **hor.**

horn,/ English a woodwind instrument, *use* **cor anglais**; **— French** a brass instrument

hornblende a mineral, *not* -d

hornpipe a dance, music for it (one word)

horology abbr. **horol.**

horresco referens (Lat.) I shudder to mention it

hors/ (Fr.) beyond, out of; *— concours* not for competition (*not* de); *— de combat* out of the fight, disabled; *-de-la-loi* outlaw (hyphens); *— de pair* without an equal

hors d'oeuvre an appetizer, pl. **-s**; in Fr. m. *hors d'œuvre*, pl. same

Horse Artillery (caps.) abbr. **HA**

horse/back, -box (one word)

horse brass (two words)

horse chestnut *not* chesnut (two words)

horse/flesh (one word), **-fly** (hyphen)

Horse Guards abbr. **HG** (two words, caps.)

horse/hair, -play (one word)

horsepower a unit of power (746 watts), abbr. **hp**

horse rac/e, -ing (two words), *but* **Horserace** (one word) **Betting Levy Board** and **Horserace Totalisator Board**

horse/radish, -shoe (one word) *but* **horse-shoeing** (hyphen)

Horseshoe Falls Niagara river, Ont.; **Horse Shoe Falls** Guyana

horse/tail, -whip, -woman (one word)

horsey horselike, *not* -sy (US)

horst (geol.) a raised elongated block of land bounded by faults on both sides

'Horst Wessel Song' the song of the German Nazi *Sturm-Abteilung*, after the writer of the words

hort. horticulture

hortus siccus an arranged collection of dried plants

Hos. Hosea

hosanna a shout of praise, 'save, we pray'; *not* -ah (not ital.); **Hosanna Sunday** Palm Sunday

Hosea (OT) abbr. **Hos.**

hospital/ abbr. **hosp.**, **-ize** *not* -ise

hospitaller one of a charitable brotherhood (one l in US)

hostell/er, -ing (one l in US)

hostler a stableman at an inn, *use* **ostler** (except in US); (US) a person who services machines, esp. railway engines

hotbed (one word)

hotchpot (law) the reunion and blending of properties for the purpose of securing equal division (one word); *not* hodgepodge (US)

hotchpotch a confused mixture, a jumble; a dish of many mixed ingredients; *not* hodge-podge (US)

hotdog perform ostentatious stunts, e.g. while skiing or surfing; a person who does this (one word); a frankfurter sandwiched in a soft roll (two words)

hôte (Fr. m.) innkeeper, host; *also* guest

hotel preceded by *a*, not *an*; name is roman, quoted *only* where necessary to avoid ambiguity: 'The Farmhouse'

Hôtel des Invalides Paris, founded 1670 as a hospital for disabled soldiers; contains Napoleon's tomb (caps.)

hôtel/ de ville (Fr. m.) town hall; *-Dieu, l'* chief hospital of a town (one cap.); *— garni, — meublé* furnished lodgings

hotelier a hotel-keeper (not ital., no accent)

hot/foot, -head, -house (one word)

hot metal (typ.) type made from molten metal

hot/plate, -pot (cook.), **-shot** (one word)

Hottentot *use* **Khoikhoi**

houdah *use* **how-**

Houdan a breed of fowls

Houdin, Jean Eugène Robert (1805–71) French conjuror

Houdini, Harry b. **Erik Weisz** (1874–1926) US escapologist

Houdon, Jean Antoine (1741–1828) French sculptor

Houghton-le-Spring Tyne & Wear (hyphens)

hoummous *see* **hummus**

hour/, -s abbr. **hr., hrs.**, *but* **h** (no point, same in pl.) in scientific and technical work; **-glass** (one word)

houri/ a beautiful young woman, esp. in the Muslim Paradise; pl. **-s**

Housa *use* **Hau-**

house the number of, in a street, has no comma after, as '6 Fleet Street'; abbr. **ho.**

House, the Christ Church (Oxford), the House of Commons, the Stock Exchange

house/ agent, — arrest (two words)

houseboat (one word)

housebote (law) a tenant's right to wood to repair house (one word)

housebreak/er, -ing (one word)

housecarl (hist.) a member of the bodyguard of a Danish or English king or noble, *not* -e

housecoat (one word)

house flag the distinguishing flag of a shipping company (two words)

house/fly, -holder, -keeper, -keeping, -maid (one word)

house martin (two words)

house-mother (hyphen, one word in US)

House of Keys in the Isle of Man, the elected chamber of Tynwald

House of Representatives (US) the lower house of the US Congress and other legislatures (cf. **Senate**), abbr. **HR**

house party (two words)

house physician abbr. **HP** (two words)

house style (typ.) a printer's or publisher's preferred way of presenting text

house surgeon abbr. **HS** (two words)

house-to-house performed at or carried to each house in turn (hyphens)

house/wife, -work (one word)

Housman,/ A(lfred) E(dward) (1859–1936) English scholar and poet; **— Laurence** (1865–1959) his brother, English writer and artist

Houssaye,/ Arsène (1815–96) French novelist and poet; **— Henri** (1848–1911) his son, French historian

Houyhnhnm in Swift's *Gulliver's Travels*, one of a race of horses with noble human characteristics, pron. 'hwinnim'; contrasted with **Yahoo**

hovercraft (not cap.) pl. same

Hövsgöl lake, Mongolia

Howards End a novel by E. M. Forster, 1910 (no apos.)

howdah an elephant-seat; *not* -a, houda, -ar

how-do-you-do *or* **how-d'ye-do** awkward situation (hyphens)

howitzer a short cannon for high-angle firing of shells at low velocities

howsoever *not* howsoe'er (except in poet. contexts)

Hoxha, Enver (1908–85) Prime Minister of Albania 1944–54, First Secretary of the Labour Party in Albania 1954–85

Hoxnian (geol.) (designating or pertaining to) an interglacial state of the Pleistocene in Britain, identified with the Holsteinian of northern Europe

hoyden tomboy, *not* hoi-

Hoyle/, Edmond (1672–1769) English writer on card games; **according to —** correctly, exactly

HP high pressure (*also* **h.p.**), high priest, hire purchase (*also* **h.p.**), house physician, Houses of Parliament

h.p. horsepower (*also* **HP, hp**)

HQ Headquarters

HR Home Rule, (US) House of Representatives

hr. (Norw., Swed.) *herr* (Mr); (Dan.) *herre* (Mr); hour, pl. **hrs.** (non-technical use)

Hradec Králové Czech Republic, *not* König-grätz

Hrdlička, Aleš (1869–1943) Bohemian-born US anthropologist

HRE Holy Roman Empire

H. Rep. (US) House of Representatives Report (space)

H. Res. (US) House of Representatives Resolution (space)

HRH Her, *or* His, Royal Highness

HRIP (Lat.) *hic requiescit in pace* (here rests in peace)

Hrsg. *Herausgeber* (editor)

hrsg. (Ger.) *herausgegeben* (edited)

Hrvatska (Croat) **Croatia**

HS *hic sepult/us, -a* (here buried), house surgeon; symbol for sesterce, a Roman coin equivalent to a quarter of a denarius

Hs. (Ger.) *Handschrift* (manuscript)

h.s. (Lat.) *hoc sensu* (in this sense)

HSE *hic sepult/us, -a est* (here lies buried)

HSH His, *or* Her, Serene Highness

HT high tension

ht. height

h.t. *hoc tempore* (at this time), *hoc titulo* (in, *or* under, this title), (elec.) high tension

HTML (comput.) Hypertext Mark-up Language

HTTP (comput.) Hypertext Transport (*or* Transfer) Protocol

ht. wkt. (cricket) hit wicket

HU Harvard University

Huanghe *see* **Hwang-Ho**

huarache a leather-thonged sandal, *not* gua-

Hubble/, Edwin Powell (1889–1953) US astronomer, **— classification, — constant, — Space Telescope**, *but* **—'s law**

hubble-bubble a rudimentary hookah; confused talk (hyphen)

Huberman, Bronisław (1882–1947) Polish violinist

hübnerite a manganese tungstate, *not* hue-

hubris/ (Gr. drama) presumptuous pride that invites disaster, *not* hy- (not ital.); **-tic**

huckaback a rough-surfaced linen fabric, *not* hugga-

Hucknall Notts., where Byron is buried

Hudibras a satiric poem by S. Butler, 1663–80

hudibrastic in the style of *Hudibras*, in octosyllabic couplets with comic rhymes, mock-heroic (not cap.)

Hudson Bay N. America, *but* **Hudson's Bay Company**

Hueffer *see* **Ford Madox Ford**

huggaback *use* **huck-**

hugger-mugger secret(ly) (hyphen)

Hughenden Bucks., *not* -don

Hugli *use* **Hooghly**

Hugo, Victor (**Marie**) (1802–85) French poet, novelist, and playwright

Huguenot (hist.) a 16th–17th-c. French Protestant, *not* -onot

huissier (Fr. m.) bailiff, doorkeeper

huîtres (Fr. f. pl.) oysters

huius/ anni (Lat.) of this year, abbr. **h.a.**; — **mensis** of this month, abbr. **h.m.**

hullabaloo uproar, *not* the many variants

Hullah, John Pyke (1812–84) English musician

hullo *use* **he-**

Hulsean Lectures Cambridge

Humanae vitae (Lat.) of human life, name of an encyclical on contraception, by Pope Paul VI, 1968

Humaniora (Lat.) the humanities, abbr. **Hum.**; *see also* **Lit. Hum.**

humanize *not* -ise

humankind (one word)

Humberside a county of England

humble-bee *use* **bumblebee**

humble pie (to eat), *not* umble (two words)

Humboldt,/ Friedrich Heinrich Alexander, Baron von (1769–1859) German naturalist; **— Karl Wilhelm, Baron von** (1767–1835) his brother, German philologist, statesman, and poet

humdrum commonplace (one word)

Humean of **David Hume** (1711–76) Scottish historian and philosopher, *not* -ian

humer/us the upper-arm bone, pl. **-i** (not ital.)

hummingbird (one word)

hummum a Turkish bath, *use* **hammam**

hummus a purée of chickpeas and sesame oil, *often* **houmous**; *not* hoummos; in Turk. *humus*

humor *use* **-our** (except in US)

humoral (med.) relating to body fluids, esp. (hist.) of the four bodily humours

humoresque a musical caprice, *not* humour-

humor/ist, -ize *not* -ise

humorous/, -ly, -ness

humoursome capricious

humous *see* **humus**

humpback(ed) (one word)

Humperdinck, Engelbert/ (1854–1921) German composer; **— —** adopted name of **Arnold** (**Gerry**) **Dorsey** (b. 1935) British popular singer

Humphrey, Duke of Gloucester (1391–1447) son of Henry IV of England, Protector during minority of Henry VI; *but* **Duke Humfrey's Library** in the Bodleian

Humphrey's Clock, Master by Dickens, 1840

Humphry (*not* -ey) **Clinker** by Smollett, 1771

Humpty-Dumpty (hyphen)

hum/us the organic constituent of soil, adj. **-ous**

hunchback(ed) (one word)

hundert (Ger.) hundred

hundred symbol **C**

hundred-and-first etc. (hyphens)

hundred-per-cent (adj.) entire

hundredweight (one word), pl. same, abbr. **cwt.**

Hundred Years War between England and France, 1337–1453 (caps., no apos.)

hung *see* **hanged**

Hung. Hungar/y, -ian

Hungary abbr. **Hung.**; in Hung. (Magyar) **Magyarország**; in Fr. **Hongrie**, in Ger. **Ungarn**

Hunstanton Norfolk

Hunter's Quay Strathclyde (apos.)

Huntingdon Cambs.

Huntington/ Cheshire, Hereford, E. Lothian, Staffs., N. Yorks., W. Virginia; **— Library** San Marino, Calif.

Huntley Glos., Staffs.

Huntly/ Grampian; **Marquess of —**; *not* -ey

Hunyadi János a Hungarian mineral water

Hunyadi, János (1387–1456) Hungarian general of Romanian descent, *not* -ady; in Hung. the order is **Hunyadi János**

hurds *use* **ha-**

hurdy-gurdy (mus.) *not* hi-, gi-

hurly-burly a commotion; *not* hi-, bi-

hurrah *or* **hurray** *not* hoo-, except in **Hooray Henry**

hurry-curry *use* **hara-kiri**

hurry-scurry pell-mell, *not* -sk-

Hurstmonceux E. Sussex, *use* **Herst-**

Hurstpierpoint W. Sussex (one word)

Husák, Gustáv (1913–91) Czechoslovak politician, leader of the Communist Party of Czechoslovakia 1969–87, President 1975–89

husband abbr. **h.**

Husbands Bosworth Leics. (no apos.)

Huss/, **John** (1369–1455) Bohemian religious and nationalist reformer, in Czech **Jan Hus**, in Ger. **Johann Hus**; **-ite**

hussar a soldier of a light cavalry regiment; a Hungarian light horseman of the 15th c., in Magyar *huszár*

hussy impudent or immoral woman, *not* -zzy

Huxley/ **Aldous** (**Leonard**) (1894–1963) English novelist; **— Sir Julian Sorell** (1887–1975) his brother, biologist and scientific administrator; **— Thomas Henry** (1825–95) their grandfather, biologist and essayist

Huygens, Christiaan (1629–95) Dutch mathematician and astronomer, *not* -ghens

Huysmans, Joris Karl (1848–1907) French novelist

huzzy *use* **-ssy**

h.w. (cricket) hit wicket

h/w herewith

Hwang-Ho the Yellow River, China, *not* Hoangho; in Pinyin **Huanghe**; either

'Hwang-Ho' *or* 'the River Hwang', *but not* 'the Hwang-Ho River'

HWM high water mark

Hy Henry (man's name) (no point)

Hyacinthe, Père born **Charles Jean Marie Loyson** (1827–1912), French priest

Hyades a group of stars in Taurus

hyaena *use* **hye-**

hybernate *use* **hi-**

hybrid (bot.) symbol ×

hybridize etc., *not* -ise

hybris *use* **hu-**

hyd. hydrostatics

Hyderabad Deccan, India; Sind, Pakistan; *not* Haidar-, Hydar-

hydrangea a shrub, *not* -ia

hydro/ (colloq.) hydropathic establishment, hydroelectric plant (no point); pl. **-s**

hydro/**carbon, -dynamics, -electric** (one word)

hydrogen symbol **H**

hydro/**lysis** decomposition by water, **-lyse** *not* -lyze (US)

hydrophobia rabies, aversion to water

hydroplane a kind of motor boat (one word)

hydrostatics abbr. **hyd.**

hydrotherapy (one word)

hyena *not* hyae-

Hyères dép. Var, France

Hy/**gieia** (Gr.) goddess of health, **-geia** *or* **-gīa** the later Rom. spelling; *not* -gea, -giea

hygien/**e** the science of health, **-ic**

hying *use* **hie-**

Hyksos rulers of Egypt, 17th–16th cc. BC

Hylton-Foster, Sir Harry (1905–65) Speaker of the House of Commons 1959–65

Hymen (Gr. and Rom. myth.) the god of marriage, **hymeneal**

hymen/ (anat.) virginal membrane (not ital.), **-al**

hymn book (two words, one word in US)

hyp. hypothesis, hypothetical

hypaesthesia diminished capacity for sensation, *not* hypes- (US)

hypaethral open to the sky, roofless; *not* hype- (US)

hypallage (rhet.) the transposition of the natural relations of two elements in a proposition (e.g. 'Theo shook his angry curls')

hyperaem/**ia** an excess of blood, **-ic**; *not* -rhaemia, -remia (US)

hyperaesthesia excessive physical sensibility, *not* hyperes- (US)

hyperbaton (rhet.) the separation or rearrangement of the normal order of words, esp. for the sake of emphasis (e.g. 'This I must see')

hyperbol/a a curve, **-ic**

hyperbol/e exaggeration, **-ical**

hypercritical excessively critical

hypermarket (Brit.) a very large supermarket, usually outside a town (one word)

hyphen (typ.) sign (-) used to join words, indicate word breaks at the end of a line, or indicate a missing implied element (e.g. hard- and paperback)

hypnotize *not* -ise

hypochondria a morbid anxiety about health, *not* -condria

hypocri/sy, -te, -tical

hypota/xis (gram.) the explicit subordination of one clause to another, **-ctic**; cf. **parataxis**

hypotenuse (geom.) *not* hypoth-

hypothecate to mortgage

hypothermia abnormally low body temperature

hypothes/is a provisional explanation, pl. **-es**; abbr. **hyp.**

hypothesize form a hypothesis; *not* -ise, -tize

hysterectomy (med.) the removal of the womb

hysteresis (phys.) a lagging of variation in effect behind variation in cause

hysteron proteron (rhet.) a figure of speech in which what should come last is put first (e.g. 'I die! I faint! I fail!') (not ital.)

hysterotomy (med.) cutting into the womb

Hz hertz, an SI unit of frequency (no point)

I iodine, (roman numeral) one (no point), the ninth in a series, Elizabethan spelling of *ay* (meaning 'yes'), (Dan.) familiar or solemn nom. pl. of 'you'

I. Island, -s; Isle, -s; *imperator* (emperor), *imperatrix* (empress)

i (med. prescriptions) one, (math.) square root of minus one

i. *id* (that)

I *or* **i** (ital.) symbol for electric current

I, the (metaphysics) the ego

ı (typ.) undotted *i*, a sort used in Turk.

ι (Gr.) iota (no dot)

IA Indian Army, infected area, Iowa (postal abbr.)

Ia. Iowa (off. abbr.)

IAA indoleacetic acid

IAAF International Amateur Athletic Federation

IAEA International Atomic Energy Agency

IAHM Incorporated Association of Headmasters; *see also* **AHMI**

IAM Institute of Advanced Motorists

iamb/us a foot of two syllables (˘ -), *not* iamb (US); pl. **-uses** *not* -bi (except in context of classical Greek poetry); adj. **-ic**; **-ics** iambic verse

Iaşi Romania, in Ger. **Jassy**

IATA International Air Transport Association

IBA Independent Broadcasting Authority

Ibáñez, Vicente Blasco (1867–1928) Spanish novelist

Ibárruri Gómez, Dolores (1895–1989) Spanish communist politician and Republican leader, known as **La Pasionaria**

I-beam a girder with an I-shaped section (use a serif typeface to approximate actual shape)

Iberian pertaining to the Spanish peninsula (including Portugal)

ibex/ a wild mountain-goat, pl. **-es**

ibidem (Lat.) in the same place, abbr. **ibid.** (*preferred*), **ib.** (not ital., not cap. except to begin sentence or note); *see also* **idem**

ibis/ a wading bird, pl. **-es**

Ibiza Balearic Islands, *not* Iv-; in Catalan **Eivissa**

Iblis *use* **E-**

IBM International Business Machines

ibn *also* **bin** (Arab.) son of (used in personal names), abbr. **b.**

ibn Abdul Aziz,/ Saud (1902–69) son of Abdul Aziz ibn Saud, King of Saudi Arabia 1953–64, succeeded by his three brothers: — — — **Feisal** (1904–75) King of Saudi Arabia 1964–75; — — — **Khalid** (1913–82) King of Saudi Arabia 1975–

82; — — — **Fahd** (b. 1923) King of Saudi Arabia 1982–

ibn Saud, Abdul Aziz (1880–1953) King of Saudi Arabia 1932–53

Ibo (of or relating to) (a member of) a people of SE Nigeria, or their Kwa language; *not* Ig-

IBRD International Bank for Reconstruction and Development (UN), also known as the **World Bank**

Ibsen, Henrik (1828–1906) Norwegian writer and playwright

IC (comput.) integrated circuit

i/c in charge, in command

ICA Institute of Contemporary Arts

ICAN International Commission for Air Navigation

ICAO International Civil Aviation Organization (UN)

Icarian of Icarus, *not* -ean

ICBM intercontinental ballistic missile

ICE Institution of Civil Engineers, internal-combustion engine

Ice. Iceland, -ic

ice age a glacial period (not cap.)

ice axe (two words)

ice/berg, -block, -box (one word)

ice/ bucket, — cap (two words)

ice-cold (hyphen)

ice/ cream, — cube, — hockey (two words)

ice house (two words, one word in US)

Icelandic/ (typ.) roman alphabet now used, **Old —** called **Old Norse** in its lit. form

ice lolly (two words)

Iceni an ancient people of E. England

ice/ pack, — pick, — rink (two words)

ice-skate(r) (hyphen, two words in US)

ice station (two words)

ICFTU International Confederation of Free Trade Unions

ich (Ger.) I (cap. only at the beginning of a sentence)

Ich dien (Ger.) I serve (motto of the Princes of Wales)

I.Chem.E. Institution of Chemical Engineers

I Ching an ancient Chinese manual of divinations (caps.)

ichneumon a wasp, a N. African mongoose

ichor (Gr. myth.) a fluid flowing like blood in the veins of the gods

ichthyology the study of fishes, abbr. **ichth.**

ichthyosaur/us an extinct marine animal, pl. **-i**

Ichthys (Gr. 'fish', early Christian symbol) initial letters of *Iesous Christos Theou Uios Soter* (Jesus Christ, Son of God, Saviour)

ICI Imperial Chemical Industries

ici (Fr.) here, — *on parle français* French spoken here (no caps.)

Icknield/ Street, — Way, etc.

icky *not* ikky

ICN *in Christi nomine* (in Christ's name)

icon/ pl. **-s; -ic;** *not* ik-, eik- (not ital.)

icon. iconograph/y, -ic

ICS Indian Civil Service

ictus (prosody) rhythmical or metrical stress, (med.) a stroke or seizure; pl. same

ICU Intensive Care Unit

ICV International Code Use (signals)

ID (US) identification, identity, (mil.) Intelligence Department, (postal abbr.) Idaho

id (psychol.) not cap.

id. *idem*

i.d. inner diameter

id (Lat.) that, abbr. **i.**

IDA International Development Association (UN)

Idaho off. abbr. **Ida.,** postal **ID**

IDB (S. Afr.) illicit diamond buy/er, -ing

idea'd having ideas, *not* -aed

idealize *not* -ise

idealogical etc., *use* **ideo-**

idée/ fixe (Fr. f.) fixed idea, — *reçue* accepted opinion

idem/ (Lat.) the same (man), as mentioned before; abbr. **id.** (not ital., not cap. except to begin sentence or note); **id.** generally used to avoid repetition of male author's name in bibliographic matter when citing more than one work in uninterrupted succession; *use* **ead.** (for *eadem*) for a female author, pl. **eaed.** (for *eaedem*), and **eid.** (for *eidem*) for two or more authors of whom at least one is male and one female; *see also **ibidem***; — *quod* the same as, abbr. *i.q.*

identikit (propr.) a system for producing a composite drawing of a face; cf. **photofit**

ideo/gram, -graph a character symbolizing the idea of a thing without expressing its name

ideologue a visionary

ideolog/y the study of ideas, a way of thinking; **-ical, -ist;** *not* ideal-

ides (pl.) in Roman calendar the fifteenth day of March, May, July, October, the thirteenth of other months

id est (Lat.) that is, abbr. **i.e.** (not ital., lower case, comma before)

id genus omne (Lat.) all of that kind

idiolect the linguistic system of one person, *not* ideo-

idiosyncra/sy a peculiarity of temperament, *not* -cy; **-tic**

idl/ing, -y *not* -eing, -ey

IDN *in Dei nomine* (in God's name)

Ido an artificial universal language based on Esperanto

idolater *not* -or

idolize *not* -ise

idol/um a false mental image, pl. **-a**

Idumaea *not* -mea

idyll a work of art depicting innocence or rusticity; a blissful period, *not* -yl

IE (Order of the) Indian Empire, Indo-European

i.e. *id est* (that is)

IEA International Energy Agency

IEE Institution of Electrical Engineers

IEEE (US) Institute of Electrical and Electronics Engineers

Ieper (Fl.) **Ypres**

IERE Institution of Electronic and Radio Engineers

Iesu (Lat.) Jesus (vocative)

IF intermediate frequency

IFC International Finance Corporation (UN)

iff (conjunction, logic and math.) if and only if (no points)

IG Indo-Germanic, (mil.) Inspector-General

I. Gas E. Institution of Gas Engineers

Igaunija Latvian for **Estonia**

Igbo *use* **Ibo**

igloo/ an Inuit snow hut, pl. **-s**

ign. *ignotus* (unknown)

igneous of, *or* like, *or* produced by, fire; *not* -ious

ignis fatuus a will-o'-the-wisp, pl. **ignes fatui** (not ital.)

ignitable *not* -ible

ignoramus/ an ignorant person, pl. **-es**

ignoratio elenchi (Lat.) refuting a proposition differing from that one professes to be refuting

ignotum per ignotius (Lat.) the unknown by means of the more unknown, *not* ignotus

ignotus (Lat.) unknown, abbr. **ign.**

IGO intergovernmental organization

IGY International Geophysical Year

i.h. *iacet hic* (here lies)

IHC same as **IHS**, *C* being a form of the Gr. cap. S

ihm (Ger.) to him

Ihnen (Ger.) to you (cap.); (not cap.) to them

i.h.p. indicated horsepower

Ihr (Ger.) your (cap.); to her, her, their, (familiar) you (not cap.)

IHS abbr. of Gr. *Iesous* (*H* being Gr. cap. long *E*); later interpreted as Lat. *Iesus Hominum Salvator* (Jesus Men's Saviour); *In Hoc Signo* (*vinces*) in this sign (thou shalt conquer); *In Hac* (*Cruce*) *Salus*, in this (cross) is salvation

IHVE Institution of Heating and Ventilation Engineers

II (roman numeral) two (no point)

III (roman numeral) three (no point)

IIII (roman numeral) *use* **IV** (except in classical or medieval texts)

IJ a water area (in the Netherlands); (typ.) a (one-piece) capital letter; *not* Ij, Y

ij (typ.) a (one-piece) lower-case letter in Du. used instead of **y** *but* alphabetized as *y*

ij (med.) two

i. J. (Ger.) *im Jahre* (in the year) (spaces in Ger.)

i. J. d. W. (Ger.) *im Jahre der Welt* (in the year of the world) (spaces in Ger.)

IJ/muiden town, **-ssel** river, **-sselmeer** *formerly* Zuider Zee, **-stein** a town, the Netherlands; *not* Ij-, Y-

Ijo (of or relating to) (a member of) a people of SE Nigeria, or their Kwa language; *not* -aw

ikky *use* **icky**

ikon *use* **ic-**

IL Illinois (postal abbr.)

il (Fr.) he, it; (It., m. sing.) the

ilang-ilang *use* **ylang-ylang**

île (Fr. f.) island

Île-de-France a French region, province, Paris square

Île-de-Montréal a county in Quebec

Île-Jésus a county in Quebec

Île-St-Louis a Paris square

ile/um (anat.) a part of the intestine, pl. **-a**

ilex/ the holm oak, pl. **-es**

Iliad of Homer (ital.)

Ilium (Lat.) Troy

ili/um (anat.) a part of the pelvis, pl. **-a**

ilk, of that (Sc.) of the same place, name, or estate; (colloq.) of family, class, or set, often considered derogatory

Ill. Illinois (off. abbr.)

ill. *illustrissimus* (most distinguished)

ill/-advised, -advisedly, -affected, -assorted (hyphens)

ill at ease (hyphens when attrib.)

ill/-behaved, -bred (hyphens)

ill breeding (two words)

ill/-considered, -defined, -disposed (hyphens)

Ille-et-Vilaine a dép. of France

illegalize *not* -ise

illegible (of handwriting, print, etc.) not clear enough to read; cf. **unreadable**

illegitimize *not* -atize, -ise

ill-equipped (hyphen)

ill fame (two words)

ill/-fated, -favoured *not* -favored (US) (hyphens)

ill feeling (hyphen when attrib.)

ill/-founded, -gotten (hyphens)

ill/ health, — humour (two words)

ill-humoured *not* -humored (US) (hyphen)

illimitable limitless

Illinois off. abbr. **Ill.**, postal **IL**

ill/-judged, -mannered (hyphens)

ill nature (two words)

ill/-natured, -omened, -starred (hyphens)

ill temper (two words)

ill/-tempered, -timed, -treat, -treatment (hyphens)

illuminati (pl.) enlightened people, cap. with reference to particular historical movements (not ital.)

ill use (two words)

ill-used (hyphen)

illusory of more apparent than real value, *not* -ive; cf. **elusive**

illustrat/ed, -ion abbr. **illus.**

illustrator *not* -er

ill will (two words)

il n'y a pas de quoi (Fr.) don't mention it

ILO International Labour Organization

ILP Independent Labour Party

'Il Penseroso' a poem by Milton, 1632

ILR Independent Local Radio

ILS instrument landing system

ILTF International Lawn Tennis Federation; *see also* **tennis**

IM intramuscular

imag/o a winged insect, pl. **-ines**; idealized mental picture, pl. **-s**

imam a leader of prayers in a mosque; a title of various Muslim leaders; *not* -âm, -aum

I.Mar.E. Institute of Marine Engineers

imbed *use* **em-**

imbrication an overlapping of tiles, scales, feathers, etc.; cf. **embrocation**

imbroglio/ a tangle, pl. **-s**; *not* em- (not ital.)

imbrue to stain, dye; *not* em-

imbue to saturate, inspire; *not* em-

IMCO Inter-Governmental Maritime Consultative Organization (UN), *now* **IMO**

I.Mech.E. Institution of Mechanical Engineers

IMF International Monetary Fund (UN)

imfe *use* **-phee**

I.Min.E. Institution of Mining Engineers

im Jahre (Ger.) in the year, abbr. **i. J.**

IMM Institution of Mining and Metallurgy

immanent indwelling, inherent, the antonym of transcendent; cf. **imminent**; **eminent**

Immelmann a kind of looping aircraft turn (cap.)

immesh *use* **en-**

immigra/te come as a permanent resident to a country other than one's native land, **-nt** one who does this; cf. **emigrate**

imminent impending; cf. **eminent**; **immanent**

immobiliz/e *not* -ise; **-ation**

immortalize *not* -ise

immortelle an everlasting flower (not ital.)

Immortels, Les the members of the French Academy

immov/able, -ability, -ableness, -ably *not* -eab- (except for feasts and (law) property); *see also* **movable**

immunize render immune, *not* -ise

immutable unchangeable

IMO International Maritime Organization

imp. imperative, imperfect, imperial, impersonal; import/ed, -er; impression, imprimatur

imp. (Fr.) *imprimeur* (printer); (Lat.) *imperator* (emperor), *imperatrix* (empress)

impanel *use* **em-**

impassable that cannot be traversed

impasse a deadlock (not ital.)

impassible that cannot feel, passive

impassion/ stir emotionally, **-ed**; *not* em-

impasto/ the thick laying-on of colour, pl. **-s**

impayable (Fr.) invaluable, priceless

impeccable *not* -ible

impedance (elec.) hindrance to alternating current

impedimenta (pl.) encumbrances, baggage

impel/, -led, -ler *not* -lor, **-ling**

imperative (gram.) mood expressing command, abbr. **imp.**

imperat/or (Lat.) f. *-rix* absolute ruler, emperor; abbr. **I.**, *imp.*

imperf. imperfect, (stamps) imperforate

imperfect abbr. **imp.**, **imperf.**

imperial abbr. **imp.**

imperil/, -led, -ling (one *l* in US)

imperium absolute power (not ital.)

imperium in imperio (Lat.) an empire within an empire

impermeable that cannot be passed through

impersonal abbr. **imp.**

impetus/ momentum, incentive; pl. **-es**

imphee a sugar cane; *not* -fe, -phie

impi (S. Afr.) an armed band, (hist.) a Zulu regiment

imping/e make an impact, encroach, **-ing**

implacable *not* -ible

impolder reclaim from the sea; *not* em-

import/ed, -er abbr. **imp.**

impose (typ.) arrange pages so that they will read consecutively when the printed sheet is folded

impost/or *not* -er, **-orous** *not* -rous

impracticable that cannot be effected or accomplished; *see also* **practical**

impractical not practical, **unpractical**; *see also* **practical**

impregn/able that cannot be taken by force, **-atable** that can be impregnated

impresa (It.) an undertaking

impresario/ a manager of operatic or other cultural undertakings (one *s*, not ital.); pl. **-s**

impressa (It.) an imprint (obs.)

impression (print.) the product from one cycle of a printing machine; all the copies of a book etc. printed at one press-run from the same type, plates, etc.; abbr. **imp.**; *see also* **edition**; **imprint**; **reprint**

impressionable *not* -ible

Impressionis/m, -t, -tic a specific artistic movement or style of music or writing (cap.); a general tendency or style (not cap.)

imprimatur an official licence to print, sanction; abbr. **imp.** (not ital. except in a RC context)

imprimatura (It.) coloured transparent glaze

imprim/er (Fr.) to print, **-erie** (f.) printing office, **-eur** (m.) printer

imprimi potest (Lat.) a formula giving imprimatur (ital.)

imprimis (Lat.) in the first place, not *in primis* (ital.)

imprint/ the name and address of the printer; **publisher's —** the name of the publisher or publishing division, place of publication, and date

impromptu pl. **-s** (not ital.)

improvable *not* -eable, -ible

improvis/e *not* -ize; **-ator** one who speaks or plays music extempore; **-er** in general, one who improvises

improvvisat/a (It.) improvisation; *-ore* improvisator, pl. *-ori*; f. *-rice*, pl. *-rici*

I.Mun.E. Institution of Municipal Engineers

IN Indiana (postal abbr.)

In indium (no point)

in. inch, -es

in (Ger.) in, into

in- (Fr.) prefix in stating book sizes, as *in-8°*, octavo *in/ absentia* (Lat.) in (one's) absence, — *abstracto* in the abstract

inadmissible *not* -able

inadverten/t (of people) negligent, (of actions) unintentional; **-ce**

inadvisable (of thing or course of action) not recommended; cf. **unadvisable**

in aeternum for ever

inamorat/o f. **-a** a lover, pl. **-i** (not ital.); in It. *innamorat/o, -a*; *not* en-

in articulo mortis (Lat.) at the moment of death

inartistic not following the principles of art, lacking artistic skill or talent; cf. **unartistic**

inasmuch (one word)

Inauguration Day (of the US President) 20 Jan.; before 1937, 4 Mar.

in banco (Lat.) as a full court of judges

Inbegriff (Ger. m.) epitome, embodiment (cap.)

in/board, -born, -bred, -built (one word)

INC *in nomine Christi* (in Christ's name)

Inc. (US) Incorporated

Inca/ (one of) the pre-Columbian people of Peru, **-n**

incage *use* en-

in camera not in open court

in/capsulate, -case *use* en-

in/ cathedra (Lat.) in the chair of office, — *cautelam* for a warning

inch/ in metric system 25.4 mm (not now in scientific use), pl. **-es**; abbr. **in.** (sing. and pl.); sign ″

inchase *use* en-

Inchcape Rock *or* **Bell Rock**, North Sea (two words)

incidentally *not* -tly

incipient beginning, in an initial stage; *not* insi-

incipit the first words (of book etc.)

incise cut into, engrave; *not* -ize

incl. including, inclusive

inclose *use* en-

includible *not* -able

inclu/ding, -sive abbr. **incl.**

'In Coena Domini' a former annual papal bull against heretics

Incogniti a cricket club

incognito/ with one's name or identity concealed or disguised, the pretended identity; pl. **-s**; abbr. **incog.** (not ital.)

income/ group, — tax (two words)

in/ commendam (Lat.) temporarily holding a vacant benefice

incommunicado without means of communication (not ital.), in Sp. *incomunicado*

in concreto in material form, definite

incondensable *not* -ible

inconnu/ (Fr.) f. **-e** unknown

incontrovertible *not* -able

incorrigible *not* -eable

increas/ed, -ing abbr. **incr.**

incredible *not* -able

incroach *use* en-

incrust *use* en-, *but* **incrustation**

incubous (bot.) having the upper leaf-margin overlapping the leaf above

incub/us a person or thing that oppresses like a nightmare, esp. a male demon believed to have sexual intercourse with sleeping women; pl. **-uses** (in extended meaning), **-i** (of demons); cf. **succubus**

incumber etc., *use* en-

incunable (Fr.) = **incunabulum**

incunabul/a (sing. **-um**) the earliest examples of any art, (bibliog.) books printed before 1501

incur/, -red, -ring, -rable

incurable that cannot be cured

in curia (Lat.) in open court

incu/s (anat.) a bone in the ear, pl. **-des**

IND *in nomine Dei* (in God's name)

Ind poetical for India (no point)

Ind. India, -n; Indiana (off. abbr.)

ind. independen/ce, -t; index, indication, industrial

Ind Coope an English brewer

indebted *not* en-

indeclinable (gram.) having no inflections, abbr. **indecl.**

indefatigabl/e tireless, **-y**

indefeasible that cannot be forfeited, *not* -able

indefensible that cannot be defended, *not* -cible, -able

indefinite abbr. **indef.**

indelible that cannot be rubbed out; *not* -able, -eble

indemni/fy protect against harm or loss; **-ty**; *not* en-

indent (typ.) begin a line, or lines, with a blank space; *not* en-; *see also* **hanging**

indenture a sealed agreement, esp. one binding apprentice to master; *not* en-

independen/ce, -t abbr. **ind., indep.**

Independence, Declaration of USA, 4 July 1776 (caps.)

Independence Day a day celebrating national independence, esp. (US) 4 July

independency a country that has attained independence

Independent a person who is politically independent, (hist.) Congregational (cap.)

Independent Order of Odd Fellows *not* Oddfellows, abbr. **IOOF**

in deposito (Lat.) in deposit

indescribable *not* -eable, -ible

ind/ex pl. **-exes**, abbr. **ind.**; (sci., math.) pl. **-ices**; (print.) *see* **fist**

'Index/ Expurgatorius' (Lat.) an index of the passages to be expunged; **'— Librorum Expurgandorum'** (RC) a list of books that might be read only in expurgated editions; **'— Librorum Prohibitorum'** (RC) a list of books that the Church forbade to be read

index/ nominum (Lat.) index of names; **— locorum** index of places, **— rerum** subject index, **— verborum** index of words; pl. **indices —** (not ital.)

India/, -n abbr. **Ind.**

India/man a large ship in the Indian trade, pl. **-men**

Indiana off. abbr. **Ind.**, postal **IN**

Indianapolis Ind.

Indian/ clubs, — corn, — file, — ink (two words, one cap.), *not* India ink (US)

Indian summer a period of warm weather in late autumn, a tranquil late period of life

India paper/ a thin book paper, *not* -ian (no hyphen); **Oxford — —** very thin, strong bible paper made only for OUP

India rubber (two words, no cap. in US)

Indic (of) the group of Indo-European languages comprising Sanskrit and its modern descendants

indication abbr. **ind.**

indicative (gram.) abbr. **indic.**

indicia (pl.) signs, identifying marks (not ital.)

indict/ accuse formally by legal process, cf. **indite**; **-er** *not* -or

indiction (later Rom. Empire and Middle Ages) a cycle of fifteen years, used for administrative and dating purposes; 'first [etc.] indiction' = the first (etc.) year of the cycle, *not* the first cycle

indie (colloq.) an independent record or film company, *not* -dy

indigestible *not* -able

indiscreet injudicious

indiscrete not divided into distinct parts

indispensable *not* -ible

indite put into written words; cf. **indict**

indium symbol **In**

individualize *not* -ise

individu/um (Lat.) the indivisible, pl. **-a**

Indo-Aryan (of or relating to) a member of any of the Aryan peoples of India, the Indic group of languages

Indo-Chin/a an unofficial collective name for the countries of the SE peninsula of Asia (hyphen; one word, one cap. in US), **-ese**

Indo-European (of or relating to) the family of languages spoken over the greater part of Europe and Asia as far as N. India, the hypothetical parent language of this family; abbr. **IE, Indo-Eur.**

Indo-Germanic *use* **Indo-European**

Indo-Iranian (of or relating to) the subfamily of Indo-European languages spoken chiefly in N. India and Iran

Indonesia indep. 1950; *formerly* Dutch East Indies, with W. New Guinea added 1962 and E. Timor annexed 1974; abbr. **Indon.**; *see also* **Bahasa Indonesia**

indoor/, -s (one word)

indorse etc., *use* **en-**

Indostan *use* **Hindu-**

indraught a drawing in, *not* -aft (US)

indubitabl/e *not* -ible; **-y**

inducement (often followed by *to*) an attraction that leads one on, a thing that induces

induction *not* -xion

indu/e, -re *use* **en-**

Indulgence, Declaration of proclamation of religious liberties, esp. under Charles II in 1672 and James II in 1687 (caps.)

industrial abbr. **ind.**

Industrial Revolution (two caps.)

inédit/ f. *-e* (Fr.) unpublished, *not* unedited

inedita (Lat.) unpublished compositions

inedited not published, *or* published without editorial alterations or additions

ineducable incapable of being educated; *not* -atable, -ible

ineffaceable that cannot be effaced

inefficacious ineffective

ineligible *not* -able

inequable not fairly distributed, not uniform

inequitable unfair, unjust

inertia (not ital.) but *vis inertiae*

in esse (Lat.) actually existing

inessential (something) not necessary, dispensable

in/ excelsis in the highest (degree); **— extenso** in full, at length; **— extremis** at the point of death, in great difficulties

in f. in fine (finally)

inf. infantry, inferior, infinitive

inf. (Lat.) *infra* (below)

infallib/le *not* -able; **-ilist** a believer in the Pope's infallibility, *not* -blist

infant/a daughter of the King and Queen of Spain; **-e** a younger son of the same (not ital., cap. as title); cf. **príncipe**

infantry abbr. **inf.**

infantryman (one word)

infected area abbr. **IA**

infer/, -red, -ring

infer/able *not* -rr-; **-ence**

inferior abbr. **inf.**

inferior (typ.) a small character set below the baseline, usually to the side of ordinary characters, e.g. $_{1\,2\,a\,b}$; *also called* **subscript**; cf. **superior**

inferno/ a raging fire, a scene of horror, pl. **-s**; (cap. and ital.) the first part of Dante's *Divina Commedia*

in fieri (Lat.) in course of completion

infighting boxing at close quarters, internal conflict (one word)

infill/ fill in, **-ing**

infin. infinitive

in fine finally, abbr. **in f.** (not ital.)

infinitive abbr. **inf., infin.**

infinity symbol ∞

in flagrante delicto in the very act of committing an offence (not ital.)

inflamma/ble easily set on fire, flammable; *not* non-flammable; **-tory** *not* flammatory; *see* **flammable**

inflatable *not* -eable

inflater one who, *or* that which, inflates, *not* -or

inflection modulation of voice, grammatical termination; *not* -xion

inflexible *not* -able

inflexion *use* **-ction**

infold etc., *use* **en-**

inforce etc., *use* **en-**

in forma pauperis (Lat.) as a pauper

infra/ (Lat.) below, abbr. *inf.*; — *dignitatem* undignified, abbr. *infra dig.*, (colloq.) **infra dig**

infra/red, -sonic, -sound, -structure (one word)

inful/a each of the ribbons of a bishop's mitre, pl. **-ae**

infuser one who, *or* that which, steeps something in a liquid; *not* -or

infusible that cannot be melted

in futuro (Lat.) in, *or* for, the future

Inge, William Ralph, Dean (1860–1954) English divine

Ingelow, Jean (1820–97) English poet

in genere (Lat.) in kind

ingenious inventive

ingénue an artless girl (not ital.)

ingenuity inventiveness

ingenuous/ free from guile, **-ness**

inglenook a chimney corner (one word)

Ingoldsby Legends by R. H. Barham, 1840

ingraft, ingrain (verb) *use* **en-**

ingrain/ (adj.) dyed in the yarn; **-ed** (adj., less specific) deeply rooted, inveterate; cf. **engrain**

Ingres/, Jean Auguste Dominique (1780–1867) French painter (no accent), *violon d'*— an additional skill

ingross *use* **en-**

in-group a small exclusive group of people (hyphen)

ingulf *use* **en-**

inhabitant abbr. **inhab.**

in hac parte (Lat.) on this part

in hoc/ (Lat.) in this respect, — — *salus* safety in this

in-house (adj. and adv., hyphen)

INI *in nomine Iesu* (in the name of Jesus)

in infinitum for ever

Inishfail poetical for Ireland, *not* Inn-

init. (Lat.) *initio* (in the beginning), *initium* (beginning)

initial/, -led, -ling (one l in US)

initial letter (typ.) a large letter used at beginning of chapter

Initial Teaching Alphabet (caps.) abbr. **i t a** (spaced lower case, no points)

initium (Lat.) beginning (as of a work), abbr. *init.*

injuri/a (law) a wrong, pl. **-ae**

ink-blot test (one hyphen; inkblot one word in US)

Inkerman Crimea, *not* -ann

ink-jet printer (hyphen)

inkling a slight knowledge or suspicion

Inklings, the an Oxford group, 1930s–1960s, composed of C. S. Lewis, J. R. R. Tolkien, C. Williams, and others

ink/pot, -stand, -well (one word)

in-laws relatives by marriage (hyphen)

in/ limine (Lat.) at the outset, abbr. *in lim.*; — *loco* in place of; — *loco citato* in the place cited, abbr. *loc. cit.*; — *loco parentis* in the position of parent; — *medias res* into the midst of affairs; — *medio* in the middle; — *medio tutissimus ibis* the middle course is safest; — *memoriam* to the memory (of)

inn, name of *see* **hotel**

innamorat/o f. *-a see* **inam-**

inner (typ.) the side of a sheet containing the second page

innervate supply (an organ etc.) with nerves; cf. **ener-**

Innes,/ Cosmo (1798–1874) Scottish historian, — **James Dickson** (1887–1914) British painter, — **Michael** pseud. of **John Innes Mackintosh Stewart** (1906–94) British novelist, — **Thomas** (1662–1744) Scottish historian

Inness, George (1825–94) US painter

innings a portion of a game played by one side, pl. same; *not* inning (except in US)

Innisfail *use* **Inishfail**

Inniskilling/ Dragoon Guards, — Fusiliers; *see also* **Enniskillen**

innkeeper (one word)

Innocents' Day 28 Dec. (caps.)

innoculate *use* **ino-**

in nomine (Lat.) in the name (of a person)

Innsbruck Austria

Inns of Court, the Inner Temple, Middle Temple, Lincoln's Inn, Gray's Inn

in/- nubibus (Lat.) in the clouds, — *nuce* in a nutshell

innuendo/ an oblique, disparaging, or suggestive remark; pl. **-es**; *not* inu- (not ital.)

Innuit *use* **Inuit**

inoculate inject an immunizing serum into; *not* en-, inn-

in/ pace (Lat.) in peace; — *pari materia* in an analogous case; — *partibus infidelium* in the regions of unbelievers, abbr. **i.p.i.**, *in partibus*; cf. **Bishop**

in-patient (hyphen, one word in US)

in petto (It.) secretly

in/ pontificalibus in pontifical vestments; — *posse* potentially; — *potentia* potentially; — *primis* use **imprimis**; — *principio* in the beginning, abbr. *in pr.*; — *propria persona* in his, *or* her, own person; — *puris naturalibus* naked

input/ (verb) **-ting,** past and past part. **-ted** or **input**

inquir/e undertake a formal or intellectual investigation; **-y** such an investigation; cf. **enquire**

inquorate lacking a quorum

in/ re (Lat.) in the matter of, — *rem* (law) relating to a matter, — *rerum natura* in the nature of things

INRI *Iesus Nazarenus Rex Iudaeorum* (Jesus of Nazareth, King of the Jews) (John 19: 19)

in/road, -rush (one word)

INS Immigration and Naturalization Service

ins. insurance

in saecula saeculorum (Lat.) for ever and ever

insconce *use* **en-**

in se (Lat.) in itself, in themselves

Insecta (zool.) (Lat. pl.) insects, *not* -ae

inselberg an isolated hill or mountain rising abruptly from its surroundings (not cap.)

insert (bind.) a bookmark, advertisement, etc., slipped loose inside bound pages; a folded section of book printed separately but bound in with the book, *formerly* inset

inset (typ.) a small map etc. printed within the borders of a larger one

inshallah (Arab.) if Allah wills

insign/ia (pl. and sing.); badges of office (not ital.); **-e** (rare) sing. form

insipient unwise, foolish; *not* inci-

insisten/ce, -t *not* -ance, -ant

in situ (Lat.) in position

insnare *use* **en-**

in so far (three words, one word in US)

insomuch to such an extent; inasmuch (one word)

insoucian/ce lack of concern, **-t** unconcerned (not ital.)

Inspector abbr. **Insp.**

Inspector-General abbr. **IG, Insp.-Gen.**

INST *in nomine Sanctae Trinitatis* (in the name of the Holy Trinity)

inst. instant; institut/e, -es, -ion

Inst. Act. Institute of Actuaries

install/, -lation (two *l*s), **-ment** (one *l* except in US)

instant of this month, abbr. **inst.**

instantaneous occurring or done instantly

instanter at once (joc.) (not ital.)

in statu/ pupillari (Lat.) in a condition of pupillage, — — *quo* (*ante, prius; nunc*) in the same state (as formerly; as now)

instauration (formal) restoration, renewal

Inst./D. Institute of Directors, **—F.** Institute of Fuel

instil/ inculcate gradually (one *l* except in US); **-led, -ling**

Institut de France the association of five French academies: Académie des beaux-arts, Académie française, Académie des inscriptions et belles-lettres, Académie des sciences, Académie des sciences morales et politiques

Institute *see* separate entries beginning **I.** or **Inst.** (Institute of), **FI** (Fellow of the Institute of), **RI** (Royal Institute of)

Institut français du Royaume-Uni the French Institute, London

Institution *see* separate entries beginning **I.** (Institution of), **FI** (Fellow of the Institution of), **RI** (Royal Institution of)

institutionalize *not* -ise, -ionize

institutor *not* -er

Inst./P. Institute of Physics, **—R.** Institute of Refrigeration

instruct/or *not* -er; f. **-ress**

instrument/, -al abbr. **instr.**

insurance when effected against a risk, *but* **assurance** of life

insur/e provide for a possible contingency, **-er** (spelling in all insurance senses); abbr. **ins.**; cf. **assurance; assure; ensure**

inswathe *use* **en-**

int. interest, interior, interjection, internal, international, interpreter

intaglio/ an incised design, pl. **-s** (not ital.); (typ.) a printing process based on an etched or incised plate

intailed *use* **en-**

intangible *not* -able

intarsia mosaic woodwork

integration, sign of (math.) ∫

intelligentsia (collective noun) the intellectual part of a population, *not* -zia

Intelpost International Electronic Post

Intelsat International Telecommunications Satellite Consortium

in tenebris (Lat.) in darkness, in doubt

inter/ bury; **-red, -ring**

inter (Lat.) between

inter intermediate

inter/ *alia* among other things, — *alios* among other persons

intercity (*but* 'InterCity' (propr.), a type of train) (one word)

inter-class (hyphen, one word in US)

inter/**collegiate, -colonial, -com** (no point), **-continental** (one word)

interdict/, **-ion, -ory**

interest abbr. **int.**, in Fr. m. *intérêt*

interface (comput.) a boundary or link between two computer units (one word)

interim (not ital.)

interior abbr. **int.**

interjection abbr. **int., interj.**

interlea/**f** an extra leaf inserted between the regular leaves of a book; pl. **-ves**; **-ve** insert such a leaf

interlinear matter (typ.) small type between lines of larger type

intermarr/**iage, -y** (one word)

intermedi/**ate** abbr. **inter.**

intermezz/**o** a short piece of entertainment, pl. **-i**; (cap., ital.) an opera by Richard Strauss, 1924

intermission a pause or cessation; interval between parts of a play, film, etc.

intermit/ stop for a time; **-ted, -tent, -ting**

internal/ abbr. **int.**; **-combustion engine** (one hyphen)

Internal Revenue Service (US) = **Inland Revenue Service**

international abbr. **int., internat.**, (US) **internat'l, int'l**

International,/ **the first** an association of working classes of all countries (Marxist 1862–73); — **the second** ('Socialist' 1889–); — **the third** (Russian Communist 1919–43)

also called the Comintern; — **the fourth** (Trotskyist 1938–)

'Internationale, The' French poem adopted internationally as a socialist hymn, until 1944 the Soviet anthem

internationalize *not* -ise

Internet (comput.) (cap., one word)

internist (med.) a specialist in internal diseases, (US) a general practitioner

inter nos (Lat.) between ourselves

internuncio/ a papal ambassador, pl. **-s** (not ital.)

interoceanic (one word)

interpellate (parl.) interrupt to demand explanation

interplanetary (one word)

Interpol International Criminal Police Commission

interpolate make insertions

interpret/, **-ed, -er** abbr. **int.**, **-ing**; **-ative** (adj.) *not* -pretive; **-atively** (adv.)

interregnum/ a period between one ruler and another, pl. **-s** *or* (esp. in classical contexts) **-a** (not cap.); **the** — in Germany (1254–73), in England (1649–60) (cap.)

interrelat/**ed, -ionship** (one word)

interrog. interrog/ation, -ative, -atively

in terrorem (Lat.) as a warning

interrupter *not* -or

inter se (Lat.) among, *or* between, themselves

inter vivos from one living person to another

inter-war in the period between two wars, esp. the two world wars (hyphen, one word in US)

in testimonium (Lat.) in witness

inthral *use* **en-**

inthrone *use* **en-**

intitule etc., *not* en-; *but* **entitle**

intonaco (It.) a plaster surface for fresco painting, *not* -ico

in toto (Lat.) entirely

intra/ (Lat.) within, — *muros* privately

intramuscular within a muscle (one word), abbr. **IM**

intrans. intransitive

intransigent (adj.) uncompromising, in Fr. *intransigeant* (m. and adj.) (no accent)

intrap *use* **en-**

intrauterine within the womb (one word)

intravenous within a vein (one word), abbr. **IV**

intra vires (Lat.) within one's powers

in-tray (hyphen)

intreat *use* **en-**

intrench *use* **en-**

intrigant/ f. **-e** an intriguer (not ital.)

introduction abbr. **introd.**

introvert *not* intra-

intrust *use* en-

intubate *not* en-

intussusception (physiol.) the taking in of foreign matter by living organism, withdrawal of one portion of a tube into another (double *s*)

intwine, intwist *use* **en-**

Inuit (of or relating to) (a member of) a Canadian Native American people, or the language of this people (*properly* **Inupiaq**); *not* Inn-; *see also* **Eskimo; Inuk; Yupik**

Inuk/ (of or relating to) (a member of) a Canadian or Greenland Native American people, or the language of this people (*properly* **-titut**); *not* Inn-

Iñupiat (of or relating to) (a member of) an Alaskan Native American people, or the language of this people; *not* Inn-

inure accustom, (law) take effect; *not* en-

in/ usu (Lat.) in use, — ***utero*** in the womb, — ***utroque iure*** under both laws (canon and civil)

inv. invent/ed, -or; invoice

inv. *invenit* (designed this)

in vacuo (Lat.) in empty space

Invalides, Hôtel des Paris, *see* **Hôtel**

invenit (Lat.) designed this, abbr. **inv.**

invent/ed, -or *not* -er, abbr. **inv.**

Inveraray Strathclyde, *not* -ry

inverness a sleeveless coat with removable cape (not cap.)

Inverness-shire a former county of Scotland (hyphen)

Invertebrata (collective noun) all animals other than vertebrates

inverted commas *see* **quotation marks**

inverter *not* -or

Inverurie Grampian

investor *not* -er

in vino veritas (Lat.) a drunken person speaks the truth

invita Minerva (Lat.) uninspiredly

in/ vitro (Lat.) in the test tube, — ***vitro fertilization*** abbr. **IVF** (caps.), — ***vivo*** (Lat.) in the living organism

invoice abbr. **inv.**

involucre (anat., bot.) a covering, envelope (not ital.)

inwards *use* **inward**

inweave *not* en-

inwrap, inwreathe *use* **en-**

inyala a large S. African antelope, *not* ny-

I/O (comput.) input/output

io (Gr., Lat.) an exclamation of triumph or strong emotion (ital.)

IOC International Olympic Committee

iodine symbol **I**

IOF Independent Order of Foresters

IOGT International Order of Good Templars

IoM Isle of Man (*also* **IOM, IM**)

Ion. Ionic

Ion/ian (hist.) of Ionia, (mus.) the mode; **-ic** (of) the dialect and architectural order (cap.)

ioni/c of, relating to, *or* using, ions; **-ze** to convert into ions, *not* -ise

IOOF Independent Order of Odd Fellows

IOP Institute of Painters in Oil Colours

IOR Independent Order of Rechabites

iota/ the ninth letter of the Gr. alphabet (*I*, *ι*); — **adscript** printed after lower-case alpha, eta, and omega: αι, ηι, ωι; — **subscript** printed beneath alpha, eta, and omega: ᾳ, ῃ, ῳ

IOU I owe you

IoW Isle of Wight (*also* **IOW, IW**)

Iowa off. abbr. **Ia.**, postal **IA**

IP input primary

IPA India Pale Ale, International Phonetic Alphabet, International Phonetic Association

IPCS Institution of Professional Civil Servants

IPD (Sc. law) *in praesentia Dominorum* (in the presence of the Lords [of Session])

ipecacuanha (bot., med.) a purgative root

IPI International Press Institute

i.p.i. *in partibus infidelium* (in the regions of unbelievers)

IPM Institute of Personnel Management

I.Prod.E. Institution of Production Engineers

i.p.s. inches per second

ipse dixit (Lat., 'he himself has said it') a dogmatic statement resting merely on the speaker's authority

ipsissima verba (Lat.) the precise words

ipso facto (Lat.) by that very fact or act, thereby; *prefer* **eo ipso**

IPTS International Practical Temperature Scale

IQ intelligence quotient

i.q. *idem quod* (the same as)

Iqbal, Sir Muhammad (1875–1938) Punjabi poet and philosopher, 'father of Pakistan'

Iquique Chile

IR infrared, Inland Revenue

Ir iridium (no point)

Ir. Irish

IRA Irish Republican Army

irade (Turk.) a written decree signed by the Sultan himself

Iran/, -ian, -ic; abbr. **Iran.**

Iraq/ *not* Irak; adj. **-i**

Irawadi *use* **Irrawaddy**

IRBM intermediate-range ballistic missile

IRC International Red Cross

Ireland abbr. **Ire.**, in Gaelic **Éire**

Irena Ireland personified

irenic (lit.) aiming or aimed at peace; *not* -ical, ei-

irenicon *use* **ei-**

Irian Jaya Indonesian for **W. New Guinea**

iridescen/ce the play of rainbow colours, **-t**; *not* irr-

iridium symbol **Ir**

iris/ (anat., bot.) pl. **-es**

Irish abbr. **Ir.**

Irishism *not* Iricism, *but prefer* **Hibernicism**

Irkutsk E. Siberia; *not* Irkoo-, Irkou-

IRO Inland Revenue Office, International Refugee Organization

iron symbol **Fe** (ferrum)

ironclad (one word)

Iron Curtain (two words, caps.)

ironic *not* -ical

iron mould (two words) *not* -mold (US)

iron ration (two words)

Ironside/ the sobriquet of Edmund II, —, **William Edmund, Baron** (1880–1959) British soldier; **-s** Cromwell's troops in the Civil War

Ironsides, Old nickname of the USS *Constitution*, a forty-four-gun frigate

iron/ware, -work (one word)

Iroquoian (of or relating to) a language family of eastern N. America

Iroquois a Native American Indian confederacy of peoples formerly inhabiting New York State; (of or relating to) a member of any of these peoples or their languages (pl. same)

Irrawaddy a river in Burma, *not* Irawadi

irreconcilable *not* -eable, -iable

irredentist one who (re)claims regions for his country, esp. (cap.) Italian

irrefragable unanswerable, *not* -ible

irreg. irregular, -ly

irregardless *use* **regardless**

irreparable *not* -pairable

irreplaceable *not* -cable

irresistibl/e, -y *not* -able, -ably

irridescen/ce, -t *use* **iri-**

irrupt/ enter forcibly or suddenly; cf. **erupt**; **-tion**

IRS Inland Revenue Service, (US) Internal Revenue Service

Irtysh a river in Cent. Asia

Irún Spain

Irvine Strathclyde

IS input secondary, Irish Society

is. island, -s; isle, -s

Isa. Isaiah

Isaiah (OT) abbr. **Isa.**

Isaian of the prophet Isaiah, *not* Isaiahian

ISBN International Standard Book Number

Isère a river and dép. SE France

Iseult Tristram's lady-love; the many variants reflect different retellings (e.g. **Isode** in Malory, **Isolde** in Wagner's opera)

Isfahan Iran, *not* Isp-

Isherwood, Christopher (William Bradshaw) (1904–86) English novelist

ISI International Statistical Institute, Iron and Steel Institute

Isidore of Seville (570–636) Archbishop of Seville and encyclopedia writer

isl. island, -s (*prefer* **I.** *or* **is.**); isle, -s

Islam literally 'surrender (to God)', the Muslim religion; *see also* **Muslim**

island/, -s abbr. **I., is.**; when with name to have cap., as Cape Verde Islands; in Fr. f. *île*

Island (Ger., Dan. n.) Iceland, **Isländer** (Ger. m.) an Icelander

Ísland Icelandic for **Iceland**

Islay Strathclyde, *not* Isla

isle/, -s abbr. **I., isl.**

Isle of/ Man abbr. **IoM, IOM, IM;** — **Wight** abbr. **IoW, IOW, IW**

Isleworth London

ISM Imperial Service Medal, Incorporated Society of Musicians

ism the suffix used as generic noun (no hyphen)

Ismaili (a member) of a Muslim sect

ISO (Companion of the) Imperial Service Order, International Organization for Standardization

isobar (meteor.) *not* -are (not ital.)

Isocrates (436–338 BC) Athenian orator

isola (It.) island

Iso/ld, -lde, -lt, -lte, -ulde *see* **Iseult**

isosceles (geom.) of a triangle, having two sides equal

isotop/e a form of an element differing from other forms in the mass of its atoms, **-ic**

isotron a device for separating isotopes by accelerating ions

isotrop/ic (phys.) having same properties in all directions, **-y**

ISP (comput.) Internet service provider

Ispahan *use* **Isfa-**

Israel/i (noun and adj.) (a citizen) of the modern state of Israel, est. 1948; **-ite** (noun) one of the ancient Jewish people, adj. **-itic, -itish** (in Bible only)

ISSN International Standard Serial Number

issue, second (bibliog.) state resulting from sheets of same edition being bound up with new title page and additional matter, or in a different order; the original state of that edition is then called the first issue; *see also* **impression**

Istanbul Turkey

isth. isthmus

isthmian of or relating to an isthmus, esp. (cap.) to the Isthmus of Corinth in S. Greece

Isthmian games one of the four principal Panhellenic festivals

I.Struct.E. Institution of Structural Engineers

It. Italian, Italy

i t a (spaced lower case, no points) Initial Teaching Alphabet

ital. italic

Italian abbr. **It.**

italic (typ.) abbr. **ital.**

italice (Lat.) in Italian

italicize to print in italic type, *not* -ise

italienne, à l' (Fr.) in Italian style (lower-case *i*)

Italiote of the ancient Greek colonies in S. Italy, *not* -ot

Italy abbr. **It.**; in Fr. f. *Italie*, Ger. n. *Italien*, It. *Italia*

ITAR-TASS the official news agency of Russia, renamed from **TASS** 1992; *see also* **TASS**

item a separate thing (as in a list)

item (Lat.) also, likewise

itemize give item by item, *not* -ise

itin. itinerary

ITN Independent Television News

ITO International Trade Organization

its possessive pronoun (no apos.)

it's it is, it has

itsy-bitsy *or* **itty-bitty**

ITU International Telecommunication Union (UN), Intensive Therapy Unit

ITV Independent Television

IU international unit

IUD intrauterine (contraceptive) device, intrauterine death (of the fetus before birth)

Iun. Lat. abbr. for **Iunius**

IUPAC International Union of Pure and Applied Chemistry

IV intravenous, (roman numeral) four (no point); *see also* **IIII**

Ivanovich, Ivan a nickname for a Russian, as in English 'John Bull'

Iveagh, Earl of

IVF *in vitro* fertilization

ivied clothed with ivy, *not* ivyed

Iviza *use* **Ib-**

Ivory Coast W. Africa

ivy pl. **ivies**

Ivybridge Devon (one word)

Ivy League a group of universities in the E. USA, usually considered to consist of Brown, Columbia, Cornell, Dartmouth, Harvard, Princeton, University of Pennsylvania, and Yale

IW Isle of Wight

IWES Institution of Water Engineers and Scientists

Iwo Jima an island in N. Pacific, taken by the US Marines 1945

IWW Industrial Workers of the World (US)

IX (roman numeral) nine (no point)

I Zingari a cricket club

izmir Turkey, *formerly* Smyrna

J (at cards) jack, (phys.) joule, Joule's mechanical equivalent of heat, (after judge's name) justice; traditionally (and often still) not used in the numeration of series

J. Journal (in abbr. title), judge, *judex* (judge), (Ger.) *Jahr* (year)

j (med. prescriptions) one, (math.) square root of minus one

JA Judge Advocate

Jabalpur Madhya Pradesh, India; *formerly* Jubbulpore

Jac. *Jacobus* (James)

jacana a small tropical wading bird; *not* jaç-, jass-

jacaranda any tropical American tree of the genus *Jacaranda* or *Dalbergia*

jacconet *use* **jaco-**

jack (naut.) a small ship's flag, esp. one showing nationality; *see also* **Union Jack**

jack, every man each and every person (three words, not cap.)

jackanapes (sing.) a pert or insolent fellow (one word)

Jack and Jill *not* Gill

jackaroo (Austral. sl.) originally a newcomer (usually from England), now a novice on a sheep- or cattle-station; *not* -eroo

jackass a male ass, a stupid person

jack/boot, -daw (one word)

jacket/, -ed, -ing

Jack Frost frost personified (two caps.)

jack/fruit, -hammer (one word)

jack-in-the-box (hyphens)

Jack Ketch the hangman; *not* Ca-, Ki-

jackknife (one word)

jack of all trades (four words)

jack-o'-lantern (hyphens) *not* -a-

jack/pot, -rabbit (one word)

Jack Russell a breed of terrier (caps.)

Jackson/, Andrew, 'Old Hickory' (1767–1845) US President 1829–37, **-ian**; **—, Thomas Jonathan, 'Stonewall'** (1824–63) Confederate general at the first battle of Bull Run, 1861

jack/staff, -stone, -straw (one word)

Jack tar a sailor (one cap.)

Jacob/ean of or relating to the reign of James I of England; of St James the Less, of the apostle St James or the Epistle of St James; *see also* **Jacobi**

Jacobethan (design) displaying a combination of Elizabethan and Jacobean styles

Jacobi, Karl Gustav Jakob (1804–51) German mathematican, hence (in math.) **Jacobian, Jacobi polynomial**; *see also* **Jacobean**

Jacobin/ (hist.) a French Dominican friar, a member of a radical democratic club established in Paris in 1789, any extreme radical; **-ic, -ism**; *see also* **Jacobean**

jacobin a pigeon with reversed feathers on the back of its neck like a cowl, *not* -ine

Jacobit/e an adherent of James II of England/ James VII of Scotland after his departure, or of the Stuarts; **-ical, -ism**

Jacob's/ ladder a plant, *Polemonium caeruleum*; **— staff** a surveyor's iron-shod rod

Jacobus Lat. for James, abbr. **Jac.**

jacobus a gold coin of James I

jaconet a medium cotton cloth, *not* jacc-

Jacquard/, Joseph Marie (1752–1834) French weaver, hence **— loom** (not cap.)

jacquerie any brutal peasant revolt; (cap.) that in France, 1358

Jacques/ Fr. for **James**; **— Bonhomme** James Goodfellow, a popular name for a French peasant; *cf.* **Robin Goodfellow**

jacta est alea (Lat.) the die is cast

jactation boasting

jactitation (med.) restless tossing of the body, (law) the offence of falsely claiming to be someone's husband or wife

jacuzzi/ (propr.) a large bath with underwater jets of water to massage the body, pl. **-s** (*properly*, and in US, cap., often used lower case)

j'adoube (Fr.) 'I adjust', said by a chess player touching, but not moving, a man

Jaeger (propr.) a woollen clothing material from which vegetable fibres are excluded (cap.)

jaeger a hunter; a seabird of the skua family; *not* ya-; *see also* **Jäger**

JAG Judge Advocate General

Jäger (Ger. m.) huntsman, rifleman

Jag/gernaut, -anath *use* **Juggernaut**

jaghire Indian land tenure; *not* -gheer, geer, -gir

Jago Cornish for **James**

Jahr/ (Ger. n.) year, pl. **-e** (*not* Jä-) abbr. **J.**; **-buch** (n.) yearbook, abbr. **Jb.**, pl. **-bücher**, abbr. **Jbb.**; **-esbericht** (m.) annual report; **-gang** (m.) year's issue, number, etc., abbr. **Jg.** (caps., one word)

jährlich (Ger. adj.) annual

Jahveh *use* **Yahweh**

jai alai (Sp.) a game like pelota

jail/, -bird, -break, -er (one word) *not now* gaol (except in hist. contexts)

Jaime Sp. for **James**

Jain (of or relating to) (an adherent of) a non-Brahmanical Indian religion

Jaipur Rajasthan, India; *see also* **Jeypore**

Jakarta Indonesia, *not* Da-, Dj-

Jakob Ger. for **Jacob**, **James**

Jakutsk Siberia, *use* **Yak-**

Jalalabad Afghanistan; Uttar Pradesh, India

Jalandhar *use* **Jullundur**

jalapeño/ a hot green chilli pepper, pl. **-s**

jalopy a dilapidated motor car, *not* -ppy

jalousie an external window shutter

Jam (hist.) (a hereditary title of) any of certain princes and noblemen in the Indian subcontinent (ital.)

jam/ pack tightly; **-med**, **-ming**; cf. **jamb**

Jamaica a Caribbean island, abbr. **Jam.**

jamb a side post, as of a door; cf. **jam**

jambon/ (Fr. cook. m.) ham, **-neau** a small ham

jamboree a celebration or merrymaking, a large rally of Scouts

James abbr. **Jas.**

Jamesone, George (1588–1644) Scottish painter

Jameson/ Raid S. Africa, 1895–6; from **Sir Leander Starr —** (1853–1917) S. African statesman

James's Day, St 25 July (caps., apos.)

jamia (Urdu) university, as Jamia Millia Islamia

Jamieson, John (1759–1838) Scottish lexicographer; *see also* **James-**

jam satis (Lat.) enough by this time

Jan. January

Janáček, Leoš (1854–1928) Czech composer

Jane Doe (US) a hypothetical average woman; *see also* **John Doe**

Jane Eyre a novel by C. Brontë, 1847

Janeite an admirer of Jane Austen's writings

Jane's yearbooks on aircraft, ships, etc. (apos.); italicize as part of title

Janglish *use* **Japl-**

janizary *not* -issary; in Turk. **yeniçeri**

Jan Mayen an Arctic island (Norw.)

Jansen/, Cornelius (1585–1638) RC Bishop of Ypres, **-ist** (cap.)

janséniste (Fr. m., f.) (of or relating to) a Jansenist (not cap.)

Janssen,/ Cornelius (**Otto**) (1590–1665) Dutch painter, **— Johannes** (1829–91) German historian, **— Pierre Jules César** (1824–1907) French astronomer

Janssens, Abraham (1569–1631) Dutch painter

January abbr. **Jan.**

Janus the Roman god of doors and beginnings, depicted as having two faces

janvier (Fr. m.) January, abbr. **janv.** (not cap.)

Jap/ (colloq., usually derog.) (a) Japanese, pl. **-s** (no point)

Jap. Japan/, -ese

Japan abbr. **Jap.**, in Jap. **Nippon**

japan/ to lacquer with a hard varnish; **-ned**, **-ner**, **-ning**

Japanese/ abbr. **Jap.**; **— paper** handmade (usually in Japan), used for proofs of etchings and engravings

Japheth the third son of Noah, *not* -et

Japlish a blend of Japanese and (pseudo-)English, used in Japan, *not* Jang-

Jaques a character in Shakespeare's *As You Like It*; *not* -cq-

jar/, -red, -ring

Jardin/ d'Acclimatation, — des Plantes Paris, botanical and zoological gardens

jardinière an ornamental flowerpot, a dish of mixed vegetables (not ital.)

jargon words or expressions used by a particular group or profession; a translucent, colourless, or smoky variety of zircon; *not* -oon

jargonelle a pear, *not* -el (not ital.)

jarl (hist.) a Norse or Danish chieftain, *not* y-

Järnefelt, (Edvard) Armas (1869–1958) Finnish composer

Jaroslav (Russ.) *use* **Yaroslavl'** (place), **Yaroslav** (person); in Pol. **Jarosław**

jarrah an Australian mahogany gum tree

Järvefelt, Göran (1947–89) Swedish opera director

Jarvie, Bailie Nicol a character in Scott's *Rob Roy*

Jas. James

jasmine (bot.) *not* -in, jessamine, -in

jaspé mottled, veined, of materials and floor coverings (not ital.)

jassana *use* **jac-**

Jassy Ger. for **Iaşi**

Jaume Catalan for **James**

Jaunpur Uttar Pradesh, India

Jaurès, Jean Léon (1859–1914) French socialist

Javanese of or relating to Java in Indonesia, its people, or its language; *not* Javan; abbr. **Jav.**

Javelle water a bleach or disinfectant; *not* -el, -elle's

jawbone (one word)

jawohl (Ger.) yes, certainly (one word); *not* -woll

Jaycees (US) a national and international civic organization

jaywalk/, -er, -ing (one word)

Jb. (Ger.) *Jahrbuch* (yearbook)

JC Jesus Christ, Julius Caesar, Justice Clerk

J.-C. (Fr.) *Jésus-Christ* (hyphen)

JCB (propr.) a type of mechanical excavator

JCL (comput.) job-control language

JCR Junior Common Room, (Cambridge University) Junior Combination Room

JD Junior Deacon, Junior Dean, *Jurum Doctor* (Doctor of Laws)

je (Fr.) I (cap. only at beginning of sentence)

Jeaffreson, John Cordy (1831–1901) English historical writer

Jean (Fr.) **John**

Jeanne d'Arc (Fr.) Joan of Arc

Jean Paul pseud. of **J. P. F. Richter**

Jedda *use* **Jiddah**

jee-ho *use* **gee-**

Jeejeebhoy, Sir Jamsetjee (1783–1859) Indian philanthropist

jeep a small sturdy esp. military motor vehicle with four-wheel drive; (propr.) a similar civilian vehicle (cap.)

jee-up *use* **gee-**

Jefferies, Richard (1848–87) English naturalist

Jefferson, Thomas (1743–1826) third US President

Jefferys, Thomas (*fl.* 1732–71) English cartographer

Jeffrey, Francis, Lord (1773–1850) Scottish jurist and literary critic

Jeffreys, George, Baron (1648–89) the infamous judge

jehad *use* **ji-**

Jehlam *use* **Jhelum**

Jehovah traditional form of **Yahweh**

jejune meagre, insipid (not ital.)

Jekyll and Hyde the eponymous character in *The Strange Case of Dr Jekyll and Mr Hyde*, by R. L. Stevenson, 1886

Jelalabad, Jellalabad *use* **Jala-**

jellaba accepted spelling var. of **djellaba**

jellify convert into jelly, *not* -yfy

Jell-o (US propr.) a fruit-flavoured gelatin dessert, = **jelly**

jelly/ baby, — bean (two words)

jellyfish (one word)

Jemappes, battle of Belgium, French victory over Austrians, 1792; *not* Jemm-

jemmy a short crowbar, *not* ji- (US)

je ne sais/ quoi (Fr.) an indescribable something, — — — *trop* I don't exactly know

Jenghis Khan *use* **G-**

Jenis/esi *use* **Yeniseisk**, **-sei** *use* **Yenisei**

Jenkins's Ear an incident that precipitated war with Spain, 1739

jennet a small Spanish horse; *not* genit, gennet, -tt; cf. **genet**

Jenůfa opera by Janáček, 1904; originally *Její pastorkyňa*

jeopardize endanger, *not* -ise

Jephthah a judge of Israel; *Jephtha* an oratorio about him by Handel, 1752

jequirity an Indian shrub with ornamental and medicinal seeds, *not* -erity

Jer. Jeremiah

jerbil *use* **ger-**

jerboa any small desert rodent of the family Dipodidae, distinct from the **gerbil**

jeremiad a doleful complaint or lamentation, a list of woes; *not* -de

Jeremiah (OT) abbr. **Jer.**

Jerez Spain, Mexico (no accent); *not* Xerez, in Fr. **Xérès**

jerfalcon *use* **gyr-**

jeroboam a wine bottle of four times the ordinary size (not cap.); a king of Israel (cap.) (1 Kgs. 12–14)

Jérôme Bonaparte (1784–1860) brother of Napoleon I

jerry/-builder a builder of unsubstantial houses (hyphen); **-building, -built**

jerrycan *not* jerri-

jerrymander *use* **ge-**

Jersey/ a light brown dairy cow from Jersey; (US colloq.) New Jersey (cap.); a knitted (usually woollen) pullover or similar garment, a plain-knitted (originally woollen) fabric (not cap.); pl. **-s**

Jerusalem artichoke (one cap.)

Jervaulx Abbey N. Yorks.

Jes. Jesus

Jespersen, Jens Otto Harry (1860–1943) Danish philologist, *not* -son

jessamin/, -e *use* **jasmine**

Jesse the father of David (OT)

Jesuits, Order of *Societas Jesu* (Society of Jesus), abbr. **SJ**

Jesus abbr. **Jes.**, in vocative (arch.) **Jesu**

jet black (two words, hyphen when attrib.)

jeté (ballet) a spring or leap with one leg forward and the other stretched backwards (not ital.)

jet/ engine, — lag (two words)

jet-propelled (hyphen)

jet propulsion (two words)

jetsam (naut.) goods thrown overboard; *not* -som, -some, -son; *see also* **flotsam and jetsam**

jet/ set (two words), **-setter** (hyphen)

jet stream (two words)

jeu/ (Fr. m.) game, pl. **-x**; — *de mots* a play on words; — *de paume* real tennis (court); **Musée du Jeu de Paume** (caps.) Paris; — *d'esprit* a witty (usually literary) trifle

jeune fille (Fr. f.) a girl

jeune/ premier (Fr.) a stage lover, f. — *première*

jeunesse dorée (Fr. f.) gilded youth

Jewel, John (1522–71) English bishop

jewel/, -led, -ler, -lery (one *l* in US)

jew's harp a small lyre-shaped instrument played against the teeth (initial cap. in US)

Jeypore Orissa, India; *see also* **Jaipur**

Jezebel a shameless or immoral woman (cap.)

Jg. (Ger.) *Jahrgang* (year's issues etc.)

Jhelum Pakistan, *not* Jehlam

Jhind *use* **Jind**

JHS *use* **IHS**

-ji in India, an honorific suffix attached to names, e.g. *guruji*

jiao a monetary unit of China, pl. same

jib of horse, also a sail; *not* -bb

jibba a Muslim man's long coat; *not* dj-, -bah

jibber *use* g-

jibe (US) agree, be in accord (usually followed by *with*); cf. **gibe**; **gybe**

Jibuti *use* **Djibouti**

JIC Joint Industrial Council

Jiddah Saudi Arabia, *not* Jedda

jiffy a short time, *not* -ey

jigger *use* **chigoe**

jigot *use* **gi-**

jigsaw/ (one word), **— puzzle** (two words)

jihad a holy war undertaken by Muslims against unbelievers, *not* je-; in Arab. *jihād*

Jilin Chinese province (Pinyin), in Wade–Giles **Kirin**

jillaroo (Austral. sl.) female station hand, *not* -eroo

jilliflower *use* **gilly-**

jimcrack *use* **g-**

Jim Crow/ (US) the practice of segregating blacks, **-ism**; (offens.) a black person; an implement for straightening iron bars or bending rails by screw pressure

Jiménez, Juan Ramón (1881–1958) Spanish poet

jimmy (US) = **jemmy** (crowbar)

Jind a town and former state, India; *not* Jh-

Jingis Khan *use* **Ge-**

jingo/ in declaration **'by —!'**; a fanatical patriot, pl. **-es**; **-ism, -istic**

jinnee (Muslim myth.) *not* djinn, ginn; pl. **jinn**; in Arab. *jinnī*, pl. *jinn*; *see also* **genie**

jinricksha *use* **rickshaw**

JIT, JiT *see* **Just in Time**

jiu-jitsu *use* **ju-**

JJ Justices

Jno. John, but use only in exact reprints of documents etc.

jnr. junior

JO *Journal Officiel*

Joan Catalan for **John**

joannes *use* **johan-**

Joan of Arc (1412–31) French national heroine, in Fr. **Jeanne d'Arc**

João Port. for **John**

jobcentre (Brit.) government offices displaying information about available jobs (one word)

job lot (two words)

job/sheet, -work (one word)

'Jock o' Hazeldean' a ballad mainly by Scott

jockstrap (one word)

jodel *use* **y-**

Jodhpur Rajasthan, India

jodhpurs riding breeches, *not* jhod-

Joe Blow (US colloq.) a hypothetical average man, = **Joe Bloggs**; *see also* **John Doe**

Joel (OT) not to be abbr.

johannes a gold coin of John V of Portugal, *not* joa-

Johannesburg S. Africa

Johannine of the apostle John, *not* -ean

Johannisberg Hesse, Germany

Johannisberger a Rhine wine, *not* -berg (not ital.)

John abbr. **J.**; *see also* **Jno.**; (NT) not to be abbr.

John Doe (US) a hypothetical average man, = **Joe Bloggs**; an anonymous man; *see also* **Jane Doe**

John Dory a fish, *not* -ey; also **dory**

Johnian (a member) of St John's College, Cambridge

johnny a fellow, man (not cap.)

John o' Groat's (**House**) a Highland site; the possessive apostrophe is often omitted

Johns Hopkins/ University, — — Medical Center Baltimore, Md.; *not* John (no apos.)

Johnson/, Lyndon Baines (1908–73) President of USA 1963–9, abbr. **LBJ** (no points); **—, Samuel** (1709–84) English prose-writer and lexicographer, **-ian**; *see also* **Jonson**

Johnsonese a florid style, *not* Jon-

John the Baptist (caps.)

Johore *see* **Malaya, Federation of**

joie de vivre (Fr.) joy of living (no hyphens)

joint/ capital, — stock etc. (hyphen when attrib.)

Jökulsárgljúfur (lit. 'Glacier River Gulch') **National Park** Iceland

jolie/ laide (Fr. f.) a fascinatingly ugly woman, pl. **-s laides**

Jon. Jonathan

Jonah, Book of (OT) not to be abbr.

Joneses/ as in 'keeping up with the —'; *not* Jones', -s's

jongleur (hist.) an itinerant minstrel (ital.)

jonquil a narcissus (not ital.)

Jonson, Benjamin ('Ben') (1572–1637) English playwright; *see also* **Johnson**

Joppa ancient name of **Jaffa**, Israel

Jordaens, Jakob (1593–1678) Dutch painter

Jordan/ adj. **-ian**

Jorrocks' Jaunts by R. S. Surtees, 1831–4

Jos. Joseph

Josephine, the Empress b. **Marie Josèphe-Rose Tascher de la Pagerie**, (1763–1814) widow of Viscount Beauharnais, married Napoleon I 1796, divorced 1809

Josh. Joshua (OT)

Josquin/ des Prez, b. — **Lebloitte** (d. 1521) Franco-Flemish composer and musician; the shortened form is 'Josquin', *not* 'des Prez'; *not* Prés

jostl/e push; **-er, -ing**

jot/, -ted, -ting

joule (phys.) an SI unit of energy, abbr. **J**

jour. journal, journey

jour/ (Fr. m.) day, abbr. **jr.**; — *de fête* a festival; — *de l'an* New Year's Day; — *des morts* All Souls' Day, 2 Nov.; — *gras* flesh day; — *maigre* fish day

journal abbr. **jour., J.** (in abbr. title)

journ/al (Fr. m.) newspaper, pl. **-aux**; — *intime* a private diary

Journal officiel the French and EU daily publications of legislation, abbr. **JO**

Journals, the a record of daily proceedings in Parliament (cap.)

journey abbr. **jour.**

joust a knightly combat, *not* just

Jovian of or like the god or pianet Jupiter

jowar a kind of sorghum = **durra**, in Hindi *jawār*

Joycean of or characteristic of **James (Augustine Aloysius) Joyce** (1882–1941) Irish novelist and poet, or his writings; a specialist in or admirer of Joyce's works

joy/ful, -ride, -stick (one word)

JP Justice of the Peace

JR *Jacobus Rex* (King James)

Jr. junior

jr. (Fr.) *jour* (day)

jt. joint

Juan Sp. for John

Juárez, Benito Pablo (1806–72) Mexican President 1861–5, 1867–72

Jubbulpore *use* **Jabalpur**

Jubilate Deo Ps. 100 as canticle (99 in Vulg.)

jud. judicial

Judaean of Judaea, *not* -ean

Judaeo- Jew(ish), *not* Judeo (US)

Judaize follow Jewish customs or rites, make Jewish; *not* -ise

Judg. Judges (OT)

Judge/ abbr. **J.**; — **Advocate** (no hyphen), abbr. **JA**; — **Advocate General** (no hyphen), abbr. **JAG** (caps.)

judgement/, -al a moral, practical, or informal deduction *but* **judgment/, -al** (law) a judge's or court's formal ruling; and in US in all contexts

Judgement Day, Last Judgement (caps.)

Judges (OT) abbr. **Judg.**

judicial abbr. **jud.**

Judith (Apocr.) not to be abbr.

judo/ a form of ju-jitsu, **-ist**

jug/, -ged, -ging, -ful

juge/ d'instance (Fr. m.) a legally trained justice of the peace, *formerly* — *de paix*; — *d'instruction* examining magistrate

Jugendstil (Ger.) art nouveau (ital., cap.)

Juggernaut an institution or notion to which persons blindly sacrifice themselves or others (cap.); *not* Ja-; in Hindi *Jagannath*; (Brit.) a large heavy motorized vehicle (not cap.)

Jugoslav/, -ia *use* Y-

juillet (Fr. m.) July (not cap.)

Juilliard/ Quartet, — **School of Music** New York City

juin (Fr. m.) June (not cap.)

ju-jitsu a Japanese system of unarmed combat and physical training; *not* jiu-, -jutsu; in Japanese *jūjutsu*; *see also* **judo**

ju-ju a charm or fetish of some W. African peoples, or its supernatural power (hyphen)

jukebox (one word)

julep a medicated drink; (US) a drink of spirits, sugar, ice, and mint; *not* -ap, -eb

Julian/ (331–63) Emperor of Rome, 'the Apostate'; — **Alps** Italy–Slovenia; — **calendar**

Julien, Saint- a claret (hyphen)

julienne (not ital.)

Juliet cap (two words, one cap.)

Jullundur India, *not* Jalandhar

July not to be abbr.

jumble sale (two words)

jumbo/ pl. **-s**; — **jet** (two words)

jumelles (Fr. f. pl.) opera glasses

jump rope (US) = **skipping rope**

jumpsuit (one word)

Jun. Junius, as Latin month *use* **Iun.**

jun. junior

junction abbr. **junc.**

June not to be abbr.

Juneau Alaska

Jung/, Carl Gustav (1875–1961) Swiss psychologist, **-ian**

junior abbr. **Jr., jun.**; *not* jnr., jr., junr. Use **Jr.** when it forms part of the bearer's name: 'J.

Doe, Jr.'; the comma preceding it is sometimes left out: follow the bearer's preference, if known. Use **jun.** where it is an ad hoc designation (like *fils*); here a comma always precedes it: 'J. Doe, jun.'

Junker (Ger. m.) a young squire or noble, a member of an exclusive (Prussian) aristocratic party (cap.)

junket/, -ed, -ing

junk food (two words)

junkie a drug addict

junk/ mail, — shop (two words)

junky of or like junk

junkyard (US) = **scrapyard**

Juno (Rom. myth.) wife of Jupiter, = **Hera**

junr. junior; *see* **junior**

junta a political or military clique; a council in Spain, Portugal, or S. America (not ital.)

Junto the Whig chiefs in reigns of William and Anne

jupe (Fr. f.), **jupon** (m.) a skirt or petticoat

jural of law, of rights and obligations

Jurassic (of or relating to) the second period of the Mesozoic era (cap., not ital.)

jure/ divino (Lat.) by divine right, — *humano* by human law

jurisp. jurisprudence

Juris utriusque Doctor (Lat.) Doctor of both civil and canon law, abbr. **JUD**

jury box (two words)

jury/man, -woman (one word)

jury-rigged (hyphen)

jus (Fr. cook. m.) natural juices from cooking

jus/ (Lat.) law, — *canonicum* canon law, — *civile* civil law, — *divinum* divine law, — *gentium* law of nations, — *gladii* the right of the sword

jusjurandum (Lat.) an oath, pl. *jurajuranda*

jus/ mariti (Lat.) right of husband to wife's property, — *naturae* law of nature, — *primae*

noctis droit de seigneur, — *relictae* right of the widow

Jussieu,/ Adrien de (1797–1853) and his father — **Antoine Laurent de** (1748–1836) French botanists

Just. Justinian

just a knightly combat, *use* **jou-**

juste milieu (Fr. m.) the golden mean

Justice a judge; abbr. **J**, pl. **JJ**; outside court the form of address or reference to a Supreme Court judge is **Mr**, *or* **Mrs**, **Justice**, followed by the surname

Justice Clerk, Lord the second highest Scottish judge (caps.), abbr. **JC**

Justice General, Lord the highest Scottish judge (caps.)

Justice of the Peace abbr. **JP**

justiciar/, -y a judge; *not* -er, -itiar (not ital.)

Justiciary, High Court of the supreme Scottish criminal court

justify (print.) put equal spaces between the words in a line of type so that they range on the measure; *see also* **full/ left, — right, — out**; **ragged left/, — right**

Justinian (483–565) Roman Emperor of the East, codified Roman law; abbr. **Just.**

Just in Time a Japanese manufacturing strategy designed to minimize stockpiling raw materials or finished product, in Jap. *kanban*; abbr. **JIT, JiT**

justitiar *use* **-ciar**

jut/, -ted, -ting

Juvenal (in Lat., **Decimus Junius Juvenalis**) (*c.*60–140) Roman poet, abbr. **Juv.**

juvenescen/ce, -t (the process of) passing from infancy to youth

juvenilia (pl.) works produced in one's youth (not ital.)

Jylland (Dan.) **Jutland**

j'y suis, j'y reste (Fr.) here I am, here I stay

K *kalium* (potassium), Kelvin (temperature scale), kelvin (unit of temperature), (chess) king (no point), the tenth in a series, thousand (*prefer* **k**)

K. (assaying) carat, king(s), King('s), Köchel (Mozart thematic catalogue number); *see also* **Kp.**

k (as prefix) kilo-, thousand; *see also* **kilo-**

k. (meteor.) cumulus

k (phys.) Boltzmann constant

K2 the second highest mountain in the world, in Karakoram Mountains

Kaaba the most sacred shrine at Mecca, in Arab. *al-Ka'bah*; *not* Caaba

kaan *use* **khan**

kabbala *use* **c-**

kabuki a popular traditional Japanese drama with highly stylized song

Kabul Afghanistan, *not* C-

kabushiki kaisha (Jap.) = public limited company, abbr. **KK**

Kádár, János (1912–89) Hungarian politician, Prime Minister 1956–8, 1961–5

kadi *use* **c-**

Kaffeeklatsch (Ger. m.) an informal gathering for coffee and conversation (not cap. or ital. in US)

Kaffir *use* **Xhosa**; (S. Afric. offens.) any black African; *not* Caffre, Kafir

kaffiyeh *use* **ke-**

Kaffraria S. Africa

Kafir a native of the Hindu Kush mountains of NE Afghanistan; *not* Caffre, Kaffir

kāfir (Arab.) infidel

Kafka/, Franz (1883–1924) Czech-born Austrian novelist and poet, **-esque**

kaftan long, belted garment worn in the Near East; *not* **c-**

kagoule *use* **c-**

Kahn-Freud, Sir Otto (1900–79) German-born English lawyer and scholar

kail Scots for **kale**

kaiman *use* **cay-**

Kainozoic *use* **Ceno-**

Kaisar-i-Hind/ (Anglo-Ind.) (the Caesar of India) former Indian title of the English monarch; *not* Q-, -er-; — **medal**, abbr. **K.i.H.**, **KIH**

Kaiser (Ger. m.) emperor (cap., not ital.)

kal. *kalendae*

kala-azar a tropical disease (hyphen)

Kalamazoo Mich.

kalarippayat an Indian martial art (ital.)

Kalashnikov any of various Russian automatic rifles, esp. the AK-47

kale the cabbage genus; *see also* **kail**; **kaleyard**

kalendae (Lat.) the calends (first day of the month), not *c-*; abbr. **kal.**

kalend/ar, -er, -s *use* **c-**

Kalevala the national epic of Finland, *not* -wala

kaleyard/ (Sc.) a kitchen garden, **kail-** in strict Scots; — **school** a group of 19th-c. fiction writers including J. M. Barrie, who described local town life in Scotland; *not* kailyard school

kali/f, -ph more learned forms of **caliph**, in Arab. *kalīfa*

Kalimantan Indonesian name for part of Borneo

Kaliningrad Russia, *formerly* Königsberg

kalium (Lat.) potassium, symbol **K**

kalmia (bot.) American evergreen shrub, *not* c-

Kalmyck a member of a Buddhist Mongolian people, their Ural-Altaic language; of this people; *not* -muck, -muk, C-

Kama the Hindu god of love (cap.)

kamarband *use* **cummerbund**

Kamboja *use* **Cambodia**

Kamchatka E. Siberia; *not* Kams-, -mtchatka, -mtschatka

Kamerun *use* **Cameroon**

kamikaze (the pilot of) a Japanese suicide aircraft (not ital.)

Kampuchea off. name of **Cambodia** 1975–89

kamsin *use* **kh-**

Kan. Kansas (off. abbr.)

kana any of various Japanese syllabaries

kanaka a South Sea Islander, esp. an indentured labourer; *not* canaker

Kanar/a a district of W. India, *not* C-; **-ese** a member of a Dravidian people in this area, their language; *see also* **Kannada**

kanaster *use* **c-**

Kanchenjunga a mountain in Himalayas, *not* Kinchin-

Kandahar Afghanistan, *not* C-

Kandy Sri Lanka

Kannada the Kanarese language written in the Kannada alphabet

Kanpur Uttar Pradesh, India; *not* Cawnpore

Kans/as off. abbr. **Kan.**, postal **KS**; **-an**

Kansas City Mo., Kan.

Kant, Immanuel (1724–1804) German philosopher

KANU Kenya African National Union

kaolin a fine white clay

kaon (phys.) a meson having a mass several times that of a pion, *not* K-meson

Kap. (Ger.) *Kapitel* (chapter)

kapellmeister a director of orchestra or choir (not cap., not ital.)

kappa the tenth letter of the Gr. alphabet (*K*, *κ*)

Kapurthala E. Punjab, India

kaput (sl.) broken, ruined (not ital.); from Ger. *kaputt*

karabiner a mountaineer's coupling link with a safety closure, *not* ca- (US)

Karachi Pakistan, *not* Kurrachee

Karafuto *use* **Sakhalin**

Karaite a member of Jewish sect that interprets scriptures literally

Karajan, Herbert von (1908–89) Austrian conductor

Karakoram Mountains Kashmir, *not* -um

karakul (fur of) Asian sheep; *not* c-, -cul

karaoke a form of entertainment in which people sing popular songs against a pre-recorded backing, *not* kari- (not ital.)

karat *use* c- (except in US as a measure of gold purity)

karate/ the Japanese art of unarmed combat, **-ka** an expert in this (one word)

kari *use* **karri**

Karl-Marx-Stadt the former name of **Chemnitz** during E. German sovereignty (hyphens)

Karlovingian *use* **Carolin-**

Karlovy Vary Czech Republic (no accent); *not* Carlsbad (except in historical contexts), Karlsbad

Karlsbad *use* **Karlovy Vary**

Karls/krona (Sweden) **-ruhe** (Germany) etc., *not* C-

karma (Buddhism) destiny (not ital.)

Kármán, Theodor von (1881–1963) Hungarian-born US physicist

Karnatic *use* **C-**

Kärnten (Ger.) **Carinthia**, Austria and Slovenia

Karoo a high pastoral plateau in S. Africa, *not* Karr- (cap.)

karoshi in Japan, death through overwork; in Jap. *karōshi*

Karpathian Mountains *use* **C-**

karri an Australian blue gum tree, *not* kari; *see also* **kauri**

Kartoum *use* **Kh-**

kasbah the citadel of a N. African city, or an Arab quarter near this; *not* c-

Kashmir/ NW India, *not* Cashmer(e); **-i** (of or relating to) (a native or the Dardic language of) Kashmir

Kassel Germany, *not* C-

kataboli/sm, -c *use* c-

katakana an angular form of Japanese kana

katana a long samurai sword

katharevousa *also* **katharévusa** (not cap.) a form of Greek favoured for official, learned, and technical writing (but not literature) before 1976, then combined with demotic to form Modern Greek

Katharina a character in Shakespeare's *The Taming of the Shrew*

Katharine/ characters in Shakespeare's *Love's Labour's Lost, Henry V*, and (**— of Aragon**) in *Henry VIII*; *see also* **Catherine**

Kathāsaritsāgara a Sanskrit epic

Kathay *use* C-

Katherine *see* C-; **Katharine**

kathism/a a section of the Greek Psalter, pl. *-ata*; not ca-

Kathmandu capital of Nepal, *not* Katm-

kathode *use* c-

kation *use* c-

Kattegat (Dan.), **Kattegatt** (Swed.) the strait between Denmark and Sweden, *not* C-

Kauffmann, Angelica (1741–1807) Swiss-born English painter

Kaufman, George Simon (1889–1961) US playwright

Kaunas Lithuania, *not* Kovno

kauri New Zealand coniferous tree etc., *not* the many variants (not ital.); cf. **cowrie**; **karri**

Kavafis *use* **Cavafy** in Eng. use

kavass a Turkish armed attendant, *not* the many variants

Kawabata, Yasunari (1899–1972) Japanese novelist

kayak/ an Eskimo canoe, *not* the many variants; **-er, -ing**

Kaye-Smith, Sheila (1889–1955) English novelist (hyphen)

Kazakhstan a former Soviet Socialist Republic; adj. **Kazakh**

Kazan′ Russia (prime accent), *not* Kas-

Kazantzakis, Nikos (1885–1957) Greek writer

KB kilobyte, (chess) king's bishop (no points), King's Bench, Knight Bachelor, Knight of the Order of the Bath

Kb kilobit

KBD King's Bench Division

KBE Knight Commander of the Order of the British Empire

KBP (chess) king's bishop's pawn (no points)

Kbps kilobits per second

KC King's College, King's Counsel

kc kilocycle; *see also* **kc/s**

KCB Knight Commander of the Order of the Bath

KCIE Knight Commander of the Order of the Indian Empire

KCL King's College London

KCMG Knight Commander of the Order of St Michael and St George

kc/s *prefer* **kHz**

kčs koruna (Czechoslovakia), since 1993 commonly abbr. **kč** (Czech Republic) and **ks** (Slovakia)

KCSI Knight Commander of the Order of the Star of India

KCVO Knight Commander of the Royal Victorian Order

KD knocked down

KE kinetic energy

Keats House Hampstead (no apos.)

Keäwe a character in R. L. Stevenson's *The Bottle Imp*

kebab *not* the many variants, *not* **kabob** (US)

keblah *use* **ki-**

Kedah *see* **Malaya, Federation of**

kedgeree *not* the many variants (not ital.)

Kedron *see* **Kidron**

Keele Staffs.

keelhaul a naval punishment (one word)

keelson (naut.) a line of timber fastening a ship's floor-timbers to its keel, *not* kelson

keepsake (one word)

keep standing (typ.) keep type or film stored in page from after first printing for possible reprint, abbr. **KS**

Kees, Weldon (1914–55) US poet and author

keeshond/ a Dutch breed of dog, pl. **-en**

kef a drowsy state induced by marijuana etc., the substance smoked to produce this state; the enjoyment of idleness; *not* kif (not ital.)

keffiyeh a Bedouin Arab headdress; in Arab. *keffiyya, kūfiyya*

kefir (Russ.) a drink of fermented cow's milk

Kelantan *see* **Malaya, Federation of**

kell/eck, -ick (naut.) *use* **killick**

Kellner/ (Ger.) f. **-in** waiter (cap.)

Kellogg College Oxford, *formerly* Rewley House

Kellogg Pact Paris 1928, fifteen leading nations renounced war

Kelly's Directories (apos.)

Kelmscott Press 1891–8, founded by W. Morris

kelpie a water spirit, *not* -y

kelson *use* **keel-**

Kelt/, -ic, -icism *use* **C-**

kelter *use* **ki-**

kelvin (sci.) symbol **K** (no point); *see also* **Thomson**

Kemal, Mustafa *see* **Atatürk**

Kempis, Thomas à (1379–1471) German monk, reputed author of *Imitatio Christi*

kendo the Japanese art of fencing with bamboo swords

Kenmare Co. Kerry

Kenmore Highland, Tayside

kennel/, -led, -ling (one *l* in US)

Kenney, James (1780–1849) Irish playwright

kentle *use* **quintal**

Kents Bank Cumbria (no apos.)

Kentucky off. abbr. **Ky.**, postal **KY**

Kenwigs a family in Dickens's *Nicholas Nickleby*

Kenya/ E. Africa; **-n**

Kenyatta, Jomo (1893–1978) Kenyan statesman

kephalic *use* **c-**

kepi (no accent, not ital.) Anglicized form of Fr. m. *képi* military cap

Kepler/, Johann (1571–1630) German astronomer, *not* Kepp-; **-ian**

keramic etc., *use* **c-**

kerb/, -side, -stone (one word); cf. **curb**

Kerch Crimea, *not* Kertch

kerfuffle disorder, fuss; *not* cur-, ge-, kur-

Kerguelen Island Indian Ocean

keris *see* **kris**

Kerkyra Modern Gr. name of **Corfu**

kermis *not* -ess, kirmess

kern/ (typ.) modify spacing between characters to allow for each letter's shape, **-ed**; (hist.) a light-armed Irish foot-soldier; *not* kerne

kernel/ a seed within a hard shell; **-led, -ly**

Kernow Cornish for Cornwall

keros/ene paraffin oil; *also* **-ine** (except in US)

Kerouac, Jack (1922–69) US novelist

kerseymere twilled woollen cloth, *not* cassi-; cf. **cashmere**

Kertch *use* **Kerch**

keskidee *use* **kiska-**

ketch (naut.) a two-masted vessel

Ketch, Jack the hangman; not Ca-, Ki-

ketchup *not* cat-, catsup

kettledrum (one word)

Keuper (geol.) the upper division of the Trias

keV kilo-electronvolt

key a wharf, *use* **quay**

keyboard/ (comput., mus., etc.) (one word); **-er** one who uses a computer keyboard, **-ist** one who plays a keyboard musical instrument

key-bugle (hyphen)

keyhole (one word)

Keynes/, John Maynard, Baron (1883–1946) British economist; **-ian** (adj.) of Keynes's economic theories; (noun) an adherent of these theories; **-ianism**

key/note, -pad, -punch, -ring (one word)

Keys, House of IoM (caps.), abbr. **HK**

key signature (mus.) (two words)

key/stone, -stroke, -way (one word)

Key West Fla. (two words)

keyword (one word)

KG Knight of the Order of the Garter, (Ger.) *Kommanditgesellschaft* (limited partnership)

kg kilogram(s) (no point)

KGB USSR state secret police, 'Committee of State Security' 1953–92; earlier post-revolution manifestations: **Cheka** 1917–22, **GPU** 1922–3, **OGPU** 1923–34, **NKVD** 1934–43, **NKGB** 1943–6, **MGB** 1946–53, **MVD** 1953–60; *see also* **FSB**

Kgotla an assembly of Bantu elders, the place for this; *not* kotla

Kgs., 1, 2 First, Second Book of Kings

Khachaturyan, Aram (Ilich) (1903–78) Armenian composer

khaddar an Indian homespun cloth

Khaibar Oasis Saudi Arabia

Khaiber Pass *use* **Khyber**

khaki (not ital.)

khal/eefate, -ifat *use* **caliphate**

khalif/, -a *use* **caliph**

khamsin an Egyptian hot wind in March, April, and May; *not* ha-, ka-, -seen

khan/ a title given to rulers and officials in Cent. Asia, Afghanistan, etc.; (hist.) the supreme ruler of the Turkish, Tartar, and Mongol tribes, *or* the emperor of China in the Middle Ages; **-ate**; **-um** a lady of high rank; a polite form of address affixed to a Muslim woman's name

khan an inn in an Eastern town or village, *not* kaan; *see also* **caravanserai**

Khan, Muhammad Ayub *see* **Ayub Khan, Muhammad**

Khanty (of or relating to) (a member of) a people living in the Ob River basin in W. Siberia, or (of) the Ob-Ugrian language of this people; *formerly* Ostyak

kharaj (Turk.) a tax on Christians; not -ach, -age, caratch

Kharoshthi one of the two oldest alphabets in the Indian subcontinent; cf. **Brahmi**

Khartoum capital of Sudan; *not* Ka-, -tum

Khaskura the Nepali language

Khayyám, Omar *see* **Omar Khayyám**

Khediv/e a viceroy of Egypt under Turkish rule 1867–1914; **-a** his wife; **-ate** his office; **-al** *not* -ial

khidmutgar (Ind.) a male waiter (*not* the many variants)

Khmer/ (of) a native of the ancient Khmer kingdom or of modern Cambodia, *or* (of) their language; **— Republic** name of Cambodia 1970–5; **— Rouge** Cambodian communists

Khoikhoi a S. African people (pl. same), *formerly* called Hottentot; their language is **Nama**

Khomeini, Ayatollah Ruhollah (1908–89) Iranian religious and political leader, head of state 1979–89

Khrushchev, Nikita (Sergeevich) (1894–1971) Soviet politician, Secretary-General of the Communist Party 1953–64, Prime Minister 1958–64

Khyber Pass NW Frontier Province, Pakistan; *not* Khai-

kHz kilohertz, 1,000 hertz (no point, cap. H); *not* kc/s

kiak *use* **kayak**

kiang a wild Tibetan ass

kibbutz/ an Israeli communal agricultural (etc.) settlement, pl. **-im**; **-nik** a member of it

kibitz/ look on at cards, be meddlesome; **-er** one who does this; *not* -bb-

kiblah the direction of the Kaaba, to which Muslims turn in prayer; a niche or slab in a mosque showing this direction (= **mihrab**); *not* ke-; in Arab. *ḳibla, qibla*

kibosh/ nonsense, *not* ky-; **put the — on** put an end to, finish

kickback a recoil, a payment for collaboration (one word)

kick-off (noun, football) (hyphen, one word in US)

kick/shaw, -sorter, -stand (one word)

kick-start (noun and verb) (hyphen)

kiddie (colloq.) a young child, *not* -y

kidmutgar *use* **khid-**

kidnap/, -ped, -per, -ping

kidney bean (two words)

Kidron (*or* **Ce-**) Palestine, **Ke-** in NEB; in Arab. **Wadi en Nar**

Kierkegaard, Søren (Aabye) (1813–55) Danish philosopher

Kiev capital of Ukraine, *not* -eff; **Kyiv, Kyjiw** are alt. Ukrainian forms

kif *use* **kef**

K.i.H. (*or* **KIH**) Kaisar-i-Hind medal

Kikuyu (of) the largest Bantu-speaking group in Kenya, or their language; pl. same

kil. kilderkin(s)

Kilauea a volcano in Hawaii, *not* -aua

Kilbracken, Baron (1847–1932) Sir Arthur Godley, of the India Office

kilderkin/ a cask for liquids etc., holding 16 or 18 gallons; pl. **-s**; abbr. **kil.**

Kilimanjaro extinct volcano, E. Africa (one word, divide Kilima-njaro)

Killala Co. Mayo, also Bishop of

Killaloe Co. Clare, also Bishop of

Killaloo Co. Londonderry

Killea Co. Donegal

Killeagh Co. Cork

Killen Highland

Killianwala *use* **Chili-**

killick a stone used as anchor; *not* -ock, kelleck, -ick

Killiecrankie Tayside

Killin Central

Killylea Co. Armagh

Killyleagh Co. Down

'Kilmansegg, Miss' a poem by T. Hood, 1828; *not* -eg

kilo/ shortened form of kilogram or kilometre (no point), pl. **-s**

kilo- usually indicates 1,000 (10³) times a unit of measurement, e.g. *kilometre, kilowatt*, but in computing it indicates a multiple of 1,024 (2¹⁰), e.g. *kilobit, kilobyte*; abbr. **k**, *not* K

kilobit (comput.) 1,024 (2¹⁰) bits, abbr. **Kb**

kilobyte (comput.) 1,024 (2¹⁰) bytes, as a measure of memory size; abbr. **KB**

kilocycle a former measure of frequency = 1 kilohertz, abbr. **kc**; *but use* **kHz** for **kc/s**

kilogram an SI unit of mass, *not* -me; abbr. **kg** (no point)

kilojoule 1,000 joules, esp. as a measure of the energy value of foods; abbr. **kJ**

kilolitre 1,000 litres, abbr. **kl** (no point); *not* -er (except in US)

kilometre/ 1,000 metres, *not* -er (except in US); **-age** *not* -rage; abbr. **km** (no point)

kiloton a unit of explosive power equivalent to 1,000 tons of TNT, *not* -tonne; abbr. **kT**

kilowatt/ 1,000 watts, abbr. **kW**; **-hour** (hyphen) abbr. **kWh**

kilter/ good condition, alignment (usually used in the phrase **out of —**); *not* ke-

Kimeridgian (geol.) (*not* -mm-) an Upper Jurassic clay found at Kimmeridge, Dorset (cap.)

Kim/ Il Sung (1912–94) Prime Minister and President of N. Korea 1948–94, father of — **Jong Il** (b. 1942) President of N. Korea 1994–

kimono/ a kind of gown, pl. **-s**

Kimric Welsh, *use* **Cym-**

kinaesthesia the sense of muscular effort, *not* kine (US)

Kincardine(shire) a former county of Scotland

Kincardine O'Neil Grampian (three caps.)

Kinchinjunga *use* **Kanchen-**

kindergarten/ a school for young children (not ital., not cap.), **-er** a student (*formerly* the teacher)

kinesthesia *use* **kinae-** (except in US)

kinfolk *use* **kins-** (except in US)

King/ abbr. **K.** (in chess, no point); (typ.) print as e.g. Edward VII, *or* the Seventh, *not* the VII,

VIIth; — **Charles's head** an obsession; — **Charles spaniel** (two caps.), *not* -s's

kingd. kingdom

kingmaker (one word)

King of Arms (her.) a chief herald, at the College of Arms: **Garter, Clarenceux,** and **Norroy and Ulster**; in Scotland: **Lyon** (three words); *not* King at Arms

kingpin (one word)

King's abbr. **K.**

Kings, First, Second Book of (OT) abbr. **1 Kgs., 2 Kgs.**

Kingsale, Baron *see also* **Kinsale**

King's Bench (apos.) abbr. **KB**

Kingsbridge Devon, Som. (one word)

King's/ College London (no comma) abbr. **KCL**; — **Counsel** abbr. **KC**; — **Cross** London and Sydney (apos.)

king-size(d) (hyphen)

King's/ Langley Herts., — **Lynn** Norfolk (apos.)

Kings Norton/ Leics., **Baron — —** (no apos.)

King's Printer *see* **printer**

Kings Sutton Oxon.

Kingsteignton Devon (one word)

Kingston Australia, Canada, Jamaica, USA

Kingstone Hereford, Som., Staffs., S. Yorks.

Kingston/ upon Hull Humberside, — **upon Thames** London (no hyphens)

Kingstown Dublin, off. **Dun Laoghaire**

Kingswinford W. Midlands (one word)

Kington Glos., Worcs.

Kinloss, Baroness

Kinnoull, Earl of

Kinross/, Baron, -shire a former county in Scotland (hyphen)

Kinsale Co. Cork; *see also* **Kingsale**

kinsfolk *not* kinfolk (US)

Kinshasa the capital of the Democratic Republic of Congo (Zaire)

kintle *use* **quintal**

Kintyre Strathclyde, *not* Cantire

Kioto Japan, *use* **Kyoto**

kip the basic monetary unit of Laos, *properly* **New —**

Kirchhoff, Gustav Robert (1824–87) German physicist

Kirghiz/ *use* **Kyrgyz**; **-ia** a former Soviet Socialist Republic, *now* **Kyrgyzstan**

Kiribati W. Pacific; adj. same

kirk/ a church (not cap.), **the — of Scotland** the Church of Scotland (cap.)

Kirkby in Ashfield Notts. (three words)

Kirkbymoorside N. Yorks. (one word)

Kirkcaldy Fife

Kirkcudbright Dumfries & Galloway

Kirkpatrick, Ralph (1911–84) US harpsichordist, compiler of catalogue of Domenico Scarlatti's keyboard works; catalogue abbr. usually **K.**

kirmess *use* **kermis**

kirschwasser a cherry liqueur, *not* kirschen-

Kishinev *use* **Chișinău**

kiskadee a tyrant flycatcher, *not* keski-

kissogram (not cap.) *but* **Kissagram** (propr.)

kist *use* c-

Kiswahili one of the six languages preferred for use in Africa by the Organization for African Unity

kitbag (one word)

kit-cat a portrait 36 × 28 in., like those painted of members of the Kit-Cat Club in the reign of James II

Kitch, Jack *use* Ke-

kitchen garden/, -er, -ing (two words)

kitchen-sink (in art forms) depicting extreme realism (e.g. '— school of painting', '— drama') (hyphen)

Kitemark the official kite-shaped mark on goods approved by the British Standards Institution (cap.)

kitmutgar use *khid-*

kitsch *not* -itch

Kit's Coty House Aylesford, Kent, a dolmen; *not* Coity, Cotty

Kitzbühel Austria

KK (Jap.) *kabushiki kaisha* (public limited company)

KKK Ku Klux Klan

KKt (chess) king's knight (no points)

KKtP (chess) king's knight's pawn (no points)

Klang (Ger. m.) quality of musical sound

klaxon a horn or warning hooter (not cap.)

Kleenex (cap., propr.)

kleistogam/ic, -ous *use* c-

Klemperer, Otto (1885–1973) German conductor

klepht a member of the original body of Greeks who refused to submit to the Turks in the 15th c., their descendants (not cap.)

klepsydra *use* c-

kleptomania an irresistible tendency to theft, *not* c-

klieg light an arc light used in making motion pictures (not cap.)

klinometer *use* c-

Klischograph (typ., propr.) an electronic photoengraving machine

KLM Koninklijke Luchtvaart Maatschappij NV (Royal Dutch Air Lines)

Klondike Yukon, Canada; *not* -yke

Klopstock, Friedrich Gottlieb (1724–1803) German poet

kludge (originally US sl.) an ill-assorted collection of poorly matching parts; (comput.) put a machine, system, or program together badly, the result of this

Klytaimestra wife of Agamemnon, in non-Gr. contexts usually **Clytaemestra**

km kilometre(s) (no point)

K Mart US retail chain (no hyphen)

K-meson *use* **kaon**

K.Mess. King's Messenger

KN (chess) king's knight (no points)

kn. knot, -s

kneecap the patella (one word)

kneel/, knelt *or* (esp. US) **kneeled, -ing**

Knesset the Israeli Parliament

knickerbocker (in pl.) loose-fitting breeches gathered at the knee or calf (not cap.); a New Yorker (cap.)

knickers a woman's or girl's underpants; (esp. US) knickerbockers, *or* a boy's short trousers

knick-knack (hyphen) *not* nick-nack

knight abbr. **K., Knt., Kt.**, (chess) **Kt** *or* **N** (no point); *see also* **KB**; **KBE**; **KCB**; **KCIE**; **KCMG**; **KCSI**; **KCVO**; **KG**; **KP**; **KT**

Knightbridge a Cambridge professorship, *not* Knights-

knight errant pl. **knights errant** (two words), *but* **knight-errantry** (hyphen)

Knightsbridge London

Knights/ Hospitallers a charitable military brotherhood (otherwise **— of St John, — of Rhodes, — of Malta**)

knit/, -ted, -ting

knitting/ machine, needle (two words)

knobby knob-shaped

knobkerrie (S. Afr.) a short stick with knobbed head; *not* -kerry, -kiri, -stick; in Afrik. **knopkierie**

knockabout (noun and adj., one word)

knock-down (adj.) (hyphen)

knocking shop (two words)

knock/ knees (two words) *but* **-kneed** (hyphen)

knock on wood (US) = **touch wood**

knockout (noun) (one word) abbr. **KO**

Knole Kent, Som.

knopkierie *use* **knobkerrie** (except in Afrik.)

Knossos Crete, *not* Cnossus

knot/, -ted, -ting

knot (naut.) abbrs. **kn., kt.**

know-how (noun, hyphen)

Knowl W. Yorks.

Knowle Avon, Devon, Shropshire, Som., W. Midlands

knowledgeable *not* -dgable

KNP (chess) king's knight's pawn (no points)

Knt. Knight, *use* **Kt.**

knur/ a knot, — **and spell** a game; *not* -rr

knurl a small projection, *not* nurl

Knut (Ger.) **Cnut**, in Dan. **Knud**, in Old Norse **Knútr**; *see also* **Canute**

Knutsford Ches.

KO *or* **k.o.** kick-off (football), knockout (boxing); **KO'd**

koala/ *not* — **bear**

København Dan. for **Copenhagen**

Koblenz Germany; *not* C-, -ce

Koch,/ Ludwig (1881–1974) German-born, English-domiciled musician and recorder of birdsong; — **Robert** (1843–1910) German bacteriologist

Köchel, Ludwig von (1800–77) Austrian scientist and music bibliographer, cataloguer of Mozart's works; abbr. **K.**

Kock, Charles Paul de (1794–1871) French novelist

Kodaikanal Observatory Madras, India

Kodály, Zoltán (1882–1967) Hungarian composer

koedoe *use* **kudu**

Koestler, Arthur (1905–83) Hungarian-born British novelist

Koh-i-noor diamond *not* -núr, -nûr (hyphens, one cap.)

kohlrabi a turnip-rooted vegetable of the cabbage family

koine (not cap.) a lingua franca, (cap.) that of the Greeks *c.*300 BC–AD 500

Kokoschka, Oskar (1886–1980) Austrian-born painter

kola *use* **cola**

kolkhoz a collective farm in the former USSR (not ital.)

Kołłątaj, Hugo (1750–1812) Polish politician, writer, and reformer, 'the Polish Machiavelli'

Köln Ger. for **Cologne**

Komi (of or relating to) (a member of) an Autonomous Republic, NW Russia; *also* the Finnic language of this people, *formerly* called Zyryan

Komintern *use* **C-**

komitadji, komitaji *use* **comitadji**

Komsomol a Soviet youth organization, *not* C-

Kongfuze *see* **Confucius**

kongo *use* **congou**

Königgrätz Czech Republic, *use* **Hradec Králové**

Königsberg *now* **Kaliningrad**

Konrad *see* **Conrad**

Konstanz Ger. for **Constance**

kontaki/on a liturgical hymn in the Eastern Church, pl. **-a**; *not* c-

Konzert/meister (Ger. m.) orchestra leader, **-stück** (n.) concert piece (one word)

koodoo *use* **kudu**

kookaburra an Australian bird

Koord *use* **Kurd**

koori an indigenous generic term for an Australian aborigine (from the Awabakal)

Kootenai Ida., Mont.

Kootenay BC, Canada

kopeck, kopek *use* **copeck**

koppa the Gr. letter Ϙ, ϙ

koppie (S. Afr.) a small hill, *not* kopje

kopro- *use* **copro-**

Koran the Islamic sacred book; *not* Coran, Q'ran; *see also* **Qur'ān**

Korea/ since 1948 divided into South Korea (off. the **Republic of Korea**) and North Korea (off. the **People's Democratic Republic of Korea**); adj. **-n**, *not* C-

Kortrijk Fl. for **Courtrai**

koruna major unit of currency in the former Czechoslovakia (abbr. **kčs**), in the Czech Republic (abbr. **kč**), and in Slovakia (abbr. **ks**); pl. same in English, in Czech the form varies with the amount; *see also* **krona**; **króna**; **krone**

Kos Greek island, *but* **cos lettuce**

KOSB King's Own Scottish Borderers

Kosciusko, Thaddeus (1746–1817) Polish patriot, in Pol. **Tadeusz Andrzej Bonawentura Kościuszko**

kosher (of food) prepared according to the Jewish law; *not* coshar, -er, koscher

Kosygin, Aleksei (**Nikolaevich**) (1904–80) Soviet Prime Minister 1964–80

kotow *use* **kow-**

Kotzebue, August Friedrich Ferdinand von (1761–1819) German playwright

koumiss a preparation from mare's milk; *not* ku-, -mis

kourbash a whip used for punishment in Turkey and Egypt, *not* kur-; in Arabic **kurbāj**

kourie *use* **kauri**

Koussevitsky, Serge Alexandrovich (1874–1951) Russian conductor

Kovno Lithuania, *use* **Kaunas**

kowrie *use* **kauri**

kowtow/ a Chinese form of submissive bow, act obsequiously; *not* kot-; in Pinyin **ketou**; **-ed, -ing**

KP (chess) king's pawn (no points), (US mil.) kitchen duty, Knight of the Order of St Patrick

k.p.h. kilometres per hour

KR (chess) king's rook (no points), King's Regiment, King's Regulations

Kr krypton (no point)

kr. kreuzer, krona, króna, krone

kraal (Afrik.) an enclosure, a native village

Krafft-Ebing, Richard von, Baron (1840–1902) German physician and psychiatrist

kraft paper a strong brown wrapping paper, *not* c-

Krakat/au volcano, Sunda Strait; common Western spelling **-oa**; *not* -ao

Kraków Pol. for **Cracow**

krans (Afrik.) a cliff, *not* krantz

Krapotkine, Prince *use* **Kropotkin**

K ration an emergency field ration (one cap., two words)

kreese *use* **kris**

Krefeld Germany, *not* C-

Kreisler, Fritz (1875–1962) Austrian-born US violinist

kremlin/ a citadel within a Russian town (not cap.); **the** — the citadel in Moscow, (hist.) the USSR Government housed within it (cap.)

kreosote *use* c-

Kreutzer, Rodolphe (1766–1831) German-French violinist; **'Kreutzer' Sonata** by Beethoven, 1803; *The Kreutzer Sonata* a novella by Tolstoy, 1889, also nickname of Janáček's String Quartet No. 1 (1923–4), inspired by Tolstoy's work

kreuzer an Austrian and old German copper coin, abbr. **kr.**

kriegspiel a war game, a form of chess with an umpire; in Ger. n. *Kriegsspiel*

Krio/ an English creole spoken in Sierra Leone, **-s** those who originally developed it

Kriol an English creole spoken in N. Australia

kris a Malay or Indonesian dagger, *also* **keris**; *not* creese, kreese

Krishnaism (Hinduism) the worship of Krishna as an incarnation of Vishnu (cap.)

kromesky a Russian dish of minced meat or fish, fried in bacon; in Fr. m. *cromesquis*

kron/a a Swedish silver coin, pl. **-or**; abbr. **kr.**; *see also* **koruna**

krón/a an Icelandic silver coin, pl. **-ur**; abbr. **kr.**; *see also* **koruna**

kron/e a silver coin, Austrian (pl. **-en**), Danish (pl. **-er**), Norwegian (pl. **-er**); all abbr. **kr.**; *see also* **koruna**

Kronos (Gr. myth.) *not* C-, -us

Kroo *use* **Kru** (not ital.)

Kropotkin/, Pyotr (Alekseevich), Prince (1842–1921) Russian geographer, revolutionist, and author; *not* Kra-, -ine

KRP (chess) king's rook's pawn (no points)

Kru (of or relating to) (a member of) a black seafaring people on the coast of Liberia; *not* -oo, -ou, (not ital.)

Kruger, Stephanus Johannes Paulus (1825–1904) S. African statesman

krugerrand a S. African gold coin (one word, not cap.)

krummhorn a medieval wind instrument, often spelt **crumhorn** in Eng.

krypton symbol **Kr** (no point); *not* c-

KS Kansas (postal abbr.), King's Scholar

Kshatriya the warrior caste of the Hindus (cap., not ital.)

K. St. J. Knight of the Order of St John of Jerusalem

KT Knight of the Order of the Thistle, Knight Templar

Kt (chess) knight (no point)

kT kiloton (no point)

Kt. Knight (Bachelor)

kt. knot

Kt. Bach. Knight Bachelor

κτλ (Gr.) *kai ta loipa* (and the rest *or* etc.)

Ku kurchatovium (no point)

Kuala Lumpur capital of Malaysia

Kublai Khan (1214–94) first Mongol Emperor of China

'Kubla Khan' a poem by Coleridge, 1816

Kuch Behar *use* **Cooch**

kudos (Gr.) renown (sing., not ital.)

kudu a S. African antelope, *not* koodoo; in Afrik. **koedoe**

Kufic (of) an early angular form of Arabic writing, *not* C-

Ku Klux Klan a US secret society (no hyphens, not ital.), abbr. **KKK**

kukri (Ind.) a curved knife, *not* the many variants (not ital.)

kulak (hist.) a Russian peasant proprietor

Kultur/ (Ger. f.) culture; (derog.) German civilization and culture, seen as racist, authoritarian, and militaristic; **-kampf** (Ger. m.) the war of culture (between Bismarck's Government and the Catholic Church, *c*.1872–7)

Kumasi Ghana; *not* Coo-, -assie

kumis(s) *use* **koumiss**

kümmel a sweet liqueur

kummerbund *use* c-

kumquat an orange-like fruit; *not* c-

Kung (of or related to) (the language of) a San people of the Kalahari Desert, *properly* **!Kung** (exclamation mark, close up)

kung fu a Chinese unarmed martial art

K'ung Fu-tzŭ *see* **Confucius**

Kunstlied (Ger. n.) art-song

Kuomintang the Chinese nationalist people's party, founded 1912; abbr. **KMT**; in Pinyin **Gwomindang**

kupfernickel (mineralogy) (one *f*, not cap.)

kupfferite (mineralogy) (two *f*s)

kurbash *use* **kour-**

kurchatovium symbol **Ku**

Kurd/ (an inhabitant) of Kurdistan, pl. **-s**; *not* Koo-; **-ish**

kurdaitcha (Austral.) the tribal use of a bone in spells intended to cause sickness or death, a man empowered to point the bone at a victim (not ital.)

kurfuffle *use* **ker-**

Kurile Islands NW Pacific

kursaal a hall for visitors at a spa or resort

Kursiv, Kursivschrift (Ger. typ. m., f.) italic type

kurta a loose shirt or tunic worn by esp. Hindu men and women, *not* -tha

Kutch India, *not* C-

kutch *use* **c-**

Kutchuk-Kainardja (Treaty) 1774, *properly* **Küçük-Kaynarca**

Kuwait/ Persian Gulf, adj. **-i**

Kuyp *use* **C-**

kV kilovolt (no point)

kVA kilovolt-ampere (no point)

kvass rye beer, *not* quass; in Russ. *kvas*

kW kilowatt (no point)

Kwa a branch of the Niger–Congo language family

KWAC (comput., indexing, etc.) keyword and context

kwacha chief monetary unit of Zambia

KwaNdebele a former black homeland in Transvaal, S. Africa (one word, two caps.)

KwaThema (S. Afric.) a township (one word, two caps.)

KwaZulu/Natal a S. African province, *formerly* Natal, incorporating the former homeland of KwaZulu

Kweyol the preferred name in Dominica and St Lucia for their French-based patois

kWh kilowatt-hour

KWIC (comput., indexing, etc.) keyword in context

KWOC (comput., indexing, etc.) keyword out of context

KY Kentucky (postal abbr.)

Ky. Kentucky (off. abbr.)

kybosh *use* **ki-**

Kyd, Thomas (1558–94) English playwright

kylie (W. Austral.) a boomerang

Kymric Welsh, *use* C-

Kyoto Japan, *not* Ki- in Jap. **Kyōto**

Kyrgyz a Mongol people living in Cent. Asia, *not* Kirghiz

Kyrgyzstan *formerly* Soviet Republic of Kirghizia

Kyrie eleison (eccl.) 'Lord, have mercy', abbr. **Kyrie**; *not* elee-

Kyrle, John (1637–1724) English philanthropist, 'the Man of Ross'

Kyzylkum a desert, Kazakhstan and Uzbekistan

Kyzyl-Orda Kazakhstan

L I

L fifty, Lake; learner (motor vehicle), Liberal; (biol.) Linnaeus; lir/a, -e; the eleventh in a series

L. Lady, Latin, (theat.) left (from actor's point of view), (Lat.) *liber* (book), licentiate; (Fr.) *livre* (book, pound); Loch, (Lat.) *locus* (place), London, Lough, prefix to enumeration of D. Scarlatti's works (*see* **Longo**)

l left, (mech.) symbol for length; litre, -s (spell out word when there is danger of confusion)

l. leaf, league, (Ger.) *lies* (read), (meteor.) lightning, line, link

l. (hist.) pound, to be placed *after* figures, as 50*l.* (ital.); *see also* **£**

L (elec.) symbol for inductance

£ pound, to be placed *before* figures, as £50; **£E** Egyptian pound (100 piastres); **£m.** (one) million pounds, with figure inserted after symbol, as £3m.

Ł, ł Polish letter 'the Polish l'

LA law agent, Legislative Assembly, Library Association, Local Authority, Los Angeles, Louisiana (postal abbr.)

La lanthanum (no point)

La. Lane, Louisiana (off. abbr.)

la (mus.) *use* **lah**

laager an encampment, esp. in a circle of wagons; in Afrik. *laer*

Lab. Labour (party), Labrador

lab (no point) laboratory

label/, -led, -ling

labi/um (anat.) a lip or liplike structure, pl. **-a**

Labor Day (US, Canada) the first Monday in September, *not* Labour

Labor Party (Austral.) *not* Labour

lab/our, -orious

Labour Day (UK and other countries) 1 May

Labourers Act (caps., no apos.)

labourite a supporter of the Labour Party (not cap.)

labour market (two words, hyphen when attrib.)

Labrador/ abbr. **Lab., — retriever** a breed of retriever (one cap.)

labr/um (Lat.) the lip of a jug etc., pl. **-a**

La Bruyère, Jean de (1645–96) French writer and moralist

labyrinth/, -ian, -ic, -ine

LAC Leading Aircraftman, Licentiate of the Apothecaries' Company, London Athletic Club

lac a resin; cf. **lakh**

Laccadive/ Sea off the Malabar Coast, India; **— Islands** *use* **Lakshadweep Islands**

lace-up (adj. and noun) (shoe) having laces (hyphen)

lace/wing, -wood, -work (one word)

Lachaise, Père a Paris cemetery (two words, caps.)

lâche (Fr.) lax, cowardly (ital.)

laches (law) negligence or unreasonable delay (not ital.)

Lachesis (Gr. myth.) the Fate that spins the thread of life

lachryma Christi any of various wines from the slopes of Mount Vesuvius

lachrym/al of tears; **-ation, -atory, -ose**; *not* lacry-; *but* **lacri-** usual in scientific use

lackadaisical listless

lacker *use* **-cquer**

lackey a servile person; *not* -kay, -quey

Lackland sobriquet of King John

lacklustre *not* -er (US)

Laconian Spartan

laconic concise (not cap.)

lacquer a varnish, *not* -ker

lacquey *use* **-key**

lacrimal etc., *use* **lachry-**

La Crosse Wis.

lacrosse a ball game

lacrymal etc., *use* **lachry-**

lacuna/ a missing portion, esp. in an ancient MS; pl. **-e**, (esp. in US) **-s** (not ital.)

LACW Leading Aircraftwoman

lacy lacelike, *not* -ey

ladanum a plant resin used in perfumery etc.; *not* labd-; cf. **laud-**

laddie a young fellow, *not* -y

la-di-da (someone) pretentious or snobbish

Ladies, the a women's lavatory (cap., no apos.)

ladies' fingers okra; cf. **ladyfinger, lady's finger**

Ladies' Gallery House of Commons

ladies' man (apos., two words)

Ladies' Mile Hyde Park, London

ladies' night (apos., two words)

Ladikia *use* **Latakia**

Ladin the Rhaeto-Romanic dialect of the Engadine in Switzerland

Ladino/ the Spanish dialect of the Sephardic Jews, also called **Judaeo-Spanish**; a mestizo or Spanish-speaking non-Indian in Cent. America; pl. **-s**

Ladismith Cape Province; *see also* **Ladysmith**

Lady abbr. **L.**

Lady, Our (caps.)

ladybird (one word), *not* -bug (US)

Lady Bountiful a patronizingly generous lady of the manor etc., after a character in Farquhar's *The Beaux' Stratagem*, 1707

Lady Day/ 25 Mar. (two words, caps.), — — **in Harvest** 15 Aug.

lady-fern (hyphen)

ladyfinger (US) a finger-shaped sponge cake; cf. **ladies' fingers**, **lady's finger**

ladyf/y make a lady of, **-ied**; *not* ladi-

lady-in-waiting (hyphens)

lady/killer, -like (one word)

lady-love a man's sweetheart (hyphen, one word in US)

Lady Margaret Hall Oxford, abbr. **LMH**

lady's finger kidney vetch; cf. **ladies' fingers**, **ladyfinger**

lady's maid pl. **ladies' maids** (no hyphen)

Ladysmith Natal; *see also* **Ladismith**

lady's slipper (apos.)

lady's smock cuckoo flower (two words)

laemergeier *use* **lammergeyer**

laer (Afrik.) *use* **laager**

laesa majestas (Lat.) *lèse-majesté*

Laetare Sunday fourth in Lent

laevo- prefix meaning left, *not* levo- (except in US)

Lafayette/, Marie Joseph, marquis de (1757–1834) French general, aided Americans in Revolution (one word); — **College** Easton, Pa.

Laffitte, Jacques (1767–1844) French statesman

Lafite, Chateau a claret (two words)

Lafitte, Jean (1780–*c*.1826) buccaneer of unknown origin

La Follette, Robert Marion (1855–1925) US politician

La Fontaine, Jean de (1621–95) French writer

LAFTA Latin-American Free Trade Association

lagan goods or wreckage lying on the bed of the sea; *not* li-

lager a light, effervescent beer

Lagerkvist, Pär (1891–1974) Swedish novelist

Lagerlöf, Selma Ottilia Lovisa (1858–1940) Swedish novelist

lager lout (two words)

Lagrange, Joseph Louis, comte (1736–1813) French mathematician

Lagting the Upper House of the Norwegian Parliament

La Guaira Venezuela, *not* -yra

LaGuardia/, Fiorello (Henry) (1882–1947) mayor of New York (one word, two caps.); — **Airport** New York

LAH Licentiate of Apothecaries' Hall, Dublin

lah (mus.) *not* la

La Hague, Cape NW France

La Haye (Fr.) The Hague

La Hogue a roadstead, NW France; in Fr. **La Hougue**

Lahore Pakistan, *not* -or

Laibach Slovenia, Ger. for **Ljubljana**

laic/ (someone) non-clerical, lay, secular; **-ity, -ize**

laid paper that which when held to the light shows close-set parallel lines; cf. **wove paper**

Laïs (4th c. BC) Greek courtesan and beauty

laissez/-aller (Fr.) absence of restraint; **-faire** letting people do as they think best, let well alone!; **-passer** (m.) pass, permit (for persons and things) (hyphens, not ital.); *not* laisser-

Lake cap. as part of the name, as Bala Lake, Lake Superior; abbr. **L**

Lakeland the Lake District in Cumbria (one word)

Lake Poets, the Coleridge, Southey, and Wordsworth

Lake Windermere *use* **Windermere**, as 'Lake Windermere' is a tautology

Lake Wobegon a fictional US town in the stories of Garrison Keillor, *not* Woe-

lakh/ (Ind.) one hundred thousand, 100,000; *not* -ck, -c (not ital.); in quantities of rupees, pointing above one lakh is with a comma after the number of lakhs: thus 25,87,000 is 25 lakhs 87 thousand rupees; *see also* **crore**

Lakshadweep Islands in the Laccadive Sea, SW coast of India

Lalitpur Uttar Pradesh, India; *not* Lalat-

Lallan/ of or concerning the Lowlands of Scotland; the Lowland Scots dialect, now usually **-s**

Lalla Rookh a novel by Moore, 1817

'L'Allegro' a poem by Milton, 1632

Lam. Lamentations (OT)

lama a Tibetan or Mongolian Buddhist monk (cap. when part of title); *not* lla-

Lamarck/, Jean Baptiste Pierre Antoine de Monet, chevalier de (1744–1829) French naturalist; **-ian, -ism**

Lamarque, comte Maximilien (1770–1832) French general

Lamartine, Alphonse Marie Louis de (1790–1869) French poet and statesman

lamasery a monastery of lamas

lambada a fast Brazilian dance

lambaste thrash, criticize; *not* -bast

lambda the eleventh letter of the Gr. alphabet (Λ, λ). (phys.) the symbol for wavelength

Lamborghini an Italian make of sports car

lamb's fry (cook.) (apos., two words)

lambskin (one word)

lamb's lettuce (apos., two words)

lambswool *not* lamb's-wool

LAMDA London Academy of Music and Dramatic Art

lamé (adj. and noun) (a material) with inwoven gold or silver thread (not ital.)

lamell/a a thin plate, pl. **-ae**

Lamentations, Book of (OT) abbr. **Lam.**

lamin/a a thin plate, pl. **-ae**

Lammas/ (in full — **Day**) 1 Aug., formerly observed as a harvest festival

lammergeyer the bearded vulture; *not* lae-, le-, -geier

lampblack (one word)

lamp holder (two words)

lamplight/, -er (one word)

lamp-post (hyphen)

lampshade (one word)

Lancashire abbr. **Lancs.**

Lancaster, County *or* **County palatine, of** the formal name of Lancashire

Lance Bombardier abbr. **L.Bdr.** *or* **L/Bdr.**

Lance Corporal abbr. **L/Cpl.**

lancelet a small fish-like chordate

lancet small surgical knife

lancewood a tough W. Indian wood (one word)

Lancing College W. Sussex

Lancs. Lancashire

Land (Ger. n.) a province of Germany or Austria, pl. *Länder* (ital., cap.)

landau/ pl. **-s**; **-let** a small landau (not ital.)

landdrost (S. Afr.) a district magistrate (not ital.)

landfall (one word)

landgrav/e (hist.) a count having jurisdiction over a territory, the title of certain German princes; f. **-ine**; **-iate** a landgrave's territory, *not* -vate

landholder (one word)

ländler an Austrian dance

land/locked, -lord, -lubber, -mark, -mine (one word)

Landor, Walter Savage (1775–1864) English poet and prose writer

landowner (one word)

Land-Rover (hyphen) *but* **Range Rover** (two words)

landscape (typ.) book, page, or illustration of which the width is greater than the depth, in US **broadside**; cf. **portrait**

Land's End Cornwall

landslide (one word)

landsmål *formerly* Landsmaal; *see* **nynorsk**

lands/man pl. **-men**

land tax (two words)

Lane abbr. **La.**

Lang,/ Andrew (1844–1912) Scottish man of letters, **— Cosmo Gordon** (1864–1945) Archbishop of Canterbury

lang. language

Langeberg Mountains S. Africa, in Afrik. **Langeberge**

langouste the spiny lobster, rock lobster, or crawfish; in Fr. f. *langouste*

langoustine the Norway lobster, in Fr. m. *langoustine*

langsam (Ger. mus.) slowly

lang syne long ago (two words)

Langtonian (an inhabitant) of Kirkcaldy, Fife

language abbr. **lang.**

langue de chat (Fr. f.) a finger-shaped biscuit or chocolate

Languedoc/ a former French province, between the Loire and the Pyrenees; **-ian** dialect of *langue d'oc* spoken in Languedoc

langue/ d'oc (Fr. f.) any of the dialects of medieval France spoken south of the Loire (*see also* **Occitan**; **Provençal**); **— d'oïl** any of the dialects of medieval France spoken north of the Loire, largely equivalent to Old French and forming the basis of modern French

languor/ lassitude, **-ous**

langur an Asian long-tailed monkey

laniard *use* **lany-**

Lankester, Sir Edwin Ray (1847–1929) English zoologist

lanolin the fat in sheep's wool, *not* -ine

Lansdown Avon, Glos.; battle, 1643

Lansdowne, Marquess of

Lansing Mich.

lansquenet a card game of German origin, a German mercenary soldier in the 16th–17th cc. (not ital.)

lantern slide (two words)

lanthanum symbol **La**

lanyard a short rope attached to something, *not* lani-

Lao a SE Asian people, the Tai language spoken in Laos and Thailand, *not* Laotian

Laocoön a Trojan priest, subject of a famous sculpture

Laodicean lukewarm (of feelings)

Laois a county of Ireland

Lao/s adj. **-tian**

Lao-tzu (*fl.* 6th c. BC) founder of Taoism (hyphen), in Pinyin **Laoze**; *not* the many variants

Lap. Lapland; *see also* **Lapp**

La Paz Bolivia

lapdog (one word)

lapel/ *not* -elle, lappelle; **-led**

Laphroaig an Islay village and Scotch whisky

lapis lazuli a rich blue stone or its colour (two words, not ital.)

Laplace, Pierre Simon, marquis de (1749–1827) French astronomer

Lapland in Norw. the same, in Fr. **Laponie**, in Ger. and Swed. **Lappland**; abbr. **Lap.**

Lapp/ a native of Lapland, (adj. and noun) **-ish**

lappelle use **lapel**

lapsus/ (Lat.) a slip; — *calami* a slip of the pen; — *linguae* a slip of the tongue; — *memoriae* a slip of memory, pl. same; a person who falls from a high standard, pl. *lapsi*

laptop a portable microcomputer suitable for use while travelling (one word)

Laputa/ a flying island in Swift's *Gulliver's Travels*; **-n** visionary, absurd

lar/ a Roman household god, pl. **-es**; **lares and penates** one's home

la Ramée, Marie Louise de (1839–1908) French writer of English novels (l.c. *la*), pseud. **Ouida**

lardon bacon for larding, *not* -oon

lardycake, lardy-cake a cake made with lard, currants, etc.

lares *see* **lar**

La Reyne/ le veult, — *— s'avisera* forms of *Le Roy* etc. when a queen is reigning

largesse a free gift, generosity; *not* -ess (not ital.)

larghetto (mus.) fairly slow

largo (mus.) slow, broad

lariat a rope for tethering animals; *not* -iette, -rriet (not ital.)

Larissa Greece, in Gr. **Lárisa**

larkspur (bot.) (one word)

La Rochefoucauld, François, duc de (1613–80) French writer

La Rochelle dép. Charente-Maritime, France

Larousse/, Pierre Athanase (1818–75) French lexicographer, — French publishers

larrikin (Austral.) a hooligan, *not* lari-

larv/a pl. **-ae** (not ital.)

laryn/x (anat.) pl. **-ges**; **-geal**, **-gitis**

lasagne (It. pl.) pasta in wide sheets or ribbons, *not* -na (It. sing.) (US)

Lasalle, Antoine Chevalier Charles Louis, comte de (1775–1809) French general; *see also* **Lassalle**

La Salle,/ Antoine de (*c.*1400–60) French soldier and poet, — **René Robert Cavelier** (1643–87) French explorer, — **St Jean Baptiste de** (1651–1719) French founder of the order of Christian Brothers

Lascar an E. Indian sailor (not ital.)

Las Casas, Bartolomé de (1474–1566) Spanish missionary

Las Cases, Emmanuel Augustin Dieudonné, comte de (1766–1842) friend of Napoleon I on St Helena

Lascaux SW France, site of palaeolithic cave art

laser a device using light amplification by stimulated emission of radiation (acronym); *see also* **maser**

laser/disc an optical disc for reproducing sound and pictures (one word), **-Vision** a system for the reproduction of video signals recorded on a disc with a laser (one word, two caps.)

lashkar a body of Indian irregular troops (not ital.)

Las Meninas by Velázquez and Picasso (after Velázquez), *not* -iñas

La Spezia NW Italy, *not* -zzia

Lassa/ Nigeria, source of — **fever**; *see also* **Lhasa**

Lassalle, Ferdinand (1825–64) German Socialist (one word); *see also* **Lasalle**; **La Salle**

Lassell, William (1799–1880) English astronomer

lassie (Sc. and N. Eng.) a young girl, *not* -y

lasso/ pl. **-s**; as verb **-ed**, **-es**, **-ing**

Lassus, Orlandus (1532–94) Belgian-born composer

'Last Post' (caps.) it is sounded, not played

Last Supper, the (caps.)

Lat. Latin

lat. latitude

Latakia Syria; *not* Ladi-, -ieh, -yah

latchkey (one word)

latecomer (one word)

lateish use **latish**

La Tène of or relating to the second Iron Age culture of Cent. and W. Europe

Lateran/, St John a church in Rome, — **Council** one of five held there

latex/ a fluid derived esp. from rubber trees, a synthetic material resembling this; pl. **-es**

lath a thin strip of wood

lathe a machine for turning wood, metal, etc.

lathi a heavy stick carried by the Indian police

Latin abbr. **L.**, **Lat.**

Latin America/ the parts of Cent. and S. America where Spanish or Portuguese is the main language, **-n** (two words, no hyphen even when attrib.)

Latin Cross †

latine (Lat.) in Latin

Latinity the quality of one's Latin

Latinize make Latin, *not* -ise

latish fairly late, *not* late-

latitude abbr. **lat.** (no point in scientific work)

Latour, Chateau a claret (two words)

La Tour, Maurice Quentin de (1704–88) celebrated French painter of pastel portraits

La Trobe University, Melbourne

Latrobe Pa.; Tasmania, Australia

latten a metal like brass (not ital.)

latter the second of two, *not* the last of a series (for which *use* **last**); *see also* **former**

Latter-Day Saints the Mormons' name for themselves

lattice-work (hyphen)

Latvia a Baltic republic; in Latvian **Latvija**, in Fr. **Lettonie**; adj. **Latvian, Lettish**

Latymer Upper School Hammersmith, London

laudanum a solution formerly used as a narcotic painkiller; cf. **lad-**

laudator temporis acti (Lat.) a praiser of past times

laughing/ gas, — stock (two words)

launderette *not* -drette

laura/ (hist.) a group of hermits' cells, pl. **-s**

laurel/, -led, -ling (one *l* in US)

Laurence, Friar a character in Shakespeare's *Romeo and Juliet*; *see also* **Law-**

Laurentian mountains and (geol.) rocks, near the St Lawrence River, Canada

laurustinus an evergreen; *not* laures-, lauris-

Laus Deo (Lat.) Praise (be) to God, abbr. **LD**

lav (colloq.) lavatory (no point)

Lavoisier, Antoine Laurent (1743–94) French chemist (one word)

law agent abbr. **LA**

law/ binding *or* **— calf, — sheep** a binding in smooth pale brown calfskin or sheepskin, formerly much used for law books

law court (two words)

Law Courts, the (caps., no hyphen)

lawgiver (one word)

lawnmower (one word)

Lawrence/, D(avid) H(erbert) (1885–1930) English novelist; **—, Sir Thomas** (1769–1830) English painter; **—, T(homas) E(dward), 'Lawrence of Arabia'** (1888–1935) English archaeologist and soldier, (from 1927) Aircraftman Shaw; adj. **Lawrentian** *or* **Lawrencian**; St — Canadian river; *see also* **Lau-**

lawrencium symbol **Lw**

Laws abbr. **LL**

law sheep *see* **law binding**

law-stationer (hyphen)

lawsuit (one word)

Laxness, Haldór Kiljan (b. 1902) Icelandic writer

lay untilled land, *use* **lea**

layabout (one word)

Layamon (*fl.* late 1200) English priest and author of the *Brut, properly* **Laȝamon**

layaway (US) a system of paying a deposit to secure an article for later purchase, in Austral. and NZ **lay-by**

lay brother etc. (two words)

lay-by/ pl. **-s** (hyphen)

layette a complete outfit for a baby (not ital.)

lay/man, -out (noun), **-person** (one word)

lay/ reader, — sister (two words)

laywoman (one word)

lazaretto/ a place for quarantine (not ital.), pl. **-s**

lazybones (one word)

lazy-tongs (hyphen, two words in US)

lazzaron/e one of a low class at Naples, *not* lazar-; pl. *-i*

lb pound, -s (weight) (not in scientific use)

l.b. (cricket) leg-bye

L.Bdr., L/Bdr. Lance Bombardier

lbs (US) pounds

lbw (cricket) leg before wicket (no points)

LC (theat.) left centre, Legislative Council, (US) Library of Congress, Lord Chamberlain, Lord Chancellor, letter of credit

l.c. *loco citato* (in the place cited); (typ.) lower case, that is *not* caps.

LCB Lord Chief Baron

LCD liquid crystal display

L.Ch. Licentiate in Surgery

LCJ Lord Chief Justice

LCM (math.) least common multiple, London College of Music

l.c.m. (math.) least common multiple

LCP Licentiate of the College of Preceptors

L/Cpl. Lance Corporal

LD Lady Day, *Laus Deo* (praise be to God), Low Dutch

Ld. Lord

LDC (econ.) less developed country

Ldg. (naval) Leading

L.d'H. Légion d'honneur

Ldp. Lordship

LDS Licentiate in Dental Surgery

£E Egyptian pound(s)

lea untilled land; *not* lay, lee; *see also* **ley**

lead (typ.) a strip of metal used to separate lines of type

lead (chem.) symbol **Pb**

leaded/ matter, — type (typ.) having the lines separated by leading

leader *see* **leading article**

leaders (typ.) dots used singly or in groups to guide the eye across the page

leading (typ.) extra spacing between lines of type

leading article newspaper article expressing editorial opinion; *also called* **leader**

leaf (typ.) single piece of paper, two pages back to back; abbr. **l.**, pl. **ll.**

leaflet (typ.) a minor piece of printing, usually two, four, or six pages

leaf mould (two words), *not* mold (US)

league abbr. **l.**

Leakey,/ Louis (**Seymour Bazett**) (1903–72) English palaeontologist and anthropologist, — **Mary Douglas** (1913–96) his wife, — **Richard** (**Erskine Frere**) (b. 1944) his son

Leamington Spa War.; *see also* **Lem-**; **Lym-**

lean/, -ed *or* **-t**

lean-to (hyphen)

leap/, -ed *or* **-t**

leapfrog/, -ged, -ging

leap year (two words)

learn/, -ed *or* **-t**

leasehold/, -er (one word)

leatherette imitation leather

leatherneck a member of the US Marine Corps. (not cap., one word)

'Leatherstocking Tales' the collective name for five novels by J. F. Cooper

leaves abbr. **ll.**

Leban/on no longer The Lebanon; **-ese**

Lebensraum (Ger. m.) territory for natural expansion

Lebesgue/, Henri Léon (1875–1941) French mathematician, — **theory of integration** (math.)

Lebewohl! (Ger. n.) farewell!

Lecocq, Alexandre Charles (1832–1918) French composer

Leconte de Lisle, Charles Marie René (1818–94) French poet

Le Corbusier pseud. of **Charles Édouard Jeanneret-Gris** (1887–1965), Swiss architect and town planner

Lecouvreur, Adrienne (1692–1730) French actress; (ital.) play (1849) by E. Scribe and E. Legouvé; *Adriana Lecouvreur* an opera by Cilea, 1902

lect. lecture

lectern a church reading desk, *not* -urn

lecture/ship the post of lecturer (as at Cambridge), *but* **-rship** at Oxford University (cap. as title)

LED light-emitting diode

lederhosen leather shorts (not ital.)

ledger/ a book of accounts, — **tackle** in fishing; *see also* **leger line**

lee untilled land, *use* **lea**

Lee, Laurie (1914–97) English writer and poet

Leeuwenhoek, Anton van (1632–1723) Dutch microscopist

leeward (the region) on or towards the side sheltered from the wind; cf. **windward**

leeway (one word)

Le Fanu, Joseph Sheridan (1814–73) Irish writer and newspaper proprietor

left/ (theat., from actor's point of view) abbr. **L**; — **centre** abbr. **LC**

left/-hand, -handed adjs. (hyphens)

left wing (hyphen as adj.), **left-winger** (hyphen)

Leg. legislat/ive, -ure

leg. legal; (Lat.) *legit* (he, *or* she, reads), *legunt* (they read, present tense)

legalize *not* -ise

Le Gallienne,/ Richard (1866–1947) English author and journalist; — — **Eva** (1899–1991) his daughter, US actress

legato (mus.) smooth

leg-bye (cricket) abbr. **l.b.**

legenda (Lat.) things to be read

Léger, Alexis St-Léger (1887–1975) French poet, pseud. **St John Perse**

legerdemain sleight of hand (not ital.)

leger line (mus.) *not* led-

leges (Lat.) laws, abbr. **ll.**

leggiero (mus.) light, swift, delicate

Legh the family name of Baron Newton; *see also* **Leigh**

Leghorn the former English name for the Italian port **Livorno**; a straw plait, a breed of domestic fowl (not cap.)

Légion d'honneur, la a French order of merit

legionnaire/ a member of a legion, a legionary (not ital.); **-s' disease** a form of bacterial pneumonia (not cap.)

legislat/ive, -ure abbr. **Leg.**

Legislative Assembly abbr. **LA** (no points)

legit (Lat.) he, *or* she, reads; abbr. **leg.**

legitim/ate (verb) (law) render (a child) legitimate, **-ation**; elsewhere use **-ize, -ization**; *not* -atize, -ise

leg/-pull, -rest (hyphens)

legroom (one word)

legume the seed pod of a leguminous plant, esp. as used for food

legunt (Lat.) they read (present tense), abbr. **leg.**

Le Havre dép. Seine-Maritime, France

Lehigh University Bethlehem, Pa.

lei a Polynesian garland; *see also* **leu**

Leibniz, Gottfried Wilhelm, Baron von (1646–1716) German mathematician and philosopher, *not* -itz

Leicester: the signature of the Bishop of Leicester (colon)

Leicestershire abbr. **Leics.**

Leiden the Netherlands, in Fr. **Leyde**; *see also* **Leyden**

Leigh, Baron *see also* **Legh**

Leighton Buzzard Beds. (two words)

Leipzig Germany; abbr. **Lpz.**, **Leip.**

leishmaniasis a disease caused by a parasite

leitmoti/v *or* **-f** (mus.) a theme associated with person, situation, or sentiment; *not* -ive; pl. **-vs, -fs** (one word, not ital.)

Leix a county of Ireland, formerly Queen's County; *now* **Laois**

le juste milieu (Fr.) the golden mean; *see also* **milieu**

L.E.L. pseud. of **Letitia Elizabeth Landon** (1802–38)

Lely, Sir Peter (1618–80) Dutch-English painter

Lemberg Ger. for **Lvov**

Lemington Glos., Tyne & Wear; *see also* **Lea-**; **Ly-**

lemm/a a title or theme, proposition taken for granted, pl. **-as**; heading of an annotation, pl. **-ata** (not ital.)

lemmergeyer *use* **la-**

Lemprière, John (1765–1824) English lexicographer

Le Nain,/ Antoine (1588–1648), — — **Louis** (1593–1648), and — — **Mathieu** (1607–67) brothers, French painters

Lenclos, Ninon de (1616–1706) a French beauty

lending library (two words)

length abbr. **l.**, (mech.) symbol **l**

Lenin assumed name of **Vladimir Ilich Ulyanov** (1870–1924) Russian political leader

Leningrad *see* **St Petersburg**

len/is (Gr.) a smooth-breathing mark ('), typographically largely equivalent to the Arab. *hamza* or Heb. *alef*; pl. **-es** (not ital.)

Lennoxtown Strathclyde (one word)

Lenox Library New York

lens/ *not* lense; pl. **-es**

Lent from Ash Wednesday to Easter (cap.)

lento (mus.) slow

Leonardo da Vinci (1452–1519) Italian painter, sculptor, engineer; a work by him is 'a Leonardo' *not* 'a da Vinci'

Leoncavallo, Ruggiero (1857–1919) Italian composer

Leonid/ a meteor, pl. **-s** (not ital.)

Lepcha the language of Sikkim

Lepidoptera (zool.) butterflies and moths

LEPRA British Leprosy Relief Association

leprechaun an Irish sprite; *not* lepra-, -awn

Le Queux, William Tufnell (1864–1927) English novelist and traveller

Lermontov, Mikhail (Yurevich) (1814–41) Russian poet

Le Roy/ le veult the royal assent to bills in Parliament, — — *s'avisera* the royal dissent to bills in Parliament; cf. *La Reyne*

lès or lez (Fr. topographical) near (with names of towns)

Le Sage, Alain René (1668–1747) French novelist and dramatist

Lesbian (an inhabitant) of Lesbos

lesbian a homosexual woman (not cap.)

lèse-majesté (Fr. f.) treason (ital.), Anglicized as **lese-majesty** (not ital.)

L. ès L. *Licencié ès lettres* (Licentiate in, *or* of, Letters)

Lesotho S. Africa

L. ès S. *Licencié ès sciences* (Licentiate in, *or* of, Science)

Lethe/ a river in Hades, **-an**

let-in notes (typ.) those set inside the text area (usually in a smaller-size type), as distinct from side notes

Letraset (propr.) a system of lettering using transfers

letter/, -ed, -ing

letterhead (typ.) printed (heading on) stationery (one word)

letter/press, -set (typ.) one word

letters of distinction as FRS, LLD, etc., are usually put in large caps., although even small caps. can improve the general effect in contexts laden with them

letterspacing (typ.) shown in copy by short vertical dashes between letters (one word)

letters patent a formal writing conferring patent or privilege (two words)

Lettish *see* **Latvia**

lettre/ de cachet (Fr. f.) warrant for imprisonment, bearing the royal seal, pl. *-s de cachet*; — *de créance*, — *de crédit* letter of credit, pl. *-s de créance*, *-s de crédit*; — *de marque* letter of marque, pl. *-s de marque*

Letzeburgesch Ger. dialect of Luxembourg

leu a unit of currency in Romania, pl. **lei**

leucotomy a brain operation, *not* -k-

leukaemia an excess of white corpuscles in blood; *not* -c-, -ch-, -kemia

Leuven in Fl. the same, Fr. **Louvain**, Ger. **Löwen**; the Katholieke Universiteit Leuven is separated into two distinct bodies, one Flemish (Katholieke Universiteit Leuven, at Leuven) and one French (Université Catholique de Louvain, at Louvain-la-Neuve)

Leuwenhoek *use* **Leeu-**

Lev. Leviticus

lev/ a Bulgarian monetary unit, pl. **-a**

Levant/, the (arch.) the eastern part of the Mediterranean with its islands and neighbouring countries (cap.), *not* -ante; **-er** a strong easterly Mediterranean wind (not cap.), a native or inhabitant of the Levant (cap.); **-ine** of or trading in the Levant, a native or inhabitant of the Levant; — **morocco** (bind.) a superior quality leather with prominent grain (one cap.)

Levante the collective name for four Mediterranean provinces of Spain, forming two autonomous regions, Comunidad Valenciana and Murcia

levee an assembly (no accent, not ital.), (US) a river embankment

level/, -led, -ler, -ling (one medial *l* in US), **-ly**

lever de/ rideau (Fr. m.) opening piece at the theatre; — — *séance* closing of a meeting

leviable that may be levied

Leviathan a book by Hobbes, 1651

leviathan a sea monster

Levi's (cap., propr.) jeans manufactured by Levi Strauss

Lévi-Strauss, Claude (b. 1908) French anthropologist and ethnographer

Leviticus (OT) abbr. **Lev.**

Levittown NY, Pa.

Levkosia Gr. for **Nicosia**

levo- a prefix, *use* **laevo-** (except in US)

Lewes E. Sussex

Lewes,/ Charles Lee (1740–1803) English actor, — **George Henry** (1817–78) English philosopher and critic; *see also* **Lewis**

Lewis Western Isles

Lewis/, Cecil Day (1904–72) Poet Laureate 1968–72, *see* **Day-Lewis**; —, **Clive Staples** (1898–1963) English writer; —, **Sir George Cornewall** *not* Cornw- (1806–63) English statesman and man of letters; —, **Harry Sinclair** (1885–1951) US novelist; —, **Isaac Newton** (1858–1931) US soldier, inventor of — **gun**; —, **Matthew Gregory, 'Monk' (1775–1818)** English writer of romances; —, **Meriwether** (1774–1809) US explorer; *see also* **Lewes**; **Wyndham Lewis**

lex (Lat.) law, pl. *leges*

lexicog. lexicograph/er, -y, -ical

lexicon/ a dictionary, esp. of Greek, Hebrew, Arabic; pl. **-s**; abbr. **lex.** (not ital.)

lex/ loci (Lat.) local custom, — *non scripta* unwritten law, — *scripta* statute law, — *talionis* 'an eye for an eye', — *terrae* the law of the land

ley/ untilled land, *use* **lea**; *but* — **farming** alternate growing of grass and crops; — **line** the supposed straight path connecting prehistoric sites

Leyden/ the Netherlands, *use* **Lei-**; *but* — **jar** (elec.)

leylandii Leyland cypress (not cap., pl. same)

Leys School Cambridge

lez *see* **lès**

LF *or* **l.f.** low frequency

Lfg. (Ger.) *Lieferung*

LG (gunpowder, leather, wheat) large grain, Life Guards, Low German

L.Ger. Low German

L.Gr. Late Greek, Low Greek

LGSM Licentiate of the Guildhall School of Music

LGU Ladies' Golf Union

l.h. left hand

LHA Lord High Admiral

Lhasa Tibet, *not* -ssa; *see also* **Lassa**

Lhasa apso a breed of dog (one cap.)

LHC Lord High Chancellor

LHD *Literarum Humaniorum Doctor* (literally doctor of the more humane letters)

LHT Lord High Treasurer

LI Light Infantry, Long Island (NY)

Li lithium (no point)

Liadov, Anatoli (Konstantinovich) (1855–1914) Russian composer; *not* Lya-

liais/e, -on *not* -as-

Líakoura Greece, modern name of **Mount Parnassus**

liana a tropical climbing plant, *not* -ne

Liapunov, Sergei (Mikhailovich) (1859–1924) Russian composer; *not* Lya-

Lib colloq. abbr. of (Men's, Women's, etc.) Liberation (cap., no point)

lib./ librarian, library; — **cat.** library catalogue

lib. (Lat.) *liber* (a book)

libel/ (law) a published false statement damaging to a person's reputation (cf. **slander**); the act of publishing such a statement; **-led, -ler, -ling, -lous** (one medial *l* in US)

liber (Lat.) a book, abbr. **L.**, *lib.*

Liberal/ abbr. **L.**, — **Unionist** (caps., no hyphen)

liberalize *not* -ise

Liberia W. Africa

libertarian an advocate of liberty, a believer in free will; cf. **necessitarian**

libertine (one who is) dissolute, licentious

libid/o sex drive, pl. **-os**; **-inal**

libr/a (Lat.) pound, pl. *-ae*; abbr. **£, l., lb**

librair/e (Fr. m.) bookseller, *-ie* (f.) bookshop

librar/ian, -y abbr. **lib.**

library sigla abbreviated references to libraries and other archives, for use in MS citations on music etc.

librett/o (It.) the text of an opera etc.; pl. **-os, -i** (not ital.); **-ist** writer of this

libris, ex- *see* **ex-libris**

libr/o (It.) a book, pl. *-i*

Libya/ N. Africa; **-n** of ancient N. Africa or modern Libya

licence (noun) a permit, *not* -se (US)

licens/e (verb) authorize; **-ee, -er, -ing**

licensed victualler

licentiate abbr. **L.**

licet (Lat.) legal, it is allowed

lichee *use* **lychee**

lichen epiphytic vegetable growth

Lichfield Staffs.; *see also* **Litch-**

Lichfield: the signature of the Bishop of Lichfield (colon)

lich-gate a roofed gateway at the entrance to a churchyard, *not* lych- (US)

lichi *use* **lychee**

lickerish desirous, greedy; cf. **liquorice**

Lick Observatory Calif.

licorice *use* **liquor-** (except in US)

Liddell, Henry George (1818–98) English lexicographer, father of the original of *Alice in Wonderland*

Lido a famous bathing beach near Venice

lido/ an open-air swimming pool or bathing beach, pl. **-s**

Lie,/ Jonas Lauritz Edemil (1833–1908) Norwegian novelist, — **Trygve Halvdan** (1896–1968) Secretary-General of UN 1946–53

Liebfraumilch a hock, in Ger. f. *Liebfrauenmilch*

Liebig/, Justus, Baron von (1803–73) German chemist, — a beef extract first prepared by him; — **condenser** (cap.)

Liechtenstein a principality on the Upper Rhine

lied/ a song, pl. **-er** (not ital.)

Lieder ohne Worte songs without words

Lieferung (Ger. f.) a part of a work published in instalments, abbr. **Lfg.**

Liège Belgium, *formerly* Lié- (in Belgian Fr. till 1946); in Fl. **Luik**, Ger. **Lüttich**, Lat. **Leodium**; **Liégeois/** f. **-e** an inhabitant of Liège

lieu, in in place (of) (not ital.)

Lieutenant/ abbr. **Lt., Lieut.;** — **Colonel** abbr. **Lt. Col., Lieut. Col.;** — **Commander** abbr. **Lt. Com., Lieut. Com.;** — **General** abbr. **Lt. Gen., Lieut. Gen.; Governor** abbr. **Lt. Gov., Lieut. Gov.** (two words)

life/belt, -blood, -boat, -buoy (one word)

life/ cycle, — **force,** — **form** (two words)

life-giving (hyphen)

lifeguard (one word)

Life Guards a regiment of the Household Cavalry (two words), **Life-guardsman** (hyphen)

life insurance is the general (though technically incorrect) term; *see also* **assurance**

life jacket (two words)

life/like, -line (one word)

lifelong lasting for life (one word); cf. **live-**

life/-preserver, -raft (hyphens, two words in US)

life-saver (Austral., NZ, and alt. US) = **lifeguard**

life-size(d) (adj., hyphen)

life/span, -style, -time (one word)

ligature (typ.) two or more letters joined together and forming one character or type as Æ, fl, ffi

liger the hybrid offspring of a lion and tigress; cf. **tigon**

light bulb (two words)

lightening making less heavy, esp. (med.) a drop in the level of the womb during the last weeks of pregnancy

light/-headed, -hearted (hyphens)

lighthouse (one word)

Light Infantry abbr. **LI, Lt. Inf.**

lighting-up time (one hyphen)

light meter (two words)

lightning/ (meteor.) abbr. **l.,** — **bug** (US) = **firefly**

light-o'-love a fickle woman (hyphens, apos.)

light/proof, -ship (one word)

light show (two words)

light/weight, -wood (one word)

light year (astron.) the distance light travels in one year, nearly 6 million million miles (two words)

ligneous of wood, woody

-like use a hyphen in formations intended as nonce-words, or not generally current, and with nouns ending in 'l'; omit the hyphen when the first element is of one syllable

likeable *not* lika- (US)

likeli/hood *not* -lyhood, *but* **-ly**

Lilienthal, Otto (1849–96) German aviator

Liliput, liliputian *use* **Lilli-, lilli-**

lillibullero a 17th-c. song refrain, *not* the many variants (not ital.)

Lilliput the country of the pygmies in Swift's *Gulliver's Travels*, **lilliputian** diminutive (not cap.)

Lilo (propr.) type of inflatable mattress

lily of the valley (no hyphens)

lima bean a tropical American plant, *Phaseolus limensis*; its flat, pale-green seeds are different from, but sometimes confused with, those of the broad bean, *Vicia faba*

limbo/ the borderland of Hell, a place of oblivion; a W. Indian dance; pl. **-s** (not ital.)

Limburg province of Belgium, province of the Netherlands; in Fl. and Du. the same, in Fr. **Limbourg**

limbus/ fatuorum (Lat.) a fool's paradise, — *infantum* limbo of unbaptized children, — *patrum* limbo of pre-Christian good men

lime-green (hyphen)

lime juice (two words)

lime/kiln, -light, -pit (one word)

limerick a humorous or comic form of five-line stanza with a rhyme scheme *aabba* (not cap.)

limes (Lat.) Roman frontier (ital.)

limestone (one word)

Limey (derog., US sl.) a British sailor, an Englishman; cf. **limy**

limn/ (arch.) paint (esp. a miniature portrait), (hist.) illuminate (MSS); **-er**

limy limelike, sticky; cf. **Limey**

lin. line/al, -ar

linable able to be covered on the inside, *not* linea-

linage number of lines, payment by the line; cf. **lineage**

linament *use* **linea-** *or* **lini-**

linchpin *not* ly- (one word)

Linch's law *use* **lynch law**

Lincoln: the signature of the Bishop of Lincoln (colon)

Lincoln Center New York, a nexus of theatres, opera house, concert hall, etc.

Lincoln green (one cap.)

Lincolnshire abbr. **Lincs.**

Lindbergh, Charles (Augustus) (1902–74) US aviator

linden a lime tree of the genus *Tilia*

Lindley, John (1799–1865) English botanist

Lindsay,/ Earl of family name Lindesay-Bethune, — **Sir Coutts** (1824–1913) English artist, — **Sir David** (1490–1555) Scottish poet, — **(Nicholas) Vachel** (1879–1931) US poet; *see also* **Lindsey**

Lindsey, Earl of family name Bertie

line abbr. **l.**, pl. **ll.**

lineage ancestry; cf. **linage**

line/al, -ar abbr. **lin.**

lineament a distinctive feature or characteristic, *not* lina-; cf. **liniment**

Linear/ A the earlier of two forms of ancient Cretan writing; — **B** the later form, found also on the Greek mainland (no hyphens)

line block (typ.) a letterpress block for lines and solids

line drawing (two words)

linen-draper (hyphen)

linenfold a type of carved scroll (one word)

line printer (two words)

linga/, -m a phallus, esp. as the Hindu symbol of Śiva; in Skt. (nominative sing.) *liṅgam*, (noun) *liṅga*, a distinguishing feature

lingerie women's underwear collectively (not ital.)

lingo/ a (foreign) language, pl. **-s**

lingua/ franca an international language (not ital.); pl. **— francas**

liniment an embrocation, *not* lina-; cf. **lineament**

lining numerals (typ.) those that align (or range) at top and bottom, as 1234567890

lining paper (bind.) a paper glued inside the cover

link 7.92 in., one-hundredth of a chain; abbr. l.

Linn/aean abbr. **Linn.**; *but* **-ean Society** London (off. spelling), abbr. **LS**

Linnaeus, Carolus (1707–78) Swedish naturalist; in Swed. **Carl von Linné**; abbr. **L.**, **Linn.**

Linnhe, Loch Highland

linocut (a print from) a design or form carved in relief on a block of linoleum (one word)

Linotype (propr.) abbr. **Lino**

linsey-woolsey a thin coarse fabric of linen and wool, gibberish; *not* linsy-, -wolsey

Linson (propr.) (bind.) a strong paper used in place of bookcloth

lintel/, -led

liny full of lines, *not* -ey

Lion, Gulf of the *or* **Lion Gulf** off the Mediterranean French coast; in Fr. **golfe du Lion**; *not* Lions, Lyon, Lyons

Lionardo da Vinci *use* **Le-**

lionize *not* -ise

lipography the omission of letters or words in writing

Lippi,/ Fra Filippo *or* **Lippo** (*c*.1406–69) and — **Filippino** (*c*.1457–1504) his son, Italian painters

Lippizaner a horse of a fine white breed used esp. in displays of dressage, *not* Lipizzaner

lipsalve (one word)

lip-service (hyphen)

lipstick (one word)

liq. liquid, liquor

lique/faction, -factive, -fiable, -fy *not* liqui-

liqueur a strong alcoholic liquor, sweetened and flavoured (not ital.)

liquid abbr. **liq.**

liquidambar a genus of balsam-bearing trees, *not* -er (one word, not ital.)

liquid crystal display a form of visual display in electronic devices (no hyphen), abbr. **LCD**

liquidize *not* -ise

liquor/ (esp. US) = **spirits** (in common usage), abbr. **liq.**; **— on draught** *not* draft (US)

liquorice *not* licor- (US)

liquorish desirous, greedy; *use* **licker-**

lir/a a unit of Italian (pl. **-e**) or Turkish (pl. same) currency; abbr. **L.**

Lisbon Portugal; in Port. **Lisboa**, in Fr. **Lisbonne**, Ger. **Lissabon**, It. **Lisbona**

LISP (comput.) a list-processing programming language (caps. or even small caps.)

lissom lithe, supple; *not* -e

Liszt, (Abbé) Franz (1811–86) Hungarian pianist and composer

lit. literal, -ly; literary, literature, litre, little

Litchfield/ Hants.; Conn.; **Earl of —**.; *see also* **Lich-**

litchi *use* **lychee**

Lit.D. *Literarum Doctor* (Doctor of Letters); *see also* **D.Lit.; D.Litt.; Litt.D.**

lite pendente (Lat.) during the trial

liter *use* **-re** (except in US)

liter/al, -ally, -ary, -ature abbr. **lit.**

literal (typ.) printing of wrong sort, of turn, or of sort in battered state or wrong font

literalize etc., render literal; *not* -ise

litera (*or* *littera*) *scripta manet* (Lat.) the written word remains

literat/i the learned as a class, sing. **-us**; *not* litt-

literatim (Lat.) letter for letter, textually, literally

Lith. Lithuanian

lithium symbol **Li**

lithography (typ.) a planographic printing process from a smooth plate, originally a stone; abbr. **litho** (no point)

Lithuania/ a Baltic country; in Lithuanian **Lietuva**, Fr. **Lituanie**, Ger. **Litauen**, **-n** (of or relating to) (the people or language) of Lithuania

Lit. Hum. *Literae Humaniores* Faculty (Classics and Philosophy) at Oxford

litmus/ paper, — test (two words)

Litolff, Henri Charles (1818–91) French pianist, composer, music-publisher

litotes (rhet.) a form of meiosis, esp. one using ironical negative, e.g. 'no mean feat', 'I shan't be sorry'

litre/ abbr. **I** (no point), **lit.**; one-thousandth of a cubic metre, 1.76 pints; **-age** a number of litres

Litt.B. *Literarum Baccalaureus* (Bachelor of Letters)

Litt.D. *Literarum Doctor* (Doctor of Letters, Camb. and TCD); *see also* **D.Lit.; D.Litt.; Lit.D.**

littera *see* **litera**

littérateur a literary man (not ital.)

litterati *use* **lite-**

Little England/, -er (two words, caps.)

Littlehampton W. Sussex (one word)

Little Russian (hist.) (a) Ukrainian

Littleton/ the family name of Baron Hatherton; **—, Sir Thomas** (?1407–81) English jurist; *see also* **Lyttelton**

littoral (of or on) the shore region of the sea, a lake, etc.

Littré, Maximilien Paul Émile (1801–81) French lexicographer

liturg. liturg/ies, -ical, -y

liv. (Fr.) *livre* (m. book, f. pound)

liveable *not* liva-

livelong intensive and emotional form of long; cf. **life-**

Liverpool: the signature of the Bishop of Liverpool (colon)

Liverpudlian (an inhabitant) of Liverpool, *also* **Liverpolitan**

livestock (one word)

Livingston Lothian

Livingstone, David (1813–73) Scottish explorer and missionary

Livorno an Italian seaport

livraison (Fr. f.) a part of a work published in instalments

livre (Fr. m.) book, (f.) pound; abbr. **L.**, *liv.*

Livy (in Lat., **Titus Livius**) (59 BC–AD 17) Roman historian

LJ Lord Justice, pl. **L JJ** Lords Justices (thin space, no points)

Ljubljana Slovenia, in Ger. **Laibach**

LL late, law, *or* Low, Latin; Lord Lieutenant, -s

ll a separate letter in Sp. and Welsh, not to be divided; in Catalan not alphabetized separately, but also not to be divided

l·l a letter group in Catalan, which is divided l-|l over a line; distinguish from **ll**

ll. leaves, lines, (Lat.) *leges* (laws)

-ll (words ending in) followed by -ful *or* -ly, usually omit one *l*

llama a S. American ruminant; *not* la-

Llandeilo/ Dyfed, **— Group** (geol.) (caps.)

Llandrindod Wells Powys

Llanelli Dyfed (*not now* -y)

Llanfairpwllgwyngyllgogerychwyrndrobwllllantysiliogogogoch Gwynedd, usually shortened to **Llanfairpwllgwyngyll** (the original name, the rest being 19th-c. whim) or **Llanfair P. G.**

llano/ a treeless grassy S. American plain or steppe, pl. **-s**

Llantwit Major S. Glam., in Welsh **Llanilltud Fawr**

LL B *Legum Baccalaureus* (Bachelor of Laws) (no points, thin space)

LL D *Legum Doctor* (Doctor of Laws) (no points, thin space)

LL M *Legum Magister* (Master of Laws) (no points, thin space)

Llosa, Mario Vargas *see* **Vargas Llosa**

Lloyd, Norddeutscher the North German Lloyd Steamship Co. (two words), abbr. **NDL**

Lloyd George, David (1863–1945) British Prime Minister 1916–22; created Earl Lloyd-George of Dwyfor; *properly* 'George' is the surname, *but* double-barrelled through usage

Lloyd's/ an incorporated society of underwriters, *not* -s; **Lloyd's List** a daily publication devoted to shipping news (ital.); **Lloyd's Register of Shipping** an institution, ital. for published annual of the same name; *see also* **Loyd**

Lloyds Bank, plc (no apos.)

Llull, Ramon (*c.*1233–*c.*1315) Catalan lay missionary and philosopher; in Sp. **Ramón Lull**, older Eng. **Raymond Lull(y)**; adj. **Lullian** (Eng. from the Lat.)

LM Licentiate in Midwifery, (mus.) long metre

£m. (one) million pounds; figure follows symbol, e.g. £3m.

l. M. (Ger.) *laufenden Monats* (of the current month)

lm lumen(s) (no point)

LMBC Lady Margaret Boat Club (St John's College), Cambridge

LMD long metre double

LMH Lady Margaret Hall (Oxford)

LMSSA Licentiate in Medicine and Surgery, Society of Apothecaries

LMT Local Mean Time

ln natural logarithm (no point)

LO Liaison Officer

loadline (one word) *see* **Plimsoll line**

load/star, -stone *use* lode-

Loanda Angola, *not* St Paul de –; *but use now* **Luanda**

loath averse, disinclined, reluctant; *not* loth

loath/e regard with disgust, detest; **-some** *not* loth-

LOB Location of Offices Bureau

Lobachevsky, Nikolai (**Ivanovich**) (1793–1856) Russian mathematician

'Lobgesang' Mendelssohn's 'Hymn of Praise', 1840

lobscouse a sailor's stew; *see also* **Scouse**

lobworm (one word)

locale a scene or locality

localize *not* -ise

loc. cit. *loco citato* (in the place cited), pl. **locc. citt.** *or* **ll. cc.** (not ital.)

loch a Scottish lake, *not* -ck; cap. when with name, abbr. **L.**

Lochalsh Highland

lochan a small Scottish lake, *not* lock-

Loch Awe Strathclyde

Lochearnhead Central (one word)

Lochgilphead Strathclyde

Loch Leven Highland, Tayside

Lochnagar a mountain in Grampian (one word)

loci pl. of **locus**

lock (naut.) a confined section of a canal or river where the water level can be raised or lowered by the use of gates and sluices, *not* loch

Lock/e, John (1632–1704) English philosopher; **-ian, -ean**

lockjaw (one word)

lock-keeper (hyphen)

lockout/ an employers' refusal of work, pl. **-s** (one word)

locksmith (one word)

lock-up/ (noun or adj.; hyphen, one word in US)

loco/ locomotive, pl. **-s** (no point)

loco/ (Lat.) in the place; — **citato** in the place cited, abbr. **l.c., loc. cit.**, pl. **locc. citt.** *or* **ll. cc.** (not ital.); — **laudato** in the place cited with approval, abbr. **loc. laud.**; — **sigilli** in the place of the seal, abbr. **LS**; — **supra citato** in the place cited above, abbr. **l.s.c.** (not ital.)

Lok Sabha the lower house of the Indian parliament; cf. **Rajya Sabha**

locum/-tenency (hyphen); — **tenens** a substitute, pl. — **tenentes** (not ital.)

locus/ (Lat.) a written passage, a curve, pl. **loci**; — **citatus** the passage quoted; — **classicus** an authoritative passage from a standard book, pl. **loci classici**; — **communis** a commonplace; — **delicti** the place of a crime; — **in quo** the place in which; — **poenitentiae** a place of repentance; — **sigilli** the place of the seal, abbr. **LS**; — **standi** a recognized position, (law) right to appear

LOD *Little Oxford Dictionary*

lode/star a star steered by, **-stone** (a piece of) magnetite (one word); *not* load-

lodg/e, -eable, -ement, -ing

Lodge, Henry Cabot (1850–1924) US senator, author, and scholar; also his grandson (1902–85) diplomat

lodging house (two words)

Łódź Poland

Loeb/, James (1867–1933) US banker, founder of the — **Library** of classical authors

loess (geol.) a deposit of fine yellowish loam in certain valleys; *not* loëss, löss

L. of C. line of communication

Lofoten Islands Norway, *not* -den, -fföden

log logarithm (no point)

log. logic

logan-stone a rocking stone; *not* loggan-, logging-

logarithm/ abbr. **log**; **natural —** to base *e*, abbr. **ln** *or* **log**_e

logbook (one word)

log cabin (two words)

loge (Fr. f.) theatre stall (not ital.)

loggia/ (It.) a gallery, pl. **-s**

logi/on a saying of Christ not in the Gospels, pl. **-a** (not ital.)

logo/ a device used as a printed identifier of an organization, pl. **-s** (no point)

logogram a sign or character representing a word, esp. in shorthand

logomachy a dispute about words, controversy turning on merely verbal points

logorrhoea an excessive flow of words, esp. in mental illness; *not* -hea (US)

logroll/, -er, -ing (give, one who gives) mutual aid among politicians or reviewers (one word)

logwood (one word)

Lohengrin a German hero; (ital.) an opera by Wagner, 1850

Loir, Loire, Loiret different forms used for various French rivers and déps.

Lollard any of the followers of the 14th-c. religious reformer John Wyclif

lollipop/ a large boiled sweet on a small stick, *not* lolly-; **— lady, — man** (Brit. colloq.) a traffic controller for schoolchildren

Lombard/ (of or relating to) (a member of) a Germanic people who conquered Italy in the 6th c., a native or the dialect of Lombardy in N. Italy; **-ic**; **-y** in It. **Lombardia**, in Fr. **Lombardie**, in Ger. **Lombardei**

Lombroso, Cesare (1836–1909) Italian criminologist

Lomé Togo

Londin: the signature of the Bishop of London (colon)

Londinii (Lat.) at London

Londini Scanorum (Lat.) at Lund

London/ abbr. **L., Lond.;** in Du. **Londen**, Fr. **Londres**, It. **Londra; — Apprentice** a hamlet in Cornwall

long. longitude

long/board, -boat -bow (one word)

long-distance (adj., hyphen)

longe *use* **lu-**

long/eval long-lived, *not* -aeval; **-evity**

Longfellow, Henry Wadsworth (*not* Words-) (1807–82) US poet

long/hair, -hand, -horn, -house (one word)

Long Island NY, abbr. **LI**

longitude abbr. **long.** (no point in scientific work), symbol *λ*

long jump (two words)

Longleat House Wilts.

long/ letter (typ.) *ā, ē*, etc.; **— mark** that placed over the long letter; the macron

Long Mynd, The Shropshire, **Longmynd Group** (geol.) (caps.)

Longo, Alessandro (1864–1945) compiler of edition of Domenico Scarlatti's keyboard works, abbr. **L.**

longo intervallo (Lat.) at a long interval

long page (typ.) one having a line or lines more than its companion pages

Longridge Lancs.

long s (typ.) former letter ſ, italic *ſ*, *not* set in final position

Longshanks sobriquet of Edward I

Longships islands and lighthouse off Cornwall

longshore/ (adj.) *not* 'long-, **-man** (US noun, one word) = **docker**

long-sighted having long sight; cf. **far-sighted**

long/-sleeved, -standing (hyphens, one word in US)

Longton Lancs., Staffs.

long ton 2,240 lb, abbr. **l.t.**

Longtown Cumbria, Hereford

longueur a tedious passage in book, play, film, usually pl. (ital.)

long vowel (typ.) *ā, ē*, etc.

long/ways, -wise = **lengthways** (one word)

loof *use* **luff**

loofah *not* luffa

lookalike (as noun, one word)

Look Homeward, Angel autobiographical novel by Thomas Wolfe, 1929 (comma)

looking glass (two words)

lookout/ pl. **-s** (one word)

loophole (one word)

Loos,/ Adolf (1870–1933) Austrian architect, **— Anita** (1893–1981) US author

loosestrife (bot.) (one word)

lop-eared (hyphen)

Lope de Vega *see* **Vega Carpio**

loping with long strides, *not* lope-

lopsided (one word)

loquitur (Lat.) he, *or* she, speaks, with the speaker's name following, used as a stage direction or to inform the reader; abbr. **loq.**

Lorca, Federico García *see* **García Lorca**

Lord (with name) may be substituted for Marquess, Earl, or Viscount, and is more often used than Baron; also prefixed to the given name of the younger son of a duke or marquess; abbr. **Ld.**

Lord/ Chamberlain, — Chancellor abbr. **LC; — Chief Baron** abbr. **LCB; — Chief Justice** abbr. **LCJ; — Justice** abbr. **LJ**, pl. **LJJ** (thin space); **Lieutenant** pl. **Lord Lieutenants,**

abbr. **LL**; — **Mayor** (two words, caps.); — **of hosts, — of lords** as Deity (one cap.); — **President of the Council** abbr. **LPC**; — **Privy Seal** abbr. **LPS**; — **Provost** abbr. **LP**

Lord's Cricket Ground London (apos.)

Lord's Day (caps.)

Lordship abbr. **Ldp.**

Lord's/ Prayer, — Supper, — Table (caps.)

Lorelei the siren of the Rhine; *not* Lurlei/, -berg; *Die Lore Lay*, poem by Brentano, 1802; *Die Loreley*, poem by Heine, 1823

Lorentz/, Hendrik Antoon (1853–1928) Dutch theoretical physist, — **force, — transformation**; Lorentz–FitzGerald contraction (en rule) *preferred* to FitzGerald–Lorentz contraction

Lorenz, Konrad Zacharias (1903–89) Austrian zoologist and ethnologist

Lorenzo *see* **Lourenço**

Loreto Colombia, Italy, Mexico, Peru

Loretto Anglicized version of the It. **Loreto**; also a Scottish school

lorgnette opera glass, or pair of eyeglasses with a long handle

loris a small tailless lemur; *not* lori, lory

Lorrain, Claude born **Gelée** (1600–82) French painter, *not* -aine

Lorraine in Ger. **Lothringren**; *see also* **Alsace-Lorraine**

lory one of the parrots; cf. **loris**

losable *not* -eable

Los Angeles Calif.

löss (geol.) *use* **loess**

lost generation a generation with many of its men killed in war, esp. that of 1914–18; an emotionally and culturally unstable generation coming to maturity, cap. esp. with reference to 1915–25

Lot-et-Garonne a dép. of France

loth/ averse, *use* **loath**; **-some** *use* **loathsome**

Lothario/ a rake in Nicholas Rowe's *The Fair Penitent*, 1703; pl. **-s**

Lothian a region of Scotland

Loti, Pierre pseud. of **Julien Viaud** (1850–1923) French writer

lotus/ Egyptian and Asian water lily, pl. **-es**

lotus-eater *not* lotos-, *but* 'The Lotos-Eaters' by Tennyson

louche disreputable, shifty (not ital.)

loudspeaker (one word)

lough an Irish lake, cap. with name, abbr. **L.**

louis d'or (hist.) a former French gold coin worth about 20 francs, pl. same

Louisiana off. abbr. **La.**, postal **LA**; *not* Lou.

Louis-Philippe (1773–1850) French king

Louis/-Quatorze reign 1643–1715; **-Quinze** 1715–74; **-Seize** 1774–93; **-Treize** 1610–43 (Louis XIV, XV, XVI, XIII), art styles (hyphens)

loung/e, -er, -ing

lounge/ bar, — lizard, — suit (two words)

loupe a small magnifying glass used by jewellers etc., *not* loop

loup-garou (Fr. m.) a werewolf, a surly man or recluse; pl. *loups-garous*

lour/ to frown, **-y**; *not* lower/, -y (US)

Lourenço Marques Mozambique, *now* **Maputo**; *not* Lorenzo Marques, -ez

Louvain Fr. and hist. for **Leuven**

louvre a shutter, ventilator; *not* -er (US)

lovable *not* -eable

love affair (two words)

love/bird, -bite (one word)

love child (two words)

love–hate relationship (en rule)

love letter (two words)

love/lock, -lorn, -making (one word)

love/ match, — nest, — seat (two words)

lovesick (one word)

Love's Labour's Lost a play by Shakespeare, 1598 (two apos.)

love song, — story (two words)

loving/ cup, — kindness (two words)

lowboy (US) a low chest or table with drawers and short legs; cf. **highboy**

Low/ Church (two words, no hyphen even when attrib.) — **Churchman** (two words, caps.)

low/-cut, -down (adj., hyphens)

low-down, the (noun, colloq.) the relevant information (hyphen, one word in US)

lower to frown, *use* **lour**

Lower California (caps.)

lower case (typ.) the small letters 'a–z' (hyphen when attrib.), abbr. **l.c.**

Lowland a region of Scotland

Low Sunday the first after Easter (caps.)

low water/ (two words), — — **mark** (three words) abbr. **LWM**

lox liquid oxygen, (US) smoked salmon

Loyd, Sam (1841–1911) US puzzle composer; *see also* **Lloyd; Lloyd's; Lloyds**

LP large paper, long-playing record, Lord Provost, low pressure, (paper) large post

l.p. low pressure

LPC Lord President of the Council

LPG liquefied petroleum gas

L-plate a learner driver's sign (hyphen)

LPO London Philharmonic Orchestra

L'pool Liverpool

LPS Lord Privy Seal

Lpz. (Ger.) Leipzig

lr. lower

LRAD Licentiate of the Royal Academy of Dancing

LRAM Licentiate of the Royal Academy of Music

LRCP Licentiate of the Royal College of Physicians

LRCS Licentiate of the Royal College of Surgeons

LRCVS Licentiate of the Royal College of Veterinary Surgeons

LRSC Licentiate of the Royal Society of Chemistry

LS Leading Seaman, Linnean Society; *loco* or *locus sigilli*, (in) the place of the seal

l.s. left side

LSA Licentiate of the Society of Apothecaries

l.s.c. *loco supra citato* (in the place cited above)

LSD least significant digit; Lightermen, Stevedores, and Dockers; lysergic acid diethylamide

l.s.d. (hist.) *librae, solidi, denarii* (pounds, shillings, and pence, also **£.s.d.**)

LSE London School of Economics and Political Science

L-shape (cap., hyphen); *see also* **sans serif**

LSI (comput.) large-scale integration

LSO London Symphony Orchestra

Lt. Lieutenant

l.t. long toll, low tension

LTA Lawn Tennis Association, London Teachers' Association

LTCL Licentiate of Trinity College of Music, London

Lt. Col. Lieutenant Colonel

Lt. Com. Lieutenant Commander

Ltd Limited

LTE London Transport Executive

Lt. Gen. Lieutenant General

Lt. Gov. Lieutenant Governor

L.Th. Licentiate in Theology (Durham)

Lt. Inf. Light Infantry

LTM Licentiate in Tropical Medicine

Lu lutetium (no point)

Luanda Angola, *not* Lo-

Luang Prabang Laos

Lübeck Germany, *not* Lue-

lubricious *not* -cous

Lubumbashi Zaire (Democratic Republic of Congo)

Lucan of St Luke, *not* Luk-; (in Lat., **Marcus Annaeus Lucanus**) (39–65) Roman poet

lucarne a dormer window

Lucayo (of or relating to) (a member of) an extinct aboriginal Arawakan tribe of the Bahamas, or their language

Lucerne Switzerland; in Fr. same, in Ger. **Luzern**

lucerne alfalfa, *not* -ern

Lucian (2nd c.) Greek writer

Lucknow Uttar Pradesh, India

Lucullan profusely luxurious (cap.), from **Licinius Lucullus** (1st c. BC) Roman general famous for his lavish banquets

lucus a non lucendo (Lat.) *approx.* inconsequent or illogical

Ludd/ite, -ism (cap.)

ludo a board game, a simplified form of parcheesi (not cap.); *see also* **pachisi**

LUE (theat.) left upper entrance

Luebeck *use* **Lü-**

luff *not* loof

Luftwaffe (hist.) the German air force 1935–45 (not ital. in contemporary use)

Luger a type of German automatic pistol (cap.), named after **George Luger** (1849–1923) German engineer and firearms expert

Luggnagg an island in Swift's *Gulliver's Travels*

lug/hole, -sail, -worm (one word)

Luik Fl. for **Liège**

Lukács, György (1885–1971) Hungarian philosopher, literary critic, and politician

Luke (NT) not to be abbr., **Lucan** *not* Luk-

lukewarm/, -ness tepid(ity) (one word)

Lull/, -ian *see* **Llull, Ramon**

Lulsgate Airport Bristol

lumbar (anat.) of the loins, esp. the lower back

lumber move clumsily; unused furniture etc.; (US) = **timber**

lum/en (anat.) a cavity, pl. **-ina**; (phys.) the unit of luminous flux, pl. **-ens**, abbr. **lm**

lumpenproletariat the lowest elements of the proletariat (beggars, drifters, etc.), a term originally used by Karl Marx (one word, not cap., not ital.)

lunate/ crescent-shaped, a crescent-shaped prehistoric implement etc. — **sigma** a form of sigma (*C, c*)

lunation the time from one new moon to next, about $29\frac{1}{2}$ days

lunge a long rope for exercising horses, *not* lo-

lunging *not* longeing

lunula/ a crescent-shaped mark, esp. the white area at the base of the fingernail; a crescent-shaped Bronze Age ornament; pl. **-e**

lupin a garden plant, *not* -e

lupine of or like a wolf or wolves

lur a bronze S-shaped trumpet; *not* -e

Lurlei/, -berg *use* **Lorelei**

Lusatian *use* **Sorbian**

Lusiads, The a poem by Camões, 1572; original title *Os Lusíadas* ('The Sons of Luso')

Lusitania Portugal

Luso- of Portugal, Portuguese; cap. in e.g. 'Luso-Brazilian' (hyphen), 'Lusophile'; *but* 'lusophone'

lustre *not* -er (US)

lustr/um a five-year period, pl. **-a**

lusus naturae (Lat.) a freak of nature, pl. same

lutenist a lute-player, *not* -anist

lutetium *not* -tec-, symbol **Lu**

Luth. Lutheran

Luthuli (*also* **Lutuli**), **Albert John** (*c.*1898–1967) S. African political leader

Lutine bell a bell rung at Lloyd's, once to announce the loss, twice for the arrival, of a vessel overdue

Lutosławski, Witold (1913–94) Polish composer

lux (phys.) unit of illuminance, abbr. **lx**

Luxembourg/ city, district, province, airport of Belgium; *also* **Grand Duchy of** — (sometimes spelt -*burg* to avoid French influence); *also* Gardens and Palace, Paris; in Fr. the same, in Letzeburgesch **Letzeburg**, in Ger. **Luxemburg**; **-er**

Luxemburg Wis.

Luxemburg, Rosa (1870–1919) German socialist

luxuriant lush, profuse in growth; (of literary or artistic style) florid, richly ornate

luxurious supplied with luxuries, self-indulgent, voluptuous

Luzern Ger. for **Lucerne**

LV luncheon voucher

L´viv Ukraine, in Eng. **Lvov** (after 1945), in Ger. and Yiddish **Lemberg**, in Pol. **Lwów**, in Russ. **L´vov**

Lw lawrencium (no point)

LWL load-water-line

LWM low water mark

lx lux (no point)

LXX the Septuagint, seventy

Lya/dov, -punov *use* **Lia-**

lycée (Fr. m.) higher secondary school

Lyceum/, the (cap.) the Aristotelian school of philosophy; (not cap.) a college of literary studies, pl. **-s**

lychee a sweet fleshy fruit and tree; *not* the many variants (not ital.)

lych-gate *use* **lich-** (except in US)

Lycra (propr.) an elastic fibre or fabric used for close-fitting clothing (cap.)

lyddite an explosive (two *d*s)

lyke wake a night watch over a dead body (hyphen); **'Lyke Wake Dirge'** medieval English song (three words)

Lyly, John (*c.*1554–1606) English author; *see also Euphues*

Lymington Hants.; *see also* **Lea-**; **Le-**

lymphoma/ any malignant tumour of the lymph nodes, excluding leukaemia; pl. **-ta**

lynch law *not* -'s, Linch's (two words)

lynchpin *use* **li-**

lynx/ a medium-sized wild cat, pl. **-es**; **-eyed** keen-sighted (hyphen), **-like** (one word)

Lyon King of Arms the chief Scottish herald

Lyonnais, Crédit French banking corporation

Lyons in Fr. **Lyon**; *see also* **Lion**

lyricist a person who writes the words to a song

lyrist a person who plays the lyre, a lyric poet

lysin (chem.) a lysing substance

lysine (chem.) an amino acid

Lyte, Henry Francis (1793–1847) English hymn writer

Lytham St Annes Lancs. (no apos.)

Lyttelton/ family name of Viscounts Chandos and Cobham (*see also* **Littleton**); —, **Humphrey** (**Richard Adeane**) (b. 1921) English jazz musician

Lytton *see* **Bulwer-Lytton**

Mm

M 1,000, (typ.) em, (as prefix) mega-, (chem.) molar, motorway, sea mile, the twelfth in a series

M. Majesty, Marquess, Marquis, Member, metronome, middle, militia, (in Peerage) minor, Monday; (Fr.) *main* (hand), *mille* (a thousand), monsieur; (It.) *mano* (hand), *mezzo, -a* (half); (Lat.) *magister* (master), *medicinae* (of medicine)

Mʻ *see* **Mac-, Mc-**

m metre, -s; (as prefix) milli-; minute, -s

m. male, married, masculine, meridian, meridional; mile, -s; mill, million; (meteor.) mist; month, -s; moon, (Lat.) *meridies* (noon), *metrum* (verse metre)

m (mech.) mass, (Fr.) *mois* (month)

m- (chem. prefix) *meta-* (ital., hyphen)

ɯ minim (drop)

MA *Magister Artium* (Master of Arts), Massachusetts (postal abbr.), Military Academy

mA (elec.) milliampere (no point)

m/a (bookkeeping) my account

Ma, Yo Yo (b. 1955) French-born Chinese cellist

ma (It.) but

ma'am *see* **madam**

Maartens, Maarten pseud. of **Joost Marius van der Poorten-Schwartz** (1858–1915) Dutch novelist, wrote in English

Maas *see* **Meuse**

Maasai *see* **Masai**

Maastricht the Netherlands, *not* Maes-

Mabinogion a collection of ancient Welsh romances

Mac-, Mc-, Mʻ- the spelling depends on the custom of the name's bearer, and this must be followed, as: MacDonald, Macdonald, McDonald, MᶜDonald, M'Donald (*properly* turned comma, *not* apos.); however spelt, alphabetize as *Mac*

mac (colloq.) mackintosh, *not* mack (no point)

macadam/ a material for road-making; from **John Loudon McAdam** (1756–1836) Scottish engineer; **-ize** *not* -ise; *see also* **tarmac**

Macao E. Asia, *not* -au

macao a parrot, use **-aw**

macaron/i (*not* macc-) long tubes of pasta; an 18th-c. dandy, pl. **-ies**; **-ics** (in pl.) burlesque verses containing Latin (or other foreign) words and vernacular words with Latin etc. terminations

MacArthur, Douglas (1880–1964) US general

Macassar/ (in full **— oil**) oil formerly used on hair (cap.), *but* **antimacassar** (not cap.)

Macaulay,/ Dame Rose (1881–1958) British novelist, **— Thomas Babington, Baron** (1800–59) British writer

macaw a parrot, W. Indian palm; *not* -ao, -cc-

Macc., 1, 2 First, Second Book of Maccabees (Third and Fourth are in the Greek Bible)

Maccabean of the Maccabees, *not* -baean

Maccabees/ (in full **Books of the —**) four books of Jewish history and theology, abbr. **Macc.**

McCarthy,/ Eugene Joseph (b. 1916) US politician; **— Joseph Raymond** (1909–57) US politician, responsible for **McCarthyism**; **— Mary** (1912–89) US writer

MacCarthy, Sir Desmond (1878–1952) British writer

McCormack, John (1884–1945) Irish-born US singer

McCoy, the real the genuine article

McCullers, Carson (1917–67) US novelist and playwright

MacCunn, Hamish (1868–1916) Scottish composer

MacDiarmid, Hugh pseud. of **Christopher Murray Grieve** (1892–1978) Scottish poet

MacDonald,/ George (1824–1905) Scottish novelist and poet; **— Rt. Hon. James Ramsay** (1866–1937) British Prime Minister 1924, 1929–35

Macdonald,/ Alexandre (1765–1840) Duke of Taranto, French marshal; **— Flora** (1722–90) Jacobite heroine

McDonald's (one of) a fast-food restaurant chain; *not* Mac-, despite e.g. its product named 'Big Mac'

McDonnell Douglas US aircraft manufacturer (no hyphen)

Macdonnell Ranges Northern Territory, Australia

MacDowell, Edward Alexander (1861–1908) US composer

macédoine mixed fruit or vegetables, esp. cut up small or in jelly (not ital.)

Macedonia/ a republic of the former Yugoslavia, in Serbo-Croat **Makedonija**; *properly*, the 'Former Yugoslav Republic of Macedonia' to distinguish it from the Greek province of that name; **-n** (of or related to) (the people or language) of Macedonia; abbr. **Maced.**

MʻFingal (*also* **Mʻ**) a mock epic by John Trumbull, the first two cantos of which were published separately 1775–6, complete work published 1782

McGill University Montreal, Canada

Macgillicuddy's Reeks mountains in Co. Kerry

McGonagall, William (1830–1902) Scottish poet noted for his bad verse

McGraw-Hill publishers (hyphen)

MacGregor family name of Rob Roy

ma chère (Fr. f.) my dear; *see also* **mon cher**

machete a broad, heavy large knife, *not* matchet

Machiavell/i, Niccolò dei (1469–1527) Florentine statesman, playwright, writer on political opportunism, *not* Macch-; **-ian** (cap. only in literal or hist. usage); noun, **-ianism**, *not* -ism

machicolation (archit.) openings between supporting corbels

machina (Lat.) a machine; *see also* **deus ex machina**

machinab/le, -ility *not* machine-

machine abbr. **M/C**

machine gun (noun two words, verb and adj. hyphen), abbr. **MG**; *see also* **sub-machine gun**

machine-readable in a form that a computer can process

machine tool *but* **machine-tooled**

machismo (a show of) exaggeratedly assertive manliness (not ital.)

Mach/ number ratio of speed of a body to speed of sound in surrounding atmosphere (one cap.), expressed as e.g. Mach 1, Mach 2; **-meter** instrument indicating air speed in the form of a Mach number (one word); from **Ernst Mach** (1838–1916) Austrian physicist

macho (a person) showily manly or virile (not ital.)

M'Choakumchild, Mr and Mrs (*also* **M'-**) schoolmaster and -mistress in Dickens's *Hard Times*, 1854

Machpelah the burial place of Abraham, *not* Macp-

Machtpolitik power politics (cap.)

Machu Picchu Peru, site of ancient Incan city

Macià, Francesc (1859–1933) Catalan leader and founder of Estat Català

McIntosh a variety of apple

Macintosh/ (propr.) a make of computer; **—, Charles Rennie** (1868–1928) Scottish architect and designer

Mackenzie, Sir Edward Montague Compton (1883–1972) British novelist

Mackinac an island, fort, and straits, Great Lakes, USA

Mackinaw city, Mich., and river, Ill.

mackinaw a heavy woollen blanket, a short thick coat (not cap.)

McKinley, William (1843–1901) US President 1896–1901

mackintosh a waterproof, (colloq.) **mac** (no point), patented by **Charles Macintosh** (1766–1843) Scottish chemist; *not* maci-

mackle (print.) a blurred impression

Mackmurdo, Arthur H(eygate) (1851–1942) Scottish architect and designer, worked in England

macle a twin crystal, spot in a mineral

MacLeish, Archibald (1892–1982) US poet

Macleod, Fiona pseud. of **William Sharp** (1856–1905) Scottish poet and novelist

McLuhan, (Herbert) Marshall (1911–81) Canadian sociologist

MacMahon, Marie Edmé Patrice Maurice de (1808–93) Duke of Magenta, French marshal, President 1873–9

McMaster University Hamilton, Ont., Canada

Macmillan, Maurice Harold (Earl of Stockton) (1894–1986) British statesman

Macmillan/ Publishers Ltd London, **— Publishing USA** New York

McNaghten rules on insanity as defence in criminal trial (one cap.); *not* named after the English judge **Edward Macnaghten** (1830–1913), but after **Daniel McNaghten** (also spelt **M'Naghten** *or* **Macnaughton**), the murderer of Sir Robert Peel's private secretary, 1843

MacNeice, Frederick Louis (1907–63) Anglo-Irish poet, critic, traveller

Macon Ga.

Mâcon dép. Saône-et-Loire, France; *also* a burgundy; *not* -çon

Macpelah *use* Mach-

Macquarie University Sydney

macramé lace a trimming of knotted thread, *not* -mi

Macready, William Charles (1793–1873) English actor

macroeconomics the study of large-scale or general economic factors (one word); cf. **microeconomics**

macron a mark (¯) to indicate a long or stressed vowel or syllable

macroscopic visible to the naked eye

macrurous (zool.) long-tailed, *not* -rour-

McTaggart, John McTaggart Ellis (1866–1925) British philosopher

macul/a a spot, pl. **-ae**

Madagascar off SE coast of Africa

madam/ pl. **-s**; colloq. abbr. **'m, ma'am** (cap. for the correct form of address to the Queen)

Madame (Fr.) abbr. **Mme**, *not* Mdme; pl. **Mesdames**, abbr. **Mmes** (no point after abbrs.)

Mädchen (Ger. n.) young girl, pl. same (cap.)

mad cow disease (colloq.) BSE

Madeira an island, fortified wine, cake

madeleine a small sponge cake

Mademoiselle (Fr.) abbr. **Mlle**, *not* Mdlle; pl. **Mesdemoiselles** abbr. **Mlles**, *not* Mdlles (no point after abbrs.)

Madhya Pradesh an Indian state; abbr. **MP**

madonna (a representation of) the Virgin Mary (cap. as name)

madonna (It.) my lady, madam (not cap.)

madrasah (Ind.) a school or college, in Arab. *madrasa*

Maecenas/ a generous patron of literature or the arts, *not* Me-; pl. **-es**, Lat. pl. **Maecenates**; from **Gaius Maecenas** (*c.*74–8 BC) Roman statesman and patron of Horace and Virgil

maelstrom a great whirlpool; *not* mahl-, mal-; *but Descent into the Maelström* by E. A. Poe, 1841

Maelzel, Johann Nepomuk (1772–1838) German musician; *see also* **metronome**

maenad/ a female follower of Bacchus, *not* me-; pl. **-s**

maestoso (mus.) majestic, stately

Maestricht the Netherlands, *use* **Maas-**

maestr/o (mus.) master, composer, conductor; pl. **-i** (not ital.)

Maeterlinck, Count Maurice (1862–1949) Belgian poet, playwright, essayist, philosopher

Mae West an inflatable life jacket named after the film actress (two words, caps.)

MAFF Ministry of Agriculture, Fisheries, and Food

Mafia a Sicilian secret society, extending to the USA and elsewhere (*see also* **Camorra**); (not cap.) a group regarded as exerting a hidden, sinister influence

Mafikeng S. Africa; **Mafeking** is the hist. spelling, e.g. for the Boer War siege, retained for the town in Manitoba, Canada

mafios/o a member of the Mafia, pl. **-i** (not cap.)

ma foi! (Fr.) upon my word!

Mag. Magyar (Hungarian)

mag. magazine, magnetism

Maga (colloq.) *Blackwood's Magazine*

magazine abbr. **mag.**

magazines, titles of (typ.) when cited, to be in italic

magdalen a repentant prostitute, a home for such; *but* **Mary Magdalene**

Magdalen College Oxford

Magdalene College Cambridge

Magdalenian (archaeol.) (of or relating to) the latest palaeolithic culture or period in Europe

Magellan, Ferdinand (1480–1521) Portuguese explorer, in Port. **Fernão de Magalhães**

maggot a grub; *cf.* **magot**

Maghrib/ countries of N. Africa joined in economic cooperation 1964–5: Algeria, Libya, Morocco, Tunisia, and Western Sahara; Mauritania became involved in 1970, Chad and Mali are sometimes associated; *not* -eb; **-i** inhabitants of this region or the form of Arabic spoken by them

magi pl. of **magus**

magic/ (verb) **-ked, -king**

magilp *use* **meg-**

magister (Lat. m.) master, abbr. **M.**; — *artium* Master of Arts, abbr. **MA**; — *chirurgiae* Master of Surgery, abbr. **M.Ch.**

magistrand an arts student ready for graduation, esp. now at Aberdeen University; at St Andrews a fourth-year student

Maglemosian (archaeol.) (of or relating to) a N. European mesolithic culture

magma/ a mass; pl. **-ta**, or **-s** in general use

Magna Carta (1215) *not* Cha-, *not* preceded by 'the'

magnalium an alloy of magnesium and aluminium

magnesium symbol **Mg**

magnetism abbr. **mag.**

magnetize *not* -ise

magneto/ a type of electric generator, pl. **-s**

magnificat a song of praise, (cap.) the hymn of the Virgin Mary (Luke 1: 46–55) used as a canticle

magnification sign × (followed by a numeral)

magnifico/ a Venetian grandee, pl. **-es** (not ital.)

magnif/y, -ied, -ying

magnifying glass (two words)

magnum a wine bottle about twice the standard size

magnum bonum a large, good variety, esp. of plums or potatoes; pl. **magnum bonums** (two words, not ital.)

magn/um opus (Lat.) an author's chief work, pl. **-a opera**; cf. *opus magnum*

magot an ape; a Chinese or Japanese figure; cf. **magg-**

Magritte, René (1898–1967) Belgian painter

mag/us a member of a priestly Zoroastrian caste of ancient Persia, a sorcerer, pl. **-i**; **the** (**three**) **Magi** the wise men from the East who brought gifts to the infant Christ (Matt. 2: 1) (one cap.)

Magyar (of or relating to) a member of a Ural-Altaic people now predominant in Hungary, the language of this people; a Hungarian; abbr. **Mag.**

magyar a type of blouse or the style of its sleeves

Mahabharata an Indian epic (accent on third syllable), *Mahābhārata* in specialist contexts

Mahame/dan, -tan *see* **Muhammad**

mahara/ja (hist.) an Indian prince, *not* -jah (cap. as title); **-ni** (hist.) the wife of a maharaja, *not* -nee (not ital.)

maharishi a Hindu sage

mahatma in esoteric Buddhism one possessing supernatural powers; (with cap.) title prefixed to exalted persons, esp. **Gandhi**

mahaut *use* **-out**

Mahayana a school of Buddhism practised in China, Japan, and Tibet

Mahdi a spiritual and temporal leader expected by Muslims, (esp. hist.) a leader claiming to be this person

Mahican (a member of) a Native American people between the Hudson River and Narragansett Bay; *see also* **Mohegan**; **Mohican**

mah-jong a Chinese game played with tiles, *not* -ngg (hyphen)

Mahler, Gustav (1860–1911) Austrian composer

mahlstick *use* **maul-**

mahlstrom *use* **mael-**

Mahomet *not* -ed; *use* **Muhammad** for the Prophet except when reproducing hist. spelling

mahout an elephant-driver, *not* -aut

Mahratta *use* **Maratha**

Mahratti *use* **Marathi**

mahseer a large Indian freshwater fish, *not* the many variants

mahwa an Indian tree

mai (Fr. m.) May (not cap.)

Maia (Gr. myth.) the mother of Hermes

maidan (Ind., Pers.) a plain, an esplanade; *not* -aun

maiden/hair, -head (one word)

maiden name (two words)

maieutic of Socratic method of educing latent ideas

maigre day (RC) one when no flesh is eaten

mail carrier postman or -woman (two words)

Maillol, Aristide (1861–1944) French sculptor

maillot a dancer's tights *or* a woman's one-piece bathing suit (not ital.)

main/ (Fr. f.) a hand, a quire, abbr. **M.**; — *droite* right hand, abbr. **MD**; — *gauche* left hand, abbr. **MG**

Maine off. abbr. **Me.**, postal **ME**

Maine-et-Loire dép. of France (hyphens)

mainframe the central processing unit and primary memory of a computer, (often attrib.) a large computer system (one word)

mainland a large continuous extent of land, excluding neighbouring islands etc.; (cap.) the largest island in Orkney and in Shetland, *or* the continental USA, as from Hawaii

main line (hyphen when attrib.)

mainline (verb) inject drugs intravenously

main/sail, -spring, -stay (one word)

mainstream the principal current of a river; (attrib.) the prevailing trend in opinion, fashion, etc., esp. a type of jazz

Mainz am Rhein Germany (no hyphens); *not* Mayence, Mentz (local form)

mai/olica a white tin-glazed earthenware decorated with metallic colours; *use* **maj-** for the 19th-c. trade name for such earthenware

maisonette a small house, a flat; Anglicized form of Fr. f. *maisonnette*

maison garnie (Fr. f.) furnished house

Maisur *see* **Mysore**

maître title of French advocate

maître d'hôtel/ head steward (not ital.), *à la* — — plainly prepared with parsley (ital.) (no hyphen)

maîtresse (Fr. f.) mistress

maiuscol/a (It. typ.) capital letter, *-etto* small capital letter

maize a cereal plant, *Zea mays*, commonly called **corn** in N. America and Australia

Maj. Major

maj. majority

Majesté, Sa (Fr. f.) His, *or* Her, Majesty; *not* Son —

Majesty abbr. **M.**

Majlis the parliament of various N. African and Middle Eastern countries, esp. Iran

majolica *see* **maiolica**

Major/ abbr **Maj.**; **-General** (caps. as title, hyphen except in US) abbr. **Maj.-Gen.**

Major, John (1470–1550) Scottish humanist; — — (b. 1943) British politician, Prime Minister 1990–7

Majorca Balearic Islands, in Sp. and Catalan **Mallorca**

major-domo/ a house steward, pl. **-s** (hyphen)

majority abbr. **maj.**

majuscule a cap. or uncial letter

make-believe (hyphen as noun)

Makedonija Serbo-Croat for **Macedonia**

makeready (typ.) the preparation of forme or plate, fitting of new offset blankets, on printing machine (one word)

makeshift (one word)

make-up cosmetics, (typ.) arrangement of matter into pages (hyphen)

makeweight (one word)

Mal. Malachi, Malayan

Malabo Equatorial Guinea, *formerly* Santa Isabel

Malacca *see* **Malaya, Federation of**

Malachi (OT) abbr. **Mal.**

malacology study of molluscs, abbr. **malac.**

maladroit clumsy (not ital.)

mala/ fide (Lat.) treacherously, — *fides* bad faith

Málaga Spain (accent); a sweet, fortified wine from there (no accent)

Malagasy a native or the language of Madagascar

Malagasy Republic *now* **Madagascar**

malagueña a fandango-like dance from Málaga

mala in se (Lat.) acts that are intrinsically wrong

malaise discomfort, uneasiness

malamute an Inuit dog, *not* male-

malanders *use* **mallen-**

malapropism the mistaken use of a word in place of one that sounds similar, to comic effect, from **Mrs Malaprop**, a character in *The Rivals* by Sheridan, 1775

malapropos inopportunely, in Fr. *mal à propos*

Malawi/ Cent. Africa, in Chichewa **Malawi; -an**; **Lake** — *formerly* Lake Nyasa

Malay the language and people predominating in Malaysia and Indonesia

Malaya, Federation of till 1957 consisted of nine states (Johore, Kedah, Kelantan, Negri Sembilan, Pahang, Perak, Perlis, Selangor, Trengganu) and the two British settlements of Penang and Malacca; adj. **Malayan**; abbr. **Mal.**; *see also* **Malaysia**

Malayalam a Dravidian language of the State of Kerala, Malabar coast, SW India

Malayo-/ a combination form of Malayan, e.g. *Malayo-Chinese* (hyphen); **-Polynesian** Austronesian

Malaysia/ since 1957 an independent state within the Commonwealth, consisting of Malaya, Sabah, and Sarawak; **-n**; *formerly* (Federation of) Malaya

Malcolm X assumed name of **Malcolm Little** (1925–65) US black nationalist leader

malcontent *not* male-

mal de mer (Fr. m.) seasickness

Malden Surrey

mal de tête (Fr. m.) headache

Maldiv/es, The SW of Sri Lanka, **-ian**

Maldon Essex

mal du pays (Fr. m.) homesickness

male (bot., zool., sociology) abbr. **m.**, sign ♂

maleable *use* **mall-**

malecontent *use* **malc-**

malee *use* **mall-**

maleficence (lit.) evildoing, harmfulness

malemute *use* **mala-**

malentendu (Fr. m.) misunderstanding (one word)

Malesherbes, Chrétien Guillaume de Lamoignon de (1721–94) French statesman; *see also* **Malherbe**

malfeasance (law) evildoing; cf. **misfeasance**

malgré (Fr.) in spite of

Malherbe, François de (1555–1628) French writer; *see also* **Malesherbes**

Mali/ NW Africa; **-an**

mali a member of the Indian gardener caste, a gardener; cf. **mallee**

Malines Belgium, in Flemish **Mechelen**; *see also* **Mechlin**

Mallarmé, Stéphane (1842–98) French poet

malleable *not* male-

mallee the Australian eucalyptus; cf. **mali**

mallemuck *use* **mollymawk**

mallenders an eruption behind a horse's knee, *not* malan-

Mallorca Sp. and Catalan for **Majorca**; the local language (a dialect of Catalan) is *Mallorquí*

Mallow Co. Cork

Malmaison near Paris (one word)

Malmesbury Wilts.

malmsey a sweet wine; *not* malv-, -sie, -esie, -asye

Malone, Edmond (*not* -und) (1741–1812) British literary critic

Malplaquet, battle of 1709

malpractice misbehaviour, *not* -se

malstrom *use* **mael-**

Maltese/ (of or related to) (a native or the language) of Malta, — **cross** ✠; *see also* **cross**; **crux**

Malthus/, Thomas Robert (1766–1834) English writer on population, **-ian**

Malton N. Yorks.

maltster a person who makes malt, *not* -ser

Maluku Indonesian islands, *not* Moluccas

malvoisie *use* malmsey

mama var. of **mamma**

mamba any venomous African snake of the genus *Dendroaspis*

mambo a Lat. American dance like the rumba, the music for this

mameluco in Brazil, the offspring of a white and an Indian

Mameluke (hist.) a member of the military caste that ruled Egypt 1254–1811; *not* the many variants; in Arab. *mamlūk*

mamill/a a nipple, pl. **-ae**; **-ary**; *not* mamm- (US)

mamma a child's name for mother, *also* **mama**

mamm/a a breast, pl. **-ae**; **-ary**

mammee a tropical American tree, *not* the many variants

Mammon wealth personified (cap.)

Man. Manila, Manitoba

man. manual

Man, Isle of *see* **Isle of Man**

mana (Maori) might, authority, prestige; supernatural or magical power; cf. **manna**

man about town (three words)

manacle a fetter, *not* -icle

Manacles rocks off Cornish coast

manage/able, -ment

manakin a tropical American bird; cf. **manikin**; **mannequin**; **mannikin**; **minikin**

Manama the capital and free-trade port of Bahrain, in Arabic **Al Manamah**

mañana (Sp.) tomorrow *or* an indefinite future time

Manassas Va.; scene of two American Civil War battles, 1861, 1862; named **Bull Run** by the North

Manasseh, tribe of

Manasses, Prayer of (Apocr.) abbr. **Pr. Man.**

man-at-arms pl. **men-at-arms** (hyphens)

manatee the sea cow

Manaus Brazil, *formerly* Manáos

Manche a dép. of France

Manche, La (Fr.) the English Channel

manche (Fr. m.) handle, (f.) sleeve

Manchester abbr. **Manch., M/c**

Manchester: the signature of the Bishop of Manchester (colon)

man-child pl. **men-children** (hyphens)

Manchu a member of a Mongolian people in China, who formed the last imperial dynasty (1644–1912); the language of the Manchus, now spoken in part of NE China (Manchuria); of or relating to the Manchu people or their language; *not* -choo, -chow

Manchukuo Japanese puppet state 1932–45, formed out of Manchuria, Chinese Jehol, and part of Inner Mongolia

Manchuria a region in NE China, named (1643) after an invading Mongolian people (*see* **Manchu**)

Mancunian (an inhabitant) of Manchester

Mandaean (of or concerning) (a member of) a Gnostic sect surviving in Iraq and claiming descent from John the Baptist; the language of this sect

mandala a symbolic circular figure representing the universe in various religions; (psychol.) such a symbol in a dream, representing the dreamer's search for completeness and self-unity

Mandalay Burma, *not* Mande-

mandamus a writ issued from a higher court to a lower, *not* -emus (not ital.)

mandarin a person of importance, esp. reactionary or secretive bureaucrat; a small orange; official language of China (cap.); *not* -ine

mandatary (law, hist.) one to whom a mandate is given

mandatory (adj.) compulsory

Mandelay, mandemus *use* -da-

mandioc *use* mani-

mandolin a stringed instrument, *not* -ine

mandoria *use* **vesica**

mandrel a spindle, *not* -il

mandrill a baboon

maneater (one word)

manège horsemanship, riding school; cf. **menage**

Manes the classical form of **Mani**; *see also* **Manichee**

Manet, Édouard (1832–83) French painter; cf. **Monet**

man/et (Lat., theat.) he, *or* she, remains; pl. *-ent*

maneuver *use* **manoeuvre**

manganese symbol **Mn**

mangel-wurzel a large beet; *not* mangle-, mangold-

mango/ a tropical fruit, *not* -oe; pl. **-es**

mangold-wurzel *use* **mangel-**

mangosteen a tropical fruit; *not* -an, -ine

mangy having mange, *not* -gey

manhaden *use* **men-**

manhandle (one word)

manhattan a cocktail (not cap.)

Manhattan Island borough, New York City

Manhattan Project the production of the first atomic bombs in USA

Manheim Germany, *use* **Mann-**

man/hole, -hood (one word)

man-hour/ the work of one person per hour, pl. **-s** (hyphen)

manhunt (one word)

Manich/ee originally a religious follower of the Persian **Mani** (also **Manes**) (*c*.216–76); **-aeism, -aean** *not* -chean (US); used generally to describe an adherent of any dualist religious system; (philos.) (often **Manichaean**) any dualist or dualistic system of conflict

manicle a fetter, *use* **-acle**

manifesto/ a declaration of policy, pl. **-s**

manikin a dwarf, an anatomical model; *not* mana-, manni-; cf. **manakin**; **mannequin**; **mannikin**; **minikin**

Manila/ Philippine Islands, abbr. **Man.**; — **cigar, — hemp** (cap.); *not* -illa

man/illa a type of sturdy paper (*also* **-ila**), an African metal bracelet used as a medium of exchange (not cap.)

manille the second best trump or honour in ombre or quadrille

manioc the cassava plant, flour made from it; *not* the many variants

maniple a subdivision of a Roman legion, a Eucharistic vestment

manipulator *not* -er

Manipur NE India, *not* Munnepoor

Manitoba a Canadian province, abbr. **Man.**

manitou (Amer. Ind.) a good or evil spirit as an object of reverence; something regarded as having supernatural power

man-made (hyphen)

manna unexpected benefit; cf. **mana**

mannequin a dressmaker's (live) model, a window dummy; *not* mani-; cf. **manakin; manikin; mannikin; minikin**

manner born, to the *not* manor (*Hamlet* I. iv. 17)

Mannheim Germany, *not* Manh-

mannikin any small finchlike bird of the genus *Lonchura*; cf. **manakin; manikin; mannequin; minikin**

Mannlicher rifle invented by **Ferdinand Ritter von Mannlicher** (1848–1904) (no umlaut)

mano (anthrop.) a primitive stone implement (not ital.)

mano/ (It. f.) a hand, abbr. **M.**, pl. *mani*; — *destra* right hand, abbr. **MD**; — *sinistra* left hand, abbr. **MS**

manoeuvrab/le, -ility (no ligature) *not* man-euverable, -ility (US)

manoeuvr/e, -ed, -ing (no ligature) *not* man-euver, -ed, -ing (US)

man-of-war an armed ship, pl. **men-of-war** (hyphens)

man-of-war's-man (apos., hyphens)

ma non troppo (mus.) but not too much so (qualifying a tempo indication)

manpower the power generated by a man working (one word); for the number of people available for work etc., *prefer* **workers, staff, personnel, people, human resources**

manqu/é (Fr.) f. *-ée* unsuccessful, unfulfilled (placed after the noun)

Man Ray pseud. of **Emmanuel Radinski** (some sources **Rudnitsky**) (1890–1977) US artist, photographer, and film-maker; usually alphabetized thus

Mansard/, François (1598–1666) French architect, — **roof** lower part steeper than upper (not cap.)

Mansfield, Katherine pseud. of **Kathleen Beauchamp**, later **Murry** (1888–1923) New Zealand-born British writer of short stories; *see also* **Murry**

Mansion House, the off. residence of the Lord Mayor of London (caps.); the house of a lord mayor or a landed proprietor (no caps.)

mansuetae naturae (law, adj.) tame (of animals), literally, of a tame nature

mantel a shelf above a fireplace

mantelet a short cloak, a movable screen to protect gunners; *not* mantlet

mantelpiece *not* mantle-

mantilla (Sp.) a veil covering head and shoulders

mantis an orthopterous insect, pl. same

mantissa the part of a logarithm after the decimal point

mantle a cloak

mantlet *use* **-telet**

mantling (her.) (a representation of) ornamental drapery etc. behind and around a shield

mantrap (one word)

Mantua Italy, in It. **Mantova**

mantua (hist.) a woman's loose gown of the 17th–18th cc.

manual an organ keyboard, abbr. **man.**

manual alphabet *use* **sign language** except when differentiating finger spelling

manufactur/e, -er abbr. **mfr.; -ed** abbr. **mfd.; -ers, -es** abbr. **mfrs.; -ing** abbr. **mfg.**

Manufacturers Hanover Corp. a US bank (no apos.)

manum/it set (a slave) free; **-itted, -itting; -ission**

manu propria (Lat.) with one's own hand

manus (Lat. f.) a hand, pl. same

manuscript abbr. **MS** (**a** *not* an, as it is pronounced 'manuscript' *not* 'em-ess'), pl. **MSS** (*but* spell out except in bibliog. enumeration)

manuscrit (Fr. m.) manuscript; abbr. *ms.*, pl. *mss.*

Manuskript (Ger. n.) printer's copy; MS is usually *Handschrift*

Manutius,/ Aldus (1450–1515) in It. **Aldo Manuzio**, — **Aldus** 'the younger' (1547–97), — **Paulus** (1512–72) Italian printers

Manx/ of the Isle of Man, of the Celtic language formerly spoken there; — **cat** (two words), **-man, -men, -woman, -women** (one word)

many-sided (hyphen)

manzanilla a dry sherry, a type of dive (not cap.)

manzanilla (Sp. f.) camomile tea

Mao/ism the doctrine of Mao Zedong, **-ist**

Maori/ *properly* **Māori** (of or relating to) (a member of) the Polynesian aboriginal people of New Zealand, or their language; pl. same

Mao/ Zedong (Pinyin), — **Tse-tung** (traditional) (1893–1976) Chairman of Chinese Communist Party 1954–76, **-ism**

Mapplethorpe, Robert (1947–89) US photographer

Maputo Mozambique, *formerly* Lourenço Marques

maquillage (the application of) make-up

Maquis the resistance movement in France 1940–5

Mar, Earl of family name: of Mar (no other family name); *see also* **Mar and Kellie**

Mar. March

mar/, -red, -ring

mar. maritime

marabou/ feather, — stork *not* -bout, -bu

marabout a Muslim monk or hermit, esp. in N. Africa, *or* a shrine marking a marabout's burial place; *not* -but

Maracaibo Venezuela, *not* -ybo

maranatha (Syriac) 'our Lord cometh'

Mar and Kellie, Earl of family name Erskine; *see also* **Mar**

maraschino/ a strong sweet liqueur made from Dalmatian cherries; **— cherry** cherry preserved in maraschino (not cap.)

Marat, Jean-Paul (1743–93) French revolutionary

Maratha a member of a warrior people native to the modern Indian State of Maharashtra, *not* Mahratta

Marathi the Indo-European language spoken in Maharashtra, NW India; *not* Mahratti

Marazion Cornwall

marbling (bind.) staining endpapers or book edges to resemble marble

marbly marble-like, *not* -ley

marbré (Fr.) marbled, the marbled edges of books

Marcan of St Mark or the Gospel according to him, *not* Mark-

marcato (mus.) emphasized

March (month of) abbr. **Mar.**

Märchen (Ger. n.) a fairy tale, pl. same

marches/e (It.) marquis, f. **-a** marchioness

marchioness the wife or widow of a marquess, *or* a woman holding the rank of marquess in her own right; abbr. **march.** (cap. as title)

Marcobrunner a hock

Marconi, Guglielmo, Marchese (1874–1937) inventor of radio telegraphy; **marconigram** a message sent by his system (not cap.)

Marcuse, Herbert (1898–1979) German-born US philosopher

Mardi Gras Shrove Tuesday

mare (Lat.) sea, (astr.) lunar plain, pl. *maria*

maréchal/ (Fr. m.) field marshal, **-e** his wife

Maréchal Niel a rose

mare/ clausum (Lat.) a sea under one country's jurisdiction; **— liberum** a sea open to all countries

mare's/-nest, -tail (apos., hyphen)

marg. margin, -al

margarine a butter substitute, colloq. **marge**

margarita a tequila-based cocktail

margarite a mineral or rock-formation

Margaux, Chateau a claret (two words)

marge colloq. for margarine, *not* marg

marge (Fr. f.) margin

margin/, -al abbr. **marg.**

marginalia (pl.) marginal notes (not ital.)

margins (typ.) the four are called back or gutter (at binding) head (top), foredge (opposite binding), and tail (foot); an acceptable ratio for the size of margins, in order as above, is $1 : 1\frac{1}{2} : 2 : 2\frac{1}{2}$

Margoliouth, David Samuel (1858–1940) British orientalist

Margrethe (b. 1940) Queen of Denmark 1972–

marguerite the ox-eye daisy

mariage de convenance (Fr. m.) marriage in order to keep up appearances, *not* marr-

Mariamne the name of two wives of Herod the Great

Marian (RC) of or relating to the Virgin Mary

Marianne a woman symbolizing France

Mariánské Lázně Czech Republic, in Ger. **Marienbad**

Marie/ de' Medici (1573–1642) wife of Henry IV of France (*not* de), in Fr. **— de Médicis**

Marienberg Germany

Marienbourg Belgium

Mariënburg Suriname

marijuana *not* -huana

marin/ade (cook.) a liquid in which food is cooked, **-ate** steep in it

Mariolatry (derog.) worship of the Virgin Mary, *not* Mary-

marionette a puppet worked by strings, in Fr. f. *marionnette*

maritime abbr. **mar.**

Maritimes, the the Canadian provinces of New Brunswick, Nova Scotia, Prince Edward Island, and sometimes Newfoundland; in full **Maritime Provinces**

marivaudage (Fr. m.) daintily affected style, from **Pierre Carlet de Chamblain de Marivaux** (1688–1763) French playwright and novelist

marjoram either of two herbs, *Origanum majorana* (or *hortensis*) *or O. onites*, used for seasoning; *see also* **oregano**

Mark (NT) not to be abbr.; **Marcan** *not* Mark-

mark/ German coin, pl. in English contexts **-s**; *see also* **Deutsche Mark**; **Ostmark**

markdown (noun) a reduction in price (one word)

Market, the (hist.) the European Economic Community (cap.)

market/ abbr. **mkt.**; **-ed, -ing**

market day (two words)

Market Drayton Shropshire

market garden/, -er (two words)

Market Harborough Leics.

Marketors, Worshipful Company of

market overt (law) open market

marketplace (one word)

market/ research, — town, — value (two words)

Market Weighton Humberside

markka the basic monetary unit of Finland

marks of reference (typ.) *, †, ‡, §, ||, ¶

mark-up (noun) an increase in price, (typ.) final copy preparation (hyphen, one word in US)

Marlburian (a member) of Marlborough College

marlin any marine fish of the family *Istiophoridae*

marline (naut.) a thin line of two strands

marlinspike for separating strands of rope in splicing; *not* -ine-, -ing- (one word)

Marlow Bucks.

Marlowe, Christopher (1564–93) English playwright

Marmara, Sea of *not* -ora

Marmite (Brit. propr.) a preparation made from yeast extract and vegetable extract (cap.); an earthenware cooking vessel (not cap.)

marmoset a monkey

Marocco *use* Mor-

Maronite a member of a sect of Syrian Christians dwelling chiefly in Lebanon

Marprelate Controversy, the a war of pamphlets 1588–9, between Puritan 'Martin Marprelate' and defenders of the Established Church

marq. marquis

marque/ the make (not type or model) of a car; **letters of —** a licence to fit out an armed vessel and employ it in the capture of an enemy's merchant shipping at sea, as a form of reprisal

marque de fabrique (Fr. f.) trade mark

marquee a large tent, (US) a canopy of the entrance to a building

Marquesas Islands S. Pacific

marquess a British nobleman ranking between a duke and an earl (cap. as title); abbr. **M.**, **marq.** Some British peers of this rank prefer **marquis**; *see also* **marchioness**

marquetry inlaid work, *not* -terie

Márquez, Gabriel García *see* **García Márquez, Gabriel**

marquis/ a (usually Continental) nobleman ranking between a duke and a count, abbr. **M.**, **marq.**; **-e** the wife or widow of a marquis, *or* a woman holding the rank of marquis in her own right, *not now* marchioness; during 16th and 17th cc. a marquis could be a woman (cap. as title only in Eng.); in Fr. *marquis/* abbr. **Mis**; f. **-e**, abbr. **M^{ise}**

Marrakesh Morocco; *not* Mara-, -kech

marriageable *not* -gable

Marriage-à-la-Mode a tragicomic play by Dryden, 1672

married abbr. **m.**

marron (Fr. m.) chestnut, **marron glacé** a sugared chestnut (not ital.)

Marsala a dark sweet fortified dessert wine (cap.)

'Marseillaise, La' French national anthem

Marseilles Bouches-du-Rhône, France; in Fr. (and increasingly in Eng.) **Marseille**, *but* **Marseilles** Ill.

marshal/ (noun and verb) *not* -ll (US); **-led, -ler, -ling** (one *l* in US)

Marshall/, General George (**Catlett**) (1880–1959) US soldier and statesman, initiator of **— Plan** for W. European recovery, 1947

Marshall Islands W. Pacific

Marsham, Viscount eldest son of the Earl of Romney; *see also* **Masham**

martellato (mus.) played with heavy strokes

Martello/ a small circular fort, pl. **-s** (cap.)

marten a weasel; cf. **martin**

Martens, Dr *or* **'Doc'** (propr.) a brand of footwear, before 1960 spelt **Maertens** (no apos.)

Martha's Vineyard an island, Mass.

Martial (in Lat. **Marcus Valerius Martialis**) (*c.*40–*c.*102) Roman poet, abbr. **Mart.**

martin a bird; *see also* **marten**

Martineau, Harriet (1802–76) English writer

martingale the strap from a horse's noseband to girth, *not* -gal

Martini (propr.) a vermouth

martini a cocktail made from gin and dry vermouth

Martinique W. Indies

Martinmas 11 Nov.

martlet (her.) an imaginary footless bird borne as a charge, (arch.) a swift or house-martin

martyrize etc., *not* -ise

marvel/, -led, -ling, -lous (one *l* in US)

Marvell, Andrew (1621–78) English poet and satirist

Marx/, Karl (1818–83) German socialist, author of *Das Kapital*; **-ism** *not* -ianism; **-ian** a student of Marx or Marxism; **-ist** an ideological follower of Marx's doctrines

Marxism-Leninism Marxism as developed by Lenin (hyphen)

Mary Turkmenistan, *formerly* Merv

Maryland off. abbr. **Md.**, postal **MD**

Marylebone/ London, **St —** parliamentary constituency

Marymass 25 Mar.

Maryolatry *use* Mari-

mas (Lat.) a male, pl. *mares*

Masai (of or relating to) (a member of) a pastoral people living in Kenya and Tanzania, their language; pl. same; *properly* **Maasai**

Masaryk,/ Tomáš (Thomas) Garrigue (1850–1937) first President of Czechoslovakia; **— Jan Garrigue** (1886–1948) his son, Czechoslovak politician

masc. masculine

Mascagni, Pietro (1863–1945) Italian composer

masculine abbr. **m., masc.**

Masefield, John (1878–1967) Poet Laureate 1930–67

maser microwave *a*mplification by *s*timulated *e*mission of *r*adiation (acronym); cf. **laser**

mashallah! (Arab., Pers., Turk.) an exclamation of wonder (lit. 'what God wills!')

Masham/, Baron family name Lister, **— of Ilton, Baroness** family name Cunliffe-Lister; *see also* **Marsham**

mashie a golf club, *not* -y

Mashona/, -land Zimbabwe

Mashraq Arab countries of the E. Mediterranean: Egypt, Jordan, Lebanon, Sudan, and Syria; cf. **Maghrib**

masjid (Arab.) a mosque; *not mes-, mus-*

maskinonge a large N. American pike; *not* muskellunge

masochism perversion in which a person delights in being cruelly treated; from **Leopold von Sacher-Masoch** (1835–95) Austrian novelist

Mason/, -ic, -ry (Freemasonry) (cap.)

Mason–Dixon line USA, separated slave-owning South from free North; surveyed 1763–7 by English astronomers Charles Mason and Jeremiah Dixon (en rule)

Masor/ah a body of trad. information and comment on the text of the Hebrew Bible, *not* the many variants; **-ete** a Jewish scholar contributing to the Masorah; **-etic Text** abbr. **MT**, 𝕸

masque a dramatic and musical entertainment esp. of the 16th and 17th cc.

mass/ (mech.) symbol **m** (not cap.); (esp. RC mus.) the Eucharist, **high —, low —** (often initial caps. in liturgical contexts)

Massachusetts off. abbr. **Mass.**, postal **MA**

massé a stroke at billiards

Masséna, André (1758–1817) French marshal

Massenet, Jules Émile Frédéric (1842–1912) French composer

Massereene, Viscount

masseu/r f. **-se** (not ital.)

massif (geol.) a mountain mass (not ital.)

Massora *use* **Masorah**

mastaba/ (archaeol.) an ancient Egyptian tomb, a stone bench attached to a house in Islamic countries; pl. **-s**

Master/ abbr. **M. — of Arts** abbr. **MA; — — Commerce** abbr. **M.Com.; — — Dental Surgery** abbr. **MDS; — — Education** abbr. **M.Ed.; — — Laws** abbr. **LL M; — — Letters** abbr. **M.Litt.; — — Music** abbr. **M.Mus.**, (Camb.) **Mus.M.; — — Philosophy** abbr. **M.Phil.; — — Science** abbr. **M.Sc.**, (US) **MS; — — Surgery** abbr. **M.Ch., M.Chir., MS, Ch.M.; — — Theology** abbr. **M.Th.**

master-at-arms (naut.) first-class petty officer (hyphens)

master mariner the captain of a merchant vessel (two words)

mastermind (noun, adj., and verb, one word)

Master of courtesy title of the eldest son of a Scottish viscount or baron, e.g. The Master of Lovat

Master of Ceremonies abbr. **MC**

Master of the Rolls abbr. **MR**

masterpiece (one word)

master printer head of a printing firm

Master Printers Association abbr. **MPA**

master/ stroke, — switch (two words)

masterwork (one word)

masthead (one word)

mastic a gum resin; *not* -ich, -ick

mat dull, *use* **matt**

Matabele/ pl. same, *now* officially **Ndebele; -land** Zimbabwe (one word)

matador a bullfighter, *not* -ore

match/board, -box (one word)

matchet *use* **machete**

match/lock, -maker (one word)

match point (two words)

match/stick, -wood (one word)

maté an infusion; in Sp. m. *mate*, in Quechua *mati*

matelot (sl.) a sailor, a shade of blue (not ital.); *not* matlo, matlow

matelot (Fr. m.) a sailor

matelote (Fr. cook. f.) a rich fish stew

mat/er (Lat.) mother, pl. *-res*

materialize *not* -ise

materia medica the science of drugs, the drugs themselves (not ital.)

matériel (mil.) everything except personnel (ital.)

matey sociable, *not* -ty

math. mathemat/ics, -ical, -ician

mathematics abbr. **math.**

Mather,/ Cotton (1663–1728), son of **— Increase** (1639–1723), American Puritan theologians and writers

Mathew, Lord Justice (1830–1909)

Mathews,/ Charles (1776–1835) English actor; **— Charles James** (1803–78) his son, English actor and playwright; **— Shailer** (1863–1941)

US educator and theologian; *see also* **Matthews**

matin (Fr. m.) morning

matinée an afternoon entertainment (no accent in US); **matinée musicale** an afternoon entertainment with music (ital.)

matins sometimes in Prayer Book **mattins**

matlo/, -w *use* **matelot**

matriculator *not* -er

matr/ix pl. **-ices**

matronymic a name taken from a female ancestor, as *Margisson, Dvorin; not* me-

matt/ (of colour, surface) dull, without lustre; a mount for a picture; *not* mat; **-e** an impure product of smelting, a mask used in film-making

Matt. St Matthew's Gospel

Mattei, Tito (1841–1914) Italian composer

matter (typ.) MS or TS copy to be printed, type that has been set

Matterhorn an Alpine peak; in Fr. **Mont Cervin**, It. **Monte Cervino**

Matthew (NT) abbr. **Matt.**

Matthew Paris *see* **Paris, Matthew**

Matthews the usual spelling, *but see* **Mathews**

mattins *see* **matins**

maty *use* **-tey**

matzo/ unleavened bread; pl. **-s**, (more correctly) **-th**

Mau Uttar Pradesh, India; *see also* **Mhow**

Maugham, (William) Somerset (1874–1965) English novelist and playwright

Maugrabin, Hayraddin a character in Scott's *Quentin Durward*

Maulmain Burma, *but* **Moulmein** in Kipling

maulstick a painter's hand rest, *not* mahl-

Mau Mau a Kikuyu secret society in Kenya, rebelled 1952 (two words)

Maundy Thursday the day before Good Friday, *not* Maunday (two words)

Maupassant, Guy de (1850–93) French writer

Mauresque *use* **Mor-**

Mauretania an ancient region of NW Africa; cf. **Mauri-**

Mauretania name of two successive Cunard liners

Maurist a member of the reformed Benedictine congregation of St Maur (Fr.)

Mauritania NW Africa; cf. **Maure-**

Mauriti/us in Indian Ocean, **-an**

mausoleum/ a magnificent tomb, pl. **-s**

mauvaise honte (Fr. f.) shyness

mauvais/ goût (Fr. m.) bad taste; — *pas* a difficulty; — *quart d'heure* a bad quarter of an hour, a short unpleasant time; — *sujet* a ne'er-do-well; — *ton* bad style

maverick an unbranded animal, masterless person, rover (not cap.)

Má Vlast (My Country) a cycle of six symphonic poems by Smetana, 1874–9

Max. Maximilian I or II, Holy Roman Emperors

max. maxim, maximum

maxill/a the jaw, pl. **-ae**

maximize *not* -ise

maxim/um the greatest, pl. **-a**; abbr. **max.** (not ital.)

maxwell a unit of magnetic flux, abbr. **Mx**

Maxwell, James Clerk (1831–79) Scottish physicist, *not* Clerk-Maxwell

Maxwell-Lyte, Sir Henry Churchill (1848–1940) English historical writer

May (month of) not to be abbr.

may (tree) (not cap.)

Maya/ one of an Indian people of Cent. America and S. Mexico, pl. same; **-n**

maya (Hindu philos.) illusion

maybe perhaps (one word)

May-bug (hyphen)

May Day 1 May (caps., two words)

mayday international radio distress signal (one word, not cap.)

Mayence on the Rhine *use* **Mainz am Rhein**

Mayfair London (one word), *but* **May Fair Intercontinental Hotel** London

may/flower, -fly (one word)

mayor cap. only as title or in the City of London

maypole (one word)

May queen (two words, one cap.)

mayst (no apos.)

mazagran (Fr. m.) black coffee served in a glass

Mazarin Bible 42-line, first book printed from movable type, by Gutenberg and Fust, *c.*1450; **Cardinal Mazarin** (1602–61) had 25 copies

mazarine deep blue

Mazatlán Mexico

mazel tov (Yiddish) congratulations! (lit. 'good luck!')

Mazepa, Ivan (1644–1709) Cossack chief, hero of Byron's poem *Mazeppa*, 1819

mazurka a Polish dance, not mazou-

Mazzini, Giuseppe (1805–72) Italian patriot

MB *Medicinae Baccalaureus* (Bachelor of Medicine), megabyte

Mb megabit

mb millibar

MBA Master of Business Administration

Mbabane Swaziland

mbar millibar

MBCS Member of the British Computer Society

MBE Member of the Order of the British Empire

MBIM Member of the British Institute of Management

MC Master of Ceremonies, Master of Surgery, (US) Member of Congress, Member of Council, Military Cross

Mc *see* **Mac-, Mc-, Mᶜ-**

M/c Manchester, machine

MCC Marylebone Cricket Club

M.Ch., M.Chir. *Magister Chirurgiae* (Master of Surgery)

mCi millicurie, -s

M.Com. Master of Commerce

MCP male chauvinist pig, Member of the College of Preceptors

MCR Middle Common Room

MCS Military College of Science

Mc/s *use* **MHz**

MCSP Member of the Chartered Society of Physiotherapy

MD managing director, Maryland (postal abbr.), (Lat.) *Medicinae Doctor* (Doctor of Medicine), mentally deficient, Middle Dutch, (It. mus.) *mano destra* (right hand), (Fr. mus.) *main droite* (right hand)

Md mendelevium (no point)

Md. Maryland (off. abbr.)

Mdlle *use* **Mlle** (Mademoiselle)

MDMA methylenedioxymethamphetamine; *see also* **ecstasy**

Mdme *use* **Mme** (Madame)

MDS Master of Dental Surgery

MDT (US) Mountain Daylight Time

MDu. Middle Dutch

ME Maine (postal abbr.), Marine Engineer, Mechanical Engineer, Middle English, Military Engineer, Mining Engineer, Most Excellent, myalgic encephalomyelitis

Me. Maine (off. abbr.)

Mᵉ (Fr.) *maître* (title of a French advocate)

me (mus.) *not* mi

me, it is, it is I both are used in speech, but the former should not be printed, except as a colloquialism

mea culpa (Lat.) by my fault

meagre *not* -er (US)

mealie/ (S. Afr.) an ear or grain of maize, pl. **-s**

meal ticket (two words)

mealtime (one word)

mealy-mouthed hypocritical (hyphen)

mean time that based on mean sun (two words)

meantime (adv.) *but* 'in the mean time'

meanwhile (adv.) *but* 'in the mean while'

measur/e, -able, -ing abbr. **meas.**; (typ.) the width to which type is set, usually stated in 12-pt. (pica) ems; (US mus.) = a bar or its time-content

measuring/ cup, — device, — glass, — jug, — line, — tape (two words)

meatball (one word)

Mebyon Kernow (Corn.) 'sons of Cornwall', movement for Cornish independence

MEC Member of Executive Council

Mecca the capital of Hejaz, and one of the federal capitals of Saudi Arabia; *not* Mekka, -ah, -eh; *see also* **Riyadh**

Mecenas *use* **Mae-**

mech. mechan/ics, -ical

mechanics is sing. as name of the science

Mechelen Belgium, in Fr. **Malines**

Mechlin lace etc., *but see* **Mechelen; Malines**

Mecklenburgh Square London, WC

Mecklenburg/-Schwerin, -Strelitz Germany

Mec Vannin (Manx) 'sons of Man', movement for Manx independence

M.Ed. Master of Education

med. medical, medicine, medieval, medium

medal/, -led, -lion, -list *not* -ist (US)

Mede a member of an Indo-European people that established an empire in Media in Persia in the 7th c. BC

Médecin malgré lui, Le a play by Molière, 1666

media pl. of **medium**, remains plural in all senses.

mediaeval *use* **medie-**

medic (sl.) a doctor or medical student (no point)

Medicaid (US) a government programme of health insurance for those requiring financial assistance

medical/ abbr. **med.**; **— signs** ʒ drachm, ♏ minim, ℳ *misce* (mix), ℥ ounce, ○ pint, ℞ *recipe*, ℈ scruple

Medicare (US) government programme of medical care, esp. for the aged

Medic/i Florentine ruling family, 15th–18th cc.; **-ean**; individual names are *de' Medici*, *see also* **Catherine de' Medici**

medicinae (Lat.) of medicine, abbr. **M.**

medicine abbr. **med.**

medico/ (colloq.) a doctor or medical student, pl. **-s**

medieval/ abbr. **med.**; **-ism, -ist, -ize**, etc., *not* mediae-

Medina a river, IoW; Arabia, in Arab. **al-Madinah**

Medit. Mediterranean

meditatio fugae (Lat., Sc. law) contemplation of flight

medi/um pl. **-a**, in spiritualism **-ums** (not ital.); abbr. **med.**; *see also* **media**

med. jur. medical jurisprudence

Médoc SW France, a claret from this region

meerschaum (not cap.)

Meerut Uttar Pradesh, India; *not* Merath, Mirat

mega- a prefix meaning a million or very large; abbr. **M**

megabit (comput.) a unit of size or speed, equal to 1,048,576 bits, abbr. **Mb**

megabyte (comput.) a unit of information, equal to 1,048,576 bytes, abbr. **MB**

Megaera (Gr. myth.) one of the Furies

megahertz a million hertz, esp. as a measure of radio-transmission frequency, abbr. **MHz**

Megara a city and port, ancient Greece

megaton a unit of explosive power equal to one million tons of TNT, *not* -tonne; abbr. **MT**

megavolt (elec.) a million volts, abbr. **MV**

megawatt (elec.) a million watts, abbr. **MW**

megilp an artist's medium, a vehicle for oil colours; *not* mag-, -ilph

megohm (elec.) a million ohms, abbr. **MΩ**

Mehmetçik (Turk.) a general name (lit. 'Little Mehmet'), equivalent to 'Tommy Atkins' or 'GI Joe'

mehrab *use* **mi-**

Meiji Tenno born **Mutsuhito** (1852–1912) emperor of Japan, **Meiji** the period of his rule

Meilhac, Henri (1831–97) French playwright

mein Herr (Ger.) a form of address, as 'sir'; pl. *meine Herren*; f. *meine Dame*, pl. *meine Damen*

meios/is (rhet.) diminution, understatement (*see also* **litotes**); (biol.) cell division before fertilization, pl. **-es**

Meiringen Switzerland, *not* Mey-

Meirionnydd a district of Gwynedd

Meissen a porcelain, from German town

Meissonier, Jean Louis Ernest (1815–91) French painter

Meissonnier, Juste Aurèle (1693–1750) French goldsmith, architect, designer

Meistersinger a member of one of the 14th- to 16th-c. German guilds for lyric poets and musicians, pl. same

Meistersinger von Nürnberg, Die an opera by Wagner, 1867

Méjico Sp. for **Mexico**, in Amer. Sp. **México**

me judice (Lat.) in my opinion

Mekk/a, -ah, -eh *use* **Mecca**

Melanchthon, Philip Graecized form of **Philipp Schwarzerd** (1497–1560) Luther's associate

Melanesia/ the islands between the Equator and the Tropic of Capricorn, and between New Guinea and Fiji (a region and archbishopric, *not* a political unit); **-n** (of or relating to) (a member of) the dominant Negroid people of Melanesia or their group of

Oceanic languages (the pidgin is officially **Neo-Melanesian**)

mélange (Fr. m.) a mixture, medley

Melchior, Lauritz (1890–1973) Danish tenor

Melchi/zedek (OT) King of Salem; **-sedec** in NT, *but* **-zedek** in NEB

mêlée a fray (not ital., no accents in US)

Meliboean (poet.) alternating; *not* -aean, -bean

Melos a Greek island; *see also* **Milo**

Melpomene (Gr. myth.) the muse of tragedy

melt spleen, *use* **milt**

meltdown (noun, one word)

melting/ point, — pot (two words)

Melton Mowbray Leics. (two words)

mem. memento, memorial

Member abbr. **M.**

Member of Parliament (caps.) abbr. **MP**, pl. **MPs**

memento/ a souvenir, pl. **-es**; abbr. **mem.** (not ital.)

memento mori (Lat.) an object reminding one of death, 'remember that you must die', pl. same (not ital.)

Meml/ook, -uk *use* **Mameluke**

memo/ memorandum, pl. **-s** (no point)

mémoire (Fr. m.) bill, report, treatise; (f.) memory

memorabilia (pl.) noteworthy things

memorand/um a written note, pl. **-ums**; pl. **-a** things to be noted; *see also* **memo**

memorial abbr. **mem.**

Memorial Day (US) the last Monday in May

memorialize to commemorate by a memorial, *not* -ise

memoria technica a system or contrivance used to assist the memory, mnemonics (not ital.)

memorize *not* - ise

memsahib *see* **sahib**

menad *use* **mae-**

ménage a household (not ital.), cf. **manège**; **ménage à trois** an arrangement in which three people live together, typically a married couple and the lover of one of them

menagerie (a place for) a collection of wild animals, *not* -ery

menarche the onset of menstruation

Mencken, H(enry) L(ouis) (1880–1956) US author, critic, and editor

mendacity falsehood

Mendel/, Gregor Johann (1822–84) Austrian botanist; **-ian, -ism**

Mendeleev, Dmitri (Ivanovich) (1834–1907) Russian chemist

mendelevium symbol **Md**

Mendelssohn(-Bartholdy), Jacob Ludwig Felix (1809–47) German composer

mendicity begging

meneer (Afrik.) Mr, sir

menhaden N. American fish of herring family, *not* man-

menhir (archaeol.) a tall, upright, usually prehistoric monumental stone

meningitis an inflammation of the meninges

Mennonite a member of a Protestant sect

meno (It. mus.) less

Menorca Sp. for Minorca

mensa (Lat.) a table; *a mensa et toro* from bed and board (a kind of divorce), not *thoro*

Mensa a constellation, an organization for those with a high IQ (one cap.)

Menshevik a member of the non-Leninist wing of the Russian Social Democratic Party before 1917; *see also* **Bolshevik**

Men's Lib (caps., no point)

mens/ rea (Lat.) criminal intent, the knowledge of wrongdoing; — *sana in corpore sano* a sound mind in a sound body.

menstru/um a solvent, pl. **-a**

mensur. mensuration

menswear (one word, no apos.)

menthe (Fr. cook. f.) mint, not *mi-*

Menton French Riviera, in It. **Mentone**

mentor an experienced and trusted adviser (not cap.)

menu/ pl. **-s**

Menuhin, Sir Yehudi (1916–99) US-born British violinist

meow *use* **miaow**

MEP Member of the European Parliament

m.e.p. mean effective pressure

Mephistophele/s; **-an** a fiendish person like Mephistopheles (cap.); malicious, cynical (not cap.); *not* -ian

mer. meridian, meridional

Merano Italian Tyrol

Merath *use* **Meerut**

Mercator projection a method of map making (one cap.); *not* -'s

Mercedes(-Benz) a German make of car (hyphen); **Mercédès** (Fr.), **Mercedes** (Sp.) a woman's name

mercerize *not* -ise

merchandise (noun and verb) *not* -ize

Merchant/ Company Schools Edinburgh, — **Taylors Company**, *but* — **Taylors' School** (apos.)

merci (Fr. m.) thanks; no, thank you; (f.) mercy

mercur/y symbol **Hg**; **-ial** swift, volatile, (cap.) of the planet Mercury

Meredith/, George (1828–1909) English novelist and poet, adj. **-ian**; —, **Owen** *see* **Bulwer-Lytton, Edward Robert**

meretricious befitting a prostitute, showy

meridian abbr. **m.**, **mer.**

meridies (Lat.) noon, abbr. **m.**

meridional of a meridian; abbr. **m.**, **mer.**; (noun) an inhabitant of S. Europe, esp of S. France

Mérimée, Prosper (1803–70) French novelist and historian

merino/ a sheep, pl. **-s**

merissa a Sudanese drink made from fermented maize

meritocracy government by the best people

meritorious deserving reward or praise

merle the common blackbird, *not* merl

merlin a small falcon

merlon the solid part of an embattled parapet

Merovingian (a king) of a Frankish dynasty in Gaul and Germany, *c*.500–700

Merrimack town and river in NH; (ital.) the name of the Confederate ironclad warship that fought the *Monitor* during the US Civil War

merry andrew a buffoon (two words, not cap.)

merry-go-round (hyphens)

merrythought the wishbone (one word)

Merseyside a metropolitan county

Merthyr Tydfil Mid Glam. (two words), *not* -vil

Merv Turkmenistan, *now* **Mary**

mesa a flat-topped mountain

mésalliance (Fr. f.) marriage with a social inferior, in Eng. *use* **misalliance**

mescal/ a maguey, or the liquor obtained from this (cf. **tequila**); — **buttons**; **-ine**, *not* -in

Mesdames (Fr.) pl. of **Madame**, abbr. **Mmes**

Mesdemoiselles (Fr.) pl. of **Mademoiselle**; abbr. **Mlles**, *not* Mdlles

mesjid *use* **mas-**

mesmerize hypnotize, fascinate; *not* -ise

Mesolongi *use* **Missolonghi**

Mesozoic (geol.) (of or relating to) an era of geological time marked by the development of dinosaurs, and with evidence of the first mammals, birds, and flowering plants (cap.)

mesquite/ a N. American tree, *not* -it; — **bean** (two words)

Messeigneurs pl. of **Monseigneur**

Messerschmitt, Willy (Wilhelm Emil) (1898–1978) German aircraft designer, *not* -dt

Messiaen, Olivier (Eugène Prosper Charles) (1908–92) French organist and composer

Messia/h, -nic a (would-be) liberator of an oppressed people, the promised deliverer of the Jews (caps.); *Messiah* oratorio by Handel, 1742, *not* The —

Messieurs (Fr.) pl. of **Monsieur**; abbr. **MM.**

mess/ jacket, — kit (two words)

Messrs pl. of **Mr** (no point)

mess tin (two words)

messuage (law) a dwelling house with out-buildings and land assigned to its use

mestiz/o a person of Spanish and American Indian blood, *not* -ino; pl. **-os**; f. **-a**, pl. **-as**

Met, the (UK) the Meteorological Office, the Metropolitan Police in London, (US) the Metropolitan Opera House in New York

met. metallurg/y, -ical, -ist; metronome

meta- combination form (usually **met-** before a vowel or *h*)

metal/, -led, -ling, -lize (one *l* in US), *not* -ise

metallurg/y, -ical, -ist abbr. **met.**, **metall.**

metamorphos/e transform; *not* -ise, -ize; noun **-is**, pl. **-es**

metaph. metaphys/ics, -ical, -ically, -ician; metaphor, -ical, -ically

metaphras/e (noun) a literal translation, (verb tr.) put into other words; (adj.) **-tic**

metathes/is pl. **-es**

meteor/, -ite, -oid

meteor. meteorology

meter measuring device, (US) = **metre**

Meth. Methodist

methodize *not* -ise

Methuselah a very old person or thing, from the name of an OT patriarch said to have lived 969 years (Gen. 5: 27); a wine bottle of about eight times the standard size (not cap.)

métier (Fr. m.) one's trade, profession, or forte

Metis a person of mixed race, esp. the offspring of a white person and a Native American in Canada; pl. same; f. **Metisse/**, pl. **-s**; in Fr. *métis*, f. *métisse*

metonymy abbr. **meton.**

metre/ SI unit of length, 39.37 in.; *not* -er (US); abbr. **m** (no point); **-age** number of metres, *not* -rage

Métro, Le (no point) abbr. of *Le Métropolitain*, the Paris underground railway

metrology the science of weights and measures, abbr. **metrol.**

metronome/ (mus.) an instrument for fixing tempos; abbr. **M.**, **met.**; **Maelzel's —** abbr. **MM**

metronymic *use* **ma-**

metropol/is pl. **-ises**; **-itan**; abbr. **metrop.**

metr/um (Lat. verse) metre, abbr. **m.**; pl. **-a**, abbr. **mm.**

meubl/é (Fr.) f. **-ée** furnished

meum/ (Lat.) mine; **— and *tuum*** mine and thine, *not* et tuum

meunière (esp. of fish) floured and cooked or served in lightly browned butter with lemon juice and parsley (not ital.)

Meuse a river of France, Belgium, and the Netherlands; in Du. **Maas**

MeV mega-electronvolt

meV milli-electronvolt

mews a street of stables converted into garages or houses, pl. same

Mex. Mexic/o, -an

Mexican (noun) a native or national of Mexico, a person of Mexican descent; a language spoken in Mexico, esp. Nahuatl; (adj.) of or relating to Mexico or its people, *or* of Mexican descent

Mexico/ in Amer. Sp. **México**, in Sp. **Méjico**; **— City** in Amer. Sp. **Ciudad México**, often shortened to **México**; **Mexican**

Meynell,/ Alice (1847–1922) English poet, **— Sir Francis** (1891–1975) English typographer, **— Wilfrid** (1852–1948) English writer

Meyringen *use* **Mei-**

MEZ (Ger.) *Mitteleuropäische Zeit* = **Central European Time**, one hour in advance of GMT

mezereon (bot.) a spring-flowering shrub, *not* -eum

mezuz/ah a parchment inscribed with religious texts and attached in a case to the doorpost of a Jewish house as a sign of faith, pl. **-oth**

mezzanine a low storey between two others; (UK) a floor or space beneath the stage, (US) a dress circle

mezza voce (It. mus.) not with full strength of sound, abbr. *m.v.*

mezzo/ short for mezzo-soprano, pl. **-s**

mezz/o (It. mus.) f. **-a** half, medium; abbr. **M.**

mezzo-relievo half-relief

mezzo-soprano (mus., hyphen)

mezzotint (typ.) an intaglio illustration process from a roughened plate

MF (paper) machine finish, medium frequency, (typ.) modern face

mf (mus.) mezzo forte (fairly loud)

mfd. manufactured

mfg. manufacturing

MFH Master of Foxhounds

MFHom. Member of the Faculty of Homoeopathy

MFN most favoured nation

MFr. Middle French

mfr. manufactur/e, -er

mfrs. manufactur/ers, -es

m.ft. *mixtura* (or, in early modern texts, *mistura*) *fiat* (let a mixture be made)

MG (paper) machine glazed, machine gun, (Fr. mus.) *main gauche* (left hand), Morris Garages (as a make of car)

Mg magnesium (no point)

mg milligram (no point)

MGB USSR 'Ministry of State Security', 1946–53; *see also* **KGB**

M.Glam. Mid Glamorgan

MGM Metro-Goldwyn-Mayer, US film studio

Mgr Monseigneur, Monsignor (no point)

MGr. Middle Greek

Mgr. Manager, pl. **Mgrs.**

MH Master of Hounds (usually beagles or harriers)

MHG Middle High German

MHK Member of the House of Keys (IoM)

mho (elec.) a former unit of conductance, the reciprocal of an **ohm**

M.Hon. Most Honourable

Mhow Madhya Pradesh, India; *see also* **Mau**

MHR Member of the House of Representatives

MHz megahertz (no point, two caps.)

MI Michigan (postal abbr.), Middle Irish, Military Intelligence, Mounted Infantry

MI5 Military Intelligence department concerned with state security, **MI6** Military Intelligence department concerned with espionage (neither is in official use) (no points)

MIAE Member of the Institute of Automobile Engineers

M.I.Ae.E. Member of the Institute of Aeronautical Engineers (also without points)

mi. mile(s)

miaow the cry of a cat; *not* meow (US), miaou (Fr.), miau (Sp.), miaul

miasm/a (Gr.) a noxious emanation, pl. **-ata** (not ital.)

M.I.Biol. Member of the Institute of Biology

Mic. Micah (OT)

micaceous pertaining to mica, *not* -ious

Micawber/, Wilkins a character in Dickens's *David Copperfield*, **-ish** unpractical but hopeful; **-ism**

MICE Member of the Institution of Civil Engineers

Mich. Michaelmas, 29 Sept.; Michigan (off. abbr.)

Michelangelo Buonarroti (1475–1564) Italian sculptor, painter, architect, poet (two words, not three)

Michelson/, Albert Abraham (1852–1931) German-American physicist; **–Morley** experiment (en rule)

M.I.Chem.E. Member of the Institution of Chemical Engineers

Michener, James (**Albert**) (1907–97) US novelist

Michigan off. abbr. **Mich.**, postal **MI**

mickey/ (to take the — out of) to make fun of, *not* micky

Mickey Finn (US) a drugged drink

Mickiewicz, Adam (1798–1855) Polish poet

Micmac (of or relating to) (a member of) a Native American tribe (one word)

micro- a prefix meaning very small, or one-millionth; symbol μ, e.g. **microhm**, **μΩ**; **micrometre** (*preferred* to **micron**), **μm**; **microvolt**, **μV**

microchip (one word)

microeconomics the branch of economics dealing with individual commodities, producers, etc. (one word); cf. **macroeconomics**

microelectronics (one word)

microfiche a sheet of film, suitable for filing, containing microphotographs of pages of book, periodical, manuscript, etc.; pl. same

microfilm film bearing microphotographs

microgram one-millionth of a gram, abbr. **μg**

micrography the description or delineation of microscopic objects

micrometer an instrument for measuring minute distances or angles; cf. **micrometre**, *see also under* **micro-**

micromillimetre *or* **millimicron** abbr. **mμ**, *but use* **nanometre** abbr. **nm**

micron symbol **μ**, *but use* **micrometre** (*see under* **micro-**)

Micronesia islands north of Melanesia

micro-organism (hyphen)

microphotograph a photograph reduced to microscopic size; cf. **photomicrograph**

microprocessor (one word)

micros. microscop/y, -ist

microsecond one-millionth of a second, abbr. **μs**

Microsoft (propr.) (the manufacturer of) an operating system for microcomputers, abbr. **MS**

microwave oven (two words)

mid. middle

midbrain (one word)

Mid Calder Lothian (caps., no hyphens)

midday (one word)

middle abbr. **M.**, **mid.**

middle age (two words) *but* **middle-aged** (hyphen)

Middle Ages, the roughly from the fall of the Western Roman Empire to the Renaissance and the Reformation (two words, caps.)

middle class (two words, hyphen when attrib.)

middle common room a common room for the use of graduate members of a college who are not Fellows, abbr. **MCR**

Middle East *not* Mideast (US)

Middle English the English language in use *c*.1150–1500, abbr. **ME**

Middle French the French language in use 12th–15th cc. (the French do not make this distinction), abbr. **MFr.**

Middle Greek the Greek language in use 7th–15th cc., abbr. **MGr.**

Middle High German the High German language in use *c*.1100–1500, abbr. **MHG**

Middle Irish the Irish language in use 11th–15th cc., abbr. **MI**

Middle Low German the Low German language in use *c*.1100–1500, abbr. **MLG**

middleman (one word)

middle-of-the-road (adj.) moderate, avoiding extremes (no hyphens as a noun)

Middlesbrough Cleveland, *not* -borough

Middle Scots the Scots language in use late 15th–early 17th cc., abbr. **MS**

Middlesex a former county of England, abbr. **Middx.**

Middleton,/ Baron family name Willoughby; **— Thomas** (*c*.1570–1627) English playwright; *see also* **Midleton; Mydd-**

Middle Welsh the Welsh language in use *c*.1150–1500, abbr. **MW**

Middle West (US) N. Cent. states as geographical area; *see also* **Midwest**

Middx. Middlesex

Mideast (US) = **Middle East**

midfield/ (noun and adj., one word), **-er**

Midgard (Norse myth.) abode of human beings

Mid Glamorgan a county of Wales, abbr. **Mid Glam., M.Glam.**

MIDI musical instrument digital interface

midi a thing of medium length or size

Midianite member of an ancient N. Arabian people

midinette a Parisian shop girl (not ital.)

Midland Bank plc

Midlands, the inland counties of central England, the region south of the Humber and Mersey and north of the Thames, excepting Norfolk, Suffolk, Essex, Middlesex, Hertfordshire, Gloucestershire, and the counties bordering on Wales; in hunting, the champaign country including parts of Leicestershire, Northamptonshire, Warwickshire, Nottinghamshire, and Derbyshire

Mid Lent the fourth Sunday in Lent (two caps., two words)

Midleton, Viscount family name Brodrick; *see also* **Midd-; Mydd-**

mid-life (hyphen, one word in US)

Midlothian former county of Scotland (one word)

mid/night, -rib, -ship (one word)

Midsomer Norton Avon

midsummer (one word)

Midsummer Day 24 June (two words, caps.)

midway (one word)

Midwest/, the (US) N. Cent. states considered as a single political or social region (one word); *see also* **Middle West; -erner**

midwi/fe pl. **-ves; -fery**

midwinter (one word)

MIEE Member of the Institution of Electrical Engineers

mielie *use* **meal-**

Miers, Sir Henry Alexander (1858–1942) English mineralogist; *see also* **Myers; Myres**

Mies van der Rohe, Ludwig (1886–1969) German-born US architect

MiG any of several aircraft designed by Mikoyan and Gurevich; individual models are cited with a hyphen, e.g. MiG-15, MiG-21 (two caps.)

mightest *not* mightst

mignonette a fragrant plant, in Fr. f. *mignonnette*

Mihailović, Draža (b. **Dragoljub**) (1893–1946) Yugoslav soldier, sometimes Anglicized as **Drazha Mihailovich**

mihrab a niche or slab in a mosque, indicating the direction of Mecca; *not* me-, mirh-; in Arab. *miḥrāb*; *see also* **kiblah**

MIJ *use* **MJI**

mijnheer (Du.) Sir, Mr; cf. **mynheer**

mil one-thousandth of an inch (no point)

mil. military, militia

Milan Italy, in It. **Milano**

milch cow a source of easy profit, *not* milk (two words)

mile/ abbr. **m.**, pl. **mls.; nautical —** = 6,076 feet; **statute —** = 5,280 feet; in Fr. m. *mille*, pl. *milles*

mileage a number of miles, *not* -lage

Milesian (an inhabitant) of ancient Miletus in Asia Minor, (joc.) an Irishman

milestone (one word)

milieu/ environment (not ital.), pl. **-x**; *see also* ***juste milieu***

military abbr. **mil.**

Military Academy abbr. **MA**

militate have effect; cf. **mitigate**

militia abbr. **M., mil.**

milk/ bar, — chocolate, — float (two words)

milkman (one word)

milk/ pudding, — round, — run, — shake (two words)

milksop (one word)

Milky Way (astr.) (caps.)

mill abbr. **m.**

Mill,/ James (1773–1836) Scottish historian and economist; **— John Stuart** (1806–73) his son, English economist and political philosopher

Millais, Sir John Everett (1829–96) English painter; *see also* **Millet**

Millay, Edna St Vincent (1892–1950) US poet, 'St.' (point) in US use

millboard a stout pasteboard for bookbinding etc. (one word)

mille/ (Fr. m.) a thousand, pl. same, abbr. **M.**; also a mile, pl. **-s**; **-feuille** (m.) a confection, (f.) a plant (one word)

millenar/y of a thousand, (celebration of) the thousandth anniversary; **-ian**

millenni/um a thousand years; pl. **-a** in literal senses, **-ums** in general contexts (two ls, two ns), **-al**

mille passus (Lat.) 1,000 paces of 5 feet, or the Roman mile; abbr. **MP, m.p.**; pl. *milia passuum*

millepede *see* **millipede**

Milles-Lade family name of Earl Sondes; *see also* **Mills**

Millet,/ Aimé (1819–91) French sculptor, — **Jean-François** (1814–75) French painter; *see also* **Millais**

milli- prefix meaning one-thousandth; abbr. **m**, e.g. **milliampere** abbr. **mA**

milliard one thousand million; *see* **billion**

millibar a unit of pressure, one-thousandth of a bar; abbr. **mbar**, (meteor.) **mb** (no point)

milligram one-thousandth of a gram; abbr. **mg** (no point); *not* -gramme

millilitre one-thousandth of a litre, abbr. **ml** (no point)

millimetre one-thousandth of a metre, 0.039 in.; abbr. **mm** (no point)

millimicron *use* **nanometre**

million abbr. **m.**; for millions of pounds use e.g. £150m.

millionaire not -onnaire

millipede (zool.) *not* mille- (though most correct)

Mills the family name of Baron Hillingdon; *see also* **Milles-Lade**

Milngavie Strathclyde

Milo Fr. and It. for **Melos**, a Greek island, esp. in Venus de Milo

M.I.Loco.E. Member of the Institute of Locomotive Engineers

Milošović, Slobodan (b. 1941) president of Serbia 1992–7, president of the Federal Republic of Yugoslavia 1997–

milt the spleen, *not* melt

Milton Keynes Bucks.

Milwaukee Wis.

M.I.Mech.E. Member of the Institution of Mechanical Engineers

mimeograph (noun) (often attrib.) a duplicating machine that produces copies from a stencil, a copy produced in this way; (verb) produce copies by this process; abbr. **mimeo**

mimic/, -ked, -king, -ry

M.I.Min.E. Member of the Institution of Mining Engineers

MIMM Member of the Institution of Mining and Metallurgy

Min any of the Chinese languages or dialects spoken in Fukien province, SE China

min. minim, minimum, mining, minister, ministry, minor; minute, -s (no point in scientific and technical work)

min/a an ancient Greek unit of weight and currency, pl. **-ae**; for the bird, *use* **mynah**

minac/ious threatening, **-ity**

minatory threatening

minauderie affected, simpering behaviour (not ital.)

mincemeat (one word)

mince pie (two words)

Mindanao one of the Philippine Islands, *not* -oa

Mindererus/ Latinized name of **R. M. Minderer** (c.1570–1621) German physician, — **spirit** a diaphoretic

mine-detector (hyphen, two words in US)

mine/field, -hunter, -layer (one word)

mineralog/y, -ical abbr. **mineral.**; *not* minerological, -ology

minever *use* **mini-**

mingy mean, *not* -ey

Mini (propr.) a make of car (cap.); a short skirt or dress (not cap.)

mini/bus, -cab, -car, -computer (one word)

Minié, Claude Étienne (1814–79) inventor of a type of bullet and rifle

minikin a diminutive person or thing; cf. **manakin; manikin; mannequin; mannikin**

minim a drop, one-sixtieth of fluid drachm; abbr. **min.**; sign ♏; (mus.) a halfnote

minimize *not* -ise

minim/um pl. **-a** (not ital.), abbr. **min.**

mining abbr. **min.**

miniscule *use* **minu-**

miniseries a short series of television programmes on a single theme (one word)

miniskirt (one word)

minister abbr. **min.**

Minister without Portfolio (two caps.)

minium a red oxide of lead

miniver a plain white fur, *not* -ever

minke a small baleen whale

Minn. Minnesota (off. abbr.)

Minneapolis Minn.

Minnehaha wife of Hiawatha in Longfellow's poem

minnesinger one of a school of medieval German lyric poets (not cap. or ital.)

Minnesota off. abbr. **Minn.**, postal **MN**

Minoan pertaining to the Bronze Age civilization, language, or scripts of ancient Crete, *c.*3000–1100 BC (from King Minos)

minor abbr. **min.**, (in Peerage) **M.**

Minorca Balearic Islands, in Sp. **Menorca**

Minories a street in London

Minotaur (Gr. myth.) the monstrous offspring of a bull and Pasiphaë, wife of King Minos

Min./ Plen. *or* **Plenip.** Minister Plenipotentiary, **— Res.** Minister Residentiary

M.Inst.P. Member of the Institute of Physics

Mint, the (cap.)

minthe *use* **menthe**

minuet a dance, its music; *not* -ette

minus/ sign −; pl. **-es**

minuscule (palaeography) a kind of cursive script developed in the 7th c.; a small or lower-case letter; (adj.) tiny; *not* mini-

minute/, -s abbr. **m., min.** (no point in scientific and technical work); sign ′; **— mark** (′) symbol for feet, minutes, also placed after a stressed syllable

minuti/ae small details, sing. **-a** (not ital.)

MIOB Member of the Institute of Building

Miocene (geol.) (of or relating to) the fourth epoch of the Tertiary period (cap., not ital.)

mi/osis the contraction of the pupil of the eye, *not* my-; **-otic**

MIPA Member of the Institute of Practitioners in Advertising

mirabile/ dictu (Lat.) wonderful to relate, **— visu** wonderful to see

MIRAS mortgage interest relief at source

Mirat *use* **Meerut**

mirepoix (Fr. cook. m.) sautéd chopped vegetables

mirhab *use* **mihr-**

mirky dark, *use* **mur-**

Miró, Joan (1893–1983) Catalan painter

MIRV multiple independently targeted re-entry vehicle (a type of ballistic missile)

miry mirelike, *not* -ey

Mirzapur Uttar Pradesh, India; *not* -pore

mis/advice bad counsel, **-advise** give it (one word)

misalliance marriage with a social inferior, in Fr. f. *mésalliance*

misan/dry the hatred of men, **-thropy** the hatred of humankind

misc. miscellaneous, miscellany

miscellanea miscellaneous matter, is plural

miscellany a mixture, medley, collection

mischievous *not* -ious

miscible capable of being mixed, esp. in scientific and technical contexts; *see also* **mixable**

misdemeanour *not* -or (US)

M^{ise} (Fr.) **marquise** (marchioness) *not* Mise

mise en abyme (Fr. lit. f.) an internal duplication of (part of) a literary work; *not abîme*, no hyphens

mise-en-scène (Fr. f.) scenery, stage effect (no hyphens as Eng. lit. term)

misère a declaration to win no tricks in cards

Miserere (a musical setting of) the 50th Psalm of the Vulgate

miserere (*properly* **misericord**) a bracket on a turn-up seat used as support for a person standing

misfeasance a wrongful act; (law) a transgression, esp. the wrongful exercise of lawful authority; cf. **malfeasance**

mishmash a mixture (one word)

Mishna/h a collection of Jewish precepts forming the basis of the Talmud, and embodying Jewish oral law; **-ic**

misle *use* **mizz-**

misletoe *use* **mistle-**

misogam/y the hatred of marriage, **-ist**

misogyn/y the hatred of women, **-ist**

misprint (typ.) a typographical error

Miss (cap. as title, no point)

Miss. Mission, -ary; Mississippi (off. abbr.)

missal (RC) a book containing the texts used in the service of the mass throughout the year; a book of prayers

missel thrush *use* **mistle**

misseltoe *use* **mistle-**

mis/send, -sent (one word)

misshape/, -n (one word)

Mission/, -ary abbr. **Miss.**

missis (sl.) **Mrs**, *not* -us (US sl.)

Mississippi a river and state, USA; off. abbr. **Miss.**, postal **MS**

Missolonghi Greece

Missouri a river and state, USA; off. abbr. **Mo.**, postal **MO**

mis/spell, -spend, -spent, -state, -step (one word)

missus (US sl.) = **missis**

mist (meteor.) abbr. **m.**

mistakable *not* -eable

Mister abbr. **Mr**

Mistinguett pseud. of **Jeanne Marie Bourgeois** (1875–1956) French entertainer, *not* -e

mistle *use* **mizzle**

mistle thrush *not* missel

mistletoe *not* missel-, misle-

Mistral,/ Frédéric (1830–1914) Provençal poet, **— Gabriela** pseud. of **Lucila Godoy de Alcayaga** (1889–1957) Chilean poet

mistral (not ital.)

Mistress abbr. **Mrs**

M.I.Struct.E. Member of the Institution of Structural Engineers

MIT Massachusetts Institute of Technology

miter *use* **mitre** (except in US)

Mithra/s the Persian sun-god; **-ic, -ism**

Mithridat/es (VI, 136–63 BC) King of Pontus, *not* Mithra-; **-ize, -ic, -ism** (not cap.)

mitigate (verb) moderate; cf. **militate**

Mitilini *see* **Mytilene**

mitre/ *not* miter (US); **-block, -board, -box** (hyphens)

mitre wheels (two words)

mitring *not* mitreing

Mitterrand, François (1916–96) President of France 1981–95

mixable in gen. use, *not* -ible; *see also* **miscible**

Mizen Head Co. Cork

mizzen/ the aftermost of the fore-and-aft sails; **-mast** the aftermost mast of a three-masted ship (one word); *not* miz-

mizzle a fine rain; *not* misle, mistle

MJI Member of the Institute of Journalists, *not* MIJ

Mk. identifying a particular design, as Mk. V; mark (Ger. coin), *use* **DM**

mks metre-kilogram-second (no points)

mkt. market

ML Licentiate in Midwifery, Medieval Latin, Middle Latin, motor launch

Ml. mail

ml millilitre, -s (no point)

MLA Member of the Legislative Assembly, Modern Languages Association

MLC Member of the Legislative Council

MLD minimum lethal dose

MLF Multilateral Nuclear Force

MLG Middle Low German

M.Litt. Master of Letters

Mlle/ Mademoiselle, pl. **-s** (no point)

MLR minimum lending rate

MLS Member of the Linnean Society

mls. miles

MM 2,000, (mus.) Maelzel's metronome, (Their) Majesties, (Fr.) Messieurs, Military Medal

mm millimetre, -s (no point)

mm. (Lat.) *metra* (verse metres)

m.m. *mutatis mutandis* (with the necessary changes)

Mme/ (Fr.) Madame, pl. **-s** (no point)

m.m.f. magnetomotive force

M.Mus. Master of Music

MN Merchant Navy, Minnesota (postal abbr.)

Mn manganese (no point)

Mn. Modern (with names of languages)

M'Naghten rules *use* **McNaghten rules**

mnemonics (pl. noun treated as sing.)

MO mass observation, Medical Officer, Missouri (postal abbr.), money order

Mo molybdenum (no point)

Mo. Missouri (off. abbr.)

mo. (US) month

mob/, -bed, -bing

Mobilian Jargon a Native American pidgin used as a lingua franca among different tribes in south-eastern USA, and as a contact language between tribes and European settlers (caps.)

mobilize *not* -ise

Möbius/, August Ferdinand (1790–1868) German mathematician, discoverer of the — **strip**

Mobutu Sese Seko (full name **Mobutu Sese Seko Kuku Ngbendu Wa Za Banga**, b. **Joseph-Désiré Mobutu**) (1930–97) president of Zaire 1965–97

Moby-Dick a novel by H. Melville, 1851 (hyphen)

MOC mother of the chapel; *see* **chapel**

moccasin a Native American shoe, a N. American venomous snake; *not* the many variants

Mocha an Arabian port on the Red Sea

mocha a coffee, a sheepskin (not cap.)

mock turtle soup (three words)

MOD Ministry of Defence, *formerly* M.o.D.

mod. moderate, modern

mod. moderato (mus.)

mode (Fr. m.) method, (gram.) mood; (f.) fashion

model/, -led, -ler, -ling (one l in US)

modem (comput.) (not cap.)

moderate abbr. **mod.**

Moderations the first public examination in some faculties for the Oxford BA degree

moderato (mus.) in moderate time, abbr. **mod.**

modern abbr. **mod.**, (with names of languages) **Mn.**

modern English the English language from about 1500 onwards

modern face (typ.) a type design with contrasting thick and thin strokes and serifs at right angles; abbr. **MF**

modernism (not cap.).

modernismo a school of 19th-c. Spanish-American poetry

modernize *not* -ise

modicum/ a small quantity, pl. **-s** (not ital.)

modif/y, -iable, -ied, -ier, -ying

Modigliani, Amedeo (1884–1920) Italian painter and sculptor

modiste a milliner, dressmaker (not ital.)

modo praescripto (Lat.) as directed

Mods. Moderations

modus/ operandi (Lat.) the particular way a person performs a task or action, a plan of working; **— vivendi** a way of living or coping, a temporary compromise

Moët et Chandon champagne manufacturers

mœurs (Fr. f. pl.) manners, customs

Mogadishu Somalia

mogul (colloq.) an important or influential person; (cap., hist.) any of the emperors of Delhi in the 16th–19th cc. (often **the Great Mogul**); cf. **Mughal**

MOH Master of Otter Hounds, Medical Officer of Health

Mohammed the Prophet, *use* **Muhammad**

Mohammedan *use* **Muslim**

Mohave Desert *use* **Moj-**

Mohawk (of or relating to) (a member of) a Native American tribe, their language; also a skating step; *not* -hock

Mohegan (of or relating to) (a member of) the eastern branch of the Native American Mahican tribe, *or* their language

Mohican (of or relating to) (a member of) the western branch of the Native American Mahican tribe, *or* their language

Mohocks 18th-c. London ruffians, *not* -hawks

Moholy-Nagy, László (1895–1946) Hungarian-born US painter, sculptor, and photographer

Mohorovičić discontinuity *or* **moho** (geol.); named after **Andrija Mohorovičić** (1857–1936) Yugoslav geophysicist

moidore (hist.) a Portuguese gold coin

moire (noun) a watered fabric, usually silk (not ital.)

moiré (adj.) (of silk etc.) watered, (noun) a patterned appearance like watered silk (not ital.)

mois (Fr. m.) month, abbr. **m** (no point)

Mojave Desert Calif.; *not* Moh-

mol (chem.) abbr. of **mole**

molar (chem.) abbr. **M**

molasses an uncrystallized syrup from raw sugar, (US) = **treacle**, *not* moll-

Mold Clwyd

mold/, -er, -ing, -y (US) = **mould/, -er, -ing, -y**

Moldau the Ger. name for two rivers, the Moldova and the Vltava

Moldavia a province of Romania (in Rom. **Moldova**)

Moldova an independent state, *formerly* the **Moldavian Soviet Socialist Republic**

mole (chem.) an SI unit of amount of substance, abbr. **mol**

Molière pseud. of **Jean Baptiste Poquelin** (1622–73) French playwright

moll (hist. sl.) a gangster's female companion, a prostitute

moll (Ger. mus.) minor

mollah *use* **mu-**

mollasses *use* **mola-**

mollusc *not* -sk (US)

mollymawk any of various small kinds of albatross or similar birds, *not* mallemuck

Molnár, Ferenc (1878–1952) Hungarian playwright

Mol/och a Canaanite idol to whom children were sacrificed (often fig.); sometimes **-ech** in the OT; *not* -eck (cap.); a spiny Australian reptile (not cap.)

Molotov/, Vyacheslav (Mikhailovich) assumed name of **V. M. Skriabin** (1890–1986) Soviet statesman; **— cocktail**

molt *use* **moult** (except in US)

Moltke,/ Count Helmuth Karl Bernard von (1800–91) Prussian field marshal; **— Helmuth Johannes Ludwig von** (1848–1916) his nephew, German general in the First World War

molto (mus.) much, very

Moluccas Indonesian islands, *use* **Maluku**

mol. wt. molecular weight

molybdenum symbol **Mo**

MoMA Museum of Modern Art, New York City (three caps.)

Mombasa Kenya, *not* -assa

momentarily lasting only a moment; *also* (US) at any moment, instantly

moment/um impetus, mass × velocity; pl. **-a** (not ital.)

Mommsen, Theodor (1817–1903) German historian

Mon. Monday

Monaci (Lat.) Munich

Monaco a principality adjoining Mediterranean France, adj. **Monégasque**

Monaco di Baviera (It.) Munich

Mona Lisa a portrait by Leonardo da Vinci, also called **La Gioconda**

mon/ ami (Fr.) f. **— amie** my friend

monandry marriage with one husband at a time

monarch, the (not cap.) *but* **the Sovereign**, **the Crown** for the British monarch

monaural of reproduction of sound by one channel, *also* **monophonic**

Mönchen-Gladbach Germany

mon cher (Fr. m.) my dear; *see also* **ma chère**

Monck,/ Viscount; **— George, Duke of Albemarle** (1608–70) English general; *see also* **Monk**

Monckton,/ Lionel (1861–1924) English composer, **— Walter Turner, Viscount** (1891–1963) British lawyer and politician

Moncreiff, Baron different from **Moncreiffe of that Ilk**

Moncrieff the more usual spelling

Moncton NB, Canada

mondaine (Fr. f.) (a woman who is) of the fashionable world, worldly

Monday abbr. **M., Mon.**

Mondrian, Piet(er Cornelis) (1872–1944) Dutch painter

Monégasque from or of Monaco

Monel metal (propr.)

Monet, Claude Oscar (1840–1926) French painter; cf. **Manet**

monetar/y, -ist

money/, -ed *not* monied; pl. **-s**, *but* **monies** in legal contexts and in Acts of Parliament

money/bags, -lender, -maker (one word)

money/ market, — order abbr. **MO** (no point), **— spider** (two words)

money/-spinner, —'s-worth (hyphens)

moneywort a trailing evergreen plant (one word)

Monghyr Bihar, India

Mongol/ a member of an Asian people; **-ian**; **-oid** (cap.); *see also* **Down syndrome**

mongoos/e an Indian animal, pl. **-es**; *not* mun-

moniker (sl.) a name; *not* -icker

Monk Bretton, Baron; *see also* **Monck**

monkey business (two words), *not* — shine/, -s (US)

monkshood a poisonous garden plant (one word, no apos.)

Mono *see* **Monotype**

mono/ short for monaural; as noun, pl. **-s**

monochrom/e in one colour (one word), **-atic**

monocle a single eyeglass

monocoque/ an aircraft or vehicle with body of single rigid structure, pl. **-s**

monocycle *use* uni-

Monoecus Lat. for **Monaco**

monogam/y marriage with one person at a time, **-ist**

monogyny marriage with one wife at a time

monologue *not* -log (US)

monomark a combination of letters, with or without figures, registered as an identification mark for goods, articles, etc.

mononucleosis (med.) (US) = **glandular fever**

monophonic *see* **monaural**

Monophoto (typ.) (propr.) a filmsetting system (cap.)

Monophysite a person who holds that there is only one nature in the person of Christ (cap.)

monopol/ism, -ist, -istic, -ize, -y

Monotype (typ.) (propr.) a hot-metal composition system; abbr. **Mono**

Monroe Doctrine that European powers should not interfere in American affairs, from **James Monroe** (1758–1831) US President

Mons Belgium, in Fl. **Bergen**

Mons. incorrect abbr. for **Monsieur**

Monseigneur a title of an eminent French person, esp. a prince, cardinal, archbishop, or bishop; abbr. **Mgr**; pl. **Messeigneurs**, abbr. **Mgrs**; *see also* **Monsignor**

Monserrat Leeward Islands, *use* **Mont-**

Monsieur/ (Fr.) Mr, Sir; abbr. (to be used in third person only) **M.**; pl. **Messieurs** abbr. **MM.**; **— Chose** Mr So-and-so; *see also* **Mons.**

Monsignor/ (RC title) abbr. **Mgr**; pl. **-s**, abbr. **Mgrs**; It. **-e**, pl. **-i** (ital.); *see also* **Monseigneur**

mons/ pubis (not cap.), **— Veneris** (one cap.)

Mont. Montana (off. abbr.)

montage (not ital.)

Montagu, Lady Mary Wortley (1689–1762) English writer

Montague Romeo's family in Shakespeare's *Romeo and Juliet*

Montagu of Beaulieu, Baron

Montaigne, Michel Eyquem de (1533–92) French essayist

Montana Switzerland; USA, off. abbr. **Mont.**, postal **MT**

Montaña/ a forest, **La —** a region, Peru

Mont Blanc (caps.)

mont-de-piété (Fr. m.) a government pawnshop, pl. *monts-de-piété* (hyphens)

Monte Albán Mexico

Monte Cristo *not* Christo

Montefiascone an Italian wine, *not* -sco (one word)

Montenegr/o a republic *formerly* in Yugoslavia, **-in**; in Serbo-Croat **Crnagora**

Monterey Calif.

Monte Rosa Switzerland (caps., two words)

Monterrey Mexico

Montesquieu, Charles Louis de Secondat, baron de (1689–1755) French jurist and political philosopher

Montesquiou, Pierre de, comte d'Artagnan (1645–1725) marshal of France

Montesquiou(-Fezensac), comte Robert de (1855–1921) aesthete and dandy

Monteverdi, Claudio Giovanni Antonio (1567–1643) Italian composer

Montevideo capital of Uruguay (one word)

Montgomorie/ family name of the Earl of Eglinton, **—, Alexander** (1556–1610) Scottish poet

Montgomery second title of the Earl of Pembroke, a town and former county in Wales, also towns in Ala. and W. Va., and in Pakistan

Montgomery of Alamein, Bernard Law, Viscount (1887–1976) British field marshal in the Second World War

month/, -s abbr. **m.**; **day of the —** to be thus: 25 Jan., *not* Jan. 25 (US). When necessary, months to be abbreviated thus: Jan., Feb., Mar., Apr., Aug., Sept., Oct., Nov., Dec.; spell out May, June, and July. In Fr. and many other languages the names of months do not take caps., as *janvier*

Montpelier Vt.

Montpellier dép. Hérault, France

Mont-Saint-Michel dép. Manche, France (caps., hyphens); in Cornwall, **Mount Saint Michael**, *use* **St Michael's Mount**

Montserrat Leeward Islands, Spain; *not* Mons-

Montyon prizes of French Academy, *not* Month-

mooch (colloq.) loiter or saunter desultorily, (esp. US) beg or steal

Moodkee *use* **Mudki**

Moog/, Robert (b. 1934) US inventor, creator of — **synthesizer** electronic musical instrument (one cap.)

Mooltan *use* **Mu-**

moolvi/ a Muslim doctor of the law, pl. **-s**; *not* -vee, -vie

moon cap. only in astr. or anthrop. contexts, and in list of planets; abbr. **m.**; sign for new ●; first quarter ☽; full ○; last quarter ☾

moon/beam, -calf (one word), **-fish** *use* **opah**

Moonie (sl.) a member of the Unification Church

moon/light, -lit, -quake, -rise, -scape, -set (one word)

moonshee an Indian writer or teacher, *not* munshi (not ital.)

moon/shine, -shot, -stone, -struck (one word)

Moor/ (of or relating to) a member of a Muslim people of mixed Berber and Arab descent, inhabiting NW Africa; **-ish**

Moore,/ George (1852–1933) Irish novelist; — **Sir John** (1761–1809) British general, killed at Corunna; — **Thomas** (1779–1852) 'the bard of Erin'; *see also* **More**

Moosonee, Archbishop of Ont., Canada

mop/e, -ed, -ing, -ish

mopoke the boobook, a brown spotted owl native to Australia and New Zealand; *not* morepork

Mor. Morocco

moral (adj.) concerned with principles of right and wrong, virtuous; (noun) a moral lesson or principle, in Fr. f. *morale*

morale state of mind, esp. in respect of confidence and courage, in Fr. m. *moral*

moralize *not* -ise

Moral Re-Armament *see* **Oxford Group**

moratorium/ pl. **-s**

Moravia/ part of the Czech Republic; **-n Brethren** (members of) a Protestant sect

Moray/ a former Scottish county, *not* Morayshire; **Earl of —**

morbidezza (It. art) extreme delicacy

morbilli (med.) measles, *not* -bilia

morbus, cholera (not ital.)

morceau/ (Fr. m.) a morsel, a short music piece; pl. **-x**

mordant biting, pungent, corrosive; (a substance) fixing dye

mordent (mus.) a type of ornament, a pralltriller

more (Lat.) in the manner of

More,/ Hannah (1745–1833) English religious writer; — **Sir Thomas** (1478–1535) English writer and statesman, canonized 1935; *see also* **Moore**

Morea medieval name for ancient and modern **Peloponnese**

'more honoured in the breach than the observance' (*Hamlet*, I. iv. 14) 'more honourable to breach it than observe it', *not* 'more often breached than observed'

moreish so pleasant one wants more, *not* -rish

morel an edible fungus, *not* -lle

morello/ a bitter dark cherry, pl. **-s**

more majorum (Lat.) in the style of one's ancestors

morendo (mus.) dying away

morepork *use* **mopoke**

mores (Lat. pl.) social customs (not ital.)

Moresco an Italian dance (cap.); cf. **Morisco**

Moresque Moorish, *not* Mau-

more suo (Lat.) in his, *or* her, own peculiar way

Moretonhampstead Devon (one word)

Moreton-in-Marsh Glos. (hyphens), *not* -in-the-Marsh

morganatic marriage between royalty and commoner, the children being legitimate but not heirs to the higher rank (not cap.)

morgue a mortuary

morgue (Fr. f.) haughtiness

MORI Market & Opinion Research Institute, *not* Mori

Morisco/ Moorish, a Moor; pl. **-s**; cf. **Moresco**

morish *use* **moreish**

Morison,/ James (1816–93) Scottish founder of the Evangelical Union 1843, — **James Augustus Cotter** (1832–88) English historical writer, — **Stanley** (1889–1967) typographer

Morisot, Berthe (1841–95) French Impressionist painter

Morland, George (1763–1804) English painter

Mormon a member of Church of Jesus Christ of Latter-Day Saints; *not* -an

morn. morning

mornay (cook.) a sauce flavoured with cheese

Morny, Charles, duc de (1811–65) French statesman

Moro a Muslim living in the Philippines

Morocc/o abbr. **Mor.**; **-an**; *not* Ma-; in Fr. **Maroc**

morocco leather/ (bind.) (not cap.), **french —** — a low grade with small grain; **levant —** — a high grade with large grain; **persian —** — the best, usually finished on the grain side

morphemics (linguistics) study of word structure (noun pl., usually treated as sing.)

morphology the study of forms (bot., linguistics), abbr. **morph.**

Morpheus Roman god of sleep, *not* -aeus

morphia a drug (pop. for **morphine**)

Morrell, Lady Ottoline (1873–1938) English hostess

Morrells (hist.) an Oxford brewer (no apos.)

Morris,/ Gouverneur (1752–1816) US statesman, and his great-grandson (1876–1953) US writer; **— William** (1834–96) English craftsman, poet, and socialist; **— William Richard, Lord Nuffield** (1877–1963) English industrialist and philanthropist

Morris chair an adjustable-backed easy chair (cap.)

morris dance (two words, not cap.)

Morrison, Toni (b. **Chloe Anthony Wofford**) (b. 1931) US novelist

mortgag/ee the creditor in a mortgage; **-er** the debtor; in law, **-or**

mortice *use* **-ise**

mortician (US) = undertaker, funeral manager

mortis causa (Lat., Sc. law) in contemplation of death

mortise/ hole for receiving tenon in joint, **— lock** one recessed in frame etc. (two words); *not* -ice

Morton/, John (*c.*1420–1500) English statesman, deviser of **—'s Fork**

Morvan, Le a French district

Morven Grampian

Morvern Highland

MOS (comput.) metal oxide semiconductor

Mosaic of Moses

mosaic/ a representation using inlaid pieces of glass, stone, etc.; as verb **-ked, -king**; **-ist** a maker of mosaics

Moscow Russia, in Russian **Moskva**

Moseley a Birmingham suburb; *see also* **Mossl-**

Moseley, Henry Gwyn Jeffreys (1887–1915) English physicist; *see also* **Mosl-**

Moselle a river, France–Germany; a white wine; in Ger. **Mosel**

moshav/ a cooperative association of Israeli smallholders, pl. **-im**

Moslem *use* **Muslim**

Mosley, Sir Oswald Ernald, Bt. (1896–1980) English politician; *see also* **Mose-**

mosquito/ pl. **-es**, *not* mu-

Mossley Ches., Gr. Manchester, Staffs.

mosso (mus.) 'moved' (e.g. più mosso, more moved = quicker)

Most/ High as Deity (caps.), **— Honourable** a title given to marquises and to members of the Privy Council and the Order of the Bath, **— Reverend** a title given to archbishops and to RC bishops

Moszkowski, Moritz (1854–1925) Polish composer

MOT Ministry of Transport, *now* Department of Transport, but still used colloq. in **MOT test** for motor vehicles

mot/ (Fr. m.) a word; **— à —** word for word, abbr. **m. à m.**; **le — juste** the most appropriate expression, pl. *les mots justes*

Mother Carey's chicken the storm petrel

Mother Hubbard a character in a nursery rhyme, a gown such as she wore

Mother Hubberds Tale by Spenser, 1591

Mothering Sunday the fourth Sunday in Lent

mother-in-law pl. **mothers-in-law** (hyphens)

motherland (one word)

mother-of-pearl (hyphens)

Mother's Day (US) second Sunday in May (for commercial purposes), = Mothering Sunday (for traditional purposes)

motif/ (not ital.); pl. **-s** (*not* motives)

motley a mixture, *not* -ly

moto/ (It. mus.) motion, **— continuo** constant repetition, **— contrario** contrary motion, **— obbliquo** oblique motion, **— perpetuo** a piece of music speeding without pause from start to finish, **— precedente** at the preceding pace, **— primo** at the first pace

motorbike (one word)

motor boat (two words, hyphens when attrib., one word in US)

motorcade (one word)

motor/ car, — coach (two words, hyphens when attrib.)

motorcycle (one word)

moto retto (It. mus.) direct or similar motion

motorized *not* -ised

motorway (one word)

Motown music with rhythm-and-blues elements, associated with Detroit

mottl/ed, -ing

motto/ pl. **-es**

motu proprio (Lat.) of his, *or* her, own accord (usually of the Pope)

moue pout (not ital.)

mouezzin *use* **mue-**

moufflet/ (Fr. m.) small child, scamp; f. *-te*

mouflon a wild sheep; *not* mouffl-, muf-

mouillé (Fr.) softened, wet, (phonetics) pal-atalized (of consonant)

moujik *use* **muzhik**

mould/, -er, -ing, -y *not* mol- (US)

moulin (Fr. m.) mill, a nearly vertical shaft in a glacier

Moulmein *see* **Maulmain**

moult a shedding, *not* molt (US)

Mount/, -ain abbr. **Mt.**, pl. **Mts.**

Mountain Ash Mid Glam.

Mount Auburn Mass., a noted cemetery

Mount Edgcumbe, Earl of *not* Edge-

Mountevans, Baron (one word)

Mountgarret, Viscount (one word)

Mountie (colloq.) a member of the Royal Can-adian Mounted Police

Mount Saint Michael Corn., *use* **St Michael's Mount**; *see also* **Mont-Saint-Michel**

Mourne Mountains Ireland

Mourning Becomes Electra a play by E. O'Neill, 1931

mourning cloak (US) a butterfly, *Nymphalis antiopa*; = **Camberwell beauty**

mousetrap (one word)

Mousquetaire a French musketeer, esp. one of the 17th- to 18th-c. royal musketeers

moussaka a Greek dish, *not* -s-

mousseline/ a muslin-like fabric; **-de-laine** a wool and cotton muslin; **-de-soie** a muslin-like silk (hyphens)

mousseu/x (Fr.) f. *-se* foaming or sparkling, as wine

moustache *not* mu- (US)

Mousterian (archaeol.) of or relating to the flint workings of the middle palaeolithic epoch; in Fr. *moustérien*

mousy mouselike, *not* -ey

mouth organ (two words)

mouth/piece -wash (one word)

mouton (Fr. m.) sheep, mutton

movable (something) that can be moved

moveable a form of *movable* used in legal work (for property) and the Prayer Book (for feasts); E. Hemingway's memoir is *A Moveable Feast*, 1964

moyen/ (Fr. m.) medium, — **âge, le** the Middle Ages

moyenne (Fr. f.) average

Mozambi/que SE Africa; in Port. **Moçambique**; **-can**

Mozart/, Wolfgang Amadeus (1756–91) Aus-trian composer, **-ian**

mozzarella an Italian curd cheese

MP Madhya Pradesh, Member of Parliament (pl. **MPs**), Metropolitan Police, Military Police

m.p. melting point, *mille passus*

mp (mus.) mezzo piano (fairly soft)

MPA Master Printers Association

mpg miles per gallon

mph miles per hour

M.Phil. Master of Philosophy

MPO Metropolitan Police Office ('Scotland Yard')

MPS Member of the Pharmaceutical Society

MR Master of the Rolls, Municipal Reform

Mr Mister, pl. **Messrs**

MRA Moral Re-Armament

MRAC Member of the Royal Agricultural Col-lege

M.R.Ae.S. Member of the Royal Aeronautical Society

MRAS Member of the Royal Asiatic Society

MRBM medium-range ballistic missile

MRC Medical Research Council

MRCA multi-role combat aircraft

MRCO Member of the Royal College of Organ-ists

MRCOG Member of the Royal College of Obstet-ricians and Gynaecologists

MRCP Member of the Royal College of Phys-icians, London

MRCS Member of the Royal College of Sur-geons, England

MRCVS Member of the Royal College of Vet-erinary Surgeons, London

MRE Microbiological Research Establishment

MRGS Member of the Royal Geographical Soci-ety

MRH Member of the Royal Household

MRI Member of the Royal Institution

MRIA Member of the Royal Irish Academy

MRICS Member of the Royal Institution of Chartered Surveyors

MRINA Member of the Royal Institution of Naval Architects

mRNA messenger RNA

Mrs Missis, Missus (corruptions of Mistress)

MRSC Member of the Royal Society of Chem-istry

MRSH Member of the Royal Society of Health

MRSL Member of the Royal Society of Lit-erature

MRSM Member of the Royal Society of Medi-cine, Member of the Royal Society of Musicians of Great Britain

MRST Member of the Royal Society of Teachers

MS *manuscriptum, manu scriptus* (manuscript, codex, narrative, etc.); pl. **MSS** (no point); *see also* **typescript**

MS Master of Science (esp. US), Master of Surgery, multiple sclerosis, (Lat.) *memoriae sacrum* (sacred to the memory of), Middle Scots, Mississippi (postal abbr.), (It. mus.) *mano sinistra* (the left hand)

Ms the title of a woman whether or not married (no point)

m/s metres per second, SI unit of speed

ms. (Fr.) *manuscrit* (= **MS**)

MSA Member of the Society of Apothecaries (of London), Mutual Security Agency

M.Sc. Master of Science

MS-DOS (comput.) Microsoft disk operating system (caps. or even small caps.)

MSF Manufacturing, Science, and Finance (union)

MSH Master of Staghounds

MSI (comput.) medium-scale integration

MSIAD Member of the Society of Industrial Artists and Designers

m.s.l. mean sea level (points)

MSM Meritorious Service Medal

MSP Member of the Scottish Parliament

MSS *manuscripta* (manuscripts)

mss. (Fr.) *manuscrits* (= **MSS**)

MT Masoretic Text (of OT), Mechanical (Motor) Transport, megaton, Montana (postal abbr.)

Mt. Mount, Mountain

MTB motor torpedo-boat

M.Tech. Master of Technology

M.Th. Master of Theology

Mts. Mounts, Mountains

mu the twelfth letter of the Gr. alphabet (M, μ), (math.) modulus, (phys.) symbol for magnetic permeability, micron, (as prefix) micro-; **µm** micrometre; **mµ** millimicron, *use* **nm**

muc/us a slimy substance, adj. **-ous**

Muddiford Devon

mud/dy (verb), **-died, -dying**

Mudeford Dorset

Mudford Som.

Mudki E. Punjab, India; *not* Moodkee

muesli a breakfast food (not ital.)

muezzin a Muslim crier, *not* mou-

muffetee a worsted cuff worn on the wrist

muffin/ a light, flat, round spongy cake, eaten toasted and buttered; (US) a round cake made from batter or dough; a British — = US **English** — (savoury), a US — = British **American** — (sweet)

muflon *use* **mou-**

mufti/ (Arab.) a magistrate, not -tee (not ital.); **in** — in civilian dress (not ital.)

Mughal a Mongolian; (attrib.) denoting the Muslim dynasty in India in the 16th–19th cc.; *not* Mog/hal, -hul, -ul; cf. **Mogul**

Muhammad the preferred form, but a compromise between the literary 'Mohammed' and the learned 'Muḥammad' (with subscript dot); adj. ending '-an' is both incorrect and often regarded as offensive; replace by the more correct **Muslim** or **Islamic**. Older forms such a 'Mahometan' and 'Mohammedan' are acceptable only in reproducing older texts

Mühlhausen Thuringia, Germany; cf. **Mulhouse**

mujahid/ a guerrilla fighter in Islamic countries, esp. one supporting Muslim fundamentalism; pl. **-in**; *not* -edin, -deen; in Arab. and Pers. *mujāhidīn*

mujik a Russian peasant, *use* **muzh-**

Mukden China

mulatto/ the offspring of one white and one black parent, pl. **-s**

mulch (treat soil with) a mixture of wet straw, leaves, etc.; *not* -sh

Mulhouse Alsace, France; in Ger. **Mülhausen**

mull (bind.) coarse muslin glued to the backs of books

mullah (Muslim) a learned man (not cap.); *not* moll-, mool-, -a

mullein a tall yellow-flowered plant, *not* -en

Müller, Friedrich Max (1823–1900) German-born English philologist; *also* later **Max-Müller** (hyphen)

mulligatawny a soup; *not* muli-, mulla-

mullion a vertical bar dividing the lights in a window, *not* munn-

mulsh *use* **-ch**

Multan Pakistan, *not* Moo-

multangular having many angles, *not* multi-

Multatuli pseud. of **Edward Dowes Dekker** (1820–87) Dutch writer

multiaccess (comput.) the simultaneous connection to a computer of a number of terminals (one word)

multiaxial of or involving several axes (one word)

multimillionaire (one word)

multinational (one word)

multipartite divided into many parts (one word)

multiple mark (typ.) the sign of multiplication ($\times$); if a medial full point is to be used instead, ensure that sufficient instruction is given

multiplepoinding (Sc. law) a process which safeguards a person from whom the same funds are claimed by more than one creditor (one word)

multiplication point to be set medially, as m·s (metre-second)

multiprocess/er, -ing (one word)
multiprogramm/er, -ing (one word)
multi-purpose (hyphen, one word in US)
multiracial (one word)
multi/-role, -stage, -storey, -user (hyphens, one word in US)
multi/valent, -valve, -vocal (one word)
multi-way (hyphen, one word in US)
multum in parvo (Lat.) much in small compass
Mumbai Maratha for **Bombay**
mumbo-jumbo/ a meaningless ritual or language; pl. **-s** (hyphen)
Munch, Edvard (1863–1944) Norwegian artist
Munchausen, Baron (1720–97) Hanoverian nobleman whose extravagant adventures are the theme of *Adventures of Baron Munchausen*, collected by Rudolph Eric Raspe *c*.1785; in Ger. **Münchhausen**
München (Ger.) Munich
Mundt, Theodor (1808–61) German journalist and writer
municipalize etc., *not* -ise
muniment (usually in pl.) a document kept as evidence of rights or privileges etc.
Munnepoor *use* **Manipur**
munnion *use* **mull-**
Munro,/ General character in J. F. Cooper's *Last of the Mohicans* based on Lieutenant Colonel Monro; **— H(ector) H(ugh)** *see* **Saki**
munshi (Ind.) *use* **moonshee**
Munster Ireland
Münster Germany, Switzerland
muntjac a S. Asian deer; *not* -jack, -jak
Muntz (metal) an alloy of copper and zinc for sheathing ships etc., *not* Muntz's
Murdoch,/ (Jean) Iris (1919–1999) British writer, **— John** (1747–1824) friend of Burns
Murdock, William (1754–1839) inventor of coal-gas lighting, *not* -och
Murfreesboro, Battle of US Civil War, 1863
murky dark, *not* mi-
Murphy's Law any of various maxims about the perverseness of things (caps.)
Murray,/ (George) Gilbert (Aimé) (1866–1957) Australian-born British classical scholar, **— Sir James (Augustus Henry)** (1837–1915) Scottish lexicographer and chief editor of the *OED*; *see also* **Murry**
Mürren Oberland, Switzerland
murrey the colour of a mulberry, a deep red or purple
murrhine fluorspar ware; *not* murrine, myrrh-
Murrumbidgee a river in New South Wales, Australia
Murry,/ John Middleton (1889–1957) English writer, *not* -ay; **— Kathleen** wife of above, *see* **Mansfield**; *see also* **Murray**

Murshidabad W. Bengal, India
mus. museum; music, -al
musaeo/graphy, -logy *use* **museo-**
Musalman *see* **Mussul-**
Mus.B., Mus. Bac. *Musicae Baccalaureus* (Bachelor of Music)
musc/a (Lat.) a fly, pl. *-ae*
Muscadet a dry white wine from Brittany, made from muscadine grapes; cf. **muscatel**
Muscat the capital of Oman, S. Arabia
muscatel a raisin from a muscadine grape, the general name for a sweet wine made from the muscadine grape; *not* -del; *also* **muscat**; cf. **Muscadet**
Muschelkalk (geol.) shell limestone (cap.)
Musc/i the true mosses, sing. *-us*
muscovado/ unrefined sugar, pl. **-s**
Muscovite a native or citizen of Moscow, of or relating to Moscow; (arch.) a Russian, of or relating to Russia
muscovite a silver-grey form of mica
Muscovy (arch.) Russia
Mus.D., Mus. Doc. *Musicae Doctor* (Doctor of Music)
museo/graphy museum cataloguing, **-logy** the science of arranging museums; *not* musae-
Muses, the nine Calliope, Clio, Erato, Euterpe, Melpomene, Polyhymnia, Terpsichore, Thalia, Urania
musette a kind of small bagpipe; a small oboe-like instrument; a dance; (US) a small knapsack
museum abbr. **mus.**
Music/, Bachelor of abbr. **Mus.B., B.Mus.; —, Doctor of** abbr. **Mus.D., D.Mus.; —, Master of** abbr. **M.Mus., (Camb.) Mus.M.**
music/, -al abbr. **mus.**
music/ drama, — hall, — paper, — stand, — stool (two words)
Musigny a red burgundy
musique concrète (Fr. f.) music constructed from recorded sounds
musjid *use* **mas-**
muskellunge *use* **maskinonge**
Muslim (a member) of the faith of Islam; *not* Moslem, Muhammadan
muslin-de-lain *use* **mousseline-de-laine**
Mus.M. Master of Music (Camb.)
musquito *use* **mos-**
muss (US) (throw into) a state of disorder
Mussadeq, Muhammad (1881–1967) Iranian Prime Minister 1951–3
Mussalman *see* **Mussul-**
Musselburgh Lothian, *not* -borough
Mussolini, Benito (Amilcaro Andrea) (1883–1945) Italian Fascist politician, Prime

Minister 1922–43; known as **Il Duce** ('the leader')

Mussorgsky (common Eng. form, more exact form **Musorgski**) **Modest** (**Petrovich**) (1839–81) Russian composer

Mussul/man (arch.) a Muslim, from Pers. *musulmān*; *not* the many variants; pl. **-mans**, *not* -men

mustache *use* **mous-** (except in US)

Mustafa Algeria

Mustafabad Uttar Pradesh, India

Musulman *see* **Mussul-**

mutable likely to change

mutand/um (Lat.) anything to be altered, pl. *-a*

mutatis mutandis (Lat.) with the necessary changes, abbr. **m.m.**

mutato nomine (Lat.) with the name changed

mutual fund (US) = **unit trust**

mutuel (US) a totalizer, a pari-mutuel

muu-muu a (Hawaiian) woman's loose-fitting dress

Muybridge, Eadweard (1830–1904) English photographer

Muzaffarabad Kashmir

Muzaffarpur Bihar, India

Muzak (propr.) a system of piped music (cap.); any (recorded) light background music (not cap.)

muzhik a Russian peasant; *not* moujik, mujik

MV megavolt, -s; motor vessel, muzzle velocity

mV (elec.) millivolt, -s (no point)

m.v. (It. mus.) *mezza voce*, muzzle velocity

MVD USSR 'Ministry of Internal Affairs' 1953–60; *see also* **KGB**

MVO Member (of fourth or fifth class) of the Royal Victorian Order

M.V.Sc. Master of Veterinary Science

MW medium wave; megawatt, -s; Middle Welsh, Most Worshipful, Most Worthy

mW milliwatt, -s (no point)

Mx maxwell, -s; Middlesex (no point)

MY motor yacht

myalism a W. Indian witchcraft, adj. **myal**

myall an Australian acacia, an Australian Aboriginal living in the traditional way

myceli/um (bot.) the thallus of a fungus, pl. **-a**

Mycenaean of or relating to the late Bronze Age civilization in Greece; its inhabitants (c.1500–1100 BC)

Myddelton Square Clerkenwell, London; *see also* **Mi-**

Myddleton, Sir Hugh (1560–1631) London merchant

Myers,/ Frederic William Henry (1843–1901) English poet, essayist, spiritualist; — **Leopold Hamilton** (1881–1944) English novelist; *see also* **Miers**; **Myres**

mynah/ a starling of SE Asia, pl. **-s**; *not* mina, myna

mynheer (hist.) Eng. term for a Dutchman, from *mijnheer* (Du.) sir, Mr

myop/ia shortness of sight, adj. **-ic**

myosis *use* **mi-**

myosotis the forget-me-not

Myres, Sir John Linton (1869–1954) English archaeologist; *see also* **Miers**; **Myers**

myriad (of) an indefinitely great number, innumerable, *or* 10,000; 'myriad of' is correct

Myriapoda the centipedes and millepedes, *not* Myrio-

myrobalan a plum, *not* -bolan

myrrhine *use* **murrh-**

myrtle *not* -tel

Mysore Deccan, India (common form); *properly* **Maisur**

myst. mysteries

myth. mytholog/y, -ical

mythopoei/a the construction of myths; **-c** myth-making; *not* -pae-, -pei-, -poeit-

myth/us (lit.) a myth, pl. **-i**

Mytilen/e Lesbos, Greece; **-aean**; Mitylene in AV NT; **Mitilíni** the modern city

myxoedema a metabolic disease, *not* myxed- (US)

myxomatosis a contagious and fatal viral disease in rabbits

Nn

N (typ.) en; (chess) knight; newton(s); nitrogen; the thirteenth in a series

₦ naira (currency of Nigeria)

N. Norse; north, -ern; (Lat.) *nom/en, -ina* (name, -s); *noster* (our)

(N.) (naval) navigat/ing, -ion

n (math.) an indefinite integer, whence (gen.) **to the nth** (**degree**); (as prefix) nano-

n. name, nephew, neuter, new, nominative, noon, note, noun

n (chem.) symbol for amount of substance

n. (Lat.) *natus* (born), *nocte* (at night)

ñ (Sp.) called 'n with tilde', or 'Spanish *n*'; pron. as *n* in 'cognac' or 'onion'; follows *n* without tilde in Spanish alphabetical sequence

NA National Academ/y, -ician; Nautical Almanac, Naval Auxiliary; North America, -n

Na *natrium* (sodium) (no point)

n/a (banking) no account, not applicable, not available

NAACP (US) National Association for the Advancement of Colored People

NAAFI Navy, Army, and Air Force Institutes

naamloze vennootschap (Du.) public limited company, abbr. **NV**

Naas Co. Kildare

nabob (hist.) an official or governor under the Mogul empire, a person of conspicuous wealth or high rank; cf. **nawab**

Nabuchodonosor *see* **Nebuchadnezzar**

nach *use* **nautch**

nach/ Christi Geburt, — Christo (Ger.) AD, abbr. **n. Chr.**

Nachdruck (Ger. typ. m.) reprint, pirated edition; **nachdrucken** to reprint, or pirate

nacho/ (usually in pl. **-s**) a tortilla chip, usually topped with melted cheese, guacamole, etc.

nach und nach (Ger.) little by little

nacre/ mother-of-pearl (not ital.), **-ous** *not* -rous

nacré (Fr.) like mother-of-pearl (ital.)

Na-Dene (*also* **Na-Déné**) a linguistic group of more than twenty Amerind languages spoken in N. America

nadir the lowest point, as opposed to **zenith**

naev/us a form of birthmark, pl. **-i**; *not* nevus (US)

Naga Hills Assam, India; Burma

Nagaland an Indian state

Nagar W. Bengal, Mysore, E. Punjab, Kashmir, India

-nagar (in Indian place names) a town, as Ahmadnagar; *not* -naggore, -nagore, -nugger, -ur

Nagpur Maharashtra, India; *not* -pore

Nah. Nahum

Nahuatl (*also* **Nahua**) (of or concerning) (a member of) a group of peoples native to S. Mexico and Cent. America, including the Aztecs, and their Uto-Aztecan language

Nahum (OT) abbr. **Nah.**

naiad/ (Gr. myth.) a water nymph, an aquatic plant; *not* naid; pl. **-s, -es**

naïf *use* naive; in Fr. **naï/f** f. **-ve**

Naini Tal Uttar Pradesh, India

nainsook an Indian muslin, *not* -zook

Nairne, Baroness b. **Caroline Oliphant** (1776–1845) Scottish poet

Nairnshire a former county of Scotland

naive/ artless; *not* naï-, naïf; **-ty**

naïveté (Fr. f.) artlessness

Najd a province of Saudi Arabia

NALGO National and Local Government Officers' Association

Nama a member of the Khoikhoi people (pl. same) *or* their language; *not* Hottentot

namable *use* name-

Namaqualand S. Africa (one word)

namby-pamby weakly sentimental (hyphen)

name abbr. **n.**

nameable *not* namable (US)

namely *preferred to* viz.

N. Amer. North America(n)

namesake (one word)

names of periodicals *see* **periodicals**

names of ships to be italic: the *Cutty Sark*, RMS *Titanic*, USS *New Jersey*, the *Charles W. Morgan*

Namibia *formerly* South West Africa

namma *use* gn-

N&Q Notes and Queries

nankeen a fabric, *not* -kin

nano- prefix meaning one-thousand-millionth (10⁻⁹), abbr. **n**

nanometre one-thousandth of a micrometre, abbr. **nm**

nanosecond one-thousandth of a microsecond, abbr. **ns**

Nansen/, Fridtjof (1861–1930) Norwegian diplomat and Arctic traveller, **— passport** a document of identification given to stateless persons after the First World War

Nantasket Beach Mass.

Nantucket Island Mass.

Nap. Napoleon

nap/, -ped, -ping

Napa Calif.

napa *use* -ppa

naphtha an inflammable oil

naphthal/ene a crystalline substance used in the manufacture of dyes etc.; **-ic**

Napierian logarithms from **John Napier** (1550–1617) Scottish mathematician, *not* -perian

Naples Italy; in It. **Napoli**, Ger. **Neapel**; adj. **Neapolitan**

napoleon/ a gold 20-franc piece of Napoleon I, **double —** a 40-franc piece; in Fr. m. *napoléon*

Napoleonic of, relating to, *or* characteristic of, Napoleon I (1769–1821) or his time

napolitaine, à la (Fr. cook.) in the Neapolitan style (not cap. *n*)

nappa a soft leather made by a special process from the skin of sheep or goats, *not* napa

Narbada an Indian river, *not* Nerbudda

narciss/us a flower, pl. **-i**; **-ism** excessive admiration of oneself

narcos/is a stupor induced by narcotics, pl. **-es**

narghile a hookah, *not* the many variants; in Pers. *nārgīleh*

Narragansett Bay RI; *not* -et

narrow measure (typ.) type composed in narrow widths, as in columns

narrow-minded (hyphen)

narwhal/ the sea unicorn; *not* -e, -wal; **— tusk** *not* horn

NAS National Association of Schoolmasters, Noise Abatement Society

NASA, Nasa (US) National Aeronautics and Space Administration

nasalize *not* -ise

NASD National Amalgamated Stevedores and Dockers

Nash,/ Ogden (1902–71) US poet; **— Richard, 'Beau'** (1674–1762) Bath Master of Ceremonies

Nash *or* **Nashe, Thomas** (1567–1601) English pamphleteer and playwright

Nasirabad Pakistan

Nasmith, James (1740–1808) English theologian and antiquary

Nasmyth/, Alexander (1758–1840) Scottish painter, **—, James** (1808–90) Scottish engineer, **— hammer** *not* -th's

nasturtium/ (bot.) *not* -ian, -ion; pl. **-s**

NAS/UWT National Association of Schoolmasters and Union of Women Teachers

Nat. Natal; Nathanael, -iel; National, -ist

nat. natural, -ist

Natal *now* **KwaZulu/Natal**

natch (colloq.) naturally; cf. **nautch**

NATFHE National Association of Teachers in Further and Higher Education

nat. hist. natural history

national abbr. **nat.**, (US) **nat'l**

National/ — Academy, — Academician abbr. **NA**; **— Bureau of Standards** (USA) abbr. **NBS**; **— Engineering Laboratory** East Kilbride, abbr. **NEL**

National Enquirer US publication, *not* — *Inquirer*

National Graphical Association abbr. **NGA**

nationalist not cap.; *but* cap. with reference to a particular party or institution, abbr. **Nat.**

nationalize *not* -ise

National/ Physical Laboratory Teddington, abbr. **NPL**; **— Playing Fields Association** abbr. **NPFA**; **— Research Council** abbr. **NRC**; **— Research Development Corporation** abbr. **NRDC**; **— Rifle Association** abbr. **NRA**; **— Rivers Authority** abbr. **NRA**

National Westminster Bank plc abbr. **NatWest** (one word)

nationwide (one word)

NATO, Nato North Atlantic Treaty Organization

nat./ ord. natural order, **— phil.** natural philosophy

natrium sodium, symbol **Na**

NATSOPA National Society of Operative Printers, Graphical and Media Personnel (*originally* Printers and Assistants)

nattier blue a soft blue, from **Jean-Marc Nattier** (1685–1766) French painter

natt/y trim; **-ier, -ily, -iness**

natura (Lat.) nature

natural/ abbr. **nat.**; **-ism -ist**; cf. **naturism**

natural (mus.) sign ♮

naturalize *not* -ise

natura non facit salt/um, -us (Lat.) Nature makes no leap, -s

nature the processes of the material world (cap. only when personified)

natur/ism the worship of nature, (advocacy of) (collective) nudism; **-ist**; cf. **naturalism**

natus (Lat.) born, abbr. **n.**

naught nothing, *but* HMS *Dreadnought*; (US) = **nought**

Nauheim, Bad Hesse, Germany

Nauru/ W. Pacific, **-an**

nause/a sickness, esp. with an inclination to vomit; **-ate** affect with nausea; **-ous** causing nausea, offensive in taste or smell

Nausicaa a character in Homer's *Odyssey* (no accent)

nautch/ an Indian dancing entertainment, **— girl**; *not* nach, natch

nautical abbr. **naut.**

Nautical Almanac abbr. **NA**

nautical mile *see* **mile**

nautil/us a shell; pl. **-uses, -i**

nav. naval, navigation

Nava/jo (of or relating to) (a member of) a Native American people, or their language; pl. **-jos**; *also* **-ho, -hos**

navarin a stew of mutton or lamb

Navarrese of Navarre

navigat/ing, -ion abbr. **(N.), nav.**

navv/y (Brit.) (work as) a labourer employed in building or excavating roads, canals, etc.; **-ies, -ied**

Navy, Army, and Air Force in toasts etc. the Navy precedes, being the senior service

navy blue (not cap.)

Navy List (two words)

navy yard (US) a government shipyard with civilian labour (not cap.)

nawab a distinguished Muslim in Pakistan, (hist.) a governor or nobleman in India; cf. **nabob**

Nazarene/ a Christian, a native of Nazareth; *not* -arite, -irite; **-s** a group of early 19th-c. German religious painters

Nazarite (hist.) a Hebrew who had taken vows of abstinence; *not* -arene, -irite

Nazi/ a member of the German National Socialist Party; **-fy, -ism** not -sm

NB New Brunswick, North Britain, (Lat.) *nota bene* (mark well)

Nb niobium (no point)

n.b. (cricket) no ball

NBA (US) National Basketball Association, (hist.) Net Book Agreement

NBC National Book Council, *now* **NBL**; (US) National Broadcasting Company; National Bus Company

NBG no bloody good

NBL National Book League

NBS National Broadcasting Service (of New Zealand)

NC North Carolina (off. and postal abbr.)

NCB (hist.) National Coal Board, since 1987 **British Coal**

NCCL National Council for Civil Liberties

n. Chr. (Ger.) *nach Christo* or *nach Christi Geburt* (AD)

NCL National Carriers, Ltd.

NCO non-commissioned officer

NCR no carbon (paper) required

NCU National Communications Union, National Cyclists' Union

NCW National Council of Women

ND North Dakota (postal abbr.)

N.D. (Fr.) *Notre Dame*

Nd neodymium (no point)

n.d. (bibliog.) no date given

N. Dak. North Dakota (off. abbr.)

N'Djamena Chad

NDL Norddeutscher Lloyd

NE Nebraska (postal abbr.), new edition, New England; north-east, -ern

Ne neon (no point)

né (Fr.) f. **née** born (not ital.)

n/e new edition, (banking) no effects

Neal,/ Daniel (1678–1743) English Puritan writer, — **John** (1793–1876) US writer; *see also* **Neele; Neill**

Neale, John Mason (1818–66) English hymnologist; *see also* **Neele; Neill**

Neanderthal/ common name for a subspecies of palaeolithic hominid; individuals are **-er** *not* — men; *not* -tal-

Neapel (Ger.) **Naples**

Neapolitan/ (an inhabitant) of Naples, — **ice** ice cream layered in different colours, — **violet** sweet-scented double viola

neap tide a tide when there is least difference between high and low water (two words)

near abbr. **nr.; near by** (adv., two words), **nearby** (adj., one word)

Nearctic (zool.) of northern N. America, *not* Neoarctic

near letter quality (comput.) abbr. **NLQ**

nearside (Brit.) the left side of a vehicle, animal, etc.; cf. **offside**

nearsighted (US) = **short-sighted**

neat's-foot oil (one hyphen)

NEB National Enterprise Board, New English Bible

Nebraska off. abbr. **Nebr.**, postal **NE**

Nebuchadnezzar King of Babylon, destroyed Jerusalem in 586 BC; a wine bottle of about twenty times the standard size (not cap.); **Nabuchodonosor** in the AV Apocrypha and the Vulgate; **Nebuchadrezzar** is the spelling in Jer. 43: 10 etc.

nebula/ pl. **-ae**

nebuly (her.) wavy in form, cloud-like

necess/ary, -arily

necessitarian (philos.) (of or concerning) a person who holds that all action is predetermined and free will is impossible (cf. **libertarian**); *not* necessarian

necess/itate, -ity

Neckar river in Württemberg, Germany

Necker, Jacques (1732–1804) French statesman

nec pluribus impar (Lat.) a match for many (motto of Louis XIV)

NED *New English Dictionary*, original name for the **OED** (*Oxford English Dictionary*)

NEDO National Economic Development Office

née (Fr. f.) born

needle/cord, -craft, -fish, -point (one word)

needle time an agreed maximum allowance of time for broadcasting commercially recorded music (two words)

needle/woman, -women, -work (one word)

Neele, Henry (1798–1828) English poet; *see also* **Neal; Neale; Neill**

neelghau *use* **nilgai**

ne'er/ never, **-do-well** (hyphens)

ne exeat regno (law) a writ to restrain a person from leaving the kingdom

nefasti (*dies*) (Lat.) black (ill-omened) days

Nefertiti (*fl.* 14th c. BC) Egyptian queen; *also* **Nofretete**

neg. negative, -ly

Negev, the a desert region of S. Israel, *not* -eb; in Fr. **Néguev**

neglig/ee a woman's dressing gown of diaphanous fabric; *not* neglige; in Fr. m. **négligé**

negligible *not* -eable

negotiate *not* -ciate

nègre (Fr. m.) Negro, black; (lit.) ghost writer

Negrillo/ (of or relating to) a member of a dwarf Negroid people in Cent. and S. Africa, pl. **-s** (cap.)

Negri Sembilan *see* **Malaya, Federation of**

Negrito/ (of or relating to) a member of a dwarf Negroid people in the Malayo-Polynesian region, pl. **-s** (cap.)

Negritude the quality of being black, African-ness (cap.)

négritude (Fr. f.) a cultural movement launched by black students in Paris, 1932, to reassert traditional African values (ital.)

Negro/ pl. **-es**, a member of a dark-skinned race originally native to Africa (cap.); outside the field of ethnology *use* **black** (q.v.); *see also* **African-American**

Negroid *not* -rooid

Negus (hist.) the title of the Emperor of Abyssinia (Ethiopia), in Amharic **n'gus**

negus (hist.) a hot drink of port or sherry, sugar, lemon, and spice, invented by **Col. Francis Negus** (d. 1732)

Neh. Nehemiah (OT)

Nehru/, Jawaharlal, 'Pandit' (1889–1964) Indian nationalist leader, Prime Minister 1947–64; **-vian**

n.e.i. *non est invent/us, -a, um* (he, she, *or* it, has not been found)

neice *use* **niece**

neige (Fr. f.) snow, (Fr. cook. f.) whisked white of egg

neighbour/, -hood, -ly *not* -or (US)

Neilgherry Hills *use* **The Nilgiris**

Neill,/ A(lexander) S(utherland) (1883–1973) British educationist; — **Patrick** (d. 1705) first printer in Belfast, of Scottish birth; — **Patrick**

(1776–1851) Scottish naturalist, *see also* **Neal; Neale; Neele**

neither (of two) *is*; neither he nor she *is*; but neither he nor they *are*, neither these nor those *are*

Nejd *use* **Na-**

nekton aquatic animals able to swim independently; cf. **plankton**

NEL National Engineering Laboratory

nematode (noun or adj.) (of) a roundworm or threadworm, *not* -oid

nem./ con. *nemine contradicente*, — *diss.* *nemine dissentiente*

Nemean/ (adj.) of the vale of Nemea in ancient Argolis, — **games** one of the four principal Panhellenic festivals, — **lion** (Gr. myth.) slain by Hercules

nemes/is (cap. when personified) pl. **-es**

nemine/ contradicente (Lat.) unanimously, abbr. *nem. con.*; — *dissentiente* no one dissenting, abbr. *nem. diss.*

nemo/ (Lat.) nobody, — *me impune lacessit* no one attacks me with impunity (motto of Scotland, and of the Order of the Thistle)

nemophila (bot.) a garden flower, *not* -phyla

N. Eng. New England

ne nimium (Lat.) shun excess

nenuphar the great white water lily; cf. **Nuphar**

neo- freely added (usually with hyphen) to names of philosophies and institutions and to their adjectival forms, to designate their revivals or new forms (retain caps. of words that have them), e.g. neo-Christianity, *but* neo-classical, Neoplatonism

Neoarctic *use* **Near-**

neocolonial/, -ism, -ist (one word)

Neocomian (geol.) (cap.)

neodymium symbol **Nd**

Neogaea (zool.) the land mass including S. and Cent. America; cf. **Arctogaea; Notogaea**

neolithic (archaeol.) of or relating to the later Stone Age (not cap.)

neolog/ize use new terms, *not* -ise; **-ism** abbr. **neol.**; **-ist**

neon symbol **Ne**

Neoplaton/ism a philosophical and religious system developed in the 3rd c., combining Platonic thought with oriental mysticism; **-ic** (one word, one cap.)

Nep. Neptune

Nepal/ a kingdom between Tibet and India, *not* -aul; adj. **-i** *not* -ese; the Nepali language is also called **Gurkhali**

neper unit for comparing power levels

nephew abbr. **n.**

ne plus ultra (Lat.) the furthest attainable point, perfection; *not* non

neptunium symbol **Np**

ne quid nimis (Lat.) be wisely moderate, nothing too much

Nerbudda *use* **Narbada**

NERC Natural Environment Research Council

nerd (esp. US sl.) a foolish, feeble, or uninteresting person; *not* nu-

nereid/ (Gr. myth.) a sea nymph; pl. **-s**, (with cap.) **-es**

Neri, Saint Philip (1515–95) Italian founder of the Congregation of the Oratory

nero antico (It.) a type of black marble

Neruda,/ Jan (1834–91) Czech writer; — **Pablo** pseud. of **Neftali Ricardo Reyes** (1904–73) Chilean poet

nerve/ cell, — centre, — gas (two words)

nerve-racking *not* wr-

Nesbit (**Bland**), **E**(**dith**) (1858–1924) English poet, novelist, and writer of children's stories

Nesbitt, Cathleen (1890–1982) English actress

nescien/t (followed by *of*) lacking knowledge, ignorant; **-ce**

Nessler's reagent (chem.) after **Julius Nessler** (1827–1905) German chemist

n'est-ce-pas? (Fr.) is it not so? aren't you?

Nestlé Rowntree part of **Société des Produits Nestlé SA** (accent)

net not subject to deduction; *not* nett

net/, -ted, -ting

net curtain (two words)

Netherlands, the formerly Holland was only part of, not equal to, the Netherlands (*or* Low Countries), which also included Belgium and Luxembourg. Now, however, these three countries are known collectively as Benelux, and the Netherlands is the official name of the province of Holland only. The definite article in 'the Netherlands' is lower case in running text, unlike that of its seat of government, The Hague; abbr. **Neth.**; (Du.) **Nederland**, (Fr.) **les Pays-Bas**

netsuke a carved Japanese button-like ornament, pl. same

nett *use* **net**

nettlerash (one word)

network (one word)

Neuchâtel Switzerland, or a white or red wine from there

Neue Folge (Ger.) new series, abbr. **NF** (small caps.)

Neufchâtel déps. Aisne and Seine-Maritime, France; a kind of cheese

Neuilly dép. Seine, France

neuma (mus.) passages sung to a single vowel, e.g. the final vowel of *alleluia*

neume (mus.) a written note in medieval music, often used specifically of staffless notation; the symbol indicating this (a ligature); *not* neum

neuralgia an intense intermittent pain in a nerve (a symptom, not a disease)

neurasthenia a general term for nervous prostration, chronic fatigue, etc. (not in medical use)

neurine a poisonous ptomaine, *not* -in

neuritis an inflammation of nerve fibres

neuron a nerve cell and its appendages, *not* -one

Neuropter/a an order of insects, sing. **-on**

neuros/is a functional derangement through nervous disorder, pl. **-es**

neurotic/ (adj. and noun), **-ally, -ism**

neurotransmitter (one word)

neuter abbr. **n., neut.**

neutralize *not* -ise

neutrino/ (phys.) an uncharged particle with very small mass, pl. **-s**

neutron/ (phys.) an uncharged particle, pl. **-s**

Nevada off. abbr. **Nev.**, postal **NV**

névé (Swiss Fr. m.) an expanse of granular snow not yet compressed into ice at the head of a glacier (not ital.)

never/-ending, -failing (hyphens)

nevermore (one word)

never-never (colloq.) hire purchase (hyphen)

nevertheless (one word)

Nevill the family name of the Marquess of Abergavenny

Neville the family name of Baron Braybrooke

new abbr. **n.**

Newbery/, John (1713–67) English printer, — **Medal** (USA)

Newbiggin Cumbria, Durham, Northumb., N. Yorks.

Newbigging Strathclyde, Tayside

new-blown (hyphen)

newborn (one word)

Newborough, Baron

New Brunswick Canada, New Jersey; abbr. **NB**

Newburgh/ Fife, Grampian, Lancs.; **Countess of —**

New Castle Ind., Pa.

Newcastle: the signature of the Bishop of Newcastle (colon)

Newcastle/ upon Tyne Tyne & Wear; — **under Lyme** Staffs. (no hyphens)

newcomer (one word)

New Criticism an approach to the analysis of literary texts concentrating on the organization of the text itself (caps.)

New Deal/, the a US programme of social and economic reform in the 1930s (caps.), **-ish**

Newdigate, Sir Roger (1719–1806) founder of the Oxford prize for English verse

new edition abbr. **NE, n/e**

New England/ (US) NE states of Maine, New Hampshire, Vermont, Massachusetts, Rhode Island, and Connecticut; **-er**

New English Bible, The first part (the NT) pub. 1961, completed 1970; abbr. **NEB**

New English Dictionary original name for the **Oxford English Dictionary**

newfangled (one word)

New Forest Hants. (two words)

Newfoundland/ (one word) Canada; abbr. **NF, Nfld.; -er** an inhabitant

New Greek the Greek language in use since the end of the Middle Ages, called **Romaic** in the 19th c.; *prefer* **Modern Greek**

New Guinea *see* **Papua**

New Hall Cambridge

Newham a borough of Gr. London (one word)

New Hampshire off. and postal abbr. **NH**

New Haven Conn. (two words)

Newhaven Lothian, E. Sussex (one word)

New Hebrew the Hebrew language used in modern Israel, *prefer* **Modern Hebrew**

New Hebrides *use* **Vanuatu**

Ne Win (b. 1911) Burmese general and politician, Prime Minister 1958–60, head of state 1962–74, President 1974–81.

New Jersey off. and postal abbr. **NJ**

New Journalism a style of journalism characterized by the use of subjective and fictional elements so as to elicit an emotional response from the reader (caps.)

new-laid egg (one hyphen)

New Latin the Latin in use since the close of the Middle Ages, esp. in the sciences; *also called* **Neo-Latin**

New Mexico off. abbr. **N. Mex.**, postal **NM**

New Mills Ches., Powys

Newmilns Strathclyde

Newnes, Sir George (1851–1910) English publisher

Newnham College Cambridge

New Orleans La., abbr. **NO**

new paragraph (typ.) abbr. **n.p.**

New Quay Dyfed, Essex (two words)

Newquay Corn. (one word)

New Red Sandstone (geol.) (caps.)

newsagent (Brit.) (one word) *but* **news agency** (two words)

news/boy, -break, -brief (one word)

news bulletin (two words)

newscaster (one word)

newsdealer (US) = **newsagent**

new series abbr. **NS** (small caps. in refs.)

newsflash (one word)

news-gather/er, -ing (hyphen, one word in US)

news/girl, -letter, -man, -monger (one word)

New South Wales Australia (three words, caps., no hyphens), abbr. **NSW**

newspaper/boy, -girl, -man (one word)

Newspaper Publishers' Association abbr. **NPA**

newspapers, titles of *see* **periodicals**

Newspeak ambiguous euphemistic language (one cap.)

newsprint a low-quality paper on which newspapers are printed

news/reader, -reel, -room (one word)

news/-sheet, -stand (hyphens, one word in US)

news theatre (two words)

New Style according to the Gregorian calendar, adopted in 1752; abbr. **NS** (full caps., no point); *see also* **Old Style**

new-style numerals (typ.) ranging, lining numerals, with uniform ascenders and no descenders

news/vendor *not* **-er, -woman, worthy** (one word)

New Testament abbr. **NT, New Test.**

newton an SI unit of force, abbr. **N**

Newton Abbot Devon

Newton-le-Willows Merseyside, N. Yorks. (hyphens)

Newtonmore Highland (one word)

Newton Poppleford Devon

Newton Stewart Dumfries & Galloway (two words); *see also* **Newtownstewart**

Newtown Powys

Newtownabbey Co. Antrim (one word)

Newtownards Co. Down (one word)

Newtownbutler Co. Fermanagh (one word)

Newtowncunningham Co. Donegal (one word)

Newtownforbes Co. Longford (one word)

Newtownmountkennedy Co. Wicklow (one word)

Newtownsands Co. Limerick (one word)

Newtownstewart Co. Tyrone (one word); *see also* **Newton Stewart**

New Wav/e the *nouvelle vague*, or a form of 1970s–1980s rock music (caps.); **-er, -ish**

New Year's Day (caps.) always 1 Jan. even when the year is reckoned from some other day

New York US state, abbr. **NY**; the city, often abbr. **NYC**, but officially **New York, NY**

New Yorker a person born or living in New York (City)

New Yorker, The a US magazine (ital.)

nexus (Lat.) a tie, a linked group; pl. same, *not* nexi

Ney, Michel (1769–1815) French marshal

Nez Percé (of or pertaining to) a Native American people of Idaho, Oregon, and Washington, or their Penutian language

NF National Front, Newfoundland, New French, Norman French

NF (Ger.) *Neue Folge* (new series) (small caps.)

NFL (US) National Football League

Nfld. Newfoundland

NFU National Farmers' Union

NFWI National Federation of Women's Institutes

NG National Giro, National Guard, New Granada

ng in Welsh usually a separate letter, following g in alphabetical sequence; not to be divided

n.g. no good

ngaio/ a small New Zealand tree, with edible fruit and light white timber; pl. **-s**

Ngbaka (of or related to) a group of related languages spoken in Cent. Africa

Ngbandi (of or related to) a Niger–Congo language

NGO non-governmental organization

Ngoko the form of Javanese used in Indonesia among intimates and when addressing certain people of lower status

ngoma a dance, or a night of dancing, in E. Africa

Ngoni a member of an Nguni people now living chiefly in Malawi

N.Gr. New Greek

Nguni (of or related to) (a member of) a Bantu-speaking people living mainly in southern Africa, or a group of closely related Bantu languages

ngwee a monetary unit of Zambia, pl. same

NH New Hampshire (off. and postal abbr.)

N.Heb. New Hebrew, New Hebrides

NHG New High German

NHI National Health Insurance

n.h.p. nominal horsepower

NHS National Health Service

NI National Insurance, Northern Ireland

Ni nickel (no point)

Niagara/ a river separating Ontario, Canada, from New York State, **— Falls** the waterfalls of the Niagara river, also towns in NY and Ontario

Nibelungenlied a German epic, 12th–13th c.

niblick a golf club

NiCad a nickel-cadmium battery (one word, two caps.), (US propr.) **Nicad** (one cap.)

Nicam a digital stereo system used in British television; also **NICAM**

Nicar. Nicaragua

Nicene Creed issued in 325 by the Council of Nicaea (in Asia Minor); to be distinguished from the longer **Niceno-Constantinopolitan Creed** of the Thirty-Nine Articles, issued in 371

niche a recess, *not* -ch

Nicholas Anglicized spelling of the names of five popes, two Russian emperors, and the patron saint of Russia; in Russ. **Nikolai**, in Fr. **Nicolas**

Nicholson the usual spelling, *but see* **Nicolson**

nicht wahr? (Ger.) is it not so?

nickel/ (US) a 5-cent coin; (chem.) symbol **Ni**; **-plated, -plating** (hyphen); **— silver** (two words)

nick-nack *use* **knick-knack**

nickname (one word)

Nicobar Islands Indian Ocean, *not* Nik-

niçois/ (Fr.) of Nice, f. **-e** (not cap.); a native of Nice, f. **-e** (cap.)

nicol prism from **William Nicol** (1768–1851) Scottish physicist

Nicolson, Hon. Sir Harold George (1886–1968) British politician and man of letters

Nicomachean Ethics by Aristotle, *not* Nicho-

Nicosia Cyprus (Gr. **Levkosia**), Sicily; *not* Nik-

NID Naval Intelligence Division

nid/us (Lat.) a nest, pl. **-i**

Niebelungenlied *use* **Nib-**

Niebuhr,/ Barthold Georg (1776–1831) German historian and philologist, **— Karsten** (1733–1815) German traveller, **— Reinhold** (1892–1971) US theologian

niece *not* nei-

niell/o Italian metalwork, pl. **-i** (not ital.)

nien hao (part of) the reign of a Chinese emperor, used in imperial China as a system of dating; a dating mark on Chinese pottery or porcelain; pl. same; in Chinese **niánhào**

Niepce/, Joseph Nicéphore (1765–1833) French physicist, originator of photography; **— de Saint-Victor, Claude Marie François** (1805–70) his nephew, inventor of heliographic engraving

Niersteiner a Rhine wine

Nietzsche/, Friedrich Wilhelm (1844–1900) German political philosopher; **-an, -anism**

Nièvre a dép. of France

Niger, Republic of W. Cent. Africa; adj. **Nigérien**

Nigeria/, Republic of W. coast of Africa; adj. **-n**, in Fr. **nigérian**

night-blindness (hyphen, two words in US)
night/cap, -clothes, -club, -dress, -fall, -gown (one word)
night-hawk (hyphen, one word in US)
nightlife (one word)
night light (two words)
night-long (adj. and adv., hyphen)
nightmarish *not* -reish
night nurse (two words)
night owl (two words, one word in US)
night/ safe, — school (two words)
nightshade (bot.) (one word)
night shift (two words)
night/shirt, -spot (one word)
nightstick (US) = **truncheon** (one word)
night-time (hyphen, one word in US)
night watch (two words)
nightwatchman (one word)
night-work (hyphen, two words in US)
nihil/ (Lat.) nothing, — *ad rem* nothing to the purpose, — *obstat* no objection is raised (to publication etc.)
Nihon *use* **Nippon**
Nijinsk/y, Vaslav (1890–1950) Russian ballet dancer; **-a, Bronislava** (1891–1972) his sister, Russian choreographer
Nijni Novgorod, Russia, *use* **Nizhni Novgorod**
Nikobar Islands, Nikosia *use* **Nic-**
nil/ (Lat.) nothing; — *admirari* wondering at nothing (*not* admiring nothing); — *conscire sibi* to be conscious of no fault; — *desperandum* despair of nothing, *not* never despair
nilgai a short-horned Indian antelope; *not* neelghau, nylghau
Nilgiris, The hills, S. India; *not* Neilgherry Hills
nil nisi bene (speak) only well (of the dead)
Nilotic of or relating to the Nile, the Nile region, or a group of E. African Negroid peoples or their languages
ni l'un (or une f.) *ni l'autre* (Fr.) neither the one nor the other
nimbostrat/us (meteor.) a low grey layer of cloud, pl. **-i**
nimb/us a halo, a rain cloud; pl. **-i, -uses**; adj. **-used**
niminy-piminy affectedly delicate, *not* -i -i
n'importe! (Fr.) never mind!
Nin, Anaïs (1903–77) French-born US writer
nincompoop a simpleton (one word)
ninepins a game (one word)
ninja (Jap.) a person skilled in the Japanese martial art of **ninjutsu**
ninth *not* -eth
niobium symbol **Nb**
nip/, -ped, -per, -ping

Nippon the native name for Japan, *not* Nihon
NIREX Nuclear Industry Radioactive Waste Executive
nirvana (not cap., not ital.)
nisi (Lat.) unless, — *prius* unless before
Nissen/, Peter Norman (1871–1930) British mining engineer, inventor of — **hut**
nisus (Lat.) an effort, pl. same
nitrate a salt of nitric acid
nitre saltpetre (potassium nitrate), *not* -er (US)
nitrite a salt of nitrous acid
nitrogen symbol **N**
nitrogenize *not* -ise
nitrogenous *not* -eous
nitroglycerine an explosive yellow liquid, *not* -in (one word)
nizam a Turkish soldier, (cap.) title of the ruler of Hyderabad; pl. same
Nizhni Novgorod Russia, named Gorky during the Soviet era
NJ New Jersey (off. and postal abbr.)
NKGB (hist.) Soviet 'People's Commissariat of State Security' 1943–6; *see also* **KGB**
Nkrumah, Dr Kwame (1909–72) Ghanaian politician, President 1960–6
NKVD (hist.) Soviet 'People's Commissariat for Internal Affairs' 1934–43; *see also* **KGB**
NL New Latin, Neo-Latin
n.l. (Lat.) *non licet* (it is not allowed), *non liquet* (it is not clear), (typ.) new line
N. lat. north latitude
NLC National Liberal Club
NLQ (comput.) near letter quality
NM New Mexico (postal abbr.)
n. M. (Ger.) *nächsten Monats* (next month)
nm nanometre
N. Mex. New Mexico (off. abbr.)
NMR nuclear magnetic resonance
nn. notes
NNE north-north-east
NNW north-north-west
NO Navigation Officer, New Orleans
No Japanese drama, *use* **Noh** (q.v.)
No nobelium (no point)
No., no. number, from It. *numero*; pl. **Nos., nos.**; in Fr. **n°**, pl. **n°s**; in Ger. **Nr.**
no (the negative) pl. **noes**
n.o. (cricket) not out
Noachian pertaining to Noah
Nobel/, Alfred (Bernard) (1833–96) Swedish inventor of dynamite; — **Prizes** (six) awarded annually for physics, chemistry, physiology or medicine, literature, peace, economics
nobelium symbol **No**

nobiliary/ of the nobility, — **particle** a preposition forming part of a title of nobility, e.g. in Fr. *de*, in Ger. *von*.

noblesse/ (Fr. f.) nobility, — **oblige** nobility imposes obligations

nobody (one word) *but* **no one** (two words)

nocte (Lat.) at night, abbr. **n.**

'Noctes Ambrosianae' articles in *Blackwood's Magazine*, 1822–35

nocturn (RC) a part of matins originally said at night

nocturne (painting) a night scene, (mus.) a night-piece (not ital. except as part of title)

NOD Naval Ordnance Department

NODE *New Oxford Dictionary of English*

nod/, **-ded, -ding**

nod/**us** a difficulty, pl. **-i**

Noel Christmas, in Fr. m. **Noël**; the Eng. **Nowel**(**l**) is obsolete except in carols

Noël the name

Noether, Emmy (1882–1935) German mathematician

noetic of the intellect

Nofretete *see* **Nefertiti**

Noh a traditional Japanese drama with dance and song, *not* No (cap.)

noisette/ a hazelnut; (cook.) in pl. **-s**, small choice pieces of meat; (bot.) a hybrid between China and moss rose

noisome noxious, ill-smelling (no connection with noise)

noisy *not* -ey

nolens volens (Lat.) willy-nilly, pl. **nolentes volentes**

noli me tangere (Lat.) don't touch me (no hyphens)

nolle prosequi (law) relinquishment of a suit by plaintiff or prosecutor, abbr. **nol. pros.**

nolo/ (Lat.) I do not wish to, — **contendere** I will not contest, — **episcopari** I do not wish to be a bishop (formula for avoiding responsible office)

nom. nominal, nominative

no man's land (apos., three words)

nombre (Fr., Catalan m.) number, (Sp. m.) name

nombril (her.) the point halfway between fess point and the base of the shield

nom de guerre (Fr. m.) an assumed name under which one fights, plays, writes, etc.

nom de plume a pseudonym under which one writes (not in Fr. usage) (not ital.), *prefer* **pen name**

nom de théâtre (Fr. m.) a stage-name

nom/en a name, pl. **-ina**; abbr. **N.**

nomen/ **genericum** a generic name, — **specificum** a specific name

nomin. nominative

nominative (gram.) the case of the subject; abbr. **n., nom.,** *or* **nomin.**

non/ (Lat.) not, — **assumpsit** a denial of any promise

nonagenarian a person from 90 to 99 years old, *not* nono-

nonce-word one coined only for the occasion (hyphen)

nonchalan/ce indifference, **-t** (not ital.)

non-commissioned officer/ abbr. **NCO**; pl. **-s** (one hyphen, two words in US)

non-committal (hyphen)

non compos mentis of unsound mind (not ital.)

non con. non-content, dissentient

Nonconform/ist an English Protestant separated from the Church of England (cap. only in this sense), **-ity**

non constat (Lat.) it is not clear

non-cooperation (one hyphen, one word in US)

none can be followed by sing. or pl. verb according to the sense

Nones (pl.) in Roman calendar the ninth day, counting inclusively, before the Ides

non est (Lat.) it is wanting; **non est invent/us**, **-a, -um** he, she, *or* it, has not been found, abbr. **n.e.i.**

nonesuch *use* **nonsuch** (except in US)

Nonesuch Press founded by Sir Francis Meynell

nonet (mus.) a composition for nine performers

nonetheless = nevertheless (one word); = not any the less (for that) (three words)

non-Euclidean (hyphen, one cap.)

nonfeasance failure to perform an act required by law (one word)

non-hero the opposite of a hero (hyphen, one word in US); cf. **anti-hero**

nonillion originally (esp. Brit.) the ninth power of a million (10^{54}), *but now* usually (originally US) the tenth power of a thousand (10^{30})

non inventus (Lat.) not found

nonjur/or a person who refuses to take an oath (one word); **-ing**

non-jury (of a trial) without a jury

non/ **libet** it does not please (me); — **licet** it is not permitted, abbr. **n.l.**

non-lining numerals (typ.) those that have ascenders and descenders, as 1234567890

non/ **liquet** (Lat.) it is not clear, abbr. **n.l.**; — **mi ricordo** (It.) I do not remember

non-net book one that a retailer may sell at less than the published price (hyphen)

non/ **nobis** (Lat.) not unto us, the first words of Ps. 115; — **obstante** notwithstanding, abbr. **non obst.**; — **obstante veredicto** notwithstanding the verdict

nonpareil unequalled

non-person a person regarded as non-existent or insignificant (hyphen, one word in US); cf. **unperson**

non placet (Lat.) it does not please (used as a negative vote in a Church or university assembly)

nonplus/ perplex; **-sed, -sing**

non plus ultra (Lat.) perfection, *use* **ne plus ultra**

non/ possumus (Lat.) we cannot; **— pro-sequitur** he does not prosecute, abbr. **non pros.**

non-resident/ , **-ial** (hyphen)

non sequitur it does not follow logically, abbr. **non seq.**

non/-skid, -slip, -stick, -stop (hyphen)

nonsuch a person or thing that is unrivalled; *not* nonesuch (US)

nonsuit the stoppage of suit by judge when plaintiff has failed to make a case (one word)

non-toxic (hyphen, one word in US)

non-U not characteristic of the upper class (hyphen, no point)

noon abbr. **n.**

noonday (one word)

no one no person (two words) *but* **nobody**

noontide (one word)

n.o.p. not otherwise provided for

Nor. Norman

Noraid Irish Northern Aid Committee (one cap.)

Norddeutscher Lloyd (two words) abbr. **NDL**

Nordenfelt gun a form of machine gun invented by the Swedish engineer **Thorsten Nordenfelt** (1842–1920)

Nordenskjöld, Nils Adolf Erik, Baron (1832–1901) Swedish Arctic explorer

Nordic of or relating to the tall blond dolichocephalic Germanic people found in N. Europe, esp. in Scandinavia or Finland

Norge Norw. for **Norway**, in New Norse (nynorsk) **Noreg**

norm/a (Lat.) a rule or measure, pl. **-ae**

normalize standardize, *not* -ise

Normanby, Marquess of

normande, à la (Fr. cook.) apple-flavoured (not cap.)

Norn any of three goddesses of destiny in Scandinavian myth.

Norroy and Ulster (her.) third King of Arms

Norse abbr. **N.**

North, Christopher pseud. of **Prof. John Wilson** (1785–1854) Scottish poet

north abbr. **N.**; *see also* **compass points**

Northallerton N. Yorks. (one word)

North Americ/a, -an abbr. **NA, N. Amer.**

Northamptonshire abbr. **Northants.**

northbound (one word)

North Britain a name for Scotland, offensive to Scots; abbr. **Scot.**, *not* NB

North Carolina off. and postal abbr. **NC**

Northd. Northumberland

North Dakota off. abbr. **N. Dak.**, postal **ND**

North Downs Kent etc.

north-east/, **-ern** (hyphen, one word in US) abbr. **NE**

northeaster a wind (one word)

northern abbr. **N.**; *see also* **compass points**

Northern Ireland abbr. **NI**

Northern Territory (Australia) abbr. **NT**

Northesk, Earl of

North-German Gazette (one hyphen)

North-Holland publisher (hyphen)

Northleach Glos. (one word)

North Pole (caps.)

Northumberland abbr. **Northumb.**, (postal) **Northd.**

North Wales abbr. **NW**

north-west/, **-ern** (hyphen, one word in US) abbr. **NW**

northwester a wind (one word)

Norvic: the signature of the Bishop of Norwich (colon)

Norw. Norway, Norwegian

Norway in Norw. **Norge**, in New Norse (nynorsk) **Noreg**, in Fr. **Norvège**, in Ger. **Norwegen**, in It. **Norvegia**

nor'wester a northwester, a glass of strong liquor, an oilskin hat (= **sou'wester**)

Nos., nos. numbers

n°ˢ (Fr.) *numéros* (numbers)

nosce teipsum (Lat.) know thyself

nose/bag, -band, -bleed (one word)

nose-cone (hyphen, two words in US)

nosedive (noun and verb, one word)

nosegay (one word)

nose job rhinoplasty (two words)

nose-piece (hyphen, one word in US)

nose wheel (two words, one word in US)

nosey *use* **nosy**

no sooner/ ... than *not* — — ... when

nostalgie/ (Fr. f.) nostalgia; **— de la boue** a desire for depravity, lit. 'mud-nostalgia'

noster (Lat.) our, our own; abbr. **N.**

Nostradamus (1503–66) French astrologer and physician, in Fr. **Michel de Nostredame**

nostrum/ a quack remedy, pl. **-s** (not ital.)

nosy *not* -ey

nosy parker an inquisitive person (not cap.)

nota bene (Lat.) mark well, abbr. **NB**

notabilia (Lat. pl.) notable things

notab/ility, -le *not* note-

notand/um (Lat.) a thing to be noted, pl. *-a*

notarize (US) certify (a document) as a notary

notar/y public a person authorized to perform certain legal formalities, esp. to draw up or certify contracts, deeds, etc. (two words); pl. **-ies public**; abbr. **NP**

notation a method of recording music or movement in written form; (US) a note or annotation, a record

note/, -s abbr. **n.**, pl. **nn.**

note/book, -case, -paper, -worthy (one word)

notic/e, -eable, -ing *not* notica-

noticeboard (one word, two words in US)

notif/y, -iable, -ied, -ying

notiti/a (Lat.) a list, pl. *-ae*

Notogaea (zool.) the land mass of Australasia; cf. **Arctogaea**; **Neogaea**

notorious well known, esp. unfavourably: 'a notorious criminal', 'notorious for its climate'; it does not mean *villainous*

not proven (Sc. law) a verdict pronouncing evidence insufficient to determine guilt or innocence

Notre Dame Ind., university and town

Notre Dame (Fr.) Our Lady, abbr. **N.D.** (no hyphen); (part of) the Fr. name of many churches (hyphen), abbr. **N.-D.**; *not* Nô-

Notre Seigneur (Fr.) Our Lord, abbr. **N.S.**

Nottinghamshire abbr. **Notts.**

Nouakchott Mauritania

n'oubliez pas (Fr.) don't forget

nougat a confection

nought the figure zero (0); *see also* **naught**

noughth immediately preceding what is regarded as 'first' in a series (e.g. 'noughth week'), also **zeroth**

noumen/on an object of intellectual intuition, not perceptible by the senses, opp. to **phenomenon**; pl. **-a**; **-al, -ally**

noun abbr. **n.**

nouns, German all have initial caps. in Ger. usage

nous (Gr.) intellect, shrewdness (not ital.); *Noûs* a journal (accent)

nous avons changé tout cela (Fr.) we have changed all that

nous verrons (Fr.) we shall see

nouveau/ riche a parvenu, pl. **-x riches** (not ital.)

nouvelle cuisine a style of cookery (not ital.)

nouvelles (Fr. f. pl.) news

nouvelle vague (Fr. f.) new wave, esp. describing French film-making of the early 1960s

Nov. November

nov/a (astr.) a new star, pl. **-ae**

Novalis pseud. of **Baron Friedrich von Hardenberg** (1772–1801) German writer

Nova/ Scotia Canada, abbr. **NS**; **— Zembla** Arctic islands, *use* **Novaya Zemlya** (two words, caps.)

Noveboracensian of New York, *not* Nova- (one word); cf. **Novi Eboraci**

novelette a short novel, (Brit. derog.) a light romantic novel, (mus.) a piano piece in free form with several themes

novella/ a short novel or narrative story, pl. **-s**

November abbr. **Nov.**; in Fr. m. *novembre*, abbr. *nov.* (not cap.)

noviciate the state or period of being a novice, *not* -tiate (US)

Nov/i Eboraci (Lat.) at New York (two words), **-um Eboracum** (Lat.) New York; *see also* **Noveboracensian**

Novotný, Antonín (1904–75) Czechoslovak politician, President 1957–68

nov/us homo (Lat.) a self-made man, pl. *-i homines*

NOW (US) National Organization for Women

nowadays (one word)

Nowel(l) *see* **Noel**

nowhere (one word)

noyade (Fr. f.) execution by drowning

noyau/ a liqueur of brandy flavoured with fruit kernels, pl. **-x**

NP New Providence, Notary Public

Np neptunium (no point)

n.p. net personalty, (typ.) new paragraph, (bibliog.) no place of publication given

NPA Newspaper Publishers' Association

NPL National Physical Laboratory

NPO New Philharmonia Orchestra (*earlier and later* **Philharmonia Orchestra**)

NR North Riding

Nr. (Ger.) *Nummer* (number)

nr. near

NRA (US) National Rifle Association, (UK) National Rivers Authority

NRC National Research Council

NRDC National Research Development Corporation

NRSV New Revised Standard Version (of the Bible)

NRT net registered tonnage

NS New Side, Newspaper Society, New Style (after 1752), Nova Scotia

ɴs New Series (small caps. in refs.)

N.S. (Fr.) *Notre Seigneur* (Our Lord)

n.s. not specified

n/s (banking) not sufficient, (advertisements) non-smoker, -ing

NSB National Savings Bank

NSC National Security Council

NSF (US) National Science Foundation

NSPCC National Society for the Prevention of Cruelty to Children

NSW New South Wales

NT National Theatre, National Trust, New Testament, (Austral.) Northern Territory, (bridge) no trumps

NTP normal temperature and pressure

nu the thirteenth letter of the Gr. alphabet (*N*, *ν*)

n.u. name unknown

nuance a shade of difference (not ital.)

NUBE National Union of Bank Employees

nucle/us pl. **-i**

nuclide (phys.) an atom having a specified type of nucleus, *not* -eide

-nugger in Indian place names, *use* **-nagar**

NUGMW National Union of General and Municipal Workers

NUI National University of Ireland

Nuits-Saint-Georges a red burgundy (two hyphens)

NUJ National Union of Journalists

Nuku'alofa Tonga

nulla bona (law) no goods that can be distrained upon

nullah (Anglo-Ind.) a dry watercourse or ravine (not ital.)

nulla-nulla an Australian club, *not* -ah -ah

nullif/y, -ied, -ying

nulli secundus (Lat.) second to none

NUM National Union of Mineworkers

Num. Numbers (OT), *not* Numb.

num. numeral, -s

number abbr. **No.**, **no.**; pl. **Nos.**, **nos.**

Numbers (OT) abbr. **Num.**

numbskull *use* **num-**

num/en a presiding deity or spirit, pl. **-ina**

numeraire (econ.) the function of money as a measure of value, a standard for currency exchange rates (no accent, not ital.)

numéraire (Fr. m.) cash, legal tender

numér/o (Fr. m.) number, abbr. **n°**, pl. **n°s**; **-oter** to number (e.g. pages), **-oteur** a numbering machine

numis. numismatic, -s; numismatology

Nummer (Ger. f.) number, abbr. **Nr.**

numskull a dunce, *not* numb-

nunatak (Inuit) a hill or mountain protruding through glacial ice, *not* -ck

Nunc Dimittis (Lat.) (the musical setting of) the Song of Simeon as a canticle

nunchaku a Japanese martial arts weapon consisting of two hardwood sticks joined together at one end by a strap or chain (not ital.)

nunci/o a papal ambassador; pl. **-os**; **-ature** the office or tenure of a nuncio

nuncupat/e declare (a will or testament) orally, not in writing; **-ion**, **-ive**

NUPE National Union of Public Employees

Nuphar (bot.) the yellow water-lily genus; cf. **nenuphar**

NUR National Union of Railwaymen (merged with the NUS to form the RMT, 1990)

nurd *use* **ne-**

Nuremberg *not* -burg, in German **Nürnberg**

Nureyev, Rudolf (**Hametovich**) (1939–93) Russian ballet dancer

nurl *use* **kn-**

Nürnberg Anglicized as **Nuremberg**

nurs/e, -ing, -ling

nursemaid (one word)

nurseryman (one word)

nursery/ rhyme, — school (two words)

NUS National Union of Seamen (merged with the NUR to form the RMT, 1990), National Union of Students

NUT National Union of Teachers

nut/, -ted, -ting, -ty

nutcrackers (one word)

NUTG National Union of Townswomen's Guilds

nut/hatch a bird, **-shell** (one word)

Nuuk Greenland, *not* Godthåb

nux vomica a seed of E. Indian tree, source of strychnine (two words, not ital.); abbr. **nux vom.**

NV *naamloze vennootschap* (public limited company), Nevada (postal abbr.), New Version

NVM Nativity of the Virgin Mary

NW north-west, -ern; North Wales

NWFP North-West Frontier Province, Pakistan

NWT North-West Territories, Canada

NY New York (City *or* State); *see also* **New York**

nyala an antelope, *use* **iny-**

Nyasaland Cent. Africa, *not* Nyassa- (one word); now **Malawi**

NYC New York City

nyctalopia night-blindness

nyet (Russ.) no (to avoid confusion the normal transliteration, *net*, is not used)

nylghau an antelope, *use* **nilgai**

nylon (not cap.)

Nymegen the Netherlands; in Du. **Nijmegen**, Fr. **Nimègue**, Ger. **Nimwegen**

nymph/ae (anat.) the *labia minora*, sing. **-a**

Nymphaea (bot.) the white water-lily genus

nymphet a young or little nymph, a sexually attractive young girl; *not* -tte

nympho/ (colloq.) a nymphomaniac, pl. **-s**

nympholep/sy ecstasy or frenzy caused by desire of the unattainable; **-t** a person inspired by violent enthusiasm, esp. for an ideal

nynorsk 'new Norwegian', a Norwegian peasant dialect given literary form *c*.1850; *formerly* landsmål (not cap.)

Nyquist/, Harry (1889–1976) Swedish-born US physicist, responsible for — **criterion**, — **diagram**, — **limit**, — **noise theorem**

Nyx (Gr. myth.) the female personification of Night, daughter of Chaos

NZ New Zealand

O (exclamation)

O oxygen (no point), (Lat.) *octarius* (a pint), the fourteenth in a series; a blood group

O. Odd Fellows, Order (as DSO), owner, (Fr. m.) *ouest* (west), (Ger. m.) *Osten* (east)

O' Irish patronymic prefix ('grandson of') (apos., *not* turned comma); o or ó, or corresponding caps., followed by thin space, also used

o. old, (meteor.) overcast

o- (chem. prefix) *ortho-* (ital., always hyphenated), *prefer to ortho-*

o' abbr. for *of*, to be set close up in common constructions (o'clock), but according to sense in reproducing archaic or dialectal constructions (cock o' th' walk)

Ö, ö in Ger., Swed., etc., may *not* be replaced by *Oe, oe* (except in some proper names), *O, o*, or *Œ, œ*

ö (Swed.), ø (Dan.) island

Ø, ø Danish and Norwegian letter

% per cent

‰ per mille

o/a on account of

oaf/ a stupid or loutish person, pl. -s

Oak-apple Day 29 May

Oaks, the annual race at Epsom (treated as sing.)

O. & M. organization and methods

OAP Old Age Pension, -er

oarlock (US) = **rowlock**

oarweed seaweed, *not* ore-weed

OAS on active service, Organization of American States, Organisation de l'Armée Secrète

oas/is pl. -es

oatcake (one word)

Oates, Titus (1649–1705) the man who fabricated the Popish Plot, 1678

oatmeal (one word)

OAU Organization of African Unity

Oaxaca Mexico

OB Old Boy, outside broadcast

ob. oboe

ob. *obiit* (he, she, *or* it, died)

Obadiah (OT) abbr. **Obad.**

obbligato (mus.) an accompaniment, *not* obl-; abbr. **obb.**

OBE Officer of the Order of the British Empire, overtaken by events

obeah W. Indian sorcery; *not* -ea, -eeyah, -i

obeisance a courtesy bow

obelisk a tapering, usually four-sided, monument or landmark; *not* -isc

obel/us (typ.) dagger-shaped reference mark in printed matter (†); **double obelus** ‡; a mark (– or ÷) used in ancient manuscripts to mark a word or passage, esp. as spurious; pl. -i; -ize mark with an obelus as spurious etc.

Oberammergau Bavaria, Germany

obi a broad Japanese sash worn with a kimono; for sorcery *use* obeah

obiit/ (Lat.) he, she, *or* it died, abbr. **ob.**; — *sine prole* died without issue, abbr. **ob.s.p.**

obit a date of death, a funeral or commemoration service; (colloq.) obituary (no point, not ital.)

obiter/ dictum (Lat.) a thing said by the way, pl. — *dicta*; — *scriptum* a thing written by the way, pl. — *scripta*

object/, -ion, -ionable, -ive, -ively abbr. **obj.**

object language a language described by means of another language (two words)

object lesson (two words)

object-oriented/ architecture abbr. **OOA**, — **design** abbr. **OOD**, — **language** abbr. **OOL**, — **planning system** abbr. **OOPS** (comput.); *not* -orientated (one hyphen)

objet/ d'art a work of artistic value, pl. -s d'art (not ital.)

objet/ trouvé (Fr. m.) thing found, pl. -s trouvés

obl. oblique, oblong

obligato *use* obb-

obligee (law) a person to whom another is bound

obliger one who does a favour

obligor (law) one who binds himself to another

oblique abbr. **obl.**

oblong abbr. **obl.**

obloquy the state of being generally ill spoken of; abuse, detraction

o.b.o. or best offer

obo/e (mus.) *not* the many variants, abbr. **ob.**; -ist *not* -eist

obol a coin and weight of ancient Greece

obole a small French coin in use 10th–15th cc.

obol/us an apothecaries' weight of 10 grains; various small coins in medieval Europe; pl. -i

O'Brien,/ Conor Cruise (b. 1917) Irish politician, — **Edna** (b. 1932) Irish writer, — **Flann** pseud. of **Brian O'Nolan** (1911–66) Irish writer, — **William Smith** (1803–64) and — **William** (1852–1928) Irish patriots

obs. observation, observatory, observed, obsolete

obscurum per obscurius (Lat.) (explaining) the obscure by means of the more obscure, *not* obscurus — —

obsequi/es funeral rites, the sing. -y *not used*; **-al**

obsequious fawning

observanda (Lat. pl.) things to be observed

observat/ion, -ory abbr. **obs.**

obsidian (mineral.)

obsolescen/t becoming obsolete; the state is **-ce**

obsolete/ disused, antiquated, abbr. **obs.**; the state is **-ness**

ob.s.p. *obiit sine prole* (died without issue)

obstetric/s abbr. **obstet.**; **-ian**

obstructor *not* -er

OC Officer Commanding, Officer of the Order of Canada

ocarina a small (usually terracotta) wind instrument, *not* och-

Occam, William (of) *see* **Ockham, William (of)**

Occidental (cap. as noun, not cap. as adj.)

occip/ut the back of the head (not ital.), **-ital**

Occitan (of or concerning) a Romance language related to Catalan, also called *langue d'oc*

Occleve *use* **Hoccleve**

occulist *use* **ocu-**

occur/, -red, -rence, -rent, -ring

Oceania the islands of the Pacific and adjacent seas

ocell/us (zool.) simple (as opp. to compound) eye (of insect), pl. **-i**

ocharina *use* **oca-**

ochlocracy mob rule

ochone (Sc., Ir.) expressing regret or lament, *not* oh-; in Gaelic and Ir. *ochóin*

ochra *use* **okra**

ochr/e a yellow pigment; *not* ocher (US), oker; **-eous, -y**

Ockeghem, Johannes (d. 1497) Franco-Flemish composer, *also* **Okeghem**

Ockham Surrey; *see also* **Occam**

Ockham/, William (of) (*c.*1285–*c.*1347) English Franciscan philosopher, deviser of **—'s razor** the principle of the fewest possible assumptions; **-ism, -ist**; *also* **Occam, Ockam**

o'clock to be printed close up (not to be abbr.)

O'Connell, Daniel (1775–1847) Irish statesman

O'Connor,/ Feargus Edward (1794–1855) Irish-born Chartist leader; **— Rt. Hon. Thomas Power** (1848–1931) Irish-born journalist and British politician

OCR (comput.) optical character recognition (reading of print etc. by electronic eye for computer input)

ocra *use* **okra**

Oct. October

octachord eight-stringed (musical instrument), *not* octo-

octahedr/on a solid figure with eight faces, pl. **-ons**; **-al**; *not* octae-, octoe-, octoh-

octaroon *use* **octo-**

octastyle (archit.) having eight columns, *not* octo-

Octateuch the first eight books of OT, *not* Octo-

octave a fencing position

octavo/ (typ.) a book based on eight leaves, sixteen pages, to the sheet; pl. **-s**, abbr. **8vo** (no point)

octet (mus.) *not* -ett, -ette

October abbr. **Oct.**; in Fr. m. *octobre*, abbr. *oct.* (not cap.)

Octobrist (Russ. hist.) *not* -erist, in Russ. *oktyabrist*

octochord *use* **octa-**

octodecimo *see* **eighteenmo**

octo/edron, -hedron *use* **octa-**

octogenarian a person from 80 to 89 years old

octop/us pl. **-uses**, formal pl. **-odes**; *not* -i

octoroon a person of one-eighth Negro blood, *not* octa-

octostyle *use* **octa-**

Octoteuch *use* **Octa-**

octroi (Fr. m.) municipal customs duties (not ital.)

OCTU *or* **Octu** Officer Cadets Training Unit

ocularist a maker of artificial eyes, *not* occ-

oculist a medical specialist in eyes, *not* occ-

Oculi Sunday third in Lent

ocul/us (Lat.) an eye, pl. *-i*

OD Old Dutch, Ordnance datum, overdose

O/D on demand, overdraft

od a hypothetical force; (arch.) God, *not* 'od

o.d. outer diameter

odal *use* **ud-**

odalisque (Turk.) a female slave or concubine, *not* -isk (not ital.)

O.Dan. Old Danish

Oddfellow a member of fraternity (off. title **Independent Order of Odd Fellows**)

oddments (typ.) parts of a book other than main text, such as contents, index; a section containing oddments

odd pages (typ.) the right-hand, or recto, pages

Odelsting the lower house of Norwegian Parliament

Odendaalsrus (off. spelling) Orange Free State, *not* -st

Odéon a Paris theatre

Oder–Neisse line between Poland and Germany (en rule)

Odets, Clifford (1906–63) US dramatist and playwright

odeum/ a building for musical performances, pl. **-s**

Odeypore *use* **Udaipur**

odi profanum vulgus (Lat.) I loathe the common herd

odium a widespread dislike

odium/ aestheticum (Lat.) the bitterness of aesthetic controversy, — *medicum* the bitterness of medical controversy, — *musicum* the bitterness of musical controversy, — *theologicum* the bitterness of theological controversy

odometer an instrument for measuring distance travelled, *not* ho-

O'Donoghue of the Glens, The (cap. *T*)

O'Donovan, The (cap. *T*)

odontoglossum/ an orchid, pl. **-s**; cap., ital., as genus

odor/iferous, -ize, -izer, -ous

odour/, -less *not* odor- (US)

Odra ancient region corresponding to the modern Indian state of Orissa

Odysseus Greek hero (spelling used in classical contexts); in Lat. **Ulixes**, Eng. **Ulysses** (e.g. Shakespeare, Tennyson, and Joyce)

Odyssey of Homer (ital., not quoted); **Odyssean** (not ital.)

odyssey a long wandering (not cap., not ital.)

OE Old English

Oe (phys.) oersted

OECD Organization for Economic Cooperation and Development

oecist the founder of a Greek colony, *not* oik-

oecology *use* **ec-**

oecumenic/, -al *see* **ecumenic**

Oecumenical Council an assembly of ecclesiastical representatives deciding on Christian matters

Oecumenical Patriarch the Archbishop of Constantinople, head of the Orthodox Church

OED *Oxford English Dictionary*, originally **NED** (*New English Dictionary*)

oedema/ a swelling, **-tous**; *not* ed- (US)

Oedipus/ the Theban hero, *not* Edi-; — **complex** (psych.) a boy's subconscious desire for his mother and hostility to his father (two words); **Oedipal**

OEEC Organization for European Economic Co-operation, *now* **OECD**

Oehlenschläger, Adam (1779–1850) Danish writer, *not* Oh-

œil (Fr. m.) eye, pl *yeux*; *œil-de-bœuf* a small round window, pl. *œils-de-bœuf*; *œil-de-perdrix* a soft corn, pl. *œils-de-perdrix*

œillade (Fr. f.) a glance

oeno/logy the study of wine, **-phile** lover of wines; *not* en- (US), oin-

oersted (phys.) unit of magnetic field strength, from **Hans Christian Oersted** (1777–1851) Danish physicist, *not* œr-; abbr. **Oe**; in SI units $1000/4\pi$ A/m

oesophag/us the gullet, pl. **-i**; **-eal** (not ital.); *not* es- (US)

Oesterreich (Ger.) Austria, *use* **Ös-**

oestrogen, oestrus *not* es- (US)

œuf (Fr. m.) egg, *œufs/ à la coque* boiled eggs, — *à la neige* whisked eggs, — *à l'indienne* curried eggs, — *de Pâques* Easter eggs, — *sur le plat* fried eggs

oeuvre work, esp. a writer's or artist's work taken as a whole, in Fr. (m.) *œuvre*

OF Odd Fellows, Old French, (typ.) old-face type

of (US) in time-keeping, used in relation to the following (*not* preceding) hour: 'quarter of three' = 2.45 *not* 3.15

O'Faoláin, Seán (1900–91) Irish writer

off. offic/e, -er, -ial, -inal

Offaly Ireland

Offa's Dike between England and Wales (apos.)

offbeat (one word)

off-centre (hyphens)

off colour not in good health, (esp. US) somewhat indecent (-or)

offcut a remnant of paper, wood, etc.

off day (two words)

Offenbach, Jacques (1819–80) German-born French composer

offence *not* -se (US)

offer/, -ed, -ing, -tory

offg. officiating

off guard (two words, hyphen when attrib.)

offhand/, -ed casual, extempore (one word)

offic/e, -er abbr. **off.**

official abbr. **off.**, **offic.**

Official Report of Parliamentary Debates, The the official name for Hansard since 1892

officiating abbr. **offg.**

officina (Lat.) workshop; *see also* *oficina*

officinal abbr. **off.**

off/-key, -licence (hyphens)

offload (one word)

off/-peak, -piste, -price (hyphens)

offprint (typ.) a separately printed copy, or small edition, of an article that originally appeared as part of a larger publication

off/-putting, -screen, -season (hyphens)

offset/ (print.) **-litho, -lithography** a planographic printing process in which ink is transferred onto an intermediate rubber blanket cylinder and then offset onto the paper (hyphens)

offshoot (one word)

offshore (adj. and adv., one word)

offside (sport); (Brit.) right side of a vehicle, animal, etc. (cf. **nearside**) (one word)

offspring (one word)

offstage (one word)

off-street (hyphen)

off-the/-cuff, -record, -shelf, -wall (adj., hyphens)

off/-time, -white (hyphen)

oficina (Sp.) a S. American factory; *see also* **off-**

Oflag a German prison camp for officers

O'Flaherty, Liam (1896–1984) Irish novelist

OFM Order of Friars Minor

OFS Orange Free State

oft-times (hyphen)

ogam *use* **ogh-**

ogee (archit.) a moulding, adj. **ogeed**

ogham an ancient alphabet, used to write Pictish and Irish; *not* -gam, -gum, -hum

ogiv/e the diagonal rib of a vault, a pointed arch; **-al**

OGPU *or* **Ogpu** the Soviet 'United state political administration for struggle against espionage and counter-revolution' 1923–34; *see also* **KGB**

O'Grady, The (cap. *T*)

ogr/e a man-eating giant, pl. **-es**; f. **-ess**; adj. **-ish** *not* -eish

OH Ohio (postal abbr.)

OHBMS On Her, *or* His, Britannic Majesty's Service

O. Henry *see* **Henry**

OHG Old High German

Ohio postal abbr. **OH**; spell out in other contexts (such as refs.)

ohm SI unit of electrical resistance; symbol Ω; *see also* **mho**; from **Georg Simon Ohm** (1787–1854) German physicist; **ohmic/ contact, — loss** (two words), **ohmmeter** (one word, two *ms*)

OHMS On Her, *or* His, Majesty's Service

oho! an exclamation of surprise; *not* O ho, Oh ho, etc.

ohone *use* **och-**

oidium a fungus, *not* oï-

oikist *use* **oec-**

oilcake (one word)

oil can (two words)

oilcloth (one word)

oil-colour (hyphen)

oilfield (one word)

oil-fired (hyphen)

oil-gauge (hyphen, two words in US)

oil/ paint, — painting (two words)

oil-press (hyphen, two words in US)

oil rig (two words)

oil/skin, -stone (one word)

oil/ tanker, — well (two words)

oino/logy, -phile *use* **oen-**

oi polloi (Gr.) the masses, *use* **hoi polloi**

O.Ir. Old Irish

Oireachtas the legislature of the Irish Republic: the President, Dáil, and Seanad

OIRO offers in the region of, only in receipt of offer; *also* **o.i.r.o.**

Oistrakh,/ David (Fyodorovich) (1908–74) and **— Igor (Davidovich)** (b. 1931) his son, Russian violinists

O.It. Old Italian

Ojibwa Wis.

Ojibway a Native American tribe

OK 'all correct'; *not* Ok, ok, okay; Oklahoma (postal abbr.)

okapi a bright-coloured African ruminant

O'Keeffe, Georgia (1887–1986) US painter

Okeghem *see* **Ockeghem**

Okehampton Devon

O'Kelly, The (cap. *T*)

oker *use* **ochre**

Oklahoma off. abbr. **Okla.**, postal **OK**

okra an African plant, its edible seed pods; *not* oc(h)-, -o

OL Old Latin

Ol. Olympiad

Olaf, St the patron of Norway

old/ abbr. **o.**, **-clothes-man** (hyphens)

Old Bailey *see* **bailey**

Old Believer dissenter from the Orthodox Church, *formerly* **Raskolnik**

Old Church Slavonic the Slavonic language from the 9th c., also called **Old Bulgarian**

Old English the English language up to *c.*1150, abbr. **OE**; (typ.) a name for the English style of black letter: 𝔒𝔩𝔡 𝔈𝔫𝔤𝔩𝔦𝔰𝔥

old face (typ.) a type design based on the original roman type of the 15th c.; abbr. **OF**

old-fashioned (hyphen)

Old French the French language before *c.*1400, abbr. **OF**

'Old Glory' the US stars-and-stripes flag

'Old Hickory' *see* **Jackson, Andrew**

Old High German the High German language up to *c.*1200, abbr. **OHG**

'Old Hundredth' a hymn tune, *not* Hundred

Old Icelandic *see* **Old Norse**

Old Ionic the Greek dialect found in Homeric epics, abbr. **OI**

Old Irish the Irish language used in the 7th–11th cc., abbr. **O.Ir.**

Old Italian the Italian language used in the 4th–10th cc., abbr. **O.It.**

Old Latin pre-classical Latin, abbr. **OL**

old maid an elderly spinster, prissy man, card game (two words); *but* **old-maidish** (hyphen)

Old Man and the Sea, The novelette by Hemingway, 1952

Old Man of the Sea a character in *Arabian Nights* (caps.)

Oldmeldrum Grampian (one word)

Old Norse the Germanic language from which the Scandinavian languages are derived, specifically the language of Norway and its colonies until the 14th c.; abbr. **ON**; its general (non-lit.) form is sometimes called **Old Icelandic**, abbr. **O.Ic.**

Old Pals Act (three words, caps., no apos.)

Old Peculier a beer, *not* -iar

Old Possum's Book of Practical Cats a collection of humorous poems by T. S. Eliot, 1939

Old Pretender, the James Stuart (1688–1766) son of James II

Old Prussian a Baltic (*not* Germanic) language used before the 17th c. in E. Prussia, abbr. **OP**

Old Red Sandstone (geol.) (caps.)

Old Saxon the Saxon language in use until *c.*12th c. in NW Germany, abbr. **OS**

old school tie (three words)

Old Style according to the Julian calendar (before 1752), abbr. **OS** (full caps., no point); cf. **New Style**

old style/ (typ.) a type design, being a regularized old face; abbr. **OS**

old-style numerals (typ.) *see* **non-lining numerals**

Old Testament abbr. **OT**, **Old Test.**

old-time/ (adj., hyphen), **-r**

Old Welsh the Welsh language found in documents up to *c.*1150, abbr. **OW**

old woman a fussy man (two words), *but* **old-womanish** (hyphen)

¡olé! (Sp.) bravo!

olefin (chem.) a hydrocarbon, *not* -ine

oleiferous oil-producing, *not* olif-

oleograph a picture printed in oil colours

O level (hist.) 'ordinary level' examination (no hyphen)

OLG Old Low German

Olifants River S. Africa (no apos.)

Oligocene (geol.) (of or relating to) the third epoch of the Tertiary period (cap., not ital.)

olive/branch, — drab, — oil (two words)

Olivetan an order of monks, *not* -tian

Olivier, Laurence (Kerr), Baron (1907–89) English actor; *see also* **Ollivier**

olla podrida the Spanish national dish; a medley (not ital.)

Ollivier, Olivier Émile (1825–1913) French statesman and writer; *see also* **Olivier**

oloroso/ (a drink of) a medium-sweet sherry, pl. **-s**

Olympiad a celebration of Olympic Games (ancient *and* modern); period of four years between celebrations; abbr. **Ol.**

Olympian of Olympus, the abode of the Greek gods; as a noun, a dweller in Olympus or a superhuman person

Olympic of Olympia in Greece, of the games held there in antiquity, of the modern games

OM (Member of the) Order of Merit

o.m. old measurement

-oma a suffix forming nouns denoting tumours and other abnormal growths

omadhaun an Irish term of contempt (*not* the many variants)

Omagh Co. Tyrone

Omaha Nebr.

Oman/ SE Arabia, adj. **-i**

Omar Khayyám (1050–1123) Persian poet, astronomer, and mathematician

ombre a card game for three, popular in Europe in the 17th–18th cc.

ombré (of a fabric etc.) having gradual shading of colour from light to dark (not ital.)

ombuds/man a parliamentary commissioner or official appointed to investigate complaints against government departments; pl. **-men**

Omdurman Sudan

omega the last letter of the Gr. alphabet (Ω, ω); Ω the symbol for **ohm**

omelette *not* -et (US)

omertà a code of silence, esp. as practised by the Mafia

omicron the fifteenth letter of the Gr. alphabet (O, o), *not* omik-

omit/, -ted, -ting

omnibus/ pl. **-es**; *see also* **bus**

omnium gatherum a confused medley (not ital.)

ON Old Norse

oncoming (one word)

oncost an overhead expense (one word)

Ondaatje, (Philip) Michael (b. 1943) Sri-Lankan-born Canadian writer

ondes martenot (mus.) electronic keyboard producing one note of variable pitch (not caps., not ital.)

on dit (Fr. m. sing./pl.) gossip, hearsay ('people say'); pl. **on dits** (not used in Fr.)

one-and-twenty etc. (hyphens)

Oneida a socialist community started at Lake Oneida, NY, 1847

one-idea'd (hyphen)

O'Neill/, Eugene (Gladstone) (1888–1953) US playwright, **—, Moira** pseud. of **Agnes Higginson Skrine** (*fl.* 1900) Irish poet; **— of the Maine, Baron** the family name of Baron Rathcavan

oneiro/critic an interpreter of dreams; **-logy, -mancy**; *not* oniro-

oneness (**a** *not* an) (one word)

one/-night stand, -off (hyphens)

oneself is reflexive or intensive, **one's self** one's personal entity

one/-sided, -upmanship (hyphens)

ONF Old Norman French

ongoing continuing (one word)

onion-skin a thin, smooth, translucent paper

onirocritic etc., *use* **oneiro-**

online (one word)

onlook/er, -ing (one word)

on ne passe pas (Fr.) no thoroughfare

o.n.o. or near(est) offer

O'Nolan, Brian *see* **O'Brien, Flann**

onomastic/ relating to names, **-on** a vocabulary of proper names, **-s** the study of the origin and formation of (esp. personal) proper names (treated as sing.)

onomatopoe/ia word-formation by imitation of sound, abbr. **onomat.**; **-ial, -ian, -ic -ical, -ically**

onomatopo/esis, -etically *not* -poë-, -poie-

onrush (one word)

on-screen (hyphen)

onshore (adj., adv., one word)

onside (sport) (one word)

onstage (one word)

on-street (adj., hyphen)

Ontario Canada, abbr. **Ont.**

onto (prep., one word, *but* two words for *on* followed by prep. *to*)

ontolog/y the metaphysical study of the essence of things, **-ize** *not* -ise

onus/ a burden, pl. **-es** (not ital.)

onus probandi (Lat.) burden of proof (ital.)

% per cent symbol; *prefer* the words to the symbol except in scientific or heavily statistical work, in notes and parenthetical matter, and in tables and captions

o-o (ornith.) a Hawaiian honeyeater; cf. **ou**

oo- (biol.) prefix denoting egg, ovum; *not* oö- (US)

Oodeypore India, *use* **Udaipur**

oolong a cured Chinese tea, *not* ou-

oomiak *use* **umiak**

‰ per mille

Oostanaula a river, Ga.

Oostende Fl. for **Ostend** (Eng. spelling)

Ootacamund Madras, India; *not* Utakamand; colloq. abbr. **Ooty**

oozy muddy, *not* -ey

OP observation post, *Ordinis Praedicatorum* (of the Order of Preachers, or Dominicans)

op. operation; optime; *opus* (work), *opera* (works)

o.p. (theat.) opposite the prompter's side, or the actor's right; (bibliog.) out of print; (typ.) overproof

opah a deep-sea fish

op art art in geometrical form giving the optical illusion of movement (no point)

op. cit. *opere citato* (in the work quoted) (not ital.)

OPEC Organization of Petroleum Exporting Countries

op-ed (US) (of or relating to) (articles) opposite the editorial page in a newspaper (hyphen, not cap.)

open-and-shut case (two hyphens)

opencast in mining, with removal of the surface layers (one word)

open-door policy an opportunity for free trade and immigration (one hyphen)

open-heart/ of surgery, **-ed** (hyphens)

open-mouthed (hyphen, one word in US)

open-plan (adj., hyphen)

open sesame (not caps., two words)

openwork/, -ed, -ing (one word)

opera *see* **opus**

operable that can be operated (on)

opera buffa comic opera, in Fr. **opéra bouffe**

Opéra-Comique a Paris theatre (hyphen)

opéra comique (Fr. m.) opera with spoken dialogue

opera/ glasses, — house (two words)

opera seria (It.) 18th-c. opera on heroic theme

operation abbr. **op.**, pl. **ops.**

opercul/um (biol.) a cover, pl. **-a** (not ital.)

opere/ citato (Lat.) in the work quoted, abbr. **op. cit.**; **— in medio** in the midst of the work

operetta/ a light opera, pl. **-s**

ophicleide (mus.) the serpent, a bass or alto key-bugle; *not* -eid

ophiolatry the worship of serpents

ophiology the study of serpents, *not* ophid-

ophthalmic of the eye

Opie,/ Amelia (1769–1853) English novelist, wife of **— John** (1761–1807) English painter; **— Iona** (b. 1923) and **— Peter** (1918–82) her husband, authors and folklorists

opinion poll (two words)

o.p.n. *ora pro nobis* (pray for us)

opodeldoc a liniment

opopanax a perfume

Oporto Portugal, in Port. **Porto**

opp. opposed, opposite

opposite font (typ.) type set in a contrasting typeface, e.g. *italic* in roman text, *or* roman *in italic text*

oppressor *not* -er

ops. operations

opt. optative, optical, optician, optics

optical centring (typ.) positioning of text on the page so that it appears to the reader to be centred, although by measurement it is not

optime at Cambridge University, one next in merit to a **wrangler** (not ital.); abbr. **op.**

optimize make the best of, *not* -ise

optim/um pl. **-a**

optometrist (esp. US) a person who practises optometry, = **ophthalmic optician**

opus (Lat.) a work, pl. **opera** (not ital.); abbr. **op.**

opus/ anglicanum a type of fine pictorial embroidery produced in England during the Middle Ages, — **anglicum** a type of lavish manuscript illumination regarded as characteristically English

opuscul/um (Lat.) a minor work; pl. **-a**; in Eng. **opuscule** pl. **opuscules**

opus Dei (eccl.) the work of God, specifically the Divine Office, or liturgical worship in general (one cap.); a RC organization founded in Spain in 1927 (two caps.)

Opusdeista (RC) a member of the Opus Dei

opus magnum a great work, pl. **opera magna**; cf. **magnum opus**

opus number (mus.) (two words)

opus/ operantis (Lat.) the effect of a sacrament resulting from the spiritual disposition of the recipient (the Donatist view); — **operatum** the effect of a sacrament resulting from the grace flowing from the sacrament itself (the RC view)

OR operating room, operational research, Oregon (postal abbr.), other ranks

or (her.) gold or yellow colour

or. oriental

o.r. owner's risk

ora (Lat. pl.) mouths, *see* **os**

oral of or relating to the mouth, spoken; cf. **verbal**

orangeade *not* -gade

orange blossom (two words)

Orange Free State a province of S. Africa (three words), abbr. **OFS**

Orange/ism *not* -gism; **-man** (one word, cap.)

Orangeman's Day 12 July

orange/ peel, — squash, — stick (two words)

orange-wood (hyphen, one word in US)

orang-utan *not* ourang-, -outang, -utang (hyphen, one word in US; not ital.)

Oranmore and Browne, Baron

ora pro nobis (Lat.) pray for us, abbr. **o.p.n.**

orat. orator, -ical, -ically

oratio/ obliqua (Lat.) indirect speech, — **recta** direct speech

oratorio/ pl. **-s**; **titles of** — when cited, to be in ital.

orca any of various whales, esp. the killer whale; *not* -ka

Orcadian of or pertaining to Orkney

orchid a member of a family of mainly exotic flowering plants; **orchis** an (esp. wild) orchid or one of genus *Orchis*

Orczy, Baroness Emmuska (Emma) (1865–1947) Hungarian-born English novelist

ord. ordained, order, ordinal, ordinance, ordinary

Order abbr. **O.**; when referring to a society, to be cap., as the Order of Jesuits

order abbr. **ord.**; for the orders of classical architecture *see* **architect**; for the orders of angels *see* **celestial hierarchy**

order/ book, — form (two words)

order paper (esp. parl.) a written or printed order of the day, an agenda (two words)

ordin/ance a regulation, **-ary**; abbr. **ord.**

ordnance artillery, military stores

Ordnance/ Survey Department (caps.) abbr. **OSD**; — **datum** (one cap.) the standard sea level of the Ordnance Survey, abbr. **OD**

ordonnance the proper disposition of parts of a building or picture (not ital.)

Ordovician (geol.) (of or relating to) the second period of the Palaeozoic era

ordre du jour (Fr. m.) agenda of a meeting

öre a Swedish coin, equal to one-hundredth of krona; pl. same

øre a Danish or Norwegian coin, equal to one-hundredth of krone; pl. same

Ore. Oregon (off. abbr.)

oregano (*Origanum vulgare*) wild marjoram used for seasoning; *see also* **marjoram**

Oregon off. abbr. **Oreg.**, postal **OR**

O'Rell, Max pseud. of **Paul Blouet** (1848–1903) French author and journalist

oreo/graphy, -logy *use* oro-

Oresteia a trilogy by Aeschylus, 458 BC

Øresund (Dan.) the sound between Denmark and Sweden, in Sw. **Öresund**

oreweed *use* oar-

orfèvrerie (Fr. f.) goldsmith's work

orfray *use* -phrey

org. organ, -ic, -ism, -ization, -ized

organdie a fine translucent cotton muslin; *not* -di, -dy (US); in Fr. m. *organdi*

organize *not* -ise

organon (Gr.) instrument of thought, esp. a means of reasoning or system of logic; title of Aristotle's logical writings (cap., ital.)

organ/um (Lat.) organ, (mus.) polyphony; pl. **-a**

organza a thin, stiff transparent dress fabric

org/y *not* -ie; pl. **-ies**

oriel a small room built out from a wall, its window

Oriel College Oxford

Orient, the the East

orientate *prefer* **orient** in all senses, and with prefixes (e.g. dis-, re-) and suffixes (e.g. -ed, -able); -tate form not used in US

oriental/ (cap. as noun), **-ist**, abbr. **or.**, **orient.**

orientalize *not* -ise (not cap.)

oriflamme *not* -flamb

orig. origin, -al, -ally, -ate, -ated

Origen (185–253) a Father of the Church

original (Sp. typ.) copy

Origin of Species, The by C. Darwin, 1859

orinasal of the mouth and nose, *not* oro-

Orinoco river, S. America; cf. **oro-**

oriole any of two genera of birds: in the Old World genus *Oriolus*, in the New World genus *Icterus*

Orissa state in NE India

Oriya a native of Orissa, or the Indic language of Orissa or Odra, an ancient region corresponding to modern Orissa

orka *use* **-ca**

Orkney a region of Scotland

Orkneys an island group

orle (her.) a narrow band or border of charges near the edge of a shield

Orléans House of; a dép. of France (accent); **Orlean/ism, -ist** (no accent in Eng. or It.)

Orme's Head, Great *and* **Little** Gwynedd (apos.)

ormolu a gilded bronze or gold-coloured alloy (one word, not ital.)

Ormonde, Marquess of

Ormuzd (Middle Pers.) the Zoroastrian spirit of good; *not* the many variants, although **Ahura Mazda** (Old Pers.) is a common early form

orn/é (Fr.) f. **-ée** adorned

ornith. ornitholog/y, -ical

ornithorhynchus duck-billed platypus

orogen/esis (geol.) the process of formation of mountains; **-etic, -ic**

oro/graphy, -logy mountain description and science, *not* oreo-

oronasal *use* **ori-**

oronoco a Virginian tobacco, *not* the many variants; cf. **Ori-**

Oroonoko a novel by Aphra Behn, *c.*1678

orotund magniloquent, imposing

orphan (typ.) first line of a paragraph at the foot of a page or column; also called **club line**; *see also* **widow**

Orphe/us (Gr. myth.) a Thracian lyrist; **-an** like his music, entrancing

Orphic pertaining to **Orphism**, the mystic cult connected with Orpheus

orphrey an ornamental border, *not* -fray

orpine a purple-flowered plant, *not* -pin

orrery a model of the solar system

orris/ lace or embroidery, an iris plant; **-powder** (hyphen), **— root** (two words)

Or San Michele a church at Florence, *not* Saint

Ortega y Gasset, José (1883–1955) Spanish philosopher

ortho- (chem. prefix) *use* **o-**

orthoepy the scientific study of the correct pronunciation of words

ortho/paedic concerned with the cure of bone deformities; **-paedics, -paedist**; *not* -ped- (US)

ortolan a small edible bird (not ital.)

Orvieto an Italian white wine

Orwell/, George pseud. of **Eric Arthur Blair** (1903–50) English novelist and essayist, **-ian**

OS Old Saxon, Old School, Old Series, Old Side, Old Style (before 1752), old style (type), ordinary seaman, Ordnance Survey, (clothing) outsize

os Old Series (small caps.)

Os osmium (no point)

o.s. only son

o/s out of stock, outstanding

os (Lat.) a bone, pl. *ossa*

os (Lat.) a mouth, pl. *ora*

OSA Order of St Augustine

Osaka Japan, *not* Oz-

OSB Order of St Benedict

Osborn, Sherard (1822–75) British rear admiral and Arctic explorer

Osborne IoW

Osborne/ family name of Duke of Leeds; **—, John James** (1929–94) British playwright

Osbourne, (Samuel) Lloyd (1868–1947) US novelist and playwright (stepson of R. L. Stevenson)

Oscan (of or written in) the ancient language of Campania in Italy, related to Latin and surviving only in inscriptions

oscill/ate move between two points (cf. vacillate); **-ation, -ator, -atory, -ogram, -ograph, -oscope**

oscul/ate kiss, adhere closely; **-ant, -ation, -atory**

oscul/um (Lat.) a kiss, pl. **-a**; *osculum pacis* the kiss of peace

OSD Ordnance Survey Department, Order of St Dominic

Oset *use* **Ossett**

OSF Order of St Francis

O.Sl. Old Slavonic

Osler, Sir William (1849–1919) Canadian physician

Oslo capital of Norway, *formerly* Christiania

Osmanlı of the family of **Osman** (1259–1326) (*not* Othman) founder of the Ottoman Empire; *not* -lee, -lie, -ly (undotted 'i', not ital.)

osmium symbol **Os**

Osnabrück Germany, the Eng. form Osnaburg(h) is obsolete

o.s.p. *use* **ob.s.p.**

ossa (Lat. pl.) bones, *see* **os**

ossein bone cartilage, *not* -eine

Ossett W. Yorks.; *not* Oset, Osset

ossia (It. mus.) or

Ossie *use* **Aussie**

osso bucco (It. cook.) shin of veal stewed with vegetables (not ital.); in It. *ossobuco*, pl. *ossibuchi*

Ossory, Ferns, and Leighlin, Bishop of

o.s.t. (naut.) ordinary spring tides

Ostend Belgium; in Fr. and Ger. **Ostende**, in Fl. **Oostende**

ostensibl/e outwardly professed, **-y**

ostensive/ indicating by demonstration, **-ly**

osteomyelitis an inflammation of the marrow of the bone (one word)

osteria (It.) an inn

Österreich/ (Ger.) Austria, *not* Oe-; **-Ungarn** Ger. for Austria-Hungary (hyphen)

Ostiak *see* **Osty-**

ostinato/ (mus.) repeated melodic figure, pl. **-s**

ostler (hist.) a stableman at an inn; *see also* **hostler**

Ostmark (hist.) W. German name for the chief monetary unit of the former Democratic Republic of Germany, correctly the **Mark der DDR**, superseded in 1990 by the **Deutsche Mark**; *see also* **mark**

Ostpolitik the foreign policy of many Western European countries with reference to the former Communist bloc (not ital.)

ostrac/on a potsherd, used in ancient Greece for inscribing and voting; pl. **-a** (*not* -k- except in Gr. contexts); **-ize** exclude from favour; *not* -ise; **-ism**

Ostrogoth/ (hist.) a member of the E. branch of the Goths, who conquered Italy in the 5th–6th cc.; **-ic**

Ostrovsky, Aleksandr (**Nikolaevich**) (1823–86) Russian playwright

Ostyak/ former name for **Khanty**, **— Samoyed** former name for **Selkup**

O.Sw. Old Swedish

Oswaldtwistle Lancs., *not* -sle

Oświęcim Pol. for **Auschwitz**

OT occupational therapy, Old Testament

Otaheite *now* **Tahiti**

OTC *now* **STC**

O temporal O mores! (Lat.) what times, what manners!

O.Teut. Old Teutonic

other-world/ly, -liness (hyphen, one word in US)

Othman *use* **Os-**

otium/ (Lat.) leisure, **— cum dignitate** leisure with dignity, **— sine dignitate** leisure without dignity

otolith any of the small particles of calcium carbonate in the inner ear, *not* -lite (not ital.)

otorhinolaryngology the study of the ears, nose, and larynx

o.t.t. over the top

ottar (of roses) *use* **attar**

ottava rima (It.) a stanza of eight lines of ten or eleven syllables, rhyming *ababababcc*, as in Byron's *Don Juan*

Ottawa Canada, *not* Otto-

otto (of roses) *use* **attar**

Ottoman/ (adj.) (hist.) of or concerning the dynasty of Osman I, the branch of the Turks to which he belonged, or the empire ruled by his descendants; (noun) an Ottoman person; a Turk; pl. **-s** (cap.); **— Turkish** Old or Middle Turkish, written in the Arabic alphabet

ottoman/ an upholstered sofa, a fabric; pl. **-s** (not cap.)

Otway, Thomas (1652–85) English playwright

OU Open University, Oxford University

ou (ornith.) a Hawaiian honeycreeper; cf. **o-o**

Ouagadougou Burkina Faso, *not* Wagadugu

oubliette a secret dungeon (not ital.)

Oudenarde Belgium; battle, 1708; in Modern Fr. **Audenarde**, in Fl. **Oudenaarde**

Oudh India, *not* Oude

OUDS Oxford University Dramatic Society

Ouessant, l'île d' an island off Brittany; in Eng. **Ushant**, in Breton **Enez Eusa**

Oughtred, William (1575–1660) English mathematician

Ouida *see* **de la Ramée**

ouï-dire (Fr. m. sing./pl.) hearsay

Ouija (propr.) a board used in spiritualistic seances (cap.)

oukaz *use* **ukase**

Ouless, Walter William (1848–1933) British painter

oulong *use* oo-

ounce/, -s (not in scientific use), abbr. **oz**

OUP Oxford University Press

ourang-outang *use* **orang-utan**

Our/ Father, — Lady, — Lord (caps.)

ours (no apos.)

Our Saviour (cap.)

ousel *use* **ouz-**

out (typ.) an accidental omission of copy in composition

out- prefixed to a verb nearly always forms a single word unless the verb begins with *t*, as *out-talk, out-turn.*

out-and-out unreserved(ly) (hyphens)

out/back (noun), **-board, -building** (one word)

outcast (person) cast out (the general word)

outcaste (Anglo-Ind.) (a person) with no caste

out/dated, -door (adj.), **-doors** (noun and adv.) (one word)

Outeniqua Mountains S. Africa

outer (typ.) the side of a sheet containing the signature and first page

Outer House (Sc. law) the hall where judges of the Court of Session sit singly

outfield (sport) (one word)

outfit/, -ted, -ter, -ting

outgeneral/ outdo in generalship; **-led, -ling** (one *l* in US)

outgo/ expenditure, pl. **-es**

outgrowth (one word)

out-Herod Herod (hyphen, two caps.)

outhouse a building, esp. a shed, lean-to, barn, etc. built next to or in the grounds of a house; (US) an outdoor lavatory (one word)

outl/ie, -ier, -ying

outmanoeuvre (one word, no lig.) *not* -neu- (US)

outmoded (one word)

out/ of date, — of doors (hyphens when attrib.); **— of sorts** unwell

outpatient (one word)

output/ (verb), **-ting**, past and past part. **output**

outrance, à (Fr.) to the bitter end, all-out; *not* à l'outrance

outr/é (Fr.) f. **-ée** eccentric

outrider (one word)

outrival/led, -ling (one *l* in US)

out/rush, -size (one word)

outspan (S. Afr.) unyoke, a place for doing this

out/standing, -station (one word)

outstrip/, -ped, -ping

out-swinger (sport) (hyphen)

out/-take, -talk, -think, -thrust, -top, -trade, -tray, -turn (hyphens, one word in US)

outv/ie, -ier, -ying (one word)

outward bound (hyphen when attrib.)

Outward Bound Trust (no hyphen)

outwit/, -ted, -ting

outwork (one word)

ouvert/ (Fr.) f. **-e** open

ouvri/er (Fr.) a workman, f. **-ère**

ouzel/ a type of thrush (**ring —**), a type of diving bird (**water —**); (arch.) a blackbird; *not* ous-

ouzo/ a Greek aniseed-flavoured spirit, pl. **-s**

oven/proof (one word)

oven-ready (hyphen)

ovenware (one word)

over/-abundant (hyphen, one word in US)

over/act, -active (one word)

overage an excess or surplus

over age above an age limit (two words, hyphen when attrib.)

overall (noun, adv., and adj., one word)

overambitious (one word)

over-anxious (hyphen, one word in US)

over/balance, -blown, -board, -book -burden, -burdensome, -careful (one word)

overcast (meteor.) abbr. **o.**

over/confidence, -confident, -critical (one word)

overcrowd/, -ed (one word)

over-curious (hyphen, one word in US)

Over Darwen Lancs., *use* **Darwen**

over-delicate (hyphen, one word in US)

overdevelop/, -ed, -ing (one word)

overemphas/is, -ize *not* -ise (one word)

overexcite (one word)

over-exercise (hyphen, one word in US)

over/exert, -familiar (one word)

overfulfil *not* -fill (US)

over/generalize, -generous (one word)

Overijssel a province of the Netherlands

over/joyed -land (one word)

over-large (hyphen, one word in US)

over/long, -look (one word)

over-many (hyphen)

overnice (one word)

overnight/, -er (one word)

over/-optimistic, -particular (hyphens)

over/pass, -populate, -produce, -rate, -reach, -react, -ride, -ripe, -rule (one word)

overrun (typ.) carry over words from one line or page to the next (one word)

overseas (one word)

oversensitive/, -ness (one word)

overset (typ.) set up (type) in excess of the available space

over/sexed, -sight, -simplify, -slaugh, -solicitous, -subscribe, -subtle, -use, -value, -view, -weight, -winter, -work (one word)

Ovid (in Lat., **Publius Ovidius Naso**) (43 BC–AD 17) Roman poet

ovol/o (archit.) a moulding, pl. **-i**

ov/um an egg, pl. **-a** (not ital.)

Owens College Manchester (no apos.)

owner abbr. **O.**

Ox. Oxford

Oxbridge Oxford and Cambridge Universities regarded collectively

Oxenstjerna, Count Axel (1583–1654) Swedish statesman

ox-eye/, — daisy (hyphen)

Oxf. Oxford

Oxfam Oxford Committee for Famine Relief

Oxford abbr. **Ox.**, **Oxf.**

Oxford Almanack not *-ac*

Oxford blue a dark blue, sometimes with a purple tinge; cf. **Blue**

Oxford comma a serial comma

Oxford corners (hist.) ruled border lines crossing and extending slightly beyond each other at the corners

Oxford Down a breed of sheep produced by crossing Cotswold and Hampshire Down sheep (two caps.)

Oxford English Dictionary, The abbr. **OED**, *not NED*

Oxford grey (US hist. sl.) a black jazz musician

Oxford Group a religious movement founded at Oxford in 1921 (two caps.), later named Moral Re-Armament

Oxford hollow (bind.) (a binding with) a flattened paper tube attached to the back of the gatherings and to the spine of the binding

Oxford Movement an Anglican High Church movement started in Oxford in 1833 (two caps.)

Oxfordshire abbr. **Oxon.**

Oxford University/ abbr. **OU**; — — **Press** only the full name is never preceded by the definite article: *not* 'the Oxford University Press' *but* 'the University Press', 'the Press', 'the OUP'; abbr. **OUP**

oxhide (one word)

oxide *not* -id, -yd, -yde

oxidation *prefer to* oxidization; *not* oxy-

oxidize etc.; *not* -ise, oxy-

Oxon. Oxfordshire; (Lat.) *Oxonia, Oxonium* (Oxford), *Oxoniensis* (of Oxford)

Oxon: the signature of the Bishop of Oxford (colon)

Oxonium (Lat.) Oxford

ox/tail, -tongue (one word)

oxychloride *not* oxi-

oxyd/e, -ation, -ize *use* oxi-

oxygen/ symbol **O**, **-ize** *not* -ise

Oxyrhynchus Egypt, a source of papyri

oxytone (Gr. gram.) (a word) with an acute accent on the last syllable

oyez! hear ye! *not* oyes

oz ounce, **-s** (no point, not in scientific use)

Ozaka Japan, *use* **Os-**

Ozalid/ (propr.) (print.) a photographic reproduction process for generating proofs on paper from film; **combined** — a proof made simultaneously from more than one Ozalid; in the USA proofs prepared by a similar process are called **blues**, from their colour

ozone-friendly (hyphen)

ozone/ hole, — layer (two words)

Ozu, Yasujiro (1903–63) Japanese film director

'Ozymandias' a sonnet by Shelley, 1818

Ozzie *use* **Aussie**

Pp

P (car) park, (chess) pawn, (as prefix) peta-, phosphorus, (phys.) poise, the fifteenth in a series

₱ Philippine peso

P. pastor, post, president, prince, (Fr.) *Père* (Father); (Lat.) *Papa* (Pope), *Pater* (Father), pontifex (a bishop), *populus* (people)

p penny, pennies, pence; (as prefix) pico-

p. page, participle, (meteor.) passing showers, passive, past, per; (Fr.) *passé* (past), *pied* (foot), *pouce* (inch), *pour* (for); (Lat.) *partim* (in part), *per* (through), *pius* (holy), *pondere* (by weight), *post* (after), *primus* (first), *pro* (for)

p- (chem. prefix) para- (ital., always hyphenated), *prefer to* para-

p (mech.) pressure, (mus.) piano (softly)

¶ (typ.) paragraph symbol, pilcrow

PA Pennsylvania (postal abbr.), personal assistant, Press Association, public address, Publishers Association

Pa (phys.) pascal, (chem.) protactinium (no point)

Pa. Pennsylvania (off. abbr.)

p.a. per annum (yearly)

Paarl Cape Province, S. Africa

pabulum (not ital.)

PABX private automatic branch exchange

pace/ (Lat.) with due respect to (one holding a different view), **— tua** by your leave

pacha *use* **pasha**

pachinko a Japanese form of pinball

pachisi a four-handed Indian board game with six cowries used like dice, in Hind. *pachīsī*; adopted in the West as **parcheesi** *or* **parchesi** (not cap.), in Sp. **parchis**; a simplified form is known in Europe as **ludo**

pachyderm any thick-skinned mammal, esp. an elephant or rhinoceros

pachymeter an instrument for measuring small thicknesses, *not* pacho-; cf. **micrometer**

pacifier (US) a baby's dummy

package/, -s abbr. pkg.; **— holiday, — tour** (two words)

pack/ animal, — drill (two words)

packet/, -ed, -ing

packhorse (one word)

packing/ box, — case (two words)

packing/-needle, -sheet (hyphens)

pack rat (two words)

pack/saddle, -thread (one word)

pad/, -ded, -ding

paddle/ boat, — steamer, — wheel (two words)

Paderewski, Ignacy Jan (1860–1941) pianist, first Premier of the Polish Republic 1919

Padishah a title applied to the Shah of Iran, the Sultan of Turkey, the Great Mogul, and the (British) Emperor of India; in Pers. *pādshāh*

padlock (one word)

padre (colloq.) a chaplain

padre (It., Port., Sp.) father, applied also to a priest

padron/e (It.) master, employer; pl. **-i**

Padua in It. **Padova**

paduasoy a strong corded silk fabric, *not* the many variants

p.ae. *partes aequales* (equal parts)

paean a song of triumph, *not* pean; cf. **paeon, peon**

paedagogy *use* ped-

paederast/, -y *use* ped-

paediatric/ (med.) relating to children (esp. their diseases); **-s** the science, usually treated as sing.; **-ian**; *not* ped- (US)

paedo/baptism, -phile, -philia (one word), *not* ped- (US)

paella a Spanish dish of rice, saffron, chicken, and seafood

paeon (Gr. and Lat. prosody) a foot of one long and three short syllables; cf. **paean, peon**

paeony *use* pe-

Paesiello, Giovanni (1740–1816) Italian composer of operas

Paganini, Niccolò (1782–1840) Italian violinist and composer

paganize *not* -ise

page (typ.) one side of a leaf; type, film, etc., made up for printing on this; abbr. **p.**, pl. **pp.**; (comput.) to present text on a VDU in static full-screen units (cf. **scroll**)

pageboy a boy serving as a page, a hairstyle (one word)

paginate to number pages

pagination (typ.) the numbering of the pages of a book, journal, etc.; may be in headline or at foot of page; generally omitted on opening pages of chapters, main sections, etc.

Pagliacci, I an opera by Leoncavallo, 1892

Pahang see **Malaya, Federation of**

Pahlanpur *use* **Pal-**

Pahlavi (of) the language and writing system of Persia under the Sassanians; *not* Pehlevi

paid abbr. pd.

pai-hua a modern form of written Chinese based on colloquial speech

paillasse (Fr. f.) a straw mattress, in Eng. **palliasse**

pailles/ (Fr. cook. f.) straws, **— de parmesan** cheese straws

Pain, Barry (Eric Odell) (1864–1928) English humorous writer; *see also* **Paine**; **Payn**; **Payne**

pain (Fr. m.) bread

Paine, Thomas (1737–1809) English-born political philosopher and American patriot, author of *The Rights of Man; see also* **Pain**; **Payn**; **Payne**

painim *use* **pay-**

painkill/er, -ing (one word)

paint. painting

paint/box, -brush (one word)

paintings, titles of when cited, to be in italic if named by the painter, roman quoted if popularly identified as such by others

paintwork (one word)

pair/, -s abbr. **pr.**

pais/a a coin of India, Pakistan, Nepal, and Bangladesh; pl. **-e**

paisano/ (in Sp.-speaking areas) a fellow-countryman, a peasant (not cap.); (Mex. and SW US) a name of the roadrunner or chaparral cock; (Mex.) a nickname for a Spaniard (cap.); pl. **-s**

Paisley (a soft woollen garment or fabric having) a distinctive detailed pattern of curved feather-shaped figures (cap. except in US)

Paiute (of or relating to) (a member of) a Native American people, originally inhabiting the south-west, or their language

pajamas (US) = **pyjamas**

Pak. Pakistan, -i

pakeha (Maori) a white man

Pakistan/ adj. **-i**; abbr. **Pak.**; *see also* **Bangladesh**

Pakhto *see* **Pashto**

Pal. Palestine

palace cap. only as part of a name (e.g. Blenheim Palace, Pardo Palace), or as an abbreviated reference to Buckingham Palace

Palaearctic (zool.) of the northern Old World, *not* Palaeoarctic

palaeo- a prefix meaning ancient, *not* -eo- (US)

Palaeocene (geol.) (of or relating to) the earliest epoch of the Tertiary period; *not* Paleocene (US)

palaeography the study of ancient writing, abbr. **palaeog.**

palaeolithic (archaeol.) *not* paleo- (US)

palaeology the study of antiquities, *not* paleo- (US)

palaeontology the study of fossils, abbr. **palaeont.**; *not* paleo- (US)

Palaeozoic (geol.) (of or relating to) an era of geological time marked by the appearance of marine and terrestrial plants and animals, esp. invertebrates; *not* Paleo- (US)

palaestra a Greek or Roman wrestling school, *not* pale-

palais (Fr. m.) palace; dance hall (not ital.)

Palanpur Rajasthan, India; *not* Pahl-

palatable *not* -eable

palate the roof of the mouth, sense of taste; cf. **palette**, **pallet**

palatinate the territory under the jurisdiction of a Count Palatine

palatine/ (hist.) (of an official or feudal lord) having local authority that elsewhere belongs only to a sovereign (Count Palatine); (of a territory) subject to this authority (cap., but often lower case in hist. contexts); (med.) of or connected with the palate, — **bone** each of two bones forming the hard palate

palazz/o (It.) palace, a grand house of a great man or family; pl. **-i**

pal/e, -ish

paleo- *use* **palaeo-** (except in US)

Palestin/e abbr. **Pal.**; **-ian**

palestra *use* **palae-**

paletot an overcoat (no accent, not ital.)

palette/ an artist's thin portable board for colour-mixing, — **knife** (two words); cf. **palate**; **pallet**

Palgrave, Francis Turner (1824–97) English anthologist

Pali an Indic language used in the canonical books of Buddhists

palimony (esp. US colloq.) an allowance made by one member of an unmarried couple to the other after separation

palimpsest a piece of writing material or manuscript on which the original writing has been effaced to make room for other writing; a monumental brass turned and re-engraved on the reverse side

palindrom/e a word or phrase that reads the same backwards as forwards, ignoring punctuation and spacing; **-ic**

Palladian characterized by wisdom or learning, after **Pallas**, epithet of the Greek goddess Athene; also a Renaissance modification of the classic Roman style of architecture, from **Andrea Palladio** (1518–80) Italian architect

palladium a safeguard or source of protection; an image of Pallas Athene; a metallic element, symbol **Pd**

pallet a mattress, projection on a machine or clock, valve in an organ, platform for carrying loads; cf. **palate**; **palette**

palliasse a straw mattress, in Fr. f. *paillasse*

palliat/e alleviate, minimize; (adj. and noun) **-ive**

palli/um an ecclesiastical pall; (hist.) a man's large rectangular cloak; (med.) the cerebral cortex; (zool.) the mantle of a mollusc or brachiopod; pl. **-ums**, **-a**

Pall Mall a London street (two words)

pall-mall (hist.) a game

pallor paleness, *not* -our

Pallottine Fathers a RC society of priests

Palmers Green London (no apos.)

palmetto/ a small palm tree, pl. **-s**

palm/ honey, — oil (two words)

Palm Sunday one before Easter (two words, caps.)

Palomar, Mount (observatory, telescope) Calif.

palp/us an insect's feeler, pl. **-i**

palsgrav/e a Count Palatinate, f. **-ine**

palstave (archaeol.) a type of bronze etc. chisel

paly (her.) divided into equal vertical shapes

pam. pamphlet

Pamir a tableland in Cent. Asia, *not* -irs

pampas grass (two words)

Pan. Panama

panacea a cure-all (not ital.)

pan-African (hyphen)

panakin *use* **panni-**

pan/-American (*but* **Pan American Union**), **-Anglican** (hyphens)

Panama/ Cent. America, abbr. **Pan.**; **-nian**; a hat of strawlike material (not cap.)

panatella a long thin cigar (not ital.)

panchayat a village council in India

Panchen/ a Tibetan Buddhist title of respect (cap.); — **Lama** the lama of the Tashi Lhunpo monastery, ranking next after the Dalai Lama; — **Rinpoche** a religious teacher held in high regard by Tibetan Buddhists

Pandaemonium the abode of all the demons in Milton's *Paradise Lost* (cap.); cf. **pande-**

Pandean pipes *not* -aean (cap.)

pandect a treatise covering the whole of a subject; the digest of Roman law made under the Emperor Justinian in the 6th c. (pl., cap.)

pandemonium (a scene of) uproar, utter confusion (not cap.); cf. **Pandae-**

Pandit, Mrs Vijaya Lakshmi (1900–90) Indian diplomat

pandit *use* **pun-**, *but* **Pandit** (cap.) as Indian title

P&O Peninsular and Oriental Steamship Company (no points)

p. & p. postage and packing

panegyr/ic a formal speech or essay of praise; **-ical**, **-ist**, **-ize** *not* -ise

panel/, -led, -ling, -list (one *l* in US)

panem et circenses (Lat.) bread and circus games

paner (Fr. cook.) dress with egg and breadcrumbs

pan-Hellen/ic, -ism (hyphen) *not* Panhellenic (except in US or in an institutional name)

panic/, -ked, -ky

panikin *use* **panni-**

pan-Islam/, -ic (hyphen)

Panizzi, Sir Antonio (1797–1879) Italian-born English librarian

Panjabi the language of Punjab (*pañjābī*)

panjandrum a mock title

pannikin a small metal drinking cup; *not* pana-, pani-, -can

panopl/y pl. **-ies**; **-ied**

pan pipe *not* Pan's (two words)

pan-Slav/ic, -ism *not* pan-Scl-

pantagraph *use* **panto-**

Pantaloon a character in Italian comedy

panta rhei (Gr.) all things are in a state of flux

pantheon the deities of a people collectively; a temple to all gods, (cap.) circular one in Rome

Panthéon Paris

panther a leopard, esp. with black fur; (US var.) a puma

panto/ (colloq.) pantomime, pl. **-s**

pantograph an instrument for copying to scale; a framework for transmitting overhead current to electric vehicle; *not* panta-, penta-

pants (US) = **trousers**

pantyhose (US) = women's tights (one word)

panzer/ armoured (not ital.), in Ger. m. *Panzer*; — **division** (two words)

Pão de Açúcar (Port.) Sugarloaf Mountain, Rio de Janeiro, Brazil

Papa (Lat.) Pope, abbr. **P.**

papabile (It.) suitable to be pope, more generally, for high office

papain an enzyme obtained from unripe papayas

papal/, -ly

Papal States, the (hist.) (caps.)

Papandreou,/ Andreas Georgios (1919–96) Greek Prime Minister 1981–9, 1993–6; — **Georgios** (1888–1968) his father, Greek statesman

paparazz/o a freelance photographer who pursues celebrities, pl. **-i** (not ital.)

papaw *use* **pawpaw** (except in US); *see also* **papaya**

papaya tropical Amer. evergreen tree and its fruit; also called **pawpaw**

papel (Sp. m.) paper; (as of an actor) role, part

paperback a softcover book (one word)

paper/ boy, — clip, — girl (two words, one word in US)

paper tiger (two words)

paper/weight, -work (one word)

papet/ier (Fr.) f. **-ière** a stationer

Papier (Ger. n.) paper (cap.)

papier (Fr. m.) paper (not cap.)

papier mâché moulded paper pulp (two words, not ital.)

papill/a a small protuberance on a living surface, pl. **-ae; -ary, -ate, -ose**

papillon (Fr. m.) butterfly; (not ital.) a breed of dog

papoose a Native American infant, *not* papp-

Pap/ smear, — test (US) test to detect cancer of the cervix or womb (cap.), from **Dr George Papanicolaou** (1883–1962) US scientist

Papst (Ger. m.) Pope (cap.)

Papua New Guinea/, -n; abbr. **PNG**

papyr/us an ancient writing material or a MS written on it, pl. **-i; -ology** the study of papyri; **-ologist**

par equality (of exchange etc.) (no point); cf. **parr**

par. paragraph, parallel, parish

par (Fr.) by, out of, in, through

Pará Brazil, *now* **Belém**

Para. Paraguay

para. paragraph, pl. **paras.**

para- (chem. prefix) (ital.)

paracetamol a drug used to reduce pain and relieve fever (not cap.)

Paraclete the Holy Spirit as advocate or counsellor (John 14: 16, 26, etc.) (cap.)

paradiddle a fast drum beat with syncopated alternate strokes, *not* tara-

paradisaical *not* -iacal

paraffin/ *not* -fine; an inflammable waxy or oily substance distilled from petroleum or shale; **— oil** its liquid form = (US) **kerosene; — wax** = (US) **paraffin**

paragraph/ a distinct section of type-matter on a page; abbr. **par., para.**; pl. **pars., paras.**; symbol ¶ (pilcrow); **— sign** symbol ¶ used in manuscripts to mark the beginning of a new section or part of a narrative or discourse until replaced by indenting; *now* used to flag marginal notes or to introduce an editorial *obiter dictum* or protest

Paraguay/ S. America, **-an**; abbr. **Para.**

parakeet *not* -quet, -oquet, -okeet, parr-

parakýisma *see* **sampi**

paralanguage elements or factors in communication that are ancillary to language proper, e.g. intonation and gesture

paralipomena things omitted from a work and added as a supplement, esp. the OT books of Chronicles; *not* -leip-

paralips/is drawing attention to a subject by affecting not to mention it, pl. **-es**; *not* -leipsis (except in specifically Hellenist contexts), -lepsis, -lepsy

parallel/ abbr. **par.; -ed, -ing**

parallelepiped a solid figure bounded by six parallelograms; *not* -ipiped, -opiped

parallel mark (‖) (typ.)

paralogize reason falsely, *not* -ise

paralyse *not* -ise, -ize, -yze (US)

Paramatta *use* **Parra-**

parameci/um (zool.) *not* -aecium, -oecium; pl. **-a**

parameter (math.) a variable factor constant in a particular case; avoid using in general senses

paranoi/a a mental disorder esp. characterized by delusions of persecution and self-importance, *not* -noea; **-ac, -d**

paraph the flourish at the end of a signature

paraphernalia (pl.) miscellaneous belongings, items of equipment, etc.

paraquat a quick-acting herbicide

paraquet *use* **-keet**

parasitize *not* -ise

parata/xis (gram.) the juxtaposition of clauses etc. one after another, without words to indicate coordination or subordination; cf. **hypotaxis; -ctic**

paratroops airborne parachute troops

par avion (Fr.) by airmail

parbleu! (Fr. colloq.) an exclamation of surprise

parcel/, -led, -ling (one *l* in US)

parcel post (two words)

parcen/ary (law) a joint heirship, **-er** joint heir

parcheesi, parchesi *see* **pachisi**

parchment/ an animal skin prepared for writing, **-paper** imitation parchment (hyphen)

parcimony etc., *use* **parsi-**

Pardo Palace a royal palace outside Madrid; cf. **Prado**

parenthes/is the upright curves ( ); pl. **-es**, abbr. **parens.**

parenthesize insert as a parenthesis, *not* -ise

parerg/on a subsidiary work, pl. **-a** (not ital.)

par excellence pre-eminently (not ital.)

par exemple (Fr.) for example, abbr. **p. ex.**

pargana in India, a parish or subdivision of a district, *not* pergunnah

parget/ed, -er, -ing (*not* -tt-)

par hasard (Fr.) by chance, *not* haz-

parheli/on a bright spot on the solar halo, *also called* **mock sun, sun dog**; pl. **-a**

pariah (Ind.) one of low or no caste, a social outcast

parietal (anat.) of the wall of the body or any of its cavities, (bot.) of the wall of a hollow structure etc., (US) relating to residence within a college

pari-mutuel a totalizator (not ital.)

pari passu (Lat.) at the same rate

Paris, Matthew (d. 1259) English monk and historian, *not* 'of Paris'

parish/ abbr. **par.**, — **priest** abbr. **PP**

Parisian of Paris (cap.), *Parisienne* (Fr. f.) a woman of Paris (cap.)

park abbr. **P, pk.**

Park, Mungo (1771–1806) Scottish traveller in Africa

parka a waterproof hooded jacket, originally worn by the Inuit

parking lot (US) = **car park**

parking/ **meter**, — **ticket** (two words)

Parkinson's/ **disease** a chronic nervous palsy, studied by **James Parkinson** (1755–1824); — **law** the law, facetiously expounded by **Cyril Northcote Parkinson** (1909–93), that work expands to fill the time available for it

parkway (US) an open landscaped highway, (UK) a railway station with extensive parking facilities

parlay/ (US) use money won on a bet as a further stake, exploit a position or circumstance successfully, an act of this, pl. **-s**; **-ed, -ing**

parley/ (hold) a conference to settle a dispute, pl. **-s**; **-ed, -ing**

Parliament/ (UK) the highest legislature, consisting of the Sovereign, the House of Lords, and the House of Commons (cap.), abbr. **Parl.** (not cap. as a general term); — **House** the Scottish Law Courts in Edinburgh

parlour *not* -or (US)

Parmesan a hard cheese made at Parma and elsewhere (cap.), in It. *parmigiano*

Parnass/**us, Mount** Greece, sacred to the Muses; now **Líakoura**; **-ian** poetic, (of or relating to) (a member of) a group of French poets in the late 19th c., emphasizing strictness of form, named from the anthology *Le Parnasse contemporain*, 1866

parochialize *not* -ise

parokeet *use* **para-**

parol (law) oral, not written; *not* -le

parol/**e** release a prisoner before the expiry of sentence; as verb, present part. **-ing**; **-ee** one paroled

paronomasia wordplay

paronym a word cognate with another, a word formed from a foreign word

paroquet *use* **parakeet**

paroxysm a fit of pain, passion, laughter

paroxytone (Gr. gram.) (a word) with acute accent on penultimate syllable

parquet/ wooden flooring, (US) the stalls of a theatre; as verb, past and past part. **-ed**; **-ry**; in Fr. f. *parqueterie*

Parr,/ **Catherine** (1512–48) last wife of Henry VIII; — **Thomas, 'Old'** (?1483–1635) English centenarian

parr a young salmon, *not* par

parrakeet *use* **para-**

Parramatta New South Wales, Australia; *not* -mata, Para-

parramatta a light dress fabric (not cap.)

Parratt, Sir Walter (1841–1924) English organist

parricid/**e** a murder(er) of a near relative or of a revered person, **-al**; *see also* **patri-**

parroquet *use* **parakeet**

pars. paragraphs

parse describe (a word in context) grammatically, stating its inflection, relation to the sentence, etc.; resolve (a sentence) into its component parts and describe them grammatically; (comput.) perform a syntax analysis on a string of input symbols

parsec (astr.) a unit of stellar distance, equal to about 3.25 light years (3.08 × 10^16 metres); abbr. **pc**; although not an SI unit, it may be used with SI units and prefixes, e.g. *megaparsec*, abbr. **Mpc**

Parsee/ a descendant of the Zoroastrians who fled from Persia to India in the 7th–8th cc., in Pers. *pārsī*; pl. **-s**

Parsifal an opera by Wagner, 1879

parsimon/**y** meanness, **-ious**; *not* parci-

parsnip (bot.) *not* -ep

part abbr. **pt.**

part. participle

partable (law) *use* **-ible**

parterre a flower bed or garden (not ital.); (US) an area in a theatre between the orchestra and audience

partes aequales (Lat.) equal parts, abbr. **p. ae.**

part-exchange (verb, hyphen), **part exchange** (noun, two words)

Parthenon the temple of Athene on the Acropolis at Athens

Parthian shot etc., a glance or remark made when turning away (one cap.)

parti (Fr. m.) party (faction), match (marriage), resolution (good *or* bad); **Parti québécois** Canadian political party (one cap., not ital)

partible (law) that must be divided, *not* -able

participator *not* -er

participle a verbal adjective, abbr. **p., part.**

particoloured variegated, *not* party- (one word)

particularize *not* -ise

partie/ (Fr. f.) part, — *carrée* a party of two men and two women

partim (Lat.) in part, abbr. **p.**

parti pris (Fr. m.) a preconceived view, a bias

partisan an adherent of a party (frequently derog.), (mil.) a member of a resistance movement; *not* -zan

partita/ (mus.) a suite, an air with variations; pl. **-s**

partout (Fr.) everywhere

part-owner (hyphen)

part-song (hyphen)

part time (hyphen when attrib.)

party (Conservative, Labour, Liberal, Communist, etc.) not cap. unless integral to the official title, as in 'Social Democratic and Labour Party'

party-coloured *use* **partic-**

party/ line, — wall (two words)

parvenu/ f. **-e** an upstart; pl. **-s, -es** (not ital.)

Pasadena Calif.

pascal (phys.) the SI unit of pressure and stress, equal to one newton per square metre (not cap.); abbr. **Pa**; (comput.) a programming language (cap. or all caps.); both named after **Blaise Pascal** (1623–62) French mathematician, physicist, and religious philosopher

paschal of or relating to the Jewish Passover, or to Easter

Pas-de-Calais a dép. of France (hyphens), **Pas de Calais** (Fr. m.) Strait of Dover (three words)

pas de/ chat a special leap in ballet, **— — deux** dance for two, **— — quatre** dance for four, **— — trois** dance for three (not ital.); *see also* **pas seul**

pasha/ (Turk.) a title placed *after* the name, *not* -cha; in Turk. *paşa*, in Fr. m. *pacha*; **-lic** a pasha's province, in Turk. *paşalık*

Pasha, Enver *see* **Enver Pasha**

Pashto the Iranian language of the Pathans, spoken in Pakistan and Afghanistan and sometimes called Afghan *or* **Pakhto** (to reflect northern pronunciation); *not* -u, Push-

Pašić, Nikola (1845–1926) Serbian statesman, Prime Minister of Serbia five times between 1891 and 1918, and of the Kingdom of Serbs, Croats, and Slovenes 1921–4, 1924–6

paso doble a ballroom dance in march style (not ital.)

pasquinade a lampoon or satire, originally one displayed in a public place

pass. passive

passable barely satisfactory, just adequate, or (of a road, pass, etc.) that can be passed; cf. **passible**

passacaglia (mus.) an instrumental piece based on an old dance

passant (her.) (of an animal) walking and looking to the dexter side, with three paws on the ground and the right forepaw raised

pass/band, -book (one word)

Passchendaele Belgium; battle, 1917

passé past, faded; abbr. **p.**; in Fr. *pass/é*, f. **-ée**

passed master *use* **past**

passementerie (Fr. f.) embroidery, *not* passi-

passepartout a master key, a picture frame consisting of glass held to a backing by adhesive tape along the edges (not ital.; hyphen in US); the valet in Verne's *Around the World in Eighty Days* (cap.)

passer-by pl. **passers-by** (hyphen, one word in US)

pas seul a dance for one person; *see also* **pas de**

Passfield *see* **Webb**

passible (theol.) capable of feeling or suffering; cf. **passable**

passim (Lat.) here and there throughout

Passion Week follows Passion Sunday (fifth in Lent)

passive abbr. **p., pass.**

pass/ key, — mark (two words)

pass/port, -word (one word)

past abbr. **p.**

pastel/ an artist's crayon, **-list**; cf. **pastille**

Pasternak, Boris (**Leonidovich**) (1890–1960) Russian novelist and poet

pasteurize sterilize, *not* -ise

pastiche a medley, esp. a work of art, made up from or imitating various sources; in It. *pasticcio*

pastille a confection, odorizer; *not* -il; cf. **pastel**

pastis an aniseed-flavoured aperitif (not cap.)

past master a former master in a guild, an expert; *not* passed

pastorale/ (mus.) a pastoral composition, pl. **-s**

past participle abbr. **past part.**

pat. patent, -ed

Pata. Patagonia

patchouli (a perfume from) a strongly scented E. Indian plant, *not* -ly

patchwork (one word)

pate (arch., colloq.) the head, esp. representing the seat of intellect

pâte the paste of which porcelain is made (not ital.)

pâté/ spread or paste of meat, fish, etc. (not ital.); **— de foie gras** a spiced paste of fatted goose liver

patell/a (anat.) kneecap, pl. **-ae**; adj. **-ar**

paten the dish used at Eucharist, a circular metal plate; *not* -in, -ine

Patent Office abbr. **Pat. Off.**

Pater (Lat.) Father, abbr. **P.**

paterfamilias the father of a family, pl. **patresfamilias**

paternoster the Lord's Prayer (esp. in Lat.), a bead in a rosary, a lift consisting of a series of doorless moving compartments

pater patriae (Lat.) father of his country

Paterson NJ

Paterson, William (1658–1719) British founder of the Bank of England

path. patholog/y, -ical

Pathan a member of a Pashto-speaking people inhabiting NW Pakistan and SE Afghanistan

Pathétique name of a sonata by Beethoven (in full *Grande sonate pathétique*) and symphony by Tchaikovsky (a subtitle authorized by him)

pathos a quality in speech, writing, events, etc. that excites pity or sadness; cf. **bathos**

Patiala E. Punjab, India

patin/, -e *use* **paten**

patio/ an inner court, paved area of garden; pl. **-s**

pâtisserie pastry (not ital.); *pâtiss/ier*, f. *-ière* (Fr.) pastry cook (ital.)

Patna a long-grain rice (cap.)

patois a (regional) dialect of the common people, differing from the literary language; pl. same (not ital.)

Patres/ (Lat.) fathers, abbr. **PP**; **— *Conscripti*** Conscript Fathers, abbr. **PP C**

patria potestas (Rom. law) a father's power over his family

patricide a murder(er) of one's own father; *see also* **parricide**

patrol/, -led, -ling

patrolman (US) = **police constable**

patronize *not* -ise

patronymic a name derived from the name of a father or ancestor, as *Johnson, O'Brien, Ivanovich*

pattée (of a cross) having almost triangular arms becoming very broad at the ends so as to form a square

Pattenmakers Company *not* Pattern-

Pattison, Mark (1813–84) Rector of Lincoln College, Oxford

Patton, George S(mith) (1885–1945) US general

PAU Pan American Union

pauca verba (Lat.) few words

pauperize *not* -ise

Pausanias (*fl. c.* AD 150) Greek traveller, author of 'Description of Greece'; abbr. **Paus.**

pavane (hist.) a stately dance, *not* -an; in Fr. f. *pavane*

pavé (Fr. m.) pavement, jewellery setting with stones close together

pavilion *not* pavill-

pavior one who lays pavements; *not* -ver, -vier, -viour; **Paviors Company** (no apos.)

Pavlov/, Ivan (**Petrovich**) (1849–1936) Russian physiologist; **-ian** of or relating to his work, esp. on conditioned reflexes

pavlova a meringue cake with cream and fruit, named after **Anna Pavlova** (1885–1931) Russian ballet dancer

pawaw *use* **powwow**

pawn (chess) abbr. **P**

pawn/broker, -shop (one word)

pawpaw a N. Amer. deciduous tree and its edible fruit; *not* papaw (US); *see also* **papaya**

PAX private automatic (telephone) exchange

pax vobiscum (Lat.) peace be with you

paxwax the neck cartilages, *not* the many variants

payback (noun) (one word)

pay/ bed, — claim (two words)

pay day (two words, one word in US)

pay dirt (US) a financially promising situation, lit. ground worth working for ore

PAYE pay as you earn, a method of tax collection

payload (one word)

paymaster abbr. **paymr., PM** (one word)

Paymaster-General (caps., hyphen) abbr. **PMG**

payment abbr. **pt.**

Payn, James (1830–98) English novelist and editor; *see also* **Pain**; **Paine**; **Payne**

Payne,/ Edward John (1844–1904) English historian; **— John Howard** (1791–1852) US playwright; *see also* **Pain**; **Paine**; **Payn**

paynim a pagan, *not* pai-

pay-off (noun, hyphen, one word in US)

pay packet (two words)

pay/phone, -roll (one word)

paysag/e (Fr. m.) a landscape (painting), *-iste* (Fr. m.) a landscape painter (ital.)

Pays-Bas (Fr. m. pl.) the Netherlands (caps., hyphen)

PB *Pharmacopoeia Britannica*, Plymouth Brethren, Prayer Book

Pb *plumbum* (lead) (no point)

PBI (mil. sl.) (poor bloody) infantry(man)

PBX private branch exchange

PC Panama Canal; Parish Council, -or; personal computer, Police Constable, politically correct, Privy Council, Privy Counsellor

pc (astr.) parsec

p.c. per cent, police constable, postcard

p/c petty cash, prices current

PCB (comput.) printed circuit board, (chem.) polychlorinated biphenyl

PCC Parochial Church Council

PCM pulse code modulation

PCS (Sc.) Principal Clerk of Session

pct. (US) per cent

PD *Pharmacopoeia Dublinensis*, (US) Police Department, Postal District (London), *privat-docent*

Pd palladium (no point)

pd. paid

p.d. per diem, (elec.) potential difference

p.d.q. pretty damn quick

PDSA People's Dispensary for Sick Animals

PDT (US) Pacific Daylight Time

PE *Pharmacopoeia Edinburgensis*, physical education, Port Elizabeth (Cape Province), potential energy, Protestant Episcopal

p.e. personal estate

p/e price/earnings ratio

PEA Physical Education Association of Great Britain and Northern Ireland

peaceable *not* -cable

peace/keeper, -maker (one word)

peace-offering (hyphen)

peace pipe (two words)

peacetime (one word)

pea-chick a young peafowl (hyphen)

peach Melba ice cream and peaches with liqueur, *not* pêche

pea/cock, -fowl (one word)

pea green (two words, hyphen when attrib.)

peahen (one word)

pea jacket a sailor's short overcoat (two words)

pean (her.) fur represented as sable spotted with or; a song of praise or triumph, *use* **paean**

pearl (knitting) *use* **purl**

Pearl Harbor a US naval base, Hawaii; *not* — Harbour

Pears, Sir Peter (1910–86) English tenor

Peary, Robert Edwin (1856–1920) US Arctic explorer, first at N. Pole 1909

pease pudding (two words)

peat/bog, -moss, -reek (one word)

peau-de-soie a smooth silky fabric (hyphens, not ital.)

pebbl/e, -y

peccadillo/ a trifling offence, pl. **-es**

peccary a S. American wild pig, *not* -i

peccavi a confession of guilt (not ital.)

pêche (Fr. f.) fish/ery, -ing; peach; **pêche Melba** in Eng. *use* **peach Melba**

péch/é (Fr. m.) sin, **-eur** (Fr.) sinner, f. **-eresse**

pêcheu/r (Fr.) fisherman, f. **-se**

peckish (colloq.) hungry, (US) irritable

peckoe, peco *use* **pekoe**

pecorino/ an Italian cheese made from ewes' milk, pl. **-s**

peculat/e embezzle, **-or**

Ped. (mus.) pedal

pedagog/ue (derog.) a pedantic teacher; **-y, -ics** the science of teaching; *not* pae-

pedal/, -led, -ling (one *l* in US)

peddler a person who sells drugs illegally; cf. **pedlar**

pederast/, -y *not* paed-

pedestal/, -led, -ling (one *l* in US)

pediatrics *use* **pae-** (except in US)

pedlar a travelling vendor of small wares, *not* peddler (US)

pedo/baptism, -philia *use* **paedo-**

Peeblesshire a former Scottish county, abbr. **Peebles.**

peekaboo (one word)

peel (hist.) a small square tower, *not* pele

Peele, George (?1558–1597) English playwright

peephole (one word)

peeping Tom a voyeur (one cap.)

peep show (two words)

peer/ f. **-ess** a member of one of the degrees of the nobility in Britain (i.e. (in descending order) a duke, marquess, earl, viscount, or baron), or a noble of any country; — **of the realm** (*or* **of the United Kingdom**) any of the class of peers whose adult members may all sit in the House of Lords; **life** — a person ennobled to the peerage, but whose title dies with him or her (unlike a **hereditary —**)

peer group (two words)

Peer Gynt a play by Ibsen, 1867; incidental music by Grieg, opera by Egk

peewit the lapwing, *not* pew-

Peggotty a family in Dickens's *David Copperfield*

Pehlevi *use* **Pahlavi**

PEI Prince Edward Island, Canada

peignoir a woman's loose dressing gown

peine forte et dure (Fr. f.) severe punishment, a medieval judicial torture

Peirce, Charles Sanders (1839–1914) US logician, founder of philosophical pragmatism

p.ej. (Sp.) *por ejemplo*, for example, e.g.

Pekinese a small dog, colloq. **peke**

Peking/ China; *not* Peip- (except during the Nationalist period), **-kin**; in Pinyin **Beijing**; **-ese** (an inhabitant) of Peking

pekoe a black tea; *not* peckoe, peco (not cap.)

Pelagian/ (of or concerning) (a follower of) the monk **Pelagius** (*c.*4th–5th cc.) or his theory denying the doctrine of original sin, **-ism**

pelagi/an inhabiting, or an inhabitant of, the open sea; **-c**

pele *use* **peel**

pell-mell confusedly, recklessly

Peloponnese S. Greece; *see also* **Morea**

pemmican a dried meat for travellers; *not* pemi-

Pen. Peninsula

penalize *not* -ise

pen-and-ink (adj., hyphens)

Penang *see* **Malaya, Federation of**

penanggalan a female vampire in Malaysian folklore

penates (pl.) Roman household gods, esp. of the storeroom; *see also* **lar**

penbardd (Welsh) a head or chief bard

pence *see* **penny**

penchant bias (not ital.)

pencil/, -led, -ling (one *l* in US)

PEN Club International Association of Poets, Playwrights, Editors, Essayists, and Novelists

pendant (noun) anything hanging

pendent (adj.) suspended

pendente lite (Lat.) during the trial

pendragon (hist.) an ancient British or Welsh prince (cap. as title)

pendulum/ pl. **-s**

penetrable that may be penetrated

penetralia (pl.) the innermost recesses (not ital.)

pen feather a quill feather; cf. **pin feather**

penfriend (one word)

pengő the chief unit of currency in Hungary 1927–46, replaced by the forint

penguin an Antarctic bird; cf. **pinguin**

pen holder (two words)

penicillin (med.)

Penicillium (bot.) a genus of fungi, mould (ital.)

Penicuik Lothian

penillion improvised stanzas sung to a harp accompaniment at an eisteddfod etc., sing. **pennill**

peninsula/ (noun) pl. **-s**, adj. **-r**

Peninsular/ Campaign SE Virginia, 1862, in the American Civil War; **— War** Spain and Portugal, 1808–14, in the Napoleonic Wars

penis/ the male organ, pl. **-es**

penknife (one word)

Penmaenmawr Gwynedd

penman/, -ship (one word)

pen name (two words)

pennant (naut.) a piece of rigging, a flag

penni/ a monetary unit of Finland; pl. **-ä**

penniless *not* penny-

pennill sing. of **penillion**

pennon a long narrow flag

penn'orth (colloq.) a pennyworth

Pennsylvania/ off. abbr. **Pa.**, postal **PA**; *not* Penn., Penna ; **— Dutch** a dialect of High German spoken by descendants of 17th–18th-c. German and Swiss immigrants to Pennsylvania etc.; (as pl.) these settlers or their descendants

penny pl. **pennies** (a number of coins), **pence** (a sum of money); abbr. **p** (sing. and pl., no point); pre-1971 penny, abbr. **d.** (sing. and pl.)

penny-a-liner (hyphens)

pennyroyal (bot.) a kind of mint (one word)

pennyweight 24 grains, abbr. **dwt.**

penny/wort, -worth (one word)

penology the science of punishment, *not* poe-

pen pal (US) = **penfriend**

Penrhyn/ Gwynedd, *also* **Baron —**

Penryn Cornwall

pensée (Fr. f.) thought, maxim; pansy

pension/ a regular payment made by a government, employer, or insurance company; based on age, length of employment, or charitable grounds; **-able, -ary, -er**

pension/ a European, esp. French, boarding house or school; *en* — as a boarder (ital.)

pensionnat (Fr. m.) a boarding school

penstemon (bot.) *not* pents-

Pent. Pentecost

pentagon/ a figure or building with five sides; the US defence headquarters (cap.); **-al**

pentagram a five-pointed star

pentagraph *use* **panto-**

pentameter (prosody) a verse of five units

Pentateuch/ the first five books of the OT, traditionally ascribed to Moses and called the **Torah** by Jews (cap.); **-al** (not cap.)

Pentecost/ Whit Sunday (cap.), abbr. **Pent.**; **-al** (not cap.)

penthouse (one word)

pentobarbital (US) = **pentobarbitone**

pentstemon *use* **pens-**

penumbr/a (astr.) a lighter shadow round dark shadow of an eclipse, pl. **-ae**

peon a Sp.-Am. day labourer or farm worker; cf. **paean**; **paeon**

peony a flower, *not* pae-

PEP Personal Equity Plan, Political and Economic Planning

pepo/ the fleshy fruit of a melon etc., pl. **-s**

pepper/box, -corn (one word)

pepper/ mill (two words)

peppermint (one word)

pepper pot (two words)

pepsin an enzyme in gastric juice, *not* -ine

Pepys, Samuel (1633–1703) English diarist and civil servant

per (Lat.) by, for (rom. when used with assimilated Eng. terms); abbr. **p.**

per. period

PERA Production Engineering Research Association of Great Britain

per accidens (Lat.) contingently, indirectly (opp. of **per se**)

perai *use* **piranha**

Perak *see* **Malaya, Federation of**

per annum yearly; abbr. **p.a.**, **per ann.**

per caput (Lat. 'by head') for each person; the pl. **per capita**, originally in contrast to **per stirpes**, has acquired the sing. form's meaning except in hist. or legal contexts (not ital.)

perceiv/e, -able, -er

per cent in every hundred (two words, one word in US, no point), symbol **%**

percentage (one word)

perceptible *not* -able

Perceval/ one of King Arthur's knights, —, **Spencer** (1762–1812) English statesman

perchance perhaps

percolat/e, -ing, -or

per contra on the other hand (not ital.)

per curiam (Lat.) by the court

perdendosi (mus.) dying away

per diem daily; (noun) daily allowance (not ital.)

perdu/ (Fr.) f. **-e** concealed, lost

Père (Fr. m.) RC father, not ital. as part of name; abbr. **P.**

père (Fr. m.) father, senior, added to a surname to distinguish a father from a son, as 'Dumas *père*'; *see also* **fils**

Père David's deer a large slender-antlered deer

Père Lachaise a Paris cemetery (two words, caps.)

Perelman, S(idney) J(oseph) (1904–79) US humorist and author

perestroika (in the former Soviet Union) the policy or practice of restructuring or reforming the economic and political system (not ital.), in Russ. *perestroïka*

perf. perfect, (stamps) perforated

perfect abbr. **perf.**

perfecta (US) a form of betting in which the first two places in a race must be predicted in the correct order

perfect binding a binding method alternative to sewing, in which the gatherings of each volume are clamped together, their back folds sheared off, and the resultant leaf edges glued to a flexible backing

perfecter one who perfects, *not* -or; (typ.) a printing press which prints both sides of the paper at one pass

perfectib/le, -ility *not* -ab-

perfecting (typ.) printing the second side of a sheet

perfecto a large thick cigar pointed at each end

perforated abbr. **perf.**

perforce of necessity (one word)

Pergamon Press publishers

Pergamum a city and kingdom in ancient Asia Minor

pergana *use* **par-**

Pergolesi, Giovanni Battista (1710–36) Italian composer

pergunnah *use* **pargana**

peri/ (Pers. myth.) a fairy, a good (originally evil) genius; a beautiful or graceful being; pl. **-s**

periagua *use* **pira-**

peridot a green semi-precious stone, *not* -te

perig/ee (astr.) abbr. **perig.**; **-ean**

Périgord (Fr. cook.) cooking based on truffles

peril/, -led, -ling (one *l* in US)

perimeter the outline of a closed figure

per incuriam (Lat.) by oversight

perine/um (anat.) pl. **-ums**, adj. **-al**

per interim (Lat.) in the mean time

period (US) = **full point**, abbr. **per.**

periodicals, titles of when cited, to be italic; as a rule the definite article should be in roman lower case, except when preceding one-word titles (e.g. *The Economist*, *The Times*)

peripatetic walking about, (cap.) Aristotelian (school of philosophy)

peripeteia a sudden reversal of fortune, *not* -tia (not ital.)

periphras/is circumlocution, pl. **-es**; **-tic**

perispomen/on (Gr. gram.) (a word) with circumflex on last syllable, pl. **-a**

peristyle (archit.) a row of columns round temple

periton/eum (anat.) pl. **-eums**; **-eal, -itis**

perityphlitis (med.)

periwig/, -ged *not* perri-

periwinkle a plant and mollusc

perlé a sparkling S. African wine

Perlis *see* **Malaya, Federation of**

perm colloq. for permanent wave, permutation, and corresponding verbs (no point)

permeable that may be permeated

per mensem for each month (not ital.)

Permian (geol.) (of or relating to) the last period of the Palaeozoic era

per mille in every thousand (not ital.), *not* mil; symbol ‰

permis de séjour (Fr. m.) a residence permit

permissible *not* -able

permit/, -ted, -ting

pernickety fastidious, over-precise; *not* persn- (US)

Perón,/ Juan Domingo (1895–1974) President of Argentina 1946–55, 1973–4; husband of — (**María**) **Eva** (**Duarte de**) (1919–52), called **'Evita'**; **Peronism** (no accent)

per pais (Norman Fr.) by jury (lit. 'by the county')

Perpendicular (archit.) of the third stage of English Gothic (15th–16th cc.), with vertical tracery in large windows (cap.)

perpetuum mobile (Lat.) something never at rest, (mus.) = **moto perpetuo**

per procurationem (Lat.) used in signatures to mean through the agency of (*incorrectly* on behalf of); the correct sequence is 'Smith *per pro.* Jones' (Jones signing for Smith); abbr. *per pro.*, **p.p.**

Perrier/ (propr.) (cap.), — **-Jouët** a champagne (hyphen)

perriwig *use* **peri-**

Pers. Persia, -n

pers. person, -al, -ally

per saltum (Lat.) at a leap (ital.)

per se by himself, herself, itself, *or* themselves, by or in itself, intrinsically (opp. of *per accidens*) (not ital.)

Perse *see* **Léger**

Perseids (astr.) a group of meteors that appear to radiate from the constellation Perseus

Persia/, -n abbr. **Pers.**; *but use* **Iran**, **Iranian**, of the modern state

Persian/ carpet, — **cat**, — **rug** (caps.) *but* — **morocco** (bind.) (no caps.)

persiflage banter (not ital.)

persil (Fr. m.) parsley

persimmon (bot.) the date-plum, *not* -simon

persist/ence (in Fr. f. *persistance*), **-ency, -ent**

persnickety *use* **pernickety** (except in US)

persona/ perceived characteristics of personality, pl. **-e** (not ital.)

persona/ grata (Lat.) an acceptable person, pl. **-e gratae**; — *gratissima* a most acceptable person, pl. **-e gratissimae**; — *ingrata*, — *non grata* an unacceptable person, pl. **-e ingratae, -e non gratae**

personalize *not* -ise

personalty (law) personal estate, *not* -ality

personnel/ staff employed in any service, members of armed forces; — **carrier,** — **manager** (two words)

persp. perspective

perspex (propr.) a tough transparent plastic (not cap.)

perspicaci/ous mentally discerning, astute; **-ty**

perspicu/ous clearly expressed; **-ity**

per stirpes (Lat.) by the number of families; cf. **per caput**

persuadable able to be induced (e.g. to do something in a particular instance)

persuasible open to persuasion or influence

persuasive able to persuade

PERT project *or* programme evaluation and review technique

pertinac/ity persistence, **-ious**

peruke a wig, *not* -que

Peruv. Peruvian

per viam (Lat.) by way of

pes (Lat.) a foot, pl. *pedes*

Pesach the Passover festival, in Heb. *Pesah*

peseta the chief monetary unit in Spain, abbr. **pta.**

Peshawar W. Pakistan, *not* -ur

peso/ the chief monetary unit in some Latin American countries and the Philippines, pl. **-s**

Pest *see* **Budapest**

Pestalozzi, Johann Heinrich (1746–1827) Swiss educationist

Pet., 1, 2 First, Second Epistle of Peter

peta- prefix meaning 10^{15}, abbr. **P**

Pétain, Henri Philippe (1856–1951) French marshal and politician, head of the Vichy government 1940–4

petal/, -led

Peter, First, Second Epistle of (NT) abbr. **1 Pet., 2 Pet.**

peterel *use* **-trel**

Peterlee Dur.

Peterloo massacre St Peter's Field, Manchester, 1819; named in ironical reference to the Battle of Waterloo

Peter Principle the jocular principle that members of a hierarchy are promoted until they reach the level at which they are no longer competent, propounded by **Laurence Johnson Peter** (1919–90) US educationist and author

Peter Schlemihl a well-meaning unlucky fellow; (ital.) novel by Chamisso, 1814

Peter's pence (hist.) an annual tax, *later* a voluntary contribution on St Peter's Day (one cap.)

petit/ (Fr. m.) small; — *bleu* (in France) a telegram, pl. *-s bleus*

petit/ bourgeois a member of the **petite bourgeoisie**, the lower middle class, pl. **-s bourgeois**; f. **-e bourgeoise** pl. **-es bourgeoises**; the Eng. form, **petty bourgeois/, -ie**, carries a more pejorative tone

petit déjeuner (Fr. m.) breakfast

petit/ four a small fancy cake, biscuit, or sweet; pl. **-s fours** (not ital.)

petitio principii (Lat.) begging the question, a logical fallacy in which a conclusion is taken for granted in the premiss *petit-maître* (Fr. m.) a dandy or coxcomb

petit/ mal a mild form of epilepsy, — point embroidery in small stitches (not ital.)

petits pois small green peas (not ital.)

petits soins (Fr. m. pl.) little attentions

petit verre (Fr. m.) a glass of liqueur

Petrarc/h, Francesco (1304–74) Italian scholar and poet, in It. -a; adj. -han

Petre, Baron

petrel a seabird, *not* -erel

Petri dish (one cap.)

Petriburg: the signature of the Bishop of Peterborough (colon)

petro/chemical, -chemistry, -dollar, -glyph (one word)

Petrograd *see* St Petersburg

petrol refined petroleum used as fuel

petroleum unrefined oil

petrology abbr. petrol.

Pettie, John (1839–93) Scottish painter

pettifog/ to cavil in legal matters; -ger, -gery, -ging

petty bourgeois/, -ie Eng. forms of petit bourgeois, petite bourgeoisie (qq.v.)

petty/ cash abbr. p/c, — officer abbr. PO (two words)

peu à peu (Fr.) little by little

Peugeot a French make of car

peut-être (Fr.) perhaps

pewit *use* pee-

p. ex. (Fr.) *par exemple* (for example)

PF Patriotic Front, Procurator-Fiscal

pF picofarad (no point)

pf (mus.) più forte (a little louder), piano forte (soft, then loud)

Pfc. (US) Private first class

Pfd. (Ger.) *Pfund* (pound)

Pfennig (Ger. m.) a small German coin, abbr. Pf.

Pfitzner, Hans (1869–1949) German composer

Pfleiderer,/ Edmund (1842–1902) and his brother — Otto (1839–1908) German philosophers

Pfund (Ger. n.) pound (cap.), abbr. *Pfd.*

PG paying guest, postgraduate

pg picogram (no point)

PGA Professional Golfers' Association

PGM (Freemasonry, Odd Fellows) Past Grand Master

pH (chem.) (one cap.)

ph phot

Phaedo (b. *c.*417 BC) a pupil of Socrates

phaenomenon etc., *use* phe-

Phaethon (Gr. myth.) son of Helios; *not* Phaë-, -ton

phaeton a light open four-wheeled carriage, (US) a type of touring car

Phalang/e a right-wing activist Maronite party in Lebanon (cf. Falange); -ism, -ist

phalan/x a line of battle or a compact body of men, pl. -xes; (biol.) a bone or stamen bundle, pl. -ges

phall/us pl. -uses, (bot., med., relig.) -i

phanariot (hist.) a member of a class of Greek officials in Constantinople under the Ottoman Empire

phantasize *use* fan-

phantasmagor/ia a shifting scene of real or imagined figures, pl. -ias; -ic; *not* fa-

phantasy *use* fan-

phantom *not* f-

Phar. Pharmacopoeia

Pharao/h *not* -oah; -nic

Pharis/ee pl. -ees; -aism, -aic, -aical

pharm. pharmaceutical, pharmacy

pharmacol. pharmacology

pharmacopoeia a book describing drugs, abbr. P. (*see* BP), Phar.; *Pharmacopoeia/ Dublinensis* (of Dublin) abbr. PD; — *Edinburgensis* (of Edinburgh) abbr. PE; — *Londiniensis* (of London) abbr. PL; *not* -peia (US)

pharos a lighthouse, (cap.) the one at Alexandria *or* the island on which it stood

pharyn/x the cavity behind the larynx, pl. -ges; -gal, -geal, -gitis

phas/e, -ic, -ing

phatic (of speech etc.) used to convey general sociability rather than to communicate a specific meaning

Ph.B. *Philosophiae Baccalaureus* (Bachelor of Philosophy)

Ph.D. *Philosophiae Doctor* (Doctor of Philosophy)

Phebe *see* Phoebe

Phèdre a play by Racine, 1677

Pheidias (5th c. BC) Athenian sculptor; *not now* Phidias except to describe an enthusiastic writer on art

Phenician *use* Phoe-

phenix *use* phoe-

phenomen/on an appearance, pl. -a; -al; *not* phae-

phial a small (usually cylindrical) glass vessel, esp. for holding liquid medicines; *see also* vial

phi twenty-first letter of the Gr. alphabet (Φ, ϕ)

Phi Beta Kappa (US) an intercollegiate honorary society to which distinguished students may be elected

Phidias *use* Phei-

Phil. Philadelphia, Philharmonic, Philippine, Philippians

philabeg *use* fili-

Philadelphia abbr. Phil., Phila.

philatel/y postage-stamp collecting; **-ic, -ically, -ist**

Philem. Philemon (NT)

philemot *use* **fi-**

philharmonic fond of music (cap. as part of the name of an orchestra or society)

philhellen/e (one) friendly to the Greeks; **-ic, -ism, -ist**

philibeg *use* **fi-**

Philip the name of five kings of Macedonia, six kings of France, and five kings of Spain; any of various French, Spanish, or Burgundian gold or silver coins issued by kings and dukes named Philip

Philippe Fr. for **Philip**

Philippians (NT) abbr. **Phil.**

Philippics (pl.) the speeches of Demosthenes against Philip of Macedon, also those of Cicero against Antony; **philippic** a bitter invective

philippina a game of forfeits, *not* the many variants

Philippine Islands abbr. **PI**

Philippines, Republic of the inhabited by Filipinos

Philipps the family name of Viscount St Davids and Baron Milford; *see also* **Phill-**

Philips/ electronics manufacturer, **—, Ambrose** (1675–1749) English writer of pastoral and nursery poems, hence 'namby-pamby'; **—, John** (1676–1709) parodist of Milton; **—, Katherine** (1631–64) English poet; *see also* **Phill-**

Philip Sparrow see *Phyllyp Sparowe*

Philister (Ger.) a townsman, a non-student; pl. same (cap.)

Philistine an inhabitant of ancient Palestine; a person indifferent to culture (not cap.); **philistinism** (not cap.)

phillipina *use* **philipp-**

Phillipps,/ James Orchard *see* **Halliwell-Phillipps, — Sir Thomas** (1792–1872) English book collector; *see also* **Philipps**

Phillips,/ Sir Claud (1846–1924) English art critic; **— Edward** (1630–94) lexicographer, and **— John** (1631–1706) Milton's nephews; **— John Bertram** (1906–82) English Bible translator; **— Stephen** (1864–1915) English poet; **— Wendell** (1811–84) US abolitionist; *see also* **Philips**

Phillpotts,/ Eden (1862–1960) English novelist and dramatist, **— Henry** (1778–1869) Bishop of Exeter; *see also* **Philpott**

philogynist a person who likes or admires women

philopoena *use* **philippina**

philosopher's stone a substance thought to change base metals to gold, *properly* **-s'**

philosophize *not* -ise

philosophy abbr. **philos.**

Philpott, Henry (1807–92) Bishop of Worcester; *see also* **Phillpotts**

Phil. Soc. Philological Society of London, Philosophical Society of America

Phil. Trans. the *Philosophical Transactions of the Royal Society of London*

philtre an aphrodisiac drink, *not* -er (US); cf. **filter**

Phiz illustrator of Dickens; *see* **Browne, Hablot Knight**

phiz, phizog (arch., colloq.) the face, *not* phizz

phlebit/is inflammation of the veins, **-ic**

Phnom Penh Cambodia

phobia/ a morbid fear, pl. **-s**

Phoebe *but* **Phebe** in Shakespeare's *As You Like It*

Phoebus 'bright', an epithet of Apollo

Phoenician *not* Phe-

phoenix a mythical bird that rose rejuvenated from its own ashes, *not* phen-

phon a unit of perceived loudness

phon. phonetics

phone/ short for telephone, *not* 'phone; **— book** (esp. US) = **telephone directory**; **-card** (one word)

phone-in a broadcast incorporating listeners' telephoned views (hyphen)

phonetics (usually treated as sing.)

phon/ey false, *not* phony; **-ier, -ily, -iness**

phonol. phonology

phosphor/us symbol P; (adj.) **-ous**

phosphuretted *not* -eted, -oretted

phot a unit of illuminance, abbr. **ph**

photo/ photograph (no point), pl. **-s**

photo/biology, -call, -chemistry (one word)

photo/composition, -setting (one word) (typ.) setting copy onto film etc. instead of in metal type

photocop/y, -ier (one word) *prefer* to **xerox** in general references

photoelectric (one word)

photo finish (two words)

photofit composite picture using photographs of facial features (one word); cf. **identikit**

photog. photograph/y, -ic

Photograph/ (Ger. m.) photographer; *-ie* (f.) photograph, -y

photograph/e (Fr. m. and f.) photographer; *-ie* (f.) photograph, -y

photogravure (typ.) the intaglio printing process; shortened as **gravure**

photojournalism (one word)

photolithography (typ.) the photographic processes for making a plate for printing by offset lithography; colloq. **photolitho**

photom. photometr/y, -ical

photomicrograph a photograph of a minute object taken with a microscope; cf. **microphotograph**

photomontage a montage of photographs

photo-offset (typ.) offset printing with plates made photographically (hyphen)

photosetting *see* **photocomposition**

photostat (propr.) a type of machine for making photocopies, (to make) such a copy

phr. phrase

phren. phrenology

phrenetic *use* **fren-**

phrenitic affected with phrenitis, inflammation of the brain

phthalic (chem.) derived from naphthalene

phthisis tuberculosis

Phyfe, Duncan (1786–1854) Scottish-born US furniture maker

phylactery a small leather box containing Hebrew texts on vellum, worn by Jewish men at morning prayer as a reminder to keep the law

Phyllyp Sparowe a poem by Skelton, 1529

phylo- (biol.) a prefix denoting a race or tribe

phyl/um a main division of the animal or vegetable kingdom, pl. **-a**

phys. physical, physician, physics

physic/, -ked, -king, -ky

Physic, Regius Professor of Cambridge University, *not* -cs

physico-chemical (hyphen, one word in US)

physiol. physiolog/y, -ical, -ist

physique constitution (not ital.)

physique (Fr. f.) physics (natural philosophy)

PI Philippine Islands

pi (typ.) *use* **pie** (except in US)

pi the sixteenth letter of the Gr. alphabet (Π, π); ∏ (math.) product; ratio of circumference to diameter of a circle, or 3.14159265 …

pianissimo (mus.) very soft, abbr. ***pp***

pianississimo (mus.) as softly as possible, abbr. ***ppp***

piano/ (mus.) softly, abbr. ***p***, pl. **piani**; instrument formally called **pianoforte** (one word), pl. **-s**; **-player, -stool** (hyphens)

piano-forte (mus.) softly, then loud (two words)

Pianola (propr.) an automatic player-piano (cap.)

piano nobile (archit.) the main floor of a building (ital.)

piassava a stout fibre from palm trees, *not* -aba

piastre a small coin of Middle Eastern countries, *not* -er (US)

piazza/ an open square, pl. **-s**

pibroch an air on the bagpipe, *not* the bagpipe itself

pica (typ.) the size of letters on some typewriters; the standard for typographic measurement, equalling 12 pt. or about one-sixth of an inch; (med.) the eating of substances other than normal food

picaninny *use* **picca-**

Picard, Jean (1620–82) French astronomer

picaresque of a style of fiction describing the life of an (amiable) rogue (not ital.)

Picasso, Pablo (**Ruiz**) (1881–1973) Spanish painter

picayune a small US coin pre-1857, (colloq.) any trifling coin, person, or thing; (adj.) trifling, mean

piccalilli a pickle of vegetables and mustard

piccaninny (offens.) a black or Australian Aboriginal infant; *not* pica-, picka- (US)

Piccard, Auguste (1884–1962) Swiss physicist

piccolo/ the smallest flute, pl. **-s**

pi character (typ.) one of a set of special sorts; *see also* **pi plaque**

pickaback *use* **piggyback**

pickaxe (one word), *not* -ax (US)

pickelhaube (hist.) a German spiked infantry helmet, in Ger. f. ***Pickelhaube***

picket/ (*also* **picq-, piq-**); as verb, **-ed, -ing; — line** (two words)

picklock (one word)

pick-me-up/ a tonic (hyphens), pl. **-s**

pickpocket (one word)

Pickwickian of or like Mr Pickwick in Dickens's *Pickwick Papers*, esp. in being jovial, plump, etc.; (of words or their sense) misunderstood or misused, esp. to avoid offence

picnic/, -ked, -ker, -king, -ky

pico- prefix meaning 10^{-12}, abbr. **p**

picquet *use* **-ket**; *see also* **piquet**

picture/ book, — card (two words)

picturegoer (one word)

picture/ hat, — postcard (two words)

pictures, titles of when cited, to be in italic if named by the artist, roman quoted if popularly identified as such by others

picture window (two words)

pidgin/ a simplified language containing vocabulary from two or more languages, used for communication between people not having a common language; **— English** a pidgin in which the chief language is English, used originally between Chinese and Europeans (two words, one cap.); a pidgin grown more sophisticated through use is a **creole**; cf. **pigeon**

pi-dog *use* **pye-**

pie (typ.) composed type that has been jumbled; *not* pi, pye

pie (hist.) former monetary unit of India, equal to one-twelfth of an anna

piebald of two colours in irregular patches, usually of horses, usually black and white; *not* pye-; cf. **skewbald**

pièce/ de résistance the most important or remarkable item, the principal dish at a meal; pl. **-s de résistance** (not ital.)

piecemeal gradually (one word)

piece-rate (hyphen)

piecework (one word)

pied/ (Fr. m.) a foot, abbr. **p.**

pied-à-terre an occasional residence, pl. **pieds-à-terre** (hyphens)

pie-dog *use* **pye-**

Pierce, Franklin (1804–69) US President 1853–7

Pierce the Ploughman's Crede anon., *c.*1394; *see also* **Piers**

Pierian Spring the fountain of the Muses in Thessaly

Pierides (Gr. myth) the nine Muses

pierr/ot a seaside entertainer derived from French pantomime, f. **-ette**

Piers Plowman, The Vision of William concerning a poem by Langland, 14th c.; *see also* **Pierce**

pietà the representation of the dead Christ in the Virgin Mary's arms

pietas (Lat.) the respect due to an ancestor, forerunner, etc.

Pietermaritzburg S. Africa

pietr/a dura (It.) a stone mosaic, pl. **-e dure**

piezoelectric/, -ity (one word)

pig (US) = **piglet**; cf. **swine**

pigeon/ common dove; a person easily swindled; (colloq.) **not my —** not my affair; cf. **pidgin**

pigeon-hol/e, -ed (hyphen, one word in US)

piggyback (one word) *not* pick-a-back

pig-headed (hyphen, one word in US)

pig iron (two words)

pigm/y, -aean *use* **pygm-**

pigpen (US) = **pigsty**

pig/skin, -sty pl. **-sties**; **-swill, -tail, -wash, -weed** (one word)

Pike's Peak Rocky Mountains (apos.)

pikestaff (one word)

Piketberg (off. spelling) Cape Province, *not* Piquet-

pilaf a dish of spiced rice or wheat with meat, fish, vegetables, etc. in the Middle East (not ital.)

pilau a dish of spiced rice or wheat with meat, fish, vegetables, etc. in India (not ital.)

pilcrow (typ. hist.) the paragraph symbol (¶)

Pilipino the national language of the Philippines, a standardized form of Tagalog; *not* Filipino

pillar box (two words)

pillbox (one word)

pill bug a type of woodlouse (two words)

pillowcase (one word)

pillow-fight (hyphen)

pillow/ lace, — lava, — talk (two words)

pillule *use* **pilule**

pilot/, -ed, -ing

pilot biscuit (US) = **ship's biscuit**

pilot/ fish, — house, — light (two words)

Piloty, Karl von (1826–86) German painter

Pilsen Czech Republic, in Czech **Plzeň**

Pilsener a light beer (cap.)

Piłsudski, Józef (1867–1935) Polish general, first President of Poland 1918

pilule a small pill, *not* pill-

pimiento/ a sweet red pepper, allspice; pl. **-s**; *not* pime- (though sometimes reserved for allspice)

PIN personal identification number

pin/ a small cask for liquids; pl. **-s**

pina colada a drink made from pineapple juice, rum, and coconut; in Sp. *piña colada*

pinball (one word)

pince-nez eyeglasses with a nose clip instead of earpieces, pl. same (not ital., hyphen)

pincushion (one word)

Pindar (518–438 BC) Greek poet, abbr. **Pind.**

Pindar, Peter pseud. of **Dr John Wolcot** (1738–1819)

pineapple (one word)

pine/ cone, — nut (two words)

Pinero, Sir Arthur Wing (1855–1934) English playwright

pin feather a small feather; cf. **pen feather**

ping-pong (hyphen)

pinguin a W. Indian plant or fruit; cf. **penguin**

pin/head, -hole (one word)

pinkie (esp. US, Sc.) the little finger

Pinkster (US) = **Whitsuntide**

pin money (two words)

pinochle (US) a card game with a double pack of forty-eight cards (nine to ace only)

pin/point, -prick (one word)

pinscher a breed of dog, *not* pinch-; *see also* **Dobermann pinscher**

pinstripe (one word)

pint (UK) 20 fl. oz (0.568 l); (US) 16 fl. oz (0.473 l); abbr. **pt.**, symbol O

pinta (Brit. colloq.) a pint of milk, (med.) a chronic skin disease endemic in tropical America

pin-table (hyphen)

pintado/ a petrel, mackerel-like fish; pl. **-s**

pinto (US, of a horse) = **piebald**

Pinturicchio the nickname of **Bernardino di Betto** (1454–1513) Italian painter

pin-up (noun; hyphen, one word in US)

pinxit (Lat.) painted this; abbr. *pnxt., pinx.*

Pinyin a system of romanized spelling for transliterating Chinese (cap.)

piob mhor the Highland pipes (not cap.), in Gael. *piob-mhór*

pion (phys.) a subatomic particle, a pi meson

pipal *use* **bo tree**

pipeclay (one word)

pipe/cleaner, — dream, — organ (two words)

pipe-rack (hyphen)

pipe rolls (hist.) the annual records of the British Exchequer 12th–19th cc.

pipe/-stem, -stone (hyphens)

pi plaque (typ.) a set of special sorts

Pippa Passes a poem by R. Browning, 1841

pipy like, or having, pipes; *not* -ey

piquan/t sharp, **-cy** (not ital.)

piqu/e resentment; a score in piquet; as a verb, irritate, **-ed, -ing**

piqué a thick cotton fabric; (mus.) short, detached (not ital.)

piqué (Fr.) (of wine) slightly sour; (cook.) larded

piquet a card game, *not* picq-; *see also* **picket**

Piquetberg *use* **Piket-**

PIRA *or* **Pira** Research Association for the Paper and Board, Printing and Packaging Industries, publishers

Piraeus the port of Athens

piragua a S. American dugout canoe, *not* the many variants

Pirandello, Luigi (1867–1936) Italian playwright

Piranesi, Giambattista (1720–78) Italian architect and etcher

piranha a ferocious S. American fish; *not* perai, piraya

pis aller (Fr. m.) a second best

piscin/a a fish pond, a swimming pool; (eccl.) a stone basin for disposing of water used in washing the chalice etc. pl. **-ae**

pisé (Fr. m.) rammed earth (ital.)

piskie *use* **pix-** (except in Cornish dialect)

Pissarro,/ Camille (1830–1903) French painter, father of **— Lucien** (1863–1944) French–British painter

pissed/ (Brit.) drunk, (US) annoyed; **off** (Brit., US) annoyed, fed up

pistachio/ a nut, pl. **-s**; *not* -acho

piste a ski track (not ital.)

pistol/, -led, -ling (one *l* in US)

pistole (hist.) a foreign (esp. Spanish) gold coin

pit (US) the stone of a fruit

pita *use* **-tta** (except in US)

pitch-and-toss (hyphens)

pitch/blende, -fork, -stone (one word)

piteous deserving pity, wretched

pitiful causing pity, contemptible

Pitman, Sir Isaac (1813–97) English inventor of shorthand

pitta a flat hollow bread that can be split and filled with salad etc., *not* pita (US)

Pitti, Palazzo an art gallery in Florence

Pitt Rivers/, Augustus Henry Lane Fox (1827–1900) English lieutenant general, archaeologist, and anthropologist, founder of the **— — Museum** Oxford (no hyphen)

Pitt-Rivers/, George Henry Lane-Fox (1890–1966) grandson of above, captain, owner/director of the former **— - — Museum** Dorset (hyphen)

Pittsburgh Pa.; *not* -burg

più (It. mus.) more; **— forte** a little louder, abbr. **pf**

pius (Lat.) holy, abbr. **p.**

pivot/, -ed, -ing

pix *use* **py-**

pixel/s (electronics) the minute areas of uniform illumination from which an image on a display screen is composed; **-ate** divide (an image) into pixels

pix/ie a small fairy or elf; *not* pisk- (except in Corn. dialect), -y; **-ilated** bewildered, *not* pixy-led

pixie/ hat, — hood (two words)

Pizarro, Francisco (*c.*1475–1541) Spanish conquistador

pizz/a pl. **-as**; **-eria** the place where pizzas are made or sold

pizzazz *not* pizazz, pzazz

pizzicato (mus.) pinched, plucked; abbr. **pizz.**

PJ presiding judge, Probate Judge

PK psychokinesis

pk. pack, park, peak, peck(s)

pkg. package, -s

PL Paymaster Lieutenant, *Pharmacopoeia Londiniensis*, Poet Laureate, Primrose League

P/L Profit and Loss

Pl. Plate, -s

pl. place, plate, platoon, plural

PLA Port of London Authority

place (UK) any of the first three or four positions in a race, esp. other than first; (US) second in a horse race

place (Fr. f.) square in a town

place aux dames! (Fr.) ladies first!

place-bet (UK) a bet on a horse to come first, second, third, or sometimes fourth in a race; (US) a bet on a horse to come second

placebo/ (med.) a medicine given with no physiological effect, (RC) the opening antiphon of vespers for the dead; pl. **-s**

place card (two words)

place mat (two words, one word in US)

place name (two words)

placent/a an organ nourishing the foetus in the womb, pl. **-ae**

place setting (two words)

placet (Lat.) it pleases, permission granted, an affirmative vote in a church or university assembly

plafond (Fr. m.) a ceiling, esp. decorated (ital.)

plagiarize take and use the thoughts, writings, inventions, etc. of another person as one's own; *not* -ise

plagu/e, -esome, -ily, -y

Plaid Cymru the Welsh nationalist party

plainchant (one word)

plain clothes (hyphen when attrib., one word in US)

plain sailing (fig.) easy work (two words); cf. **plane sailing**

plain/sman, -song (one word)

plaint (Eng. law) an accusation or charge

plaintiff (law) a person who brings a case against another in court, abbr. **plf.**

plaintive expressing sorrow

Plaisterers, Worshipful Company of

planchet a coin-blank

planchette a small board on castors with a pencil-point, used to trace letters spontaneously at spiritualistic seances (not ital.)

Planck/ constant symbol *h* (6.626 × 10⁻³⁴ J s); — **Law of Radiation** in the quantum theory, from **Max Planck** (1858–1947) German physicist; *not* -'s

plane short for aeroplane, *not* 'plane

plane sailing (naut.) the calculation of a ship's position on the assumption that it is moving on a plane surface (two words); cf. **plain sailing**

planetari/um pl. **-ums**

plankton microscopic organic life drifting in water; cf. **benthal; nekton**

planographic (typ.) of a printing process based on a flat surface, on which the image areas are made greasy so as to accept ink and the rest wet to reject it

Plantagenet family name of the English sovereigns from Henry II to Richard II, 1154–1399

Plantin, Christophe (*c*.1520–89) French printer

plasmolyse (bot.) *not* -ize, -yze (US)

plasterboard (one word)

plaster of Paris (one cap.)

plasticine (propr.) a soft modelling substance (not cap.)

plasticky plastic-like

plastic wrap (US) = **cling film**

plastron a breastplate, bodice front, etc.

plat/ (Fr. cook. m.) a dish, — *du jour* special dish of the day

Plate/, -s (typ.) abbr. **Pl.**

plate/ (typ.) planographic or typographic printing surface of complete page or sheet cast or etched in metal or polymerized resin; half-tone etc. illustration; (photog.) **whole** — 8½ × 6½ in., **half** — 6½ × 4¼ in., **quarter** — 4¼ × 3¼ in.

plateau/ area of fairly level high ground, pl. **-x** (not ital.)

plate/ glass, — rack (two words)

platinize coat with platinum, *not* -ise

platinum/ symbol **Pt**; — **black** platinum in powder form; — **blond** (a person with) silvery-blond hair, f. — **blonde**

Platon/ic (cap. in hist. or philos. contexts) *but* **platonic love** (not cap.); **-ism, -ist, -ize** *not* -ise

Plattdeutsch Low German (one word)

platteland/ (S. Afr.) remote country districts, **-er**

platypus/ the Australian duckbill, pl. **-es**

platyrrhine broad-nosed (of monkeys), *not* -yrhine

plausible *not* -able

Plautus, Titus Maccius (*c*.254–*c*.184 BC) Roman playwright, abbr. **Plaut.**

play-act/or, -ing (hyphens, one word in US)

playback (noun) (one word)

play/bill, -boy, -fellow, -girl, -goer, -ground, -group, -house (one word)

playing/ card, — field (two words)

play/let, -list, -mate (one word)

play/-off (noun; hyphen, one word in US)

playpen (one word)

plays, titles of when cited to be in italic

play/school, -thing, -time, -wright (one word)

plaza/ a public square, pl. **-s** (not ital.)

plc, PLC public limited company (no points); *use* caps. or lower case according to a company's preferred style; *see also* **AG; Inc.; KK; NV; Pty; SA; SpA**

plead past and past part. **pleaded** *or* (esp. US, Sc.) **pled**

pleased as Punch (one cap.)

pleasur/e, -able

plebeian a commoner in ancient Rome, vulgar, common; *not* -bian

plebiscit/e a vote of the people (no accent, not ital.), **-ary**

plebiscit/um (Lat.) a law passed by the *plebs*, pl. **-a**

plebs (Lat.) the general populace, pl. ***plebes***

plectr/um pl. **-ums, -a**

pled *see* **plead**

Pleiad (Gr. myth.) one of the **Pleiades**, the seven daughters of Atlas (cap.); any brilliant group of seven (not cap.)

Pleiades a star-group

plein air (Fr. m.) the open air, outside

pleinairist a painter reproducing effects of atmosphere and light (not ital.)

Pleistocene (geol.) (of or relating to) the first epoch of the Quaternary period; also called the **ice age**

Plen. plenipotentiary

pleno jure (Lat.) with full authority

plethora an excess, glut; (med.) an excess of red corpuscles in the blood; *not* a synonym for *many*

pleur/a a membrane lining the thorax or enveloping the lungs, pl. **-ae**; **-isy** inflammation of this; **-itic**

pleuropneumonia (one word)

Plexiglas (US propr.) = **perspex**, *not* -ss

plexus/ a network (of nerves etc.), pl. **-es**

plf. plaintiff

plié/ (ballet) a bending of the knees with the feet on the ground (not ital.); pl. **-s**

Plimsoll line (naut.) *properly* **loadline**, the marking on a ship's side showing the limit of legal submersion under various conditions; *not* -'s; named after **Samuel Plimsoll** (1824–98) English politician and promoter of the Merchant Shipping Act of 1876

plimsolls rubber-soled canvas shoes, *not* -es

Plinlimmon *use* **Plynlimon**

Pliny/ the Elder in Lat. **Gaius Plinius Secundus** (23–79) and his nephew — **the Younger** (**Gaius Plinius Caecilius Secundus**) (*c*.61–*c*.112) Roman writers

Pliocene (geol.) (of or relating to) the last epoch of the Tertiary period

plissé gathering, kilting, or pleating (not ital.)

PLO Palestine Liberation Organization

plod/, -der, -ding

PL/1 a (comput.) programming language (caps. or even small caps.)

plow (esp. US) = **plough**, *but* **Piers Plowman** by Langland

PLP Parliamentary Labour Party

PLR Public Lending Right

plumb vertical, determine depth using a plumb line

plumbum lead, symbol **Pb**

plummy abounding or rich in plums, (colloq.) (of a voice) sounding affectedly rich or deep in tone

plum pudding (hyphen when attrib.)

plumy plumelike, *not* -ey

plung/e, -ing

Plunket family name of Baron Plunket

Plunkett family name of the Earl of Fingall, and of Barons Dunsany and Louth

pluperfect abbr. **plup.**

plural/ abbr. **pl.**, **-ize** *not* -ise

plus/ with the addition of, sign +; an additional amount, an advantage, pl. **-es**

Plutarch (*c*.50–*c*.120) Greek philosopher and biographer, abbr. **Plut.**

Pluto (Rom. myth.) the god of the underworld, (astr.) planet, symbol ♇

plutonium symbol **Pu**

Plutus (Gr. myth.) the personification of riches

pluviometer a rain gauge, *not* pluvia-

Plymouth Brethren a religious sect formed *c*.1830, abbr. **PB**

Plynlimon a Welsh mountain; *not* Plin-, -limmon

Plzeň Czech for **Pilsen**

PM paymaster, postmaster, post-mortem, Prime Minister, Provost Marshal

Pm promethium (no point)

pm picometre (no point)

pm. premium, premolar

p.m. (Lat.) *post meridiem* (after noon) (not cap., points)

PMG Paymaster-General, Postmaster General

p.m.h. production per man-hour

PMRAFNS Princess Mary's Royal Air Force Nursing Service

PMS (US) premenstrual syndrome = **PMT**, (comput.) processor-memory switch

PMT (typ.) photo-mechanical tint, (finance) post-market trading, premenstrual tension

p.n. promissory note

PNdB perceived noise decibel(s)

PNEU Parents' National Educational Union

pneumatic relating to air or gases, abbr. **pneum.**

pneumon/ic pertaining to the lungs, **-ia**

PNG Papua New Guinea

pnxt. *pinxit* (painted this)

PO petty officer (RN), pilot officer (RAF), postal order, post office

Po polonium (no point)

po/ (colloq.) chamber pot, pl. **-s**

pocketbook (one word)

pocket handkerchief (two words, hyphen in US)

pocket knife (two words, one word in US)

pocket money (two words)

pocket-piece (hyphen)

poco/ (It.) a little, — *a poco* little by little

pococurant/e apathetic, careless (one word, not ital.); **-ism** *not* -eism

POD pay on delivery, Post Office Department

POD *Pocket Oxford Dictionary*

podestà (It. m.) municipal magistrate

Podgorica cap. of Montenegro, *formerly* **Titograd**

podiatr/ist, -y (US) = **chiropod**/ist, -y

podi/um a base or pedestal, pl. **-a**

Podsnappery English self-congratulatory philistinism, from Mr Podsnap in Dickens's *Our Mutual Friend*

podzol/ infertile acidic soil with minerals leached from the surface layers, *not* -sol; **-ization, -ize** *not* -isation, -ise

Poe, Edgar Allan (1809–49) US writer; *not* Alan, Allen

poêle (Fr. m.) stove, (f.) frying pan

poème (Fr. m.) a long poem

poems, titles of when cited to be roman quoted unless long enough to form a separate publication, in which case they are to be in italic

poenology *use* **pen-**

poésie (Fr. f.) poetry, a short poem

poet. poetic, -al; poetry

poetaster a paltry or inferior poet

poeticize *not* -ise

Poet/ **Laureate** (caps., two words); abbr. **PL**, pl. **-s Laureate**; *see also* **Austin; Betjeman; Bridges; Cibber; Lewis; Masefield; Southey; Tennyson**

Poets' Corner Westminster Abbey (caps.)

po-faced solemn (hyphen)

pogrom an organized massacre, esp. of Jews in Russia

poignard *use* **poni-**

poikilothermic (zool.) cold-blooded

poilu (Fr. m.) a French soldier, esp. of the First World War

Poincaré, Raymond (1860–1934) French statesman, President 1913–20

poiniard *use* **poni-**

poinsettia (bot.) *not* point-

point a general term for all marks of punctuation, esp. the full stop; *see also* **compass, point system**

point-blank (hyphen)

point/ *d'appui* (Fr. m.) base of operations, — *d'attaque* base of offensive operations

Point de Galle *see* **Galle**

point-device extremely precise (hyphen)

point duty (two words)

point-virgule (Fr. m.) the semicolon

pointsettia *use* **poins-**

points of omission *see* **ellipsis**

point system (typ.) an Anglo-American standard by which the bodies of all types are multiples, or divisions, of the twelfth of a pica; in the UK and USA 1 point = 0.351mm, in Europe 1 point = 0.376 mm; abbr. **pt.**

poire (Fr. f.) pear

poiré (Fr. m.) perry

poireau/ (Fr. m.) leek, pl. **-x**

poirée (Fr. f.) white beet, Swiss chard

poirier (Fr. m.) pear tree, wood from this

pois (Fr. m. sing. and pl.) pea

poise (phys.) a unit of dynamic viscosity, in SI units 10^{-1} Pa s; abbr. **P**

poisson/ (Fr. m.) fish, — *d'avril* April fool

poivre (Fr. m.) pepper

pokey (US sl.) jail

poky small and cramped, (US) annoyingly slow; *not* -ey

Pol. Poland, Polish

Poland abbr. **Pol.**

polarize *not* -ise

pole/axe, **-cat** (one word)

pol. econ. political economy

pole-jump (hyphen)

poles, the caps. when used as geographical designations, e.g. North Pole

pole vault (noun, two words; verb, hyphen)

Police (Ger.), *police* (Fr.) policy of insurance; *see also* **Polizei**

police constable (two words), abbr. **p.c.** (**PC** when used before a name)

policeman (one word)

police officer (two words)

police sergeant (two words), abbr. **p.s.** (**PS** when used before a name)

police/ **state**, — **station** (two words)

policewoman (one word)

polichinelle (Fr. m.) puppet, buffoon

poliomyelitis infantile paralysis; (colloq.) **polio**/, pl. **-s**

Polish abbr. **Pol.**

Polish notation (logic, math.) a system of formula notation without brackets and punctuation

polit. political, politics

politburo the principal policy-making committee of a Communist party, esp. (hist.) in the USSR (cap. as title); in Russ. *politbyuro*

politesse (Fr. f.) formal politeness

Politian (1454–94) Italian humanist, in It. **Angelo degli Ambrogini**, known as **il Poliziano**

politic/, **-ize** *not* -ise; **-ked**, **-king**; **-s**

political correctness abbr. **PC**

political economy abbr. **pol. econ.**

politico/ one devoted to politics, pl. **-s**

polity an organized society, form of civil government

Polizei (Ger. f.) police (cap.); *see also* **Police**

polka/, **-ed**

polka dot (hyphen when attrib.)

pollack a sea fish, *not* -ock

pollen/ analysis, — count (two words)

poll/ex thumb, pl. **-ices**

polling/ booth, — day (two words)

Pollock, Jackson (1912–56) US abstract expressionist painter

Pollok, Robert (1798–1827) Scottish poet

Pollok/shaws, -shields Glasgow

pollster a sampler of public opinion

poll tax (two words)

Pollyanna an irrepressibly cheerful optimist, from the eponymous heroine of a novel by Eleanor Porter, 1913

polonaise a dance, music, type of woman's dress, or method of cooking in the Polish style

polonium symbol **Po**

Pol Pot (*c.*1925–98) Cambodian communist leader of the Khmer Rouge, Prime Minister 1976–9, born **Saloth Sar**

Poltoratsk Turkmenistan, *now* **Ashgabat**

poly/ (colloq.) polytechnic, pl. **-s**

polyandr/y marriage to more than one husband at the same time, **-ous**

polyanthus/ (bot.) *not* -os, pl. **-es**

Polybius (*c.*200–*c.*118 BC) Greek historian, abbr. **Polyb.**

polyethylene polymerized ethylene

polygam/y marriage to more than one wife or husband at the same time, **-ous**

polygen/y the theory that humankind originated from several independent pairs of ancestors; **-ism, -ist**

polyglot/, **-tal, -tic**

polygyn/y marriage to more than one wife at the same time, **-ous**

polyhedr/on *not* polye-, pl. **-a**

Polyhymnia (Gr. myth.) the muse of rhetoric

Polynesia/ islands in central Pacific (a bishopric, not a political unit); **-n** (a native) of Polynesia; (of or concerning) the Austronesian family of languages including Maori, Hawaiian, and Samoan

polynya a stretch of open water surrounded by ice, esp. in the Arctic seas (not ital.)

Polyolbion a poem by Drayton, 1613–22

polyp/ (zool.) pl. **-s**

polyp/us (med.) pl. **-i**

polysem/y (philol.) the existence of many meanings (of a word etc.); **-ic, -ous**

polytechnic (cap. when part of name) (colloq.) **poly**

polythene the commercial name for a polyethylene

poly/urethane, -vinyl chloride synthetic resins or plastics

polyzoan *use* **bryozoan**

pomade a preparation for the hair, *not* pomm-

pomelo/ a fruit, the shaddock; pl. **-s**; *not* pomm-, pu-

pomfret-cake *see* **Pontefract-cake**

Pommard a burgundy, *not* Pomard

pommel/ a knob, saddle bow; **-led, -ling** (one *l* in US); cf. **pummel**

pommelo *use* pom-

pommes/ (Fr. f. pl.) apples, **— de terre** potatoes

Pommy Austral. and NZ term for a Briton (esp. a recent immigrant); *NODE* and *COD* 10th edn. label it 'informal, derogatory'; the *Australian COD* has no cap. and labels it 'colloq.', adding *pommy bastard* as 'a term of affectionate abuse'; abbr. **Pom**

pompano/ a W. Indian and N. American food-fish, pl. **-s**

Pompeian of Pompeii

pom-pom an automatic quick-firing gun, often on a ship

pompon an ornamental tuft or ball, as worn on a hat or brandished by cheerleaders; *not* -pom (US; hyphen in US)

poncho/ a S. American cloak or one of similar design, pl. **-s**

pondere (Lat.) by weight, abbr. **p.**

Pondicherry India, in Fr. **Pondichéry**

pongo/ an ape, (naut. sl.) a soldier, (Austral., NZ sl. offens.) an Englishman; pl. **-s**

poniard a dagger; *not* poign-, poin-

Poniatowski,/ Józef Antoni (1763–1813) Polish soldier, **— Stanisław August** (1732–98) last King of Poland

pons (Lat.) a bridge, pl. *pontes*

pons asinorum any difficult proposition, originally a rule of geometry from Euclid, lit. 'bridge of asses'

Pontacq a white wine

Pontefract-cake a small liquorice sweet originally made at Pontefract (*earlier* Pomfret) in Yorkshire; *not* pomfret-

pontif/ex (eccl.) a bishop, (Rom. hist.) a member of a priestly college; pl. **-ices**; **Pontifex Maximus** a head of college

pont/iff a bishop, esp. the Pope; **-ifical**

Pont-l'Évêque dép. Calvados, France; a cheese

Pontypridd Mid Glam.

Pooh-Bah a holder of many offices at once, from a character in Gilbert and Sullivan's *The Mikado*, 1885

pooh-pooh to scorn, ridicule; *not* poo-poo

pooja *use* **pu-**

pooka a hobgoblin, in Ir. *púca*

Pool Corn., W. Yorks.

Poole Dorset

Poole, William Frederick (1821–94) US librarian, compiler of *Poole's Index*

Poona India, *not* -ah; *also now* **Pune**

poor box (two words)

poorhouse (one word)

Poor Law (caps. when hist.)

poor rate (hist.) assessment for relief of poor (two words, no caps.)

Poorten-Schwartz *see* **Maartens**

POP (comput.) point of presence, Post Office Preferred (size of envelopes etc.)

Pop a social club and debating society at Eton College

pop/ (colloq.) popular, — **art**, — **music** that based on popular culture (two words)

pop. population

popadam, -dom *use* **poppadam**

Pope cap. as title for a specific man: 'the Pope', 'Pope John Paul II'; not cap. for general concept and in ref. to more than one person

Pope/, **Alexander** (1688–1744) English poet, satirist, and translator; **-an**

Pope Joan a card game (two words)

Popocatepetl a volcano, Mexico

poppadom a thin, crisp, spiced bread eaten with curry etc.; *not* popa-, -dum

Popsicle (US and Canadian propr.) a rectangular ice lolly with two flat handles (cap.)

popularize *not* -ise

population abbr. **pop.**

populus (Lat.) people, abbr. **P.**

porc (Fr. m.) pork, pig

Porch, the the Stoic school of philosophy

Porchester/, **Lord**; — **Terrace** London; *see also* **Port-**

Porsche a German make of car

Porson/ a sloping Greek typeface, supposedly derived from the Greek hand of **Richard** — (1759–1808) English Greek scholar

Port. Portug/al, -uese

Portakabin (propr.) a portable room or building designed for quick assembly

portament/**o** (mus.) a continuous glide (not break) from one note to another of different pitch, pl. **-i**

Portarlington, Earl of

Port au Prince Haiti

Port aux Basques Newfoundland

Portchester Hants.; *see also* **Porch-**

Portcullis (her.) one of the four pursuivants of the English College of Arms

Porte/ (hist.) the Turkish court and government, more fully **the Sublime** —

porte cochère (no accent in US)

Port Elizabeth Cape Province, abbr. **PE**

portent/, **-ous** *not* -ious

Porter, William Sydney *see* **Henry, O.**

portfolio/ pl. **-s**

Port Glasgow Strathclyde

Porthmadog Gwynedd, *formerly* Portmadoc

portico/ pl. **-es**; **-ed**

portière a door curtain (no accent in US)

Portland/ **cement**, — **stone**

portmanteau/ pl. **-s**; — **word** one blending the sounds and combining the meanings of two others, e.g. *motel*, *Oxbridge*, *smog* (not ital.)

Porto Port. for **Oporto** (*o* being the definite article), in hist. Port. and Brazilian Port. **Pôrto**

Porto Bello Panama, *use* **Puerto Bello**

Portobello/ Lothian, — **Road** London (one word)

Port of Spain Trinidad

Porto Rico *use* **Puerto Rico**

Portpatrick Dumfries & Galloway (one word)

portrait (typ.) a book, page, or illustration of which the depth is greater than the width; cf. **landscape**

Port-Royal monastery, Versailles and Paris (hyphen)

Port Royal Jamaica; SC (two words)

Port Salut a cheese (two words)

Portsmouth: the signature of the Bishop of Portsmouth (colon)

Portugal abbr. **Port.**

Portuguese abbr. **Port.**

pos. positive

pos/**e, -ed, -ing**

Posen *use* **Poznań**

pos/**er** a problem; **-eur** f. **-euse** one who behaves affectedly, pl. **-eurs, -euses**

posey *use* **posy**

posit/, **-ed, -ing**

posology (med.) the study of dosages

poss. possess/ion, -ive

posse/ a body of men, pl. **-s**; — **comitatus** (hist.) a county force of men over 15

Post, Van der *see* **Van der Post**

post (Lat.) after, abbr. **p.**

postage/ **meter** (US) = **franking machine**; — **stamp** (two words)

postal code *use* **postcode**

postal order abbr. **PO**

post/**bag, -box, -card** (one word)

post-classical (hyphen)

postcode (one word)

post-date (verb and noun, hyphen, one word in US)

postdoctoral (one word)

poste restante a post office department where letters remain till called for (not ital.)

post-exilic subsequent to the exile of the Jews in Babylon (hyphen)

postgraduate (one word)

post-haste (hyphen, one word in US)

post hoc/ (Lat.) after this; — — *ergo propter hoc* after this, therefore because of this, the fallacy of consequence for sequence

post horn (mus.) (two words)

posthumous occurring after death, *not* postu-

Posthumus a character in Shakespeare's *Cymbeline*

postilion one who guides post- or carriage-horses, riding the near one; *not* -llion

post-Impressionis/m (hyphen, one word in US; one cap.: I in UK, P in US); **-t**

post-industrial (hyphen)

post initium (Lat.) after the beginning (as of a work), abbr. *post init.*

Post-it (propr.) (one cap., hyphen)

post litem motam (Lat.) after litigation began

post/man, -mark (one word)

postmaster abbr. **PM**; *also* a scholar at Merton College, Oxford (one word)

postmaster general the head of a country's postal service, abolished as an office in the UK; pl. **postmasters general**

post medium (Lat.) after the middle (as of a work), abbr. *post med.*

post meridiem (Lat.) after noon, abbr. **p.m.**

post-millennial/, -ism, -ist (hyphen, one word in US)

postmistress (one word)

postmodern/ (one word, not cap.), **-ism, -ist**

post mortem (Lat.) after death

post-mortem (adj. and noun) abbr. **PM** (hyphen, one word in US; not ital.)

post/-natal, -nuptial (hyphens, one word in US)

post-obit taking effect, or a bond payable, after death (hyphen, not ital.)

Post Office, The (caps., two words) public corporation, replaced the government department in 1969

post office (not caps., two words) a local office of the above, abbr. **PO**; (US) a children's game = **postman's knock**

post-paid (hyphen, one word in US) abbr. **p.p.**

postpositi/on a word or particle placed after another; **-ve** designating this (one word)

postprandial after dinner (one word)

postscript (one word) abbr. **PS**, pl. **PSS**

post-structural/ (hyphen), **-ism, -ist**

post terminum (Lat.) after the conclusion

postumous *use* **posth-**

post-war use only as adj., not adv. (hyphen, one word in US)

posy a nosegay, *not* -ey

Pot, Pol *see* **Pol Pot**

pot. potential

potage a thick soup

potassium symbol **K**

potato/ pl. **-es**; — **chips** (US) = — **crisps**

pot-au-feu (Fr. cook. m.) a large cooking pot, a meat broth

poteen alcohol made illicitly, usually from potatoes; *not* pott-, poth-; in Ir. *poitín*

potential abbr. **pot.**

pothole/, -r (one word)

pot-pourri a mixture or medley (hyphen, one word in US)

potsherd a piece of broken earthenware, *not* -ard

potteen *use* **poteen**

Potteries, the general name for a group of six towns in Staffordshire associated with production of pottery and china: Burslem, Fenton, Hanley, Longton, Stoke-on-Trent, and Tunstall; also called 'the Six Towns'; *see also* **the Five Towns**

potter's field a burial place for paupers, strangers, etc. (after Matt. 27: 7); *not* -s'

potting shed (two words)

potto/ a W. African lemur-like animal, a kinkajou; pl. **-s**

pouce (Fr. m.) an inch, a thumb; abbr. **p.**

pouding (Fr. cook. m.) pudding

poudr/é (Fr.) f. **-ée** powdered

Poughkeepsie NY

Pouilly/ dép. Saône-et-Loire, France, source of **-Fuissé** white wine; **-sur-Loire** dép. Nièvre, France, source of **-Fumé** white wine (hyphens)

poulard a fattened domestic hen, in Fr. f. *poularde*

poule (Fr. f.) hen

poulet (Fr. m.) young chicken

poulette (Fr. f.) young hen

POUNC Post Office Users' National Council

pound avoirdupois, approx. 453 g; abbr. **lb**, pl. same (not in scientific use)

pound sign (money) **£** (sing. and pl.); *see also* at **l.**

pour/ (Fr.) for, abbr. **p.**; — *ainsi dire* so to speak

pourboire (Fr. m.) gratuity, tip

pourparler (Fr. m.) preliminary discussion (one word)

pousse-café (Fr. m.) liqueur (after coffee)

poussette a dance with hands joined, to do this (not ital.)

Poussin, Nicolas (1594–1665) French painter

poussin a very young chicken (not ital.)

pou sto (Gr.) standing-place

POW Prince of Wales, prisoner of war

powder/ flask, — keg, — magazine, — monkey, — puff, — room (two words)

power/ boat, — cut, — dive, — factor (two words)

powerhouse (one word)

power/ plant, — station (two words)

Powis, Earl of family name Herbert

powwow a Native American conference, or any meeting compared to this; *not* pawaw (one word)

Powys family name of Baron Lilford; a Welsh county

Poznań Poland, *not* Posen

PP parish priest, Past President, (Lat.) *Patres* (Fathers)

pp. pages

p.p. past participle, post paid, (Lat.) *per procurationem* (q.v.)

pp (mus.) pianissimo (very soft), più piano (softer)

p.p.b. parts per billion (10⁹)

PP C (Lat.) *Patres Conscripti* (Conscript Fathers) (thin space)

PPC (Fr.) *pour prendre congé*

PPE Philosophy, Politics, and Economics (Oxford degree subject)

p.p.m. parts per million

PPP Psychology, Philosophy, and Physiology (Oxford degree subject)

ppp (mus.) pianississimo (as softly as possible)

PPS Parliamentary *or* principal private secretary, *post-postscriptum* (further postscript)

PQ Parliamentary Question, previous (or preceding) question; Province of Quebec, Canada; (Fr.) Parti québécois (Quebec Party)

PR (Lat.) *Populus Romanus* (the Roman people), prize ring, Proportional Representation, Public Relations, Puerto Rico

Pr praseodymium (no point)

Pr. priest

pr. pair, -s; price

PRA President of the Royal Academy

praam a boat, *use* **pram**

Prachtausgabe (Ger. typ. f.) de luxe edition

practicable that can be done or used, possible in practice; *see also* **impracticable**

practical of, concerned with, or suited to practice or use rather than theory; *see also* **impractical, unpractical**

practice (noun, in US also verb)

practise (verb)

Practising Law Institute US legal publishers, *not* -cing

Prado a Madrid art gallery; cf. **Pardo Palace**

praecipe (law) a writ demanding action or an explanation of non-action, an order requesting a writ (ital., roman in US)

praemunire (hist.) a sheriff's writ concerned with papal jurisdiction (not ital.)

praenomen a Roman first name, *not* pren-

praepostor a school prefect; *not* prep-, -itor

praeses *use* **pre-**

praesidium *use* **pres-**

Praeterita Ruskin's (unfinished) autobiography, 1889

praetor/ a Roman magistrate, **-ian**; *not* pre-

Praga a suburb of Warsaw; It. for **Prague**

Prague the Czech Republic; Eng. and Fr. for Czech **Praha**; in Ger. **Prag**

prahu *use* **proa**

Prakrit any of the (esp. ancient or medieval) vernacular dialects of N. and Cent. India

pram a perambulator; a flat-bottomed gunboat or Baltic cargo boat, a Scandinavian ship's dinghy; *not* praam

praseodymium symbol **Pr**

Prayer Book (caps., two words) abbr. **PB**

Prayer of Manasses (Apocr.) abbr. **Pr. of Man.**

PRB Pre-Raphaelite Brotherhood (group of artists), 1848

pre-adam/ic, -ite (hyphens, not cap.)

pre-adolescent (hyphen, one word in US)

preamplifier (one word)

Préault, Antoine Auguste (1809–79) French sculptor

preb. prebend, -ary

prec. preceding, precentor

Precambrian (geol.) (of or relating to) the earliest era of geological time

precede *not* -eed

precent/or a controller of cathedral music, f. **-rix**; abbr. **prec.**

precept/or teacher, f. **-ress**

preces (Lat.) prayers

precession (astr.) the successively earlier occurrence (of the equinoxes), (dyn.) the rotation of the axis of a spinning body about another body

pre-Christian (hyphen, cap. *C*)

Précieuses ridicules, Les a play by Molière, 1659

précieu/x (Fr.) an affected man, f. **-se**

precipitate hasty

precipitous steep

précis/ (to write) a summary, pl. same (not ital.); as verb **-ed, -ing**

precisian one who is rigidly precise, esp. in religious observance, (hist., in hostile sense) a Puritan

precisionist one who makes a practice of precision

preclassical (one word)

pre-Columbian (hyphen, cap. *C*)

preconce/ive, -ption (one word)

precursor forerunner, *not* -er

pred. predicative, -ly

pre-dat/e, -ed, -ing (hyphen, one word in US)

predecease (noun and verb, one word)

predicant a preacher, esp. Dominican

predictor *not* -er

predikant (Afrik.) a preacher of the Dutch Reformed Church, esp. in S. Africa

predilection partiality

predispos/e, -ition (one word)

pre-echo/, -ing (hyphens, one word in US)

pre-elect/, -ion (hyphens, one word in US)

pre-eminen/t, -ce (hyphens, one word in US)

pre-empt/, -ion, -ive (hyphens, one word in US)

pre-exilic prior to exile of Jews in Babylon (hyphen, one word in US)

pre-exist/, -ence (hyphens, one word in US)

pref. preface, preference, preferred; prefix, -ed

prefab (colloq.) a prefabricated building (no point)

prefabricate (one word)

preface an introductory address to the reader in which the author explains the purpose, prospective readership, and scope of the book and may include a brief acknowledgement to colleagues or advisers in the absence of an acknowledgements section; abbr. **pref.**

préfecture/ (Fr. f.) the county hall in a French town, **— de police** office of the commissioner of police

prefer/, -able, -ably, -ence, -red -ring; abbr. **pref.**

préfet (Fr. m.) prefect

prefix/, -ed abbr. **pref.**

pre/form, -frontal, -heat, -historic (one word)

Preignac a white wine

prejudge/, -ment (one word), *not* prejudgment (US)

prelim. preliminary

preliminary matter (typ.) all matter preceding the main text; (colloq.) **prelims**

pre-makeready (typ.) careful preparation of the forme before it goes to the machine

pre/marital, -menstrual (one word)

premier/ (short for — minister) the first or chief minister (of a country or institution), esp. the first minister of the Crown (= **Prime Minister**); (Austral. and Canadian) the chief minister of a state or province, or (US obs.) the Secretary of State

premi/er (Fr.) f. **-ère** first; abbrs. **1ᵉʳ, 1ᵉʳᵉ**

premiere/ (give) the first performance of a film or play; as verb, **-d** (not ital., no accent)

première danseuse (Fr. f.) the principal female dancer in a ballet

premise (verb) say or write by way of introduction, or (logic) create or apply a premiss

premises (noun, pl.) a house or building with its grounds and appurtenances; (law) the houses, lands, or tenements previously specified in a document or the like

premiss/ a previous statement from which another is inferred or follows as a conclusion, a proposition; pl. **-es**; *also* **premise**

premium/ abbr. **pm.**, pl. **-s**

premolar a tooth, abbr. **pm.**

Premonstratensian (hist.) (of or relating to) (a member of) an order of regular canons founded at Prémontré in France in 1120, or the corresponding order of nuns

prenomen *use* prae-

preoccup/y, -ation (one word)

preordain (one word)

prep/ (colloq. Brit.) the preparation of school work by a pupil, the period when this is done; (colloq. US) (as or like) a student in a preparatory school, *see also* **preppy**

prep. preparat/ion, -ory; preposition

pre/paid, -pay (one word)

preparatory school a usually private school preparing pupils for a higher school, or (US) for college or university (= **public school**)

prepositor *use* praepost-

prepossess (one word)

preppy (US colloq.) (of or concerning) a person attending a private school, with conservative clothes and outlook; *not* -ie

pre-prandial (hyphen)

pre-preference ranking before preference shares (hyphen, one word in US)

Pre-Raphaelite/ (caps., hyphen), **— Brotherhood** abbr. **PRB**

prerequisite (one word)

Pres. president

Pres, Josquin des *see* **Josquin des Prez**

présalé (Fr. m.) salt-marsh sheep or mutton (one word), pl. *prés-salés* (hyphen)

Presb. Presbyterian

presbyop/ia a failing of near sight in the elderly, **-ic**

Presbyterian (cap.) abbr. **Presb.**

prescribable *not* -eable

prescribe advise the use of, recommend, lay down or impose authoritatively; cf. **proscribe**

pre-select/, -ive, -or *not* -er (hyphens)

Preseli a district of Dyfed

present author, the *prefer* **I** *or* **me**

presentiment a vague expectation or foreboding

presently soon, after a short time; *also* (esp. US and Sc.) immediately, at the present time

presentment the act of presenting information

preses (Sc.) a president or chairman, pl. same; *not* prae-

preset (one word)

pre-shrunk (hyphen)

president abbr. **P., Pres.**

presidium a standing executive committee in a Communist country, esp. in the former USSR; *not* prae-

Presocratic (philos.) prior to Socrates, *not* pre-Socratic (US)

press, the newspapers, journalists, etc., generally or collectively (not cap.); a specific printing establishment or publishing company, with or without the organization's full name: 'Athlone Press', 'the (Oxford University) Press' (cap.)

press agent (two words)

Press Association abbr. **PA**

press box a shelter for reporters at outdoor functions (two words)

press-button (hyphen)

press conference (two words)

Pressensé, Edmond Dehaut de (1824–91) French theologian and statesman

press gallery esp. in House of Commons (two words)

press-gang (hyphen)

pressman (one word)

pressmark that which shows the place of a book in a library (one word), *now usually* **shelf mark**

press-proof (typ.) the last one examined before platemaking or going to press (hyphen)

press stud (two words), colloq. known as *popper* in Britain and *snap* in the USA

press-up (hyphen)

pressure (mech.) symbol *p*

pressurize produce or maintain pressure (in something); in abstract senses *use* **pressure**

presswork (typ.) the preparation for and control of the printing-off of composed material; the work thus produced

Presteigne Powys

Prester John a mythical medieval priest-king of Cent. Asia or Abyssinia; a novel by John Buchan, 1910 (ital.)

prestissimo (mus.) very quickly

presto (mus.) quickly

Prestonpans Lothian (one word)

prestressed (hyphen)

Prestwich Gr. Manchester

Prestwick Northumb., Strathclyde

presum/e, -able, -ably, -ing

presumptive giving grounds for an inference from known facts; *see also* **heir presumptive**

presumptuous unduly or overbearingly confident and presuming

presuppos/e, -ition (one word)

pret. preterite

prêt-à-porter (Fr. m.) ready-to-wear (clothes)

pre/-tax, -teen (hyphen, one word in US)

pretence *not* -se (US)

preten/sion, -tious

preterite the past tense, *not* -it; abbr. **pret.**

preternatural etc. (one word)

pretor *use* prae-

pretzel a crisp knot- or stick-shaped salted biscuit or bread, *not* br-

Preussen Ger. for Prussia

preux chevalier (Fr. m.) a brave knight

prevail/, -ed, -ing

prevaricate speak or act evasively or misleadingly, quibble or equivocate; cf. **procrastinate**

preventive *not* -tative, -titive

previous abbr. **prev.**

Prévost, Marcel (1862–1941) French novelist

Prévost d'Exiles, Antoine François (1679–1765) French novelist, known as **Abbé Prévost**

prévôt (Fr. m.) provost

prevue *use* **preview**

pre-war use only as adj., not adv. (hyphen, one word in US)

Prez, Josquin des *see* **Josquin des Prez**

PRI *Partido Revolucionario Institucional* (Mexican governing party), President of the Royal Institute of Painters in Water Colours

PRIBA President of the Royal Institute of British Architects

Pribilof Island Bering Sea

price abbr. **pr.**

price-fixing (hyphen)

price/ list, ring (two words)

prices current abbr. **p/c**

price tag (two words)

pricey *not* -cy

prie-dieu a kneeling stool (hyphen, not ital.)

priest abbr. **Pr.**

prig/, -gery, -gish, -gism

prim. primary, primate, primitive

prima (typ.) the page of copy on which a new batch of proof begins; also a mark on copy where this begins or where reading is to be resumed after interruption; pron. 'prī-ma'

prima/ ballerina pl. **— ballerinas, — donna** pl. **— donnas** (not ital.)

primaeval use **prime-**

prima facie (adv., adj., no hyphen, not ital.)

Primate of/ All England the Archbishop of Canterbury, **— — England** the Archbishop of York

prime/ (math.) symbol ', **double —** symbol ″; a fencing position

Prime Minister (two words, caps.) abbr. **PM**

primeval of the first age of the world, *not* -aeval

primigravid/a a woman in her first pregnancy, pl. **-ae**

primipar/a a woman bearing her first child, pl. **-ae**

primitive abbr. **prim.**

primo/ (mus.) the upper part in a duet, pl. **-s**

primo (Lat.) in the first place, abbr. **1°**

primum mobile (Lat.) the central or most important source of motion or action

Primus (propr.) a portable stove (cap.)

primus the presiding bishop of the Scottish Episcopal Church

primus/ (Lat.) first, abbr. **p.**; **— inter pares** first among equals

prin. principal

prince abbr. **P.**; **Prince of/ Glory, — — Life**, *or* **— — Peace** as Deity (caps.)

Prince of Wales/ abbr. **POW, — — — Island** off Penang

princeps (Lat.) the first, pl. **principes**; *see also* **editio princeps**

Princes Town Trinidad

Princeton town and university, NJ

Princetown Devon, Mid Glam.

principal (adj.) chief; (noun) the chief person (cap. as title of an office); abbr. **prin.**

principe (Fr. m.) principle

príncipe (Sp. m.) a Spanish crown prince (not ital., cap. as title); cf. **infante**

Principe, Il (It.) Machiavelli's *The Prince*

principessa (It. f.) an Italian princess (cap., not ital., as title)

principle a fundamental truth, moral basis

print. printing

print/, in still on sale; **out of —** new copies no longer obtainable, abbr. **o.p., o/p**

printani/er (Fr. cook.) f. **-ère** with early spring vegetables

printer abbr. **pr.**; **the King's**, *or* **Queen's, Printer/ of Bibles and Prayer Books** may print bibles (AV) and prayer books (1662) to the exclusion of all other English presses, except those of the universities of Oxford and Cambridge; **— — — of the Acts of Parliament** has the duty of providing an authoritative printing of all Acts of Parliament etc., and controls their copyright

printer's error pl. **print/er's**, *or* **-ers', errors** (use hyphen to avoid ambiguity: *bad printers'-errors*)

printing abbr. **ptg., print.**

print/maker, -out, -works (one word)

Prinz/ (Ger. m.) prince (usually of the blood royal), pl. **-en**; f. **-essin** pl. **-essinnen** (cap., not ital., as part of title); cf. **Fürst**

prise force open, *not* -ize (US)

prisonbreak, -er (one word)

Prisoner's Dilemma in game theory, a non-zero-sum game invented by A. W. Tucker (caps.), *not* Prisoners' —

pristine in its original condition, unspoilt, *not* a synonym for spotless

priv. privative

privat-docent (hist.) a German university lecturer paid only by students' fees, abbr. **PD**; in Ger. m. **Privatdozent**

Private (mil.) cap. as title, abbr. **Pte.**

privative denoting the loss or absence of something, esp. in grammar; abbr. **priv.**

privileg/e, -ed

priv/y secret, **-ily, -ity** (law) a recognized relation between two parties, e.g. that of blood, lease, or service

Privy Coun/cil, -sellor (two words, caps.) abbr. **PC**

Privy Seal abbr. **PS**

prix/ (Fr. m.) prize, price; **— fixe** fixed price

prize force open, use **-ise** (except in US)

prize/fight, -fighter (one word)

prize-giving (hyphen, two words in US)

prize/ money, — ring (two words)

prize/winner, -winning (one word)

p.r.n. *pro re nata* (as occasion may require)

PRO Public Record Office, Public Relations Officer

pro/ for, abbr. **p.**; (colloq.) professional, pl. **-s** (no point)

proa a Malay outrigged boat, *not* the many variants

proactive creating or controlling a situation by taking the initiative (one word)

pro-am involving professionals and amateurs (no points, hyphen)

pro and con for and against, pl. **pros and cons** (not ital., no points)

prob. probab/le, -ly; problem

probit (statistics) a unit of probability based on deviation from the mean of a standard distribution

probity uprightness, honesty

pro bono publico (Lat.) for the public good

probosci/s a long flexible trunk or snout, pl. **-ses**; *properly* **-des**

Proc. proceedings, proctor

proceed *not* -ede

procès (Fr. m.) lawsuit

process blocks (typ.) those made by photographic and etching processes, for printing illustrations by letterpress

procès-verb/al a written report, minutes; pl. **-aux** (not ital.)

proconsul (one word)

procrastinate defer action, be dilatory; cf. **prevaricate**

Procrustean using force to impose conformity, like Procrustes (Gr. myth.) (cap.)

Procter,/ Adelaide Anne (1825–64) English poet; — **Bryan Waller** *not* Walter (1787–1874) pseud. **Barry Cornwall**, English poet

Proctor, Richard Anthony (1837–88) British astronomer

proctor a university official, an attorney in spiritual courts; abbr. **Proc.**; **King's**, *or* **Queen's**, **Proctor** an official who can intervene in divorce cases

procurator-fiscal a Scottish law officer (not cap., hyphen), abbr. **PF**

prodrome a preliminary treatise or symptom, *not* -dromus

producible *not* -able

product (math.) symbol Π

proem/ a preface or preamble, **-ial**

pro et contra (Lat.) for and against; *see also* **pro and con**

Prof. Professor, pl. **Profs.**, *but* spell out before name (except in narrow measure)

profane secular, irreverent, blasphemous

Professeur (Fr. m.) professor (masculine regardless of the person)

professoriate *not* -orate

proffer/, -ed, -ing

profit/, -ed, -ing

profiterole a confection of choux pastry and sweet filling (not ital.)

Pr. of Man. Prayer of Manasses

pro forma/ (adv. and adj.) (done) as a matter of form, (noun) an invoice sent in advance of goods supplied (in full — — **invoice**); pl. **-s**

progr/amme *but* **-am** (noun and verb) in computing and in US

pro hac vice (Lat.) on this occasion (only), *not* hâc

Prohibition the prevention by law of the manufacture and sale of alcohol, esp. in the USA 1920–33 (cap.)

projector *not* -er

Prokofiev, Sergei (**Sergeevich**) (1891–1953) Russian composer

prolegomen/a preliminary remarks, sing. (rare) **-on**; **-ary, -ous**

proleps/is anticipation, esp. of adjectives in grammar; pl. **-es**

proletari/at the poorest class in a community, *not* -ate; **-an, -anize** *not* -ise

PROLOG (comput.) a programming language (caps. or even small caps.), *also* **Prolog**

prologize deliver a prologue; *not* -ise, -uize

prologue *not* -og

PROM (comput.) programmable read-only memory (caps. or even small caps.)

prom a paved public walk along seafront; (US) a school or university ball or dance, a promenade concert, esp. (Brit.) **The Proms** the Henry Wood Promenade Concerts

prom. promontory

Promethean of or like Prometheus (Gr. myth.)

promethium symbol **Pm**

promissory note abbr. **p.n.**

promoter one who or that which promotes, *not* -or

pron. pronominal, pronoun, pronounced, pronunciation

proneur flatterer, in Fr. **prôneur**

pronoun abbr. **pron.**

pronounc/e, -eable, -ed, -ement, -ing abbr. **pron.**

pronunciamento/ a manifesto, pl. **-s** (not ital.)

pronunciamiento (Sp.) a revolt, insurrection, coup

pronunciation *not* -nounc-

proof errors *see* **errors** (**on proof**)

proofread/, -er, -ing (one word, *but* sometimes hyphenated esp. as verb)

Prop. Propertius

prop (colloq.) (stage) property, propeller (no point)

prop. proposition

propagand/a an activity for the spread of a doctrine or practice, is *singular*; **-ize**, *not* -ise; **-ism, -ist**

proparoxytone (Gr. gram.) (a word) with acute accent on last syllable but two

pro patria (Lat.) for one's country

propel/, -led, -ler, -ling

propell/ant (noun), **-ent** (adj.)

properispomen/on (Gr. gram.) (a word) with circumflex on penultimate syllable, pl. **-a**

Propertius, Sextus (*c.*50–*c.*14 BC) Roman poet, abbr. **Prop.**

prophe/cy (noun), **-sy** (verb)

proportional (math.) symbol ∝

proposition abbr. **prop.**

Proprietary (Austral., NZ, S. Afr.) after name of company, abbr. **Pty.**

proprio motu (Lat.) of his, *or* her, own accord

propter hoc (Lat.) because of this; *see also* ***post hoc***

propylae/um (Lat. from Gr.) the entrance to a temple, pl. **-a**; **Propylaea** the entrance to the Acropolis at Athens (pl., cap.)

propylon/ (Gr.) the entrance to a temple, pl. **-s**

pro rata in proportion (not ital.)

prorate allocate or distribute pro rata (one word, not ital.)

pro re nata as occasion may require (ital.), abbr. **p.r.n.**

pros. prosody

prosceni/um the front part of the stage, pl. **-ums**

proscribe banish; cf. **prescribe**

proselyt/e a religious convert; **-ize** to convert, *not* -ise

prosit! (Lat. and Ger.) your good health!; *see also* ***prost!***

prosod/y the laws of poetic metre, abbr. **pros.**; **-ic**, **-ist**

prosopograph/y a description of a person's appearance, personality, social and family connections, career, etc., or the study of such descriptions (esp. in Rom. hist.); **-er**, **-ical**

prosopopoeia (rhet.) the introduction of pretended speaker

prospector *not* -er

prospectus/ pl. **-es**

prost! (Ger.) your good health! (standard form); *see also* ***prosit!***

prostate a gland surrounding the neck of the bladder in male mammals

prostrate lying face downwards or horizontally

pros/y commonplace, *not* -ey; **-ily**

Prot. Protectorate, Protestant

protactinium symbol **Pa**

protagonist the leading character in a play, novel, or cause (*not* the opp. of antagonist)

pro tanto (Lat.) to that extent

protean assuming different shapes, like Proteus (Gr. myth.); *not* -ian

protector *not* -er

Protectorate abbr. **Prot.**

protég/é one under the protection of a patron, f. **-ée**; pl. **-és**, **-ées** (not ital.)

pro tempore (Lat.) for the time being (not ital. in US), (colloq.) **pro tem** (no point, not ital.); abbr. **p.t.**

Proterozoic (geol.) (of or relating to) the later part of the Precambrian era; in US *also* **Algonkian**

Protestant/ abbr. **Prot.**; **-ism** (cap.)

protester *not* -or

'Prothalamion' a poem by Spenser, 1596

protocol/, **-led**, **-ling**

protonotary a chief clerk, esp. to some law courts; *not* protho-

prototype an original model

protozo/on a single-cell form of life, pl. **-a** (not ital., cap. as grouping of phyla); **-al**, **-ic**

protractor a drawing instrument, *not* -er

Proudhon, Pierre Joseph (1809–65) French socialist

Prov. Proven/ce, -çal; Proverbs, Province, Provost

prov. proverbially, provincial, provisional

prov/e, -able, -ed, lit., Sc., and US **-en**

proven, not (Sc. law) a verdict pronouncing evidence insufficient to determine guilt or innocence

provenance (place of) origin (not ital.), *not* -venience

Provençal/ (of or relating to) the region of Provence in SE France; a native of Provence, or the language spoken there; **Old —** a medieval form of Provençal

provençale, à la (Fr. cook.) with garlic or onions (not cap.)

Provence SE France (no cedilla), abbr. **Prov.**

provenience *use* -nance

Proverbs (OT) abbr. **Prov.**

provinc/e abbr. **Prov.**; **-ial** abbr. **prov.**

Province of Quebec Canada, abbr. **PQ**

Provincetown Mass.

proviso/ a stipulation, pl. **-s** (not ital.)

Provo/ a member of the Provisional IRA; pl. **-s**

Provost/ abbr. **Prov.**, **— Marshal** (caps., two words) abbr. **PM**

proxime/ accessit (Lat.) he, *or* she, came nearest (to winning a prize etc.) abbr. *prox. acc.*; pl. **— accesserunt**

proximo in, *or* of, the next month; do not abbr.

PRS Performing Rights Society, President of the Royal Society

PRSA President of the Royal Scottish Academy

PRSE President of the Royal Society of Edinburgh

Prudhomme/ divide Pru|dhomme; *see also* **Sully —**

prud'homme (Fr. m.) *formerly* good and true man; *now* expert, umpire

Prufrock, J. Alfred in T. S. Eliot's 'The Love Song of J. Alfred Prufrock', 1915

prunella a throat affliction; a strong silk or worsted material; a plant (as genus name, cap. and ital.)

Pruss. Prussia, -n

PS permanent secretary, Police Sergeant (*see also* **police constable**), *postscriptum* (postscript) (pl. **PSS**), private secretary, Privy Seal, (theat.) prompt side

Ps. Psalm

p.s. police sergeant

PSA President of the Society of Antiquaries

Psalm/ abbr. **Ps.**, pl. **-s** abbr. **Pss.**, **Book of Psalms** (OT) abbr. **Ps.**

psalm-book a book containing the Psalms (not cap., hyphen, one word in US)

psalmist the author of a psalm (not cap.); **the — David or the author of any of the Psalms (cap.)**

psalter the Book of Psalms (not cap.); a specific version of this (cap.)

psaltery an ancient and medieval plucked instrument

p's and q's (apos., no points) *or* **ps and qs**

PSBR public sector borrowing requirement

psepholog/y the study of patterns in voting; **-ical, -ist**

pseud (colloq.) (an) intellectually or socially pretentious (person) (no point)

pseud. pseudonym (full point)

pseudepigraph/a (pl.) **-ic, -ical**

pseudo/ pretentious or insincere (person), pl. **-s**

pseudonym an assumed name, abbr. **pseud.**

pseudo/science, -scientific (one word)

pshaw! an exclamation; *not* psha, -h

psi the twenty-third letter of the Gr. alphabet (Ψ, ψ), the lower-case form is used to denote parapsychological factors

p.s.i. pounds per square inch

p.s.i.g. pounds per square inch gauge

psilocybin a hallucinogenic alkaloid found in some mushrooms

psittac/ine of or related to parrots, parrot-like; **-osis** a contagious disease transmissible from birds to humans

PSS *postscripta* (postscripts) (no point)

Pss. *see* **Psalm**

PST (US) Pacific Standard Time

PSV public service vehicle

psych. psychic, -al

psychedelic *not* psycho-

psycho/ (colloq.) psychotic (person), pl. **-s**

psychoanaly/sis, -se, -st, -tic, -tical (one word)

psycho/babble, -drama, -dynamics (one word)

psychokinesis movement by psychic agency, abbr. **PK**

psychol. psycholog/y, -ical

psycho/sis pl. **-ses**, adj. **-tic**

psychotherapy (one word)

PT physical training, post town, pupil teacher

Pt platinum (no point)

Pt. (geog.) Point, Port

pt. part, payment; pint, -s; (math., typ.) point

p.t. (Lat.) *pro tempore* (for the time being)

PTA Parent–Teacher Association, Passenger Transport Authority

pta. peseta

Ptah (Egyptian myth.) the creator of the world

Pte. (mil.) Private

pterodactyl *not* -le

ptg. printing

ptisan a medicated or nourishing drink, esp. of barley water; cf. **tisane**

PTO please turn over, Public Trustee Office

Ptolemaic (hist.) of or relating to **Claudius Ptolemy** (*c.* AD 100–70) Alexandrian astronomer, or his theories; of or relating to the **Ptolemies**, a dynasty of Macedonian rulers of Egypt 323–30 BC

Pty. (Austral., NZ, S. Afr.) Proprietary (company) = **Ltd**

Pu plutonium (no point)

pub/ (colloq.) a public house, (Austral.) a hotel; **— crawl** (two words)

pub./ public, -an; publish, -ed, -er, -ing; **— doc.** public document

public address/, — — system (no hyphen even when attrib.; hyphen in US in all uses), abbr. **PA**

publican the keeper of a public house, (Austral.) the keeper of a hotel

public house (two words)

publicity agent (two words)

publicize *not* -ise

Public Lending Right the right of authors to payment when their work is lent by public libraries, based on an estimate drawn from a pool of libraries; abbr. **PLR**

public limited company abbr. **plc, PLC**

public school (Brit.) a private fee-paying secondary school, esp. for boarders; (US, Austral., Sc., etc.) any non-fee-paying school (two words)

publish/, -ed, -er, -ing abbr. **pub.**

Publishers Association/ (no apos.) abbr. **PA; Scottish — —** abbr. **SPA**

publisher's/ binding (bibliog.) the standard binding in which an edition is supplied to booksellers, **— imprint** *see* **imprint**

pucka *use* **pukka**

Pudd'nhead Wilson, The Tragedy of a novel by Mark Twain, 1894

pudend/um usually pl. **-a**, genitals (usually female)

Puebla Mexico

Pueblo Col.

pueblo/ a town or village in Spain or Latin America, pl. **-s**

Pueblo Indians any of the Native American tribes of SW USA, esp. the Hopi and Zuni

Puerto/ Bello Panama; — **Rico** W. Indian island, adj. — **Rican**; *not* Porto-

puff adder (two words)

puffball (one word)

puff pastry (two words)

pug/ dog, — **nose(d)** (two words); **-gish, -gy**

puggaree an Indian turban, hat-scarf; *not* the many variants

Pugwash/ NS, Canada; site of the first — **Conference**

puîn/é (Fr.) f. **-ée** younger, opp. to *aîné* senior

puisne (law) subsequent (to)

puja a Hindu rite of worship, a prayer; *not* poo-

pukka *not* puck-, -ah; *see also* **sahib**

pul/e to whine, **-ing**

Pulitzer/, Joseph (1847–1911) US journalist, endowed thirteen — **Prizes** for various genres of literature, journalism, and music

pull (typ.) a proof

Pullman a railway carriage or motor coach (cap.)

pull-out (something) that pulls out (hyphen, one word in US)

pullover a knitted garment (one word)

pull-up (hyphen)

pulque a Mexican fermented drink made from the sap of the maguey

pulsar (astr.) a source of pulsating radio signals

pulse-rate (hyphen)

pulsimeter a pulse measurer

Pulsometer (propr.) a pumping engine

pulverize *not* -ise

pumelo *use* pom-

pumice/, — **stone** (two words); **-ous**

pummel/ pound with the fists; **-led, -ling** (one *l* in US); cf. **pommel**

pummelo *use* pomelo

pump a light shoe, a plimsoll; (US) = **court shoe**

pumpernickel a black rye bread

Punchinello (cap.) the principal character in an Italian puppet show, hence **Punch** (no point)

punctatim (Lat.) point for point

punctilio/ (scrupulous observance of) a point of behaviour, pl. **-s**; adj. **-us**

punctus/ (Lat.) a point, pl. same; (in MSS) — *elevat/us* ꞉ (like an inverted semicolon), pl. — **-i**; — *interrogativ/us* ? (like a question mark), pl. — **-i**; — *vers/us* ; (like a semicolon), pl. — **-i**

pundit a Hindu sage, (gen.) an expert; in Hind. *paṇḍit*; *see also* **pandit**

Pune India, *also* (esp. hist.) **Poona**

Punica fides (Lat.) Punic faith, treachery

Punjab/ India and Pakistan; *not* -aub; **-i** (of or relating to) (a native) of Punjab, *not* -bee; *see also* **Panjabi**

punkah (Anglo-Ind.) a large fan, *not* -a

Punkt (Ger. typ. m.) point, dot, a full stop (cap.); *punktieren* to point, dot, or punctuate; *Punktierung* (f.) punctuation

PUO (med.) pyrexia (fever) of unknown origin

pup/a (zool.) a chrysalis, pl. **-ae** (not ital.)

pupillage (two *l*s)

puppy love (US) = **calf love**

pur *use* purr

-pur (Ind.) a city, as Nagpur, Kanpur

Puran/a any of a class of Sanskrit sacred writings on Hindu mythology, folklore, etc.; **-ic**

Purchas, Samuel (1577–1626) English compiler of voyages

purchas/able *not* -eable, **-er** *not* -or

purdah (Ind.) (a curtain for) seclusion of women of rank, *not* -a

purée pulped vegetables etc. (no accent in US)

purgatory (not cap.)

Purim a Jewish spring festival commemorating the defeat of Haman's plot to massacre the Jews (Esther 9)

puritan/ one strict in religion or morals (cap. in hist. use); **-ical, -ism, -ize** *not* -ise

purl in knitting, *not* pearl

Purleigh Essex

Purley Berks., London

purlieus surroundings, a person's bounds or limits

Purple Heart (US) a decoration for those wounded in action

purpose/, -ful, -less, -ly

purpure (her.) purple

purr (verb, noun), *not* pur

pur sang (Fr. m.) pure blood; (adj.) thoroughbred, total

purslane (bot.) a salad herb, *not* -lain

pursuivant (Brit.) an officer of the College of Arms ranking below a herald, (arch.) a follower or attendant

purveyor one whose business is to supply (food), *not* -er

push-bike (hyphen)

push-button (hyphen; as noun, two words in US)

push/cart, -chair (one word)

pushover (colloq.) something that is easily done; someone who can easily be overcome, persuaded, etc. (one word)

pushrod (one word)

Pushto, Pushtu *use* **Pashto**

pushup (US) = **press-up**

put in golf, *use* **putt**

put over make acceptable or effective, express in an understandable way; also (US) postpone, achieve by deceit

putre/fy go rotten, *not* -ify; **-scent** in the process of rotting; **-scible** liable to rot

putsch a revolutionary attempt (not cap.), in (Swiss) Ger. m. *Putsch*

putt in golf, *not* put

puttees strips of cloth worn round the lower leg for protection, *not* -ies

putt/o (It.) a figure of a child in Renaissance art, pl. **-i**

Puy-de-Dôme a dép. of France (hyphens, two caps.); in phrases, *puy* (Fr. m.) a volcanic plug, to have lower-case *p* and no hyphens, as *le puy de Dôme*

PVC polyvinyl chloride

Pwllheli Gwynedd

PWR pressurized water reactor

pwt pennyweight, *use* dwt.

Pwyll (Welsh myth.) a prince of Dyfed and 'Head of Hades'

pyaemia (med.) a type of blood poisoning, *not* pyem- (US)

pycnic (anthrop.) *use* pyk-

pye (typ.) *use* **pie**

pyebald *use* **pie-**

pye-dog a vagrant mongrel, esp. in Asia; *not* pi-, pie-

pygm/y *not* pig-, **-aean** *not* -ean

pyjamas *not* pa- (US)

pyknic (anthrop.) (a person) of short, squat stature; *not* pyc-

Pylon School the nickname for a group of 1930s poets including Auden, Day-Lewis, Mac-Neice, and Spender

Pym,/ Barbara (**Mary Compton**) (1913–1980) English novelist, **— John** (1584–1643) English statesman

Pynchon, Thomas (b. 1937) US novelist

Pyongyang N. Korea

pyorrhoea a periodontal disease, or any discharge of pus; *not* -hea (US)

Pyrenees Mountains France and Spain

Pyrénées/-Atlantiques, Hautes- —, — -Orientales déps. of France

Pyrex (propr.) (cap.)

pyrit/es (in full **iron pyrites**) **-ic**; **-iferous**; **-ize** *not* -ise; **-ous**

pyro/lysis decomposition from heat, pl. **-lyses**; **-lyse** *not* -lyze

pyrotechnics abbr. pyrotech.

pyrrhic/ dance an ancient Greek war dance; **— foot** (prosody) a foot of two short syllables; **— victory** one won at too great a cost, like that of **Pyrrhus**, King of Epirus, over the Romans in 279 BC

Pyrrhon/ (*c*.300 BC) Greek sceptic philosopher, **-ism**

Pytchley Hunt, the

Pythagor/as (*c*.580–*c*.500 BC) Greek philosopher and mathematician, formulated **-as' theorem**; **-ean**

Pythian of or relating to Delphi (in Cent. Greece) or its ancient oracle of Apollo

python any of several non-venomous constricting snakes

pythoness the Pythian priestess, a witch

pyx/ (eccl.) the vessel in which the consecrated bread of the Eucharist is kept; a box at the Royal Mint in which specimen gold and silver coins are deposited to be tested annually, the **trial of the —**; *not* pix (not cap.)

Q quartermaster, Quarto (Shakespeare etc.), Queen('s), (chess) queen (no point), question, the sixteenth in a series

Q. pseud. of Sir Arthur Thomas Quiller-Couch

q. quaere, query, quintal; quire, -s; (meteor.) squalls

QAB Queen Anne's Bounty

Qaddafi, Muammar (Muhammad al-) (b. 1942) Libyan leader 1969– ; *use* Qaddāfī in specialist texts; *not* Gadafi, Gadhdhafi, Qadafy, Gaddafi (though preferred by *The Times*), Gadaffi

Qaisar-i-Hind *use* **K-**

Qantas Queensland and Northern Territory Aerial Service (Australian airline), *not* Qu-

QARANC Queen Alexandra's Royal Army Nursing Corps

QARNNS Queen Alexandra's Royal Naval Nursing Service

Qatar/ Persian Gulf, adj. **-i**

QB Queen's Bench, (chess) queen's bishop

QBD Queen's Bench Division

Q-boat (First World War) a merchant vessel with concealed guns

QBP (chess) queen's bishop's pawn

QC Queen's, *or* Queens', College; Queen's Counsel (title follows name, separated by a comma)

q.e. *quod est* (which is)

QED *quod erat demonstrandum* (which was to be demonstrated)

QEF *quod erat faciendum* (which was to be done)

QEI *quod erat inveniendum* (which was to be found out)

QF quick-firing

qibla *see* **kiblah**

QKt (chess) queen's knight, **QKtP** queen's knight's pawn

q.l. *quantum libet* (as much as you please)

Qld Queensland (no point)

QM Quartermaster

q.m. *quomodo* (by what means)

QMC Queen Mary College, London

Q.Mess. Queen's Messenger

QMG Quartermaster General

QMS Quartermaster Sergeant

QN (chess) queen's knight

QNP queen's knight's pawn

Qom a river, city, and former province, Cent. Iran (common spelling); **Qum** is a more exact transcription, **Ghom** reflects Pers. pronunciation

QP (chess) queen's pawn

q.pl. *quantum placet* (as much as seems good)

QPM Queen's Police Medal

QPR Queen's Park Rangers football club

qq.v. *quae vide* (which see) (refers to pl.) (not ital.)

QR (chess) queen's rook

qr. quarter, quire

QRP (chess) queen's rook's pawn

qrs. quarters

QS quarter sessions, Queen's Scholar

q.s. *quantum sufficit* (as much as suffices)

QSO quasi-stellar object, quasar

qt. quantity; quart(s)

q.t. (colloq.) (on the) quiet

qu. question

qua in the capacity or character of; *not* -à, -â (not ital.)

quad (colloq.) quadrangle; quadraphony; a quadruplet; (typ.) in metal setting, a piece of spacing material; in photosetting, the action of spacing out a line; (paper) a size of printing paper four times (quadruple) the basic size (no point in any sense)

quad. quadrant

Quadragesima the first Sunday in Lent

quadrant a quarter of a circle's circumference, quarter of a sphere, etc.

quadraphon/y sound reproduction using four transmission channels; **-ic, -ically**; *not* quadri-, quadro-; (colloq.) **quad**

quadrat (ecology) a small area marked out for study, *not* -te

quadrate (esp. anat., zool.) (to make) (something) square or rectangular

quadrenni/um a period of four years; pl. **-ums, -a**; **-al**; *not* quadrie-

quadrillion a thousand raised to the fifth power, 10^{15}; *formerly* (esp. Brit.) a thousand raised to the eighth power, 10^{24}

quadriplegia *not* tetra-

quadrivium (hist.) a medieval university course of arithmetic, geometry, astronomy, and music; cf. **trivium**

quaere (Lat. imperative) inquire, (as noun) a question; abbr. **q.**

quaestor an ancient Roman magistrate; cf. **que-**

quae vide (Lat.) which see (refers to plural), abbr. **qq.v.**

quag/ a marshy or boggy place, **-gy**

quagga (S. Afr.) an extinct zebra-like animal

quahog any of various edible clams of the Atlantic coast of N. America, *not* -haug

quai (Fr. m.) quay, railway platform

quaich a Scots drinking vessel, *not* -gh; in Gaelic *cuach*

Quaid-e-Azam/ College of Commerce and Business Administration Peshawar, — **Library** Lahore

Quaid-i-Azam University Islamabad

Quai d'Orsay Paris, the French Foreign Office

Quaker a member of the Society of Friends

quand même (Fr.) notwithstanding, all the same

quango/ quasi non-governmental organization, pl. **-s**

quant (propel with) a punting pole with a prong at the bottom to prevent it sinking into the mud

quantile (statistics) *not* fractile

quantity abbr. **qt.**

quantize *not* -ise

quant/um (not ital.) a natural minimum quantity of an entity, pl. **-a**; *see also* **Planck**

quantum/ (Lat.) a concrete quantity, pl. *quanta*; — *libet* as much as you please, abbr. *q.l.*; — *meruit* as much as he, *or* she, deserved; — *placet* as much as seems good, abbr. *q.pl.*; — *sufficit* as much as suffices, abbr. *q.s., quant. suff.*; — *vis* as much as you wish, abbr. *q.v.*

Qu'Appelle/ a river; **Bishop of** — Rupert's Land, Canada

Quarles, Francis (1592–1644) English poet

quarrel/, -led, -ler (*not* -lor), **-ling** (one *l* in US), **-some**

quart two pints (40 fl. oz, (US) 32 fl. oz), abbr. **qt.**; a sequence in piquet

quart. quarterly

Quart (Ger. n.) quarto (cap., not cap. if adj.)

quarte a position in fencing; *also* **quart**; *not* carte

quarter/, -s abbr. **qr., qrs.**

quarterback (one word)

quarter binding the spine in a different material from the rest of the case (two words), *but* **quarter-bound** (hyphen)

quarter day (two words)

quarterdeck (one word)

quarter-final (hyphen, one word in US)

Quarter Horse (caps.)

quarter-hour (hyphen)

quarter-light (hyphen)

quartermaster (one word) abbr. **QM, Q**; **Quartermaster/ General** (two words, caps.) abbr. **QMG**; — **Sergeant** (two words, caps.) abbr. **QMS**

quarter note (esp. US mus.) a crotchet

quarter-plate (hyphen)

quarter sessions (not caps.); abbr. **QS**

quarterstaff (hist.) a stout pole 6–8 feet long, formerly used as a weapon (one word)

quartet *not* -ette

quartier/ (Fr. cook. m.) quarter, — *d'agneau* quarter of lamb, *-général* military headquarters (hyphen), *Quartier Latin* the Latin Quarter of Paris (caps.)

quarto/ (typ.) a book based on four leaves, eight pages, to the sheet; pl. **-s**; abbr. **4to** (no point)

quasar a quasi-stellar object, abbr. **QSO**

quasi- a prefix with the sense 'seeming(ly)', 'almost'

Quasimodo/ the first Sunday after Easter (one word, cap.), a character in Hugo's *Notre-Dame de Paris*; —, **Salvatore** (1901–85) Italian poet

quass *use* **kvass**

quater/centenary (a celebration of) a four-hundredth anniversary, *not* quart-

quater-cousin *use* **cater-**

quaternary having four parts (not cap.); (geol.) (of or relating to) the most recent period in the Cenozoic era (cap.)

quatorzain any fourteen-line poem, an irregular sonnet

quatrain a stanza of four lines usually with alternate rhymes

Quatre-Bras battle, 1815

Quattrocento 1400–99, art and literature of the early Renaissance period (cap.)

quay a wharf, *not* key

QUB Queen's University, Belfast

Quebec/ Canada; abbr. **PQ, Que.**; adj. and noun **-ois**, pl. same; **Québécois** a French-speaking native or inhabitant, in Eng. **Quebecker** (cap.); **Parti québécois** Canadian political party (one cap.)

Quechua a S. American Indian language widely spoken in Peru and neighbouring countries, *not* Qui-

Queen abbr. **Q** (no point)

Queen Anne's Bounty formerly for augmenting Church of England livings (apos.), abbr. **QAB**

Queenborough Sheppey, Kent; *see also* **Queens-**

Queen Mary College London, *not* Mary's; abbr. **QMC**

Queen's abbr. **Q**

Queens a borough of New York City (no apos.)

Queensberry/ Rules the standard rules, esp. of boxing, named after **Sir John Sholto Douglas** (1844–1900) **8th Marquess of** —

Queensboro Bridge New York City, *not* -ough

Queensborough Co. Louth; *see also* **Queenb-**

Queensbury London, W. Yorks.

Queens College Charlotte, NC; Flushing, NY (no apos.)

Queen's College, The Oxford (named after one queen)

Queens' College Cambridge (named after two queens)

Queen's Counsel abbr. **QC**

Queen's County Ireland, *now* **Laois**

Queensland Australia, abbr. **Qld**

Queen's Printer *see* **printer**

Queen's University Belfast; Kingston, Ontario

queensware cream-coloured Wedgwood (one word)

Quelimane Mozambique

Quellen/angabe (Ger. f.) reference; **-forschung** (Ger. f.) source research, criticism (one word)

quelque chose (Fr. m.) some thing, a trifle

quenelle (cook.) a forcemeat ball (not ital.)

Quentin Durward a novel by Scott, 1823

¿Qué pasa? (Sp.) What's up? (turned question mark before, unturned after)

query abbr. **q.**, **qy**; sign ?

Quesnay, François (1694–1774) French economist

question/ abbr. **Q.**, **qu.**; — mark ?

questionnaire (two *n*s)

questor an official of the RC Church or French Assembly; cf. **quae-**

Quételet, Lambert Adolphe Jacques (1796–1874) Belgian mathematician and astronomer

Quetta Pakistan

quetzal a beautiful bird of Cent. America; the chief monetary unit in Guatemala

Quetzalcoatl the chief hero-god of the Toltecs and Aztecs

queu/e persons in line, to form this; **-ed**, **-ing**; *not* cue

queue/ (Fr. f.) tail, **— de bœuf** oxtail

quiche an open flan (not ital.)

Quichua *use* **Que-**

quick/-fire, **-freeze** (hyphens)

quicklime (one word)

quick march (two words)

quick/sand, **-set**, **-silver** **-step**, **-thorn** (one word)

quick time (two words)

quicumque vult (Lat.) whosoever will (be saved) (first words of the Athanasian Creed)

quid (Brit. sl.) one pound sterling, pl. same

quid (Lat.) that which a thing is

quidam (Lat.) an unknown person, pl. same

quiddity (philos.) the essence of a person or thing, what makes a thing what it is

quid pro quo something in return, an equivalent (not ital.)

¿Quién sabe? (Sp.) Who knows? (turned question mark before, unturned after)

quieten (Brit.) (verb tr. and intr., often followed by *down*) = (US) **quiet**

quietus death (not ital.)

Quijote de la Mancha, El ingenioso hidalgo don *see* **Don Quixote**

Quiller-Couch, Sir Arthur (Thomas) (1863–1944) English novelist and essayist (hyphen), pseud. **Q.**

quin (colloq.) for quintuplet (no point), *not* quint (except in US)

quincentenary (a celebration of) a five-hundredth anniversary (one word), *not* -centennial

quincun/x five arranged as on dice, pl. **-xes**; **-cial**

quinine a medicine, *not* -in

Quinquagesima the Sunday before Lent

quinquenni/um a period of five years; pl. **-ums**, **-a**; **-al** lasting for, or occurring every, five years; the word's ambiguity makes a more specific wording preferable

quinquereme an ancient Roman galley with five files of oarsmen on each side

quins/y tonsillitis; *not* -cy, -sey, -zy; **-ied**

quint a sequence of five cards in piquet, (US) = **quin**; cf. **quinte**

quint/al *not* kentle, kintle; pl. **-als** (in Fr. **-aux**); abbr. **q.**

quinte a position in fencing; cf. **quint**

quintet (mus.) *not* -ette

quintillion a thousand raised to the sixth power, 10^{18}; *formerly* (esp. Brit.) a thousand raised to the tenth power, 10^{30}

quiproquo (Fr. m.) mistake

quipu the ancient Peruvians' substitute for writing by knotting threads of various colours; *not* -po, -ppo, -ppu

quire/ four sheets of paper etc. folded to form eight leaves; any collection of leaves one within another in a manuscript or book; twenty-five (*formerly* twenty-four) sheets of paper; **in -s** unbound, in sheets; abbr. **q.**, **qr.**, pl. same

Qui s'excuse s'accuse (Fr.) to excuse oneself is to accuse oneself

quisling a traitor, from **Vidkun Quisling** (1887–1945) pro-Nazi leader in Norway

quit/, **-ted**, **-ter** (*not* -tor), **-ting**

Quito Ecuador

Qui va là? (Fr.) Who goes there?

Qui vive? (Fr.) Who goes there?

qui vive, on the on the alert (not ital.)

quixotic extravagantly romantic and visionary, like Don Quixote

quiz/, **-zed**, **-zer**, **-zes**, **-zing**

Qum *see* **Qom**

Qumran Jordan, site associated with Dead Sea Scrolls

quoad/ (Lat.) as far as, — *hoc* to this extent

quod erat demonstrandum etc., *see* **QED** etc.

quod est (Lat.) which is, abbr. **q.e.**

quodlibet/ (hist.) (exercise on) subject of philosophical or theological disputation, (mus.) a medley; **-arian, -ical, -ically**

quod vide (Lat.) which see (refers to sing.), abbr. **q.v.**

quoins (typ.) wedges or expanding devices that secure type, blocks, and furniture in the chase; pron. 'coins'

quoits a game, *not* coits

quo jure? (Lat.) by what right?

quomodo (Lat.) by what means, abbr. **q.m.**

quondam (adj.) former, sometime; from Lat. *quondam* (adv.) formerly

Quonset hut (US) a prefabricated metal building similar to a Nissen hut

quor/um the number of members whose presence is needed to make proceedings valid, pl. **-ums** (not ital.); adj. **-ate**

quot. quot/ation, -ed

quota/ a share, pl. **-s**

quotation marks (typ.) single (' '), double (" "); (colloq.) **quotes** (no point)

quot homines, tot sententiae (Lat.) there are as many opinions as there are people

quo vadis? (Lat.) where are you going?

Qur'ān Arab. and specialist rendering of **Koran**

qursh a monetary unit of Saudi Arabia, pl. same

q.v. *quod vide* (which see) (refers to sing., pl. **qq.v.**)

q.v. *quantum vis* (as much as you wish)

qwerty keyboard of typewriter or computer input (no caps., an acronym from the first letters on top row of this keyboard)

qy query (no point)

R radius, rand, *Regina*, *retarder* (on timepiece regulator), *Rex*, River, roentgen, (chess) rook, the seventeenth in a series, (elec.) symbol for resistance

R. rabbi, Radical, railway, rector, regiment, registered, reply, (US) Republican, Royal, (Fr.) *Rue* (street), (Ger.) *Recht* (law), (naut.) run (deserted), (theat.) right (from actor's point of view), (thermometer) Réaumur

® registered trade mark

℞ *recipe* (take)

℞ response (to a versicle)

r rare, recto, residence, resides, right, rises; rouble, **-s**; (meteor.) rain

RA Rear Admiral, Royal Academy, Royal Academician, Royal Artillery, (astr.) right ascension

Ra radium (no point), Egyptian god of the sun, spelt **Rē᷄** by Egyptologists

R/A refer to acceptor, return to author

RAA Royal Academy of Arts

RAAF Royal Australian Air Force, Royal Auxiliary Air Force

Rabat Morocco

Rabb. Rabbinic

rabbet/ a groove in woodwork; **-ed, -ing**; *not* -bit, rebate

rabbi/ a Jewish expounder of the law, pl. **-s**; abbr. **R.** (cap.); **Chief Rabbi** (caps.)

rabbin/ usually in pl. **-s**, Jewish authorities on the law, mainly of 2nd–13th cc.; **-ical, -ism, -ist**

rabbinic/ of or relating to rabbis; **— Hebrew** (noun) late Hebrew (caps.), abbr. **Rabb.**

rabbit/, -ed, -ing; **-duck** (philos.) *see* **hare-duck**; cf. **rabbet**

rabbit/ fever, — punch, — warren (two words)

rabdomancy *use* **rhab-**

Rabelais/, François (?1494–1553) French writer, **-ian** (cap.)

rabscallion *use* **raps-**

RAC Royal Agricultural College, Royal Armoured Corps, Royal Automobile Club

raccoon *not* rac-

race use in technical contexts to describe a genus, species, breed, stock, strain, or variety of animal, plant, or micro-organism, *but* use *people, nation, group*, or *community* to describe humans in non-technical contexts as being of a distinct ethnic stock with distinct physical characteristics

race/card, -course, -goer, -horse, -track, -way (one word)

racey *use* **-cy**

rach/is (bot., zool.) *not* rha-, pl. **-ides** (though incorrectly formed)

rachiti/s rickets, **-c**

Rachmaninov, Sergei (**Vasilevich**) (1873–1943) Russian composer

Rachmanism slum landlordism

rack/ and ruin, — one's brains; *see also* **wrack**

racket/, -eer, -s (game), **-y**; *not* -quet, *but see* **racquetball**

rackett (mus.) a Renaissance woodwind instrument; *not* -et, rank-

racont/eur f. **-euse** (not ital.)

racoon *use* **racc-**

racquet *use* **-ket**

racquetball (US) a court game similar to handball (one word), *not* racket-

RACS Royal Arsenal Co-operative Society

rac/y *not* -ey; **-ily**

RAD Royal Academy of Dancing

rad a former unit of absorbed radiation dose, = 0.01 Gy (*now use* **gray**); radian

Rad. Radical

rad. radix (root)

RADA Royal Academy of Dramatic Art

radar *radio detection and ranging* (acronym) (not cap.)

RADC Royal Army Dental Corps

Radcliffe/, Ann (1764–1823) English writer; **—, John** (1650–1714) English physician; **— College** Mass.; **— Camera, — Infirmary, — Science Library, — Observatory** Oxford; *see also* **Rat-**

Radhakrishnan, Sir Sarvepalli (1888–1975) Indian philosopher and statesman, President 1962–7

radian the SI unit of plane angle (approx. 57.296°), abbr. **rad**

radiator *not* -er

Radical (politics) abbr. **R., Rad.**

radical/ (chem.) *not* -cle, **— sign** (math.) $\sqrt{}$

radices pl. of **radix**

radicle (bot.)

radio/ pl. **-s**

radioactiv/e (one word), **-ity**

radio-assay (hyphen)

radiobiology (one word)

radio/ cab, — car (two words)

radio/carbon, -cobalt (one word)

radio-control/, -led (hyphen)

radio-element (hyphen, one word in US)

radio frequency (two words, hyphen when attrib.)

radio/gram, -graph, -immunology, -isotope, -meter, -metric, -paque, -phonic, -scopy (one word)

radio/-telegraphy, -telephony (hyphens, one word in US)

radio telescope (two words)

radio/telex, -therapy (one word)

radium symbol **Ra**

rad/ius pl. **-ii**, abbr. **R**

rad/ius vector pl. **-ii vectores**

rad/ix a root, pl. **-ices**; abbr. **rad.**

radon symbol **Rn**

RAE Royal Aircraft Establishment(s)

Rae, John (1813–93) Scottish Arctic traveller; *see also* **Ray**; **Reay**

Rae Bareli Uttar Pradesh, India; *not* Ray Bareilly

Raeburn, Sir Henry (1756–1823) Scottish painter

RAEC Royal Army Education Corps

R.Aero.C. Royal Aero Club of the United Kingdom

R.Ae.S. Royal Aeronautical Society

Raetia *use* **Rh-**

RAF Royal Air Force

RAFA Royal Air Forces Association

Rafferty's rules (Austral., NZ colloq.) no rules at all, esp. in boxing

raffia a palm fibre; *not* -fia, -phia

RAFRO Royal Air Force Reserve of Officers

RAFVR Royal Air Force Volunteer Reserve

rag/, -ged, -ging

raga (Ind. mus.) a pattern of notes used as a basis for improvisation, or a piece using a particular raga; *not* rag

ragamuffin (one word)

rag-and-bone man (two hyphens)

ragbag (one word)

rag doll (two words)

ragee a coarse Indian grain; *not* ragg-, -i; in Hind. *rāgī*

ragged/ left, — right (typ.) set text with even internal spacing to align with, respectively, the right or left margin of a page; *ragged right* is *ranged left*, and vice versa; cf. **full/ left, — right, — out**

raglan (not cap.)

ragout a rich meat stew, in Fr. m. *ragoût*

ragtag (one word) **and bobtail** (one word)

ragtime (mus.) (one word)

raguly (her.) like a row of sawn-off branches

Ragusa (It.) Dubrovnik (Croatia), also a town in Sicily

Rahman, Ziaur *see* **Ziaur Rahman**

RAI Royal Anthropological Institute

Rai (It.) Radiotelevisione Italiana (It. broadcasting corporation), *formerly* Radio Audizioni Italiane (one cap., no point)

raie (Fr. f.) skate (a fish)

Raikes, Robert (1735–1811) English originator of Sunday Schools

rail/car, -card, -head, -man, -road, -way (abbr. **R.**, **rly.**), **-wayman** (one word)

railway yard (two words)

rain/ abbr. **r.**; **-bow, -coat, -drop, -fall, -forest** (one word)

rain gauge (two words)

rain/hat, -proof, -storm, -water (one word)

raise (US noun) an increase in salary, = **pay rise**

raison/ de plus (Fr.) all the more reason, — **d'état** a reason of state, — **d'être** purpose of existence

raisonn/é (Fr.) f. **-ée** reasoned out

Raj, the (hist.) British sovereignty in India (cap.), in Hind. *rāj*

raja/ an Indian title, a Malay or Javanese chief; *not* -h (not cap.); in Hind. *rājā*; *see also* **ranee**

Rajagopalachari, Chakravarti (1878–1972) last Governor-General of India 1948–50

Rajasthan/ an Indian state; **-i** an Indo-Aryan language, spoken in Rajasthan in India and Pakistan

Rajput/ a member of the Hindu soldier caste claiming Kshatriya descent, *not* -poot; **-ana** an Indian region

Rajshahi Bangladesh, *not* -eshaye

Rajya Sabha the upper house of the Indian parliament, *not* Raja —; cf. **Lok Sabha**

raki any of various spirits made in E. Europe and the Middle East

raku a kind of Japanese lead-glazed earthenware

rale/ a noise made in difficult breathing, pl. **-s**; in Fr. m. *râle*

Ralegh, Sir Walter (1552–1618) English courtier, colonizer, soldier, and writer; *formerly* also spelt -eigh

Raleigh NC

Raleigh, Prof. Sir Walter (Alexander) (1861–1922) English writer; *see also* **Rayleigh**

Ralfs, John (1807–90) English botanist

rallentando/ (mus.) (passage performed) with decreasing pace, pl. **-s**; abbr. **rall.**

rallying point (two words)

RAM (comput.) random-access memory, Royal Academy of Music (London)

ram/, -med, -ming

Ramadan the ninth month of the Muslim year, during which strict fasting is observed from sunrise to sunset; in Arab. *ramaḍān*

Raman/, Sir Chandrasekhara Venkata (1888–1970) Indian physicist, **— effect** a change of frequency in scattering of radiation

Ramayana a Hindu epic

Ramblers' Association *not* 's

Rambouillet dép. Seine-et-Oise, France

RAMC Royal Army Medical Corps

ramchuddar an Indian shawl

Ramée, Marie Louise de la *see* **la Ramée, Marie Louise de**

ramekin a small mould, *not* -quin

Rameses the name of kings of ancient Egypt, *not* Ramses (US)

Ramillies battle, 1706

Rampur Uttar Pradesh, India

Ramsay,/ Allan (1686–1758) Scottish poet, — **Allan** (1713–84) Scottish painter, — **Sir William** (1852–1916) Scottish chemist

Ramses *use* **Rameses**

Ramsey Cambs., Essex, IoM

Ramsey,/ Arthur Michael (1904–88) Bishop of Durham 1952–6, Archbishop of York 1956–61, Archbishop of Canterbury 1961–74; — **Ian Thomas** (1915–72) Bishop of Durham 1966–72

ram/us (Lat.) a branch, pl. **-i**

RAN Royal Australian Navy

ranchero/ person who farms or works on a ranch (not ital.); pl. **-s**

ranc/our spite, *not* -or (except in US); *but* **-orous**

Rand (colloq.) the Witwatersrand, S. Africa

rand chief monetary unit of S. Africa and some neighbouring countries, pl. same; abbr. **R**

R & A Royal and Ancient (Golf Club)

R & B rhythm and blues

r. & c.c. riot and civil commotion

R & D research and development

Randolph-Macon College Ashland and Lynchburg, Va. (hyphen)

random-access memory (comput.) abbr. **RAM**

R & R rest and relaxation

ranee (hist.) a Hindu queen, the wife or widow of a raja (q.v.); *also* **rani** (not cap.); *not* rann-; in Hind. *rānī*

rangatira (NZ) a Maori chief or noble

rang/e (typ.) align vertically and/or horizontally (cf. **ragged/ left,** — **right**); **-ing numerals** lining numerals

range a large cooking stove kept continually hot, (US) an electric or gas cooker

rang/é (Fr. m.) f. **-ée** domesticated, orderly

Ranger (UK) a senior Guide (US) a commando (cap.); keeper of a royal park or forest, (not cap.)

Range Rover (two words) *but* **Land Rover** (hyphen)

Rangoon Burma, *not* -un

rani *see* **ranee**

Ranjit Singh (1780–1839) founder of the Sikh kingdom

Ranjitsinhji, Kumar Shri (1872–1933) Indian cricketer, Maharaja Jam Sahib of Nawanagar 1906–33

Ranke, Leopold von (1795–1886) German historian

ranket(t) *use* **rackett**

rannee *use* **ranee**

Ransom, John Crowe (1888–1974) US poet

Ransome, Arthur (1884–1967) English writer

ranuncul/us a buttercup, pl. **-uses**; (bot.) the genus including buttercups (cap. and ital.)

ranz-des-vaches Swiss alpenhorn melody

RAOB Royal Antediluvian Order of Buffaloes

RAOC Royal Army Ordnance Corps

rap/, -ped, -ping

RAPC Royal Army Pay Corps

rape (hist.) any of the six ancient divisions of Sussex (not ital.)

Raphael/ in It. **Raffaello Sanzio** (1483–1520) Italian painter, **-esque**

raphia *use* **raff-**

raphide (bot., zool.) a needle-like crystal, *not* rha-

rapid eye movement (three words) abbr. **REM**

rapid-fire (hyphen)

Rappahannock a river, Va.

rapparee a 17th-c. Irish freebooter

rappee a coarse snuff

rappel/ (esp. US) abseil; **-led, -ling** (one *l* in US) (not ital.)

rapport fruitful communication or relationship (not ital.)

rapporteur one who prepares account of proceedings (not ital.)

rapprochement the establishment or renewal of friendly relations (not ital.)

rapscallion a rascal, *not* rabs-

rar/a avis (Lat.) a prodigy, literally a rare bird; pl. **-ae aves**

rare abbr. **r.**

rarebit *see* **Welsh rabbit**

rarefaction *not* -efication

rarefy *not* rari-

rarity *not* -ety

RARO Regular Army Reserve of Officers

Rarotonga Cook Islands, NZ

RAS Royal Agricultural, Asiatic, *or* Astronomical, Society

RASC Royal Army Service Corps, *now* **RCT**

rase destroy, *use* **-ze**

Raskolnik/ (Russ.) pl. **-i**; *see* **Old Believer**

Rasoumoffsky *see* **Razumovsky**

Rasselas, Prince of Abyssinia, The History of a novel by S. Johnson, 1759

Rastafarian/ (a member of *or* relating to) a Jamaican religion, **-ism** the religion

Rasumovsky Quartets, the by Beethoven, 1806

rat/, **-ted**, **-ting**

ratable *use* **rateable**

ratafia a liqueur, a biscuit; *not* -afie, -ifia

ratan *use* **ratt-**

ratany (bot.) *use* **rh-**

ratatouille a vegetable stew

ratbag (one word)

ratchet/, **-ed**

Ratcliffe College Leicester

rateable *not* rata-

ratepayer (one word)

Rathaus (Ger. n.) town hall

rathskeller (US) a beer hall or restaurant in a basement (not cap.), in Ger. m. *Ratskeller* a (restaurant in the) town-hall cellar

ratifia *use* **rata-**

ratiocinat/e go through logical processes, reason, esp. using syllogisms; **-ion, -ive, -or**

rationale a logical cause, reasoned explanation

rationalize *not* -ise

Ratisbon *use* **Regensburg**

ratline (naut.) the ladder-rope on the shrouds; *not* -in, -ing

rat race (two words)

rattan a cane, *not* ratan

rattlesnake (one word)

Raumer,/ Friedrich Ludwig Georg von (1781–1873) German historian; — **Rudolf von** (1815–76) German philologist; *see also* **Réaumur**

ravage devastate, plunder

RAVC Royal Army Veterinary Corps

ravel/, **-led**, **-ling** (one *l* in US)

ravioli (not ital.)

ravish commit rape on (a woman), enrapture

Rawalpindi Pakistan, *not* Rawul-

raw sienna a brownish-yellow pigment, *not* siena

ray (mus.) in tonic sol-fa, *not* re

Ray,/ John (1627–1705) English naturalist, spelt Wray till 1670; — **Man** *see* **Man Ray**; *see also* **Rae**; **Reay**

Ray Bareilly *use* **Rae Bareli**

Rayleigh Essex

Rayleigh, John William Strutt, Baron (1842–1919) English physicist; *see also* **Ralegh**; **Raleigh**

raze destroy, erase; *not* -se

Razumovsky, Prince Andrei (**Kirillovich**) (1752–1836) Russian statesman, ambassador to Vienna; *not* Rasoumoffsky, Rasumovsky (except in Beethoven's work)

razzmatazz *not* the many variants

Rb rubidium (no point)

RBA Royal Society of British Artists

RBS Royal Society of British Sculptors

RC/ Red Cross, reinforced concrete, (theat.) right centre, Roman Catholic; — **paper** (print.) a resin-coated paper (for photosetting)

RCA Royal College of Art, (US) Radio Corporation of America

RCAF Royal Canadian Air Force

RCC Roman Catholic Church

RCDS Royal College of Defence Studies

RCM Royal College of Music (London)

RCMP Royal Canadian Mounted Police

RCN Royal College of Nursing, Royal Canadian Navy

RCO Royal College of Organists

RCOG Royal College of Obstetricians and Gynaecologists

RCP Royal College of Physicians

RCS Royal College of Science, Royal College of Surgeons, Royal Commonwealth Society, Royal Corps of Signals

RCT Royal Corps of Transport

RCVS Royal College of Veterinary Surgeons

RD Royal Dragoons, Royal Naval Reserve Decoration, Rural Dean, (US) Rural District

R/D refer to drawer (of a cheque)

Rd. road

RDC Royal Defence Corps, (hist.) Rural District Council

RD$ Dominican peso

RDF Radio Direction-Finder, -ing

RDI Royal Designer for Industry (Royal Society of Arts)

RDS Royal Drawing Society

RE Reformed Episcopal, Religious Education, Right Excellent, Royal Engineers, Royal Exchange, Royal Society of Painter-Etchers and Engravers

Re Reynolds number, rhenium, rupee (no point)

re (mus.) *use* **ray**

Re, il (It.) the King (no accent)

re with regard to (as first word in a heading, esp. of a law document); avoid using as substitute for *about, concerning* in general contexts (not an abbr., no point)

re- (prefix) *use* hyphen when followed by *e* and separately sounded (except in US), *re-ecbo, re-enact*; and when forming a compound to be distinguished from a more familiar one-word form, as with *recover* (= regain) and *re-cover* (= cover again)

react produce response (one word)

re-act act again (hyphen)

Read, Sir Herbert Edward (1893–1968) English critic; *see also* **Reade**; **Rede**; **Reed**; **Reid**

readdress (one word)

Reade, Charles (1814–84) English novelist; *see also* **Read**; **Rede**; **Reed**; **Reid**

Reader a university teacher, in some universities intermediate between Lecturer and Professor (cap. as title)

reader (print.) a proof corrector, one who reports on typescripts to a publisher (not cap.)

Reader's Digest Association Ltd publishers

reading/ desk, — lamp, — light, — room (two words)

readjourn, readjust, readmission (one word)

readmit/, -ted, -ting (one word)

read-only memory (comput.) abbr. **ROM**

read-out (noun, comput., hyphen, one word in US)

ready/-made, -to-wear (adjs., hyphens)

reafforest/ (one word) *not* reforest (US), **-ation**

reagent (one word)

real/ a former Portuguese and current Brazilian coin, pl. *reais*, *formerly* *réis*; (hist.) a Spanish and Mexican coin, then equivalent to a US 'bit' (12½ cents), pl. **-es**

realiz/e, -able *not* -is-

realpolitik politics based on realities and material needs, rather than on morals or ideals (not cap., not ital.); in Ger. f. *Realpolitik*

real tennis *see* **tennis**

realt/or (US) a real-estate agent, **-y** (law) landed property

ream of paper 500 sheets, abbr. **rm.**

reanimate, reappear, reappoint (one word)

reapprais/e, -al (one word)

Rear Admiral abbr. **RA**, **Rear Adm.** (two words, caps.)

rearguard (one word)

rearm/, -ament (one word)

rearrange, reascend, reassemble (one word)

reassert/, -ed, -ing (one word)

reassur/e, -ance (one word)

Réaumur/, René Antoine Ferchault de (1683–1757) French inventor of the thermometer scale; — the scale itself, abbr. **R.**, **Réaum**; *see also* **Raumer**

reawake etc. (one word)

Reay, Donald James Mackay, Baron (1839–1921) Dutch-born Scottish Governor of Bombay and first president of the British Academy; *see also* **Rae**; **Ray**

Reb a traditional Jewish courtesy title used preceding a man's forename or surname, as 'Mr', 'Rabbi'

rebaptize *not* -ise (one word)

rebate to reduce, a reduction; cf. **rabbet**

rebb/e a rabbi or Jewish religious leader, **-itzin** the wife of a rabbi

rebec (mus.) a medieval stringed instrument, *not* -eck

rebel/, -led, -ling

rebind bind (a book) again, past part. **rebound**

rebound spring back, have an adverse effect on doer of an action (one word)

rebus/ an enigmatic representation of a word (esp. a name), by pictures etc. suggesting its parts; (her.) a device suggesting the name of its bearer; pl. **-es**

rebut/, -tal, -ted, -ting

rec. receipt, recipe; record, -ed, -er

Récamier, Jeanne Françoise Julie Adélaïde, Madame (1777–1849) a leader of French society

recap/ (colloq.) recapitulate (no point); **-ped, -ping**

recast (one word)

recce/ (sl.) a reconnaissance, to reconnoitre; pl. **-s**

recd. received, *not* rec'd (US)

recede withdraw, shrink back (one word)

re-cede cede back to a former owner (hyphen)

receipt abbr. **rec.**

receivable *not* -eable

recension the revision of a text, a particular form or version of a text resulting from such revision

recent not long past or established, (geol., cap.) = **Holocene**

receptor (biol.) *not* -er

Rechabite a total abstainer (cap.)

réchauffé (Fr. m.) a warmed-up dish, (fig.) a rehash

recherché chosen with care, far-fetched (not ital.)

recidiv/ist one who relapses into crime, **-ism**

recipe/ pl. **-s,** abbr. **rec.**

réclame (Fr. f.) notoriety by advertisement, (journalism) an editorial announcement

recogniz/ance a bond given to a court, *not* -sance; **-ant** showing recognition or consciousness, *not* -sant

recognize *not* -ise

recollect remember (one word)

re-collect collect again (hyphen)

recolour (one word) *not* -or (US)

recommit/, -ted, -ting

recompense (noun and verb)

reconcilable *not* -eable

reconciler *not* -or

reconnaissance a preliminary survey, *not* reconnoi- (not ital.)

reconnoitre make a preliminary survey, *not* -er (US); in Fr. **reconnaître**

record/, -ed, -er abbr **rec.**

record player (two words)

recount narrate (one word)

re-count count again, a further count (hyphen)

recoup to recompense, recover, make up for

recover regain possession of, revive (one word)

re-cover cover again (hyphen)

recreate refresh, create again (one word)

recreation an amusement, pastime (one word)

re-creat/ion the act of creating again; **-or** *not* -er (hyphen)

rect. rectified

rectif/y, -iable, -ied, -ier, -ying

recto/ (print.) the right-hand page, opp. of **verso**; abbr. ʳ, **r.** (not ital.); pl. **-s**

rector/ abbr. **R., -ial**

rectri/x a strong tail-feather, pl. **-ces**

rectum/ (anat.) the straight part of the intestine, pl. **-s**

rect/us (anat.) a straight muscle, pl. **-i**

reçu (Fr. m.) a receipt

recueil (Fr. m.) a literary compilation, miscellany

reculer pour mieux sauter (Fr.) withdraw to await a better opportunity

recur/, -red, -ring

redact/ put into literary form, edit for publication; **-or**

rédact/eur (Fr.) (publisher's) editor, f. *-rice*; cf. *éditeur*

rédaction (Fr. f.) editing, editorial department

Redakteur (Ger. m.) editor (cap.)

Redbourn Herts.

Redbourne Humberside

redbreast a robin (one word)

red-brick new (university) (hyphen)

Redbridge Gr. London

redcap (Brit.) a member of the military police, (US) a railway porter

redcoat (hist.) a British soldier (so called from the scarlet uniform of most regiments) (one word, not cap.)

redcurrant (one word)

redd/en, -ish, -y

Reddish Gr. Manchester

Redditch Worc.

Rede Lecture Cambridge University; *see also* **Read; Reade; Reed; Reid**

Redeless, Ethelred the (*c.*968–1016) King of England 978–1016, 'the Unready'

Redemptionists an order of Trinitarian friars devoted to the redemption of Christian captives from slavery

Redemptorists an order of missionaries founded in 1732 by Alfonso Liguori

Redgauntlet a novel by Scott, 1824 (one word)

red-handed (hyphen)

redhead (one word) *but* **red-headed** (hyphen, one word in US)

red-hot (hyphen)

redial/, -led, -ling (one l in US)

Red Indian (offens.) *use* Native American

rediviv/us (Lat.) restored to life, pl. *-i*; f. *-a*, pl. *-ae*

red lead (two words)

red/-letter day, -light district (one hyphen)

redneck (one word)

redoubt (mil.) an outwork, *not* -out

redpoll a finch (one word)

red poll a breed of hornless red cattle (two words)

redress to remedy (one word)

re-dress dress again (hyphen)

redskin (one word)

red tape excessive (use of) formalities (two words)

reducible *not* -eable

reductio ad/ absurdum (Lat.) disproof by reaching an obviously absurd conclusion, — *impossibile* disproof by reaching an impossible conclusion

redwater a cattle disease (one word, two in US)

reebok *use* rhe-, *but* **Reebok** (propr.) for the sportswear manufacturer

re-echo (hyphen, one word in US)

Reed,/ Alfred German (1847–95) English actor; — **Edward Tennyson** (1860–1933) English caricaturist; — **Talbot Baines** (1852–93) English writer of boys' books; — **Walter** (1851–1902) US army surgeon; *see also* **Read; Reade; Rede; Reid**

re/-edit, -educate (hyphens, one word in US)

reef knot (two words)

Reekie, Auld Old Smoky (Edinburgh)

re/-elect, -election, -eligible, -embark (*not* reim-), **-emerge, -emergence, -emphasize** (not -ise), **-employ, -enact, -enactment, -enforce** (enforce again), **-enlist, -enslave, -enter, -enthrone** (hyphens, one word in US)

re-entrant (of) an angle pointing inwards, esp. in fortification (cf. **salient**); (geom.) (an angle that is) reflex (hyphen, one word in US)

re/-entry, -equip, -establish, -evaluate (hyphens, one word in US)

reeve (naut.) thread or fasten rope, past **rove**; *see also* **ruff**

re/-examine, -exchange, -exhibit, -export (hyphens, one word in US)

Ref. the Reformation

ref. referee, reference, referred; reform/ed, -er

Ref. Ch. Reformed Church

refer/, -able, -ence, -red, -rer, -ring

refer/ee, -eed abbr. ref.

reference/ book, — library (two words)

reference marks (typ.) may be used (esp. in math. setting) as an alternative to superior figures for footnote references in the order * (not used in math. works) † ‡ § ¶ ‖, repeated on the same page in duplicate ** etc. if necessary

reference point (two words)

referendum/ referring to the electorate on a particular issue, pl. **-s**

referrible use **-erable**

refit/, -ted, -ting

refl. reflect/ion, -ive; reflexive

reflectible use **reflexible**

reflection not -exion, abbr. **refl.**; in Fr. f. *réflexion*

reflective (of surfaces) giving back a reflection, abbr. **refl.**; (of people) meditative

reflector not -er

reflet lustre or iridescence, esp. on pottery (not ital.)

reflexible able to be reflected, not reflect-

reflexion use **-ction**

reflexive (gram.) implying that the action is reflected upon the doer, abbr. **refl.**

reforest/, -ation use **reafforest-** (except in US)

reform/ improve, correct; **-ation** (one word)

re-form/ form again, **-ation** (hyphen)

Reformation, the (cap.) 16th-c. movement for the reform of abuses in the RC Church; abbr. **Ref.**

Reform Bills 1832, 1867, 1884–5

reform/ed, -er abbr. ref.

refractor a type of lens or telescope

refractory stubborn, unmanageable, rebellious, difficult

refrangible that can be refracted

refuel/, -led, -ling (one *l* in US)

refund pay back, reimburse (one word)

re-fund fund again (hyphen)

refuse withhold acceptance or consent (one word)

re-fuse fuse again (hyphen)

refusenik (hist.) a Jew in the Soviet Union who had been refused permission to emigrate to Israel, also **refusnik** (not cap., not ital.)

Reg. Regent, *regina* (queen)

reg. regis/ter, -trar, -try; regular, -ly

regalia (pl.) insignia

regardless without regard, consideration, or attention; not irre-

regd. registered

regenerator not -er

Regensburg Bavaria, not Ratisbon, -berg

Regent abbr. **Reg.**

Regent's Park/ London (apos.); — — **College** Oxford

reggae a W. Indian style of music with a strong subsidiary beat

Reg. Gen. Registrar General

régie a government department that controls an industry or service, e.g. in Austria, France, Italy, Spain, and Turkey

regime/ pl. **-s, -n** pl. **-ns** (not ital., no accent)

regiment abbr. **regt., R.**

Regina (Lat.) queen; abbr. **R., Reg.**

regisseur a ballet or theatre director (not ital.)

register abbr. **reg.**; (bind.) a bookmarker; (typ.) print so that pages back one another exactly, or the separate colour printings of an illustration superimpose exactly

registered abbr. **regd.**

Registered Nurse (US) = **SRN**, abbr. **RN**

register marks (typ.) the crosses used to help achieve good register

Register Office off. name, not Registry

registrable not -erable

Registrar an official of Oxford University, not Registrary

registr/ar, -y abbr. **reg.**

Registrar General (two words, caps.) abbr. **Reg. Gen.**

Registrary an official of Cambridge University, not Registrar

Registry Office see **Register Office**

regium donum (Lat.) a royal grant

Regius professor (cap. *P* only when used to refer to a specific chair) abbr. **Reg. prof.**

règle (Fr. f.) a rule

regnal years not regal (except in hist. usage)

regret/, -ful, -fully, -table, -tably, -ted, -ting

regt. regiment

regul/a (Lat.) a book of rules, pl. **-ae**

regular/, -ly abbr. **reg.**

regulator not -er

re/hash, -heat (noun and verb, one word)

rehoboam a wine bottle of about six times the standard size, named after **Rehoboam**, a king of Israel (1 Kgs. 12)

rel (hist.) erroneous English back-formation for *real*

rei/ (Port. m.) king, pl. **-s** (no accent); **o rei** the king, but **El-Rei** His Majesty

Reich/ (hist.) the German State and Commonwealth (cap.); **Deutsches —** the official

name of Germany 1871–1945; **First** — the
Holy Roman Empire 962–1806; **Second** — the
German Empire 1871–1918; **Third** — the Nazi
regime 1933–45; of these, only *Third Reich* is
normal historical terminology

Reichsanstalt a German official institution
1871–1945

Reichsanzeiger a German gazette

Reichs/kanzler the German Chancellor;
-mark the former basic monetary unit of
Germany, abbr. **RM**; **-tag** (hist.) (the building
where met) the legislative body of the North
German Confederation 1867–71, of the German Empire 1871–1918, or of post-Imperial
Germany until 1945; **-wehr** the German army
1921–35 (one word)

Reid,/ Sir George (1841–1913) Scottish
painter, — **Capt. Thomas Mayne** (1818–83)
British novelist, — **Thomas** (1710–96) Scottish
metaphysician, — **Whitelaw** (1837–1912) US
journalist and diplomat; *see also* **Read**; **Reade**;
Rede; **Reed**

Reikiavik *use* **Reykj-**

Reilly, the life of *use* **Riley**

reimbark etc., *use* **re-embark** etc.

reimburse pay for loss or expense (one word)

réimpression (Fr. f.) a reprint

Reims dép. Marne, France, Fr. adj. **rémois**; *prefer to* Rheims (trad. Eng. spelling) *but* adj.
Rhemish

reine-claude (Fr. f.) greengage, pl.
reines-claude (hyphen)

re infecta (Lat.) with the object not attained

reinforce/ strengthen, **-ment**; *see also*
re-enforce

Reinhardt, Max (1873–1943) German theatrical producer

reinstate (one word)

reis the captain of a boat or ship; a chief or
governor; in Arab. *ra'is*

réis (hist.) pl. of *real*

Reis Effendi (Turk.) the title of the former
Secretary of State for Foreign Affairs in the
Ottoman Empire (caps.)

rejectamenta (pl.) wasted matter (not ital.)

rel. relative, -ly; religion, religious, (Fr.) *relié*
(bound), (Lat.) *reliquiae* (relics)

relabel/, -led, -ling (-ed, -ing in US)

relat/er one who relates something, **-or** (law)
one who lays information before the Attorney General

relative/, -ly abbr. **rel.**

relativity the state of being relative, Einstein's
theory of space-time

relativize *not* -ise

relator *see* **relater**

relay arrange in relay(s), to pass on, lay again
(one word)

releas/er one who releases, **-or** (law) one who
grants a release

relent abandon a harsh intention, yield to compassion (one word)

relet/ let again, **-ting** (one word)

relev/é (Fr.) f. **-ée** exalted, noble; (cook.) highly
seasoned; *not ré-*

reliable *not* -y-

relié (Fr. bibliog.) bound

relief-printing (typ.) printing from surfaces
raised to contact ink and paper, = **letterpress** (hyphen)

relievo (art) = **relief**, in It. *riliev/o*, pl. **-i**

religieuse/ (Fr. f.) a nun, pl. **-s**

religieux (Fr. m.) a monk, pl. same

relig/ion, -ious abbr. **rel.**

religionize *not* -ise

religious denominations as Baptist, Protestant, to have caps.

reliquar/y (esp. eccl.) a receptacle for relics, pl.
-ies

reliquiae (Lat. pl.) relics, fossils; abbr. **rel.**

rel/y, -ied, -ying

REM rapid eye movement

rem roentgen equivalent man

rem. remarks

remainder (print.) that part of an edition's
print-run that is unsaleable at its original
price

remanen/t (adj.) remaining, residual, esp. (of
magnetism) remaining after the mag-
netizing field has been removed; **-ce**; cf. **remnant**

Remarque, Erich Maria born **Krämer** (1898–
1970) German-born US novelist

remblai/ earth used to form a rampart, pl. **-s**

Rembrandt/ in full — (**Harmenszoon**) **van Rijn**
(1606–69) Dutch painter, **-esque**

REME Royal Electrical and Mechanical Engineers

Remembrance Sunday that nearest to 11
Nov.

remerciment (Fr. m.) thanks, *not -îement*
(except in 17th-c. spelling)

rem/ex a wing quill feather, pl. **-iges**

Reminiscere Sunday the second in Lent

remise (law) to make over, *not* -ize

remissible capable of being forgiven

remit/, -tal, -tance, -tee, -tent, -ter

remnant a small remaining quantity; cf.
remanent

remodel/, -led, -ling (one l in US)

rémois (Fr.) of Reims, f. **-e** (not cap.); a native
of Reims, f. **-e** (cap.)

remonstrator *not* -er

rémoulade or *rémolade* (Fr. f.) a salad dressing, a kind of sauce

remould *not* -mold (US)

removable *not* -eable

Rémusat,/ Charles François Marie, comte de (1797–1875) French politician and writer, **— Jean Pierre** (1788–1832) French Chinese scholar

Renaissance, the (the period of) the revival of art and literature under the influence of classical models in the 14th–16th cc. (cap.); (not cap.) any similar revival; *not* -ascence

Renaixença (Catalan f.) the revival of Catalan culture in the 19th c.

Renard the fox, *use* **Rey-** (except in a specifically French context)

renascen/ce rebirth, renewal; **-t**

Renault a French make of car

rendezvous/ sing. and pl. (one word, not ital.); as verb **-es, -ed, -ing**; in Fr. m. *rendez-vous* (hyphen)

renege renounce, abandon; *not* -gue

reniform kidney-shaped

Renoir,/ Auguste (1841–1919) French painter, **— Jean** (1894–1979) his son, French film director

renounceable *not* -cable

renouncement *use* **renunciation**

renovator *not* -er

renown fame, high distinction; *not* -known

rent-a/-car, -cop, -crowd etc. (hyphens)

rentes/ (Fr. f.) independent income, also government stocks; **— sur l'État** interest on government loans

rentier one whose income is derived from investments, in Fr. *rent/ier*, f. *-ière*

renuncia/tion, -nt, -tive, -tory

reoccup/y, -ation (one word)

reometer etc., *use* **rhe-**

re/open, -order, -organize *not* -ise (one word)

reorient/, -ate (one word); *see also* **orient, orientate**

Rep. (US) Representative, Republican

rep a fabric, *not* repp; (colloq.) representative, (theat.) repertory (no point), (US) reputation

rep. report, -er; republic, -an

rep/air, -airable (of material things); **-arable, -aration** (of amends for loss)

repartee (the making of) witty retorts (not ital.), in Fr. f. *repartie*

repêchage a contest between runners-up for a place in the final (not ital.)

repel/, -led, -lent, -ling, -ler

repertoire a stock of pieces, techniques, etc. that a company or a performer knows (not ital.)

repertorium (Lat.) a catalogue

repertory the theatrical performance of various plays for short periods by one company, or the company that performs them

repetatur (Lat.) let it be repeated, abbr. *repet.*

répétiteur a private teacher or coach, esp. of opera singers (not ital.), in Fr. *répétit/eur*, f. *-rice*

repetitorium (Lat.) a summary

replaceable *not* -cable

réplique (Fr. f.) a reply

repl/y, -ies, -ier, -ying

report/, -er abbr. **rep., rept.**

report/age (not ital.), **-orial** (US) of newspaper reporters

repoussé (ornamental metalwork) hammered from the reverse side (not ital.); cf. **retroussé**

repp *use* **rep**

repr. representing, reprint

reprehensible *not* -able

representable *not* -ible

Representative abbr. **Rep.**

Representatives, House of the lower division of the US Congress (caps.)

repress/, -ible, -or *not* -er

reprint (print.) a second or new impression of any printed work, with only minor corrections; a reimpression with no corrections at all; printed matter taken from some other publication for reproduction; or (in imprecise use) printed 'copy'; (one word) abbr. **repr., RP**; *see also* **edition; imprint**

reprisal an act of retaliation, *not* -izal

reprise (law) a yearly charge or deduction, (mus.) repeated passage; *not* -ize

reprize to prize anew

repro./ reproduction, **— pull** (typ., no point) a good proof made for camera use

reproducible *not* -eable

reprogram *not* -mme

reproof (noun) a rebuke, (verb) make waterproof again

reprove to rebuke

rept. report

republic/, -an abbr. **rep.**

Republican abbr. **R** (no point)

Republic Day in India 26 Jan.

République française (Fr. f.) French Republic (one cap.), abbr. **RF**

repudiat/e, -or *not* -er

reputable respectable

requiem/ the mass for the dead, or its musical setting; pl. **-s**

requies/cat in pace (Lat.) may he, *or* she, rest in peace; abbr. **RIP**; pl. *-cant in pace*; *-cit in pace* he, *or* she, rests in peace

reread (one word)

reredos/ an ornamental screen or panelling behind an altar, *not* the many variants; pl. **-es**

re-release (hyphen, one word in US)

re-route/ (hyphen, one word in US), **-ing**

rerun (noun and verb, one word)

res. research, reserve; resid/ence, -es; resigned

res/ (Lat.) a thing or things, — **adjudicata** a matter already decided

re/sale, -sell (one word)

res angusta domi scanty means at home

rescuable *not* -ueable

research abbr. **res.**

reserve that which is kept back, restraint, to keep back (one word); abbr. **res.**

re-serve serve again (hyphen)

Reserve, Army (caps.)

reservist *not* -eist

res gestae (Lat. pl.) things done, matters of fact

resid/ence, -es abbr. **r., res.**

residence permit (two words)

residu/e pl. **-es, -um** pl. **-a**

resign/ give up office, employment, etc.; **-ed** abbr. **res.**

re-sign sign again

resin a gum from trees or synthetically produced; cf. **rosin**

resist/ance, -ant *not* -ence, -ent

resist/er person, **-or** thing

res/ judicata (Lat.) a thing already decided, — **nihili** a nonentity

resoluble that can be resolved (one word)

re-soluble that can be dissolved again (hyphen)

resolv/able, -er

resonator an instrument responding to a certain frequency of vibrations

resorb absorb again

resort have recourse to, expedient, a holiday spot (one word)

re-sort sort again (hyphen)

resource in Fr. f. **ressource**

resp. respondent

respecter *not* -or

Respighi, Ottorino (1879–1936) Italian composer

respirator *not* -er

respondent abbr. **resp.**

response mark (print.) ℟

responsible in Fr. **responsable**

restaurateur restaurant-keeper, *not* -rant-

rest/-baulk, -cure (hyphens, two words in US)

rest day (two words)

rest-harrow (hyphen, two words in US)

rest/ home, — house (two words)

resting place (two words)

restor/able, -er

Restoration, the (hist.) the re-establishment of Charles II as king of England in 1660, or the literary period following this; also used for other countries, e.g. the period 1814–30 in France (cap.)

restrain check, hold in (one word)

re-strain strain again (hyphen)

restroom (one word)

resum/e, -able

résumé a summary (not ital., two accents), (US) = **curriculum vitae**

resurgam (Lat.) I shall rise again

resuscitat/e, -or

Reszke,/ Édouard de (1856–1917) Polish bass; **— Jean de** (1850–1925) his brother, Polish tenor

ret. retired, returned

retable a shelf or framed panels above back of altar

retd. retired, returned; *not* ret'd (US)

R. et I. (Lat.) *Rex et Imperator* king and emperor, *Regina et Imperatrix* queen and empress (points); in Eng. **RI**

retin/a the inner membrane of the eyeball; pl. (anat.) **-ae**, (gen.) **-as**

retinol vitamin A

retiral (esp. Sc.) retirement from office etc.

retired abbr. **ret., retd.**

retraceable *not* -cable

retractable *not* -ible

retractor *not* -er

retree slightly defective paper

retrial (one word)

retriever a dog

retrocede cede back again; for the sense 'move back' *prefer* **recede**

retrochoir (archit.) (one word)

retroflex (adj.) turned backwards (one word)

retrorocket (one word)

retroussé turned up (not ital.), in Fr. **retrouss/é**, f. **-ée**; cf. **repoussé**

retry (one word)

returned abbr. **ret., retd.** *not* ret'd (US)

Reuben (OT) a son of Jacob

Reubens, Peter Paul *use* **Ru-**

reunion a social gathering, in Fr. f. **réunion**

Réunion, Île de Indian Ocean

re/unite, -urge, -usable, -use (one word)

Reuters a reporting agency

Rev. Book of Revelation, Review; *see also* **Reverend**

rev. revenue, reverse; revis/e, -ed, -ion; revolution, -s

Reval the former name of (and still Ger. for) **Tallinn**

revalorize establish a new value, *not* -ise

Revd *see* **Reverend**

réveil (Fr. m.) an awaking, a morning call

reveille a morning call to troops (no accents, not ital.)

revel/, -led, -ler, -ling (one *l* in US)

Revelation, Book of (NT) *not* -ions, abbr. **Rev.**

revenons à nos moutons (Fr.) let us return to our subject (lit. '... to our sheep')

revenue/ abbr. **rev.**; **— office, — tax** (two words)

reverberator *not* -er

Reverend abbr. (**The**) **Revd**, pl. **Revds** (cap. *T* only in official title of address, not in running text); *not* Rev. (US); **Most Revd** archbishop or Irish RC bishop; **Revd Mother** Mother Superior of a convent; **Right Revd** *or* **Rt. Revd** bishop or moderator; **Very Revd** dean, provost, or former moderator

rever/end deserving reverence, **-ent** showing it

reverie a daydream, *not* -y

revers the front of a garment turned back showing the inner surface, pl. same

reverse abbr. **rev.**

reversed block (typ.) a design in which the illustration or wording appears in white against a background; a block whose contents are transposed left-to-right for offset printing

reversible *not* -able

rêveu/r (Fr.) f. *-se* (day)dreamer

review abbr. **rev.**

revis/e *not* -ize; **-able, -ing**; (print.) a proof including corrections made in an earlier proof; abbr. **rev.**

revis/ed, -ion abbr. **rev.**

Revised Standard Version of the Bible (caps.), abbr. **RSV**

Revised Statutes abbr. **RS, Rev. Stat.**

Revised Version of the Bible (caps.), abbr. **RV**

reviv/er one who revives, **-or** (law) a proceeding to revive a suit

revoir, à (Fr.) to be revised; cf. **au revoir**

revo/ke, -cable, -cation

Revolution, the American 1775–83; Chinese 1911–12; English 1688–9; French 1789–95, 1830, 1848, 1870; Russian 1905, 1917 (cap.); unless otherwise specified, 'the French Revolution' is assumed to be that of 1789–95, and 'the Russian Revolution' that of (esp. October) 1917

revolution/, -s abbr. **rev.**; *see also* **rpm**; **rps**

revolutionize *not* -ise

Rev. Stat. Revised Statutes

revue a theatrical entertainment (not ital.)

Rewley House Oxford, *now* **Kellogg College** (for matriculated students)

Rex (Lat.) king, abbr. **R.**

Rexine (propr.) imitation leather (cap.)

Reykjavik Iceland, *not* Reiki-

Reynard the fox, *not* Ren- (cap.)

Reynolds/, Osborne (1842–1912) Irish engineer and physicist; **—'s law** (two words, apos.); **— number** (two words, no apos.), abbr. **Re**

Reynolds News (no apos.)

rez-de-chaussée (Fr. m.) ground floor

Rezniček, Baron Emil Nikolaus von (1860–1945) Austrian composer

RF *République française* (French Republic)

Rf rutherfordium (no point)

r.f. radio frequency

rf. see **rinforzando**

RFA Royal Field Artillery, Royal Fleet Auxiliary

RFC Royal Flying Corps, Rugby Football Club

RGS Royal Geographical Society

RH Royal Highness

Rh rhesus, rhodium (no point)

r.h. right hand

RHA Regional Health Authority, Road Haulage Association, Royal Hibernian Academy, Royal Horse Artillery

rhabdomancy divination by rod, *not* ra-

Rhadamanth/ine stern, like **-us** (Gr. myth.) the judge of the dead

Rhaet/ia, -ian, -ic (of) the Austrian Tyrol; *not* Rae-, Rhe-

rhaphis *use* ra-

rhapsodize to be enthusiastic, *not* -ise

rhatany (bot.) a S. American shrub with an astringent root, *not* rat-

rhebok an antelope, *not* rhee-, ree-

Rheims *use* **Reims**

Rhein (Ger. m.) the Rhine

Rheingold, Das the first opera in Wagner's *Ring des Nibelungen*, 1869

Rhemish of Reims (trad. Eng. form); *use* **rémois** in specialist texts only

Rhenish (a wine) of the Rhine

rhenium symbol **Re**

rheology (phys.) the science of flow

rheo/meter, -stat, -trope instruments for (respectively) measuring, regulating, reversing electric current; *not* reo-

rhesus/ an Indian monkey; **— factor** (in the blood) abbr. **Rh-factor**; **Rh-positive, Rh-negative** (hyphens, no point)

rhet. rhetoric

Rhetia *use* **Rhae-**

RHF Royal Highland Fusiliers

RHG Royal Horse Guards (the Blues)

Rhine/ a European river; in Fr. **Rhin**, Ger. **Rhein**; **-land** (one word)

rhinestone an imitation diamond

rhinoceros pl. same; colloq. **rhino**/, pl. **-s** (no point)

R.Hist.S. Royal Historical Society

rho the seventeenth letter of the Gr. alphabet (P, ρ)

Rhode Island off. and postal abbr. **RI**

Rhod/es an island in Aegean Sea, and its capital; **-ian**

Rhodes Scholar/, -ship (at Oxford)

rhodium symbol **Rh**

rhododendron/ pl. **-s**

rhodomontade use **rodo-**

rhombus/ (geom.) pl. **-es**

Rhondda a river and town, Mid Glam.

Rhône a French dép. and river, not Rhone

RHS Royal Historical, Horticultural, or Humane, Society

rhumb any of the thirty-two points of the compass, or the angle between two successive compass points

rhumba use **ru-**

rhumb line (naut.) (two words)

rhym/e (noun and verb) not rime (except in older use); **-er** (-ester is usually derog.)

rhythm/, -ic

RI (US) Rhode Island, Royal Institute, Royal Institute of Painters in Water Colours, Royal Institution; Eng. form of *R. et I.*

RIA Royal Irish Academy

rial a monetary unit of Iran, Oman, and Yemen

Rialto Venice (cap.)

RIB a rigid inflatable boat (caps.)

rib/, **-bed, -bing**

RIBA Royal Institute of British Architects

riband see **ribbon**

ribband a light spar used in shipbuilding

ribbon not riband, except in sport and heraldry

riboflavin not -e

Ricard/o, David (1772–1823) English economist, **-ian**

Riccio use **Rizz-**

ricercar an elaborate contrapuntal instrumental composition in fugal or canonic style, esp. of the 16th–18th cc.; not -e

Richelieu, Armand Jean du Plessis, duc de, Cardinal (1585–1642) French statesman

Richepin, Jean (1849–1926) French writer

Richter/, Charles Francis (1900–85) US seismologist, devised **— scale** for expressing the magnitude of an earthquake; **—, Hans** (1843–1916) German conductor of Wagnerian opera and the Hallé Orchestra; **—, Johann Paul Friedrich** (1763–1825) German writer, pseud.

Jean Paul; **—, Karl** (1926–81) German conductor; **—, Svyatoslav** (**Teofilovich**) (1915–97) Russian pianist

Richthofen, Baron Manfred von (1882–1918) German flying ace

rick to sprain or strain, not wrick

rickets a bone disease

rickettsi/a a micro-organism such as typhus, pl. **-ae**; from **Howard Taylor Ricketts** (1871–1910) US pathologist

rickety shaky, not -tty

rickrack use **ricrac**

rickshaw a light two-wheeled vehicle, originally a shortening of the Jap. *jinrikisha*; not -sha

ricochet/ to skip or rebound (of projectile); **-ed, -ing** (not ital.)

ricrac a zigzag braid trimming, not rickrack

RICS Royal Institution of Chartered Surveyors

rid/, **-dance, -ded, -ding**

rid/e, -eable, -den, -ing

ride to hounds not — — the —

ridge piece (two words)

ridge pole (two words, one word in US)

ridge/ tile, — tree (two words)

ridgeway (one word, cap. as a specific name for a geographical feature)

Ridgway Col., Pa.

ridgy not -ey

riding each of three former administrative divisions (**East Riding, North Riding, West Riding**) of Yorkshire (caps.), an electoral division of Canada

Riemann/, Georg Friedrich Bernhard (1826–66) German mathematician, **-ian**

Riesling a white wine

Rievaulx Abbey N. Yorks., not Riv-

Rif, Er a mountainous region in N. Morocco, not Riff

rifaciment/o (It.) a remaking, pl. **-i**

Riff/ a Berber of Er Rif, pl. **-i**

riff (mus.) (play) a short repeated phrase in jazz etc.

riffle turn (pages etc.) quickly, leaf through quickly, shuffle; an instance of this

riff-raff rabble (hyphen, one word in US)

rifl/e, -ing

rifle/ range, — shot (two words)

rigadoon a lively dance, not rigaudon

right/ (theat., from actor's point of view) abbr. **R**, **— centre** abbr. **RC**

right angle symbol ∟

right ascension (astr.) abbr. **RA**

righteous

right/-hand, -handed (adjs.) (hyphens)

right-hand pages (print.) the recto pages

Right Honourable a title given to certain high officials (e.g. Privy Counsellors) and peers below the rank of marquess; abbr. **Rt. Hon.**

Right Reverend (for bishops and moderators in Presbyterian churches and Church of Scotland) abbr. **(The) Right Revd, Rt. Revd**

right wing (hyphen as adj.), **right-winger**

Rigi Swiss mountain, *not* -hi

rigor (med.) sudden shivering or rigidity (not ital.)

rigor mortis stiffening of the body after death (not ital.)

rigour severity, *not* -or (US); *but* **rigorous**

Rigsdag the former Danish Parliament

Rig Veda the oldest and principal of the Sanskrit Vedas, in specialist contexts *Rigveda, Ṛgveda; see also* **Veda**

RIIA Royal Institute of International Affairs

Riksdag the Swedish Parliament

riksmål *formerly* **Rigsmaal**; *see* **bokmål**

Riley,/ the life of (sl.) carefree existence, *not* Reilly; — **Bridget Louise** (b. 1931) British painter; — **James Whitcomb** (1849–1916) US poet

riliev/o (It.) raised or embossed work, pl. *-i*; in Eng. **relievo**

Rilke, Rainer Maria (1875–1926) German poet

rill a small stream

rille a narrow valley on the moon

rim/, -med, -ming

rim/a (It.) verse, pl. *-e*

rim/e hoar-frost, **-y**; cf. **rhyme**

Rime of the Ancient Mariner, The a poem by Coleridge, 1798

Rimsky-Korsakov, Nikolai (Andreevich) (1844–1908) Russian composer

RINA Royal Institution of Naval Architects

rinderpest pleuropneumonia in ruminants (one word)

rinforz/ando, -ato (It. mus.) with more emphasis; abbr. *rf., rinf.*

Ring des Nibelungen, Der cycle of operas by Wagner, 1869–76

ring/leader, -master (one word)

Ringling Brothers and Barnum & Bailey Circus a US circus organization

rio (Port.) river, (Venetian It.) canal

río (Sp.) river (accent)

Rio de Janeiro Brazil, *not* Rio Janeiro

Rio Grande port, Brazil; — — **do Norte,** — — **do Sul** states, Brazil (no accent)

Río Grande river, Mexico (no accent in US usage)

RIP *requiesc/at* (or *-ant*) *in pace* (may he, she (or they), rest in peace)

RIPA Royal Institute of Public Administration

RIPH & H Royal Institute of Public Health and Hygiene

ripien/o (mus.) a player or instrument additional to a leader or soloist; pl. **-os, -i**

Ripman, Walter (1869–1947) English educationist

rippl/e, -y

Rip Van Winkle by Washington Irving, 1820 (three caps.)

ris de veau (Fr. cook. m.) sweetbread

rises abbr. **r.**

rishi a Hindu sage or saint, in Skr. *ṛṣi*

risible provoking laughter, *not* -able

Risorgimento (hist.) a 19th-c. movement for the unification and independence of Italy, achieved in 1870 (also used for the ensuing period)

risotto/ rice with stock, onions, etc.; pl. **-s**

risqué slightly indecent (not ital.), in Fr. *risqu/é* f. *-ée*

rissole a fried cake of breaded minced meat (not ital.)

rissolé (Fr. cook.) well-browned

ritardando/ (mus.) holding back, pl. **-s**; abbr. **rit., ritard.**

Ritchie-Calder, Baron (hyphen)

ritenuto (mus.) with immediate reduction of speed, abbr. **riten.**

ritornello/ (mus.) a short repeated instrumental passage in a vocal work, return of full orchestra after a solo passage in a concerto; pl. **-s**

Ritter/ (Ger. m.) (the rank of) knight (cf. *Springer*) (cap.; not ital. as part of title, no comma preceding), pl. same; (f.) *-zeit* the Age of Chivalry (one word)

ritualist/ one devoted to ritual, **-ic** (cap. with hist. reference)

ritualize *not* -ise

Riv. River

rival/, -led, -ling (one *l* in US)

Rivaulx *use* **Rie-**

river abbr. **r., R., Riv.**

river (typ.) a track of white space twisting down a printed page, caused by bad word-spacing

Rivera y Orbaneja, Miguel Primo de (1870–1930) Spanish general, dictator 1923–30

river/ blindness, — capture, — dolphin, — god (two words)

river/scape, -side (one word)

Rivesaltes a French wine

rivet/, -ed, -er, -ing

Riviera the coast of France and Italy from Nice to La Spezia (cap.); a similar region elsewhere (not cap.)

Rivière, Briton (1840–1920) English painter

rivière (Fr. f.) river, (of diamonds) collar

Riyadh capital of Nejd, and one of the federal capitals of Saudi Arabia; *see also* **Mecca**

riz (Fr. m.) rice

Rizzio, David (1540–66) Italian musician, favourite of Mary Queen of Scots, assassinated; *not* Ricc-

RL Rugby League

RLO Returned Letter Office

R.L.S. Robert Louis Stevenson

RLSS Royal Life Saving Society

rly. railway

RM (hist.) Reichsmark, Resident Magistrate, Royal Mail, Royal Marines

rm. ream, room

RMA Royal Military Academy (Sandhurst)

RMCS Royal Military College of Science

R.Met.S. Royal Meteorological Society

r.m.m. relative molecular mass

r months September to April

RMP Royal Military Police

RMS Royal Mail Service, Royal Mail Steamer, Royal Microscopical Society, Royal Society of Miniature Painters

rms root mean square

RMSM Royal Military School of Music

RMT National Union of Rail, Maritime, and Transport Workers

RN Royal Navy, (US) Registered Nurse

Rn radon (no point)

RNA ribonucleic acid

RNC Royal Naval College

RNCM Royal Northern College of Music

RNIB Royal National Institute for the Blind

RNID Royal National Institute for the Deaf

RNLI Royal National Lifeboat Institution

RNR Royal Naval Reserve

RNZAF Royal New Zealand Air Force

RNZN Royal New Zealand Navy

RO Receiving Office, -r; Record Office, Relieving Officer, Returning Officer, Royal Observatory

ro. rood

Road after name to be cap., as Fulham Road; abbr. **Rd.**

road/bed, -block (one word)

road hog (two words)

roadhouse (one word)

road map (two words)

road/runner, -show, -side, -stead (one word)

road/ tax, — test (two words, hyphen when attrib.)

road/way, -works, -worthy (one word)

roan (bind.) a soft and flexible sheepskin, often imitating morocco

Roanoke Va.

Roaring/ Forties the stormy ocean tracts between latitudes 40° and 50° S., **— Twenties** the decade of the 1920s (caps.)

Robarts, Mr a character in Trollope's *Framley Parsonage*

Robbe-Grillet, Alain (b. 1922) French writer

Robben Island S. Africa

Robbia, Luca della (1399–1482) Italian sculptor; *see also* **Della Robbia**

Robespierre, Maximilien François Marie Isidore de (1758–94) French revolutionary

Robin Goodfellow a sprite, the 'Puck' of Shakespeare's *A Midsummer Night's Dream* (caps.); cf. **Jacques Bonhomme**

Robin Hood a hero of medieval legend

robin redbreast (two words)

Robinson Crusoe a novel by Defoe, 1719

Rob Roy Robert ('the Red') MacGregor (1671–1734) Scottish outlaw (caps., two words), a drink named after him

ROC Royal Observer Corps

roc a fabulous bird of eastern legend, *not* the many variants

roccoco *use* **roco-**

Roch, St

Rochefoucauld *see* **La Rochefoucauld**

roches moutonnées (geol.) a glaciated type of rock surface (not ital.)

rochet a surplice-like linen garment; *not* rotch-, -ette

Rocinante Don Quixote's steed, usually Anglicized as Rosinante

rock (US) a stone of any size

Rock, the Gibraltar

rock and roll/ *also* **rock 'n' roll/, -er** (often no hyphens as adj.)

rock-bottom (adj., hyphen; noun, two words)

rockburst (one word)

rock candy (two words)

Rockefeller/, John D(avison) (1840–1937) head of a family of US capitalists; **—, Nelson (Aldrich)** (1908–79) US statesman; **— Center** a nexus of office skyscrapers, NYC; **— Foundation** philanthropic; **— Institute** a university for medical research

rock face (two words)

rockfall (one word)

rock garden (two words)

Rockies, the (N. Amer.) the Rocky Mountains

'Rock of Ages' (caps.)

rock/ plant, — python, — salmon, — salt, — wool (two words)

rococo/ a late baroque ornamental style of decoration in 18th-c. Europe, also in music; pl. **-s**; *not* rocc-

Rod, Édouard (1857–1910) French writer

Rodd, James Rennell, first Baron Rennell (1858–1941) English diplomat and scholar

rodeo/ pl. **-s**

Roderic (d. 711) last king of the Visigoths, *not* -ick

Rodin, Auguste (1840–1917) French sculptor

rodomontade bragging talk, *not* rh-

roebuck (one word)

Roedean School Brighton

roe deer (two words)

roentgen/ former unit of ionizing radiation dose, now expressed in coulombs per kilogram; abbr. **R**; **-ography** photography with X-rays; **-ology** study of X-rays; *see also* **Röntgen**

ROF Royal Ordnance Factory

Roffen: the signature of the Bishop of Rochester (colon)

Rogation Sunday that before Ascension Day

Roget, Peter Mark (1779–1869) English physician and taxonomist, compiled *Roget's Thesaurus of English Words and Phrases*

rognons/ (Fr. m. pl.) kidneys, — *blancs* (Fr. cook) testicles

rogues' gallery *not* rogue's

Rohilkhand Uttar Pradesh, India; *not* Rohilc-, -und

Rohmer,/ Eric (b. 1920) French film director, — **Sax** pseud. of **Arthur Sarsfield Ward** (1883–1959) British mystery-writer

ROI Royal Institute of Oil Painters

roi fainéant (Fr.) do-nothing king, used specifically of any of the late Merovingians

roinek *use* **rooi-**

roisterer a noisy reveller, *not* roy-

rok *use* **roc**

Rokitansky, Karl, Baron von (1804–78) Czech-born Austrian anatomist

role an actor's part, in Fr. m. *rôle*

roll-call (hyphen, two words in US)

roller-coaster (hyphen; noun, two words in US)

roller skate (noun and verb; two words)

rolling pin (two words)

rollmop (one word)

rollock *use* **rowlock**

roll-on (noun and adj., hyphen)

Rolls-Royce (hyphen)

Rölvaag, Ole Edvart (1876–1931) Norwegian-US novelist

roly-poly a pudding, *not* the many variants

ROM (comput.) read-only memory

Rom/ a male Gypsy, pl. **-a** (cap.)

Rom. Roman, Romance, Romans (Epistle to the)

rom. roman type

Romaic the vernacular language of modern Greece, esp. its pure demotic or dialectal form

romaika a national dance of modern Greece

Romain, Jules (c.1499–1546) Italian architect, *but use* **Giulio Romano**

romain/ (Fr.) Roman, f. *-e*

romaine lettuce (US) = **cos lettuce**

Romains, Jules (1885–1972) French writer

rōmaji the Roman alphabet used to transliterate Japanese

roman (typ.) the ordinary upright letters as distinct from bold or italic, abbr. **rom.** (not cap.)

roman/ (Fr. m.) novel (*see* e.g. *roman-à-clef*, *roman-fleuve*); (medieval lit.) romance; also used of the language intermediate in time between Latin and Old French; (Fr. adj.) Romanesque (art, architecture), Romance (language, literature); f. *-e*

roman-à-clef (Fr. m.) a novel about real people under disguised identities, pl. *romans-à-clef*

romanais/ (Fr.) of or relating to the city of Romans-sur-Isère; f. *-e*

Roman Catholic/ (caps.) abbr. **RC**; — — **Church** (caps.), abbr. **RCC**

Romance (of or relating to) the languages derived from Latin regarded collectively

romance (Fr. f.) a sentimental song; (Sp. m.) an eight-syllable metre, or a ballad written in it (not ital. in Hispanic studies)

romancear (Sp.) to translate into Spanish; in Chile *also* to waste time chattering, *or* to flirt

Roman de la Rose 13th-c. French allegorical verse romance, the source of *Romaunt of the Rose*, attributed to Chaucer

Romanée-Conti a red burgundy wine

Romanes lectures at Oxford University

Romanesque the style of architecture c.900–1200, between classical and Gothic

roman-feuilleton (Fr. m.) a serial, pl. *romans-feuilletons*; *roman-fleuve* (Fr. m.) a long novel or novels about the same characters over a period, pl. *romans-fleuves*

Romania/, -n *not* Roum- or Rum- (except in hist. contexts to distinguish the modern state from the Roman world etc.)

romaniz/e *not* -ise, **-ation**

Romano a strong-tasting hard cheese

Romano- prefix meaning Roman, e.g. 'Romano-British' (hyphen, cap.)

roman/o (It., Sp.) Roman, f. *-a*

Romanov a Russian dynasty 1613–1917; *not* -of, -off

Romans, Epistle to the (NT) abbr. **Rom.**

Romansh (of) Rhaeto-Romanic, (esp.) the dialects of the Swiss canton of Grisons (*also called* **Grishun**); *not* Rou-, Ru-, -ansch, -onsch

Romantic/ of or relating to the 18th–19th-c. movement or style in the European arts (cap.), **-ism, -ist, -s**

Romany (of or concerning) a Gypsy, the Gypsies, or their Indo-European language; *not* -ncy, -mmany (cap.); in Romany *Romani*

romanza (It. f.) romance (medieval lit., music), aria

romanzesco (It.) adventurous, romantic (fiction)

romanz/o (It.) Romance, f. *-a*; (m.) romance, novel, fiction

Romaunt of the Rose see Roman de la Rose

Romeo/ a young lover, pl. **-s** (cap.)

Romney, George (1734–1802) English painter

romneya a poppy-like shrub

Romney Marsh Kent

Romsey Hants.

Ronaldsay Orkney

Ronaldshay, Earl of the Marquess of Zetland's heir

Ronaldsway Airport IoM

Ronda Spain

rondavel (S. Afr.) a round tribal hut or any similar building

rondeau/ a poem of ten or thirteen lines with only two rhymes throughout, and with the opening words used twice as a refrain; pl. **-x**

rondel a special form of the rondeau

rondo/ (mus.) a movement with a recurring main theme, pl. **-s**

rone (Sc.) a gutter for carrying off rainwater from a roof

Röntgen,/ Julius (1855–1934) Dutch composer; **— Wilhelm Konrad von** (1845–1923) German physicist, discoverer of Röntgen (or X-) rays; *see also* **roentgen**

roo (Austral. colloq.) a kangaroo, *not* 'roo

rood abbr. **ro.**

roof garden (two words)

roof rack (two words, one word in US)

rooftop/, -s (one word)

rooinek (Afrik. sl. offens.) an Englishman, *not* roi-

rook (chess) abbr. **R,** *also* a bird

Rooke, Sir George (1650–1709) English admiral

room abbr. **rm.**

rooming house (two words)

room-mate (hyphen, one word in US)

room service (two words)

Roosevelt,/ Franklin Delano (1882–1945) US President 1933–45; **— Theodore** (1858–1919) US President 1901–9

root rummage, give support, search out; cf. **rout**

root (math.) sign √

root mean square (hyphens for adj., e.g. 'root-mean-square value') abbr. **rms**

rop/e, -eable, -ing, -y

rope-dancer (hyphen, one word in US)

rope ladder (two words)

rope-walk/, -er (hyphen, one word in US)

Roquefort a French cheese

ro-ro (adj.) roll-on roll-off (of shipping practices)

rorqual a whale

Rorschach test (psychol.) a personality test using ink-blots; *not* -scharch

rosaceous of the rose family

Rosalind a character in Shakespeare's *As You Like It,* and Spenser's *Shepheardes Calendar*

Rosaline a character in Shakespeare's *Love's Labour's Lost* and *Romeo and Juliet*

Rosamond Clifford, 'Fair' (d. *c.*1176) probable mistress of Henry II

rosary (RC) (the beads for) a set of devotions; cf. **rosery**

Roscommon Ireland

rose/ (Fr. m.) pink colour, (f.) a rose; *couleur de* — roseate, attractive

rosé pink wine

Rosebery, Earl of *not* -berry, -bury

rose/bowl, -bud (one word)

rose bush (two words, one word in US)

rose-coloured (hyphen)

rose/ garden, — hip (two words)

rosella an Australian parakeet

Rosencrantz and Guildenstern characters in Shakespeare's *Hamlet*

Rosencrantz and Guildenstern are Dead a comedy by T. Stoppard, 1966

Rosenkranz, Johann Karl Friedrich (1805–79) German metaphysical philosopher

Rosenkreuz *see* **Rosicrucian**

roseola (med.) a rosy rash, German measles

rose/-pink, -red (hyphens)

rosery a rose garden; cf. **rosary**

rose-tinted (hyphen)

rose tree (two words)

Rosetta/ Egypt, **— Stone** (caps.)

rose/ water, — window (two words)

rosewood (one word)

rosey *use* -sy

Rosh Hashanah the Jewish New Year's Day (not ital.), *not* -annah

Roshi the spiritual leader of a community of Zen Buddhist monks

Rosicrucian (a member) of a secretive 17th–18th-c. order devoted to metaphysical occult lore, said to be launched by a mythical 15th-c. knight, Christian Rosenkreuz

rosin a solid residue from turpentine distillation, used esp. on the bow of musical instruments; cf. **resin**

Rosinante *see* **Rocinante**

Roskilde/ Denmark; **Treaty of** — 1658, between Denmark and Sweden

Roslin Lothian

Rosny, Joseph Henry joint pseud. of brothers **Joseph Henri Boëx** (1856–1940) and **Séraphin Justin François Boëx** (1859–1948) French novelists

rosolio/ a sweet cordial of S. Europe, pl. **-s**; *not* -oglio, -oli (not cap.)

RoSPA Royal Society for the Prevention of Accidents

Ross,/ **Sir James Clark** (1800–62) English Arctic explorer; — **Sir John** (1777–1856) his uncle, Scottish explorer; — **Sir Ronald** (1857–1932) English physician

Rosse, Earl of

Rossellini, Roberto (1906–77) Italian film director

Rossetti,/ **Christina** (**Georgina**) (1830–94) English poet; — **Dante Gabriel** (1828–82) her brother, English painter and poet; — **Gabriele** (1783–1854) Italian poet and liberal, father of the other three; — **William Michael** (1829–1919) his son, English author and critic

Rosslyn, Earl of *see also* **Roslin**

Ross-shire (hyphen) latterly **Ross and Cromarty**, now part of Highland region

Rostand, Edmond (1868–1918) French playwright

roster a list of persons, showing rotation of duties

Rösti (Ger. f. pl. cook.) thinly sliced fried potatoes

Rostropovich, Mstislav (**Leopoldovich**) (b. 1927) Russian cellist and conductor

rostr/**um** a speaker's platform, pl. **-a** (not ital.)

ros/**y** *not* -ey, **-ily**

rot/, **-ted**, **-ting**

rota/ a roster, pl. **-s**; **the** — the supreme ecclesiastical and secular court of the Roman Catholic Church (cap.)

Rotarian a member of a Rotary Club (cap.)

rotary revolving, *not* rotatory; (print.) a printing machine in which the plate(s) are mounted on a cylinder

Rotary Club a branch of Rotary International, a charitable society (caps.)

rotator a revolving part, (anat.) a muscle that rotates a limb

rotatory *use* **rotary**

Rotavator (propr.) a rotary cultivator, *not* Roto-

rotchet *use* **roch-**

rote mechanical memory or performance

Rothamsted Herts., agricultural station for soil research

Rothe, Richard (1799–1867) German theologian

Rothes/ Grampian, **Earl of** —

Rothschild a European family of bankers

rôti (Fr. m. cook.) roast meat

rotifer/ a minute aquatic animal, pl. **-s**; **Rotifera** the phylum containing them

rotogravure (print.) the printing from photogravure cylinders on a web-fed rotary press

rotor (mech.) a revolving part

rottenstone decomposed siliceous limestone (one word)

Rottingdean E. Sussex (one word)

Rottweiler a tall black-and-tan breed of dog (not cap. in US)

rotunda/ a domed circular building or hall, pl. **-s**

roturi/**er** (Fr.) f. **-ère** a commoner (as opposed to a noble)

Rouault, Georges (1871–1958) French painter

Roubiliac, Louis François (c.1705–62) French sculptor, *not* -lliac

rouble a Russian coin and monetary unit, *not* ru- (US); abbr. **r.**; in Russ. *rubl´*

rouche *use* **ru-**

roué a debauchee (not ital.)

Rouge/ **Croix**, — **Dragon** pursuivants

rouge-et-noir a game of chance (hyphens, not ital.)

Rougemont, Louis De assumed name of **Louis Grin** (1847–1921) Swiss-born adventurer and writer

Rouget de Lisle, Claude Joseph (1760–1836) composer of 'La Marseillaise', *not* l'Isle

rough trump, *use* **ruff**

rough-and/**-ready**, **-tumble** (hyphens)

rough breathing (typ.) *see* **breathing**

roughcast (one word)

rough/**-dry**, **-hew** (hyphens)

rough house (two words, one word in US)

roughneck (one word)

rough pull (print.) a proof pulled by hand on inferior paper for correction purposes

rough-rider (hyphen, one word in US) *but* Teddy Roosevelt's **Rough Riders** (caps., two words)

roughshod (one word)

Rougon-Macquart a family depicted in a cycle of novels by Émile Zola (hyphen)

roulade (cook.) a dish cooked or served in the shape of a roll, (mus.) a florid passage in solo vocal music on one syllable (not ital.)

rouleau/ a cylindrical roll of coins, pl. **-x** (not ital.)

Roumania/, **-n** *use* **Rom-**

Roumansh *use* **Rom-**

Roumelia/, -n *use* **Rum-**

round about (adv. and prep., two words) *but* **roundabout** (noun and adj., one word)

roundhouse (one word)

rounding (bind.) shaping the back of a book into a convex curve

round robin (two words)

roundworm (one word)

rouseabout (Austral., NZ) an unskilled labourer or odd jobber, esp. on a farm; *see also* **roustabout**

Rousseau,/ Henri (1844–1910) French painter, called *Le Douanier*; — **Jean Baptiste** (1670–1741) French poet; — **Jean-Jacques** (1712–72) Geneva-born French philosopher; — **Pierre Étienne Théodore** (1812–67) French painter

Roussillon a French province, a red wine from there

roustabout a labourer on an oil rig, an unskilled or casual labourer, (US) a dock labourer or deckhand; *see also* **rouseabout**

rout (verb) to put to flight; (noun) a rabble, a disorderly retreat; cf. **root**

route/ a way taken from a starting point to a destination; **-ing**

Routledge publishers

roux (cook.) a mixture of fat and flour

ROW (econ.) rest of the world

rowing boat (two words) *not* rowboat (US)

rowlock (naut.) *not* roll-, rull-

Roxburgh Borders

Roxburghe, Duke of *not* -burg

Roxburghe Club an exclusive club for bibliophiles

royal/ a former size of paper, 20 × 25 in.; — **4to** 12½ × 10 in., — **8vo** 10 × 6¼ in. (untrimmed)

Royal/ (cap.) abbr. **R.**; — **Academy,** — **Academician,** — **Artillery** abbr. **RA**

Royal Greenwich Observatory Cambridge, formerly at Herstmonceaux, originally at Greenwich; abbr. **RGO**

Royal Highness abbr. **RH**

Royal Military Academy Greenwich (no comma)

Royal Society abbr. **RS**

royal/ standard used solely by the monarch, other members of the royal family having a — **banner**

Royal/ Welch Fusiliers, — Welch Regiment (*but* **Welsh Guards**)

roysterer *use* **roi-**

RP read for press, received pronunciation, Reformed Presbyterian, reply paid, reprint, (Fr.) *Révérend Père* (Reverend Father), Royal Society of Portrait Painters

RPC Royal Pioneer Corps

RPE Reformed Protestant Episcopal

RPI retail price index

RPM resale price maintenance

rpm revolutions per minute (no points)

RPO Royal Philharmonic Orchestra

rps revolutions per second (no points)

RPS Royal Philharmonic Society, Royal Photographic Society

RQMS Regimental Quartermaster-Sergeant

RR (US) railroad, rural route

RRC (Lady of the) Royal Red Cross

RS (US) Received Standard, Revised Statutes, Royal Scots, Royal Society

Rs rupees

r.s. right side

RSA Royal Scottish Academ/y, -ician; Royal Society of Arts

RSAA Royal Society for Asian Affairs

RSC Royal Shakespeare Company, Royal Society of Chemistry

RSD Royal Society of Dublin

RSE Royal Society of Edinburgh

RSFSR Russian Soviet Federative Socialist Republic, largest republic in the former USSR

RSH Royal Society of Health

R. Signals Royal Corps of Signals

RSL Royal Society of Literature

RSM Regimental Sergeant Major, Royal School of Mines, Royal Society of Medicine, Royal Society of Musicians of Great Britain

RSMA Royal Society of Marine Artists

RSO railway sub-office, railway sorting office

RSPB Royal Society for the Protection of Birds

RSPCA Royal Society for the Prevention of Cruelty to Animals

RSRE Royal Signals and Radar Establishment

RSV Revised Standard Version (of Bible)

RSVP *répondez, s'il vous plaît* (please reply) (do not use in writings in French, or in the third person)

RT radio-telegraphy, radio-telephony, received text

rt. right

RTE Radio Telefís Éireann

Rt. Hon. Right Honourable

RTO Railway Transport Officer

RTR Royal Tank Regiment

Rt. Revd Right Reverend (of a bishop or moderator)

RTS Royal Toxophilite Society

RTYC Royal Thames Yacht Club

RU Rugby Union

Ru ruthenium (no point)

Ruanda *use* **Rw-**

rub-a-dub/ make the sound of a drum, **-bed, -bing** (hyphens)

rubai a quatrain in Persian poetry, pl. **rubaiyat**; in Pers. (and in specialist works) **rubāʿī**, pl. **rubāʿiyāt**; see also next entry

Rubáiyát of Omar Khayyám, The a collection of Persian poetry translated by E. FitzGerald, 1859

rubato/ (mus.) (performed at) tempo varied for expressive effect, pl. **-s**

rubber (Brit.) eraser, or (colloq.) condom; **-s** (US) galoshes, or (colloq.) condoms

rubber stamp (hyphen as verb)

rubef/y to make red, not -ify; **-acient, -action**

rubella (med.) German measles; cf. **rubeola**

Rubens, Peter Paul (1577–1640) Flemish painter, not Reu-

rubeola (med.) measles; cf. **rubella**

Rubicon, cross the take an irretraceable step (cap.); **rubicon** (noun and verb; in piquet, not cap.)

rubidium symbol **Rb**

Rubinstein,/ Anton (**Grigorevich**) (1829–94) Russian composer and pianist, — **Artur** (1886–1982) Polish-born American pianist

ruble use **rou-** (except in US)

RUC (hist.) Royal Ulster Constabulary

ru/c, -ck, -kh use **roc**

ruch/e a quilling or frilling, **-ing**; not rou-

rudbeckia a composite garden plant of the genus *Rudbeckia*; cf. **rutabaga**

Rüdesheimer a Rhine wine

RUE (theat.) right upper entrance

ru/e a herb, to regret; **-eful, -ing**

rue (Fr. f.) street, (herb) rue; in Fr. not cap. with street names; in Eng. cap., not ital.

ruff a frill worn round the neck, esp. in the 16th c.; a domestic pigeon; a wading bird, f. **reeve**; a perch-like fish (not ruffe); (to) trump at cards

rug/a (Lat.) a wrinkle, pl. **-ae**

Rugbeian a member of Rugby School

rugby football (not cap.) colloq. **rugger**

Ruhmkorff,/ Heinrich Daniel (1803–77) German-born French electrical inventor, — **coil**

RUKBA Royal United Kingdom Beneficent Association

rule/ (typ.) a line; dotted …; double ====; em —; en –; French – ◂—; milled ----------; parallel ====; single ———; spread or swelled ———; total ====; wavy ∿∿∿∿

'Rule, Britannia!' (comma, to denote an imperative rather than an invitation)

rullock use **row-**

Rumania/, -n use **Rom-**

Rumansh use **Rom-**

rumba/ a dance; **-ed, -ing, -s**; not rhu-

rumb-line use **rh-**

Rumelia/ an area of the Balkans, mainly in Bulgaria; **-n**; not Rou-

rumen/ a ruminant's first stomach, pl. **-s**

rumin/ant an animal that chews the cud; **-ator** one who ponders, not -er

rummage sale (US) = **jumble sale**

Rump, the (hist.) the remnant of the English Long Parliament 1648–53, or after its restoration in 1659

Rumpelstiltskin a dwarf in German folklore, in Ger. **Rumpelstilzchen**

run (naut.) deserted, abbr. **R.**; (US) = **ladder** (in hosiery)

runabout a small light vehicle (one word)

runaway (noun and adj., one word)

rune any of the letters of the earliest Germanic alphabet, used also by Scandinavians and Anglo-Saxons; a Finnish poem or a division of it

Runeberg, John Ludwig (1804–77) Finnish poet

rune-staff a magic wand inscribed with runes, or a runic calendar or almanac (hyphen)

running/ foot(line) a line of type set in margin at foot of page; see also next entry

running/ head(line) or — **title** (typ.) a line of type set in the head margin of a page

Runnymede a meadow on the River Thames where King John sealed Magna Carta, 1215

run-off (noun, hyphen, one word in US)

run-of-the-mill (hyphens)

run on (typ.) (matter) to be set without break or paragraph; the continued operation of press subsequent to first (or stated quantity of) copy

run round (typ.) to set text etc. round three or more sides of a block on a page, as with illustrations, tables, etc.

runway (one word)

Runyon,/ (Alfred) Damon (1884–1946) US journalist and author, **-esque**

rupee the chief monetary unit of India, Pakistan, Sri Lanka, Nepal, Mauritius, and the Seychelles; in Hind. **rūpiyah**; abbr. **Re**, pl. **Rs**, tens of rupees **Rx**

Rupert's Land, Prince Canada

rupiah the chief monetary unit of Indonesia, abbr. **Rp**

RUR Royal Ulster Regiment, (hist.) Royal Ulster Rifles

RUR *Rossum's Universal Robots* (title of a play by K. Čapek, 1920)

ruralize not -ise

Ruritania/ an imaginary setting in SE Europe in the novels of Anthony Hope, **-n** relating

to or characteristic of romantic adventure or
its setting

RUSI Royal United Services Institute for
Defence Studies

rus in urbe (Lat.) the country within a town

Russ. Russia, -n

**Russell/, Bertrand (Arthur William),
Earl** (1872–1970) English philosopher and
mathematician; **Baron — of Liverpool**; *also*
the family name of Duke of Bedford and
Barons Ampthill and De Clifford; **—, George**
see **A.E.**; **Jack —** a breed of terrier

Russell cord a ribbed fabric (two words)

Russia/, -n abbr. **Russ.**

Russia leather (bind.) a durable bookbinding
leather from skins impregnated with
birch-bark oil

rut/, -ted, -ting, -ty

rutabaga (US) = swede; cf. **rudbeckia**

Ruth (OT) not to be abbr.

ruthenium symbol **Ru**

Rutherford,/ Ernest, Baron (1871–1937) New
Zealand scientist; **— Mark** pseud. of **William
Hale White** (1831–1913) English writer

rutherfordium symbol **Rf**

Ruthven, Baron

Ruwenzori mountain, Uganda and Congo

Ruy Lopez a chess opening, from **Ruy López**
(16th-c.) Spanish chess master; also called
'the Spanish opening'

Ruysbroeck, Jan van (1293–1387) Flemish
mystic

Ruysdael,/ Jakob van (1628–82) and **—
Salomon van** (1600–70) Dutch painters

RV Revised Version (of the Bible)

RW Right Worshipful, Right Worthy

Rwanda/ Cent. Africa; *not* Ru-; **-n**

RWF Royal Welch Fusiliers

RWS Royal Society of Painters in Water Colours

Rx tens of rupees

Ry. railway

RYA Royal Yachting Association

ryegrass (one word)

Rye House Plot 1682–3 (no hyphens, three
caps.)

ryokan a traditional Japanese inn

ryot an Indian peasant, in Urdu *ra'īyat*

RYS Royal Yacht Squadron (a club)

Ryukyu Islands Japan, *not* the many variants

Ss

S (Lat.) *semi* (half, e.g. IIS = $2\frac{1}{2}$); siemens; sulphur; (on timepiece regulator) slow; the eighteenth in a series

S. Sabbath, Saint, school, series, *Signor*, Socialist, Society, soprano; south, -ern; sun, Sunday, surplus, (Fr.) *saint* (saint), (Ger.) *Seite* (page), (Lat.) *sepultus* (buried), *socius* or *sodalis* (Fellow)

S/. sucre (currency of Ecuador)

s second, -s (of time or angle)

s. section, see; sets, -s; shilling, -s; sign, -ed; singular, (meteor.) snow, solo, son, spherical, stem, (meteor.) stratus cloud, substantive, succeeded; (Fr.) *siècle* (century), *sud* (south); (Ger.) *siehe* (see), (It.) *sinistra* (left)

s/ (Fr.) *sur* (on) e.g. Boulogne s/M = Boulogne-sur-mer

's abbr. for Du. *des* (of the), as 's-Gravenhage (The Hague); arch. prefix (esp. in oaths) for *God's*, as 'sblood, 'struth

※ *see* **dal segno**

$ *or* **$** the dollar sign; to be before, and close up to, numerals

∫ italic form of the **long s**, (math.) sign of integration

SA the Salvation Army, sex appeal, South Africa, South America, South Australia, (Sp.) *Sociedad Anónima* (public limited company), (Port.) *Sociedade Anónima* (public limited company), (Brazilian Port.) *Sociedade Anônima* (public limited company), (Fr.) *Société Anonyme* (public limited company), (Ger.) *Sturm-Abteilung* (the paramilitary force of the Nazi Party)

sa. sable

s.a. *sine anno* (without date)

Saar/ a river and region; **-land** a province of Germany (one word)

Sabaean of ancient Yemen

Sabah a part of Malaysia

Sabaism star worship in ancient Arabia and Mesopotamia (cap.)

Sabaoth, Lord (God) of (Scripture) Lord of Hosts (cap.), in Heb ṣᵉḇāōṯ; cf. **sabbath**

Sabatini, Rafael (1875–1950) Anglo-Italian author

Sabbatarian/, -ism (caps.)

sabbath/ (day) (not cap.), **— day's journey** (Heb.) about two-thirds of a mile; cf. **Sabaoth**

Sabian (a member) of a sect classed in the Koran with Muslims, Jews, and Christians, as believers in the true God

Sabine (of or relating to) a people of the Cent. Apennines in ancient Italy

sable (her.) black

sabra a Jew born in Israel (not cap.), in Modern Heb. *sābrāh*

sabre/ *not* -er (US)

sabretache *not* -tash, -tasche

sabre-toothed/ cat, — tiger

sabreur a user of the sabre, esp. a cavalryman

SAC Senior Aircraftman, (US) Strategic Air Command

sac (med., biol.) a baglike cavity

saccharimeter an instrument for measuring sugar content by means of polarized light, *not* -ometer

saccharin a non-fattening sugar substitute

saccharine (adj.) sugary, either literally or figuratively

saccharometer an instrument for measuring sugar content by hydrometry, *not* -imeter

sachem the supreme chief of some Native American tribes, (US) a political leader

Sacheverell, Henry (?1674–1724) English ecclesiastic and politician

Sachlichkeit/ (Ger. f.) objectivity, realism; **Neue —** a German art movement

Sachs,/ Hans (1494–1576) German poet; **— Julius** (1832–97) German botanist; *see also* **Sax; Saxe**

Sachsen Ger. for Saxony

sackbut a medieval trombone

sackcloth (one word)

sack race (two words)

Sackville-West, Victoria Mary ('Vita') (1892–1962) English author

sacral (anat.) of or relating to the sacrum, (anthrop.) of or for sacred rites

sacr/é (Fr.) f. **-ée** sacred

Sacred College (RC) the body of cardinals

sacrileg/e, -ious *not* sacre-, -ligious

SACW Senior Aircraftwoman

SAD (med.) seasonal affective disorder

Saddam Hussein (al-Takriti) (b. 1937) president of Iraq 1979–

saddlebag (one word)

saddle blanket (two words)

saddle bow (two words, one word in US)

saddlecloth (one word)

saddle/ horse, — shoe, — soap (two words)

saddle-sore (hyphen, two words in US)

saddle stitch (bind.) stitching of thread or wire staple through the centre of a pamphlet or magazine placed open on a saddle-shaped support (two words)

Sadduce/e, -an

sadhu an Indian holy man, sage, or ascetic

Saʿdī (?1184–1291) Persian poet, born **Muslih Addin**

sadism a sexual perversion marked by love of cruelty, from **Donatien Alphonse François, comte ('marquis') de Sade** (1740–1814) French soldier and writer

Sadleir, Michael born **Sadler** (1888–1957) English author, bibliographer, and publisher, son of following

Sadler, Sir Michael Ernest (1861–1943) English educationist

sadomasochism (one word)

sae stamped (self-)addressed envelope

safari/ pl. **-s**

safe/ **conduct, — deposit** (hyphen when attrib.)

safety/ **belt, — catch, — curtain, — film, — glass, — lamp, — match, — net, — pin, — razor, — valve** (two words)

Saffron Walden Essex (no hyphen)

S. Afr. South Africa, -n

saga/ pl. **-s** an Old Norse (spec. Icelandic) prose narrative, hence any long or heroic story; in the original, titles of individual sagas have only an initial cap. and no possessive apos., e.g. *Kórmáks saga*, *Njáls saga*; the title may also be compounded with the preceding genitive, e.g. *Sturlungasaga*, but note e.g. *Gunnlaugs saga ormusungu* where the name has a following attribute

sagesse (Fr. f.) wisdom

Saghalien Island *use* **Sakhalin**

sago/ a palm, a starch produced from it, pl. **-s**

Sahara/ desert (in Arab. *ṣaḥrā*) *not* — Desert; **-n**

sahib (Ind.) European master, gentleman; (cap.) an honorific affix, as Smith Sahib; f. **memsahib; pukka sahib** perfect gentleman

Saidpur India, *not* Sayyid-

saignant/ (Fr. cook.) f. **-e** underdone, rare

Saigon *now* **Ho Chi Minh City**

sailboat (US) = **sailing boat** (one word)

sailcloth (one word)

sailed abbr. **sld.**

sailer a ship of specified power

sailing/ **boat, — ship** (two words)

sailor a seaman or -woman

Sailors' Home *not* -'s

sailplane (one word)

sainfoin (bot.) a leguminous fodder plant, *not* saint-

Saint abbr. **S., St**; pl. **SS, Sts**

St Abbs *but* **St Abb's Head** Borders

St Albans/ Herts.; **Bishop** *and* **Duke of — —** (no apos.)

St Albans: the signature of the Bishop (colon)

St Alban's Head Dorset (apos.)

St Aldwyn, Earl

St Andrews (**University**) Fife (no apos.)

St Andrew's/ **Cross** ×, **— — Day** 30 Nov.

St Andrews, Dunkeld, and Dunblane, Bishop of

St Anne's/ **College** Oxford; **— — Day** 26 July; **— — on Sea** Lancs. (no hyphens, apos.)

St Anthony's/ **cross** ⊤; **— — fire** erysipelas

St Antony's College Oxford

St Arvans Gwent (no apos.)

St Aubin Jersey, *not* Aubin's

St Barnabas's Day 11 June

St Barthélemy French W. Indies

St Bartholomew's Day 24 Aug.; *see also* **Bartholomew Day**

St Bees (**Head, School**) (St Begha's) Cumbria (no apos.)

St Benet's Hall Oxford

St Bernard (dog or Pass)

St Boswells Borders (no apos.)

St Catharines Ontario (no apos.)

St Catharine's College Cambridge

St Catherine's College Oxford

St Christopher Island W. Indies (no apos.); *see also* **St Kitts-Nevis**

St Clears Dyfed (no apos.)

St Clement's Day 23 Nov.

St Crispin's Day 25 Oct.

St Cross Church *and* **College** Oxford

St Davids/ **Head** Dyfed, *and* **Viscount — —** (no apos.)

St David's Day 1 Mar.

St Denis's Day 9 Oct.

St Dunstan's Day 19 May

St Ebbe's Oxford

Sainte-Beuve, Charles Augustin (1804–69) French literary critic

Sainte-Claire Deville, Henri Étienne (1818–81) French chemist (one hyphen)

St Edm. and Ipswich: the signature of the Bishop of St Edmundsbury and Ipswich

St Edmund Hall Oxford

St Edmund's House Cambridge

St Elmo's fire an electric discharge, a corposant

Saint-Émilion a claret

Saint-Estèphe a claret

Saint-Étienne dép. Loire, France

Saint-Exupéry, Antoine Jean Baptiste (**Marie Roger**) **de** (1900–44) French aviator and writer

St Fillans Tayside (no apos.)

saintfoin *use* **sain-**

St Frideswide/ patron of Oxford (city and university), **— —'s Day** 19 Oct.

Saint-Gall *or* **St Gallen** Switzerland

St George's/ Channel, — — Day 23 Apr. (apos.)

St Germans, Bishop *and* **Earl of**

St Giles' an Oxford street (apos.)

St Gotthard Switzerland, *not* Goth-

St Gregory's Day 12 Mar.

St Helens/ Cumbria, IoW, Merseyside; **Baron** — — (no apos.)

St Helier Jersey

St Ive Corn.

St Ives Cambs., Corn., Dorset (no apos.)

St James's the British court

St James's Day 25 July

St James's/ Palace, — — Park, — — Square, — — Street London

St John as proper name pron. 'sinjun' (stress on first syllable)

Saint John New Brunswick

St John Ambulance/ Association, — — — Brigade *not* John's

St John's/ Antigua; NF, Que., Canada; — — **College** Oxford, Cambridge, Durham; — — **Wood** London; — — **wort** any yellow-flowered plant of the genus *Hypericum* (three words, two hyphens in US)

St John the Baptist's Day 24 June

St John the Evangelist's Day 27 Dec.

Saint-Julien a claret (hyphen)

St Just/ Corn., **Baron** — —

Saint-Just, Louis Antoine Léon de (1767–94) French revolutionary

St Just-in-Roseland Corn. (hyphens)

St Kitts-Nevis St Christopher Island, W. Indies; *properly* **the Federation of St Christopher and Nevis** (no apos.)

St Lambert's Day 17 Sept.

St Lawrence River Canada

St Lawrence's Day 10 Aug.

St Leger a race; as surname pron. 'sillinger' *or* 'sentlejer' (stress on first syllable)

St Leonards/ Bucks., Dorset, Lothian, Strathclyde; **Baron** — — (no apos.)

St Leonards-on-Sea E. Sussex (hyphens, no apos.)

St Lucia W. Indies

St Luke's/ Day 18 Oct.; — — **summer** a warm period in mid-October

St Maarten, St Martin a Caribbean island divided between Dutch and French control respectively

St Margaret's at Cliffe Kent

St Margaret's Day 20 July

St Mark's Day 25 Apr.

St Martin-in-the-Fields a London church, *not* Martin's (hyphens)

St Martin's/ Day 11 Nov.; — — **summer** a warm period in mid-November

St Mary Abbots Kensington (no apos.)

St Mary Church S. Glam. (three words)

St Marychurch Devon (two words)

St Mary Cray London, *not* Mary's

St Matthew's Day 21 Sept.

St Matthias's Day 24 Feb., *not* Matthias'

St Mawes Corn.

St Michael and All Angels' Day 29 Sept.

St Michael's Mount Corn.; *see also* **Mont-Saint-Michel**

St Neot Corn.

St Neots Cambs. (no apos.)

St Nicholas patron of Russia, a town in Belgium

St Nicholas's clerks thieves

St Olaf the patron of Norway

St Patrick's Day 17 Mar.

St Paul Minn.

St Paul de Loanda *use* **Luanda**

saintpaulia any plant of the genus *Saintpaulia*, esp. the African violet

St Paul's/, — — Cray London; — — **Day** 25 Jan.

St Peter Port Guernsey, *not* Peter's

St Peter's/ Rome; — — **College** Oxford; — — **Day** 29 June

St Petersburg capital of Russia 1712–1918; called **Petrograd** Dec. 1914–Feb. 1924, thereafter **Leningrad**, till Oct. 1991, when it regained its original name; in Russ. **Sanktpeterburg** (one *s*), colloq. **Piter**; in Fr. **Saint-Pétersbourg**, in Ger. (**Sankt**) **Petersburg**, in It. (**S.**) **Pietroburgo**

St Philip and St James's Day 1 May

Saint-Pierre a claret

Saint-Pierre, Jacques Henri Bernardin de (1737–1814) French author

Saint-Saëns, Charles Camille (1835–1921) French composer

Saintsbury, George Edward Bateman (1845–1933) English literary critic

St Sepulchre, Church of

Saint-Simon,/ Claude Henri de Rouvroy, comte de (1760–1825) founder of French socialism, whence **-ism** a form of socialism; **— Louis de Rouvroy, duc de** (1675–1755) French diplomat and writer

St Simon and St Jude's Day 28 Oct.

St Stephen Corn.

St Stephen's/ the chapel of the Houses of Parliament; — — **Day** 26 Dec.

St Swithun *see* **Swithun**

St Thomas's Day 21 Dec.

St Valentine's Day 14 Feb.

St Vitus's dance Sydenham chorea, not Vitus'

Sakandarabad Hyderabad, India, *use* **Secunder-**; Uttar Pradesh, India, *use* **Sikandar-**

sake a Japanese fermented liquor; *not* -ké, -ki

Sakhalin an island, E. Asia; *not* Saghalien, Karafuto

Sakharov, Andrei (Dmitrievich) (1921–89) Russian physicist and dissident

Saki pseud. of **H(ector) H(ugh) Munro** (1870–1916) English writer

saki/ a S. American monkey, pl. **-s**

Sakta a member of a Hindu sect worshipping the Sakti, in Skt. *śākta*

Sakti (in Hinduism) the female principle, esp. when personified as the wife of a god (cap.); in Skt. *śakti*

Śākyamuni the title of Buddha

salaam the oriental salutation 'Peace', *not* -lam (not ital.); in Arab. *salām*

salable *use* **sale-** (except in US)

salad/ days, — dressing, — oil (two words)

salade a helmet, *use* **sallet**

salade (Fr. f.) lettuce, salad

salami/ a highly seasoned sausage, pl. **-s**; in It. *salame*, pl. *salami*; cf. *salume*

Salammbô a novel by Flaubert, 1862

salariat the salaried class, *not* -ate

saleable *not* sala- (US)

Salem Madras; Mass.

Salempur Uttar Pradesh, India

saleroom *not* salesroom (US)

Salesian (a member) of a RC order founded by Don Bosco in honour of St Francis de Sales

sales/man, -woman, -person (one word)

Salian of or relating to the Salii, a 4th-c. Frankish people living near the River Ijssel

Salic law *not* -ique

salicylic acid a chemical used as a fungicide, and in aspirin and dyestuffs

salient jutting out, conspicuous, (of an angle, esp. in fortification) pointing outwards (cf. **re-entrant**); (her.) (of a lion etc.) standing on its hind legs with the forepaws raised

Salinger,/ J(erome) D(avid) (b. 1919) US novelist, **— Pierre (Emil George)** (b. 1925) US journalist and writer

salle/ (Fr. f.) hall, **— à manger** dining room, **— d'attente** waiting room

sallenders a dry eruption on a horse's hind leg, *not* sellan-

sallet (hist.) a light helmet with an outward-curving rear part, *not* salade

Sallust in Lat., **Gaius Sallustius Crispus** (86–?34 BC) Roman historian, abbr. **Sall.**

Sally Lunn a teacake (caps., two words)

salmagundi/ a medley, a seasoned dish; pl. **-s**

salmanazar a wine bottle of about twelve times the standard size

salmi a ragout, esp. of game; in Fr. m. *salmis*

salmon trout (two words)

Salomon Brothers, Inc. a US investment bank; *not* So-, -an

salon (Fr.) reception room, hairdresser's etc. establishment (not cap.); an annual exhibition in Paris of living artists' pictures (cap.)

Salonika Greece

saloon/ — bar, — car (two words)

Salop. *now* Shropshire

Salopian (a native *or* inhabitant) of, *or* relating to, Shropshire

Salpêtrière, La a hospital, Paris

salpicon (Sp. m.) cold minced meat, *not* -çon

salsa (not ital.)

salsify (bot.) *not* -afy

SALT Strategic Arms Limitation Talks (*or* Treaty)

saltarello/ an Italian and Spanish dance, pl. **-s**

salt cellar (two words, one word in US)

salt lake (two words)

Salt Lake City Ut. (caps., three words)

salt mine (two words)

Saltoun, Baron

saltpetre *not* -peter (US)

saltus a sudden transition, a breach of continuity; pl. same

salt water (one word when attrib.)

Saltykov(-Shchedrin), M. E., pseud. of **graf Mikhail (Yevgrafovich) Saltykov** (1826–89) Russian satirical writer and journalist; pen name also **N. Shchedrin**

Saltykov-Shchedrin State Public Library St Petersburg (hyphen *not* en rule); now the **National Library of Russia**

saluki pl. **-s**

salum/e (It. cook.) salt meat (esp. pork), pl. *-i*; cf. **salami**

salutary beneficial, *not* -ory

salutatory welcoming, *not* -ary

Salvador/, El republic of Cent. America; **-ean** in Sp. *salvadoreño*

salver a tray; cf. **salvor**

salvo/ a simultaneous discharge of guns, bombs, cheers, pl. **-es**; a reservation, excuse, pl. **-s**

salvo jure (Lat.) reserving the right

sal volatile ammonium carbonate, smelling salts

salvor one who salvages; cf. **salver**

Salzkammergut Austria

SAM surface-to-air missile

Sam. Samaritan

Sam., 1, 2 First, Second Book of Samuel

samarium symbol **Sm**

Samarkand Uzbekistan; *not* -cand, -quand

samba/ a Brazilian dance; **-ed, -ing, -s**

sambok (Afrik.) *use* **sjam-**

Sam Browne an army officer's belt with a shoulder strap

sambuca an Italian aniseed-flavoured liqueur, (hist.) a triangular stringed instrument, a kind of siege engine; *not* -cca

S. Amer. South America, -n

Samhain 1 Nov., Celtic festival marking the beginning of winter; in Scots Gaelic **Samhuinn**

Samhita a continuous version of a Vedic text, any of the basic collections of Vedic texts

Sami the preferred native and scholarly term for the Lapps collectively

Samian of or relating to Samon, an Aegean island

samisen a long three-stringed Japanese guitar, played with a plectrum (not ital.)

samizdat the secret publication of banned matter, as in the former USSR (not ital.)

Samnite (of or relating to) a member of a people of ancient Italy often at war with republican Rome, or the language of this people

Samoyed/ a Mongolian of NW Siberia, a breed of dog; *not* -oied, -oide, -oyede; **-ic**

sampan a small flat-bottomed Chinese boat, *not* san-

sampi *or* **sanpi** (Gr.) modern name (derived from 'san' and 'pi') for the character ϡ, used for 900, in Byzantine times called *parakýisma*

Sampson, Dominie a character in Scott's *Guy Mannering*

samsara in Indian philosophy, the endless cycle of death and rebirth to which life in the material world is bound; in Skt. *saṃsāra*

samskara in Indian philosophy, a purificatory ceremony or rite marking an event in one's life; a mental impression, instinct, or memory; in Skt. *saṃskāra*

Samuel, First, Second Book of (OT) abbr. **1 Sam., 2 Sam.**

samurai the Japanese military class (sing. and pl., not cap.), *not* -ourai

Sana'a N. Yemen, *properly* Ṣanʿāʾ; *not* Sanaa

sanatorium/ *not* sanitarium (US), pl. **-s**

sanatory healing; cf. **sanitary**

sanbenito/ a penitential garment, pl. **-s**

Sancho Panza Don Quixote's squire

Sancho-Pedro a card game (caps., hyphen)

sanctum/ a retreat, pl. **-s**; **— sanctorum** (Lat.) the holy of holies in a Jewish temple, a special retreat, pl. **sancta sanctorum** (not ital.)

Sand, George (*not* Georges) pseud. of **Madame Amandine Aurore Lucile Dupin, baronne Dudevant** (1804–76) French novelist

sandal/, -led, -wood

sandarac realgar, resin; *not* -ach

Sandars Reader Cambridge University

sand/bag, -bank, -bar (one word)

sandblast (noun and verb, one word)

sandbox (US) = **sandpit**

sandboy, happy as a (one word)

Sandburg, Carl (1878–1967) US poet

sandcastle (one word)

sand dollar a round flat sea urchin of the order *Exocycloida* (two words)

sand/paper, -piper (bird), **-pit, -stone, -storm** (one word)

sandwich/board, — course (two words)

sangar a stone breastwork round a hollow, *not* -ga

sang-de-bœuf (Fr. m.) a deep red colour

sangfroid composure (one word, not ital.)

sangria a Spanish drink made from red wine with fruit etc. (not ital.)

Sanhedrin the supreme council and court of justice in ancient Jerusalem, *not* -im

sanitarium *use* **sanatorium** (except in US)

sanitary healthy, *not* -ory; cf. **sanatory**

sanitize *not* -ise

Sankt (Ger.) saint, abbr. **St.**

sannup (Amer. Ind.) among some Native American peoples, a married man; *not* -op

sannyasi a Hindu religious mendicant, pl. same; *not* sany-; in Hind. and Urdu **sannyāsī**

sanpan *use* **sam-**

sanpi *see* **sampi**

sans (Fr.) without

San Salvador capital of El Salvador

sans/ appel (Fr.) without appeal, **— cérémonie** informally, **— changer** without changing

Sanscrit *use* **Sansk-**

sans-culott/e in the French Revolution, a lower-class extreme republican or revolutionary, pl. **-es; -erie, -ism, -ist** (hyphen); in Fr. m. **sans-culotte** (hyphen), **sans-culottisme; -id** (hist.) each of the five (in leap year six) complementary days added at the end of the month Fructidor of the French Republican calendar

sans doute (Fr.) no doubt

sanserif *use* **sans serif**

Sansevieria (bot.) a genus of lily

sans/ façon (Fr.) informally, **— faute** without fail, **— gêne** free and easy (hyphen if used as a noun)

Sanskrit abbr. **Skt.**

sans/ pareil (Fr.) unequalled, **— peine** without difficulty; **— peur et sans reproche** fearless and blameless, — *phrase* without circumlocution

sans serif (typ.) a typeface without serifs; use to illustrate shapes only in contexts where it is important to represent actual configuration exactly (e.g. 'K-angled', 'X-joint'), but not where the shape is understood (e.g. *The L-Shaped Room*, 'a T-shirt'); use a serif typeface for *I-beam* when representing the configuration, or the sense may be lost; (two words), *not* sanserif

Sanssouci the palace of Frederick II at Potsdam (one word)

sans/ souci (Fr.) without cares, — *tache* stainless

Santa (It., Sp., Port.) a female saint, abbr. **Sta**

Santa Ana Calif.

Santa Claus *not* Kl-

Santa Fe N. Mex., Argentina (no accent)

Santa Isabel *now* **Malabo**

Santander N. Spain (one word)

Santa Trinita Florence, *not* Trinità

Santayana, George b. **Jorge Agustín Nicolás Ruiz de Santayana y Borrais** (1863–1952) Spanish-born US philosopher and novelist

Santenot a burgundy wine

Santo Domingo a former name of the Dominican Republic, W. Indies; name of its capital

Santos-Dumont, Alberto (1873–1932) Brazilian airman

sanyasi *use* **sannyasi**

São (Port.) saint, e.g. in place names, as **São Miguel** Azores, **São Paulo** Brazil

Saône/ a French river; **Haute-** — a dép. of France (hyphen); **-et-Loire** a dép. of France, abbr. **S.-et-L.** (hyphens)

São Tomé and Príncipe W. Africa

Sapho an opera by Gounod, 1851; a novel by Daudet, 1884

sapienti sat (Lat.) sufficient for a wise man; in full *verbum sapienti sat est*, a word is enough to the wise

Sapper the official term for a private of the Royal Engineers, abbr. **Spr.** (cap.)

sapph/ics verse in sapphic stanzas, **-ism** homosexual relations between women (not cap.)

Sappho (*c.*600 BC) Greek poetess of Lesbos; adj. **Sapphic** *but* **sapphic/ metre,** — **verse** (not cap.)

SAR (US) Sons of the American Revolution

Sar. Sardinia, -n

SARA (comput.) search and replace automatically, pl. **SARAs**

saraband a stately old Spanish dance, the music for this; *not* -bande

Saragossa Spain, in Catalan same, in Sp. **Zaragoza**

sarai *use* **ser-**

Sarajevo Bosnia-Hercegovina

sarape *use* **ser-**

Sarawak a state in Malaysia

sarcenet *use* **sars-**

sarcom/a (med.) a tumour, pl. **-ata**

sarcophag/us a stone coffin, pl. **-i**

Sardinia in It. **Sardegna**, abbr. **Sar.**

Sardou, Victorien (1831–1908) French playwright

saree *use* **-ri**

sargasso/ a seaweed, pl. **-s**

Sargent,/ John Singer (1856–1925) US painter, — **Sir Harold Malcolm Watts** (1895–1967) English conductor

sari/ a garment worn by Indian women, *not* -ee; pl. **-s**; in Hind. **sāṛ(h)ī**

SARL or **Sarl** (Fr.) *société à responsabilité limitée* (private limited company)

sarong a Malay or Javanese long garment for man or woman

saros (astr.) a period of about eighteen years between repetitions of eclipses

sarsaparilla a preparation of dried roots used to flavour some drinks and medicines and formerly as a tonic; *not* saspa-, sassper-

sarsen (geol.) a sandstone boulder carried by ice during a glacial period, *not* sara-

sarsenet a fabric, *not* sarc-

Sartor Resartus 'the tailor retailored', by Carlyle, 1833–4

Sartre, Jean Paul (1905–80) French philosopher

Sarum the historical name of Salisbury

Sarum: the signature of the Bishop of Salisbury (colon)

SAS Special Air Service

Sasanian *see* **Sass-**

SASC Small Arms School Corps

s.a.s.e. (US) self-addressed stamped envelope

sashay (esp. US colloq.) walk or move ostentatiously, casually, or diagonally

sash/ cord, — **weight,** — **window** (two words)

sasine (Sc. law) (an act or document granting) the possession of feudal property; cf. **seisin**

Saskatchewan Canada, abbr. **Sask.**

Sasquatch a supposed yeti-like animal of NW America, *also called* **Bigfoot**

sassafras (bot., med.) a N. American tree, an infusion from its bark; *not* sasse-

Sassan/ian, -id (a member of) a Persian dynasty ruling AD 211–651; *properly* **Sasa-**, and thus in specialist contexts

Sassenach (Sc., Ir., usually derog.) (of) an English person or the English generally; in Scots Gaelic **Sasunnoch**, in Ir. **Sasanach**

Sat. Saturday

Satan (cap.)

satanic devilish (not cap. unless directly referring to Satan)

Satan/ism, -ology (caps.)

satay in Indonesian *sate*, in Malayan *satai*

SATB (mus.) (scored for) soprano, alto, tenor, bass

sateen a shiny fabric, *not* satt-

sati *use* **suttee**

satinet a thin satin, *not* -ette

satire a literary work holding up folly or vice to ridicule

satirize *not* -ise

satisfice (esp. econ., social sci.) perform the minimum required

sat sapienti *see* *sapienti sat*

satsuma/ a variety of tangerine (not cap.); — **ware** cream-coloured Japanese pottery (cap.)

satteen *use* sat-

Saturday abbr. **Sat.**

Saturnalia (Lat. pl.) the ancient Roman orgiastic festival of Saturn (cap.), a time or occasion of wild revelry (in this sense commonly sing., not cap.); adj. **saturnalian** (not cap.)

Saturnian of the god or planet Saturn (cap.)

saturnic (med.) affected with lead poisoning

saturnine of a sluggish, gloomy temperament, or having dark and brooding looks (not cap.)

satyagraha (Ind. hist.) a policy of passive resistance, esp. to British rule, as advocated by Gandhi (not ital.); in Hind. *satyāgraha*

satyr/, -ic; -iasis

Sauchiehall Street Glasgow

saucisse (Fr. f.) fresh pork sausage

saucisson (Fr. m.) a large, highly seasoned sausage

Saudi Arabia *formerly* Hejaz, Nejd, and Asir

sauerkraut (Ger.) chopped pickled cabbage (not ital.)

Saumur a French sparkling white wine

sauna bath (two words)

sausage/ dog (colloq.) a dachshund, — **meat,** — **roll** (two words)

Saussure/, Ferdinand de (1857–1913) Swiss linguistic scholar, **-an**

saut/é (food) lightly fried, to cook in this way; **-éd** *not* -éed (except in US)

Sauternes dép. Gironde, France; a white Bordeaux wine produced in this district; *not* Sauterne

sauve qui peut (Fr.) let him save himself who can

SAVAK (hist.) the secret intelligence organization of Iran 1957–79; acronym from the Persian Sāzmān-i-Attalāt Va Amnīyat-i-Keshvar (National Security and Intelligence Organization)

savannah a treeless plain of subtropical regions, *not* -na (US)

Savannah a river and town, Ga.; a town, Tenn.

savant/ a man of learning, pl. **-s**; f. **-e**, pl. **-es** (not ital.)

Savigny a red burgundy

Savile/ the family name of the Earl of Mexborough; **Baron** —; — **Club,** — **Row** London; **—, Sir Henry** (1549–1622) founder of the Savilian chairs at Oxford; *not* -ille

savin a kind of juniper; (US) = **red cedar**; *not* -ine

savings/ bank, — **certificate** (two words)

saviour *not* -ior (US)

savoir-faire skill, tact (not ital.)

savoir-vivre (Fr.) good breeding (hyphens)

Savonarola, Girolamo (1452–98) Italian religious reformer

savory/ the herb (**summer —, winter —**)

savoury appetiz/er, -ing; *not* -ory (US)

Savoyard of Savoy (region or theatre)

saw/dust, -fish, -mill (one word)

sawn-off *not* sawed-off (US)

sawtooth (one word)

saw-wort a composite plant yielding a yellow dye (hyphen)

sax (colloq.) saxophone; a slater's chopper, *not* zax

Sax. Saxon, Saxony

Sax, Adolphe (1814–94) Belgian inventor of saxhorn and saxophone; *see also* **Sachs; Saxe**

Saxe Fr. for Saxony, in Ger. **Sachsen**

Saxe,/ Hermann Maurice, comte de (1696–1750) French marshal; — **John Godfrey** (1816–87) US poet and humorous writer; *see also* **Sachs; Sax**

saxe (Fr. m.) Dresden china

Saxe/-Altenburg, -Coburg-Gotha, -Meiningen, -Weimar (hyphens) former duchies in eastern Germany, incorporated in Thuringia (Coburg in Bavaria) 1919; in Ger. **Sachsen-**

saxhorn a brass wind instrument with a long winding tube and bell opening

Saxon/, -y abbr. **Sax.**

saxony a fine kind of wool, cloth made from this (not cap.)

saxophone a brass wind instrument with keys and a reed like that of a clarinet, colloq. **sax**

SAYE save as you earn

Saye and Sele, Baron

say-so (noun, hyphen)

Sayyidpur *use* **Said-**

Sb *stibium* (antimony) (no point)

sb stilb

sb. substantive

s.b. single-breasted

S-bend (cap., hyphen); *see also* **sans serif**

SBN *see* **ISBN**

SC South Carolina, Special Constable, Staff College, Staff Corps, Supreme Court, (Lat.) *senatus consultum* (a decree of the Senate), (law) same case, (paper) super-calendered

Sc scandium (no point)

Sc. Scotch, Scots, Scottish

sc. scene, scruple, (Lat.) *scilicet* (namely)

s.c. (typ.) small capitals

sc. *sculpsit* (carved or engraved this)

Sca Fell an English mountain, Cumbria; *not* Scaw (two words)

Scafell Pike the highest English mountain, Cumbria (two words)

scagliola an imitation marble, *not* scal-

scal/a (anat.) a canal in the cochlea, pl. **-ae**

Scala, La a theatre, Milan; in full **Teatro alla Scala**

scalable *not* -eable

scalar (math., phys.) (of a quantity) having only magnitude, not direction; a scalar quantity

scalawag use **scally-** (except in US)

scald an ancient Scandinavian composer and reciter, *use* **sk-**

scaler one who, *or* that which, scales

Scaliger,/ Joseph Justus (1540–1609) French philologist; — **Julius Caesar** (1484–1558) his father, Italian-born scholar

scaliola *use* **scagl-**

scallop/ a shellfish, a shallow pan or dish, a decorative edging; **-ed, -ing**; *not* sco-, escallop

scallywag a scamp, an ill-fed animal; *not* scalla-, scala- (US)

scampi (pl.) breaded langoustines or large prawns; (sing.) a dish of these; in It. **scamp/o**, pl. **-i**

scan/, **-ned, -ning, -sion**

Scand. Scandinavia, -n

scandalize *not* -ise

scandal/um magnatum (Lat.) defamation of high personages, pl. **-a magnatum**; abbr. **scan. mag.**

Scandinavia/, -n includes Denmark, Norway, Sweden, Iceland, and the Faeroe Islands, but not Finland; abbr. **Scand.**

scandium symbol **Sc**

SCAPA Society for Checking the Abuses of Public Advertising

Scapigliatura, La a 19th-c. Italian literary movement

s. caps. (typ.) small capitals

scar the craggy part of a cliff etc., *not* -aur

scaramouch (arch.) a boastful coward, a braggart, esp. as a stock character in Italian farce; in It. **Scaramuccia**, Fr. **Scaramouche**

Scarborough N. Yorks.

Scarbrough, Earl of

scare/crow, -monger (one word)

scar/f a strip of material worn around the neck, pl. **-ves**; (make) a join in the ends (of timber, metal, leather), pl. **-fs**

scarlatina scarlet fever, *not* scarlet-

Scarlatti,/ Alessandro (1660–1725) and — **Domenico** (1685–1757) his son, Italian composers

Scarlett family name of Baron Abinger

scaur *use* **scar**

Scaw Fell *use* **Sca Fell**

scazon (prosody) *see* **choliamb**

Sc.B. *Scientiae Baccalaureus* (Bachelor of Science)

SCC Sea Cadet Corps

Sc.D. *Scientiae Doctor* (Doctor of Science)

SCE Scottish Certificate of Education

scen/a (It., Lat.) a scene in a play or opera; It. pl. **-e**, Lat. pl. **-ae**

scenario/ an outline of a ballet, play, or film; pl. **-s**

scène/ (Fr. f.) scene, stage; **en —** on the stage

Scenes of Clerical Life by George Eliot, 1858, not *from* or *of a*

scep/sis philosophic doubt, **-tic** one inclined to disbelieve; adj. **-tical**; *not* sk- (US)

sceptre *not* -er (US)

SCGB Ski Club of Great Britain

sch. scholar, school, schooner

schadenfreude malicious glee, delight in others' misfortune; in Ger. f. **Schadenfreude**

Schadow,/ Friedrich (1789–1862) German painter; — **Johann Gottfried** (1764–1850) German sculptor, father of Rudolph and Friedrich; — **Rudolph** (1786–1822) German sculptor

Schäfer, E. A. *see* **Sharpey-Schafer**

schako *use* **sha-**

schallot, schalom *use* **sh-**

Schaumburg-Lippe Germany (hyphen)

Scheele/, Karl Wilhelm (1742–86) German chemist, **—'s green** (apos.)

Scheherazade the relater in *The Arabian Nights*; a more scholarly transliteration from Pers. is 'Shahrazād' *or* 'Šīrazād'; the symphonic suite by Rimsky-Korsakov is *Sheherazade*, 1888; the combined song cycle by Ravel and poems by Tristan Klingsor is *Shéhérazade*, 1903

Schelde a river, Belgium–Holland; *not* -dt; in Fr. **Escaut**

Schelling, Friedrich Wilhelm Joseph von (1775–1854) German philosopher

schem/a (Gr.) an outline, pl. **-ata**

schematize *not* -ise

schemozzle *use* **sh-**

Schenectady NY

scherzando/ (mus.) in a playful or lively manner; as noun, pl. **-s**

scherzo/ (mus.) a playful or vigorous piece or movement, pl. **-s**

Schiedam (cap.) Dutch gin, schnapps

Schiehallion a mountain, Tayside

Schiller, Johann Christoph Friedrich von (1759–1805) German poet

schilling the chief monetary unit of Austria

Schimmelpenninck, Mary Anne (**Mrs**) (1778–1856) English writer

Schimpf/wort (Ger.) an insulting epithet, a term of abuse; pl. **-wörter**

schipperke a breed of small black tailless dog; *not* ski-

schizanthus (bot.) the butterfly flower

schizo/ (colloq.) schizophrenic, pl. **-s**

schlemiel (US colloq.) a foolish or unlucky person (not ital.), in Yiddish **shlemiel**

Schlesinger, Arthur M(eier)/ (1888–1965) and **— — — Jr.** (b. 1917) his son, US professors and historians

Schleswig-Holstein Germany (hyphen)

Schliemann, Heinrich (1822–90) German archaeologist

schmaltz sentimentalism; *not* sh-, -alz (not ital.)

schnapps any of various spirits drunk in N. Europe, *not* -aps

schnauzer German breed of dog (not cap.)

schnitzel/ (Ger.) a veal cutlet, **Wiener** — this fried in breadcrumbs (one cap.)

Schnitzler, Arthur (1862–1931) Austrian playwright

schnorkel *use* **sn-**

Schobert, Johann (*c.*1720–67) German composer

Schoenberg, Arnold (1874–1951) Austrian-born composer, *not* Schö-

Scholar-Gipsy, The a poem by M. Arnold, 1853

scholi/um (Lat.) a marginal note or explanatory comment in a manuscript, pl. **-a**; **-ast** (hist.) an ancient or medieval scholar, esp. a grammarian

Schomberg, Friedrich Hermann, Duke of (1615–90) German-born French marshal and English mercenary officer

Schomburg Center for Research in Black Culture New York City

Schomburgk, Sir Robert Hermann (1804–65) German traveller

Schönbrunn Vienna

school an educational institution for children under 19 years; (US) any level of education, including college or university; abbr. **S.**; — **age**, — **bag**, — **board** (hyphen, one word in US) (US or hist.) a board or authority for local education (two words)

school/book, -boy (one word)

school bus (two words)

schoolchild (one word)

schooldays (one word, two words in US)

school/fellow, -girl (one word)

schoolhouse a building for school (one word); **school house** the headmaster's or housemaster's house at a boarding school (two words)

school leaver (two words)

school-leaving age (hyphen)

school/man, -master, -mate, -mistress, -room, -teacher (one word)

school time (two words, one word in US)

school year (two words)

schooner abbr. **sch.**

Schopenhauer, Arthur (1788–1860) German philosopher

Schreiner, Olive Emilie Albertina (1855–1920) S. African writer

Schrift/ (Ger. f.) (hand)writing, book, publication, paper, review, periodical, work, etc., pl. **-en**

Schriftsteller/ (Ger. m.) writer, author, f. **-in** (cf. **Dichter**, **Verfasser**); **-name** (f.) pen-name

Schrödinger/, Erwin (1887–1961) Austrian physicist, — **equation** *but* **—'s cat**

Schubart, Christian Friedrich Daniel (1739–91) German poet

Schubert, Franz Peter (1797–1828) Austrian composer

Schuman,/ Robert (1886–1963) French statesman, — **William Howard** (1910–92) US composer

Schumann, Robert Alexander (1810–56) German composer

schuss (make) a straight downhill run on skis (not ital.)

Schütz, Heinrich (1585–1672) German composer

Schutzstaffel (Ger. f.) (hist.) the Nazi elite corps, abbr. **SS**

Schuyler,/ Eugene (1840–90) US writer, — **Philip John** (1733–1804) US statesman and soldier

Schuylkill a town and river, Pa.

schwa (phonetics) the indistinct vowel sound, as in 'ago'; symbol ə; *not* sheva, shwa

Schwärmerei (Ger. f.) a sentimental enthusiasm

Schwarzerd *see* **Melanchthon**

Schwarzwald (Ger. m.) the Black Forest

Schweinfurt/ Bavaria; — **blue,** — **green,** etc.

Schweinfurth, Georg August (1836–1925) German traveller in Africa

Schweitzer, Albert (1875–1965) German philosopher, theologian, organist, and medical missionary

Schweiz, die Ger. for Switzerland

Schwyz a canton and its capital in Switzerland

sci. scien/ce, -tific

scia/graphy the art of the perspective of shadows, X-ray radiography; **-gram, -graph, -graphic; -machy** fighting with shadows; *not* scio-, skia- (US, and in Greek contexts)

science abbr. **sci.**

science fiction (two words), (colloq.) **sci-fi** abbr. **SF**

scienter (law) knowingly, intentionally (not ital.)

scientific/ abbr. **sci.**

Scientology a religious system (cap.)

sci-fi (colloq.) science fiction (hyphen)

scilicet that is to say, namely (introducing a word or an explanation of an ambiguity); abbr. **sc.** (not ital.)

Scill/y, **Isles of** off Corn., **-onian**

scimitar an oriental curved sword, *not* the many variants

Scind Pakistan, *use* **Sind**

scintilla/ a spark, a trace; pl. **-s**

sciography etc., *use* **scia-**

sciolist a superficial pretender to knowledge

scion *not* cion

scire facias (law) a writ to enforce or annul a judgment, patent, etc.

scirocco *use* **si-**

Sclavic etc., *use* **Sl-**

sclerom/a pl. **-ata** (med.) hardening

scleros/is pl. **-es** (med.) hardening

SCM State Certified Midwife, Student Christian Movement

Sc.M. *Scientiae Magister* (Master of Science)

Scolar Press publishers, *not* Sch-

scollop *use* **sca-**

Scone Tayside

SCONUL Standing Conference of National and University Libraries

score (bind.) break the surface of a board to help folding

-score (suffix, one word e.g. *threescore*)

score/board, -card (one word)

score sheet (two words)

scori/a slag, pl. **-ae**

Scot a native of Scotland

Scot. Scotch, Scotland, Scottish

Scotch use only in phrases such as — **(whisky),** — **broth,** etc.; abbr. **Sc., Scot.**

Scotch catch (mus.) a short note on the beat followed by a long one

Scotch/ **egg,** — **gambit,** — **kale**

Scotchman *use* **Scots-**

Scotch mist (two words)

Scotch pine *use* **Scots pine**

Scotch snap (mus.) = **Scotch catch**

Scotch tape (US propr.) transparent adhesive tape; *see also* **Sellotape**

Scotch terrier *use* **Scottish terrier**

Scotchwoman *use* **Scots-**

scot-free (hyphen)

scotice *use* **scott-**

Scotic/ism, -ize *use* **Scott-**

Scotism the doctrine of Duns Scotus

Scots fir = **Scots pine**

Scots Guards (no apos.)

Scotsman *not* Scotchman

Scots pine *not* Scotch pine

Scotswoman *not* Scotchwoman

Scott Fitzgerald, F. *see* **Fitzgerald, F. Scott**

scottice in the Scots dialect (no accent), *not* scotice

Scotticism a Scottish expression, *not* Scoti-

Scotticize make or become like the Scots; *not* -ise, Scoti-

Scottie (colloq.) a Scottish person or terrier

Scottish prefer to Scotch, *not* Scotish; abbr. **Sc., Scot.**

Scottish terrier (one of) a breed of rough-haired short-legged dogs, *not* Scotch terrier

Scouse (colloq.) a native of Liverpool (cap.); the Liverpool dialect, a stew (short for **lobscouse**) (not cap.)

Scout *not now* Boy Scout (cap.)

scow a flat-bottomed boat, *not* sk-

SCPS Society of Civil and Public Servants

SCR Senior Common Room, (Cambridge University) Senior Combination Room

scr. scruple, -s

scrap/book, -yard (one word)

screen (typ.) a fine grating on film or glass that breaks an illustration with various tones into dots of the appropriate size

screenplay the script of a film (one word)

screenwriter a person who writes a screenplay (one word)

screwball (a person who is) crazy or eccentric (one word)

screw cap (two words, hyphen when attrib.)

screwdriver (one word)

screw top (two words, hyphen when attrib.)

screw up bungle, muddle (hyphen when noun, one word in US)

screw valve (two words)

Scriabin(e) *use* **Skriabin**

scribes and Pharisees (cap. *P* only)

scrips/it (Lat.) wrote this; pl. *-erunt*, *-ere*

Script. Scripture

script (typ.) a type resembling handwriting

scriptori/um a writing room, pl. **-a**

scriptural (not cap.)

Scriptures, the (cap.)

scrod (US) a young cod or haddock

scroll (comput.) to move text vertically up or down screen; cf. **page**

Scrooge a miser, from the character in Dickens's *A Christmas Carol* (cap.)

scrot/um (anat.) pl. **-a**

scruple 20 grains; abbr. **sc.**, sign ℈

scrutator a scrutineer

scrutin/ize inspect closely; *not* -ise, **-y**

scry/ divine by crystal-gazing; **-er, -ing**

scuba/ self-contained underwater breathing apparatus (acronym), pl. **-s**; **-diver, -diving** (hyphens, two words in US)

Scud missile (one cap.)

sculduggery *use* **skul-**

sculp. sculpt/or, -ress, -ural, -ure

sculps/it (Lat.) engraved, or carved, this; pl. *-erunt, -ere*; abbr. **sc., sculps.**

sculptures, titles of when cited, to be in italic

scurry (noun and verb) *not* sk-

S-curve (cap., hyphen); use sans serif typeface where it is important to represent the actual configuration exactly

Scutari Albania, *not* Sk-; in Albanian **Shkodër**

scutcheon *use* **escut-**, *but A Blot in the 'Scutcheon* by R. Browning

scuttlebutt (one word)

Scylla and Charybdis (Gr. myth.) a sea monster and whirlpool in the Straits of Messina, two dangers such that avoidance of one increases the risk from the other

scymitar *use* **scim-**

SD South Dakota (postal abbr.)

sd. (books) sewed

s.d. shillings and pence, (Ger.) *siehe dies* (= q.v.), (Lat.) *sine die* (indefinitely)

S. Dak. South Dakota (off. abbr.)

SDI (US) Strategic Defense Initiative, begun 1983; commonly called **Star Wars**

SDLP (N. Ireland) Social Democratic and Labour Party

SDP (UK) Social Democratic Party

SDR special drawing right (from the International Monetary Fund)

SE south-east, -ern; (Fr.) *Son Excellence* (His, *or* Her, Excellency)

S/E Stock Exchange

Se selenium (no point)

Sea cap. with name, as North Sea, Sea of Marmara

sea/bed, -bird, -board, -borne (one word)

sea breeze (two words)

SEAC South-East Asia Command

sea/ change, — cow, — cucumber, — dog (two words)

sea/farer, -faring, -food (one word)

Seaford E. Sussex

Seaforde Co. Down

sea/going, -gull (one word)

sea horse (two words)

Seal Kent

Seale Surrey

sea/ legs, — level (two words)

sealing wax (two words)

sea lion (two words)

Sea Lord a naval member of the Admiralty Board (caps.)

sealskin (one word)

Séamas, Séamus (Anglicized as **Seamus**) Ir. Gael. for **James**; *see also* **Seumas, Seumus**

sea mile *see* **mile**

seamstress a sewing-woman, *not* semp-

Seanad Éireann the Upper House of the Irish Parliament

seance a spiritualist meeting (not ital., no accent), in Fr. f. *séance*

sea/plane, -port (one word)

SEAQ Stock Exchange Automated Quotations (a computerized access to share information)

sear scorch, wither(ed); cf. **sere**

searchlight (one word)

search/ party, — warrant (two words)

seascape (one word)

sea serpent (two words)

sea/shell, -shore, -sick, -sickness, -side (one word)

seasons, names of not cap. except when used poetically or as part of a formal appellation

season ticket (two words)

SEAT a Spanish make of car

SEATO South-East Asia Treaty Organization

sea urchin (two words)

sea/ wall, — water (two words, one word in US)

sea/way, -weed, -worthy (one word)

sebaceous fatty, *not* -ious

Sebastopol (hist.) the spelling generally used in contemporary accounts of the Crimean War; *see also* **Sev-**

SEC (US) Securities and Exchange Commission *but* Securities Exchange Act

sec (math.) secant (no point), (colloq.) second; dry (as of wine) (not ital.), in Fr. **sec**, f. **sèche**

sec. second, -s (of time or angle, no point in scientific and technical work), secondary, secretary

sec. see secundum

secateurs (pl.) a pair of pruning clippers (no accent, not ital.)

secco/ painting on dry plaster, pl. **-s**

Sec.-Gen. Secretary-General

Sechuana the language of the Bechuanas, *use* **Setswana**

Secker and Warburg publishers

second (adj.) abbr. **2nd**

second/, **-s** abbr. **s.**, **sec.** (no point in scientific and technical work); sign ″; — **mark** (″) symbol for inches or seconds; cf. **secund**

seconde a fencing parry

second-hand (adj. and adv., hyphen, one word in US)

second floor (two words, hyphen as adj.)

second lieutenant an army officer next below lieutenant or (in the US) first lieutenant

secondo (mus.) the lower part in a duet

second-rate (hyphen)

Second World War 1939–45 (caps.) is common British style; **World War II** is common US style

secrecy *not* -sy

sec. reg. *secundum regulam* (according to rule)

secretaire an escritoire (not ital.)

secretariat a permanent administrative office or department, esp. a governmental one; *not* -ate

secretary abbr. **sec.**

Secretary/-General pl. **—-Generals**, (US) **Secretaries-General**; (caps.), abbr. **Sec.-Gen.**

Secretary of State, the head of a major government department, (US) chief government official responsible for foreign affairs (caps.)

secret/e to hide, to discharge from a cell (blood, sap, etc.); **-ion, -or, -ory**

section/ abbr. **s.**, **sect.**; symbol §, pl. §§; — **mark** §, the fourth mark for footnotes

secularize *not* -ise

secund (biol.) on one side only; cf. **second**

Secunderabad Hyderabad, India; *not* Sak-, Sek-; *see also* **Sikandar-**

secundo (Lat.) in the second place, abbr. **2º**

secundum/ (Lat.) according to, abbr. **sec.**; — *artem* according to art, abbr. **sec. art.**; — *naturam* naturally, abbr. **sec. nat.**; — *quid* in a particular respect only; — *regulam* according to rule, abbr. **sec. reg.**

SED Scottish Education Department

sedan/ (US) = **saloon car**; — **chair** (two words)

Sedbergh Cumbria

se defendendo (Lat.) in defending himself, *or* herself

Seder Jewish service on the first night or two nights of Passover, *not* ceder; in Heb. **sĕder**

sederunt (Sc.) a sitting of an ecclesiastical assembly or other body (not ital.)

sede vacante (Lat.) when the see is vacant

Sedgemoor/ Som.; battle, 1685 (one word)

sedil/e a stone seat for a priest in the chancel of a church, usually one of three; pl. **-ia** (not ital.)

seduc/er *not* -or, **-ible** *not* -eable

séduisant/ (Fr.) f. **-e** bewitching

See, the Holy the Papacy

see (verb) often ital. in indexes and reference books to distinguish it from the words being treated, abbr. **s.**

Seefried, Irmgard (1919–88) German soprano

Seeing Eye dog (US propr.) = **guide dog for the blind**

Seeley, Sir John Robert (1834–95) English historian and writer

Seely family name of Baron Mottistone

see-saw (hyphen, one word in US)

seethe boil, bubble over; *not* -th

sego/ a N. American lily, pl. **-s**

segu/e go on without a pause; an uninterrupted transition; **-ed, -es, -ing**

seguidilla/ a Spanish dance, the music for this; pl. **-s**

Sehnsucht (Ger. f.) yearning, wistful longing

Seicent/o the style of Italian art and literature of the 17th c.; in It. = 600, used with reference to the years 1600–99; **-ist, -oist**

seiche a fluctuation in the water level of a lake

seigneur/ a feudal lord or lord of the manor, *not* -ior; **-ial** (not ital.)

seigniorage a superior's prerogative, the Crown's right to revenue from bullion, *not* seignor-

seigniory lordship, sovereign authority, a seigneur's domain; *not* -eury; *see also* **signory**

Seine/-et-Marne abbr. **S.-et-M.**, **-Maritime**, **-St.-Denis** déps. of France (hyphens)

seise (law) put in possession of; cf. **seize**

seisin (law) (taking) possession by freehold, *not* -zin; cf. **sasine**

seismo/gram a record given by a **seismograph**, an instrument used to record the force of earthquakes; **-logy** the study of earthquakes

Seit/e (Ger. f.) a page, pl. **-en**; abbr. **S.** in sing. and pl.

seize grasp; cf. **seise**

seizin *use* **seis-**

sejant (her.) (of an animal) sitting upright on its haunches (placed after noun)

Sejm the Polish parliament

séjour (Fr. m.) sojourn

Sekt a German sparkling white wine (cap., not ital.)

Sekunderabad *use* **Sec-**

sel. selected

Selangor *see* **Malaya, Federation of**

Selassie, Haile *see* **Haile Selassie**

Selborne, Earl of

Selborne, Natural History of by Gilbert White, 1789

selector one who, or that which, selects; *not* -er

selenium symbol **Se**

self- added (with hyphen) as a reflexive prefix to nouns, adjs., and parts., as *self-absorption*, *self-contained*, *self-evident*, *self-made*, etc.; but note *selfsame*

self-conscious (hyphen) *but* **unselfconscious** (one word)

Seljuk (a member) of the Turkish dynasties ruling in 11th–13th cc., *not* -ouk; in Turk. *Selçuk*

Selkup (of or relating to) (a member of) a Samoyedic people of N. Siberia, or (of) the Uralic language of this people; *formerly* Ostyak Samoyed

Sellafield site of a nuclear power station and reprocessing plant, Cumbria; known as Windscale 1947–81

sellanders *use* **sallen-**

sell-by date (hyphen)

selle de mouton (Fr. f.) saddle of mutton

seller's option abbr. **s.o.**

Sellindge Hythe, Kent

Selling Sittingbourne, Kent

Sellotape (propr.) a transparent adhesive tape (cap.); esp. in transatlantic writing *prefer* e.g. *sticking* or *sticky tape*; *see also* **Scotch tape**

Selsey Glos., E. Sussex; *not* -sea

seltzer a German mineral water

selvedge an edging of cloth, *not* -age

Sem. Semitic

semant/ic (adj.) concerning the meaning of words, **-ics** the branch of philology concerned with this (pl. but treated as sing.)

Semei Kazakhstan, *formerly* **Semipalatinsk**; *not* Semey

semeio- *use* **semio-**

semi/ (colloq.) a semi-detached house, (US) a semi-trailer; pl. **-s**

semi (Lat.) half; abbr. *s*, **S**

semi- prefix meaning half, partly, or almost

semi-automatic (hyphen, one word in US)

semi-barbar/ian, -ic, -ism, -ous (hyphens, one word in US)

semi-bold (typ.) a weight between light roman and bold (hyphen, one word in US)

semi/circle, -circular, -colon (**;**), **-conductor** (one word)

semi-conscious (hyphen, one word in US)

semidemisemiquaver *use* **hemi-**

semi-final/, -ist (hyphen, one word in US)

semi-monthly twice a month (hyphen, one word in US), *prefer* to bi-monthly

Seminole (of or relating to) (a member of) a Native American people, pl. same

semi-official (hyphen, one word in US)

semi/ology, -otics the branch of linguistics concerned with signs and symbols; (med.) the science of symptoms; *not* semeio-

Semipalatinsk *see* **Semei**

semi/-precious, -skilled, -skimmed, -sweet (hyphens, one word in US)

Semite *not* Sh-

Semitic abbr. **Sem.**

Semitize *not* -ise (cap.)

semi/-transparent, -tropical (hyphens, one word in US)

semi-weekly twice a week (hyphen, one word in US), *prefer to* bi-weekly

semp. (mus.) sempre

semper/ eadem (Lat. f. sing., and n. pl.) always the same; — *fidelis* always faithful, pl. — *fideles*; — *idem* (m. and n. sing.) always the same

semplice (mus.) in simple style

sempre (mus.) always, abbr. *semp.*

sempstress *use* **seams-**

Semtex a highly malleable, odourless plastic explosive (cap.)

SEN State Enrolled Nurse

Sen. Senat/e, -or; Seneca, senior

sen. senior

senari/us (prosody) a verse of six feet, esp. an iambic trimeter; pl. **-i**

Senate abbr. **Sen.**

senator cap. only when used with name

Senatus (Lat.) the Senate

Senatus Academicus the governing body in Scottish universities (not ital.)

senatus consultum a decree of the Senate, abbr. **SC**, in Fr. m. (hist.) *sénatus-consulte*

Seneca, Lucius Annaeus (*c.*3 BC–AD 65) Roman Stoic philosopher and statesman, abbr. **Sen.**

Senegal/ W. Africa; **-ese**; in Fr. **Sénégal**

seneschal the steward or major-domo of a medieval great house, a judge in Sark

senhor/ (Port.) Mr, abbr. **sr.**; **-a** Mrs, abbr. **sra.**; **-ita** Miss, abbr. **srta.** (cap. when used with name)

senior abbr. **sen.**, **Senr.**; not part of bearer's name, and therefore used only as ad-hoc designation (like *père*); set after surname, with comma preceding, and before degrees or other titles: 'J. Bloggs, sen., Esq.', *not* 'Esq., sen.'

seniores priores (Lat.) elders first

senior nursing officer the official term for a hospital matron

Sennacherib (d. 681 BC) King of Assyria

sennet (hist.) a signal call on a trumpet or cornet; cf. **sennit**; **sinnet**

sennight (arch.) a week

sennit (hist.) plaited straw, palm leaves, etc., used for making hats; cf. **sennet**; **sinnet**

se non è vero è ben trovato (It.) if it is not true, it is well invented

señor/ (Sp.) Mr, abbr. **sr.**; **-es** Messrs; **-a** Mrs, abbr. **sra.**; **-ita** Miss, abbr. **srta.** (cap. when used with name)

senr. senior

sensitize make sensitive, *not* -ise

sensori/um (Lat.) the grey matter of the brain and spinal cord, pl. **-a**

sensory pertaining to the senses or sensation

sensual concerned with the gratification of the senses, carnal

sensualize *not* -ise

sensu/ lato (Lat.) in the wide sense; — **stricto** in the narrow sense, *not* strictu

sens/um (philos.) sense datum, pl. **-a**

sensuous pertaining to or affected by the senses in aesthetic terms

sentimentalize *not* -ise

Senussi a member of a fanatic Muslim sect, pl. same

senza (It. mus.) without

Seoul S. Korea; *not* Seul, Soul; in Korean **Kyongsong**

separate (typ.) a reprint of one of a series of items, abbr. **sep.**

separator *not* -er

Sephardi/ a Jew of Spanish or Portuguese descent, pl. **-m**; adj. **-c** (cap.); *not* Sef-; cf. **Ashkenazi**

sepoy (hist.) an Indian soldier in European (esp. British) service (not cap.); cf. **spahi**

seppuku (Jap.) the formal term for ritual suicide by disembowelment with a sword; **hara-kiri** is colloq.

Sept. September, Septuagint, *not* Sep.

sept a clan, esp. in Ireland

September abbr. **Sept.**; in Fr. m. *septembre*, abbr. **sept.** (not cap.)

septemvir/ (Lat.) one of a committee of seven, pl. **-i**

septenari/us (prosody) a verse of seven feet, esp. a trochaic or iambic tetrameter catalectic; pl. **-i**

septet (mus.) *not* -ett, -ette

septfoil a seven-lobed ornamental figure

septicaemia blood poisoning, *not* -cemia (US)

septillion a thousand raised to the eighth power (10^{24}), *formerly* the fourteenth power (10^{42}); pl. same

septime a fencing parry

septuagenarian a person from 70 to 79 years old

Septuagesima Sunday the third before Lent

Septuagint the Greek version of the OT including the Apocrypha, *c.*270 BC; abbr. **Sept.**, **LXX**

sept/um (biol.) a partition, pl. **-a**

sepulchre/ a burial vault or tomb; **whited —** a hypocrite (Matt. 23: 27); *not* -er (US); **sepulchral**

Sepulchre, Church of St *not* -'s

sepultus (Lat.) buried, abbr. **S.**

seq. (sing.) (Lat.) *sequens* (the following), *sequente* (and in what follows), *sequitur* (it follows)

seqq. (pl.) (Lat.) *sequentes*, *sequentia* (the following), *sequentibus* (in the following places)

sequel/a (med.) a symptom following a disease, pl. **-ae**

sequen/s, -te *see* **seq.**

sequent/es (Lat. m., f.), **-ia** (n.), **-ibus** *see* **seqq.**

sequitur (Lat.) it follows, abbr. **seq.**

ser. series

sera pl. of **serum**

serac/ a castellated mass of ice in a glacier, pl. **-s** (not ital.)

seraglio/ a harem, (hist.) a Turkish palace; pl. **-s**

serai a caravanserai; *not* sar-, -ay

Serajevo *use* **Sa-**

serang (Anglo-Ind.) a native head of a Lascar crew

serape a Spanish-American shawl or blanket; *not* sar-, zar-

seraph/ a celestial being, pl. **-im** *not* -s

seraskier (hist.) the Turkish Commander-in-Chief and minister of war

Serb. Serbian, (no point) a native of Serbia or a person of Serbian descent

Serb/ia a republic of the former Yugoslavia, in Serbo-Croat **Srbija**

Serbo-Croat/ (of or relating to) the main official language of the former Yugoslavia, combining Serbian and Croatian dialects; also **-ian, Croato-Serbian** (hyphens)

SERC Science and Engineering Research Council

sere a gun-lock's catch, (ecology) a sequence of animal or plant communities; cf. **sear**

sere/cloths, -ments *use* **cere-**

serein (Fr. m.) a fine rain from a cloudless sky in tropical climates

serge a fabric; for candle, *use* **cie-**

sergeant (mil.; but *-j-* in some official contexts) abbr. **Sgt.** (cap. as title)

serial comma a name sometimes given to the comma before *and* in a list of three or more items, e.g. the second comma in 'red, white, and blue'

seriatim serially, point by point

series sing. and pl.; abbr. **S., ser.**

serifs (typ.) the short lines across the ends of arms and stems of letters, *not* ceriphs

Serinagar *use* **Sr-**

Seringapatam Mysore, India

serio-comic (hyphen, one word in US)

Serjeant *see* **sergeant**

sermonize *not* -ise

serra (Port.) a sierra, mountain range

ser/um the fluid that separates from clotted blood, an antitoxin; pl. **-a**

serviceable *not* -cable

service/man, -woman (one word)

serviette a table-napkin (not ital.)

servitor *not* -er

servo/ a mechanism for powered automatic control of a larger system, pl. **-s**; as a combined form denotes a machine with this function, e.g. *servomotor* (one word)

Sesotho a Bantu language, *not* Sesuto

sesquicentenary (the celebration of) a 150th anniversary, *not* -tennial (US)

sesquipedalian (of word) one and a half (metrical) feet long, many-syllabled

sess. session

Session/, Court of the supreme Scottish Court, *not* Sessions; **Parliamentary —** (caps.)

sesterce a Roman coin; in Lat. **sesterti/us** pl. **-i**, symbol **HS** (no point)

sesterti/um 1,000 sesterces, pl. **-a**

sestet the last six lines of a sonnet; cf. **sextet**

Sesuto *use* **Sesotho**

set a shoot for planting; an alignment in weaving; (typ.) amount of spacing controlling the distance between letters, the width of a piece of type or sort; *see also* **sett**

setback (noun, one word)

S.-et-L. Saône-et-Loire

S.-et-M. Seine-et-Marne

set-off (typ.) an unwanted transfer of ink from one sheet to another

set/ piece, — point (two words)

sets abbr. **s.**

Setswana the Bantu language of the Tswana

sett a badger's burrow, a granite paving block, a pattern in a tartan; *not* set

Settecento (It.) the years 1700–99 (esp. in Italy)

Settlement (Stock Exchange) (cap.)

settler one who settles

settlor (law) one who makes a settlement

set-up (adj. and noun, hyphen, one word in US)

Seul Korea, *use* **Seoul**

Seumas, Seumus (Anglicized as **Seamus**) Ir. Gael. for **James**; in Scots Gael. **Seumas** (Anglicized as **Hamish**); *see also* **Séamas, Séamus**

Seuss, Dr pseud. of **Theodor Seuss Geisel** (1904–91) US author-illustrator of children's books

Sevastopol Crimea, Ukraine; in Russ. **Sevastopol′**, in Ukrainian **Sevastopol** *or* **Sevastopil′**; *see also* **Seb-**

seven deadly sins pride, envy, anger, sloth, covetousness, gluttony, and lust

seven liberal arts *see* **quadrivium; trivium**

Sevenoaks Kent (one word)

seven seas the oceans of the world: Arctic, Antarctic, N. Atlantic, S. Atlantic, Indian, N. Pacific, and S. Pacific

Seventh-Day Adventist (three caps., one hyphen)

seven wonders of the world (from antiquity): the Egyptian Pyramids, the Mausoleum at Halicarnassus, the Hanging Gardens of Babylon, the Temple of Artemis at Ephesus, the statue of Zeus by Phidias at Olympia, the Colossus at Rhodes, and the Pharos at Alexandria (*or* alternatively the walls of Babylon)

Seven Years War 1756–63 (caps., no apos.)

Sévigné, Marie de Rabutin-Chantal, Madame de (1626–96) French writer

Sèvres fine porcelain made at Sèvres in the suburbs of Paris (no accent in US)

sewage/ the refuse that passes through sewers; **— farm, — works** (two words)

sewerage a system of sewers

sewin a salmon trout, *not* -en

sewing (bind.) the individual sewing of each book section to its neighbours; *see also* **stitching**

sewing machine (two words)

sexagenarian a person from 60 to 69 years old

Sexagesima Sunday the second before Lent

sex/ appeal, — change, — kitten (two words)

sex-linked (genetics) (hyphen)

sex/ maniac, — object, — symbol (two words)

sextet (mus.) (a work for) a group of six performers; *not* -ett, -ette; cf. **sestet**

sexto (typ.) a book based on six leaves (twelve pages) to the sheet, abbr. **6to; sextodecimo** *or* **sixteenmo** a book based on sixteen leaves (thirty-two pages) to the sheet, abbr. **16mo**

sexualize attribute sex to, *not* -ise

Seychell/es, Republic of Indian Ocean; **-ois**

Seymour, Jane (1509–37) third wife of Henry VIII of England

SF San Francisco, science fiction

s.f. *sub finem* (towards the end)

SFA Scottish Football Association

Sforza/ a Milanese ducal family, notably —, **Ludovico** (1451–1508); —, **Carlo, Count** (1873–1952) leader of anti-Fascist opposition in Italy

sforz/ando, -ato (mus.) with sudden emphasis on a chord or note, abbr. **sfz**

sfumato (It.) (the technique of painting) with indistinct outlines

SG (US) senior grade, (law) Solicitor-General, specific gravity

SGA Society of Graphic Artists

Sganarelle the name of several characters in Molière's comedies

sgd. signed

s.g.d.g. (Fr.) *sans garantie du gouvernement* (without government guarantee) (also caps.)

SGML (comput.) Standard Generalized Markup Language

sgraffit/o decorative work in which different colours are got by removing outer layers, pl. **-i**; cf. **graffito**

's-Gravenhage formal Du. for **The Hague**

Sgt. Sergeant

sh. shilling, -s

shadoof an Egyptian water-raising apparatus, in Egyptian Arab. **šādūf**

shagreen the untanned leather from the skin of fish, sharks, etc.

shah (hist.) a title of the former monarch of Iran, cap. when part of a formal title; in Pers. **šāh**

Shahabad Bengal, Hyderabad, Punjab, Uttar Pradesh, India

shaikh *see* **sheikh**

shakedown (noun and attrib. one word)

Shakespear/e, William (1564–1616) English playwright, *not* the many variants (except when approximating hist. usage); abbr. **Shak.**; **-ian, -iana** (OUP preference); *also* **-ean, -eana** (esp. in US)

Shakespeare Society, the *but* **the New Shakespere Society**

shako/ a military headdress, *not* sch-; pl. **-s**

shakuhachi/ a Japanese bamboo flute, pl. **-s**

shaky unsteady, *not* -key

shallop a small boat or dinghy; *not* shalop, -oop

shallot a kind of onion; *not* esch-, sch-, shalott

shalom a Jewish salutation, *not* sch-

Shalott, The Lady of a poem by Tennyson, 1833

sha/man pl. **-mans** *not* -men

shamefaced (one word)

shammy-leather *use* **chamois**

Shandong (Pinyin) Chinese province, also **Shantung** esp. with reference to a type of silk (not cap.)

shandrydan a rickety vehicle, *not* -dery-

Shanghai China; **shanghai/** make drunk and ship as a sailor (not cap.), **-ed**

Shangri-La an imaginary earthly paradise, from J. Hilton's novel *Lost Horizon* (hyphen, two caps.)

shanty/ a hut, a rough dwelling, a sailor's song; *not* ch-; — **town** (two words, one word in US)

shapable *not* shape-

SHAPE Supreme Headquarters, Allied Powers, Europe

Shahrazād *see* **Scheherazade**

sharecropper (one word)

share-farmer (hyphen)

shareholder (one word)

share-list (hyphen)

share-out (noun, hyphen)

shareware (comput.) (one word)

shariah the Muslim code of religious law, in Arab. **šarī'a**

sharif a descendant of Muhammad through his daughter Fatima; a Muslim leader; *not* shereef, -if; in Arab. **šarīf**

sharp/ (mus.) sign ♯, **double —** sign ×

Sharp,/ Becky a character in Thackeray's *Vanity Fair*; — **Cecil James** (1859–1924) English collector of folk songs; — **Granville** (1735–1813) English abolitionist; — **James** (1613–79) Scottish prelate; — **William** (1855–1905) Scottish poet and novelist, pseud. **Fiona Macleod**

Sharpe,/ Charles Kirkpatrick (1781–1851) Scottish antiquary and artist, — **Samuel** (1799–1881) English Egyptologist and biblical scholar

Sharpesburg Ky., Pa.

Sharpesville Pa.

Sharpeville S. Africa

Sharpey-Schafer, Sir Edward Albert b. **Schäfer** (1850–1935) English physiologist

sharpshoot/er, -ing (one word)

sharp/-tongued, -witted (hyphens)

Shasta daisy a European plant, *Chrysanthemum maximum* (one cap.)

Shastra Hindu sacred writings; in Hind. *šāstr*, in Skt. *šāstra*

shaving/-brush, -cream, -soap, -stick (hyphens, two words in US)

Shavu/oth a Jewish holiday commemorating the handing down of the Law on Mt. Sinai, in Heb. *šā̄bu̇'ō̄ṯ*; also **-ot**

Shaw/, George Bernard (1856–1950) Irish-born English playwright, adj. **Shavian**; **Aircraftman —** *see* **Lawrence, T. E.**

shawm (mus.) a medieval double-reed wind instrument

shaykh *see* **sheikh**

Shchedrin, N. *see* **Saltykov(-Shchedrin)**

shchi a Russian cabbage soup, *not* the many variants

s/he short for 'he or she', used to indicate both sexes; *not* to be used in formal writing

sheaf pl. **sheaves**

shealing *use* **shiel-**

shear/ to cut; past **-ed**, past part. **shorn** *but* **-ed** with reference to mechanical shears (cf. **sheer**); **-hulk, -legs** *use* **sheer-**

shearwater a bird (one word)

sheath/ (noun), **-e** (verb)

shebang (US sl.) a matter or affair, esp. in 'the whole —'

shebeen (Ir.) an unlicensed house selling spirits, in Ir. *síbín*

Shechinah *use* **Shek-**

sheep dip (two words)

sheep/dog, -fold (one word)

sheep run (two words)

sheepshank a type of knot (one word)

sheepskin a rug, a bookbinding leather, a parchment (one word)

sheepwalk a tract of land on which sheep are pastured (one word)

sheer (adj.) mere, very steep, very thin; (adv.) quite, vertically; (verb) deviate, swerve; cf. **shear**

sheer/hulk a dismasted ship, **-legs** a hoisting apparatus for masts (one word)

Sheer Thursday (Maundy Thursday); in Scots also **Shere, Skire**

sheet (typ.) a piece of paper of a definite size, a signature of a book

sheet/ metal, — music (two words)

sheets, in (typ.) not folded, or, if folded, not bound

sheet work (typ.) printing the two sides of a sheet from two formes

Sheffield: the signature of the Bishop of Sheffield (colon)

Shéhérazade *see* **Scheherazade**

sheikh (common Eng. spelling) a chief or head of an Arab tribe, family, or village (lit. 'old man'), a Muslim leader; more learned transliterations are **shaikh** (preferred by *The Times*), **shayk**; in Arab. *šayk*

sheiling *use* **shie-**

shekel the chief monetary unit of modern Israel, (hist.) a silver coin and unit of weight in ancient Israel and the Middle East; in Heb. *šeķel*

Shekinah the visible glory of God, *not* Shech-

sheldrake a coastal wild duck, *not* shell-; f. and pl. **shelduck** *not* sheld duck

shelf-ful/ the quantity that fills a shelf, pl. **-s** (hyphen)

shelf-life (hyphen, two words in US)

shelf-like (hyphen, one word in US)

shelf/ mark, — room (two words)

shellac/ a gum; *not* -ack, shelac, shelack; as verb **-ked, -king**

Shelley, Percy Bysshe (1792–1822) English poet

shell/fire, -fish (one word)

shell game (US) = **thimblerig**

shell jacket (two words)

shell pink (two words, hyphen when attrib.)

shellproof (one word)

shell shock/, -ed (two words)

shell suit (two words)

Shelta ancient hybrid secret language used by Irish tinkers, Gypsies, etc.

sheltie a Shetland pony or sheepdog, *not* -y

shelv/e, -ing, -y

Shemite *use* **Sem-**

shemozzle rumpus, *not* sch-

Sheol Hebrew underworld abode of the dead; in Heb. *še'ōl*

Shepheardes Calender, The a poem by Spenser, 1579; several subsequent edns. have variant spellings

Shepheard's Hotel Cairo

Shepherd Market London

Shepherd's Bush London

shepherd's/ crook, — needle, — pie, — plaid, — purse (apos.)

Sheppard, Jack (1702–24) English highwayman

Sheppey, Isle of Kent

Shepton Mallet Som.

Sheraton, Thomas (1751–1806) English furniture designer

sherbet a flavoured sweet effervescent powder or drink; (US) a water ice, sorbet; a cooling drink of sweet diluted fruit juices; (Austral. joc.) beer; *not* -bert

Sherborne Dorset, Glos.; **Baron —**

Sherbourne War.

Sherburn Dur., N. Yorks.

Sherburn in Elmet N. Yorks.

Shere Surrey

shereef, sherif *use* **sharif**

Shere Thursday *use* **Sheer Thursday**

sheriff a county officer

Sheringham Norfolk

Sherpa (a member of) a Himalayan people from borders of Nepal and Tibet, *not* -ah; pl. same

Sherpur Bangladesh

Sherrington, Sir Charles Scott (1857–1952) English physiologist

's-Hertogenbosch the Netherlands, commonly called **Den Bosch**; in Fr. **Bois-le-Duc**

Shetland/ a region of Scotland, **— Islands** *or* **-s** the main group of islands in it

sheva *use* **schwa**

shew *use* **show** except in Scots law, and biblical and Prayer Book citations

shewbread (Scripture) loaves displayed in a Jewish temple, *not* Show-

sheyk *use* **sheikh**

Shia one of the two main branches of Islam, esp. in Iran; *also* **Shiah**; *see also* **Sunni**; in Arab. **šī'a**

shiatsu therapy in which pressure is applied with the thumbs and palms to certain points on the body

shibboleth *not* shibo-

shieling a Highland hut or sheep-shelter; *not* sheal-, she-

shi/est, -ly, -ness *use* **shy-**

Shifnal Shropshire

shih-tzu a breed of dog with long silky hair (hyphen, two words in US)

shiitake an edible mushroom

Shi'ite (a member) of the Shia branch of Islam, *not* Shiite; *also* **Shi'ī** in learned contexts

shikaree (Ind.) a hunter, *not* the many variants

Shikarpur Pakistan

shiksa (offens.) a Gentile girl or woman, in Yiddish *shikse*

shillelagh an Irish cudgel, *not* the many variants

shilling/, -s abbr. *s.*, **sh.**; symbol *l-*

shilly-shally/, -ing

Shinto/, -ism the official Japanese religion

shiny *not* -ey

'ship (typ.) *see* **companionship**

ship/board, -builder, -building, -load, -mate, -owner (one word)

shipping agent (two words)

shipping/-bill, -master, -office (hyphens)

ship's biscuit sing. and pl.

shipshape (one word)

ships' names to be italic

Shipston on Stour War. (three words)

Shipton Glos., N. Yorks., Shropshire

Shiptonthorpe Humberside

Shipton under Wychwood Oxon. (three words)

ship/way, -worm, -wreck, -wright, -yard (one word)

Shiraz Iran; *not* Sheraz, Shyraz; in Pers. **Shīrāz**; also the Eng. form of **Syrah**

Shire/brook Derby., **-hampton** Avon, **-newton** Gwent (one word)

Shires, the (cap.) generally, the group of English counties ending in -*shire*, extending NE from Hampshire and Devon

shirtsleeve/, -s (one word)

shirt-tail (hyphen, one word in US)

shirtwaist/ (US) a blouse resembling a shirt, **-er** (US) a dress with a bodice like a shirt (one word)

shish kebab (two words), in Turk. **şiş kebabı**

Shiva *see* **Śiva**

shivaree *use* **charivari** (except in US)

shmaltz *use* **sch-**

shockproof (one word)

shock/ tactics, — therapy, — treatment, — troops, — wave (two words)

shoe/, -ing

shoe/black, -box (one word)

shoe buckle (two words)

shoe/horn, -lace (one word)

shoe leather (two words)

shoe/maker, -shine, -string (one word)

shoe tree (two words)

shogun/ (hist.) any of a succession of Japanese hereditary commanders-in-chief and virtual rulers before 1868, in Jap. **shōgun**; **-ate**

Sholokhov, Mikhail (**Aleksandrovich**) (1905–84) Russian novelist

Shooters Hill London (no apos.)

shooting box (two words)

shooting brake an estate car, *not* break

shooting/ coat, — gallery, — range, — star (two words)

shooting stick a walking stick with a foldable seat (two words)

shop/ assistant, — boy (two words)

shopfront (one word)

shop girl (two words)

shopkeeper (one word)

shoplift/, -er, -ing (one word)

shopping mall (two words)

shop steward (two words)

shop talk (two words, one word in US)

shopwalker (one word)

shop window (two words, one word in US)

short/bread, -cake (one word)

short-change (verb, hyphen; one word in US)

short circuit (noun, hyphen for verb)

short/coming, -crust, -fall, -hand, -horn (one word)

short mark that placed over a short vowel, a breve; *see also* **short vowel**

short-sighted lacking foresight, the inability to focus except on comparatively near objects (hyphen, one word in US)

short/ ton 2,000 lb, abbr. **s.t.**; — **vowel** ă, ĕ, etc.

shorty (colloq.) a short person or garment, *not* -ie

Shostakovich, Dmitri (**Dmitrievich**) (1906–75) Russian composer

shotgun (one word)

shoulder/ bag, — band, — blade (two words)

shoulder head(**line**) (typ.) a supplementary running head, usually of section, paragraph, or line numbers, or listing the first and last entry on a page

shoulder note (typ.) a marginal note at the top outer corner of the page

shoulder/ pad, — strap (two words)

shovel/, -led, -ler, -ling (one *l* in US), **-ful** pl. **-fuls**

shovelboard (one word)

shoveler a duck, *Anas clypeata*, with a broad shovel-like beak; *not* -ller

shovelhead (one word)

show *see* **shew**

showboat (US) a river steamer on which performances are given

Showbread *use* **shew-**

show business (two words) colloq. **showbiz** (one word)

show/case, -down, -girl (one word)

show house (two words)

showjump/, -er, -ing (one word, two words in US)

showman (one word)

show-off (noun, hyphen)

show/piece, -place, -room (one word)

show-through (typ.) the degree to which printing is visible on the other side of the paper

s.h.p. shaft horsepower

shrieval/ of or relating to a sheriff; **-ty** a sheriff's office, jurisdiction, or tenure

shrill/y, -ness

shrink-wrap (noun and verb, hyphen; one word in US)

shrivel/, -led, -ling (one *l* in US)

Shropshire *formerly* Salop

Shrovetide from the Saturday evening before to Ash Wednesday morning

Shrove Tuesday the day before Ash Wednesday

shufti/ (Brit. colloq.) a look or glimpse, pl. **-s**

shumac *use* **su-**

'shun! (colloq.) attention!

Shute, Nevil pseud. of **N. S. Norway** (1899–1960) English novelist

shuttlecock (one word)

s.h.v. *sub hac voce* or *sub hoc verbo* (under this word)

shwa *use* **sch-**

shy/er, -est, -ly, -ness *not* shi-

shyster (US) a person, esp. a lawyer, who uses unscrupulous methods

SI Sandwich Islands, (order of the) Star of India, Staten Island (NY), Système International (d'Unités)

Si silicon (no point)

si (mus.) *use* **te**

SIAD Society of Industrial Artists and Designers

sialagogue an agent inducing a flow of saliva, *not* sialo-

Siam *use* **Thailand**

Siamese/ *use* **Thai** except set phrases such as — **cat**, — **twins**

Sib. Siberia, -n

Sibeli/us, Jean (1865–1957) Finnish composer, **-an**

sibilant (adj.) hissing, (noun) letter(s) sounded with a hiss (e.g. *s*, *sh*)

sibyl/ a prophetess, **-line; the Sibylline books** (one cap.) an ancient Roman collection of oracles; cf. **Sybil**

Sic. Sicil/y, -ian

sic (Lat.) thus, so

sice the six on dice; cf. **syce**

Sichuan (Pinyin) a Chinese province, also **Szechwan**

Sicilian Vespers a massacre of the French in Sicily, 1282; subject of an opera by Verdi, *Les Vêpres siciliennes*, 1855

sick/bay, -bed (one word)

sick benefit (two words)

sick building syndrome (three words)

sick/ call, — flag, — leave (two words)

sick-making (hyphen)

sickroom (one word)

sic transit gloria mundi (Lat.) thus passes the glory of the world

sicut ante (Lat.) as before

sic vos non vobis (Lat.) thus you labour, but not for yourselves

Siddhārtha Gautama (Skt.) (*c*.490 BC–*c*.410 BC) the Buddha, founder of Buddhism; in Pali **Siddhāttha Gotama**

side arm a weapon worn at the side (two words)

sideband (one word)

side-bet (hyphen)

sideboard (one word)

sideburns = **sideboards**, side whiskers (one word)

sidecar (one word)

side/ chapel, — dish, — door, — drum, — effect (two words)

side head (typ.) a heading or subheading set full left to the margin

side issue (two words)

sidekick a close associate

side/light, -line, -long (one word)

side notes (typ.) those in margin, generally outer (two words)

side/ order, — road (two words)

side saddle (two words, one in US)

side salad (two words)

sideshow (one word)

sidestep (noun and verb) (one word)

side street (two words)

side/stroke, -swipe (one word)

side table (two words)

sidetrack (one word)

side trip (two words)

side valve of an engine (hyphen when attrib.)

side view (two words)

sidewalk (US) = **pavement**

sideways (one word)

side/ whiskers, — wind (two words)

sidewinder a N. American desert rattlesnake, (US) a sideways blow

Sidgwick & Jackson publishers

Sidney, Sir Philip (1554–86) English soldier, courtier, writer; *see also* **Syd-**

SIDS sudden infant death syndrome, cot death

siècle (Fr. m.) century, abbr. **s.**

Siegfried/ a *Nibelungenlied* hero, eponym of the third opera in Wagner's *Ring*, 1876; *not* Sig-; **— Line** the German fortified line on the Franco-German border before 1939

siehe (Ger.) see, abbr. **s.**

siehe/ dies (Ger.) see this (= q.v.), abbr. **s. d.**; **— oben** see above, abbr. **s. o.**; **— unten** see below, abbr. **s. u.** (spaces in Ger.)

Siemens,/ Werner von (1816–92) German founder of the electrical firm; **— Sir William**, born **Karl Wilhelm von** (1823–83) his brother, German-born British engineer; **— Friedrich** (1826–1904) the youngest brother, applied Sir William's open-hearth process to glass making

siemens (elec.) the SI unit of conductance, abbr. **S**

Siena Italy, *not* -nna

Sienkiewicz, Henryk (1846–1916) Polish novelist

sienna/ a pigment in paint; **burnt —, raw —**

sierra/ (Sp.) a mountain chain, pl. **-s**

Sierra/ Leone W. Africa, **— Leonean**; **— Madre** Mexican mountain chains; **— Nevada** a mountain chain in E. Calif. and in Spain

siesta/ (Sp.) afternoon rest, pl. **-s**

Sieyès, Emmanuel Joseph (1748–1836) French statesman

siffleu/r (Fr. m.) f. **-se** a professional whistler

Sig. Signor, -i

sig. signature

Sigfried *use* **Sieg-**

sight-read/, -er, -ing of music (hyphen)

sight screen (two words)

sightsee/r, -ing (one word)

sightworthy (one word)

sigill/um (Lat.) a seal, pl. **-a**

sigla *see* **library sigla**

sigl/um a sign denoting source of text, pl. **-a**

sigma the eighteenth letter of the Gr. alphabet (Σ, σ, final ς), Σ (math.) sum; **lunate —** a form of sigma (C, c)

sign abbr. **s.**

signal/, -ize *not* -ise, **-led, -ler, -ling** (one *l* in US), **-ly**

signal/book, box (two words)

signalman (one word)

signal tower (US) = **signal box**

signatory one who has signed, *not* -ary

signature (mus.) the key or time sign at beginning of the stave, abbr. **sig.**

signature (typ.) a complete part of a book printed on one sheet, usually sixteen or thirty-two pages, abbr. **sig.**

signed abbr. **s., sgd.**

Signor/ (It.) Mr, pl. **-i**, abbr. **Sig.**; **-a** Mrs, pl. **-e**, abbr. **Sig.ra**; **-ina** Miss, pl. **-ine**, abbr. **Sig.na**

signory (hist.) the governing body of a medieval Italian republic; *see also* **seigniory**

signpost (one word)

Sikandarabad Uttar Pradesh, India; *see also* **Secunder-**

Sikes, Bill a character in Dickens's *Oliver Twist*, *not* Sy-

Sikh/ a member of an Indian monotheistic sect founded in the 16th c., **-ism** the religious tenets of the Sikhs

Sikkim/ a former E. Himalayan kingdom, annexed as a state by India 1975; **-ese**

Sikorski, Gen. Władysław (1881–1943) Polish Prime Minister

silent partner (US) = **sleeping partner**

silen/us (Gr. myth.) a bearded old man like a satyr, sometimes with the tail and legs of a horse; pl. **-i** (often cap. in sing. or specific senses, not cap. in pl. or general senses)

siliceous of silica, *not* -ious

silicon a chemical element, symbol **Si**

silicone any of the many polymeric organic compounds containing silicon

siliqu/a a long narrow seed pod, pl. **-ae**

silkworm (one word)

sill (of door, window) *not* c-

sillabub *use* **syll-**

Sillanpää, Frans Eemil (1888–1964) Finnish novelist

Sillery a champagne

silo/ an airtight chamber for storing grain, pl. **-s**

Silurian (geol.) (of or relating to) the third period of the Palaeozoic era

silva/, -n *use* **syl-**

silver/ symbol **Ag** (argentum) (no point); **— age** a period regarded as inferior to a golden age, e.g. that of post-classical Latin literature in the early Imperial period

silverfish pl. same (one word)

silver Latin literary Latin of the early Imperial period (one cap.)

silver/side, -smith, -ware (one word)

silvicultur/e, -ist *not* silvi-

s'il vous plaît (Fr.) if you please, abbr. **s.v.p.**

similia similibus curantur (Lat.) like cures like

similiter (Lat.) in like manner

simitar *use* **scim-**

Simla Himachal Pradesh, India

simon-pure real, genuine (hyphen, not cap.); from (**the real**) **Simon Pure**, a character in Centlivre's *Bold Stroke for a Wife*

Simonstown Cape Province, S. Africa (one word)

simon/y the buying or selling of ecclesiastical privileges, e.g. pardons or benefices; **-iac, -iacal**

simoom a hot, dry, dust-laden wind blowing at intervals esp. in the Arabian desert; *not* -oon; in Arab. **samūm**

simpatico (It.) congenial, in Sp. **simpático**

simpliciter (Lat.) absolutely, without qualification

simulacr/um an image, a deceptive substitute; pl. **-a**

simultaneous *not* -ious

simurg (Persian myth.) a monstrous bird, in Pers. **sīmorgh**

sin (math.) sine (no point)

Sinaitic of or relating to Mount Sinai or the Sinai peninsula (cap.)

Sind/ Pakistan; *not* -e, -h, Scinde; **-hi** a native of Sind, pl. **-his**; an Indo-Aryan language spoken in Pakistan and NW India

Sindbad a character in the *Arabian Nights*, *not* Sinb-

sine (math.) abbr. **sin**

sine/ (Lat.) without; **— anno** without the date, abbr. **s.a.**; **— cura** without office; **— die** with no appointed day (of business adjourned indefinitely) abbr. **s.d.**; **— dubio** without doubt; **— invidia** without envy; **— legitima prole** without lawful issue, abbr. **s.l.p.**; **— loco, anno, vel nomine** without place, year, or name, abbr. **s.l.a.n.**; **— loco et anno** without place and date (of books without imprints), abbr. **s.l.e.a.**; **— mascula prole** without male issue, abbr. **s.m.p**; **— mora** without delay; **— nomine** without (printer's) name, abbr. **s.n.**; **— odio** without hatred; **— prole** (**superstite**) without (surviving) issue, abbr. **s.p.(s.)**

sine qua non an indispensable condition, *not* quâ

sinfon/ia (It. mus.) an overture or symphony, pl. **-ia; -ietta** a small-scaled symphony or orchestra, pl. **-iettas**

sing. singular

Singapore/ an island off S. end of the Malay Peninsula, **-an**

sing/e scorch; **-ed, -eing**

Singer Sargent, John *see* **Sargent, John Singer**

Singh/ a title adopted by the warrior castes of N. India, a surname adopted by male Sikhs; *not* -ng; **-alese** *use* **Sinhalese**

single-minded (hyphen)

sing-song (adj. and noun, hyphen, one word in US)

singular abbr. **s., sing.**

sinh hyperbolic sine (no point)

Sinha, Baron

Sinhalese (a member of the major population group or Indic language) of Sri Lanka, or (of) the Indic language spoken by this people, *also* **Sinhala**; *not* Sing-, Cing-

sinister (her.) of or on the shield-bearer's left, the observer's right, opp. to **dexter**

sinistra/ (It.) left-hand side, abbr. **s.**; **— mano** (mus.) the left hand, abbr. **SM**

sinnet (naut.) braided cordage made in flat or round or square form from three to nine cords; cf. **sennet; sennit**

Sinn Fein/ the movement and political party for Irish independence; in Ir. **Sinn Féin; -er, -ism**

Sino- a prefix denoting Chinese

sinus/ (anat.) a cavity in bone or tissue, pl. **-es**

Sion *use* **Zion**

Siou/x (of or relating to) (a member of) a group of Native American peoples, or the language of this group; pl. same; **-an**

siphon *not* sy-

si quis (Lat.) if anyone, first words of a notice of ordination

Sirach *or* **Sirah** (Apocr.) abbr. **Sir.**, *also called* **Ecclesiasticus**

sircar (Ind.) a head, the government; *not* -kar

sirdar (Ind. etc.) a person of high political or military rank, in Urdu *sardār*

siren a sea nymph, temptress, (device that emits) warning sound; *not* sy-

Sirenia an order of aquatic mammals

siringe *use* sy-

sirocco/ a Saharan wind reaching Italy and S. Europe, pl. **-s**; *not* sci-

sirup *use* sy-

sirvente (Fr. m.) a medieval Provençal narrative poem

SIS Secret Intelligence Service

sissy *not* ci-

sister german having same parents (two words)

sister/-in-law pl. **sisters-in-law, -uterine** having same mother only (hyphens)

Sistine Chapel in the Vatican, *not* Six-

Sisyphean condemned to eternal punishment, like **Sisyphus** (Gr. myth.) (cap.)

Sitapur Uttar Pradesh, India

sitcom (abbr.) a situation comedy (one word)

sitrep a situation report on the current military condition in an area (one word)

sits vac (abbr.) situations vacant (no points)

sitting room (two words)

situs (Lat. sing. and pl.) a site

Sitwell,/ Dame Edith (1887–1964) English poet; — **Sir Osbert** (1892–1969) English poet, novelist, essayist; — **Sir Sacheverell** (1897–1988) English poet and art critic

sitz bath a hip bath (two words)

Śiva/ a Hindu god; **-ism, -ite**; *also* **Shiva** in informal contexts

Siwalik Hills India, *not* Siv-

sixain (prosody) a six-line stanza

Six Day War 1967 (no hyphen)

Six Mile Bottom Cambs. (three words)

Sixmilebridge Co. Clare, Co. Limerick (one word)

Sixmilecross Co. Tyrone (one word)

six/pence, -penny (one word)

Six Road Ends Co. Down (three words)

sixte a fencing parry

sixteenmo *see* **sextodecimo**

Sixth Avenue Manhattan, New York City; former (and still trad.) name for **Avenue of the Americas**

Sixtine *use* **Sistine**

Six Towns the Potteries in Staffordshire; *see also* **Five Towns, The**

sixty-fourmo (typ.) a book based on 64 leaves, 128 pages, to the sheet (hyphen); abbr. **64mo**

sixty-fourth note (US mus.) = **hemidemisemiquaver**

sizable *use* **sizea-** (except in US)

sizeism *not* sizism

sizar an assisted student at Cambridge or Trinity College, Dublin

sizeable *not* -zable (US)

SJ Society of Jesus (Jesuits)

SJAA St John Ambulance Association

SJAB St John Ambulance Brigade

Sjælland an island, Denmark; *not* Zealand; in Ger. **Seeland**

sjambok (Afrik.) (flog with) a hide whip, *not* sam-

SJC (US) Supreme Judicial Court

sjužet (lit.) in Russian Formalism, a narrative work's plot as it is presented to the reader (cf. *fabula*); *also* (in non-specialist contexts) *syuzhet*

Skagerrak the arm of the North Sea between Denmark and Norway (one word), *not* **Skager Rack**

skald in ancient Scandinavia, a composer and reciter of poems honouring heroes and their deeds; *not* scald

Skara Brae Orkney

skateboard/, -er, -ing (one word)

skean/ (hist.) a Gaelic dagger formerly used in Ireland and Scotland, **-dhu** a dirk worn in the stocking as part of Highland costume (hyphen); *not* skene-

skein of silk etc., *not* -ain

Skelmersdale/ Lancs.; **Baron —**

skep a wooden or wicker basket or beehive, *not* skip

skep/sis, -tic, -tical *use* **sc-** (except in US)

skeuomorph *not* skew-

skewbald of two colours in irregular patches, usually of horses, usually white and a colour other than black; cf. **piebald**

ski/ pl. **-s**; as verb **-ed, -ing** (no hyphens)

skiagraphy etc., *use* **scia-** except in US, and in Greek contexts

skier a person using skis; cf. **skyer**

skiey *use* **skyey**

skiing *see* **ski**

ski-joring a sport in which the skier is towed (hyphen), in Norw. *skikjøring*

skilful *not* skill- (US)

skillet a small metal cooking pot with a long handle and (usually) legs; (US) = **frying pan**

skill-less without skill (hyphen, three *l*s)

skin-deep (hyphen)

skin div/e, -er, -ing (two words, one in US)

skinflint a miser (one word)

skin graft (two words)

skinhead (one word)

skinlike (one word)

Skinner, B(urrhus) F(rederic) (1904–90) US psychologist

skin test (two words)

skintight (one word)

skip a large container for builders' refuse etc.; *see also* **skep**

skirting board (two words)

skiver (bind.) a binding leather split from the grain side of sheepskin

Skokie a city and river, Ill.

skol a toast in drinking, *not* **skoal**; in Dan. before 1948 *skaal*, in Swed. and Dan. after 1948 *skål*

Skopje Macedonia

skow *use* sc-

Skriabin, Aleksandr (Nikolaevich) (1872–1915) Russian composer, *also* **Skryabin**

Skt. Sanskrit

skulduggery trickery; *not* scul-, skull-

skullcap (one word)

skull-less (hyphen, three *l*s)

skunk/-bear (US) a wolverine (hyphen), **— cabbage** (US) a herbaceous plant with an offensive-smelling spathe (two words)

skurry *use* sc-

Skutari *use* Sc-

skydiv/e, -er, -ing (one word)

skyer a high hit at cricket; *cf.* **skier**

Skye terrier (one cap.)

skyey *not* skiey

sky/jack, -lark, -light, -line, -sail, -scraper, -watch (one word)

skywriting (one word)

SL serjeant-at-law, solicitor-at-law

SLADE Society of Lithographic Artists, Designers, Engravers, and Process Workers

slainte a Gaelic toast: good health!; in Gael. *sláinte*

slaked lime *not* slack-

slalom ski race down zigzag course, *not* slallom

Slamannan Central

s.l.a.n. *sine loco, anno, vel nomine* (without place, year, or name)

slander/ (law) false oral defamation; *cf.* **libel**; **-er, -ous, -ously**

slapdash (one word)

slap-happy (hyphen)

slapstick (one word)

S. lat. south latitude

slate (colloq.) criticize severely; (US) schedule, plan; (US) nominate for office etc.

slaty like, or made of, slate; *not* -ey

Slav/ic (esp. in US), **-onian, -onic** (esp. in UK) of the Slavs; *not* Sc-; abbr. **Slav.**

SLBM submarine-launched ballistic missile

SLD (hist.) Social and Liberal Democrats, in 1989 officially replaced by **Liberal Democrats**

sld. sailed

s.l.e.a. *sine loco et anno* (without place or date)

sled (US) = **sledge**

sledgehammer (one word)

sleeping/ bag, — car, — partner, — pill, — sickness (two words)

sleepwalk/, -er, -ing (one word)

sleight of hand, *not* sli-

slenderize *not* -ise

Slesvig (Dan.) a province, Germany and Denmark; in Ger. **Schleswig**

sleuth-hound (hyphen, one word in US)

S level a GCE examination (no hyphen), abbr. of special *or* (hist.) scholarship level

slew *not* slue

slily *use* **slyly**

slip road a road for entering or leaving a motorway etc. (two words)

slip/shod, -stream, -way (one word)

Sloane, Sir Hans (1660–1753) English naturalist

sloe/ (fruit of) blackthorn, **— gin** a liqueur of sloes (two words); **-worm** *use* **slow-**

sloot (Du.) a ditch; *see also* **sluit**

sloping fractions (typ.) those with a solidus or oblique stroke, as ½

sloth laziness, also (zool.) a slow-moving nocturnal S. American mammal

slot machine (two words)

Slough Berks.

slough to shed

Slovak/ a member or the language of a Slavonic people inhabiting Slovakia, **-ian**

Slovene a member or the language of a Slavonic people in Slovenia, of or relating to Slovenia or its people or language; *also* **Slovenian**

Slovenia a republic in the former Yugoslavia, in Serbo-Croat **Slovenija**

slowpoke (US) = **slowcoach** (one word)

slow-worm a small European legless lizard, *not* sloe- (hyphen)

s.l.p. *sine legitima prole* (without lawful issue)

SLR single-lens reflex (camera), self-loading rifle

slue *use* **slew**

slugabed a lazy person (one word)

sluice/, -gate, -valve, -way (hyphens)

sluit (Afrik.) a deep gully formed by heavy rain; *see also* **sloot**

slyly *not* sli-

SM sadomasochism, Sergeant Major, Staff Major, (mus.) short metre, (Fr.) *Sa Majesté*, (Ger.) *Seine Majestat* (His Majesty), (It. mus.) *sinistra mano* (the left hand), (It.) *Sua Maesta*, (Sp.) *Su Majestad* (His, *or* Her, Majesty)

Sm samarium (no point)

sm. small

small arms (two words)

small-bore (of a firearm) (hyphen, two words in US)

small capitals abbr. **s.c., small caps., s. caps.**

smallgoods (Austral.) delicatessen meats

smallhold/er, -ing (one word)

small-minded (hyphen)

smallpox (one word)

Smalls the Oxford 'Responsions' Examination (cap.); small items of laundry (not cap.)

smart alec *not* -eck, -ick (two words)

SMD (mus.) short metre double

SME Sancta Mater Ecclesia (Holy Mother Church)

Smelfungus Sterne's name for Smollett (one l)

smelling/ bottle, — salts (two words)

smell-less (hyphen, three ls)

smelt past of smell, *not* smelled (US); a small sea fish; *see also* **smolt**

smetana sour cream

Smetana, Bedřich (1824–84) Czech composer

SMI (Fr.) *Sa Majesté Impériale* (His, *or* Her, Imperial Majesty)

smidgen *not* -in, -eon

Smith,/ Sydney (1771–1845) English clergyman and wit; **— Sir William Sidney** (1764–1840) English admiral, defender of St Jean d'Acre; *see also* **Smyth**; **Smythe**

Smithsonian Institution Washington, DC, *not* -tute; abbr. **Smith. Inst.**; founded 1846 from funds left by **James Smithson** (1765–1829) English chemist

SMM Sancta Mater Maria (Holy Mother Mary)

smok/e, -able, -y

smoke/screen, -stack (one word)

smoking/ jacket, — room (two words)

smolder *use* **smoulder** (except in US)

Smollett, Tobias (George) (1721–71) Scottish novelist and physician

smolt a young salmon; *see also* **smelt**

smooth/ (verb) **-s** *not* -e, -es; **— breathing** (typ.) *see* **breathing**

smorgasbord open sandwiches served with delicacies, as hors d'oeuvres or a buffet (not ital.); in Swed. *smörgåsbord*

smorzando (It. mus.) gradually dying away

smoulder *not* smol- (US)

s.m.p. *sine mascula prole* (without male issue)

smriti Hindu traditional teachings on religion etc., in Skt. *smṛti*

Smyrna the former name for **İzmir**, Turkey

Smyrniot (a native) of Smyrna

Smyth,/ Dame Ethel (1858–1944) English composer, **— John** (1586–1612) founder of the English Baptists; *see also* **Smith**; **Smythe**

Smythe, Francis Sydney (1900–49) English mountaineer; *see also* **Smith**; **Smyth**

Sn stannum (tin) (no point)

s.n. (Lat) *sine nomine* (without name), *sub nomine* (under a specified name)

snake charmer (two words)

snake-pit (hyphen, two words in US)

snap (US) (close with) a press stud

snapdragon (bot.) a plant, *Antirrhinum majus*; a Christmas game (one word)

snifter a small drink of alcohol; (US) a balloon glass for bandy etc.

snipe/ a gamebird, pl. **-s** and (collective) same

snivel/, -led, -ler, -ling (one l in US)

snorkel/ a device for underwater swimming etc., **-ler, -ling** (one l in US); *not* schn-

Snorri Sturluson (1178–1241) Icelandic historian and poet; *see also* **Heimskringla**

snow (meteor.) abbr. **s.**

snow/ball, -berry (one word)

snow-blind/, -ed, -ing, -ness (hyphen, one word in US)

snowblower (one word)

snow boot (two words)

snowbound (one word)

snow bunting a mainly white finch (two words)

snow/cap, -drift, -drop, -fall, -field, -flake (one word)

snow/ goose, — leopard (two words)

snow/line, -man, -mobile (one word)

snow/plough *not* -plow (US), **-shoe, -storm** (one word)

snowy owl (two words)

SNP Scottish National Party

Snr. *see* **senior**

snuffbox (one word)

SO Staff Officer, Stationery Office, sub-office

so (mus.) *use* **soh**

s.o. seller's option, (Ger.) *siehe oben* (see above), substance of

so-and-so/ a particular person not specified, pl. **-s** (no apos.); **Mr So-and-so** (one cap.)

Soane's, Sir John (**Museum**) London

soap/bark, -berry, -box (one word)

soap/ flakes, — opera (two words)

soap/stone, -suds, -wort (one word)

SOAS School of Oriental and African Studies

sobriquet nickname, *not* sou- (not ital.)

Soc. Socialist, Society, Socrates

socage a feudal tenure of land, *not* socc-

so-called (adj., hyphen)

Socialist cap. when referring to a political party or its members; not cap. when referring to general principles of socialism or their adherents; abbr. **S., Soc.**

socialize *not* -ise

sociedad/ (Sp. f.) society; **— anónima** public limited company, abbr. **SA**

sociedade/ (Port. f.) society; **— anónima** public limited company, abbr. **SA**; **— anônima** (Brazilian Port.) public limited company, abbr. **SA**

società/ (It. f.) society; **— per azioni** public limited company, abbr. **SpA**

société/ (Fr. f.) society; **— anonyme** public limited company, abbr. **SA**

Société des Bibliophiles françois founded 1820, *not* français (lower-case *f*); abbr. **Sté**

Society abbr. **S., Soc.**

socio/biology, -cultural (one word)

socio-economic (hyphen, one word in US)

sociolinguistic (one word)

sociology abbr. **sociol.**

socius/ (Lat.) Fellow, Associate, abbr. **S.**; **— criminis** associate in crime

Socotra Indian Ocean; *not* -ora, Sok-

Socrat/es (469–399 BC) Greek philosopher, *not* Sok-; **-ic**; abbr. **Soc.**

sodium symbol **Na** (natrium)

sodomize *not* -ise

Sodor and Man, Bishop of; Sodor & Man: his signature (one colon)

SOE Special Operations Executive

SOED *Shorter Oxford English Dictionary*

sœur/ (Fr. f.) sister, nun; **— de charité** Sister of Mercy

Sofar (acronym, one cap.)

soffit (archit.) the under-surface of an arch or eaves

Sofi *use* **Sufi**; *see also* **Sophy**

Sofia Bulgaria, in Bulgarian **Sofiya**

S. of S. Song of Solomon

softa a Muslim student of sacred law and theology (not ital.)

soft copy (comput.) the transient reproduction of keyboard input on VDU (two words); cf. **hard copy**

soft-core (hyphen, one word in US)

soft-headed/, -ness (hyphens, one word in US)

soft-hearted/, -ness (hyphens, one word in US)

S. of III Ch. Song of the Three Children

softie a soft-hearted, silly, or weak person; *not* -y

soft-pedal/, -led, -ling (one *l* in US)

soft sell (noun, two words)

soft-sell (verb, hyphen, two words in US)

soft sign (typ.) a single prime ('), used in e.g. transliterated Russ., cf. **hard sign**

soft-spoken (hyphen)

software programs and other operating information used by a computer (one word)

softwood (one word)

SOGAT *or* **Sogat** Society of Graphical and Allied Trades, from 1982 officially called **SOGAT 82**

sogenannt (Ger.) so-called, abbr. **sog.**

soh (mus.) *not* so

Soho a district of London's West End (one cap.), **SoHo** a district of Manhattan south of Houston Street (two caps.)

soi-disant (Fr.) self-styled (hyphen); do not use for 'so-called' (i.e. by others)

soign/é (Fr.) f. **-ée** carefully finished or arranged, well-groomed

soirée/ an evening party, **— dansante** one with dancing, **— musicale** one with music (not ital.)

Sokotra *use* **Socotra**

Sokrates *use* **Soc-** except in Hellenic contexts, or esp. of a Sokrates other than the philosopher

Sol (Lat.) (the personification of) the sun (cap.)

Sol. Solomon

sol. solicitor, solution

sola *see* **solus**

solan goose the gannet; cf. **solen**

solarize *not* -ise

solati/um (Lat.) compensation, pl. **-a**

sola topi an Indian sun helmet, *not* solar

solecis/m a blunder in speaking, writing, or behaviour; **-tic**

solecize *not* -ise

solemnize *not* -ise

solen a razor-shell mollusc; cf. **solan**

solenoid a cylindrical wire coil acting as a magnet

sol-fa/ (mus.) (hyphen), **-ed**

solfegg/io (mus.) a sol-fa exercise for the voice, pl. **-i**

soli pl. of **solo**

solicitor abbr. **sol., solr.**

Solicitor-General (caps., hyphen, two words in US); abbr. **SG, Sol.-Gen.**

solicitude anxiety, concern; in Fr. f. *sollicitude*

solid (typ.) text matter set without extra spacing between lines or letters

solidarność (Pol.) solidarity, cap. as name of Polish trade-union movement led by Lech Wałęsa

solid/us oblique stroke (/), pl. **-i**, abbr. **s.**

soliloqu/y a speech made alone or regardless of hearers, pl. **-ies**; **-ize** *not* -ise

solipsis/m (philos.) the view that the self is all that exists or can be known; **-t, -tic, -tically**

solmization (mus.) *not* -sation

sol/o abbr. **s.**, pl. **-os**; It. mus. pl. **-i**

Solon (638–?558 BC) Athenian lawgiver

solr. solicitor

solubilize make soluble or more soluble, *not* -ise

soluble that can be dissolved or solved

sol/us (theat.) f. **-a** alone, unaccompanied

solution abbr. **sol.**

Solutrean (the culture of) the palaeolithic period in Europe following the Aurignacian and preceding the Magdalenian, *not* -ian

solvable that can be solved; *not* -eable, -ible

solvent *not* -ant

solvitur ambulando (Lat.) the question settles itself naturally

Solzhenitsyn, Aleksandr (Isaevich) (b. 1918) Russian writer

Som. Somerset

Somali/ (of or relating to) (a member of) a Hamitic Muslim people of Somalia, or the Cushitic language of this people; pl. same

Somalia NE Africa, adj. **Somali**

Somaliland (one word)

sombre *not* -er (except in US)

sombrero/ a broad-brimmed hat, esp. the characteristic hat of Mexico; pl. **-s**; in Sp. *sombrero* a hat of any type

somebody a person (one word); an unspecified group of persons, or thing or collection of thing (two words)

somehow (one word)

someone somebody (one word); a single person or thing (two words)

Somerby Leics., Lincs.

somersault *not* -set, summer-

Somersby Lincs., birthplace of Tennyson

Somerset an English county, abbr. **Som.**

Somers Town London (two words)

Somerstown W. Sussex (one word)

something (one word)

some/what, -when, -where (one word)

sommelier a wine waiter (not ital.)

Somoza (Debayle), Anastasio (1925–80) President of Nicaragua 1967-72, 1974-9

Son, the as the Deity (cap.)

son abbr. **s.**

sonar (acronym, not cap.)

sonata/ (mus.) pl. **-s**

Sondes, Earl *not* of

son et lumière (Fr.) a night entertainment with sound and light effects

song/bird, -book (one word)

song cycle (two words)

Song/ of Solomon (OT) abbr. **S. of S.**, *also called* — **of Songs**; — **of the Three Children** (Apocr.) abbr. **S. of III Ch.**

songs, titles of (typ.) to be roman quoted when cited

song thrush (two words)

songwriter (one word)

son-in-law (hyphens) pl. **sons-in-law**

Son of/ God, — — Man (caps.)

sons/y (Sc.) plump, buxom; of a cheerful disposition; bringing good fortune; **-ier, -iest**; *not* -ie, -zy

soochong *use* **sou-**

Soofee *use* **Sufi**

Sop. soprano, -s

Sophocles (495–406 BC) Greek playwright, abbr. **Soph.**

sophomore a second-year university or (US) high-school student, *not* sophi-

Sophy English name for the Shah, 16th–17th cc.; cf. **Sufi**

sopra (It.) above

sopranino/ (mus.) an instrument higher than a soprano, pl. **-s**

sopran/o (mus.) pl. **-os**, It. pl. **-i**; abbr. **S.**, **Sop.**

sorbefacient (med.) (a drug etc.) causing absorption

Sorbian of or relating to a Slavonic people in southern Brandenburg and eastern Saxony, or to their W. Slavonic language, still spoken around Lusatia, Bautzen, and Cottbus, eastern Germany; *not* Sora-, *not* Lusatian, Wendish (q.v.)

Sorbonne the medieval theological college of Paris, now comprising three of the Paris universities with faculties of science and arts also; formally Académie Universitaire de Paris

sorcer/er f. **-ess** a wizard or magician, **-ous**

sordin/o (mus.) a mute for a bowed or wind instrument, pl. **-i**

sorehead (US) a touchy or disgruntled person (one word)

sorghum a tropical cereal grass, *not* -gum

sortes/ (Lat.) (divination by) lots; — *Biblicae or Sacrae*, — *Homericae*, — *Vergilianae* (divination from) random passages of Scripture, Homer, Virgil

sortie/ (make) a sally, esp. from a besieged garrison; (make) an operational flight by a single military aircraft; **-d, -ing, -s**

sortilege divination by sorts

sorts/ (typ.) letters or pieces of type; *see also* **special —**

SOS (a) signal for help, pl. **SOSs**

so-so passable (hyphen)

sostenuto/ (mus.) (a passage played) in sustained manner, pl. **-s**

Sotheby Parke Bernet & Co. auctioneers ('Sotheby's')

sotto/ (It.) under, **— voce** in an undertone

sou (hist.) a French coin of small value (not ital.)

Soubirous, St Bernadette (1844–79) of Lourdes, French nun

soubrette a maid or other pert female character in a (musical) comedy (not ital.)

soubriquet *use* **sob-**

souchong a fine black China tea, *not* soo-

Soudan/, **-ese** *use* **Sud-**

souffle (med.) a low murmur heard in the auscultation of various organs etc. (no accent)

soufflé a light spongy dish using egg whites (not ital.)

souffleur (Fr. m.) a theatre prompter

souk a market place in Muslim countries; *not* suk, sukh; in Arab. **sūḵ**

Soul *use* **Seoul**

soul food (two words)

soulless (one word)

soulmate (one word, two words in US)

soul music (two words)

Soult, Nicolas Jean de Dieu (1769–1851) French marshal, Duke of Dalmatia

sound barrier (two words)

sound bite a short extract from a recorded interview, chosen for its pungency or appropriateness; *not* byte

sound effect (two words)

soundhole (one word)

sounding board (mus.) (two words)

sound post (two words)

sound/proof, -track (one word)

sound wave (two words)

soup bowl (two words)

soupçon a very small quantity (not ital.)

souper (Fr. m.) supper, *not* -pe

soup/ kitchen, — plate (two words)

soup spoon (two words, one word in US)

sourcebook (one word)

source criticism (two words)

sour cream *not* -ed —

soutane (RC) a priest's cassock

souteneur (Fr. m.) a pimp

souterrain (esp. archaeol.) an underground chamber or passage

south abbr. **S.**; *see also* **compass points**

South/ Africa, — African abbr. **S. Afr., SA; — America, — American** abbr. **S. Amer., SA; South Australia, — Australian** abbr. **SA**

southbound (one word)

South/ Carolina off. and postal abbr. **SC; — Dakota** off. abbr. **S. Dak.**, postal **SD**

Southdown a breed of sheep (one word)

South Downs Hants. etc.

south-east/, **-ern** (hyphen, one word in US) abbr. **SE**

southeaster a wind from south-east (one word)

southern abbr. **S.**; *see also* **compass points**

Southern Africa a geographical term, including Zimbabwe and other countries as well as the Republic of South Africa

southernwood a species of wormwood, lad's love

Southern Yemen *see* **Yemen**

Southesk, Earl of

Southey, Robert (1774–1843) Poet Laureate 1813–43

southpaw (a person who is) left-handed (one word)

South Pole (caps.)

South Wales abbr. **SW**

Southwark *or* 'The Borough', formerly in Surrey

Southwark: the signature of the Bishop of Southwark (colon)

Southwell: the signature of the Bishop of Southwell (colon)

south-west/, **-ern** (hyphen, one word in US) abbr. **SW**

South West Africa (three words)

southwester a wind from south-west (one word)

soutien-gorge (Fr. m.) bra, brassiere; pl. **soutiens-gorge**; cf. **brassière**

souvlaki a Greek dish of pieces of meat grilled on a skewer, *not* -ia

sou'wester a sailor's oilskin hat or coat, a southwester wind

sovereign/, **-s** abbr. **sov., sovs.**

soviet (Russ.) an elected local, district, or national council, the basis of Russian governmental machinery since 1917; (hist.) a revolutionary council before 1917 (not cap.); (adj.) of or concerning the former Soviet Union (cap.); *see also* **Union of Soviet Socialist Republics**

Sowet/o a group of townships SW of Johannesburg, S. Africa; adj. **-an**

sox *use* **socks** (except in some commercial contexts, or as part of the name of certain US baseball teams)

Soxhlet (chem.) an extraction apparatus

soybean *not* soya-

Sp. Spain, Spanish

sp. species (sing.), specimen, spelling, spirit

s.p. self-propelled, starting price

s.p. *sine prole* (without issue)

SpA (It.) *Società per Azioni* (public limited company)

spacecraft (sing. and pl.) (one word)

space flight (two words)

spaceman (one word)

space rocket (two words)

spaces (typ.) blanks between words or letters

spaceship (one word)

space station (two words)

spacesuit (one word)

space-time (hyphen) *or* **spacetime** (one word)

space travel/, -ler (two words)

space/ vehicle, — walk (two words)

spacewoman (one word)

spacial *use* **spat-**

spae/ (Sc.) foretell, prophesy; **-wife** a female fortune-teller or witch (one word)

spaghetti strings of pasta (not ital.)

spahi a Turkish horse-soldier, Algerian French cavalryman; in Turk. *sipahi*; cf. **sepoy**

Spain abbr. **Sp.**

Spalato It. for **Split**

spandrel (archit.) a space between the curve of an arch and the enclosing mouldings, *not* -il

Spanish (of or relating to) (a person from) Spain or the Castilian language of Spain, abbr. **Sp.**

Spanish n (*ñ*) '*n* with the tilde' or 'curly *n*'; pron. *ng* in 'cognac' or *ni* in 'onion'

Spanish Town Jamaica

sparagmos (Gr. tragedy) the ritual tearing to pieces of a victim

spare rib/, -s (two words, one word in US)

spark plug (two words)

spatial *not* -acial

spatio-temporal (hyphen, one word in US)

spatterdash (US) = **roughcast**

SPCK Society for Promoting Christian Knowledge

SPE Society for Pure English

speakeas/y pl. **-ies**

spear/head, -man, -mint, -wort (one word)

spec (colloq.) specification, speculation (no point)

spec. special, -ly; specific, -ally, -ation; specimen

spécialité (Fr. f.) a speciality (ital.)

speciality in general senses, *not* specialty (US)

specialize *not* -ise

special sort (typ.) a character or symbol not on the standard keyboard or ASCII character set, one that must be accessed by codes during setting

specialty (law) a contract under seal, (US) = **speciality**

specie coin, as distinct from paper money; pl. same

species abbr. **sp.**; pl. same, abbr. **spp.**

specific gravity relative density, abbr. **sp. gr.**

specimen abbr. **sp., spec.**

specs (colloq.) spectacles

Spectaclemakers Society (no hyphen, no apos.)

spectre *not* -er (US)

spectr/um pl. **-a**

speculat/e, -or

specul/um (surg.) an instrument for dilating body cavities for viewing, a (polished metal) mirror, (ornith.) a bright patch on a bird's wing; pl. **-a**

speech day (two words)

speed/boat, -way (one word)

spele/an (adj.) cave-dwelling; **-ologist, -ology**; *not* spelae-

spel(l)ican *use* **spillikin**

spell past and past part. **spelled** *or* **spelt**

spell/bind, -bound (one word)

speluncar of, pertaining to, or resembling a cave

spelunker (US) a person who explores caves, esp. as a hobby

Spencer,/ Earl (*not* of), **— Herbert** (1820–1903) English philosopher, **— Sir Stanley** (1891–1959) English painter

Spengler, Oswald (1880–1936) German philosopher of history

Spenser/, Edmund (1552–99) English poet; **-ian** of the poet, his style, *or* his stanza (*ababbcbcc*)

Spetsai Greece, *not* Spezzia

spew to vomit, *not* spue

Speyer Germany, *not* Spires

Spezzia *use* **Spetsai** (Greece) *or* **La Spezia** (Italy)

sp. gr. specific gravity

spherical abbr. **s.**

sphinx/ *not* sphy-, pl. **-es** (cap. with reference to Gr. myth. or the huge sphinx near the Pyramids at Giza)

sphygmomanometer an instrument for measuring blood pressure

spianato (mus.) made smooth

spick and span (three words)

spicy not -ey

spiegando (mus.) 'unfolding', becoming louder

spiflicate (joc.) trounce, not spiff-

spiky not -ey

spill past and past part. **spilt** or **spilled** (esp. in US)

spillikin a small rod, or a game using them; not spel(l)ican

spillover (noun) (one word)

spillway a passage for surplus water from a dam (one word)

spina bifida (med.) a congenital defect of the spine (two words, not ital.)

spinach not -age

spin/-dry, -dryer (hyphens) not -drier

spine/ (bind.) that part of the case protecting the back of a book, and bearing — **lettering**

spinney a thicket, not -ny

spinning/ jenny, — machine, — top, — wheel (two words)

spin-off (noun, hyphen)

Spinon/e an Italian gun dog, pl. **-i** (cap.)

Spinoz/a, Baruch (1632–77) Dutch philosopher; **-ism, -ist, -istic**

spiraea (bot.) an ornamental shrub, not -rea (US)

spiral/, -led, -ling (one *l* in US)

Spires Germany, use **Speyer**

spirit abbr. **sp.**

spirito (mus.) life, spirit

spiritual of the spirit

spiritualize not -ise

spirituel marked by refinement and quickness of mind (not ital); in Fr. *spirituel/* f. *-le*

spirochaete any of various flexible spiral-shaped bacteria, not -hete (US)

spirt use **spurt**

spitfire a person of fiery temper (one word)

Spithead the strait between IoW and Portsmouth

Spitsbergen Arctic Ocean, not Spitz-

spiv/ (sl.) a flashy petty black marketeer; **-vish, -very, -vy**

splendour not -or (US)

Split Croatia, formerly **Spalato**

Spode/, Josiah (1754–1827) maker of — **china** at Stoke

Spohr, Louis (1784–1859) German composer

spoil past and past part. **spoilt** or **spoiled** (esp. in US)

spokes/man, -person, -woman (one word)

spolia/ (Lat.) spoils, — *opima* a trophy won by a general who killed the commander of an opposing army in single combat

spoliation not spoil-

spond/ee (prosody) a foot of two long (or stressed) syllables, **-aic**

sponge bag (two words)

sponge bath (US) = **blanket bath**

sponge/ cake, — cloth, — pudding (two words)

spongy like sponge, not -gey

sponsion (law) being a surety for another, a pledge or promise made on behalf of the State by an agent not authorized to do so

sponson a projection from the side of a warship, tank, seaplane, or paddle steamer

spontane/ity, -ous

spoonerism a transposition of the initial letters etc. of two or more words, e.g. 'You have hissed my mystery lectures' (not cap.); from the English scholar **Revd W. A. Spooner** (1844–1930)

spoon-feed (hyphen)

spoonful/ pl. **-s**

sporran a pouch worn over a kilt

spos/a (It.) bride, pl. **-e**; **-o** bridegroom, pl. **-i**

spotlight (one word)

spp. species (pl.)

SPQR *Senatus Populusque Romanus* (the Senate and Roman people, used as the emblem of the modern City), small profits and quick returns

SPR Society for Psychical Research

Spr. Sapper

Sprachgefühl (Ger. n.) a feeling for (the natural idiom of) a language

Sprechgesang (mus.) a style of dramatic vocalization between speech and song

sprezzatura (It.) ease of manner, studied carelessness, nonchalance, esp. in art or literature

sprightly lively, not spritely

spring (verb); (past) **sprang**, (US past) **sprung**

spring (season of) (not cap.)

spring balance (two words)

springboard (one word)

springbok (Afrik.) an antelope; (cap.) a South African, esp. one who plays or has played for South Africa in international sporting competitions; not -buck

spring/ chicken, — clean, — cleaning (two words)

Springer (Ger. m.) the knight at chess, not *Ritter*

spring fever (two words)

springtail any wingless insect of the order *Collembola*

spring/tide, -time the season of spring (one word)

spring tide the tide of greatest range (two words)

spring water (two words, one word in US)

sprinkled edges (bind.) the cut edges of books sprinkled with coloured ink

SPRL (Fr.) *société de personnes à responsabilité limitée* (private limited company)

spry/ active; **-er, -est, -ly, -ness**

s.p.s. *sine prole superstite* (without surviving issue)

spue *use* **spew**

spumante an Italian sparkling white wine (not cap., not ital.)

spumoni (US) a kind of ice-cream dessert (not ital.)

spurrey a slender plant, *not* -y

spurt *not* -irt

sputnik each of a series of Russian artificial satellites launched between 1957 and 1961

sput/um expectorated matter, pl. **-a**

spy/glass, -hole (one word)

sq./ square; **— ft.** square feet; **— in.** square inches; **— m.** square metres, square miles (each sing. and pl.); not used in scientific and technical work

Sqn. Ldr. *or* **Sqn/Ldr** Squadron Leader

squacco/ a small crested heron, pl. **-s**

squaddie (Brit. sl.) a recruit, a private; *not* -dy

squalls (meteor.) abbr. **q.**

square (bind.) that part of the case which overlaps the edges of a book

square back (bind.) a book whose back has not been rounded; *see* **rounding**

square brackets [ ]

square off (US) = **square up**; (Austral.) placate

square root (two words)

squeegee a rubber-edged implement for sweeping wet surfaces, *not* -ie

squirearchy landowners collectively, esp. as a class; *not* -rarchy

squirrel/, -led, -ling (one *l* in US), **-ly**

squirt gun (US) = **water pistol**

sq. yd. square yards (sing. and pl.)

SR Southern Region

Sr strontium (no point)

Sr. Sister, (Sp.) *Señor*

sr steradian

sr. *use* **sen.**

Sra. (Sp.) *Señora*

Srbija Serbo-Croat for **Serbia**

SRC Science Research Council, Students' Representative Council

Sri Lanka/ 'Resplendent Island'; **-n**

Srinagar Kashmir, *not* Ser-

SRN State Registered Nurse

sRNA soluble (transfer) RNA, *use* **tRNA**

SRO standing room only, statutory rules and orders

Srta. (Sp.) *Señorita*

SS Saints, Secretary of State, steamship, (Fr.) *Sa Sainteté* (His Holiness), (Ger.) *Schutzstaffel* (Nazi elite corps), (It.) *Sua Santità* (His Holiness)

SS, collar of the former badge of the House of Lancaster, *not* esses

ss. subsection, (med.) half

s.s. screw steamer, (mus.) *senza sordini* (without mutes)

SSAFA Soldiers', Sailors', and Airmen's Families Association

Ssangyong a Korean make of car; *also* **SsangYong** (one word)

SSC (Sc.) Solicitor to the Supreme Court

SSE south-south-east

S.Sgt., S/Sgt. Staff Sergeant

SSP statutory sick pay

SSR Soviet Socialist Republic

SSRC Social Science Research Council

SSSI Site of Special Scientific Interest

SST supersonic transport

SSW south-south-west

St Saint, alphabetize under Saint, *not* St-; stokes

St. (in Slavonic languages) *Stari* etc., old; Strait, -s; Street

st. stanza, stem, stone, strophe, (cricket) stumped

s.t. short ton (2,000 lb)

Sta (It., Sp., Port.) Santa (female saint) (no point)

Sta. Station

Staal,/ Georges Frédéric Charles, baron de (1824–1907) Russian diplomat; **— Marguerite Jeanne Cordier De Launay, baronne de** (1684–1750) French writer; *see also* **Staël; Stahl**

'Stabat Mater' 'the Mother was standing' (medieval poem, RC hymn)

stabbing (bind.) wire stitching near the back edge of a closed section or pamphlet, the piercing of a book section prior to sewing or stitching

stabilize/ *not* -ise, **-r** (US) the horizontal tailplane of an aircraft

staccato/ in an abrupt or detached manner; as noun, pl. **-s**

stadi/um (Gr. antiquity) a measure of length (about 185 metres), a racecourse, pl. **-a**; (modern use) a sports ground, pl. **-ums**

stadtholder (cap. only as part of title); in Du. *stadthouder*

Staël, Madame de in full **Anne Louise Germaine, baronne de Staël-Holstein**, b.

Necker (1766–1817) French writer; *see also* **Staal; Stahl**

staff/ a pole or stick; (mus.) a set of lines on which music is written, pl. **staves**; a body of persons under authority, pl. **-s**; cf. **stave**

Staffs. Staffordshire

Staff Sergeant abbr. **S.Sgt.**, **S/Sgt.**

stag beetle (two words)

stage/coach, -craft (one word)

stage/ **direction, — door, — fright** (two words)

stagehand (one word)

stage/-manage (hyphen), **— manager** (two words)

stage name (two words)

staghound (one word)

Stagirite, the Aristotle, *not* Stagy-

stag/ **night, — party** (two words)

stagy excessively theatrical *not* -ey

Stahl,/ **Friedrich Julius** (1802–61) German lawyer and politician; **— Georg Ernst** (1660–1734) German chemist; *see also* **Staal; Staël**

staid solemn; cf. **stayed**

stair/case, -head, -way, -well (one word)

Stakhanovite an exceptionally productive worker (esp. in the former USSR) (cap.)

stalactite a mineral deposit hanging from the roof of a cave

Stalag (hist.) a German POW camp, esp. for non-commissioned officers and privates

stalagmite a mineral deposit rising from the floor of a cave

stalemate (one word)

Stalin, Joseph (1879–1953) b. **Iosif Vissarioniovich Dzhugashvili**, General Secretary of the Communist Party of the USSR 1922–53

Stalingrad *previously* **Tsaritsyn**, *now* **Volgograd**

stalking horse (two words)

stamen/ (bot.) pl. **-s**

stamina power of endurance

stamp/ collector, — duty (two words)

stamping ground (two words)

stamp/ mill, — office (two words)

stanch (verb) check a flow; cf. **staunch**

stand-alone (of a computer) operating independently of a network or other system

standardize *not* -ise

standing type (typ.) type not yet distributed after use

stand-off/ a deadlock, **-ish** rather cold and reserved (hyphen)

stand/pipe, -point, -still (noun) (one word)

stannum tin, symbol **Sn**

Stanstead Suffolk

Stansted Essex, Kent

stanza/, -s, -ed; abbr. **st.**

stapes (anat.) a bone in the ear, pl. same

star/, -red, -ring, -ry

Starcross Devon (one word)

star/dust, -fish (one word)

star fruit the carambola (two words)

star/light, -lit (one word)

Stars and Stripes the US flag

'Star-Spangled Banner, The' the US national anthem

START Strategic Arms Reduction Treaty (*or* Talks)

starting/ block, — gate, — pistol, — point, — post, — price, — stall (two words)

Star Wars (US colloq.) **SDI**, from the science-fiction film *Star Wars*, 1977 (caps., not ital.)

stat. statics, statuary, statute

state a nation or territory considered as a political community, often cap. to denote the abstract concept: 'separation of Church and State'

State Department (US) the department of foreign affairs

Staten Island New York, *not* Staa-; abbr. **SI**

state-of-the-art (adj., hyphens; noun, four words)

stater an ancient Greek coin, *not* -or

stateroom (one word)

States, the commonly the United States of America; the legislative body in Jersey, Guernsey, and Alderney

States General (hist.) the legislative body in the Netherlands and in France before 1789

stateside (US colloq.) of, in, or towards the USA (not cap.)

statesman/like, -ship (one word)

statics the science of forces in equilibrium (sing.)

Station abbr. **Sta.**, **Stn.**

stationary not moving

Stationers' Hall the hall of the Stationers' Company in London, at which a book was formerly registered for purposes of copyright (apos. after *s*)

stationery paper etc.

Stationery Office the government's publishing house, which also provides stationery for government offices

stationmaster (one word)

station wagon (US) = **estate car**

statistics the subject is treated as sing., while the numerical facts systematized are treated as pl.

Státní tajná bezpečnost (hist.) Czechoslovak equivalent to the KGB, abbr. **STB**

stator (elec.) a stationary part within which something revolves; *not* -er

statuary abbr. **stat.**

status/ rank, pl. **-es** (not ital.)

status quo/ the same state as now, the existing state of affairs (not ital.)

status quo ante (Lat.) the same state as before (ital.)

statute a written law passed by a legislative body, e.g. an Act of Parliament; abbr. **stat.**

statute/ book, — law (two words)

statute mile *see* **mile**

statutory *not* -ary

staunch firm, loyal; cf. **stanch**

stave/ (mus.) a staff, a stanza or verse (of a song), an alliterative letter in Germanic poetry, a piece of wood in the side of a barrel; pl. **-s**; cf. **staff**

stay-at-home (adj. and noun, hyphens)

stayed stopped, remained; cf. **staid**

STB *Sacrae Theologiae Baccalaureus* (Bachelor of Sacred Theology), Státní tajná bezpečnost (q.v.)

STC Senior (Officers') Training Corps, Short-Title Catalogue

stchi *use* **sh-**

STD *Sacrae Theologiae Doctor* (Doctor of Sacred Theology), sexually transmitted disease, subscriber trunk dialling

Ste (Fr. f.) *sainte* (female saint) (no point)

Ste (Fr.) *Société* (Society)

steadfast *not* sted-

steakhouse (one word, two words in US)

steak knife (two words)

steam/ age, — bath (two words)

steamboat (one word)

steam/ boiler, — engine, — gauge, — hammer, — heat, — iron, — organ, — power (two words)

steam/roller, -ship, abbr. **SS** (one word)

steam shovel (two words)

steam/ train, — turbine (two words)

Steel, Flora Annie (1847–1929) Scottish novelist

Steele, Sir Richard (1672–1729) English essayist and dramatist

Steell,/ Gourlay (1819–94) Scottish painter; — **Sir John** (1804–91) his brother, Scottish sculptor

steel/work, -works, -yard (one word)

steenbok (Afrik.) a small antelope, *not* steinbuck; *see also* **steinbock**

steenkirk (hist.) a neckcloth, *not* stein-

steeplechase/ a cross-country horse race, **-r** the horse or rider taking part

steeplejack (one word)

Steevens,/ George (1736–1800) English Shakespearian commentator; — **George**

Warrington (1869–1900) English journalist; *see also* **Stephen**; **Stephens**; **Stevens**

Stefánsson, Vilhjálmur (1879–1962) Canadian-born US anthropologist, archaeologist, and Arctic explorer

Steinbeck, John (**Ernst**) (1902–68) US novelist

Steinberg a hock (wine)

steinbock an Alpine ibex

steinbuck *use* **steenbok**

steinkirk *use* **steen-**

stel/a (archaeol.) an upright slab or pillar, usually engraved and sculpted, esp. as a gravestone; pl. **-ae**

stem abbr. **s.**, **st.**

stemm/a a family tree or pedigree, pl. **-ata**

stencil/, -led, -ler, -ling (one *l* in US)

Stendhal pseud. of **Marie Henri Beyle** (1783–1842) French novelist

Sten gun a type of lightweight sub-machine gun (one cap.)

Stentor/ a person with a powerful voice, from Homer's herald in the Trojan War; **-ian** (not cap.)

step/brother, -child, -daughter, -father (one word)

Stephen, Sir Leslie (1832–1904) English biographer and critic; *see also* **Steevens**; **Stephens**; **Stevens**

stephengraph *use* **stev-**

Stephens,/ Alexander Hamilton (1812–83) US statesman, — **James** (1882–1950) Irish poet and novelist; *see also* **Steevens**; **Stephen**; **Stevens**

Stephenson,/ George (1781–1848) English locomotive engineer; — **Robert** (1803–59) his son, English engineer; *see also* **Stev-**

step/ladder, -mother (one word)

step-parent (hyphen, one word in US)

steppe a treeless plain, esp. of Russia

stepping stone (two words, hyphen in US)

step/sister, -son (one word)

steradian the SI unit of solid angle, abbr. **sr**

stere a unit of volume, 1 cubic metre

stereophonic of reproduction of sound by two channels, (colloq.) **stereo/**, pl. **-s**

stereotype (typ.) a duplicate plate cast from a matrix moulded from original relief printing material; (colloq.) **stereo**

sterilize *not* -ise

Sterling, John (1806–44) Scottish writer; *see also* **Stir-**

sterling/ (of money) of standard value, abbr. **stg.**; — **silver** silver of $92\frac{1}{4}$ per cent purity

Sterne, Laurence (*not* Law-) (1713–68) English novelist

stet/ (typ.) let the original form stand; **-ted, -ting**

Stetson (US propr.) a wide-brimmed, high-crowned hat (cap.)

Stettin Ger. for **Szczecin**

Steuart,/ Sir James Denham (1712–80) Scottish economist; — **John Alexander** (1861–1932) Scottish journalist and novelist; *see also* **Stewart; Stuart**

stevengraph a colourful picture made of silk, *not* steph-

Stevens,/ Alfred (1818–75) English sculptor, — **Thaddeus** (1792–1868) US abolitionist, — **Wallace** (1879–1955) US poet; *see also* **Steevens; Stephen; Stephens**

Stevenson,/ Adlai (**Ewing**) (1835–1914) US Vice-President; — **Adlai** (**Ewing**), **III** (1900–65) his grandson, US politician; — **Robert** (1772–1850) English lighthouse engineer; — **Robert Louis** (**Balfour**) (1850–94) his grandson, Scottish novelist, essayist, and poet, abbr. **R.L.S.**; *see also* **Steph-**

Stewart/ family name of the Earl of Galloway, **—, Dugald** (1753–1828) Scottish metaphysician, **—, James** (1831–1905) Scottish African missionary; *see also* **Steuart; Stuart**

Stewartry a district of Dumfries & Galloway

stg. sterling

stibium antimony, symbol **Sb**

stichometry the division into, or measurement by, lines of verse; *not* stycho-

stichomythia dialogue in alternate lines of verse

Stieglitz, Alfred (1864–1946) US photographer

stigma/ a mark or sign of disgrace; (Gr.) the name given in modern times to the character *ϛ*; pl. **-s**, *but* **-ta** with reference to Christ's wounds (pron. with stress on the first syllable)

stigmatize *not* -ise

stilb an SI unit of luminance, equal to 1 candela per cm²; abbr. **sb**

stilboestrol a powerful synthetic oestrogen, *not* -be- (US)

stile an arrangement of steps over a fence, a vertical piece in framework; cf. **style**

stiletto/ a dagger; (in full — **heel**) a long tapering heel on a woman's shoe; pl. **-s**

still/birth, -born (one word)

still life/ pl. **-s** (hyphen when attrib.)

Stillson wrench (one cap.)

stilly (adv.) in a still, quiet manner

Stilton a kind of strong rich cheese (cap.)

stilus *use* **sty-**

stimie *use* **sty-**

stimul/ate, -able

stimul/us pl. **-i**

stimy *use* **stymie**

stip. stipend, -iary

stir-fry (hyphen)

Stirling a town and district of Central

Stirling,/ J. Hutchison (*not* -inson) (1820–1909) Scottish metaphysician; — **Sir William Alexander, Earl of** (?1567–1640) Scottish poet, usually called **William Alexander**; *see also* **Ster-**

stirp/s (biol.) a classification group, (law) a branch of a family or its progenitor; pl. **-es**

stitching (bind.) the sewing together of all the sections of a book in a single operation; *see also* **sewing**

Stn. Station

stoa/ (Gr. archit.) a long building with a colonnade, pl. **-s** (not cap.); a philosophical school of Zeno and the Stoics (*see* **Stoic**) (cap.)

stock/breeder, -broker (one word)

stock company (US) a repertory company performing mainly at a particular theatre

Stock Exchange (caps.) abbr. **S/E, St. Ex., Stock Ex.**

Stockhausen, Karlheinz (b. 1928) German composer and theorist

stockholder (one word)

stockinet an elastic fabric; *not* -ette, -inget

stock/jobber, -list, -pile, -pot, -room, -yard (one word)

stodg/e, -y *not* -ey

stoep (Afrik.) a terrace attached to a house; cf. **stoop; stoup**

Stoic/ (a member) of a Greek philosophical school founded by Zeno in the 4th c. BC; **-ism**; (gen., not cap.) a person having great self-control in adversity, adj. **-al**

stoichio/logy the doctrine of elements; *not* stoechio-, stoicheio-; **-metric** (chem.) having elements in fixed proportions; **-metry** (chem.) the proportion in which elements occur in a compound

stoke/hold, -hole (one word)

Stoke-on-Trent Staffs. (hyphens)

stokes a unit of kinematic viscosity, abbr. **St**; in SI units 10⁻⁴ m²/s

STOL short take-off and landing

ston/e a unit of weight, 14 lb (6.35 kg); abbr. **st.**

stone (typ.) the table on which pages of type are imposed

stone/cutter, -fish (one word)

stone/ fly, -ground (one word, hyphen in US)

Stone House Cumbria

Stonehouse Ches., Devon, Glos., Northumb., Strathclyde

stonemason (one word)

stone/wall (verb), **-ware, -washed, -work** (one word)

stony *not* -ey

Stonyhurst College Lancs.

stoop (US) a step or small porch at a house door; cf. **stoep**; **stoup**

stop/cock, -gap (one word)

stop-go alternating progress and lack of it, esp. the alternate restriction and stimulation of economic demand (hyphen)

stop light a red traffic light (two words, one word in US)

stop/off, -over (nouns, one word)

stop press (two words, hyphen when attrib.)

stop valve (two words)

stopwatch (one word)

storable *not* -eable

storage heater (two words)

store/front, -house, -keeper, -room (one word)

storey/ a horizontal division or level of a building, pl. **-s**; *not* story (US), -ies; **-ed**

storied celebrated in story, *not* -yed

storiolog/y the scientific study of folklore, *not* story-; **-ist**

stormbound (one word)

storm petrel (two words) *not* stormy

storm troop/er, -s (two words)

Storting the legislative assembly of Norway

story (of a building) *use* **storey** (except in US)

storyboard (one word)

story book (two words, one word in US)

story/line, -teller (one word)

stoup a holy-water basin, (arch.) a flagon; cf. **stoep**; **stoup**

Stow, John (?1525–1605) English historian

stowaway (one word)

Stowe/ a village and school in Bucks.; **—, Harriet (Elizabeth)** (née) **Beecher** (1811–96) US writer

Stow-on-the-Wold Glos. (hyphens)

STP *Sacrae Theologiae Professor* (Professor of Sacred Theology), standard temperature and pressure

Str. Strait, -s

str. stroke (oar)

Strachey/ the family name of Baron O'Hagan; **—, (Giles) Lytton** (1880–1932) English biographer and essayist

Strad (colloq.) Stradivarius (violin) (cap., no point), italic as journal title

Stradbroke, Earl of

Stradivarius an instrument of the violin family made by **Antonio Stradivari** (in Latin **Antonius Stradivarius**) of Cremona (*c.*1644–1737), (colloq.) **Strad**

Strafford, Earl of

straight away immediately (two words)

straightaway (US) (of a course) straight, straight part of a racecourse (one word)

straightforward (one word)

strait/, -s cap. when with name; abbr. **St., Str.**

straitjacket *not* straight-

strait-laced *not* straight- (hyphen, one word in US)

Straits Settlements *now* part of Malaysia

Stranraer Dumfries & Galloway

strappado/ a form of torture, pl. **-s**; as verb **-ed, -ing**

Strasburg Eng. form of Fr. **Strasbourg**, Ger. **Strassburg**; if using Fr. spelling, *use* Ger. spelling for the period of German rule, 1871–1919 (but not for the Nazi occupation, 1940–5)

Stratford-upon-Avon War., *but* **Stratford-on-Avon District Council** (hyphens)

strath (Sc.) a broad mountain valley; cap. and separate word when referring to the strath itself, e.g. 'Strath Spey'

Strathclyde/ an ancient kingdom and modern region in Scotland; university; **Baron —**

strathspey a slow Scottish dance

stratigraphy (geol., archaeol.) (the study of) the order and relative position of strata, *not* strato-

stratosphere the upper atmosphere; cf. **tropo-**

strat/um a layer, pl. **-a**

strat/us a low layer of cloud, pl. **-i**; abbr. **s.**

Straus, Oskar (1870–1954) Austrian-born composer

Strauss,/ Johann I (1804–49) Austrian composer of Viennese waltzes; **— Johann II** (1825–99) his son, the best known of the family; **— Joseph** (1827–70) and **— Eduard** (1835–1916) also sons of Johann I; **— Johann III** (1866–1939) son of Johann II; **— Richard Georg** (1864–1949) German composer of operas, songs, and orchestral works

Stravinsky, Igor (Fyodorovich) (1882–1971) Russian-born composer

strawberry/ blonde, — mark, — pear, — roan (two words)

stream of consciousness (hyphens when attrib.)

Streatfeild a family name, *not* -field

street name of, to have initial cap., as in Regent Street; spell out when a number, as Fifth Avenue, *but* follow local conventions, e.g. in New York spell out numbers only for avenues, using arabic numberals for streets: 42nd Street; house number to be in arabic, not followed by any punctuation, as 6 Fleet Street; abbr. **St.**

street/walker, -wise (one word)

stretto/ (mus.) (passage played) in quicker time, pl. **-s**

strew to scatter, *not* -ow; past part. **strewed** *or* **strewn**

strewth (colloq.) God's truth (no apos.), *not* stru-

stri/a (anat., geol.) a stripe, pl. **-ae**

stride past **strode**, past part. **stridden**

strike/-bound, -breaker (hyphens, one word in US)

strike-through (typ.) the penetration of ink into paper (hyphen)

Strine a comic transliteration of Australian speech, e.g. *Emma Chissitt* ('How much is it?') (cap.)

string bass (US) = **double bass**

stringendo (mus.) pressing, accelerating the tempo

strip mine (US) = **opencast mine**

stripping-in (typ.) in filmsetting, making alterations to text by the excision and replacement of the film containing it

strip-search (hyphen; noun, two words in US, verb, hyphen)

striptease (one word)

stripy having stripes, *not* -ey

strive past **strove**, past part. **striven**

Stroganoff (cook.) (designating) a dish of meat cooked in sour cream (cap.)

strong-arm (hyphen)

strong/box, -hold, -man (one word)

strongroom (one word, two words in US)

strontium symbol **Sr**

Strood Kent

Stroud Glos., Hants.

strow *use* **strew**

struth *use* **strew-**

Struwwelpeter a German children's book, a character with straggly unkempt hair and long fingernails

strychnine *not* -in

Sts Saints

Stuart,/ House of (of or relating to) (a member of) the royal family ruling Scotland 1371–1714 and England 1603–49, 1660–1714, — **Leslie** pseud. of **Thomas Barrett** (1866–1928) English composer; *see also* **Steuart**; **Stewart**

stucco/ (apply) plaster or cement coating to wall surfaces, pl. **-es**; as verb **-es, -ed**

Stück (Ger. n.) a piece

student a graduate recipient of a stipend from the foundation of a college, esp. a Fellow of Christ Church, Oxford

studio/ pl. **-s**

stumbling block (two words)

stupa a round usually domed building erected as a Buddhist shrine, in Skt. ***stūpa***

stupefy *not* -ify

stupor *not* -our

Sturla Þórðarson (*c*.1214–84) (sometimes Anglicized as **Thord(h)arson**) Icelandic historian, author of *Sturlungasaga* and nephew of Snorri Sturluson

Sturluson *see* **Snorri Sturluson**

Sturm und Drang (Ger.) a literary and artistic movement in Germany in the late 18th c. (three words)

Sturm-und-Drang-Periode German Romanticism of the late 18th c. (three hyphens)

Stuttgart Germany; *not* Stü-, -ard

Stuyvesant, Peter (1592–1672) Dutch colonial governor

sty an inflamed swelling on eyelid, an enclosure for pigs; *not* stye; pl. **sties**

stycho/metry, -mythia *use* **sticho-**

Stygian (Gr. myth.) of or relating to the River Styx in Hades

style a custom, manner, etc.; *see also* **house style**; cf. **stile**

stylite (eccl. hist.) an ancient or medieval ascetic living on top of a pillar

stylize *not* -ise

styl/us a needle-like device; pl. **-i** *or* (esp. those used in playing gramophone records) **-uses**

stymie thwart, obstruct, an obstruction; *not* sti-, -my

Styx (Gr. myth.) a river in Hades

s.u. (Ger.) *siehe unten* (see below)

Suabia *use* **Swa-**

suable that can be sued, *not* -eable

Suakin Sudan, *not* -im

suaraj *use* **sw-**

suaviter in modo (Lat.) gently in manner; cf. ***fortiter in re***

sub/ (colloq.) subaltern, sub-editor, submarine, subscription, substitute; as verb, act as substitute, sub-edit; **-bed, -bing**

sub (Lat.) under

subahdar (Ind.) a native captain

subaltern an officer below the rank of captain, (colloq.) **sub**

subaudi (Lat.) understand, supply

sub/-basement, -branch, -breed (hyphens, one word in US)

sub/category, -class (one word)

sub-clause (hyphen, one word in US)

sub/committee, -conscious, -contract, -deacon, -dean, -divide, -division, -dominant (one word)

sub-edit/, -or, -orial (hyphens, one word in US)

sub finem (Lat.) towards the end (as of a work), abbr. **s.f., sub fin.**

subfusc/, -ous dark, esp. of formal clothing worn at some universities

subgenus (one word)

sub-heading (hyphen, one word in US)

subhuman (one word)

subj. subject, -ive, -ively; subjunctive

subject matter (two words)

sub judice (Lat.) under consideration

subjunctive abbr. **subj.**

subkingdom (one word)

sub/-lease, -let (hyphens, one word in US)

sub lieutenant abbr. **Sub-Lt.** (cap. as title; two words, one word in US)

Sublime Porte, the (hist.) the Turkish court and government

sub-machine gun (one hyphen, no hyphen in US: **submachine gun**)

submarginal (esp. econ.) not reaching minimum requirements, (of land) that cannot be farmed profitably

submarine (one word), in the Royal Navy classed as boats

submerged tenth (econ.) the supposed fraction of the population permanently living in poverty

submicroscopic (one word)

sub/ modo (Lat.) in a qualified sense; — *nomine* under a specified name, abbr. **s.n.**

subnormal (one word)

sub-plot (hyphen, one word in US)

subpoena/ (serve) a writ commanding attendance, pl. **-s**; as verb **-ed**; *not* -pena (one word, not ital.)

sub rosa in secrecy or confidence

subscript (a symbol or letter) written below the line, inferior; cf. **superscript**; *see also* **iota**

subscription (colloq.) **sub**

subsection (one word) abbr. **subsec.**

subsequence a subsequent incident, a consequence; a sequence forming part of a larger one

subsidize pay a subsidy to, *not* -ise

subsidy a grant of public money

sub/ sigillo (Lat.) in the strictest confidence, — *silentio* in silence

sub/sonic, -space (one word)

sub specie aeternitatis (Lat.) under the aspect of eternity, in a universal perspective

subspecies sing. abbr. **subsp.**, pl. abbr. **subspp.**

substance, amount of symbol **n**

sub-standard (hyphen, one word in US)

substantive abbr. **s., sb., subst.**

substitute (noun) colloq. **sub**

substrat/um pl. **-a**

sub/structure, -terranean (one word)

subtil/, -e *use* **subtle** in all senses

subtilize rarefy, *not* -ise

subtitle (one word)

subtl/e fine, rarefied, elusive, cunning; **-er, -est, -ety, -y**; *not* subtil-

subtopia suburban development regarded unfavourably

sub/total, -tropical (one word)

suburbia suburbs and their inhabitants (not cap.)

sub/ voce or — verbo (Lat.) under a specified word, preferred to *ad voc.*; abbr. **s.v.**

subway a tunnel beneath a road etc., (UK) for pedestrians, (US) for an underground railway (one word)

succeeded abbr. **s.**

succès/ de scandale (Fr. m.) success due to being scandalous, — *d'estime* success with more honour than profit, — *fou* extravagant success

Succoth the Jewish Feast of Tabernacles, *not* -ukko- (US); in Heb. **sukkōṯ**

succour *not* -or (US)

succub/us a female demon believed to have sexual intercourse with sleeping men, pl. **-i**; cf. **incubus**

suchlike (one word)

sucking pig (two words) *also* (esp. in US) **suckling pig**

sucre the basic monetary unit of Ecuador

sud (Fr. m.) south, abbr. **s.**

Süd (Ger. m.) south, abbr. **S.** (cap.)

Sudan/ N. Africa, **-ese**; in Fr. **Soudan**

sudd floating vegetation impeding the navigation of the White Nile

Sudra the Hindu labourer caste, the lowest of the four great castes; in Skt. *śūdra*

Sue, Marie-Joseph *self-styled* **Eugène** (1804–57) French novelist, *not* Suë

su/e, -ed, -ing

Suède Fr. for Sweden, adj. **suédois**

suede dull-dressed kid leather (no accent)

Suetonius, Gaius Tranquillus (*c.*70–*c.*160) Roman biographer and antiquarian, abbr. **Suet.**

suff. suffix

suffic/it (Lat.) it is sufficient, pl. *-iunt*

Sufi a Muslim ascetic and mystic; *not* Sofi, Soofee; in Arab. **ṣūfī**; *see also* **Sophy**

sugar/-bowl (hyphen, two words in US)

sugar/ beet, — cane, — daddy (two words)

sugarloaf (one word)

sugar/ maple, — pea (two words)

sugarplum (one word)

sugar soap (two words)

suggestible capable of being suggested, open to suggestion; *not* -able

suggestio falsi (Lat.) an indirect lie

sui/ generis (Lat.) (the only one or ones) of his, her, its, *or* their, own kind; **— juris** of full age and capacity

suisse (Fr. adj.) of or relating to Switzerland, (m., f., cap.) a Swiss person, (m., not cap.) a beadle of a church; **la Suisse** (Fr.) Switzerland

suite a set of rooms, attendants, *or* musical pieces (not ital.)

suivez (mus.) follow the soloist

suk(h) *use* **souk**

sukiyaki a Japanese dish of sliced meat simmered with vegetables and sauce

Sulawesi Indonesia, formerly **Celebes**

Süleyman/ I (?1495–1566) Sultan of Turkey 1520–66, called 'Kanuni' (the Lawgiver) in Turkey, 'the Magnificent' in Europe; **— II** (1641–91) Sultan of Turkey 1687–91; *not* Sulathough often **Suleiman** in hist. texts

Sully Prudhomme, René François Armand (1839–1907) French poet and critic

sulpha a class of drugs, *not* -fa (US)

sulph/ur symbol **S**, *not* -fur (US); **-ate, -ite, -uretted, -urize** *not* -ise

sultan/ a Muslim ruler, f. **-a**; **Sultan, the** of Turkey, till 1922; abbr. **Sult.**

Sultanpur India

sum (math.) symbol Σ

sumac (bot.) an ornamental tree; *not* sh-, -ach, -ack

Sumburgh Airport Shetland

Sumer/ Babylonia; **-ian** (of or relating to) the early and non-Semitic element in the civilization of ancient Babylonia, a member of this people, or their language

summ/a (Lat.) a summary of what is known of a subject, pl. **-ae** (not cap.)

summa cum laude (esp. US) (of a degree, diploma, etc.) of the highest standard, with the highest distinction (not ital.)

summarize *not* -ise

summer (not cap.)

summersault *use* **somer-**

summertime the summer season (one word); **British Summer Time** in summer only, one hour in advance of GMT 1922–67, and from 1972 (three words); *see also* **BST**; **Daylight Saving Time**

summonsed (law) issued with a summons, *not* -oned

summum bonum (Lat.) the supreme good

Sumter, Fort SC

Sun. Sunday

sun cap. only in astron. and anthropomorphic contexts, and in a list of planets; abbr. **S.**

sun/bathe, -beam, -bed, -belt, -block (one word)

sun bonnet (two words, one in US)

sunburn/, -t *or* **-ed** (one word)

sundae an ice cream dessert

Sunday abbr. **Sun.**

sun/dial, -down, -dress (one word)

sundry various, several

sun-dr/y dry in the sun, **-ied**

sunfast (US) (of dye) not subject to fading by sunlight

sun/flower, -glasses (one word)

sun-god (hyphen, two words in US)

sunhat (one word, two words in US)

sun/light, -like (one word)

Sunna a traditional portion of Muslim law based on Muhammad's words or acts; *not* -ah

Sunni/ (of or relating to) (an adherent of) one of the two main branches of Islam; *see also* **Shia**; pl. same; *not* -ee; also **-te**

sun/rise, -set, -shade, -shine -spot, -stroke, -tan (one word)

suntrap (one word, two words in US)

sunup (US) = **sunrise** (one word)

Sun Yat-sen (Pinyin **Sun Yixian**) (1866–1925) Chinese Kuomintang politician

suo/ jure (Lat.) in one's own right, **— loco** in its own place

Suomi Fin. for **Finland**

sup. superior, supine

sup. (Lat.) *supra* (above)

superannu/ate, -able (one word)

supercalendered paper highly polished but not coated, abbr. **SC**

supercargo/ an officer in a merchant ship managing sales, pl. **-es** (one word)

supercede *use* **-sede**

superego/ (psychol.) the part of mind that exerts conscience, pl. **-s** (one word)

superexcellen/ce, -t (one word)

superficies a surface, pl. same

super/fine, -glue, -highway, -human (one word)

superintendent abbr. **supt.**

superior abbr. **sup.**

superior (typ.) a small character set above the line, usually to the side, of ordinary characters, e.g. ¹ ² ª ᵇ; *also called* **superscript**; cf. **inferior**

superl. superlative

super/man, -market (one word)

supermundane superior to earthly things, *not* exceptionally tedious

super/natural, -power (one word)

superscript (a symbol or letter) written above the line, *also called* **superior**; cf. **subscript**

supersede to set aside, take the place of, *not* -cede

super/sonic, -store, -structure, -tanker (one word)

supervis/e *not* -ize, **-or** *not* -er

supine abbr. **sup.**

suppl/e, -y *not* -ely (US)

supplement abbr. **suppl.**

suppositious hypothetical, assumed

supposititious spurious

suppository *not* -ary

suppressio veri (Lat.) suppression of the truth

suppressor *not* -er

supr. supreme

supra (Lat.) above, formerly; abbr. **sup.**; in text *prefer* 'above' except in legal work

suprême (Fr. f.) a method of cooking, with a rich cream sauce

Supreme Court (two caps.)

supremo/ a leader or ruler, pl. **-s**

supt. superintendent

suq *use* **souk**

sur (Fr. prep.) upon, abbr. **s/** (close up) in addresses

sura a chapter or section of the Koran (cap. when referring to specific chapters), *not* ass-, -ah; in Arab. *sūra*

Surabaya Indonesia

surah a thin silk fabric

Surat Bombay, India

surcingle a belt

Sûreté the French CID, in Paris

surfboard (one word)

surfiction (lit.) postmodernist or metafiction

surf-riding (hyphen)

surg/eon, -ery, -ical abbr. **surg.**

Surgeon General (US) the head of a public health service or of the medical service of an army etc., pl. **Surgeons General**

Surgeons, Royal College of abbr. **RCS**

Suriname S. America

surmise conjecture, *not* -ize

surplus abbr. **S.**

surprise *not* -ize

surrealism (two *r*s) a 20th-c. movement in art and literature, often cap. to distinguish from the looser meaning of a bizarre imaginative effect

surrebutter (law) the plaintiff's reply to the defendant's rebutter

sursum corda (Lat.) (lift) up your hearts

Surtees, Robert Smith (1805–64) English fox-hunting novelist

surtitle (one word)

surtout an overcoat or greatcoat

surv. survey/ing, -or; surviving

Surv.-Gen. Surveyor-General

survivor *not* -er

Susanna (Apocr.) abbr. **Sus.**

susceptible *not* -able

suspenders a suspender belt, (US) a pair of braces; *not* -ors

sus. per coll. (Lat.) *suspen/sio* (*-sus, -datur*) *per collum*, hanging (hanged, let him be hanged) by the neck

Susquehanna River Pa., *not* -ana

suss/ slang for suspect, suspicion; **— out** to reconnoitre; **-ed, -ing**

susuhunan (hist.) (the title of) the ruler of Surakarta and of Mataram in Java

Sutlej a Punjab river

Sutra an aphorism or set of aphorisms in Hindu literature, a narrative part of Buddhist literature, Jainist scripture

suttee (the custom of) a Hindu widow immolating herself on her husband's pyre, in Hind. and Urdu *satī*

suum cuique (Lat.) let each have his own

SUV sport utility vehicle

Suwannee River Ga., Fla.; *not* Swa- (except as song title)

sužet *use* **sju-**

SV (Lat.) *Sancta Virgo* (Holy Virgin), *Sanctitas Vestra* (Your Holiness)

s.v. sailing vessel; *sub voce* or *sub verbo*

SVA Incorporated Society of Valuers and Auctioneers

Svedberg (**unit**) a unit of time equal to 10^{-13} second used in expressing sedimentation coefficients, symbol **S**; from **Theodor S. Svedberg** (1884–1971) Swedish chemist

svelte slender, lissom, graceful (not ital.)

Svendsen, Johan Severin (1840–1911) Norwegian composer

Svengali a person who exercises a controlling or mesmeric influence on another, esp. for a sinister purpose

Sverige Swed. for Sweden

s.v.p. (Fr.) *s'il vous plaît* (if you please)

SW South Wales; south-west, -ern

Sw. Swed/en, -ish

swab (clean with) a mop or other absorbent device, *not* -ob

Swabia Germany, *not* Su-

Swahili (of or relating to) (a member of) a Bantu-speaking people of Zanzibar and adjacent coasts of Tanzania, properly **Mswahili** (sing.), **Waswahili** (pl.); (of or relating to) their language, used widely as a lingua franca in E. Africa, properly **KiSwahili**

swami/ a Hindu male religious teacher, pl. **-s**; in Hind. *swāmī*

Swammerdam, Jan (1637–80) Dutch naturalist

'Swanee River' song, otherwise known as 'Old Folks at Home', by Stephen Collins Foster, 1851; in all other instances *use* **Suwannee**

swan/sdown, -song (one word)

swan-upping the annual taking up and marking of Thames swans (hyphen)

swap to exchange, *not* -op

Swapo South West Africa People's Organization, in Namibia

Swaraj (hist.) self-government or independence for India, *not* su-

swash (typ.) (of) letters with elaborate tails or flourishes

swat hit sharply; cf. **swot**

swath a line of cut grass or corn

swathe bind or enclose

Swazi/, -land S. Africa

sweat/ past and past part. **-ed** (*sweat* in US)

sweatband (one word)

sweating-sickness an epidemic fever with sweating, prevalent in England in the 15th–16th cc.

sweat/shirt, -shop, -suit (one word)

swede a kind of turnip (not cap.)

Sweden abbr. **Swed., Sw.**; (the latter is acceptable in narrow measure and where no confusion with Switzerland can arise); in Swed. **Sverige**, in Fr. **Suède**

Swedenborg, Emanuel (1688–1772) Swedish philosopher

Swedish/ abbr. **Swed., Sw.**; '— a' Å, å

sweepback (of aircraft's wings) noun and adj. (one word)

Sweet, Henry (1845–1912) English philologist; *see also* **Swete**

sweet and sour (cook. adj., no hyphen even when attrib.; no hyphens in US unless attrib.)

sweetbread (one word)

Sweet Briar Va., *not* — Brier

sweetheart (one word)

sweetie a sweet, (esp. US) a term of endearment

sweet/meal, -meat (one word)

sweet potato a tropical climbing plant, *Ipomoea batatas*, or the edible tuberous roots of this; cf. **yam**

sweet-talk (verb, hyphen)

sweet tooth (two words)

sweet william (bot.) (two words, not caps.)

swelled rule (typ.) a rule wider in centre than at ends; *see also* **rule**

Swete, Henry Barclay (1835–1917) English biblical scholar; *see also* **Sweet**

Sweyn the name of three Danish kings, in Dan. **Svend**

SWG standard wire gauge

swimming/ bath, — costume, — pool (two words)

swimsuit (one word)

Swinburne, Algernon Charles (1837–1909) English poet

Swinden N. Yorks.

Swindon Glos., Staffs., Wilts.

swine/ (US and formal Brit.) a mature pig, pl. same; cf. **hog**; **pig**; **— fever** (two words), **-herd** (one word)

swing door (two words)

swingeing hard (blow)

swing-wing (of aircraft) (hyphen)

Swinton Gr. Manchester, N. Yorks., S. Yorks., Borders

swipe card (two words)

switch/back, -board, -blade (one word)

Swithun/, St Bishop of Winchester 852–62, *not* -in; **-'s Day** 15 July

Switzerland abbr. **Switz., Sw.** (the latter is acceptable in narrow measure and where no confusion with Sweden can arise); in Fr. **la Suisse**, Ger. **die Schweiz**, It. **Svizzera**

swivel/, -led, -ling (one *l* in US)

swizz/ (sl.) a swindle, a disappointment; pl. **-es**; *not* swiz

swop *use* **-ap**

sword dance (two words)

sword/fish, -play, -sman, -stick (one word)

swot study hard; cf. **swat**

SWP Socialist Workers' Party

swung dash (typ.) ∼

SY steam yacht

Sybil woman's name; cf. **sibyl**

sycamine (NT, AV) the black mulberry tree

sycamore any of three trees: a large maple, *Acer pseudoplatanus*, grown in Europe and Asia; (US) the plane tree, *Platanus*; a fig tree, *Ficus sycomorus* (spelt **sycomore** in the Bible), growing in Egypt, Syria, etc.

syce (Anglo-Ind.) a groom; cf. **sice**

Sydney New South Wales, Australia; *see also* **Sid-**

Sykes *see* **Si-**

syllab/ication *not* -ification, **-ize** *not* -ise

syllabub *not* sill-

syllabus/ pl. **-es**

sylleps/is (gram.) application of a word in differing senses to two others ('he caught his train and a cold'), pl. **-es**; cf. **zeugma**

syllogism a logical argument of two premisses and a conclusion

syllogize argue by syllogism, *not* -ise

sylva/, -n *not* si-

Sylvester,/ James Joseph (1814–97) English mathematician, **— Josuah** (1563–1618) English poet

sylvicultur/e, -ist *use* **si-**

symbolize *not* -ise

symmetr/ic, -ical, -ize *not* -ise

sympathique (Fr.) congenial, having the right artistic feeling for

sympathize not -ise

symposi/um a conference, a collection of views on a topic (not cap.); one of Plato's Socratic dialogues (cap., ital.); pl. **-a**

syn. synonym, -ous

syn- (chem.) of isomers, *use* **cis-**

synaeres/is (gram.) the contraction of two vowels, pl. **-es**; *not* -neresis (US)

synaesthesia *not* synes- (US)

synagog/ue an assembly of Jews for worship, their place of worship; **-al, -ic**

synchronize (cause to) coincide in time, *not* -ise; colloq. **sync,** *not* synch

syndrome a group of concurrent symptoms; in medical and scientific use, avoid 's in identification of syndromes derived from names of individuals; thus e.g. *Angelman syndrome, Munchausen syndrome*

synecdoche a figure of speech in which a part is made to represent the whole or vice versa

synonym/ a word with the same meaning as another; **-ous** abbr. **syn.**; **-ize** *not* -ise; **-y** *not* -e, -ey

synops/is a summary, pl. **-es**

Synoptic Gospels Matthew, Mark, and Luke, which relate the events from the same point of view

synthes/ist, -ize *not* synthet-, -ise

syphon *use* **si-**

Syr. Syria, -c, -n

syr. syrup

Syrah a variety of grape, the wine made from this; trad. spelt **Shiraz** in Eng.

syren *use* **si-**

Syriac (in or relating to) the literary language of ancient Syria, based on W. Aramaic; abbr. **Syr.**

Syringa (bot.) the lilac genus

syringa the mock orange

syringe/ an instrument for squirting or injecting, **-ing**; *not* si-

syrin/x a pan pipe, (anat.) a narrow tube from throat to eardrum, the vocal organ of birds, (archaeol.) a narrow gallery in rock; pl. **-xes, -ges**

syrup *not* sir-, abbr. **syr.**

syst. system

system/atic methodical, **-atize** *not* -ise, **-ic** (physiol.) of the bodily system as a whole

Système International (**d'Unités**) a coherent system of scientific units based on the metre, kilogram, second, ampere, kelvin, mole, and candela; adopted by the General Conference of Weights and Measures (CGPM) and endorsed by the International Organization for Standardization (ISO); abbr. **SI**

syuzhet *see* **sjužet**

syzygy (prosody) a combination of two different feet in one measure, a dipody; (astr.) the moon being in conjunction or opposition; (philos.) a pair of connected or correlative things; a word game invented by Lewis Carroll

Szczecin Poland, in Ger. **Stettin**

Szechwan a Chinese province, in Pinyin **Sichuan**

Szent-Györgyi, Albert von (1893–1986) Hungarian-born US biochemist

Sze Yap (of or relating to) the form of Cantonese spoken in the south of Guangdong Province

Szigeti, Joseph (1892–1973) Hungarian violinist

Szilard, Leo (1898–1964) Hungarian-born US physicist and molecular biochemist

szlach/ta (hist.) the aristocratic or landowning class in Poland before 1945, **-cic** a member of this (ital.)

Szymanowski, Karol (1883–1937) Polish composer

T (as prefix) tera-, tesla, tritium, the nineteenth in a series

_T_ temperature

T. Tenor, Territory, Testament, (It. mus.) tace (be silent)

t ton, -s; tonne, -s

t. town(-ship); tun, -s; (Fr.) *tome* (volume), *tonneau* (ton); (Lat.) *tempore* (in the time of), (mus.) tempo (time); (It.) *tenor/e, -i* (tenor, -s); (meteor.) thunder

't (Du.) *het* (the, n.) as in 'van 't Hoff'

_t_ time

TA Territorial Army

Ta tantalum (no point)

Taal, the (hist.) an early form of Afrikaans

TA & VRA Territorial Auxiliary and Volunteer Reserve Association

TAB typhoid-paratyphoid A and B vaccine, (Austral.) Totalizator Agency Board

Tabago *use* **To-**

tabasco a pungent pepper, (cap., propr.) a sauce made from this

tabbouleh an Arabic vegetable salad made with cracked wheat, in Arab. *tabbūla*

Tabernacles, Feast of Succoth

tabla (Ind. mus.) a pair of small drums played with the hands

tablature (mus.) a form of notation using letters, figures, or diagrams to indicate placement of fingers on an instrument

table/ _alphabétique_ (Fr. typ. f.) index, **— _des matières_** table of contents

tableau/ a picturesque presentation, dramatic situation, pl. **-x** (not ital.); **— _vivant_** a still silent group representing a scene, pl. **-x viv-ants** (ital.)

tablecloth (one word)

table/ d'hôte a set meal for guests at hotel, pl. **-s d'hôte** (not ital.)

tableland (one word)

table mat (two words)

tablespoonful/ pl. **-s**, abbr. **tbsp**

table/ talk, — tennis (two words)

table top (two words, one word in US)

tableware (one word)

taboo/ (something) forbidden, to prohibit, a prohibition; *not* -pu (NZ), -u; in Tongan *tabu*; **-ed, -s**

tabor a small drum, *not* -our

tabouret a drum-shaped stool, *not* -oret (US)

tabul/a (Lat.) a document, pl. **-ae**; **— rasa** a blank surface, pl. **-ae rasae** (not ital.)

tabulat/e, -or

Tac. Tacitus

tac-au-tac (fencing) parry and riposte (hyphens, not ital.); but *du tac au tac* (Fr. fig.) from defence to attack (no hyphens, ital.)

tace (mus.) be silent, abbr. **T.**

tacet (mus.) is silent

tachism action painting, in Fr. m. *tachisme*

tacho/ (colloq.) tachometer, pl. **-s**

tachograph a device for recording the speed and travel-time of vehicles

tachometer an instrument for measuring the speed of rotation

tachymeter an instrument used in surveying

Tacitus, Gaius Cornelius (*c*.55–120) Roman historian, abbr. **Tac.**

taco/ (Mexican cook.) meat, vegetables, etc. in a folded, fried (maize) tortilla; pl. **-s**

Tadjikistan *use* **Taj-**

taedium vitae (Lat.) weariness of life (often as a pathological state with a tendency to suicide)

taeni/a (archit.) a fillet between a Doric architrave and frieze; (anat.) any flat ribbon-like structure; a large parasitic tapeworm; (Gr. antiquity) a fillet or headband; pl. **-ae**; *not* te- (US)

Tae-ping *use* **Taiping** (one word)

taffeta a fabric, *not* the many variants

Taffy (offens.) colloq. term for a Welshman (cap.)

taff/y (US) a confection like chewy toffee, insincere flattery; *not* tof-; pl. **-ies**

Tagalog (of or relating to) (a member of) the principal people of the Philippine Islands, or their language; *see also* **Filipino**; **Pilipino**

tag end (US) the last remaining part of something

tagetes (bot.) a type of marigold, *not* -ete; pl. same

tagliatelle (It. cook.) pasta in ribbons, *not* -elli

Tagore, Rabindranath (1861–1941) Indian poet

Tagus a river, Spain and Portugal; Sp. **Tajo**, Port. **Tejo**, Fr. **Tage**, It. **Tago**

Tahiti an island, Pacific Ocean

tahr a goatlike mammal of the Himalayas, *not* thar

tahsil an administrative area in parts of India, in Urdu *tahsīl*

Tai a language family of SE Asia, including Thai, Lao, and Shan

t'ai chi ch'uan a Chinese martial art and system of callisthenics, often abbr. as **t'ai chi** (not ital.)

taiga a coniferous forest lying between tundra and steppe, esp. in Siberia

tail (typ.) blank space at the bottom of a page; *see also* **margins**

tailback a queue of vehicles in a traffic jam (one word, two words as verb), (US) in American football, one player's position

tail/board, -gate (one word)

tail lamp (two words, one word in US)

taille/ (Fr. f.) engraving, also size etc.; *— douce* copperplate engraving

tailless (one word)

tail light (two words, one word in US)

tailpiece (typ.) the design at the end of a section, chapter, or book

tail/pipe, -plane, -spin, -stock (one word)

Tain Highland

Táin an Old Irish tale

Taine, Hippolyte Adolphe (1828–93) French historian and literary critic

taipan the head of a foreign business in China, a large venomous Australian snake

Taipei the capital of Taiwan

Taiping rebellion 1850–64, *not* Tae-

Tait,/ Archibald Campbell (1811–82) Archbishop of Canterbury; **— Peter Guthrie** (1831–1901) Scottish mathematician and physicist; *see also* **Tate**

Taiwan *formerly* Formosa

taj a tall conical cap worn by a dervish, in Arab. *tāj*

Tajik a member of the Iranian language family, spoken in Tajikistan, Uzbekistan, and Afghanistan

Tajikistan a former Soviet Socialist Republic, *not* Tadj-, Tadzh-

Taj Mahal the mausoleum at Agra, India; *not* Me-

takable able to be taken, *not* -eable

take (typ.) a single batch of copy or of proofs

takeaway (noun and adj., one word)

take back (typ.) transfer (text) to the previous line

take-home pay (one hyphen)

take-off (noun, hyphen, one word in US)

takeout (noun, US) = **takeaway**

take over (typ.) transfer (text) to the next line

takeover the assumption of control over a business, as through a buyout (one word, two words as verb)

Tal (Ger. n.) valley, before 1901 spelt *Th-*

Talbot of Malahide, Baron

talebearer (one word)

tales (law) a suit for summoning jurors to supply a deficiency (ital.); **tales/man** one so summoned, pl. **-men** (not ital.); cf. **talis-**

taletell/er, -ing (one word)

Talfourd, Sir Thomas Noon (1795–1854) English playwright, biographer, and author of the Copyright Act of 1842

Taliesin (6th c.) Welsh bard

talisman/ a charm, amulet, pl. **-s**; cf. **tales-**

talis qualis (Lat.) such as he *or* she is

talking/ blues, — book, — drum, — film, — head, — point, — shop (two words)

talking-to a sharp reprimand (hyphen)

talk show (two words)

talktime the time a mobile phone is in use (one word)

Tallahassee Fla.

Tallahatchie a river in Mississippi

tallboy a tall chest of drawers, sometimes in lower and upper sections or mounted on legs (in US **highboy**)

Talleyrand(-Périgord), Charles Maurice de (1754–1838) French politician

Tallinn capital of Estonia, *formerly* (and still in Ger.) **Reval**

Tallis, Thomas (?1505–85) English composer; *not* Talys, Tallys; **Tallis's canon** a hymn tune

tally-ho/ pl. **-s**, as verb **-ed, -es** (hyphen)

Talmud/ (cap.), **-ic** (not cap.) *not* -ical

Tal-y-llyn Gwynedd, Powys (two hyphens)

TAM television audience measurement

Tam. Tamil

tam (colloq.) tam-o'-shanter (no point)

tamable *use* **tameable** (except in US)

tamarin a S. American monkey

tamarind a tropical evergreen tree, or its fruit

tamarisk a shrub of the genus *Tamarix*

tambala a monetary unit of Malawi, pl. same

tambour a drum; a circular frame for holding fabric taut during embroidery; (archit.) the circular part of various structures, esp. those forming the shaft of a column, or a sloping buttress or projection

tamboura (mus.) an Indian stringed instrument used as a drone, in Arab. *ṭanbūra*

tambourin a long narrow drum of Provence, (music for) a dance accompanied by it

tambourine a small drum with jingling metal discs, beaten with the hand

tameable *not* -mable (US)

Tamerlane (1336–1405) Mongol conqueror (but Tamburlaine in Marlowe)

Tameside a district, Gr. Manchester

Tamil/ (concerning) (a member of) a Dravidian people inhabiting S. India and Sri Lanka, the language of this people; *not* -ul; adj. **-an**; abbr. **Tam.**

Tammany/ Hall a corrupt political organization or group, or corrupt political activities in general; **-ism**; *not* Tama-

'Tam o' Shanter' a poem by Burns, 1791 (caps., lower-case *o*, apos., no hyphens)

tam-o'-shanter a woollen cap (hyphens, apos.); colloq. **tam**

tampion a plug for the muzzle of a gun or the top of an organ pipe, *not* to-

tampon (med.) an absorbent plug

tam-tam a large metal gong (hyphen)

tan (math.) tangent (no point)

Tánaiste the deputy Prime Minister of Ireland

Tanak/ the Hebrew Scriptures, comprising the three canonical divisions of the Law, the Prophets, and the Hagiographa or Writings; pl. *-im*

Tananarive *use* **Antananarivo**

Tang a dynasty ruling China 618–*c*.906; (attrib.) designating art and artefacts of this period; in Chin. *táng*

tanga a bikini of small panels connected with thin ties

Tanger/ (Fr., Ger.) Tangier, (It.) **-i**

tangerine a citrus fruit, (cap.) a native of Tangier; *not* tangier-

tangible *not* -eable

Tangier Morocco, *not* -iers

tango/ pl. **-s**

tanh (math.) hyperbolic tangent (no point)

tanist/ (hist.) the elected heir apparent to a Celtic chief, **-ry** the system of appointing such as successor while the principal lives; cf. **Tánaiste**

Tanjor/, -e *use* **Thanjavur**

tanka a Japanese poem in 5 lines and 31 syllables, giving a complete picture of an event or mood

Tannhäuser an opera by Wagner, 1845

Tannoy (propr.) a type of public address system

tanrec *use* **ten-**

tantalize *not* -ise

tantalum symbol **Ta**

tant/ bien que mal (Fr.) with indifferent success, **— mieux** so much the better, **— pis** so much the worse

tantr/a any of a class of Hindu or Buddhist mystical and magical writings; **-ic, -ism, -ist**

Tanzania E. Africa

Taoiseach the Prime Minister of the Irish Republic

Taoism a Chinese philosophy based on the writings of Lao-tzu; *not* Tâ-, Taŏ- (one word)

tap dance (two words)

tape/ deck, — measure (two words)

tape-record (verb, hyphen)

tape record/er, -ing (two words)

tapis a tapestry or covering (not ital.)

tapis, sur le (Fr.) under consideration or discussion

tapisserie (Fr. f.) tapestry

tap pants (US) = **french knickers** (lingerie)

tap/room, -root (one word)

taps (pl., usually treated as sing.) (US) last bugle call of the night in army quarters, or a similar call blown at a military funeral

tap-water (hyphen, two words in US)

Ṭarābulus al-Ġarb (Arab.) **Tripoli**, Libya

Ṭarābulus/ ash-Shām, *properly* **— al-Ša'm** (Arab.) **Tripoli**, Lebanon

taradiddle a petty lie, pretentious nonsense; *not* para-, tarra-

tarantella a whirling Italian dance, or the music for it

tarantism (hist.) dancing mania

tarantula a large spider

Tarbert Strathclyde, Western Isles, Co. Kerry; (river) Highland

Tarbet Loch Lomond, Strathclyde, and Loch Nevis, Highland

Tardenoisian (archaeol.) (of or relating to) a mesolithic culture using small flint implements

tariff a duty on particular goods, *not* -if

tarlatan a muslin, *not* -etan

tarmac/ (propr.) tarmacadam, or a surface made of this; (verb) to cover with tarmac, **-ked** (not cap.)

tarot a card game or a trump in this, a similar deck used in fortune-telling; *not* -oc

tarpaulin a waterproof cloth, originally of tarred canvas, *not* -ing; (US and Austral. colloq.) **tarp**

Tarpeian Rock ancient Rome

tarradiddle *use* **tara-**

Tarragona Spain

tarry covered with or like tar, *not* tary; linger, stay, wait

tartan a pattern of coloured stripes crossing at right angles

Tartar/, -y *see* **Tatar**

tartar a violent-tempered or intractable person (not cap.), adj. **-ian**; a deposit on the teeth, adj. **-ic**

tartare sauce *not* -r (except in US)

Tartar/us (Gr. myth.) the place of punishment in Hades, **-ean**

Tartuff/e a religious hypocrite, **-ian**; in Fr. m. *tartufe*

Tartuffe, Le a play by Molière, 1669

tartufo (It.) truffle

Tas. Tasmania

Tashi Lama a title of the **Panchen Lama**

tashinamu (Jap.) dedicate oneself privately to some purpose or design, regardless of whether it will succeed, or one's labour will be recognized

task/master, -mistress (one word)

Tasmania abbr. **Tas.**

TASS the official news agency of the Soviet Union, renamed **ITAR-Tass** 1992; *also* **Tass**

tassel/, -led, -ling (one *l* in US)

taste bud (two words)

ta-ta (colloq.) goodbye (hyphen)

Tatar/ (of or relating to) (a member of) a group of Cent. Asian peoples including Mongols and Turks, or the Turkic language of these peoples; of or relating to Cent. Asia E. of the Caspian Sea; *not* Tartar, -y except in hist. contexts; **-stan** the Tatar Autonomous Republic

Tate/, Nahum (1652–1715) Irish poet and playwright, **—, Sir William Henry** (1842–1921) English industrialist, **— Gallery** London; *see also* **Tait**

tatterdemalion a ragged fellow, *not* -ian

tattersall check a fabric pattern of coloured lines (not cap.)

Tattersalls London (-*s*' only in the possessive case)

tattoo/ an evening drum or bugle signal, call to quarters, military parade by night; a design on the skin; *not* the many variants; **-ed, -er, -ing, -s**

tau/ the nineteenth letter of the Gr. alphabet (T, τ), **— cross** ⊤

Tauchnitz,/ Karl Christoph (1761–1836) founded at Leipzig, 1796, the publishing firm once famous for editions of Latin and Greek authors; **— Christian Bernhard, Baron von** (1816–95) founded at Leipzig, 1837, the Librairie Bernhard Tauchnitz, famous for good-quality reprints of British and US authors, banned in Britain and USA because of copyright infringements

tausend (Ger.) thousand

taut (naut.) tight, in good condition; *not* -ght

tautolog/y, -ize *not* -ise

tavern, name of *see* **hotel**

TAVR (hist.) Territorial and Army Volunteer Reserve (1967–79), *now called* **TA**

tawny tan-colour, *not* -ey

taxa pl. of **taxon**

tax-free (hyphen)

tax haven (two words)

taxi/, -ing

tax/on a taxonomic group, pl. **-a**

taxpayer (one word)

tax return (two words)

Taylor Institution Oxford, strictly *not* Taylorian, Institute

Taylour family name of the Marquess of Headfort

Tayside a region of Scotland (one word)

tazz/a a bowl or cup, pl. **-e**

TB terabyte(s) torpedo boat, tuberculosis (tubercle bacillus)

Tb terbium (no point)

Tbilisi Georgia, *formerly* Tiflis; in Georgian **T'bilisi**

T-bone (hyphen)

tbsp tablespoon(ful)

Tc technetium (no point)

TCD Trinity College, Dublin

Tchad, Lake etc., *use* **Chad**

Tchaikovsky, Pyotr (Ilich) (1840–93) Russian composer, *not* Tschaï-; those with the same surname usually transliterated **Chaïkovskiĭ**

Tchebyshev, Tchekoff etc. *use* **Che-**

TD (Ir.) *Teachta Dála* (Member of the Dáil), Territorial Decoration, touchdown

Te tellurium (no point)

te tonne, -s

te (mus.) *not* si, ti

tea/ bag, — caddy (two words)

teacake (one word, two words in US)

tea/ chest, — cosy (two words)

teacup (one word)

tea/ dance, — garden, — lady, — leaf (two words)

team/mate, -work (one word)

tea party (two words)

teapot (one word)

teapoy a small three- or four-legged table

tearaway an impetuous or reckless young person, hooligan (one word)

tearoom (one word)

tea rose (two words)

tear sheet (two words)

tease *not* -ze

teasel (bot.) *not* -sle, -zel, -zle

tea shop (two words)

Teasmade (propr., cap.)

teaspoonful/ pl. **-s** (one word), abbr. **tsp**

teatime (one word)

tea/ towel, — tray, — tree (two words)

tech. technical, -ly

technetium symbol **Tc**

Technicolor (propr.) a process of colour cinematography (cap.); (colloq.) a vivid or artificial colour (not cap.); *not* -our

technol. technological, -ly

techy *use* **tetchy**

tectonics/ (pl. treated as sing.) (archit.) the craft of producing practical and aesthetically pleasing buildings; (geol.) the study of large-scale structural features, as in **plate —**

teddy bear (two words, not cap.)

Teddy boy (two words, one cap.)

tedesc/o (It. adj.) f. **-a** German (not cap.)

Te Deum (mus.) a hymn (caps.)

teed (golf)

tee-hee a titter; *not* **tehee**

teenage/, -d, -r (one word)

teepee *use* **te-**

tee shirt *use* **T-shirt**

Teesside Cleveland

teetotal/ advocating or characterized by total abstinence from alcoholic drink; abbr. **TT**; **-ism, -ler** (one *l* in US), **-ly**

teetotum/ a four-sided top spun with the fingers, pl. **-s**

TEFL teaching of English as a foreign language

Tegnér, Esaias (1782–1846) Swedish poet

tehee *use* **tee-**

Tehran Iran, *not* -heran

Teignmouth Devon; *see also* **Tyne-**

Teil/ (Ger. m. *or* n.) a part, pl. **-e**; *not Th-* (cap.)

Teilhard de Chardin, Pierre (1881–1955) French writer

tel *use* **tell**

tel. telegraph, telephone

telaesthesia *not* tele- (US)

telamon/ (archit.) a male figure used as a supporting pillar, pl. **-es**

Tel Aviv Israel

tele/camera, -cine, -communication(s), -conference, -fax (one word)

Telegu *use* **Telu-**

tele/marketing, -message (one word)

telephone/ book, — number (two words)

tele/printer, -prompter (one word)

telesthesia *use* **telae-** (except in US)

teletex/ (propr.) an electronic text transmission system; **-t** a news and information service transmitted to televisions from a computer source

teletype (propr., cap. in US)

televis/e *not* -ize, **-ion**

Telford/ Shropshire, **—, Thomas** (1757–1834) Scottish engineer

tell (archaeol.) an artificial mound in Middle East, *not* tel

Tell-el-Amarna Egypt

telltale (one word)

tellurian (inhabitant) of the earth

tellurion an orrery, *not* -ium

tellurium symbol **Te**

Telstar a communications satellite, launched 1962

Telugu a Dravidian people of SE India, or their language; *not* -oogoo, Tele-

Téméraire, The Fighting a picture by Turner, 1839

temp. temperature, temporary

temp. *tempore* (in the time of)

tempera a method of painting using an emulsion, this paint

temperature symbol **T** (no point)

Templar a member of a religious order, the **Knights Templars**, suppressed in 1312; a student or lawyer living in the Temple, London

template a pattern or gauge, *not* -plet

Temple Bar London

temp/o (mus.) time, pl. **-os**; abbr. **t.**

tempora mutantur (Lat.) times are changing

temporar/y abbr. **temp.**, adv. **-ily**

tempore (Lat.) in the time of; abbr. **t.**, **temp.**

temporize *not* -ise

tempura a Japanese dish of fish, shellfish, or vegetables, fried in batter

tempus edax rerum (Lat.) time consumes everything

ten. tenuto

Tenasserim Burma, *not* Tenn-

Ten Commandments, the (caps.)

tendentious calculated to promote a particular cause or point of view, *not* -cious

tenderfoot a novice (one word)

tender-hearted/, -ness (hyphen, one word in US)

tenderize *not* -ise

tenderloin the middle part of a pork loin; (US) the undercut of a sirloin

Tenerife a peak and island, Canary Islands; *not* -iffe

tenia *use* **taenia** (except in US)

Teniers, David/ (1582–1649) and —— (1610–90) his son, Dutch painters

Tenison, Thomas (1636–1715) Archbishop of Canterbury; *see also* **Tennyson**

Tennasserim *use* **Tena-**

Tennessee off. abbr. **Tenn.**, postal **TN**

Tenniel, Sir John (1820–1914) English cartoonist and caricaturist

tennis/ not necessary to use 'lawn tennis', *but* see **ILTF**; **real —** a different game, played on an indoor court

tennis/ ball, — court, — racket (two words)

Tenno, Meiji *see* **Meiji Tenno**

Tennyson/, Alfred, Lord (1809–92) Poet Laureate 1850–92, **-ian**; *see also* **Tenison**

Tenochtitlán former Aztec capital, on the site of Mexico City

tenor a settled course, *not* -our; (mus.) male voice, abbr. **T.**

tenor/e (It. mus. m.) tenor voice, pl. **-i**; abbr. **t.**

tenrec a hedgehog-like mammal native to Madagascar, *not* tan-

tenson a contest between troubadours, *not* tenz-

tenuto (mus.) held on, sustained; abbr. **ten.**

Teotihuacán pre-Columbian city, near Mexico City

tepee a portable conical Native American dwelling, esp. of the Great Plains; cf. **wigwam**

tequila a mescal liquor made in Tequila in Mexico (not cap.)

Ter. Terence, Terrace

ter (Lat.) thrice

tera- prefix meaning 10¹², abbr. **T**

teraph/ a small image as a domestic deity or oracle of the ancient Hebrews, pl. **-im**; in Heb. **tᵉrāpim**

terat. teratology (study of malformations

terbium symbol **Tb**

terce (eccl.) the office said at the third daytime hour; cf. **tie-**

tercel a male hawk, *not* tier-

tercenten/ary a 300th anniversary; **-nial** occurring every, or lasting, 300 years, (US) = **tercentenary**

tercet (prosody) a triplet, *not* tier-

Terence in Lat. **Publius Terentius Afer** (190–159 BC) Roman comic playwright, abbr. **Ter.**

Teresa, St of Ávila *not* Th-

tergiversat/e to change one's principles; **-ion, -or**

termagant an overbearing or brawling woman (cap. in hist. use as imaginary deity, as in morality plays)

termination abbr. **term.**

terminator *not* -er

terminology abbr. **term.**

termin/us pl. **-i**

terminus/ ad quem (Lat.) the finish, *— a quo* the starting point

termor (law) a person who holds lands etc. for a term of years, or for life; *not* -er

Terpsichore/ (Gr. myth) the muse of dancing, **-an** of dancing

Terr. Territory

terra alba a white mineral, esp. pipeclay or pulverized gypsum

terrace cap. when with name, abbr. **Ter.**; in Fr. f. *terrasse*

terracotta (an object made of) unglazed kiln-burnt clay and sand; its colour (one word, hyphen in US)

Terra del Fuego *use* **Tierra del Fuego**

terrae/ filius (Lat.) lit. son of the soil, denoting a 'worthless nobody'; pl. *— filii* (ital.); **Terrae filius** (hist.) at Oxford University, a semi-licensed jester in the 'Act' (part of the ancient degree ceremony), permitted to make satirical remarks (but liable for punishment if he went too far) (not ital., one cap.)

terra firma dry land (two words, not ital.)

terr/a incognita (Lat.) an unexplored region, pl. *-ae incognitae* (ital.)

terramare an ammoniacal earthy deposit found in mounds in prehistoric lake-dwellings or settlements, *or* the dwelling or settlement itself (not ital.)

terrarium/ a vivarium for small land animals or growing plants, pl. **-s**

terra sigillata an astringent clay, or Samian ware (ital.)

terrazzo/ a floor of stone chips set in concrete and smoothed, pl. **-s**

terret the ring for a driving rein, *not* -it

terre-verte a soft green earth used as a pigment (hyphen, not ital.)

Territory (cap. in geog. names) abbr. **T., Terr.**

terrorize *not* -ise

Tertiary (geol.) (of or relating to) the first period in the Cenozoic era (cap., not ital.); *see also* **Eocene; Miocene; Oligocene; Palaeocene; Pliocene**

tertio (Lat.) in the third place, abbr. **3°**

tertium quid a third something, an intermediate course (not ital.)

terz/a rima (It.) a particular rhyming scheme, pl. *-e rime*

terzetto/ (mus.) a piece for three voices or instruments, pl. **-s**

TES Times Educational Supplement

TESL teaching of English as a second language

tesla the unit of magnetic induction, from **Nikola Tesla** (1856–1943) Croatian-American physicist

TESOL teaching of English to speakers of other languages

tessellate(d) pave(d) with tiles, *not* -ela-

tesser/a a small square tile, pl. **-ae**; **-act** a cube in four dimensions (not ital.)

tessitura (mus.) the ordinary range of a voice

Tess of the D'Urbervilles a novel by Hardy, 1891

Testament abbr. **T., Test.**

testamur (Lat.) examination certificate

test/ drive (hyphen as verb), *— flight* (two words)

test/is (anat.) pl. **-es**

test/ match, — paper, — pilot (two words)

test tube (two words), **test-tube baby** (one hyphen)

Testudinata *use* **Chelonia**

Tet the Vietnamese New Year, observed for three days following the first new moon after 20 Jan. (cap.); in Vietnamese *tết*

tetchy peevish, *not* techy

tête-à-tête (adv., adj., *and* noun, hyphens, accents, not ital.)

tête-bêche (of a postage stamp) printed upside down or sideways relative to another (ital.)

Tetragrammaton the Hebrew name of God written in four (usually small-cap.) letters (YHVH, YHWH), articulated as Yahweh, Jehovah, etc.

tetralogy a group of four related literary or operatic works, (Gr. antiquity) a trilogy of tragedies with a satyric drama

tetrameter (prosody) a verse of four measures

tetraplegia *use* **quadri-**

Teufelsdröckh, Herr Diogenes a character in Carlyle's *Sartor Resartus*

Teut. Teuton, -ic

Teutonic/ relating to or characteristic of the Germanic peoples or their languages; **-ism**

Tevere It. for the Tiber river

Tex. Texas (off. abbr.), Texan (originally Texian)

textbook (one word)

textus receptus (Lat.) the received text, abbr. **text. rec.**

Teyte, Maggie (1888–1976) English soprano

t.g. type genus

TGV (Fr.) *Train à Grande Vitesse*

TGWU Transport and General Workers' Union

Th thorium (no point)

Th. Thomas, Thursday

th a separate letter in Welsh, not to be divided

thagi *use* **thuggee**

Thai of or relating to Thailand, or (a member of) its people; pl. same

Thailand adj. **Thai**

Thaïs (4th c. BC) Greek courtesan

thaler (hist.) a German silver coin

Thalia (Gr. myth.) the muse of comedy

thallium symbol **Tl**

thalweg (geog.) the deepest point or lowest line along a river bed or valley, (law) a boundary between states along the centre of a river etc.; in Modern Ger. m. *Talweg*

Thames a river; in Du. **Theems**, Fr. **Tamise**, Ger. **Themse**, Sp. **Támesis**

Thanjavur India; *not* Tanjor, -e

Thanksgiving Day (US) the fourth Thursday in November, (Canada) second Monday in October

Thant, U (1909–74) Burmese diplomat; 'U' is a Burmese honorific (equivalent to 'Mr') and not a first name

thar *use* **tahr** (except for despot)

Tharrawaddy Burma, *not* Tharawadi

thé/ (Fr. m.) tea, — *dansant* afternoon tea with dancing

Theaetetus a dialogue by Plato, named after a disciple of Socrates

theat. theatrical

theatre/ *not* -er (US), **— -in-the-round** (hyphens), **— nurse, — sister** (two words); in Fr. m. *théâtre*; *Théâtre français* Paris (one cap.)

thec/a (anat., bot.) a case, sheath, sac; pl. **-ae**

thegn (hist.) an English thane

theirs (no apos.)

them/a (Gr.) a theme, pl. **-ata**

Theo. Theodore

theocracy a priest- or god-governed state (cap. with hist. ref. to Jews), *not* -sy

theocrasy the mingling of several divine attributes in one god, *not* -cy

Theocritus (3rd c. BC) Greek poet, abbr. **Theoc.**

theodicy (an instance of) the vindication of divine providence in view of the existence of evil

theodolite a surveying instrument

theol. theolog/y, -ian, -ical

theologize *not* -ise

Theophrastus (*c*.370–*c*.288 BC) Greek philosopher and botanist, abbr. **Theoph.**

theor. theorem

theoret. theoretic, -al, -ally

theorize *not* -ise

theosoph/y a philosophy professing knowledge of God by inspiration; **-ical, -ist, -ize**

Theoto/copuli, -kopoulos *see* **Greco, El**

therapeutic/ healing, **-s** the study of healing agents; abbr. **therap.**

Theravada a conservative form of Buddhism, in Pali *theravāda*

thereanent (Sc.) about that matter

therefor (arch.) for that object or purpose

therefore for that reason, accordingly, consequently; (math.) sign ∴

therein/ in that place or respect, **-after** later in the same document etc., **-before** earlier in the same document etc. (one word)

theremin an electronic musical instrument with a tone varied by the proximity of the hand etc. to the sounding rod (not cap.)

Theresa, St of Ávila, *use* **Ter-**

Thérèse (Fr.)

thereto/ to that or it, in addition; **-fore** before that time (one word)

thereupon in consequence of that, soon or immediately after that (one word)

therm a unit of heat

thermodynamics (one word, pl. usually treated as sing.)

thermomet/er, -ric abbr. **thermom.**

thermonuclear (one word)

Thermopylae, Pass of Greece; battle, 480 BC

thermos (propr.) a vacuum flask

THES *Times Higher Education Supplement*

thesaur/us pl. **-i**

thes/is pl. **-es**; titles to be printed in roman, quoted

Thess./ Thessaly, **1, 2** — Thessalonians (NT)

theta the eighth letter of the Gr. alphabet (Θ, θ)

THI temperature-humidity index

thiamine a vitamin, *not* -in

thias/os (Gr. antiquity) a gathering to worship a deity, *not* -us; pl. **-oi**

thicken/, **-ed**, **-er** *not* -or, **-ing**

thickset (one word)

thick space (typ.) a third of an em space

thimblerig/ (play) a swindling trick or game; **-ger**, **-ging** (one word)

thin/, **-ner**, **-nish**

thing/amy, **-umabob**, **-umajig**, **-ummy**, **-y** are the usual British variants; **-amabob**, **-amajig** are the usual US versions

think tank an advisory organization (two words)

thin space (typ.) a fifth of an em space, symbol ‡ *or* ⸶

third/ (adj.) abbr. **3rd**, **— country** (econ.) a country that does not participate in a customs union, specifically the EU

Third World (caps., no hyphen when attrib.)

Thirty-Nine Articles, the (hyphen, caps.)

thirty-second note (US mus.) a demisemiquaver

thirty-twomo (typ.) a book based on thirty-two leaves, sixty-four pages to the sheet; abbr. **32mo** (no point)

thirty-year rule (hyphen)

Thirty Years War 1618–48 (caps., no apos.)

tho' though

thole-pin (naut.) one of two which keep an oar in position; *not* -owl, -owel (hyphen)

thol/os (Gr. archit.) a dome-shaped building, esp. a tomb; pl. **-oi**

Thomas abbr. **Th.**, **Thos.**

Thom/ism the doctrine of St Thomas Aquinas, **-ist**

Thompson,/ **Sir Benjamin, Count von Rumford** (1753–1814) American-born founder of the Royal Institution, London; **—** **Sir D'Arcy Wentworth** (1860–1948) Scottish biologist; **—** **Sir Edward Maunde** (1840–1929) English librarian and palaeographer; **—** **Francis** (1859–1907) English poet; **—** **Silvanus** (*not* Sy-) **Phillips** (1851–1916) English physicist

Thomson/, **Prof. Arthur** (1858–1935) Scottish anatomist; **—**, **Sir Charles Wyville** (1830–82) Scottish zoologist; **—**, **James** (1700–48) Scottish poet, 'The Seasons'; **—**, **James** (1834–82) Scottish poet, pseud. **B.V.**, 'City of Dreadful Night'; **—**, **Prof. Sir John Arthur** (1861–1933) Scottish zoologist and writer; **—**, **Joseph** (1858–95) Scottish African traveller; **—**, **Prof.**

Sir Joseph John (1856–1940) English physicist; **—**, **Sir William, Baron Kelvin** (1824–1907) British mathematician and physicist (hence **kelvin**); **Barons — of Fleet** *and* **of Monifieth**

thor/ax (anat., zool.) the part of the body between neck and abdomen or tail, pl. **-aces**; adj. **-acic**

Thord(h)arson *properly* **Þórðarson** *see* **Sturla Þórðarson**

Thoreau, Henry David (1817–62) US author and philosopher

thorium symbol **Th**

thorn a runic letter, = *th*; in OE þ, Þ; by the late medieval period similar in form to y; in Icelandic Þ, þ. Distinguish from **eth** and **wyn**

thorough bass (mus.) harmony above bass indicated by system of numerals (two words)

thorough/bred, **-fare**, **-going** (one word)

Thos. Thomas

thou (colloq.) thousand, -th (no point or apos.)

though abbr. **tho'**

thousand-and-first etc. (hyphens)

thow(e)l-pin *use* **thole-**

thr. through

thral/l slave, bondage; **-dom** bondage

thrash/ beat soundly, strike the waves, make way in water; **— out** discuss exhaustively; cf. **thresh**

thread/bare, **-fin** (one word)

thread mark (in banknote paper)

Threadneedle Street/ London (two words), **The Old Lady of — —** the Bank of England

threadworm (one word)

three/fold, **-pence**, **-penny** (one word)

three-point turn (one hyphen)

three-quarter(s) (adj., hyphen)

three quarters (noun, two words)

three Rs, the reading, writing, arithmetic (no point, no apos.)

threescore (one word)

threescore and ten seventy (three words)

threesome (one word)

thresh beat and separate grain from corn etc.; cf. **thrash**

threshing/ floor, **— machine** (two words)

threshold *not* -hhold

thrips a plant pest (sing.)

thrive past **thrived** *or* **throve**, past part. **thrived**

thro' *use* **through**

Throckmorton, Sir Nicholas (1515–71) English diplomat

throes violent pangs

Throgmorton/ Avenue, **— Street** London

Throndhjem *use* **Trondheim**

throne a chair of State for a sovereign or bishop etc. (not cap.)

through *not* thro'; (US) up to and including, e.g. *Monday through Friday*, abbr. **thr.**

Thucydides (*c*.460–*c*.400 BC) Greek historian, abbr. **Thuc.**

thug/ a brutal ruffian (cap. with hist. ref. to assassins in India); **-gee** (hist.) the practice of the Thugs (*not* thagi except in modern specialist contexts), **-gery**

thuja Eng. form of the botanical *Thuya*, the arbor-vitae genus

Thule/ Greenland; **Southern —** S. Atlantic

thulium symbol **Tm**

thumb index (two words, hyphen as verb)

thumb/nail, -print, -screw, -tack (one word)

thunder (meteor.) abbr. **t.**

thunder/bolt, -box, -clap, -cloud, -head, -storm, -struck (one word)

Thüringen Austria; in (hist.) Eng. **Thuringia**, Fr. **Thuringe**, It. **Turingia**

Thursday abbr. **Th., Thur., Thurs.**

thuya *see* **thuja**

THWM Trinity High-Water Mark

thym/e the herb, adj. **-y** *not* -ey

Thynne family name of the Marquess of Bath

Ti titanium (no point)

ti (mus.) *use* **te**

Tiananmen Square Beijing, China

Tian-Shan a mountain range, Kyrgyzstan and China

tiara/ a turban, diadem, ornamental coronet; **-ed** *not* -'d

Tiber a river, Italy; in It. **Tevere**, Fr. **Tibre**

Tiberias ancient Palestine, *now* **Teverya** Israel

Tiberius (**Claudius Nero Caesar**) (42 BC–AD 37) second Emperor of Rome 14–37

Tibet/ in Tibetan **Bod**, in Pinyin **Xizang**; **-an** of or relating to Tibet, or (a member of) its people or its Tibeto-Burman language

Tibeto-Burman a family of languages distributed throughout Cent. and SE Asia

tibi/a (anat.) the inner bone from knee to ankle, pl. **-ae**

Tibullus, Albius (*c*.50–19 BC) Roman poet, abbr. **Tib.**

tic douloureux facial neuralgia, *not* dol-, not ital. (two words)

ticket/, **-ed, -ing**

ticket office (two words)

tickety-boo (hyphen)

tick-tack a regular beat, racecourse semaphore; *not* tic-tac

tick-tack-toe *or* **tic-tac-toe** (US) = **noughts and crosses**

Ticonderoga NY; a battleship (ital.)

t.i.d. (med.) *ter in die* (three times a day)

tidbit *use* **tit-** (except in US)

tiddly (sl.) tiny, slightly drunk; *not* -ey

tiddlywink/ a counter, **-s** the game; *not* tiddle(d)y- (US)

tideland (US) land that is submerged at high tide (one word)

tidemark (one word)

tide mill (two words)

tide table (two words)

tide/waiter, -water, -wave, -way (one word)

tie, tying *not* tieing

tie/-back, -break, -dye, -in (hyphen)

tiepin (one word)

tierce/ (arch.) a wine measure, (mus.) an interval of two octaves and a major third, a fencing position, a sequence of three cards; **-d** (her.) divided into three parts of different tinctures; cf. **terce-**

tierc/el, -et *use* **terc-**

Tierra del Fuego S. America, *not* Terra

Tiers/ État (Fr. m.) third estate, the common people; **— Monde** (Fr. m.) Third World (caps.)

Tietjens, Therese Cathline Johanna (1830–77) German-born Hungarian soprano, *not* Titiens

Tiffany,/ Charles Lewis (1812–92) US jeweller, founder of the New York jewellery store; his son **— Louis Comfort** (1848–1902) US interior designer

tiffany a gauze muslin (not cap.)

tiffin (Anglo-Ind.) a light lunch, *not* -ing

Tiflis *use* **Tbilisi**

tigerish *not* tigr-

Tighnabruaich Strathclyde

tight back (bind.) the cover glued to the back, so that it does not become hollow when open

tightrope (one word)

tigon the hybrid offspring of a tiger and lioness, *not* -glon (US); cf. **liger**

Tigre, Tigrinya two different Semitic languages of N. Ethiopia

tigrish *use* **tiger-**

TIH Their Imperial Highnesses

tike *use* **ty-**

tiki/ (NZ) a large wooden or small ornamental greenstone image representing a human figure, pl. **-s**

tilde a mark (˜) over a letter, e.g. in Sp. over *n* when pron. *ny* (as in *señor*), in Por. over *a* or *o* when nasalized (as in *São Paulo*); in Sp. may mean 'accent' in general; in Port. *til*

Tilsit/ a cheese (cap.); **Treaty of —** 1807; *not* -tt

Tim., 1, 2 First, Second Epistle to Timothy

timar/ (hist.) a fief held by military service under the feudal system of Turkey, in Pers. *tīmār*; **-iot** one holding a timar (not ital.)

timbal (arch.) the kettledrum

timbale/ (biol.) a drum-shaped membrane in certain insects (e.g. cicada), used to produce a shrill chirping sound; (cook.) a drum-shaped dish of minced meat or fish cooked in pastry or a mould; **-s** (mus.) a pair of single-headed drums played with drumsticks

timber dressed lumber for building etc., (US) rough (undressed) wood, forest

timbre the characteristic quality of sounds of a voice or instrument (not ital.)

Timbuktu Mali, *not* -buctoo; *but* **'Timbuctoo'** in Tennyson's prize-poem, 1829, and usually in a figurative sense; in Fr. **Tombouctou**

time symbol *t*

timeable *not* -mable

time-and-motion (adj., hyphens)

time/ bomb, — capsule, — clock, — exposure (two words)

time/-fuse, -honoured *not* -ored (US) (hyphens)

time immemorial (two words)

timekeeper (one word)

time/ lag, — limit (two words)

time of day (typ.) to be in numerals, with full point (colon in US) where time includes minutes and hours: 9.30 a.m. *or* 09.30; *but* phrases such as 'half past two', 'a quarter to four' to be spelt out

timeout (comput.) (one word)

timepiece (one word)

Times, The established 1788 (caps.), *not* The London Times. The (cap. T, ital.) is traditionally included in references, *but note* e.g. the *Sunday Times*, the *New York Times* do not follow this rule

time/scale -share (one word)

time/ sheet, — signal (two words)

time-stratigraphic unit (geol.) name given to a specific rock formation formed during a given time in a type area (e.g. Devonian); units of the higher orders (e.g. Cambrian, Ordovician) are given as headwords in this book

time switch (two words)

timetable (one word)

time warp (two words)

time-worn (hyphen, one word in US)

time zone (two words)

Timothy (NT) abbr. **Tim.**

timpan/o (mus.) the orchestral kettledrum, *not* ty-; pl. **-i**; cf. **tympanum**

tin symbol **Sn** (*stannum*)

tinct. tincture

Tindal, Matthew (1656–1733) English theologian, *not* -all; *see also* **Tyn-**

tinfoil (one word)

tingeing *not* -ging

tinhorn (US colloq.) a contemptible person (one word)

tin Lizzie a Model T Ford, hence any old motor car (one cap.)

Tin Pan Alley the world of popular music (three words, caps.), also with reference to the (hist.) district in New York City

tin plate (two words)

tinpot having poor leadership or organization (one word)

tinsel/, -led, -ling

Tintagel Corn., *not* -il

tintinnabulation the ringing sound of bells

tip in (bind.) to insert a plate etc. by pasting its inner margin to the next page

tip-off (noun, hyphen)

Tipperary a town and county, Ireland

tippet a cape, *not* tipet

tipstaff/ a bailiff, pl. **-s**

tip/toe, -toeing (one word)

tip-top (hyphen)

TIR international road transport, esp. with ref. to EU regulations (*transport international routier*)

tirailleur a sharpshooter or skirmisher (not ital.)

Tiranë Albania, *not* -na

tire of a wheel, *use* **ty-** (except in US)

tiré à part (Fr. typ. m.) an offprint

Tir-nan-Og (Ir. myth.) a land of perpetual youth, equivalent to Elysium (two caps., two hyphens)

tiro/ a novice, a new recruit; pl. **-s**; *not* ty- (US)

Tirol(o) *see* **Tyrol**

'tis for *it is* (apos., close up)

tisane an infusion of dried herbs etc.; cf. **ptisan**

Tisiphone (Gr. myth.) one of the Furies

'Tis Pity She's a Whore a play by John Ford, 1633, *not* 'Tis a …

Tit. Titus

tit. title

titanic of titanium, colossal (not cap., except with ref. to Titans)

Titanic the White Star liner sunk by an iceberg, 1912

titanium symbol **Ti**

titbit (one word) *not* tid- (US)

Titel/ (Ger. typ. m.) the title, ***-blatt*** (n.) title page, ***-zeile*** (f.) headline (caps.)

titer *use* **titre** (except in US)

tit for tat (three words)

titi a S. American monkey, an American evergreen shrub (one word)

ti-ti the New Zealand mutton-bird (hyphen)

Titian in It. **Tiziano Vecellio** (1477–1576) Venetian painter

Titiens *use* **Tietjens**

titillate excite pleasurably

titivate smarten up, *not* titt-

title deed (two words)

title/ page (typ.) properly the *full-title page*, as distinct from the *half-title page*; — **piece**, — **role** (two words)

titles (**cited**) articles, chapters, shorter poems, songs to be roman, quoted; series of books etc. to be roman, no quotes; books, periodicals, newspapers, epic poems, plays, operas, symphonies, ballets, works of art to be italic

title verso (typ.) the reverse of a title page (two words)

Tito/ pseud. of **Josip Broz** (1892–1980) President of Yugoslavia 1953–80, **-ism, -ist**; **-grad** former name of **Podgorica**

titre (chem.) the strength of a solution determined by titration, *not* -ter (US)

titre (Fr. typ. m.) title

tittivate *use* **titi-**

tittup/ behave or move in a lively way; **-ed, -ing, -py**

Titus/, Epistle to (NT) abbr. **Tit.**; — (Rom. praenomen) abbr. **T.**

T/-joint, -junction (caps., hyphens); *use* a sans serif typeface only where important to represent the actual configuration exactly

TKO technical knockout

Tl thallium (no point)

Tlemcen NW Algeria

TLS Times Literary Supplement

TLWM Trinity Low-Water Mark

TM transcendental meditation

Tm thulium (no point)

tmes/is (gram.) the division of a compound word by intervening word(s), pl. **-es**

TN Tennessee (postal abbr.)

tn (US) ton, town

TNT trinitrotoluene

TO Telegraph Office, turn over

toad/fish, -flax (one word)

toad-in-the-hole (hyphens)

toad/stone, -stool (one word)

to and fro (adv., three words)

toast/-master, -mistress (hyphens, one word in US)

toastrack (one word)

Toba Batak *see* **Batak**

Tobago island, part of Trinidad and Tobago; *not* Ta-

Tobermore Co. Londonderry

Tobermory Isle of Mull, Strathclyde

Tobit (Apocr.) not to be abbr.

toboggan/ *not* -ogan; **-er, -ing**

toby/ collar, — **jug** (two words, not cap.)

Toc H a society, orig. of ex-service personnel founded after the First World War (no point)

Tocharian (of or in) an extinct Indo-European language of a Cent. Asian people in the first millennium AD, or a member of the people speaking this language

Tocqueville, Alexis Charles Henri Maurice Clérel, comte de (1805–59) French statesman and political writer

tocsin an alarm bell or signal

to-do commotion (hyphen)

toe/ (verb), **-d, -ing**

toe/cap, -nail, -rag (one word)

toffee *not* -y

toga/ an ancient Roman mantle, pl. **-s**

together with takes a singular verb if the subject is singular

Togo/ Cent. W. Africa; adj. **-lese**

toile linen cloth

toilet *not* -ette

toilet/ paper, — powder, — roll, — set, — soap, — table (two words)

toilette (Fr. f.) toilet

toilet-train/, -ing (hyphen, two words in US)

toilet water (two words)

toing and froing (three words, no hyphens); (US) to-ing and fro-ing (hyphens)

Toison d'or (Fr. f.) the Golden Fleece

Tokaj Hungary; trad. Eng. **Tokay**, also for the region's **Tokaji** wine

Tokyo Japan, *not* -io; in Jap. **Tōkyō**; in Eng. formerly **Edo**, previously **Yeddo**

Toler in the family name of the Earl of Norbury

Tolkien, J(ohn) R(onald) R(euel) (1892–1973) English writer and scholar, *not* -ein

tollbooth (one word), *not* tol-

toll call (US) a long-distance (non-local) telephone call

Tolstoy, Count Leo (**Lev Nikolaevich**) (1828–1910) Russian novelist, *not* -oi

Toltec (of or related to) (a member of) an American Indian people that flourished in Mexico before the Aztecs, or their language

tomahawk a Native American war-axe, a hatchet

tomato/ pl. **-es**

tombola a kind of lottery using a drum-shaped container

tombolo a spit joining an island to the mainland

Tombouctou Fr. for **Timbuktu**

tom/boy, -cat (one word)

Tom Collins a gin-based iced cocktail

tome a large book or volume, usually thought of as a massive work of obscure learning

tome (Fr. m.) a volume, abbr. **t.**

tomfool/, **-ery** (one word)

Tommy a British private soldier (cap.)

tommy gun (not cap.; noun, two words; verb, hyphen)

tommyrot (one word)

Tompion, Thomas (?1639–1713) English clock maker

tompion *use* **tam-**

tomtit a small bird (one word)

tom-tom a kind of drum (hyphen)

ton/ (weight), **-s**; abbr. **t**

ton (Fr. m.) style

Tonbridge *but* **Tunbridge Wells** Kent

tond/**o** (It.) a painting or relief of circular form, pl. **-i** (not ital.)

tone poem (mus.) (two words)

tong a Chinese guild, association, or secret society

tongu/**e** (verb), **-ed**, **-ing**

tonic sol-fa (one hyphen)

Tonkin Vietnam; *not* Tongking, Tonquin, Tun-

tonn. tonnage

tonne a metric ton, equal to 1,000 kg, 0.984 long tons, or 1.102 short tons; abbr. **t**, **te**

tonneau the rear of a motor car

tonneau (Fr. m.) ton, tun, or cask; abbr. **t.**

tonsil/, **-lar**, **-lectomy**, **-litis**

ton/**y** (US colloq.) having 'tone', stylish or fashionable; *not* -ey; **-ier**, **-iest**

toolbox (one word)

tooling (bind.) impressing a design or lettering on the (usually leather) binding by hand

toolmaker (one word)

tooth/**ache**, **-brush**, **-comb**, **-paste**, **-pick**, **-some**, **-wort** (one word)

topcoat (one word)

topgallant (naut.) the mast, sail, yard, or rigging immediately above the topmast and topsail (one word)

top-heavy (hyphen)

Tophet (Scripture) hell, in Heb. *tōpet*

topi (Anglo-Ind.) a hat, *not* -pee

top/**knot**, **-less**, **-mast** (one word)

top-notch first-rate (hyphen)

topog. topograph/y, -ical

top/**os** a stock theme in literature etc., pl. **-oi**

topsail (one word)

tops and tails (typ.) preliminary matter and index etc.

topside (naut.) the ship's side between waterline and deck, also of beef (one word)

topsoil (one word)

Topsy a character in Stowe's novel *Uncle Tom's Cabin*

topsy-turvy (hyphen)

Torah, the the Jewish term for the Pentateuch, in Heb. *tōrāh*

Tor Bay Devon

Torbay a town, Devon

torc (hist.) a necklace of twisted metal, esp. of the ancient Gauls and Britons; cf. **torque**

torchère a tall stand with a small table for a candlestick etc. (not ital.)

torchlight (one word)

tori pl. of **torus**

torii the gateway of a Shinto shrine; pl. same

Torino It. for **Turin**

tormentor *not* -er

tornado/ pl. **-es**

torniquet *use* **tour-**

torpedo/ pl. **-es**

Torphichen, Baron

torque (mech.) the moment of a system of forces tending to cause rotation; cf. **torc**

Torquemada, Tomás de (1420–98) Spanish Inquisitor

torr (phys.) a unit of pressure, with numbers **Torr** (no point); its use is now discouraged

Torres Vedras a fortified town near Lisbon, Portugal; battle, 1810

torse (her.) a wreath

torso/ (a representation of) the human trunk; something unfinished or mutilated; pl. **-s**

tort/ (law) a breach of duty (other than under contract) leading to liability for damages; **-feasor** a person guilty of tort; **-ious** constituting a tort, wrongful; cf. **tortuous**; **torturous**

torte/ an elaborate sweet cake or tart, pl. **-n**

tortilla (Mexican cook.) a thin flat unleavened maize or wheat cake

tortoiseshell (one word)

tortue/ (Fr. f.) turtle, — *claire* clear turtle soup

tortuous full of twists and turns, devious, circuitous, crooked; cf. **tortious**; **torturous**

torturous concerning torture; cf. **tortious**; **tortuous**

Tory (of or related to) the British Conservative Party; (US hist.) a loyal colonist during the American Revolution

Toscana It. for **Tuscany**

Toscanini, Arturo (1867–1957) Italian conductor

Tosk one of two main dialects of Albanian, the basis for standard Albanian; *see also* **Geg**

total/, **-led**, **-ling** (one *l* in US)

totalizator a betting device, colloq. 'the tote'; *but* **Horserace Totalisator Board**

totalize collect into a total, *not* -ise

t'other (colloq.) the other, *not* tother

totidem verbis (Lat.) in so many words

toties quoties (Lat.) the one as often as the other

toto caelo (Lat.) diametrically opposed, *not* coe-

touchdown (one word) abbr. **TD**

touché acknowledging a hit (not ital.)

touchline (one word)

touch/-tone, -type (hyphen)

touchwood readily inflammable wood (one word)

Toulouse-Lautrec, Henri Marie Raymonde de (1864–1901) French painter

toupee a wig; *not* -ée, -et

tour/ (Fr. m.) a tour; (f.) tower; — *à tour* alternately, in turn (ital.)

touraco *use* tur-

tour de force a feat of strength or skill (not ital.)

tour/ de main (Fr. m.) sleight of hand, *-d'horizon* a broad survey or summary; pl. *-s* — — (ital.)

touring car (two words)

tourmaline a mineral, sometimes cut as a gem; *not* -in

Tournai Belgium; in Fl. **Doornik**, *formerly* in Eng. **Tournay**

Tournay France

tournedos a small round thick cut from a fillet of beef, pl. same

tourney (take part in) a tournament

tourniquet a bandage etc. for stopping flow of blood, *not* torn-

Toussaint L'Ouverture, François (1743–1803) Haitian general and liberator, in Fr. **Louverture** (no apos.)

tout/ à coup (Fr.) suddenly; — *à fait* entirely; — *court* abruptly, or simply; — *de même* all the same; — *de suite* immediately; — *d'un coup* all at once; *le* — *ensemble* the general effect; — *le monde* all the world, everybody (no hyphens)

tovarishch/ (Russ. m. or f.), comrade, pl. *-i*; in Eng. **tovarish** (not ital.); *see also* **grazhdanin**

towel/, -led, -ling (one *l* in US)

town abbr. **t.**

town councillor *not* -ilor, abbr. **TC** (two words)

town/hall, — house (two words)

townie *not* -ee

Townshend, Marquess

township abbr. **t.**

toxaemia blood poisoning, *not* -xemia (US)

toxicol. toxicolog/y, -ical

toxin a poison, *not* -ine

toxophilite a student or lover of archery

Toys "Я" Us a retail chain (double quotes, reverse *R*)

Tpr. Trooper

Tr. trustee

tr. transitive, translat/ed, -ion, -or; transfer, -red

Trabzon Turkey

tracasserie a fuss or state of annoyance (not ital.)

trace/able, -ability *not* -cable

trache/a the windpipe, pl. **-ae**

track/ record, — shoe (two words)

tracksuit (one word)

Tractarian/, -ism the Oxford or High Church Movement of the mid-19th c. (cap.)

tractor *not* -er

trad (colloq.) traditional (music, no point), also as abbr. (with point)

tradable *not* -eable

trade/ book, — cycle, — edition, — gap (two words)

trademark (one word, *but* two in law)

trade/ name, — secret, — wind (two words)

trades/man, -people, -woman (one word)

trade/ union (*not* trades union) pl. — **unions** (two words), abbr. **TU**; *but* **Trades Union Congress** abbr. **TUC**; — **unionism, — unionist** (two words)

trade wind (two words)

trading post (two words)

traduction (Fr. f.) translation

traffic/, -ked, -ker, -king

traffic circle (US) = **roundabout**

traffic/ jam, — light *or* — **signal, — sign, — warden** (two words)

trag. tragedy, tragic

tragedi/an a writer of tragedies, a tragic actor; **-enne** a tragic actress

tragicomedy a drama of mixed tragic and comic elements (one word)

trahison des clercs (Fr. f.) the betrayal of standards, scholarship, etc. by the intellectuals

trailer an unpowered vehicle towed by another, (US) = **caravan**

train-bearer (hyphen, one word in US)

train/man, -men (one word)

train oil oil obtained from whale blubber (two words)

trainsick (one word)

trainspott/er, -ing (one word)

traipse trudge, *not* -apes

trait a characteristic

trait d'union (Fr. typ. m.) the hyphen

Trajectum ad Rhenum *see* **Utrecht**

tram/, -car, -lines (one word)

trammel/ entangle; **-led, -ling** (one *l* in US)

tramontana a cold north wind in the Adriatic (not ital.)

tramontane (a person) situated or living on the other side of mountains, foreign; *not* trans-; in It. *tramontano*

trampoline a sprung canvas sheet used by acrobats, gymnasts, etc.; *not* -in

tranche a portion of income etc. (not ital.)

tranny (colloq.) a transistor radio, a transparency; *not* -ie

tranquil/, -lity, -lize *not* -ise (one l in US), **-ly**

trans. transactions, transitive; translat/ed, -ion, -or

transact/, -or

transalpine beyond the Alps, esp. from the Italian point of view (one word, not cap.); cf. **cisalpine**

transatlantic beyond or crossing the Atlantic, esp. (Brit.) American, and (US) European (one word, not cap.)

transcontinental (one word)

transcript a written or recorded copy (usually of speech)

transexual *use* **transs-**

transf. transferred

transfer/, -able, -ee, -ence, -red, -rer, -ring

transgress/ pass beyond the limit of; **-ible, -or**

tranship/, -ment *use* trans-s-

transition a literary monthly 1927–38 (not cap.)

transitive (gram.) (of verb) taking a direct object; abbr. **trans., transit.**

Transkei S. Africa

translat/ed, -ion, -or abbr. **tr., trans.; -able**

trans/missible (med.), **-mittable** (physics)

transmogrify *not* -morg-

transmontane *use* **tram-**

transonic relating to speeds close to that of sound, *not* trans-sonic

transpacific beyond or crossing the Pacific (one word)

transpontine on the other side of a bridge, esp. on the south side of the Thames; *see also* **cispontine**

transpose/ (typ.) to interchange letters, words, lines of type, etc.; — **mark** ⌐

transsexual *not* transexual

trans-ship/, -ment (hyphens, one word in US), *not* transh-

trans-sonic *use* **transonic**

Transvaal a province of S. Africa, abbr. **Tvl.**

transverse (adj.) situated, arranged, or acting in a crosswise direction; cf. **traverse**

Transylvania a part of Romania, before 1919 part of Hungary; Romanian **Transilvania**, Hung. **Erdély**, Ger. **Siebenbürgen**

trapes *use* **traipse**

trapezi/um a quadrilateral with only one pair of sides parallel; (US) a quadrilateral with no two sides parallel; pl. **-a**

trapezoid/ a quadrilateral with no two sides parallel; (US) a quadrilateral with only one pair of sides parallel; pl. **-s**

trash/ (US) refuse, rubbish; — **can** (US) = **dustbin** (two words)

trattoria an Italian-style restaurant (not ital.)

trauma/ a wound or shock, pl. **-s**

travail/, -ed, -ing

travel/, -led, -ler, -ling (one l in US)

travel agent (two words)

Travellers' Club London (*not* 's)

travelogue *not* -og (US)

traverse (verb) travel, lie across, turn horizontally, consider or discuss the whole extent, thwart or oppose, (law) deny; (noun) a sideways movement, a thing that crosses another, an act of traversing; cf. **transverse**

travois a drag sledge used by Native Americans, pl. same

Trawsfynydd Gwynedd

TRC Thames Rowing Club

tread past **trod**, past part. **trodden**

treadmill (one word)

Treas. treasurer, treasury

trecent/o 1300–99, and the Italian art and literature of that century; **-ist** (not ital.)

tre corde (mus.) direction in piano-music to release soft pedal; cf. **una corda**

treen (treated as pl.) small domestic wooden objects, esp. antiques

trefa *or* **tref** not kosher, *not* the many variants; in Heb. ṭᵉrēpāh

Treitschke, Heinrich von (1834–96) German historian

trek/ (to make) an arduous journey; *not* -ck; **-ked, -ker, -king**

trellis/ *not* -ice, **-work** (hyphen, one word in US)

trematode (noun or adj.) (of) a flatworm, *not* -oid

tremolo/ (mus.) a tremulous effect or device producing this, pl. **-s**

tremor *not* -our

Trengganu *see* **Malaya, Federation of**

trente-et-quarante (Fr. m.) a game of chance, *rouge-et-noir* (hyphens)

Trento Italy; in hist. contexts the older Eng. form **Trent** is still used, e.g. for the Council of Trent and the Trent Codices; in Fr. **Trente**, Ger. **Trient**

trepan/ (to use) a surgeon's cylindrical saw, a borer; to trap; **-ation, -ned, -ning**

trepang bêche-de-mer, a sea cucumber

Tresco Scilly

Trescowe Corn.

Tresilian Bay S. Glam.

Tresillian Corn.

Tressell, Robert pseud. of **Robert Noonan** (?1870–1911) English novelist

Trèves Fr. for **Trier**

trevet *use* tri-

TRH Their Royal Highnesses

Triassic (geol.) (of or relating to) the earliest period of the Mesozoic era

trib. tribal, tribun/e, -al, tributary

tribrach (prosody) a foot of three short or unstressed syllables

tricolour (a flag) having three colours, esp. the French flag; in Fr. m. *drapeau tricolore*

tricorne (an imaginary animal) with three horns, a cocked hat; *not* -n

Tridentine of or relating to the Council of Trent, held at Trento in Italy 1545–63, esp. as the basis of RC doctrine; a RC adhering to this trad. doctrine and practice (cap.)

trienni/al lasting, or occurring every, three years; **-um** a period of three years, pl. **-ums**

Trier Germany; *not* -rs, Trèves

trig. trigonometry

trigesimo-secundo *use* **thirty-twomo**

trigon. trigonometr/y, -ical

trillion a million million (10^{12}); in France (since 1948), Germany, and formerly in Britain, a million million million (10^{18}); corresponds to the change in use of **billion**; avoid ambiguity

trimeter (prosody) a verse of three measures

Trin. Trinidad, Trinity

Trinidad and Tobago W. Indies

Trinity Sunday the one after Whit Sunday

triphthong a union of three vowels (letters *or* sounds) pron. in one syllable (as in *fire*), or three vowels representing the sound of a single vowel (as in *beau*)

Tripitaka the sacred canon of Theravada Buddhism, written in Pali

Tripoli/ Libya, in Arab. **Ṭarābulus al-Ġarb** ('Tripoli of the West'); Lebanon, in Arab. **Ṭarābulus ash-Shām**; *properly* **Ṭarābulus al-Ša'm** ('Tripoli of Syria'), in local pronunciation **Trâblous**; **-tania** the coastal region surrounding Tripoli in Libya

tripoli rottenstone (not cap.)

tripos the honours examination for the BA degree at Cambridge

triptych a set of three painted or carved panels, hinged together; or a similarly associated set of pictures

triptyque a customs permit serving as a passport for a motor vehicle

triquetr/a a symmetrical ornament of three interlaced arcs, pl. **-ae**; **-al**

trireme an ancient Greek ship with three banks of oars on each side

Tristan da Cunha S. Atlantic, *not* d'Acunha

Tristan und Isolde an opera by Wagner, 1865

Tristram a knight of the Round Table; also spelt Tristran, Tristrand, Trystan, etc.

tritium symbol **T**

triturat/e grind finely, **-or**

triumvir/ one of a committee of three; Eng. pl. **-s**; Lat. pl. **-i** (the earlier and more correct Lat. pl. is **tresviri** (three men)); collective noun **-ate**

trivet an iron tripod or bracket, *not* tre-

trivia trifles, is pl.

trivium (hist.) a medieval university course of grammar, rhetoric, and logic; cf. **quadrivium**

tri-weekly produced or occurring three times a week or every three weeks; to avoid confusion, spell out what is meant

tRNA transfer RNA, *not* sRNA

trocar (med.) an instrument for withdrawing fluid from the body, *not* troch-

troche (med.) a medicated lozenge

troch/ee a foot of two syllables (- ˘); **-aic**

Troilus and Cressida a play by Shakespeare, c.1602; *but* **Troilus and Criseyde** a poem by Chaucer, c.1387

trolley *not* -lly

trollop a disreputable girl or woman, a prostitute

Trollope,/ Anthony (1815–82) and — **Frances** (1780–1863) his mother, English novelists

trompe-l'œil (Fr. m.) an illusion, esp. in still-life painting or plaster ornament (pl. same)

Trondheim Norway; *not* Th-; in Ger. **Dront-**; in Dan. **-hjem**

troop/ an assembly of soldiers etc.; in pl. of armed forces generally; **-er** abbr. **Tpr.**; **-ing the colour** *not* of the colours; cf. **troupe**

tropaeolum/ a trailing plant, pl. **-s**; as a botanical genus, *Tropaeolum*

trop/e a figurative (e.g. metaphorical or ironical) use of a word or words, **-ology**

trophic of or concerned with nutrition

tropical (not cap.)

tropic/ of Cancer, — of Capricorn; the -s region between these two (one cap.)

troposphere the lower atmosphere; cf. **strato-**

troppo/ (mus.) too much, **ma non** — but not too much so

Trotsky/, Leon pseud. of **Lev Davidovich Bronstein** (1879–1940) Russian revolutionary; *not* -tz-, -ki; **-ism, -ist, -ite**

trottoir (Fr. m.) footway, pavement

trouble/maker, -shooter (one word)

troup/e a company of performers; **-er** one of these, or a staunch colleague; cf. **troop**

trousseau/ the clothes collected by a bride for her marriage, pl. **-s** (not ital.)

trouvaille (Fr. f.) a lucky find

trouvère a medieval poet in N. France in the 11th–14th cc., composing in *langue d'oïl*

trowel/, -led, -ling (one *l* in US)

troy weight (not cap.) 1 troy pound (approx. 373 g) = 12 troy ounces or 5,760 grains; 1 troy ounce = 20 pennyweights

TRRL Transport and Road Research Laboratory

trs. (print.) transpose, trustees

Trucial States former name of the United Arab Emirates

Trudeau, Pierre (**Elliott**) (b. 1919) Canadian Prime Minister 1968–79, 1980–4

Truffaut, François (1932–84) French film director

Truman, Harry S (1884–1972) US politician, President 1945–53 (no point after the *S*, as it stands for nothing: he had no middle name)

trumpet/, -ed, -ing

Truron: the signature of the Bishop of Truro (colon)

Trustee abbr. **Tr.**, pl. **Trs.**

TS (paper) tub-sized, typescript

tsar/ (hist.) the title of the former emperor of Russia; **-evich** his eldest son, *not* cesarevitch; **-evna** his daughter; **-ina** his wife (in Russ. *tsaritsa*) (caps. as titles); *not* cs-, cz- (US), tz-

Tsaritsyn Russia, *now* Volgograd

Tsarskoe Selo the imperial residence near St Petersburg; renamed Detskoe Selo and, later, Pushkin; *not* Tz-, Z-

TSB Trustee Savings Bank

Tschaikowsky, P. I. *use* **Tchaikovsky**

tsetse African fly, *not* tzetze

TSH Their Serene Highnesses, thyroid-stimulating hormone

T-shirt (hyphen) *not* tee shirt

Tsigane (Fr. m. and f.) a Hungarian Gypsy, a tzigane

tsp teaspoon(ful)

T-square (hyphen) *not* tee-

TSS typescripts

tsunami/ a long tidal wave (not ital.); pl. **-s**

t.s.v.p. (Fr.) *tournez s'il vous plaît*, = PTO

Tswana (a member of) a southern African people living in Botswana and neighbouring areas; *see also* **Setswana**

TT teetotal, Tourist Trophy, tuberculin tested

TTS (typ., compositing) teletypesetting

TU trade union, -s

tuba/ the bass saxhorn, pl. **-s**

Tube, the the London Underground system

Tübingen a town and university, Germany

TUC Trades Union Congress

tuck/-box, -net (hyphens)

tuck shop (two words, one word in US)

Tudor (hist.) of, characteristic of, or associated with the royal family of England ruling 1485–1603, or this period

Tuesday abbr. **Tu.**, **Tue.**, **Tues.**

tugrik a monetary unit of Mongolia, pl. same

Tuileries Paris (one *l*)

tularaemia a severe infectious disease of animals transmissible to man, *not* -remia (US)

tulle a fine silk fabric

tumble/down, -weed (one word)

tumbrel a cart, *not* -il

tumour a morbid growth, *not* -or (US)

tumul/us an ancient burial mound, pl. **-i** (not ital.)

tun/ a large beer or wine cask, or a brewer's fermenting vat; a measure of capacity; pl. **-s**; abbr. **t.**

Tunbridge Wells *but* **Tonbridge** Kent

tuneable *not* tunable

Tungking *use* **Tonkin**

tungsten wolfram, symbol **W**

Tunisia N. Africa; capital Tunis

tunnel/, -led, -ling (one *l* in US)

Tupamaro a Marxist urban guerrilla in Uruguay

Tupi (of or relating to) (a member of) a Native American people living in the Amazon valley, or their language; pl. same

tu quoque! (Lat.) so are you!

turaco/ a large African bird, pl. **-s**; *not* tou-, -cou, -ko

Turanian (of or relating to) the group of Asian languages that are neither Semitic nor Indo-European, esp. the Ural-Altaic family

turbid muddy, thick, unclear; (of a style) confused or disordered

turbo/charger, -fan, -jet, -prop, -shaft (one word)

Turco/ (hist.) an Algerian soldier in the French army, pl. **-s**; *not* -ko

Turco- a prefix meaning *Turkish*, *not* Turko-

Turcoman *use* **Turkoth**

Turcophile one friendly to the Turks

Turgenev, Ivan (**Sergeevich**) (1818–83) Russian novelist, *not* the many variants

turgid swollen, inflated, enlarged; (of language) pompous, bombastic

Turin Italy, in It. **Torino**

Turk, Young *see* **Young Turk**

Turk. Turk/ey, -ish

Turkey in Turk. **Türkiye**, Fr. **Turquie**, Ger. **Türkei**, It. **Turchia**

Turkey red (one cap.)

Turki (of or relating to) a group of Ural-Altaic languages (including Turkish), and the people speaking them

Turkic a group of languages spoken in Asia Minor

Turkish the language of Turkey

Turkish/ bath, — carpet, — coffee, — delight, — towel (two words, one cap.)

Turkistan a region of Cent. Asia, *not* Turke-

Turkmenistan Cent. Asia, a former Soviet Socialist Republic

Turko- *use* **Turco-**

Turkoman/ an inhabitant or language of Turkmenistan, *not* Turco-; pl. **-s** *not* -men

Turku Finland, in Swed. **Åbo**

turn/coat, -cock (one word)

turned/ comma (typ.) an opening quote produced (as if) by printing a comma upside down ('); **— sort** (typ.) a sort printed upside down or on its side

Turner, Joseph Mallord William *not* Mallad, -ard (1775–1851) English painter

turning/ circle, — point (two words)

turnkey (one word)

turn-line (typ.) a line wider than the measure, which finishes on a following line; the second or subsequent line of a paragraph (hyphen)

turn/-off, -on (nouns, hyphens, one word in US)

Turnour family name of Earl Winterton

turn-out (noun, hyphen, one word in US)

turn over abbr. **TO**

turnover/ (noun and adj., one word); **— line** *see* **turn-line**

turn/pike, -side (one word)

turn signal (US) = **indicator** (vehicle)

turn/spit, -stile, -stone, -table (one word)

turn-up/ an unexpected surprise (hyphen, one word in US), **-s** cuffs on trouser legs (hyphen)

turtle dove (two words, one in US)

turtleneck (one word)

Tuscany Italy; in It. **Toscana**, Fr. **Toscane**, Ger. **Toskana**

Tuskar Rock a lighthouse, Co. Wexford

Tuskegee Institute Ala.

tussock a clump of grass, *not* -ac(k)

tussore an Indian or Chinese silk(worm); *not* -ah (US), -er

Tutankhamun an Egyptian pharaoh, *not* -amen

Tutsi (of or relating to) a people of Rwanda and Burundi, pl. same; *not* Watusi, Watutsi

tutti/ (mus.) (passage performed with) all instruments or voices together, pl. **-s**

tutti-frutti a confection flavoured with mixed fruits (hyphen)

tutu a ballet dancer's skirt, NZ shrub (one word)

tuum (Lat.) thine; *see also* **meum**

Tuvalu/ W. Pacific; **-an**

tu-whit, tu-whoo (make) an owl's cry

tuxedo/ (US) a dinner jacket, black tie; pl. **-s**

tuyère a furnace nozzle, *not* twyer

TV television

TVA (US) Tennessee Valley Authority

Tvl. Transvaal

TVP (propr.) textured vegetable protein

Twain, Mark *see* **Clemens**

'twas for *it was* (apos., close up)

Tweeddale/ a district of Borders; **Marquis of —**

Twelfth/ Day 6 Jan., **— Night** 5–6 Jan.

twelvemo *see* **duodecimo**

twenty-fourmo (typ.) a book based on twenty-four leaves, forty-eight pages, to the sheet; abbr. **24mo**

twentymo (typ.) a book based on twenty leaves, forty pages, to the sheet; abbr. **20mo**

'twere, 'twill for *it were, it will* (apos., close up)

twerp a stupid or objectionable person, *not* -irp

twilit illuminated (as if) by twilight

Twisleton-Wykeham-Fiennes the family name of Baron Saye and Sele (two hyphens); *see also* **Fiennes**

'twixt for *betwixt* (apos.)

two/-bit (US) cheap, petty (hyphen); **— bits** a quarter of a dollar (two words)

two-faced (adj., hyphen)

twofold (one word)

two/pence, -penny (one word)

twosome (one word)

two/-step, -stroke, -time, -timer, -ton, -tone (hyphens)

'twould for *it would* (apos., close up)

two-way (hyphen)

TX Texas (postal abbr.)

TYC Thames Yacht Club

tyke an objectionable fellow, a mongrel, a small child, (sl.) a Yorkshireman; *not* ti-

Tyler,/ John (1790–1862) US President 1841–5; **— Wat** (d. 1381) English rebel

Tylers and Bricklayers livery company

Tylor, Sir Edward Burnett (1832–1917) English anthropologist

tympan (print.) an appliance in a printing press used to equalize pressure between the platen etc. and a printing sheet

tympan/um (med.) the eardrum, (archit.) a vertical triangular space forming the centre of a pediment or arch; pl. **-a**; cf. **timpano**

Tyndale, William (1484–1536) English priest and translator of the Bible, burnt at the stake

Tyndall, John (1820–93) English physicist

Tyne and Wear a metropolitan county

Tynemouth Tyne & Wear; *see also* **Teign-**

Tynwald/ the parliament of the Isle of Man, **— Day** 5 July

typ. typograph/er, -ic, -ical, -ically

type/**cast, -face** (one word)

type/ **founder, — foundry** (two words, one word in US)

type metal an alloy of lead, antimony, and tin (two words)

typescript prefer to *manuscript* for any document typewritten, printed by computer or typesetter, or otherwise not written by hand; abbr. **TS**, pl. **TSS** (no points)

type/**setter, -setting, -writer, -written** (one word)

tyrannize *not* -ise

Tyre Lebanon; in Arab. **Ṣūr**, Fr. **Tyr**, Ger. **Tyrus**

tyre (of a wheel) *not* ti- (US)

Tyrian/ (a native or citizen) of, *or* relating to, ancient Tyre in Phoenicia; — **purple** a crimson dye obtained from some molluscs

tyro *use* **tiro** (except in US)

Tyrol/ a region of Austria and Italy; in Ger. **Tirol**, It. **Tirolo**; adj. **-ean, -ese**; **South —** a region belonging to Italy since 1919; in Ger. **Südtirol**, It. **Alto Adige**

Tyutchev, Fyodor (**Ivanovich**) (1803–73) Russian lyric poet and diplomat

tzar etc., *use* **ts-**

Tzarskoye Selo *use* **Tsarskoe Selo**

tzatziki a Greek side dish of yogurt with cucumber

Tzeltal, Tzotzil the names for two distinct American Indian peoples inhabiting parts of S. Mexico, or the Mayan language of each

tzetze *use* **tsetse**

tzigane a Hungarian Gypsy, or characteristic of the tziganes or (esp.) their music; in Magyar *cigány*, Fr. m. and f. **Tsigane**, Ger. m. **Zigeuner**

tzolkin the cycle of 260 days constituting a year in the Mayan sacred calendar

Tz'u Chou a district in NE China; the pottery made there from the Sui dynasty onwards; in Pinyin **Cizhou**

U upper class (*see also* **non-U**), uranium, a film-censorship classification, the twentieth in a series; Burmese title of respect before a man's name (e.g. U Nu, U Thant), equivalent to 'Mr' (not an abbr.); (Du.) you (polite, sing. and pl.)

U. Unionist

u unified atomic mass unit

u. (meteor.) ugly, threatening weather; (Ger.) *und* (and), *unter* (among)

Ü, ü in German etc., is not to be replaced by *Ue, ue*, except in some proper names and historical spellings, or *U, u*

u. a. (Ger.) *unter anderem* (among other things)

u. ä. (Ger.) *und ähnliche(s)* (and the like) (space in Ger.)

UAE United Arab Emirates

u. a. m. (Ger.) *und andere(s) mehr* (and so on) (spaces in Ger.)

UAR (hist.) United Arab Republic 1958–71

U-bend (cap., hyphen) *use* a sans serif typeface only where it is important to represent the actual configuration exactly

Übersetzung (Ger. f.) translation

ubique (Lat.) everywhere

ubi supra (Lat.) in the place (mentioned) above, abbr. **u.s.**

U-boat a German submarine (hyphen), in Ger. n. (colloq.) **U-Boot**, in full **Unterseeboot**

UC University College

u.c. (typ.) upper case, (It. mus.) una corda

UCATT Union of Construction, Allied Trades, and Technicians

UCC Universal Copyright Convention

UCCA Universities Central Council on Admissions (no apos.)

UCD University College, Dublin

UCH University College Hospital, London

UCL University College London

UCLA University of California at Los Angeles

UCS University College School

UCW Union of Communications Workers, University College of Wales

UDA Ulster Defence Association

Udaipur India; *not* Odeypore, Oodey-, Ude-

udal a freehold right based on uninterrupted possession; *not* od-; **-ler, -man** (one word)

Udall, Nicholas (1505–56) English playwright

UDC Universal Decimal Classification, (hist.) Urban District Council

UDI unilateral declaration of independence

UDR Ulster Defence Regiment

UEA University of East Anglia

UEFA Union of European Football Associations

UFC United Free Church (of Scotland)

Uffizi Gallery *and* **Palace** Florence, *not* -izzi

UFO/ unidentified flying object; pl. **-s**

ufology the study of UFOs (not cap.)

Ugand/a Africa; **-an**

UGC University Grants Committee

Ugley Essex

Ugli/ (propr.) a citrus fruit, pl. **-s** (cap.)

Ugric of or relating to a branch of the Finno-Ugric language family, *also* **Ugrian**

UHF ultra-high frequency

UHT ultra heat treated (esp. of milk, cream, etc. for keeping long)

u.i. *ut infra* (as below)

Uitlander (Afrik.) a foreigner, esp. before the Boer War

UJD *Utriusque Juris Doctor* (Doctor of Laws)

uji/ in feudal and pre-feudal Japan, a name indicating to which ancestral family the bearer belonged; a patriarchal lineage group of all those with the same *uji*; **-gami** the ancestral deity of an *uji*, or (later) a tutelary deity (one word)

UK United Kingdom

UKAEA United Kingdom Atomic Energy Authority

ukase an arbitrary command, (hist.) an edict of the tsarist Russian government; *not* oukaz; in Russ. **ukaz**

ukiyo-e a style and school of Japanese art (hyphen)

Ukrain/e E. Europe; a former republic of the USSR; abbr. **Ukr.**; *not* -ia, Little Russia, the Ukraine (which implies a region rather than a state); **-ian** (of or relating to) (a native or the language of) Ukraine

ukulele a small guitar, *not* uke-

Ulan Bator *properly* **Ulaanbaatar**; **Ulaangom, Ulaanhus** Mongolia

Ulan-Burgasy mountains, Russia

ulema (a member of) a body of Muslim doctors of sacred law and theology; in Arab. (pl.) ʿ**ulamā**

Ullswater Cumbria, *not* Ulles-

uln/a lower-arm bone, pl. **-ae** (not ital.)

ulotrich/an (a person) having tightly curled hair, esp. denoting a human type; also **-ous**

Ulster/ Ireland, comprises the present N. Ireland and the counties of Cavan, Donegal, and Monaghan; **-man, -woman** (one word)

ulster a coat (not cap.)

ult. *see* **ultimo**

ultima ratio/ (Lat.) the final sanction, last resource; —— **regum** resort to arms

ultima Thule a distant unknown region (one cap., ital.)

ultimatum/ a final proposal, pl. **-s**

ultimo in, or of, the last month; better not abbr.

ultimum vale (Lat.) the last farewell

ultimus haeres (Lat., the final heir) the Crown or the State

ultra/ (Lat.) beyond, extreme; — **vires** beyond legal power

ultra-high (of frequency) (hyphen)

ultra/ist, -ism

Ultrajectum *see* **Utrecht**

ultramontane (a person) situated or living on the other side of the Alps from the point of view of the speaker, (a person) advocating supreme papal authority in matters of faith and discipline

ultramundane lying beyond the world or the solar system, *not* extremely dull

ultra/sonic, -violet (one word)

Uluru *see* **Ayers Rock**

Ulyanov *see* **Lenin**

Ulysses *see* **Odysseus**

Um/bala, -balla *use* **Ambala**

umbel/ (bot.) a flower cluster; **-lar, -late**

umble pie *use* **humble**

umbo/ the boss of a shield, pl. **-s**

umbr/a (astr.) a shadow, pl. **-ae**

UMI University Microfilms International

umiak an Inuit skin-and-wood open boat used by women, *not* oom-

UMIST University of Manchester Institute of Science and Technology

umlaut mark (¨) used over a vowel, esp. in Germanic languages to indicate a vowel change

Umritsur *use* **Amritsar**

UN United Nations; *not* UNO, Uno

'un/ colloq. for *one* (as in *good 'un, young 'un*), pl. **-s** (apos.)

UNA United Nations Association

una corda (mus.) direction in piano music to use soft pedal; cf. **tre corde**

unadvisable (of person) not open to advice; cf. **inadvisable**

un-American (hyphen, cap.)

unanim/ous, -ity (**a** *not* an)

unartistic not concerned with or appreciating art; cf. **inartistic**

una voce (Lat.) unanimously

unberufen (Ger.) *absit omen*

unbiblical (one word)

unbusinesslike (one word)

uncared-for (hyphen)

unchristian (one word, not cap.)

uncome-at-able inaccessible (two hyphens)

uncooperative (one word)

uncoordinated (one word)

UNCSTD United Nations Conference on Science and Technology for Development

UNCTAD United Nations Conference on Trade and Development

unctuous greasy (usually of manner), *not* -ious

under- (prefix) when joined to nouns, adjs., advs., and verbs, normally forms one word (*see* entries below), *but note* **under-secretary**.

under/achieve, -act (one word)

under age below an age limit (two words, hyphen when attrib.)

under/brush (US) = **undergrowth, -carriage, -clothes, -coat, -cover** (adj.), **-current, -cut, -developed, -dog, -emphasis, -emphasize** *not* -ise, **-employed, -estimate, -expose, -ground, -growth, -hand** (one word)

underlie *but* **underlying**

underline (typ.) former term for a caption to illustration, diagram, etc. (regardless of position)

under/manned, -mentioned (one word)

Under Milk Wood a radio drama by Dylan Thomas, 1954 (three words)

under/part, -pass, -privileged (one word)

underproof containing less alcohol than proof spirit does (one word); abbr. **u.p.**

underrate (one word)

under-runners (typ.) an excess of marginal notes, which are continued below the body of text, generally at foot of page (hyphen, one word in US), cf. **shoulder note**

undersea (one word)

under-secretary (caps. as title, hyphen, one word in US)

under/sell, -sexed (one word)

under-sheriff a deputy sheriff (hyphen)

undershirt (US) = **vest**

under/shrub, -side, -signed, -sized, -skirt, -staffed, -surface, -tone, -value, -water (adj.) (one word)

under way in motion (two words)

underweight (one word)

underwrite/, -r (one word)

undies (colloq.) (women's) underclothing

undine a female water-spirit

UNDRO United Nations Disaster Relief Organization

un-English (hyphen, cap.)

unequivocal not ambiguous, plain, unmistakable; *not* uni-

UNESCO United Nations Educational, Scientific, and Cultural Organization; also **Unesco**

unexception/able that cannot be faulted, **-al** not unusual

Ungarn Ger. for Hungary

unget-at-able inaccessible (two hyphens)

unguent ointment

ungul/a hoof, talon; pl. **-ae**; **-ate** hoofed, a hoofed mammal

unheard-of (hyphen)

uni/ (colloq.) university, pl. **-s**

Uni/ate (of or relating to) (a member of) any community of Christians in E. Europe or the Near East that acknowledges papal supremacy but retains its own liturgy etc., *also* **-at**; in Russ. *uniyat*; the term is resented by many of those concerned, who would rather be called Greek Catholics

UNICEF United Nations (International) Children's (Emergency) Fund, also **Unicef**

unidea'd having no ideas, *not* -aed

Unido United Nations Industrial Development Organization

uninterested not interested; cf. **disinterested**

Union/ flag the national ensign of the United Kingdom (one cap.), *see also* **— Jack**

Unionist abbr. **U.**

unionize *not* -ise (one word)

un-ionized not ionized; *not* -ised (hyphen)

Union Jack a small Union flag flown from a ship (two caps.)

Union of Soviet Socialist Republics (hist.) abbr. **USSR**

unisex (one word)

Unit. Unitarian, -ism

United Arab Emirates group of seven Emirates on Persian Gulf, namely: Abu Dhabi, Ajman, Dubai, Fujaira, Ras al Khaima, Sharja, Umm al Qaiwain; abbr. **UAE**

United Arab Republic Egypt and Syria 1958–61, Egypt alone 1961–71; abbr. **UAR**

United/ Brethren the Moravians, **— Free Church of Scotland** (caps.) abbr. **UFC**

United Kingdom (caps.) Great Britain and N. Ireland, abbr. **UK**; *see also* **Britain**

United Nations abbr. UN

United Presbyterian/ abbr. **UP, — — Church** (caps.) abbr. **UPC**

United Service Club (*not* Services)

United States of America abbr. (noun) **USA**, (adj.) **US**

Univ. University, (in Oxford) University College

Univers (typ.) a sans serif font, *not* a generic term for sans serif face

universal (a *not* an) abbr. **univ.**

Universal Copyright Convention adopted 1952, effective in USA from 1955, in UK 1957, and in USSR 1973; each of the more than 90 member states extends benefit of its own copyright law to works by citizens of other member states; abbr. **UCC**; *see also* **Berne Convention**

universalize *not* -ise

Universal Time = Greenwich Mean Time, abbr. **UT**

university (colloq. **uni/**, pl. **-s**), abbr. **univ.**

University College London (no comma) abbr. **UCL**

unjustified setting (typ.) composition with a single invariable word space, giving an uneven (ragged) margin, usually on the right

Unknown Soldier an unidentified soldier representing casualties in war (caps.)

unlicensed *not* -ced

unlisted (US) of a telephone number = **ex-directory**

un/lived-in, -looked-for (hyphens)

unm. unmarried

UNO *or* **Uno** United Nations Organization, *use* **UN**

uno animo (Lat.) unanimously

unperson a person whose identity is denied or ignored (one word); cf. **non-person**

unpractical not suitable for actual conditions, *not* im-; cf. **impracticable; impractical**

unpractised *not* -ced (US)

unputdownable (of a book) (one word)

unreadable too dull or too difficult to be worth reading; cf. **illegible**

UNRRA United Nations Relief and Rehabilitation Administration, also **Unrra**

UNRWA United Nations Relief Works Agency, also **Unrwa**

unselfconscious (one word)

unsewn binding (bind.) = **perfect binding**

unshakeable *not* -kable

unwieldy cumbersome, *not* -ldly

UP United Presbyterian, United Press; Uttar Pradesh (*formerly* United Provinces), India

up. upper

u.p. underproof, (colloq.) all up (with someone)

up-and/-coming (colloq.) likely to succeed; **-over** (adj.) of a door; **-under** a type of high kick in League Rugby, in Rugby Union called a **garryowen** (hyphens)

Upanishad each of a series of Sanskrit philosophical compositions concluding the exposition of the Vedas

upbeat (colloq.) optimistic or cheerful (one word)

up-beat (mus.) an unaccented beat (hyphen)

up-country (hyphen)

Updike, John (**Hoyer**) (b. 1932) US author, poet, and critic

up/field, -hill (one word)

up/ish, -ity *use* **upp-**

upmarket (adj., one word)

upper case (typ.) capital letters

upper class the highest social class in society, including the aristocracy (but technically not royalty) (two words, hyphen when attrib.)

upper crust (two words, hyphen when attrib.)

uppercut (strike with) an upwards blow delivered with the arm bent

Upper House the higher house in a legislature, esp. the House of Lords (caps.)

Upper Volta *now* **Burkina Faso**

upper works the part of a ship that is above the water when fully laden

upp/ish self-assertive; **-ity** arrogant, snobbish; *not* upi-

Uppsala Sweden; in Ger. **Upsala**, Fr. **Upsal**

upright (one word)

Upsala Minn.; Ont., Canada

upside down (two words, hyphen when attrib.)

upsilon the twentieth letter of the Gr. alphabet (Y, v)

upskill/, -ed, -ing (econ.) (one word)

up/stage, -stairs (one word)

upstate (US) in, to, of, or relating to part of a state remote from its large cities, esp. the northern part, e.g. 'upstate New York' (one word)

upstream (one word)

upsy-daisy encouragement spoken to child who has fallen over, *also* **ups-a-**

uptight (colloq.) nervously tense, rigidly conventional (one word)

up to date (hyphens when attrib.)

uptown (US) (of or in) the more northerly or residential part of a town or city; (cf. **downtown**)

UPU Universal Postal Union

upwind (one word)

uraemia (med.) *not* ure- (US)

Ural-Altaic of or relating to a family of Finno-Ugric, Turkic, Mongolian, and other agglutinative languages of N. Europe and Asia; of or relating to the Ural and Altaic mountain ranges in E. Europe and Cent. Asia

Urania (Gr. myth) the muse of astronomy

uranium symbol **U**

Uranus (Gr. myth., astr.)

urari (hist.) *now* **curare**

urbanize *not* -ise

urbi et orbi (Lat.) to the city (Rome) and the world

Urdu a language related to Hindi but with many Persian words, an official language of Pakistan also used in India

urethr/a (anat.) pl. **-ae**

URI (med.) upper respiratory infection

urim and thummim in Exod. 28: 30, are plurals

Uruguay/ abbr. **Uru.**, adj. **-an**

urus *use* **aurochs**

US Under-Secretary, United Service, United States (adj.)

u.s. (Lat.) *ubi supra* (in the place (mentioned) above), *ut supra* (as above)

u/s unserviceable

USA United States of America

usable *not* -eable

USAF United States Air Force

USAFA United States Air Force Academy

USCL United Society for Christian Literature

USDAW Union of Shop, Distributive, and Allied Workers

usf. (Ger.) *und so fort* (= etc., and so on)

Ushant an island off Brittany; in Breton **Enez Eusa**, Fr. **l'île d'Ouessant**

Usher Hall Edinburgh

USI United Service Institution (*not* Services)

USIS United States Information Service

Üsküp Turkey

USN United States Navy

USPG United Society for the Propagation of the Gospel

usquebaugh (Gaelic) whisky, in Gaelic *uisge beatha*

USS United States Ship, Universities Superannuation Scheme

Ussher, James (1581–1656) Irish divine, Archbishop of Armagh

US spellings differences from British usage, such as *aluminum, maneuver,* and *pajamas,* are given under headwords in their alphabetical places

USSR (hist.) Union of Soviet Socialist Republics

usu. usual, -ly

usucaption in Roman and Scots law, acquisition of a title or right to property by uninterrupted and undisputed possession for a prescribed term; *not* -capion

usufruct/ in Roman and Scots law, the right of enjoying the use and advantages of another's property short of the destruction or waste of its substance; **-uary**

usurper *not* -or

usw. (Ger.) *und so weiter* (= etc., and so on)

UT Universal Time, Utah (postal abbr.)

Utah off. abbr. **Ut.**, postal **UT**

Utakamand *use* **Ootacamund**

Utd. United

ut dictum (Lat.) as directed, abbr. *ut dict.*

U Thant *see* **Thant, U**

UTI (med.) urinary tract infection

utilize *not* -ise

ut infra (Lat.) as below, abbr. *u.i.*

uti possidetis (Lat.) as you now possess (opposed to *status quo ante*)

utmost *not* utter-

Utopia/ an imagined perfect place or state of things, from the title of a book by Thomas More, 1516; adj. **-n** (caps.); not cap. when referring to a general concept rather than the specific work

Utrecht city and province, the Netherlands; in old imprints sometimes referred to as **Trajectum ad Rhenum** or **Ultrajectum**

UTS ultimate tensile strength

ut supra (Lat.) as above, abbr. *u.s.*

Uttar Pradesh India, *formerly* United Provinces; abbr. **UP**

U/-tube, -turn (caps., hyphens); *use* a sans serif typeface only where it is important to represent the actual configuration exactly

ut videtur (Lat.) as it seems

UU Ulster Unionist

UV ultraviolet

U/W underwriter

UWIST University of Wales Institute of Science and Technology

UWT Union of Women Teachers

uxor (Lat.) wife, abbr. *ux.*

uxor/ial of or relating to a wife; **-icide** the killing of one's wife, or a person who does this; **-ious** greatly or excessively fond of one's wife

Uzbek/ a member (or the language) of a Turkic people living mainly in **Uzbekistan**, *not* Uzbeg-

Vv

V five, vanadium, (elec.) volt(s), (Ger.) *Vergeltungswaffe* (reprisal weapon: **V1** flying bomb, **V2** rocket); traditionally (and often still) not used in the numeration of series

V. Vice, Volunteers

℣ sign for versicle

v velocity, verse, verso, versus, very, (meteor.) unusual visibility, volume (*prefer* **vol.**), (Ger.) *von* (of)

v italic 'v', in some typefaces may appear identical to Greek nu or upsilon; to avoid confusion where both are used, specify an alternative with a pointier or rounder base

v. (Lat.) *vice* (in place of), *vide* (see), (It. mus.) *violino* (violin), *voce* (voice)

VA (US) Veterans' Administration, Vicar Apostolic, vice admiral, (Order of) Victoria and Albert (for women), Virginia (postal abbr.)

Va. Virginia (off. abbr.)

va. (mus.) viola

v.a. verb active, (Lat.) *vixit ... annos* (lived (so many) years)

vaccinat/e inoculate with vaccine; **-ion, -or**

vacillat/e move from side to side, waver; **-ion, -or**; cf. **oscillate**

vacu/um pl. **-ums**, *or* **-a** in scientific and technical use

vacuum/ brake, — cleaner, — flask, — gauge (two words)

vacuum-packed (hyphen)

vacuum pump (two words)

VAD Voluntary Aid Detachment (for nursing)

vade mecum/ a handbook or other article carried on the person, pl. **-s** (two words)

vae victis! (Lat.) woe to the vanquished!

vaille que vaille (Fr.) whatever it may be worth, at all events

vainglor/y, -ious (one word)

Vaishnava (Hinduism) a devotee of Vishnu, in Skt. *vaiṣṇavá*

Vaisya (a member of) the third of the four great Hindu castes, comprising merchants and farmers; in Skt. *vaiśya*

valance a short curtain or drapery; cf. **valence; valency**

vale (arch. or poet. except in place names) a valley, e.g. 'Vale of White Horse'

vale! (Lat.) farewell!, pl. *valete!*; **vale** (noun) a farewell (not ital.)

valence (US) = **valency**, esp. as adj.; cf. **valance**

Valencia Ecuador; island, Ireland; cities, Philippines; autonomous territory, city, and gulf, Spain; N. Mex., Pa.; city and lake, Venezuela

Valenciennes a rich kind of lace (cap.)

valenc/y (chem.) the combining power of an atom, measured by the number of hydrogen atoms it can displace or combine with; pl. **-ies**; *see also* **valence**; cf. **valance**

Valentia, Viscount *not* -cia

valentine a sweetheart, a card or message sent to or received by one (not cap.)

Valentine's Day, St 14 Feb. (apos.)

Valéra, Éamon de *see* **de Valéra, Éamon**

valet a man's personal attendant etc. (not ital.)

valeta *use* **vel-**

Valetta *use* **Vall-**

valgus a deformity involving the outward displacement of the foot or hand from the midline; cf. **varus**

Valhalla (Norse myth.) the palace in which souls of dead heroes feasted, in Old Norse **Valhǫll**; *not* W-; *see also* **Hel**

valise a kitbag, (US) a small portmanteau

Valkyrie/ (Norse myth.) each of Odin's twelve handmaidens, pl. **-s**; (the opera *The Valkyrie* refers to a single handmaiden); in Norse **Valkyrja**, pl. **Valkyrjur**; in Ger. f. **Walküre**, pl. **Walküren**

Valladolid Spain

Valletta Malta; *not* Vale-, -eta

valley/ pl. **-s**

Vallombrosa N. Italy, *not* Vallam-

valorize artificially raise or fix a price, *not* -ise

valour *not* -or (US), *but* **valorous**

Valparaiso Ind.

Valparaíso Chile

valse waltz (not ital.); **valse/ à deux temps, — à trois temps** (Fr.) variations of the waltz (ital., no hyphens)

valuate (esp. US) estimate the worth of a thing, esp. by a professional

value added tax (three words, no hyphen) abbr. **VAT**

valuta (econ.) the value of one currency with respect to another, a currency considered in this way

van, van den, van der in Du. prefixes to proper names, usually not initial cap. except at beginning of a sentence, and alphabetized under the main name; in Fl. may be cap. V, and alphabetized under V; in Afrik. may be either; in UK and US alphabetize under V

vanadium symbol **V**

Van Allen/ belt *or* **layer** of radiation surrounding the earth, named after **James Alfred —— —** (b. 1914), US physicist

Vanbrugh, Sir John (1664–1726) English architect and playwright

Van Buren, Martin (1782–1862) US President 1837–41

Vancouver system a reference system in which each bibliographical source is assigned a number, which is then used to cite that source in text

V&A Victoria and Albert Museum (no points)

Vandal (a member) of, *or* relating to, a Germanic people of 4th–5th cc. (cap.); a wilful destroyer of art or property (not cap.)

vandalize *not* -ise

van de Graaff/, Robert Jemison (1901–67) US physicist; — — — accelerator, — — — generator

Vanderbilt/, Cornelius (1794–1877) US businessman and philanthropist, founded — University Nashville, Tenn.

Van der Hum a South African liqueur

Van der Post, Sir Laurens (**Jan**) (1906–96) South African explorer, writer, and conservationist

van der Rohe *see* **Mies van der Rohe**

van der Waals/, Johannes (1837–1923) Dutch physicist; — — — forces, — — — equation

van de Velde *see* **Velde, van de**

Van Diemen's Land *not* Dieman's (apos.), *now* **Tasmania**

Van Dijck, Christoffel *see* **Dijck**

V&V verification and validation (to be set close up)

Van Dyck, Sir Anthony (1599–1641) Flemish painter (two words); Anglicized form **Vandyke/** (one word) used to denote a work by him, and in — **beard,** — **brown; vandyke** each of a series of points bordering lace etc. (not cap.)

Vane-Tempest-Stewart family name of the Marquess of Londonderry (hyphens)

Van Eyck,/ Hubert (1366–1426) and — — **Jan** (1385–1440) his brother, Flemish painters

Van Gogh, Vincent *see* **Gogh, Vincent Van**

Vanhomrigh, Esther (1692–1723) Swift's 'Vanessa'

Van Nostrand Reinhold publishers

van 't Hoff, Jacobus Hendricus *see* **Hoff**

Vanuatu SW Pacific, *formerly* New Hebrides

Van Vleck/, John Hasbrouck (1899–1980) US physicist (cap. *V*); — — paramagnetism

vaporiz/e *not* -ise, **-er** *not* -or

vapour *not* -or (US); *but* **vapor/ific, -iform, -imeter, -ish, -ous**

Var a river and dép. of France

var. (biol.) variety

Varanasi *see* **Benares**

Varèse, Edgar(d) (1883–1965) French-born US composer

Vargas/ (y Chávez), (Joaquín) Alberto (1896–1982) Peruvian-born US surrealist painter who worked under the name **Varga**; **—, Getúlio Dornelles** (1883–1954) President of Brazil 1930–45, 1951–4; **— Llosa, (Jorge) Mario (Pedro)** (b. 1936) Peruvian novelist, dramatist, and essayist

variables (math.) normally to be set in italics

vari/a lectio (Lat.) a variant reading, abbr. **v.l.**; pl. **-ae lectiones** abbr. **vv.ll.**

variety (biol.) abbr. **var.**

variorum (of an edition of a text) having notes by various editors or commentators, (of an edition of an author's works) including variant readings

variorum notae (Lat.) notes by commentators

Varna Bulgaria, *formerly* Stalin

varna each of the four main Hindu castes, in Hind. *varṇa*

varus a deformity involving the inward displacement of the foot or hand from the midline; cf. **valgus**

vas/ (anat.) a duct, pl. **-a**

vascul/um a botanist's specimen case, pl. **-a**

vas deferens the spermatic duct, pl. **vasa deferentia**

vasectomy the excision of vas deferens

Vaseline (propr.) a type of petroleum jelly (cap.)

vassal (hist.) a holder of land by feudal tenure on conditions of homage and allegiance

Vassar College Poughkeepsie, NY

VAT/ value added tax, **-man** a customs and excise officer who administers VAT (one word)

Vatican/ the palace and official residence of the Pope in Rome; — **City** the independent Papal State in Rome, instituted in 1929; — **Council** an ecumenical council of the Roman Catholic Church; abbr. **Vat.**

Vaudois (of or relating to) a native of Vaud in W. Switzerland, or its French dialect; *see also* **Waldenses**

Vaughan Williams, Ralph (1872–1958) English composer

Vauvenargues, Luc de Clapiers, marquis de (1715–47) French writer

v. aux. verb auxiliary

Vaux of Harrowden, Baron

vb. verb

VC vice-chairman, vice-chancellor, vice-consul, Victoria Cross

VCH Victoria County History

v. Chr. (Ger.) *vor Christo* or *vor Christi Geburt*, BC

VCR video cassette recorder, (US) the machine colloq. called **video** in the UK

VD venereal disease, Volunteer (Officers') Decoration

v.d. various dates

v. dep. verb deponent

VDH valvular disease of the heart

VDU (comput.) visual display unit

VE/ victory in Europe; — **Day** 8 May 1945; *not* V-E (US)

vᵉ (Fr.) *veuve* (widow), *cinquième*

veau (Fr. m.) calf, (cook.) veal; (bind.) calf, calf-skin

VEB (hist.) *Volkseigener Betrieb* (state-owned company) (GDR)

Veblen, Thorstein (**Bunde**) (1857–1929) US economist

vectors (math.) to be set in bold

Ved/a (sing. and pl.) the most ancient Hindu scriptures, esp. the four collections called *Rig Veda*, *Sama Veda*, *Yajur Veda*, and *Atharva Veda* (caps.; one word, one cap. in specialist contexts); adj. **-ic**

Vedanta the Upanishads, or the Hindu philosophy based on these, esp. in its monistic form

Vedda (of or relating to) an aboriginal of Sri Lanka

vedette a mounted sentinel, patrol boat; *not* vi-

veg (colloq.) vegetable(s) (no point)

Vega, Garcilaso de la *see* **Garcilaso**

Vega Carpio, Lope Félix de known as **Lope de Vega** (1562–1635) Spanish playwright and poet

Vehmgericht (not ital.), adj. **Vehmic**; *see* **Fehmgericht**

veille (Fr. f.) the day before, eve; cf. *vieille*; **vielle**

Velázquez, Diego Rodríguez de Silva y (1599–1660) Spanish painter, *not* Velas-

Velcro (propr.)

veld (Afrik.) open country, *not* -dt

Velde,/ Willem van de (**the Elder**) (1611–93) Dutch marine painter; father of — **Willem van de** (**the Younger**) (1633–1707) Dutch marine painter; brother of — **Adriaen van de** (1636–72) Dutch landscape and portrait painter; — **Henri** (**Clemens**) **van de** (1863–1957) Belgian architect, designer, and teacher

veleta a dance in triple time, *not* val-

Velikovsky, Immanuel (1895–1979) Russian-born writer on astronomy

vellum/ fine parchment, — **paper** that imitating vellum

veloce (mus.) quickly

velocity (mech.) symbol **v** (ital.)

velour a plushlike fabric, *not* -ours

velouté (cook.) a sauce of white stock mixed with cooked butter and flour (not ital.)

vel/ simile (Lat.) or the like; pl. — *similia* abbr. *vel sim.*

vel/um a membrane, pl. **-a**

velveteen a velvet-like cotton fabric

velvety *not* -tty

Ven. Venerable (used for archdeacons only)

ven/a cava (med.) each of the veins carrying blood to heart, pl. **-ae cavae**

venal/ (of person) bribable, (of conduct) sordid; **-ity, -ly**; cf. **venial**

venation the arrangement of veins in a leaf

Vendée, La a dép. of France; adj. **Vendean** of the royalist party 1793–5, specifically of a royalist and Catholic rebellion supressed with great brutality

vendee the person to whom one sells

vendetta/ a blood feud, pl. **-s** (not ital.)

vendeuse (Fr. f.) saleswoman

vendible that may be sold, *not* -able

Vendôme/ dép. Loir-et-Cher, France; **Colonne** —, and **Place** — (l.c. *p* in Fr.), Paris

vendor a seller, *not* -er

vendue (US) a public auction

venepuncture (med.) a puncture of a vein, *not* veni-

venerat/e, -or

venere/al, -ology

venery (arch.) hunting, sexual indulgence; *not* -ary

venesection phlebotomy, *not* veni-

Venet. Venetian

venetian blind (not cap.)

Venetian/ glass, — red, — window (one cap.)

Venezuela abbr. **Venez.**

venial (of sin) pardonable; cf. **venal**

Venice Italy; in It. **Venezia**, Fr. **Venise**, Ger. **Venedig**

Venn diagram a set of circles representing the relation of logical categories (one cap.)

venose having prominent veins

ven/ous of the veins, **-osity**; *not* vein-

ventilat/e, -or

ventre à terre (Fr.) at full speed, lit. 'belly to the ground'

ventriloquize *not* -ise

Venus de Milo the Melian Aphrodite, in Fr. f. *Vénus de Milo*

Venus flytrap an insect-eating plant (two words); in US, **Venus's-flytrap** (apos., hyphen)

Venus's/ comb shepherd's needle (a plant), — **looking glass** any of various plants of the genus *Legousia*, — **girdle** a ribbon-like jellyfish, — **slipper** lady's slipper (a plant) (one cap.); *not* Venus'

ver (Du. name prefix) combined form of **van der**, usually cap. and run in: as Vermeer; *see also* **van, van den, van der**

veranda *not* -ah

verb abbr. **vb.**

verb. (Ger.) *verbessert* (improved, revised)

verbal of or concerned with words; (gram.) of, or in the nature of, a verb; literal

verbalize put into words, *not* -ise

verbatim (Lat.) word for word (not ital.)

verboten (Ger.) forbidden

verbum satis sapienti (Lat.) a word to the wise suffices, abbr. **verb. sap.**

verd-antique an ornamental marble, *not* verde- (hyphen)

verderer a judicial officer of royal forests, *not* -or

verdigris green rust on copper, *not* verde-

Verein (Ger. m.) Association (cap.)

Vereinigte Staaten/ (Ger. f.) United States (of America), *but* **die Vereinigten Staaten**

Vereshchagin, Vasili (Vasilevich) (1842–1904) Russian painter

Verey/ light, — pistol *use* **Very**

Verfasser/ (Ger. m.) author (of a specific work), f. **-in**; abbr. **Verf.**; cf. ***Dichter, Schriftsteller***

verger an attendant in a church; *see also* **vir-**

Vergil, Polydore (1470–1555) Italian humanist and historian

Vergilius Maro, Publius (70–19 BC) Roman poet; trad. Anglicized as **Virgil**, in modern classical contexts as **Vergil**; *see also* **Virgilius Maro**

verglas a thin layer of ice or sleet (not ital.)

vergleiche (Ger.) compare, abbr. **vgl.**

verism/ realism in literature or art, pl. **-s**; **-o** realism, esp. in opera (not ital.)

verkrampte (Afrik.) (a person who is) politically or socially conservative or reactionary

Verlag (Ger. m.) publishing house

verligte (Afrik.) (a person who is) progressive or enlightened

vermilion *not* -llion

Vermillion Kan., S. Dak.

Vermont off. abbr. **Vt.**, postal **VT**

vermouth an aperitif wine flavoured with aromatic herbs (not cap.)

vernal of, in, *or* appropriate to, spring

Verner's law (phonetics) relating to voicing of fricatives in Germanic languages (one cap.)

Veronese, Paolo (1528–88) Italian painter, real surname **Cagliari**

Verrazano-Narrows Bridge New York City (hyphen)

Verrocchio, Andrea del (1435–88) Italian painter and sculptor, *not* the many variants

verruc/a a wart or similar growth, pl. **-ae**

Versailles near Paris

vers de société (Fr. m.) society verses

verse abbr. **v.**, **ver.**; pl. **vv.** *but* avoid confusion with lower-case roman numerals

versicle a short verse in liturgy said or sung by minister, followed by the people's (or choir's) response; (typ.) the sign ℣ used in liturgical works; *see also* ℟ (response)

vers libre (Fr. m.) free verse

verso/ (typ.) the left-hand page, opp. of **recto**; abbr. **v.**, **v.** (not ital.); pl. **-s**

verst a Russian measure of length, about 1.1 km (0.66 mile); in Russ. ***versta***

versus against (not ital.); abbr. **v.**, **vs.** (esp. in sport); in law often in opposite font

vert. vertical

vertebr/a a segment of the backbone, pl. **-ae** (not ital.)

vertebrate an animal with a spinal column, of the subphylum Vertebrata (*or* Craniata)

vert/ex the highest point, angular point of triangle etc.; pl. **-ices**

vertical abbr. **vert.**

vertig/o giddiness, pl. **-os**; **-inous**

vertu *use* **virtu**

Vertue, George (1684–1756) English engraver

verve spirit (not ital.)

vervet a small African monkey

Verwoerd, Hendrik Frensch (1901–66) Dutch-born Prime Minister of the Republic of South Africa 1958–66

Very Large Array astronomic apparatus, New Mex.; abbr. **VLA**

Very/ light a flare fired from a **— pistol**, *not* Verey

Very Revd Very Reverend (for deans, provosts, and former moderators)

vesica piscis (art) a pointed oval used as an aureole in medieval sculpture and painting, *not* mandorla (not ital.)

Vespucci, Amerigo (1454–1512) Italian navigator

vest an undergarment worn on the upper part of the body, (US, Austral.) = **waistcoat**

vestigia (Lat. pl.) traces

vet/ (colloq.) veterinary surgeon (no point); examine carefully; **-ted**, **-ting**; (US colloq.) a veteran

veterinarian (US) a veterinary surgeon

veto/ a ban, pl. **-es**

veuf (Fr. m.) widower

veuve (Fr. f.) widow; abbr. **vᵉ**, **Vve**

Veuve Clicquot a champagne

Vevey Switzerland, *not* -ay

vexata quaestio (Lat.) a disputed question

vexillology the study of flags (three ls)

vexill/um an ancient Roman military standard, esp. of a maniple; pl. **-a** (not ital.)

v.f. very fair

VG Vicar General

v.g. very good

vgl. (Ger. for cf.) *vergleiche* (compare)

VHF very high frequency (no points)

VHS video home system (no points)

v.i. verb intransitive

v.i. (Lat.) *vide infra* (see below)

via by way of, *not* -â (not ital.)

vial (Brit. poet. and US) = **phial**

via media (Lat.) a middle course (ital.)

Viaud *see* **Loti**

vibrato/ (mus.) rapid variation of pitch, pl. **-s**

vibrator *not* -er

Vic. vicar, -age; Victoria

vicar/, -ial

Vicar/ Apostolic abbr. **VA**, — **General** abbr. **VG**

Vicar's College a cathedral residence

vice a tool, *not* vise (US)

vice/ abbr. **V.**; — **admiral** abbr. **VA** (two words, caps. as title); **-chairman, -chairperson, -chairwoman** abbr. **VC**; **-chamberlain; -chancellor, -consul** abbr. **VC** (hyphens, caps. as titles)

vice in place of (ital.)

vicegerent a deputy (one word)

vice-president abbr. **VP** (hyphen, two words in US, caps. as title)

viceregent (cap. as title) (one word, hyphen in US)

vicereine a female viceroy or a viceroy's wife (cap. as title)

viceroy (cap. as title), adj. **viceregal**

vice versa the order being reversed, *not* visa (no hyphen or accent, not ital.); abbr. **v.v.**

vichyssoise a chilled soup of leeks and potatoes

Vichy water (one cap.)

vicomt/e (Fr.) Viscount, f. *-esse* (not cap., not ital. as part of name)

victimize *not* -ise

Victoria/ abbr. **Vic.**; — **and Albert, Order of** for women, abbr. **VA**; — **Cross** abbr. **VC**; — **Nyanza** *use* **Lake Victoria**

victoria a type of carriage, a S. American water lily, a pigeon, a large plum (not cap.)

Victoria County History abbr. **VCH**

victor ludorum the overall champion in a sports competition (not ital.)

victual/, -led, -ler, -ling (one *l* in US)

vicuña a llama-like S. American mammal, the cloth made from its wool or an imitation of it

vide (Fr. mus.) open (of strings)

vide/ (Lat.) see, consult (a reference or passage in a text etc.); abbr. **v.**; — *ante* see above; — *infra* see below, abbr. **v.i.**

videlicet (Lat.) namely (one word), abbr. **viz.**

video/ pl. **-s**; (colloq. for) — **cassette** (two words), — **cassette recorder** abbr. **VCR**

videodisc (one word); *see also* **disc**

video/ game, — nasty (two words)

videophone (one word)

VideoPlus (propr.) (one word, two caps.)

video recorder (two words)

video/tape, -tex (one word)

vide/ post see below; — *supra* see above, abbr. **v.s.**

vidette *use* **ve-**

videtur (Lat.) it seems

vide ut supra (Lat.) see as above

vidimus (Lat. 'we have seen') a certified copy of accounts etc. (not ital.)

vie compete, rival; **vying**

vieille (Fr. f.) an old woman; cf. *veille*

vielle a hurdy-gurdy; cf. *veille*

Vienn/a in Ger. **Wien**, in Fr. **-e**; adj. **-ese**; in classical and scholarly Latin **Vindobona**

Vienne dép. Isère, France; also a river, tributary of River Loire; *see also* **Haute-Vienne**

viennoise, à la (Fr.) in Viennese style (not cap.)

vient de paraître (Fr.) just published

Vientiane Laos

Vierkleur (Afrik.) the flag of the former Transvaal Republic

vi et armis (Lat.) by force and arms

Vietcong a former guerrilla force in S. Vietnam

Vietnam/ SE Asia, divided into N. and S. Vietnam 1954–79; **-ese**

vieux jeu (adj., noun; Fr. m.) (an) outworn, hackneyed (subject)

view/data, -finder, -graph (one word)

view halloo (hunting) a shout on seeing a fox break cover, *not* the many variants

viewpoint (one word)

vif (Fr. mus.) lively, briskly

vigesimo (typ.) *use* **twentymo**

vigesimo-quarto (typ.) *use* **twenty-fourmo**

vigilante/ a member of a vigilance body, pl. **-s** (not ital.)

vignettes (typ.) illustrations with undefined edges

vigoro (Austral.) a team ball game combining elements of cricket and baseball

vigour *not* -or (US), *but* **vigorous**

vihara a Buddhist temple or monastery

Viking (of or relating to) any of the Scandinavian seafaring pirates and traders in the 8th–11th cc.

vilayet a Turkish province, abbr. **vila.**

vilif/y disparage, *not* vill-; **-ied, -ier, -ying**

village abbr. **vil.**

villain/ an evildoer, (colloq.) a rascal; **-ous, -y**; cf. **villein**

Villa-Lobos, Heitor (1887–1959) Brazilian composer

villanell/a a rustic Neapolitan part song, pl. **-e**

villanelle a usually pastoral or lyrical poem of nineteen lines, with only two rhymes throughout, and some lines repeated

Villa-Villa (propr.) a kind of Havana cigar (hyphen)

villeggiatura (It. f.) a country holiday

villégiature (Fr. f.) a country holiday

villein/ a serf, **-age**; cf. **villain**

Villiers/ family name of the Earls of Clarendon and Jersey; **— de l'Isle Adam, Jean Marie Mathias Philippe Auguste, comte de** (1838–89) French writer

Vilnius Lithuania

vinaigrette a salad dressing, an ornamental smelling-bottle; *not* vineg(a)r-

Vinci,/ Leonardo (1690–1730) Italian composer, **— Leonardo da** *see* **Leonardo**

vin de/ pays (Fr. m.) country wine, **— — table** table wine; *not du*

vineg(a)rette *use* **vinaigrette**

vineyard *not* vinyard

vingt-et-un (Fr. m.) a card game, pontoon

vin ordinaire (Fr. m.) cheap (usually red) wine as drunk in France mixed with water, now called *vin de table*

vintager a grape gatherer

vintner a wine merchant, *not* -ter

viola/ da braccio a Renaissance term for any member of the violin family played 'on the arm', but now pertaining to an instrument similar to the viola; **— da gamba** any viol held between the player's legs, esp. the bass viol; **— d'amore** a sweet-toned 18th-c. bowed instrument like a modern viola (not ital.)

viol/ate, -able, -ator *not* -er

violencia (Sp.) in Colombia, the decade of violent political conflict 1948–58

violino (It.) violin, abbr. **v.**

Viollet-le-duc, Eugène Emmanuel (1814–79) French architect

violoncell/o *not* violin-; pl. **-os**; usually shortened to **cello** (no apos.); **-ist**

VIP very important person

virago/ a termagant, pl. **-s**

Virchow, Rudolf (1821–1902) German pathologist

virelay a short (esp. Old Fr.) lyric poem

virger the spelling of **verger** traditional at certain cathedrals, such as St Paul's and Winchester

Virgil *see* **Vergilius**

Virgilius Maro (7th c.) Irish-born grammarian

Virginia/ off. abbr. **Va.**, postal **VA**; **— creeper** (bot.) *not* -ian

virginibus puerisque (Lat.) for girls and boys; (with two caps) book by R. L. Stevenson, 1881

virg/o intacta (a) virgin with hymen intact, pl. **-ines intactae** (not ital.)

virgule (typ.) a solidus, stroke

virgule (Fr. typ. f.) comma

virtu/ the knowledge of or expertise in fine arts, virtuosity; in It. *virtù*; **article of —** an artistic article of interesting workmanship, antiquity, or rarity; *not* ve-, -ue (not ital.)

virtuos/o one skilled in an art, pl. **-i**

virus/ a submicroscopic infective agent, pl. **-es**

Vis. Viscount

vis (Lat. f.) force, pl. *vires*

visa/ a permit or endorsement on a passport (not ital.), pl. **-s**; as verb **-ed** *not* -'d

vis a tergo force from behind

vis-à-vis (Fr.) face to face, as regards, compared to; (US) a social partner (hyphens, not ital.)

visc/era (pl.) interior organs, esp. in the abdomen; sing. **-us**

viscount/, -ess a British nobleman or -woman ranking between an earl and a baron (cap. as title), abbr. **Vis.**

viscount/cy, -ship the rank or jurisdiction of a viscount; **-y** only in hist. use

viscous sticky

vise (US) a tool = **vice**

Vishnu a Hindu god, in Skt. *Viṣṇu*

visier *use* **viz-**

Visigoth a member of the branch of the Goths who settled in France and Spain in the 5th c., and ruled much of Spain until 711

vis inertiae (Lat.) force of inanimate matter

visit/, -ed, -ing

visiting nurse (US) = **district nurse**

visitor/ *not* -er, **-s'** book *not* -or's

vis/ major superior force, **— medicatrix naturae** nature's power of healing

visor part of a helmet, the peak of a cap, the sun shield in a car, (hist.) a mask, etc.; *not* viz-

vista/ a view, pl. **-s**

visualize *not* -ise

vis viva (Lat.) living force

vitalize *not* -ise

vitell/us the yolk of an egg, pl. **-i**

vitiat/e impair the quality or efficiency of, make invalid or ineffectual; **-or**

viticulture the culture of vines

Vitoria Spain; battle, 1813

vitriol,/ oil of sulphuric acid, **— blue** copper sulphate, **— green** ferrous sulphate, **— white** zinc sulphate

vituperat/e revile, **-or**

viva/ short for **viva voce**, pl. **-s**; as verb **-ed** *not* -'d (not ital.)

vival (It.) long live!, *also evvival*

vivace (mus.) lively, quickly

vivandi/er (Fr.) f. *-ère* army sutler

vivant rex et reginal (Lat.) long live the King and Queen!

vivari/um an enclosure for living things, pl. **-a**

vivat/ reginal (Lat.) long live the Queen! — *rexl* long live the King!

viva/ voce orally, *not* vivâ; (noun) an oral examination, pl. — **voces**; (with hyphen) verb (not ital.); *see also* **viva**

vive/l (Fr.) long live! — *la bagatellel* long live trifles! — *la différencel* long live the difference! (usually between the sexes), — *la Républiquel* long live the Republic!

vivisect/, -ion, -or

vixit ... annos (Lat.) lived (so many) years, abbr. **v.a.**

viz. *videlicet* (namely) (not ital., comma before), *but use* **namely**

vizier (hist.) a high official in some Muslim countries, esp. in Turkey under Ottoman rule; *not* -ir, -sier

vizor *use* **vis-**

VJ/ victory over Japan; — **Day** 15 Aug. 1945; in USA 2 Sept. 1945; *not* V-J (US)

v.l. *varia lectio* (a variant reading)

Vlaanderen Fl. for **Flanders**

Vlach Bulgarian for **Wallachian**

Vlaminck, Maurice de (1876–1958) French painter

vlei (S. Afr.) a hollow in which water collects during the rainy season (not ital.)

VLF very low frequency (no points)

Vlissingen Du. for **Flushing**

Vltava a Czech river, in Ger. **Moldau**

v. M. (Ger.) *vorigen Monats* (last month)

VMH Victoria Medal of Honour

v.n. verb neuter

V-neck (cap., hyphen)

VO Veterinary Officer, Royal Victorian Order

voc. vocative

vocab. vocabulary

vocalize *not* -ise (except when noun as mus. term, *but not* in US)

vocative abbr. **voc.**

voce (It. mus.) voice, abbr. **v.**

Vogüé, Eugène Melchior, vicomte de (1848–1910) French essayist

vogue la galèrel (Fr.) happen what may!

voice box (two words)

voicemail (one word, two in US)

voice-over narration without picture of speaker (hyphen)

voiceprint (one word)

voilà/ (Fr.) see there! — *tout* that is all

voile a thin semi-transparent dress material (not ital.)

vol. volume

Volapük an artificial international language, invented by J. M. Schleyer, 1879

volatilize *not* -ise

vol-au-vent (Fr. cook. m.) a filled puff pastry case (not ital.)

volcano/ pl. **-es**; **-logy** (US) = **vulcanology**

volet a panel or wing of a triptych

Volgograd Russia, *formerly* **Tsaritsyn**, *later* **Stalingrad**

Völkerwanderung (Ger. f.) the 2nd–11th-c. migration of Germanic and Slavic peoples into Europe

Volksausgabe (Ger. f.) popular edition

Volkslied/ (Ger. n.) folk song, pl. **-er** (cap.)

Volkswagen a German make of car, abbr. **VW**

vols. volumes

volt/ (fencing) make a volte; (elec.) abbr. **V**, SI unit of potential difference; **-ampere** (hyphen)

Voltairean *not* -ian

volte (fencing) a quick movement to escape a thrust, (equestrian) a sideways circular movement of a horse; *not* volt

volte-face a turning about (not ital.)

volti subito (It. mus.) turn over quickly, abbr. **v.s.**

voltmeter a device for measuring electric potential in volts, *not* volta-

volume abbr. **vol.**, pl. **vols.**

voluntarism the doctrine of the financial independence of the Church; (philos.) belief in dominance of will; belief in importance of voluntary action; *not* -aryism

Volunteer(s) abbr. **V.**

vom *see* **von**

von/ as Ger. prefix to a proper name, usually not cap. except at the beginning of a sentence, omitted when surname stands alone, and ignored during alphabetization, *but* cap. in some Swiss names; — **dem**, — **den**, — **der**, and **vom** are also not cap. *but* are retained when the surname stands alone, and form the basis for alphabetization

von Neumann, John (b. **Johann**) (1903–57) Hungarian-born US computer scientist and mathematician, usually alphabetized thus

voodoo the use of, or belief in, religious witchcraft as practised esp. in the W. Indies; *not* voudou, vodu, vudu

voortrekker (Afrik.) pioneer

vor/ Christi Geburt, — Christo (Ger.) BC, abbr. **v. Chr.**

vort/ex a whirlpool, whirling mass, engrossing system; pl. **-exes** (*but* **-ices** in scientific and technical use)

vorticist (art) a painter, writer, etc., of a school influenced by Futurism (often cap.); (metaphysics) a person regarding the universe as a plenum in which motion propagates itself in circles

votable *not* -eable

vouch/er a coupon, one who vouches; in law **-or**

voussoir (archit.) a wedge-shaped or tapered stone forming an arch (not ital.)

vowelize *not* -ise

vox/ (Lat. f.) voice, pl. *voces*; — *angelica* an organ stop with a soft, tremulous tone; — *et praeterea nihil* voice and nothing else; — *humana* an organ stop with a voice-like tone; — *populi* public sentiment, colloq. abbr. **vox pop** (no point, not ital.)

voyager one making a voyage

voyageur a Canadian boatman, esp. (hist.) one employed in transporting goods and passengers between trading posts (not ital.)

voyeur one who spies on sexual activity (not ital.)

voyez! (Fr.) see! look!

VP vice-president

VR variant reading, Victoria Regina (Queen Victoria), Volunteer Reserve

vraisemblance the appearance of truth (not ital.)

Vratislavia/ Latin for **Breslau/Wrocław**; locative (used in place-dates) **-e**; *not* to be Anglicized as Bratislava

VRD Royal Air Force Volunteer Reserve Officers' Decoration, Royal Naval Volunteer Reserve Officers' Decoration

v. refl. verb reflexive

VRI Victoria Regina et Imperatrix (Victoria Queen and Empress)

VS Veterinary Surgeon

vs. versus

v.s. (Lat.) *vide supra* (see above), (It. mus.) *volti subito* (turn over quickly)

V-sign (cap., hyphen, two words in US)

VSO Voluntary Service Overseas

VSOP very special old pale (brandy)

VT Vermont (postal abbr.)

Vt. Vermont (off. abbr.)

v.t. verb transitive

VTOL vertical take-off and landing

vudu *use* **voodoo**

Vuillard, Jean Édouard (1868–1940) French painter

Vuillaume, Jean Baptiste (1798–1875) most important of French family of makers of bowed instruments

vulcan/ize treat rubber with sulphur at high temperature, *not* -ise; **-ology** the study of volcanoes, *not* vo- (except in US)

vulg. vulgar, -ly

vulgarize *not* -ise

Vulgate the Latin version of the Bible prepared mainly by St Jerome in the late 4th c., the official RC Latin text as revised in 1592; abbr. **Vulg.**; the accepted text of an author (not cap.)

vulgo (Lat.) commonly

vv. verses, volumes (*prefer* **vols.**), (mus.) first and second violins

v.v. vice versa

Vve (Fr.) Veuve (widow)

vv.ll. (Lat.) *variae lectiones* (variant readings)

VW Very Worshipful, Volkswagen

v.y. (bibliog.) various years

Vyborg Russia

Východočeský a region of the Czech Republic

Východoslovenský a region of Slovakia

vying *see* **vie**

Vyrnwy a lake and river, Powys

Ww

W watt, -s; wolfram (tungsten); traditionally (and often still) not used in the numeration of series

W. Wales, warden, Wednesday, Welsh; west, -ern

w week, -s; (cricket) wicket, wide, wife

w. war, (meteor.) wet dew, width, word, work

WA Washington State (postal abbr.), Western Australia

WAAC (hist.) Women's Army Auxiliary Corps; in Britain, 1917–19; in USA, 1942–8

WAAF Women's Auxiliary Air Force, 1939–48; *earlier* and *later* **WRAF**

wabbl/e, -y *use* **wo-**

WAC (US) Women's Army Corps

waddy an Australian war-club

wad/e, -able *not* -eable

Wade–Giles (en rule, for Sir Thomas Wade and Herbert Giles) a system of transcribing Chinese sounds into Latin alphabet

wadi/ (Arab.) the dry bed of a torrent, *not* -y; pl. **-s**; in Arab. **wādī**

w.a.f. with all faults

waffle (indulge in) verbose but ignorant talk or writing; (esp. US) avoid committing oneself, prevaricate

W. Afr. West Africa

wag/ a joker; **-gery, -gish**

Wagadugu Burkina Faso, *use* **Ouagadougou**

wage earner (two words)

wagon/, -er, -ette *not* wagg-

wagon/ (Fr. m.) a railway carriage; ***wagon-lit*** a sleeping car, pl. ***wagons-lits*** (hyphen, not ital. in Eng. usage)

wagtail a bird (one word)

Wahabi a sect of Muslim puritans formed by **Muhammad ibn ʿAbd-al-Wahhab** (1691–1787), following strictly the original words of the Koran; *not* -bees; *properly* **Wahh-**

Wahrheit, Dichtung und (Ger.) ('fiction and truth') by Goethe, 1811–33

wah-wah (mus.) a fluctuating muted effect achieved on brass and electric instruments, *not* wa-wa

Waiapu, Bishop of New Zealand

Wai-hai-wei *use* **Weihaiwei** (one word)

Waikiki Beach Hawaii

Wain, John (**Barrington**) (1925–94) British poet, critic, and novelist

Wainfleet Lincs.

wainscot/ panelled woodwork on an interior wall; **-ed, -ing**

waist/band, -belt, -coat, -line (one word)

waiting/ list, — room (two words)

wake past **woke**, past part. **woken**

Wakefield: the signature of the Bishop of Wakefield (colon)

Wakley, Thomas (1795–1862) English doctor, founded the *Lancet* in 1823; *see also* **Walkley**

Wal. Walloon

Walachia/, -n *use* **Walla-**

Waldenses a much persecuted puritan religious sect, founded *c.*1170; *not* Vaudois

Waldteufel, Émile (1837–1912) French composer

wale *use* **weal**

wale knot (two words) *not* wall-

Waler a horse from New South Wales

Wal/es abbr. **W.**, **-ian** *not* -ean

Wałęsa, Lech (b. 1943) Polish trade union leader, President of Poland 1990–

Walhalla *use* **V-**, in Old Norse *use* **Valhǫll**

walkabout (one word)

walkathon (one word)

walkie-talkie a two-way portable radio, *not* -y -y

walking/ frame, — stick, — tour (two words)

Walkley, Arthur Bingham (1855–1926) English drama critic; *see also* **Wakley**

Walk/man (propr.) a type of compact portable personal stereo equipment, pl. **-mans**

walkover an easy victory (one word), abbr. **w.o.**

Walküre, Die the second part of Wagner's *Ring des Nibelungen*, 1870

walkway (one word)

Walkyrie *use* **V-**

walla *use* **wallah**

wallaby a variety of small kangaroo, *not* the many variants

Wallace,/ Alfred Russel *not* -ell (1823–1913) English naturalist; **— Sir Donald Mackenzie** (1841–1919) English writer; **— George Corley** (b. 1919) US politician; **— Henry Agard** (1888–1965) US politician; **— Lewis ('Lew')** (1827–1905) US general and author; **— Sir Richard** (1818–90) English art collector and philanthropist (Wallace Collection, London); **— Prof. Robert** (1853–1939) Scottish agricultural writer; **— Sir William** (1272–1305) Scottish hero; **— William Vincent** (1812–65) Irish composer; *see also* **Wallas; Wallis**

Wallachia/ a former principality, now part of Romania; **-n** of or concerning Wallachia or a native of Wallachia, one of a non-Slav people of SE Europe; *not* Wala-

wallah (Anglo-Ind., *now* sl.) a man (usually in some specified connection)

Wallas, Graham (1858–1932) English socialist writer; *see also* **Wallace; Wallis**

wall eye(d) (two words, one in US)

wallflower (one word)

Wall Game, the a form of football played at Eton (two caps.)

Wallis,/ Sir Barnes (1887–1979) British inventor; — **George Harry** (1847–1936) English art writer; — **John** (1616–1703) English mathematician, a founder of the Royal Society; *see also* **Wallace**; **Wallas**

wall knot *use* **wale-**

Walloon a member of a French-speaking people inhabiting S. and E. Belgium and neighbouring N. France (cf. **Fleming**); the French dialect spoken by this people; abbr. **Wal.**

Wallop family name of the Earl of Portsmouth

wall painting (two words)

wallpaper (one word)

Wall Street New York City

Walpurgis night the eve of 1 May, when witches are alleged to meet and hold revels with the Devil; in Ger. f. *Walpurgisnacht*

Walton, Izaak *not* Isaac (1593–1683) English author of *The Compleat Angler*

waltz a dance (not ital.), in Fr. f. *valse*, Ger. m. *Walzer* (ital.)

Walvis Bay Namibia

WAN (comput.) wide area network

wanderlust (one word, not ital.)

W. & M./ William and Mary (King and Queen); *also* — **College** Williamsburg, Va.

wangle (colloq.) obtain (a result) by scheming, altering, or faking, or the act of this; cf. **wrangle**

wannabe (sl.) an avid fan or follower who tries to emulate the admired person, *not* -bee

wapiti a N. American deer, *not* wapp-

War. Warwickshire

Warboys Cambs.

war/ bride, — chest, — cloud, — correspondent, — crime, — cry (two words)

Ward,/ Artemas (1727–1800) American Revolutionary general, — **Artemus** pseud. of **Charles Farrar Browne** (1834–67) US humorist, — **Mrs Humphry** *not* -rey (1851–1920) English novelist, b. **Mary Augusta Arnold**

war/ damage, — dance (two words)

warden abbr. **W.**

Wardour Street London

war game (two words)

war-god (hyphen, two words in US)

war grave (two words)

war/head, -horse, -like (one word)

Warlock, Peter pseud. of **Philip Heseltine** (1894–1930) English composer

war/lock, -lord, -monger (one word)

War Office abbr. **WO**, *now* **MOD**

war/paint, -path (one word)

warrant/er one who authorizes or guarantees, **-or** (law) one who gives warranty

warrant officer (two words)

warrigal (Austral.) (noun) a dingo dog, an untamed horse, a wild Aborigine; (adj.) wild, untamed; *not* warra-

Warrnambool Victoria, Australia

Warsaw in Pol. **Warszawa**, Fr. **Varsovie**, Ger. **Warschau**

Warsaw Pact a military and economic alliance between the E. European Communist countries, originally signed in 1955 by Albania, Bulgaria, Czechoslovakia, E. Germany, Hungary, Poland, Romania, and the USSR

warship (one word)

warthog (one word)

wartime (one word)

war-torn (hyphen)

Warwickshire abbr. **War.**

war zone (two words)

Wash. Washington State (off. abbr.)

wash/bag, -basin, -board (one word)

washbowl (US) = **washbasin, washing-up bowl**

washday (one word)

wash drawing one made with a brush and black or grey watercolour (two words)

washerwoman (one word)

wash house (two words, one in US)

Washington a US state; off. abbr. **Wash.**, postal **WA**

Washington, DC the US capital

washing-up (noun) dirty crockery and cutlery ready for cleaning

wash out (noun, one word)

washroom (US) a room with washing and toilet facilities (one word)

wash/stand, -tub (one word)

wash up (Brit.) wash (crockery and cutlery) after use, (US) wash one's (face and) hands

Wasp, WASP (US, usually derog.) white Anglo-Saxon Protestant

Wassermann a blood test for syphilis, from **August von Wassermann** (1866–1925) German bacteriologist

wastable *not* -eable

wastebasket (US) = **waste-paper basket**

wasteland (one word) *but* **The Waste Land** a poem by T. S. Eliot, 1922

watch case (two words, one in US)

watch chain (two words)

watch/dog, -maker, -man, -tower, -word (one word)

water bailiff an official enforcing fishing laws, (hist.) a customs house official at a port

water/bed, -bird (one word)

water/ biscuit, — bottle, — butt (two words)

water closet abbr. **WC** (two words)

watercolour (one word; -or in US) *but* the Royal Society of Painters in Water Colours

water-cool/ cool with water (hyphen), **-ed**

water cooler (two words)

water/course, -cress, -fall, -fowl, -front, -gate, -hole (one word)

watering/ can, — place (two words)

water/ jump, — level, — lily (two words)

water/line, -log, -logged (one word)

water main (two words)

waterman (one word)

watermark (typ.) a design in the paper itself (one word)

water meadow (two words)

water/melon, -mill (one word)

water/ nymph, — pistol, — polo (two words)

waterproof (one word)

water rates (two words)

watershed a divide or line of separation between waters flowing to different catchments (e.g. basins, rivers, seas); (US) the catchment itself

waterside (one word)

water strider (US) = **pond skater** (insect)

water/ski (one word, two in US), **-skied, -skiing** *not* ski'ing, **-skier** (one word)

waterspout (one word)

water/ supply, — table (two words)

watertight (one word)

water/ torture, — tower (two words)

water/way, -works (one word)

Watling Street a Roman road between Dover and Shropshire, passing through London

watt (phys.) a unit of power, abbr. **W**

Watteau/, Jean Antoine (1684–1721) French painter, whence **— hat** etc.

Watts-Dunton, Walter Theodore (1832–1914) English man of letters

Watusi, Watutsi *use* **Tutsi**

Waugh,/ Alec (1898–1981); **— Auberon** (b. 1940) son of **— Evelyn** (**Arthur St John**) (1903–66) English writers

waul a loud cat-cry, *not* -wl

wave/band, -guide (one word)

wavelength (one word) symbol λ (lambda)

wave number (two words)

wavy *not* -ey

wax/cloth, -work (one word)

Waynflete, William of *see* **William of Waynflete**

-ways suffix forming adjs. and advs. of direction or manner (*crossways, sideways*); *see also* **-wise**

wayzgoose/ (orig. **waygoose**) an annual summer dinner or outing held by a printing house for its employees (one word); pl. **-s,** *not* -geese

Waziristan India, *not* **Wazar-**

Wb weber

WBA West Bromwich Albion

WC water closet, West Central (postal district of London), without charge

WCC World Council of Churches

W/Cdr. Wing Commander

WD War Department, Works Department

w/e week ending

WEA Workers' Educational Association

weak abbr. **wk.**

weal a flesh mark, *not* wale

Weald/, the a formerly wooded district including parts of Kent, Surrey, and East Sussex (cap.); (not cap.) **-clay** beds of clay, sandstone, limestone, and ironstone, forming the top of Wealden strata (hyphen)

Wealden (adj.) of the Weald, resembling it geologically; (noun) a series of Lower Cretaceous freshwater deposits above Jurassic strata and below chalk, best exemplified in the Weald

wear a dam, *use* **weir**

weasel/, -lled, -lling (one *l* in US)

weather/ chart *or* **— map** (two words)

weather/cock, -man, -proof (one word)

weather station (two words)

weather/vane, -woman (one word)

weather-worn (hyphen, one word in US)

weazen *use* **wizened**

Web, the (abbr.) the World Wide Web (cap.)

Webb,/ Beatrice (1858–1943) wife of **— Sidney James, Baron Passfield** (1859–1947) English economists and sociologists; **— Mary** (1881–1927) English novelist

Weber,/ Carl Maria (**Friedrich Ernst**) **von** (1786–1826) Austrian-born German composer and pianist; **— Ernst Heinrich** (1795–1878) German physiologist and psychologist, **Weber-Fechner law** (en rule) *use* **Weber's law**; **— Max** (1864–1920) German sociologist; **— Max** (1881–1961) Russian-born US painter

weber (phys.) the SI unit of magnetic flux, abbr. **Wb**; named after **Wilhelm Eduard Weber** (1804–91) German physicist, brother of **Ernst Heinrich Weber** (q.v.)

Webern, Anton (**Friedrich Ernst**) **von** (1883–1945) Austrian composer

web/-fed (typ.) presses that receive paper from a reel and not as separate sheets (hyphen); **— letterpress, — offset** (two words)

Webster,/ Daniel (1782–1852) US statesman and orator; **— Noah** (1758–1843) US lexicographer

Weddell/, James (1787–1834) British navigator; discovered — **Sea** (two caps.), — **seal** *Leptonychotes weddelli* (one cap.)

wedding/ breakfast, — cake, — day, — march, — night, — ring (two words)

Wedgwood ware a superior kind of pottery, invented by **Josiah Wedgwood** (1730–95); *not* Wedge-

Wednesday abbr. **W.**, **Wed.**

week/, -s abbr. **w.**, **wk.**

week/day, -end (one word)

week-long (hyphen, one word in US)

Weelkes, Thomas (*c.*1575–1623) English composer

weepie (colloq.) a sentimental film, play, etc.

weepy (colloq.) tearful

weever a spiny marine fish, *not* weav-

weevil a destructive beetle

w.e.f. with effect from

Wehrmacht (Ger. hist. f.) the German armed forces, esp. the army, 1921–45 (cap., ital.)

Weidenfeld (George) & Nicolson publishers

weighbridge (one word)

weight abbr. **wt.**

weightlift/er, -ing (one word)

weights use numerals; abbr. as cwt, g, lb, oz, no *s* added for the plural

Weihaiwei China, *not* **Wai-hai-wei**

Weil,/ Adolf (1848–1916) German physician, — **Simone** (1909–43) French philosopher

Weill, Kurt (1900–50) German-born US composer

Weimar Republic the German republic 1919–33

Weimaraner a breed of dog

Weingartner, Paul Felix (1863–1942) German conductor and composer

Weinstein, Nathan Wallenstein *see* **West, Nathanael**

weir a dam across a river, *not* -ar

weird *not* wie-

Weismann/, August (1834–1914) German zoologist, **-ism** a theory of heredity

Weissnichtwo (Ger. for Know-not-where) in Carlyle's *Sartor Resartus*

Weizmann/, Chaim (1874–1952) Polish-born chemist and Zionist leader, — **Institute** Israel

Weizsäcker,/ Carl Friedrich Freiherr von (b. 1912) German philosopher and physicist, — **Julius** (1828–89) German historian, — **Karl** (1822–99) German theologian

welch *use* -sh

Welch Fusiliers, Royal *but* **Welsh Guards**

Welfare State (two words, caps.)

welk *use* whe-

well- prefix joined to participles in *-ed* or *-ing*, takes hyphens when the compound is used attributively, and to preserve the unity of the sense when it is used predicatively, e.g. 'a well-known book', 'the book is well known', 'the action was not well-advised', 'he has not been well advised'

well/-being, -doer (hyphens)

Welles, Orson (1915–85) US actor and director

Wellesley town and college, Mass.

wellington a waterproof rubber or plastic boot (not cap.), colloq. **welly** *not* -ie

well-known *see* **well-**

well-nigh (hyphen)

well-to-do (hyphens)

well-wisher (hyphen)

Welsh abbr. **W.**

welsh/ default in payment, (esp. US) break one's word; *not* -lch; **-er**; *but prefer* another term to avoid offence

Welsh/ corgi, — dresser, — harp, — onion (one cap.)

Welsh rabbit melted cheese on toast; *not* rarebit

Welt/anschauung (Ger.) world-philosophy, **-politik** participation in international politics, **-schmerz** world-sorrow (one word)

Wemyss/ Bay Strathclyde, — **Castle** Fife, **Earl of** —

wen *see* **wyn**

Wend, -ic, -ish (hist.) (a member of) a Slavonic people of N. Germany, now inhabiting E. Saxony; in modern contexts *use* **Sorb**; *see also* **Sorbian**

Wensleydale a variety of white or blue cheese, a breed of long-wool sheep (cap.)

werewol/f a mythical being who at times changes from a person to a wolf, pl. **-ves**; *not* werw-

West, Nathanael pseud. of **Nathan Wallenstein Weinstein** (1903–40) US writer

west abbr. **W.**; *see also* **compass points**

West Africa abbr. **W. Afr.**

westbound (one word)

West Bridgford Notts., *not* Bridge-

Westchester NY

West Chester Del., Pa.

West Country the south-western counties of England (two caps.)

West End London (caps.)

westeria *use* wis-

Westermarck, Edward Alexander (1862–1939) Finnish anthropologist

Western a cowboy film (cap.)

western abbr. **W**; *see also* **compass points**

Western Australia abbr. **WA**

Western Isles the formal name for the Hebrides

Westfalen Ger. for **Westphalia**

Westhoughton Gr. Manchester (one word)

Westmeath/ a county of Ireland (one word), **Earl of** —

Westmorland/ a former county of England, **Earl of** — *not* -eland

Westonzoyland Som. (one word)

West Virginia off. abbr. **W. Va.**, postal **WV**

wetlands (one word)

w.f. (typ.) wrong font

WFEO World Federation of Engineering Organizations

WFTU World Federation of Trade Unions

W.G. W. G. Grace (1848–1915) English cricketer

Wg. Comdr., Wg/Cdr. Wing Commander

Wh watt-hour

whalebone (one word)

whallabee *use* **wallaby**

whar/f a landing stage, abbr. **whf.**; pl. **-ves**

Wharfedale Yorks.

Wharncliffe, Earl of

whatchamacallit (US colloq.) (one word)

what-d'you-call-it? (colloq.) (hyphens, apos.)

Whately, Richard (1787–1863) Archbishop of Dublin, *not* -ey

whatever (one word)

Whatman paper a first-quality English handmade drawing paper (cap.)

whatnot an indefinite or trivial thing, a piece of furniture with shelves (one word)

what not many other similar things, e.g. 'pens, pencils, and what not' (two words, one word in US)

what's/-her-name, -his-name, -its-name (hyphens)

whatso (arch.) whatever

whatsoever (one word)

wheal *use* **weal**

wheatear a small migratory bird (one word)

Wheatstone bridge an apparatus for measuring electrical resistances

wheel/barrow, -base, -chair (one word)

wheel clamp (two words)

wheelhouse (one word)

wheel lock (two words)

wheelwright (one word)

whelk a predatory mollusc, a pimple; *not* we-

whence from which (place), and thence; 'from whence' is a tautology

when/ever, -soever (one word)

whereas (law) a word that introduces the recital of a fact (one word)

where/ver, -soever (one word)

whether or not *not* or no

whf. wharf

whidah *use* **why-**

whiffletree (US) = **whippletree**

Whig/, -gish, -gism (cap.)

whimbrel a small curlew, *not* wim-

whimsy caprice, *not* -ey

whing/e, -er, -ing, -y

whinny (give) a gentle neigh, *not* -ey

whip/cord, -lash (one word)

whipper/-in (hunting) pl. **-s-in**

whippersnapper (one word)

whippletree a swingletree, the crossbar to which the traces of a harness are attached; *not* whiffle- (US)

whippoorwill an American nightjar (one word)

whirligig a child's spinning toy, a merry-go-round

whirl/pool, -wind (one word)

whirlybird (colloq.) a helicopter

whirr (make) a continuous buzzing sound, *not* whir

whisk/ey (Irish and US); **-y** (Scotch and Canadian)

Whistler, James Abbott McNeill, *not* -eil (1834–1903) US painter and etcher

Whitaker & Sons, J. publishers of the Almanack (*not* -ac) etc.

white/ a white person, (typ.) any space of paper not printed upon; **line of** — a line not printed upon (not cap.)

whitebait (one word)

Whitechapel London (one word)

Whitefield, George (1714–70) English preacher, *not* Whitf-; *but* pron. 'Wit-'

Whitehall London (one word)

Whitehorse Yukon (one word)

White Horse, Vale of Oxon. (*formerly* Berks.), *not* of the

White House official residence of the US President, Washington, DC

Whiteing, Richard (1840–1928) English journalist and novelist

white-out a polar blizzard (hyphen, one word in US)

White Paper a Government report giving information or proposals on an issue (caps.) cf. **Blue Book**; **Green Paper**

White Russian Soviet Socialist Republic a former Soviet Socialist Republic, *properly* **Belorussian Soviet Socialist Republic**, *now* **Belarus**'; avoid 'White Russian' in this sense, since it was the standard term for anti-Bolsheviks

White's Club London

whitewash (one word)

Whitey derog. for a white person, or white people collectively (cap.); cf. **white**; **whity**

whitish *not* -eish

Whitman, Walt (1819–92) US poet

Whit/ Monday, — Sunday seventh after Easter, *but* **Whitsun/, -tide** (one word)

Whittier, John Greenleaf (1807–92) US poet

Whittlesey, Cambs. *not* -sea

whity whitelike, *not* -ey; cf. **Whitey**

whizz/ *not* whiz (US); **-zed, -zing**

whizz-kid (colloq.) (hyphen, **whiz kid** in US)

WHO World Health Organization

whoa/ a command to stop; **-ed, -ing, -s**

whodunit a novel or play of crime detection, *not* -nnit (one word)

whole-bound (bind.) full-bound

whole/food, -grain, -hearted, -meal (one word)

whole note (US) = **semibreve**

whole/sale, -some (one word)

wholewheat (one word, two words in US)

whoopee/, — cushion *not* -ie

whooping cough *not* hooping

whore/house, -monger, -son (one word)

whose of whom *or* of which

Who's Who, **Who Was Who** reference books

whydah an African weaver-bird, *not* whidah

why ever (two words)

Whymper, Edward (1840–1911) British climber and writer

Whyte-Melville, George John (1821–78) Scottish novelist (hyphen)

WI West Ind/ies, -ian; Windward Islands; Wisconsin (postal abbr.); Women's Institute

wich alder *use* **witch alder**

wich elm *use* **wych elm**

wich hazel *use* **witch hazel**

Wicliffe *use* **Wyclif**

widdershins (Sc.) anticlockwise, opp. to **deasil**; *not* wither-

wide (cricket) abbr. **w.**

wide awake fully awake, (colloq.) alert, knowing (hyphen when attrib.)

wideawake a kind of hat (one word)

widespread (one word)

widgeon a bird, *use* **wigeon**

widow (typ.) the last line of a paragraph at the top of a page or column, *or* word or part of a word at the end of a paragraph on a line by itself; *see also* **orphan**

Wieland, Christoph Martin (1733–1813) German poet and novelist

Wien Ger. for **Vienna**

Wiener, Norbert (1894–1964) US mathematician and writer on cybernetics

Wiener Neustadt Austria (two words)

Wiener schnitzel a veal cutlet dressed with breadcrumbs (two words, one cap.)

Wieniawski,/ Henri (1835–80) Polish violinist and composer; **— Joseph** (1837–1912) his brother, Polish pianist and composer

Wiesbaden Germany

wife abbr. **w.**

wigeon a dabbling duck, *not* widg-

Wiggin, Kate Douglas (1856–1923) US educator and novelist

Wight, Isle of abbr. **IOW, IoW, IW**

Wigorn: the former signature of the Bishop of Worcester (colon)

Wigton Cumbria

Wigtown a district and town, Dumfries & Galloway

wigwam an arched or conical dwelling of the eastern Native American peoples; cf. **tepee**

Wilamowitz(-Mullendorf), **Ulrich von** (1848–1931) German classical scholar, *not* Moe-

wildcat a hot-tempered person, reckless or sudden, (US) a bobcat (one word)

Wilde,/ Henry (1833–1919) English physicist, **— Oscar** (**Fingal O'Flahertie Wills**) (1854–1900) Irish playwright, author, and poet

wildebeest a gnu, in Afrik. **wildebees/** pl. **-te**

wild/fire, -fowl (one word)

wild-goose chase (one hyphen)

wildlife (one word)

wilful/, -ly, -ness *not* will- (except in US)

Wilhelmj, August Emil Daniel Ferdinand (1845–1908) German violinist

Wilhelmshaven a city, Lower Saxony, and former German naval station (one word)

Wilhelmstrasse Berlin, the diplomatic quarter, named **Otto-Grotewohl-Straße** under Communist rule

William of Waynflete (1395–1486) Bishop of Winchester, Lord Chancellor

Willkie, Wendell (**Lewis**) (1892–1944) US politician

will-o'-the-wisp the ignis fatuus, an elusive person, a delusive hope (apos., hyphens)

willowware (US) willow-pattern pottery (one word)

will-power (hyphen, one word in US)

willy-nilly whether one likes it or not, haphazardly (hyphen)

willy-willy (Austral.) a cyclone or dust storm (hyphen)

Wiltshire abbr. **Wilts.**

Wimborne, Viscount

Wimborne Minster Dorset

wimbrel *use* wh-

Wimpey a British construction company

Wimpy a fast-food hamburger chain

Wimsey, Lord Peter in the novels by Dorothy Sayers

winable *use* **winn-**

wincey/ a cloth, *not* -sey; **-ette** a lightweight flannelette

Winchelsea E. Sussex

Winchilsea,/ Earl of; — **Anne Finch, Countess of** (1661–1720) English poet

Winckelmann, Johann Joachim (1717–68) German art critic

wind/age, -bag, -bound, -break (one word)

windbreaker (US) = **windcheater** (jacket)

Windermere *not* Lake —

windfall (one word)

Windhoek Namibia

Wind. I. Windward Islands

winding sheet a shroud (two words)

window/ box, — dressing, — ledge (two words)

window pane (two words, one word in US)

window seat (two words)

window-shop/, -per, -ping (hyphens)

window sill (two words)

window tax (hist.) a tax on windows or similar openings (abolished in 1851)

wind/mill, -pipe, -screen (one word)

Windscale *see* **Sellafield**

wind shear (two words)

windshield (US) = **windscreen** (car)

windsurf/, -er, -ing (one word)

windward (the region) on or towards the side from which the wind is blowing; cf. **leeward**

wine bottle (two words)

wine/glass, -glassful, -press (one word)

winery an establishment where wine is made

wineskin (one word)

winey winelike, *not* winy

Winged Victory (Gr. antiquity) (a statue of) Nike (Athena) (caps.)

winnable able to be won, *not* wina-

Winnie-the-Pooh (hyphens)

wino/ (sl.) an alcoholic, pl. **-s**

winsey *use* **-cey**

wint/er, -ry (not cap.)

wintergreen an aromatic plant (one word)

winterize adapt for use in cold weather, *not* -ise

Winton: the signature of the Bishop of Winchester (colon)

winy *use* **winey**

wipe-out (noun, hyphen, one word in US)

WIPO World Intellectual Property Organization

wireless/ (in full — **set**) a radio receiving set; superseded by **radio**

Wis. Wisconsin (off. abbr.)

Wisbech Cambs., *not* -each

Wisconsin off. abbr. **Wis.**, postal **WI**

Wisden Cricketers' Almanack *not* -'s, -ac

Wisdom of Solomon (Apocr.) abbr. **Wisd.**

-wise suffix forming adjs. and advs. of manner (e.g. *crosswise, clockwise, lengthwise*) or respect (*moneywise*); *see also* **-ways**

wiseacre (one word)

wisent the European bison, *Bison bonasus*; *not* aurochs (q.v.)

wishbone (one word)

wishy-washy (hyphen)

Wislicenus, Johannes (1835–1902) German chemist

Wistar/, (*also* **-er**), **Caspar** (1761–1818) US anatomist; — **rats** (from the Wistar Institute, Philadelphia, founded by Caspar's grand-nephew)

wisteria (bot.) *not* -taria

witch alder *not* wich, wych (except in US)

witch elm *use* **wych elm**

witchetty (Austral.) the larva of beetle or moth, *not* -ety

witch hazel (two words) *not* wich-, wych-

witch-hunt (hyphen)

withal *not* -all

with/e pl. **-es**, *or* **-y** pl. **-ies** a flexible twig, often of willow; *not* wy-

withershins *use* **widder-**

withhold etc. (one word, two *hs*)

without abbr. **w/o**

witness box (two words) *not* -stand (US)

Wittenberg Germany

Witwatersrand University Johannesburg, S. Africa

wivern *use* **wy-**

wizened shrivelled; *not* weaz-, -en

Wk Walk (in place names)

wk. weak; week, -s; work

W. long. west longitude

Wm. William

WMO World Meteorological Organization

WNW west-north-west

WO War Office (*now* **MOD** (q.v.)), Warrant Officer, Wireless Operator

w.o. walkover

w/o without

wobbl/e, -y *not* wa-

Wodehouse/ the family name of the Earl of Kimberley, —, **P. G. (Sir Pelham Grenville)** (1881–1975) English humorous novelist; *see also* **Woodhouse**

woebegone dismal-looking (one word), *but* 'Lake Wobegon' in the novels of Garrison Keillor

Wolcot, Dr John (1738–1819) **'Peter Pindar'**, English writer; *see also* **Wolcott**; **Woollcott**

Wolcott, Oliver (1726–97) and — — (1760–1833) his son, American statesmen; *see also* **Wolcot**; **Woollcott**

Wolf,/ Friedrich August (1759–1824) German classical scholar, — **Hugo** (1860–1903) Austrian composer

Wolfe,/ Charles (1791–1823) Irish poet; — **Humbert** (1885–1940) English poet; — **James** (1727–59) British general, took Quebec; — **Thomas** (**Clayton**) (1900–38) US novelist; — **Tom** (**Thomas Kennerley**) (b. 1931) US journalist and writer

Wolff,/ Sir Henry Drummond Charles (1830–1908) British politician and diplomat; — **Christian von** (1679–1754) German philosopher and mathematician; — **Joseph** (1795–1862) German-born, English-domiciled traveller; — **Kaspar Friedrich** (1733–94) German embryologist; **-ian**

Wolf-Ferrari, Ermanno (1876–1948) Italian composer

wolfhound (one word)

Wollstonecraft/ (**Godwin**), **Mary** (1759–97) English writer, mother of **Mary — Godwin, Mrs Shelley** (1797–1851) English writer

wolverine a voracious weasel-like animal, called **glutton** in Europe; *not* -ene

womanize *not* -ise

womankind *not* women- (one word)

Women's Lib (caps., no point)

wonky (Brit. sl.) crooked, loose, unsteady, unreliable; *not* -ey

woo/, **-ed**, **-er**, **-s**

Wood, Anthony à (1632–95) English antiquary

Woodard Foundation of a number of English public schools, named after **Nathaniel Woodard** (1881–91) English Anglican priest; *not* Woodw-

woodbine honeysuckle, *not* -bind

woodchuck a N. American marmot, a groundhog (one word)

woodcock/ (m. and f.) a bird, pl. same

woodcut (typ.) a design cut in the side grain of a type-high block of wood (one word)

wood engraving (typ.) a design cut in the end grain of a type-high block of wood (two words)

Woodhouse the surname of Emma in Jane Austen's *Emma*; *see also* **Wodehouse**

wood/land, **-lark**, **-louse**, **-man** (one word)

wood nymph (two words)

wood/pecker, **-pile**, **-shed**, **-wind** (mus.), **-work**, **-worm**, **-yard** (one word)

wool/, **-len** (one *l* in US), **-ly**

Woolacombe Devon

Wooler Northumb.

Woolf,/ (**Adeline**) **Virginia** née **Stephen** (1882–1941) English novelist and essayist; — **Leonard Sidney** (1880–1969) her husband, English writer

Woollcott, Alexander (**Humphreys**) (1887–1943) US author and drama critic; *see also* **Wolcot**; **Wolcott**

Woolloomooloo Sydney, Australia

woolpack a fleecy cumulus cloud, (hist.) a bale of wool (one word)

Woolsack the official seat of the Lord Chancellor in the House of Lords (one word)

wool-sorters' disease anthrax, *not* -er's

woolverine *use* wolv-

Worcester: the signature of the Bishop of Worcester (colon)

Worcestershire/ a county of England, abbr. **Worcs.**; — **sauce** (US) = (what is in Britain commonly called) **Worcester sauce**

Worde *see* **Wynkyn**

Word of God, the (caps.) *but* in NT a lower-case w

word/play, **-smith** (one word)

work abbr. **wk.**

workaday (one word)

work and turn (typ.) the printing of two sides of a sheet of paper from one forme

work/bench, **-box**, **-day**, **-force**, **-horse** (one word)

workhouse (hist.) a public institution in which the destitute of a parish received board and lodging in return for work done, (US) a house of correction for petty offenders (one word)

working class (hyphen when attrib.)

work/load, **-man**, **-manlike**, **-manship**, **-mate** (one word)

work off (typ.) actually to print the paper

work/out (noun), **-sheet**, **-shop**, **-station** (one word)

work study a system of assessing methods of working (two words)

work-study a programme or course combining work with classroom time (hyphen)

worktop (one word)

work-to-rule (noun, hyphens)

World,/ the New America; — **the Old** Europe, Asia, and Africa, known to the ancients (two caps.)

World Bank *formally*, the **International Bank for Reconstruction and Development**, a UN agency administering economic aid between member nations

world/-famous, **-shaking** (hyphens)

World War I 1914–18, **World War II** 1939–45 are preferred US forms; **First World War** and

Second World War are preferred British forms

worldwide (one word) *but* (comput.) **World Wide Web, World Wide Fund for Nature** (caps.)

worm-eaten (hyphen)

worm's-eye view (apos., one hyphen)

wormwood (bot.) *Artemisia*, (fig.) bitterness

Wormwood Scrubs a prison, London

worry beads (two words)

worry-guts (colloq.) (hyphen)

worrywart (US colloq.) (one word)

worship/, -ped, -per, -ping (one *p* in US)

Wörterbuch (Ger. n.) dictionary

worthwhile (one word, *formerly* two words predicatively, one word attributively)

Wotton, Sir Henry (1568–1639) English diplomat and poet

would-be adj. (hyphen)

Woulfe/, Peter (1727–1803) English chemist, hence — **bottle** for passing gas through liquid

wove paper that which does not show wire marks; cf. **laid paper**

Wozzeck an opera by Berg, 1925, based on **Woyzeck**, a play by Büchner, 1837

WP weather permitting

w.p.b. waste-paper basket

WPC woman police constable

w.p.m. words per minute

WR Western Region, West Riding

WRAC Women's Royal Army Corps

wrack destruction; a seaweed; *see also* **rack**

WRAF (hist.) Women's Royal Air Force, since 1994 integrated into the RAF

Wrangel Island Arctic Ocean

Wrangell Island Alaska

wrangle (engage in) a noisy argument or (US) herd cattle; cf. **wangle**

wrangler one who wrangles, (US) a cowboy, (Cambridge University) one placed in the first class of the mathematical tripos

wraparound (one word)

wrap-round (bind.) a folded section placed outside another section, so that sewing passes through both

wrath (noun) great anger; *see also* **wro-**

Wray *see* **Ray**

wreath/ (noun), **-e** (verb)

Wren a member of the Women's Royal Naval Service

wrick *use* **rick**

wrist/band, -watch (one word)

writable *not* -eable

write/-back, -down, -off, -protect, -up (nouns, hyphens)

writer's cramp *not* -ers' cramp

writing/ desk, — paper, — table (two words)

WRNS Women's Royal Naval Service, a member is a **Wren**

Wrocław Poland; in Ger. **Breslau**, Lat. **Vratislavia**

wrongdo/er, -ing (one word)

wrong font (typ.) said of letter(s) set in wrong size or cut of type, abbr. **w.f.**

wroth (poet. or joc.) angry; *see also* **wra-**

Wrottesley/ a cape, NW Canada; **Baron —**

WRVS Women's Royal Voluntary Service, *formerly* **WVS**

wry/bill, -mouth, -neck (one word)

WS (Sc.) Writer to the Signet (= attorney)

WSW west-south-west

WT *or* **W/T** wireless telegraphy

wt. weight

wunderkind one who achieves success in youth, *not* wo- (not ital.); in Ger. n. **Wunderkind**

Württemberg a German state (two ts); *see also* **Baden-Württemberg**

Wuthering Heights a novel by E. Brontë, 1846

WV West Virginia (postal abbr.)

W. Va. West Virginia (off. abbr.)

WVS Women's Voluntary Service, *now* **WRVS**

w/w weight for weight

WWW World Wide Web

WY Wyoming (postal abbr.)

Wyandot (of) (a member of) a Native American subgroup of the Hurons

wyandotte a breed of domestic fowl, *not* -ot

wych alder *use* **witch alder**

wych elm (two words) *not* wich, witch

Wycherley, William (1640–1716) English playwright

wych hazel *use* **witch hazel**

Wyclif/, John (c.1324–84) English religious reformer and translator of the Bible, *not* the many variants; **-fite**

Wycliffe/ College Stonehouse; — **Hall** Oxford, a theological college

Wykeham/, William of (1324–1404) English prelate, **-ist** a member of Winchester College (cap.)

Wymondham Leics., Norfolk

wyn the Old English Þ, ρ (distinguish from **eth** and **thorn** (qq.v.)); in modern editions *w* is normally substituted

Wyndham/ the family name of Baron Leconfield; **—, Sir Charles** (1837–1919) English actor, **—, George** (1863–1913) English statesman, **—'s Theatre** London

Wyndham Lewis,/ Dominic Bevan (1894–1969) British writer, **— — Percy** (1882–1957) English writer and painter

Wyndham-Quin family name of the Earl of Dunraven

Wynkyn de Worde (1471–1534) early printer in London

Wyoming off. abbr. **Wyo.**, postal **WY**

Wyredrawers, Gold and Silver a livery company

WYSIWYG (comput.) 'what you see is what you get' (caps.), pron. 'wizziwig'

wyth/e, -y *use* **wi-**

Wythenshawe Manchester

wyvern (her.) a winged two-legged dragon with a barbed tail, *not* wi-

X x

X cross; ten; the twenty-first in a series; former film-censorship classification (replaced in the UK in 1983 by **18**, and in 1990 by **NC-17** in the USA)

X (usually **XP** or **Xt.**) the Greek letter chi, for *Christos*, Christ

x (math.) the first unknown quantity

x. (meteor.) hoar frost

Xaime Galician for **James**

Xanthippe the wife of Socrates, used allusively for a shrewish woman

Xavier, St Francis (1506–52) Jesuit missionary

Xbre (Fr.) December

XC 90

XCIX 99

x.cp. ex (without) coupon

x.d. ex (without) dividend

Xe xenon (no point)

xebec a small Mediterranean boat, *not* z-

Xenocrates (396–314 BC) Greek philosopher

xenon symbol **Xe**

Xenophanes (*c.*570–*c.*500 BC) Greek philosopher and poet

Xenophon (*c.*438–*c.*354 BC) Greek historian, abbr. **Xen.**

Xérès Fr. for **Jerez**

xeric (ecology) having or characterized by dry conditions

xerograph a copy produced by **xerography**, a dry copying process using electrically charged powder after exposure

Xerox (propr.) a xerographic copying machine (cap.); produce (copies) from such a machine (not cap.); *prefer* **photocopy** in general references

Xerxes (519–465 BC) King of Persia

x-height (typ.) the distance between top and bottom of those lower-case letters of a given font that have no ascenders or descenders (e.g. n, x)

Xhosa (of or relating to) (a member of) a Bantu people of Cape Province, S. Africa; or their language (*formerly* called Kaffir)

xi the fourteenth letter of the Gr. alphabet (Ξ, ξ)

x.i. *or* **ex int.** ex (without) next interest

Xianggang Pinyin for **Hong Kong**

Xiaoping, Deng *see* **Deng Xiaoping**

xiphoid (biol.) sword-shaped

Xizang Pinyin for **Tibet**

XL 40

XLIX 49

Xmas Christmas (no point)

XML (comput.) Extended Mark-up Language

Xn. Christian

x.n. (ex new) (without) the right to new shares

Xnty. Christianity

Xoán Galician for **John**

xoan/on (Gr. antiquity) a primitive (usually wooden) image of a deity, supposed to have fallen from heaven; pl. **-a**

Xosa *use* **Xho-**

XP (as monogram ☧) the Gr. letters *chi rho*, the first two of *Khristos*

X-ray (hyphen)

Xt. Christ

XX 20

XXX 30

XXXX 40 in Roman and early-modern use, though modern writers favour **XL**

xylograph/ a woodcut or wood engraving; **-y** making woodcuts or wood engravings, the use of wood blocks in printing

Xylonite (propr.) a kind of celluloid

xylophon/e, -ist

xyst/us an ancient Greek portico used by athletes, pl. **-i**; in archaeological (rather than literary) contexts *also* **-os**, pl. **-oi**

Yy

Y yen (q.v.), yttrium; the twenty-second in a series

Y, y (**Ӯ**, **ÿ**) in mod. Dutch *use* **IJ**, **ij**, as in IJmuiden, Nijmegen

y. year, -s; (meteor.) dry air

y (math.) the second unknown quantity

yacht/, -sman (one word)

yager *use* **jaeger**

Yahoo in Swift's *Gulliver's Travels*, an animal with human form but brutish instincts (cap.); a lout or hooligan (not cap.)

Yahweh the probable pronunciation of the Hebrew Tetragrammaton, the consonants YHVW, YHWH, which are traditionally transliterated as **Jehovah**; *not* Jahveh, Yaveh

Yakö (of or relating to) (a member of) a Nigerian people of the Cross River region, *not* Yache

Yakutsk Siberia, *not* J-

yakuza a Japanese gangster or racketeer, pl. same (not ital.)

Yale university, New Haven, Conn.; (propr.) a kind of lock (cap.)

yam any tropical or subtropical climbing plant of the genus *Dioscorea*, or the edible starchy tuber of this; in US also called **sweet potato**

Yamato-e the style or school of art in Japan, culminating in the 12th and 13th cc., that dealt with Japanese subjects in a distinctively Japanese (rather than Chinese) way

Yangtze Kiang a Chinese river (*kiang* = river), in Pinyin **Yangzijiang**

Yank/, -ee *not* -i

Yankey in England a comedy by David Humphreys, 1814

Yanomami (of or relating to) (a member of) an Amazonian people, pl. same; *also* **-mö**

yanqui (Sp.) a citizen of the USA

Yaoundé Cameroon, *not* Yasun-

yaourt *use* **yogurt**

yapp a form of bookbinding with a limp leather cover projecting to fold over the edges of the leaves

yarborough a hand in whist or bridge with no card above 9 (not cap.)

yard/, -s = 3 feet (0.9144 metre); abbr. **yd**, **yds**

yardarm (naut.) (one word)

yardbird (US sl.) a new military recruit, a convict (one word)

Yarde-Buller family name of Baron Churston

yardstick (one word)

Yarkand Cent. Asia; *not* -end, -und

yarl *use* **j-**

yarmulke/ a Jewish skullcap, pl. **-s**; *not* yarme-, -ka

Yaroslavl'/, — Oblast Russia, *not* J-

Yates/, Dornford pseud. of **Cecil William Mercer** (1885–1960) English novelist; **—, Frank** (1902–94) English statistician, **—'s correction**

YB Year Book

Yb ytterbium (no point)

YC Young Conservative

yclept (arch., joc.) called, named (one word)

Yding Skovhøj a peak, Denmark

yd yard, pl. **yds**

yᵉ the; in approximating 15th- to 17th-c. works, the second letter to be superior (no point); *see also* **yᵗ**

Yeames, William Frederick (1835–1918) English painter

year/, -s abbr. **y.**; **a**; **yr.**, **yrs.**

yearbook (one word), **Year Book** (law reports) (caps., two words) abbr. **YB**

year-long (hyphen, one word in US)

year-round (hyphen)

years when in figures, to be elided except in titles; no apos. except as possessive, e.g. 'the 1940s' *but* '1940's population figure'

Yeats, William Butler (1865–1939) Irish poet

Yeats-Brown, Francis (1886–1944) English author

Yeddo/ a former name (later **Edo**) for Tokyo: **— hawthorn, — spruce**

yellowhammer a bird, *not* -ammer (one word)

Yellowknife NW Territories, Canada

Yellow Pages (caps.)

Yellowplush Papers (two words) by Thackeray, 1841

Yellowstone/ (one word) **National Park, — River**

Yemen/ S. Arabia; **North —** officially **— Arab Republic; South —** officially **People's Democratic Republic of —**; adj. **-i**

yen the chief monetary unit of Japan, pl. same; abbr. **Y**, symbol **¥**

Yeniseisk Siberia, on the **River Yenisei**

Yeo. Yeomanry

Yeoman/ Usher, — Warder; pl. **— Ushers, — Warders**; *not* Yeomen

yerba maté = **maté**

Yerevan Armenia; *not* E-, -iv-

yes-man (colloq.) (hyphen)

yesteryear (one word)

yeux *see* **œil**

Yevtushenko, Yevgeni (**Aleksandrovich**) (b. 1933) Russian writer

Y-fronts (propr.) men's or boys' briefs with a Y-shaped seam at the front

Yggdrasil (Scandinavian myth.) the ash tree binding heaven, earth, and hell; Anglicized from Old Norse **yg(g)drasill**; *not* Ygd-

YHA Youth Hostels Association, (US) Youth Hostels of America

YHVH *or* **YHWH** the Tetragrammaton, the Hebrew name of God written in four (usually small-capital) letters, articulated as Yahweh, Jehovah, etc.

Yiddish/ (of or relating to) a vernacular used by Jews in or from Cent. and E. Europe; also called *Judaeo-German* by linguists; **-ist** a scholar of the subject

yield point (two words)

yippee an exclamation of delight

ylang-ylang (the oil from) a Malayan tree (hyphen), in Tagalog *ilang-ilang*

YMCA Young Men's Christian Association

Ymuiden *use* **IJm-**

Ynca *use* **I-**

Ynys Môn Welsh for Anglesey

yob/ (colloq.) a lout, hooligan; *also* **-bo**; pl. **-s**; **-bish**

yod the tenth and smallest letter in the Hebrew alphabet

yodel/ a song, *or* to sing, with inarticulate partly falsetto voice that carries over long distances; **-led, -ling** (one *l* in US); *not* -dle, jodel

yog/a Hindu system of philosophic meditation; **-i** a person proficient in yoga; adj. **-ic**

yogh the ME letter ð, ȝ; normally *use* ȝ, ȝ; standing for certain values of *g* and *y*

yogurt a semi-solid sour fermented-milk food; *not* -hurt, -ourt; in Fr. **yaourt**

Yoknapatawpha County a fictional setting in Mississippi in the novels and stories of William Faulkner

Yokohama Japan (one word)

Yom Kippur (Jewish relig.) Day of Atonement

Yonge,/ **Charles Duke** (1812–91) English historian; **— Charlotte Mary** (1823–1901) English novelist; pron. 'Young'; *see also* **Young**

Yorke family name of the Earl of Hardwicke

Yorkshire a former county of England, abbr. **Yorks.**

Yorktown Va. (one word)

Yoruba a Kwa language spoken in SW Nigeria, Benin, and Togo

Yosemite Valley Calif., pron. 'Yo-sem-itty'

Youcon *use* **Yukon**

Youghal Co. Cork

Youl, Sir James Arndell (1809–1904) Tasmanian colonist

Young, Brigham (1801–77) US Mormon leader; *see also* **Yonge**

younger abbr. **yr.**

Young Men's Christian Association abbr. **YMCA**

Young Turk a member of a revolutionary party in Turkey in 1908; a young person eager for radical change to the established order (cap.); (offens.) a violent child or youth (not cap.)

young 'un (colloq.) a youngster

Young Women's Christian Association abbr. **YWCA**

your abbr. **yr.**

yours (no apos.) abbr. **yrs.**

yo-yo/ a kind of toy, pl. **-s** (hyphen, orig. propr. and cap.)

Ypres/ Belgium, in Fl. **Ieper; Earl of —**

Yquem/ a vineyard, dép. Gironde; **—, Château-d'** a Sauterne (hyphen)

yr. year, younger, your

YRA Yacht Racing Association, *now* **RYA**

Yriarte, Charles (1832–98) French writer

yrs. years, yours

Ysaye, Eugène (1858–1929) Belgian violinist

Yseult etc., *use* **Is-**

Yssel *use* **IJssel**

YT Yukon Territory, Canada

yᵗ that; in approximating 15th- to 17th-c. works, the second letter to be superior (no point); *see also* **yᵉ**

ytterbium symbol **Yb**

yttrium symbol **Y**

Y2K (comput.) year 2000 (caps.)

yuan chief monetary unit of China, pl. same

Yucatán Mexico (accent)

yucca an American white-flowered liliaceous plant, *not* yuca

Yue another name for **Cantonese**

yugen in trad. Japanese court culture and Noh plays, a hidden quality of graceful beauty or mystery; profound aestheticism

Yugoslavia *not* J-; adj. **Yugoslav**, *not* -avian

Yuk a dialect of Yupik

Yukon/ River Alaska, USA; and Canada; **— Territory** Canada; *not* Youcon, -kon

yule log (two words, cap. Y in US)

Yuletide (one word, cap.)

Yupik an Eskimo or Eskimos of NE Siberia, the Aleutian Islands, and Alaska; the language spoken by them; *not* Yuit; *see also* **Eskimo; Inuit; Inuk**

yupp/ie *also* **-y**

Yvetot dép. Seine-Maritime, France

YWCA Young Women's Christian Association

Z the twenty-third in a series, pron. (UK) 'zed', (US) 'zee'

z. (meteor.) haze

z (math.) the third unknown quantity

zabaglione an Italian sweet of whipped and heated egg yolks, sugar, and (esp. Marsala) wine (not ital.)

Zach. Zachary

Zacynthus the ancient name of **Zante**

Zaehnsdorf, Joseph (1819–86) Austrian-born English-domiciled bookbinder

zaffre an impure cobalt oxide used as a blue pigment, *not* -er (US)

Zagreb Croatia, *not* -ab; in Ger. **Agram**, Hung. **Zágráb**, It. **Zagabria**

Zaharoff, Sir Basil (1849–1936) Greek-born British financier

Zaire name of the Democratic Republic of Congo 1960–97

Zaïre a major river in the Congo, *formerly* the **Congo** (accent, cap.); the monetary unit of the Congo (no accent, not cap.)

Zaïre a tragedy by Voltaire, 1732

zajčyk monetary unit of Belarus'

Zambezi an African river, *not* -si

Zambia Africa

Zamenhof, Ludwig Lazarus (1859–1917) Polish physician, inventor of Esperanto

zamindar *use* **zemin-**

zanana *use* **ze-**

Zangwill, Israel (1864–1926) English novelist and playwright

Zante a Greek island, ancient name **Zacynthus**

ZANU Zimbabwe African National Union

Zanzibar/ island, Tanzania; **-i**

zapateado a flamenco dance with rhythmic stamping of the feet (not ital.)

ZAPU Zimbabwe African People's Union

Zaragoza Sp. for (Catalan and Eng.) **Saragossa**

zarape *use* **ser-**

Zarathustra (Avestan) (6th c. BC) Persian founder of the Magian system of religion; in Gr. **Zoraster**

zariba (Arab.) a fortified enclosure, *not* the many variants

Zarskoe Selo *use* **Tsarskoe Selo**

zarzuela a trad. Spanish form of musical comedy, a fish stew (not cap., not ital.)

zax *use* **s-**

z. B. (Ger.) *zum Beispiel* (for example)

Zealand Denmark, *use* **Sjælland**

Zealand NB, Canada

zealot an uncompromising or extreme partisan, a fanatic (not cap.); (hist.) a member of an ancient Jewish sect aiming at a world Jewish theocracy and resisting the Romans until AD 70 (cap.)

zebec *use* **x-**

Zech. Zechariah (OT)

Zeeland the Netherlands, *not* Zea-; in Fr. **Zélande**, Ger. **Seeland**

Zeitgeist the spirit of the time, the trend of thought of a period (cap., not ital.); in Ger. m. **Zeitgeist**

Zeitschrift (Ger. f.) periodical (cap.)

Zeltinger a Moselle wine

zemindar an official in India under the Mogul empire, an Indian landowner paying tax to Britain; *not* zamin-

Zen a meditative form of Mahayana Buddhism (cap.)

zenana the part of a house for the seclusion of women of high-caste families in India and Iran, *not* za-; in Hind. **zenāna**

Zend/ an interpretation of the Avesta, each Zend being part of the **-Avesta**, the Zoroastrian sacred writings of the Avesta (text) and Zend (commentary)

Zener cards used in ESP research (one cap.)

zenith the highest point, opp. to **nadir**

Zeph. Zephaniah (OT)

Zeppelin/ (hist.) a large German dirigible airship of the early 20th c.; named after **Count Ferdinand von —** (1838–1917) German airman, its first constructor

Zermatt Switzerland

zero/ pl. **-s**

zeroth immediately preceding what is regarded as 'first' in a series, *also* **noughth**

zeta the sixth letter of the Gr. alphabet (Z, ζ)

Zetinje *use* **C-**

Zetland/ former off. name of Shetland county; **Marquess of —**

zeugma/ (gram.) a figure of speech in which a verb or adj. is used with two nouns, to only one of which it is strictly applicable, e.g. 'with weeping eyes and [sc. 'grieving'] hearts'; pl. **-s**, adj. **-tic** cf. **syllepsis**

zho *use* **dzo**

Zhou Enlai (1898–1976) Chinese statesman, Wade–Giles **Chou En-lai**

Zhu De (1886–1976) founder and commander of the Chinese People's Liberation Army 1930–54, *also spelt* **Chu Teh**

Zia/ ul-Haq, Mohammad (1924–88) President of Pakistan 1978–88; *properly* **— al-Haq**

Ziaur Rahman (1935–81) Bengali nationalist, President of Bangladesh 1977–81

zibet an Asian or Indian civet, *not* -eth (US)

Ziegfeld, Florenz (1869–1932) US theatre manager

ziggurat an ancient Mesopotamian tower, *not* zikk-

zigzag/, -ged, -ging (one word)

Zimbabwe/ Africa, **-an**

zinc symbol **Zn**

zinco/ (typ.) a relief block, usually in line, made from zinc; pl. **-s**

zincography the art of engraving and printing from zinc

zingara, à la (Fr. cook.) in the Gypsy style

zingar/o (It.) a Gypsy, pl. **-i**; f. **-a** pl. **-e**

Zinjanthropus an E. African fossil hominid

Zion/, -ism, -ist *not* Si-

zip/, -ped, -per, -ping, -py

zip/-bag (hyphen)

Zip code (US) = **postcode** (one cap., originally **ZIP**)

zip fastener (two words)

zirconium symbol **Zr**

zloty/ monetary unit of Poland, pl. **-s**, abbr. **zl**

Zn zinc (no point)

zo *use* dzo

Zoffany, John (1734–1810) German-born English-domiciled painter

Zollverein (Ger. m.) customs union

zombie a revived corpse, a person in a stupor; *not* -i, -y

zoolog/y genera, species, and subspecies to be italic, all other divisions roman, e.g. Carnivora (order), Felidae (family), *Felis* (genus), *Felis catus* (species); specific epithets, even when derived from names of persons, should be lower case: *Myotis daubentoni*; **-ical, -ist**; abbr. **zool.**

zo/on (biol.) an animal, pl. **-a**

zôon politikon (Gr. antiquity) the political animal, man

Zorast/er Gr. form of **Zarathustra**; **-rian** of or relating to Zoroaster, or the religion taught

by him or his followers (*see also* **Zend**); a follower of Zoroaster

Zouave a member of a French light-infantry corps, originally formed of Algerians and retaining their uniform (cap., not ital.)

Zou-Zou (hist.) a Zouave

ZPG zero population growth

Zr zirconium (no point)

ZS Zoological Society

ZST zone standard time

zucchetto/ (RC) a skullcap, pl. **-s**

zucchini (esp. US, Austral.) a courgette, pl. same; in It. **zucchin/o**, pl. **-i**

zugzwang (chess) a blockade, a position in which any move is undesirable yet some move must be made (not ital.)

Zuider Zee (hist.) the Netherlands, after enclosure **IJsselmeer**

Zuleika/ Potiphar's wife in the Koran, in Arab. *zuleḵhā*; also the heroine of Byron's *The Bride of Abydos*; — **Dobson** a femme fatale, eponymous heroine of a novel by Max Beerbohm, 1911

Zulu (of or relating to) a member of a black S. African people originally inhabiting Zululand and Natal, or the language of this people

Zululand (one word) annexed by S. Africa 1897, *now* **KwaZulu/Natal**

Zuñi (of or relating to) a member of a Pueblo Indian people inhabiting the valley of the River Zuñi

Zurich Switzerland; in Ger. **Zürich**, Romansh **Türich**, Lat. **Turicum**

zwieback a kind of biscuit rusk (not ital.)

Zwingli, Ulrich (*also* **Huldrych**) (1484–1531) Swiss Protestant reformer

zydeco a form of Cajun dance music originating in S. Louisiana (not cap.)

zymurgy originally the art of fermentation in winemaking, brewing, and distilling, *now* the branch of biochemistry dealing with this

Zyryan *use* **Komi**

zythum (hist.) a fermented-malt drink made in ancient times, esp. in Egypt

The Oxford
Guide to Style
Index

Index

Note: The index entries appear in word-by-word alphabetical order. Page references in italics indicate illustrations.